D0806040

# TEXAS CIVIL PROCEDURE: PRETRIAL LITIGATION

## FOURTH EDITION

**William V. Dorsaneo III**

*Chief Justice John and Lena Hickman*
*Distinguished Faculty Fellow*
*and Professor of Law*
*Southern Methodist University School of Law*

**David Crump**

*Newell H. Blakeley Professor of Law and*
*Faculty Director of Continuing Legal Education*
*University of Houston*

**Elaine A. Carlson**

*Professor of Law*
*South Texas College of Law*

**Elizabeth G. Thornburg**

*Professor of Law*
*Southern Methodist University School of Law*

**CASEBOOK SERIES**

**1999**

MATTHEW BENDER

## QUESTIONS ABOUT THIS PUBLICATION?

For questions about the **Editorial Content** reprint permission, please call:

Andrew D. Watry, J.D. .................................................. (800) 424-0651 ext. 268
Ann Gidden Bowman, J.D. .................................................. (800) 424-0651 ext. 216
Outside the United States and Canada please call .................................................. (415) 908-3200

To order a copy of this book, or for assistance with shipments, billing or other customer service matters, please call:

Customer Services Department at .................................................. (800) 533-1646
Outside the United States and Canada, please call .................................................. (518) 487-3000
Fax number .................................................. (518) 487-3584

For information on other Matthew Bender publications, please call
Your account manager or .................................................. (800) 223-1940
Outside the United States and Canada, please call .................................................. (518) 487-3000

Library of Congress Card Number: 99–21944



ISBN 0-8205-3124-3

MATTHEW BENDER

MATTHEW BENDER & COMPANY, INCORPORATED
Editorial Offices
Two Park Avenue, New York, NY 10016-5675 (212) 448-2000
201 Mission Street, San Francisco, CA 94105-1831 (415) 908-3200

# TABLE OF CONTENTS



## CHAPTER 1
## The Pre-Litigation Phase of a Civil Dispute

## CHAPTER 2

## Emergency and Interim Relief (Special Remedies)

## CHAPTER 3
## The Subject Matter Jurisdiction of the Texas Trial Courts

## CHAPTER 4
## Jurisdiction of Persons and Property

## CHAPTER 5
## Pleadings

## CHAPTER 6
## Venue

## CHAPTER 7
## Parties

## CHAPTER 8
## The Effects of Prior Adjudication (Res Judicata)

## CHAPTER 9
## Discovery: Purposes, Scope, and Uses

## CHAPTER 10
## Discovery: Methodology of the Individual Devices

## CHAPTER 11
## Disposition Without Trial

# Preface to the Second Edition

This text was conceived in 1978 when I attempted (with mixed results) to teach a pretrial procedure course at the University of Texas School of Law. Since that time the text has been written and rewritten in order to make the treatment of the subjects covered more understandable and, consequently, more teachable. Although many persons have contributed to the text, special thanks must be extended to four of them for the first and second editions. Celia Lee, then a law student at the University of Texas and now an Austin attorney, performed many tedious hours organizing, scrutinizing, and improving the original text. Paula Miller, a third year law student at the law school at Southern Methodist University, deserves a large amount of credit for the improvement made by this second edition. Although I have been working on the second edition for several years, without her assistance I doubt that I would have had the energy to make the necessary modifications in the original text. Much of what I had done mentally probably would not have ever gotten down on paper. Finally Beverly Mack and Edna Coplin, secretaries at the University of Texas School of Law and at the SMU School of Law, provided skillful assistance in preparing the manuscript.

This edition of the text contains many modifications. Major changes are made in the chapters concerning jurisdiction and discovery. The chapter on claim and issue preclusion also has been redone. All chapters have been updated and honed to a finer edge.

The demonstrations included in the appendices are designed to help the student make the transition from one who knows the law to one who appreciates how a lawyer functions in the context of the litigation process. Professor Crump and I continue to think that they are among the best teaching vehicles available to illustrate the legal principles discussed in the cases and textual material.

I want to pay thanks to the membership of the Committee on Administration of Justice, the Supreme Court Advisory Committee, the Supreme Court of Texas, and especially, to the Chief Justice of the Texas Supreme Court, the Honorable Jack Pope. By their influence on the subjects themselves, we have all been enriched. By their influence on me, my comprehension of the subjects covered in the text has been improved greatly. My friends, for all you do, this book is for you.

William V. Dorsaneo, III

## Preface to the Third Edition

The third edition of *Texas Civil Procedure: Pre-Trial Litigation* provides substantially complete coverage of significant procedural developments that have occurred since the publication of the second edition of the text. During the past five years, the Texas Supreme Court has been especially active in developing and refining the pre-trial and discovery phase of modern civil litigation. In this same period, numerous statutory changes, recodifications of existing law and procedural rule changes have altered the subject matter jurisdiction of Texas trial courts, Texas venue law, and modified a whole range of matters concerning the pre-trial litigation process.

We have also taken the opportunity to improve the text by adding better and more recent cases and by replacing decisions of intermediate appellate courts with Texas Supreme Court decisions. As with previous editions, however, our aim has been to teach lawyering skills to the users of the text.

The persons who have contributed useful suggestions and assistance in the revision process are too numerous to mention by name. We do hope, however, that our teaching colleagues at all Texas law schools as well as our nonacademic colleagues understand how much we do appreciate their help. We do thank you one and all.

August 1989
William V. Dorsaneo, III
David Crump

## Preface to the Fourth Edition

Now that the 1999 Discovery Rules have been promulgated we have decided to go ahead with the publication of the fourth edition of *Texas Civil Procedure: Pretrial Litigation.* We had planned to wait for the complete recodification of the Texas Rules of Civil Procedure to complete the fourth edition. However, we now believe that the best way to handle this development—when and if—it occurs in "about a year"—is to prepare a fifth edition. Much of what will be contained in the fourth edition will be readily adaptable to the recodified rules, as long as the Texas Supreme Court remains reasonably faithful to the Recodification Draft submitted to the Court by the Supreme Court Advisory Committee in late 1997.

The principal thrust of the textual changes made in the fourth edition involves the incorporation of the 1999 Discovery Rules throughout the text and particularly in new Chapters 9 and 10. The new "no evidence" summary judgment provision and related procedural developments is also given special attention in a revised Chapter 11 of the text. Recent developments in the law of Texas venue are also covered in an improved Chapter 6. In addition, the coverage of statutes of limitation, service of process, and the treatment of the pleadings, the pleading process, and the subject of frivolous pleadings have been improved and expanded.

Many persons have contributed useful comments and suggestions for improvement of the book. In addition to our new co-authors, Professors Elaine Carlson and Elizabeth Thornburg, special thanks are extended to Professor Ruth Cross of Southern Methodist University School of Law for her many useful questions and suggestions. We also want to pay special thanks to Ms. Sarah Rous, SMU Class of 1999, whose work on the new text has been significant and outstanding, Ms. Sharon Magill, my most able and professional legal assistant, and Mr. Andrew D. Watry, a very capable and diligent member of the publisher's editorial staff, without whom this fourth edition would not have been possible.

May 1999
William V. Dorsaneo, III
Chief Justice John and Lena Hickman Distinguished Faculty Fellow and Professor of Law
Dallas, Texas

# CHAPTER 1

## THE PRE-LITIGATION PHASE OF A CIVIL DISPUTE

### SCOPE

This chapter examines the early phases of a civil dispute before litigation has been instituted. It covers such considerations as initiating the attorney-client relationship including making fee arrangements, case evaluation, fact gathering, interviewing techniques, client relations, managing a litigation matter, and attorney malpractice.

### § 1.01 An Introduction to the Pre-Litigation Phase of a Civil Dispute

The majority of disputes that arise are settled without the filing of suit, and the majority of those disputes that result in the filing of suit are settled without trial. Finally, the vast majority of cases that are tried are not appealed.

As lawyers and law students, we tend to forget these statistics. But what they indicate, or should indicate to us, is that there are other skills than the ability to handle a case at the appellate or even the trial level that lawyers must have. One of these is the ability to handle a dispute properly when it is at the pre-litigation stage. Proper interviewing, fact-gathering, and counseling are essential. The ability to evaluate the case is probably even more important. The ability to negotiate and draft a fair contract of employment with one's own client may be the most important skill of all—for both lawyer and client. The ability to perform these tasks is important not just in cases that settle before the appellate level; if not properly performed, they will make even the best trial or appellate lawyer less able to serve the client.

Accordingly, this chapter begins with material on setting fees, negotiating and drafting a fee contract with the client, and the ethical considerations attending those processes.

Next, the chapter contains materials on case evaluation and settlement, including case evaluation problems. A lawyer cannot properly counsel a client on the worth of a claim or the advisability of settlement of the dispute without a sensible evaluation of it. In addition, because many cases are accepted on a contingent fee basis by plaintiff's lawyers, one cannot properly initiate or reject the litigation unless one can evaluate the claim properly. This evaluation process is quite different from appellate case analysis. It involves traditional "legal" issues only incidentally, as part of the calculus of liability, damages, collectability, and expense.

The chapter also adresses litigation management. What is the lawyer trying to do with the client's problem, and in the context of what limitations? Efficient, economical solution of the client's concerns is the aim. Beautifully detailed lawyering is valueless unless it addresses itself to this aim. These materials serve to introduce the student to the relevant concerns in litigation management. That process begins with, and is heavily influenced by, the pre-litigation phase of the suit.

There are at least two subjects in this chapter that relate closely to material covered in later chapters. First, interviewing and investigation is introduced here because of its importance at the pre-litigation phase. However, it cannot be completely understood except in the context of discovery, and so some materials related to it appear in the discovery chapters as well. Second, coverage of certain subjects related to settlement is delayed until the chapter on disposition without trial. This organization should not minimize the importance of either of these subjects at the pre-litigation phase.

## § 1.02 Initiating the Attorney-Client Relationship

### W. Dorsaneo, TEXAS LITIGATION GUIDE

*§ 3.04[2] (1999)*[*]

[2] Fees

[a] Propriety of Fee

Lawyers are prohibited from entering into an arrangement for, charging, or collecting illegal or unconscionable fees [State Bar Rules, Art. 10 § 9, Rule 1.04(a); *cf.* former DR 2-106(A)—illegal or clearly excessive fees may not be charged; *see also* Sutton & Newton, *Proposed Texas Disciplinary Rules of Professional Conduct: Commonly Asked Questions,* 52 Tex. B.J. 561, 563 (1989)—new, more stringent standard for discipline on basis of improper fee derived from pre-Code cases]. In this regard, a fee is *unconscionable* if a competent lawyer could not form a reasonable belief that the fee is reasonable [State Bar Rules, Art. 10 § 9, Rule 1.04(a)].

Among the factors that may be taken into account in determining the reasonableness of a fee are the following [State Bar Rules, Art. 10 § 9, Rule 1.04(b)]:

1. The time and labor required.
2. The novelty and difficulty of questions involved.
3. The skill needed to perform the legal service properly.
4. The likelihood, if apparent to the client, that the acceptance of the particular employment will preclude other employment by the lawyer.
5. The customary fee in the locality for similar legal services.
6. The amount involved in the matter and the results obtained by the lawyer.
7. The time limitations imposed by the client or by circumstances.
8. The nature and length of the professional relationship between the lawyer and the client.
9. The ability, experience, and reputation of the lawyer or lawyers performing the services.
10. Whether the fee is fixed or contingent.

When a lawyer has not regularly represented the client, the basis or rate of the fee must be communicated to the client, preferably in writing. This should be done before or shortly after the representation commences [State Bar Rules, Art. 10 § 9, Rule 1.04(c)].

Lawyers who are not members of the same firm are prohibited from dividing a fee or entering into agreements to divide a fee unless they comply with certain requirements. A fee division is permitted only when the division is one of the following: [State Bar Rules, Art. 10 § 9, Rule 1.04(f)(1); *see* former DR 2-107—comparable rule]:

1. In proportion to the professional services performed by each lawyer.

2. Made with a forwarding lawyer.

3. Made, by written agreement with the client, with a lawyer who assumes joint responsibility for the representation.

In addition, the client must be advised of the participation of all the lawyers involved, and must not object [State Bar Rules, Art. 10 § 9, Rule 1.04(f)(2); Polland & Cook v. Lehmann, 832 S.W.2d 729, 736 (Tex. App.—Houston [1st Dist.] 1992, den.)—under former rule, corporation had authority to consent to referral fee on behalf of investors; *see* Lemond v. Jamail, 763 S.W.2d 910, 914 (Tex. App.—Houston [1st Dist.] 1988, den.)—under former Code of Professional Responsibility, court refused to enforce referral and fee-splitting agreement of which client was never informed]. Finally, the aggregate fee must not be an illegal or unconscionable fee [State Bar Rules, Art. 10 § 9, Rule 1.04(f)(3)].

Rule 1.04 does not require that an attorney disclose his or her intention to divide the legal fees, or that the lawyer obtain the client's consent to employment. Under Rule 1.04, if a lawyer acts as a forwarding attorney, the client need only be advised of and not object to the participation of all the lawyers involved. In these respects, Rule 1.04 differs from the former Code of Professional Responsibility [Polland & Cook v. Lehmann, 832 S.W.2d 729, 736 (Tex. App.—Houston [1st Dist.] 1992, den.)—former rule applied].

[b] Contingent Fee Contracts

Contingent fee contracts are prohibited in criminal defense matters [State Bar Rules, Art. 10 § 9, Rule 1.04(e)]. Unless prohibited under this provision or by other law, contingent fees are permissible. Such agreements must be in writing and must state the method by which the fee is to be determined [State Bar Rules, Art. 10 § 9, Rule 1.04(d); *see also* Gov. C. § 82.065—contingent fee contracts must be in writing and must be signed by attorney and client]. Section 82.065 of the Government Code (requiring contingent fee agreements to be in writing) has been construed to operate in a manner similar to the statute of frauds [Enochs v. Brown, 872 S.W.2d 312, 317–318 (Tex. App.—Austin 1994, no writ)—contingent fee contract signed by client not void even though it lacked attorney's signature]. If different percentages are to be paid to the lawyer in the event of settlement, trial, or appeal, those percentages must be stated in the contract. The agreement must state the expenses, litigation or otherwise, that will be deducted from the recovery, and whether the expense deduction is taken before or after the contingent fee is calculated. When a contingent fee matter comes to a conclusion, the lawyer must provide the client with a written statement that describes the outcome of the matter, and, in the case of a recovery, shows the remittance to the client and the method of determining that amount [State Bar Rules, Art. 10 § 9, Rule 1.04(d); *see* § 3.100—sample contingent fee contract].

The rule does not prohibit the use of contingent fee arrangements in family law cases [*see* State Bar Rules, Art. 10 § 9, Rule 1.04; Newton, *Proposed Texas Disciplinary Rules of Professional Conduct Should be Adopted,* 52 Tex. B.J. 557, 559 (1989)]. However, such contingent fee arrangements are not favored. It is thought that they tend to promote divorce and create a conflict of interest between lawyer and client regarding the appraisal of assets obtained for the client. Moreover, family law matters such as child custody and adoption do not create any res that would fund a fee. "Because of the human relationships involved and the unique character of the proceedings, contingent fee arrangements in domestic relations cases are rarely justified" [State Bar Rules, Art. 10 § 9, Rule 1.04, Comment 9—contingent fees may tend to promote divorce; *see* Twyman v. Twyman, 855 S.W.2d 619, 625 n.18 (Tex. 1993)—when cause of action for tort of intentional infliction of emotional distress is brought in divorce proceeding, counsel should enter into two separate fee arrangements, one for divorce and one for tort claim].

A contingent fee contract is voidable by the client if it results from conduct that violates Texas laws or state bar rules regarding barratry, the improper institution of litigation, or improper solicitation of employment by attorneys or other persons [Gov. C. § 82.065(b); *see* Pen. C. § 38.12—barratry; State Bar Rules, Art. 10 § 9, Rule 8.04(a)(8)—lawyer may not engage in conduct that is defined as barratry under state laws].

[c] Informing Client of Fee

An attorney should not hesitate to discuss fees with the client on the first visit [*see* State Bar Rules, Art. 10 § 9, Rule 1.04, Comment 2]. Surveys have indicated that although attorneys typically do not discuss fees during a client's first visit, most clients want to discuss fees at that time but are hesitant to initiate the discussion.

If the amount to be charged the client is not based on an agreement that specifies the fee, but rather is based on an understanding that the attorney is entitled to a reasonable fee for services, collection will be facilitated if the statement sent to the client contains details of the services rendered. An itemization of the fee may also be helpful in some instances. The attorney should keep detailed records indicating precisely what he or she has done (particularly with regard to telephone calls and office conferences that are often overlooked) so that the statement for services can be specific and detailed and the amount of the bill can be readily justified should any question arise.

The attorney should bill the client promptly, because the longer the delay after the completion of the services, the greater the likelihood that the client will have forgotten the services actually rendered. If prolonged litigation is not being handled on a contingent fee basis, the attorney ordinarily will want to bill the client at regular monthly intervals rather than waiting until completion of the litigation.

---

## ARCHER v. GRIFFITH

*390 S.W.2d 735 (Tex. 1964)*

WALKER, Justice.

This is an action to set aside a deed executed by Mrs. Nova Dean Griffith, respondent, to her attorney, Fancher Archer, Esq., petitioner, pursuant to the provisions of a contingent fee contract between the parties. The case was tried before the court without a jury, and judgment was rendered cancelling the deed and awarding petitioner $400.00 in addition to the amounts previously received by him for his services to respondent. No findings of fact or conclusions of law were filed or requested. The Court of Civil Appeals affirmed. Archer v. Blakemore, 367 S.W.2d 402.

Respondent originally employed the law firm of Archer & Archer in January, 1959, to institute divorce proceedings in her behalf. She made a deposit for court costs and gave them $100.00 at the time, but according to her testimony they said their fee would be collected from the husband. According to their testimony she orally agreed to pay a contingent fee of one-fourth of any property recovered for her in the suit. After a preliminary investigation of the property rights involved, the divorce action was instituted by filing an original petition which was verified by respondent and signed by petitioner as her attorney. She there prayed for a temporary restraining order, temporary alimony, divorce, custody of the minor child born to the marriage, an allowance for the support of the child, and attorney's fees in the amount of $1,000.00. Prior to the issuance of a restraining order, however, respondent notified her attorneys that she and her husband had effected a reconciliation and were living together again. No further action was taken in the suit at that time, and no additional payment was requested from her.

About eighteen months later respondent again consulted the Archers and insisted on going forward with the suit. She then signed a written contract employing petitioner to represent her "in preserving, keeping and managing my separate property and my community property . . . and . . . to file suit and take such other action and steps by suit or otherwise to preserve and protect my property." It was further stipulated that in consideration of services rendered and to be rendered, petitioner would be entitled to one-fourth of "whatever property either personal, real or money which shall be determined to be mine either through settlement or suit."

[Adversary processes resulted in the case being set on the jury docket, but then settled. Negotiations lasted several weeks. The settlement agreement gave the husband a number of valuable properties, including the home, a business enterprise, and stocks. The wife was given household furnishings, and the husband was to pay $500 of her attorney's fees. Other interests, including realty, were divided between the husband and wife.]

. . . .

The hearing in the divorce action was held the following day, and judgment was entered awarding respondent a divorce and custody of the child. According to the recitals of the judgment, the settlement agreement was explained to the court, which found that there was no necessity for adjudicating the property rights of the parties. Immediately after the divorce was granted and before the parties left the court house, respondent executed and acknowledged the following three deeds: (1) a conveyance of the home to her former husband; (2) a deed establishing their interests in the 13th Street property in accordance with the settlement agreement; and (3) the instrument now in controversy, which conveyed to petitioner one-fourth of respondent's undivided one-half interest in the 13th Street property. The husband later paid petitioner the $500.00 fee as provided in the settlement agreement.

Petitioner insists that the trial court erred in setting aside the deed because there is no evidence of any fraud in connection with its execution and delivery. It was stipulated by the parties that the relationship of attorney and client existed between petitioner and respondent when the deed was executed and delivered. That fact has an important bearing on the controversy. The relation between an attorney and his client is highly fiduciary in nature, and their dealings with each other are subject to the same scrutiny, intendments and imputations as a transaction between an ordinary trustee and his cestui que trust. "The burden of establishing its perfect fairness, adequacy, and equity, is thrown upon the attorney, upon the general rule, that he who bargains in a matter of advantage with a person, placing a confidence in him, is bound to show that a reasonable use has been made of that confidence; a rule applying equally to all persons standing in confidential relations with each other." Story, Equity Jurisprudence, 7th ed. 1857, § 311. This principle has always been recognized by the Texas courts. [footnote omitted] Cooper v. Lee, 75 Tex. 114, 12 S.W. 483; Holland v. Brown, Tex. Civ. App., 66 S.W.2d 1095 (writ ref.); Bell v. Ramirez, Tex. Civ. App., 299 S.W. 655 (writ ref.).

The general rule mentioned above applies to a contract or other transaction relating to compensation provided the attorney-client relationship was in existence at the time. "Although an attorney is not incapacitated from contracting with his client for compensation during the existence of the relation of attorney and client, and a fair and reasonable settlement of the compensation to be paid is valid and enforceable, if executed freely, voluntarily, and with full understanding by the client, the courts, because of the confidential relationship, scrutinize with jealousy all contracts between them for compensation which are made while the relation exists. There is a presumption of unfairness or invalidity attaching to the contract, and the burden of showing its fairness and reasonableness is on the attorney." Pomeroy, Equity Jurisprudence, 5th ed. 1941, § 960d. . . . .

. . . .

Aside from one deficiency in proof which will be noticed later, the validity of the deed in the present case turns upon whether the preexisting agreement was, in fact, so unfair and unreasonable that a court of equity should intervene and set the conveyance aside. Since there are no findings of fact or conclusions of law, it must be presumed that the trial court found that it was. The question for us to decide then is whether the record shows conclusively that such implied finding is erroneous. We take it for granted that petitioner acted in good faith, but that does not entitle him to prevail as a matter of law. The issue here is constructive or legal fraud and not actual fraud. Actual fraud usually involves dishonesty of purpose or intent to deceive, whereas constructive fraud is the breach of some legal or equitable duty which, irrespective of moral guilt, the law declares fraudulent because of its tendency to deceive others, to violate confidence, or to injure public interests. 37 C.J.S. Fraud § 2; 23 Am. Jur. Fraud and Deceit § 4.

. . . .

Entirely aside from that problem, it is our opinion that the record will support the conclusion that the contingent fee contract was so exorbitant and unreasonable as to require that the conveyance be set aside. There is no direct evidence as to the value of the 13th Street property when the contract was executed on September 20, 1960. It was purchased in 1951 for a total consideration of $60,500.00, and there is testimony indicating that property values in the area have increased since 1951. About five months after the divorce, petitioner wrote respondent that he had told some people, apparently real estate agents, "that if they had a proposition to make with a definite amount of $110,000.00 with earnest money to pay down, we would then listen to their proposition and make a decision as to whether or not we would sell." The record also contains a notation in petitioner's handwriting that the estimated value of the 13th Street property on December 1, 1960, was $90,000.00. Petitioner testified that the notation was made in connection with the settlement negotiations and had no meaning as far as value was concerned, but the trial court was not required to accept this explanation. In the light of the foregoing evidence and in view of the absence of any other proof of value, the court was entitled to conclude that the property was worth at least $90,000.00 at the time the contract was made. On the basis of such valuation and after deducting the amounts unpaid on the outstanding encumbrance and the lien imposed on respondent's interest in favor of her former husband, the computed value of the one-eighth interest conveyed to petitioner is more than $6,400.00. To this must be added the $600.00 he was paid by respondent and her husband, which means that his total compensation was in excess of $7,000.00.

One member of the Travis County Bar, who represented the husband in the divorce action and who was thus familiar with the issues and property involved in the suit, testified that from $500.00 to $750.00 would have been a reasonable fee for the services rendered by petitioner. This evidence is not necessarily controlling, because the witness was speaking of a fee that would be paid without regard to the outcome of the litigation. If accepted by the trial court, however, it shows that the contingent fee agreement yielded petitioner approximately ten times what he could reasonably have expected to receive under a fixed fee agreement.

The schedule of fees recommended by the State Bar of Texas, which was introduced in evidence, does not recognize contingent fee arrangements in divorce actions. There is a section dealing with contingent fees, but it is prefaced by a paragraph which states, in effect, that such section does not apply to divorce suits and certain other types of cases that are dealt with specifically elsewhere in the schedule. In the section applicable to divorce actions, a minimum fee of $250.00 is recommended in an uncontested case with $100.00 to be added if the custody of children is involved and an agreement is reached. It further states that: "For the legal services rendered in connection with the property settlement, the additional charge, based on the fair net value of the property allocated or set aside to the attorney's client, should be 10 per cent on the first $5,000.00 and five per cent on the excess; where unusual or complex problems are involved or where the parties cannot agree and the matter must be decided by litigation, a higher charge should be made." The trial judge, who was familiar with the problems involved in the divorce action, was entitled to conclude that the contract now under attack provided for a fee three and one-half times greater than the minimum fee recommended in such schedule.

The certainty or contingency of the compensation is one of the factors to be considered by an attorney in fixing his fee. See Canon 11, Article XIII, Section 3, of the State Bar Rules, Vernon's Ann. Civ. St. We are not concerned here, however with the ordinary contingent fee arrangement where there is considerable doubt that the attorney will receive anything for his services. The contract obligated respondent to pay petitioner one-fourth of all property determined to be hers, whether by settlement or suit. She and her husband owned a large amount of community property, and the record does not establish that there was any serious question as to her right to a divorce. Even if they were permanently reconciled, petitioner would have been entitled to recover the reasonable value of his services despite the agreement for a contingent fee. Kelly v. Gross, Tex. Civ. App., 4 S.W.2d 296 (writ ref.). Subject to this one contingency, a substantial recovery was reasonably certain even after making allowance for the husband's separate funds used to purchase the real estate. It was very likely, therefore, that petitioner would receive either the reasonable value of his services or one-fourth of the property set apart to his client when the divorce was granted. In this respect his situation was quite different from that of an attorney employed to prosecute a damage suit or establish a constructive trust.

It is a matter of common knowledge, moreover, that divorce cases are frequently settled, and that the lawyers usually do less work in such instances than where the issues are contested through the trial and appellate courts. The attorney who represented the husband in the divorce action testified that the contract was unfair to respondent in that no provision was made for a reduction of the fee in the event of a settlement. He regarded one-fourth of the recovery as a reasonable contingent fee if petitioner had been required to try a contested case, but it was his opinion that "twenty-five per cent straight across the board is too high." He thought the contract was "wrong" and that "they took advantage of her, just to be plain about it."

After reading the entire statement of facts and carefully considering all of the evidence, we are unable to say that either party to this suit is entitled to prevail as a matter of law. Whether the contingent fee contract and the conveyance executed pursuant thereto were so unfair and inequitable as to warrant the intervention of a court of equity is a question of fact, and that issue was resolved by the trial judge in respondent's favor.

Petitioner also contends that respondent ratified the contract and deed by allowing him to look after the 13th Street property and consulting him regarding its sale after the divorce was granted. These dealings apparently are referable to the contract of employment and occurred while the attorney-client relationship existed between the parties. Although there is a conflict in the evidence, respondent's testimony will support the conclusion that she did not realize until May, 1961, that she had signed a contract entitling petitioner to one-fourth of the recovery or a deed conveying him an interest in the real estate. She "just signed what they thought I should sign," and originally it was her understanding that petitioner's fee would be collected from the husband. After the property settlement was worked out and before the divorce was granted, she was advised that there would be an additional fee. She told her attorneys that if she owed them anything, it would have to be paid at the time the property was sold "and they said that was all right." There were no further dealings between them after she discovered that petitioner had a deed to an interest in the real estate. Aside from the fact that there is no pleading of ratification, it is our opinion that such defense is not conclusively established by the evidence and that the judgment setting aside the deed must be affirmed.

By cross-point in the Court of Civil Appeals, respondent contended that the trial court erred in awarding petitioner $400.00 in addition to the $600.00 he had already received. She asserted that such recovery is without support in either the pleadings or the evidence. The intermediate court refused to consider the question because respondent did not perfect an appeal from the judgment in so far as it is adverse to her.

Petitioner attempted to limit the scope of his appeal to the portion of the judgment which set aside the conveyance. See Rule 353, Texas Rules of Civil Procedure. Such attempt was ineffectual in this instance, however, because the judgment is not severable in that manner. The $400.00 award is predicated on respondent's offer, in her petition, to pay petitioner any additional fee to which he might be entitled in the event the conveyance should be set aside. It is dependent upon her right to the relief she sought, and could not be allowed to stand if it had been determined that the trial court erred in cancelling the deed. When petitioner perfected his appeal, therefore, the entire judgment was brought to the appellate court for review and respondent was entitled to urge her cross-point attacking the portion of such judgment which is adverse to her. See Dallas Electric Supply Co. v. Branum Co., 143 Tex. 366, 185 S.W.2d 427, and authorities there cited.

Since respondent offered to do equity, it was unnecessary for petitioner to seek a recovery on the *quantum meruit* in the event the deed was set aside. There is ample testimony to support the additional $400.00 award in his favor, and the cross-point is accordingly overruled.

The judgment of the Court of Civil Appeals is affirmed.

GRIFFIN, SMITH, GREENHILL and STEAKLEY, JJ., dissenting.

GREENHILL, Justice (dissenting).

This is not a case in which the trial court was called upon to fix a reasonable attorney's fee. Nor is it a suit by an attorney for his fees in which the amount thereof is an ordinary issue of fact. This is a suit to set aside a deed, one which had been executed more than a year before suit was brought, and the ground alleged for setting the deed aside is fraud. [footnote omitted] In my opinion, there is absolutely no evidence of fraud, actual or constructive.

. . . .

I would reverse the judgments of the courts below and render judgment that the plaintiff take nothing.

GRIFFIN, SMITH and STEAKLEY, JJ., join in this dissent.

---

## NOTES AND QUESTIONS

(1) *Contingent Fees.* Contingent fee arrangements in divorce cases are not prohibited in Texas, although they are in many other states. Is there something about a divorce case that distinguishes it from other types of litigation in which contingent fees are legitimate?

(2) *Fiduciary Relationship.* What if no attorney-client relationship had existed at the time that the contingent fee contract was made? At what point in time does an attorney owe a fiduciary duty to another party to a fee contract? Does the principal case mean that attorneys are not permitted to make favorable fee contracts with non-clients?

---

**ROYDEN v. ARDOIN**, 331 S.W.2d 206, 209 (Tex. 1960). An attorney's license was suspended before the completion of his contingent fee contract entered into with his client. He sued the client in quantum meruit for services rendered before the suspension, but the court denied any relief. Citing an Arkansas case, the Texas Supreme Court stated that "If an attorney, without just cause, abandons his client before the proceeding for which he was retained has been conducted to its termination, or if such attorney commits a material breach of his contract of employment, he thereby forfeits all right to compensation."

Thus, fee forfeiture is recognized as an appropriate remedy against counsel who has breach its fiduciary duty to the client. *Arce v. Burrow, 958 S.W.2d 239, 247 (Tex. App.—Houston [1st Dist.] 1997, writ granted).*

In some jurisdictions, an attorney who is discharged for cause has no right to recover a fee and may be forced to remit a retainer paid in advance. *See* Coclin Tobacco Co. v. Griswell, 408 F.2d 1338 (1st Cir. 1969). In other jurisdictions an attorney who has a contingent fee contract with a client, who has been discharged for sufficient cause, is allowed to recover the reasonable value of services rendered up to the time of discharge. *See* Fracasse v. Brent, 6 Cal. 3d 784, 100 Cal. Rptr. 385, 494 P.2d 9 (1972); *see generally* Howell v. Kelly, 534 S.W.2d 737, 739 (Tex. Civ. App.—Houston (1st Dist.) 1976, no writ)—summarizing conflicting authorities.

Despite the quotation from the Texas Supreme Court's opinion in the *Ardoin* case, Texas law is not completely clear on the availability of a recovery in quantum meruit. For example, in *Rocha v. Ahmad,* 676 S.W.2d 149 (Tex. App.—San Antonio 1984, writ dism'd), an attorney was allowed to collect fees in quantum meruit when he was discharged for good cause. Because the former client proved good cause for discharge of the attorney, the attorney could not recover under the contract, but could recover in quantum meruit.

What is the difference, if any, from being discharged for good cause or for committing a material breach of the contract? Notice that the *Ardoin* court says that a material breach by an attorney forfeits all right to compensation. Is not returning a client's phone calls a material breach? What about procrastination in working up a file for trial? While *Ardoin* was an abandonment case and therefore the material breach language is dictum, the point is that there is a risk of no compensation for ignoring the client or his or her file.

Further, in regard to material breaches of attorney-client contracts, what implied provisions might be made a part of the contingency fee contract? Might some or all of the provisions of the Disciplinary Rules of Professional Conduct be read into the contract?

---

## W. Dorsaneo, TEXAS LITIGATION GUIDE

*§ 3.100[1], [2] (1999)**

§ 3.100 General Contingent Fee Agreement

[1] Comment

[a] Use of Form

This form is a contingent fee contract between an attorney and a client for the representation of the client on a specific matter such as a claim for unliquidated damages. Although it can be used for any type of claim, the most common use of this type of agreement is with regard to claims for personal injury and property damage arising out of automobile accidents. For a discussion of the Disciplinary Rules applicable to fees in general, see § 3.04[2].

[b] Contingent Fees

Contingent fee arrangements (defined as an agreement to undertake representation in litigation in exchange for a percentage share of the claim or recovery) developed as a method of financing legal services for working-class persons who had suffered personal injuries. They have long been legal in Texas [*see* DeHay v. Cline, 5 F. Supp. 630, 631 (N.D. Tex. 1933)]. They are expressly permitted under the Disciplinary Rules of Professional Conduct in civil matters [State Bar Rules, Art. 10 § 9, Rule 1.04(d), (e)].

The percentage of recovery that constitutes the fee generally varies depending on the stage at which recovery is made [*see* State Bar Rules, Art. 10 § 9, Rule 1.04(d)]. For example, a lower fee is usually charged when the case settles before trial than if the matter is fully litigated.

Contingent fee arrangements may be appropriate in any situation involving unliquidated damages or an uncertain recovery, such as will contests, suits for recovery of real property, collections, and condemnation proceedings. Contingent fees are permitted, although discouraged, in family law matters [*see* § 3.04[2][b]].

A contingent fee contract, since it involves a risk depending on the result, may properly provide for a larger compensation than would otherwise be reasonable. Most contingent fee contracts provide for fees varying between 25 percent and 40 percent. The lawyer should, however, keep in mind the basic prohibition against charging an unconscionable fee [*see* State Bar Rules, Art. 10 § 9, Rule 1.04(a); *see* § 3.04[2][a]].

A contingent fee contract is voidable by the client if it was procured as a result of conduct violating the laws of Texas or the state bar Disciplinary Rules regarding barratry [Gov. C. § 82.065(b)].

[c] Requirements for Contract

A contingent fee contract must be in writing and signed by the client and by the attorney [Gov. C. § 82.065(a); State Bar Rules, Art. 10 § 9, Rule 1.04(d)]. The agreement must state the method by which the fee is to be determined. If different percentages will be applicable depending on whether the matter settles, goes to trial, or is appealed, those percentages must be stated in the agreement. The agreement must state the litigation and other expenses to be deducted from the recovery, and whether such expenses are to be deducted before or after the contingency is calculated [State Bar Rules, Art. 10 § 9, Rule 1.04(d)].

After a contingent fee matter is concluded, the lawyer must provide the client with a written statement explaining the resolution of the matter and if there is a recovery, showing the remittance to the client and the method of its determination [State Bar Rules, Art. 10 § 9, Rule 1.04(d); *see* § 3.101].

[2] Form

CONTINGENT FEE CONTRACT

__________ [*Name of client*], of __________ [*address*], referred to as the Client, and __________ [*name of attorney or law firm or professional corporation*], of __________ [*address*], referred to as the Attorney, agree as follows:

I. Purpose of Representation

The Client retains and employs the Attorney to: __________ [*state purpose of contractual relationship, e.g.,* sue for and recover all damages and compensation to which the Client may be entitled as well as to compromise and settle all claims arising out of the __________ (*specify, e.g.,* automobile accident) that occurred on or about the ______ day of __________, 19_____, at __________ (*location of occurrence*) *or* represent the Client in contesting the will of __________ (*name*), deceased, dated __________, 19_____]. To secure the performance of Client's obligations, as set forth below, the Client hereby transfers and assigns to the Attorney an undivided interest in the Client's claim, such interest being equivalent to the amount or percentage that the Client, by this agreement, promises to pay for the services of the Attorney.

II. Attorney's Fees

In consideration of services rendered and to be rendered by the Attorney, the Client agrees to pay to the Attorney __________ [*specify percentage, e.g.,* forty (40)] percent of all money and property collected, whether from the proceeds of any suit and judgment or from a settlement after trial. However, if the claim and cause of action is such that the fee allowed to an attorney is set by law, the amount payable to the Attorney shall be limited to the maximum so allowed by law. In the event the case is settled before trial, the Client agrees to pay __________ [*specify percentage, e.g.,* thirty-three and one-third (33⅓)] percent of the amount recovered as attorney's fees.

[*OR*]

II. Attorney's Fees

In consideration of the services to be rendered by the Attorney, Client hereby agrees to pay to Attorney a sum of money equal to:

__________ [*Specify percentage, e.g.,* Twenty-five (25)] percent of all money and property collected __________ [prior to the filing of an action *or* prior to the commencement of trial].

__________ [*Specify percentage, e.g.,* Thirty-three and one-third (33⅓)] percent of all money and property collected __________ [after the filing of an action *or* after the commencement of trial].

__________ [*Specify percentage, e.g.,* Forty (40)] percent of all money or property collected after either the commencement of a second trial or the filing of an appeal by either party.

However, if the claim is such that the fee allowed to an attorney is set by law, the fee assigned to the Attorney shall be limited to the maximum so allowed by law.

The Attorney will be compensated for __________ [his *or* her] services only if a recovery is actually obtained by the Client.

[*OR*]

[*If a will contest is contemplated, the following fee provision may be used*]

II. Attorney's Fees

The Attorney will be compensated at __________ [*specify percentage, e.g.,* twenty-five (25)] percent of the fair market value of whatever cash or property the Client receives from the estate of the decedent. The Attorney will be compensated for services rendered only if a recovery is obtained for the Client. In the event that the Attorney and the Client are unable to agree on the value of the property recovered, the fair market value of any recovery, other than cash, will be ascertained by the written appraisal of three appraisers, one to be selected by the Client, one to be selected by the Attorney, and the third to be selected by the first two. The appraisers are to render the appraisal within _______ days after the date of recovery. The Client agrees to pay the fees of the appraisers.

III. Approval Necessary for Settlement

No settlement of any nature shall be made for any of the claims of the Client without the complete approval of the Client.

IV. Deduction of Expenses

The costs of court and all reasonable expenses advanced or incurred by the Attorney in the handling of this claim shall be deducted by the Attorney from the Client's share of any recovery that is obtained. The Client shall remain liable for all expenses in the event that a recovery is not obtained or in the event that the recovery obtained is less than the expenses incurred.

[*Optional. Add in personal injury cases*]

All medical expenses and charges of any nature will be paid by the Client. In the event of a recovery, the Client agrees that the Attorney may pay any unpaid bills from the Client's share of the recovery, but the Attorney is not bound to pay any of these expenses or charges.

V. Calculation and Explanation of Contingency

The percentage paid to the attorney shall be calculated ________ [before *or* after] expenses and costs are deducted from the amount of the recovery. At the conclusion of the matter, the Attorney will provide the Client with a statement clearly detailing the determination of the fee and any remittance to Client.

VI. Cooperation of Client

The Client shall keep the Attorney advised of the Client's whereabouts at all times, shall appear on reasonable notice at any and all depositions and court appearances, and shall comply with all reasonable requests of the Attorney in connection with the preparation and presentation of the claim.

VII. Permission to Withdraw

In case the Attorney shall determine, after conducting a preliminary investigation, that the Client's claim should not be pursued further, the Client agrees that the Attorney may withdraw from the representation of the Client by sending written notice of the Attorney's intention to withdraw to the Client at the Client's last known address. In such event, the Client shall not be obligated to pay any fees to the Attorney, but the Attorney shall be entitled to reimbursement of any expenses, charges, or costs that the Attorney may have advanced or incurred during the course of the representation.

VIII. Texas Law to Apply

This agreement shall be construed in accordance with the laws of the State of Texas, and all obligations of the parties are performable in ________ County, Texas.

IX. Parties Bound

This agreement shall be binding on and inure to the benefit of the parties and their respective heirs, executors, administrators, legal representatives, successors, and assigns.

X. Legal Construction

In case any one or more of the provisions contained in this agreement shall be held to be invalid, illegal, or unenforceable in any respect, such invalidity, illegality, or unenforceability shall not affect any other provision, and this agreement shall be construed as if such invalid, illegal, or unenforceable provision did not exist.

XI. Prior Agreements Superseded

This agreement constitutes the only agreement of the parties and supersedes any prior understandings or written or oral agreements between the parties respecting the subject matter.

SIGNED AND AGREED on __________, ______.

By: ______________________________ [*signature*]
______________________________ [*typed name*], Client

By: ______________________________ *signature*]
______________________________ [*typed name*], Attorney

---

**Foonberg, HOW TO START AND BUILD A LAW PRACTICE 219–224, 232–238 (4th ed. 1999)***

*(Published by the Law Student Division and the Section of Law Practice Management of the American Bar Association)*

*How to Set Your Fees*

The importance of the fee-representation-engagement agreement cannot be overemphasized. It will help eliminate disputes between you and your client more effectively than any other procedure.

The fee letter can best be explained by using an all-inclusive example and then exploring the importance of the various parts:

John Client
123 Main Street
Anytown, U.S.A.

[1] RE: Jones vs. Smith; breach of contract
Dear Mr. Jones:

[2] This letter will confirm our office discussion of Thursday, January 4.

[3] It was a pleasure meeting with you in our office. As I explained to you, it is my opinion that you defi–
[4] nitely need the assistance of a lawyer, whether it be our
[5] firm or another lawyer. In my opinion, the matter with you in our office is too complex for you to represent yourself.
[6] As I explained to you, if you wish us to repre-
[7][8] sent you, our fee will be $1,500 to prepare the complaint, do written interrogatories, take the deposition of Mr. Smith if necessary, and appear for the first day in
[9] court. If any additional work is required for such things as motions, additional depositions, or additional days in court, you will be charged at our hourly rate of $115
[10] per hour. If the case is settled short of trial, the fee will still be a minimum of $1,500.
[11] The above does not include any out-of-pocket costs that may be incurred, such as court filing fees, sheriff's fees, deposition costs, photocopying, etc. We estimate, but cannot

* Available from American Bar Association, 750 N. Lake Shore Drive, Chicago, IL 60611. Reprinted with permission of the author, copyright © 1999.

guarantee, that these costs will run between $250 and $350, and, explained, these costs are in addition to our fee and are not included in the $1,500 fee.

[12] We shall have the right to engage other attorneys to assist us at our sole expense and at no additional cost to you.

[13] You indicated that you wished to pay in installments of $350 fees and $ 100 costs to begin work, and $150 fees and $50 costs the first of each month you are current, and then, additional fees and costs will be paid monthly, as billed.

[14] This schedule is acceptable to us, so long as you

[15] understand that if you terminate payments, we may terminate our services and withdraw from the case.

[16] You are also agreeing to cooperate and participate in the conduct of your case and to truthfully and immediately notify us as to anything that may occur that could affect the case. You understand we axe relying on the facts as given to us by you.

[17] As I indicated to you, based on the facts as you related them to me in the office, you should win, and you should be awarded a judgment of between $9,500 and $15,000, unless the case is settled at a different sum. Obviously, depending upon the facts as they are developed, our opinion could change you could be

[18] awarded more or less, or even lose. You also understand that getting a judgment is not the same as getting cash and that you may have to expend additional costs and fees to collect the judgment.

You asked me if spending money on legal fees in this case is throwing good money, after bad, and I told you that at this point, I couldn't give you an answer,

[19] and that you should understand that there are no guarantees of winning or collecting. It is my opinion, however, that whether you use our firm or other lawyers, you should proceed with your

[20] case. Please do not delay. If you delay the commencement of your suit, you may at some point be barred from bringing it.

[21] If the above properly sets forth our agreement, please sign and return the enclosed copy of this letter, along with a check in the amount of $450, payable to my trust account. I will draw $350 toward my fees, and

[22] leave $100 toward costs as outlined above. Trust account funds are deposited to out Trust Account in accordance with the rules governing lawyers in our state including IOLTA (Interest On Lawyer Trust Accounts) rules as well as our fiduciary duty to you as a client. If the funds are significant enough to earn net interest for the period of time held, we will consult with you for instructions. A self-addressed, postage-paid envelope is enclosed for your convenience.

[23] If we do not receive the signed copy of this letter, and your check, within 30 days, I shall assume that you have obtained other counsel, and shall mark my file "closed" and do nothing further. If any of the above is not clear, or if you have any questions, please do not hesitate to call.

Very truly yours,

________________________

To be typed on the copy of the letter:

The above is understood and agreed to, and my check in the amount of $450, payable to Jane Attorney Client Trust Account is enclosed.

Dated:

John Client

Essential Points to the Fee and Representation Letter

Obviously, the fee-representation letter must be tailor-made to the particular facts of the matter and the fee. Whatever form you decide to use, your letter should include the following:

[1] The Matter Involved. Perhaps your client has several legal matters, and has not told you about any of them except the Smith matter. This should prevent a later claim their for more than this matter.

[2] Your Interview Date. This establishes when you had an interview to get the facts. This is for your protection in the event you are sued by you client or another party.

[3] Whether or Not a Lawyer Is Required. This avoids the interviewee claiming that you said no lawyer was necessary and that he or she should "forget about it."

[4] Suggesting Other Lawyers. Suggest that the client may wish to see another lawyer. This relates to not representing the client until the agreement is returned. (See point 21 below.)

[5] If You Wish Us to Represent You. This reinforces that you are not yet the lawyer, and don't yet have responsibility.

[6] The Amount of the Fee. This establishes what I call the "Basic Fee."

[7] Describing the Work the Fee Covers. This discusses what you will do for the Basic Fee.

[8] What the Basic Fee Does NOT Cover. This describes what is not included in the Basic Fee.

[9] Additional Work Fee Arrangement. How you will charge for the work that is not included in this Basic Fee.

[10] Minimum Fee. What the minimum fee will be.

[11] Out-of Pocket Costs. The client will not understand the difference between costs and fees, unless you explain it. This reinforces your explanation.

[12] Addition to Fees. Reinforce that out-of-pocket costs are in addition to fees.

[13] Engaging Other Attorneys to Assist. This allows you to get help at your expense if you are in over your head and need help.

[14] Payment Schedule. Set forth the cash flow that you have agreed upon, to avoid later misunderstandings

[15] Right to Terminate Services. It is important that the client understands your right to terminate services for nonpayment. In some jurisdictions there may be ethical considerations in domestic relations and criminal matters. This portion should satisfy the requirements of DR 2-110(C)(1)(e) so that you can withdraw when the client stops paying.

[16] Agreeing to Cooperate and Be Truthful. This may be the basis of your motion to be relieved as counsel at a later time.

[17] Your Opinion of the Merits of the Case. Repeat in a letter what you told the client in the office, and that what you said was based upon the facts that were given you. (Obviously, you may use this part of your letter to state that you are not yet in a position to express an opinion as to the outcome, or that you won't be able to express an opinion until research is done or

until discovery is underway or completed.) In some types of work, you can quote dollar amounts. In some types, such as personal injury, you should not. Always repeat in writing what you did or did not say in the office to prevent later problems when the client claims you quoted a large recovery.

[18] Explain Judgments. Be sure the client is aware that winning a case and getting a judgment for fees and costs is not the same as getting cash, and that many judgments are uncollectible.

[19] No Guarantees. The client should understand that you have not guaranteed the outcome, and that it is possible that the funds expended on legal fees won't guarantee results.

[20] Tell Client Not to Delay. Warn the prospective client in lay language not to delay. Warn the prospective client that laches or a statute of limitations can prejudice the case if there are delays. Do not express an opinion on the statute date, unless you are engaged to do so. If you gave the client the wrong date, you could have malpractice liability.

[21] Signing and Returning Copy of Letter. Obviously, the signed copy in effect becomes a fee contract when returned to you.

[22] Trust Account Rules—Explain IOLTA. IOLTA rules may vary from state to state. You have to comply with your IOLTA rules and also comply with your fiduciary duties to your client. In some states IOLTA is mandatory. In some states it is optional or "opt out." Be careful when the amount of net interest that could be earned on your client's funds might exceed bank charges. Refer to your local IOLTA rules and The ABA
Guide to Lawyer Trust Accounts, which I wrote.

[23] Repeat that both letter and check should be returned.

[24] Set Date for Return of Engagement Letter. Clearly indicate that you will assume the "client" has obtained other help to prevent the "client" coming in two years later claiming you undertook the case even though you never heard from the client again. Let there be no misunderstanding that you are doing nothing further until you receive the signed fee agreement and the check.

[25] Clarify Any Loose Ends. Give the client an opportunity to ask if anything is not clear.

[26] Have the Client Sign the Fee Agreement, and Get Your Retainer for Fees and Costs. Upon execution and return of the fee agreement, you have a client, and the client has a lawyer.

Other items to consider in your fee agreement:

1. Existence or nonexistence of malpractice insurance. This disclosure may be required in some states.

2. Possibly include a schedule of anticipated fees and costs, including faxes, photo reproduction, possible experts, depositions, and charges for file retrieval and copying after the case is closed.

3. Special provisions for potential conflict waivers.

4. Special provisions for multiple client representation.

5. Late payment penalties.

6. Who does or does not get copies of correspondence.

7. Where and how communications can be sent.

8. Requirement that fee disputes be arbitrated if allowed or re quired by local rules.

9. Relationship to third parties who guarantee or pay fees.

. . . .

*How to Set Your Fees*

No matter how long you practice law you'll make a lot of mistakes when you set fees. As a new lawyer you are obviously more vulnerable to making mistakes in fee setting than the more experience lawyers.

There are no simple formulas for fee setting. Platitudes are plentiful and concrete advice is hard to come by. Acknowledging in advance my inability to give you a simple panacea, I'll try in this chapter to give you general rules for fee setting, emphasizing the problems you'll encounter in the early part of your career. Hopefully you won't quote $3,000 for a fee when you should have quoted a $300 fee, or vice versa.

Fee Surveys

The Law Practice Management committee or section of your state or local bar association probably conducts periodic surveys of prevailing fees being charged by firms for given types of work. These fee surveys are typically done by firm size. Bar associations don't like to disseminate these survey results for fear they will be equated with the old minimum fee schedules, which are generally not used anymore. You may have to ask the Economics Chair of your bar association to get this information.

Other Lawyers

In my opinion the smartest thing you can do to get a handle on fee setting is to ask another lawyer. The other experienced lawyer give you some help in ascertaining the important factors that will affect fees and costs. If you explain to the other lawyer that you don't know what you are doing he or she will help you. Obviously you will get only generalizations. These generalizations are much better than nothing.

Contingency Fees

Contingency fees are common in some types of work such as personal injury and are absolutely prohibited in other areas such as criminal matters or domestic relations.

1. *Personal Injury/Auto Accident.* Fees are commonly quoted by formulas such as "one-third if no lawsuit is necessary or 40 percent if a lawsuit is necessary" or "one-fourth if settled before filing of suit or 40 percent if settled after suit is filed but before 30 days of trial date and 50 percent if tried or settled within 30 days of trial."

2. *Personal Injury/Assault and Battery.* Fees of 40 percent to 50 percent with a cash minimum fee of $300 to $600 or more paid in advance are common. Collection of judgments is difficult as there is often no insurance.

3. *Personal Injury/Slip Fall.* Fees of 45 percent to 50 percent are common due to difficulty of establishing liability.

4. *Personal Injury/Medical Negligence.* Usually slightly higher than personal injury auto accident due to high cost of preparation of case and difficulty of settlement until you are "on the courthouse steps."

5. *Workers' Compensation.* Depends on local practice. Private fee contracts not permitted or valid in some jurisdictions. A private fee agreement may even be illegal.

6. *Commercial Collections.* Usually 25 percent to one-third of collections, based upon amount involved.

Lump Sum Fees

This involves setting a lump sum fee regardless of how little or how much work is involved. This is very common in criminal matters and domestic relations. Although this method has the greatest potential for being grossly unfair to either the client or the lawyer, it seems to be the most desired by clients who prefer a fixed fee. Since both you and the client will be relatively unsophisticated, this method is probably best for both of you.

A word of advice. If you grossly underestimated the fee, that's your mistake, not the client's. Continue doing the very best, job you can on the case. When you finish the case tell the client what you should have charged. About one time in twenty-five a client will offer to pay the difference to bring the fee to the proper amount. Be careful not to suggest that the difference be paid. As with friends and relatives, the client has no way of knowing the value of the services unless you tell him or her. If you did $4,000 of work for $1,500 tell the client. The client should know the value of what has been received and that you're a person of your word. The client will respect you and use you again.

Minimum-Maximum Lump Sum Fees

For the new lawyer this method is also good when you can't get an accurate handle on the exact amount. Give the client a range of minimum to maximum. For example: "I cannot give you an exact fee quotation at this time since the amount of work required will depend upon how aggressively the other side fights. The minimum fee will be $500 and the maximum, to and including trial, will be $5,000." Minimum fees must be "reasonable" or they will be refundable.

Hourly Rates

I don't recommend the use of hourly rates in the first several months for new lawyers for two reasons:

1. The time you devote to a matter in many instances will be inordinate due to your inexperience. It's not unusual for something to take you twelve hours the first time, including research and drafting, because you are starting from ground zero. The second time, using your form file as an aid, it may only take six hours; the third time perhaps only three hours and the fourth time one hour or less. There are many things I can do now in an hour that took me from ten to thirty hours the first time I did it. Based on purely hourly rates the inexperienced lawyer will be more highly compensated than the more experienced lawyer.

2. You'll frighten the client away. It is difficult if not impossible to quote an hourly rate of $150 per hour to someone who earns $85 per day. There simply is no communication between you. If you estimate that the work should reasonably take ten to fifteen hours and you want $100 per hour, then tell the client the cost will be between $1,000 and $1,500 and don mention time.

Sophisticated business executives are used to being charged on an hourly rate; lower-and middle-class people are not used to paying on an hourly rate.

After you've been in practice six months or so you'll have enough back round to be able to quote hourly rates where appropriate.

Fee by Stages

There will be cases where you simply cannot quote lump sum fees and where you don't want to quote hourly rates. You should try to break the work into "stages," estimating the work for each stage and then setting a fee for each stage as you go. An example would be as follows:

1. Research as to merits of case and written opinion: $350

2. If I believe the case is meritorious and collectible, our fee will be one-third of recovery, giving you credit for $350 paid.

3. If I believe the case has uncertain merit or uncertain collectability, you may use other counsel with no further obligation to us or you may proceed further as set forth.

4. Drafting of complaint: $350.

5. Law and motion appearances (prior to answer): $750 (includes two appearances if necessary; additional preparation and appearances $300 each if required).

6. Propounding or answering written interrogatories (four sets anticipated): each $100.

7. Deposition preparation and attendance: $300 per deposition of less than four hours, or $650 if more than four hours and less than ten hours.

8. Trial estimated (five days): $750 per day.

9. All other services not covered above: $100 per hour.

10. You may stop using our services at any stage simply by so notifying us. If we accept the case on a contingency basis and you subsequently discharge us, our fee will be the greater of one-third of any offers received prior to or within five days of being terminated or $100 per hour. If we decide not to proceed further after taking the case on a contingency, then you will have no further obligation past the $350 and out-of-pocket costs advanced.

Bonuses

I personally believe that fees should be related to results. I pay substantial bonuses to employees based upon money they earn for the firm or money they save the firm with management suggestions and secretarial productivity. I also believe in billing clients over and above the agreed hourly rate when we accomplish unusually good results for the client. On the other hand I sometimes reduce a fee below the agreed hourly rate when the results are poor for the client. I have rejected substantial fees based upon purely hourly compensation where the client was not agreeable to a bonus. I have refused to accept a case based on a purely hourly basis, where I would have earned between $25,000 and $50,000, because the client was not agreeable to a bonus of 10 percent of the amount saved. The amount in the case was in excess of $1,200,000, with another $300,000 in interest and penalties involved. I was not about to accept professional responsibility for $1,500,000 for 2 percent to 3 percent of the amount involved. I would have been happy to accept the fee arrangement if the amount involved had been about $500,000.

While the numbers involved here may be beyond what you can reasonably expect in your first year or two, the concept is the same for smaller amounts.

It goes without saying that the "bonus" must be agreed to in concept if not in exact amount as soon as possible in the case. The concept of a fee predicated in part upon the results obtained and the amount involved is recognized by most existing state bar rules.

Setting Fees after the First Year or Two

After you've been in practice a year or two, much of the mystery in the fee-setting process will be removed, although some will always remain. You may wish to use different methods. examples of which follow (these methods are not necessarily recommended):

1. *Supply and Demand.* Charge all you can get in each case, subject to the fee not being unconscionable or "clearly excessive."
2. *Follow the Leader.* Charge what your contemporaries charge on the theory that they know what they are doing (a premise of doubtful reliability).
3. *Take What the Client Pays and Be Grateful.* This is a sure way to bankruptcy court (your personal bankruptcy). Remember that even churches doing the work of God have to close when their parishioners don't give enough.
4. *Decide Your Own Value:*
   a. Estimate the number of chargeable hours you work per year (Factor CH).
   b. Set the net dollar profit you wish to earn per year (Factor P).
   c. Estimate your overhead per year (Factor 0).
   d. Hourly rate = (P + 0) divided by CH.
5. *The Big Mac Formula of Fee Charging.* McDonald's is one of the world's most sophisticated marketing companies. They operate thousands of stores all over the world. Their prices in any given store reflect local labor, food, and other operating costs. Their prices also reflect the economic abilities of local buyers to pay for their products. The product is uniform; it is the price that changes depending on local costs and the local economy.

It has been suggested that a law firm in a community could base their hourly rates on the price that McDonald's charges for a Big Mac in the community.

Guidelines might be as follows:

| | Price of a big Mac/$1.50 |
|---|---|
| Clerk Not Yet Admitted: | 50 times price = $75 per hour |
| Brand New Lawyer: | 100 times price = $150 per hour |
| After One Year: | 110 times price = $165 per hour |
| After Two Years: | 120 times price = $180 per hour |
| After Three Years: | 130 times price = $195 per hour |
| After Four Years: | 140 times price = $210 per hour |
| Five to Ten Years: | 150 times price = $225 per hour |

It goes without saying that prices of many goods and services including lawyers is going to be higher in Manhattan than in a small community in Montana or North Dakota. Many large multinational companies get much of their legal work done in smaller communities throughout the United States where hourly rates and operating costs are lower than in their headquarters city.

The new lawyer should also not be afraid to raise his or her hour rate to reflect experience levels.

You might wish to play with the numbers based on local hourly rates, but this method may be of help to you.

Legal Fees and the Code of Professional Responsibility

The ABA Model Rules of Professional Conduct cover fees in Model Rules 1.15(a) and (d). Unfortunately, the code is of limited help to the new lawyer. It is very helpful in analyzing a situation in retrospect, but isn't very helpful to the new lawyer who wants to quote a fee to the client sitting across a desk.

I suggest you read Model Rule 1.15 and try to apply it within the context of the suggestions in this chapter.

Should You Charge for the Initial Consultation?

Our firm does not charge separately for the first consultation. We feel that the public should not be afraid to see a lawyer when they want to find out if they need professional help. After we have gotten the facts we advise them that they do or that they don't require professional help. (See points 3 and 4 in sample fee representation letter in "The Fee and Representation Letter" chapter.) We include the initial consultation services in the first bill if we do further services for the client.

Other lawyers tell the prospective client to bring a check to the initial interview. I feel that demanding a fee in advance for the first consultation leaves the public and potential clients with the impression that the lawyer is more interested in making money than in helping the client.

I have no proof, but I feel that our method gives the clients respect and confidence and encourages candor in relating the facts. I also feel that the client understands that we are sincerely trying to help.

Costs

Be sure to cover the subject of out of pocket costs. Filing fees, medical reports, depositions, expert witnesses,)jury fees etc., can cost more than a potential recovery. To the client, fees and costs may be indistinguishable. Be sure you look up your local ethics rules on advancing litigation related costs such as filing fees and non litigation related costs such as car rental. If you advertise "No Recovery No Fee" you may be required to warn a client about costs if the case is lost.

---

## NOTES AND QUESTIONS

(1) *Retainer Agreement.* Does it appear to you that the advice offered by Foonberg reflects an excessive preoccupation with money? On its face, it may give that impression. On the other side of the question, it may be worth considering that lawyers surprisingly earn lower average annual incomes than individuals in other professions requiring similar education (physicians earn roughly double the average). Does this factor change the picture? Additionally, one might take

the position that a lawyer who follows Foonberg's advice can "clear the decks" so as to be able to do the best possible job for the client rather than working at an excessive number of marginally paying matters, and can also take on more matters solely because of the principles involved in them. Do these arguments support the approach of Foonberg?

Even if you disagree with Foonberg, it is probably good that you are exposed to his ideas.

(2) *Establishing the Relationship and the Fee Agreement.* A major portion of the advice offered by Foonberg concerning the fee and representation letter is an effort to avoid professional malpractice or even accusations of malpractice. Can you see how this is so? Why, for example, is it important to state in writing that a lawyer is required to handle the client's problem? Why is it important to get across to the client (or rather, potential client) that the lawyer does not yet represent the client? Why is it necessary to tell the client not to delay?

(3) *The Scope of the Representation.* A portion of the representation letter is also concerned with avoiding misunderstandings about the obligations of the lawyer if representation is undertaken. Why is it important to spell out carefully the matter on which the lawyer is considering accepting responsibility? What could happen if the contract did not specify? Why does the contract so carefully indicate the monetary aspects of the fee arrangement? Why is it important to indicate in the contract itself that the lawyer has the ability to withdraw?

There are some lawyers who take the position that any disagreement between lawyer and client over the fee or nature of the representation is the lawyer's own fault. While this position is extreme, it does (correctly) embody the principle that many misunderstandings over such matters are preventable.

(4) *The Client's Obligations.* How much of the fee and representation letter should be concerned with obligations of the client? For example, does the client have an obligation to keep in touch with the lawyer if the client changes his or her address (a frequent and serious problem)? What does the lawyer do if the client is "too nervous" to have a deposition taken by the opponent and refuses to appear (a not unheard-of problem)? Finally, what does the lawyer do if, in a contingent fee case in which the lawyer has invested considerable time and money, the client insists on perjury or requests an unethical course of conduct for the lawyer? Can these matters be covered in a written document, and is it worthwhile to do so?

Note that the form contract from W. Dorsaneo, *Texas Litigation Guide*, excerpted above, has a section covering "Cooperation of Client." There are varying schools of thought as to whether it is best to set forth a general duty to cooperate or whether it is better to specify by listing a number of duties the client is to perform, together with an explicit statement that the attorney may withdraw and collect the earned portion of the fee on breach.

(5) *Discuss Fees Sooner Rather Than Later.* Professor Dorsaneo indicates that "an attorney should not hesitate to discuss fees with the client on the first visit." You may be surprised to learn that there is virtual unanimity among writers on this conclusion. The reason is apparently that clients themselves wish to have the matter clarified. Of course, the problem with discussing fees at the first visit is that the attorney generally does not yet know how much effort it will take to solve the client's problem. Accordingly, the setting of fees is an art, and a very important one for the lawyer to learn. What disadvantageous consequences can occur if a lawyer overestimates the time and effort required and quotes a fee arrangement that is too high? What disadvantages flow from setting a fee that is too low?

What techniques can be used to avoid the "shot-in-the-dark" approach to fee setting?

(6) *Adversarial Client Relationships*. Does it appear from these materials that the lawyer may sometimes have an adversarial relationship with his or her own client?

If that thought seems disturbing, consider the matter this way. A stranger to the lawyer has just contacted the lawyer and has asked him or her to spend time and money to pursue a claim, the merits of which the lawyer has heard only from the prospective client, a stranger. The lawyer has no accurate way to judge whether the stranger is telling the truth. The action the stranger is requesting is that the lawyer initiate a suit, an act which, by itself, will cause harm and expense to another party, the defendant. The lawyer also does not know whether the stranger will pay for the lawyer's efforts, will fulfill his or her own obligations, or will look for opportunities to accuse the lawyer of wrongdoing. It is not that the lawyer assumes the worst about these matters, it is simply that the lawyer does not know.

Is this picture overdrawn?

(7) *Enforcing the Fee Contract*. What should be done about the situation in which the lawyer does considerable work and spends money on a case only to find that the client has previously hired another lawyer? What of the lawyer who is "fired" by the client after spending considerable effort and money? Does the device of assigning an interest in the litigation provide adequate protection? How else can a lawyer protect himself or herself? Note that the situation of the client who hires two separate lawyers without telling either about the other is not unknown. The problem can be an acute one for personal injury lawyers who loan money to their clients!

(8) *Suing the Client*. In *Jamail v. Thomas,* 481 S.W.2d 485 (Tex. Civ. App.—Houston [1st Dist.] 1972, writ ref'd n.r.e.), an attorney sued several persons, including an insurance company and a husband and wife alleged to be his former clients. The gist of the claim was the allegation that the insurer and the putative clients had entered into a settlement without the lawyer's assent, thus creating an alleged breach of contract with the clients and an alleged tortious interference with the contract by the insurer.

The court refused the claim, largely because it upheld jury findings to the effect that there was no contract. The contract, which had been signed by the husband, assigned a 40 percent interest in "my (our) cause of action." The injury, however, had been to the wife, and the court held that the right to compensation was a right over which she had management and control under Texas law. The jury's findings established that the wife had not ratified the contract, nor was the husband her agent.

The fact pattern of *Jamail v. Thomas* may be unusual, but the dilemma it poses is not. An attorney generally undertakes representation of a client without knowledge of the full situation. The attorney may make a considerable investment in the case only to find that it has been wasted. How could the result in *Jamail v. Thomas* and in similar situations be avoided? The problem of the client who does not have the rights he or she purports to assert is not an uncommon one. The following notes deal with the dilemma that is posed.

(9) *Withdrawal of Counsel*. One of the problems (from the lawyer's standpoint) about the attorney-client relationship is that it can, at times, be a difficult one to terminate. If one is attorney of record in a litigation matter, termination is not accomplished merely by the attorney's unilateral decision, nor is it accomplished even by the agreement of the client. A motion to withdraw should be filed with the court, accompanied by a proposed form of order, indicating whether the withdrawal is with the client's consent and, if not, the reasons. Although such a motion will ordinarily be granted, the court is not required to grant it (except in exceptional circumstances

such as those posing a conflict of interest). In particular, a tardy motion may be denied if it would result in delay. A lawyer may be required to spend valuable time and money when previous time and money have been uncompensated (or worse, be forced to represent the views of a client with whom the attorney has serious personality or ethical differences).

Foonberg advises a series of steps leaving a clear record of communications when the lawyer anticipates the need to withdraw. J. Foonberg, *How to Start and Build a Law Practice* 102–109 (4th ed. 1999).

## § 1.03 Case Evaluation, Acceptance, and Settlement

The vast majority of cases (probably in excess of 90 percent of cases filed) are settled without trial. Another very substantial proportion of litigation is settled without suit being filed. Consequently, ascertaining the "settlement value" of a case is integral to proper case evaluation. It is important to realize that this process is not a low form of intellectual endeavor, and it is not done without effort and work.

These materials cover the techniques involved in evaluating a case and negotiating for fair settlement value. The procedure involved in the settlement process and the documents produced thereby will be covered in Chapter 11, *Disposition Without Trial.*

### D. Reneker, GEARY, STAHL AND SPENCER LITIGATION SECTION ORIENTATION*

. . . .

*Settlements.* The majority of the litigation matters the firm handles are concluded by means of compromise settlements that are negotiated by the lawyers with the consent of the clients. Accordingly, the prospects of settlement should be borne in mind throughout each stage of the litigation process.

The client makes the final decision as to whether a case is to be settled, and on what basis. For this reason, it is never appropriate for us to commit to a settlement without the client's express authorization. The client's decision, however, as to whether and on what terms to settle should not be made on the basis of his layman's view of the case; to the contrary, it should be made only after we have given the client the benefit of our recommendations.

In order for us to make appropriate recommendations about settlement, we must make an analysis of the case for the purpose of determining its "settlement value." The "settlement value" of a case is the amount a reasonable plaintiff would accept or a reasonable defendant would pay to avoid the risks inherent in a trial, given a full understanding of all significant factors in the case.

The significant factors to be analyzed in determining the reasonable settlement value of a case are (1) liability, (2) damages, and (3) ability to pay. The manner in which these factors relate to each other is best described by the use of several examples of situations that may arise within a general factual framework. Assume a personal injury case involving a two-car automobile collision. One of the cars was driven by our client, the plaintiff, who is a wealthy businessman, age 45, with a demonstrated ability to earn over $100,000 per year. The other car was driven by the defendant, a retired schoolteacher, age 75, who has no non-exempt assets and whose income consists of a pension and social security benefits.

---

* Reprinted by permission of Geary, Stahl & Spencer.

EXAMPLE NO. 1

*Liability:* Undisputed evidence shows that defendant ran a red light.

*Damages:* Plaintiff suffered severe brain damage, can no longer work and requires constant medical care.

*Ability to Pay:* Defendant carries liability insurance that provides coverage up to $1,000,000.

*Settlement Value:* Very high.

EXAMPLE NO. 2

*Liability:* Evidence conflicts as to which party ran red light.

*Damages:* Plaintiff suffered severe brain damage, can no longer work and requires constant medical care.

*Ability to Pay:* Defendant carries liability insurance that provides coverage up to $1,000,000.

*Settlement Value:* Moderate; discount due to reduced liability factor.

EXAMPLE NO. 3

*Liability:* Undisputed evidence shows that defendant ran a red light.

*Damages:* Plaintiff suffered cuts and bruises and no lost time from work and required minimal medical care.

*Ability to Pay:* Defendant carries liability insurance that provides coverage up to $1,000,000.

*Settlement Value:* Nominal; discount due to reduced damages.

EXAMPLE NO. 4

*Liability:* Undisputed evidence shows that defendant ran a red light.

*Damages:* Plaintiff suffered severe brain damage, can no longer work and requires constant medical care.

*Ability to Pay:* Defendant uninsured.

*Settlement Value:* Nominal; discount due to lack of ability to pay.

We normally make our recommendations with a view toward the reasonable settlement value of a case. This is not to say, however, that the client is bound to accept our recommendations. As you will learn, however, the client will be more likely to accept our recommendations if he has been conditioned to do so from the outset and has been given reason to have confidence in our ability to give sound advice.

Settlements are normally reached through the process of negotiation, which involves offers and counter-offers. No attempt will be made here to review all the tactics that may be involved in negotiating with another lawyer. Several broad principles, however, are generally applicable. First of all, the opposing lawyer is not likely to want to "talk settlement" until he is generally familiar with the strengths and weakness of his case. Secondly, it is usually incumbent on the claimant to make the first offer. Thirdly, an offer once made, to which no response is given, should be withdrawn within a reasonable time; or, conversely, a time frame within which the offer must be accepted or rejected may be established when the offer is made. Finally, once an offer is made, a counter-offer is appropriate; accordingly, we should not "bargain with ourselves" by making a lower offer, if the first offer is rejected and no counter-offer is made.

Once a settlement is orally agreed to between the lawyers and the parties, it must be fully documented in writing as soon as practicable. Settlement documents may consist, in some cases, of no more than a release from one party to the other. Ordinarily, however, they are much more involved because many settlements contain terms that require actions other than the payment of money. The nature and extent of the settlement documents will depend on the nature of the case. The objective, of course, is to resolve all disputes between the parties, leaving no "loose ends," and to fully and fairly set forth the terms that have been agreed on, so that there can be absolutely no question about what is intended, what constitutes performance, what constitutes default and what rights and remedies are available to the parties upon performance or default, as the case may be.

. . . .

---

## D. Crump, FACTORS IN CASE EVALUATION, ACCEPTANCE OR SETTLEMENT

*Law Practice Skills Advice and Problem Book A-44 (1977)**

1. *Cost of suit or defense* is a major factor. Is the suit going to be one that can be adequately prepared by ordinary discovery, or is it in a complex area of the law, with expert testimony probably required, in a distant forum?
2. *Probability of Establishing Liability.* How likely is it that the defendant will be held liable?
3. *Damages.* A clearcut case on liability is not useful if the cost of winning will exceed the amount of damages you can reasonably expect.
4. *Solvency of the Defendant.* A judgment for one million dollars will do you no good if you can't collect it. For this reason, suits against most individuals are less attractive prospects to plaintiff's lawyers than suits against so-called "target" defendants.
   In addition to these four major factors—cost of litigation, probability of liability, damages and collectability of the judgment—there are several subsidiary questions:
5. *The Nature of the Suit.* The lawyer may take on a litigation matter without expecting to make a fair fee (but if he does, he should do so with his eyes open).
6. *Principle or Reputation.* The client may be willing to pay more than it is worth to bring the suit—because there is other "worth" to the plaintiff in not allowing the defendant to get away with what he has done. Or a defendant may desire to spend millions for defense but not one cent for tribute.
7. *The Lawyer's Situation.* The lawyer can sometimes afford to fill marginal time with matters that pay less than the bulk of his practice (but the tendency to do so on long-term matters should be avoided).

A host of subsidiary matters affects these considerations. Lawyers become adept at recognizing that slip-and-falls are not good plaintiff's cases because liability is hard to establish, "emotional-harm" cases are not good because they do not usually prompt large damage awards, medical malpractice cases are very expensive to litigate, collection of professional accounts is difficult

---

because the debtors are often unable to pay or have resistance because they did not like the service, etc. The lawyer does well to refuse such matters as plaintiff's counsel even if there seems an outside chance of success.

---

## NOTE

*Case Evaluation.* Lawyers who have had litigation experience tend to recognize kinds of cases and clients that should be avoided. In general, the cases fall into two categories: those in which the facts, regardless of the initial appearance, are likely to turn out adversely, and those in which the kind of case or client is likely to create more headaches for the lawyer than the worth of the case would justify.

Foonberg, for example, lists cases in which there have been two or three prior lawyers, cases involving "hurt feelings," landlord-tenant cases, and slip and fall cases, among others. He advises not taking divorce cases for people heavily in debt or criminal cases or bankruptcy cases unless paid in advance. Clients who claim they are suing out of "principle," clients who use the lawyer's secretary or office to do their personal business and clients who proclaim that the opposition will settle because they can't afford the "publicity" are among the kinds of people, according to Foonberg, to avoid. J. Foonberg, *How to Start and Build a Law Practice* 202–205 (4th ed. 1999).

In some such cases, the problem is that liability or damages will be difficult to establish before a jury. "Emotional harm" cases, for some reason, simply do not appeal to juries as deserving high damages nearly as often as they do to new law school graduates. An assault between neighbors is likely to evoke the reaction, "A pox on both their houses." *See generally* H. Kalven and H. Zeisel, The American Jury (1966).

In other cases, the problem is a client who will require hand-holding or other attention out of proportion to the value of the claim or who will be dissatisfied no matter what the outcome. A client who presumptuously uses the lawyer's facilities for personal business and a client who is overly concerned about principle when the real dispute is over money are likely to fall into this category.

Of course, there are exceptions. Sometimes, high verdicts are won in emotional harm or slip and fall cases and sometimes a client who has had two prior lawyers will get along famously with the third. The point is to recognize the danger signals.

---

## D. Crump, CASE ANALYSIS AND EVALUATION PROBLEMS

*Law Practice Skills Advice and Problem Book A-42–A-43 (1977)**

In each of the following instances, decide what you would say to the potential client who has consulted you. Consider theories, investigation, expense of suit, probable responses by opponents, likelihood of success, etc.

1. Your potential client maintained a brokerage account with Simpson, Marwell & Co. in New York City where the account was serviced by a friend, John Starke. When Starke quit work at Simpson, Marwell, and moved to Baker, Putnam & Co., your client moved the account there. Starke has now disappeared. It now appears that Starke was addicted to drugs and "churned" the account while at Simpson, Marwell. ("Churning" means that he sold and purchased stocks for the purpose of getting commissions.) By the time that Starke had moved to Baker, Putnam & Co., he had apparently caused a portfolio worth $25,000 to decrease to $12,000. Simpson, Marwell has since become insolvent and has been taken over by the Securities Investors' Protective Corporation. However, before insolvency and while Simpson, Marwell was operating, though on the brink of insolvency, Baker, Putnam & Co. transferred $5,000 in commissions to Simpson, Marwell upon being billed by Simpson, Marwell against your client's account, without his authorization. Your client has now moved to Texas and consults you in your Houston office, relating to you the facts given here. What do you do?
2. Your potential client was driving down the Gulf Freeway one afternoon when a cloud of dust blew across the road. She slowed and stopped, or nearly stopped, because her visiblity was severely limited. Suddenly she was struck from behind by another automobile, which in turn was struck by another, and then by another. Your client suffered a broken arm and a broken ankle and hit her chest against the steering wheel. The woman in the car behind her suffered a broken nose and cheekbone, requiring a series of painful operations and continuing disability. Your client says that there was a sign about a half mile or so before the site of the accident that said, "Slow. Work on Highway," and because of this sign she had slowed to about 40 miles an hour before seeing the cloud of dust. These are the facts related to you by your potential client; what do you do?
3. Your potential client sold his business to one John Doakes, who gave him cash and a promissory note in response. The promissory note required payments of $2,500 a year for five years. Doakes has not made a payment now for three years. Your client is quite angry because Doakes drives an expensive car and eats in all the fanciest restaurants, and he owes your client $7,500 which he has not and will not pay. These are the facts as your client gives them to you; what do you do?
4. Decedent J was 16 years old and was in the pit crew area of the Lone Star International Motor Speedway when the Cyclops, a jet-powered racing car, started its run down the track as a special, unannounced crowd-pleaser event. When the Cyclops reached the pit area along the track, it suddenly veered sharply to the left, careened into the pit crew, and killed the decedent and two other people. No one knows exactly what happened. The Cyclops is a mass of twisted wreckage. Some persons on the scene saw the parachute open and say that it opened prematurely; others say it got fouled in an overhead walkway; others say there was an explosion and cloud of dust emanating from the left side of the Cyclops; many who saw it happen can't describe it very well because "it all happened too fast." J's parents have consulted you. They weren't there, but they have just told you these facts as they know them. What do you do?
5. Your client is a member of the New Saints Church, a religion claiming several hundred thousand members throughout the world. She met and married her now-deceased husband through the church. Both were regular in their attendance and attempted to follow the teachings of the faith in their regular lives. The New Saints Church is a Christian religion,

and it follows most of the teachings of other Christian sects, but it also seeks simplicity in all phases of life and death. The New Saints custom, which is a "law" of the Church, is that upon death the body is to be buried without embalming. Upon the death of her husband of a heart attack at the Hazelhurst Hospital, your client was given a sedative. She was also told that she would need to make arrangements to have his body transferred to a funeral home. Having heard of the Smithers Funeral Home, your client asked a nurse to call that institution; an ambulance driver came from there and picked up the body, giving her a form to sign releasing the body to the Home. She read it three times to ensure that it only released the body and did not allow embalming, and then signed it. A relative then took her home. Upon arriving home, she called the Smithers Funeral Home to ensure that the body would not be embalmed; she was assured that it had not. Three months later, while paying her bill, she discovered that Smithers had embalmed the body immediately upon its arrival at the Home. She has been seeing a psychiatrist regularly and has had increased difficulties with her hypoglycemia, and she says of the funeral home: "I would like to put them out of business." She cannot stop thinking about the incident and cries easily at inappropriate moments. These are the facts she relates to you; what do you do?

6. Your client was struck by a motorist who left the scene with tires squealing. Your client was a pedestrian and suffered paraplegic injuries. He is able to give you the last three digits of the license number, and say that the car was a maroon Chevrolet with a dent in the rear—and the year model was about four years ago. What do you do?

## § 1.04 Pre-Litigation Fact-Gathering: Investigation and Interviewing

### [A] Interviewing Techniques

THE CLIENT INTERVIEW

Interviewing is an art, but there is some science to it. Consider the following:

(1) In one of the case evaluation problems in this chapter, the lawyer was able to develop a claim against a defendant readers do not commonly see from the facts provided. Having learned from the client that she slowed and stopped on the freeway, the lawyer was able to prove causative fault of a company spreading lime dust nearby. The claim was discovered through careful interviewing.

(2) In *People v. Newton,* 8 Cal. App. 3d 359, 87 Cal. Rptr. 394 (1970), the defendant, accused of murder, testified that his stomach wound had felt as though "boiling hot soup" had been poured over him. The testimony probably affected the jury's verdict and was quoted by the appellate court, which reversed because the charge failed to instruct on an issue of voluntariness raised by this and other testimony. How do you suppose the defendant happened to use words of such vividness?

(3) In *Stevens v. Travelers Ins. Co.,* 563 S.W.2d 223 (Tex. 1978), the plaintiff's attorney found, through his client, a letter written by her deceased husband prior to his death. The lawyer was able to use this letter, together with a psychiatrist's testimony interpreting it, to rebut an insurer's defense of suicide. (The lawyer also uncovered four insurance

policies issued by separate companies, including one that was an incident of membership in an automobile club.) Would you have found these items?[1]

Good interviewing requires proper preparation, proper questioning, and proper interview structure. It requires the ability to break communications barriers. It requires the ability to detect and deal with intended or unintended falsehood.

*Structure: Beginning the Interview.* If the interviewee is a client, it is generally useful to begin the interview by finding out what the client wants.[2]

The point appears obvious and most lawyers observe it intuitively to some degree, but proper interviewing means encouraging the client to express, and express completely, what he or she wants, before moving on. "I want a divorce" may mean just that, or it may mean the opposite. "I've been sued and I don't know what to do" may lead to the conclusion that the client wants a little more time to pay and is fearful that this supplier will tell others of the default.

The best beginning may be to ask the client, "How may I serve you?" or some similarly broad question. It is equally important, though, to realize that the initial response may be incomplete. Probing may be in order. "How do you feel about that?" or "Tell me what consequences you see that this might have for you personally?" might be the kind of follow-up that would be appropriate.

Before discussing the structure of the remainder of the interview, it may be useful here to distinguish between "hard" and "soft" information, because the structure sometimes depends on that distinction.

*"Hard" and "Soft" Information.* Evidence that is clear, definite, and unlikely to be successfully disputed may be called "hard" evidence. Other information is "soft." In a contract dispute, for instance, an order form sent by one party and stamped with the other party's indication that it was received is relatively hard information. The recollection of one of the parties as to the contents of a telephone call, on the other hand, is relatively soft information.

Generally speaking, it is best to assemble hard points of data first to the extent they are available and then fill in the gaps with soft information. That is to say, the best approach may be to collect all pieces of paper related to the dispute, put them in chronological order and then attempt to reconstruct the remainder of the story with the aid of the chronology thus established.

Several further points about this principle need explanation. First, it is important to realize that "hard" and "soft" are relative terms. A document may turn out to be false, misleading, or ambiguous. A telephone conversation may become a hard data point if it is the subject of identical and positive recollection by both parties. One must, therefore, be willing to consider even the "hard" structure as changeable. Second, "soft" information may be just as valuable as "hard." The most important issues in the case may be, and frequently are, controlled more by soft than by hard evidence; this is because soft evidence is susceptible to differing versions. The versions naturally take the shape of the disputants' interests and become the battleground of the case. Third, although every case has some hard information, there are great differences in the degree to which hard information controls the interview process.

---

[1] Conversely, each of the authors of this book has had the experience of discovering, after having filed suit, a document signed by the client destroying the claim—an experience that will be shared in the future by some readers of this book!

[2] As to interview structure, *see, e.g.*, T. Shaffer, E. Polen & J. Elkins, *Legal Interviewing and Counseling*, 72–74 (1997).

If the case is one in which hard information is voluminous, the collection of that hard information ordinarily must precede an in-depth reconstruction of the event. It may be possible to have the client collect the hard data in advance. If not, sequential interviews will likely be necessary. It may be advisable in any event to obtain an overview before looking for hard information.

*Structure: The Interview as a Whole.* The structure of the interview thus depends somewhat on whether the available hard data have been assimilated. After the problem identification stage at the beginning of the interview, it may be advisable to pause to collect further hard information or it may not, depending on the situation. If the interview is continued, the remainder of the interview may be concerned with three categories of activity: "Getting out the story," formulating theories or proposed courses of action, and testing the theories.

First, getting the story: This aspect of the interview is usually best conducted in a chronological manner. There are essentially two problems with a chronological approach: finding an appropriate starting point, and proceeding, step-by-step, without getting sidetracked or missing an important item. These are more formidable problems than they appear. For example, if the lawyer asks, "When did this all begin?" and the response is, "In 1969, when I met my partner," does the lawyer develop the story chronologically by asking for a complete statement of the relationship between the client and the partner, or does the lawyer do better to say, "And what was the next important event?"

Second, formulating courses of action: It is important to be tentative at this stage. In the litigation context, this step generally consists of formulating theories about the situation.

Third, testing the theories: If the lawyer has tentatively identified a defense of self-defense to an assault suit, or a fraud claim against the partner, the lawyer should not conclude the interview without comparing the elements of that legal theory against the facts the client can furnish. In other words, the lawyer should test the theory.

To recapitulate: A well-structured client interview would begin with a complete examination of the client's own conception of his or her desires. "What can I do to help you?" "Have you told me everything about this that bothers you?" The next step would be a chronological development of the story. "Suppose we go back to the beginning and you tell me what happened." "Is that really where it started?" This development may require careful direction to keep from getting sidetracked. Next, there should be formulation of integrating theories in a tentative way and the testing of these theories against the client's perceptions.

*Questioning Techniques.* There are many different kinds of questions. One of the most fundamental distinctions is that between leading and non-leading questions. "You were frightened, right?" is more leading than "Tell me how you felt." The leading question is susceptible to a greater danger of producing misleading information, but it is sometimes necessary for direction of the interview or to test a hypothesis.

Sometimes, "questioning" may be done by utterances that do not seem to involve questions at all. Reflecting the client's statements back to him or her, or what is called "active listening" (consisting of reactions indicating absorption of the client's statements) may be considered questioning techniques in that they prompt the client to provide further information. "Let me see whether I understand what you're saying . . ." or simply "I see, uh-huh," are examples of these techniques. At the opposite end of the spectrum, urging a position or rejecting one ("Oh, no, I certainly wouldn't say that") are techniques akin to questioning. The different approaches might be thought of as falling along a continuum from least leading or suggestive to most leading with silence (or active listening) at the lower end of the spectrum, non-leading questioning or reflection in the middle, and urging or rejection at the higher end.

*The Funnel Sequence.*[3] It follows from this discussion of question types that some should be used in some situations, others in other situations. It is inadvisable to begin a client interview pertaining to a complex event by asking the client a highly leading question. Likewise, once the client has exhausted the narrative possibilities, it is not appropriate to say, "Uh-huh, I see" and leave the matter at that. The sequence that is usually best is the opposite of this example: a sequence from less-leading to more-leading questions. To be more descriptive, a proper sequence often resembles a funnel, in that it starts with broad questions and proceeds to narrower ones. Writers in the area describe the sequence as "funnelling" or "T-funnelling" (the latter signifying that one questions broadly, across the bar of the "T," before zeroing in on particulars). An upside-down metaphor to similar effect is the pyramid, which has a broad base and builds to a narrow point.

The technique is easier to describe than it is to apply. The trickiest part is to know when and how to switch from broad to narrow questions. Switching too early may well cause important details to be missed. Switching too late can cause a half-hour interview to consume an afternoon, and it can mean failure to get to necessary subjects. The most common problem, however, is missed details because the lawyer does not know of them and the client does not see their relevance. "Why didn't you tell me that?" "Because you didn't ask," is the result that a switch too early from broad to narrow questions may produce.

As in the beginning of the interview, it is important in the funnel sequence to "squeeze" the client (here the metaphor being that of a sponge), albeit gently. The message should be, "Have you told me everything?" Example:

> Tell me what happened.
>
> I went in the bar and he hit me.
>
> Can you tell me a little more about how it happened?
>
> Well, I was walking to my table, and he come up to me and says, "What did you say?" and I says, "I didn't say anything."

Notice that the interviewer has resisted the temptation, after the first question and answer, to proceed to narrower questions, because the "squeezing" process has only begun. The squeeze produces more, but still incomplete, information. What should be the next question? An interviewer might ask: "Do you suppose he might have mistaken you for someone else?," but that would not be the sort of question the funnel sequence would dictate. "What led up to his saying that?" or better yet, "Can you tell me more about what happened?" would be more in line with the funnel sequence. The dangers of the leading question at this stage are twofold: it detracts from the client's free-form narrative, which may uncover useful information to which it is unlikely the lawyer will direct a specific question, and furthermore, it may suggest to the client a direction the interviewer wants the client to take with all subsequent responses.

After the client has been thoroughly squeezed, the interviewer is ready to explore aspects the lawyer has seen but the client has not. For instance, the setting. What was the bar like? The

---

[3] For a discussion of the funnel sequence and of questioning types, *see, e.g.,* R. Gorden, *Interviewing: Strategy, Techniques and Tactics* 265–289 (1969).

questioning should begin at that level of generality, not with "How many people were there in the bar?" or "Was it dark?" The question, "What was the bar like?" is intermediate in the funnel sequence. It is important, eventually, to ask about the number of people and the lighting after the client's narrative potential has been exhausted by broader questions and careful squeezing.

*Preparation; Interviewing Forms.* Interview forms or checklists are useful, but there is a wide variety of views about their proper place. Some lawyers use long and detailed checklists. Some use forms to be filled out by clients. Others use neither or use checklists only as a vague guide.

The degree to which interview forms can be useful depends on several factors, including the kind of information to be gathered, the frequency with which the attorney gathers this kind of information, the nature of the clientele and the personality of the individual client. For gathering personal data on the client, forms are quite useful. Thus, in obtaining the client's name, address, telephone, employment location, next of kin, and the like, forms are a means of ensuring complete, accurate, and efficient data collection. For certain information in certain types of cases—property and income information in a divorce case, the factors necessary for a commercial collection suit, the damage and liability factors in an automobile collision case—forms may likewise be extremely useful.

Should the client be asked to fill out a form, or should the attorney question from it? The answer depends on the complexity of the questions and the nature of the client. If the form is longer than one or two pages, the sheer intimidation factor, surprisingly, may dictate against its use. Many clients, even intelligent ones, will be incapable of filling in a form of any complexity without assistance—and clients who are intelligent enough are sometimes offended. A few lawyers are successful in sending interview forms in the mail in advance of the interview. Doing so requires great sensitivity and willingness to consider that the client may appear without the form filled in (or may be offended or intimidated by it), but pays great dividends if done successfully.

The obtaining of information or documents by the client in advance is another important problem. In general, it is better to tell the client to be inclusive in bringing documents. Don't say, "Bring me that life insurance policy." Instead, say: "Go through your house from top to bottom and bring me everything that has the word insurance on it or has anything to do with insurance." Deciding that a homeowner's policy, or a liability policy, or some other kind of insurance policy does not cover the event is a task to be done by the lawyer, not the client.

In the office, the lawyer may interview the client in free-flow fashion and then have the client fill in a form or write a narrative. Another alternative may be to have a legal assistant conduct a more in-depth interview or assist the client to fill in a form. Forms and free-flow interviewing should be viewed as complementing each other. It is important to keep in mind that a form cannot substitute for a free-flow interview. It is equally important, but less obvious, to recognize that a free-flow interview is sometimes not a substitute for a systematic form.

Interviewing structure requires some problem-identification at the beginning. It also requires the building of some rapport. These factors may explain the difficulty of mailed interview forms. They also, in all probability, dictate that the free-flow interview should be placed before the use of a form (unless the form is used in a limited fashion to gather such information as name and address).

*Reluctance.*[4] In some instances, obtaining information from a client may be difficult not because the interviewer uses the wrong questioning sequence, but because the interviewee has a reluctance to express something important. There are several kinds of blocking factors that may be at work.

To see what they might be, we will consider a simple example. Assume that the client (the husband) is being interviewed in connection with potential divorce proceedings. He is on the brink of insolvency because of a parasitic illness. He does not particularly wish to discuss either the insolvency or the illness. The reasons may include:

(1) *Fear that disclosure may hurt his legal position.* He may feel that admitting these facts will hurt his legal position. (Actually, the opposite may be true if, for example, he is concerned about property division or holding child support to a reasonable amount; or it may be that the facts would indeed hurt him but would best be known by his lawyer, such as if, for example, a custody dispute is possible.) In either event, the client does not perceive the need for disclosure as a lawyer would.

(2) *Social embarrassment.* It is not easy for anyone except a clinician to discuss a parasitic disease, and then only if it is someone else's. Many people do not feel it is the kind of thing one brings up in polite conversation. Even if the client sees the purpose of the interview, he may unconsciously refrain from disclosure.

(3) *Self-esteem.* The client may have higher self-esteem if he refuses to recognize these facts.

(4) *Desire to talk about other subjects.* In a divorce situation, a client often wishes to catalogue completely his complaint about the other spouse and may do so to the exclusion of subjects he sees as less important.

(5) *Differences in status.* Sometimes communication is inhibited because the client perceives himself as of a different social class from the lawyer. Personal matters may be difficult to discuss with one of another social class.

(6) *Failure to recognize relevance.* Clients often think of information as categorized into "legal" and "non-legal" or they may simply fail to see the relevance of the issue. Indeed, unless one has either a curious mind or awareness of legal issues, it may be hard to see how a disease or insolvency relates to divorce. If the lawyer asks, after the proceeding, "Why didn't you tell me that?" a client who failed to see its relevance will reply, "Because you didn't ask me."

(7) *Concern for confidentiality.* The client may fear that the lawyer will disclose the matter carelessly. (Such a fear is not totally unfounded.)

These factors may operate singly or in tandem. The most insidious thing about them is that they do not operate in the open and they operate to mask subjects about which the lawyer may not know to ask in the first place. Thus there are two kinds of problems that may affect each other: (1) the lawyer does not broach the subject; and (2) even if the lawyer does, the client resists providing the information.

---

[4] For a discussion of "inhibiting" factors creating reluctance and "facilitators" for removing them, *see* D. Binder and S. Price, *Legal Interviewing and Counseling: A Client-Centered Approach*, Ch. 2 (1977). Additional coverage of the subject may be found in Amsterdam, Segal and Miller, 2 *Trial Manual for the Defense of Criminal Cases*, Ch. 5 (1968); Benjamin, *The Helping Interview* (1969); DeCotiis & Steele, *The Skills of the Lawyering Process*, 41 Tex. B.J. 483 (1977).

*Dealing With Reluctance.* There are many means of dealing with these problems, including:

— *Expression of Understanding.* "In a divorce, there are usually things we have to talk about that are embarrassing. I understand that. You're probably feeling embarrassed just talking to a complete stranger about the whole thing, right?" The same technique can be used in response to the revelation of a traumatic event: "I can imagine how upset you must have been when she asked you for money and you didn't have any."

— *Praise.* "These are hard things to talk about and you're doing pretty well at telling me about them."

— *Assurance Against Certain Harms.* Explicit expression of, and explanation of, the attorney-client privilege, together with a statement of a determination to follow it, is sometimes useful, as is an expression of loyalty. In some instances, the statement "Sometimes people think they may be hurt by information they give me. I'm not going to hurt you" is useful.

— *Statement of Expectation.* "I know that if you try, you can remember at least something about it, and whatever you remember will help." Acting as though the interviewer expects the client to make disclosure often produces the disclosure.

— *Explanation of Law or Analogy.* Explaining the legal elements of a claim or defense is a way of preventing the "failure-to-recognize-relevance" blocking factor from operating. "We don't recover anything unless we prove the defendant was 'negligent.' 'Negligent' means the defendant was 'careless.' Any information you have that might possibly show that would be useful." The technique is subject to the criticism that it may produce falsehood. However, it often operates to extract truthful information that would otherwise have remained buried. A related idea is to give an example: "In the so-and-so case, we were able to find out that the defendant had done such-and-such. That's the sort of thing that would be useful to find out here."

— *Helpfulness to Legal Position.* With respect to the "legal position" blocking factor, sometimes the best antidote is to convince the client that disclosure not only will not hurt the case, but it will help the case. "I can't defend you until I know everything you know." "Even the most seemingly irrelevant detail might help." Explaining forthrightly that even harmful information should be disclosed so that it can be dealt with in the adversary context, together with an example or analogy illustrating this principle, is useful.

— *Appeal to Pride.* Sometimes an appeal to higher values helps. This is particularly true of disinterested witnesses ("You don't want to see a horribly injured man unable to pay his medical bills, do you?"), but sometimes it is useful as to the client as well. "You owe it to every physician who is wrongly sued, as you are, to search your memory carefully."

The careful development of rapport and respect, of course, is the best way around some blocking factors. For some of them patience and persistence are also the best curatives.

*Falsehood.* Clients fabricate more than beginning lawyers usually expect they will. In a way, falsehood is human. Some falsehood is necessary to normal living, as an incident of common courtesy. Other falsehood is necessary to defend the ego. The experienced lawyer, although not completely accepting falsehood, learns to expect it and tends to judge it slightly less harshly than the beginning lawyer.

The easiest and most effective method of detecting fabrication is also the most obvious. A story that is unreasonable, inconsistent with human nature, filled with physical improbabilities, or inconsistent with social custom to a marked degree should be recognized as a red flag. "So you say that, although you usually don't do it, on this occasion, you looked to the left side, then looked to the right side, then turned back and looked to the other side again, and the first time you saw this car was when it hit you?" "You say you were never angry when you spanked little Johnny?"

The obviousness of the technique, however, does not mean that it is easy to employ. In the first place, litigators are usually dealing with extraordinary situations; those are the kinds of situations that create litigation. Recognizing the unusual that is also unreasonable is harder than it sounds. Second, the recognition that the interviewee is one's client and is lying is difficult. Third, a trusting relationship between lawyer and client is a good thing, and disbelief interferes with that relationship. Fourth, the most effective technique for dealing with the falsehood may not be to confront it directly (indeed, in the short run, it may be to ignore it), and it is easier to ignore it if one fails to recognize it in the first place. Finally, a great deal of popular wisdom ("A lawyer's got to believe his client") tells the lawyer to suspend disbelief. Hence, while the statement, "You say you were never angry when you spanked little Johnny?" may bring broad smiles from parents who know otherwise, when it is put forth sincerely by a credible client who has paid a fee, it tends not to raise a red flag.

There are other means of detecting deception. One is recognizing reluctance. Reluctance to talk about the subject may indicate falsehood (it may also indicate blocking factors, of course; falsehood is not always indicated). A story that shifts and contains internal inconsistencies is another. Yet another method is to ask the client what hostile persons will say about him or her, under the ostensible guise of obtaining information for the case. "Of course, the driver of the car doesn't necessarily always tell the story the same way. Even if he's not going to tell the truth, we want to know what he's going to say. You might know or have some idea. Do you think he's going to say you looked both ways?"

The methods of dealing with fabrication are also varied. One is to ignore the matter at first, waiting until rapport has been built before confronting it. As an alternative to direct confrontation, the lawyer may ask the client to explain an inconsistent version given by a third person; in this situation, the third party, not the lawyer, does the confronting, so that the relationship is not damaged. Another means of indirect confrontation is to explore areas of reluctance by probing questions. Understand that case relation or similar "blockbreakers" should accompany the use of these techniques. Non-verbal communication, such as a cold stare or a start of surprise can sometimes be effective. Sometimes the best approach is direct confrontation, which can be done by an expression of the reasons for disbelief in a polite manner, or can be done by the conclusory statement, "Look, you're lying your head off to me and I can't represent you in that situation." Which technique to use depends on the magnitude of the falsehood, the motivation for its use, and the attorney's concern for the trusting relationship that is needed.

*Conclusion.* The techniques of interviewing are simple to describe, intuitively obvious to many, but hard to employ in practice. A good interview is one that is properly structured, uses different questioning types in funnelling sequence where appropriate, recognizes inhibitions and deals with them, and recognizes and deals with falsehood. The use of forms can often enhance interviewing if it does not take over the interviewing process.

---

## NOTES AND QUESTIONS

(1) *Example of Poor Interview.* Consider the following interview, which is designed to provide a bad example, though there are a few things the interviewer does right. Discuss the techniques used.

Lawyer: Come in, Mr. Client. As I understand it, you want to file a lawsuit against somebody?

Client: That's right, if you think that's what I ought to do.

L: All right. I see you've got a cast on your leg. Broken, I guess?

C: In six places.

L: Who did it to you?

C: This guy who was driving about fifty miles an hour.

L: He was going over the speed limit, huh?

C: I think so.

L: Well, let's consider what sort of damages you might have. Tell me everything you know of that's wrong.

C: Well, the leg hurts like hell, for one thing.

L: Anything else?

C: I can't play tennis now and I probably won't ever be able to like I used to.

L: That's terrible. To somebody else that'd probably be no big deal, but I really feel for you because I like to play tennis myself and once I was pretty good. But let me get back to the subject: anything else about the leg bother you?

C: Not that I think of.

L: Does it affect your employment?

C: Oh, I see. Sure. I'm a truck driver and I haven't been able to work for the last month. I probably can't go back to work after this for another three months and then I have to take it easy.

L: How much have you had to pay for all this, to doctors and so forth?

C: I don't know. Don't have any idea.

L: Well, that's all right. Tell you what. Take this sheet and fill it in. Go in the library there and have a seat. Just holler when you have it done. Okay?

C: Okay.

(2) *More Coverage of Interviewing.* The description of interviewing techniques given here is brief. More complete coverage can be obtained from the following: Freeman and Weihofen, *Clinical Law Training: Interviewing and Counseling* (1972); Gorden, *Interviewing: Strategy, Techniques and Tactics* (1969); M. S. Heller, E. Polen and S. Polsky, *An Introduction to Legal Interviewing* (1960); Binder and Price, *Legal Interviewing and Counseling* (1977).

(3) *Techniques Applicable to Witnesses.* Many of the techniques described here for interviewing clients are also applicable to interviewing of witnesses; to some extent, they are applicable to the taking of depositions. Advice on taking depositions is contained in Appendix B to the Chapter 10, *Discovery: Methodology of the Individual Devices.*

(4) *Sample Interview Form.* A sample interviewing form is contained in the materials that follow.

### [B] What to Look for: Organizing the Pre-Litigation Fact-Gathering Effort

Much information can be gotten from friendly third parties without revealing information to an opponent or witness to cross examination. In such a situation, "self-help" discovery may be more appropriate than a deposition. In addition, information of several kinds can be gotten from the secretary of state (e.g., the name of the defendant's agent for service of process, corporate organizational documents, etc.), from the Department of Public Safety (accident reports), from police agencies or medical examiners (autopsies), and from many other governmental agencies. More important, the client is often the best source of information, provided the attorney uses proper interview techniques.

The following excerpt gives insight into investigation of strict liability claims. The student should consider how this advice could be adapted to other kinds of litigation.

### Sales and Perdue, THE LAW OF STRICT TORT LIABILITY IN TEXAS

*14 Hous. L. Rev. 1, 158–167 (1977)**

Initial Investigation of the Products Case—Plaintiff's View

Product liability cases are difficult, time consuming, and expensive to prosecute. Therefore, the preliminary investigation of the case should focus on whether the facts justify the large investment of the attorney's resources that the case will require. Since these cases are often taken on a contingent fee basis by plaintiff's attorneys, it is important that the case have substantial potential for successful prosecution. In order to properly analyze and determine whether the case is meritorious and "winnable", the attorney must be intimately familiar with the basic legal concepts involved.

. . . .

*A. The Client Interview*

The client interview is the plaintiff attorney's initial source of information. Often, particularly in the industrial situation, the injured party can furnish little information regarding the source of the product involved in the accident. Likewise, in death cases, the surviving spouse may have a paucity of information regarding the product. The attorney must therefore be prepared to supplement the client's information with information obtained through independent investigation.

All salient facts regarding the product and the injury-producing incident should be meticulously gathered. Generally, the essential facts sought are as follows:

1. *The incident.*

---

* Reprinted with permission of the Houston Law Review, copyright © 1977.

(a) The date and time of the injury;

(b) The place where the injury occurred;

(c) Names and addresses of all persons present at the time of occurrence;

(d) Names and addresses of all persons or bodies who subsequently investigated the occurrence; and

(e) A complete description of what occurred including:

(1) How the product was being used at the time of injury;

(2) The use to which it had been put immediately prior to injury; and

(3) Complete details of the product failure, malperformance, or misadventure.

2. *The product.*

(a) A full description of the product, including:

(1) Manufacturer (make);

(2) Seller;

(3) Model;

(4) Optional equipment;

(5) Rated capacities (performance limitations); and

(6) Type (some manufacturer's models are supplied in different types for different usages).

(b) Details regarding the purchase of the product including:

(1) By whom purchased;

(2) From whom;

(3) When;

(4) All written information and sales literature which accompanied the product should be obtained; and

(5) All alterations or changes made before injury, including identity of person or entity making change.

(c) Present details, including:

(1) The present location of the product;

(2) The persons who have examined or photographed it; and

(3) The persons who have custody of any part or portions.

Of course, other information pertaining to damages and related matters should be obtained. A sample information sheet or case history follows this discussion. As the interview progresses other avenues of inquiry will become apparent. In any event, it must at all times be recognized that no checklist can substitute for imagination, hard work, and experience.

Sample Form

Date ______________________

PRODUCTS LIABILITY CASE HISTORY

Client ______________________ Age ________ Sex ________

Husband/Wife ______________________ Age ________

Residence Business

Address ______________________

Phone ______________________

Adverse Party:

Name ______________________

Address ______________________ Phone ______________________

. . . .

Client's Personal Information

Education ______________________

Prior Claims Under This or Any Other Name: ______________________

______________________

Do you or does your spouse have a criminal record? ______________________

If so, please give details ______________________

______________________

. . . .

Client's History

Name and Address of Employer ______________________

______________________

Salary ________ Jobs & Duties ______________________

Former Employer ______________________

Spouse's Employer ______________________

How Long Employed ______________________

Jobs & Duties ______________________

Salary ______________________

Names, Addresses, Business Address & Phone Numbers of Persons who can reach you at all times ______________________

______________________

Member of What Church or Lodge ______________________

Social Security No. ________ Name of Spouse ____________________

| Former Marriages: | Divorced/Deceased | Date |
| --- | --- | --- |
| ____________ | ____________ | ____________ |

| Children: | Age | Married |
| --- | --- | --- |
| ____________ | ____________ | ____________ |

Names and Addresses of Living Parents:

Mother ____________________________________________

Name Address

Father ____________________________________________

Name Address

. . . .

Cause of Action

Date or dates when injury due to product occurred ____________________

____________________________________________

Who owned product (you, employer, etc.)? ____________________

Full description of product, make, model, optional equipment, etc. ____________

____________________________________________

Describe generally what occurred ____________________

____________________________________________

When was product purchased? ____________________

Who bought it? ____________________

Had any changes or alterations been made on it before injury? ____________

____________________________________________

Where is product presently located? ____________________

____________________________________________

Who has examined or photographed it? ____________________

____________________________________________

Name all doctors seen ____________________

____________________________________________

| Hospitals | Admitted/Discharged | Amount of Bill |
| --- | --- | --- |
| ____________ | ____________ | ____________ |

Prior Medical History ____________________

____________________________________________

. . . .

Client's Insurance

Do you have insurance? ______ If so, answer the following:

Name of Company ______________________________

Name of Agent ______________________ Policy No.______________________

Military

Were you in the service? __________ What Branch? ______________________

Date: __________ Type of Discharge ______________________

Do you now or have you ever drawn any pension or disability payments?

______________________________________________

______________________________________________

When and how much? ______________________________

Referring Attorney ______________________________

Address ______________________________

Phone ______________________________

### *B. Obtaining the Product*

The most essential step in the preparation of a products liability case is to obtain the product involved in the incident. The product is not only important for testing, but it will also provide information pertaining to date and place of manufacture and warnings or directions for use. It is imperative that the product be secured as soon as possible. In this vital aspect the consumer plaintiff enjoys an advantage over the defense. The manufacturer generally does not know that one of its products has caused injury and hence is making no effort to retrieve its product. The product commonly will have been purchased by the plaintiff, a member of his family, or a friend. Obviously, the plaintiff's attorney should have no difficulty in obtaining the product under these conditions. In the industrial or medical situation, the task is manifestly more difficult. The product in the industrial situation is usually a specialty item. Where the product has failed and is no longer serviceable it may be found in the custody of the company's safety department or in the offices of the workmen's compensation carrier. Early contact should be made with the appropriate office to secure the product. If the company, however, refuses to cooperate, an appropriate discovery motion would be necessary.

. . . .

When the product is obtained, all written materials, including packaging, should be obtained. These materials will reveal the information that the manufacturer sought to impart to the user regarding warnings and directions for use. In the event that the product experienced a physical or structural failure, any similar new or unused products in the owner's possession should be secured.

### *C. Testing*

A myriad of concepts is covered under this denomination. It is beyond the scope of this work to list and analyze all the types of testing available. Generally, testing involves any type of analysis performed by an expert on the involved product to determine the cause or explanation for the failure. Testing may be destructive or nondestructive in nature.

The product should not be destroyed if at all possible. If destructive testing is necessary, a substitute product should be utilized. Where destructive testing of the product is indicated, opposing counsel should be afforded an opportunity to be represented during such procedure. Of course, photographs should be made to document each phase of the testing procedure.

In addition to testing the product involved, it may be appropriate to test competitive products. The expert should begin an investigation into competitive products as soon as possible. A visit to suppliers and retail outlets to obtain comparable products and accompanying written materials is recommended. . . .

*D. The Expert's Preliminary Report*

Following the examination, analysis, and testing procedures, the expert should prepare a preliminary report. Counsel should instruct the expert in this regard at the outset. After receiving the preliminary report, counsel is then in a position to make a knowledgeable determination of whether to pursue the case. Likewise, if the report is favorable, plaintiff's counsel may then proceed in his prosecution of the case secure in his knowledge that there is a reasonable basis for the action. The report may also be used as a roadmap for his further discovery and development.

. . . .

THE ROLE OF THE EXPERT IN INITIAL INVESTIGATION AND DISCOVERY

. . . .

The importance of the expert cannot be overestimated. The expert should be viewed as much more than a trial witness. An expert can provide the attorney with an analysis of the product and a scientific investigation of the occurrence. Although eyewitness reports are often unreliable, discussions with eyewitnesses can help the expert increase his factual understanding of the occurrence and verify scientific calculations. The expert should carefully examine the product, evaluate the circumstances of the occurrence, and prepare a research report for the attorney on the product's characteristics. This report should include a detailed defect analysis. The attorney may also utilize the expert's technical advice in the drafting of interrogatories, in the preparation for depositions, and in the evaluation of the other party's answers.

The reports of experts are subject to pretrial discovery, unless the attorney guarantees that the experts will not be called as witnesses in any capacity at the trial. For this reason, the attorney may consider limiting reports from expert witnesses.

. . . .

## § 1.05 Managing a Litigation Matter

All too often, practicing attorneys find themselves being managed by—rather than managing—their litigation docket. The number of separate matters that attorneys in this area typically handle, the time requirements of client and other contacts, the haphazard nature of scheduling in a litigation practice, the volume of paper to be handled, and the cost considerations all contribute to this state of affairs. "Most trial lawyers," says Professor Garey Spradley, "are like one giant nerve. They react." Rather than being in control, they do what is necessary to handle the immediate situation.

It must be remembered that litigation procedure is a means to an end. Actions taken by an attorney are ultimately to be tested by whether they move the litigation closer to that desired end. Such is the task of litigation management.

## D. Reneker, GEARY, STAHL AND SPENCER LITIGATION SECTION ORIENTATION*

### *I. The Concept of Litigation*

For our purposes, the term "litigation" means the process of resolving disputes between the firm's clients and others. This process may take place in the courts through the vehicle of a lawsuit, but this is not always the case. As you will learn, many "litigation matters" ultimately do not involve a lawsuit. Furthermore, a very small percentage of the "litigation matters" that do involve a lawsuit are actually resolved by a trial. This is especially true with respect to the types of major litigation that this firm handles. As a result, while eloquence and the ability to persuade a court or jury are important characteristics for a litigation lawyer to possess, they are certainly not the only important characteristics for a litigation lawyer to possess, and, in fact, ability in other areas may be more important. This will become more and more apparent during the course of your development as a litigation lawyer.

. . . .

### *III. Administration and Assignment of Litigation Matters*

Among the materials you have been furnished is a specimen of the Litigation Section's "Case Status Report" form. [form omitted] This form is used for a number of purposes in the administration of the section's business.

At the time each litigation file is opened, the lawyer opening the file must fill out a Case Status Report. At this point, only the items above the double lines are filled in with the exception of the item designated "Attorney in Charge" which is left blank. In the area styled "Nature of Case" the lawyer provides a one sentence description of what is involved in the case and an indication of the amount in controversy. In "Evaluation of Case and Special Comments" the lawyer should indicate anything that is out-of-the-ordinary about the case, such as problems that are apparent with the case from the face of the information the lawyer has, any especially favorable aspects of the case, any requests for handling by a specific lawyer, and any appropriate comments about the credit-worthiness of the client.

. . . .

### *IV. The Handling of Litigation Matters*

*General Comments.* To some degree, each experienced litigation lawyer uses some procedures and methods that are peculiar to him or to his practice. Nevertheless, the basic framework for the proper handling of a litigation matter should not be and is not a matter of personal preference. To the contrary, there are certain identifiable phases of the litigation process that must be recognized and dealt with in almost every case. It is essential, therefore, that the firm's new litigation lawyers begin learning the basics about the proper way to handle a litigation matter as rapidly as possible. By understanding this process, new lawyers are benefited in at least two

* Reprinted by permission of Geary, Stahl and Spencer.

ways: (1) They understand why they are being asked to do certain work on a case and how their work fits into the overall plan for handling the case. (2) They begin preparing for the time when they will have the responsibility of being an Attorney in Charge.

*Four Important Principles.* Before we begin our discussion of the proper method of handling a litigation matter you should become aware of four related principles that must be considered and applied in virtually every litigation matter. The first such principle is: *"The best file is a closed file."* In other words, the client employs us and pays us fees to solve his problem or resolve his dispute. It is apparent, therefore, that the client's objective is not obtained until his file is closed. Accordingly, all work that is done in a case should be part of a systematic plan to obtain the desired result and get the file closed in the most expedient fashion and in the shortest time.

The second important principle is: *"It is almost always wrong to do nothing."* More specifically, it takes work to get a litigation matter into a posture from which it can be concluded, and we know that our opposition is not likely to do our work for us. Accordingly, there is no time like the present to begin working toward closing the file. Also, it is rarely advantageous to be on the defensive. Therefore, an aggressive approach that leaves you on the offensive most of the time is preferred. This applies to plaintiff's and defendant's cases alike.

This brings us to the third principle, which is: *"Any action taken must be economically feasible."* The problem addressed here is that clients are almost always primarily concerned with the economic "bottom line" of litigation, and the fees and expenses they incur contribute to that bottom line. For this reason, unless there is sufficient economic inducement, clients are not likely to desire to incur high costs in prosecuting or defending a matter. By way of example, a plaintiff's case with an amount in controversy of $500 may involve significant issues of constitutional law and fact issues that would, absent economic considerations, require the taking of ten depositions. The client, however, is not likely to want to pay us for the necessary legal research or the taking of the depositions in order to recover his $500; to the contrary, he would probably rather we telephone the other lawyer and negotiate a settlement for $250 or, in some instances, advise him at the outset that the handling of his matter is not economically feasible for him or for us.

The final, and perhaps most important principle is: *"Keep the client advised."* We are working for our clients, and we expect them to pay us for what we do. The least we can do, therefore, is let them know what we are doing for them on a regular basis. In fact, one of the major causes of conflicts and fee disputes between lawyers and clients is a breakdown in communications.

We can keep the clients advised, in part, by sending them copies of all correspondence we write in their behalf and all pleadings and briefs we file for them. In most cases, however, this will not be enough because the clients, in all likelihood, will not understand the significance of each letter or pleading. For this reason, we need to advise the client of each major development or strategy decision in his case by letter or telephone. It should be remembered, however, that clients, being human, sometimes forget advice that is given orally, so it is best to "put it in writing" whenever possible.

*The Phases of Litigation.* With these principles firmly in mind, we are ready to discuss the mechanics of handling a litigation matter. In this connection, we can refer to the "Goals" section of the Case Status Report form which serves as an outline of the various steps in the litigation process. These are described at length below.

*Goal 1.* The purpose of Goal 1 is that of making sure the file is opened properly and that we have all the materials and co-operation from the client necessary to begin working on the case. "Opening File Materials" refers to the Opening File Form and the Case Status Report that must be filled out when the file is opened. "Initial Case Report" and "Initial Evaluation Report" are usually combined, since they are both part of Goal 1. This report usually contains some or all of the following, depending on the nature of the case: the facts, as related by the client; the client's objectives; the issues of law and fact that are apparent at the outset; a list of relevant documentary evidence; a list of persons who will probably be witnesses; an indication of any special problems that are apparent; and an indication of any immediate deadlines or time limitations. "Fee Contract" refers to a written statement of the fee arrangement, preferably signed by the client. "Documents" refers to any relevant documentary evidence that is in the client's possession.

Some lawyers prepare these reports on printed forms that are available through the section, and some lawyers dictate the report in the form of a memorandum. Examples of both are in the materials you have received. Goal 1 usually must be accomplished within a week to ten days after the file is opened. It is generally unwise to begin actual work on the case before Goal 1 is accomplished.

*Goal 2.* As is apparent, this goal is accomplished by preparing a "Pre-Litigation Plan" and by "Assignment" of any of the work to be done in this regard. A "Pre-Litigation Plan" contains an analysis of the case in terms of what are the elements of the parties' claims and defenses, including what special problems are present, and a statement of what is to be done in the pre-litigation period. The pre-litigation period is the time before suit is filed or before formal discovery begins, as the case may be. The kinds of things normally listed in the Pre-Litigation Plan to be done during the pre-litigation period are investigation, photographing, interviewing witnesses and taking statements, obtaining documents from persons other than the client and preparing the initial pleadings. Depending on the nature of the case and the client's desires, the pre-litigation period may be an appropriate time to make a demand on the opposing party and discuss settlement. For convenience, the Pre-Litigation Plan may be combined with the Initial Case Report as has been done in one of the examples you were furnished. Goal 2 is normally accomplished within a week to ten days from the date the file is opened and work on the items listed in the Pre-Litigation Plan is begun immediately after the Plan is prepared.

*Goal 3.* This Goal is accomplished by the preparation of a "Pre-Trial and Discovery Plan" and the "Assignment" by the Attorney in Charge of the tasks, if any, to be performed by another lawyer. Goal 3 is usually accomplished at the beginning of the pre-trial and discovery period, which is the period between the times formal discovery is begun and completed.

As you learned in law school, discovery is the process of gathering evidence by means of the various methods allowed under the applicable Rules of Civil Procedure, such as interrogatories, requests for admissions, production of documents, and depositions. The Pre-Trial and Discovery Plan, therefore, sets forth the methods of discovery to be employed, the parties or other persons to whom they are to be directed, and the time within which they will be completed. An example of a Pre-Trial and Discovery Plan is included in your materials.

The pre-trial and discovery period is, more often than not, the most significant period in the litigation process because it is during the course of discovery that the strengths and weaknesses of the various parties' positions normally begin to become apparent. Accordingly, the sooner discovery is completed, the better you will be able to analyze your case, and, therefore, the better positon you will be in to make final recommendations to the client. Accordingly, it is important to begin pursuing discovery at an early date and to continue in a systematic fashion until discovery is completed. It is, of course, difficult to do this without a proper Pre-Trial and Discovery Plan.

[Discussion of discovery techniques and tactics at this point is omitted.]

. . . .

Good practice dictates that all discovery be completed at least a month before trial. This is not always possible because you continually turn up new leads through the discovery process. Nevertheless, it is difficult to plan for trial if discovery is not complete.

*Goal 4.* After the conclusion of the pre-trial and discovery phase of the lawsuit, the lawyer should be ready to accomplish Goal 4, which contemplates the preparation of a "Trial Plan." In preparing the Trial Plan the lawyer decides what witnesses he will call at trial, what documents he will attempt to introduce, what objections to evidence he contemplates will be raised, what witness he must subpoena, what will be said to the jury during *voir dire*, how the opening statement and closing argument will be framed, what charge will be submitted by the court to the jury, and the like. The Trial Plan is the framework within which the lawyer prepares for trial.

. . . .

Actual materials generated during the trial preparation process, such as testimony outlines, deposition summaries, legal memoranda, and the like, are placed and organized in a "Trial Notebook," which the lawyer will actually use in the presentation of his case at trial.

. . . .

Preferred trial preparation techniques are so numerous that it is virtually impossible to provide a list of them all. As you will see from your review of the various trial notebooks that are available, however, certain basic rules should be followed. These are as follows: A "Proof Outline" setting forth the elements you must prove and the methods by which you will prove them should be prepared. All testimony should be outlined in writing, so that important elements will not be overlooked during the trial. All depositions should be summarized, so that you will be able to find relevant passages on short notice. The *voir dire* and arguments should be outlined, so that important questions or points will not be forgotten. Responses to evidence objections that are contemplated should be set forth, so that you will be ready to respond when the objection is made. All authorities upon which you rely should be readily available, so that you will have support for your legal positions in case they are questioned.

The number of trial techniques that are alleged to be effective are as numerous as the state's trial lawyers. For this reason, no attempt will be made here to discuss how to examine a witness, how to cross-examine a witness, how to make a jury argument, or other matters that involve individual techniques and preferences. In any event, our purpose in this orientation program is not that of teaching you how to try a lawsuit but of introducing you to the litigation process as it operates in the real world. You should, however, take every opportunity that is reasonably presented to watch the firm's litigation lawyers and their opponents in action at the courthouse in order to see various trial techniques being applied.

. . . .

*Goal 5.* After a case has been tried to conclusion and a verdict rendered, the post-trial phase of litigation begins. It is at this time that you should begin formulating a "Post-Trial and Appellate Plan." The nature of the Post-Trial or Appellate Plan will depend, in large measure, on whether you won or lost the case.

If you lost the case, the burden is upon you, within some fairly strict time limits, to decide whether you will pursue further proceedings in the case. This will involve, at the outset, a conference with the client to determine whether he desires to pursue post-trial and appellate proceedings and, if so, to agree on a fee arrangement under which this will be done or to confirm the previous fee arrangement. Assuming the client wishes to proceed, the Post-Trial and Appellate Plan should contain the following: a statement as to whether a Motion for New Trial is required in the case or, if it is not, whether one should be filed as a matter of strategy or otherwise; a list of the points you believe should be brought forward in the post trial and appellate process and your evaluation of their strengths and weaknesses; a schedule of the various dates on the appellate timetable by which each step in the appellate process must be accomplished; and a statement as to which lawyers will be responsible for the various tasks involved in the further proceedings. The latter requirement, of course, should be supplemented by one or more Assistance Memos from the Attorney in Charge to the lawyer who will be asked to assist.

In the event you won the case, your Post-Trial and Appellate Plan will be similar to the above, although it will normally be necessary to determine what points will be raised in the appellate process by the appealing party before you determine how to respond. It should be noted, however, that it is sometimes expedient to urge a cross-appeal with respect to certain matters, which may require some steps independent of those undertaken by the appealing party. An indication of a cross-appeal and the matters to be included therein, along with an appropriate timetable, should be included in the prevailing party's Post-Trial and Appellate Plan.

During the proceedings in the appellate court, the parties file briefs and submit the case on oral argument. Naturally, a considerable amount of additional planning goes into deciding on the content of the briefs and the oral argument. These decisions are normally made on a final basis as the case progresses in the appellate process, but the framework within which they are made is the original Post-Trial and Appellate Plan.

*Goal 6.* In a Plaintiff's case, after a judgment is obtained and becomes final, or in rare instances while the case is on appeal, we begin our attempts to collect the judgment. The methods and means we will use to collect the judgment are set forth in the "Execution Plan."

The first items that are set forth in the Execution Plan are the steps that are taken as a matter of course under the Litigation Section's systems. These are as follows: obtaining an abstract of judgment and recording same in the counties in which we believe the judgment debtor does now or may in the future own property subject to execution, especially real property; obtaining an execution and having same levied by the Sheriff or Constable; upon return of the execution, assuming the judgment is not collected, determining whether the client wishes us to place the file in our execution system and, if so, placing same in the system.

In many cases, however, it is advisable to take additional steps in an attempt to collect the judgment. These steps include post-judgment discovery, which may be in the form of interrogatories, oral depositions, or other methods allowable under the applicable Rules of Civil Procedure. Accordingly, in formulating the Execution Plan, you should decide whether the case warrants additional efforts to collect the judgment, and, if so, what methods should be undertaken, and you should determine whether the client wishes us to undertake these and is willing to pay for them. A statement as to each of these matters should also be set forth in the Execution Plan. The Plan should also contain an indication as to the lawyers who will carry out the various steps in the Execution Plan and should be supplemented with Assistance Memos to the extent appropriate.

*Goal 7.* The final phase in the litigation process is that of "Collection and Closing." During this stage of the case we are concerned with several forms of collection: collection of any judgments we may have obtained; collection of reimbursement of any court costs that may have been taxed against the adverse party; and collection of any amounts still owed with respect to our fee and expenses. By the time the case reaches this period the file should be ready for closing, and it should be promptly closed in accordance with the procedures previously discussed.

. . . .

## D. Crump, MANAGING A LITIGATION MATTER

*Law Practice Skills Advice and Problem Book A-44–A-46 (1977)**

### *I. INITIAL STEPS*

1. *Opening and Organizing the File.* At the time the file is opened, a number in the filing system should be assigned to it and a reference card prepared for it.

One method for preparing the file itself might be as follows:

— *On the upper right side* as the file is opened, put a paper fastener to hold pleadings and papers.

— *On the lower right side,* another paper fastener to hold evidence and similar materials.

— *On the upper left side,* correspondence and notes.

— *On the lower left side,* financial materials such as copies of checks, etc.

. . . .

This system is designed to organize the various papers efficiently for availability—and, not coincidentally, to avoid undue expense in preparing and storing files. Believe it or not, office supplies—even files—run into great expense, and it is worth being frugal with them.

Some lawyers use expansion files (accordion files) for each case. That is fine for matters containing enough material to fit into several manila folders; however, it means that everything must be pulled out of the file in order to be examined—and the files cost up to just under $2 a piece. The system outlined above is cheaper and superior in efficiency unless the file is large.

2. *Filing.* The file has to be read from the bottom up, because most recent matters are added as they arrive. Otherwise, every new addition to the file would require everything else to be removed. Consequently, the petition is at the bottom or near the bottom of the pleading file, etc.

3. *Fee Contract.* The fee contract should be in writing; it may be in the form of a letter; and it should be part of the file.

4. *Index.* Some law firms put an index at the top of the pleading file. The index usually has the style of the case at the top and lists all the pleadings and other court papers in the order in which they were filed. When a new pleading is added, the title of it is typed on the index and it is placed under the index. Some lawyers place tabs indicating each pleading on a sheet that is placed above the pleading itself. These steps are useful if the file is to be referred to by a number of different lawyers in the office; if not, they may be unnecessary.

---

5. *Tickler System.* When a litigation matter is opened, it should be immediately noted on the lawyer's tickler system—if only to note when the statute of limitations runs and a fair interval before it for filing of suit.

6. *Client Interview and Information.* Be sure to have several ways to get in touch with the client—home, work, through relatives. This information and other information can be systematically obtained through the use of interview forms or check lists.

7. *Client Communications.* It is a good idea in many types of litigation (as in other types of lawyering) to send the client copies of every paper generated by your activity. The client appreciates knowing what you are doing for him. Many lawyers have canned sets of information for the client—a "client handbook" or similar device.

8. *Scheduling Discovery.* As soon as the other side answers, or as soon as you answer, have your discovery planned. If you are not sending initial interrogatories, contact the other side with reference to scheduling of depositions if you are in state court.

9. *Motions to Compel and Other Discovery Motions.* If you conduct much litigation practice at all, you need to have a form motion to compel answers ready to go, as well as a form motion for protective order. There will be much evasion, failure to answer, and delay. However, it is best to try to work it out and to use the motion practice as a last resort.

10. *Delay.* You should advise your client early that the process will take a long time. Otherwise, your client will call the next week to see where his check is. . . .

---

## NOTES AND QUESTIONS

(1) *Closing the File.* Why does Reneker say that "the best file is a closed file"? Is this always true? Imagine, for example, that you represent a defendant who, if the case is tried, will probably be found liable and is more likely than not to have a judgment taken against him or her. Why not simply allow the matter to remain unresolved? Are there disadvantages to the lawyer or client in doing so?

(2) *Taking Action.* Why does Reneker say that "it is almost always wrong to do nothing"? (This is one part of Reneker's advice that seems open to some dispute. If, for example, the litigation is of a type that cannot be resolved until time for trial approaches, does not economically justify expenditures for large amounts of attorney activity, and will not be reached for trial for a year, it may be unwise to take action now. But Reneker qualifies his statement by the adverb "almost.")

(3) *Legal Economics.* In a suit for a maximum amount of $5,000, in which the probable actual recovery is difficult to estimate but will probably be around $2,000, and in which there is a chance of no recovery at all, what sort of action is "economically feasible" within the meaning of Reneker's statement that "any action taken must be economically feasible?" What amount should the plaintiff's lawyer be ready to expend if the attorney has contracted with the client to be paid at $150 per hour? What kind of retainer (if any) should be asked for? What sort of pretrial activity could likely be conducted by plaintiff in such a case?

What does this example tell you about the economics of law practice? (Can such a piece of litigation be efficiently handled by a lawyer today?)

Might it be reasonable to approach the case with relatively little preparation other than securing witnesses for trial? What other alternative do you see?

(4) *The Importance of Keeping the Client Informed.* Reneker says that the lawyer should "keep the client advised." As is indicated by his and other materials in this chapter, one way to do so is to send copies of all papers concerning the case to the client. What should the lawyer do if (as sometimes happens) the client requests that the lawyer explain what all the papers mean and the lawyer knows that the fee necessary to do so would be large enough that the client would be unwilling to pay it?

Failure to keep the client advised is a major area of malpractice liability, particularly when a settlement offer has been received. The worst situation is when a settlement offer is received and the attorney fails to communicate it, or fails adequately to explain it or to explain the risk of trial, and the case is then tried and lost. Reneker advises that "clients sometimes forget advice that is given orally." Advice concerning a settlement offer that is rejected is the sort of advice that is likely to be forgotten. Can you see why?

(5) *Use of Forms.* To open and maintain a file under the system Reneker prescribes requires filling out a number of forms. Does this itself create disadvantages? Why?

(6) *Litigation Phases.* Is it helpful to think of litigation, as Reneker does, as a series of "phases" rather than in the traditional mold of procedure courses? Note that the phases are frequently not as discrete as the materials might tend to indicate. There is no one "phase" at which one interviews, or assesses the case, or conducts settlement negotiations, or prepares for trial. Nevertheless, these activities do tend to group themselves into certain patterns, and the phases Reneker describes are a useful means of looking at the problem.

## § 1.06 Avoiding Malpractice

### [A] Standards, Causes, and Incidence of Malpractice

#### Cross, SPECTRE OF THE MALPRACTICE SUIT: INCREASINGLY VISIBLE

*Houston's Legal Advocate, March, 1979, p. 3, col. 1*[*]

"The insurance policy is America's No. 1 least read bestseller. Almost everybody has some form of coverage but no one (and this includes attorneys) reads the fine print until it is needed and then it is too late."

The speaker was Richard Cross, J.D., a professional liability law professor, who has five years as a senior partner in a firm with a substantial amount of medical malpractice defense work behind him. He now serves as president of the Houston-based Insurance Corporation of America, called "the nation's fastest growing writer of professional malpractice insurance in the nation" by Best's Review, the leading insurance industry trade publication.

"The cost of liability insurance protection for legal professionals is rapidly increasing nationwide," said Cross. "If this trend continues, lawyers will find themselves facing their own 'malpractice insurance crisis' with already skyhigh premium rates rising comparable to those paid by doctors."

### Read The Fine Print

"Already premiums have increased more than five hundred percent in the past five years," added Cross, "but the biggest rip off by insurance companies for the legal profession is lack of coverage". Most lawyers overlook the fine print which may require an attorney:

1. to pay his own defense cost up to the amount of the deductible;
2. to agree to any settlement which is acceptable to the claimant and the insurance company, or the company will not accept liability for amounts exceeding the proposed settlement;
3. to swallow the fact that all claims expenses will be deducted from the total limits of liability and only what remains will be applied to a judgment.

"Also, the coverage is written on a 'claims made' form which means the claim must be presented during the policy term or there is no coverage. What happens to a lawyer who retires and gives up his policy? He has no coverage." . . .

Cross then presented some frightening statistics. "Probably 85 percent of potential legal malpractice cases get settled quietly out of court, with the average paid claim being $28,000. This is a 200 percent higher settlement than a year ago. . . ."

### Malpractice Causes

"According to statistics some 60 percent of malpractice suits are caused by carelessness of action or statement by the attorney involved, and range from not keeping the client informed of what's going on to failure to keep an up-to-the minute docket. There is no viable excuse for such non-professional actions," said Cross.

He then presented a short list of Do's and Don'ts that can help keep a process server away from the attorney's door.

1. Don't ever neglect your client. He is paying you for your services and he is entitled to be kept informed on what's going on. Send him copies of all correspondence pertaining to his case. If you can't write a separate letter to him, put a stamped notation on his copy reading "No action required—for your information only."
2. Don't build up your client's expectations. NEVER tell him that he has a "sure thing" or that he will get "a lot of money." In other words, don't predict outcomes.
3. Put your agreement in writing and give him a copy for his files. This agreement lists the exact activities you are contracting for with him.
4. If you promise results and the client doesn't get them you may be liable for breach of contract and the client has four years to sue you rather than the two year tort limit.
5. Bill your client on a regular monthly basis—don't hand it to him all at once. Especially if you have not won anything for him he will feel that he is being overcharged for services not rendered.
6. Do proper research before giving legal opinions. An attorney is immune from "mistakes in judgment" only if he can demonstrate he has done his homework before advising a client.
7. Keep careful records of what services you have performed for your client, the time involved and dates, to avoid fee disputes.

8. Return ALL phone calls. If you are too busy, have your secretary or a clerk call for you.
9. Advise your client of any possible choices he may have in his cause of action. Do not arbitrarily decide for him.
10. Don't bring in outside legal or other professional help without consulting him first—he is paying for it, not you.
11. Remember that EVERYTHING your client tells you is in the strictest confidence.
12. Don't ever let your docket system fall behind. If you miss an important filing date you are liable. (A prominent Houston attorney paid a $450,000 malpractice suit recently because he missed a statute of limitations deadline.)
13. Carefully review any case to see if you could be liable for conflict of interest. (A Harris county attorney was hit for an $800,000 law suit last year by a woman who alleged an interest conflict because the same law firm represented both her and her husband in her divorce action.)
14. ALWAYS disclose adverse interests—don't try to be both business partner and lawyer to your client.
15. Don't try to settle your own case.

"If a client accuses you of malpractice never try to settle your own case. There are both ethical and legal considerations that prohibit this type of activity."

"After all, you should remember that you are in a fiduciary relationship with your client. If a mistake is made, he is entitled to an independent evaluation of the situation as well as independent counsel."

---

## PATTERSON & WALLACE v. FRAZER

*79 S.W. 1077 (Tex. Civ. App. 1904, no writ)*

This suit was brought by Ella Frazer against Patterson & Wallace, a firm of lawyers composed of C. B. Patterson and G. E. Wallace, to recover damages for alleged negligence in the conduct and prosecution of a suit in her behalf, under their contract of employment, against John Moore and his wife, for $10,000 damages, for uttering slanderous words of and concerning plaintiff. The substance of the allegations in plaintiff's petition is: That on the 1st day of February, 1901, she employed defendants (paying them a cash fee of $250) as attorneys at law to institute and prosecute a suit, through all the courts it might be carried, against John Moore and his wife, Ellen, for slander.

. . . That in pursuance of their employment the defendants, Patterson & Wallace, filed suit in the district court of Reeves county, Tex., where Moore and wife resided, and the slanderous language was spoken, for the plaintiff, against John Moore and wife, to recover of and from them $10,000 damages by reason of the utterance and publication by Mrs. Moore of and concerning plaintiff the slanderous language above stated. That after such suit was instituted, and defendants therein cited, and had filed their answer, the clerk of the court filed a motion in the case asking the court to require the plaintiff to enter into a bond for the costs that had accrued and might accrue in said suit. That such motion was granted, and a rule for costs entered on the minutes against the plaintiff on the 5th day of March, 1901, and the cause continued until the September term of the court. That, after the rule for costs had been granted, defendants herein, Patterson & Wallace, promised plaintiff that they would make satisfactory arrangements with the clerk of the court in regard to securing the costs, and told her that she need not bother herself about that matter, for one of the firm would be in attendance upon the court on the first day of its September term, and attend to the matter. That, being ignorant of the rules of judicial procedure in such matters, and relying upon the promise of defendants, made as her attorneys in the case, she never made nor tendered to the clerk on the first day of September term of the court a bond for costs, as was required by the order made by the court at its prior term, and, neither member of the firm of Patterson & Wallace being present or in attendance on the court on the first day of its September term, the fact that no bond or security for costs in the case had been given by plaintiff was called to the court's attention by its clerk, whereupon the court then entered an order dismissing the cause from its docket. That defendants, Patterson & Wallace, were guilty of negligence, after promising her that they would see that security for costs was given at the proper time, and that one of them would be in attendance on the court at its September term, in not seeing that the proper bond or security for costs was given in time to prevent a dismissal of the cause, and in not being present and in attendance on court at the first day of its September term, and then taken such steps as were necessary to prevent the cause from being dismissed. That afterwards, during the September term, 1901, of said court, the defendants filed a motion to set aside the order of dismissal and reinstate the cause upon the docket, but that, in drawing up such motion and its amendment, they negligently failed to incorporate therein such grounds therefor, which, when addressed to the sound judicial discretion of the court, would have authorized the court in granting it, and that by reason of such negligence said motion was overruled, and the order of dismissal thereby became the final judgment of the court, and her cause of action against Moore and wife lost, because then barred by the statute of limitations. . . .

[On the jury's verdict, judgment for $500 was awarded to plaintiff. In reviewing the evidence, the court found it insufficient to prove the claim for slander itself. For that reason, the court reversed; part of the burden of plaintiff in recovering against her attorneys was to show that she had a valid claim that was lost through their negligence. Having found that no claim was lost, the court went on to discuss the standard of care applicable to attorneys, including trial attorneys, in Texas.]

. . . Plaintiff's cause of action against Moore and wife, if any she had, was for the alleged slanderous words charged to have been spoken in the presence of Mrs. Shertz in May, and, as there was no legal evidence introduced upon the trial of this cause that such language was ever used, no cause of action was shown in this case against appellants. In an action for tort the injured party is entitled to recover such damages as will compensate him for the injury received, so far as it might reasonably have been expected to flow from the circumstances—such as, according to common experience and the usual course of events, might have been reasonably anticipated. He who is responsible for a negligent act must answer for all injurious results which flow therefrom by ordinary, natural sequence, without the interpretation of any other negligent act or overpowering force. The damage is not too remote, if, according to the usual experience of mankind, the result was to be expected. If, therefore, plaintiff had a cause of action against Moore and wife for slander—which is a question of fact—for which suit was pending, the loss of her action would inevitably follow from the negligence of her counsel causing the dismissal of her suit, when barred by limitations, and, after its dismissal, in so negligently preparing and presenting a motion to reinstate the suit as would not authorize the court to grant it. If, then, were it not for such negligence, it can be reasonably shown that she would have recovered judgment, and collected anything on it, she has lost by such negligence of defendants what she would have otherwise collected; and the fact that a part of the judgment which might reasonably have been expected to be recovered and collected might have been for exemplary damages would make no difference. It is known that judgments for damages, actual and exemplary, are recovered and collected for slander, and it will not do to say that attorneys at law are not liable to their clients for negligence in managing such cases, because of the difficulty a jury may have in arriving at the damages occasioned by such negligence, for this would absolve them from all liability for negligence in such cases.

For reason of the errors indicated, the judgment is reversed, and the cause remanded.

## [B] Frequent Problems Causing Malpractice Litigation

### [1] Whom to Sue: Inadequate Representation at One Extreme, Malicious Prosecution at the Other

**COOK v. IRION**, 409 S.W.2d 475 (Tex. Civ. App.—San Antonio 1966, writ ref'd n.r.e.). Plaintiff Cook had had a take-nothing judgment rendered against her in a slip-and-fall case. She had been represented by an attorney named John C. Akard, who, in turn, associated defendant James C. Irion, an attorney with "wide experience in the trial of personal injury actions." There had been three potential defendants in the claim of Ms. Cook for her injuries: the owner of the shopping center where Ms. Cook fell; a television station that owned a television cable over which she fell; and the merchants' association of the tenants and landlord in the center, which engaged in promotional activities which brought both Ms. Cook and the television station to the center. On the advice of defendant Irion, the case was pursued against the merchant's association only. An instructed verdict was rendered for defendant, from which no appeal was taken.

After stating the facts, the court analyzed the case as follows:

> Appellants alleged that appellees were grossly negligent in suing only the Merchants Association instead of proceeding against all three of the possible defendants. More than two years had elapsed before the first trial was h[illegible] and appellants assert that the statute of limitations would have barred any subsequent suit against the Center and/or KROD TV. There is no allegation of lack of good faith on the part of appellees or any allegation that the trial was mishandled. Mrs. Cook did testify that appellees failed to "brief" or "prepare" her prior to testifying at the original trial, although she was "briefed" prior to the taking of her deposition, and there is no showing that this failure resulted in any harm to appellants.
>
> John E. Allen, Esq., a duly licensed attorney who was practicing in Alpine, Texas, testified as an expert witness on behalf of appellants. He had never tried a jury or any other type case in El Paso County, and therefore did not profess to testify as to the degree of care, skill and diligence customarily exercised by attorneys practicing in El Paso County. He was permitted to testify, over the objection of appellees, that appellees had failed to exercise the standard of care of the average general practitioner in the State of Texas in not suing all three of the possible defendants. In substance he testified that "when there is room for doubt in your mind as to whether some party might or might not be liable as to whether some party or concern might or might not have operation and control of the premises, *all*

(or) one have operation, the other have control, they may be joint tort feasors, and those doubts would necessarily, I think, in the proper representation of a client would be resolved in making those people parties-defendants." He admitted that he might later have dismissed one or more of the defendants after full investigation, and that the plaintiff would be at a real disadvantage in giving the defendants 18 peremptory challenges.

The duty of the attorney in representing his client is well stated by the Supreme Court of North Carolina in Hodges v. Carter, 239 N.C. 517, 80 S.E.2d 144, 45 A.L.R.2d 1 (1954), as follows: "Ordinarily when an attorney engages in the practice of the law and contracts to prosecute an action in behalf of his client, he impliedly represents that (1) he possesses the requisite degree of learning, skill, and ability necessary to the practice of his profession and which others similarly situated ordinarily possess; (2) he will exert his best judgment in the prosecution of the litigation entrusted to him; and (3) he will exercise reasonable and ordinary care and diligence in the use of his skill and in the application of his knowledge to his client's cause." Patterson & Wallace v. Frazer, Tex. Civ. App., 79 S.W. 1077, charge approved by Supreme Court, 100 Tex. 103, 94 S.W. 324 (1906); Collins v. Wanner, Sup. Ct. of Okl., 382 P.2d 105 (1963); 7 Am. Jur. 2d Attorneys at Law § 168; Restatement of the Law of Torts 2d, § 299A. He is thus subject to the same general rules of law as are physicians, dentists, and other professional people. Prosser, Torts, 3d Ed., p. 164; Theobald v. Byers, 193 Cal. App. 2d 147, 13 Cal. Rptr. 864, 87 A.L.R.2d 986.

The attorney is not liable, however, for an error in judgment if he acts in good faith and in an honest belief that his advice and acts are well founded and in the best interest of his client. . . .

[The court also stated that "an attorney practicing in a vastly different locality would not be qualified to second-guess the judgment of an experienced attorney of the El Paso County Bar as to who [sic] should be joined as additional party defendants." Allen practiced in a community of only 6,434 persons. He admitted, further, that the probable makeup of the jury panel is an important consideration in deciding whom to sue. The court pointed out that for reasons such as these, there is a well-recognized practice of associating local counsel.]

[The court affirmed a take-nothing judgment against Ms. Cook.]

---

## NOTES AND QUESTIONS

(1) *Duties to Third Parties.* What obligations does an attorney have to avoid suing a potential defendant who may be innocent of wrongdoing? Ironically, the cases indicate that the attorney has no duty to third parties, with certain exceptions. *Bryan & Amidei v. Law,* 435 S.W.2d 587 (Tex. Civ. App.—Fort Worth 1968, no writ). Of course, these cases are concerned only with civil recovery against an attorney by the third party; they do not obviate possible obligations under the Disciplinary Rules of Professional Conduct or moral obligations not to oppress the innocent.

Discovery may, indeed, show more facts than are known at that time pleadings are filed. But the attorney's usual situation is that of having to decide with only sketchy information. Where should the line be drawn: should the attorney sue anyone who might conceivably be liable and sort things out later, or should the attorney look for a certain threshold of evidence (and if so, what threshold)? If the attorney elects not to sue someone and facts later develop showing that the omitted defendant is the only one liable, what will the attorney's position be?

(2) *Missed Deadlines.* It is worth noting that both of the two preceding cases involved the statutes of limitation. The failure to observe time deadlines, including the statutes of limitation, is a great source of actionable attorney malpractice in the trial area. Trial attorneys typically have from 100 to 300 ongoing matters at any one time. New information is obtained daily and must be assimilated. Each matter involves not just one deadline, but rather a series of deadlines. In cases in which suit has not yet been filed, the attorney may be engaged in settlement negotiations, cogitation on theories of suit, investigation, or the like. If these problems are not enough, time considerations change with the life of the lawsuit, and questions of economic feasibility frequently nudge the lawyer into less preparation than would be preferable. Missing a deadline under these conditions is not something that happens only to the slovenly. It happens even to skilled, conscientious lawyers.

(3) *Good Faith Does Not Excuse Negligence.* The Texas Supreme Court has determined that there is no subjective good faith excuse for attorney negligence, but rather a lawyer is held to the standard of care that would be exercised by a reasonably prudent attorney. *Cosgrove v. Grimes,* 774 S.W.2d 662, 664 (Tex. 1989). The Court has also held that a client represented in a criminal case must prove that he or she has been exonerated from the criminal conviction, either by direct appeal, post-conviction relief, or otherwise, in order to successfully prosecute a malpractice claim against criminal defense counsel. *Peeler v. Hughes & Luce,* 909 S.W.2d 494, 497–498 (Tex. 1995).

---

## LAUB v. PESIKOFF

*979 S.W.2d 686 (Tex. App.—Houston [1st Dist.] 1998, pet. denied)*

TAFT, Justice.

Appellant, Levi Lee Laub (Levi), appeals from summary judgments granted to appellees in these cases, Dr. Richard Pesikoff and Dr. Rita Justice, Ph.D. We consider (1) whether Levi's claims are barred by the judicial communication privilege and (2) whether the trial court's award of sanctions against Levi was appropriate. We reform the trial court's judgments, and as reformed, affirm.

### Factual and Procedural Background

These appeals arise out of a divorce proceeding styled *In the Matter of the Marriage of Mary Maher Laub and Levi Lee Laub*, filed by Mary Laub (Mary) on January 4, 1995. [footnote omitted] On January 9, 1996, Levi filed a motion for partial summary judgment, requesting the court to uphold certain gifts allegedly made by Mary to Levi during their marriage. Levi alleged that, on or about September 7, 1984, Mary signed a quitclaim gift deed conveying to him a one-half interest in parcels of real property located in Houston. Levi also alleged that, on or about June 7, 1990, he and Mary signed a memorandum of gift to "confirm" that, in 1984, Mary had made a gift to Levi of a one-half interest in a securities portfolio that she inherited from her father. In his motion, Levi argued that he owned a one-half interest in the real property and the securities portfolio as his sole and separate property.

On January 29, 1996, Mary filed a response to Levi's motion for partial summary judgment. She argued that, at the time she executed the quitclaim gift deed and the memorandum of gift, she did not possess the requisite donative intent to make those transfers. In support of this position, Mary attached the affidavits of Dr. Richard Pesikoff, her treating psychiatrist, and Dr. Rita Justice, her treating psychologist. In their affidavits, both Dr. Pesikoff and Dr. Justice expressed opinions concerning Mary's mental health and its effect on her ability to enter into the 1984 and 1990 agreements. Specifically, the affidavits stated that Mary revealed to the doctors that Levi had physically abused her in the past. Both affidavits concluded that, if not for her reduced mental capacity resulting from Levi's abusive behavior, she would never have entered into the agreements at issue in the divorce proceeding.

On February 14, 1996, Levi filed an amended cross-petition in which he asserted third-party actions against Dr. Pesikoff and Dr. Justice based on the statements contained in their affidavits. Levi asserted multiple claims against both Dr. Pesikoff and Dr. Justice, including (1) "intentional" libel and slander; (2) intentional infliction of emotional distress; (3) engaging in a conspiracy to defraud Levi of his property by making false statements; (4) denial of due process under the United States and Texas Constitutions; and (5) tortious interference with the contractual relationship between Levi and Mary. In addition, Levi asserted a negligence claim against Dr. Justice, based on an alleged doctor-patient relationship arising from therapy sessions he attended in conjunction with Mary's treatment.

. . . .

Sanctions

In his second, third, and fourth points of error, Levi claims that the trial court erred in (1) awarding sanctions against him in favor of Drs. Pesikoff and Justice, (2) denying him an opportunity to present a defense to the rule 13 sanctions, and (3) awarding attorney's fees to Drs. Pesikoff and Justice as sanctions.

Hearings were conducted on the sanctions issue on August 13, September 13, and September 20, 1996. During those hearings, Drs. Pesikoff and Justice attempted to show that, because Levi's claims were groundless, brought in bad faith, and for the purpose of harassment, attorney's fees should be awarded against Levi as sanctions. The doctors alleged that Levi's claims were groundless because they were clearly barred by the judicial communication privilege, and that his arguments did not request a reasonable extension or modification of existing law. The doctors claimed the suits were brought in an attempt to coerce them into changing their sworn affidavit testimony.

Levi's counsel and counsel for both doctors testified at the hearings. Counsel for Dr. Pesikoff testified that he had been approached by Levi's counsel, who offered to nonsuit Dr. Pesikoff if he would modify his earlier affidavit to state that he could not render opinions regarding Mrs. Laub's condition prior to the date his treatment began. Dr. Justice's counsel testified that Levi's counsel made a similar offer to her client in writing. [footnote omitted] Upon reading the proposed affidavit language submitted to Dr. Justice by Levi's counsel, the trial court informed Levi's counsel of his right to remain silent, in response to accusations that the witness tampering statute may have been violated. *See* Tex. Penal Code Ann. § 36.05 (Vernon 1994). Levi's counsel denied these allegations, and contends on appeal that the proposed affidavit merely clarified issues raised in the original affidavit, and was suggested as part of a settlement offer.

On September 20, 1996, the trial court granted summary judgments to both Dr. Pesikoff and Dr. Justice. In separate orders, the court awarded $27,973.04 as sanctions against Levi in favor of Dr. Justice, and $86,251.26 against Levi in favor of Dr. Pesikoff. These amounts represent the attorney's fees incurred by counsel for Drs. Pesikoff and Justice, as found by the court. The trial court's orders state that the sanctions were awarded pursuant to rule 13 of the Texas Rules of Civil Procedure and chapter 10 of the Texas Civil Practice and Remedies Code. Tex. R. Civ. P. 13; Tex. Civ. Prac. & Rem. Code Ann. §§ 10.001–.006.

. . . .

B. Rule 13 as a Basis for Sanctions

In his second point of error, Levi alleges that the trial court erred in awarding sanctions against him in favor of Drs. Pesikoff and Justice. We review a court's order of rule 13 sanctions under an abuse of discretion standard. *Lawrence v. Kohl*, 853 S.W.2d 697, 699 (Tex. App.—Houston [1st Dist.] 1993, no writ). The test for determining if the trial court abused its discretion is whether the trial court acted without reference to any guiding rules or principles. *Aldine Indep. Sch. Dist. v. Baty*, 946 S.W.2d 851, 852 (Tex.App.—Houston [14th Dist.] 1997, no writ).

Pursuant to rule 13, a court may impose sanctions against a party, a party's attorney, or both, if they file pleadings, motions, or other papers that are both groundless and either (1) brought in bad faith or (2) for the purpose of harassment. *Lawrence*, 853 S.W.2d at 699. The rule further provides that the court may impose any appropriate sanction available under Tex.R.Civ.P. 215(2)(b), including the assessment of attorney's fees. *Lawrence*, 853 S.W.2d at 699. "Groundless" means without basis in law or fact and not warranted by a good faith argument for an extension, modification, or reversal of existing law. *Miller v. Armogida*, 877 S.W.2d 361, 365 (Tex. App.—Houston [1st Dist.] 1994, writ denied).

Drs. Pesikoff and Justice argue that Levi's claims were groundless because the judicial communication privilege clearly bars the claims which Levi has raised in this case. They refer us to a series of letters, in which defense counsel notified Levi's counsel of this fact, exchanged between the parties prior to the filing of the motions for summary judgment. They also argue that Levi never specifically argued for an extension, modification, or reversal of Texas law. In addition, they claim that, because the evidence shows that Levi's claims were brought only to intimidate Drs. Pesikoff and Justice and to coerce them into changing their testimony, the suit was brought in bad faith and for an improper purpose.

Clearly, rule 13 is a tool that must be available to trial courts in those egregious situations where the worst of the bar uses our system for ill motive without regard to reason and the guiding principles of the law. *Dyson Descendant Corp. v. Sonat Exploration Co.*, 861 S.W.2d 942, 951 (Tex. App.—Houston [1st Dist.] 1993, no writ). The rule, however, cannot become a weapon used to punish those with whose intellect or philosophic viewpoint the trial court finds fault. *Id.* Innovative changes in the law or applications of the law must by necessity come from creative and innovative sources. *Id.* By their very definition, changes in the law are different from and in disagreement with what has been historically accepted. *Id.* We cannot allow rule 13 to have a chilling effect on those who seek change in legal precedent. *Id.*

Before reaching the issue of whether harassment or bad faith existed in any given case, the trial court must first find that the claims brought by the party to be sanctioned are groundless. Tex. R. Civ. P. 13. Although Levi has not specifically argued that adopting his position would call for a modification, extension, or reversal of existing law, his claims are not patently unmeritorious or frivolous, with no arguable basis in law or fact. Although we hold today that Levi's claims are barred by the judicial communications privilege, he has argued that they are not, based in part on Justice Gammage's concurrence in *Bird* and on other cases and statutes which he claims support his position.

As stated earlier, most Texas decisions in this area involve claims of defamation. Levi correctly points out that many Texas decisions involve negligent conduct, as opposed to intentional conduct, as alleged here. In addition, Justice Gammage's concurrence in *Bird* may not constitute a "directive," but it did urge that a qualified privilege, not an absolute privilege, should apply. Based on the state of the law surrounding the judicial communication privilege, Levi's arguments, although unsuccessful, are not "groundless" as contemplated by rule 13. As this Court stated in *Dyson*, we should not allow rule 13 to have a chilling effect on those who seek change in legal precedent. 861 S.W.2d at 951. Therefore, we hold that, to the extent that the court based its award of sanctions on rule 13, it abused its discretion.

We sustain Levi's second point of error. Because we so hold, we need not address Levi's third and fourth points of error which also challenge the sanctions award.

. . . .

Conclusion

We reform the trial court's judgment in cause number 95-00198A by deleting both the $86,251.26 in sanctions awarded to Dr. Pesikoff and the findings of fact upon which those sanctions were based. Likewise, we reform the trial court's judgment in cause number 95-00198B by deleting both the $27,973.04 in sanctions awarded to Dr. Justice and the findings of fact upon which those sanctions were based. As reformed, we affirm both judgments of the trial court.

---

## NOTES AND QUESTIONS

(1) *Sanctions for Frivolous Pleadings.* In addition to Civil Procedure Rule 13, Civil Practice and Remedies Code, Chapter 10, Sanctions for Frivolous Pleadings and Motions, provides another basis for sanctioning attorneys or parties for filing baseless suits or motions. If a court finds a violation of the requirements related to good faith filing of pleadings and motions in C.P.R.C. § 10.001, it may impose a sanction on the attorney, the party, or both. Sanctions may include paying a penalty into the court or paying the amount of reasonable expenses incurred by the other party due to the filing. *See* C.P.R.C. §§ 10.001–10.006. In *Laub*, the court did not address C.P.R.C. Chapter 10 because the initial claims and counterclaims had been filed before the effective date of Chapter 10. *See Laub v. Pesikoff*, 979 S.W.2d 686, 692 (Tex. App.—Houston [1st Dist.] 1998, pet. denied), *above*.

(2) *Malicious Prosecution.* Before the advent of rules such as Civil Procedure Rule 13 and the analogous federal rule, Federal Rule of Civil Procedure 11, recourse was limited for

defendants who believed they had been sued unjustifiably. The doctrine of malicious prosecution provided a remedy, but only if the defendant had suffered some "interference, by reason of the suit, with his person or property." *Martin v. Trevino,* 578 S.W.2d 763, 766 (Tex. Civ. App.—Corpus Christi 1978, writ ref'd n.r.e.). Proving the requisite "interference" is not easy, as a groundless suit, filed with intent to harass, is not sufficient. In *Martin,* the defendant doctor was sued for medical malpractice. After he countersued for malicious prosecution, the plaintiff moved to voluntarily dismiss her claim. The court found against the doctor on the malicious prosecution claim, finding mere harassment would not sustain the claim and stating "[a] pleading which does not allege some interference with the complainant's person or property fails to state a cause of action for malicious prosecution and is fatally defective." *Martin v. Trevino,* 578 S.W.2d 763, 766 (Tex. Civ. App.—Corpus Christi 1978, writ ref'd n.r.e.). The rationale for such a strict approach is that to permit malicious prosecution claims too readily will deter good faith plaintiffs from seeking redress in the courts.

### [2] Conflict of Interests

**EMPLOYERS CAS. CO. v. TILLEY**, 496 S.W.2d 552 (Tex. 1973). Employers Casualty brought this declaratory judgment action against its insured, Tilley, requesting exoneration of liability on its contract of insurance with Tilley on the alleged ground that Tilley's late giving of notice violated the policy conditions. At the same time, Employers undertook to defend Tilley in the primary suit, a personal injury claim, under a standard "non-waiver agreement" (i.e., an agreement that provision of defense shall not be a waiver of the right to assert policy defenses in the declaratory judgment action). The attorney engaged by Employers to defend Tilley did indeed perform services in his defense, but, at the same time, for a period of 18 months, he also performed services for Employers Casualty that were adverse to Tilley in that they sought to establish Employers' defense of late notice.

Tilley was led to make his employees available for statements, sometimes on his own time and at his own expense, with no reason to think that his attorney was working in other than his own interests. At least one statement taken from his foreman had as its admitted purpose the establishment of the late notice defense. Tilley's attorney took the deposition of the foreman, and this deposition, the court concluded, was the source of many of the questions and answers in the deposition of the same witness taken in this declaratory judgment action on the late notice question. The attorney engaged by Employers to represent Tilley did not inform him of the conflict and did not withdraw until nearly 18 months had passed.

Under these circumstances, the trial court granted summary judgment in Tilley's favor, holding that Employers was obligated to defend him in the personal injury action and would be liable for the payment of any judgment up to the limits of the policy. The Supreme Court of Texas affirmed this holding.

The Supreme Court held that the facts proven showed prejudice to the insured as a matter of law by the failure of both Employers and the attorney to perform their legal duty of informing Tilley of the conflict. These circumstances created an estoppel preventing the insurer from asserting the policy defense. Furthermore, the non-waiver agreement, which was a general reservation of rights, did not obviate the duty to inform the insured. In the course of articulating this holding, the Court stated the following:

> These are serious questions involving legal ethics and public policy with which this Court has not dealt under like circumstances. Counsel for both parties apparently concede that

similar situations often confront insurers and attorneys employed by them to represent insureds under comprehensive liability insurance policies and that guidelines from this Court would be welcomed, even though the parties disagree as to what the guidelines and consequences should be. At the outset, it should be stated that the impeccable reputation of the attorney engaged by Employers to represent Tilley, Mr. Dewey Gonsoulin, and the fact that his conduct may be representative of the customary conduct of counsel employed by insurance companies in similar situations, is not questioned by counsel for Tilley nor by this Court. However, as stated by courts of other jurisdictions which have dealt with the problem, custom, reputation, and honesty of intention and motive are not the tests for determining the guidelines which an attorney must follow when confronted with a conflict between the insurer who pays his fee and the insured who is entitled to his undivided loyalty as his attorney of record. Van Dyke v. White, 55 Wash. 2d 601, 349 P.2d 430 (1960); Hammett v. McIntyre, 114 Cal. App. 2d 148, 249 P.2d 885 (1952).

*Duties of Insurers and Attorneys Employed to Represent Insureds*

Under the policy in question (comprehensive liability) the insurance company's obligation to defend the insurer provides that the attorney to represent the insured is to be selected, employed and paid by the insurance company. Nevertheless, such attorney becomes the attorney of record and the legal representative of the insured, and as such he owes the insured the same type of unqualified loyalty as if he had been originally employed by the insured. If a conflict arises between the interests of the insurer and the insured, the attorney owes a duty to the insured to immediately advise him of the conflict. . . .

. . . .

*Effect of the Non-Waiver Agreement*

The above guiding principles are not diluted or nullified by a general non-waiver agreement. The printed non-waiver form signed by Tilley on October 6, 1969, did not authorize Employers to use the same attorney to represent Tilley in the personal injury suit and to actively work against Tilley on the conflicting coverage question, without informing Tilley of the specific conflict and affording him the opportunity to employ his own counsel. Non-waiver agreements are strictly construed against the insured and will not be extended by implication beyond their exact terms. . . .

. . . .

---

## NOTES AND QUESTIONS

(1) *Legal Ethics.* According to Professor Garey Spradley, an experienced defense counsel, the reaction of many in the insurance defense bar to the *Tilley* case was: "Gee! I guess that's right. We just never thought about it." The industry has responded, however, by generally hiring two separate attorneys in the event of a policy coverage defense, one of whose sole loyalty is owed to the insured. Note, however, that the attorney employed in the first place is often the one who has the responsibility to notice.

What should an attorney do if employed by an insurer to fulfill its obligations to provide a defense to an insured and the attorney uncovers serious evidence of a policy defense? (Is there a completely satisfactory answer to this question?)

The non-waiver agreement was Tilley's expression of assent to the insurer's reservation of its rights to assert the policy defense. The insurer argued that this expression of assent should have carried the day. Why didn't it? (*Hint:* Did it waive the right to a completely loyal attorney? For that matter, did it apprise Tilley that he might not have a completely loyal attorney?)

(2) *Conflict of Interest Is Common.* The court's opinion, although finding a failure of duty on the part of the attorney, takes great pains to cite the honesty and good reputation of the same attorney. It is important to realize that a conflict of interest is not rare or something that happens only to marginal practitioners.

(3) *Representing Multiple Parties.* The other side of the coin is that it is often economically or strategically preferable for parties with a nominal conflict to have only one attorney. Such situations create tension, because the attorney may not wish to cause the parties to hire separate attorneys if it is not necessary. Common situations involving allegations of conflict of interest include uncontested divorce cases (in which the attorney should take great pains to ensure that the opposing spouse does not believe that the attorney is representing both spouses), corporate situations in which shareholders have disputes with management or with the corporation, among others. In these situations, if there is a conflict, the attorney has the obligation of disclosure and withdrawal in the absence of consent.

### [3] Statutes of Limitation

CIVIL PRACTICE AND REMEDIES CODE
CHAPTER 16. LIMITATIONS

C.P.R.C. § 16.002. *One-Year Limitations Period.* (a) A person must bring suit for malicious prosecution, libel, slander, or breach of promise of marriage not later than one year after the day the cause of action accrues.

. . . .

C.P.R.C. § 16.003. *Two-Year Limitations Period.* (a) Except as provided by Sections 16.010 and 16.0045, a person must bring suit for trespass for injury to the estate or to the property of another, conversion of personal property, taking or detaining the personal property of another, personal injury, forcible entry and detainer, and forcible detainer not later than two years after the day the cause of action accrues.

(b) A person must bring suit not later than two years after the day the cause of action accrues in an action for injury resulting in death. The cause of action accrues on the death of the injured person.

C.P.R.C. § 16.004. *Four-Year Limitations Period.* (a) A person must bring suit on the following actions not later than four years after the day the cause of action accrues:

(1) specific performance of a contract for the conveyance of real property;

(2) penalty or damages on the penal clause of a bond to convey real property; or

(3) debt.

(b) A person must bring suit on the bond of an executor, administrator, or guardian not later than four years after the day of the death, resignation, removal, or discharge of the executor, administrator, or guardian.

(c) A person must bring suit against his partner for a settlement of partnership accounts, and must bring an action on an open or stated account, or on a mutual and current account concerning the trade of merchandise between merchants or their agents or factors, not later than four years after the day that the cause of action accrues. For purposes of this subsection, the cause of action accrues on the day that the dealings in which the parties were interested together cease.

C.P.R.C. § 16.0045. *Five-Year Limitations Period.* (a) A person must bring suit for personal injury not later than five years after the day the cause of action accrues if the injury arises as a result of conduct that violates:

(1) Section 22.011, Penal Code (sexual assault); or

(2) Section 22.021, Penal Code (aggravated sexual assault).

(b) In an action for injury resulting in death arising as a result of conduct described by Subsection (a), the cause of action accrues on the death of the injured person.

(c) The limitations period under this section is tolled for a suit on the filing of a petition by any person in an appropriate court alleging that the identity of the defendant in the suit is unknown and designating the unknown defendant as "John or Jane Doe." The person filing the petition shall proceed with due diligence to discover the identity of the defendant and amend the petition by substituting the real name of the defendant for "John or Jane Doe" not later than the 30th day after the date that the defendant is identified to the plaintiff. The limitations period begins running again on the date that the petition is amended.

C.P.R.C. § 16.051. *Residual Limitations Period.* Every action for which there is no express limitations period, except an action for the recovery of real property, must be brought not later than four years after the day the cause of action accrues.

C.P.R.C. § 16.001. *Effect of Disability.* (a) For the purposes of this subchapter, a person is under a legal disability if the person is:

(1) younger than 18 years of age, regardless of whether the person is married;

(2) imprisoned; or

(3) of unsound mind.

(b) If a person entitled to bring a personal action is under a legal disability when the cause of action accrues, the time of the disability is not included in a limitations period.

(c) A person may not tack one legal disability to another to extend a limitations period.

(d) A disability that arises after a limitations period starts does not suspend the running of the period.

C.P.R.C. § 16.063. *Temporary Absence From State.* The absence from this state of a person against whom a cause of action may be maintained suspends the running of the applicable statute of limitations for the period of the person's absence.

C.P.R.C. § 16.062. *Effect of Death.* (a) The death of a person against whom or in whose favor there may be a cause of action suspends the running of an applicable statute of limitations for 12 months after the death.

(b) If an executor or administrator of a decedent's estate qualifies before the expiration of the period provided by this section, the statute of limitations begins to run at the time of the qualification.

C.P.R.C. § 16.065. *Acknowledgment of Claim.* An acknowledgment of the justness of a claim that appears to be barred by limitations is not admissible in evidence to defeat the law of limitations if made after the time that the claim is due unless the acknowledgment is in writing and is signed by the party to be charged.

C.P.R.C. § 16.068. *Amended and Supplemental Pleading.* If a filed pleading relates to a cause of action, cross action, counterclaim, or defense that is not subject to a plea of limitation when the pleading is filed, a subsequent amendment or supplement to the pleading that changes the facts or grounds of liability or defense is not subject to a plea of limitation unless the amendment or supplement is wholly based on a new, distinct, or different transaction or occurrence.

C.P.R.C. § 16.069. *Counterclaim or Cross Claim.* (a) If a counterclaim or cross claim arises out of the same transaction or occurrence that is the basis of an action, a party to the action may file the counterclaim or cross claim even though as a separate action it would be barred by limitation on the date the party's answer is required.

(b) The counterclaim or cross claim must be filed not later than the 30th day after the date on which the party's answer is required.

C.P.R.C. § 16.010. *Misappropriation of Trade Secrets.* (a) A person must bring suit for misappropriation of trade secrets not later than three years after the misappropriation is discovered or by the exercise of reasonable diligence should have been discovered.

(b) A misappropriation of trade secrets that continues over time is a single cause of action and the limitations period described by Subsection (a) begins running without regard to whether the misappropriation is a single or continuing act.

C.P.R.C. § 16.070. *Contractual Limitations Period.* (a) Except as provided by Subsection (b), a person may not enter a stipulation, contract, or agreement that purports to limit the time in which to bring suit on the stipulation, contract, or agreement to a period shorter than two years. A stipulation, contract, or agreement that establishes a limitations period that is shorter than two years is void in this state.

(b) This section does not apply to a stipulation, contract, or agreement relating to the sale or purchase of a business entity if a party to the stipulation, contract, or agreement pays or receives or is obligated to pay or entitled to receive consideration under the stipulation, contract, or agreement having an aggregate value of not less than $500,000.

---

There are many other statutes of limitation; only a few are reproduced here. For example, C.P.R.C. § 16.004 (four-year period for actions on executor, administrator or guardian bond); C.P.R.C. § 16.066 (action on foreign judgment barred by statute of place where obtained); C.P.R.C. § 16.004(a)(1) (four-year period of specific performance of contract to convey realty); C.P.R.C. § 16.008 (architects', engineers', and contractors' liability for real property construction limited to ten years from substantial completion). C.P.R.C. § 16.064, which is dealt with in the chapter on jurisdiction, provides for the contingency that a suit may be dismissed for want of jurisdiction after limitations have run. *See also* C.P.R.C. §§ 16.068, 16.069, *above*. In addition, there are special statutes applicable to particular legislation, such as Bus. & Com. C. § 2.725, providing a four-year period for actions based on sales of goods.

A number of limitation problems, however, are dealt with by court interpretation rather than by statute. Consider the following case regarding application of the discovery rule to a statute of limitations question.

---

## S.V. v. R.V.

*933 S.W.2d 1 (Tex. 1996)*

HECHT, Justice.

R. intervened in her parents' divorce proceeding, alleging that her father, S., was negligent by sexually abusing her until she was seventeen years old. (Given the sensitive nature of these allegations, we refer to the parties only by initials to avoid the use of proper names.) Because R. did not sue her father within two years of her eighteenth birthday as required by the applicable statutes of limitations, her action is barred as a matter of law unless the discovery rule permits her to sue within two years of when she knew or reasonably should have known of the alleged abuse. R. contends that the discovery rule should apply in this case because she repressed all memory of her father's abuse until about a month after she turned twenty, some three months before she intervened in the divorce action. The district court directed a verdict against R. on the grounds that the discovery rule does not apply in this case, and that R. adduced no evidence of abuse. A divided court of appeals reversed and remanded for a new trial. 880 S.W.2d 804. We reverse the judgment of the court of appeals and affirm the judgment of the district court on limitations grounds.

### I

Before we review the evidence in this case it is important to have clearly in mind the issue that is crucial in determining whether to apply the discovery rule. To pose that issue we begin with an analysis of our discovery rule jurisprudence.

We have long recognized the salutary purpose of statutes of limitations. In *Gautier v. Franklin,* 1 Tex. 732, 739 (1847), we wrote that statutes of limitations

> are justly held "as statutes of repose to quiet titles, to suppress frauds, and to supply the deficiencies of proof arising from the ambiguity, obscurity and antiquity of transactions. They proceed upon the presumption that claims are extinguished, or ought to be held extinguished whenever they are not litigated in the proper forum at the prescribed period. They take away all solid ground of complaint, because they rest on the negligence or laches of the party himself; they quicken diligence by making it in some measure equivalent to right. . ." [Joseph P. Story, Conflicts of Law 482.]

More recently, we explained:

> Limitations statutes afford plaintiffs what the legislature deems a reasonable time to present their claims and protect defendants and the courts from having to deal with cases in which

> the search for truth may be seriously impaired by the loss of evidence, whether by death or disappearance of witnesses, fading memories, disappearance of documents or otherwise. The purpose of a statute of limitations is to establish a point of repose and to terminate stale claims.

*Murray v. San Jacinto Agency, Inc.,* 800 S.W.2d 826, 828 (Tex. 1990).

The enactment of statutes of limitations is, of course, the prerogative of the Legislature. At the time this case was filed and tried, the applicable statute was the one governing personal injury actions generally, which provided: "A person must bring suit for . . . personal injury . . . not later than two years after the day the cause of action accrues." Act of May 17, 1985, 69th Leg., R.S., ch. 959, § 1, 1985 Tex. Gen. Laws 3242, 3252, *formerly codified as* Tex. Civ. Prac. & Rem. Code § 16.003(a). The code contains two other provisions relevant to this case. One is: "If a person entitled to bring a personal action is under a legal disability when the cause of action accrues, the time of the disability is not included in the limitations period." Tex. Civ. Prac. & Rem. Code § 16.001(b). The other is: "For the purposes of this subchapter, a person is under a legal disability if the person is: (1) younger than 18 years of age. . ." *Id.* § 16.001(a). Thus, a person has until his or her twentieth birthday (or the next business day, *id.* § 16.072) to bring suit for personal injury from sexual assault if—and here we come to the root of the problem in the case before us—the cause of action "accrued" while the person was a minor.

In 1995, the Legislature enacted a special five-year statute of limitations for sexual abuse cases: "A person must bring suit for personal injury not later than five years after the day the cause of action accrues if the injury arises as a result of conduct that violates: (1) Section 22.011, Penal Code (sexual assault); or (2) Section 22.021, Penal Code (aggravated sexual assault)." Tex. Civ. Prac. & Rem. Code § 16.0045(a); Act of May 27, 1995, 74th Leg., R.S., ch. 739, 1995 Tex. Gen. Laws 3850. This new statute was not enacted until long after the present case was filed and tried and therefore does not govern. *Raley v. Wichita County,* 123 Tex. 494, 72 S.W.2d 577, 579 (1934). We mention it here to point out that under both the new statute and its predecessor, the prescribed period begins to run on the day the cause of action "accrues".

Many other statutes peg the beginning of the limitations period on the date the cause of action "accrues". Occasionally the date of accrual is defined. *E.g.,* Tex. Civ. Prac. & Rem. Code § 16.003(b) (a wrongful death cause of action "accrues on the death of the injured person"). More often, however, the definition of accrual is not prescribed by statute and thus has been left to the courts. As a rule, we have held that a cause of action accrues when a wrongful act causes some legal injury, even if the fact of injury is not discovered until later, and even if all resulting damages have not yet occurred. *Trinity River Auth. v. URS Consultants, Inc.,* 889 S.W.2d 259, 262 (Tex. 1994); *Quinn v. Press,* 135 Tex. 60, 140 S.W.2d 438, 440 (1940). We have not applied this rule without exception, however, and have sometimes held that an action does not accrue until the plaintiff knew or in the exercise of reasonable diligence should have known of the wrongful act and resulting injury. *Trinity River Auth.,* 889 S.W.2d at 262. (Deferring accrual and thus delaying the commencement of the limitations period is distinct from suspending or tolling the running of limitations once the period has begun.)

We first referred to this exception as the "discovery rule" in *Gaddis v. Smith,* 417 S.W.2d 577, 578 (Tex. 1967). We have sometimes used the phrase to refer generally to all instances in which accrual is deferred, including fraud and fraudulent concealment. [citations omitted] At other times we have distinguished between fraudulent concealment and the discovery rule. [citations omitted] Strictly speaking, the cases in which we have deferred accrual of causes of action for limitations purposes fall into two categories: those involving fraud and fraudulent concealment, and all others. The deferral of accrual in the latter cases is properly referred to as the discovery rule. We observe the distinction between the two categories because each is characterized by different substantive and procedural rules. *Weaver,* 561 S.W.2d at 793–794. *See American Petrofina, Inc. v. Allen,* 887 S.W.2d 829 (Tex. 1994); *Woods v. William M. Mercer, Inc.,* 769 S.W.2d 515, 518 (Tex. 1988).

We have considered the applicability of the deferred accrual exception to the legal injury rule in an assortment of settings. [citations omitted]

The justifications we have offered for deferring accrual have been diverse, somewhat inconsistent, and often overly broad. Fraud, we have said, in and of itself prevents running of the statute of limitations, as does fraudulent concealment. [citations omitted] We have applied the discovery rule because of a special relationship between the plaintiff and defendant. *E.g., Willis,* 760 S.W.2d at 645–646 (attorney and client); *Slay,* 187 S.W.2d at 388–393 (trustee and beneficiary). Even apart from such a relationship, we have indicated that the discovery rule applies when it is otherwise difficult for the injured party to learn of the wrongful act. *Gaddis,* 417 S.W.2d at 580 (leaving surgical sponge in plaintiff's body). We have characterized barring claims before plaintiffs knew they had them "shocking results". *Id.* at 581. On the other hand, we have observed:

> Statutes of limitations are not directed to the merits of any individual case, they are a result of legislative assessment of the merits of cases in general. The fact that a meritorious claim might thereby be rendered nonassertible is an unfortunate, occasional by-product of the operation of limitations. All statutes of limitations provide some time period during which the cause of action is assertible. However, preclusion of a legal remedy alone is not enough to justify a judicial exception to the statute. The primary purpose of limitations, to prevent litigation of stale or fraudulent claims, must be kept in mind.

*Robinson,* 550 S.W.2d at 20. A principal factor in deciding whether to apply the discovery rule has been to what extent the claim was objectively verifiable. *E.g., Gaddis,* 417 S.W.2d at 581 (leaving a surgical sponge in a body "is a peculiar type of case which is not particularly susceptible to fraudulent prosecution"); *Robinson,* 550 S.W.2d at 21 ("Unlike *Gaddis v. Smith* there exists in the present case [alleging misdiagnosis of herniated intervertebral disc] no physical evidence which in-and-of-itself establishes the negligence of some person."); *Kelly,* 532 S.W.2d at 949 (credit defamation clear from written report).

While the language in the opinions in these cases varies, a general principle unites them. *Computer Associates International, Inc. v. Altai, Inc.,* 918 S.W.2d 453 (Tex. 1996). Accrual of a cause of action is deferred in two types of cases. In one type, those involving allegations of fraud or fraudulent concealment, accrual is deferred because a person cannot be permitted to avoid liability for his actions by deceitfully concealing wrongdoing until limitations has run. The other type, in which the discovery rule applies, comprises those cases in which "the nature of the injury incurred is inherently undiscoverable and the evidence of injury is objectively verifiable." *Id.* at 456. These two elements of inherent undiscoverability and objective verifiability balance the conflicting policies in statutes of limitations: the benefits of precluding stale or spurious claims versus the risks of precluding meritorious claims that happen to fall outside an arbitrarily set period. Restated, the general principle is this: accrual of a cause of action is deferred in cases of fraud or in which the wrongdoing is fraudulently concealed, and in discovery rule cases in which the alleged wrongful act and resulting injury were inherently undiscoverable at the time they occurred but may be objectively verified. This principle, while not expressed in every deferred accrual case, is derived from them and best defines when the exception to the legal injury rule has been and should be applied.

We have considered the "inherently undiscoverable" element of the discovery rule in several cases. [citations omitted] The common thread in these cases is that when the wrong and injury were unknown to the plaintiff because of their very nature and not because of any fault of the plaintiff, accrual of the cause of action was delayed.

To be "inherently undiscoverable", an injury need not be absolutely impossible to discover, else suit would never be filed and the question whether to apply the discovery rule would never arise. Nor does "inherently undiscoverable" mean merely that a particular plaintiff did not discover his injury within the prescribed period of limitations; discovery of a particular injury is dependent not solely on the nature of the injury but on the circumstances in which it occurred and plaintiff's diligence as well. An injury is inherently undiscoverable if it is by nature unlikely to be discovered within the prescribed limitations period despite due diligence. *Computer Associates,* 918 S.W.2d at 456.

We have also considered the "objectively verifiable" element of the rule in a number of cases. In *Gaddis,* a patient claimed that her doctors were negligent in leaving a sponge inside her body after surgery. The presence of the sponge in her body—the injury—and the explanation for how it got there—the wrongful act—were beyond dispute. The facts upon which liability was asserted were demonstrated by direct, physical evidence. In contrast, *Robinson* involved a claim by a patient against his doctors for misdiagnosis of his back condition. We summarized the issue this way:

> Plaintiff, to prove his cause of action, faces the burden of proving both a mistake in professional judgment and that such mistake was negligent. Expert testimony would be required. Physical evidence generally is not available when the primary issue relevant to liability concerns correctness of past judgment. Unlike *Gaddis v. Smith* there exists in the present case no physical evidence which in-and-of-itself establishes the negligence of some person. What physical evidence was to the cause of action alleged in *Gaddis v. Smith,* expert testimony is to the cause of action in the present case. Even the fact of injury is a matter of expert testimony.

550 S.W.2d at 21. Expert testimony, we concluded, did not supply the objective verification of wrong and injury necessary for application of the discovery rule.

We have adhered to the requirement of objective verification fairly consistently in our discovery rule cases, although we have not always emphasized the requirement because the alleged injury was indisputable. [citations omitted]

In the present case plaintiff R. claims that her father sexually abused her and that she unconsciously repressed all memory of it for years. If the legal injury rule were applied, R.'s claims against S. would each have accrued on the date the alleged incident of abuse occurred. In applying the statute of limitations, however, the years of her minority are not included. In effect, then, under the legal injury rule, R. is in the same position as if her claims all accrued on her eighteenth birthday and limitations began to run on that date, expiring about four months before she filed suit. R.'s claims are therefore barred unless she is entitled to an exception to the legal injury rule. R. does not allege fraud or fraudulent concealment.... For the discovery rule to apply, R.'s claim must have been inherently undiscoverable within the limitations period and objectively verifiable.

We have twice held a fiduciary's misconduct to be inherently undiscoverable. *Willis,* 760 S.W.2d at 645 (attorney); *Slay,* 187 S.W.2d at 394 (trustee). The reason underlying both decisions is that a person to whom a fiduciary duty is owed is either unable to inquire into the fiduciary's actions or unaware of the need to do so. [citations omitted] While a person to whom a fiduciary duty is owed is relieved of the responsibility of diligent inquiry into the fiduciary's conduct, so long as that relationship exists, when the fact of misconduct becomes apparent it can no longer be ignored, regardless of the nature of the relationship. Because parents generally stand in the role of fiduciaries toward their minor children, *see Thigpen v. Locke,* 363 S.W.2d 247, 253 (Tex. 1962), R. was not obliged to watch for misconduct by her father as long as she was a minor. Again, however, R. does not claim to have been misled.

Nevertheless, given the special relationship between parent and child, and the evidence reviewed in detail below that some traumas are by nature impossible to recall for a time, we assume without deciding that plaintiff can satisfy the inherent undiscoverability element for application of the discovery rule. We therefore focus on the second element of objective verifiability. The question is whether there can be enough objective verification of wrong and injury in childhood sexual abuse cases to warrant application of the discovery rule. To answer this question, we look first at the facts of this case and then at the general nature of such cases.

II

[The court reviews the family's history, R.'s delayed recall of allegedly repressed memories of repeated sexual abuse by S., R.'s experiences in counseling, and psychological testing of both R. and S.]

III

R. sued S. for negligence "[d]uring the years 1973 through 1988, inclusively," in engaging or attempting to engage in sexual acts or contacts with her, and exposing himself to her while he was nude and aroused. She alleged that S.'s negligence was a breach of her right to privacy and caused her damages not in excess of $10 million. . . As we have already explained, R.'s claims were subject to the two-year statute of limitations which did not begin to run until R.'s eighteenth birthday, October 15, 1988. R. has not complained of any occurrence after her eighteenth birthday. R.'s claims were thus barred by limitations after October 15, 1990, more than four months before she filed suit. She pleaded, however, that she was entitled to the benefit of the discovery rule.

Trial commenced to a jury. At the close of plaintiff's case, S. moved for directed verdict on two grounds: that the discovery rule did not apply and R.'s action was therefore barred by limitations as a matter of law; and that R. had failed to offer any evidence of sexual abuse. The district court granted S.'s motion without explanation and rendered judgment accordingly. The court of appeals, by a divided vote, reversed the judgment of the district court and remanded the case for further proceedings. 880 S.W.2d 804. . . .

. . . .

The balancing test formulated by the court of appeals plurality [in *L.C. v. A.D.K., available in* 1994 WL 59968 (Tex. App.—Dallas 1994, no writ), relied on by the court of appeals in this case]—weighing the availability of objective evidence against the injustice of requiring that suit be filed before injury is discovered—does not correctly state Texas law. As we have already noted, for the discovery rule to apply a plaintiff's claim must be inherently undiscoverable and objectively verifiable. The concern that meritorious claims will be barred is already taken into account in fashioning these two elements. The two elements strike the proper balance between the beneficial purposes of statutes of limitations and the real concern that a person's rights may be cut off. To reweigh this concern, which is of course a legitimate one, against the very balance it has produced would be to make it the determinative factor. As we stated in *Robinson,* the "preclusion of a legal remedy alone is not enough to justify a judicial exception to the statute. The primary purpose of limitations, to prevent litigation of stale or fraudulent claims, must be kept in mind." 550 S.W.2d at 20. Allowing late-filed claims that are inherently undiscoverable while requiring objectively verifiable injury reduces the likelihood of injustice in cutting off valid claims while affording some protection against stale and fraudulent claims.

The only physical evidence to support R.'s allegations consists of her symptoms and to a lesser extent her behavioral traits, as described by her and the experts who testified on her behalf. In every instance this evidence was inconclusive. The experts testified that R.'s symptoms could have been caused by other things than sexual abuse by her father. While R. fit a behavioral profile for someone who has been sexually abused, the experts acknowledged that that did not mean she had actually been abused. Tests on S. were also inconclusive. While he had many of the characteristics of a sex abuser, he did not match a characteristic profile, and even if he had, it would not prove that he abused R. Thus, there is no physical or other evidence in this case to satisfy the element of objective verifiability for application of the discovery rule.

The kinds of evidence that would suffice would be a confession by the abuser, *e.g. Meiers-Post v. Schafer,* 170 Mich. App. 174, 427 N.W.2d 606, 610 (1988); a criminal conviction, *e.g. Petersen v. Bruen,* 106 Nev. 271, 792 P.2d 18, 24–25 (1990); contemporaneous records or written statements of the abuser such as diaries or letters; medical records of the person abused showing contemporaneous physical injury resulting from the abuse; photographs or recordings of the abuse; an objective eyewitness's account; and the like. Such evidence would provide sufficient objective verification of abuse, even if it occurred years before suit was brought, to warrant application of the discovery rule.

Although we indicated in *Robinson* that expert testimony would not alone provide the objective verification of a claim necessary to invoke the discovery rule, we have not held that such testimony can never suffice, at least in connection with other evidence, such as the symptoms of a survivor of abuse. We have held only that the bar of limitations cannot be lowered for no other reason than a swearing match between parties over facts and between experts over opinions. It is quite possible that recognized expert opinion on a particular subject would be so near consensus that, in conjunction with objective evidence not based entirely on the plaintiff's assertions, it could provide the kind of verification required. That is not true in this case, but we must explain why.

IV

. . . .

In sum, the literature on repression and recovered memory syndrome establishes that fundamental theoretical and practical issues remain to be resolved. These issues include the extent to which experimental psychological theories of amnesia apply to psychotherapy, the effect of repression on memory, the effect of screening devices in recall, the effect of suggestibility, the difference between forensic and therapeutic truth, and the extent to which memory restoration techniques lead to credible memories or confabulations. Opinions in this area simply cannot meet the "objective verifiability" element for extending the discovery rule.

V

As the court of appeals observed in *L.C.*, other states are divided over whether to apply the discovery rule in childhood sexual abuse cases. The caselaw of other jurisdictions is a confusing patchwork that does not seem to indicate any overwhelming trend.

. . . .

Legislatures have been far more active than courts in addressing the problem. Though fewer than fifteen state supreme courts have addressed the problem of limitations and childhood sexual abuse, since the mid-1980s, over half of the state legislatures have enacted or amended statutes of limitations to specifically address the problem of childhood sexual abuse claims. [citations omitted]

. . . .

The Texas Legislature entered this area just last year, enacting a special statute of limitations for civil actions for sexual abuse which extends the period for filing suit from two years to five years. However, the new limitations period, like the old one, begins on the day the cause of action accrues. The Legislature did not define accrual for purposes of the new statute, although it certainly could have done so, just as it could have chosen a different starting date altogether. It could also have prescribed application of the discovery rule as it has done in other statutes. *E.g.*, Tex. Bus. & Com. Code § 17.565 ("All actions brought under [the Deceptive Trade Practices—Consumer Protection Act, *Id.* §§ 17.41–.63] must be commenced within two years after the date on which the false, misleading, or deceptive act or practice occurred or within two years after the consumer discovered or in the exercise of reasonable diligence should have discovered the occurrence of the false, misleading, or deceptive act or practice.") It did not do so, just as it has not done so in criminal sexual abuse cases. Tex. Code Crim. Proc. arts. 12.01(2)(D) & 12.03 (criminal action must be brought within ten years from the date of the commission of the offense). We must assume that the Legislature did not intend for sexual abuse cases to be treated differently from any other case in applying the discovery rule. The Legislature is in the best position to determine and accommodate the complex and conflicting policies involved in determining an appropriate limitations period, and it has done so.

. . . .

VII

Accordingly, we conclude that the discovery rule does not apply in this case. . . .

We do not, of course, impose any additional requirements on proof of a childhood sexual abuse case brought within the applicable limitations period. The objective verifiability requirement of the discovery rule does not apply in proving the case on the merits.

. . . .

The judgment of the court of appeals is reversed and the judgment of the district court is affirmed.

[The concurring opinions of Justice Gonzalez and Justice Cornyn are omitted.]

[The dissenting opinion of Justice Owen is omitted.]

---

## NOTES AND QUESTIONS

(1) *Legal Injury Rule.* The legal injury rule provides that a cause of action accrues when all facts come into existence that authorize a claimant to seek a judicial remedy, even if all damages have not yet occurred or become apparent. Accrual does not depend on when the plaintiff learns of the injury (except in those cases in which the discovery rule applies). *Murphy v. Campbell,* 964 S.W.2d 265, 270 (Tex. 1997). Thus, when the defendant's act is a legal injury in itself, the cause of action accrues at the time of the act. For example, defamation is treated as an act that is wrongful in itself. An action for libel accrues on the date the defamatory material is published, not from the date of its damaging consequences. *Langston v. Eagle Pub. Co.,* 719 S.W.2d 612, 615 (Tex. App.—Waco 1986, writ ref'd n.r.e.).

(2) *Latent Disease Cases.*. The discovery rule applies to cases in which an injured party was exposed to a latent disease and remained asymptomatic for an extended time, beyond the statute of limitations. *Childs v. Haussecker,* 974 S.W.2d 31, 36–45 (Tex. 1998) (latent occupational diseases silicosis and asbestosis); *cf. Howard v. Fiesta Texas Show Park, Inc.*, 980 S.W.2d 716, 720–722 (Tex. App.—San Antonio 1998, pet. denied) (plaintiff's injury arose from single event and was not inherently undiscoverable notwithstanding fact that injured party did not immediately know extent of injuries). Although the Texas Supreme Court has not squarely addressed this issue, under the "single-action" rule there is only one accrual date for the separate asbestos-caused diseases asbestosis and cancer (mesothelioma) even though the cancer does not manifest itself until a number of years after the asbestosis. *Pustejovsky v. Pittsburgh Corning Corp.*, 980 S.W.2d 828, 831–833 (Tex. App.—San Antonio 1998, pet. granted).

(3) *Accounting Malpractice.* Professional liability in areas such as accounting or law (*See* Note (4)) may require application of the discovery rule, which delays the accrual of a cause of action until the earliest date when the plaintiff should be aware of a legal injury through the exercise of reasonable diligence. In *Murphy v. Campbell,* 964 S.W.2d 265 (Tex. 1997), the Court held that a person suffers legal injury from faulty professional advice when the advice is taken, but also found that the discovery rule may apply, given the difficulty a layperson would typically have in recognizing the faulty advice. 964 S.W.2d at 270. Thus, a cause of action based on accounting malpractice rendered to the *Murphy* plaintiffs accrued when they received a deficiency notice from the Internal Revenue Service, which was when they first should have known of their injury. *Murphy v. Campbell,* 964 S.W.2d 265, 269–271 (Tex. 1997).

(4) *Legal Malpractice.* The discovery rule applies to cases of legal malpractice. *Willis v. Maverick,* 760 S.W.2d 642, 645 (Tex. 1988). In addition, a special tolling doctrine applies in legal malpractice cases such that the limitations period is suspended until all appeals are exhausted in the underlying action if it is alleged that legal malpractice occurred in the prosecution or defense of that suit. *Hughes v. Mahaney & Higgins,* 821 S.W.2d 154, 157 (Tex. 1991).

(5) *Medical Malpractice.* A special limitations statute applies in medical malpractice cases:

R.C.S. Art. 4590i. Medical Liability and Insurance Improvement Act.

> Section 10.01. Limitation on Health Care Liability Claims. Notwithstanding any other law, no health care liability claim may be commenced unless the action is filed within two years from the occurrence of the breach or tort or from the date the medical or health care treatment that is the subject of the claim or the hospitalization for which the claim is made is completed; provided that, minors under the age of 12 years shall have until their 14th birthday in which to file, or have filed on their behalf, the claim. Except as herein provided, this subchapter applies to all persons regardless of minority or other legal disability.

Under this statute, suit must be brought within two years of the date of the occurrence of the breach or tort, or within two years from the date the medical or health care that is the subject of the claim is completed. R.C.S. Art. 4590i § 10.01. The Texas Supreme Court has explained that "the Legislature's intent in passing Art. 4590i, § 10.01 was to abolish the discovery rule in cases governed by the Medical Liability Act." *Morrison v. Chan,* 699 S.W.2d 205, 208 (Tex. 1985). In addition, the Texas Supreme Court has interpreted the Medical Liability Act to mean that "[w]hen the precise date of the specific breach or tort is ascertainable from the facts of the case . . ., section 10.01 requires the limitations period to run from the date of the breach or tort" rather than from the date the patient's health care treatment was completed. *Kimball v. Brothers,* 741 S.W.2d 370, 372 (Tex. 1987).

The statutory phrase "notwithstanding any other law" eliminates a number of the statutory tolling provisions contained in Chapter 16 of the Civil Practice and Remedies Code, including Sections 16.001 (Effect of Disability) and 16.063 (Temporary Absence From State) and casts others in doubt, such as, for example, Section 16.062, which provides that the limitation period for causes of action against or in favor of a decedent is suspended for one year after his or her death, or until the time of qualification of an executor or administrator of the decedent's estate, whichever is earlier. *See Bala v. Maxwell,* 909 S.W.2d 889, 892–893 (Tex. 1995) (statute does not toll limitation period in survival action arising from medical malpractice); *but see Valdez v. Texas Children's Hospital,* 673 S.W.2d 342, 344–345 (Tex. App.—Houston [1st Dist.] 1984, no writ) (former R.C.S. Art. 5538 (now C.P.R.C. § 16.062) tolled limitation period for health care liability claim brought by estate representative).

Although the common law discovery rule does not apply, the "Open Courts" provision of Article 1, Section 13 of the Texas Constitution (". . . All courts shall be open, and every person for an injury done him, in his lands, goods, person or reputation, shall have remedy by due course of law") precludes the legislature from making a remedy contingent on an impossible condition, such as bringing suit when the nature of the injury could not have been discovered before limitations ran. *See Diaz v. Westphal,* 941 S.W.2d 96, 99 (Tex. 1997) (distinction between discovery rule and open courts doctrine explained); *see also Nelson v. Krusen,* 678 S.W.2d 918, 923 (Tex. 1984) (claimant who could not have discovered injury has "reasonable time" after injury could have reasonably been discovered to bring suit).

(6) *Fraudulent Concealment.* A separate doctrine, called fraudulent concealment, suspends the limitations period if a defendant makes fraudulent representations or conceals facts that would reveal the existence of a cause of action, until the time the defendant's wrongful conduct is discovered or should have been discovered in the exercise of reasonable diligence. *See American Petrofina, Inc. v. Allen,* 887 S.W.2d 829, 830 (Tex. 1994).

## FIRST NAT. BANK OF EAGLE PASS v. LEVINE

*721 S.W.2d 287 (Tex. 1986)*

WALLACE, Justice

This is a suit by Mrs. Ben Levine against First National Bank of Eagle Pass, Texas, for tortious interference with business relations. The sole issue is whether the two-year or four-year statute of limitations applies to this cause of action. The trial court granted a summary judgment for the Bank on the basis that the two-year statute applies. The court of appeals, based upon a holding that the four-year statute applies, reversed the judgment of the trial court and remanded the cause for trial. 706 S.W.2d 749 (Tex. App. 1986). We reverse the judgment of the court of appeals and affirm the judgment of the trial court.

The petition of Mrs. Levine alleged that she had made an application for a loan from the Small Business Administration and gave the Bank as a credit reference. The loan was refused. She submitted another application without the Bank as a reference and the second application was granted. She further alleged the Small Business Administration told her that the Bank had given a negative credit reference. The parties stipulated that the events made the basis of this suit occurred more than two years, but less than four years, prior to the filing of the suit.

The applicable statute of limitations in effect at the time the case was filed was Tex. Rev. Civ. Stat. Ann. art. 5526, now Tex. Civ. Prac. & Remed. Code Ann. § 16.003 (Vernon 1986) (the two-year statute) and art. 5529, now Tex. Civ. Prac. & Rem. Code § 16.004 (Vernon 1986) (the four-year statute). Article 5526 stated in pertinent part:

> There shall be commenced and prosecuted within two years after the cause of action shall have accrued, and not afterward, all actions or suits in court of the following description:
>
> 1. Actions of trespass for injury done to the estate or the property of another.

Article 5529 stated in pertinent part:

> Every action . . . for which no limitation is otherwise prescribed, shall be brought within four years next after the right to bring same shall have accrued and not afterward.

The dispositive question in this case is whether a suit for tortious interference with business relations is an action of trespass for injury done to the estate or property of another. To determine the answer to that question we must look to judicial history and its treatment of the tort of "trespass."

The Constitution of the Republic of Texas, 1836, Art. IV, Sec. 13, 1 Laws of Texas 1074, provided that Congress should as early as practicable enact by statute the Common Laws of England. In response to that constitutional mandate, the Congress of the Republic of Texas, on January 20, 1840, declared that "the Common Law of England . . . should continue in force until altered or repealed by Congress." 2 Laws of Texas 177.

In reviewing the history of English Common Law, we find that the original meaning of the term "trespass" was that "a defendant 'with force and arms' and 'against the peace of our Lord the King' had interfered with a plaintiff's land or goods." B. Lyon, *A Constitutional & Legal History of Medieval England*, 634 (2d ed. 1980). By the thirteenth century, however, the definition of "trespass" had been expanded to include what, in our jurisprudence, is known as a tort. S.F.C. Milsom, *Historical Foundation of the Common Law*, p. 261 (1969).

Following the English Common Law, this Court in 1885, in interpreting "trespass" as used in the two year statute of limitations stated:

> The word "trespass" as here used, is used, not in the technical sense, but broadly, and means any act violative of the right of another through which injury is done to his estate or property. *Bear Bros. & Hirsch v. Marx & Kempner*, 63 Tex. 298 (1885).

Tortious interference with a contract was held to be controlled by the two-year statute in *Atomic Fuel Extraction Corp. v. Estate of Slick*, 386 S.W.2d 180 (Tex. Civ. App.—San Antonio 1964) *writ ref'd n.r.e. per curiam*, 403 S.W.2d 784 (Tex. 1965). In *National Founders Corp. v. Central National Bank*, 521 S.W.2d 92 (Tex. Civ. App.—Houston [14th Dist.] 1975, writ ref'd n.r.e.), the plaintiff alleged a tortious interference with business relations by the defendant bank by wrongful foreclosure of stock pledged to secure a loan. The court of civil appeals upheld a summary judgment based upon a holding by the trial court that suit was barred by the two-year statute of limitations.

In *Citizens State Bank of Dickinson v. Shapiro*, 575 S.W.2d 375 (Tex. Civ. App.—Tyler 1978, writ ref'd n.r.e.), a former client of a law firm alleged that the firm actively "interfered with [his] interest in the family business." The trial and appellate courts held the action to be barred by the two-year statute of limitations.

Black's Law Dictionary defines "trespass" as:

> *Trespass*. An unlawful interference with one's person, property, or rights. At common law, trespass was a form of action brought to recover damages for any injury to one's person or property or relationship with another.

*Black's Law Dictionary* 1347 (5th ed. 1979).

The court of appeals in this case relied on *Phillips Chemical Co. v. Hulbert*, 301 F.2d 747 (5th Cir. 1962), in holding that the case is controlled by the four-year statute. In *Hulbert*, the court, without discussng the issue, stated that the four-year statute of limitations applied to an action for interference with business relations. The court cited *Brown v. American Freehold Land Mortgage Co.*, 97 Tex. 599, 80 S.W. 985 (1904) as authority. The *Brown* case merely held that the plaintiff's cause of action was not limited to libel and slander; thus the one-year statute of limitations did not apply. It is inapplicable both to the *Hulbert* facts and to this case. For this reason, the court in *Hulbert* incorrectly held the four-year statute applied to wrongful interference with business relations.

The Fifth Circuit case which correctly interprets Texas law is *Coastal Distributing Co., Inc. v. NGK Spark Plug Co., Ltd.*, 779 F.2d 1033 (5th Cir. 1986), which held that the two-year statute of limitation applied to a case alleging unfair competition. The court stated:

> The unfair competition claim, based on NGK's wrongful acquisition and use of Coastal's trade secrets, is a tort governed by the two-year limitations period of article 5526.

779 F.2d at 1038.

We hold that trespass, within the meaning of article 5526, includes suits for tortious inteference with business relations. Accordingly, we reverse the judgment of the court of appeals and affirm the judgment of the trial court.

## NOTES AND QUESTIONS

(1) *Statutory Interpretation.* What part of Section 16.003 of the Civil Practice and Remedies Code provides the broadest coverage as a result of Justice Wallace's opinion in the preceding case? If the term "trespass" is equivalent to the term "tort," what kinds of tort cases involve "injury done to the estate or the property" of another? What kind of recovery is obtainable in a tortious interference case?

(2) *A Word of Caution.* Why do the Texas limitation statutes speak so confusingly about these important issues? Consider the following discussion of the subject from W. Dorsaneo, "The Texas General Limitation Statutes: Dealing with Mumbo Jumbo," 1 *Pers. Inj. Rptr.* 145 (1987).*

*The Texas General Limitation Statutes: Dealing With Mumbo Jumbo*

Hardly anything is more worrisome than the prospect of dueling unsuccessfully with a statute of limitation. A lawyer who misconstrues the law of limitations has a difficult time explaining the matter. There are few trial lawyers on the plaintiff's side of the docket who have not had nightmares about this problem area.

Currently, the general limitation statutes are located in Chapter 16 of the Civil Practice and Remedies Code. A general review of the code sections indicates that the provisions were not drafted by a modern lawyer who thinks in terms of negligence cases, strict liability in tort cases, breach of contract cases, etc. These types of cases are not mentioned in the code sections. As a result of the way the sections are drafted, it is not always easy to apply them. For example, although it is clear that a two year period is applicable to "personal injury" cases [C.P.R.C. § 16.003], when a case does not involve personal injuries (and perhaps when recovery is not so limited), clarity diminishes. This is so because Chapter 16, like its statutory predecessors, prescribes particular periods for commencing suit in terms of the types of actions that existed in Anglo-American law when Chapter 16's statutory predecessors were first enacted in Texas. Consequently, some of the limitations sections contain what can be called mumbo jumbo. Where did we get this mumbo jumbo?

*The Sources of Texas Limitation Laws*

On February 5, 1841, a comprehensive statute of limitations was approved by the Fifth Congress of the Republic of Texas. The legislation appears to have been directed toward resolving problems created by the repeal of the statutes of limitation in force prior to the legislative adoption of the common law in 1840. Dr. Anson Jones, President pro tem of the Senate at that time (and the last President of the Republic) introduced the bill in the Senate but it is not clear who drafted it. The end product seems to have been borrowed because it bears some substantial resemblance to limitation statutes then in effect in Alabama and Mississippi.

One thing is clear. Despite the fact that Texas had previously rejected the common law system of pleading and the forms of action in favor of a more simplified and less formalistic model, when it became necessary to enact a comprehensive limitations statute, the draftsmen copied from common law jurisdictions. In these jurisdictions, limitation statutes prescribed particular periods for commencing suit in terms of the type or form of action. Consequently, while this borrowing may have seemed to be a good idea at the time, because of the arcane way in which actions were identified, it is a bad idea now.

*Recent Developments and Interpretive Problems*

The Texas Supreme Court has recently had occasion to grapple with the general limitations statutes in *National Bank of Eagle Pass v. Levine*, 721 S.W.2d 287 (Tex. 1986). The case involved the question of whether the two year limitation statute [C.P.R.C. § 16.003 (formerly R.C.S. Art. 5526)] or the general and residual four year statute [C.P.R.C. § 16.051] applied in a tortious interference case, *i.e.*, a case not involving personal injuries. The San Antonio Court of Appeals had held that former Article 5529 applied because those actions "enumerated in article 5526 do not include tortious interference with business or prospective contractual relations" and, therefore, "the general four year period found in article 5529 controls." *Levine v. First Nat. Bank of Eagle Pass*, 706 S.W.2d 749, 751–752 (Tex. App.—San Antonio 1986, *rev'd* 721 S.W.2d 287 (Tex. 1986). The Texas Supreme Court reversed. The Court held that the residual four year statute did not apply to the claim because it was included within the two year statute's coverage of "[a]ctions of trespass for injury done to the estate or property of another." *See* former R.C.S. Art. 5526(1) now contained in C.P.R.C. § 16.003(a). The primary justification for the Court's holding is an historical interpretation of the meaning of the term "trespass" under which "trespass" encompasses virtually all torts, regardless of the nature of the interference with another's rights. This historical explanation is buttressed by the definition of "trespass" that is contained in *Black's Law Dictionary* 1347 (5th ed. 1979) and by case law that had applied the two year statute to business tort cases involving economic losses. These cases applied an earlier version of the two year statute without analysis of the statutory language. Moreover, the cited cases do not reflect an appreciation of the overall problem of statutory construction that is presented by the terminology of the general limitations statutes.

The statutory interpretation set forth in *Levine* may indicate that the Court has made the sound policy choice that all tort cases are covered by the two year statute whether or not they are explicitly mentioned by it. This choice is a sound one because a clear rule is needed in light of the procedural penalty that is imposed on persons who wait too long to file suit. Unfortunately, neither the statutory language nor precedent necessarily compels this result in other business tort cases.

*Prior Tinkering With Mumbo Jumbo: The 1979 Amendments*

As a result of amendments to the general limitations statutes made in 1979, in several contexts, Texas cases suggest that not all tort cases are covered by the two year statute. *See, e.g.*, *Anderson v. Sneed*, 615 S.W.2d 898, 903–904 (Tex. App.—El Paso 1981, no writ)—legal malpractice case involving negligent failure to file suit covered by four year statute, not two year statute.

Prior to the 1979 amendments to former articles 5526 (two years) and 5527 (four years), fraud claims for damages in non-personal injury cases were considered "actions for debt" covered by subsection 4 of former article 5526 because it encompassed "[a]ctions for debts where the indebtedness is not evidenced by a contract in writing." *See Steele v. Glenn*, 57 S.W.2d 908, 910 (Tex. Civ. App.—Eastland 1933), writ dism'd, 61 S.W.2d 810 (Tex. 1933); *Blondeau v.*

*Sommer*, 139 S.W.2d 223, 225 (Tex. Civ. App.—Galveston 1940, writ ref'd). As a result of the 1979 amendments, all actions for "debt" were moved to the four year limitation statute. *See* former R.C.S. Art. 5527(1) now codified as C.P.R.C. § 16.004(a)(3). Hence, the prior cases suggest that such actions including certain business fraud cases (of the sort cited in *Levine*) and negligence cases not involving personal injuries would be governed by the four year limitations period provided by former article 5527(1). This reasoning is the rationale for the El Paso Court's conclusion in *Anderson v. Sneed, supra.*

*Dealing With Mumbo Jumbo After Levine*

In light of the broad interpretation that is given to the statutory language construed by the Texas Supreme Court in the *Levine* case, too much reliance should not be placed on *Anderson v. Sneed* (or its antecedents) because after *Levine* "trespass" equals "tort" and, hence, all tort cases (except for malicious prosecution, libel, and slander, which must be brought no later than one year after the day the cause of action accrues) are covered by the two year statute. In other words, as a general rule, the best way to deal with this mumbo jumbo is to bring all tort cases within two years. Try very hard not to convince yourself that you have more time. Think about it.

(3) *Subsequent Supreme Court Action*. The "tort equals trespass" reasoning in the *Levine* opinion has been undercut by the Texas Supreme Court's subsequent opinion in *Williams v. Khalaf,* 802 S.W.2d 651 (Tex. 1990). In that case, the court held that the four-year statute applied to fraud claims because they are considered actions for debt, rather than trespasses. After *Williams,* only torts that involve some form of violence (even if it is exceedingly small) are trespasses and governed by the two-year statute. In *Williams*, after concluding that fraud is not a trespass, the Court reasoned that the four-year statute applied because the modern fraud cause of action developed from an action on the case for deceit, and was related to debt as an evolution from the action of assumpsit.

At least two things are clear from the *Williams* decision. First, the four-year statute is applicable to fraud actions and has been since August 27, 1979. Second, it is no longer sufficient to rely on the rule of thumb that if an action sounds in tort the two-year statute is applicable. Each cause of action must be carefully analyzed to determine which, if any, statute of limitation refers to it. If the action is not expressly mentioned, then the common law origin of the cause of action must be researched to determine which action referred to in the statutes of limitations, if any, is analogous. If the cause of action has not been held to be analogous to an action that is referred to in the statutes, then the four-year residual statute is applicable. It is likely, however, that the Texas Supreme Court will hold that any action that can be classified as a tort will be considered a trespass action under the two-year statute, unless it can be demonstrated that it had a different common law development. *See* Thomas and Brooks, *The 1979 Amendments Revolutionized the Texas Statutes of Limitation. . . . But It Was Not Recognized Until Almost 11 Years Later,* 54 Tex. B.J. 325, 328 (1991).

## [C] Methods of Avoiding Malpractice

### [1] Systems for Dealing With Time Deadlines

#### Hanson, LAUGHING ALL THE WAY HOME . . . A "TICKLER" SYSTEM THAT WORKS

*29 Tex. B.J. (1966)*[*]

No lawyer who has practiced long has failed to be plagued by his subconsciousness as he closes his office of an evening with the nagging doubt of having left some matter unattended. How many of us have gone through a day with the persistent thought that there is an important deadline needing attention? But, which file? Sometimes, the lack of a simple and efficient reminder system finds lawyers in an embarrassing position, either with the court or client.

Lawyers handling many cases or numerous files have found it difficult, if not impossible, to keep themselves abreast of happenings and deadlines attendant to each case or file unless some type of reminder system is utilized. Recognizing the obvious need, lawyers have devoted many hours to devising a satisfactory method of file reminder or "tickler" system. Numerous involved and time-consuming methods have been promulgated, but the true value of any such system lies in its simplicity of operation. It has been found that the reminder system set out in this article is so simple that it can be utilized by any law office, regardless of the number of lawyers, secretaries, files and filing systems employed.

*NECESSARY MATERIALS*

Each matter coming under the system must be placed in a FILE FOLDER customarily used by the lawyer. The only other materials necessary for the use of the system are TWO inexpensive and readily available DESK CALENDARS, one for the lawyer and one for his secretary. Although any type of calendar can be used, and each lawyer may have his own preference, it is desirable to use an 11½-inch by 10-inch page calendar with one month on each page, divided into blank squares for each day of the month. This enables the lawyer to summarize at a glance and organize the work required for any given day, week or month.

*THE PULL DATE*

After the client's file folder is established for a particular matter and the lawyer has performed his initial work, he merely writes a date on the upper righthand portion of the outside of the file folder, such date being a day in the future on which he anticipates further work to be performed or information obtained on the matter. The date notation made on the file folder, which may be called the "pull date," provides the secretary with necessary information for proper and complete posting of the file to her calendar. In addition to marking the pull date on the file folder, the lawyer may also note thereon the work he anticipates performing on that certain date.

The determination of the pull date by the lawyer is entirely within his discretion and depends upon the type and importance of the matter involved, his foreseeable commitments and the desires of his client. Generally, every active file should be marked for pulling monthly, if for no reason other than to advise the client of its unchanged status. Although particularly active files should

[*] Reprinted with permission of the Texas Bar Journal, copyright © 1966.

be pulled every ten days, the determination of the pull date may follow the time limits set out in the Rules of Civil Procedure. Statutes, such as those dealing with probate, workmen's compensation, and mechanic's liens, may also provide a guide to determining the pull date for a file.

After marking the pull date on the file folder, the lawyer then posts the file on his own desk calendar by making a simple notation such as "#65015—Acme v. George" on the calendar square provided for that particular pull date. Calendar notations of extremely important matters are made in red ink to denote that it is imperative that such file have attention on that day.

After the lawyer has posted the pull date on his calendar, the file folder is placed in his "out" basket, from which the secretary will remove the folder, post the file on her calendar in the same manner as the lawyer posted the file and return the file folder to the filing cabinet.

*PULLING THE FILE*

Each day the secretary will check her calendar, remove from the filing cabinet each file folder posted for that particular day and cross off that matter from her calendar. The file folder, which is placed on the lawyer's desk, is examined by him and crossed off his calendar as he completes the additional work on such file. File folders are also pulled by the secretary prior to the assigned pull date upon receipt by the lawyer of correspondence or new information necessitating additional work to be performed.

*UP-DATING THE FILE*

After performing the required work on the matter, the lawyer up-dates the file by marking a new pull date on the upper right-hand corner of the folder. Thereafter, the above process is repeated until the file is ultimately retired upon conclusion of the matter. As with any office system, this "tickler" method requires clear instruction to the secretary that no file will be removed from the out-basket without a new pull date noted thereon or a notation that the file be retired.

This basic revolving reminder system provides a series of simple steps which can be varied, not only with the wishes and desires of each lawyer, but also with the particular type of legal work involved. Its doublecheck concept insures that no file is overlooked and that no deadline passes without the lawyer's full knowledge. Additionally, it demonstrates that a valuable by-product of any adequate reminder system is the organization of legal work enabling conservation of a lawyer's time and improved legal service to his clients.

### [2] The "Conflict of Interest" Letter

FORM LETTER FOR UNCONTESTED DIVORCE

Mr. Harry P. Hobbs
2031 Landry Lane
London, TX 60106

Dear Sir:

The purpose of this letter is to express in writing your relationship with this law office.

In connection with divorce proceedings contemplated between yourself and your spouse, you should be aware that the undersigned and this office represent Ms. Hobbs. In a divorce action, just as in any other action, both parties have the right to have lawyers of their choice. We encourage you to consider exercising that right.

In connection with this proceeding, we cannot render legal advice or act on your behalf. We can only act on your spouse's behalf and in her interest. To be more specific, we cannot act as your lawyer, but only as your spouse's.

Please understand that this letter is not meant to be impolite or to create bitter feelings between you and us or between you and your spouse. We have a duty under the Texas Disciplinary Rules of Professional Conduct to make you aware of these matters, and it is for that reason that we have written this letter.

Very truly yours,

Received:

____________________

Lawrence A. Lawyer

______________________________

Harry P. Hobbs

---

## NOTES AND QUESTIONS

(1) *Defining the Relationship.* What are the advantages of a letter such as this? The disadvantages? Do the advantages outweigh the disadvantages? What is the last paragraph designed to accomplish, and does it do so?

Many professionals working in the marriage counseling area take the position that when lawyers enter the picture, they create disputes between spouses that never would have otherwise existed and need not be created. Does this sort of letter justify that complaint? If it does, should it be used anyway, on the theory that the lawyer has a duty to clarify such matters irrespective of such consequences?

(2) *Drafting Exercise.* How would you adapt this communication in the event of a potential conflict between two business people who nevertheless wish to employ you jointly to handle their defense in a stockholder's derivative suit? If there is such a conflict, should you write a letter of this sort? What action would you take in the event of a conflict of the nature shown in *Employers Cas. Co. v. Tilley*?

# CHAPTER 2

## EMERGENCY AND INTERIM RELIEF (SPECIAL REMEDIES)

### SCOPE

Emergency judicial intervention involves procedural problems that must be considered in the context of the need to obtain interim relief before final adjudication. As a general principle, interim relief is used to preserve the status quo pending a determination of the primary proceeding. Although coverage of extraordinary creditors' remedies is provided in more specialized courses devoted to them, this chapter provides overview coverage of the most important special remedies.

## § 2.01 Temporary Restraining Orders and Injunctions

*Read Tex. R. Civ. P. 680–689, 692.*

### J. Weber, SO YOU NEED A TEMPORARY RESTRAINING ORDER?

*41 Tex. B.J. 728 (1978)**

Imagine this situation:

*You are sitting at your desk at 2:00 P.M. on Friday. The telephone rings. One of your better clients, Sam Successful, is frantic! Sam has recently purchased a beautiful 50-acre tract of woodlands on which he and his wife plan to build a summer home. Today Sam received word from an adjoining landowner that Landeater Lumber Company has cut his fence, and begun cutting the timber on his homesite. Landeater has a timber deed by which it claims the right to cut the timber. Landeater refused to cease operations and hopes to have the land cleared before the weekend is over. Sam wants you to stop Landeater immediately, before the entire tract is ruined. You need a temporary restraining order!*

The facts always differ, but two things are always the same: there is a crisis, and both you and your client are in a hurry. This note will not deal with the substantive issue of whether Sam is entitled to a TRO (temporary restraining order). Instead, it presents the practical aspects of: (a) preparing the proper pleadings; (b) "greasing the skids"; and (c) effectively pursuing the TRO through so as to fully accomplish your purpose: to halt the cutting of trees pending a determination of the parties' rights.

The process of obtaining a TRO is complex. There are many details, legal and practical, all of which *must* be taken into account if you are to reach your objective.

---

I. What Papers Do We Need?

These are the items the lawyer must have ready when he or she applies for his temporary restraining order:

A. The petition or complaint.

B. The temporary restraining order itself.

C. The restraining order bond.

D. The filing fee.

These items will be discussed in detail but remember—by now *it is 2:30* on Friday afternoon. You must make the practical arrangements to see that the necessary people are available to issue and serve the writ. This is "greasing the skids."

II. Greasing the Skids

You cannot issue and serve the temporary restraining order yourself. You will need the cooperation of the district judge (state or federal), the district clerk (state or federal), and the county sheriff or federal marshal. Each of these persons has a role to play and each must be available.

A. *Call the District Clerk:* A personal call to the clerk's office and a conversation with the deputy who will be handling the application for the TRO is a must. Give the clerk an estimate of when the papers will be prepared and the application filed. In counties with multiple judges, one judge may be designated the injunction judge. The clerk can give you this information. Rule 685, T.R.C.P., provides for presentment of the application for TRO to the judge *prior* to filing the petition with the district clerk. Therefore, especially on weekends and after hours, a hearing can be arranged with the judge prior to filing the pleadings with the clerk. Since the clerk does not issue citation and writ until after the order has been signed and the bond posted, this procedure will require the clerk to make only one special trip to the courthouse. The clerk can file the application when you meet him at his or her office for preparation of the citations and writ.

B. *Contact the Judge:* You should immediately contact the injunction judge to determine his availability. Has he or she left for the weekend? Where can he or she be reached? Can another judge hear the matter? If it is necessary to present the application to the court at home, arrangements should be made in advance. The judge may want you to advise Landeater or his lawyer to be present. Furthermore, an advance call to the judge emphasizes the urgency of the proceeding. During this conference you may apprise the court of the circumstances of the case, thus minimizing the actual time required to present the matter to the court. Also, the judge might be asked the amount of the bond he or she is inclined to set so you can have it prepared in advance.

C. *Contact the Marshal or Sheriff:* The TRO is worthless to the lawyer unless he can get it served on Landeater and its employees. The lawyer must confer with the sheriff or marshal to schedule service of the restraining order after it is issued. If after hours, do not ask the sheriff or marshall to meet you at the courthouse at the same time you have arranged to meet the clerk. The filing of the petition, issuance of citation and preparation of copies of the order to be served may take some time, especially if there are many persons to be served, (as, in a labor strike), and the marshal and sheriff may not be needed for an hour or so.

III. Preparing the Papers

A. *The Bond.* The bond is the last instrument you will need, but the first you need to prepare. Both the state and federal rules (Rule 684, T.R.C.P.; Rule 65c, F.R.C.P.) require posting of a bond in almost all cases before issuance of a restraining order.[1]

If you intend to post a corporate surety bond, you should contact the bonding or insurance agent immediately. By now *it is 3:30 P.M.* and the bond must be prepared quickly, before the bonding company closes. The clerk will probably honor your own personal or firm check for the bond, but it [is] preferable that if your client intends to post cash, he should make arrangements to have the cash available or to have the district clerk approve his personal check.

B. *Prepare the Facts.* Who and where are the parties? Sam must supply you with basic information concerning Landeater Lumber Company, including some address where the sheriff or marshal can find its management, in order to serve the TRO.

Get a good factual summary of the events giving rise to your case. Hard, specific facts are needed for the application for temporary restraining order, to show that Sam owns the property in question, that Landeater has actually begun cutting timber without permission, and that, unless Landeater is restrained, Sam will suffer irreparable harm for which there is no adequate remedy at law. *Remember* you or your client must swear to the factual allegations (Rule 682, T.R.C.P., Rule 65(b), F.R.C.P.) and, under the Texas Rules, an affidavit based only on information and belief is not sufficient.

C. *The Petition or Complaint.* The petition or complaint will contain five parts, many of which are common to any original petition or original complaint:

(1) *The names of the parties* and places where the defendant can be served with citation;

(2) *The factual allegations* giving rise to your right to relief, i.e., that Sam owns the land and that Landeater is cutting the timber without right or authority. Sam must further allege and show that irreparable harm will result if the temporary restraining order is not granted, to-wit: that the land upon which he is hoping to build his summer home is being ruined by the cutting of the timber, that his remedy at law of money damages is not adequate to protect him, and that Landeater is unable to respond in money damages anyway. These allegations must be of specific facts—pleading legal conclusions is not sufficient.[2]

(3) *The prayer* should ask for not only a temporary restraining order but also that Landeater be cited to appear and show cause why the restraining order should not be converted into a temporary injunction. The prayer should further request a permanent injunction upon final hearing on the merits.

(4) *The affidavit:* Both the state and federal rules require verified pleading, or alternatively, in the federal court, supporting affidavits. Although Rule 14, T.R.C.P.,

---

[1] A bond need not be posted by the United States Fed. R. Civ. P. 65(e). In the discretion of the court no bond may be required in Texas in a divorce case. Tex. R. Civ. P. 693a. A limited and conditional exception to the bond requirement is offered to the State of Texas, its subdivisions, and a number of federal agencies by Tex. Rev. Civ. Stat. Ann. art. 279a (1973).

[2] *Wilson v. Whittaker,* 353 S.W.2d 945, 947 (Tex. Civ. App.—Houston 1962, no writ); *Texas State Board of Medical Examiners v. McKinney,* 315 S.W.2d 387, 390 (Tex. Civ. App.—Waco 1958, no writ).

allows the applicant's attorney to make the affidavit, it is not sufficient (in state court) that the affidavit be upon information and belief.[3] Further, an affidavit made by the applicant's attorney must state his authority to do so.[4] In federal court either affidavits or verified pleading may be used as evidence supporting issuance of a TRO.[5]

(5) *Certificate of Counsel:* Texas Rule 680 provides that no temporary restraining order shall be granted without notice unless it clearly appears from specific facts shown by affidavit or the complaint that immediate and irreparable harm will result before notice can be served. The allegations made in your state court petition should satisfy this requirement. In federal court a certificate of counsel is usually included at the conclusion of the application for TRO to satisfy the requirements of Federal Rule 65(b)(2). A form of certificate is set out in the footnote.[6]

D. *Temporary Restraining Order.* The requirements of the order itself are set out in Rules 680 and 683, T.R.C.P. and Rules 65(b) and (d), F.R.C.P. The order should track the complaint or petition in:

(1) defining the injury in specific factual terms;

(2) stating specifically why the injury is irreparable; mere conclusory statements will not suffice;[7]

(3) stating why the order was granted without notice;

(4) providing for the posting of a bond as a prerequisite to the clerk's issuing writs of injunction. (*Note:* the amount of the bond can be left blank to be filled in by the judge when the order is signed.)[8]

(5) *specifically* setting out the act or acts being enjoined.[9]

---

[3] *Durrett v. Boger,* 234 S.W.2d 898, 900 (Tex. Civ. App.—Texarkana 1950, no writ).

[4] *Kern v. Treeline Gulf Club, Inc.,* 433 S.W.2d 215, 216 (Tex. Civ. App.—Houston [14th Dist.] 1968, no writ).

[5] The Fifth Circuit prefers personal affidavits but does not rule out consideration of hearsay evidence, or affidavits based upon information and belief, in the proper case. *See Marshall Durbin Farms, Inc. v. National Farmers Org., Inc.,* 446 F.2d 353, 357–358 (5th Cir. 1971).

[6] "Pursuant to Rule 65(b)(2), Federal Rules of Civil Procedure, counsel for plaintiff certifies that the temporary restraining order sought herein is necessary to halt and prevent immediate, ongoing, and threatened injury for which plaintiff has no adequate remedy at law. Because of the emergency conditions described in the foregoing complaint, there is not sufficient time to effect service upon the defendant [*or plaintiff's counsel has given oral notice to defendant that a temporary restraining order will be sought* ] prior to its issuance and the necessity for relief is immediate. Counsel will furnish notice to defendant of plaintiff's complaint as expeditiously as possible and will effect appropriate service of notice and citation upon defendant prior to any hearing on application for a preliminary injunction."

[7] Tex. R. Civ. P. 683; *see Charter Medical Corp. v. Miller,* 547 S.W.2d 77, 78 (Tex. Civ. App.—Dallas 1977, no writ); *see also State v. Cook United, Inc.,* 464 S.W.2d 105, 106 (Tex. 1971); *Transport Co. of Texas v. Robertson Transports,* 261 S.W.2d 549 (Tex. 1953).

[8] The bond may be a useful defensive tool if you represent the person or entity being enjoined. The bond must be posted prior to the clerk's issuance of the writ. If your client's damages will be significant, the court can, at anytime, entertain a motion to increase the amount of bond.

[9] Legions of cases dismiss restraining orders and injunctions which are too broad to inform what acts were prohibited. Tex. R. Civ. P. 683; *Villalobos v. Holguin,* 208 S.W.2d 871, 875 (Tex. 1948); *Fastex Wildlife Conservation Ass'n v. Jasper, Et Al.,* 450 S.W.2d 904, 918 (Tex. Civ. App.—Beaumont 1970, writ ref'd n.r.e.). On the other hand, the order must be broad enough to encompass every shade and phase of the prohibited conduct. *Cf. San Antonio Bar Ass'n v. Guardian Abstract & Title Co.,* 291 S.W.2d 697, 702 (Tex. 1956). If you have a labor injunction involving picketing, the acts prohibited in the order are even more important. The language must be specific enough to be easily

(6) specifically stating that the order is binding on the parties, their officers, agents, servants, employees, attorneys, and those persons in active concert with them who receive actual notice of the order by personal service or otherwise;[10]

(7) setting a date, within ten days, for a hearing on application for temporary injunction.

[Effective Jan. 1, 1988, the time for setting a hearing was extended from 10 days to 14 days for state court proceedings. *See* Tex. R. Civ. P. 680.]

IV. Hearing, Filing and Followup

A. *The Hearing.* Now that the skids are greased and the pleadings prepared, you are ready for the hearing. The judge may have instructed you to advise Landeater. He or she may not have. At any rate, you should appear wherever you have arranged to meet the judge with your client, Sam Successful. Sam should be prepared to testify to the matters set out in your pleadings. If the judge grants your TRO, he will (a) fill in the amount of the bond; (b) set a date, within ten days for hearing the application for temporary injunction; and (c) sign the order.

B. *Don't Forget the Filing Fee.* Check state or federal cost schedules to determine the amount of the filing fee. In state court, you should give consideration to the number of citations to be served and include in the filing fee an amount sufficient for service of enough citations to serve Landeater and its employees out on the land. In federal court this is unnecessary, since the marshall will send his bill for services after the fact.

C. *Copies of Pleadings.*

(1) Copies of Petition or Complaint: The lawyer will need sufficient copies of his or her original petition or complaint to serve one on each named defendant.

(2) . Certified Copies of TRO: You will need sufficient certified copies of the TRO for service upon all defendants. Further, if you contemplate serving Landeater's unnamed employees out in the woods (John Doe citations) you will need additional certified copies of the TRO for service on these agents and employees.

D. *Federal Court—A Special Reminder*

(1) In federal court you will need the Form JS-44c, Civil Cover Sheet, the form for institution and filing of a new lawsuit.

(2) In addition to a copy of the complaint and the TRO, the lawyer should have prepared, for each named defendant:

(a) a Marshal's Form 285, and

(b) a summons.

(3) If the lawyer intends to have the marshall serve John Doe citations on whoever may be found at the site, he or she should have a supply of forms (Marshal's Form 285) as well as a sufficient number of certified copies of the TRO.

---

understood. On the other hand, it must be broad enough to encompass the cumulative imaginations of forty or fifty striking workers who will spend the day conjuring up alternatives by which the strike may continue without being in literal violation of the court's order. The order should authorize the marshal to seize or confiscate any picket signs or plaques in order to prevent the passing on of the sign from one restrained picketer to another, as yet unrestrained, picketer.

[10] Tex. R. Civ. P. 683; Fed. R. Civ. P. 65(d).

E. *Get the TRO Served.* The sheriff or marshal should be given any assistance necessary to find the defendants and have them served. Furthermore, the lawyer should usually go to the site of the activity. Many times problems may come up at this stage which might thwart the restraining effort if the lawyer is not there to respond immediately.

In the rare instance where a party may defy the restraining order, the lawyer's presence is even more necessary. He or she can prepare, on the spot, the affidavit which will support a citation for contempt. The affidavit will set out what the offending defendant or person has done and is continuing to do in disregard of the court's order after service of same upon him. The lawyer can obtain the officer's signature on the affidavit and present it to the court with an order requiring that the contemptuous person be brought into Court to show cause why he should not be held in contempt.

F. *Prepare for the Temporary Injunction Hearing.* Finally, the lawyer must prepare for the hearing on temporary injunction to be held at the date and time set out in the TRO.

V. Congratulations!

By noon Saturday all is peaceful. Landeater has withdrawn from Sam's land. Sam lost a few trees, but serious damage has been averted. If you have obtained the TRO, had it served, and stopped the cutting smoothly and without a hitch, you have done an outstanding job of legal planning and organization. Sam should be pleased and impressed with a job well done.

---

## NOTE

A temporary restraining order may only be extended once, *for a like period,* absent an agreement to the contrary. Tex. R. Civ. P. 686. The extension order must be made in writing. An oral extension of a temporary restraining order is ineffective and will not support an order of contempt absent notice to the contemnor of the written extension before the alleged contemptuous conduct occurs. *Ex Parte Lesikar,* 899 S.W.2d 654 (Tex. 1995).

---

## CHARTER MEDICAL CORP. v. MILLER

*547 S.W.2d 77 (Tex. Civ. App.—Dallas 1977, no writ)*

ROBERTSON, Justice.

This appeal is from a temporary injunction, enjoining appellants, Charter Medical Corporation, Mesquite Memorial Hospital, Inc., and Howard Mulcay, and all others acting in concert with them, from attempting to enforce the provisions of the amended bylaws of Mesquite Memorial Hospital or in any manner attempting to interfere with or limit the appellees' rights to practice podiatry in the hospital as they existed prior to the adoption of the amendment. The order granting the temporary injunction set forth the reasons for its issuance as follows:

> . . . Plaintiffs have established by full and satisfactory proof all elements required for such injunction, including their probable right to recovery and irreparable damage herein and injury by virtue of the Defendants' conduct;

. . . .

We hold that the recital in this order does not comply with the requirement of Tex. R. Civ. P. 683 that every order granting an injunction shall set forth specific reasons for its issuance. Accordingly, we dissolve the temporary injunction.

In *State v. Cook United, Inc.,* 464 S.W.2d 105, 106 (Tex. 1971), the supreme court stated that a trial court need not explain its reasons for believing an applicant has shown a probable right of recovery on the merits, but must give the reasons why injury will be suffered if the temporary injunction is not ordered. *See Transport Co. of Texas v. Robertson Transports,* 152 Tex. 551, 261 S.W.2d 549 (1953). The specific reasons are to be stated in lieu of mere conclusory statements. *Schulz v. Schulz,* 478 S.W.2d 239, 244–45 (Tex. Civ. App.—Dallas 1972, no writ); *Round Mountain Community v. Fulkes,* 501 S.W.2d 474, 475 (Tex. Civ. App.—Austin 1973, no writ); and *Charton Corp. v. Brockette,* 534 S.W.2d 401, 405 (Tex. Civ. App.—Corpus Christi 1976, writ ref'd n.r.e.). When a temporary injunction order is issued which does not conform to the requirements of the rule, it necessarily constitutes an abuse of the trial court's discretion and requires reversal. *Crouch v. Crouch,* 164 S.W.2d 35, 38 (Tex. Civ. App.—Waco, 1942, no writ). The recital of "irreparable damage herein and injury by virtue of the Defendants' conduct" lacks the specificity required by Rule 683 and by the above decisions. Accordingly, we hold that the trial court abused its discretion.

In view of this holding it would be inappropriate for us to decide the points raised concerning appellees' probable right to permanent injunctive relief, and thus to render, in effect, an advisory opinion. A hearing on an application for temporary injunction does not serve the same purpose as a trial on the merits, nor should an appeal from a preliminary order be used to obtain an advance ruling thereon. Neither should it delay a trial on the merits.

Finally, as we have observed in *Crawford Energy, Inc. v. Texas Industries, Inc.,* 541 S.W.2d 463, 468 (Tex. Civ. App.—Dallas 1976, no writ); *Irving Bank & Trust Co. v. Second Land Corp.,* 544 S.W.2d 684, 689 (Tex. Civ. App.—Dallas 1976, no writ); and *Town Plaza Fabrics, Inc. v. Monumental Properties of Texas, Inc.,* 544 S.W.2d 775 (Tex. Civ. App.—Dallas 1976, no writ); this appeal, like many other temporary injunction appeals, appears to be entirely unnecessary. Presumably, the trial judge, after granting the temporary injunction, would have given the case a preferred setting for an early trial on the merits on request of either party so that the substantial questions involved in this litigation could be decided finally and expeditiously, as directed by the supreme court in *Texas Foundries, Inc. v. International Moulders & Foundry Workers' Union,* 151 Tex. 239, 248 S.W.2d 460, 464 (1952). We see no reason why the case could not have been prosecuted to final judgment in less time than that required by this interlocutory appeal, which decides nothing except whether the status quo should be preserved pending trial on the merits. The most expeditious way of obviating the hardship of an unfavorable preliminary order is to try the case and thus secure a hearing in which both facts and law may be fully developed, and then both trial and appellate courts can render judgment finally disposing of the controversy. *Southwest Weather Research, Inc. v. Jones,* 160 Tex. 104, 327 S.W.2d 417, 422 (1959).

Accordingly, we reverse the judgment of the trial court and dissolve the temporary injunction order.

## § 2.02 Interim Relief for Secured Creditors and Other Claimants

### [A] Sequestration

Sequestration is a purely ancillary statutory procedure. The purpose of the procedure is to take specified property, in which the claimant asserts a preexisting property interest, out of the possession of a party to a suit and place it in the custody of the court pending final judgment on the issue of who is entitled to the property. *Harding v. Jesse Dennett, Inc.*, 17 S.W.2d 862, 864 (Tex. Civ. App.—San Antonio 1929, writ ref'd). The procedure is designed to preserve the property until a final determination on this issue has been made. *See Radcliff Fin. Corp. v. Industrial State Bank of Houston*, 289 S.W.2d 645, 649 (Tex. Civ. App.—Beaumont 1956, no writ). Sequestration is available only when provided for by statute, and strict compliance with the statute and applicable rules of procedure is required. *See American Mortgage Corp. v. Samuell*, 130 Tex. 107, 111–112, 108 S.W.2d 193, 196 (1937); *Hunt v. Merchandise Mart, Inc.*, 391 S.W.2d 141, 144–145 (Tex. Civ. App.—Dallas 1965, writ ref'd n.r.e.).

CIVIL PRACTICE AND REMEDIES CODE

CHAPTER 62. SEQUESTRATION

SUBCHAPTER A. AVAILABILITY OF REMEDY

C.P.R.C. § 62.001. *Grounds.* A writ of sequestration is available to a plaintiff in a suit if:

(1) the suit is for title or possession of personal property or fixtures or for foreclosure or enforcement of a mortgage, lien, or security interest on personal property or fixtures and a reasonable conclusion may be drawn that there is immediate danger that the defendant or the party in possession of the property will conceal, dispose of, ill-treat, waste, or destroy the property or remove it from the county during the suit;

(2) the suit is for title or possession of real property or for foreclosure or enforcement of a mortgage or lien on real property and a reasonable conclusion may be drawn that there is immediate danger that the defendant or the party in possession of the property will use his possession to injure or ill-treat the property or waste or convert to his own use the timber, rents, fruits, or revenue of the property;

(3) the suit is for the title or possession of property from which the plaintiff has been ejected by force or violence; or

(4) the suit is to try the title to real property, to remove a cloud from the title of real property, to foreclose a lien on real property, or to partition real property and the plaintiff makes an oath that one or more of the defendants is a nonresident of this state.

C.P.R.C. § 62.002. *Pending Suit Required.* A writ of sequestration may be issued at the initiation of a suit or at any time before final judgment.

C.P.R.C. § 62.003. *Available for Claim Not Due.* A writ of sequestration may be issued for personal property under a mortgage or a lien even though the right of action on the mortgage or lien has not accrued. The proceedings relating to the writ shall be as in other cases, except that final judgment may not be rendered against the defendant until the right of action has accrued.

## SUBCHAPTER B. ISSUANCE

C.P.R.C. § 62.021. *Who May Issue.* A district or county court judge or a justice of the peace may issue writs of sequestration returnable to his court.

C.P.R.C. § 62.022. *Application.* The application for a writ of sequestration must be made under oath and must set forth:

(1) the specific facts stating the nature of the plaintiff's claim;

(2) the amount in controversy, if any; and

(3) the facts justifying issuance of the writ.

C.P.R.C. § 62.023. *Required Statement of Rights.* (a) A writ of sequestration must prominently display the following statement on the face of the writ:

> YOU HAVE A RIGHT TO REGAIN POSSESSION OF THE PROPERTY BY FILING A REPLEVY BOND. YOU HAVE A RIGHT TO SEEK TO REGAIN POSSESSION OF THE PROPERTY BY FILING WITH THE COURT A MOTION TO DISSOLVE THIS WRIT.

(b) The statement must be printed in 10-point type and in a manner intended to advise a reasonably attentive person of its contents.

## SUBCHAPTER C. DISSOLUTION AND REPLEVY

C.P.R.C. § 62.041. *Motion for Dissolution; Stay.* (a) The defendant may seek dissolution of an issued writ of sequestration by filing a written motion with the court.

(b) The right to seek dissolution is cumulative of the right of replevy.

(c) The filing of a motion to dissolve stays proceedings under the writ until the issue is determined.

C.P.R.C. § 62.042. *Hearing on Motion.* Unless the parties agree to an extension, the court shall conduct a hearing on the motion and determine the issue not later than the 10th day after the motion is filed.

C.P.R.C. § 62.043. *Dissolution.* (a) Following the hearing, the writ must be dissolved unless the party who secured its issuance proves the specific facts alleged and the grounds relied on for issuance.

(b) If the writ is dissolved, the action proceeds as if the writ had not been issued.

C.P.R.C. § 62.044. *Compulsory Counterclaim for Wrongful Sequestration.* (a) If a writ is dissolved, any action for damages for wrongful sequestration must be brought as a compulsory counterclaim.

(b) In addition to damages, the party who sought dissolution of the writ may recover reasonable attorney's fees incurred in dissolution of the writ.

C.P.R.C. § 62.045. *Wrongful Sequestration of Consumer Goods.* (a) If a writ that sought to sequester consumer goods is dissolved, the defendant or party in possession of the goods is entitled to reasonable attorney's fees and damages equal to the greater of:

(1) $100;

(2) the finance charge contracted for; or

(3) actual damages.

(b) Damages may not be awarded for the failure of the plaintiff to prove by a preponderance of the evidence the specific facts alleged if the failure is the result of a bona fide error. For a bona fide error to be available as a defense, the plaintiff must prove the use of reasonable procedures to avoid the error.

(c) In this section, "consumer goods" has the meaning assigned by the Business & Commerce Code.

C.P.R.C. § 62.046. *Liability for Fruit of Replevied Property.* (a) In a suit for enforcement of a mortgage or lien on property, a defendant who replevies the property is not required to account for the fruits, hire, revenue, or rent of the property.

(b) This section does not apply to a plaintiff who replevies the property.

---

In addition to the statutory requirements, the rules of civil procedure must be consulted. See Civil Procedure Rules 696–716.

*Issuance of the Writ of Sequestration.* The application for the issuance of the writ must be made under oath and must set forth specific facts stating the nature of the plaintiff's claim, the amount in controversy, the statutory grounds relied on, and specific facts relied on by the plaintiff to justify findings of fact that support the statutory ground or grounds relied on. Tex. R. Civ. P. 696. Under Civil Procedure Rule 696, the application must comply with all statutory requirements and must be supported by affidavits. The supporting affidavits may be based on information and belief only if the grounds for such belief are specifically stated. The application for the writ must also include a sufficient description of the property to be sequestered to identify it and to distinguish it from similar property. The application must state the value of each article of property and the county in which it is located. Tex. R. Civ. P. 696.

The clerk may issue the writ only on a written order following a hearing, which may be ex parte. The court's written order granting the application must contain specific findings of fact to support the statutory grounds which support the application and the writ. Property to be sequestered must be described in the court order with sufficient certainty to distinguish it from other similar property; in addition to this identification, the order must state the value of each item to be sequestered and the county in which it is located. Tex. R. Civ. P. 696. Before the writ of sequestration can issue, the plaintiff must file a sufficient bond with the court. Tex. R. Civ. P. 698. The court must specify the amount of bond required of the plaintiff in the court order granting the writ. The bond must, in the opinion of the court, be sufficient to "adequately compensate defendant in the event plaintiff fails to prosecute his suit to effect and pay all damages and costs as shall be adjudged against him for wrongfully suing out the writ." Tex. R. Civ. P. 696. Either party may challenge the amount of the bond or the sufficiency of the sureties. Tex. R. Civ. P. 698. The court must also indicate in its order the amount of bond required of the defendant to replevy. Tex. R. Civ. P. 696. Civil Procedure Rule 696 establishes the amount of the bond at the value of the property sequestered or the amount of the plaintiff's claim plus interest if allowed by law on the claim, whichever is less, plus court costs.

*Contents of the Writ and Service on the Defendant.* Civil Procedure Rule 700a requires that the copy of the writ served on the defendant prominently display in 10-point type, in a manner calculated to advise a reasonably attentive person, the following message:

> YOU HAVE A RIGHT TO REGAIN POSSESSION OF THE PROPERTY BY FILING A REPLEVY BOND. YOU HAVE A RIGHT TO SEEK TO REGAIN POSSESSION OF THE PROPERTY BY FILING WITH THE COURT A MOTION TO DISSOLVE THIS WRIT.

Tex. R. Civ. P. 700a. This language, and the rights of dissolution and modification granted under Civil Procedure Rule 712a, help protect the Texas sequestration procedure from constitutional attack.

The writ of sequestration must be directed to a sheriff or any constable within the State of Texas and must command him or her to take possession of the property, subject to the right of replevy and further order of the court. Tex. R. Civ. P. 699. The defendant must be served with a copy of the writ, the application of the plaintiff, accompanying affidavits, and orders of the court. Service may be made in any manner prescribed for service of citation or as provided in Civil Procedure Rule 21a. Service must occur as soon as practicable following the levy of the writ. Tex. R. Civ. P. 700a. On the face of the writ, before the required 10-point language quoted above, the writ must state:

> To ______, Defendant:
>
> You are hereby notified that certain properties alleged to be claimed by you have been sequestered. If you claim any right in such property, you are advised: [The quoted language above in 10-point type must be placed here]. Tex. R. Civ. P. 700a.

*Dissolution or Modification of the Writ of Sequestration.* Under Civil Procedure Rule 712a, the defendant may, for any extrinsic or intrinsic ground or cause, seek by sworn written motion to vacate, dissolve, or modify the writ and the order directing the issuance of the writ. The motion to dissolve, modify, or vacate must admit or deny each finding in the court order authorizing the issuance of the writ. If, however, the moving party is unable to admit or deny a finding contained in the order, that party must state the reasons for the inability to admit or deny it. The motion must then be heard promptly, after reasonable notice to the plaintiff (which may be less than three days) and the issue shall be determined not later than 10 days after the motion is filed. Tex. R. Civ. P. 712a.

Once a Rule 712a motion has been filed, all other proceedings under the writ are stayed except for orders relating to the care and preservation of the property. This stay remains in effect until a hearing is had on the motion and the issue is decided. Tex. R. Civ. P. 712a.

Generally, the writ of sequestration is to be dissolved if the plaintiff fails to prove the grounds relied on for issuance of the writ. The movant, however, has the burden of proving, if he or she so contends, that the reasonable value of the property sequestered exceeds the amount necessary to secure the sum total of the debt, interest for one year, and probable costs. Tex. R. Civ. P. 712a.

In ruling on a motion, the court may make its determination on the basis of uncontroverted affidavits that set forth facts that would be admissible in evidence. If the affidavits are controverted, the court must make its determination on the basis of evidence submitted by the parties in the normal manner. In addition to dissolving the writ, the rules give the court great latitude in modifying its previous order on the writ if dissolution is not appropriate. If the court determines that the order or the writ should not be vacated or dissolved, but only modified, it may make further orders with respect to a replevy bond filed by the defendant that are consistent with the modification. Tex. R. Civ. P. 712a.

*Replevy.* The defendant may replevy the property at any time before judgment. Tex. R. Civ. P. 701. "If the movant has given a replevy bond, an order to vacate or dissolve the writ shall vacate the replevy bond and discharge the sureties." Tex. R. Civ. P. 712a. Replevin requires that the defendant give bond with sufficient sureties; the surety or sureties must be approved by the officer who levied the writ and must be payable to the plaintiff. The amount of the bond is the amount fixed by the original court order; that is, an amount equivalent to the value of the property or the amount of the plaintiff's claim and one year's interest, whichever is the lesser amount, and the probable costs of court. Tex. R. Civ. P. 701. *See* Tex. R. Civ. P. 702, 703 (condition of bond for personal property and real estate).

If the bond is objectionable to either party, that party, on motion and notice to the opposing party, has the right to a prompt judicial review of the amount of the bond required, denial of bond, sufficiency of sureties, or to the estimated value of the property in question. Judicial review of these issues is to be made by the court that authorized the issuance of the writ on the basis of evidence submitted, or uncontroverted affidavits setting forth facts that would be admissible. Tex. R. Civ. P. 701.

If the defendant fails to replevy the property within 10 days after levy of the writ and the service of notice, the plaintiff may replevy by giving bond payable to the defendant in an amount not less than the amount fuxed by the court's order, with sufficient sureties to be approved by the levying officer. Tex. R. Civ. P. 708. Under Rule 708, if the property to be replevied is personalty, the bond must provide that the plaintiff will either preserve the property in the same condition as when it is replevied, together with the value of the fruits or revenue thereof, to abide the decision of the court, or that the plaintiff will pay the value thereof, or the difference between its value at the time of replevy and the time of judgment. If the property is realty, the bond must provide that the plaintiff will not injure the property and will pay the value of the rents if required to do so. On proper notice by either party, the complaining party can obtain judicial review of the plaintiff's replevy, just as in the case of defendant's replevy.

For further discussion and forms, see W. Dorsaneo, *Texas Litigation Guide*, Ch. 40, *Sequestration* (1998). See also Soules, *Attachment, Sequestration, and Garnishment: The 1977 Rules,* 32 Sw. L.J. 753 (1978).

### [B] Notice of Lis Pendens

Another method of preserving the subject matter of the litigation pending final resolution is the notice of lis pendens. The procedure is controlled by the following statutes.

PROPERTY CODE

Prop. C. § 12.007. *Lis Pendens.* (a) After the plaintiff's statement in an eminent domain proceeding is filed or during the pendency of an action involving title to real property, the establishment of an interest in real property, or the enforcement of an encumbrance against real property, a party to the action who is seeking affirmative relief may file for record with the county clerk of each county where a part of the property is located a notice that the action is pending.

(b) The party filing a lis pendens or the party's agent or attorney shall sign the lis pendens, which must state:

(1) the style and number, if any, of the proceeding;

(2) the court in which the proceeding is pending;

(3) the names of the parties;

(4) the kind of proceeding; and

(5) a description of the property affected.

(c) The county clerk shall record the notice in a lis pendens record. The clerk shall index the record in a direct and reverse index under the name of each party to the proceeding.

Prop. C. § 13.004. *Effect of Recording Lis Pendens.* (a) A recorded lis pendens is notice to the world of its contents. The notice is effective from the time it is filed for record, regardless of whether service has been made on the parties to the proceeding.

(b) A transfer or encumbrance of real property involved in a proceeding by a party to the proceeding to a third party who has paid a valuable consideration and who does not have actual or constructive notice of the proceeding is effective, even though the judgment is against the party transferring or encumbering the property, unless a notice of the pendency of the proceeding has been recorded under that party's name in each county in which the property is located.

---

The following excerpt from *King v. Tubb,* 551 S.W.2d 436, 443–444 (Tex. Civ. App.—Corpus Christi 1977, no writ), sets out the purpose and the effect of the notice of lis pendens:

> The ultimate effect of lis pendens is to prevent either party to certain litigation from alienating the property that is in dispute. *Black v. Burd,* 255 S.W.2d 553 (Tex. Civ. App.—Fort Worth 1953, writ ref'd n.r.e.). It is a well settled rule of law in this State that a purchaser of land pendente lite stands in no better attitude than his vendor. *Rio Bravo Oil Co. v. Hebert,* 130 Tex. 1, 106 S.W.2d 242 (1937); *Randall v. Snyder,* 64 Tex. 350 (1885); *Willis v. Ferguson,* 59 Tex. 172 (1883) and cases cited therein. The very purpose of the statutory *lis pendens* notice is to put those interested in the land on inquiry as to the status of the land. *Kropp v. Prather,* 526 S.W.2d 283 (Tex. Civ. App.—Tyler 1975, writ ref'd n.r.e.). Therefore, it is apparent that the filing of the *lis pendens* notice by Tubb and Allison rendered King's title to the land defective and justified Middlebrook's failure to consummate the sale, resulting in his claim for the return of his $20,000.00 earnest money. . . . Since the trial court was correct in holding that the lis pendens rendered the contract unperformable, it is unnecessary for us to consider the propriety of the trial court's findings that the property description in the contract was too vague and indefinite and was incapable of being located on the ground.

For a discussion of the relationship of the lis pendens statutes to receivership, see *First S. Properties, Inc. v. Vallone,* 533 S.W.2d 339, 342–343 (Tex. 1976) (holding property in receivership in custodia legis. "We hold that compliance with Articles 6640 and 6642 is not required to prevent lands in receivership from being acquired under attempted sales by third parties . . ." without court approval).

### [C] Self-Help Repossession by Secured Party

Section 9.503 of the Texas Business and Commerce Code provides, "Unless otherwise agreed a secured party has on default the right to take possession of the collateral. In taking possession a secured party may proceed without judicial process if this can be done without breach of the peace or may proceed by action. If the security agreement so provides the secured party may require the debtor to assemble the collateral and make it available to the secured party at a place to be designated by the secured party which is reasonably convenient to both parties. Without removal a secured party may render equipment unusable, and may dispose of collateral on the debtor's premises under [Business and Commerce Code] Section 9.504." Bus. & Com. C. § 9.503. The scope of this statute depends on a number of definitions of terms set out elsewhere in the code (*see* Bus. & Com. C. §§ 1.201 (action; party), 9.105 (collateral; debtor; secured party; security agreement), 9.109 (equipment)) and on the definition of two terms (default, breach of the peace), which the code does not define.

## § 2.03 Interim Relief for the General (Unsecured) Creditor

### [A] Attachment

The purpose of attachment is to impound and fix a lien on the nonexempt property of a debtor before judgment. Property of a debtor that is exempt from attachment, execution, or other seizure for the satisfaction of liabilities is set forth in Property Code Sections 41.001–41.004. The remedy is structured primarily to prevent a debtor from making himself or herself judgment proof during the pendency of litigation. *Midway Nat'l Bank of Grand Prairie v. West Tex. Wholesale Co.*, 447 S.W.2d 709, 710–711 (Tex. Civ. App.—Fort Worth 1969), writ ref'd n.r.e. per curiam, 453 S.W.2d 460 (Tex. 1970). Attachment is in the nature of execution before judgment. When the writ of attachment is levied on the nonexempt property of the debtor, the creditor obtains a lien on the property. In other words, the general (unsecured) creditor becomes a judicial lien creditor from the date of levy. The type of suit that will normally support the issuance of the writ is a suit for a debt, which is defined as an obligation to pay a liquidated sum on an express or implied contract. C.P.R.C. § 61.001. *El Paso Nat'l Bank v. Fuchs*, 89 Tex. 197, 201, 34 S.W. 206, 207 (1896).

CIVIL PRACTICE AND REMEDIES CODE

CHAPTER 61. ATTACHMENT

SUBCHAPTER A. AVAILABILITY OF REMEDY

C.P.R.C. § 61.001. *General Grounds.* A writ of original attachment is available to a plaintiff in a suit if:

(1) the defendant is justly indebted to the plaintiff;

(2) the attachment is not sought for the purpose of injuring or harassing the defendant;

(3) the plaintiff will probably lose his debt unless the writ of attachment is issued; and

(4) specific grounds for the writ exist under Section 61.002.

C.P.R.C. § 61.002. *Specific Grounds.* Attachment is available if:

(1) the defendant is not a resident of this state or is a foreign corporation or is acting as such;

(2) the defendant is about to move from this state permanently and has refused to pay or secure the debt due the plaintiff;

(3) the defendant is in hiding so that ordinary process of law cannot be served on him;

(4) the defendant has hidden or is about to hide his property for the purpose of defrauding his creditors;

(5) the defendant is about to remove his property from this state without leaving an amount sufficient to pay his debts;

(6) the defendant is about to remove all or part of his property from the county in which the suit is brought with the intent to defraud his creditors;

(7) the defendant has disposed of or is about to dispose of all or part of his property with the intent to defraud his creditors;

(8) the defendant is about to convert all or part of his property into money for the purpose of placing it beyond the reach of his creditors; or

(9) the defendant owes the plaintiff for property obtained by the defendant under false pretenses.

SUBCHAPTER B. ISSUANCE

C.P.R.C. § 61.021. *Who May Issue.* The judge or clerk of a district or county court or a justice of the peace may issue a writ of original attachment returnable to his court.

---

To obtain a writ of attachment, the plaintiff must make an affidavit and execute a bond. The affidavit must state three things (C.P.R.C. § 61.022):

(1) general grounds for issuance under C.P.R.C. § 61.001 (1), (2) and (3);

(2) the amount of the demand; and

(3) specific grounds for issuance under C.P.R.C. § 61.002.

The writ of attachment may also be issued in suits based on tort or unliquidated demands if personal service on the defendant cannot be obtained within Texas. C.P.R.C. § 61.005. A writ of attachment may be issued either at the initiation of the suit or during its pendency but may not be issued before suit has been initiated (C.P.R.C. § 61.003) and it may be issued even though the plaintiff's debt or demand is not due. C.P.R.C. § 61.004. However, a final judgment may not be rendered against the defendant until the debt or demand becomes due.

The rules of civil procedure supplement the statutes concerning the remedy of attachment. *See* Tex. R. Civ. P. 592–609.

*Issuance of the Writ of Attachment.* Civil Procedure Rule 592 establishes specific procedures governing the plaintiff's application for, and the court's issuance of, a writ of attachment. Rule 592 was designed to meet the constitutional demands of due process. The specificity requirements are similar to the requirements for the application for the writ of sequestration described above.

Civil Procedure Rule 592a requires that the plaintiff file an attachment bond before the writ will be issued and provides for judicial review, if requested by either party, of the amount of the bond or the sufficiency of the sureties. The bond required of the plaintiff is designed to compensate the defendant adequately in the event the plaintiff fails to prosecute the suit to effect and to compensate the defendant sufficiently for all damages and costs that may be adjudged against the plaintiff for wrongfully suing out the writ of attachment. Tex. R. Civ. P. 592. If the attachment is wrongful, there are remedies available to the defendant. If none of the grounds stated in the plaintiff's affidavit for the issuance of the writ is true, then the attachment is wrongful. *See, e.g., Petty v. Lang*, 81 Tex. 238, 242, 16 S.W. 999, 1000 (1891). This is true notwithstanding the plaintiff's good faith. *See, e.g., Christian v. H. Seeligson & Co.*, 63 Tex. 405, 406 (Tex. Comm'n App. 1885, opinion adopted). The party whose property was wrongfully attached must prove interference with his or her property rights to be entitled to more than nominal damages. *Bartley v. J.M. Radford Grocery Co.*, 15 S.W.2d 46 (Tex. Civ. App.—Amarillo 1929, writ ref'd). When, however, the attachment creditor has acted maliciously and without probable cause, exemplary damages may be available. *See, e.g., Craddock v. Goodwin*, 54 Tex. 578, 586–589 (1881). The attachment bond requirement is almost identical to the bond required by the rules for sequestration.

*Contents of the Writ and Service on the Defendant.* The writ of attachment must be directed to a sheriff or any constable within the state. The instructions to the sheriff or constable direct the officer to attach property "of a reasonable value in approximately the amount fixed by the court." Tex. R. Civ. P. 593. The levy of the writ fixes a lien on personalty. A lien on real estate is affixed by an "office levy." This procedure involves endorsement of the writ with a description of the realty and recordation of the writ and the return in the county in which the realty is located. The writ of attachment must inform the defendant of the right to replevy and regain possession by filing a motion to dissolve the writ. *See* Tex. R. Civ. P. 598a.

*Dissolution or Modification of the Writ of Attachment.* Civil Procedure Rule 608 governs dissolution and modification of the writ of attachment. Rule 608 provides for a prompt hearing at which the burden of persuasion is on the attaching creditors.

*Replevy.* Civil Procedure Rule 599 provides that the defendant may replevy on the filing of the required bond. The amount of the bond required of the defendant is the amount of the plaintiff's claim, one year's accrued interest if allowed by law, and the estimated costs of court. At the election of the defendant, however, the bond may be set at the value of the property the defendant seeks to replevy. Either party is entitled to judicial review of the amount of the bond, denial of bond, sufficiency of the sureties, and the estimated value of the property attached. Tex. R. Civ. P. 599. Rule 599 further provides that the defendant may move to have property of equal value substituted for the property attached.

### [B] Prejudgment Garnishment

Prejudgment garnishment is also provided for by statute and is available (1) when an original attachment has issued; or (2) when suit is brought for a debt owed and an affidavit is made by the plaintiff to the effect that the debt is just, due and unpaid and that the defendant does not possess property in Texas subject to execution sufficient to satisfy the debt and the plaintiff is not seeking to injure or harass the defendant or the garnishee with the garnishment. C.P.R.C. § 63.001. The debt must be liquidated. *See Cleveland v. San Antonio Bldg. & Loan Ass'n*, 148 Tex. 211, 215, 223 S.W.2d 226, 228 (1949).

The effect of the service of the writ is set forth in the following statute.

C.P.R.C. §. 63.003. *Effect of Service.* (a) After service of a writ of garnishment, the garnishee may not deliver any effects or pay any debt to the defendant. If the garnishee is a corporation or joint-stock company, the garnishee may not permit or recognize a sale or transfer of shares or an interest alleged to be owned by the defendant.

(b) A payment, delivery, sale, or transfer made in violation of Subsection (a) is void as to the amount of the debt, effects, shares, or interest necessary to satisfy the plaintiff's demand.

---

Only personalty (tangible or intangible) can be "seized" by the service of the writ. Moreover, certain property is exempt from garnishment. *See* C.P.R.C. § 63.004. Tex. Const. Art. 16, § 28 provides, "No current wages for personal service shall ever be subject to garnishment, except for the enforcement of court-ordered child support payments" an exemption that is repeated by Section 63.004 of the Civil Practice and Remedies Code.

The rules of civil procedure also must be consulted on the subject of prejudgment garnishment. *See* Tex. R. Civ. P. 657–679.

*Issuance of the Writ of Garnishment.* The requirements of an application for and issuance of the writ of garnishment are essentially the same as for the writ of attachment. A prejudgment garnishment bond is required. *See* Tex. R. Civ. P. 658a. The bond must be sufficient to cover any potential damages for wrongful garnishment. Tex. R. Civ. P. 658. The remedies for wrongful garnishment remain. Garnishment is wrongful if the prescribed allegations set forth in the garnishor's affidavit are untrue. *See Peerless Oil & Gas Co. v. State*, 138 S.W.2d 637, 640 (Tex. Civ. App.—San Antonio 1940), *aff'd,* 138 Tex. 301, 158 S.W.2d 758 (1942). As in attachment, good faith is no defense. *Massachusetts v. Davis*, 160 S.W.2d 543, 554 (Tex. Civ. App.—Austin 1942), *aff'd in part and rev'd in part on other grounds,* 140 Tex. 398, 168 S.W.2d 216 (1942). Although good faith is not a defense, the garnishee cannot recover exemplary damages unless he or she can prove that the garnishment was obtained maliciously and without probable cause. *See, e.g., Biering v. First Nat'l Bank*, 69 Tex. 599, 7 S.W. 90 (1888); *Pegues Mercantile Co. v. Brown*, 145 S.W. 280, 281 (Tex. Civ. App.—El Paso 1912, no writ). Third parties whose property interests are wrongfully garnished as belonging to the garnishment debtor may also maintain an action against the erring creditor. *See Stevens v. Simmons*, 61 S.W.2d 122, 125 (Tex. Civ. App.—El Paso 1933, no writ).

After the writ of garnishment is served on the garnishee, the garnishee must answer as in other civil actions. If the garnishee's uncontroverted answer reflects that he or she is indebted to the defendant or has possession of property of the defendant, after due notice to the defendant, the court in which the garnishment is pending may, on hearing, reduce the required amount of the bond to double the sum of the garnishee's indebtedness to the defendant, plus the value of the property in his or her possession that belongs to the defendant. Tex. R. Civ. P. 658a.

Garnishment involves a separate ancillary lawsuit between the garnishor and the garnishee (the third party). The garnishment action cannot be concluded with a judgment against the garnishee until the primary action for the debt between the plaintiff (garnishor) and the defendant (debtor) ends. The court dockets the case in the name of the plaintiff as plaintiff and of the garnishee as defendant. Tex. R. Civ. P. 659. The court must immediately issue a writ of garnishment if the application and the bond requirements are fulfilled. Tex. R. Civ. P. 659, 661. Under Civil Procedure Rule 659, the writ should command the garnishee to appear and answer under oath what, if anything, is owed to the defendant-debtor, and what the debt was to the defendant-debtor at the time the writ was served. The garnishee must also reveal what property of the defendant-debtor is in his or her possession presently, and what property was possessed when the writ was served. Finally, the garnishee must reveal any other persons known who are indebted to the defendant-debtor, or have property belonging to that person, in their possession. Tex. R. Civ. P. 659.

*Contents of the Writ and Service on the Defendant.* After the court orders issuance of the writ, which may be in the form prescribed by Civil Procedure Rule 661, the defendant-debtor is required to be served with a copy of the writ, the application, accompanying affidavits, and orders of the court as soon as practicable following the service of the writ on the garnishee. Tex. R. Civ. P. 663a. As in the case of attachment, the writ must inform the defendant of the right to replevy and to regain possession by filing a motion to dissolve the writ. Tex. R. Civ. P. 663a.

*Dissolution or Modification of the Writ.* Civil Procedure Rule 664a controls dissolution or modification of the writ and the order directing its issuance. It is similar to counterpart rules concerning dissolution or modification of the writs of sequestration and attachment.

*Replevy.* The defendant-debtor may replevy at any time before judgment if the garnished property has not been previously claimed or sold. Tex. R. Civ. P. 664. The defendant-debtor may replevy the property, any part thereof, or the proceeds from the sale of the property if it has been sold under a court order. The procedure necessary to entitle the defendant-debtor to replevy in garnishment is the same as in attachment. Also, as in attachment, the defendant-debtor may move to have property substituted for the garnished property. Tex. R. Civ. P. 664.

*Garnishment After Judgment Distinguished.* Garnishment after judgment is also available. Post-judgment garnishment is a procedure available to a judgment-creditor to satisfy a money judgment from the judgment-debtor's nonexempt personal property in the possession of a third person. Post-judgment garnishment is only available when the plaintiff has a valid, subsisting judgment and the judgment-debtor does not have property in his or her possession within the state subject to execution to satisfy the judgment. C.P.R.C. § 63.001(3). This statute governing post-judgment garnishment has been found constitutional notwithstanding that post-judgment garnishment does not require that a writ of execution be issued, or issued and returned unsatisfied. No bond is required for post-judgment garnishment.

---

## BANK ONE, TEXAS, N.A. v. MOODY

*800 S.W.2d 280 (Tex. App.—El Paso 1990), rev'd on other grounds, 830 S.W.2d 81 (Tex. 1992)*

OSBORN, Chief Justice.

This is an appeal from the overruling of a motion for new trial following the entry of a Default Judgment on a Writ of Garnishment. We affirm.

Robert L. Moody, Jr. obtained a judgment in the 56th judicial District Court against Apex Natural Resources, Inc. and Joe Richardson for $79,000.00, plus $3,000.00 in attorney's fees and for cost and post-judgment interest. A month later, Moody filed an Application for Writ of Garnishment in the same court and the Writ was served upon the Bank's senior vice-president fourteen days later. No answer was filed and a Default Judgment was entered against the Bank for $82,000.00, plus $1,000.00 for attorney's fees, interest and cost. The Bank filed a motion for new trial and a hearing was had, but the trial court never acted on the motion and it was overruled by operation of law.

. . . .

. . . Appellant contends a default judgment for the full amount of the judgment held by the garnishee violates its right to due process. The basic complaint is that the Writ served upon the Bank only required it to answer as to what, if anything, the Bank was indebted to its two customers. It argues that it was not put on notice that it could be held liable for a sum in excess of the balance of its customers' accounts and could not know that judgment could be rendered against it for $82,000.00. No authority is cited to support this contention. The Writ is a basic standard form similar to those found in *Moffett's Texas Civil Form Book,* Form No. 362 (Ninth Ed. 1948) or *West's Texas Forms,* Vol. 1, Chapter 23, Post-Judgment Garnishment, section 23.4 (1977) and in Tex. R. Civ. P. 661. This question is discussed in Dorsaneo, *Texas Litigation Guide,* Vol. 2, § 42.103[1][g] as follows:

> Traditionally, a garnishee who fails to answer the writ of garnishment is subject to a default judgment. The amount may be in excess of the amount owed by the garnishee to the judgment debtor. The constitutionality of holding a garnishee liable when no notice that such a consequence may result from a default is subject to considerable doubt.

*See also* Dorsaneo, *Texas Litigation Guide,* Vol. 2, § 42.05[2][b]. We, likewise, have considerable doubt about holding one liable for more than it has in its possession without adequate notice. But, in this case, we need not reach that issue. This issue has been raised for the first time on appeal, was not presented to the trial court and under Tex. R. App. P. 52(a), has not been preserved for appellate review. Point of Error No. Two is overruled.

[NOTE: The judgment against the garnishee (Bank One) was reversed by the Texas Supreme Court, 830 S.W.2d 81 (Tex. 1992), which found that the trial court erred in denying an equitable motion for new trial. Proof of the bank's mistaken belief that it was not required to file a written answer if it froze the subject account supported its argument that its failure to answer was not intentional or due to conscious indifference.]

---

## NOTES AND QUESTIONS

(1) *Case Evaluation.* Decide what prelitigation special remedy or other action, if any, would be appropriate in each of the following situations. Take into account both legal and practical considerations (that is, try to decide on the most expeditious and inexpensive method, but one that is legally justified under the circumstances).

(a) Big-Hearted Ben, a car dealer, sold a new Hellcat Spyder automobile to Dan Deadbeat. Dan has stopped making payments to Ben. He keeps the car parked on the street at night; Ben, of course, has no key to it. The contract of sale provides Ben with a lien and with all remedies allowed under the Uniform Commercial Code. What can Ben do?

(b) Assume the same situation as in (a), but with the additional fact that Dan keeps the car in his locked garage at night, is a light sleeper; can see the garage door from his bedroom window and has a loaded shotgun nearby. In addition, Dan has announced to Ben his intention to drive the car to California to get it where Ben cannot get to it and to "take a sledgehammer to it" if Ben does. What can Ben do now?

(c) Don Debtor has defaulted on an unsecured promissory note to Carl Creditor. He has told Carl that he intends to remove all his non-exempt property to California, and has, to Carl's knowledge, already begun doing so.

(d) Diane Debtor owes $10,000 to Carol Creditor and Carol has learned that Diane has $100,000 in one bank account and $200,000 in another. Both accounts have maintained that balance for the past year. Diane disputes the debt and has refused to pay for that reason.

(e) Assume the same situation as (d), except that Diane's accounts total only $15,000, her cash requirements for her business are about $20,000 per month, her balance has been steadily diminishing, and Diane has stated to Carol that she owes the debt but "can't pay it because I need the money for other things."

## § 2.04 Wrongful Use of Special Remedies

### [A] Due Process Problems

#### MONROE v. GENERAL MOTORS ACCEPTANCE CORP.

*573 S.W.2d 591 (Tex. Civ. App.—Waco 1978, no writ)*

McDONALD, Chief Justice.

This is an appeal by defendant from judgment against him for the unpaid balance of a retail installment contract, secured by a 1976 Chevrolet, and foreclosure of security interest of plaintiff in such automobile.

On October 26, 1977 plaintiff GMAC, sued defendant Monroe on a retail installment contract executed by defendant in the credit purchase of a 1976 Chevrolet automobile; alleging plaintiff is owner of such contract; that defendant is in arrears in his payments; that plaintiff has declared the entire principal balance due as provided in the contract; and sought judgment for the balance of principal and interest due, attorney's fees, and foreclosure of security interest in the automobile.

On the same date plaintiff filed the affidavit of its manager A. B. Rich for writ of sequestration of the automobile, and on such date the Judge of the 74th District Court issued writ of sequestration commanding the Sheriff to take possession of the automobile and keep same subject to further order of the court. On October 29, 1977 the Sheriff took possession of the automobile pursuant to the writ of sequestration.

On October 31, 1977 defendant filed Motion to Dissolve the Writ of Sequestration, and the trial court after hearing, on November 4, 1977 overruled same.

Trial on the merits was to a jury which found:

(1) Plaintiff GMAC requested defendant Monroe to surrender possession of the 1976 Chevrolet.

(2) The unpaid balance of the installment contract was $4,597.34.

(3) It was necessary for GMAC to secure an attorney.

(4) GMAC declared the entire principal balance of the installment contract due.

(5) GMAC did not waive its right to accelerate maturity.

(6) A. B. Rich made the sequestration affidavit at a time when he had reasonable knowledge to fear defendant would conceal, dispose of, ill treat, waste, destroy, or remove the 1976 Chevrolet from the jurisdiction of the court.

It was stipulated a reasonable attorney's fee would be $1000.

The trial court rendered judgment on the verdict for plaintiff for $5,597.34 (unpaid balance of the installment contract plus $1000. attorney's fee); and for foreclosure of security interest in the automobile.

Defendant appeals on 11 points which we summarize as 4 main contentions.

(1) The trial court erred in issuing the writ of sequestration because plaintiff's affidavit was insufficient as a matter of law in not setting forth:

a) specific facts as to the amount in controversy;

b) specific facts justifying issuance of the writ;

c) sufficient facts from which a reasonable conclusion may be drawn that defendant would conceal, dispose, ill treat, waste, destroy or remove the property during pendency of suit.

(2) The trial court erred in overruling defendant's motion to dissolve the writ because:

a) there was no evidence of any grounds and specific facts relied on by plaintiff for issuance of the writ as required by statute;

b) the evidence was insufficient to prove the grounds and specific facts relied on for issuance of the writ.

(3) The trial court erred in not assessing attorney's fees and damages against plaintiff.

(4) The Sequestration Statute [Article 6840] is unconstitutional in that it fails to provide for notice and opportunity for a hearing at a meaningful time and in a meaningful manner before depriving a defendant of his property, thereby depriving the defendant of procedural due process.

. . . .

Contention 1 asserts plaintiff's affidavit insufficient as a matter of law.

Section 2 Article 6840 requires the affidavit to state the nature of plaintiff's claim, the amount in controversy, and the facts justifying the issuance.

Plaintiff's affidavit for writ of sequestration filed herein states "Plaintiff sues for the title and possession of the hereinafter described property and for foreclosure of a security interest therein [describing the 1976 Chevrolet] of the value of $6,987.96; the said property is now in the possession of the defendant . . . and the plaintiff fears that there is immediate danger that the defendant in possession thereof will conceal, dispose of, ill treat, waste or destroy such property, or remove the same out of the jurisdiction of this court during the pendency of this suit."

We think the affidavit is in substantial and sufficient compliance with the statute to authorize the judge to issue the writ.

Contention 2 asserts the trial court erred in overruling defendant's motion to dissolve the writ because there was no evidence or insufficient evidence of any grounds or specific facts to sustain issuance of the writ.

At the hearing on the motion to dissolve it was undisputed that defendant owed a debt (the installment contract), secured by a lien (security interest) on the automobile, and that defendant was delinquent 3 monthly payments of $166.38 each; that defendant had been in default before; that plaintiff's agents had contacted defendant by telephone and personally urged him to pay up; that he said "he didn't have the money and there was no way we could get the car at his place of business or at his home." Defendant at other times agreed to pay up his delinquent payments by times certain, but failed to do so. An automobile is a rapid depreciation chattel, and in the hands of defendant who did not make his payments but was continuing to use the vehicle, we think the trial court authorized to overrule the motion to dissolve the writ, and that the evidence is ample to sustain such order.

Contention 3 asserts the trial court erred in not assessing damages and attorney's fees against the plaintiff. Attorney's fees and damages against the plaintiff are authorized only if the writ is dissolved.

Contention 4 asserts the sequestration statute is unconstitutional in that it does not provide for notice and hearing at a meaningful time and in a meaningful manner before depriving defendant of his property.

Defendant relies on *Fuentes v. Shevin,* 1972, 407 U.S. 67, 92 S. Ct. 1983, 32 L. Ed. 2d 556, which held statutes in Florida and Pennsylvania invalid which permitted a creditor to obtain a prejudgment writ of replevin through summary process of ex parte application upon posting a bond. The court held that procedural due process requires an opportunity for a hearing before the State authorizes its agents to seize property from the party in possession.

The same court in *Mitchell v. W. T. Grant Co.,* (1974) 416 U.S. 600, 94 S. Ct. 1895, 40 L. Ed. 2d 406, held a Louisiana sequestration statute valid, which like the Texas statute provides that the debtor may immediately seek dissolution of the writ, which must be ordered unless the creditor proves grounds for issuance. The court held "it comports with due process to permit the initial seizure on sworn ex parte documents, followed by the early opportunity to put the creditor to his proof."

And the court recognizes the distinction between *Fuentes* and *Mitchell* in the 1975 case of *North Georgia Finishing, Inc. v. Di-Chem, Inc.,* 419 U.S. 601, 95 S. Ct. 719, 42 L. Ed. 2d 751.

All defendant's points and contentions have been considered and are overruled.

AFFIRMED

### [B] The Tort of Wrongful Attachment, Garnishment, and Sequestration

#### CHANDLER v. CASHWAY BUILDING MATERIALS, INC.

*584 S.W.2d 950 (Tex. Civ. App.—El Paso 1979, no writ)*

OSBORN, Justice.

This is an appeal from a summary judgment entered against a party seeking to recover damages in a suit for wrongful garnishment. We reverse and remand.

In June, 1977, Cashway Building Materials, Inc., sued Richard L. Chandler dba Skyline Hardware in Cause No. 39938-1 in County Court at Law No. 1 in El Paso to recover a debt of $1,276.24. In September, a default judgment was entered for $1,583.75, which amount included the amount of the debt, interest in the amount of $57.51 and attorney fees of $250.00. Execution was issued in November, 1977, for $1,833.75 (recited as being $1,583.75 and $250.00). Another execution was issued in March, 1978, for $1,583.75. The record does not reflect the return on those writs.

In March, 1978, Cashway filed in Cause No. 41705-1 in the County Court at Law No. 1 an Application for Writ of Garnishment after Judgment. El Paso National Bank was named garnishee and the writ was served on it on March 20, 1978. It answered on March 23, 1978, that the account of Skyline showed a balance of $5,945.35. On hearing Chandler's "Motion to Dismiss Garnishment," the Court authorized the Bank to release to Chandler any and all amounts over the sum of $1,150.00 which was required to be paid into the registry of the Court and the sum of $275.00 as attorney fees which were awarded to the garnishee.

Subsequently, the attorneys approved an "Agreed Judgment" styled Cashway Building Materials, Inc., Plaintiff, v. Richard L. Chandler d/b/a Skyline Hardware, Defendant, in No. 39938-1, in the County Court at Law No. 1, El Paso County, Texas. That judgment then recites:

> "On this day the 24th day of April, 1978, came on to be heard the above styled cause and the parties appeared by and through their attorneys of record and announced to the Court that they had compromised and settled all of the issues of fact and of law in dispute.
>
> On the 4th day of April, 1978, the Court issued an order modifying the writ of garnishment in the case styled CASHWAY BUILDING MATERIALS, INC., Garnishor v. EL PASO NATIONAL BANK, Garnishee No. 41705-1 ordering the Garnishee to pay into the registry of the Court the sum of $1,150.00 to be taken from the garnished funds. The parties now wish to settle cause No. 39938-1 in the following manner:
>
> 1. The sum of $1,000.00 is to be paid from the funds in the registry of the Court to the Plaintiff CASHWAY BUILDING MATERIALS, INC. as an all inclusive settlement.
> 2. The remaining $150.00 is awarded to the Defendant RICHARD L. CHANDLER d/b/a SKYLINE HARDWARE.
>
> A jury having been waived, the Court proceeded to hear the evidence and argument of counsel supporting such settlement agreement and is of the opinion and finds that such settlement agreement should be and is hereby, approved and made a part of this judgment.
>
> It is accordingly ORDERED, ADJUDGED, AND DECREED that Plaintiff recover from the Defendant the sum of $1,000.00 in accordance with the settlement agreement and that the Defendant be awarded the remaining $150.00. All other relief prayed for is denied."

The trial judge struck through the cause number as typed on the judgment and with a pen changed the cause number to 41705-1. Thus, we have a judgment reciting "came on to be heard the above styled cause" in which Chandler is named as defendant, being entered in another cause in which he is not defendant and in which the El Paso National Bank is garnishee. That judgment recites that "The parties now wish to settle cause No. 39938-1 . . ." but makes no mention of settling No. 41705-1 in which the judgment was actually entered. Of course, the original judgment in No. 39938-1 became final many months earlier and no new judgment could be entered in that case. Thus, the trial judge entered the judgment in the only pending case between these parties. It appears the parties should have prepared a release of judgment to be filed in No.

39938-1 and an agreed judgment in No. 41705-1 reciting a desire or intention to settle that case. They, of course, did neither.

In May, 1978, Chandler filed this suit against Cashway seeking damages for wrongful garnishment. Cashway answered and filed a motion for summary judgment on the grounds that (1) there was no final judgment, but merely an agreed judgment in the garnishment case, (2) the suit was barred under the doctrine of res judicata, and (3) the claim is barred under the doctrine of estoppel by judgment. Chandler also filed a motion for summary judgment. The trial Court entered judgment as follows:

> "IT IS THEREFORE ORDERED, ADJUDGED AND DECREED as follows:
>
> 1. The Motion for Summary Judgment filed by Plaintiff CHANDLER is in all things denied;
>
> 2. The Amended Motion for Summary Judgment filed by Defendant CASHWAY in in all things granted;
>
> 3. Plaintiff CASHWAY be dismissed and costs of suit be taxed against Plaintiff CHANDLER."

We don't know if the Court intended to say "Plaintiff Chandler" or "Defendant Cashway" at the beginning of paragraph 3 of the judgment. The judgment never recites that the Plaintiff take nothing from the Defendant as it should. . . .

The Appellant presents twelve points of error and in the sixth point urges that the trial Court erred in granting summary judgment when the proof did not establish, as a matter of law, that there was no genuine issue of fact as to one or more of the essential elements of Appellant's claim. We first consider the contention by the Appellee that there was no wrongful garnishment because there was no final judgment but only an agreed judgment entered in the garnishment case. Whether a garnishment is wrongful depends upon whether the steps taken by the parties seeking the writ comply with the statute authorizing such relief, and not the type of judgment entered. Article 4076, Tex. Rev. Civ. Stat. Ann., authorizes the issuance of a writ of garnishment:

> "Where the plaintiff has a valid, subsisting judgment and makes affidavit that the defendant has not, within his knowledge, property in his possession within this State, subject to execution, sufficient to satisfy such judgment."

The garnishment is wrongful if the facts set forth in the affidavit prescribed by Art. 4076, Tex. Rev. Civ. Stat. Ann. (1966), are untrue. *Peerless Oil & Gas Co. v. Teas,* 138 S.W.2d 637 (Tex. Civ. App.—San Antonio 1940), *aff'd* 138 Tex. 301, 158 S.W.2d 758 (1942); *Sayeg v. Federal Mortgage Co.*, 54 S.W.2d 238 (Tex. Civ. App.—Waco 1932, no writ); 27 Tex. Jur. 2d Garnishment sec. 141. In this case, Cashway obtained a judgment against Chandler for $1,583.75 but the Application for Writ of Garnishment, which was sworn to as being true and correct, asserted it was based upon a judgment for $1,833.75, "that said judgment is valid and existing," and that after payment of $500.00 the balance of $1,333.75 remains unsatisfied and that defendant has not, within the knowledge of plaintiff, property in his possession within this state, subject to execution, sufficient to satisfy said judgment. The affidavit incorrectly stated the amount of the judgment and the amount due after the payment.

In Plaintiff's Original Petition, it is alleged that Cashway's attorney was advised by the deputy sheriff, who had attempted to complete a writ of execution, as to the location and value of sufficient nonexempt property to satisfy the judgment. If that be true, the affidavit was incorrect in that regard. In order to be entitled to a summary judgment, the burden was on Cashway to conclusively rebut as a matter of law this allegation. *Zale Corporation v. Rosenbaum,* 520 S.W.2d 889 (Tex. 1975). There is no such proof in this case. In addition, Cashway in its motion for summary judgment assumed all of the facts of the plaintiff's original petition to be true. Thus, the Appellee's first contention fails to support the granting of the motion for summary judgment.

. . . .

Certainly, the suit for wrongful garnishment was not a compulsory counter-claim under Rule 97(a), Tex. R. Civ. P., because that claim did not arise out of the transaction or occurrence that is the subject matter of the opposing party's claim, in this case a debt for goods sold. . . .

. . . .

It should be noted that a 1971 amendment to Rule 97(a) provides:

> ". . . that a judgment based upon a settlement or compromise of a claim of one party to the transaction or occurrence prior to a disposition on the merits shall not operate as a bar to the continuation or assertion of the claims of any other party to the transaction or occurrence unless the latter has consented in writing that said judgment shall operate as a bar."

We believe that amendment was to provide for the problem arising from such cases as *Akers v. Simpson,* 445 S.W.2d 957 (Tex. 1969). See Texas Procedure, 48 Texas L. Rev. 978 (1970), and McElhaney, Texas Civil Procedure, 24 Sw. L.J. 179 at 184 (1970). But it appears that even if this claim for wrongful garnishment did arise out of the opposing party's claim, the compulsory counterclaim rule would not be applicable under the 1971 amendment of the Rule as set forth above. Clearly, the agreed judgment which was based upon a settlement of Cashway's claim does not reflect that Chandler has consented in writing that the judgment shall bar his claim.

In *Hardeman & Son v. Morgan,* 48 Tex. 103 (1877), the court recognized the right of a defendant in an attachment suit to file a cross-action for wrongful attachment but concluded that he is not compelled to seek redress in this way. The court said: "He may undoubtedly, if he prefers it, bring his separate suit in the court having jurisdiction of such a demand, without regard to the tribunal in which the plaintiff's action may be pending." In this connection, we note that Chandler's suit for wrongful garnishment which seeks 1.5 million dollars in damages was not within the jurisdiction of the County Court at Law where the garnishment proceedings had been filed by Cashway. See 2 McDonald, Texas Civil Practice sec. 7.49—(III)(a)(1970).

. . . .

We sustain the Appellant's Point of Error Number Six, and reverse and remand the case to the trial Court.

---

## BARFIELD v. BROGDON

*560 S.W.2d 787 (Tex. Civ. App.—Amarillo 1978, no writ)*

ROBINSON, Chief Justice.

The trial court entered judgment for defendant on a jury verdict on his cross-claim for actual and exemplary damages for wrongful sequestration. Affirmed subject to a remittitur.

Plaintiff, Robert E. Barfield, an attorney, took his lawn mower to Profitt's Lawn Mower Service owned by defendant, J. Darrell Brogdon, for a tune-up. Barfield testified that the price of the tune-up was agreed to be $14.00. Brogdon testified that (1) the agreed price was $14.50 plus the cost of parts; (2) he wrote "14.50 plus parts" on the repair order in the presence of Mr. Barfield; and (3) a large poster inside the shop showed that the standard tune-up charge was $14.50 plus parts. Barfield returned to pick up his lawn mower after the tune-up had been completed. Barfield refused to pay the $24.32 charges ($14.50 plus $9.82 for parts), and Brogdon refused to relinquish possession of the lawn mower. The following day Barfield filed suit by a sworn petition, alleging that he was the owner and entitled to possession of the lawn mower, seeking return of the lawn mower and $500.00 attorney's fees. Barfield later amended his petition to allege that Brogdon withheld the lawn mower for the purpose of defrauding Barfield and extorting money from him and asked for an additional $3,000.00 as exemplary damages. No affidavit for sequestration meeting the statutory requirements for issuance of sequestration as set out in Rule 696, Tex. R. Civ. P. and Art. 6840, Tex. Rev. Civ. Stat. was filed.

Rule 696 provides:

Rule 696. Applicant's Affidavit

No sequestration shall issue in any cause until the party applying therefore shall file an affidavit in writing stating:

(a) That he is the owner of the property sued for, or some interest therein specifying such interest, and is entitled to the possession thereof; or,

(b) If the suit be to foreclose a mortgage or enforce a lien upon the property, the fact of the existence of such mortgage or lien, and that the same is just and unsatisfied, and the amount of the same still unsatisfied, and the date when due.

(c) The property to be sequestered shall be described with such certainty that it may be identified and distinguished from property of a like kind, giving the value of each article of the property and the county in which the same is situated.

(d) It shall set forth one or more of the causes named in Art. 6840 of the Revised Civil Statutes of Texas, 1925, entitling him to the writ. The writ shall not be quashed because two or more grounds are stated conjunctively or disjunctively.

The relevant part of Art. 6840 at that time provided:

Judges and clerks of the district and county courts, and justices of the peace shall, at the commencement or during the progress of any civil suit, before final judgment, have power to issue writs of sequestration, returnable to their respective courts, in the following cases:

. . . .

> 2. When a person sues for the title or possession of any personal property of any description, and makes oath that he fears the defendant or person in possession thereof will injure, ill-treat, waste or destroy such property, or remove the same out of the limits of the county during the pendency of the suit.

Despite Barfield's failure to comply with the statute, a writ of sequestration was issued and served. Barfield obtained possession of the lawn mower by filing a replevy bond. He has since worn out and discarded the mower. Brogdon answered and cross-claimed for actual and exemplary damages alleging that Barfield acted "willfully, intentionally, unlawfully and maliciously" in causing the writ of sequestration to be issued when he knew or should have known that he was not entitled to it.

Trial was held and the jury answered the corresponding numbered special issues as follows:

(1) Brogdon did not agree to repair the lawn mower for $14;

(2) The reasonable value of parts and labor to repair the lawn mower was $24.32;

(3) $74.32 would compensate Brogdon for his damages as a result of the wrongful issuance and execution of the writ of sequestration;

(4) Barfield knew or should have known that he had no right to possession of the lawn mower;

(5) Barfield knew or should have known that he violated the statutory sequestration procedures in causing the writ to be issued and executed;

(6) Barfield knew or should have known of the unconstitutionality of the sequestration statute; An exemplary damage issue was submitted conditioned on an affirmative answer to Issue 4, 5, or 6. The jury found:

(7) Brogdon is entitled to $3,000 as exemplary damages for the wrongful sequestration of the lawn mower.

The trial court entered judgment for Brogdon for $3,074.32 based on the verdict of the jury. Barfield appeals.

On appeal Barfield contends that jury findings on which the exemplary damage issue was conditioned, i.e., that he knew or should have known that he did not have a right to sequester the property, are insufficient to support a judgment for exemplary damages.

It is well settled that to justify the recovery of exemplary damages, the issuance of a writ of sequestration must not only be wrongful, but procured without probable cause and maliciously. *O'Hara v. Ferguson Mack Truck Co.,* 373 S.W.2d 507 (Tex. Civ. App.—San Antonio 1963, writ ref'd n.r.e.); *Mathes v. Williams,* 134 S.W.2d 853 (Tex. Civ. App.—Amarillo 1939, no writ). In the case of *Hamlett v. Coates,* 182 S.W. 1144, 1148 (Tex. Civ. App.—Dallas 1915, writ ref'd) the court discussed the requirement for malice as follows:

> Malice is where the facts and circumstances show not only that the grounds upon which the writ of sequestration issued were untrue and that there was no probable cause for believing them to be true, but evidences bad motives or such reckless disregard of the rights of the party against whom it is sued out as satisfies the mind that the unlawful act was willfully and purposely done to the injury of such party.

. . . .

We conclude that Issues 4, 5, and 6 were each defective or improper submissions of a controlling issue necessary for an award of exemplary damages.

However Barfield did not object to the charge for its failure to submit an issue expressly inquiring if he acted with malice. He did not object at all to Special Issue No. 4 inquiring if he knew or should have known that he had no right to possession of the lawn mower and he did not object at all to the issue inquiring as to the amount of exemplary damage which should be awarded for wrongful sequestration. He did not object to Special Issue No. 5 or Special Issue No. 6 on the ground that they would not support exemplary damages.

Therefore, we consider Brogdon's reply point that Barfield waived his right to complain of the issues submitted by his failure to make pertinent objections to the charge as required by Rules 272 and 274.

. . . .

. . . We conclude that Barfield's points of error contending that jury findings in Special Issues Nos. 4, 5, and 6 are insufficient to support a judgment for exemplary damages are not properly before us.

Plaintiff next contends that as a matter of law Brogdon sustained no actual damages because plaintiff had posted adequate sequestration and replevy bonds. We overrule the contention. The filing of a sequestration bond does not preclude actual damages. On the contrary it guarantees the payment of damages and costs in case it is decided that the sequestration was wrongfully issued. Rule 698. *See Kelso v. Hanson,* 388 S.W.2d 396, 399 (Tex. 1965). The undisputed evidence establishes that Brogdon suffered actual damage in that he lost possession of the lawn mower which he was entitled to hold as security for the repair bill. There is no point of error that the jury finding of actual damages is excessive. There was no objection to the charge challenging the elements of damage which the jury was instructed that it could consider in connection with Special Issue No. 3.

. . . .

After considering the evidence in the light most favorable to the verdict and judgment and in the light of the authorities already cited we overruled plaintiff's contention that there was no evidence that plaintiff acted with malice, ill will, or reckless disregard for the rights of others in causing the writ of sequestration to be issued.

As above stated, certain of appellant plaintiff's points of error are not properly before us. We have considered and overrule each point of error before us except for the point of error presenting his contention that the jury finding of $3,000.00 exemplary damages is excessive. After consideration of the record as a whole, we are of the opinion that the verdict and judgment is excessive in the amount of $2,000.00.

If appellee files a remittitur of $2,000.00 within 15 days, the judgment will be reformed and affirmed. Otherwise, the judgment will be reversed and the cause remanded to the trial court for a new trial. Rule 440, Tex. R. Civ. P.

REYNOLDS, Justice, concurring and dissenting.

Otherwise agreeing with the majority's disposition of this appeal, I respectfully dissent to the award of exemplary damages. It is my view that, under the circumstances of this cause, J. Darrell Brogdon waived his ground of recovery for exemplary damages.

. . . .

---

## NOTES AND QUESTIONS

(1) *Client Counseling.* Assume that, in the context of a bitter dispute, your client is considering sequestration of goods sold a consumer-debtor. How would you counsel this client? What

cautionary advice would you offer? Try to create an informal, mental "checklist" of pre-sequestration considerations.

(2) In view of Barfield's ownership of the lawn mower, why did he not have the right to its possession? What does this have to do with the outcome of the case?

If Barfield had peaceably and privately obtained possession, would Brogdon have had the right to sequestration himself?

(3) Cashway's application was defective. In what respect? What does this fact have to do with the outcome?

(4) Of what relevance is the applicant's good faith?

CHAPTER 3

# THE SUBJECT MATTER JURISDICTION OF THE TEXAS TRIAL COURTS

SCOPE

This chapter covers the subject matter jurisdiction of Texas state courts. Topics examined include an overview of the Texas court system, constitutional and statutory provisions controlling courts, the various types of courts and their particular jurisdiction, shared jurisdiction, transfer and concurrent jurisdiction, appellate jurisdiction, competing jurisdiction, the amount in controversy requirement, justiciability, and the consequences of lack of jurisdiction.

## § 3.01 An Overview of the Texas Court System

### [A] A Simplified Diagram of the Texas Trial Courts

The following diagram illustrates the jurisdiction of four kinds of trial courts in Texas. The district, county, and justice courts are established by the Texas Constitution. The Texas Legislature has varied the constitutional pattern in many counties by the creation of additional courts by legislative enactment. These courts are important to an understanding of the jurisdictional scheme and are included in the diagram as a separate kind of court. Note that while the most common jurisdictional range for such courts is shown on the diagram, the subject matter jurisdiction of "legislative" county courts can vary substantially. Other legislative courts, such as small claims courts (which are conducted by justices of the peace), have been omitted for the sake of simplicity.

The statutory basis for the diagram will be set forth in the next section. As the diagram illustrates, the amount in controversy is the main factor that determines a court's subject matter jurisdiction. However, jurisdiction over certain categories of cases is conferred on specific courts regardless of the amount in controversy. Also notice the areas on the diagram where the jurisdiction of two or more courts overlaps.

# THE TEXAS TRIAL COURTS: A SIMPLIFIED DIAGRAM

The Texas Trial Courts: A Simplified Diagram

| Amount in controversy | Proper court or courts, plus jurisdiction not dependent on amount in controversy | | | |
|---|---|---|---|---|
| Infinity - | | | | DISTRICT COURTS |
| $100,000* | | | LEGIS-LATIVE COUNTY COURTS | plus: land title; defamation; family law cases; certain trials of right of property; eminent domain; probate etc. (varies with county) |
| $ 5,000 - | JUSTICE COURTS | COUNTY COURTS | plus: eminent domain; appeals of workers' compensation rulings and decisions; probate; family law cases (varies with county) | |
| | plus: forcible entry & detainer | plus: probate (varies with county) | | |
| $ 500 | | | | |
| $ 200 | | | | |
| $ 0 | | | | |

* NOTE: Many county courts at law have specific amount in controversy jurisdiction provided by particular statutes. These specific jurisdictional grants take precedence by virtue of amended Civil Practice & Remedies Code § 25.0001(a). For example, Tex. Gov't Code Ann. § 25.2222 provides that Tarrant County Courts at law have civil jurisdiction that does not exceed $100,000 . . . excluding mandatory damages and penalties, attorney's fees, interest, and costs."

### [B] A View of the Texas System as a Whole

The following diagram illustrates the relationships between the trial and appellate courts in Texas.

COURT STRUCTURE OF TEXAS: A SIMPLIFIED DIAGRAM

January 1, 1982

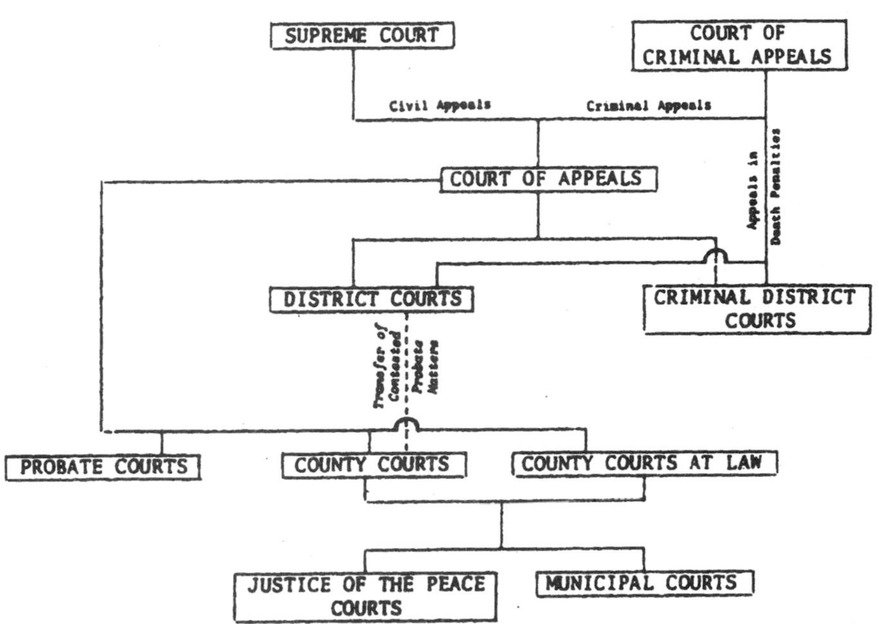


Review of a court of appeals' decision in the Texas Supreme Court is not a matter of right, but involves a petition for review (Tex. R. App. P. 53, 56), which may be denied in the court's discretion if the court is of the opinion that the error, if any, of the court of appeals is not of such importance to the jurisprudence of the state that it requires correction. Gov. C. § 22.001(a)(6). There are situations in which the Texas Supreme Court has discretion to hear an appeal directly from an order of the trial court.

## § 3.02 Constitutional and Statutory Provisions: An Explanation

Article 5, Section 1 of the Texas Constitution provides that "[t]he judicial power of this State of Texas shall be vested in one Supreme Court, in one Court of Criminal Appeals, in Courts of Appeals, in District Courts, in County Courts, in Commissioners Courts, in Courts of Justices of the Peace, and in such other courts as may be provided by law."

Article 5, Section 1 further provides: "The Legislature may establish such other courts as it may deem necessary and prescribe the jurisdiction and organization thereof, and may conform the jurisdiction of the district and other inferior courts thereto."

Of these courts, three are primarily appellate. The courts of appeals have intermediate appellate jurisdiction in civil and criminal cases. The Texas Supreme Court is the highest court in Texas for civil cases; the Texas Court of Criminal Appeals is the highest court for criminal cases. The "commissioners courts" are not really courts but rather county legislative branches.

The remaining courts noted in Article 5—the "District Courts," "County Courts," "Courts of Justices of the Peace," and "such other courts" as "the Legislature may establish"—are the principal Texas trial courts. The jurisdiction of these courts is the subject of this chapter.

### [A] Justice Courts

*Read Tex. Const. Art. 5 § 19; Gov. C. §§ 27.031, 27.032.*

Unless another court has been granted jurisdiction over the subject matter of a case, justice courts have exclusive original jurisdiction over civil cases when the amount in controversy is $200 or less. Tex. Const. Art. 5, § 19. The justice courts share concurrent original jurisdiction with the county courts in civil cases in which the amount in controversy exceeds $200 but does not exceed $5,000, exclusive of interest, and with district courts in civil cases in which the amount in controversy exceeds $500 but does not exceed $5,000, exclusive of interest. *See* Tex. Const. Art. 5, §§ 8, 16, 19; Gov. C. §§ 26.042(a), 27.031(a)(1).

Justice courts have original jurisdiction over forcible entry and detainer cases (i.e., actions in which the issue is the right of possession but not involving title to the premises). *See* Gov. C. § 27.031(a)(2), (b)(4). Jurisdiction over forcible entry and detainer actions exists regardless of the value of the land and occasionally a large commercial lease in which millions of dollars are potentially at stake becomes the basis of a detainer action in a justice court. A claim for unpaid rent or other damages is not part of the claim for possession, therefore the rent or damages sought must be within the jurisdiction of the court.

The court may also foreclose mortgages and enforce liens on personal property when the amount in controversy is within the court's jurisdiction. *See* Gov. C. § 27.031(a)(3).

The justice courts may issue writs of attachment, garnishment, and sequestration in cases otherwise within their jurisdiction (*See* Gov. C. § 27.032) but have no authority to issue writs of mandamus or injunction. Justice courts are expressly denied jurisdiction of suits on behalf of the state to recover penalties, forfeitures and escheats, suits for divorce, suits to recover damages for slander or defamation of character, suits for the trial of title of land and suits for the enforcement of liens on land. *See* Gov. C. § 27.031(b).

### [B] Constitutional County Courts

*Read Gov. C. §§ 26.042, 26.043, 26.044, 26.051; C.P.R.C. §§ 51.001, 51.002, 61.021, 62.021.*

Constitutional county courts (to be distinguished from legislative county courts, which are created by statute and are generally referred to as "county courts at law") occupy the next rung on the trial court ladder. The Texas Constitution provides that "The County Court has jurisdiction as provided by law." *See* Tex. Const., Art. 5, § 16. This constitutional provision has been implemented by statutes contained in the Government Code. These courts usually have jurisdiction in cases in which the amount in controversy is $200.01 through $5,000. Unless a cause is specifically assigned to another court because of its subject matter, a constitutional county court has concurrent jurisdiction with the justice courts in civil cases in which the amount in controversy exceeds $200 but does not exceed $5,000, exclusive of interest, and with the district court in civil cases in which the amount in controversy exceeds $500 but does not exceed $5,000, exclusive of interest. *See* Gov. C. §§ 26.042(a), (d), 27.031(a)(1).

A county court has civil appellate jurisdiction over cases arising in the justice courts or small claims court when the judgment rendered exceeds $20, exclusive of costs. Review is by a trial de novo. *See* Tex. Const. Art. 5, § 16; C.P.R.C. § 51.001; Gov. C. § 28.052. Original and appellate judgments of the county court may be appealed to the court of appeals if the judgment or amount in controversy exceeds $100, exclusive of interest and costs. *See* C.P.R.C. § 51.012.

Constitutional county courts have limited probate jurisdiction in many counties, but ordinarily these courts do not have authority to resolve contested probate matters. This jurisdiction is summarized in [D][2], *below*.

A constitutional county court may issue writs of injunction, mandamus, certiorari, and all other writs necessary to enforce its jurisdiction. *See* Tex. Const. Art. 5, § 16; Gov. C. §§ 26.044, 26.051; C.P.R.C. §§ 61.021, 62.021, 63.002, 65.021.

In addition to the general grants of statutory jurisdiction, many constitutional county courts are granted additional jurisdiction by statutory provisions which apply only to those courts. *See* Gov. C. §§ 26.101–26.354.

Constitutional county courts have no jurisdiction in (1) a suit to recover damages for slander or defamation of character; (2) a suit for the enforcement of a lien on land; (3) a suit in behalf of the state for escheat; (4) a suit for divorce; (5) a suit for the forfeiture of a corporate charter; (6) a suit for the trial of the right to property valued at $500 or more and levied on under a writ of execution, sequestration, or attachment; (7) an eminent domain case; or (8) a suit for the recovery of land. *See* Gov. C. § 26.043.

### [C] District Courts

The district courts are the primary Texas trial courts, and are constitutional courts of general jurisdiction. Article 5, Section 8 of the Texas Constitution states broadly that district courts have jurisdiction over all proceedings except those reserved exclusively to other courts.

District court jurisdiction consists of exclusive, appellate, and original jurisdiction of all actions, proceedings, and remedies, except in cases where exclusive, appellate, or original jurisdiction may be conferred by the Texas Constitution or other law on some other court, tribunal, or administrative body. Tex. Const. Art. 5, § 8; *see also* Gov. Code §§ 24.007, 24.008, 24.011.

The amount in controversy jurisdiction of the district courts is probably limited to controversies involving at least $500. *See Peek v. Equipment Serv. Co. of San Antonio*, 779 S.W.2d 802, 803 n.4 (Tex. 1989); *see also Gulf, C. & S.F. Ry. Co. v. Rainbolt,* 67 Tex. 654, 4 S.W. 356 (1887) (interpreting conflict in former constitutional provisions). There is no maximum jurisdictional limit. This means that district courts have concurrent amount in controversy jurisdiction with justice courts, constitutional county courts, and statutory courts (i.e., county courts at law) in cases in which the amount in controversy exceeds $500, up to the other courts' maximum jurisdictional limits. *See* Gov. C. §§ 26.042(d), 27.031. More recently, the Texas Supreme Court has held that Article 5, Section 8 of the Texas Constitution no longer prohibits trial courts from resolving an insurer's duty to indemnify an insured prior to a determination of the insured's liability to a third party. Along the way to concluding that indemnity issues are justiciable before the insured's liability is resolved, despite the constitutional prohibition against "advisory opinions," the Court had some curious things to say about Article 5, Section 8, as follows:

> Our holding in *Burch* was based upon Article V, Section 8 of the Texas Constitution, which prohibits advisory opinions. *Burch*, 442 S.W.2d at 333. At that time, Article V, Section 8 provided [a specific jurisdictional minimum of "five hundred dollars exclusive of interest"]. Thus, until the underlying lawsuit was concluded, a district court could only speculate that the value of the matter in controversy exceeded five hundred dollars. Since our decision in *Burch*, however, Section 8 has been amended to create original jurisdiction in the district courts over "all actions, proceedings, and remedies." Tex. Const. art. V, § 8. This amendment to Article V, Section 8 significantly broadened the scope of district court jurisdiction. The language of the amended version is broad enough to allow district courts jurisdiction to resolve declaratory judgment actions on the duty to indemnify.

*Farmers Texas County Mut. Ins. Co. v. Griffin,* 955 S.W.2d 81, 83–84 (Tex. 1997).

As provided in the Texas Constitution, district courts have original jurisdiction over all types of claims over which justice and constitutional county courts do not have jurisdiction. This concept is called "residual jurisdiction." In other words, *the district court's jurisdiction is ascertainable by the process of elimination.* In addition, Section 26.043 of the Government Code provides that a constitutional county court does not have jurisdiction in:

(1) A suit to recover damages for slander or defamation of character;

(2) A suit for the enforcement of a lien on land;

(3) A suit in behalf of the state for escheat;

(4) A suit for divorce;

(5) A suit for the forfeiture of a corporate charter;

(6) A suit for the trial of the right to property valued at $500 or more and levied on under a writ of execution, sequestration, or attachment;

(7) An eminent domain case; or

(8) A suit for the recovery of land.

Gov. C. § 26.043.

Similarly, Section 27.031(b) states that a justice court does not have jurisdiction of:

(1) A suit in behalf of the state to recover a penalty, forfeiture, or escheat;

(2) A suit for divorce;

(3) A suit to recover damages for slander or defamation of character;

(4) A suit for trial of title to land; or

(5) A suit for the enforcement of a lien on land.

Gov. C. § 27.031(b).

Therefore, because the constitution and the statutes define the district court's jurisdiction by exclusion, a review of the constitutional and statutory provisions regarding the jurisdiction of the district court should include a comparison with other constitutional and statutory grants of jurisdiction to other trial courts.

### [D] Legislative Courts

The above discussion deals primarily with the constitutional jurisdictional scheme. The following subsections pertain to statutory county courts at law, probate courts, and family district courts created by the Texas legislature pursuant to its constitutional authorization. *See* Tex. Const. Art. 5, § 1, as well as statutory alteration of the constitutional jurisdictional pattern.

### [1] Legislative Courts Exercising District Court Jurisdiction

The Texas Supreme Court has held that the legislature may not restrict the jurisdiction of a district court. *See Lord v. Clayton*, 163 Tex. 62, 352 S.W.2d 718, 721–722 (1962). On the other hand, the constitutional power to establish "other courts" permits the creation of legislative district courts with limited jurisdiction. *See Cook v. Nelius*, 498 S.W.2d 455 (Tex. Civ. App.—Houston [1st Dist.] 1973, no writ). The legislature can also change a "statutory" court into a constitutional district court by increasing its jurisdiction to constitutional proportions. For example, the legislature has established family district courts that have primary responsibility for family law matters such as divorce, annulment, child conservatorship and support and with jurisdiction "concurrent with that of other district courts in the county in which it is located." Gov. C. § 24.601(a). At one time, these courts were called "domestic relations" and "juvenile" courts and had more rigidly defined jurisdiction. Now, as family district courts, they can exercise jurisdiction over all matters within the competence of district courts without impediment.

### [2] Legislative County Courts

Because the Texas legislature is empowered by the Texas Constitution to "establish such other courts as it may deem necessary," to prescribe the jurisdiction of such statutory courts, and because the legislature "may conform the jurisdiction of the district and other inferior courts thereto" (Tex. Const., Art. 5, § 1), the jurisdiction of legislative county courts can be confusing. The basic jurisdictional provision is contained in Government Code at Section 25.0003.

GOVERNMENT CODE

CHAPTER 25. STATUTORY COUNTY COURTS

SUBCHAPTER A. GENERAL PROVISIONS

Gov. C. § 25.0003. *Jurisdiction.* (a) A statutory county court has jurisdiction over all causes and proceedings, civil and criminal, original and appellate, prescribed by law for county courts.

(b) A statutory county court does not have jurisdiction over causes and proceedings concerning roads, bridges, and public highways and the general administration of county business that is within the jurisdiction of the commissioners court of each county.

(c) In addition to other jurisdiction provided by law, a statutory county court exercising civil jurisdiction concurrent with the constitutional jurisdiction of the county court has concurrent jurisdiction with the district court in:

(1) civil cases in which the matter in controversy exceeds $500 but does not exceed $100,000, excluding interest, statutory or punitive damages and penalties, and attorney's fees and costs, as alleged on the face of the petition; and

(2) appeals of final rulings and decisions of the Texas Workers' Compensation Commission, regardless of the amount in controversy.

(d) Except as provided by Subsection (e), a statutory county court has, concurrent with the county court, the probate jurisdiction provided by general law for county courts.

(e) In a county that has a statutory probate court, a statutory probate court is the only county court created by statute with probate jurisdiction.

---

Section 25.0003(a) of the Government Code is an important general provision that provides simply that statutory county courts have jurisdiction over all causes and proceedings prescribed by law for county courts. Gov. C. § 25.0003(a). Accordingly, statutory county courts have amount in controversy jurisdiction in cases in which there is an amount in controversy that exceeds $200, unless a specific statute provides otherwise. Gov. C. §§ 25.0003(a), 26.042(a). Similarly, because Section 25.0003(a) embraces the jurisdiction prescribed by law for county courts, it appears that statutory county courts do not have jurisdiction in those civil matters set forth in Section 26.043 of the Government Code unless a specific statute provides otherwise. *See* Gov. C. § 26.043.

The jurisdiction of statutory county courts is governed by both general provisions contained in Subchapter A of Chapter 25 of the Government Code and by specific provisions relating to particular statutory county courts on a county-by-county basis set forth in Subchapter C of Chapter 25. If a general provision conflicts with a specific provision for a particular court or county, the specific provision controls. Gov. C. § 25.0001(a). In order to determine the exact contours of a particular statutory county court's jurisdiction, the particular statute should first be consulted to determine what it provides about a statutory county court's jurisdictional role in the county in which it operates. *See* Gov. C. § 25.0032 et seq. For those counties for which detailed provisions have been enacted (*See, e.g.*, Gov. C. § 25.2222 (Tarrant County Court at Law Provisions)), the specific statutory provisions will contain most of the pertinent information. For other counties, very little information is contained in the specific provisions and, consequently, the general provisions must be consulted to determine a statutory county court's jurisdictional role. *See, e.g.*, Gov. C. § 25.0592 (Dallas County Court at Law Provisions).

### [E] Shared Jurisdiction and Jurisdiction Varying From County to County: Effects on Filing and Transfer

When jurisdiction is shared between courts of the same or different levels, a number of questions arise. For example, in a county containing two district courts, where should an action appropriate for district court adjudication be filed? Can the case be transferred from one district court to the other? What happens when the provisions creating constitutional and/or legislative county courts for a given county result in shared jurisdiction between county courts or between the county courts and a district court, as may occur in the areas of probate and eminent domain? Where should the action be filed? When can the action be transferred? The following subsections discuss the procedural rule and statutory provisions which pertain to the division of adjudicative responsibilities among courts of overlapping jurisdiction.

#### [1] Adjudicative Responsibility and Transfer Between District Courts and Legislative Courts Exercising Concurrent Jurisdiction With District Courts

*Read Tex. R. Civ. P. 330(e).*

When a county contains two district courts having civil jurisdiction, responsibilities for adjudication are not located exclusively in one court or the other. Civil Procedure Rule 330(e) provides that in such counties, the district court judges may, in their discretion, exchange benches or districts, and may transfer cases or proceedings from one court to another. Any judge may in his or her own courtroom try and determine any case or proceeding pending in another court without having the case transferred, or may sit in any other district court and hear and determine any case pending there. The rule applies strictly to district courts. *See G.C.D. v. State,* 577 S.W.2d 302, 303–304 (Tex. Civ. App.—Beaumont 1978, no writ) (Justice Keith's concurring opinion).

A comprehensive plan for judicial administration in individual counties is contemplated by the Court Administration Act, originally enacted by the 69th Legislature in 1985 and amended and recodified by the 70th Legislature in 1987. The state is divided into nine administrative judicial regions (Gov. C. § 74.042), with one judge appointed by the governor, with the advice and consent of the senate, as presiding judge of each region. Gov. C. § 74.005(a). There is a local administrative judge in each county (Gov. C. § 74.091), whose duties include the assignment, docketing, transfer, and hearing of cases. Gov. C. § 74.092(1). Section 74.093 authorizes the district and statutory county court judges in each county to adopt local rules, such rules to provide for the "assignment, docketing, transfer, and hearing of all cases, subject to jurisdictional limitations of the district courts and statutory county courts." Gov. C. § 74.093(b)(1). The statute also provides that a rule "relating to the transfer of cases and proceedings shall not allow the transfer of cases from one court to another unless the cases are within the jurisdiction of the court to which it is transferred." Gov. C. § 74.093(d).

As amended in 1989, Section 74.094(a) of the Court Administration Act provides that district and county court judges may hear and determine a matter pending in any district or statutory court in the county and may sign a judgment or order regardless of whether the case has been transferred. Gov. C. § 74.094(a). Apparently, as a result of the repeal of a provision limiting a statutory county court judge's ability to act for a district judge in a case in which the statutory county court lacked jurisdiction, section 74.094(a) "allow[s] a statutory county court judge to hear, determine, and sign a judgment in a matter pending in district court outside his court's jurisdiction." *Camacho v. Samaniego*, 831 S.W.2d 804, 811 (Tex. 1992); *see also Texas Animal Health Comm'n v. Garza*, 980 S.W.2d 776, 777 (Tex. App.—San Antonio 1998, no pet. h.).

Section 74.121 provides that judges of constitutional county courts, statutory county courts, justice courts, and small claims courts in a county may transfer cases to and from the dockets of their respective courts, as long as the judge of the court to which it is transferred consents and the case is within the jurisdiction of the court to which it is transferred. Gov. C. § 74.121(a). Section 74.121(b) provides that statutory county court judges may transfer a case to the district court docket, as long as the district judge consents and the case is within the district court's jurisdiction. Gov. C. § 74.121(b).

A complete understanding of the system requires a consideration of the Rules of Judicial Administration. Rule 3 creates a "council of presiding judges," which is composed of the Chief Justice of the Texas Supreme Court and the nine presiding judges of the administrative regions. This council's task is to oversee dockets and case loads and to promote such uniformity in local rules as is practicable and consistent with local conditions. *See* Tex. R. Jud. Admin. 3.

Rule 4 creates a "council of judges" within each administrative region, which is composed of the presiding judge and all qualified district and statutory county court judges for the region, including retired and former judges. This council's main goals include monitoring case loads and the promulgation of regional rules. *See* Tex. R. Jud. Admin. 4.

Rule 6 establishes the time standards for the disposition of various categories of cases. For example, the rule provides that civil jury cases other than family law cases should be brought to trial or final disposition within 18 months from appearance date, and that civil nonjury cases other than family law cases should be brought to trial or final disposition within 12 months from appearance date. *See* Tex. R. Jud. Admin. 6(b).

### [2] Adjudicative Responsibility and Transfer in Cases Involving Eminent Domain, Probate, and Divorce

The legislative county courts are an integral part of the jurisdictional scheme in cases involving eminent domain, probate, and divorce.

*Eminent Domain*

District courts have jurisdiction concurrent with the county courts at law in eminent domain cases. The constitutional county courts do not have jurisdiction over such cases. *See* Gov. C. § 26.043 (7). Since not all county courts of law have eminent domain jurisdiction, the statutes pertaining to the relevant county must be consulted. The relevant sections of the Property Code provide:

PROPERTY CODE

CHAPTER 21. EMINENT DOMAIN

SUBCHAPTER A. JURISDICTION

Prop. C. § 21.001. *Concurrent Jurisdiction.* District courts and county courts at law have concurrent jurisdiction in eminent domain cases. A county court has no jurisdiction in eminent domain cases.

Prop. C. § 21.002. *Transfer of Cases.* If an eminent domain case is pending in a county court at law and the court determines that the case involves an issue of title or any other matter that cannot be fully adjudicated in that court, the judge shall transfer the case to a district court.

Prop. C. § 21.013. *Venue; Fees and Processing for Suit Filed in District Court.* (a) The venue of a condemnation proceeding is the county in which the owner of the property being condemned resides if the owner resides in a county in which part of the property is located. Otherwise, the venue of a condemnation proceeding is any county in which at least part of the property is located.

(b) Except where otherwise provided by law, a party initiating a condemnation proceeding in a county in which there is one or more county courts at law with jurisdiction may file the petition with any clerk authorized to handle filings for that court or courts.

(c) A party initiating a condemnation proceeding in a county in which there is not a county court at law must file the condemnation petition with the district clerk. The filing fee shall be due at the time of filing in accordance with Section 51.317, Government Code.

(d) District and county clerks shall assign an equal number of eminent domain cases in rotation to each court with jurisdiction that the clerk serves.

---

*Probate.* In counties without a statutory probate court, county court at law, or other statutory court exercising probate jurisdiction, probate cases are filed in the county court. If probate matters are contested, the county judge may (and on motion of a party, must) either request the assignment of a statutory probate judge to hear the contested part of the proceeding or transfer the contested matters to the district court. In such transferred contested matters the district court has the general jurisdiction of a probate court, concurrently with the county court. *See* Prob. C. § 5(b).

In counties that do have a statutory probate court, county court of law, or other statutory court exercising the jurisdiction of a probate court, probate cases are filed and heard in those courts and in the constitutional county court, rather than in the district court, unless otherwise provided by the legislature. The judge of a constitutional county court may not determine contested matters, but may (and on motion of a party, must) transfer the proceeding to the statutory probate court, county court at law, or other statutory court exercising probate jurisdiction. The transferee court then hears the proceeding as if it were originally filed in that court. *See* Prob. C. § 5(c). Probate jurisdiction is discussed further at § 3.03[B][2].

*Divorce and Related Matters.* All district courts and some county courts at law have subject matter jurisdiction to litigate divorce cases and related matters such as custody, visitation, and child support. Certain district courts have been established as family district courts, which have concurrent jurisdiction with other district courts in the county in which they are located. Gov. C. § 24.601(a).

A review of statutory provisions governing jurisdiction of the county courts at law is necessary to determine whether the legislative courts have concurrent jurisdiction with the district court in family law cases in a given county. *See, e.g.*, Gov. C. §§ 25.0032 (Anderson county court at law), 25.0132 (Bastrop county court at law), 25.0222 (Brazoria statutory county court).

### [F] Other Courts

In addition to the statutory courts discussed above, there are statutory provisions creating municipal courts, only some of which are courts of record. "Small claims" jurisdiction allows justice courts to use simplified procedures when the amount in controversy does not exceed $5,000. *See* Gov. C. § 28.003.

To summarize: As a result of legislative action, many counties have unique provisions governing their courts. The reason may be the county's special needs, its population, the particular mix of cases, or simply the county's political situation. As a result, the jurisdiction of Texas trial courts resembles a patchwork quilt: confusing, overlapping, and not always consistent or rationally based. The Texas Supreme Court has voiced concern over the difficulties created "for the bench, the bar, and the public by the patchwork organization of Texas' several trial courts" (*Continental Coffee Prods. v. Cazarez*, 937 S.W.2d 444, 449 (Tex. 1996)), acknowledging that "confusion and inefficiency are endemic to a judicial structure with different courts of distinct but overlapping jurisdiction." *Camacho v. Samaniego*, 831 S.W.2d 804, 811 (Tex. 1992).

## § 3.03 Appellate Cases Concerning Trial Court Jurisdiction

### [A] Cases Illustrating the Trial Court System as a Whole

**CONNELL v. SHANAFELT**, 446 S.W.2d 126 (Tex. Civ. App.—Fort Worth 1969, no writ). Plaintiff sued on an indebtedness secured by a mechanic's and materialmen's lien on real property.

He prayed for judgment on the debt and foreclosure of the lien. Because the indebtedness was less than $500 but more than $200, the plaintiff brought the suit in county court. The trial judge rendered judgment for the indebtedness only, refusing to adjudge foreclosure.

The court of civil appeals reversed and remanded with instructions to dismiss unless the petition was amended to show county court jurisdiction. Why?

---

**SUPER-X DRUGS OF TEXAS, INC. v. STATE**, 505 S.W.2d 333 (Tex. Civ. App.—Houston [1st Dist.] 1974, no writ). The state and the city of Houston brought suit to enjoin the defendant from selling certain items on Sundays in alleged violation of Sunday closing laws. The suit was brought in district court, and the trial judge issued a temporary injunction. Defendant appealed, claiming that the district court lacked jurisdiction because the value of the items shown to have been sold was under $500.

The court of civil appeals rejected this argument, holding that "This is . . . a case . . . [that] does not involve an 'amount in controversy'. . . ." Accordingly, the court held that the district court did, indeed, have jurisdiction. Why?

---

**AMIGO HELICOPTERS, INC. v. JONES**, 488 S.W.2d 473 (Tex. Civ. App.—Houston [14th Dist.] 1972, no writ). Plaintiff filed suit for an indebtedness of just over $4,200, including attorney's fees, in the county court in Brazoria County. The county court was a constitutional county court. Defendant filed a plea to the effect that Brazoria County was not the proper venue for the action and prayed that it be transferred to Bexar County, where there were legislative county courts. The trial judge found against defendant on this venue plea and refused the transfer. Defendant appealed this venue ruling.

The court of civil appeals reversed. However, it did not consider the venue question except to hold that the trial judge had no jurisdiction to rule on it. The court therefore remanded the case with directions to dismiss.

It might be added that because Bexar County had legislative county courts, one of these courts might well have been able validly to exercise jurisdiction over the case had it been brought there originally. Why? But the court of civil appeals indicated, by its holding, that the trial judge in Brazoria County would have no authority even to transfer the case to one of these legislative courts; instead, the judge's only authority was to dismiss. Why?

---

## NOTES AND QUESTIONS

(1) *Determining Jurisdiction.* For each of the following claims, identify what court or courts would have jurisdiction. If there is more than one court, specify each. Give the basis for your

answer, and if there is another court that at first glance seems to have jurisdiction but for some special reason does not, explain why. (Adapted from a Texas Bar Examination question.)

(a) Suit for $495.00 for libel (Note: Libel is a type of defamation).

(b) Suit for forcible entry and detainer on the ground the defendant has failed to pay rent amounting to $3,000.00.

(c) Suit for divorce, in which the community estate is alleged to be worth $495.00.

(d) Suit for specific performance of a contract for the sale of land worth $495.00.

(e) Suit for an oil and gas pipeline easement in which the owner has refused an offer of $10,000.00. (Note: What type of power do utilities have to secure land necessary to their endeavors that ordinary citizens do not have?)

(f) Suit on an indebtedness of $495.00 and to foreclose on an automobile worth $3,000.00, which is the subject of a lien to secure the indebtedness. (Note: When suit is brought for foreclosure of a lien and on the indebtedness it secures, the amount in controversy is the larger of the debt or property value.)

(g) Suit for $495.00 against a fire insurance company for fire damage to a building. (Note: Although the building is real property, this is not a suit concerning either title to it or a lien on it.)

(h) Suit on an indebtedness of $495.00 and to foreclose on a parcel of real property worth $200.00, which is the subject of a lien securing the indebtedness.

(i) Suit in trespass to try title and to oust defendant's tenant from the land in question. (Note: "Trespass to try title" is the manner of disputing title to land in Texas.)

(j) Suit to determine who holds title to a leasehold interest in realty.

(k) Probate of a will.

(2) *Good Neighbors Are Hard to Find.* One of the authors of this book once had an acquaintance who filed suit to enjoin his neighbor from allowing his dog to bark (a true story!). What court or courts would have jurisdiction over such an action, assuming one were inclined to bring it? Why?

(3) *Strategic Considerations.* What sort of strategic considerations would govern the choice of court in each of the following situations?

(a) Suit for $750 on an indebtedness.

(b) Same as (a), except that the action is based on the federal Truth in Lending Act (for which there is a special statute conferring federal jurisdiction without regard to amount in controversy, but not exclusive jurisdiction).

(4) *Family District Courts.* Can a judge of a family district court issue an injunction? If the family law docket slackens in the district in question (an unlikely occurrence, but hypothesize it for purposes of this question), can the presiding judge of the district authorize cases from the ordinary civil docket to be transferred to the family district court? *See* Gov. C. § 74.092.

## [B] Competing Jurisdictional Grants: Particular Controversies

### [1] The District Court Land-Title Grant Collides With the Justice Court: Forcible Entry and Detainer

*Read Tex. R. Civ. P. 738, 739, 746, 748, 749.*

## ORANGE LAUNDRY CO. v. STARK

*179 S.W.2d 841 (Tex. Civ. App.—Amarillo 1944, no writ)*

PITTS, Chief Justice.

This is a suit for forcible detainer and damages instituted by appellee, H. J. L. Stark, in the Justice Court of Precinct No. 1, Orange County, against appellants, Orange Laundry Company, Inc., and Edna Comeaux Smith and husband, C. B. Smith. From an adverse judgment in the justice court appellants perfected their appeal to the County Court of Orange County. Upon a trial in the county court the jury was instructed by the trial judge to find for the appellee for possession of the premises and against appellant and to find for appellee for damages in a sum to be fixed by them. The jury returned a verdict for appellee as instructed and allowed appellee the sum of $100 per month from January 9, 1943, to April 13, 1943, as damages for the withholding of the possession of the property in question from appellee by appellants for the said period of time. Judgment was rendered on April 13, 1943, for appellee for possession of the property and $313.28 as damages, from which judgment appellants perfected their appeal to the Court of Civil Appeals of the Ninth Supreme Judicial District at Beaumont and the same was transferred to this court by the Supreme Court of Texas.

Appellants predicate their appeal upon four points of error which, in effect, are as follows: That the county court was without jurisdiction to hear the case because the question of title to real estate was in issue and that appellee had failed to discharge the burden of proof on the issue of title and that appellee was not the legal owner of the land and the premises in question because the sale of the same to appellee by his predecessor was void, for all of which reasons the trial court erred in rendering judgment against appellants and for appellee.

The record discloses that the First National Bank in Orange owned a part of Block 7 in the Wingate Addition to the City of Orange, Orange County, and leased the same for a period of one year from April 6, 1937, to April 6, 1938, by a written contract to appellants for the purpose of maintaining a laundry by appellants thereon; that the written lease was not renewed when it expired but appellants remained in possession of the property and paid rent to the said bank until July 6, 1942; that on December 28, 1942, the said bank sold by warranty deed the property in question to appellee; that on January 9, 1943, the said bank notified appellants in writing of the sale of the said property to appellee and asked for possession of the same for appellee; that on January 9, 1943, appellee asked appellants in writing for possession of the property; that suit was filed in the justice court for possession and damages on January 20, 1943; that appellee made proof of the above facts at the trial in county court and made further proof that $150 to $175 per month was a reasonable rental value of the property in question at the time and that appellants had never paid any rent to appellee. Appellee then closed his evidence and appellants likewise closed without offering rebuttal testimony.

In his pleadings appellee made the usual allegations in a suit of this character and alleged further the purchase of the land and premises by him from the bank and that he was the owner of the same but the only relief he prayed for was to recover restitution of the premises, for damages, cost of suit and for general relief. The judgments of the justice court and county court adjudicate nothing more than the issues of possession, rents, damages and cost of suit.

Appellants answered in county court with a general denial and in their reply they endeavored to raise the question of legal title to the land in question and make it an issue in the case by alleging that the bank as the predecessor in title to the said land had acquired the same more than five years prior to the purported sale of the same to appellee; that a national bank should not hold title to or possession of real estate for more than five years; that the said bank was attempting to hold the said property at the time of the sale for more than five years in violation of the Federal Statutes and that the said purported sale was therefore void.

Appellee excepted in a supplemental answer to appellants' pleadings raising the question of legal title to the land in question and to the charge of a violation of the Federal Statutes by the said bank as the predecessor to the title to the said land. The trial court sustained appellee's exceptions and ordered all of such pleadings stricken, to which action of the trial court appellants excepted.

In our opinion the trial court properly sustained appellee's exceptions to appellants' answer raising the questions above mentioned. In a forcible detainer suit the merits of the title to land shall not be inquired into. Rule 746, Texas Rules of Civil Procedure. Farrell v. Sien, Tex. Civ. App., 145 S.W.2d 606.

In such cases proof of title may be received, not to determine title, but in connection with possession. *Young Women's Christian Ass'n of Austin, Tex. v. Hair*, Tex. Civ. App., 165 S.W.2d 238; Holcombe et al. v. Lorino, 124 Tex. 446, 79 S.W.2d 307.

If the sale made by the bank to appellee is to be attacked as being invalid, it must be done in a suit filed in the district court for that purpose and such is not permissible in a suit for forcible detainer. Scott et ux. v. Hewitt, 127 Tex. 31, 90 S.W.2d 816, 103 A.L.R. 977; Holcombe et al. v. Lorino, supra.

[The court concluded that it lacked appellate jurisdiction to consider the merits of a forcible entry and detainer judgment because a statute provided that county court judgments could not be appealed in detainer cases on the issue of possession.]

. . . .

For the reasons stated above, we believe appellee had the right to allege and prove ownership of the property in question in connection with the issue of forcible detainer but the question of legal title to the real estate involved was properly excluded by the trial court; that this court does not have jurisdiction over the question of forcible detainer since the trial court's judgment was conclusive and final as to that part of the judgment and that this court has jurisdiction over that part of the judgment awarding appellee $313.28 in money, but the power to review that part of the judgment was not conferred upon us by the appeal since there was no complaint or assignment of error about the money part of the judgment.

We therefore overrule all of appellants' assignments of error and dismiss that part of the appeal from the trial court's judgment awarding restitution of the property and premises in question to appellee and affirm that part of the trial court's judgment awarding the sum of $313.28 to appellee as damages.

## RODRIGUEZ v. SULLIVAN

*484 S.W.2d 592 (Tex. Civ. App.—El Paso 1972, no writ)*

PRESLAR, Justice.

This is an appeal from an order of the District Court denying a temporary injunction against the Sheriff of El Paso County, Texas, to prevent him from executing a writ of possession issued by a Justice of the Peace in a Forcible Entry and Detainer Case. We are of the opinion that the injunction should have issued, and therefore reverse the order of the trial Court.

In the Justice Court, the plaintiff, Juan Sandoval, sought the writ of possession on pleadings that he had sold the property to the defendant, Ricardo Rodriguez, under a purchase-sale contract in 1961, for a consideration of $5,650.00, payable $250.00 down and monthly payments of $47.00, and that the defendant had become delinquent in his payments as of June, 1970; that the plaintiff had given the defendant notice of the default and his intention to accelerate the indebtedness, pursuant to Art. 1301b, Vernon's Ann. Civ. St.; that the defendant had failed to comply with the contract; and that plaintiff was entitled to possession of the property.

> "An action of forcible entry and detainer is a special proceeding and as such is governed by the special statutes and rules applicable thereto. See Lowe and Archer, Texas Practice, Injunctions and Extraordinary Proceedings (1957), Section 121; Rules 738 through 755, Texas Rules of Civil Procedure; Ringgold v. Graham, Com. App., 13 S.W.2d 355 (1929); Simmons v. Brannum, Tex. Civ. App., 182 S.W.2d 1020 (1944), no wr. hist.; Ragsdale v. Ward, Tex. Civ. App., 173 S.W.2d 765 (1933), no wr. hist. Under the provisions of Article 3973, Vernon's Annotated Civil Statutes, an action of forcible entry and detainer must be instituted in the Justice Court. Forcible entry and detainer is an action for possession and the question of right of possession is the only issue involved in the Justice Court."

As seen from this quotation from Haginas et ux. v. Malbis Memorial Foundation, 163 Tex. 274, 354 S.W.2d 368 (1962), the right of possession is the issue. In the case before us, it is apparent that the determination of the right of possession issue in the Justice Court depended on who owned the real estate involved. The defendant, Ricardo Rodriguez, is the plaintiff in this injunction action, and he contends that the original contract is lost, but that under it he has paid an amount which entitles him to a deed.

We are of the opinion that the judgment of the Justice Court is void as it necessarily was based on a determination to the title to realty. The entry was under the contract, so only forcible detainer could be the case. Justice Courts have no jurisdiction of suits for title to land, and hence have no jurisdiction to try a case in forcible detainer, which necessarily involves trial of title to land, or to render judgment therein. American Spiritualist Ass'n v. Ravkind et al. 313 S.W.2d 121 (Tex. Civ. App.—Dallas 1958, writ ref'd n.r.e.). Article 2387, V. A.T.C.S., provides that Justice Courts have no jurisdiction for the trial of title to land.

Since the Justice Court judgment was void, it follows that the District Court erred in not enjoining execution of the writ of possession. Proper application of the law to the facts was not made. The judgment of the trial Court is reversed with instructions to that Court to issue the temporary injunction as prayed for by Appellant.

---

## NOTES AND QUESTIONS

(1) *What is a Title Dispute?* Are the two decisions above, *Orange Laundry Co. v. Stark* and *Rodriguez v. Sullivan,* consistent? In *Orange Laundry,* the tenants, the parties objecting to jurisdiction, would not be entitled to possession even if correct in the contention that Stark, their landlord, did not have title because the bank's sale of the property was invalid. In *Rodriguez,* the party complaining of improper jurisdiction, Rodriguez, would be entitled to possession if correct that he was entitled to a deed. Does this distinction make a difference?

(2) *Incidental Determinations of Title.* There is a line of Texas cases that deals with title questions that are merely "incidental" to other, more substantial issues within the jurisdiction of a county or justice court. For example, in *Johnson v. Fellowship Baptist Church,* 627 S.W.2d 203 (Tex. App.—Corpus Christi 1981, no writ), justice and county courts ordered a writ of restitution in a forcible detainer action against a tenant, Johnson. Johnson sought an injunction from the district court on issuance of the writ. She argued that the justice and county courts, in deciding whether restitution should be made to Fellowship Baptist Church or Mayfair Park Baptist Church, both of whom could assert title to the property, had impermissibly determined a title issue. The Court of Civil Appeals affirmed the district court's denial of injunctive relief. The court stated, "In the case before us, there was never a claim of title by Mrs. Johnson. The only dispute involving title arose between Fellowship Baptist Church and Mayfair Park Baptist Church. It was not beyond the authority of the county court to determine title on this collateral matter." *Johnson v. Fellowship Baptist Church,* 627 S.W.2d 203, 204 (Tex. App.—Corpus Christi 1981, no writ).

Another example is to be found in *Smith v. Armes,* 208 S.W.2d 409 (Tex. Civ. App.—Fort Worth 1948, no writ). The essential nature of the case is shown by the following excerpt:

> Plaintiff, J. C. Armes, sued defendants, A. J. Smith and his wife, Ethel P. Smith, in a Justice Court of Jack County, Texas, to recover $125.
>
> The case was appealed from the Justice Court to the County Court of Jack County, Texas.
>
> Written pleadings were filed in the County Court, and from plaintiff's petition his suit appears to be based on allegations that he purchased from defendants "a lot or parcel of land in the City of Jacksboro, Jack County, Texas, eighty feet wide and one hundred and fifty feet long," . . . .
>
> Allegations are made that by a survey the lot so purchased by plaintiff was only 70 ft. wide and deficient in width by 10 ft.; that defendants, by warranty deed, had made the conveyance and did not keep their covenant as contained in the deed; that plaintiff paid $600 for the lot and because of the deficiency in quantity he was damaged $125. He prayed for recovery of that amount and for costs of suit.
>
> . . . .
>
> The general rule seems to be that even though title to real estate be incidentally involved, if it be a mere auxiliary or collateral matter incident to the primary cause of action, the district court would have no original jurisdiction, but any inferior court having jurisdiction of the amount in controversy would be the proper forum in which to litigate the issue.

In Kegans v. White et al., Tex. Civ. App., 131 S.W.2d 990, 992, a suit was instituted in the County Court for the recovery of the reasonable rentals for the use of real estate claimed by plaintiff. The amount sued for was within the jurisdiction of the County Court. The defendant denied owing any attornment to plaintiff upon the ground that plaintiff had no interest in the real estate for which he sought rentals. The case is rather a complicated one and much ado was had over the result of several law suits, but the question of ownership of title was only incidental to the claim for rentals. The court said: "If the title is involved in no other way than that suggested, clearly the trial court had jurisdiction to hear and determine the case as established by the authorities relied upon by appellees. *Kalteyer v. Wipff*, Tex. Civ. App., 65 S.W. 207; *Putty v. Putty*, Tex. Civ. App., 6 S.W.2d 136; *Robinson v. Clymer*, Tex. Civ. App., 170 S.W. 107; *Melvin v. Chancy*, 8 Tex. Civ. App. 252, 28 S.W. 241; *Southwestern Bell Co. v. Burris*, Tex. Civ. App., 68 S.W.2d 542, 543." The cited authorities lead us to conclude that trial of the title of property was not involved and that the County Court had appellate jurisdiction.

. . . .

---

Can this "incidental title question" concept be used to distinguish the *Orange Laundry* case, above (in which the justice court was held to have jurisdiction), from the *Rodriguez* case, above (in which it did not)?

(3) *Equitable Title and Equitable Rights*. Under Texas law, a purchaser under a contract for the conveyance of land acquires equitable title once the purchaser has performed the contractual obligations. *Johnson v. Wood,* 138 Tex. 106, 157 S.W.2d 146 (1941); *Trans-World Bonded Whses. & Storage v. Garza*, 570 S.W.2d 2, 5 (Tex. Civ. App.—San Antonio 1978, writ ref'd n.r.e.). In *Haith v. Drake,* 596 S.W.2d 194, 197 (Tex. Civ. App.—Houston [1st Dist.] 1980, no writ), a case similar to *Rodriguez* in which the grant of the temporary injunction was reversed on appeal, the court of appeals distinguished between "equitable title" and an "equitable right" to possession. Because the defendant in the justice court was held to have no "equitable title," the justice court had jurisdiction to determine the question of possession. "Until he has fully performed his obligations under the contract [for deed] Dr. Drake possesses only equitable rights, not equitable title."

(4) *Concurrent Jurisdiction*. It has been held that the district courts have concurrent jurisdiction with justice courts in trying possession rights to land. *McCloud v. Knapp,* 507 S.W.2d 644 (Tex. Civ. App.—Dallas, 1974, no writ).

(5) *Appeals to County Court*. A final judgment of a county court in a forcible entry and detainer suit may not be appealed on the issue of possession unless the premises in question are being used for residential purposes only. Prop. C. § 24.007. The same statute provides that a county court judgment may not be stayed unless the appellant files a supersedeas bond in the amount set by the county court, within 10 days of the signing of the judgment.

### [2] Problems With Probate Jurisdiction

## SEAY v. HALL

*677 S.W.2d 19 (Tex. 1984)*

KILGARLIN, Justice.

The issue in this case is whether statutory probate courts have jurisdiction over survival and wrongful death actions. Because of her husband's death from injuries received when a boiler safety valve released scalding water and steam onto him, Willia Rhoneta Seay sued the various respondents[1] in this case. Suit was initially brought in a Dallas County district court under the provisions of Tex. Rev. Civ. Stat. Ann. art. 4671 (wrongful death action) and Tex. Rev. Civ. Stat. Ann. art. 5525 (survival action). Five days after filing suit in that court, Mrs. Seay brought the same causes of action against the same defendants in the probate court of Dallas County.[2] The various defendants filed motions to dismiss in the probate court, claiming that court lacked jurisdiction over the two causes. Dismissal for want of jurisdiction was ordered. However, the court of appeals held that the probate court did have jurisdiction of the survival action, and reversed that part of the cause. It affirmed the probate court judgment that it had no jurisdiction over the wrongful death cause. 663 S.W.2d 468. We affirm that part of the appellate court's judgment that the probate court had no jurisdiction over the wrongful death action, and reverse that part of the judgment holding that the probate court did have jurisdiction over the survival cause of action. We affirm the dismissal order of the probate court.

The basis of Mrs. Seay's argument that the probate court has jurisdiction over both causes of action is found in Tex. Prob. Code Ann. §§ 3, 5, and 5A.

Section 5(d) provides that "[a]ll courts exercising original probate jurisdiction shall have the power to hear all matters incident to an estate." Section 5A(b) provides that "[i]n situations where the jurisdiction of a statutory probate court is concurrent with that of a district court, any cause of action appertaining to estates or incident to an estate shall be brought in a statutory probate court rather than in the district court." Further, section 5A(b) defines "appertaining to estates and incident to an estate" as including:

> [T]he probate of wills, the issuance of letters testamentary and of administration, and the determination of heirship, and also include, but are not limited to, all claims by or against an estate, all actions for trial of title to land and for the enforcement of liens thereon, all actions for trial of the right of property, all actions to construe wills, the interpretation and administration of testamentary trusts and the applying of constructive trusts, and generally all matters relating to the settlement, partition, and distribution of estates of wards and deceased persons.

Section 3(c) provides that " 'claims' include liabilities of a decedent which survive, including taxes, whether arising in contract or in tort or otherwise, funeral expenses, the expense of a

---

[1] William K. Hall, William K. Hall & Associates, William K. Hall and Company: engineers and consultants in the design and construction of the boiler and boiler room; Charles R. Freeburg, Charles R. Freeburg and Associates: architects and consultants in the design and construction of the boiler and boiler room; Henry C. Beck Company: general contractor in the construction of the boiler room; Travelers Indemnity Company: boiler inspector; and, Gaston Episcopal Hospital: Seay's employer.

[2] Houston General Insurance Company subsequently intervened seeking recovery of compensation benefits paid Seay.

tombstone, expenses of administration, estate inheritance taxes, liabilities against the estate of a minor or incompetent, and debts due such estates."

The pivotal issue is whether the statutory terms "appertaining to estates and incident to an estate," "all matters relating to the settlement . . . of estates," and "claims" are broad enough to confer upon probate courts jurisdiction over survival or wrongful death actions. This is necessary because the probate code does not expressly name wrongful death or survival causes of action as being claims by an estate or claims appertaining to or incident to an estate. If the statutory language is sufficiently broad, then section 5A(b) makes plain that the statutory probate court will have dominant jurisdiction over the two causes of action.

Understanding the history of the current statutes is necessary in determining if the probate courts have jurisdiction. In 1973, Texas adopted an amendment to article V, section 8, of the Texas Constitution. That amendment empowered the legislature "to increase, diminish or eliminate the jurisdiction of either the district court or the county court in probate matters." . . . Anticipating voter approval of the constitutional amendment, the legislature also enacted an amendment to section 5 of the probate code. This amendment provided that in counties having statutory probate courts, "all applications, petitions and motions regarding probate, administrations, guardianships, and mental illness matters" should be filed and heard in such courts. The 1973 Probate Code § 5 amendment further provided:

> All courts exercising original probate jurisdiction shall have the power to hear all matters incident to an estate, including but not limited to, all claims by or against an estate, all actions for trial of title to land incident to an estate and for the enforcement of liens thereon incident to an estate and of all actions for trial of the right of property incident to an estate.
>
> . . . .

Realizing that there was uncertainty among the bench and bar as to what were matters incident to probate, the Speaker of the Texas House, in 1977, charged the House Judiciary Committee to return to the 66th Legislature recommendations for changes in the probate code. That committee did report and made as its third recommendation that there be "clarification of the phrases 'appertaining to estates' and 'incident to an estate' in Probate Code Sections 4 and 5(d)." Interim Report, Tex. House Judiciary Comm.: Proposed Revision of the Texas Probate Code 13. 66th Leg. (1978). The committee report observed "the question of jurisdiction 'incident to probate' is still an unsettled one in the Texas legal community." *Id.* at 15. . . .

Following the committee report, the legislature, in 1979, adopted H.B. 329, which struck part of the language of Texas Probate Code section 5(d) and created a new section 5A. In addition to the old section 5(d) provisions of (1) claims by or against an estate; (2) actions for trial of title to land incident to an estate; (3) enforcement of liens thereon incident to an estate; (4) all actions for trial of the right of property incident to an estate; and (5) actions to construe wills, new section 5A added to the probate court's original jurisdiction the following: (1) probate of wills, (2) issuance of letters testamentary and of administration, (3) determination of heirship, (4) the interpretation and administration of testamentary trusts and applying of constructive trusts, and (5) generally, all matters relating to the settlement, partition, and distribution of estates of wards and deceased persons. The bill as it passed the House contained no authorization for constitutional county courts and statutory county courts at law to probate wills, issue letters testamentary and administration, determine heirship, or have jurisdiction of all matters relating to the settlement, partition, and distribution of estates of wards and deceased persons. The Senate, however, added in committee an amendment, which ultimately became law, bestowing upon constitutional county courts and statutory county courts at law under section 5A(a) much of the same authority given statutory probate courts in section 5A(b).

If there is any legislative intent to be gleaned from the 1979 proceedings as to what appertains to an estate, it would seemingly be that the legislature did not intend to expand probate court jurisdiction to matters other than those in which the controlling issue was the settlement, partition, or distribution of an estate. It is of significance that the language "appertaining to estates" appeared previous to 1979 in only section 4, having to do with jurisdiction of county courts to hear probate matters. Previously, section 5 language granted authority to probate courts "to hear all matters incident to an estate . . ." The Judiciary Committee recommended the "appertaining to estates" language be added to section 5. This recommendation comes directly from Schwartzel and Wilshusen, who urged the "appertaining to an estate" language so that the phrase would be construed "as limiting probate jurisdiction to the probate of the will, the issuance of letters testamentary, and the settlement, partition, and distribution of estate assets." 53 Texas L. Rev. at 358.

Further, in ascertaining legislative intent, one must look to the stated purpose of the committee report: "minimizing the possibility of overboard [sic] construction of the phrases 'appertaining to an estate' and 'incident to an estate'. . . ." Interim Report at 15. The "appertaining to" and "incident to" language recommended and subsequently enacted was unquestionably designed to limit probate court jurisdiction to matters in which the *controlling issue* (emphasis added) was the settlement, partition, or distribution of an estate. Thus, we conclude that neither wrongful death nor survival actions are, or were intended to be, matters appertaining to or incident to estates.

Next, we consider whether Tex. Prob. Code Ann. § 5A language "Claims by or Against an Estate" can be construed so as to confer probate court jurisdiction over survival and wrongful death causes. Texas Prob.Code Ann. § 3(c) defines "claims" in terms of certain enumerated liabilities of a decedent and debts due the estate. Obviously, the deceased's liabilities language would not confer jurisdiction. Therefore, we must determine if wrongful death or survival actions constitute debts due the estate. A debt is a "specified sum of money owing to one person from another, including not only [an] obligation of [a] debtor to pay but [the] right of [a] creditor to receive and enforce payment." Black's Law Dictionary 363 (5th ed. 1979). In survival and wrongful death actions we have no specified sums of money owed, because the damages are for the most part unliquidated. Moreover, at this time no one is obligated to pay anything.

Further justification for holding that "claims" are limited to those of a liquidated nature can be found throughout the probate code. Tex. Prob. Code Ann. § 322 classifies and sets priorities for claims against a decedent's estate. Claims specified include funeral expenses, expenses of administration and other claims significantly different from the unliquidated expectancy contemplated by wrongful death and survival personal injury claims. Although section 322 only addresses claims against an estate, there is no reason to believe that the legislature intended one definition for "claims by an estate" and a different definition for "claims against an estate." A limited definition of the word "claims" is also suggested by the language in Tex. Prob. Code Ann. § 233 which addresses responsibilities for collecting claims and recovering property on behalf of the estate. Therefore, we conclude these two causes of action do not constitute a claim by an estate.

The third statutory term in the trinity upon which Ms. Seay relies is the section 5A(b) language "and generally all matters relating to the settlement, partition, and distribution of estates of wards and deceased person." As noted, however, *Zamora v. Gonzalez* restricted these types of cases to those in which the controlling issue is the settlement, partition or distribution of an estate. More recently, when called upon to interpret similar language in a predecessor statute to section 5A, the court in *Wolford v. Wolford*, 590 S.W.2d 769, 771 (Tex. Civ. App.—Houston [14th Dist.] 1979, writ ref'd n.r.e.), held that a probate court lacked jurisdiction to try a personal injury case. The appeals court said that while it was apparent that the legislature intended to broaden the jurisdiction of probate courts, the phrase " 'all matters incident to an estate' applies only to those matters in which the controlling issue is the settlement, partition, or distribution of an estate . . . ." *Accord Bell v. Hinkle*, 562 S.W.2d 35 (Tex. Civ. App.—Houston [14th Dist.] 1978, writ ref'd n.r.e.), *cert. denied*, 454 U.S. 826 (1981); *Sumaruk v. Todd*, 560 S.W.2d 141 (Tex. Civ. App.—Tyler 1977, no writ). We approve interpretations that allow a probate court to exercise jurisdiction only if the controlling issue of the case is the settlement, partition or distribution of an estate. It is hornbook law that neither in a survival cause of action nor a wrongful death cause of action are the controlling issues, even arguably the settlement, partition, or distribution of an estate.

. . . .

The legislature has thrice amended Probate Code § 5 since its original enactment. In none of the bill analyses, reports, recorded committee or floor debates, or law review articles has there been a hint that the legislature intended probate court jurisdiction over survival or wrongful death actions. Further, the legislature has thrice broadened probate court jurisdiction in specifically named areas, but has not chosen to single out the two causes under consideration.

The legislature's failure to discuss wrongful death and survival causes of action clearly illustrates that the legislature never contemplated or intended the jurisdictional step which Mrs. Seay proposes. While this court may properly write in areas traditionally reserved to the judicial branch of government, it would be a usurpation of our powers to add language to a law where the legislature has refrained. Intrusion into the legislative arena without regard for traditional constitutional and legal safeguards of legislative power would violate a fundamental judicial rule. Courts should carefully search out a statute's intent, giving full effect to all of its terms. "But they must find its intent in its language and not elsewhere. They are not the law-making body. They are not responsible for omissions in legislation." *Simmons v. Arnim*, 110 Tex. 309, 324, 220 S.W. 66, 70 (1920). *See also General Elec. Credit Corp. v. Smail*, 584 S.W.2d 690 (Tex. 1979); *Jefferson County Drainage Dist. No. 6 v. Gary*, 362 S.W.2d 305 (Tex. 1962).

The wisdom in following legislative intent is reinforced by those problems that would be created by a judicial expansion of probate jurisdiction. Multiple plaintiffs, some injured and some killed in the same accident, would necessarily be forced into different courts. This would create needless litigation, potential appeal and res judicata problems and could conceivably frustrate a litigant's ability to protect his interest. These problems underscore this court's justification for remaining outside the legislative realm.

Absent the legislature's express mandate that these two causes of action appertain to an estate and are within the jurisdiction of the statutory probate courts, we conclude that the proper forum for the trial of such cases is in the state district courts. Accordingly, the judgment of the court of appeals affirming the probate court's dismissal of the wrongful death action is affirmed; the judgment of the court of appeals reversing the probate court's dismissal of the survival action is reversed; and, the order of dismissal of the probate court is affirmed.

---

## IN RE GRAHAM

*971 S.W.2d 56 (Tex. 1998)*

HANKINSON, Justice.

In this original proceeding, we decide whether a statutory probate court has the authority to transfer to itself from district court a divorce action when one spouse is a ward of the probate court. Section 608 of the Texas Probate Code authorizes a statutory probate court to transfer to itself a matter appertaining or incident to a guardianship estate. The court of appeals conditionally issued a writ of mandamus compelling the probate court to vacate its order transferring Gitta and Richard Milton's divorce, filed in a Travis County district court, to Travis County Probate Court Number One, where a guardianship of Mr. Milton's estate and person is pending. 947 S.W.2d 737. Because we conclude that the Miltons' divorce proceeding is a matter appertaining and incident to Mr. Milton's guardianship estate, we conditionally grant Relator's petition for writ of mandamus and direct the court of appeals to vacate its order.

Gitta and Richard Milton married in July 1991 and had one child. In April 1995, Mr. Milton attempted suicide; he is now incapacitated and resides in an Austin nursing home.

Following Mr. Milton's attempted suicide, the probate court appointed Mrs. Milton guardian of her husband's person and estate. But after discovering a deed in which Mrs. Milton had transferred title to the community homestead to herself, the probate court appointed Nancy Scherer as Mr. Milton's attorney ad litem. Scherer then filed a motion to show cause why Mrs. Milton should not be removed as guardian of her husband's estate. During a hearing on the motion, the probate court instructed Mrs. Milton on her duties as guardian and directed her to take corrective actions. After the hearing, however, Mrs. Milton filed for divorce in a Travis County district court; she resigned as guardian the next day. The probate court then appointed Scherer guardian of Mr. Milton's estate, and on Scherer's motion, the probate court transferred the divorce proceeding to itself under Probate Code section 608.

Mrs. Milton responded by filing a petition for writ of mandamus in the court of appeals, alleging that the transfer was improper. The court of appeals conditionally granted the writ, ordering the probate court to withdraw its transfer order, and the probate court complied. Scherer moved for rehearing at the court of appeals. After being informed of the rehearing motion, the probate court reinstated its transfer order and resumed the show cause proceeding. The court of appeals issued a substitute opinion, overruling Scherer's motion for rehearing and again directing the probate court to vacate its transfer order. 947 S.W.2d at 742. The same day, the probate court informed the parties by letter of its conclusion that certain property characterized as community property in probate pleadings by Mrs. Milton was Mr. Milton's separate property and that his separate estate owned certain reimbursement claims against the community property estate. In addition, the probate court awarded Scherer attorney's fees.

Mrs. Milton then filed an application for writ of prohibition and injunction in the court of appeals, requesting the court to "direct the probate court to vacate its orders [awarding Scherer attorney's fees and characterizing property in the marital estate] . . . and enjoin [it] from further attempts to interfere with . . . the jurisdiction of . . . the district court." The application is still pending in the court of appeals.

Following the mandamus proceeding and the filing of the application for writ of prohibition and injunction in the court of appeals, Scherer resigned as successor guardian of Mr. Milton's estate, and the probate court appointed Samuel Graham, Relator before this Court, successor guardian. Thereafter, the parties began mediated settlement negotiations of the divorce proceedings. As a result, they signed a written agreement, pursuant to Texas Rule of Civil Procedure 11, settling the property division and support issues.

Because the guardianship remained pending in the probate court, Graham moved to approve the settlement with that court. The probate court issued an order approving the settlement, conditioned on the inclusion of certain amendments. The district court rendered a final decree of divorce, but Graham filed a motion for new trial in the district court, asserting that the decree did not comport with the rule 11 agreement or the probate court's amendments. Graham also filed this original proceeding, seeking relief from the court of appeals' mandamus order and arguing that the probate court's transfer of the Miltons' divorce was proper. The question presented for our review is whether the probate court acted without authority in transferring the divorce.

Section 608 of the Probate Code authorizes a statutory probate court to transfer to itself a matter appertaining to or incident to a pending guardianship estate:

> A judge of a statutory probate court on the motion of a party to the action or of a person interested in a guardianship, may transfer to the judge's court from a district, county, or statutory court a cause of action appertaining to or incident to a guardianship estate that is pending in the statutory probate court and may consolidate the transferred cause of action with the other proceedings in the statutory probate court relating to the guardianship estate.

Tex. Prob. Code § 608. A cause of action is appertaining or incident to an estate if section 607 of the Probate Court explicitly defines it as such or if the controlling issue in the suit is the settlement, partition, or distribution of an estate. *See Palmer v. Coble Wall Trust Co., Inc.*, 851 S.W.2d 178, 182 (Tex. 1992). Section 607 defines the term "appertaining to or incident to an estate" to include, among other things, "all actions for trial of the right of property incident to a guardianship estate, and generally all matters relating to the settlement, partition, and distribution of a guardianship estate." Tex. Prob. Code § 607(b). Relying on *English v. Gregory*, 714 S.W.2d 443 (Tex. App.—Houston [14th Dist.] 1986, orig. proceeding), and *Williams v. Scanlan*, 714 S.W.2d 38 (Tex. App.—Houston [14th Dist.] 1986, orig. proceeding), and notwithstanding the language of sections 607 and 608, Mrs. Milton argues that the probate court does not have authority to transfer to itself a divorce proceeding because only district courts have the power to grant all requested relief in family matters. We disagree.

Although *Williams* and *English* imply that district court jurisdiction over divorces is exclusive, both cases were decided before the Legislature narrowed the exclusive jurisdiction of district courts in 1987. *See* Act of May 21, 1987, 70th Leg., R.S., ch. 148, § 1.36, 1987 Tex. Gen. Laws 538. Before 1987, the Government Code specified that district courts had exclusive jurisdiction over divorces. *Id.* The revised section states that "[t]he district court has the jurisdiction provided by Article V, Section 8, of the Texas Constitution." Tex. Gov't Code § 24.007. In turn, article V, section 8 bridles the exclusive jurisdiction of district courts when jurisdiction is conferred on another court:

> District Court jurisdiction consists of exclusive, appellate, and original jurisdiction of all actions, proceedings, and remedies, *except in cases where exclusive, appellate, or original jurisdiction may be conferred by this Constitution or other law on some other court. . . .*

Tex. Const. art. V, § 8 (emphasis added).

The Probate Code confers jurisdiction on statutory probate courts to hear matters appertaining to or incident to a guardianship estate. *See* Tex. Prob. Code § 607(b) ("In a situation in which the jurisdiction of a statutory probate court is concurrent with that of a district court, a cause of action appertaining to or incident to a guardianship estate shall be brought in a statutory probate court rather than in the district court."); Tex. Prob. Code § 606(c) ("In those counties in which there is a statutory probate court . . . all applications, petitions and motions regarding guardianships . . . or other matters addressed by this chapter shall be filed and heard in those courts. . . ."); Tex. Prob. Code § 606(e) ("A court that exercises original probate jurisdiction has the power to hear all matters incident to an estate."). Thus, current Texas law does not impede a probate court from providing all necessary relief in a divorce action when it properly transfers to itself a cause of action appertaining or incident to a guardianship estate.

We must next determine whether the divorce proceeding itself is appertaining to or incident to the guardianship estate. Courts have determined that a variety of matters are appertaining or incident to an estate. *See Lucik v. Taylor*, 596 S.W.2d 514, 516 (Tex. 1980) (holding that suits "incident to an estate" include determining whether property was part of marital estate); *Potter v. Potter*, 545 S.W.2d 43, 44 (Tex. Civ. App.—Houston [1st Dist.] 1976, writ ref'd n.r.e.) (concluding that probate court has jurisdiction to determine whether shares of stock were part of community estate or separate property); *see also Bailey v. Cherokee County Appraisal Dist.*, 862 S.W.2d 581, 582 (Tex. 1993) (recovery of delinquent ad valorem taxes); *English v. Cobb*, 593 S.W.2d 674, 674 (Tex. 1979) (conversion of estate's bank account); *Parr v. White*, 543 S.W.2d 440, 444 (Tex. Civ. App.—Corpus Christi 1976, writ ref'd n.r.e.) (probate court determines who has the right to control, transfer, and vote the stock of decedent). To determine whether this is such a proceeding, we review Mrs. Milton's pleadings. In her original divorce petition, she requested (1) a disproportionate share of the parties' estate, (2) reimbursement to the community estate for funds used to benefit Mr. Milton's separate estate, (3) reimbursement to her separate estate for funds used to benefit Mr. Milton's separate estate, and (4) reimbursement to her separate estate for funds used to benefit the community estate. Mrs. Milton also sought temporary orders (1) awarding her exclusive control of all community property, (2) enjoining Mr. Milton's guardian from entering, operating, or exercising control over the community property, (3) ordering the guardianship estate to pay child support, and (4) ordering Mr. Milton's separate estate to pay interim attorney's fees. Thus, the outcome of this divorce proceeding, which involves child support but not child custody or visitation, necessarily appertains to Mr. Milton's estate because it directly impacts the assimilation, distribution, and settlement of his estate. *See* Tex. Prob. Code § 607; *Palmer*, 851 S.W.2d at 182; *see also* Tex. Fam. Code § 3.63 ("In a decree of divorce . . . the court shall order a division of the estate of the parties. . . ."); *In re Johnson*, 595 S.W.2d 900, 903 (Tex. Civ. App.—Amarillo 1980, writ dism'd w.o.j.) (explaining that without a property division, a divorce is not final).

The Probate Code provides that these claims may be resolved in the same court by the same judge. *See* Tex. Prob. Code §§ 607–608. This interpretation comports with legislative intent as evidenced by the Legislature's persistent expansion of statutory probate court jurisdiction over the years. *See Palmer*, 851 S.W.2d at 181 ("In 1985, the legislature responded to *Seay* by amending the Texas Probate Code to broaden statutory probate court jurisdiction."); *Seay v. Hall*, 677 S.W.2d 19, 21, 25 (Tex. 1984) (noting that the Legislature recognizes probate court expertise in handling estate matters but concluding that statutory probate courts do not have jurisdiction to hear wrongful death and survival claims).

That this case involves child support issues does not alter our conclusion. The Probate Code affirmatively grants probate courts the authority to order child support payments after balancing the child's interests with the ward's interests. See Tex. Prob. Code § 776A(a)–(b) (granting probate courts broad authority to order expenditure of funds from ward's estate for the education and maintenance of ward's spouse or dependents after considering, among other things, the circumstances of ward, ward's spouse, and ward's dependents). The Probate Code also charges the probate court with monitoring payments from the guardianship estate. *See, e.g.*, Tex. Prob. Code § 671(a) (requiring courts to determine whether guardian is performing all duties that pertain to ward and ward's estate); Tex. Prob. Code § 741 (requiring the probate court to review guardian's accounting of ward's estate at least annually); Tex. Prob. Code § 742 (describing when court may authorize payments of claims made against the guardianship estate after reviewing guardian's accounting); Tex. Prob. Code § 743 (requiring probate court to review guardian's annual report of "disbursements for the support and maintenance of the ward and . . . the ward's dependents"). Because Mr. Milton's child support obligations will be paid from his guardianship estate, the probate court can effectively and efficiently supervise the payments to ensure that the interests of both Mr. Milton and his child are protected.

Accordingly, we hold that a statutory probate court has authority under Probate Code section 608 to transfer to itself from district court a divorce proceeding when one party to the divorce is a ward of the probate court. Because the court of appeals exceeded its mandamus power when it disturbed the probate court's judgment absent an abuse of discretion, exercise of our mandamus authority is proper. *See Johnson v. Fourth Court of Appeals*, 700 S.W.2d 916, 917 (Tex. 1985, orig. proceeding). We therefore conditionally grant the writ of mandamus, which will issue only if the court of appeals does not vacate its mandamus judgment.

---

## NOTE

In 1985, the legislature amended § 5A(b) of the Probate Code by adding a sentence that provided that "[i]n actions by or against a personal representative, the statutory probate courts have concurrent jurisdiction with the district court." Prob. C. § 5A(b) (1985). As the Texas Supreme Court has explained, the purpose of the amendment was to overrule *Seay v. Hall*. *Palmer v. Coble Wall Trust Co., Inc.*, 851 S.W.2d 178, 181 (Tex. 1992) ("We agree with the court of appeals' assessment in *Pearson v. K-Mart*, 755 S.W.2d 217, 219 (Tex. App.—Houston [1st Dist.] 1988, no writ) that 'it is readily apparent that the purpose of [House Bill 479] was to overrule *Seay v. Hall*.' "). In 1987, the legislature modified the last sentence of § 5A(b) to read: "In actions by or against a personal representative, or in matters involving an inter vivos trust, the statutory probate courts have concurrent jurisdiction with the district courts." 70th Leg. R.S. Ch. 459, § 1, 1987 Tex. Gen. Laws 2043, 2044. In 1989, the jurisdiction of statutory probate courts was broadened even further to cover claims by or against personal representatives "whether or not the matter is appertaining to or incident to an estate." *See* Prob. C. § 5A(c)–(e). Nevertheless, the "controlling issue" test established in *Seay*, to determine whether a claim is "appertaining to" or "incident to" an estate, is still the principal test regarding probate jurisdiction in many counties. Which ones? Why?

In counties having a statutory probate court, the *Seay v. Hall* interpretation of the terms "incident to an estate" or "appertaining to an estate" is relevant in at least two important respects.

First, the ability of a statutory probate court to "pull down" a proceeding from a district court or from a county-level court is limited by Probate Code Section 5B to "a cause of action appertaining to or incident to an estate pending in the statutory probate court." Of course, the statute that specifically pertains to the particular legislative court must always be consulted to determine whether more or less jurisdiction is accorded that court. For example, Government Code Section 25.1034(a) gives a statutory probate court in Harris County expanded authority to transfer to itself "a cause of action in which a personal representative of an estate pending in [the] statutory probate court is a party." Gov. C. § 25.1034(a); *see In re J7S Inc.*, 979 S.W.2d 374 (Tex. App.—Houston [14th Dist.] 1998, mand. requested). Second, the statutory command contained in the last sentence of Probate Code Section 5A(b) ("In situations where the jurisdiction of a statutory probate court is concurrent with that of a district court, any cause of action appertaining to estates or incident to an estate shall be brought in a statutory probate court rather than in the district court.") does not apply unless the cause of action satisfies the standard set forth in *Seay v. Hall.*

## § 3.04 Amount in Controversy

The amount in controversy is the determinative factor in cases not otherwise assigned by statute and the Constitution to a particular court. In the one-plaintiff, one-defendant case, the amount claimed by the plaintiff in good faith is the amount in controversy. Unless otherwise provided by statute, exemplary damages, attorney's fees, penalties, and like recoveries are counted as part of the amount in controversy, provided the claim for them is not invalid on its face. *See Bybee v. Fireman's Fund Ins. Co.*, 331 S.W.2d 910, 913–914 (Tex. 1960). By statute, however, statutory county courts exercising civil jurisdiction must not include "interest, statutory or punitive damages and penalties, and attorney's fees and costs, as alleged on the face of the petition" in the amount in controversy calculus. *See* Gov. C. § 25.0003(c); *cf* Gov. C. § 25.2222 (Tarrant County).

Interest and costs are not included in computing amount in controversy. However, this principle is subject to a confusing exception: it is only interest "eo nomine" ("interest under the name of interest") that is excluded; interest "as damages" is included. *See Binge v. Gulf Coast Orchards Co.*, 93 S.W.2d 813, 814 (Tex. Civ. App.—San Antonio 1936, dis.).

"Interest eo nomine" includes conventional interest provided for by agreement (such as a promissory note) as well as certain kinds of interest provided for by statute. It is considered an incident of the debt. "Interest as damages" exists when the dollar value of the loss is fixed by the conditions as of the time of the injury giving rise to the cause of action. Prejudgment interest was not recoverable in personal injury cases until 1985 when the Texas Supreme Court decided *Cavnar v. Quality Control Parking, Inc.*, 696 S.W.2d 549, 551–556 (Tex. 1985). Now, wrongful death, personal injury, and property damage actions filed or retried after September 1, 1987, must include statutory prejudgment interest (Fin. C. § 304.102), though it is probable that this statutory interest constitutes "interest as damages" rather than "interest eo nomine." In *Johnson & Higgins of Tx v. Kenneco Energy*, 962 S.W.2d 507, 530 (Tex. 1998), the Texas Supreme Court concluded that the prejudgment interest statute applies only to wrongful death, personal injury, and property damage cases. However, the Court also modified the rules for common law prejudgment interest (those cases that are outside the prejudgment interest statute) to conform with the rules governing prejudgment interest in wrongful death, personal injury, and property damage cases. *See Johnson & Higgins of Tx v. Kenneco Energy*, 962 S.W.2d 507, 531 (Tex. 1998). It is clear that such common law prejudgment interest is interest as damages, not interest eo nomine.

On the other hand, an award of prejudgment interest in accordance with another statutory provision that applies when no specified rate of interest is agreed on by the contracting parties, on all accounts and contracts "ascertaining the amount payable," probably is "interest eo nomine" rather than "interest as damages." *See* Fin. C. § 302.002; *see also Federal Life Ins. Co. of Chicago v. Kriton,* 112 Tex. 532, 249 S.W. 193 (Comm. App. 1923, approved); *Great Am. Ins. Co. v. MUD,* 950 S.W.2d 371, 372–373 (Tex. 1997).

What court has jurisdiction if the claim is not for the recovery of money damages? For example, what of an action to recover possession of personalty? The fair market value of the personalty controls. *Fath v. Newman,* 4 S.W.2d 193 (Tex. Civ. App.—Eastland 1927, no writ). What of a foreclosure on personalty? The amount in controversy is either the value of the property sought to be foreclosed on or the amount of the underlying debt, whichever is larger. *Walker Mercantile Co. v. J.R. Raney Co.,* 154 S.W. 317, 318 (Tex. Civ. App.—Austin 1913, no writ). Claims for injunctive relief or mandamus, too, may involve an amount in controversy. *See, e.g., City of Lubbock v. Green,* 312 S.W.2d 279, 283–284 (Tex. Civ. App.—Amarillo 1958, no writ) (suit to enjoin foreclosure upon property of the value of $400 could be brought in county court). Remember, however, that it is possible for a suit to involve no amount in controversy, and in that event, as we have seen, jurisdiction is in the district court. *Super-X Drugs, Inc. v. State,* 505 S.W.2d 333, 336 (Tex. Civ. App.—Houston [1st Dist.] 1974, no writ) (residual jurisdiction).

Actions involving multiple parties and multiple claims are more complex. Pursuant to statute (Gov. C. § 24.009) ("If two or more persons originally and properly join in one suit, the suit for jurisdictional purposes is treated as if one party is suing for the aggregate amount of all their claims added together . . ."), it has been held that an action by 88 plaintiffs for approximately $25 apiece was proper in district court. *Texas Employment Comm'n v. International Union of Elec. Radio and Mach. Workers,* 352 S.W.2d 252, 254 (Tex. 1961). In the absence of a comparable statutory provision, claims against multiple defendants are *not* aggregated. It is somewhat unsettled as to whether the claim of an intervening plaintiff should be aggregated with the claims of the "persons (who) originally join in one suit." The commentators think that the intervention should not work an ouster of jurisdiction. *See* W. Dorsaneo, *Texas Litigation Guide*, Ch. 82, *Intervention* (1998). The Texas Supreme Court has also held that the aggregation statute does not apply to require that multiple counterclaims be aggregated to determine the amount in controversy. *See* Smith v. Clary Corp., 917 S.W.2d 796, 797 (Tex. 1996).

Texas courts have a species of "ancillary jurisdiction" for claims that could not originally be filed in a particular court because they are too small. "Counterclaims" or "cross-claims" (*see* Tex. R. Civ. P. 97) and "third party actions" (*see* Tex. R. Civ. P. 38) that would not satisfy amount in controversy requirements as "original claims" are within the trial court's ancillary jurisdiction if they are *less than* the minimum jurisdictional limits *and* if they arise from the same set of events ("same transaction or occurrence or series"). *See, e.g., Andel v. Eastman Kodak Co.,* 400 S.W.2d 584, 586 (Tex.App.—Houston 1966, no writ). The amount in controversy in an interpleader action is the value of the fund or property that is the subject of the interpleader. *See* W. Dorsaneo, *Texas Litigation Guide*, Ch. 81, *Interpleader* (1998).

Finally, what of an increase or decrease in the amount in controversy after the suit is filed? The general rule appears to be that increase or decrease after filing does not oust the court of jurisdiction, provided it had jurisdiction initially—at least this appears to be the rule if the increase or decrease is due solely to passage of time. *Flynt v. Garcia,* 587 S.W.2d 109, 109–110 (Tex. 1979).

## PEEK v. EQUIPMENT SERVICE CO.

*779 S.W.2d 802 (Tex. 1989)*

PHILLIPS, Chief Justice.

These cases present the question of whether a plaintiff seeking damages under the wrongful death and survival statutes invokes the jurisdiction of a district court by filing a petition which fails to allege either a specific amount of damages or that the damages sustained exceed the court's minimum jurisdictional limits. The district court held that its jurisdiction was not invoked by such a pleading. Because plaintiffs did not file a pleading properly alleging damages until after the applicable statute of limitations had run, the district court dismissed the suit. The court of appeals, in two unpublished opinions, affirmed.[footnote omitted] We reverse the judgments of the court of appeals and remand this consolidated cause to the trial court because the original pleading, although defective, was sufficient to invoke the court's jurisdiction and prevent the running of limitations.

. . . .

The Peeks amended their petition on December 16, 1986, but made no changes in their defective allegations of damages. In a second amended pleading, filed January 14, 1987, the Peeks sought $3,750,000 actual damages and $5,000,000 exemplary damages against the defendants, jointly and severally. This pleading, however, came more than two years after Clyde's death. All defendants except Oshman's Sporting Goods, Inc. filed motions to dismiss, alleging that the Peeks had failed to invoke the jurisdiction of the district court prior to the running of the two-year statute of limitations. [footnote omitted] Tex. Civ. Prac. & Rem. Code Ann. 16.003(b) (Vernon 1986). The trial court granted these motions at various times, and severance orders were signed so that these judgments became final. [footnote omitted]

The Peeks timely appealed to the court of appeals, which affirmed the judgments of the trial court in two opinions. From both judgments of the court of appeals, the Peeks applied to this court for writ of error. After granting both writs, we consolidated the two causes for oral argument and decision.

The parties here have assumed the minimum monetary jurisdictional limit of the district court to be $500.00. Although recent constitutional and legislative changes call this assumption into question,[4] we will also assume, for purposes of our decision, that the jurisdiction of the district court does not extend to controversies involving sums of less than $500.00.

---

[4] The minimum monetary limit was formerly found in article V, section 8 of the Texas Constitution and article 1906 of the Texas Revised Civil Statutes. Both limited the jurisdiction of the district court to controversies involving at least $500.00. In 1985, however, this provision of the constitution was amended to delete any reference to the minimum monetary jurisdiction of the district court. Also in 1985, article 1906 was repealed and recodified with the enactment of the Government Code. In the recodification of article 1906, the legislature deleted the specific description of the district court jurisdiction, including the minimum monetary limit of $500.00. Tex. Gov. Code Ann. § 24.007 (Vernon 1988). One commentator has suggested that a $500.00 minimum remains a limitation of the jurisdiction of the district courts despite its removal from the constitution and statute. *See* W. Dorsaneo, 1 *Texas Litigation Guide* § 2.01[3][b][ii] (1989). We do not decide this question because it is not necessary to our decision in this matter.

In this case, all parties agree that the trial court's jurisdiction was invoked not later than the filing of the Peeks' second amended petition. The respondents, however, argue that the Peeks did not invoke jurisdiction by the first two pleadings, and hence did not obtain jurisdiction until after limitations had run. The Peeks, on the other hand, asserted that their original petition did invoke the trial court's jurisdiction. Although the petition did not expressly allege that the amount sought was within the court's jurisdiction. In fact, the Peeks argue that the nature of the loss sustained and the claims asserted made it absolutely apparent that plaintiffs sought damages far in excess of five hundred dollars.

. . . .

In the instant case, however, the Peeks' original and first amended petitions did not affirmatively demonstrate an absence of jurisdiction. Under these circumstances, a liberal construction of the pleadings is appropriate. As we wrote in *Pecos & Northern Texas Railway Co. v. Rayzor,* 106 Tex. 544, 548, 172 S.W. 1103, 1105 (1915): "In any doubtful case all intendments of the plaintiff's pleading will be in favor of the jurisdiction." Unless it is clear from the pleadings that the court lacks jurisdiction of the amount in controversy, it should retain the case. *Dwyer v. Bassett & Bassett,* 63 Tex. 274, 276 (1885). As one court recently said: "[W]e must presume in favor of the jurisdiction unless lack of jurisdiction affirmatively appears on the face of the petition." *Smith v. Texas Improvement Co.*, 570 S.W.2d 90, 92 (Tex. Civ. App.—Dallas 1978, no writ).

The failure of a plaintiff to state a jurisdictional amount in controversy in its petition, without more, thus will not deprive the trial court of jurisdiction. *See* W. Dorsaneo, 1 *Texas Litigation Guide* 11.02(4)(a) (1989); Newton, *Conflict of Laws,* 33 Sw. L.J. 425, 431–32 (1979). Even if the jurisdictional amount is never established by pleading, in fact, a plaintiff may recover if jurisdiction is proved at trial. Dorsaneo, *supra,* § 2.01(4)(b); 2 R. McDonald, *Texas Civil Practice in District and County Courts* § 6.09.1 (rev. 1982). This result is consistent with our holdings in cases when a plaintiff has failed to plead facts which state a cause of action. Unless the petition affirmatively demonstrates that no cause of action exists or that plaintiff's recovery is barred, we require the trial court to give the plaintiff an opportunity to amend before granting a motion to dismiss or a motion for summary judgment. *Texas Dept. of Corrections v. Herring,* 513 S.W.2d 6, 10 (Tex. 1974), *Kellebrew v. Stockdale,* 51 Tex. 529, 532 (1879); *Southern Sur. Co. v. Sealy I.S.D.*, 10 S.W.2d 786, 789 (Tex. Civ. App.—Austin 1928, writ ref'd). And unless defendant objects, the plaintiff may proceed to trial, however defective its allegations. So it is here. In the absence of special exceptions or other motion, defendant waives the right to complain of such a defect if plaintiff establishes the trial court's jurisdiction before resting its case. *See Olivares v. Service Trust Co.*, 385 S.W.2d 687 (Tex. Civ. App.—Eastland 1964, no writ). [footnote omitted]

In summary, we hold that the omission of any allegation regarding the amount in controversy from plaintiff's petition did not deprive the court of jurisdiction, but was instead a defect in pleading subject to special exception and amendment. Although defective, the original petition filed in this cause was sufficient to invoke the jurisdiction of the district court. The court of appeals therefore erred in affirming the judgments of dismissal, as the Peeks amended their petition and cured the defect prior to the rendition of the judgments which dismissed their claims. Accordingly, the judgments of the court of appeals are reversed and the causes remanded to the trial court for further proceedings.

---

**SEARS, ROEBUCK v. BIG BEND MOTOR INN,** 818 S.W.2d 542 (Tex. App.—Fort Worth 1991, writ denied). Appellant Sears, Roebuck & Co. appealed a Tarrant County Court at Law judgment on the grounds that the case should have been dismissed for want of subject matter jurisdiction. Specifically, Sears alleged that the amount in controversy exceeded the jurisdiction of the trial court because the appellee requested attorney's fees and treble damages under the DTPA which would take the damages beyond the court's maximum jurisdiction.

The court of appeals affirmed, holding that the DTPA damages are excluded from the computation of the amount in controversy under the language of the Tarrant County Court at Law statute, which excludes "mandatory damages and penalties, attorney's fees, interest, and costs . . ." from the amount in controversy. The court reasoned as follows:

> Since the DTPA treble damages award provision was amended in 1979, [footnote omitted] no cases have directly addressed the issue of whether treble damages should be included when calculating the amount in controversy for the purpose of jurisdiction. Before 1979, the award of treble damages in a DTPA action was mandatory. [footnote omitted] *See Pennington v. Singleton,* 606 S.W.2d 682, 691 (Tex. 1980); *Mytel Int'l, Inc. v. Turbo Refrigerating Co.*, 689 S.W.2d 315, 319 (Tex. App.—Fort Worth 1985, no writ). Therefore, the treble damages amount was included in the amount in controversy. *Allright Inc. v. Guy,* 590 S.W.2d 734, 735 (Tex. Civ. App.—Houston [14th Dist.] 1979, writ ref'd n.r.e.). *See also Long v. Fox,* 625 S.W.2d 376, 378–79 (Tex. App.—San Antonio 1981, writ ref'd n.r.e.) (agreeing with holding in *Allright* but never stating effective date of statute). However, Big Bend asserts that neither *Allright* nor *Long* is applicable to the present case because the Tarrant County Courts at Law statute excludes mandatory damages from its jurisdictional amount. Tex. Gov't Code Ann. 25.2222 (Vernon Supp. 1991). In addition, commentators also suggest that *Allright* and *Long* are outdated due to the present non-mandatory nature of the treble damages. *See* Bragg, Maxwell & Longley, Texas Consumer Litigation 2.10 (2d ed. 1983). For cases governed by the 1979 amendment, as we are in this case, only a portion of the damages is automatically trebled; thus, a plaintiff would only use this amount in calculating the amount in controversy. *Id.*

. . . .

> We need to address the language of the Tarrant County Courts at Law statute. *See* Tex. Gov't Code Ann. 25.2222 (Vernon Supp. 1991). The legislature chose to exclude "mandatory damages and penalties, attorney's fees, interest, and costs . . ." from the jurisdictional amount. It is the word "mandatory" which presents a dilemma. "Mandatory" may modify "damages" and "penalties," or only "damages." Thus, the statute may be interpreted as having excluded "mandatory penalties" or as excluding all penalties. This court takes the position that "mandatory" only modifies "damages" and, therefore, the statute excludes all penalties from the amount in controversy. In this regard, we think the disposition of this case is most appropriately controlled by an examination of the nature of treble damages.
>
> The treble damages provision, after the 1979 amendment, provides that the award of treble damages is purely discretionary with the finder of fact and is allowed only if the DTPA violation was committed knowingly. *See* Act of June 13, 1979, 66th Leg., R.S., Ch. 603 § 4, 1979 Tex. Gen. Laws 1327, 1330. *See also Martin v. McKee Realtors, Inc.*, 663 S.W.2d

446, 448 (Tex. 1984); *Pena v. Ludwig,* 766 S.W.2d 298, 301 (Tex. App.—Waco 1989, no writ). The legislature initially provided the treble damages remedy so that consumers could discourage, and hopefully deter, deceptive practices in consumer transactions. *Pennington,* 606 S.W.2d at 690–91; *Woods v. Littleton*, 554 S.W.2d 662, 670 (Tex. 1977). Because the mandatory trebling of damages was harsh, the legislature amended the statute to consider the culpability of the defendant's conduct and provided mandatory trebling only for knowing violations. *Pennington,* 606 S.W.2d at 691. Therefore, the award of treble damages is clearly punitive in nature. *First Nat'l Bank of Kerrville v. Hackworth,* 673 S.W.2d 218, 220 (Tex. App.—San Antonio 1984, no writ). *See also Singleton v. Pennington,* 568 S.W.2d 367, 376 (Tex. Civ. App.—Dallas 1977); *rev'd on other grounds,* 606 S.W.2d 682 (Tex. 1980). Moreover, the issue of treble damages is submitted to the jury, and was likewise in this case, as an issue whereby the jury decides an amount to award the plaintiff "as a penalty or by way of punishment." *See* Bragg, Maxwell & Longley, Texas Consumer Litigation § 10.17 (2d ed. 1983). Therefore, since treble damages are punitive in nature, such damages are properly excluded from the amount in controversy under the Tarrant County Courts at Law statute as a penalty. *See* Tex. Gov't Code Ann. 25.2222 (Vernon Supp. 1991).

[Affirmed.]

---

## SMITH v. CLARY CORP.

*917 S.W.2d 796 (Tex. 1996)*

PER CURIAM.

. . . .

The issue in this case is whether counterclaims of multiple defendants should be aggregated to determine whether the amount in controversy in a county court at law exceeds that court's maximum statutory jurisdictional limit and divests it of jurisdiction. The court of appeals held that a statute required aggregation. We hold that the legislature enacted Tex. Gov't Code section 24.009, the aggregating statute, to allow multiple plaintiffs to aggregate their claims to achieve the minimum jurisdictional amount for a court, not to defeat jurisdiction for multiple defendants each of whose counterclaims is within the jurisdictional limit. Accordingly, the statute does not apply to require that multiple counterclaims be aggregated to determine the amount in controversy for statutory county court jurisdiction. Without hearing argument, the Court reverses the judgment of the court of appeals and remands the cause to that court for further proceedings. *See* Tex. R. App. P. 170.

Daniel Smith and Michael Smith formed Fairfield Distributors and contracted with Clary Corporation to sell Clary's pallet products. Clary sued the Smiths, individually, and d/b/a Fairfield Distributors in Tarrant County Court at Law Number Three for a $19,821.85 balance on an open account. The Smiths and Fairfield counterclaimed against Clary alleging deceptive trade practices, negligent misrepresentation, and tortious interference with business relations.

In their original counterclaims, the Smiths and Fairfield generally alleged damages in excess of the minimum jurisdiction of the Tarrant County Court at Law. Later, the three parties amended their counterclaims to allege damages of $100,000 each, for an aggregate of $300,000. A jury awarded Clary $14,155.57 on its open account claim. However, the jury found for the Smiths and Fairfield on their counterclaims. After deducting the $14,155.57 plus attorney's fees, the court rendered a net judgment for the Smiths and Fairfield for $264,270.61, including pre-judgment interest, statutory penalties, treble damages, attorney's fees and costs. Clary appealed this judgment arguing that the aggregate amount of the counterclaims exceeded the jurisdictional limit of the county court's authority. The court of appeals reversed the judgment and remanded the cause. 886 S.W.2d 570.

County courts at law generally have statutorily prescribed jurisdiction in civil cases where the amount in controversy exceeds $500 but does not exceed $100,000, excluding mandatory damages and penalties, attorney's fees, interest, and costs. [footnote omitted] Tex. Gov't Code Ann. § 25.0003(c) (Vernon Supp. 1995). A counterclaim, whether permissive or compulsory, must be within the court's jurisdiction. 2 Roy W. McDonald, Texas Civil Practice § 9.76 (rev. 1992); *see* also *Wyatt v. Shaw Plumbing Co.,* 760 S.W.2d 245, 247 (Tex. 1988) (counterclaim is compulsory if "it is within the jurisdiction of the court."). A counterclaim is not within the court's jurisdiction when the amount in controversy exceeds the maximum jurisdictional limit of the court. *Kitchen Designs, Inc. v. Wood,* 584 S.W.2d 305, 307 (Tex. Civ. App.—Texarkana 1979, writ ref'd n.r.e.); 2 Roy W. McDonald, Texas Civil Practice § 9.77 (rev. 1992); 16 Tex. Jur. 3d *Courts* § 70 (1981). Daniel Smith, Michael Smith, and Fairfield individually pleaded $100,000 in damages. Each claim is within the jurisdictional purview of Tarrant County Court at Law Number Three. However, the court of appeals held that the counterclaim amounts should be aggregated under § 24.009 of the Government Code . . . .

. . . .

The legislature enacted the aggregating statute in 1945 to statutorily overrule this Court's holding in *Long v. City of Wichita Falls,* 142 Tex. 202, 176 S.W.2d 936, 940 (1944). *Long* involved two plaintiffs' claims against the same defendant, properly subject to joinder under Rule 40 [footnote omitted], one of which was below the minimum jurisdictional amount of the trial court. We held the trial court lacked jurisdiction over the smaller claim. The legislature sought to overturn what we quoted as the majority rule prevailing in 1944: "Where several claimants have separate and distinct demands against a defendant or defendants, and join in a single suit to enforce them, they cannot be added together to make up the required jurisdictional amount but each separate claim furnishes the jurisdictional test." *Long*, 176 S.W.2d at 940. Thus, Clary Corporation's reliance on *Long* is misplaced because neither *Long* nor any case cited in *Long* considered aggregation of counterclaims of separate defendants to defeat jurisdiction.

For statutory construction we begin with the words of the statute itself. *Cail v. Service Motors, Inc.,* 660 S.W.2d 814, 815 (Tex. 1983). The statute provides it applies when "two or more persons *originally* and properly *join* in *one suit.*" (Emphasis supplied.) The words indicate the parties must volitionally join at the outset, for purposes of jointly presenting claims. The words clearly apply to co-plaintiffs jointly asserting related claims against a common defendant. In those circumstances the claims aggregate to reach the jurisdictional minimum. [footnote omitted] This conclusion is consistent with the legislature's desire to overturn *Long*. The words do not appear to apply when separate defendants answer and file their individual counterclaims. Because the legislature did not define the terms otherwise, we should give the words this ordinary meaning. [citations omitted] The jurisdictional and procedural statutes and rules in effect when the legislature enacted the aggregating statute recognized the county court's ancillary jurisdiction to entertain each defendant's counterclaim up to the jurisdictional maximum of the court, and we do not favor construing statutes to repeal such law by implication. *Twin City Fire Ins. Co. v. Cortez,* 576 S.W.2d 786, 789 (Tex. 1978).

The courts have not and should not apply aggregation to divest a court of jurisdiction on counterclaims asserted by multiple defendants, whose joinder normally is not voluntary, and who have not chosen the forum. *See* Tex. R. Civ. P. 38, 39. Moreover, co-defendants have no control over the number of defendants joined or the amounts of their counterclaims. Permitting aggregation of counterclaims to defeat jurisdiction under such circumstances would encourage races to the courthouse and forum shopping by parties to set arbitrary limits on anticipated claims by adversaries.

We reverse the judgment of the court of appeals and remand the cause to that court for further proceedings.

---

## ANDEL v. EASTMAN KODAK COMPANY

*400 S.W.2d 584 (Tex. Civ. App.—Houston 1966, no writ)*

BELL, Chief Justice.

Appellants, who are husband and wife, sued appellee on their own behalf and as next friends for their two minor children, to recover damages allegedly resulting to Mrs. Andel and the children when the automobile Mrs. Andel was driving was in collision on March 6, 1964 with an automobile driven by an agent of appellee. Suit was for an amount exclusively within the jurisdiction of the District Court. Appellee, in addition to its answer setting up a denial, contributory negligence and unavoidable accident, filed a counter-claim to recover damages to its automobile in the amount of $183.98. The basis of recovery on the counter-claim was negligence on the part of Mrs. Andel.

When the case was reached for trial, the appellants' motion for continuance was overruled and they were required to proceed to trial. Appellants thereupon took a nonsuit. They then filed a plea to the District Court's jurisdiction over the counter-claim, it being in an amount normally within the exclusive jurisdiction of the Justice Court. The plea was overruled and the trial was had to a jury on the counter-claim.

. . . .

We conclude that the court did have jurisdiction of the counter-claim, which was a compulsory one. It seems to be held in Texas that where a court by the plaintiff's pleading obtains jurisdiction over the case, a defendant may assert against the plaintiff a counter-claim in an amount that is below the minimum jurisdiction of the court where the case is filed. [citations omitted]

Once the court has obtained jurisdiction over the controversy between the parties by the filing of a counter-claim, dismissal of plaintiff's case does not deprive the court of jurisdiction of the counter-claim. Bartholomew v. Shipe, 251 S.W.1031 (Tex. Com. App.); Kirby v. American Soda Fountain Co., 194 U.S. 141, 24 S. Ct. 619, 48 L. Ed. 911; Cammack v. Prather, 74 S.W. 354 (Tex. Civ. App.), no writ hist.

. . . .

[Affirmed.]

---

**BARNES v. UNITED STATES FIDELITY & GUARANTY CO.**, 279 S.W.2d 919 (Tex. Civ. App.—Waco 1955, no writ). Appellant Barnes attacked a district court judgment as void for want of jurisdiction. The petition of the appellee, U.S. Fidelity & Guaranty, had been to the effect that it had furnished a fidelity bond to Barnes' former employer, that it had been required, under that bond, to pay the employer an amount of $471.53, and that Barnes had an obligation to indemnify it for this amount plus 6 percent interest from the date of payment. The petition set forth the indemnity agreement in full; it required Barnes to indemnify against any "loss, damage or expense . . . in consequence of such guarantee on my behalf . . . to repay the amount so paid, and all other losses, costs, damages and expense." The district court had held for U.S. Fidelity & Guaranty, awarding it judgment for $660.07, representing the $471.53 plus 6 percent interest from date of payment. Barnes' claim was that the interest was to be excluded from determining the amount in controversy, and that when it was so excluded, the amount in controversy was below the minimum jurisdictional limits of the court, since the action had been brought in district court.

The court of civil appeals affirmed, rejecting Barnes' argument. In essence, its reasoning was that the 6 percent was not really interest, but rather recovery of damages under an indemnity agreement. The court explained its holding by distinguishing between "interest eo nomine" (i.e., interest under the name of interest) and "interest as damages," as follows:

> By the terms of Art. V, § 8 of the *Vernon's Ann. St. Constitution of Texas*, and of Art. 1906, Subd. 6 of Vernon's Tex. Civ. Stats., the district courts of this State are vested with original jurisdiction over civil suits "when the matter in controversy shall be valued at or amount to five hundred dollars exclusive of interest." For jurisdictional purposes, the amount in controversy must be determined from the allegations of fact contained in the pleadings of the party seeking to invoke the court's jurisdiction, unless the adverse party alleges and proves that the allegations of his adversary with respect to the amount in controversy were falsely made for the fraudulent purpose of wrongfully conferring jurisdiction. *Dwyer v. Bassett*, 63 Tex. 274; Clonts v. Johnson, 116 Tex. 489, 294 S.W. 844, pt. 7. It also appears to be well settled that the word "interest," as used in the Constitutional and statutory provisions above referred to, means interest *eo nomine* as distinguished from interest as an element of recoverable damages. [citations omitted]
>
> From the allegations of fact contained in its original petition . . . it appears that appellee was legally entitled at the time when that suit was instituted on February 9, 1940, to a recovery from appellant of such sum of money as was necessary to indemnify it at that time against the loss and damage it had sustained as a result of appellant's breach of fidelity to his former employer, Atlas Supply Co. The two elements of recoverable damages . . . were (1) a sum equal to the amount appellee had paid to Atlas Supply Co. on March 10, 1937 and (2) an additional sum equal to interest at the rate of 6% per annum on the $471.53 so paid from the date when such payment was made. The elements of damages thus recoverable exceeded the sum of $500 so that the amount in controversy . . . was within the jurisdiction of the district court. Since appellee was not entitled to any recovery . . .

for interest *eo nomine*, the amount of interest sought by it as an element of recoverable damages constituted a part of the amount in controversy . . . American Surety Co. of New York v. Ritchie, Tex. Civ. App., 191 S.W.2d 137, pt. 5; Ritchie v. American Surety Co. of New York, 145 Tex. 422, 198 S.W.2d 85, pt. 1.

---

**FLYNT v. GARCIA**, 587 S.W.2d 109 (Tex. 1979). Sue Ann Flynt sued Julian Garcia on a contract for alimony pursuant to a marital settlement agreement. When she brought suit, the amount of arrearage that had accrued was less than $5,000. Accordingly, Ms. Flynt alleged an amount in controversy within the jurisdictional limits of the county court at law at the time, and she brought suit in that court.

After the filing of suit, but before judgment, additional delinquent amounts accrued under the terms of the settlement agreement. At trial, Ms. Flynt sought and obtained a trial amendment to include these amounts. The resulting total was $6,242.40 claimed, and the trial court rendered judgment for this amount.

The court of civil appeals concluded that the trial court had no jurisdiction to render judgment for an amount exceeding its jurisdictional limits and reversed. The Texas Supreme Court, however, reinstated the judgment of the trial court.

The Supreme Court quoted the general rule that once a court's jurisdiction has been "properly acquired, no subsequent fact . . . in the particular case serves to defeat that jurisdiction." This rule applied, said the Court, in a case in which the original suit was within the trial court's jurisdiction "and subsequent amendments seek only additional damages that are accruing because of passage of time."

---

**CONTINENTAL COFFEE PRODUCTS CO. v. CAZAREZ,** 937 S.W.2d 444 (Tex. 1996). A county court at law had subject matter jurisdiction of a case brought under the antiretaliation law (Lab. C. § 451.001) despite reference in the statute to district court (because statute did not confer *exclusive* jurisdiction on the district court), given an amount in controversy within the county court at law's monetary limit of $100,000. The court could render judgment for an amount in excess of jurisdictional limits under the principle that "[i]f a plaintiff's original petition is properly brought in a particular court, but an amendment increases the amount in controversy above the court's jurisdictional limits, the court will continue to have jurisdiction if the additional damages accrued because of the passage of time." In response to defendant's challenge to plaintiff's amended pleadings, which increased damages above the jurisdictional limit due to passage of time, plaintiff testified regarding her state of mind: "[i]t's getting worser [sic], everyday."

## NOTES AND QUESTIONS

(1) *Awards in Excess of Jurisdictional Limits After an Initial Claim Within Jurisdictional Limits.* Does the result in *Flynt v. Garcia* follow if the additional damages are not the result of mere "passage of time?" *Cf. Dews v. Floyd,* 413 S.W.2d 800 (Tex. Civ. App.—Tyler 1967, no writ) (holding justice court award for $443.64, at time when justice court jurisdiction was limited to $200, void for want of jurisdiction when pleadings and facts did not affirmatively show increase after filing). But several courts have reached results different from that in *Dews.* In *Cook v. Jaynes,* 366 S.W.2d 646 (Tex. Civ. App.—Dallas 1963, no writ), the case was brought in the county court at law when its jurisdiction did not exceed $1,000. Under the original petition, plaintiff sought title and possession of a boat, motor, and trailer with an alleged total value of $500. By amended petition, plaintiff added claims for exemplary damages, loss of use, and attorney's fees, raising the amount in controversy to $1,700. The court of civil appeals held that the trial court properly retained jurisdiction. *See also Smith v. Texas Improvement Co.,* 570 S.W.2d 90 (Tex. Civ. App.—Dallas 1978, no writ) ("[t]he fact that an amended petition alleges damages in excess of the jurisdictional limits of the county court does not deprive that court of the jurisdiction it properly acquired when the original petition was filed").

(2) *Initial Pleading That Fails to Show Jurisdiction.* The above cases deal with the situation in which the court initially acquires jurisdiction by a proper pleading, but is asked subsequently to act on a matter that would appear ordinarily to be outside its jurisdiction. The opposite situation is that in which an initial petition fails to show jurisdiction, but a later amendment cures the defect by properly showing a claim within the court's authority. What should happen in such a situation? In *Byke v. City of Corpus Christi,* 569 S.W.2d 927 (Tex. Civ. App.—Corpus Christi 1978, writ ref'd n.r.e.), plaintiffs sued in district court but alleged an amount in controversy below the minimum jurisdictional limits of that court. They later amended to claim an amount within district court limits. The court of civil appeals held that the trial court should have dismissed for want of jurisdiction: "As a general rule, if the original petition does not affirmatively allege jurisdictional facts . . ., the only jurisdiction which the court has is to dismiss the suit for want of jurisdiction." Chief Justice Nye dissented, saying: "The majority says that if you do not file your first petition with properly joined parties whose claims aggregate the minimum jurisdictional amount, the trial court can do nothing but dismiss the lawsuit. I disagree." *Compare Byke with Connell v. Shanafelt,* 446 S.W.2d 126 (Tex. Civ. App.—Fort Worth 1969, no writ) (cause remanded with directions to dismiss unless petition was amended to show proper jurisdiction).

(3) *Liquidated Versus Unliquidated Damages.* Other principles may also limit a party's ability to amend a pleading so as to state an amount within the court's jurisdiction. The Dallas Court has expressed the traditional rule this way:

> If a party . . . alleges an amount of damages in excess of a trial court's jurisdictional limits and the damages as alleged are liquidated and nonseverable, then the party cannot freely amend its pleading to reduce its liquidated damage claim to an amount to be within the trial court's jurisdiction. [citations omitted] The opposite generally holds true if the claimed damages are unliquidated. A party may freely reduce its unliquidated claim if the party pleads in good faith.

*Smith Detective Agency & Nightwatch Serv., Inc. v. Stanley Smith Sec., Inc.*, 938 S.W.2d 743, 747 (Tex. App.—Dallas 1996, writ denied).

(4) *Computing Amount in Controversy.* Decide what would be the proper computation of the amount in controversy, and the proper court for the action, in each of the following situations:

(a) A suit to enjoin the foreclosure of a lien on a chattel alleged to be worth $750, when the lien secures an indebtedness of $300.

(b) A suit by two plaintiffs against a single defendant, each claiming $150.

(c) A suit by a single plaintiff against two defendants, allegedly each owing the plaintiff $150.

(d) A class action by a group of plaintiffs, each claiming approximately $5, with the class including more than 1,000 persons.

(e) A suit on a note for $495 plus $50 interest, which has accrued in accordance with the interest provisions of the note, plus $50 attorney's fees, which are expressly payable under the terms of the note.

(f) A suit on an indebtedness of $495 and to foreclose a lien on an automobile alleged to be of a value of $3,000, which lien secures the indebtedness.

(g) A suit against Jones as administrator of Smith's estate for $10,000 or, in the alternative, against Jones personally if the estate is not liable due to the fraudulent conduct of Jones.

(h) A suit to enjoin the operation of a house of prostitution.

(i) A counterclaim of $200, when plaintiff's claim is for $4,500 and is filed in a legislative county court.

(j) A cross-claim for $150,000 in the situation in item (i), above.

## § 3.05 Justiciability and Related Doctrines

If the decision of the court will not actually resolve a meaningful conflict between the parties, the court will not entertain the dispute. This general prohibition against advisory opinions has several consequences of importance. For example, petitions requesting declaratory judgments are often given special scrutiny. Although Texas has a declaratory judgment statute, the courts look with some care to the effect the declaration will have. The Texas Supreme Court is permitted to answer questions of law certified to it by any federal appellate court if that court is presented with determinative questions of Texas law on which there is no controlling Texas Supreme Court precedent. *See* Tex. R. App. P. 58.

The mootness doctrine is also a variant of the justiciable controversy doctrine. If a case or controversy existed at one time, but by the time of suit, the requested relief would not redress the alleged wrong, Texas courts (like other courts throughout the nation) will consider the matter "moot" and dismiss it. In *Ben Robinson Co. v. Texas Workers' Comp. Com'n,* 934 S.W.2d 149, 152 (Tex. App—Austin 1996, writ denied), the plaintiff-company challenged the Commission's designation of the company as an "extra hazardous employer." The Commission alleged the complaint was moot, because the designation had been lifted before the trial court's judgment was rendered. The court disagreed; the requested relief would effectively purge the designation from state records and reverse the detrimental consequences to the company due to the designation (such as higher insurance premiums), whereas the mere lifting of the designation did not bring such relief. Because removal of the designation did not "leave the Company in the position it was in before being labelled extra-hazardous," the controversy was not moot. The court went further and suggested that even if the case were moot, it would fall within the "capable of repetition yet evading review" exception to the mootness doctrine. Under this exception, the court will review a moot controversy so as to assure the plaintiff has judicial review that would otherwise not be available to the plaintiff due to the circumstances of the controversy. In the case of an extra hazardous designation, an employer is required to take certain actions to immediately remedy the allegedly hazardous workplace conditions. Given severe penalties for noncompliance, the result is that in most cases the designation lasts for less than 10 months. If mootness were applied in such a situation to dismiss a plaintiff's claim, the plaintiff would never be able to obtain review of an allegedly erroneous designation. The court concluded, "Because the short duration of an employer's extra-hazardous status renders it nearly impossible for an employer to obtain judicial review while that status remains pending, we would hold that this case falls within the 'capable of repetition yet evading review' exception to the mootness doctrine." *Ben Robinson Co. v. Texas Workers' Comp. Com'n,* 934 S.W.2d 149, 153 (Tex. App.—Austin 1996, writ denied).

Likewise, if the suit is not "ripe" (i.e., if a matter essential to the claim has not yet occurred or may never occur), the courts will find that there is no justiciable controversy. A court's abstention on grounds of ripeness is based on the prohibition against issuing advisory opinions. To rule on a case in which the claim depends on the occurrence of future events that may or may not occur "would be the essence of an advisory opinion, advising what the law would be on a hypothetical set of facts." *See Patterson v. Planned Parenthood,* 971 S.W.2d 439, 444 (Tex. 1998) (holding not ripe for review a suit for declaratory judgment to declare a legislative appropriations rider unconstitutional because the state had not yet implemented the rider and was considering a plan under which plaintiff's funding would not be affected anyway).

The doctrine of standing is related, but slightly different. If a case or controversy exists, but the person who is bringing the suit is not the proper person to assert the rights at issue, it is sometimes said that the claimant lacks "standing" to sue. The Texas courts, in harmony with federal and other state courts, hold that a court lacks jurisdiction over a controversy asserted by a claimant without standing. *Texas Ass'n of Business v. Texas Air Control Bd.,* 852 S.W.2d 440, 443 (Tex. 1993) ("standing is implicit in the concept of subject matter jurisdiction").

The "political question" doctrine and the doctrine of "primary jurisdiction" are also jurisdictional concepts followed in Texas. A political question is one that is entrusted to the judgment of a governmental branch other than the judiciary. If a person disagreed with an appointment made by the governor of the state, for example, the person probably could not bring suit against the governor to rescind it (at least if the governor had acted within his or her legitimate political authority).

The doctrine of "primary jurisdiction" is related. It deals with disputes that the law has entrusted to administrative agencies or other tribunals other than the courts for the formulation of the initial decision. One court described the primary jurisdiction doctrine as follows:

> Primary jurisdiction is a judicially created doctrine of abstention, whereby a court that has jurisdiction over a matter nonetheless defers to an administrative agency for an initial decision on questions of fact or law within the peculiar competence of the agency." The purpose behind primary jurisdiction is to assure that the administrative agency will not be bypassed in a matter which has been especially committed to it by the legislature. Where the legislature has committed a matter to an agency, the agency's primary jurisdiction is exclusive. In other words, "a court does not have jurisdiction to determine administrative

questions or to adjudicate controversies involving them until they have been determined by the appropriate administrative agency. [citations omitted]

*In re Luby's Cafeterias, Inc., 979 S.W.2d 813, 816 (Tex. App—Houston [14th Dist.] 1998, no pet. h.).*

The following materials show the application of some of these doctrines in Texas.

CIVIL PRACTICE AND REMEDIES CODE

CHAPTER 37. DECLARATORY JUDGMENTS

C.P.R.C. § 37.003. *Power of Courts to Render Judgment; Form and Effect.* (a) A court of record within its jurisdiction has power to declare rights, status, and other legal relations whether or not further relief is or could be claimed. An action or proceeding is not open to objection on the ground that a declaratory judgment or decree is prayed for.

(b) The declaration may be either affirmative or negative in form and effect, and the declaration has the force and effect of a final judgment or decree.

. . . .

---

## FARMERS TEXAS COUNTY MUTUAL INS. v. GRIFFIN

*955 S.W.2d 81 (Tex. 1997)*

PER CURIAM.

This is a declaratory judgment action. Farmers Texas County Mutual Insurance Company sought a declaration that it had no duty to defend or indemnify its insured, James Royal III, in a suit brought by Robert Griffin. The trial court granted summary judgment for Farmers. The court of appeals reversed, holding that Farmers has a duty to defend Royal but not to indemnify him. We hold that, under the facts alleged against Royal, Farmers has no duty to defend Royal in the underlying suit. We further hold that Farmers' duty to indemnify Royal constituted a justiciable controversy properly reached and decided by the trial court. Accordingly, we reverse the judgment of the court of appeals and render judgment for Farmers.

After issuing our original opinion, we recognized an issue regarding the justiciability of the duty to indemnify, which we must raise *sua sponte. Central Sur. & Ins. Corp. v. Anderson*, 445 S.W.2d 514, 515 (Tex. 1969). We requested further briefing from the parties on this question, and now withdraw our former opinion and substitute this one in its stead.

On October 22, 1991, gunshots from a passing vehicle hit and injured Robert Griffin as he walked down the street in Beaumont, Texas. Griffin sued the driver of the vehicle, James Royal III, and others for negligence and gross negligence resulting in injury to his right leg. [footnote omitted] Griffin alleged that Royal drove the vehicle while his two passengers fired the shots. Royal invoked Farmers' duty to defend him under his personal automobile liability insurance policy. Farmers defended Royal subject to a reservation of rights and then filed this declaratory judgment action to challenge its duty to defend and indemnify Royal. The record shows that the suit between Griffin and Royal remains pending.

Farmers' policy provides that Farmers "will pay damages for bodily injury or property damage for which any covered person becomes legally responsible because of an *auto accident*. . . . We will settle or defend, as we consider appropriate, any claim or suit asking for these damages." (Emphasis added.) The policy defines a "covered person" as "you or any family member for the *ownership, maintenance, or use* of any auto or trailer." (Emphasis added.) The policy excludes coverage for any person "[w]ho intentionally causes bodily injury or property damage."

An insurer's duty to defend and duty to indemnify are distinct and separate duties. *Trinity Universal Ins. Co. v. Cowan*, 945 S.W.2d 819, 821–22 (Tex. 1997). Thus, an insurer may have a duty to defend but, eventually, no duty to indemnify. For example, a plaintiff pleading both negligent and intentional conduct may trigger an insurer's duty to defend, but a finding that the insured acted intentionally and not negligently may negate the insurer's duty to indemnify. We therefore address these two duties separately.

. . . .

Before determining whether Farmers has a duty to indemnify Griffin, we must first address whether this duty is properly justiciable by declaratory judgment before the rendition of a judgment in the underlying suit. *Bonham State Bank v. Beadle*, 907 S.W.2d 465, 467 (Tex. 1995). In *Firemen's Insurance Co. v. Burch*, 442 S.W.2d 331 (Tex. 1968), we held that there was no justiciable controversy regarding the insurer's duty to indemnify before a judgment has been rendered against an insured. Thus, a declaratory judgment to determine whether the insurer had a duty was premature. Based in part on the amended language of Article V, Section 8 of the Texas Constitution and our decision in *State Farm Fire & Cas. Co. v. Gandy*, 925 S.W.2d 696 (Tex. 1996), we now hold that parties may secure a declaratory judgment on the insurer's duty to indemnify before the underlying tort suit proceeds to judgment.

In *Burch*, Dorothy Burch was injured in a collision between the car in which she was riding and a car driven by Sarah Buttler. At the time, Sarah was separated from her husband, Larry Buttler, and they afterward divorced. Before the accident, when the Buttlers were still living together, they purchased a family automobile policy, but only Larry Buttler was listed as a named insured. Firemen's Insurance took the position that since the Buttlers had separated, Sarah was not covered. The trial court ruled that Firemen's Insurance was obliged to defend Larry Buttler and pay any judgment rendered against him, but that it was not obliged to defend Sarah Buttler or pay any judgment rendered against her. The court of appeals affirmed. 426 S.W.2d 306 (Tex. Civ. App.—Austin 1968). This Court held that whether Firemen's Insurance was obliged to defend the Buttlers was a justiciable issue, but whether it was obliged to indemnify the Buttlers was not justiciable until judgment was rendered against them in favor of the Burches. *Burch*, 442 S.W.2d at 332–34.

Our holding in *Burch* was based upon Article V, Section 8 of the Texas Constitution, which prohibits advisory opinions. *Burch*, 442 S.W.2d at 333. At that time, Article V, Section 8 provided:

> *The District Court shall have original jurisdiction* in all criminal cases of the grade of felony; in all suits in behalf of the State to recover penalties, forfeitures and escheats; of all cases of divorce; of all misdemeanors involving official misconduct; of all suits to recover damages for slander or defamation of character; of all suits for trial of title to land and for the enforcement of liens thereon; of all suits for the trial of the right of property levied upon by virtue of any writ of executions, sequestration or attachment when the property levied on shall be equal to or exceed in value five hundred dollars; *of all suits, complaints or pleas*

> *whatever, without regard to any distinction between law and equity, when the matter in controversy shall be valued at or amount to five hundred dollars exclusive of interest;* of contested elections, and said court and the judges thereof, shall have power to issue writs of habeas corpus, mandamus, injunction and certiorari, and all writs necessary to enforce their jurisdiction.
>
> The District Court shall have appellate jurisdiction and general control in probate matters, over the County Court established in each county, for appointing guardians, granting letters testamentary of administration, probating wills, for settling the accounts of executors, administrators and guardians, and for the transaction of all business appertaining to estates; and original jurisdiction and general control over executors, administrators, guardians and minors under such regulations as may be prescribed by law. The District Court shall have appellate jurisdiction and general supervisory control over the County Commissioners Court, with such exceptions and under such regulations as may be prescribed by law; and shall have general original jurisdiction over all causes of action whatever for which a remedy or jurisdiction is not provided by law or this Constitution, and such other jurisdiction, original and appellate, as may be provided by law.

Tex. Const. art. V, § 8 (amended 1985) (emphasis added). Thus, until the underlying lawsuit was concluded, a district court could only speculate that the value of the matter in controversy exceeded five hundred dollars. Since our decision in *Burch*, however, Section 8 has been amended to create original jurisdiction in the district courts over "all actions, proceedings, and remedies." Tex. Const. art. V, § 8. This amendment to Article V, Section 8 significantly broadened the scope of district court jurisdiction. The language of the amended version is broad enough to allow district courts jurisdiction to resolve declaratory judgment actions on the duty to indemnify.

Our decision in *Gandy*, handed down after the amendment of Article V, Section 8, hinted that indemnity issues are not always nonjusticiable before liability is resolved. Gandy requires an insurer to either accept coverage or make a good faith effort to resolve coverage before adjudication of the plaintiff's claim, and also suggests that the plaintiff may wish to participate in that litigation. *Gandy*, 925 S.W.2d at 714. If, as *Burch* held, coverage issues other than the duty to defend are always nonjusticiable, it would be impossible for an insurer to make a good faith effort to fully resolve coverage before a judgment has been rendered in the underlying claim.

It may sometimes be necessary to defer resolution of indemnity issues until the liability litigation is resolved. In some cases, coverage may turn on facts actually proven in the underlying lawsuit. For example, the plaintiff may allege both negligent conduct and intentional conduct; a judgment based upon the former type of conduct often triggers the duty to indemnify, while a judgment based on the latter usually establishes the lack of a duty. In many cases, however, the court may appropriately decide the rights of the parties before judgment is rendered in the underlying tort suit.

We now hold that the duty to indemnify is justiciable before the insured's liability is determined in the liability lawsuit when the insurer has no duty to defend *and the same reasons that negate the duty to defend likewise negate any possibility the insurer will ever have a duty to indemnify.* Based on the facts and the rule we announce today, Farmers has no duty to indemnify Royal. No facts can be developed in the underlying tort suit that can transform a drive-by shooting into an "auto accident." Farmers has no duty to defend, and, for the same reasons, has no duty to indemnify Royal.

Accordingly, the Court grants Farmers' application for writ of error and, under Texas Rule of Appellate Procedure 59.1, without hearing oral argument, reverses the judgment of the court of appeals and renders judgment for Farmers. Griffin's application for writ of error is denied.

---

**TEX. ASS'N OF BUSINESS v. AIR CONTROL BD.,** 852 S.W.2d 440 (Tex. 1993). The Texas Association of Business (TAB) brought a declaratory judgment action, on behalf of its members, seeking a ruling that statutes authorizing administrative agencies to assess fines for violations of environmental laws violate the Texas Constitution. The Texas Supreme Court first addressed the matter of standing, concluding that standing is implicit in subject matter jurisdiction; therefore it cannot be waived by the parties and may be raised for the first time on appeal. In favorably assessing TAB's standing, the Court adopted the *Hunt* test (*See Hunt v. Washington State Apple Advertising Comm'n*, 432 U.S. 333, 343 (1977)), which provides that an association may sue if its members would otherwise have standing to sue in their own right, if the interests the association seeks to protect are germane to its purpose, and if neither the claim asserted nor the relief requested requires participation of association members. Turning to the merits, the court affirmed the administrative agencies' authority as not inconsistent with the constitutional right to jury trial, concluding the Constitution's grant of power to the legislature to enact laws includes the power to delegate certain judicial functions (including fact finding) to administrative agencies. However, the court struck down forfeiture provisions in the statutes providing that an offender who fails to either tender a cash deposit or post a supersedeas bond forfeits the right to judicial review. The Court found they imposed an unreasonable financial barrier to access to the courts, thereby violating the Open Courts provision of the Texas Constitution.

## § 3.06 Consequences of Lack of Jurisdiction Over the Subject Matter and Related Problems

The textbook law in Texas is that a court lacking jurisdiction over the subject matter of an action has jurisdiction to do nothing but dismiss. However, given the ambiguity of some jurisdictional grants, it is to be expected that some cases will be filed in the wrong court even when an attorney is well informed and careful. It may take months or years to determine the jurisdictional issue; the statute of limitations may run in the meantime. What should happen in such a situation? The following materials deal with that question.

CIVIL PRACTICE AND REMEDIES CODE

CHAPTER 16. LIMITATIONS

SUBCHAPTER C. RESIDUAL LIMITATIONS PERIOD

C.P.R.C. §. 16.064. *Effect of Lack of Jurisdiction.* (a) The period between the date of filing an action in a trial court and the date of a second filing of the same action in a different court suspends the running of the applicable statute of limitations for the period if:

(1) because of lack of jurisdiction in the trial court where the action was first filed, the action is dismissed or the judgment is set aside or annulled in a direct proceeding; and

(2) not later than the 60th day after the date the dismissal or other disposition becomes final, the action is commenced in a court of proper jurisdiction.

(b) This section does not apply if the adverse party has shown in abatement that the first filing was made with intentional disregard of proper jurisdiction.

---

## VALE v. RYAN

*809 S.W.2d 324 (Tex. App.—Austin 1991, no writ)*

JONES, Justice.

Margaret Portz Vale sued Vernon McKenzie, Lanny Ryan, and others for false arrest, false imprisonment, and malicious prosecution. The trial court rendered a take-nothing summary judgment on the ground that the limitations period for Vale's cause of action had expired before she filed suit. Vale appeals, asserting that the trial court erred in granting summary judgment because sixty days had not passed between the dismissal of her identical federal action and the filing of this suit in state court. The issues in this appeal are whether: (1) a federal court's refusal to exercise jurisdiction over pendent state claims constitutes a dismissal for lack of jurisdiction under the Texas "saving statute," Tex. Civ. Prac. & Rem. Code Ann. § 16.064 (1986); and (2) the dismissal here was final for purposes of the same statute on the date of the federal district court's dismissal order. We will reverse the summary judgment and remand the cause.

The facts are undisputed. McKenzie, a Temple police sergeant, had participated in a drug "sting" operation. [footnote omitted] Apparently as the result of a name error, McKenzie incorrectly testified to a Bell County grand jury that Vale was a known drug offender and had received delivery of controlled substances. After hearing only McKenzie's testimony, the grand jury indicted Vale. She was arrested and jailed on November 17, 1982. The following day McKenzie's misidentification was discovered, and Vale was released.

On June 28, 1984, Vale brought suit in federal court against various defendants, including McKenzie, alleging violations of federal civil rights statutes. Vale also alleged, under the doctrine of federal courts' "pendent jurisdiction," state-law causes of action arising from the same facts. McKenzie was not initially a defendant in the federal suit; Vale filed a motion for leave to add him on November 20, 1984.[2] On August 15, 1985, the federal district court granted McKenzie's motion to dismiss her action as to him on the basis of limitations. However, the court refused to sever Vale's cause against McKenzie from those against the other defendants, effectively preventing the summary judgment in McKenzie's favor from becoming final and appealable. As a result, Vale did not obtain appellate review of the dismissal until 1989, when the United States Court of Appeals for the Fifth Circuit held that the district court should have preserved her pendent state claims for prosecution in state court. *Vale v. Adams*, 885 F.2d 869 (5th Cir. 1989). The Fifth Circuit modified the district court's judgment to reflect that, as to McKenzie, the dismissal was "without prejudice." On April 16, 1990, the United States Supreme Court denied certiorari. *Vale v. Cooke*, — U.S. —, 110 S. Ct. 1814, 108 L. Ed. 2d 944 (1990).

---

[2] Vale contends that, under federal law, once her motion for leave to add McKenzie was granted, his addition to the suit related back to the date she filed the motion, November 20, 1984. We agree. *See Canion v. Randall & Blake*, 817 F.2d 1188 (5th Cir. 1987).

While the federal cause was still wending its way through the federal appellate system, Vale began to seek relief in state court. On October 18, 1985, following the federal district court dismissal but before its disposition on appeal, Vale filed the present state-court suit, asserting the same state claim she had previously alleged as pendent to her federal action. On August 21, 1986, the state district court granted McKenzie's motion for partial summary judgment on the ground that limitations had run on Vale's state claim. The parties agreed to continue the matter without a final judgment until the Fifth Circuit's disposition of the federal appeal.

Despite the Fifth Circuit's holding that Vale's pendent state claim should have been dismissed as a matter of judicial discretion, and without prejudice to its being refiled in state court, the state court refused to reconsider its earlier summary-judgment ruling. On February 23, 1990, the state district court severed the summary judgment in McKenzie's favor from the remainder of the state suit, allowing it to become final. Vale appeals from this judgment.

McKenzie obtained his summary judgment in state court by asserting the defense of limitations, arguing that Vale had filed her suit more than two years after the events giving rise to her cause of action. *See* Tex. Civ. Prac. & Rem. Code Ann. § 16.003 (1986). In response, Vale invoked a state tolling statute. *See* Tex. Civ. Prac. & Rem. Code Ann. § 16.063 (1986). McKenzie had been out of the state for at least three days during the limitations period. Therefore, Vale contended, the statute of limitations was tolled for the days of his absence. Consequently, her state-court lawsuit, which "related back" to the date she filed her motion for leave to add McKenzie in the federal suit, was timely filed.[3]

A summary-judgment movant has the burden to show that no genuine issue of material fact exists and that he is entitled to judgment as a matter of law. *Nixon v. Mr. Property Management Co.*, 690 S.W.2d 546, 548–49 (Tex. 1985). A defendant claiming entitlement to summary judgment on limitations grounds must, therefore, show that there is no genuine issue of material fact on his defense of limitations in order to obtain a summary judgment. Once a plaintiff has asserted the applicability of a tolling provision, the moving defendant bears the burden of showing its inapplicability as a matter of law. *Zale Corp. v. Rosenbaum*, 520 S.W.2d 889, 891 (Tex. 1975); *Hill v. Milani*, 678 S.W.2d 203, 204 (Tex. App. 1984), aff'd, 686 S.W.2d 610 (Tex. 1985).

Vale asserts that the trial court incorrectly interpreted a portion of the saving statute, section 16.064, and erroneously concluded that her limitations period had expired before she filed suit. Section 16.064 and its predecessor statute, 1931 Tex. Gen. Laws, ch. 81, § 1, at 124 [Tex. Rev. Civ. Stat. art. 5539a, since amended and codified], were designed to protect litigants from the running of limitations in certain circumstances. Section 16.064 provides:

> The period between the date of filing an action in a trial court and the date of a second filing of the same action in a different court suspends the running of the applicable statute of limitations for the period if:
>
> (1) because of *lack of jurisdiction* in the trial court where the action was first filed, the action is dismissed or the judgment is set aside or annulled in a direct proceeding; and
>
> (2) not later than the 60th day after the date the dismissal or other disposition *becomes final*, the action is commenced in a court of proper jurisdiction.

---

[3] At oral argument, counsel for McKenzie conceded that the record raised a fact issue that his client had been absent from the state for the three days in question; therefore, we consider the matter to have been admitted for purposes of this decision.

(Emphasis added.) These tolling provisions are remedial in nature and are to be liberally construed. *Republic Nat'l Bank v. Rogers*, 575 S.W.2d 643, 647 (Tex. Civ. App. 1978, writ ref'd n.r.e.).

First, McKenzie asserts that section 16.064 does not apply because the federal court dismissed appellant's state claims "as a matter of judicial discretion," rather than for "lack of jurisdiction" as required by the statute. This distinction, he argues, removes Vale's state claims from the umbrella of the saving statute's protection. We disagree.

When state and federal claims arise from a common nucleus of operative facts, a federal court may hear and determine the state claims as well as the federal ones by exercising its pendent jurisdiction. *United Mine Workers v. Gibbs*, 383 U.S. 715, 725, 86 S. Ct. 1130, 1138, 16 L. Ed. 2d 218 (1966). However, the federal court's power to hear a pendent state claim does not create for the plaintiff a right to federal-court disposition of such state-law claims. The federal court. in its discretion, may decline to hear pendent state claims based on "considerations of judicial economy, convenience and fairness to litigants." *Id.* at 726, 86 S. Ct. at 1139. The first question, then, is whether such a dismissal constitutes a dismissal for "lack of jurisdiction" within the meaning of section 16.064.

One commentator has observed that the saving statute "applies whether the dismissed action was filed in the state or the federal court, and whether the dismissal is one for want of jurisdiction of the subject matter or one based upon the *impropriety of exercising jurisdiction in a particular action*." 4 McDonald, *Texas Civil Practice* § 17.20, at 123 (rev. ed. 1984) (emphasis added); *see also* Annotation, *Statute Permitting New Action after Failure of Original Action Commenced within Period of Limitation, as Applicable in Cases Where Original Action Failed for Lack of Jurisdiction*, 6 A.L.R.3d 1043 (1966).

This Court has previously held the tolling provision to apply in cases like the present one. In *Burford v. Sun Oil Co.*, 186 S.W.2d 306 (Tex. Civ. App. 1944, writ ref'd w.o.m.), this Court considered whether the predecessor to section 16.064 applied to toll limitations in circumstances almost identical to those in the present cause. In concluding that the saving statute applied, this Court stated in *Burford* that

> the governing factor in determining whether [the saving statute] applies, is the same in any event—appellees were denied the right to litigate their suit as to state law issues in the federal court because the state courts afforded the appropriate remedy. The effect of the order as one of dismissal for want of jurisdiction cannot be obviated by means of nomenclature. And this is true in the instant case regardless of the distinction in a proper case between want of jurisdiction and refusal to exercise it.

186 S.W.2d at 318. We believe, as did the court in *Burford*, that a litigant who chooses the federal forum in good faith should not suffer a penalty merely for having made that selection. *Id.* at 309. We conclude that, for purposes of the applicability of section 16.064, a federal court's refusal to exercise jurisdiction over a pendent state claim is tantamount to a dismissal for lack of jurisdiction.

McKenzie also contends that Vale did not file her state court action within sixty days of the federal district court's dismissal. Therefore, he argues, she cannot avail herself of the saving statute because she has not satisfied the second requirement of section 16.064. We disagree.

Until September 6, 1989, when the Fifth Circuit ruled that the federal district court's dismissal of the pendent state claims should have been discretionary rather than on the merits, Vale did not have a cause to which the saving statute could apply. Therefore, the earliest date from which the sixty-day period could begin to run was September 6, 1989. Vale filed her cause in state district court on October 18, 1985, well before the date of the Fifth Circuit's opinion. Therefore, she has met the saving statute's second requirement.[4]

We conclude that the saving statute applied to toll limitations during the pendency of Vale's federal suit. Consequently, we sustain her first point of error. Because of our disposition of Vale's first point, it is unnecessary for us to address her remaining points. That portion of the cause relating to appellee Lanny Ryan is severed, and the judgment is affirmed as to him. We reverse the summary judgment in McKenzie's favor and remand that portion of the cause to the trial court for further proceedings.

---

[4] We do not address the question of when a disposition becomes final for purposes of section 16.064 where, for example, a district-court dismissal for lack of jurisdiction is later *affirmed* on appeal.

# CHAPTER 4

## JURISDICTION OF PERSONS AND PROPERTY

### SCOPE

This chapter examines courts' jurisdiction over people and property, including in personam and in rem jurisdiction, long-arm statutes that provide for jurisdiction over people outside Texas, service of process, and challenges to jurisdiction.

## § 4.01 Traditional Principles Governing In Personam and In Rem Jurisdiction

### [A] Evolution of the "Minimum Contacts" Doctrine

This chapter concerns the interpretation and application of statutes and rules of procedure involving the proper methods for the exercise of jurisdiction over residents and nonresidents of Texas. Since the most complicated problems are encountered in securing jurisdiction of nonresidents, the principal focus of the first part of the chapter is the "minimum contacts" doctrine and its relationship to the applicable Texas rules and statutes.

The "minimum contacts" doctrine supplanted the concept of territoriality embedded in *Pennoyer v. Neff*, 95 U.S. 714, 24 L. Ed. 565 (1877), under which in-state service was required before a court could exercise personal jurisdiction over a nonresident because "[t]he authority of every tribunal is necessarily restricted by the territorial limits of the State in which it is established." 95 U.S. at 720. *Pennoyer* sharply limited the availability of in personam jurisdiction over defendants not resident in the forum state.

### [B] Fleshing Out the "Minimum Contacts" Doctrine

Justice Stone's opinion in the landmark case of *International Shoe* tells us that the defendant must have "certain minimum contacts [with the forum state] such that the maintenance of the suit does not offend traditional notions of fair play and substantial justice." *International Shoe Co. v. Washington*, 326 U.S. 310, 316, 60 S. Ct. 154, 90 L. Ed 95 (1945). On the other hand, "The unilateral activity of those who claim some relationship with a non-resident defendant cannot satisfy the requirement of contact with the forum State. . . . [I]t is essential in each case that there be some act by which the defendant purposely avails [him]self of the privilege of conducting activities within the forum State . . ." *Hanson v. Denckla,* 357 U.S. 235, 253, 78 S. Ct. 1228, 2 L. Ed. 2d 1283 (1958). In grappling with these relatively cryptic quotations, lower courts have developed more specific formulations. United States Supreme Court decisions have refined the jurisdictional analysis by dividing personal jurisdiction into two categories: general jurisdiction and specific jurisdiction.

General jurisdiction exists when the nonresident's contacts are "continuous and systematic." *See Helicopteros Nacionales de Colombia, S.A. v. Hall*, 466 U.S. 408, 414–415, 104 S. Ct. 1868, 80 L. Ed. 2d 404 (1984); *Perkins v. Benguet Consolidated Mining Co.*, 342 U.S. 437, 72 S.

Ct. 413, 96 L. Ed. 485 (1952). The activity must be substantial and of the right type. General jurisdiction is the state's exercise of personal jurisdiction "in a suit not arising out of or related to the defendant's contacts with the forum." *Burger King Corp. v. Rudzewicz*, 471 U.S. 462, 473 n.15, 105 S. Ct. 2174, 85 L. Ed. 2d 528 (1985), quoting *Helicopteros.* As stated in *Helicopteros* "we hold that mere purchases, even if occurring at regular intervals, are not enough to warrant a State's assertion of *in personam* jurisdiction over a nonresident corporation in a cause of action not related to those purchase transactions." *Helicopteros Nacionales de Colombia*, 466 U.S. at 418.

In contrast, specific jurisdiction requires the litigation to "arise out of or relate to" the defendant's "minimum contacts" in the forum state. *Burger King Corp. v. Rudzewicz*, 471 U.S. 462, 472, 105 S. Ct. 2174, 85 L. Ed. 2d 528 (1985). "[T]he constitutional touchstone remains whether the defendant purposefully established 'minimum contacts' in the forum state. . . . This 'purposeful availment' requirement ensures that a defendant will not be haled into a jurisdiction solely as a result of 'random,' 'fortuitous,' or 'attenuated' contacts . . . or the 'unilateral activity of another party or a third person.' . . . Jurisdiction is proper, however, where the contacts proximately result from actions by the defendant himself that create a 'substantial connection' with the forum state. . . . Jurisdiction in these circumstances may not be avoided merely because the defendant did not physically enter the forum state." *Burger King Corp.*, 471 U.S. at 474–476. For a more detailed discussion of these concepts, see Carlson, *General Jurisdiction and the Exercise of In Personam Jurisdiction Under the Texas Long-Arm Statute,* 28 S. Tex. L. Rev. 307 (1986).

As evidenced in *Asahi Metal Ind. Co., Ltd. v. Superior Court*, the Supreme Court remains divided on the application of the jurisdictional standard, thereby leaving the lower federal courts and the several states to work out solutions to common dilemmas.

---

## ASAHI METAL INDUSTRY CO. v. SUPERIOR COURT

*480 U.S. 102, 107 S. Ct. 1026, 94 L. Ed. 2d 92 (1987)*

O'CONNOR, Justice.

This case presents the question whether the mere awareness on the part of a foreign defendant that the components it manufactured, sold, and delivered outside the United States would reach the forum State in the stream of commerce constitutes "minimum contacts" between the defendant and the forum State such that the exercise of jurisdiction "does not offend 'traditional notions of fair play and substantial justice.' " International Shoe Co. v. Washington, 326 U.S. 310, 316, 66 S. Ct. 154, 158, 90 L. Ed. 95 (1945), quoting Milliken v. Meyer, 311 U.S. 457, 463, 61 S. Ct. 339, 342, 85 L. Ed. 278 (1940).

I

[Gary Zurcher was injured when his motorcycle went out of control and collided with a tractor. He sued Cheng Shin Rubber Industrial Company, Ltd. (Cheng Shin), a Taiwanese corporation, in California Superior Court in and for Solano County, claiming that the accident was caused in part by a defective tube Cheng Shin manufactured. Cheng Shin in turn sought indemnification from Asahi Metal Industry Co., Ltd. (Asahi), the manufacturer of the tube's valve assembly. Zurcher's claims against Cheng Shin and the other defendants were eventually settled and dismissed, leaving only Cheng Shin's indemnity action against Asahi.]

California's long-arm statute authorizes the exercise of jurisdiction "on any basis not inconsistent with the Constitution of this state or of the United States." Cal. Civ. Proc. Code Ann. § 410.10 (West 1973). Asahi moved to quash Cheng Shin's service of summons, arguing the State could not exert jurisdiction over it consistent with the Due Process Clause of the Fourteenth Amendment.

In relation to the motion, the following information was submitted by Asahi and Cheng Shin. Asahi is a Japanese corporation. It manufactures tire valve assemblies in Japan and sells the assemblies to Cheng Shin, and to several other tire manufacturers, for use as components in finished tire tubes. Asahi's sales to Cheng Shin took place in Taiwan. The shipments from Asahi to Cheng Shin were sent from Japan to Taiwan. Cheng Shin bought and incorporated into its tire tubes 150,000 Asahi valve assemblies in 1978; 500,000 in 1979; 500,000 in 1980; 100,000 in 1981; and 100,000 in 1982. Sales to Cheng Shin accounted for 1.24 percent of Asahi's income in 1981 and 0.44 percent in 1982. Cheng Shin alleged that approximately 20 percent of its sales in the United States are in California. Cheng Shin purchases valve assemblies from other suppliers as well, and sells finished tubes throughout the world.

. . . .

[The Superior Court denied the motion to quash. The appellate court required the lower court to quash service. The California Supreme Court reversed, finding the exercise of jurisdiction over Asahi to be consistent with due process.] [The California Supreme Court] concluded that Asahi knew that some of the valve assemblies sold to Cheng Shin would be incorporated into tire tubes sold in California, and that Asahi benefited indirectly from the sale in California of products incorporating its components. The court considered Asahi's intentional act of placing its components into the stream of commerce—that is, by delivering the components to Cheng Shin in Taiwan—coupled with Asahi's awareness that some of the components would eventually find their way into California, sufficient to form the basis for state court jurisdiction under the Due Process Clause.

We granted certiorari, 475 U.S. 1044, 106 S. Ct. 1258, 89 L. Ed. 2d 569 (1986), and now reverse.

II

A

The Due Process Clause of the Fourteenth Amendment limits the power of a state court to exert personal jurisdiction over a nonresident defendant. "[T]he constitutional touchstone" of the determination whether an exercise of personal jurisdiction comports with due process "remains whether the defendant purposefully established 'minimum contacts' in the forum State." Burger King Corp. v. Rudzewicz, 471 U.S. 462, 474, 105 S. Ct. 2174, 2183, 85 L. Ed. 2d 528 (1985), quoting International Shoe Co. v. Washington, 326 U.S., at 316, 66 S. Ct., at 158. Most recently we have reaffirmed the oft-quoted reasoning of Hanson v. Denckla, 357 U.S. 235, 253, 78 S. Ct. 1228, 1239, 2 L. Ed. 2d 1283 (1958), that minimum contacts must have a basis in "some act by which the defendant purposefully avails itself of the privilege of conducting activities within the forum State, thus invoking the benefits and protections of its laws." Burger King, 471 U.S., at 475, 105 S. Ct., at 2183. "Jurisdiction is proper . . . where the contacts proximately result from actions by the defendant *himself* that create a 'substantial connection' with the forum State." Ibid., quoting McGee v. International Life Insurance Co., 355 U.S. 220, 223, 78 S. Ct. 199, 201, 2 L. Ed. 2d 223 (1957) (emphasis in original).

Applying the principle that minimum contacts must be based on an act of the defendant, the Court in World-Wide Volkswagen Corp. v. Woodson, 444 U.S. 286, 100 S. Ct. 559, 62 L. Ed. 2d 490 (1980), rejected the assertion that a *consumer's* unilateral act of bringing the defendant's product into the forum State was a sufficient constitutional basis for personal jurisdiction over the defendant. It had been argued in World-Wide Volkswagen that because an automobile retailer and its wholesale distributor sold a product mobile by design and purpose, they could foresee being haled into court in the distant States into which their customers might drive. The Court rejected this concept of foreseeability as an insufficient basis for jurisdiction under the Due Process Clause. Id., at 295–296, 100 S. Ct. at 559. The Court disclaimed, however, the idea that "foreseeability is wholly irrelevant" to personal jurisdiction, concluding that "[t]he forum State does not exceed its powers under the Due Process Clause if it asserts personal jurisdiction over a corporation that delivers its products into the stream of commerce with the expectation that they will be purchased by consumers in the forum State." Id., at 297–298, 100 S. Ct. at 559 (citation omitted). The Court reasoned:

> "When a corporation 'purposefully avails itself of the privilege of conducting activities within the forum State,' Hanson v. Denckla, 357 U.S. [235,] 253 [78 S. Ct. 1228, 1239, 2 L. Ed. 2d 1283] [(1958)], it has clear notice that it is subject to suit there, and can act to alleviate the risk of burdensome litigation by procuring insurance, passing the expected costs on to customers, or, if the risks are too great, severing its connection with the State. Hence if the sale of a product of a manufacturer or distributor . . . is not simply an isolated occurrence, but arises from the efforts of the manufacturer or distributor to serve, directly or indirectly, the market for its product in other States, it is not unreasonable to subject it to suit in one of those States if its allegedly defective merchandise has there been the source of injury to its owners or to others." Id., at 297, 100 S. Ct. at 559.

In World-Wide Volkswagen itself, the state court sought to base jurisdiction not on any act of the defendant, but on the foreseeable unilateral actions of the consumer. Since World-Wide Volkswagen, lower courts have been confronted with cases in which the defendant acted by placing a product in the stream of commerce, and the stream eventually swept defendant's product into the forum State, but the defendant did nothing else to purposefully avail itself of the market in the forum State. Some courts have understood the Due Process Clause, as interpreted in World-Wide Volkswagen, to allow an exercise of personal jurisdiction to be based on no more than the defendant's act of placing the product in the stream of commerce. Other courts have understood the Due Process Clause and the above-quoted language in World-Wide Volkswagen to require the action of the defendant to be more purposefully directed at the forum State than the mere act of placing a product in the stream of commerce.

The reasoning of the Supreme Court of California in the present case illustrates the former interpretation of World-Wide Volkswagen. The Supreme Court of California held that, because the stream of commerce eventually brought some valves Asahi sold Cheng Shin into California, Asahi's awareness that its valves would be sold in California was sufficient to permit California to exercise jurisdiction over Asahi consistent with the requirements of the Due Process Clause.

The Supreme Court of California's position was consistent with those courts that have held that mere foreseeability or awareness was a constitutionally sufficient basis for personal jurisdiction if the defendant's product made its way into the forum State while still in the stream of commerce. See Bean Dredging Corp. v. Dredge Technology Corp., 744 F.2d 1081 (CA5 1984); Hedrick v. Daiko Shoji Co., 715 F.2d 1355 (CA9 1983).

Other courts, however, have understood the Due Process Clause to require something more than that the defendant was aware of its product's entry into the forum State through the stream of commerce in order for the State to exert jurisdiction over the defendant. In the present case, for example, the State Court of Appeal did not read the Due Process Clause, as interpreted by World-Wide Volkswagen, to allow "mere foreseeability that the product will enter the forum state [to] be enough by itself to establish jurisdiction over the distributor and retailer." App. to Pet. for Cert. B5. In Humble v. Toyota Motor Co., 727 F.2d 709 (CA8, 1984), an injured car passenger brought suit against Arakawa Auto Body Company, a Japanese corporation that manufactured car seats for Toyota. Arakawa did no business in the United States; it had no office, affiliate, subsidiary, or agent in the United States; it manufactured its component parts outside the United States and delivered them to Toyota Motor Company in Japan. The Court of Appeals, adopting the reasoning of the District Court in that case, noted that although it "does not doubt that Arakawa could have foreseen that its product would find its way into the United States," it would be "manifestly unjust" to require Arakawa to defend itself in the United States. Id., at 710–711, quoting 578 F. Supp. 530, 533 (ND Iowa 1982). See also Hutson v. Fehr Bros., Inc., 584 F.2d 833 (CA8 1978); see generally Max Daetwyler Corp. v. R. Meyer, 762 F.2d 290, 299 (CA3 1985) (collecting "stream of commerce" cases in which the "manufacturers involved had made deliberate decisions to market their products in the forum state").

We now find this latter position to be consonant with the requirements of due process. The "substantial connection," Burger King, 471 U.S., at 475, 105 S. Ct., at 2184; McGee, 355 U.S., at 223, 78 S. Ct., at 201, between the defendant and the forum State necessary for a finding of minimum contacts must come about by *an action of the defendant purposefully directed toward the forum State*. Burger King, supra, 471 U.S., at 476, 105 S. Ct., at 2184; Keeton v. Hustler Magazine, Inc., 465 U.S. 770, 774, 104 S. Ct. 1473, 1478, 79 L. Ed. 2d 790 (1984). The placement of a product into the stream of commerce, without more, is not an act of the defendant purposefully directed toward the forum State. Additional conduct of the defendant may indicate an intent or purpose to serve the market in the forum State, for example, designing the product for the market in the forum State, advertising in the forum State, establishing channels for providing regular advice to customers in the forum State, or marketing the product through a distributor who has agreed to serve as the sales agent in the forum State. But a defendant's awareness that the stream of commerce may or will sweep the product into the forum State does not convert the mere act of placing the product into the stream into an act purposefully directed toward the forum State.

Assuming arguendo, that respondents have established Asahi's awareness that some of the valves sold to Cheng Shin would be incorporated into tire tubes sold in California, respondents have not demonstrated any action by Asahi to purposefully avail itself of the California market. Asahi does not do business in California. It has no office, agents, employees, or property in California. It does not advertise or otherwise solicit business in California. It did not create, control, or employ the distribution system that brought its valves to California. Cf. Hicks v. Kawasaki Heavy Industries, 452 F. Supp. 130 (MD Pa. 1978). There is no evidence that Asahi designed its product in anticipation of sales in California. Cf. Rockwell International Corp. v. Costruzioni Aeronautiche Giovanni Agusta, 553 F. Supp. 328 (ED Pa. 1982). On the basis of these facts, the exertion of personal jurisdiction over Asahi by the Superior Court of California [footnote omitted] exceeds the limits of due process.

B

The strictures of the Due Process Clause forbid a state court to exercise personal jurisdiction over Asahi under circumstances that would offend " 'traditional notions of fair play and substantial justice.' " International Shoe Co. v. Washington, 326 U.S., at 316, 66 S. Ct., at 154; quoting Milliken v. Meyer, 311 U.S., at 463, 61 S. Ct., at 339.

We have previously explained that the determination of the reasonableness of the exercise of jurisdiction in each case will depend on an evaluation of several factors. A court must consider the burden on the defendant, the interests of the forum State, and the plaintiff's interest in obtaining relief. It must also weigh in its determination "the interstate judicial system's interest in obtaining the most efficient resolution of controversies; and the shared interest of the several States in furthering fundamental substantive social policies." World-Wide Volkswagen, 444 U.S., at 292, 100 S. Ct., at 559 (citations omitted).

A consideration of these factors in the present case clearly reveals the unreasonableness of the assertion of jurisdiction over Asahi, even apart from the question of the placement of goods in the stream of commerce.

Certainly the burden on the defendant in this case is severe. Asahi has been commanded by the Supreme Court of California not only to traverse the distance between Asahi's headquarters in Japan and the Superior Court of California in and for the County of Solano, but also to submit its dispute with Cheng Shin to a foreign nation's judicial system. The unique burdens placed upon one who must defend oneself in a foreign legal system should have significant weight in assessing the reasonableness of stretching the long arm of personal jurisdiction over national borders.

When minimum contacts have been established, often the interests of the plaintiff and the forum in the exercise of jurisdiction will justify even the serious burdens placed on the alien defendant. In the present case, however, the interests of the plaintiff and the forum in California's assertion of jurisdiction over Asahi are slight. All that remains is a claim for indemnification asserted by Cheng Shin, a Taiwanese corporation, against Asahi. The transaction on which the indemnification claim is based took place in Taiwan; Asahi's components were shipped from Japan to Taiwan. Cheng Shin has not demonstrated that it is more convenient for it to litigate its indemnification claim against Asahi in California rather than in Taiwan or Japan.

Because the plaintiff is not a California resident, California's legitimate interests in the dispute have considerably diminished. The Supreme Court of California argued that the State had an interest in "protecting its consumers by ensuring that foreign manufacturers comply with the state's safety standards." 39 Cal. 3d, at 49, 216 Cal. Rptr., at 392, 702 P.2d, at 550. The State Supreme Court's definition of California's interest, however, was overly broad. The dispute between Cheng Shin and Asahi is primarily about indemnification rather than safety standards. Moreover, it is not at all clear at this point that California law should govern the question whether a Japanese corporation should indemnify a Taiwanese corporation on the basis of a sale made in Taiwan and a shipment of goods from Japan to Taiwan. Phillips Petroleum Co. v. Shutts,

472 U.S. 797, 821–822, 105 S. Ct. 2965, 86 L. Ed. 2d 628 (1985); Allstate Insurance Co. v. Hague, 449 U.S. 302, 312–313, 101 S. Ct. 633, 66 L. Ed. 2d 521 (1981). The possibility of being haled into a California court as a result of an accident involving Asahi's components undoubtedly creates an additional deterrent to the manufacture of unsafe components; however, similar pressures will be placed on Asahi by the purchasers of its components as long as those who use Asahi components in their final products, and sell those products in California, are subject to the application of California tort law.

. . . .

Considering the international context, the heavy burden on the alien defendant, and the slight interests of the plaintiff and the forum State, the exercise of personal jurisdiction by a California court over Asahi in this instance would be unreasonable and unfair.

III

Because the facts of this case do not establish minimum contacts such that the exercise of personal jurisdiction is consistent with fair play and substantial justice, the judgment of the Supreme Court of California is reversed, and the case is remanded for further proceedings not inconsistent with this opinion.

It is so ordered.

BRENNAN, Justice, concurring in part and concurring in the judgment. [Joined by Justice WHITE, Justice MARSHALL, and Justice BLACKMUN.]

I do not agree with the interpretation in Part II-A of the stream-of-commerce theory, nor with the conclusion that Asahi did not "purposely avail itself of the California market." Ante, at 112. I do agree, however, with the Court's conclusion in Part II-B that the exercise of personal jurisdiction over Asahi in this case would not comport with "fair play and substantial justice," International Shoe Co. v. Washington, 326 U.S. 310, 320, 66 S. Ct. 154, 90 L. Ed. 95 (1945). This is one of those rare cases in which "minimum requirements inherent in the concept of 'fair play and substantial justice' . . . defeat the reasonableness of jurisdiction even [though] the defendant has purposefully engaged in forum activities." Burger King Corp. v. Rudzewicz, 471 U.S. 462, 477–478, 105 S. Ct. 2174, 85 L. Ed. 2d 528 (1985). I therefore join Parts I and II-B of the Court's opinion, and write separately to explain my disagreement with Part II-A.

Part II-A states that "a defendant's awareness that the stream of commerce may or will sweep the product into the forum State does not convert the mere act of placing the product into the stream into an act purposefully directed toward the forum State." Ante, at 112. Under this view, a plaintiff would be required to show "[a]dditional conduct" directed toward the forum before finding the exercise of jurisdiction over the defendant to be consistent with the Due Process Clause. Ibid. I see no need for such a showing, however. The stream of commerce refers not to unpredictable currents or eddies, but to the regular and anticipated flow of products from manufacture to distribution to retail sale. As long as a participant in this process is aware that the final product is being marketed in the forum State, the possibility of a lawsuit there cannot come as a surprise. Nor will the litigation present a burden for which there is no corresponding benefit. A defendant who has placed goods in the stream of commerce benefits economically from the retail sale of the final product in the forum State, and indirectly benefits from the State's laws that regulate and facilitate commercial activity. These benefits accrue regardless of whether that participant directly conducts business in the forum State, or engages in additional conduct directed toward that State. Accordingly, most courts and commentators have found that jurisdiction premised on the placement of a product into the stream of commerce is consistent with the Due Process Clause, and have not required a showing of additional conduct. [footnote omitted]

The endorsement in Part II-A of what appears to be the minority view among Federal Courts of Appeals [footnote omitted] represents a marked retreat from the analysis in *World-Wide Volkswagen v. Woodson,* 444 U.S. 286, 100 S. Ct. 559, 62 L. Ed. 2d 490 (1980). In that case, "respondents [sought] to base jurisdiction on one, isolated occurrence and whatever inferences can be drawn therefrom: the fortuitous circumstance that a single Audi automobile, sold in New York to New York residents, happened to suffer an accident while passing through Oklahoma." Id., at 295, 100 S. Ct., at 566. The Court held that the possibility of an accident in Oklahoma, while to some extent foreseeable in light of the inherent mobility of the automobile, was not enough to establish minimum contacts between the forum State and the retailer or distributor. Id., at 295–296, 100 S. Ct., at 566. The Court then carefully explained:

> "[T]his is not to say, of course, that foreseeability is wholly irrelevant. But the foreseeability that is critical to due process analysis is not the mere likelihood that a product will find its way into the forum State. Rather, it is that the defendant's conduct and connection with the forum State are such that he should reasonably anticipate being haled into Court there." Id., at 297, 100 S. Ct., at 567.

The Court reasoned that when a corporation may reasonably anticipate litigation in a particular forum, it cannot claim that such litigation is unjust or unfair, because it "can act to alleviate the risk of burdensome litigation by procuring insurance, passing the expected costs on to consumers, or, if the risks are too great, severing its connection with the State." Ibid.

To illustrate the point, the Court contrasted the foreseeability of litigation in a State to which a consumer fortuitously transports a defendant's product (insufficient contacts) with the foreseeability of litigation in a State where the defendant's product was regularly *sold* (sufficient contacts). The Court stated:

> "Hence if the *sale* of a product of a manufacturer or distributor such as Audi or Volkswagen is not simply an isolated occurrence, but arises from the efforts of the manufacturer or distributor to serve, *directly or indirectly*, the market for its product in other States, it is not unreasonable to subject it to suit in one of those States if its allegedly defective merchandise has there been the source of injury to its owner or to others. The forum State does not exceed its powers under the Due Process Clause if it asserts personal jurisdiction over a corporation that delivers its products into the stream of commerce *with the expectation that they will be purchased by consumers* in the forum State." *Id.,* at 297–298, 100 S. Ct., at 567 (emphasis added).

The Court concluded its illustration by referring to *Gray v. American Radiator & Standard Sanitary Corp.,* 22 Ill. 2d 432, 176 N.E.2d 761 (1961), a well-known stream-of-commerce case in which the Illinois Supreme Court applied the theory to assert jurisdiction over a component-parts manufacturer that sold no components directly in Illinois, but did sell them to a manufacturer who incorporated them into a final product that was sold in Illinois. 444 U.S., at 297–298, 100 S. Ct., at 567.

The Court in World-Wide Volkswagen thus took great care to distinguish "between a case involving goods which reach a distant State through a chain of distribution and a case involving goods which reach the same State because a consumer . . . took them there." Id., at 306–307, 100 S. Ct., at 584 (BRENNAN, J., dissenting). [footnote omitted] The California Supreme Court took note of this distinction, and correctly concluded that our holding in World-Wide Volkswagen preserved the stream-of-commerce theory. *See* App. to Pet. for Cert. C-9, and n. 3, C-13–C-15; cf. Comment, Federalism, Due Process, and Minimum Contacts: World-Wide Volkswagen Corp. v. Woodson, 80 Colum. L. Rev. 1341, 1359–1361, and nn. 140–146 (1980).

In this case, the facts found by the California Supreme Court support its finding of minimum contacts. The court found that "[a]lthough Asahi did not design or control the system of distribution that carried its valve assemblies into California, Asahi was aware of the distribution system's operation, and it knew that it would benefit economically from the sale in California of products incorporating its components." App. to Pet. for Cert. C-11. [footnote omitted] Accordingly, I cannot join the determination in Part II-A that Asahi's regular and extensive sales of component parts to a manufacturer it knew was making regular sales of the final product in California is insufficient to establish minimum contacts with California.

STEVENS, Justice, concurring in part and concurring in the judgment.

[Joined by Justice WHITE and Justice BLACKMUN.]

The judgment of the Supreme Court of California should be reversed for the reasons stated in Part II-B of the Court's opinion. While I join Parts I and II-B, I do not join Part II-A for two reasons. First, it is not necessary to the Court's decision. An examination of minimum contacts is not always necessary to determine whether a state court's assertion of personal jurisdiction is constitutional. See Burger King Corp. v. Rudzewicz, 471 U.S. 462, 476–478, 105 S. Ct. 2174, 85 L. Ed. 2d 528 (1985). Part II-B establishes, after considering the factors set forth in World-Wide Volkswagen Corp. v. Woodson, 444 U.S. 286, 292, 100 S. Ct. 559, 62 L. Ed. 2d 490 (1980), that California's exercise of jurisdiction over Asahi in this case would be "unreasonable and unfair." Ante, at 1035. This finding alone requires reversal; this case fits within the rule that "minimum requirements inherent in the concept of 'fair play and substantial justice' may defeat the reasonableness of jurisdiction even if the defendant has purposefully engaged in forum activities." Burger King, 471 U.S., at 477–478, 105 S. Ct., at 2184–2185 (quoting International Shoe Co. v. Washington, 326 U.S. 310, 320, 66 S. Ct. 154, 160, 90 L. Ed. 95 (1945)). Accordingly, I see no reason in this case for the plurality to articulate "purposeful direction" or any other test as the nexus between an act of a defendant and the forum State that is necessary to establish minimum contacts.

Second, even assuming that the test ought to be formulated here, Part II-A misapplies it to the facts of this case. The plurality seems to assume that an unwavering line can be drawn between "mere awareness" that a component will find its way into the forum State and "purposeful availment" of the forum's market. Ante, at 1033. Over the course of its dealings with Cheng Shin, Asahi has arguably engaged in a higher quantum of conduct than "[t]he placement of a product into the stream of commerce, without more . . . ." Ibid. Whether or not this conduct rises to the level of purposeful availment requires a constitutional determination that is affected by the volume, the value, and the hazardous character of the components. In most circumstances I would be inclined to conclude that a regular course of dealing that results in deliveries of over 100,000 units annually over a period of several years would constitute "purposeful availment" even though the item delivered to the forum State was a standard product marketed throughout the world.

---

**BURNHAM v. SUPERIOR COURT,** 495 U.S. 604, 110 S. Ct. 2105, 109 L. Ed. 2d 631 (1990). In addition to modern articulations of the bases for personal jurisdiction, the traditional bases—such as consent to personal jurisdiction, domicile in the forum, and physical presence in the forum—remain valid. In *Burnham*, the United States Supreme Court held that temporary presence in the forum state, even if unrelated to the suit, suffices for the forum state's exercise of personal jurisdiction. Mr. Burnham had been served with a divorce petition while in California to conduct business and visit his children. After returning to his home in New Jersey, he made a special appearance in California Superior Court to challenge personal jurisdiction, asserting his only contacts with California were a few short visits to the State for business purposes and visits with his children. The Court stated: "Among the most firmly established principles of personal jurisdiction in American tradition is that the courts of a State have jurisdiction over nonresidents who are physically present in the State . . . no matter how fleeting [the] visit." 495 U.S. at 610–611.

---

**SHAFFER v. HEITNER,** 433 U.S. 186, 97 S. Ct. 2569, 53 L. Ed. 2d 683 (1977). After tracing the development of the minimum contacts doctrine and quoting *International Shoe*, the United States Supreme Court recast the doctrine in the following terms: "Thus the relationship *among the defendant, the forum, and the litigation*, rather than the mutually exclusive sovereignty of the States on which the rules of *Pennoyer* rest, became the central concern of the inquiry into personal jurisdiction." 433 U.S. at 204 (emphasis added). This new formulation of the minimum contacts doctrine lends a slightly different emphasis to the method of analysis. This approach is compatible with traditional in rem jurisdictional analysis, under which ownership interests in property located within a state can be adjudicated there, regardless of the property owner's whereabouts, because the State is said to have sovereignty over property located within its borders. In *Shaffer*, the Court held that there must be a relationship between the defendant, the forum, and the litigation in quasi in rem actions, based on attachment or seizure of the defendant's property within the State, as well as in personam actions. "[A]lthough the presence of the defendant's property in a State might suggest the existence of other ties among the defendant, the State, and the litigation, the presence of the property alone would not support the State's jurisdiction. . . . For in cases such as . . . this one, the only role played by the property is to provide the basis for bringing the defendant into court . . . . In such cases, if a direct assertion of personal jurisdiction over the defendant would violate the Constitution, it would seem that an indirect assertion of that jurisdiction should be equally impermissible." 433 U.S. at 209.

## § 4.02 The General Long-Arm Statute

### [A] Statutory Construction

CIVIL PRACTICE AND REMEDIES CODE

CHAPTER 17. PARTIES; CITATION; LONG-ARM JURISDICTION

SUBCHAPTER C. LONG-ARM JURISDICTION IN SUIT ON BUSINESS TRANSACTION OR TORT

C.P.R.C. § 17.041. *Definition.* In this subchapter, "nonresident" includes:

(1) an individual who is not a resident of this state; and

(2) a foreign corporation, joint-stock company, association, or partnership.

C.P.R.C. § 17.042. *Acts Constituting Business in This State.* In addition to other acts that may constitute doing business, a nonresident does business in this state if the nonresident:

(1) contracts by mail or otherwise with a Texas resident and either party is to perform the contract in whole or in part in this state;

(2) commits a tort in whole or in part in this state; or

(3) recruits Texas residents, directly or through an intermediary located in this state, for employment inside or outside this state.

C.P.R.C. § 17.043. *Service on Person in Charge of Business.* In an action arising from a nonresident's business in this state, process may be served on the person in charge, at the time of service, of any business in which the nonresident is engaged in this state if the nonresident is not required by statute to designate or maintain a resident agent for service of process.

C.P.R.C. § 17.044. *Substituted Service on Secretary of State.* (a) The secretary of state is an agent for service of process or complaint on a nonresident who:

(1) is required by statute to designate or maintain a resident agent or engages in business in this state, but has not designated or maintained a resident agent for service of process;

(2) has one or more resident agents for service of process, but two unsuccessful attempts have been made on different business days to serve each agent; or

(3) is not required to designate an agent for service in this state, but becomes a nonresident after a cause of action arises in this state but before the cause is matured by suit in a court of competent jurisdiction.

(b) The secretary of state is an agent for service of process on a nonresident who engages in business in this state, but does not maintain a regular place of business in this state or a designated agent for service of process, in any proceeding that arises out of the business done in this state and to which the nonresident is a party.

(c) After the death of a nonresident for whom the secretary of state is an agent for service of process under this section, the secretary of state is an agent for service of process on a nonresident administrator, executor, or personal representative of the nonresident. If an administrator, executor, or personal representative for the estate of the deceased nonresident is not appointed, the secretary of state is an agent for service of process on an heir, as determined by the law of the foreign jurisdiction, of the deceased nonresident.

(d) If a nonresident for whom the secretary of state is an agent for service of process under this section is judged incompetent by a court of competent jurisdiction, the secretary of state is an agent for service of process on a guardian or personal representative of the nonresident.

C.P.R.C. § 17.045. *Notice to Nonresident.* (a) If the secretary of state is served with duplicate copies of process for a nonresident, he shall require a statement of the name and address of the nonresident's home or home office and shall immediately mail a copy of the process to the nonresident.

(b) If the secretary of state is served with process under Section 17.044(a)(3), he shall immediately mail a copy of the process to the nonresident (if an individual), to the person in charge of the nonresident's business, or to a corporate officer (if the nonresident is a corporation).

(c) If the person in charge of a nonresident's business is served with process under Section 17.043, a copy of the process and notice of the service must be immediately mailed to the nonresident of the nonresident's principal place of business.

(d) The process or notice must be sent by registered mail or by certified mail, return receipt requested.

(e) If the secretary of state is served with duplicate copies of process as an agent for a person who is a nonresident administrator, executor, heir, guardian, or personal representative of a nonresident, the secretary shall require a statement of the person's name and address and shall immediately mail a copy of the process to the person.

---

## NOTES AND QUESTIONS

(1) *"Nexus Requirement."* Although the Texas general long-arm statute as originally enacted (former R.C.S. Art. 2031b) clearly contained a nexus requirement, the alteration of the statutory language as a result of the recodification of the statute in the Civil Practice and Remedies Code has confused this matter. C.P.R.C. § 17.043 still contains an explicit nexus requirement in its first sentence as follows: "In an action arising from a nonresident's business in this state; . . . ." But doesn't the phrase "or engages in business in this state" in C.P.R.C. § 17.044(a)(1) authorize service of process on the secretary of state for nonresidents who are "doing business" under Section 17.042, even though the nonresident is not required by another statute to designate a resident agent? If it does so provide literally, why then does Section 17.044(b) contain an explicit nexus requirement?

(2) *"Doing Business" Concept.* What sorts of cases fall under the notion of "doing business" in Texas? Contract or tort cases are mentioned, but notice that the reach of the statute is not limited to them. What kinds of "contacts" are sufficient? What does the phrase "[i]n addition to other acts that may constitute doing business" in C.P.R.C. § 17.042 mean? *See Reul v. Sahara Hotel*, 372 F. Supp. 995 (S.D. Tex. 1974), in [C], *below* (control over a subsidiary may be sufficient if the latter is doing business in Texas). Where does the language "doing business" come from? What does this source indicate about the intended breadth of the statute?

(3) *Other Long-Arm Statutes.* There are other Texas long-arm statutes. For example, the nonresident motorist statute, Sections 17.061–17.067 of the Civil Practice and Remedies Code,

provides for service on the Chairman of the Texas Transportation Commission for civil actions arising from the operation of a motor vehicle in Texas. Articles 1.14.1 and 1.14.2 of the Insurance Code permit service on the Insurance Commissioner when a foreign insurance company engages in insurance business in violation of the Code.

(4) *Service on the Secretary of State.* The mechanics of serving a nonresident by serving the secretary of state are complex. First, the citation must be prepared by the proper court clerk or by the plaintiff or the plaintiff's attorney. *See* C.P.R.C. § 17.027. Second, the petition and citation must be served on the secretary by the clerk or by the plaintiff or the plaintiff's representative or by a sheriff or constable in accordance with the Texas Rules of Civil Procedure. *See* C.P.R.C. § 17.026. Third, the secretary must send the papers to the defendant at the address provided by the person requesting service.

(5) *Other Provisions on Service.* Subchapter B of Chapter 17 of the Civil Practice and Remedies Code contains miscellaneous statutory provisions concerning service on noncorporate business agents (C.P.R.C. § 17.021), partnerships (C.P.R.C. § 17.022), joint-stock associations (C.P.R.C. § 17.023), and political subdivisions (C.P.R.C. § 17.024). Unfortunately, the Civil Practice and Remedies Code is only a partial recodification of the statutes concerning service and personal jurisdiction. Other codes dealing with specific subjects may contain additional provisions that supplement or effectively supersede the general jurisdictional provisions. *See, e.g.*, Fam. C. §§ 6.305, 102.011.

### [B] "Arising Out of Business Done": Scope of the Texas Long-Arm Statute

*Read Tex. R. Civ. P. 108.*

## U-ANCHOR ADVERTISING, INC. v. BURT

*553 S.W.2d 760 (Tex. 1977)*

STEAKLEY, Justice.

This is a suit for breach of contract. It was instituted in the 47th District Court of Potter County, Texas by U-Anchor Advertising, Inc., Petitioner, against N. H. Burt, doing business as Granot Lodge, Respondent. U-Anchor is a Texas corporation domiciled in Amarillo, Potter County, Texas. Burt is a resident of Clinton, Custer County, Oklahoma. Citation was served upon the Secretary of State of Texas as the presumed agent of Burt for service of process pursuant to Article 2031b, Tex. Rev. Civ. Stat. Ann., the Texas "long-arm" statute. Burt entered a special appearance to contest the jurisdiction of the Texas court pursuant to Rule 120a of the Texas Rules of Civil Procedure. The trial court sustained Burt's Motion to the Jurisdiction, and this was affirmed by the Court of Civil Appeals. It was the view of the court that while Burt was unquestionably doing business in Texas within the terms of Article 2031b, his contacts with Texas fell short of the requirements of due process. 544 S.W.2d 500. We affirm the judgment of the Court of Civil Appeals.

Certain additional facts bearing upon the question of jurisdiction appear undisputed. The written contract upon which suit was brought was executed by the parties in Clinton, Oklahoma. It resulted from solicitation by a salesman for U-Anchor who signed the contract for U-Anchor. The contract called for U-Anchor to place five advertising displays for Burt at various Oklahoma highway locations for a period of 36 months. Burt agreed to pay U-Anchor $80 monthly at its office in Amarillo, Potter County, Texas. U-Anchor constructed the signs in Amarillo and erected them at the Oklahoma locations. Burt mailed six and perhaps seven monthly payment checks to U-Anchor at its office in Amarillo, but he had no other contacts with Texas.

The controlling provisions of Sections 3 and 4 of Article 2031b are as follows:

> Sec. 3. *Any . . . non-resident natural person that engages in business in this State,* irrespective of any Statute or law respecting designation or maintenance of resident agents, and does not maintain a place of regular business in this State or a designated agent upon whom service may be made upon causes of action arising out of such business done in this State, the act or acts of engaging in such business within this State shall be deemed equivalent to an appointment by such . . . non-resident natural person of the Secretary of State of Texas as agent upon whom service of process may be made in any action, suit or proceedings arising out of such business done in this State, wherein such . . . non-resident natural person is a party or is to be made a party.
>
> Sec. 4. For the purpose of this Act, *and without including other acts that may constitute doing business,* any . . . non-resident natural person shall be deemed doing business in this State *by entering into contracts* by mail or otherwise *with a resident of Texas to be performed in whole or in part by either party in this State,* . . . (Italics are added for emphasis).

Article 2031b provides that a non-resident entering into a contract with a Texas resident performable in part by either party in Texas shall be deemed to be doing business in Texas. The contract in question obligated Burt to perform his payment obligations at the office of U-Anchor in Amarillo, Texas, and thus he was "doing business" in Texas within the meaning of the statute. We agree that in this respect, as well as with respect to "other acts that may constitute doing business," Article 2031b reaches as far as the federal constitutional requirements of due process will permit. We let stand the statement in *Hoppenfeld v. Crook,* 498 S.W.2d 52 (Tex. Civ. App.—Austin 1973, writ ref'd n.r.e.) "that the reach of Art. 2031b is limited only by the United States Constitution." *See also National Truckers Service, Inc. v. Aero Systems, Inc.*, 480 S.W.2d 455 (Tex. Civ. App.—Fort Worth 1972, writ ref'd n.r.e.).[1] The federal courts have similarly construed Article 2031b. *See Product Promotions, Inc. v. Cousteau*, 495 F.2d 483 (5th Cir. 1974), and the cases there cited. Furthermore, such a construction is desirable in that it allows the courts to focus on the constitutional limitations of due process rather than to engage in technical and abstruse attempts to consistently define "doing business." *See* Thode, *In Personam Jurisdiction; Article 2031b, the Texas "Long Arm" Jurisdiction Statute; and the Appearance to Challenge Jurisdiction in Texas and Elsewhere,* 42 Tex. L. Rev. 279, 307 (1964).

The question, then, becomes one of due process. . . .

. . .

The facts of this case bring it within the literal reach of Art. 2031b, but, as detailed above, the due process clause of the Fourteenth Amendment prohibits Texas courts from exercising

---

[1] It may be noted that in 1975 Rule 108 of the Texas Rules of Civil Procedure was amended to add the words shown in italics:

> A defendant served with such notice shall be required to appear and answer in the same manner and time and under the same penalty as if he had been personally served with citation within the State *to the full extent that he may be required to appear and answer under the Constitution of the United States in an action either in rem or in personam.*

We stated that the purpose of the amendment is to permit acquisition of in personam jurisdiction to the constitutional limits.

jurisdiction over Burt in a suit arising out of his contract with U-Anchor [because the contract was negotiated and executed in Oklahoma and Burt did not avail himself of the privilege of doing business in Texas; rather, he was merely a passive customer of a Texas corporation who had only one single and fortuitous contact with Texas]. The nature and extent of the contacts of a non-resident with the forum state determine whether or not the forum may exercise in personam jurisdiction over the non-resident, but the infinite variety of such contacts and the vagueness of the constitutional standard render a more definitive articulation of due process requirements impossible. As noted in *Cousteau, supra,* no one formulation of the constitutional test could possibly encompass all the potentially important factors, nor could a formula perform the crucial task of weighing and balancing the relevant considerations. Narrow factual distinctions will often suffice to swing the due process pendulum. Here, as elsewhere, important constitutional questions prove immune to solution by checklist. *See* Annot., 20 A.L.R.3rd 1201 (1968); Thode, *supra*; Kurland, *The Supreme Court, the Due Process Clause and the In Personam Jurisdiction of State Courts—From Pennoyer to Denckla: A Review,* 25 U. Chi. L. Rev. 569 (1958); Comment, *The Texas Long-Arm Statute, Article 2031b: A New Process Is Due,* 30 Sw. L.J. 747 (1976); Comment, *Long-Arm and Quasi in Rem Jurisdiction and the Fundamental Test of Fairness,* 69 U. Mich. L. Rev. 300 (1970); Note, 34 U. La. L. Rev. 691 (1974).

The judgment of the Court of Civil Appeals is affirmed.

---

## NOTES AND QUESTIONS

In reviewing each of these notes and questions, please note that former Article 2031b has been superseded by Sections 17.041–17.045 of the Civil Practice and Remedies Code. Although the Civil Practice and Remedies Code purports to be a nonsubstantive revision of Texas law, its provisions do not literally correspond to the former statutory provisions.

(1) *The Reach of the Texas Long-Arm Statute.* Despite the broad language used by the Texas Supreme Court in *U-Anchor Advertising, Inc. v. Burt,* several subsequent federal cases reached the conclusion that Section 3 of Revised Civil Statutes Art. 2031b required the cause of action to arise from the nonresident's contacts with the State of Texas. *Prejean v. Sonatrach, Inc.,* 652 F.2d 1260, 1266–1267 (5th Cir. 1981). In *Prejean,* Judge Sam Johnson criticized a prior district court opinion (*Navarro v. Sedco, Inc.,* 449 F. Supp. 1355 (S.D. Tex. 1978)) in the following terms: "Article 2031b demands what due process merely takes into account; a nexus between the contacts with the forum and the cause of action of such a kind as to make the cause of action arise from those contexts. *Navarro* thus took the U-Anchor language out of context. This Court expressly disapproves *Navarro's* language refusing to require a nexus, and henceforth it should not be followed." It is noteworthy that Judge Johnson also concluded that "due process allows the state to assert jurisdiction over a nonresident defendant that carries on continuous and systematic activities in the state unrelated to the cause of action." The Texas Supreme Court, in *Hall v. Helicopteros Nacionales de Colombia, S.A.*, 677 S.W.2d 19 (Tex. 1984), withdrew its earlier opinion, 638 S.W.2d 870, 872–873 (Tex. 1982), "pursuant to the judgment of the United States Supreme Court" which held that Helicopteros's contacts with Texas were insufficient to satisfy due process requirements. The earlier opinion had rendered the narrow reading of Article 2031b in *Prejean* insupportable. Based on the now-withdrawn opinion, the Fifth Circuit itself,

as reflected in *Placid Investments, Ltd. v. Girard Trust Bank*, 689 F.2d 1218 (5th Cir. 1982), reluctantly retreated from the position it took in *Prejean*. As shown in the following cases in this chapter, it is now clear that the Texas long-arm statute reaches "as far as the federal constitutional requirements of due process will allow." *Guardian Royal Exchange Assurance v. English China Clays*, 815 S.W.2d 223, 226 (Tex. 1991); *CSR Limited v. Link*, 925 S.W.2d 591, 594 (Tex. 1996).

(2) *Civil Procedure Rule 108.* What is the relevance of the footnote reference in *U-Anchor* to Civil Procedure Rule 108? Is Rule 108 a functional equivalent of the Texas long-arm statutes? In *Aamco Automatic Transmissions, Inc. v. Evans Advertising Agency, Inc.*, 450 S.W.2d 769 (Tex. Civ. App.—Houston [14th Dist.] 1970, writ ref'd n.r.e.), the Court of Civil Appeals concluded that the rule was not a long-arm statute. It has been considered to be applicable only to service of absent domiciliaries and as a notice to non-residents of the pendency of a suit involving property in Texas (in rem situations).

The following is Professor Hans Baade's letter styled *Rule 108: A Dissent*, which appeared in 38 Tex. B.J. 988 (1975).* It should be noted that the rule was revised in 1975. Please read Civil Procedure Rule 108.

## RULE 108: A DISSENT

Dear Editor:

In your current issue (Oct. '75), you report an amendment to Rule 108 of the Texas Rules of Civil Procedure.

I submit that this amendment is an impermissible extension of the Texas long-arm statute. The rule-making power of the Supreme Court of Texas may only be used for the establishment of rules "not inconsistent with the laws of this State" (Tex. Const. Art. V, § 25).

At the present, the scope of the long-arm jurisdiction of the Texas courts is determined by *legislatively* enacted long-arm statutes, *i.e.*, primarily Tex. Civ. Stat. art. 2031b (contracts and torts); and Tex. Fam. Code §§ 3.26 & 11.051 (matrimonial actions and suits affecting the parent-child relationship). These statutes are of course subject to the due process clause of the fourteenth amendment, but they are not mandated by that clause. The Legislature could, at any time, repeal or restrict the Texas long-arm statutes that are currently in effect.

Rule 108, as presently interpreted, is not an additional long-arm statute, but merely a provision for service of process on absent defendants and non-residents. *Aamco Automatic Trans. Inc. v. Evans* App.—Houston [14th Dist.], writ ref. n.r.e., and sources there cited.

The Constitution of the United States indicates the limits within which States, if they so choose, may enact long-arm statutes. As a matter of Texas practice and, perhaps, Texas constitutional law, the power to enact and to amend long-arm statutes for this State is a legislative function. Under the constitution of this State, the rule-making power of the Supreme Court of Texas may not be exercised in a manner "inconsistent with the laws of the State." In simple terms, this means that the Texas Rules of Civil Procedure should *implement* the legislatively enacted Texas long-arm statutes, but not amend or enlarge them. The proposed amendment of Rule 108 is an attempt to amend and to enlarge, rather than to implement, the existing framework of Texas long-arm statutes. For that reason, it is constitutionally defective.

Hans W. Baade
Austin

What do you think of Professor Baade's argument? Why does the Supreme Court refer us to Civil Procedure Rule 108 in *U-Anchor?* If Article 2031b goes to due process limits, is there a modification or enlargement of substantive law by Rule 108? If so, what is it?

In *Paramount Pipe & Supply Co. v. Muhr*, 749 S.W.2d 491, 495 (Tex. 1988), the Texas Supreme Court wrote the following:

> First, Muhr complains of improper service of citation. Muhr admits he was served with citation in Arizona pursuant to Tex. R. Civ. P. 108. However, according to Muhr, service under Rule 108 was insufficient to subject him to personal jurisdiction in the district court below. We agree that service under Rule 108 does not, by itself, confer jurisdiction over non-resident defendants. However, Rule 108 is a valid procedural alternative to service under the long-arm statute. Tex. Civ. Prac. & Rem. Code §§ 17.041–17.045 (Vernon 1986). We further reject Muhr's contention that Rule 108 impermissibly abridges substantive rights. *See* Carlson, *General Jurisdiction and the Exercise of In Personam Jurisdiction Under the Texas Long-Arm Statute*, 28 S. Tex. L. Rev. 307, 328–30 (1986).

(4) *The Limits of U-Anchor.* Several Texas cases indicate that a narrow interpretation of *U-Anchor's* holdings regarding the execution and performance of contracts is warranted. In *Gubitosi v. Buddy Schoellkopf Products, Inc.*, 545 S.W.2d 528, 536 (Tex. Civ. App.—Tyler 1976, no writ), an action was instituted by Texas corporations against a New York resident who had signed two guaranty agreements that made him individually liable for payment of two notes. The notes were payable in Dallas, Texas, and evidenced the obligation of a New York corporation to the Texas plaintiffs. The obligation arose from an on-going business relationship between the New York corporation and the Texas corporation and represented an arrearage on an open account for merchandise. The idea for the notes originated from the New York corporation of which Gubitosi was the president and major stockholder. Under these circumstances, the court held that Gubitosi did "purposefully consummate some transaction in the forum State."

In *Diversified Resources Corp. v. Geodynamics Oil & Gas, Inc.*, 558 S.W.2d 97 (Tex. Civ. App.—Corpus Christi 1977, writ ref'd n.r.e.), plaintiff instituted suit against a nonresident to recover on an agreement and note given in connection with a settlement of litigation pending in a Texas court. The court concluded:

> [T]he defendant by executing the note, which clearly reflected the payments were due in the State of Texas, and by executing the agreement which settled the lawsuit on file in the Southern District of Texas wherein the settlement was to be performed in the State of Texas, not only purposefully conducted business in the State of Texas but it also contracted to perform its obligations within the State of Texas, thus invoking the benefits and protections of this State's law.

Several cases reflect that negotiation of the contract in Texas may be sufficient to satisfy the requirement that the nonresident engage in purposeful activity. For example, in *Motiograph, Inc. v. Check-Out Systems, Inc.*, 573 S.W.2d 606 (Tex. Civ. App.—Eastland 1978, writ ref'd), in addition to sending two payments to the plaintiff's office in Texas, the nonresident corporate defendant had initiated the contract that gave rise to the obligation in suit and had sent employees to Texas to learn the use of equipment sold to the nonresident. "Defendant's corporate officer testified that defendant 'proceeded to represent' plaintiff [as a dealer] in South Carolina even though the [dealership] contract was not signed." Under these circumstances, the court held:

> [The defendant] conducted business within this state by virtue of its affirmative acts in "representing" a Texas corporation and in sending its employees to Texas to learn how to sell and service the equipment. We also note that defendant ordered the equipment from Texas and sent payments for the equipment to Texas. We hold that it would be fair and reasonable to require [the defendant] to defend the action in this state.

*See also Wright Waterproofing Co. v. Applied Polymers,* 602 S.W.2d 67, 71 (Tex. Civ. App.—Dallas), writ ref'd n.r.e. per curiam, 608 S.W.2d 164 (Tex. 1980) (defendant's coming to Texas to discuss his product and meeting with architect and subcontractor were purposeful acts in Texas).

---

## GUARDIAN ROYAL EXCH. v. ENGLISH CHINA

*815 S.W.2d 223 (Tex. 1991)*

HIGHTOWER, Justice.

The issue before this court is whether it is consistent with the requirements of due process of law under the United States Constitution for Texas courts to assert in personam jurisdiction over Guardian Royal Exchange Assurance, Ltd. ("Guardian Royal"), an English insurance company. Southern Clay products, Inc. ("Southern Clay"), Gonzales Clay Corporation ("Gonzales Clay"), English China Clays Overseas Investments Ltd. ("Overseas Investments") and English China Clays, P.L.C. ("English China")[1] sued Guardian Royal in Gonzales County, Texas. The trial court granted Guardian Royal's special appearance and dismissed the cause. The court of appeals reversed the judgment of the trial court and remanded the cause for trial. 762 S.W.2d 927. We reverse the judgment of the court of appeals and affirm the judgment of the trial court.

Guardian Royal is an English insurance company with its office and principal place of business in England. English China is an English company with American subsidiaries including Southern Clay and Gonzales Clay, which are Texas corporations. In 1980–81, Guardian Royal issued an insurance policy including several endorsements[2] to English China providing coverage for third party liability occurring anywhere in the world English China and its subsidiary companies did business. These transactions occurred in England between an English insurer and an English insured. All acts concerning the negotiation, implementation and performance of the policy and endorsement (including the payment of premiums) occurred in England between Guardian Royal and English China.

---

[1] In this opinion these parties are collectively referred to as the "English China entities."

[2] The endorsements substantially altered the terms of the original policy. Among other things, the endoresements (1) extended coverage to English China's subsidiaries including Southern Clay and Gonzales Clay, (2) extended the definition of "Insured" to include any associated or subsidiary company of English China anywhere in the world, and (3) deleted the policy's geographical limits.

Guardian Royal asserts that the coverage was extended to the American subsidiaries on the understanding that they would obtain underlying liability insurance from American insurers. Although the endorsement to the policy listed Southern Clay and Gonzales Clay as located in the "U.S.A.," there was no indication that these subsidiaries were located in Texas. [footnote omitted] Furthermore, Guardian Royal did not know whether English China or its American subsidiaries did business in Texas or sent products to Texas. Subsequently Southern Clay acquired liability coverage from United States Fire Insurance Company ("U.S. Fire") and others.

In 1982, an employee of Southern Clay was killed in an on-the-job accident in Gonzales County, Texas. The deceased's family filed wrongful death lawsuits against the English China entities and others in federal and state courts in Texas. The English China entities settled the lawsuits and U.S. Fire contributed approximately $600,000 to the settlement. Asserting that the policy covered English China and its subsidiaries only for liability in excess of the coverage provided by American insurers, Guardian Royal declined to participate in or contribute to the settlement of the lawsuits. The English China entities asserted that Guardian Royal should "reimburse" U.S. Fire[4] for its settlement contribution on their behalf because Guardian Royal was the "primary insurer." After Guardian Royal refused to "reimburse" U.S. Fire, the English China entities sued Guardian Royal. Guardian Royal filed a special appearance pursuant to Rule 120a of the Texas Rules of Civil Procedure asserting that it did not have such minimum contacts with Texas as would allow the court to exercise personal jurisdiction without offending traditional notions of fair play and substantial justice. The trial court granted the special appearance and dismissed the cause. The court of appeals reversed the judgment of the trial court and remanded the cause for trial. 762 S.W.2d 927.

Guardian Royal argues that it is inconsistent with federal constitutional requirements of due process for Texas courts to assert *in personam* jurisdiction over Guardian Royal in this cause. We agree.

The Texas long-arm statute authorizes the exercise of jurisdiction over nonresidents "doing business" in Texas, Tex. Civ. Prac. & Rem. Code Ann. section 17.042 (Vernon 1986). Although it lists particular acts which constitute "doing business," the statute also provides that the nonresident's "other acts" may satisfy the "doing business" requirement. *Id. See Schlobohm v. Schapiro,* 784 S.W.2d at 357; *U-Anchor Advertising, Inc. v. Burt,* 553 S.W.2d 760, 762 (Tex. 1977). As a result, we consider only whether it is consistent with federal constitutional requirements of due process for Texas courts to assert in personam jurisdiction over Guardian Royal. *See Helicopteros Nacionales de Columbia v. Hall,* 466 U.S. 408, 413–14, 104 S. Ct. 1868, 1871–72, 80 L. Ed. 2d 404, 410–11 (1984).

Federal constitutional requirements of due process limit the power of the state to assert personal jurisdiction over a nonresident defendant such as Guardian Royal. In *Helicopteros,* 466 U.S. at 413–14, 104 S. Ct. at 1872. The United States Supreme Court divides the due process requirements into two parts: (1) whether the nonresident defendant has purposely established "minimum contacts" with the forum state; and (2) if so, whether the exercise of jurisdiction comports with "fair play and substantial justice." *Burger King Corp. v. Rudzewicz,* 471 U.S. 462, 475–76, 105 S. Ct. 2174, 2183–84, 85 L. Ed. 2d 528, 542–43 (1985). *See Helicopteros,* 466 U.S. at 414, 104 S. Ct. at 1872.

[4] As a result of the settlement, U.S. Fire has been subrogated to the rights of the English China entities in this cause. Therefore, U.S. Fire is the real party in interest.

I.

Under the minimum contacts analysis, we must determine whether the nonresident defendant has purposefully availed itself of the privilege of conducting activities within the forum state, thus invoking the benefits and protection of its laws. *Burger King,* 471 U.S. at 474–75, 105 S. Ct. at 2183. This "purposeful availment" requirement ensures that a nonresident defendant will not be haled into a jurisdiction based solely upon "random," "fortuitous" or "attenuated" contacts or the "unilateral activity of another party or a third person." *Burger King,* 471 U.S. at 475, 105 S. Ct. at 2183; *Helicopteros,* 466 U.S. at 417, 104 S. Ct. at 1873; *World-Wide Volkswagen Corp. v. Woodson,* 444 U.S. 286, 298, 100 S. Ct. 559, 567, 62 L. Ed. 2d 490, 502 S. Ct. at 2182; *Zac Smith & Co. v. Otis Elevator Co.*, 734 S.W.2d 662, 633 (Tex. 1987).

The exercise of personal jurisdiction is proper when the contacts proximately result from actions of the nonresident defendant which create a substantial connection with the forum, state, *Burger King,* 471 U.S. at 474–75, 105 S. Ct. at 2183–84. The substantial connection between the nonresident defendant and the forum state necessary for a finding of minimum contacts must come about by action or conduct of the nonresident defendant purposefully directed toward the forum state. *Burger King,* 471 U.S. at 472–76, 105 S. Ct. at 2182–84. However, "the constitutional touchstone remains whether the [nonresident] defendant purposefully established 'minimum contacts' in the forum State." *Burger King,* 471 U.S. at 474, 105 S. Ct. at 2183.

Foreseeability is also an important consideration in deciding whether the nonresident defendant has purposely established "minimum contacts" with the forum state. However, "foreseeability" is not necessarily determinative when considering whether the nonresident defendant purposefully established "minimum contacts" with the forum state. Although not an independent component of the minimum contacts analysis, the concept of "foreseeability" is implicit in the requirement that there be a "substantial connection" between the nonresident defendant and Texas arising from action or conduct of the nonresident defendant purposefully directed toward Texas. *World-Wide Volkswagen,* 444 U.S. at 297, 100 S. Ct. at 567; *Burger King,* 471 U.S. at 474, 105 S. Ct. at 2183. "Foreseeability" is especially pertinent when the nonresident defendant is an insurance company. . . . . Thus, when the nonresident defendant is an insurance company, the following factors, when appropriate, should be considered when determining whether the nonresident defendant has purposely established "minimum contacts" with the forum state: (a) the insurer's awareness that it was responsible to cover losses arising from a substantial subject of insurance regularly present in the forum state; and (b) the nature of the particular insurance contract and its coverage.

The United States Supreme Court has refined the minimum contacts analysis into specific and general jurisdiction. When specific jurisdiction is asserted, the cause of action must arise out of or relate to the nonresident defendant's contact with the forum state in order to satisfy the minimum contacts requirement. *Helicopteros,* 466 U.S. at 414 n.8, 104 S. Ct. at 1872 n.8. *See World-Wide Volkswagen,* 444 U.S. at 293–94, 100 S. Ct. at 565. However, the contact must have resulted from the nonresident defendant's purposeful conduct and not the unilateral activity of the plaintiff or others. *See Helicopteros,* 466 U.S. at 417, 104 S. Ct. at 1873; *World-Wide Volkswagen,* 444 U.S. at 298, 100 S. Ct. at 567–68. Furthermore, the nonresident defendant's activities must have been "purposefully directed" to the forum and the litigation must result from alleged injuries that "arise out of or relate to" those activities. *Burger King,* 471 U.S. at 472, 105 S. Ct. at 2182; *Zac Smith & Co.*, 734 S.W.2d at 663. When specific jurisdiction is asserted, the minimum contacts analysis focuses on the relationship among the defendant, the forum and the litigation. *Helicopteros,* 466 U.S. at 414, 104 S. Ct. at 1872; *Schlobohm,* 784 S.W.2d at 357.

General jurisdiction may be asserted when the cause of action does not arise from or relate to the nonresident defendant's purposeful conduct within the forum state but there are continuous and systematic contacts between the nonresident defendant and the forum state. *Helicopteros,* 466 U.S. at 414–16, 104 S. Ct. at 1872–73; *Schlobohm,* 784 S.W.2d at 357. When general jurisdiction is asserted, the minimum contacts analysis is more demanding and requires a showing of substantial activities in the forum state. *Schlobohm,* 784 S.W.2d at 357.

II.

Once it has been determined that the nonresident defendant purposefully established minimum contacts with the forum state, the contacts are evaluated in light of other factors to determine whether the assertion of personal jurisdiction comports with fair play and substantial justice. *Asahi Metal Indus. Co. v. Superior Court,* 480 U.S. 102, 113–15, 107 S. Ct. 1026, 1033–34, 94 L. Ed. 2d 92, 105 (1987); *Burger King,* 471 U.S. at 476, 105 S. Ct. at 2184. These factors include (1) "the burden on the defendant," (2) "the interests of the forum state in adjudicating the dispute," (3) "the plaintiff's interest in obtaining convenient and effective relief,"[7] (4) "the interstate judicial system's interest in obtaining the most efficient resolution of controversies," and (5) "the shared interest of the several States in furthering fundamental substantive social policies." *World-Wide Volkswagen,* 444 U.S. at 292, 100 S. Ct. at 564; *Burger King,* 471 U.S. at 477, 105 S. Ct. at 2184; *Asahi,* 480 U.S. at 113, 107 S. Ct. at 1033–34. "These considerations sometimes serve to establish the reasonableness of jurisdiction upon a lesser showing of minimum contacts than would otherwise be required." *Burger King,* 471 U.S. at 477, 105 S. Ct. at 2184. However, regardless of these factors, it must be established that the nonresident defendant purposely established minimum contacts with the forum state. Even if the nonresident defendant has purposely established minimum contacts with the forum state, the exercise of jurisdiction may not be fair and reasonable under the facts in a particular case. *Burger King,* 471 U.S. at 477–78, 105 S. Ct. at 2185.

When the defendant is a resident of another nation, the court must also consider the procedural and substantive policies of other nations whose interests are affected by the assertion of jurisdiction by a state court:

> *World-Wide Volkswagen* also admonished courts to take into consideration the interests of the "several States," in addition to the forum State, in the efficient judicial resolution of the dispute and the advancement of substantive policies. In the present case, this advice calls for a court to consider the procedural and substantive policies of other nations whose interests are affected by the assertion of jurisdiction by the California court. The procedural and substantive interests of other nations in a state court's assertion of jurisdiction over an alien defendant will differ from case to case. In every case, however, those interests, as well as the Federal Government's interest in its foreign relations policies, will be best served by a careful inquiry into the reasonableness of the assertion of jurisdiction in the particular case, and an unwillingness to find the serious burdens on an alien defendant outweighed by minimal interests on the part of the plaintiff or the forum State. "Great care and reserve

---

[7] This factor was fully described in *World-Wide Volkswagen* as "the plaintiff's interest in obtaining convenient and effective relief . . . at least when that interest is not adequately protected by the plaintiff's power to choose the forum. . . ." 444 U.S. at 292, 100 S. Ct. at 564 (citations omitted).

> should be exercised when extending our notions of personal jurisdiction into the international field." *United States v. First National City Bank,* 379 U.S. 378, 404 (1965) (Harlan, J., dissenting).

*Asahi,* 480 U.S. at 115, 107 S. Ct. at 1034–35 (emphasis in original). "The unique burdens placed upon one who must defend oneself in a foreign legal system should have significant weight in assessing the reasonableness of stretching the long arm of personal jurisdiction over national borders." *Asahi,* 480 U.S. at 114, 107 S. Ct. at 1034. Thus, when an "international dispute" is involved, the following factors, when appropriate, should also be considered: (a) the unique burdens placed upon the defendant who must defend itself in a foreign legal system; and (b) the procedural and substantive policies of other nations whose interests are affected as well as the federal government's interest in its foreign relations policies.

The state's regulatory interests are also an important consideration in deciding whether the exercise of jurisdiction is reasonable. Other courts have recognized that the states have a legitimate concern in areas in which the state possesses a manifest regulatory interest such as insurance, securities and hazardous and toxic waste. *See Shaffer v. Heitner,* 433 U.S. 186, 222–26, 97 S. Ct. 2569, 2589–91, 53 L. Ed. 2d 683, 708–12 (1977) (Brennan, J., concurring in part and dissenting in part).[8] Traditionally, regulation of the "business of insurance" has been delegated to the states by the federal government. *See McCarran-Ferguson Act,* 15 U.S.C. 1012 (1976); Reyes, *Insurance Company Liquidation in Texas—"The Basics",* 51 Tex. B.J. 957 (1988).

The State of Texas has a special interest in regulating certain areas such as insurance, and the Texas courts have implicitly recognized the role of that interest for purposes of determining personal jurisdiction. *See First National Bank of Libby, Montana v. Rector,* 710 S.W.2d 100, 106 (Tex. App.—Austin 1986, writ ref'd n.r.e.); *Texas Commerce Bank v. Interpol'80 Ltd.*, 703 S.W.2d 765, 773–74 (Tex. App.—Corpus Christi 1985, no writ); *GRM v. Equine Inv. & Management Group,* 596 F. Supp. 307, 317 (S.D. Tex. 1984); *but see Beecham v. Pippin,* 686 S.W.2d 356, 360–61 (Tex. App.—Austin 1985, no writ). We find that a state's regulatory interest in a certain area or activity such as insurance is an important consideration in deciding whether the exercise of jurisdiction is reasonable and that a state's regulatory interest may establish the reasonableness of jurisdiction upon a lesser showing of minimum contacts than would otherwise be required. However, a state's regulatory interest alone is not in and of itself sufficient to provide a basis for jurisdiction.

III.

In *O'Brien v. Lanpar Co.*, 399 S.W.2d 340 (Tex. 1966), this court adopted the following "formula" articulated by the Supreme Court of Washington in *Tyee Construction Co. v. Dullen*

[8] A "State's valid substantive interests are important considerations in assessing whether it constitutionally may claim jurisdiction over a given cause of action." *Shaffer*, 433 U.S. at 233, 97 S. Ct. at 2589 (Brennan, J., concurring in part and dissenting in part). "State courts have legitimately read their jurisdiction expansively when cause of action centers in an area in which the forum State possesses a manifest regulatory interest." 433 U.S. at 223, 97 S. Ct. at 2590 (Brennan, J., concurring in part and dissenting in part). *See, e.g., McGee v. International Life Ins. Co.*, 355 U.S. 220, 223, 78 S. Ct. 199, 201, 2 L. Ed. 2d 223, 226 (1957) (insurance regulation: "It cannot be denied that California has a manifest interest in providing effective means of redress for its residents when their insurers refuse to pay claims."); *O'Neil v. Picillo*, 682 F. Supp. 706, 714 n.1 (D.R.I. 1988) (heavily regulated activities—hazardous/toxic substances); *Wichita Federal Savings & Loan Ass'n v. Landmark Group, Inc.*, 674 F. Supp. 321, 326 (D. Kan. 1987) (securities regulation: "It is also relevant to this inquiry that the defendants are engaging in a highly regulated activity, making it more foreseeable that they might have to litigate in a distant forum.").

*Steel Products, Inc.*, 62 Wash. 2d 106, 381 P.2d 245, 251 (1963), to determine when assertion of jurisdiction over a nonresident defendant is proper:

(1) the nonresident defendant or foreign corporation must purposefully do some act or consummate some transaction in the forum state;

(2) the cause of action must arise from, or be connected with, such act or transaction; and

(3) the assumption of jurisdiction by the forum state must not offend traditional notions of fair play and substantial justice, consideration being given to the quality, nature, and extent of the activity in the forum state, the relative convenience of the parties, the benefits and protection of the laws of the forum state afforded the respective parties, and the basic equities of the situation.

*O'Brien v. Lanpar Co.*, 399 S.W.2d at 342. This jurisdictional formula[9] was designed in an effort to ensure compliance with the federal constitutional requirements of due process. *Schlobohm,* 784 S.W.2d at 358. Since 1966, this court has dutifully repeated this jurisdictional formula. *See, e.g., U-Anchor Advertising,* 553 S.W.2d at 762; *Siskind v. Villa Foundation for Education, Inc.*, 642 S.W.2d 434, 436 (Tex. 1982); *Hall v. Helicopteros Nacionales De Columbia,* 638 S.W.2d 870, 872 (Tex. 1982), *rev'd on other grounds*, 466 U.S. 408 (1984); *Zac Smith & Co.*, 734 S.W.2d at 664; *Schlobohm,* 784 S.W.2d at 358. However, during the past 24 years, the parameters of personal jurisdiction have evolved as the United States Supreme Court has continued to examine, develop and refine the permissible reach of federal due process. [footnote omitted] Therefore, under appropriate circumstances, the jurisdictional formula may be reviewed, and, if necessary, modified to ensure compliance with federal constitutional requirements of due process. This court recently acknowledged the necessity to review the jurisdictional formula, and, as a result, modified the second part of the formula to include the concept of general jurisdiction. *Schlobohm,* 784 S.W.2d at 358.

## IV.

Today, we further clarify the jurisdictional formula to ensure compliance with federal constitutional requirements of due process. First, the nonresident defendant must have purposefully established "minimum contacts" with Texas.[11] There must be "substantial connection"[12] between the nonresident defendant and Texas arising from action or conduct of the nonresident defendant purposefully directed toward Texas. When specific jurisdiction is asserted, the cause of action must arise out of or relate to the nonresident defendant's contacts with Texas. When general jurisdiction is alleged, there must be continuous and systematic contacts between the

[9] In *Schlobohm,* the second part of the jurisdictional formula was modified to incorporate the concept of general jurisdiction:

> (2) The cause of action must arise from, or be connected with, such act or transaction. Even if the cause of action does not arise from a specific contact, jurisdiction may be exercised if the defendant's contacts with Texas are continuing and systematic.

784 S.W.2d at 358.

[11] In analyzing minimum contacts, it is not the number, but rather the quality and nature of the nonresident defendant's contacts with the forum state that is important. *Texas Commerce Bank v. Interpol '80 Ltd.*, 703 S.W.2d 765, 772 (Tex. App.—Corpus Christi 1985, no writ).

[12] "So long as it creates a 'substantial connection' with the forum, even a single act can support jurisdiction." *Burger King*, 471 U.S. at 475 n.18, 105 S. Ct. at 2184 n.18. *See McGee*, 355 U.S. at 223, 78 S. Ct. at 201.

nonresident defendant and Texas. General jurisdiction requires a showing of substantial activities by the nonresident defendant in Texas.

Second, the assertion of personal jurisdiction must comport with fair play and substantial justice. In this inquiry, it is incumbent upon the defendant to present "a compelling case that the presence of some consideration would render jurisdiction unreasonable." *Burger King,* 471 U.S. at 477, 105 S. Ct. at 2185; *see also Zac Smith & Co.,* 734 S.W.2d at 664.[13] . . . .

Only in rare cases, however, will the exercise of jurisdiction not comport with fair play and substantial justice when the nonresident defendant has purposefully established minimum contacts with the forum state. *See Burger King,* 471 U.S. at 477–78, 105 S. Ct. at 2185; *see also Schlobohm,* 784 S.W.2d at 358 ("it has become less likely that the exercise of jurisdiction will fail a fair play analysis."). [footnote omitted] The stringent standard to be applied is set forth in *Burger King*:

> [W]here a defendant who purposefully has directed his activities at forum residents seeks to defeat jurisdiction, he must present a compelling case that the presence of some other considerations would render jurisdiction unreasonable. Most such considerations usually may be accommodated through means short of finding jurisdiction unconstitutional. For example, the potential clash of the forum's laws with the *fundamental substantive social policies* of another State may be accommodated through application of the forum's choice-of-law rules. Similarly, a defendant claiming substantial inconvenience may seek a change of venue.

471 U.S. at 477, 105 S. Ct. at 2185 (emphasis added) (footnotes omitted); *see also Zac Smith & Co.*, 734 S.W.2d at 664 (quoting same language). Nor is distance alone ordinarily sufficient to defeat jurisdiction: "modern transportation and communication have made it much less burdensome for a party sued to defend himself in a State where he engages in economic activity." *McGee,* 355 U.S. at 223, 78 S. Ct. at 201.

V.

. . . .

We must first determine whether Guardian Royal purposefully established "minimum contacts" with Texas; in other words, whether there was a "substantial connection" between Guardian Royal and Texas arising from action or conduct of Guardian Royal purposefully directed toward Texas. The policy and endorsements provided coverage for third party liability occurring anywhere in the world English China did business. Among other things, the policy stated that "[t]he words 'The Insured' wherever they appear shall apply to each party described in the Schedule as if a separate insurance policy had been issued to each. . . ." [footnote omitted] The endorsements to the policy (1) extended coverage to English China's subsidiaries including Southern Clay and Gonzales clay, (2) extended the definition of "Insured" to include any associated and subsidiary company of English China anywhere in the world, and (3) deleted the policy's geographical limits. Furthermore, under these facts and circumstances, it is apparent that the nature of the insurance contract between Guardian Royal and English China and its coverage are sufficient to establish that Guardian Royal purposefully established "minimum contacts" with Texas.[16] As the insurer

---

[13] We have previously held that the nonresident defendant must negate all bases of personal jurisdiction. *Zac Smith & Co.*, 734 S.W.2d at 664; *Siskind v. Villa Foundation for Education, Inc.*, 642 S.W.2d at 438.

[16] Since we have determined that Guardian Royal has purposefully established "minimum contacts" with Texas based upon the nature of the insurance contract between Guardian Royal and English China and its coverage, it is not necessary to consider whether Guardian Royal was aware that it was responsible to cover losses arising from a substantial subject of insurance regularly present in Texas.

of English China and its approximately 120 subsidiary companies located in many countries in the world including the United States and the issuer of an insurance policy providing coverage for third party liability occurring anywhere in the world English China and its subsidiary companies did business, Guardian Royal could reasonably anticipate the significant risk (if not the probability) that a subsidiary would become involved in disputes and litigation in many countries in the world including any state in the United States. In addition, Guardian Royal could reasonably anticipate the significant risk concerning the litigation brought in one of many countries including any state in the United States. Furthermore, the policy language that "the words 'The Insured,' wherever they appear, shall apply to each [subsidiary] . . . as if a separate insurance [policy] had been issued to each [subsidiary]" acknowledges the formation of a significant relationship between Guardian Royal and each subsidiary including Southern Clay. Under these facts and circumstances, we find that Guardian Royal purposefully established "minimum contacts" with Texas.

VI.

Second, we must determine whether the assertion of personal jurisdiction comports with fair play and substantial justice . . . .

Requiring Guardian Royal, an English insurer unaffiliated with American companies, to submit its dispute with its English insured to a foreign nation's judicial system is burdensome. All acts concerning the negotiation, implementation and performance of the policy and endorsements (including the payment of premiums) occurred in England. Frequently the interests of the forum state and the plaintiff will justify the severe burden placed upon the nonresident defendant. *See Asahi,* 480 U.S. at 114, 107 S. Ct. at 1033. In this case, however, the interests of Texas in adjudicating the dispute and the English China entities in obtaining convenient and effective relief are minimal. Like California, Texas "has a manifest interest in providing effective means of redress for its residents when their insurers refuse to pay claims. These residents would be at a severe disadvantage if they were forced to follow the insurance company to a distant State in order to hold it legally accountable." *McGee,* 355 U.S. at 223, 78 S. Ct. at 201. However, this is a dispute between two insurers—Guardian Royal and U.S. Fire as subrogee to the rights of the English China entities. Among other things, U.S. Fire is seeking "reimbursement" for its contribution to the settlement of the wrongful death lawsuits against the English China entities. The family of the deceased employee of Southern Clay has been compensated and the English China entities, the insureds, were defended and indemnified. Thus, in reality, U.S. Fire is the real party in interest and neither the family of the deceased employee nor the English China entities have an interest in the outcome of this lawsuit. In addition, since Guardian Royal and U.S. Fire are neither Texas consumers nor insureds, Texas' interest in adjudicating the dispute (including its special interest in regulating insurance) is considerably diminished. While Texas "has a manifest interest in providing effective means of redress for its residents when their insurers refuse to pay claims," Texas does not have a compelling interest in providing a forum for resolution of disputes between these insurers. Under these facts and circumstances, we find that the assertion of personal jurisdiction over Guardian Royal is unreasonable and does not comport with fair play and substantial justice. Accordingly, we hold that it is inconsistent with federal constitutional requirements of due process for Texas courts to assert in personam jurisdiction over Guardian Royal in this case.

For the reasons explained herein, we reverse the judgment of the court of appeals and affirm the judgment of the trial court.

[Justice Mauzy dissented by arguing that it was reasonably foreseeable that Guardian Royal would be haled into court in Texas. He reasoned that "Guardian Royal's willingness to being haled into court in a foreign state was an express, and very marketable, feature of its policy. [citation omitted] The company's contacts with the state of Texas cannot be viewed as 'random' or 'fortuitous.' Since Guardian Royal purposefully availed itself of the privilege of conducting business with English China and its Texas subsidiaries, it now has the burden of presenting 'a compelling case that the presence of some other considerations would render jurisdiction unreasonable.' *Burger King Corp. v. Rudzewicz,* 421 U.S. 462, 477 (1985). [footnote omitted] There is no such compelling case here . . . . The fact that United States Fire Insurance Company subrogated to the interest of the insured should not be relevant. A subrogee 'stands in the shoes' of his subrogor . . . . The result here should be no different than if Gonzales Clay and Southern Clay brought this lawsuit directly . . . ."]

---

## CSR LTD. v. LINK

*925 S.W.2d 591 (Tex. 1996)*

SPECTOR, Justice.

This original proceeding concerns the exercise of personal jurisdiction over a foreign corporation by Texas courts. . . . In this case, we find that mandamus is appropriate and conditionally grant the writ.

I.

CSR Limited is a corporation organized under the laws of New South Wales, Australia, with its principal place of business in Sydney, Australia. For a period of time before 1967, CSR was the agent for sales of raw asbestos fiber mined by a subsidiary, Australian Blue Asbestos Proprietary, Limited. The Johns-Manville Corporation purchased this raw asbestos fiber and resold it in the United States. Johns-Manville was the only company marketing CSR's fiber in this country.

On August 23, 1957, CSR sold 363 tons of raw Australian blue asbestos to Johns-Manville. CSR sold the asbestos to Johns-Manville F.O.B. Fremantle, Australia, so that title to the fiber passed to Johns-Manville when Johns-Manville loaded the fiber onto the ship in Australia. Johns-Manville shipped the asbestos to Houston; the fiber was eventually used for the manufacture of transite pipe. The plaintiffs in the underlying suit allege that they were injured by exposure to CSR asbestos used to manufacture pipe.

Because of the large number of asbestos cases that have been filed, the Harris County district courts have created a Master Asbestos File under the authority of local rule. Harris County (Tex.) Dist. Ct. Loc. R. 3.2.3(c); *In re: Asbestos Cases*, Cause No. 90-23333. The judge presiding over the Master Asbestos File rules on issues common to the individual asbestos cases in Harris County. Those rulings in the Master Asbestos File control all asbestos cases currently pending or that may be filed in Harris County. See Standing Order No. 2, *In re: Asbestos Cases*, Cause No. 90-23333 (Dist. Ct. of Harris County). CSR filed a special appearance in the Master Asbestos

File asserting that the trial court lacked personal jurisdiction over the company. Judge Link, the respondent in this case, overruled the motion. The court of appeals denied CSR leave to file its petition for writ of mandamus. CSR now seeks mandamus relief in this Court to prevent the trial court from asserting personal jurisdiction over it.

II.

A court must possess both subject matter jurisdiction over a case and personal jurisdiction over a party to issue a binding judgment. *See Insurance Corp. of Ireland, Ltd. v. Compagnie des Bauxites de Guinee*, 456 U.S. 694, 701–03, 102 S. Ct. 2099, 2103–05, 72 L. Ed. 2d 492 (1982). While subject matter jurisdiction refers to the court's power to hear a particular type of suit, personal jurisdiction concerns the court's power to bind a particular person or party. See 1 Casad, Jurisdiction In Civil Actions § 1.01 (2d ed. 1991). This case involves the trial court's personal jurisdiction over CSR.

A court may assert personal jurisdiction over a nonresident defendant only if the requirements of both the Due Process Clause of the Fourteenth Amendment to the U.S. Constitution and the Texas long-arm statute are satisfied. *See* U.S. Const. amend. XIV, § 1; Tex. Civ. Prac. & Rem. Code § 17.042; *Helicopteros Nacionales de Colombia v. Hall*, 466 U.S. 408, 413–14, 104 S. Ct. 1868, 1871–72, 80 L. Ed. 2d 404 (1984). The long-arm statute allows a court to exercise personal jurisdiction over a nonresident defendant that does business in Texas. In addition to a discrete list of activities that constitute doing business in Texas, the statute provides that "other acts" by the nonresident can satisfy the requirement. *See* Tex. Civ. Prac. & Rem. Code § 17.042; *Guardian Royal Exch. Assurance, Ltd. v. English China Clays, P.L.C.*, 815 S.W.2d 223, 226 (Tex. 1991). Our Court has repeatedly interpreted this broad statutory language "to reach as far as the federal constitutional requirements of due process will allow." *Guardian Royal*, 815 S.W.2d at 226; *see also U-Anchor Advertising, Inc. v. Burt*, 553 S.W.2d 760, 762 (Tex. 1977). Consequently, the requirements of the Texas long-arm statute are satisfied if the exercise of personal jurisdiction comports with federal due process limitations. *See Guardian Royal*, 815 S.W.2d at 226.

Under the Due Process Clause of the Fourteenth Amendment, a defendant must have certain minimum contacts with the forum "such that the maintenance of the suit does not offend 'traditional notions of fair play and substantial justice.' " *International Shoe Co. v. Washington*, 326 U.S. 310, 316, 66 S. Ct. 154, 158, 90 L. Ed. 95 (1945) (quoting *Milliken v. Meyer*, 311 U.S. 457, 463, 61 S. Ct. 339, 343, 85 L. Ed. 278 (1940)). A nonresident defendant that has purposefully availed itself of the privileges and benefits of conducting business in the foreign jurisdiction has sufficient contacts with the forum to confer personal jurisdiction. *See Burger King Corp. v. Rudzewicz*, 471 U.S. 462, 475–76, 105 S. Ct. 2174, 2183–84, 85 L. Ed. 2d 528 (1985). A defendant should not be subject to the jurisdiction of a foreign court based upon "random," "fortuitous," or "attenuated" contacts. *Id.* Minimum contacts are particularly important when the defendant is from a different country because of the unique and onerous burden placed on a party called upon to defend a suit in a foreign legal system. *See Asahi Metal Industry Co., Ltd. v. Superior Court*, 480 U.S. 102, 114, 107 S. Ct. 1026, 1033, 94 L. Ed. 2d 92 (1987).

A defendant's contacts with a forum can give rise to either general or specific jurisdiction. General jurisdiction is present when a defendant's contacts are continuous and systematic, permitting the forum to exercise personal jurisdiction over the defendant even if the cause of action did not arise from or relate to activities conducted within the forum state. *See Schlobohm v. Schapiro*, 784 S.W.2d 355, 357 (Tex. 1990). General jurisdiction requires a showing that the defendant conducted substantial activities within the forum, a more demanding minimum contacts analysis than for specific jurisdiction. *See Guardian Royal*, 815 S.W.2d at 228. In contrast, specific jurisdiction is established if the defendant's alleged liability arises from or is related to an activity conducted within the forum. *See id.* at 227.

CSR is an Australian company headquartered in Sydney. It has no offices in Texas, no employees in Texas, and no bank accounts in Texas. CSR has not solicited business in Texas and has not sent any correspondence to Texas. CSR has never owned property in Texas and has never paid taxes in Texas. CSR has never entered into a contract in Texas. Under these facts, CSR did not have systematic and continuous contacts with Texas sufficient to support general jurisdiction. [footnote omitted]

CSR also argues that the trial court does not have specific jurisdiction in this case because the company conducted no activity in or related to Texas. It is undisputed that CSR sold Johns-Manville a shipment of 363 tons of raw asbestos that was sent directly to Houston in August of 1957. But title to the asbestos passed to Johns-Manville in Australia and there is no evidence that CSR controlled or participated in the decision to ship the fiber to Texas. The plaintiffs contend, however, that CSR knew that one of Johns-Manville's plants was in Denison, Texas. The plaintiffs argue that CSR could have foreseen that its raw asbestos fiber would be used in Texas. Therefore, they argue, CSR should be subject to the personal jurisdiction of Texas courts.

Although foreseeability is a factor to consider in a minimum contacts analysis, foreseeability alone will not support personal jurisdiction. *See Guardian Royal*, 815 S.W.2d at 227. The defendant must take an action "*purposefully directed* toward the forum state" to be subject to the jurisdiction of its courts. *Asahi*, 480 U.S. at 112, 107 S. Ct. at 1032 (emphasis added). Assuming that CSR could have known that the raw asbestos it sold to Johns-Manville might be distributed in Texas, "a defendant's awareness that the stream of commerce may or will sweep the product into the forum state does not convert the mere act of placing the product into the stream into an act purposefully directed toward the forum State." *Id.* Additionally, CSR's knowledge that there was a Johns-Manville plant in Texas is not determinative in establishing jurisdiction because there are also Johns-Manville plants located in at least four other states: Louisiana, New Jersey, Illinois and California. *See State ex rel. CSR Ltd. v. MacQueen*, 190 W.Va. 695, 441 S.E.2d 658, 660 (1994). There must be some indication that CSR intended to serve the Texas market.

CSR did not advertise its asbestos in Texas. CSR did not provide advice to Texas buyers or have any sales agents in Texas. CSR did not "create, control, or employ" the distribution system that brought the asbestos into Texas. *Asahi*, 480 U.S. at 112, 107 S. Ct. at 1032. There is no direct evidence that CSR knew that Johns-Manville would distribute its fiber in Texas. In short, the record contains no evidence that CSR took any act purposefully directed toward selling or distributing the raw asbestos fiber in Texas. Absent such a purposeful act, foreseeability alone cannot create minimum contacts between CSR and Texas. The Harris County courts, therefore, cannot exercise personal jurisdiction over CSR consistent with due process.

In Texas, a nonresident defendant must negate all bases of personal jurisdiction to prevail in a special appearance. *See Kawasaki Steel Corp. v. Middleton*, 699 S.W.2d 199, 203 (Tex. 1985). CSR has demonstrated that it had no systematic and continuous contacts with Texas, that it did not purposefully direct any act toward Texas, and that it took no act within Texas that gave rise to the plaintiffs' cause of action. We therefore conclude that CSR has carried its burden to negate all bases of personal jurisdiction.

. . . .

[The concurring opinion of Justice Gonzalez and the dissenting opinion of Justice Baker are omitted.]

---

## CMMC v. SALINAS

*929 S.W.2d 435 (Tex. 1996)*

HECHT, Justice.

The sole question in this case is whether the Fourteenth Amendment permits a state court to take personal jurisdiction over a foreign manufacturer merely because it knew its allegedly defective product would be shipped to that state. We answer no, and thus reverse the judgment of the court of appeals, 903 S.W.2d 138, and affirm the judgment of the trial court.

Hill Country Cellars, a small winery located in Cedar Park, Texas, ordered a winepress from KLR Machines, Incorporated, an independent distributor of equipment used in the wine and juice industries. KLR, in turn, ordered the winepress for Hill Country Cellars from CMMC, a French manufacturer, instructing CMMC to wire the press for electrical use in the United States. KLR quoted the price to Hill Country Cellars in deutch [sic] marks, although it would accept payment in U.S. dollars at the current exchange rate. KLR instructed CMMC to arrange with A. Germaine, a freight forwarder paid by KLR, to transport the press from the CMMC's factory in Chalonnes, France, to the ship on which it would travel to the United States, and to arrange for the press to be shipped FOB the port of Houston. CMMC complied and thus knew that the destination of the press was Texas. Hill Country Cellars took title to the winepress in Houston and paid for transportation to its winery. Shortly after it began to use the press, Hill Country Cellars made a warranty claim to KLR. KLR satisfied the claim by having an electrical motor rewound for proper use in the United States, for which it paid $529.57. KLR in turn presented the claim to CMMC, which agreed to credit KLR.

CMMC, a French corporation owned since 1986 by a German manufacturer, sells wine production equipment primarily in Europe. It does not directly market or advertise its equipment in the United States, other than by providing promotional materials to KLR. A buyer may acquire products from CMMC directly or through KLR. CMMC and KLR have no contractual arrangement and share no employees. KLR advertises CMMC products, but CMMC does not specifically authorize or approve the ads. CMMC has sold equipment in the United States, including a direct sale to another winery in Texas. CMMC has never had a place of business, distributor, or representative in Texas, or any other contacts with Texas. Hill Country Cellars never had any direct contact with CMMC.

KLR, a New York corporation with offices in Sebastopol, California, and Bath, New York, has never had offices or employees in Texas. In the ten years preceding this case it made only three or four equipment sales in Texas. It has never had any other contacts with Texas. KLR sells the equipment of numerous manufacturers, only one of which is CMMC. KLR directs its marketing efforts primarily toward California but also advertises in nationally circulated wine industry magazines. KLR advertisements have never pictured the particular press Hill Country Cellars purchased, although it was a KLR ad that led to the sale to Hill Country Cellars.

Ambrocio Salinas, a Hill Country Cellars employee, injured his arm while cleaning the press and filed this lawsuit for damages against CMMC, asserting strict product liability and negligence claims. The district court sustained CMMC's special appearance and dismissed the case for want of personal jurisdiction. The court of appeals reversed and remanded, holding that a Texas court's assertion of personal jurisdiction over CMMC could be based solely on CMMC's knowledge that the winepress would be shipped to Texas, and that this assertion would not offend traditional notions of fair play and substantial justice. 903 S.W.2d 138, 142–145.

We have so frequently and so recently reiterated the constitutional standards for determining personal jurisdiction that we need not restate them yet again here. *CSR Ltd. v. Link*, 925 S.W.2d 591 (Tex. 1996); *National Indus. Sand Ass'n v. Gibson*, 897 S.W.2d 769, 772 (Tex. 1995); *In re S.A.V.*, 837 S.W.2d 80, 85–86 (Tex. 1992); *Guardian Royal Exch. Assurance, Ltd. v. English China Clays, P.L.C.*, 815 S.W.2d 223, 226–228 (Tex. 1991); *Schlobohm v. Schapiro*, 784 S.W.2d 355, 357 (Tex. 1990); *Zac Smith & Co. v. Otis Elevator Co.*, 734 S.W.2d 662, 663–664 (Tex. 1987). Our polestar must be, of course, the United States Supreme Court. *Asahi Metal Indus. v. Superior Court*, 480 U.S. 102, 107 S. Ct. 1026, 94 L. Ed. 2d 92 (1987); *Burger King Corp. v. Rudzewicz*, 471 U.S. 462, 105 S. Ct. 2174, 85 L. Ed. 2d 528 (1985); *Helicopteros Nacionales de Colombia v. Hall*, 466 U.S. 408, 104 S. Ct. 1868, 80 L. Ed. 2d 404 (1984); *World-Wide Volkswagen Corp. v. Woodson*, 444 U.S. 286, 100 S. Ct. 559, 62 L. Ed. 2d 490 (1980); *International Shoe Co. v. Washington*, 326 U.S. 310, 66 S. Ct. 154, 90 L. Ed. 95 (1945). Suffice it to say that the rule in these cases is that a state court can take personal jurisdiction over a defendant only if it has some minimum, purposeful contacts with the state, and the exercise of jurisdiction will not offend traditional notions of fair play and substantial justice.

CMMC's only contacts with Texas are that it made isolated sales of equipment to customers here, and that it knew the machine it sold KLR was being shipped here. Salinas argues, and the court of appeals agreed, that CMMC's release of its winepress into the stream of commerce with knowledge of the intended destination is sufficient to subject it to personal jurisdiction under our decisions in *Keen v. Ashot Ashkelon, Ltd.*, 748 S.W.2d 91 (Tex. 1988), and *Kawasaki Steel Corp. v. Middleton*, 699 S.W.2d 199 (Tex. 1985) (per curiam), which follow the rule of *World-Wide Volkswagen Corp. v. Woodson*, 444 U.S. at 286, 100 S. Ct. at 561–562, and *Asahi Metal Industry v. Superior Court*, 480 U.S. at 102, 107 S. Ct. at 1026–1027.

In *World-Wide Volkswagen*, the United States Supreme Court stated a basis for personal jurisdiction that has come to be referred to as the stream-of-commerce doctrine:

> [I]f the sale of a product of a manufacturer or a distributor . . . is not simply an isolated occurrence, but arises from the efforts of the manufacturer or distributor to serve, directly or indirectly, the market for its product in other States, it is not unreasonable to subject it to suit in one of those States if its allegedly defective merchandise has there been the source of injury to its owner or to others. The forum State does not exceed its powers under the Due Process Clause if it asserts personal jurisdiction over a corporation that delivered its products into the stream of commerce with the expectation that they will be purchased by consumers in the forum State.

*World-Wide Volkswagen*, 444 U.S. at 297–298, 100 S. Ct. at 567. Applying this rule, the Court held that a car distributor and a retail dealer, both doing business in New York, did not have minimum contacts with Oklahoma simply because cars they sold ended up in that state.

Seven years later, the Court was unable to agree on the scope of the rule stated in *World-Wide Volkswagen*. In *Asahi*, a motorcyclist filed suit in a California court to recover damages for personal injuries. Settlements among the parties left pending only a cross-claim between two defendants: a claim for indemnity by a Taiwanese tire tube manufacturer, Cheng Shin Rubber Industrial Company, against a Japanese manufacturer of the tube's valve assembly, Asahi Metal Industry Company. Cheng Shin argued that the state court had jurisdiction over Asahi because Asahi was aware that its valve assemblies sold to Cheng Shin and others would be incorporated in their products and would end up in the United States, generally, and in California, in particular. Asahi did not design its products specifically for use in California and did not attempt to market them there. Asahi had no other contacts with California.

Justice O'Connor, writing for a four-Member plurality, concluded that Asahi did not have sufficient contacts with California to be subject to personal jurisdiction in state court. Asahi's mere awareness that its products might end up in California was not enough to show that it purposely availed itself of the California market. Regarding the stream-of-commerce doctrine of *World-Wide Volkswagen*, Justice O'Connor explained:

> Since *World-Wide Volkswagen*, lower courts have been confronted with cases in which the defendant acted by placing a product in the stream of commerce, and the stream eventually swept defendant's product into the forum State, but the defendant did nothing else to purposefully avail itself of the market in the forum State. Some courts have understood the Due Process Clause, as interpreted in *World-Wide Volkswagen*, to allow an exercise of personal jurisdiction to be based on no more than the defendant's act of placing the product in the stream of commerce. Other courts have understood the Due Process Clause and the above-quoted language in *World-Wide Volkswagen* to require the action of the defendant to be more purposefully directed at the forum State than the mere act of placing a product in the stream of commerce.
>
> * * *
>
> We now find this latter position to be consonant with the requirements of due process. The "substantial connection" between the defendant and the forum State necessary for a finding of minimum contacts must come about *by an action of the defendant purposefully directed toward the forum State*. The placement of a product into the stream of commerce, without more, is not an act of the defendant purposefully directed toward the forum State. Additional conduct of the defendant may indicate an intent or purpose to serve the market in the forum State, for example, designing the product for the market in the forum State, advertising in the forum State, establishing channels for providing regular advice to customers in the forum State, or marketing the product through a distributor who has agreed to serve as the sales agent in the forum State. But a defendant's awareness that the stream of commerce may or will sweep the product into the forum State does not convert the mere act of placing the product into the stream into an act purposefully directed toward the forum State.

*Asahi*, 480 U.S. at 110–112, 107 S. Ct. at 1031–1032 (citations omitted). Justice Brennan expressed the opposing view:

> I see no need for [a showing of additional conduct directed toward the forum]. The stream of commerce refers not to unpredictable currents or eddies, but to the regular and anticipated flow of products from manufacture to distribution to retail sale. As long as a participant

> in *this process* is aware that the final product is being marketed in the forum State, the possibility of a lawsuit there cannot come as a surprise. Nor will the litigation present a burden for which there is no corresponding benefit. A defendant who has placed goods in the stream of commerce benefits economically from the retail sale of the final product in the forum State, and indirectly benefits from the State's laws that regulate and facilitate commercial activity. These benefits accrue regardless of whether that participant directly conducts business in the forum State, or engages in additional conduct directed toward that State. Accordingly, most courts and commentators have found that jurisdiction premised on the placement of a product into the stream of commerce is consistent with the Due Process Clause, and have not required a showing of additional conduct.

*Asahi*, 480 U.S. at 117, 107 S. Ct. at 1034–1035 (Brennan, J., concurring in part) (emphasis added, footnote omitted).

Even if a defendant has substantial contacts with a state, the state court cannot exercise personal jurisdiction over the defendant if to do so would offend traditional notions of fairness. In *Asahi*, the Supreme Court was unanimous in holding that it was unfair to subject Asahi to the jurisdiction of a California court.

For now, we need not take sides in the *Asahi* debate over the stream-of-commerce doctrine because of the difference in the factual circumstances of that case and the one now before us. Asahi's products were regularly sold in California, although not by Asahi. CMMC's wine-producing equipment did not regularly find its way to Texas. Neither CMMC nor KLR made any effort to market CMMC's equipment in Texas, other than by advertisements in magazines with national circulation. Hill Country Cellars' purchase was an isolated event. KLR did not contact Hill Country Cellars; Hill Country Cellars contacted KLR. Hill Country Cellars never had any contacts at all with CMMC. CMMC's mere knowledge that its winepress was to be sold and used in Texas and its wiring the machine for use in the United States were not sufficient to subject CMMC to the jurisdiction of Texas courts. This evidence simply does not show that CMMC designed products for use in Texas, or that it made any effort to market them here, or that it took any other action to purposely avail itself of this market. Even Justice Brennan's view of the stream-of-commerce doctrine would not allow jurisdiction absent a "regular and anticipated flow of products from manufacture to distribution to retail sale." *Id.* There is no flow of products from CMMC to Texas; there is scarcely a dribble.

The court of appeals cited two Fifth Circuit cases recognizing that even one act by a defendant can support jurisdiction. *Ruston Gas Turbines, Inc. v. Donaldson Co.*, 9 F.3d 415, 419 (5th Cir. 1993); *Irving v. Owens-Corning Fiberglas Corp.*, 864 F.2d 383, 385 (5th Cir. 1989), *cert. denied*, 493 U.S. 823, 110 S. Ct. 83, 107 L. Ed. 2d 49. Still, that act must be purposefully directed at the forum state so that the defendant could foresee being haled into court there. *See, e.g., Burger King*, 471 U.S. at 475, 105 S. Ct. at 2183–2184; *World-Wide Volkswagen*, 444 U.S. at 297–298, 100 S. Ct. at 567–568; *Ruston*, 9 F.3d at 419; *Irving*, 864 F.2d at 385–386. Single or even occasional acts are not sufficient to support jurisdiction if, as here, " 'their nature and quality and the circumstances of their commission' create only an'attenuated' affiliation with the forum." *Burger King*, 471 U.S. at 475, n. 18, 105 S. Ct. at 2184, n.18 (citing *International Shoe*, 326 U.S. at 318, 66 S. Ct. at 159).

This Court has followed the United States Supreme Court's stream-of-commerce rule, as of course we must. In *Kawasaki*, we held that a foreign steel manufacturer that confirmed orders for millions of dollars of steel annually to be shipped to Texas consumers had sufficient contacts to be subject to suit here. 699 S.W.2d at 201. The result would have been the same under either of the views expressed in *Asahi*. We cited *Kawasaki* and *Asahi* in *Keen*, stating: "A defendant's delivering of its product into the stream of commerce with the expectation that the product will enter the forum state will ordinarily satisfy the due process requirement of minimum contacts so as to afford that state personal jurisdiction over the defendant." *Keen*, 748 S.W.2d at 93. We did not by this one sentence extend the reach of Texas jurisdiction beyond that allowed by *World-Wide Volkswagen*, or even beyond that which Justice Brennan would have allowed in *Asahi*. Indeed, we could not have done so even if we had wanted to, bound as we are in this area by the decisions of the United States Supreme Court. To the contrary, we cited Justice O'Connor's plurality opinion twice and did not mention Justice Brennan's concurring opinion. If anything, *Keen* suggests that we would follow Justice O'Connor's formulation of the stream-of-commerce rule in Texas.

It is neither unfair nor unjust to require Salinas to litigate his disputes with CMMC at CMMC's place of business when neither he nor his employer ever had any contact whatever with CMMC in Texas. A manufacturer cannot fairly be expected to litigate in every part of the world where its products may end up; its contacts with the forum must be more purposeful, even in Justice Brennan's view, before it can constitutionally be subjected to personal jurisdiction. As we recently stated, echoing *Burger King Corp. v. Rudzewicz*, "[a] defendant should not be subject to the jurisdiction of a foreign court based upon 'random,' 'fortuitous,' or 'attenuated' contacts." *CSR*, 925 S.W.2d at 594 (quoting *Burger King*, 471 U.S. at 475, 105 S. Ct. at 2183). "Minimum contacts are particularly important when the defendant is from a different country because of the unique and onerous burden placed on a party called upon to defend a suit in a foreign legal system." *Id.* at 595. Here, those contacts are missing.

Accordingly, the judgment of the court of appeals is reversed and the judgment of the district court dismissing CMMC is affirmed.

---

## NOTES AND QUESTIONS

(1) *The O'Brien Test.* Given the discussion of the *O'Brien* test in Parts III and IV of the Court's opinion in *Guardian Royal,* what is the continuing significance of the test to the law of personal jurisdiction in Texas?

(2) *Expansion of General Jurisdiction?* The Texas Supreme Court has taken an expansive view of general jurisdiction in *Schlobohm v. Schapiro,* 784 S.W.2d 355, 359 (Tex. 1990), a case in which an investor was sued for a corporate rental obligation owed by his corporation to a Texas landlord, despite the fact that the investor had not guaranteed that obligation. The following excerpt from the opinion indicates the Court's reasoning:

> Our first inquiry centers on the second part of the formula, the question whether jurisdiction in this case is premised on continuing and systematic activity or on a cause of action that arises from isolated and sporadic activity. The Schlobohms rely on the number and continuity of Schapiro's actions to support their proposition that an activity in which Schapiro did not directly participate, that is, the negotiation and signing of their lease, subjects him to jurisdiction. Their claim of jurisdiction is, therefore, based on continuing

> and systematic activity. Schapiro further agrees that he did maintain a number of contacts with Texas. Despite this concession, however, he insists that his "primary" contacts amount to nothing more than his negotiation for the equipment loan and his status as sole stockholder of Hangers.
>
> . . . .
>
> Schapiro became actively involved in a Texas business and voluntarily continued his commitment for almost two years. He was investor, stockholder, director, advisor, lender, and guarantor for Hangers. He visited the state and maintained regular communication with some of its citizens. When we consider the degree of his involvement, we regard it difficult to believe that anyone in Schapiro's position could have been surprised by the call to litigation in Texas. It is clear that he purposefully availed himself of the benefits of this forum. We hold that Schapiro's minimum contacts with Texas were continuing and systematic enough to subject him to the jurisdiction of a Texas court.

Another expansive view of the state's long-arm power under general jurisdiction, is found in *Project Engineering USA, Corp. v. Gator Hawk, Inc.*, 833 S.W.2d 716 (Tex. App.—Houston [1st Dist.] 1992, no writ). General jurisdiction was found proper because the defendant had visited Texas for business purposes on a few occasions and signed a contract in Texas. Defendant had objected on the basis that it had no employees, servants, or agents in Texas, had no place of business in Texas, and conducted the majority of its business with Texas companies in California.

(3) *Stream of Commerce.* Do the Texas Supreme Court's opinions in the *CSR* and *CMMC* cases accurately reflect the disagreement between the justices of the United States Supreme Court in *Asahi* about "stream of commerce" cases? Does *CMMC* create a new "isolated occurrence" test?

### [C] Interrelated Businesses and the Scope of the General Texas Long-Arm Statute

Corporations or other business entities that have parent-subsidiary relationships, control over one another, joint venture agreements or simply patterns of dealing present frequent, and knotty, due process issues under long-arm statutes. Consider the cases below and their divergent results.

---

**REUL v. SAHARA HOTEL**, 372 F. Supp. 995 (S.D. Tex. 1974). A Texas husband and wife filed a products liability claim in federal district court in Texas after they were injured in a chlorine tank explosion at the Sahara Hotel in Las Vegas, Nevada. The tank had been furnished to the hotel by a California corporation, which was a wholly owned subsidiary of a New York corporation. The New York corporation was a closely held family corporation and was qualified to do business in Texas. The California corporation had never sold or solicited the sale of any product or service on its own behalf in Texas, had received no income from the sale of any products or services in the state, had not been granted a permit to do business in Texas, owned no property in the state, and maintained no offices or personnel in Texas. The California corporation filed a motion to quash service and to dismiss the case. As one basis for its motion, the corporation alleged lack of personal jurisdiction.

In sustaining both service and jurisdiction, the court first focused on the meaning and application of the phrase, "without including other acts that may constitute doing business," in

Section 4 of the general Texas long-arm statute (at the time of the case, R.C.S. Art. 2031b; *see now* C.P.R.C. § 17.041 et seq.):

> Most courts have been faced with the rather clear-cut question of finding a tort or a contract upon which to base the finding that the corporation was "doing business" in Texas. As Professor Thode pointed out in his historical treatise on Article 2031(b), however, the words "without including other acts that may constitute doing business," contained in § 4 of the article, were perhaps an inelegant attempt to keep the statute from being limited to torts and contracts. Thode, *In Personam Jurisdiction; Art. 2031(b), The Texas "Long Arm" Statute; and the Appearance to Challenge Jurisdiction in Texas and Elsewhere*, 42 Tex. L. Rev. 279 (1964). This court believes that that language is perfectly suited to the instant case. While the California corporation has clearly not committed a tort in Texas nor entered into a contract to be performed in Texas, its very relationship with its parent corporation gives rise to a situation in which its "acts . . . constitute doing business." Since there is no question that the New York parent is amenable to process in Texas and is within the court's jurisdiction, this court is convinced that the actual relationship between parent and subsidiary permits the California subsidiary to be amenable to process in Texas via 2031(b).

*Reul v. Sahara Hotel*, 372 F. Supp. 995, 998 (S.D. Tex. 1974)

The facts the court deemed relevant in finding a single enterprise for jurisdictional purposes included: (1) the closely held nature of the enterprise, (2) common ownership, (3) common directors and management, (4) the interchangeability of employees, (5) common offices in New York, (6) common advertisement which did not distinguish among the corporations, and (7) central administration of business out of New York. The court noted:

> [T]he fact pattern as presented in the depositions taken relating to the questions before the court at this time leads to the conclusion that there is present here more than that amount of control of one corporation over another which mere common ownership and directorship would indicate.
>
> . . . .
>
> [T]he five subsidiary corporations are not autonomous units but constitute completely integrated subsidiaries which exist for the convenience of the parent corporation, its stockholders, officers, and directors. Except for the actual sales and services to their local customers, the corporations carry on no local activities. Everything else is done for them in New York just as everything for the sales and service aspect of the New York corporation's business is done for it in New York.
>
> The evidence presented to the court at this point has revealed a situation of complete control of the subsidiary California corporation by the parent New York corporation. Since the New York corporation clearly does business in Texas, the court holds, accordingly, that the activities of the New York corporation in Texas can be imputed to the California corporation. For purposes of Article 2031(b) in personam jurisdiction, the California corporation can be said to be "doing business" in Texas.

*Reul v. Sahara Hotel*, 372 F. Supp. 995, 998–1002 (S.D. Tex. 1974)

The court then addressed the provision in sec. 3 of art. 2031(b) allowing service of process in actions "arising out of such business" and the second prong of the *O'Brien v. Lanpar* test:

> In the case at hand, any doubt about whether or not the cause of action "arises from" or is "connected with" the activities carried on in Texas by Jones Chemicals can best be

> answered by the fact that the activities of Jones Chemicals are carried out on a nationwide scale. The activities which are performed in Texas by the New York parent are the same activities which are performed in Nevada by the California subsidiary. These activities are the same activities which are alleged to have caused the explosion of the chlorine tank in Nevada; and in that sense, the cause of action is connected with the parent's activities in Texas.

*Reul v. Sahara Hotel*, 372 F. Supp. 995, 1002 (S.D. Tex. 1974)

---

**PRODUCT PROMOTIONS, INC. v. COUSTEAU**, 495 F.2d 483 (5th Cir. 1974). Product Promotions entered into a contract with Centre d'Etude Marines Advancees ("CEMA"), one of a group of entities that the court described as "spinoffs from [Jacques] Cousteau's oceanic exploits." On alleged breach, Product Promotions brought suit in Texas and, as is frequently the case in such situations, attempted to join Cousteau and related entities (the "Cousteau Group Companies") on the theory that they were "doing business" in Texas through CEMA, as their agent, alter ego or subsidiary. The court analyzed the contention as follows:

> Under this theory the alleged agency and parent-subsidiary relationships were facts on which jurisdiction was predicated, and appellant had the burden of making a *prima facie* showing of their existence. It is here that appellant founders from the confusion surrounding the identity of and relationship between the parties defendant. We can find no evidence in the record before us that CEMA was, as appellant argues, a subsidiary of the "Cousteau Group Companies," even assuming such a separate corporate entity existed. And even were we to assume the existence of a parent-subsidiary relationship, we can find no evidence that the parent exercised the type of control necessary to ascribe to it the activities of the subsidiary. Nor can we find any support for the assertion that the Cousteau Group Companies, either individually or collectively, were the "alter-egos" of Jacques Cousteau. [footnote omitted] Certainly the hearsay testimony regarding Horton's statement to Ross that Cousteau does business through the Cousteau Group Companies does not suffice. We concede that the evidence in the record shows that the so-called Cousteau Group Companies were, at least at the time this contract was executed, related in some way to each other and to Jacques Cousteau. Unfortunately, that is not enough; it was for appellant to sort out those business relationships, and the failure to do so is jurisdictionally fatal.
>
> We are likewise convinced that appellant failed to carry the burden of establishing by prima facie evidence the existence of any agency relationship between CEMA and the other defendants other than that based on parent-subsidiary or alter-ego status. Under well-settled principles of law, appellant had to make a *prima facie* showing that in this contractual dealing CEMA acted with either actual or apparent authority on behalf of the others. [footnote omitted] Both types of authority depend for their creation on some manifestations, written or spoken words or conduct, by the principal, communicated either to the agent (actual authority) or to the third party (apparent authority).

*Product Promotions, Inc. v. Cousteau*, 495 F.2d 483, 492–493 (5th Cir. 1974), *overruled on other grounds*, *Insurance Corp. of Ireland v. Compagnie des Bauxites de Guinee*, 456 U.S. 694, 702–703, 102 S. Ct. 2099, 72 L. Ed. 2d 492 (1982), as stated in *Burstein v. State Bar of Ca.*, 693 F.2d 511, 518 n.12 (5th Cir. 1982).

---

**NATIONAL INDUS. SAND ASS'N v. GIBSON,** 897 S.W.2d 769 (Tex. 1995). The National Industrial Sand Association (NISA), a nonprofit lobbying association representing the interests of the sandblasting industry and headquartered in Maryland, was sued in Texas as one of several defendants in plaintiffs' silicosis suit. Plaintiffs alleged NISA was engaged in a conspiracy with Texas Mining Company to suppress information on the dangers of silica. The trial court found sufficient basis for exercising personal jurisdiction over NISA; the court of appealst denied mandamus relief, holding that NISA had an adequate remedy by way of appeal from a final judgment, rather than by immediate mandamus relief. However, the Texas Supreme Court conditionally issued mandamus. Finding NISA's contacts within Texas insufficient, the court "decline[d] to recognize the assertion of personal jurisdiction over a nonresident defendant based solely upon the effects or consequences of an alleged conspiracy with a resident of the forum state." 897 S.W.2d at 773. The dissent took issue with NISA's failure to demonstrate that ordinary appeal would not be an adequate remedy—a " 'fundamental tenet' of mandamus practice." The dissent cited *Canadian Helicopters Ltd. v. Wittig*, 876 S.W.2d 304 (Tex. 1994), for the principle that mandamus should issue for the denial of a special appearance only if the harm to the defendant is irreparable, involving more than increased cost and delay.

### [D] TBCA Provisions and the General Texas Long-Arm Statute

Consider the following sections of the Texas Business Corporation Act (TBCA). What relationship do they bear to the general Texas long-arm statute? What bearing, if any, do they have on the problem of a corporation that does business in Texas but is sued on a claim unrelated to that business? Do the exceptions to the requirement of a certificate of authority constitute exceptions from the general Texas Long-Arm Statute?

BUSINESS CORPORATION ACT

Bus. Corp. Act Art. 8.01. *Admission of Foreign Corporation*

A. No foreign corporation shall have the right to transact business in this State until it shall have procured a certificate of authority so to do from the Secretary of State.

. . . .

B. Without excluding other activities which may not constitute transacting business in this state, a foreign corporation shall not be considered to be transacting business in this state, for the purposes of this Act, by reason of carrying on in this state any one (1) or more of the following activities:

. . . [The statute contains 13 subsections listing such activities as being a party to a suit, holding corporate meetings, maintaining bank accounts, maintaining transfer agents, voting stock, using independent contractors to effect sales, creating debts or mortgages, collecting debts, "transacting any business in interstate commerce," conducting an isolated transaction, acting as executor or administrator, and acquiring certain property such as accounts payable or mineral interests.]

Bus. Corp. Act Art. 8.10. *Service of Process on Foreign Corporation*

A. The president and all vice presidents of a foreign corporation authorized to transact business in this State and the registered agent so appointed by a foreign corporation shall be agents of such corporation upon whom any process, notice, or demand required or permitted by law to be served upon the corporation may be served.

B. Whenever a foreign corporation authorized to transact business in this State shall fail to appoint or maintain a registered agent in this State, or whenever any such registered agent cannot with reasonable diligence be found at the registered office, or whenever the certificate of authority of a foreign corporation shall be revoked, then the Secretary of State shall be an agent of such corporation upon whom any such process, notice, or demand may be served. Service on the Secretary of State of any such process, notice, or demand shall be made by delivering to and leaving with him, or with the Assistant Secretary of State, or with any clerk having charge of the corporation department of his office, duplicate copies of such process, notice, or demand. In the event any such process, notice or demand is served on the Secretary of State, he shall immediately cause one of such copies thereof to be forwarded by registered mail, addressed to the corporation at its principal office in the state or country under the laws of which it is incorporated. Any service so had on the Secretary of State shall be returnable in not less than thirty days.

C. The Secretary of State shall keep a record of all processes, notices and demands served upon him under this Article, and shall record therein the time of such service and his action with reference thereto.

D. Nothing herein contained shall limit or affect the right to serve any process, notice, or demand required or permitted by law to be served upon a foreign corporation in any other manner now or hereafter permitted by law.

---

## NOTES AND QUESTIONS

(1) *The Significance of an Appointed Agent.* In *Juarez v. United Parcel Service de Mexico S.A. de C.V.*, 933 S.W.2d 281 (Tex. App.—Corpus Christi 1996, no writ), the court declined to exercise personal jurisdiction in a personal injury suit between Mexican citizens and a Mexican corporation, arising out of an accident that took place wholly in Mexico. The defendant corporation had regular contacts in Texas (though the contacts were unrelated to the accident) and had appointed an agent for service of process in Texas. Nonetheless, the court of appeals held that an appointed agent for service was, of itself, insufficient to indicate consent to general jurisdiction, but rather was only one factor to be considered in the overall jurisdictional analysis. Furthermore, considering the defendant's minimal contacts, the court found that the exercise of jurisdiction would offend traditional notions of fair play and substantial justice, emphasizing the lack of connection to Texas, the burden on the defendants of defending in Texas, and Mexico's interest in providing a forum and a remedy for disputes between its citizens.

(2) When does the general Texas long-arm statute apply to a corporation "authorized to transact business" in Texas?

(3) Does the TBCA provision permit service when a corporation should be "authorized" but is not "authorized to transact business"? *Compare* Bus. Corp. Act Art. 8.01 *with* Bus. Corp. Act Art. 8.10.

## § 4.03 Other Long-Arm Statutes: The Family Code

The long-arm provisions of the Texas Family Code are contained in Sections 6.305 and 102.011. As you will see below, Section 6.305 deals with the exercise of personal jurisdiction over a nonresident respondent in a suit to dissolve the matrimonial relationship whereas section 11.051 concerns suits affecting the parent-child relationship:

FAMILY CODE

Fam. C. § 6.305. *Acquiring Jurisdiction Over Nonresident Respondent*

(a) If the petitioner is a resident or a domiciliary of this state at the time the suit for dissolution is filed, the court may exercise personal jurisdiction over the respondent, or the respondent's personal representative, although the respondent is not a resident of this state if:

(1) this state is the last marital residence of the petitioner and the respondent and the suit is commenced within two years after the date on which marital residence ended; or

(2) there is any basis consistent with the constitutions of this state and the United States for the exercise of the personal jurisdiction.

(b) A court acquiring jurisdiction under this section also acquires jurisdiction over the respondent in a suit affecting the parent-child relationship.

Fam. C. § 102.011. *Acquiring Jurisdiction Over Nonresident*

(a) The court may exercise status or subject matter jurisdiction over the suit as provided by Chapter 152 [containing provisions of the Uniform Child Custody Jurisdiction Act].

(b) The court may also exercise personal jurisdiction over a person on whom service of citation is required or over the person's personal representative, although the person is not a resident or domiciliary of this state, if:

(1) the person is personally served with citation in this state;

(2) the person submits to the jurisdiction of this state by consent, by entering a general appearance, or by filing a responsive document having the effect of waiving any contest to personal jurisdiction;

(3) the child resides in this state as a result of the acts or directives of the person;

(4) the person resided with the child in this state;

(5) the person resided in this state and provided prenatal expenses or support for the child;

(6) the person engaged in sexual intercourse in this state and the child may have been conceived by that act of intercourse; or

(7) there is any basis consistent with the constitutions of this state and the United States for the exercise of the personal jurisdiction.

To interpret these provisions and understand their application, you must bring to bear your understanding of the full faith and credit clause and due process. *See* Dorsaneo, *Due Process, Full Faith and Credit, and Family Law Litigation,* 36 Sw. L. J. 1085 (1983). Because of considerations associated with full faith and credit and due process, the treatment of custody and termination has bedeviled the courts at all levels. Neither the teachings of *Pennoyer* (*See* § 4.01[A]) nor the conceptual scheme embodied in the *International Shoe* opinion (prior to its reformulation in *Shaffer v. Heitner*) handled custody litigation easily. Thus, lower courts have struggled with custody cases more than virtually any other species of domestic relations litigation. One result of the confusion has been the passage of uniform state legislation such as the Uniform Child Custody Jurisdiction Act, passed by the Texas state legislature in 1983.

---

## IN INTEREST OF S.A.V.

*837 S.W.2d 80 (Tex. 1992)*

COOK, Justice.

This case involves complex jurisdictional issues arising from a Texas trial court's modification of a Minnesota divorce decree. We must decide whether the Texas court could exercise jurisdiction to modify the decree with respect to four areas: child support, visitation expense, custody, and actual visitation arrangements. The court of appeals determined that the Texas court could exercise jurisdiction to modify child support and visitation expense but that the Texas court could not exercise jurisdiction to modify custody or visitation. 798 S.W.2d 293. Because we hold that the trial court could exercise jurisdiction over all these issues, we affirm in part and reverse in part the judgment of the court of appeals.

### I. FACTS AND PROCEDURAL HISTORY

The mother and the father, both physicians, were married on June 7, 1980 in Minnesota. They continued to reside in Minnesota throughout their marriage. The mother and the father entered a stipulated divorce decree in 1986. The decree contained specific provisions relating to the two minor children of the marriage. The decree provided for joint custody of the children with the mother having physical custody. The decree also provided for visitation. In addition, the decree set out each parent's child support obligation. Each parent was obligated to pay child support when the children resided with the other parent for more than one week.

The mother moved to Amarillo in the spring of 1987. The children joined her there in August 1987. The father has continued to reside in Minnesota since the divorce.

On October 22, 1987, the Minnesota court modified its divorce decree. The court implemented a provision in the original decree which provided that the mother's child support obligation would be increased if her annual income reached $60,000. In addition, the Minnesota court held that the parties could deduct their visitation expenses from their child support obligation. This modification was made to allow for the visitation expenses the father incurred when traveling to Amarillo to see the children.

On January 19, 1989, the mother brought the instant action in Texas to modify the Minnesota court's October 1987 order. The mother asked the trial court to terminate the offset for visitation expenses. Additionally, she asked that she not be required to pay any child support to the father and that the court modify the joint conservatorship of the children.

The next day the father filed a motion to modify the same decree in a Minnesota court. The father asked that the mother be ordered to pay additional child support and that the offset for visitation expenses be maintained.

Simultaneous modification proceedings in Texas and Minnesota resulted.

In order to object to the Texas trial court's exercise of jurisdiction, the father entered a special appearance pursuant to Rule 120a of the Texas Rules of Civil Procedure. The father's challenge to the Texas court's jurisdiction took two forms. First, the father objected to the trial court's exercise of subject matter jurisdiction to modify custody. Second, the father objected to the trial court's exercise of personal jurisdiction over him to modify his child support obligation. The trial court denied his special appearance and determined that it had subject matter jurisdiction over the case and personal jurisdiction over the father.

Before the Texas court reached the merits of the case, the Minnesota court issued an order modifying the Minnesota decree. The Minnesota order modified the parties' child support obligations and terminated the offset of visitation expenses. The Minnesota order did not alter custody or visitation.

After the Minnesota court had rendered its order, the Texas trial court issued an order modifying the Minnesota decree. The Texas court's order mirrored the Minnesota order with respect to child support and visitation expenses. However, the Texas order dissolved the joint conservatorship and appointed the mother as sole managing conservator. The order also narrowed and specified the father's visitation rights. The father appealed the Texas court's order modifying the Minnesota decree arguing that the trial court did not have subject matter jurisdiction over the case or personal jurisdiction over him. Additionally, the father challenged the merits of the trial court's modification of visitation and custody.

On April 5, 1989, while the case was pending beforc the Texas court of appeals, the Minnesota trial court entered a separate order that unconditionally asserted jurisdiction over child support issues. The order also conditionally asserted continuing jurisdiction over the custody issues involved in this case. The Minnesota trial court's assertion of jurisdiction over custody was expressly conditioned on an appellate court ruling. On December 24, 1990, the Minnesota court of appeals issued an opinion affirming the April 5th order of the Minnesota trial court.

In the appeal of the Texas order, the court of appeals determined that, by raising the issue of subject matter jurisdiction in his special appearance, the father made a general appearance before the trial court. Therefore, the court held that the father had subjected himself to the personal jurisdiction of the Texas court. As a result, the court of appeals determined that the trial court's modification of the father's support obligation and offset of visitation expenses was proper. The court determined, however, that the Texas court's modification of the Minnesota order as it related to custody and actual visitation arrangements was improper under the Parental Kidnaping Prevention Act of 1980 (PKPA), 28 U.S.C.A. § 1738A (West Supp. 1990).

## II. DUE PROCESS REQUIREMENTS

We begin our examination of the issues presented in this case by examining the distinct due process requirements necessary for the proper exercise of jurisdiction over child support, visitation expense, child custody, and visitation.

### A. Child Support and Visitation Expenses

Claims for child support and visitation expenses are like claims for debt in that they seek a personal judgment establishing a direct obligation to pay money. *See Creavin v. Moloney,* 773 S.W.2d 698, 703 (Tex. App.—Corpus Christi 1989, writ denied); *Perry v. Ponder,* 604 S.W.2d 306, 312–13 (Tex. Civ. App.—Dallas 1980, no writ). Therefore, a valid judgment for child support or visitation expenses may be rendered only by a court having jurisdiction over the person of the defendant. *See Kulko v. Superior Court of California,* 436 U.S. 84, 91, 98 S. Ct. 1690, 1696, 56 L. Ed. 2d 132 (1978).

### B. Custody and Visitation

A "custody determination" means a court decision providing for the custody of a child, including visitation rights. Tex. Fam. Code Ann. § 11.52 (Vernon 1986). Unlike adjudications of child support and visitation expense, custody determinations are status adjudications not dependent upon personal jurisdiction over the parents. *See Creavin,* 773 S.W.2d at 703; *Perry,* 604 S.W.2d at 313; *see also Shaffer v. Heitner,* 433 U.S. 186, 208 n.30, 97 S. Ct. 2569, 2582 n.30, 53 L. Ed. 2d 683 (1977).

Generally, a family relationship is among those matters in which the forum state has such a strong interest that its courts may reasonably make an adjudication affecting that relationship even though one of the parties to the relationship may have had no personal contacts with the forum state. *See Creavin,* 773 S.W.2d at 703; *Perry,* 604 S.W.2d at 313. Consequently, due process permits adjudication of the custody and visitation of a child residing in the forum state without a showing of "minimum contacts" on the part of the nonresident parent. *See Creavin,* 773 S.W.2d at 703; *Perry,* 604 S.W.2d at 313.

The Texas legislature recognized the state's strong interest in determining the custody of children by adopting the Uniform Child Custody Jurisdiction Act (UCCJA). Tex. Fam Code Ann. § 11.51 *et seq.* (Vernon Supp. 1992). To acquire jurisdiction over custody issues, no connection between the nonresident parent and the state is required. Instead, jurisdiction can be established by demonstrating that Texas has become the child's "home state." *Id.* at § 11.53. Texas will become the child's home state when the child has resided here for six months, or since birth if the child is young than six months. *Id.* at § 11.52(5). Alternatively, a Texas court may assert jurisdiction to modify custody when the best interests of the child will be served because the child and at least one contesting parent have a significant connection with Texas and substantial evidence concerning the child's care exists in Texas. *Id.* at § 11.53(a)(2).

If the requirements of the Family Code are satisfied, the state's interest in determining custody has been demonstrated. That is, the state has acquired a sovereign's interests in and responsibility for the child's welfare. In such a situation, the state's interest in the child's welfare outweighs the nonresident parent's interest in avoiding the burden and inconvenience of defending the suit in Texas. Therefore, due process does not require that a connection exist between the nonresident parent and this state. In adjudications of custody, once these jurisdictional provisions have been satisfied, the court can properly exercise jurisdiction over the nonresident. Satisfaction of these provisions confers "personal jurisdiction" over the nonresident as well as subject matter jurisdiction over the case. *See Creavin,* 773 S.W.2d at 703; *Perry,* 604 S.W.2d at 313–14.

### III. JURISDICTION OVER CHILD SUPPORT AND VISITATION EXPENSE

Because custody adjudications do not require minimum contacts with the forum state, disputes involving both custody and child support create a unique jurisdictional problem for courts. A custody adjudication may be made by a court that has no jurisdiction to render a personal judgment for support against a nonresident parent. This difficulty, however, is inherent in our system of jurisdiction as a result of the separate due process requirements for adjudications of custody and adjudications of child support. With this inherent difficulty in mind, we must now attempt to reach a result that is both fair to the parties and in the best interest of the children.

. . .

#### B. Minimum Contacts Analysis

Because the father properly preserved his right to challenge the trial court's exercise of personal jurisdiction over him, we must determine whether that exercise of jurisdiction was proper. For a Texas court to properly exercise jurisdiction in suits seeking to impose a personal obligation to pay money, such as child support modification proceedings, two conditions must be met. First, a Texas long-arm statute must authorize the exercise of jurisdiction. Second, the exercise of jurisdiction must be consistent with federal and state constitutional guarantees of due process. *Schlobohm v. Schapiro,* 784 S.W.2d 355, 356 (Tex. 1990).

Section 11.051 of the Family Code provides the Texas courts with personal jurisdiction over nonresident parents with regard to child support. Subsection 4 of that provision requires only "any basis" consistent with due process. Tex. Fam. Code Ann. § 11.05(4) (Vernon 1986).

. . . .

With the federal and state guidelines in mind, we hold that the Texas trial court's exercise of jurisdiction did not violate the father's right to due process.

First, the father purposefully established minimum contacts with Texas. There was a substantial connection between the father and Texas arising from his repeated visits to Texas. Although it is unclear exactly how often the father came to Texas, the record reflects that he visited Amarillo so often between September 1987 and January 1989, that there were many months in which he was able to virtually eliminate his entire child support payment ($1800 per month) through his visitation expense offset.

In analyzing minimum contacts, we recognize that it is not the number of the contacts with the forum state that is important. Rather, the quality and nature of the nonresident defendant's contacts are important. *Guardian Royal,* 815 S.W.2d at 230 n.11. The record reflects that during his numerous trips to Texas, the father visited the children and sought employment in Amarillo. At the special appearance hearing, the father testified that on one trip to Amarillo he spent four hours with doctors at the Amarillo Diagnostic Clinic. During the visit, he inquired into the opportunities available at the clinic and expressed an interest in any openings that might arise. The father testified that on one trip to Amarillo he spent two hours making the rounds with another doctor at the clinic. This testimony indicates that the father's contacts with Texas included a continuing job search as well as visits with the children. Based on these facts, we find that the father purposefully established minimum contacts with Texas.

. . . .

Second, the Texas court's asserting of personal jurisdiction comports with fair play and substantial justice. The burden on the father of adjudicating the suit in Texas is not an extremely heavy one. Although there are many miles between Texas and Minnesota, modern transportation and communication have made it much less burdensome for a party sued to defend himself in a state where he has minimum contacts. *See generally McGee v. International Life Insurance Co.*, 355 U.S. 220, 223, 78 S. Ct. 199, 201, 2 L. Ed. 2d 223 (1957). Moreover, the father's repeated trips to Texas indicate that traveling to this state does not present an undue hardship on him. Additionally, Texas has asserted its particularized interest in adjudicating child support by enacting a special jurisdictional statute. *See* Tex. Fam. Code Ann. § 11.051 (Vernon 1986); *see also Kulko,* 436 U.S. at 98, 98 S. Ct. at 1700. Finally, Texas has a vital interest in protecting the rights of children within its borders and providing for their support. For these reasons, we hold that the Texas court's exercise of jurisdiction comports with fair play and substantial justice.

## IV. JURISDICTION OVER CUSTODY AND VISITATION

The UCCJA creates a system of concurrent jurisdiction in custody determinations. That is, two states may have subject matter jurisdiction to modify custody of the same children. This is true in the instant case. Because the children lived in Texas for a period in excess of six months before the proceedings in question, Texas is their "home state" under the Texas UCCJA and has acquired subject matter jurisdiction over the children's status. Tex. Fam. Code Ann. §§ 11.52(5), 11.53. Minnesota also had subject matter jurisdiction over the original custody determination made in the 1986 divorce decree and continues to have jurisdiction concerning the custody of the children. Min. Stat. Ann. § 518A.03 (West 1990). Therefore, Texas and Minnesota have concurrent jurisdiction over the same child custody question.

In order to prevent jurisdictional conflicts and competition over could custody, the United States Congress passed the Parental Kidnapping Prevention Act of 1980 (PKPA), 28 U.S.C.A. § 1738A (West Supp. 1990). The PKPA requires every state to give full faith and credit to child custody determinations of other states. 28 U.S.C.A. § 1738A(a). However, the PKPA provides that:

> A court of a State may modify a determination of the custody of the same child made by a court of another State, if
>
> (1) it has jurisdiction to make such a child custody determination; and
>
> (2) the court of the other State no longer has jurisdiction, or it has declined to exercise such jurisdiction to modify such determination.

28 U.S.C. § 1738A(f). In case of any conflict, the PKPA takes precedence over state law.

The court of appeals rejected the mother's argument that the Minnesota court declined to exercise its jurisdiction. The mother bases her argument on the April 5, 1990 order rendered by the Minnesota trial court while this case was pending before the Texas court of appeals. The Minnesota order states:

> CONCLUSIONS OF LAW
>
> 1. This Court has jurisdiction over all dissolution matters, including child support and visitation expenses.
>
> 2. This Court has continuing jurisdiction over child custody and visitation based on the children's best interests pursuant to Minnesota's version of the Uniform Child Custody Jurisdiction Act.

3. Minnesota is not an inconvenient forum.

4. This Court will decline to exercise its jurisdiction over child custody and visitation if Texas insists on exercising jurisdiction pursuant to an appellate court decision.

IT IS HEREBY ORDERED:

1. [The father's] motion for this Court to exercise jurisdiction is granted with respect to child support and visitation expenses and partially granted with respect to child support and visitation.

2. [The mother's] motion for this Court to decline jurisdiction is granted with respect to child custody and visitation issues if an appellate court rules this Court should not be exercising jurisdiction.

3. [The father] shall provide the Texas Court of Appeals and District Court with a copy of this Order and Memorandum.

The court of appeals determined that, although the Minnesota court appeared to decline jurisdiction in paragraph 4 of the above conclusions of law and paragraph 2 of the decree, when considered as a whole, the order did not decline jurisdiction within the meaning of the PKPA. Instead, the court of appeals concluded, those recitations were only a "praiseworthy attempt" by that Minnesota court to shorten the "period of uncertainty" by deferring to the Texas court of appeals' decision. 798 S.W.2d at 297. We disagree.

In its order, the Minnesota court recognizes that it has jurisdiction over all dissolution matters, i.e., child support, visitation expenses, child custody and visitation. The order, however, *asserts* jurisdiction only over child support and visitation expenses, those matters for which "minimum contacts" are required. The Minnesota court declines to exercise its subject matter jurisdiction over custody and visitation.

Our view is supported by the Minnesota court of appeals' opinion in the appeal of the April 1990 order. That opinion was issued following the Texas court of appeals' disposition of the case. The Minnesota court of appeals affirmed the Minnesota trial court's order and held that, if no appeal was taken from the Texas court of appeals' judgment, or this Court upheld the court of appeals, Minnesota would exercise jurisdiction over custody and visitation issues to assure that a "jurisdictional vacuum" would not occur. The Minnesota court went on to hold that if this Court affirmed the Texas trial court's exercise of jurisdiction over child custody and visitation, Minnesota "will *continue to decline* to exercise the jurisdiction it has over these issues." (emphasis added). In interpreting the actions of the Minnesota trial court, we respect the determination made by the Minnesota court of appeals that the trial court had declined to exercise jurisdiction over custody and visitation.

This case presents the difficulties inherent in the resolution of all interstate custody disputes. The cooperation of the Minnesota court of appeals has allowed us to resolve the jurisdictional questions with careful regard for the rights of the parties and the best interests of the children.

Because we determine that Minnesota had declined to exercise its jurisdiction over custody and visitation matters, the Texas court's exercise of jurisdiction over custody and visitation was proper under the PKPA.

## V. CONCLUSION

For the above reasons we affirm in part and reverse in part the judgment of the court of appeals. We hold that the trial court could exercise jurisdiction to modify the Minnesota decree as it related to child support, visitation expense, custody and visitation. The court of appeals determined that the trial court could not properly exercise jurisdiction over visitation and custody and, therefore, did not address the merits of the trial court's order modifying these aspects of the Minnesota decree. Because the father properly challenged the trial court's modification of visitation and custody, we remand this cause to the court of appeals so that it may address the merits of the father's challenges to the modification order.

---

## NOTES AND QUESTIONS

(1) *Civil Status Determinations*. In *Pennoyer v. Neff*, 95 U.S. 714, 24 L. Ed. 565 (1877) (*See* § 4.01[A]), the United States Supreme Court stated "that we do not mean to assert, by anything we have said, that a State may not authorize proceedings to determine the *status* of one of its citizens towards a non-resident, which would be binding within the State . . . ." *See also Shaffer v. Heitner*, 433 U.S. 186, 97 S. Ct. 2569, 53 L. Ed. 2d 683 (1977), in § 4.01[B]. Consider the following excerpt from *Dosamantes v. Dosamantes*, 500 S.W.2d 233, 236 (Tex. Civ. App.—Texarkana 1973, writ dism'd):

> JURISDICTION
>
> It is urged that the District Court of Titus County lacked jurisdiction to grant appellee a divorce, irrespective of whether or not appellant was properly served, because the jurisdiction of the Texas court could not extend beyond Texas' territorial borders to affect the rights or the status of a citizen of Mexico.
>
> Historically, it has been recognized that a state court in the United States has the jurisdiction to determine or alter the status of a marriage relationship when one of the parties thereto is a domiciliary of that state, even though the other party thereto is a nonresident or a citizen of another state. Williams v. North Carolina, 317 U.S. 287, 63 S. Ct. 207, 87 L. Ed. 279; Williams v. North Carolina, 325 U.S. 226, 65 S. Ct. 1092, 89 L. Ed. 1577; Maynard v. Hill, 125 U.S. 190, 8 S. Ct. 723, 31 L. Ed. 654, 27A C.J.S. Divorce § 71, p. 246; 27A C.J.S. Divorce § 73, pp. 250, 251. The basis for this power is that domicile in itself creates a relationship to the state which is sufficient for the exercise of state power. It has been said that domicile implies a nexus between person and place of such permanence as to authorize the control of the legal status, relationships and responsibilities of the domiciliary. The state, as sovereign, has an important and legitimate interest in the marital status of persons domiciled within its borders and consequently, it may determine, regulate and alter that status. As held by the United States Supreme Court in the case of Williams v. North Carolina, 317 U.S. 287, 63 S. Ct. 207, 87 L. Ed. 279:
>
> > "Thus it is plain that each state by virtue of its command over its domiciliaries and its large interest in the institution of marriage can alter within its own borders the marriage status of the spouse domiciled there, even though the other spouse is absent."
>
> Divorce actions are not mere in personam actions, but are quasi in rem. Williams v. North Carolina, 317 U.S. 287, 63 S. Ct. 207, 87 L. Ed. 279. In such cases the court is not exercising personal jurisdiction over the nonresident, but is exercising jurisdiction over the subject

> matter—that is, the marital status of its citizen. Thus, in this case, Texas was not attempting to extend its laws so as to give them extraterritorial effect in Mexico. Rather, it was exercising jurisdiction over the legal status and relations of its own citizen. The fact that such action affects a citizen of another sovereign does not prevent the exercise of such power any more than the exercise of jurisdiction over a true "res" located within the borders of the acting sovereign would be prohibited simply because the adjudication affects the rights of nonresidents of whom the sovereign has no personal jurisdiction.
>
> Most of the cases decided on this question involve divorces where one of the parties is a citizen of another state of the United States, but the rule applies with equal force when the nonresident is a resident of a foreign nation. Risch v. Risch, 395 S.W.2d 709 (Tex. Civ. App., Houston 1965, dism'd).

Is this consistent with *Shaffer?* What about division of marital property located within the state? What of suits affecting (terminating) the parent-child relationship? *See May v. Anderson*, 345 U.S. 528 (1953), which sets forth the traditional rule that custody awards require in personam jurisdiction. *See also Spitzmiller v. Spitzmiller*, 429 S.W.2d 557 (Tex. Civ. App.—Houston [14th Dist.] 1968, writ ref'd n.r.e.), which is to the same effect. Before the adoption of the parent-child long-arm provision of the Texas Family Code, personal jurisdiction of the parents was not sufficient unless the child was either domiciled in Texas or physically present. *See Ex parte Birmingham*, 150 Tex. 595, 244 S.W.2d 977 (1952). As stated by Professor Jack Sampson, "This disability is what the parent-child long-arm statute is designed to correct to the maximum extent possible." Sampson, *Jurisdiction in Divorce and Conservatorship Suits*, 8 Tex. Tech L. Rev. 159, 1973 (1976).

In *Perry v. Ponder*, 604 S.W.2d 306, 313–314, 320 (Tex. Civ. App.—Dallas 1980, no writ), the court of appeals found:

> [D]ue process permits adjudication of the custody of a child residing in the forum state without a showing of "minimum contacts" on the part of the nonresident parent, and we also hold that if the requirements of due process and applicable procedural rules are met, a Texas court has "personal jurisdiction" over the nonresident within subdivision (4) of section 11.051 to adjudicate the custody issue, even though it may not have such jurisdiction to render a personal judgment enforcing or imposing affirmative duties [such as child support obligations] on the nonresident.

The Dallas court concluded "that *May* [*May v. Anderson, above*] need not be interpreted as imposing . . . [a 'minimum contacts'] requirement in cases like the present, when the child and one parent reside in the forum state."

(2) What if the controversy involves claims to the property?

(3) *Spell It Out.* In *Kulko v. Superior Court*, 439 U.S. 84, 98 S. Ct. 1690, 56 L. Ed. 2d 132 (1978), there is a suggestion that long-arm provisions should enumerate the specific fact situation in which jurisdiction may be obtained. "California has not attempted to assert any particularized interest in trying such cases in its courts by, e.g., enacting a special jurisdictional statute." 98 S. Ct. at 1700, 56 L. Ed. 2d at 145. For an attempt at the drafting of a specific statute, see Mowrey, *Article 2031b: A New Process is Due*, 30 Sw. L.J. 747 (1977).

(4) *In Interest of S.A.V.* discusses the Uniform Child Custody Jurisdiction Act (UCCJA). Virtually all jurisdictions have adopted the act, Texas doing so in 1983. UCCJA Section 3, codified in Section 152.003 of the Family Code, provides that a court may make a binding custody

determination if the forum state is the child's "home state"; or if the forum state was the child's "home state" within six months before the commencement of the proceeding and a parent or person acting as a parent continues to reside in the state; or if it is in the best interest of the child that the court exercise jurisdiction because (1) the child and his or her parents or at least one "contestant" have a significant connection with the state, and (2) substantial evidence is available within the state concerning the child's present or future care, protection, training and personal relationships; or if the child is physically present in the state and (1) has been abandoned or (2) an emergency situation involving mistreatment or abuse arises; or no other court has jurisdiction or another state has declined to exercise it on the ground that the forum state is the more appropriate forum to determine custody of the child and it is in the child's best interest that the court in the forum state exercise jurisdiction.

The binding effect of a custody adjudication is set out in Section 12 of the UCCJA (codified in Section 152.012 of the Texas Family Code): "A custody decree rendered by a court of this State which has jurisdiction under section 3 binds all parties who have been served in this State or notified in accordance with section 5 or who have submitted to the jurisdiction of the court, and who have been given an opportunity to be heard."

The comment to Section 12 of the UCCJA states expressly, "There is no requirement for technical personal jurisdiction, on the traditional theory that custody determinations, as distinguished from support actions . . ., are proceedings in rem or proceedings affecting status." Under the 1983 amendment quoted at the beginning of this note, is it clear whether the satisfaction of the situational requirements of UCCJA Section 3 (Fam. C. § 152.003) will be sufficient to make the binding child custody determination addressed in Section 12 (Fam. C. § 152.012)?

The Texas statute may differ from the UCCJA in another way. Commentators have debated about provisions of the UCCJA having to do with continuing jurisdiction. *See* Bodenheimer, *Interstate Custody: Initial and Continuing Jurisdiction Under the UCCJA,* 14 Fam. L. Q. 203, 215 (1981). "Exclusive continuing jurisdiction is not affected by the child's residence in another state for six months or more. Although the new state becomes the child's home state, significant connection jurisdiction continues in the state of the prior decree where the court record and other evidence exists and where one parent or another contestant resides. *Only when the child and all parties have moved away is deference to another state's continuing jurisdiction no longer required*" (emphasis added). For the same interpretation *but* criticizing the UCCJA for it, *see* Sampson, *Jurisdiction in Divorce and Conservatorship Suits,* 8 Tex. Tech L. Rev. 159, 232–235 (1976). Compare a more restrained interpretation of the UCCJA concerning continuing jurisdiction in Bodenheimer, *Progress Under the Uniform Child Custody Jurisdiction Act and Remaining Problems: Punitive Decrees, Joint Custody, and Excessive Modifications,* 65 Cal. L. Rev. 978, 989 (1977) (suggesting outer limits of "three or four years, depending upon the circumstances").

The statutory basis of the Bodenheimer view is Section 14 of the UCCJA (codified in Section 152.014 of the Texas Family Code), which provides:

> If a court of another state has made a custody decree, a court of this state may not modify the decree unless:
>
> (1) it appears to the court of this state that the court which rendered the decree does not now have jurisdiction under jurisdictional prerequisites substantially in accordance with this Act or has declined to assume jurisdiction to modify the decree; and
>
> (2) the court of this state has jurisdiction.

While the length of the continuing jurisdiction of *another* state's courts over a custody determination may still be debated, Texas seems to have settled the question for *its own* courts. The Texas Family Code adaptation of the UCCJA contains a provision not found in the uniform act:

> Except on written agreement of all the parties, a court may not exercise its continuing jurisdiction to modify custody if the child and the party with custody have established another home state unless the action to modify was filed before the new home state was acquired.

Fam. C. § 152.003(d). "Home state" is defined in Tex. Fam. Code § 152.002(b):

> "Home state" means the state in which the child immediately preceding the time involved lived with his parents, a parent, or a person acting as parent, for at least six consecutive months, and in the case of a child less than six months old, the state in which the child lived from birth with any of the persons mentioned. Periods of temporary absence of any of the named persons are counted as part of the six-month or other period.

How long, then, can a Texas court exercise continuing jurisdiction after a child, the subject of a Texas custody adjudication, has left the state?

(5) The Parental Kidnaping Prevention Act of 1980 (PKPA) contains a section that requires that decrees rendered by sister states be enforced, generally without modification. The following summary of the federal act is taken from Dorsaneo, *Interstate Modification and Enforcement: A Pilgrim's Progress Through UCCJA, PKPA and Section 14.10,* State Bar of Texas, Marriage Dissolution Institute, Chapter B (1981).*

*PARENTAL KIDNAPING PREVENTION ACT (1980)*

*FULL FAITH AND CREDIT GIVEN TO CHILD CUSTODY DETERMINATIONS*

1. *Child Custody Determination.* This term is defined as follows: " 'Custody determination' means a judgment, decree, or other order of a court providing for the custody or visitation of a child, and includes permanent and temporary orders, and initial orders and modifications." 28 U.S.C.A. § 1738A(b)(3).

2. *When Enforcement Mandatory.* "The appropriate authorities of every State shall enforce according to its terms, and, shall not modify except as provided in subsection (f) of this section, any child custody determination made consistently with the provisions of this section by a court of another State." 28 U.S.C.A. § 1738A(a).

3. *When Modification Permissible.* Subsection (f) permits modification if: (a) the court of the State in which modification is sought has jurisdiction to make a child custody determination, and (b) the court of the State which made the decree no longer has jurisdiction, or it has declined to exercise it. 28 U.S.C.A. § 1738A(f).

4. *When Determination Made Consistently with PKPA Requirements.*

(a) The court must have jurisdiction under the law of the state in which it sits to make the child custody determination. If it does not, then the determination is not consistent with PKPA.

(b) In addition, one of the following conditions must be met before a state court's exercise of jurisdiction is consistent with PKPA.

(1) the state is the child's "home state" [" 'home state' means the State in which, immediately preceding the time involved, the child lived with his parents, a parent, or a person acting as a parent for at least six consecutive months . . ." 28 U.S.C.A. § 1738A(b)(4)]; or

(2) the state had been the "home state" within six months of the date suit was brought and one "contestant" [" 'contestant' means a person, including a parent, who claims a right to custody or visitation of a child" 28 U.S.C.A. § 1738A(b)(2)] "continues to live in such State"; or

(3) if and only if there is no "home state" and the second alternative also does not apply, *and* it is in the child's best interest that the state assume jurisdiction because the child and at least one contestant have a significant connection with the State and substantial evidence exists in the State; or

(4) the child is physically present in the State *and* has been abandoned *or* requires emergency treatment as a result of actual or threatened mistreatment or abuse; or

(5) none of the above are applicable *or* another state has declined to exercise jurisdiction on the ground that the State whose jurisdiction is in issue is the more appropriate forum *and* it is in the best interest of the child for it to exercise jurisdiction; or

(6) "the court has continuing jurisdiction pursuant to subsection d of this section." 28 U.S.C.A. § 1738A(c)(2)(e). Subsection d provides: "The jurisdiction of a court of a State which has made a child custody determination consistently with the provisions of this section continues as long as the requirement of subsection (c)(1) ['such court has jurisdiction under the law of such State'] of this section continues to be met and such State remains the residence of the child or of any contestant."

(6) *Concurrent Jurisdiction: Comity.* The PKPA also provides that: "A court of a State shall not exercise jurisdiction in any proceeding for a custody determination commenced during the pendency of a proceeding in a court of another State where such court of that other State is exercising jurisdiction consistently with the provisions of this section to make a custody determination." 28 U.S.C.A. § 1738A(g).

## § 4.04 Service of Process

### [A] Due Process Requirements

**PERALTA v. HEIGHTS MEDICAL CTR, INC.,** 485 U.S. 80, 108 S. Ct. 896 (1988). In this case, the United States Supreme Court related due process notice requirements to the requirements for setting aside a default judgment. Peralta sought relief in Texas state court to set aside a default judgment entered against him two years earlier and void a subsequent sale of his property to satisfy the judgment. He alleged that because the original service of process itself showed it was defective and, in fact, he had never been personally served, the judgment was void under Texas law. The Texas courts denied relief on the ground that Peralta failed to show he would have had a meritorious defense, even if he had had notice. The appellate court rejected Peralta's contention that the meritorious defense requirement violated his due process rights under the Fourteenth Amendment, finding the requirement "not onerous."

The Supreme Court unanimously reversed. The Court first noted that all parties agreed Peralta had never been personally served and had no notice of the judgment. "[U]nder our cases, a judgment entered without notice or service is constitutionally infirm. 'An elementary and fundamental requirement of due process in any proceeding which is to be accorded finality is notice reasonably calculated, under the circumstances, to apprise interested parties of the pendency of the action and afford them the opportunity to present their objections.' *Mullane v. Central Hanover Bank & Trust Co.,* 339 U.S. 306, 314 (1950). Failure to give notice violates the most rudimentary demands of due process of law." *Armstrong v. Manzo,* 380 U.S. 545, 550 (1965). The Court rejected the argument that without a meritorious defense the same judgment would again be entered against Peralta, and therefore he suffered no harm from the judgment. "[T]his reasoning is untenable. . . . [H]ad he notice of the suit, [Peralta] might have impleaded the employee whose debt had been guaranteed, worked out a settlement, or paid the debt. He would also have preferred to sell his property himself in order to raise funds rather than to suffer it sold at a constable's auction."

### [B] Texas' Strict Compliance Standard

#### WILSON v. DUNN

*800 S.W.2d 833 (Tex. 1990)*

HECHT, Justice.

The district court in this case authorized substitute service of suit papers upon defendant without an affidavit or other evidence justifying such service as required by Rule 106(b) of the Texas Rules of Civil Procedure. [footnote omitted] Defendant nevertheless received citation and plaintiff's petition, but did not answer, and the trial court rendered default judgment against him. The court of appeals reversed the default judgment because of the defect in service and remanded the case to the trial court for further proceedings. 752 S.W.2d 15. We affirm.

I

Jesse Wilson sued Michael Dunn for damages resulting from Dunn's negligent operation of a motor vehicle. [footnote omitted] Wilson alleged that Dunn could be served with citation at his apartment, where, in fact, Dunn was then residing and has resided at all times material to this case. Repeated, sustained efforts to serve Dunn there, however, both in person and by mail, proved unsuccessful.

After several months, Wilson's attorney filed a motion for substitute service under Rule 106(b). Rule 106(b) states:

> Upon motion *supported by affidavit* stating the location of the defendant's usual place of business or usual place of abode or other place where the defendant can probably be found and stating specifically the facts showing that service has been attempted under either (a)(1) or (a)(2) at the location named *in such affidavit* but has not been successful, the court may authorize service
>
> (1) by leaving a true copy of the citation, with a copy of the petition attached, with anyone over sixteen years of age at the location specified *in such affidavit*, or
>
> (2) in any other manner that the *affidavit* or other evidence before the court shows will be reasonably effective to give the defendant notice of the suit.

(Emphasis added.) Contrary to the explicit requirement of the rule, Wilson's motion was not verified or supported by affidavit or other evidence. Nonetheless, the judge of the 236th District

Court to which the case was assigned granted the motion and ordered that citation be served upon Dunn either by attaching it to the door of his apartment or by delivering it to the apartment manager at Dunn's address. However, the judge instructed the clerk to attach a note to the docket sheet stating that no default judgment was to be taken. [footnote omitted] The return of citation authorized by the district court stated that it had been served by a deputy constable "by delivering to the within named Michael Donell [sic] Dunn by delivering to his agent for service, Carol Berlinger, apartment manager" [footnote omitted] a copy of the citation and plaintiff's original petition. Dunn actually received the papers, as he later acknowledged in a sworn statement given to Wilson's attorney:

> . . . I received some suit papers from [Wilson's attorney]. These papers were placed in my apartment by the apartment manager where I live after the Constable served the papers on her. Within five days from the date that I received the suit papers, I hand delivered them to my insurance agent. . . .

Within a few weeks an adjuster for Dunn's insurer telephoned Wilson's attorney to discuss the case. Following up their conversation, the adjuster wrote Wilson's attorney requesting him to agree that, pending efforts to obtain Dunn's cooperation and to settle Wilson's claim, Dunn would not be required to file an answer in the case and no default judgment would be taken without ten days' notice. Wilson's attorney wrote at the bottom of the letter, "I agree to the above", signed it, and returned it to the adjuster. Shortly thereafter the adjuster retained an attorney to monitor the case. The attorney telephoned the clerk of the court on at least two occasions and was told that at the court's instruction a note had been attached to the file that no default judgment could be taken in the case. The attorney did not contact Dunn but the adjuster finally did, and obtained a statement from him. About the same time, however, the insurer transferred the case to another adjuster, and Wilson's attorney was not informed that Dunn had been contacted.

Concerned that the second anniversary of the accident was approaching, Wilson's attorney wrote Dunn a letter dated February 19, 1987, urging him to cooperate with his insurer and warning him of the possible consequences of failing to do so. [footnote omitted] Specifically, the letter stated, "we are going to ask the Court for the Default Judgment against you during the second week of March, 1987." Wilson's attorney sent a copy of the letter to the adjuster and the attorney retained by the adjuster. In response to the letter, the sometimes elusive Dunn contacted Wilson's attorney and arranged to meet with him. Dunn gave Wilson's attorney a sworn statement in which he indicated that he had not failed to communicate with his insurer.

Convinced that the adjuster had not been fully candid with him, Wilson's attorney went to the 236th District Court on February 27, 1987, to obtain a default judgment. Finding that the judge of that court was not available, Wilson's attorney requested the file from the clerk so that he could take it to another judge for hearing on his request for a default judgment. The clerk was reluctant to give Wilson's attorney the file because the judge had told her that default judgment was not to be taken in the case. She pointed out to Wilson's attorney the note the judge had instructed her to attach to the file, but he insisted on taking it, and she finally relented. On the way to a hearing before the judge of the 67th District Court, [footnote omitted] Wilson's attorney removed the note from the file and threw it away.

Wilson's original petition requested $144 damages for past medical expenses, and unspecified amounts for future medical expenses, lost wages, loss of earning capacity, and past and future physical pain and mental anguish. After hearing, the judge of the 67th District Court rendered default judgment for Wilson for $475,000. [footnote omitted] Later the same day Wilson's attorney told the judge who granted the default judgment that he had removed the prior judge's note from the file because Dunn had actual knowledge of the suit and default was therefore appropriate. The judge who granted the default judgment strongly reproved Wilson's attorney but did not set aside the judgment.

Neither Dunn nor his insurer learned of the default judgment until after it was signed. Dunn filed a motion for new trial, which was also presented to the judge of the 67th District Court. The motion did not complain of the defect in service. After hearing evidence, the trial court denied the motion. The trial court concluded that substitute service was appropriate, [footnote omitted] and that Dunn had received actual notice of the suit. The trial court also concluded that Dunn's failure to file an appearance was due to the conscious indifference of his insurer.

On appeal, Dunn argued that service was defective and could not support the default judgment. Dunn also argued that the trial court's conclusion that he was not entitled to a new trial was against the great weight of the evidence and manifestly unjust. The appeals court agreed with Dunn's defective service argument and did not address his other arguments. Thus, the only issue presented to us is the sufficiency of service.

II

For well over a century the rule has been firmly established in this state that a default judgment cannot withstand direct attack by a defendant who complains that he was not served in strict compliance with applicable requirements. *See, e.g., Uvalde Country Club v. Martin Linen Supply Co.*, 690 S.W.2d 884, 886 (Tex. 1985) (per curiam); *McKanna v. Edgar*, 388 S.W.2d 927, 929 (Tex. 1965); *Sloan v. Batte*, 46 Tex. 215, 216 (1876); *see also* R. McDonald, Texas Civil Practice in District and County Courts § 17.23.2, at 134–144 (F. Elliott rev. 1984). This Court only recently reasserted:

> There are no presumptions in favor of valid issuance, service, and return of citation in the face of a [direct] attack on a default judgment . . . Moreover, failure to affirmatively show strict compliance with the Rules of Civil Procedure renders the attempted service of process invalid and of no effect.

*Uvalde*, 690 S.W.2d at 885. *See Higginbotham v. General Life & Acc. Ins. Co.*, 796 S.W.2d 695, 697 (Tex. 1990).

In this case, Dunn was not strictly served in compliance with Rule 106(b) because substitute service was not properly authorized absent the affidavit explicitly required by the rule. The express requirement of an affidavit in support of a motion for substitute service was added effective in 1981. 599–600 S.W.2d xxxviii–xxxix (Tex. Cases 1980). It appears, however, that prior to that change in the text of the rule the courts uniformly held that substitute service could be authorized only upon probative evidence of the impracticality of personal service. [citations omitted] Since the 1981 change in Rule 106(b) the courts have consistently held that substitute service may not properly issue on a motion supported by an affidavit that is conclusory or otherwise insufficient. [citations omitted] We agree and hold that substitute service is not authorized under Rule 106(b) without an affidavit which meets the requirements of the rule demonstrating the necessity for other than personal service.

Wilson acknowledges that service on Dunn was defective because of the failure to comply with Rule 106(b), but argues that the default judgment rendered against Dunn should nevertheless stand because Dunn actually received the suit papers and actually knew of the pendency of the suit. We disagree. Actual notice to a defendant, without proper service, is not sufficient to convey upon the court jurisdiction to render default judgment against him. *See Harrell v. Mexico Cattle Co.*, 73 Tex. 612, 11 S.W. 863, 865 (1889). Rather, jurisdiction is dependent upon citation issued and served in a manner provided for by law. *Id.*; *Panhandle Constr. Co. v. Casey*, 66 S.W.2d 705, 707 (Tex. Civ. App.—Amarillo 1933, writ ref'd); *see C.W. Bollinger Ins. Co. v. Fish*, 699 S.W.2d 645, 655 (Tex. App.—Austin 1985, no writ). Absent service, waiver, or citation, mere knowledge of a pending suit does not place any duty on a defendant to act. *See Harrell*, 11 S.W. at 865; *Panhandle Constr. Co.*, 66 S.W.2d at 707. Consequently, Dunn's knowledge that Wilson had sued him and his actual receipt of suit papers is not sufficient to invoke the district court's jurisdiction to render default judgment against him.

Wilson relies heavily upon section 3 of the Restatement (Second) of Judgments (1982), which states: "When actual notice of an action has been given, irregularity in the content of the notice or the manner in which it was given does not render the notice inadequate." Wilson fails to note, however, that this rule does not apply to default judgments. As comment d to section 3 explains:

> The objection to the regularity of notice also often arises in the context of an application for relief from a default judgment. Here again there is a rational basis for treating an irregularity in notice-giving as significant even though actual notice has been conferred. To do so is to apply a rule of parity among the parties concerning formal defects in procedure.
>
> A default judgment is awarded not because the court is entirely satisfied that the claim has substantive merit . . . . but because the party in default was derelict in complying with the rules of procedure governing how he may make his defense. An applicant for relief from such dereliction must show that he acted with due diligence after having become aware of the default and that he has a good case on the merits. . . . Assuming he makes such a showing, the only ground supporting the judgment is that the defendant has failed to respond to the action in conformity with applicable procedure for doing so. If the defendant can then show that the person commencing the action was guilty of comparable nonconformity with procedural rules, under a principle of equality the derelictions offset each other and the merits of the controversy may be brought forward for consideration.

This authority contradicts, rather than supports, Wilson's position.

Wilson also contends that Dunn is foreclosed from complaining that service was defective because he has admitted receipt of the suit papers. We agree that Dunn could have waived his complaint of defective service by conceding the issue, but he has not done so. Dunn has admitted receipt, not service. Indeed, the issue presented is whether actual receipt can cure defective service in this context. The two cases upon which Wilson relies demonstrate this distinction. In both *First Nat'l Bank v. Peterson*, 709 S.W.2d 276, 280 (Tex. App.—Houston [14th Dist.] 1986, writ ref'd n.r.e.), and *Hurst v. A.R.A. Manufacturing Co.*, 555 S.W.2d 141, 142 (Tex. Civ. App.—Fort Worth 1977, writ ref'd n.r.e.), the defendant admitted not simply that process was received, but that it was "duly served". The distinction between actual receipt and proper service is precisely what gives rise to the issue we address here. We hold that a default judgment is improper against a defendant who has not been served in strict compliance with law, even if he has actual knowledge of the lawsuit. *See Higginbotham v. General Life & Acc. Ins. Co.*, 796 S.W.2d 695, 697 (Tex. 1990).

Finally, Wilson argues that Dunn has failed to preserve any complaint of defective service by not raising the issue in his motion for new trial. Rule 324 imposes no such requirement for preservation of such error. Tex. R. Civ. P. 324; *see Bronze & Beautiful, Inc. v. Mahone*, 750

S.W.2d 28, 29 (Tex. App.—Texarkana 1988, no writ); *American Universal Ins. Co. v. D.B. & B., Inc.*, 725 S.W.2d 764, 765 (Tex. App.—Corpus Christi 1987, writ ref'd n.r.e.). We hold that Dunn's complaint was preserved for appeal. [footnote omitted]

III

Accordingly, we conclude that the default judgment against Dunn was improper. We therefore affirm the judgment of the court of appeals reversing the judgment of the district court and remanding the case to that court for further proceedings.

---

## NOTE

(1) *Strict Compliance*. As *Wilson* indicates, Texas courts require strict compliance with the requirements for service. Actual receipt will not cure defective service, as it will in many other jurisdictions. *See also Primate Construction, Inc. v. Silver*, 884 S.W.2d 151, 153 (Tex. 1994) ("It is the responsibility of the one requesting service, not the process server, to see that service is properly accomplished. . . . This responsibility extends to seeing that service is properly reflected in the record.").

### [C] Waiver of Process

*Read Tex. R. Civ. P. 119, 329b.*

## DEEN v. KIRK

*508 S.W.2d 70 (Tex. 1974)*

WALKER, Justice.

This is an original mandamus proceeding. It was instituted by Betty L. Deen, relator, against F. Edgar Deen, Jr., and the Honorable Stanley C. Kirk, Judge of the 78th Judicial District of Wichita County, to require the latter to expunge an order purporting to set aside a divorce judgment previously rendered by him. We agree with relator that the judgment in question had become final and that Judge Kirk had no power to set it aside as he attempted to do. In accordance with our usual procedure in cases of this nature the writ of mandamus will be granted conditionally.

On June 22, 1973, F. Edgar Deen, Jr., hereinafter referred to as respondent, instituted suit for divorce against relator in Cause No. 94,536-B in the 78th District Court of Wichita County. At the same time he filed a waiver of citation previously executed by relator. The jurat on the waiver is dated June 21, 1973. On August 22, 1973, without further notice, citation or waiver, Judge Kirk rendered judgment granting respondent a divorce and approving an undescribed property settlement agreement. Relator first learned of these proceedings on October 27, 1973.

. . . .

On December 3, 1973, relator filed in Cause No. 95,544-B in the 78th District Court of Wichita County a petition in the nature of a bill of review, praying that the judgment in Cause No. 94,536-B be set aside. On December 13, 1973, Judge Kirk on his own motion entered an order in Cause No. 94,536-B setting aside the judgment previously rendered in that case. A few days later relator was served with citation in the original divorce case. Respondent then filed in Cause No. 95,544-B a motion to dismiss, alleging that since the judgment in Cause No. 94,536-B had been set aside, the bill of review proceeding was moot. On January 3, 1974, the motion was granted and the bill of review proceeding was dismissed. The original divorce case was also set for trial on the merits.

. . . .

Under the provisions of Rule 119, Texas Rules of Civil Procedure, a defendant may waive the issuance and service of citation by filing among the papers of the cause a verified written memorandum "signed by him, or by his duly authorized agent or attorney, after suit is brought." Article 2224, Vernon's Ann. Civ. St., prohibits the waiver of process by an instrument executed prior to institution of suit. It is clear then that the waiver executed by relator prior to institution of the divorce suit in Wichita County did not subject her to the jurisdiction of the court. McAnelly v. Ward, 72 Tex. 342, 12 S.W. 206.

[However, the Supreme Court also considered the question whether Judge Kirk had jurisdiction to vacate the order. The Court held that the time for the judge's jurisdiction to vacate a judgment had expired and he had no jurisdiction to do so. After reviewing the cases, the court concluded as follows:]

. . . [T]he 78th District Court of Wichita County had jurisdictional power to determine the validity and effectiveness of the waiver and to render a judgment for divorce. Relator's petition for a bill of review was never heard but was dismissed. In these circumstances and under the provisions of Rule 329b, the order of December 13, 1973, purporting to set aside the divorce judgment previously rendered in Cause No. 94,536-B is void and should itself be set aside. We are not to be understood as saying that a bill of review was the only effective remedy available to relator when she learned of the divorce judgment. See Art. 2255, V.A.C.S.; Whitney v. L & L Realty Corp., Tex., 500 S.W.2d 94; Flynt v. City of Kingsville, 125 Tex. 510, 82 S.W.2d 934. It was, however, the only remedy then available to her in the trial court.

We assume that Judge Kirk will set aside his order of December 13, 1973, promptly after our judgment in this proceeding becomes final. In the event he fails to do so, a writ of mandamus will issue.

---

## NOTES AND QUESTIONS

(1) *Waiver vs. Consent.* What is the difference between pre-suit waiver of service of process, which is impermissible under Section 30.001 of the Civil Practice and Remedies Code and Civil Procedure Rule 119, and statutory or contractual consent to jurisdiction, which may be permissible? Contractual consent to jurisdiction satisfies due process unless the consent is not valid because it is not voluntarily, knowingly or intelligently made. *See National Equipment Rental, Ltd. v. Szukhent,* 375 U.S. 311, 84 S. Ct. 411, 11 L. Ed. 2d 354 (1964) (Michigan residents validly consented to substituted service on a named person in New York—someone they did not know personally—when they entered into a lease that named that person as their agent); *see also D.H. Overmeyer, Inc. v. Frick Co.*, 405 U.S. 174, 92 S. Ct. 775, 31 L. Ed. 2d 124 (1972).

A forum selection clause contained in an employment contract was held to be enforceable by the Dallas Court of Appeals such that dismissal of a Texas action was required because the clause required the parties to litigate employment disputes in New Jersey. *Barnette v. United Research Co., Inc.,* 823 S.W.2d 368, 369–370 (Tex. App.—Dallas 1991, writ denied).

(2) *Waiver and Termination of Parental Rights.* Note that exceptions to the holding in *Deen v. Kirk* are found in cases arising under Texas Family Code provisions pertaining to termination of parental rights. *See Brown v. McLennan County Children's Protective Services,* 627 S.W.2d 390 (Tex. 1982), which upheld the constitutionality of the Code's provisions authorizing a parent's waiver of citation prior to filing of suit for termination of parental rights where such waiver was voluntarily, intelligently, and knowingly made.

(3) *Counterclaims and Cross-Claims.* Is service of citation necessary for a counterclaim? How about for a cross-claim? *See* Tex. R. Civ. P. 124; *see also Galloway v. Moeser,* 82 S.W.2d 1067, 1069 (Tex. Civ. App.—Eastland 1935, no writ).

(4) *Amended Pleadings.* If the opposing party has not appeared, new service of citation is required when an amended pleading states a new cause of action or seeks a more onerous judgment. *See Sanchez v. Texas Industries, Inc.,* 485 S.W.2d 385, 387 (Tex. Civ. App.—Waco 1972, writ ref'd n.r.e.). On the other hand, if an opposing party has appeared, new service of citation is not required. *See Sanders v. Fit-All Pricing Corp.,* 417 S.W.2d 886, 888 (Tex. Civ. App.—Texarkana 1967, no writ). Read Tex. R. Civ. P. 21a and 124. *See also* Tex. R. Civ. P. 92 (second paragraph).

## [D] The Technique of Service

### [1] Issuance and Service of Citation

*Read Tex. R. Civ. P. 99.*

Section 17.027 of the Civil Practice and Remedies Code allows the plaintiff to prepare the appropriate citation for the defendant as long as the citation is prepared in the form prescribed in Tex. R. Civ. P. 99(b) and served in the manner prescribed by law. Although the clerk may charge for the issuance of a citation, the clerk may not charge for signing his/her name and affixing the seal to a citation that is prepared by the plaintiff or his/her attorney in accordance with Section 17.027.

### [2] Serving Persons in Texas

*Read Tex. R. Civ. P. 103, 106, 107.*

Unless the citation otherwise directs, it may be served by either of two alternate methods:

a. *Persons Who May Serve Citations*

Civil Procedure Rule 103 provides that citation may be served by any sheriff or constable, any person authorized by law, and any person authorized by written court order who is not less than 18 years of age. The language of Rule 106 speaks in terms of service by "any person authorized by Rule 103." Sheriffs and constables also are not restricted to their counties for purposes of service of process. In addition, "[t]he order authorizing a person to serve process may be made without written motion and no fee shall be imposed for issuance of such order." Tex. R. Civ. P. 103.

b. *Basic Methods of Service*

Service by mail is authorized "by any person authorized by Rule 103 by . . . mailing to the defendant by registered or certified mail, return receipt requested, a true copy of the citation with a copy of the petition attached thereto." Tex. R. Civ. P. 106(a)(2). No court order is necessary to authorize service by certified mail under Civil Proceudre Rule 106(a)(2).

Service on a non-natural person (e.g., a corporation) is ordinarily accomplished by the delivery of citation to one of its authorized agents. Hence, the addressee to whom delivery is restricted under Civil Procedure Rule 106(a)(2) should be the defendant or an agent authorized to accept service of citation.

Various Texas statutes have provided for service upon resident defendants by serving some person other than the named defendant. A few are noted here:

1. *Domestic Corporations.* Service agents are the president, vice-president, or registered agent for service. Bus. Corp. Act Art. 2.11; R.C.S. Art. 1396—2.07. If a domestic corporation fails to appoint a registered agent, the secretary of state serves as the registered agent.
2. *Partnerships.* Service on a partner *or* local agent of partnership in county in which local agent transacts business, in all suits or actions growing out of or connected with such business and brought in the county in which office, place of business or agency is located. C.P.R.C. §§ 17.021, 17.022 ("Citation served on one member of a partnership authorizes judgment against the partnership and the partner actually served"). *See also* C.P.R.C. § 31.003 (no personal judgment against partner not served).
3. *Limited Liability Companies.* Service agents are the managers, if any, and the registered agents for service of process. R.C.S. Art. 1528n art. 2.08 § A.
4. *Joint Stock Associations.* Service agents are the president, vice president, secretary, cashier, assistant cashier, treasurer, or general agent. C.P.R.C. § 17.023.
6. *Real Estate Investment Trusts.* Service agents are the president, all vice presidents, and the registered agent. R.C.S. Art. 6138A, §§ 5.10, 5.20.
6. *Domestic Insurance Companies.* Service agents are the president, active vice president, secretary, and attorney in fact. Ins. C. Art. 1.36, § 2(a).
7. *Counties.* Service agent is the county judge. C.P.R.C. § 17.024(a).
8. *Municipalities.* Service agents are mayor, clerk, secretary, or treasurer. C.P.R.C. § 17.024(b).
9. *School Districts.* Service agents are the president of school board or the superintendent. C.P.R.C. § 17.024(c).
10. *State of Texas.* The secretary of state is the service agent for the State of Texas. C.P.R.C. § 101.102(c).

c. *Alternate Service in Texas*

When "service has been attempted" under either Civil Procedure Rule 106(a)(1) or 106(a)(2), but has not been successful, the court, on motion, may authorize service in some other reasonably effective manner. *See* Tex. R. Civ. P. 106(b). Particular methods suggested by the rule are as follows:

1. Leaving a true copy of the citation, with a copy of the petition attached with anyone over 16 years of age at the location of the defendant's usual place of business or usual place of abode or other place where the defendant can probably be found; or

2. Any other manner that is shown by affidavit or other evidence to be reasonably effective to give the defendant notice of the suit.

The party requesting alternate service must file a motion supported by an affidavit that sets forth the location of the defendant's usual place of business, abode, or other place and that states service was attempted either in person or by certified mail and that this attempt failed. The affidavit must specifically state factual propositions and not be conclusory. *Sgitcovich v. Sgitcovich,* 150 Tex. 398, 241 S.W.2d 142, 146 (1951). A trial court should not sign an order authorizing alternate service without hearing and considering evidence to the effect that it was impractical to obtain personal service. A record of the hearing should be made. *See Kirkegaard v. First City Nat'l of Binghamton, N.Y.,* 486 S.W.2d 893, 894 (Tex. Civ. App.—Beaumont 1972, no writ). Affidavits will suffice. *Smith v. Texas Discount Co.,* 408 S.W.2d 804, 806 (Tex. Civ. App.—Austin 1966, no writ). Failure to make a record may result in the reversal of a default judgment. *Spencer v. Texas Factors, Inc.,* 366 S.W.2d 699, 700 (Tex. Civ. App.—Dallas 1963, writ ref'd n.r.e.). *Cf. Smith v. Smith,* 544 S.W.2d 121 (Tex. 1976).

Service may be made on the secretary of state by certified mail by the clerk of the court, the party, or a representative of the party. C.P.R.C. § 17.026. This method of service is in addition to any other method authorized by statute or by the Texas Rules of Civil Procedure.

Note that service on the secretary of state does not require that the secretary of state be served in person. *Capital Brick, Inc. v. Fleming Mfg. Co.,* 722 S.W.2d 399, 401 (Tex. 1986) (service effected by delivery of citation and petition to clerk having charge of corporation division of secretary of state's office).

---

## EICHEL v. ULLAH

*831 S.W.2d 42 (Tex. App.—El Paso 1992, no writ)*

LARSEN, Justice.

This is a personal injury suit stemming from an automobile accident which occurred May 26, 1985. On May 22, 1987, plaintiffs Thomas and Lea Eichel filed suit in Harris County District Court against Wazi Ullah. Mr. Ullah was not served with process, however, until August 12, 1988. The issue presented is whether the failure to serve process upon defendant for 14 months after the statute of limitations expired established lack of due diligence, thus preventing the mere filing of suit from tolling the running of limitations. The trial court held that the failure to use due diligence was established as a matter of law. We affirm.

To "bring suit" within the two-year limitations period prescribed by Section 16.003 of the Texas Civil Practice and Remedies Code, plaintiff must not only file suit within the applicable limitations period, but must also use diligence in having the defendant served with process. *Gant v. DeLeon,* 786 S.W.2d 259, 260 (Tex. 1990) (per curiam); *Rigo Manufacturing Company v. Thomas,* 458 S.W.2d 180, 182 (Tex. 1970). When plaintiff files a petition within the limitations period, as here, but does not serve the defendant until after the statutory period has expired, the date of service relates back to the date of filing only if the plaintiff exercises diligence in effecting service. *Zale Corporation v. Rosenbaum,* 520 S.W.2d 889, 890 (Tex. 1975) (per curiam).

To obtain summary judgment on the grounds that an action was not served within the applicable limitations period, the movant must show that, as a matter of law, diligence was not used to effectuate service. *Zale,* 520 S.W.2d at 891. Generally, the exercise of due diligence in obtaining service of citation is a question of fact. *Valdez v. Charles Orsinger Buick Company,* 715 S.W.2d at 126 (Tex. App.—Texarkana 1986, no writ). The issue can be determined as a matter of law, however, if no valid excuse exists for plaintiffs' failure to timely serve notice of process. *Gant,* 786 S.W.2d at 260; *Rigo,* 458 S.W.2d at 182. The two controlling factors which decide due diligence are: (1) whether plaintiffs acted as ordinary prudent persons would act under the same circumstances; and (2) whether plaintiffs acted diligently up until the time defendant was actually served. *Perry v. Kroger Stores, Store No. 119,* 741 S.W.2d 533, 535 (Tex. App.—Dallas 1987, no writ). The duty to use due diligence continues from the date suit is filed until the defendant is served. *Martinez v. Becerra,* 797 S.W.2d 283, 284 (Tex. App.—Corpus Christi 1990, no writ).

In this case, the uncontroverted summary judgment evidence establishes that plaintiffs failed to use due diligence during a period of time from October 1987 until July 1988, a lapse of nine months duration. It is undisputed that the accident here occurred on May 26, 1985, and plaintiffs filed their suit on May 22, 1987, four days before the statute of limitations expired. Plaintiffs did not request issuance of citation when they filed suit; rather they waited until August 6, 1987 to do so. The only other citation issued was dated July 27, 1988. [footnote omitted] Service upon Wazi Ullah was not achieved until August 12, 1988.

Plaintiffs assert that because Mr. Ullah initially fled the scene of the accident without identifying himself, and that plaintiffs did not learn his name until three weeks after the accident, that those three weeks should be deleted from the calculation of the statute of limitations.

Further, plaintiffs maintain that they have satisfactorily explained any delay in service of citation because at the time suit was filed, both plaintiffs and their counsel believed that the only home address available for defendant Ullah was no longer valid. This belief was based upon the return of a certified letter mailed to defendant's purported residence address. The returned letter did not actually indicate that defendant had moved or that he was unknown at that address; the envelope simply noted that the letter was unclaimed. Likewise, counsel did not seek service at Ullah's employment address because the telephone number for that business had been disconnected. It also appears that Mr. Ullah's business address was incorrect on the police accident report, the numbers of his street address having been transposed. These asserted reasons seem to this Court inadequate to excuse the failure for over two months to request that citation issue. A reasonably diligent person in plaintiff's circumstance would not assume that an "unclaimed" letter meant a bad address; even if the address was not defendant's residence, some investigation might have revealed where defendant could be found. Further, the Court notes that although plaintiffs knew who Mr. Ullah's insurance carrier was, and actually received payment from the carrier, their summary judgment evidence is silent as to any attempt to locate Mr. Ullah through his insurer, or to attempt substituted service or service by publication, as allowed by Tex. R. Civ. P. 109 and 109a. These obvious avenues apparently remained completely unexplored by plaintiffs and their counsel.

Plaintiffs' prior counsel, by affidavit, detailed the efforts he did make to find and serve defendant Ullah after suit was filed. These efforts included: (1) requesting Ullah's motor vehicle record from the Texas Department of Public Safety; (2) requesting any forwarding address from the postal service; (3) mailing letters to Mr. Ullah's forwarding address; (4) requesting issuance of the first citation for service at the forwarding address provided by the U.S. Postal Service; and (5) asking plaintiffs to confirm whether Mr. Ullah lived at the new address (which, strangely, was across the street from plaintiffs' home). In October 1987, counsel's efforts to find Mr. Ullah and effect service ceased. His affidavit states:

> At this point I did not know what to do. I did not know where Mr. Ullah lived nor where he worked. The occupation listed on the police report in my mind was unintelligible. . . . Therefore I did not even know what he even did for a living. He had an unlisted phone number [and] had left no proper forwarding address. From what I could see, he had failed to notify the Department of Public Safety of his current address. Those facts combined with the fact that initially he fled the scene of the accident, and that he had an unusual and foreign sounding name caused me to believe that he may have left the area.

In April 1988, counsel sent plaintiffs a letter advising that his firm no longer wished to represent them. The firm did not withdraw, however, as plaintiffs requested that they keep the file for "a while longer." No activity aimed at perfecting service took place between October 1987 and July 1988. Fortuitously, in July 1988, plaintiff Thomas Eichel met defendant Ullah at a computer fair. Mr. Ullah was served with process within two weeks following this meeting.

Texas courts have consistently held that due diligence was lacking as a matter of law based on unexplained lapses of time between filing of suit, issuance of citation and service. *See, e.g., Rigo,* 458 S.W.2d at 180 (approximately seventeen months between filing and service); *Liles v. Phillips,* 677 S.W.2d 802 (Tex. App.—Fort Worth 1984, writ ref'd n.r.e.) (two years and one month between filing and service); *Williams v. Houston-Citizens Bank and Trust Company,* 531 S.W.2d 434 (Tex. Civ. App.—Houston [14th Dist.] 1975, writ ref'd n.r.e.) (approximately eight months between expiration of first citation and issuance of second); *Buie v. Couch,* 126 S.W.2d 565, 567 (Tex. Civ. App.—Waco 1939, writ ref'd) (almost four months between filing and issuance of citation and another month between issuance and service). Plaintiffs' delay here of over two months between filing suit and issuance of citation, and nine months without any activity at all aimed at finding or serving Mr. Ullah, established lack of diligence as a matter of law, and the trial court correctly entered summary judgment against plaintiffs.

Regarding plaintiffs' argument that Mr. Ullah fraudulently concealed his identity following the accident, it is true that concealment of a party's identity is a factor which weighs heavily in favor of finding due diligence. *Martinez v. Becerra,* 797 S.W.2d 283, 285 (Tex. App.—Corpus Christi 1990, no writ). Limitations begin to run only from the time the fraudulent concealment is discovered or, in the exercise of reasonable diligence, should have been discovered by the wronged party. *Estate of Stonecipher v. Estate of Butts,* 591 S.W.2d 806, 809 (Tex. 1979). Here, for summary judgment purposes, an inference was raised that defendant Ullah did conceal his identity when he fled the scene of the accident. However, he apparently called the police to report his name and insurance information that same day. Plaintiffs admit that they actually learned Ullah's identity three weeks later, when Ullah voluntarily called them, gave them a residence address and telephone number and assured them that his insurance would take care of everything. Plaintiffs made a claim on Ullah's liability insurance and received payment for medical expenses from the carrier during the two years before the limitations period expired. Mr. Ullah's initial brief concealment of his identity, therefore, had no bearing upon plaintiffs' failure to obtain service. Even assuming that for three weeks following the accident, the statute of limitations was tolled, there remains over eight months for which plaintiffs have failed to explain their lack of effort to diligently pursue service.

The Court is concerned with a potential public policy issue here: That a defendant who fled the scene of an automobile accident may now reap some reward from his refusal to take responsibility for his actions. Here, however, Mr. Ullah apparently realized his error promptly, and made efforts to correct it by reporting the accident to the police the very day it happened, and by telephoning plaintiffs personally. Plaintiffs contacted Mr. Ullah's liability insurance carrier and received medical benefits from that company. It was plaintiffs who opted not to hire an attorney until almost two years after the collision occurred. Mr. Ullah's initial failure to stop at the scene had nothing to do with the decision. This does not appear to be a case in which defendant willfully avoided revealing his identity to avoid service of process, and the outcome here should not be read as holding that such irresponsible conduct, in an appropriate case, would not toll the statute of limitations. Points of Error Nos. One and Two are overruled.

The judgment of the trial court is affirmed.

### [3] Proof of Service: The Return

*Read Tex. R. Civ. P. 102, 103, 105, 107, 109a, 124.*

#### [a] Personal Service

Any sheriff or constable, a person authorized by law, or any other disinterested person authorized by written order of the court who is not less than 18 years of age, may serve citation anywhere. In addition, service by registered or certified mail and citation by publication may be made by the clerk of the court in which the case is pending. Tex. R. Civ. P. 103. Alternative methods of service are provided in Civil Procedure Rule 106(b). In any event, the person serving process must make a return of service that shows:

(1) The day and hour on which citation was received. Tex. R. Civ. P. 105.

(2) The day on which citation was served and the manner of service. Tex. R. Civ. P. 107. *See Brown-McKee, Inc. v. J. F. Bryan & Associates,* 522 S.W.2d 958, 959 (Tex. Civ. App.—Texarkana 1975, no writ).

#### [b] Certified or Registered Mail

If service is by registered or certified mail, the return must also contain the return receipt with the addressee's signature. Tex. R. Civ. P. 107, 109a.

#### [c] Alternative Service

If service is made pursuant to court order, strict compliance with the court order is required. *Broussard v. Davila,* 352 S.W.2d 753, 754 (Tex. Civ. App.—San Antonio 1961, no writ). When service is by disinterested person or in some other manner reasonably effective to give defendant notice of the suit (Tex. R. Civ. P. 106(b)), proof of service must be made in the manner ordered by the court. Tex. R. Civ. P. 107.

### [d] First Aid for Flawed Returns

## BAVARIAN AUTOHAUS, INC. v. HOLLAND

*570 S.W.2d 110 (Tex. Civ. App.—Houston [1st Dist.] 1978, no writ)*

PEDEN, Justice.

Bavarian Autohaus, Inc. and BMW of North America, Inc. (BMW) appeal . . . from a default judgment in favor of David Holland, who claimed unliquidated damages under the Deceptive Trade Practices and Consumer Protection Act (Tex. Bus. & Com. Code, Chapter 17) as a result of the defendants' alleged misrepresentations concerning the quality of their automobiles and their repair service. The trial court heard testimony on the plaintiff's damages and entered a judgment of $5,000 plus costs against the defendants jointly and severally. Bavarian Autohaus asserts error in the trial court's finding that citation was served on it, and both appellants contend that the plaintiff did not offer adequate proof of damages. The appellee has not responded. We reverse and remand.

. . . .

Bavarian Autohaus argues under its first eight points of error that the default judgment should be set aside because the record does not affirmatively show that citation was properly served upon it. Ordinarily, presumptions are made in support of due service when it is recited in the judgment but not when a direct attack is made upon a default judgment. *McKanna v. Edgar,* 388 S.W.2d 927, 929 (Tex. 1965). In that case, jurisdiction must affirmatively appear on the face of the record. *Flynt v. City of Kingsville,* 125 Tex. 510, 82 S.W.2d 934 (1935).

The citation recites that it was to be issued to Bavarian Autohaus, Inc., a Texas corporation, by serving its agent, Charles Vann. The original sheriff's return states that it was delivered to "Clint Hughes—V. Pres."

The amended return states:

> "Received this writ on the *3* day of *FEB,* 1977, at 10:49 o'clock A.M., and executed the same in Harris County Texas, on the *9* day of *FEB,* 1977, at 2:50 o'clock P.M., by summoning the *BAVARIAN AUTOHAUS, INC.*, a corporation by delivering to *Clint Hughes,* in person *Vice President* of the said *Corporation* a true copy of this writ, together with accompanying certified copy plaintiff's original petition."

The amended return relates back and is regarded as filed when the original return was filed. *Lafleaur v. Switzer,* 109 S.W.2d 239, 241 (Tex. Civ. App. 1937, no writ); *Nash v. Boyd,* 225 S.W.2d 649 (Tex. Civ. App. 1949, no writ); 2 McDonald, Texas Civil Practice 406, § 9.19 (1970).

Article 2.11 of the Texas Business Corporation Act makes the president, all vice presidents and the registered agent of a corporation agents for service of process. The original officer's return did not state that Bavarian Autohaus was served by serving "Clint Hughes—V. Pres." It did not recite, as it must, that process was delivered to the defendant, Bavarian Autohaus, through its named agent. *Brown-McKee, Inc. v. J. F. Bryan & Associates,* 522 S.W.2d 958, 959 (Tex. Civ. App. 1975, no writ); *Firman Leather Goods Corp. v. McDonald & Shaw,* 217 S.W.2d 137, 140 (Tex. Civ. App. 1948, no writ).

This original return was fatally defective, but the appellee procured an amended return sometime prior to the day of the hearing. Rule 118, Texas Rules of Civil Procedure, provides:

"At any time in its discretion and upon such notice and on such terms as it deems just, the court may allow any process or proof of service thereof to be amended, unless it clearly appears that material prejudice would result to the substantial rights of the party against whom the process issued."

When this case was before the trial judge for assessment of damages, he noted that the court file did not show service of citation on Bavarian Autohaus, whereupon the appellee produced the amended return described above from his file and related that his secretary had taken it to the constable's office for correction. Further discussion followed, outside the hearing of the court reporter.

It is obvious that the trial court allowed the amended return to be filed before entering judgment next day. Although the statement of facts does not show that the provisions of Rule 118 were specifically invoked in the trial court, it appears that they were complied with. Bavarian Autohaus has not asserted that it was misled by the earlier return on the citation. We cannot say the trial court erred in allowing the already-amended return to be filed or in not requiring that notice of the amendment be given to Bavarian Autohaus.

Bavarian Autohaus argues that the amended return fails to comply with Rule 107, Texas Rules of Civil Procedure, because it does not show the manner of service. More specifically, Bavarian Autohaus asserts that the use of the words "writ" and "summoning" in the return render it defective, pointing out that "writ" was used prior to the adoption of the Rules of Civil Procedure and is still being used when referring to citations. See 2 McDonald, Texas Civil Practice 398. § 9.16 (1970). A return should be given a fair, reasonable and natural construction to its plain intent and meaning. *Brown-McKee, Inc. v. J. F. Bryan & Associates,* 522 S.W.2d 958, 959 (Tex. Civ. App. 1975, no writ). In our case the citation was directed by the clerk to the defendant; it referred both to service of "this citation" and to service of "this writ." We hold that the return in this case fairly states the manner of service as required by Rule 107.

. . . .

The judgment of the trial court is reversed and remanded for a new hearing on the issue of damages.

### [4] Citation by Publication

*Read Tex. R. Civ. P. 109–117a, 244, 329.*

#### [a] Generally

The pejorative term "constructive service" is frequently employed to describe citation by publication. It also has been accurately described as a "sham upon due process." Johnson, *Citation by Publication: A Sham Upon Due Process* 36 Tex. B.J. 205 (Mar. 1975). Traditionally, it has been restricted to proceedings that are classifiable as in rem or quasi in rem. *Pennoyer v. Neff,* 95 U.S. 714, 24 L. Ed. 565 (1877). *See* § 4.01[A]. Modern due process notions reject the idea that a determination of the type of action as either in rem or in personam controls the availability of publication. *See Mullane v. Central Hanover Bank & Trust Co.,* 339 U.S. 306, 314 (1950). On the other hand, the application of the traditional categories has led courts to conclude that publication is ordinarily not available *unless* the action is *in rem,* at least where non-domiciliaries are concerned. Some older cases indicate that it is not available in actions to obtain personal judgments against non-domiciliaries of Texas. *Sgitcovich v. Sgitcovich,* 150 Tex. 398, 241 S.W.2d

142, 146 (1959). Compare Tex. R. Civ. P. 117a. *See also Mullane v. Central Hanover Bank & Trust Co.,* 339 U.S. 306, 314 (1950).

### [b] Specific Uses

Citation by publication is specifically authorized in the following circumstances:

(1) *Partition.* In an action to partition when some portion of the land described in the petition is owned by a person who is unknown to the plaintiff or whose residence is unknown to the plaintiff. Tex. R. Civ. P. 758.

(2) *Defunct Corporations.* In an action against unknown heirs or stockholders of a defunct corporation. Tex. R. Civ. P. 111; C.P.R.C. § 17.004.

(3) *Land.* In an action against unknown owners or claimants of interests in land. Tex. R. Civ. P. 112, 113; C.P.R.C. § 17.005.

(4) *Marriage Dissolution.* In an action for divorce or annulment of marriage in which the defendant cannot be notified by personal service or registered or certified mail. Fam. C. § 3.521.

(5) *Ad Valorem Taxes.* In suits for the collection of delinquent ad valorem taxes. Tex. R. Civ. P. 117a.

(6) *Whereabouts of Defendant Unknown.* When the defendant's residence is unknown and cannot be ascertained after reasonable diligence, or the defendant is a transient person whose whereabouts are unknown and cannot be ascertained, or the defendant is absent from or a nonresident of Texas and service under Tex. R. Civ. P. 108 has been attempted unsuccessfully. Tex. R. Civ. P. 109.

Whenever citation by publication is authorized, the court may, on motion, prescribe a different method of service if the court finds, and so recites in its order, that the method so prescribed would be as likely as publication to give the defendant actual notice. Tex. R. Civ. P. 109a. *See also* Tex. R. Civ. P. 329.

---

## NOTES AND QUESTIONS

(1) *Notice Reasonably Calculated.* In light of the standard articulated in *Peralta, above*, when will you use publication?

(2) *Publication and Default Judgments.* Can there be a true default judgment when citation is by publication? How long does the nonresident have to reopen a default under Civil Procedure Rule 329?

### [5] Special Requirements for Substituted Service Under the General Texas Long-Arm Statute

#### [a] Pleading Requirements

## McKANNA v. EDGAR

*388 S.W.2d 927 (Tex. 1965)*

[Edgar sued McKanna in Travis County, Texas on a promissory note payable by its terms in Austin. Service was purportedly done through the secretary of state pursuant to the general Texas long-arm statute. A default judgment was rendered against McKanna, which the court of civil appeals affirmed. McKanna attacked the judgment on appeal on the ground that the record failed to show the conditions required by the general Texas long-arm statute. The Texas Supreme Court agreed and reversed.]

Section 3 of [the general Texas long-arm statute], here to be construed, reads in part as follows:

> "Any . . . non-resident natural person that engages in business in this State . . . and does not maintain a place of regular business in this State or a designated agent upon whom service may be made . . ., the act or acts of engaging in such business . . . shall be deemed equivalent to an appointment . . . of the Secretary of State of Texas as agent upon whom service of process may be made . . . ."

. . . .

Edgar alleged in his petition that Eileen Ann McKanna resided in Orange County, California, and that she executed and delivered to Edgar her note "payable to the order of plaintiff at 1210 Perry-Brooks Building, Austin, Texas . . . ." These allegations comply with the requirements of Section 3 of [the general Texas long-arm statute] that McKanna be a nonresident and, as stipulated, be doing business in this State. But there are no allegations that McKanna "does not maintain a place of regular business in this State or a designated agent upon whom service may be made." The nonexistence of those two conditions is shown to be a necessary prerequisite to the applicability of Section 3 because of the language used in Section 2. Section 2 provides:

> "When any . . . non-resident natural person . . . shall engage in business in this State . . . service may be made by serving a copy of the process with the person who . . . is in charge of any business in which the defendant or defendants are engaged . . . ."

If the defendant had a regular place of business or a designated agent in Texas, we doubt that it could be successfully contended that service of process could be made on the Secretary of State. We hold under the clear language of [the general Texas long-arm statute] that "the intent is to permit resort to Section 3 only if Section 2 is not available." Counts, More on Rule 120a, 28 Tex. B.J. 95, 137 (Feb. 1965). This holding is in accord with the established law of this State that it is imperative and essential that the record affirmatively show a strict compliance with the provided mode of service.

[The Court next rejected two arguments relied on by the court of civil appeals. First, although there is a presumption in favor of most judgments, that rule does not apply to default judgments or to jurisdictional allegations subjected to direct attack. Secondly, although the cases indicate that actual *proof* of certain kinds of jurisdictional facts need not be made on default, they must at least be *alleged.*]

. . . .

The judgments of the courts below are reversed, and the cause remanded to the District Court for a trial on the merits.

---

**PARAMOUNT PIPE & SUPPLY CO. v. MUHR**, 749 S.W.2d 491 (Tex. 1988). Because the defendant has the burden of *disproving* contacts, it seems logical to require notice of the contacts on which plaintiff relies. Should this sort of notice be required to appear in the petition, and if so, what degree of specificity should be required? In *Paramount*, the Court upheld two default judgments after addressing the adequacy of the jurisdictional allegations:

> So long as the allegations confronting Muhr were sufficient to satisfy due process requirements, the trial court had jurisdiction to render judgment by default against him. The only question, then, is whether the jurisdictional allegations in the petitions were sufficient, under the Constitution of the United States, to require Muhr to answer. Tex. R. Civ. P. 108.
>
> The petitions in both cases alleged that the defendants, including Muhr, engaged in business in Texas and further that the causes of action arose from and were connected with "purposeful acts committed by Defendant Western International Petroleum Corporation, acting for itself and as agent for Defendant Ulrich Muhr." The petitions went on to allege, in substance, that Western International made and breached contracts in Texas as Muhr's agent and on his behalf. These allegations against Western International (which, by default, admittedly was acting for Muhr) are sufficient to satisfy the rule stated in *Siskind v. Villa Foundation for Education, Inc.*, 642 S.W.2d 434 (Tex. 1982), and we perceive no due process violation. We conclude that the trial court did have in personam jurisdiction and constitutionally rendered judgments by default on the allegations made against Muhr.

### [b] Method of Service

*The Mechanics of Service on the Secretary of State.* Section 17.026 of the Civil Practice and Remedies Code provides that in an action in which citation may be served on the secretary of state, service may be made by certified mail, return receipt requested, by the clerk of the court in which the case is pending or by the party or the representative of the party. C.P.R.C. § 17.026. When a nonresident is served through the Secretary of State pursuant to this statute, the following steps are required:

(a) Send two copies of petition and citation by certified mail to:

Secretary of State
Statutory Document Section
P.O. Box 12887
Austin, Texas 78711

together with check for $35.

(b) The secretary of state's office will send one copy of the petition and citation to the defendant by certified mail. When the secretary of state's office receives the "return receipt" in the mail, it will send the plaintiff's counsel a certificate indicating that the defendant has been served.

There is no provision in C.P.R.C. § 17.026 for a "citation return" but in an abundance of caution, counsel may want to prepare a return substantially in the following form and file it with the court after the green return receipt card is received.

OFFICER'S RETURN

Came to hand this 10th day of December, 1998, at 8:30 a.m. Executed December 10, 1998, at 9:30 a.m., pursuant to Section 17.026, Civil Practice and Remedies Code, by mailing to the Secretary of the State of Texas, Statutory Documents Section, P.O. Box 12887, Austin, Texas 78711, by certified mail, return receipt requested, two copies of Citation with attached Original Petition for Declaratory Judgment with instructions that one copy of the process should be mailed to the defendant ________ at his/her home address located at 7020 South Woodland Road, Route 87, Novelty, Ohio 44072.

Proof of service (the green return receipt card), is attached to this return, indicating that the Secretary of State of Texas received the above described documents on the ______ day of December, 1998.

______________________________
Printed Name: ________________
Representative of Plaintiff

SUBSCRIBED AND SWORN TO BEFORE ME on this ________ day of December, 1998, to certify which witness my hand and seal of office.

______________________________
Notary Public in and for the State of Texas
My commission expires ____________

### [c] Proof of Long-Arm Service

If a defendant is served pursuant to the general Texas long-arm statute, the service is actually on the secretary of state. The nonresident defendant's time to answer begins to run when the secretary is served, not when the defendant receives the certified mailing. *See Bonewitz v. Bonewitz*, 726 S.W.2d 227, 230 (Tex. App.—Austin 1987, writ ref'd n.r.e.) (service on Secretary triggered defendant's answer date). Accordingly, the return will show that it was served on the secretary, the date and hour, etc. Should this be sufficient? Consider the following.

---

## WHITNEY v. L & L REALTY CORPORATION

*500 S.W.2d 94 (Tex. 1973)*

GREENHILL, Chief Justice.

These suits by a landlord to collect rent from former tenants raise a question concerning the proof needed to support a default judgment where service of process was upon the Secretary of State. The solution turns upon the construction, and the requirements as to service, of Article 2031b, the Texas long-arm statute. [footnote omitted] The immediate question is whether, as a matter of jurisdiction, the long-arm statute involved requires not only service upon the Secretary of State but also requires a showing in the record that he forwarded the service to the defendant. We hold that it does.

Plaintiff, L & L Realty Corporation, leased apartments in Dallas to defendants Whitney and Parnass for one year terms. During the term, defendants moved out of the state, abandoned their apartments, and ceased rental payments. Plaintiff took default judgments against them after serving process on the Secretary of State of Texas, as authorized by Article 2031b. Nothing in the record indicates whether or not the Secretary of State forwarded a copy of the process to either defendant.

. . . .

A record showing of jurisdiction necessary to support a default judgment upon substituted service, such as we have here, must meet two major requirements: (1) The pleadings must allege facts which, if true, would make the defendant responsible to answer,—or in the language of Rule 120a, contain allegations making the defendant "amenable to process" by the use of the long-arm statute; and (2) there must be proof in the record that the defendant was, in fact, served in the manner required by statute.

We have no problem here as to the responsibility to answer, or "amenability to process." The allegations are sufficient, under Section 6 of Article 2031b, to require the defendants to answer if they have in fact been served in accordance with the requirements of that statute. McKanna v. Edgar, 388 S.W.2d 927 (Tex. 1965). The fact of service, however, must be shown by proof appearing in the record. Flynt v. City of Kingsville, 125 Tex. 510, 82 S.W.2d 934 (1935); Roberts v. Stockslager, 4 Tex. 307 (1849); De Proy v. Progakis, 269 S. W. 78 (Tex. Com. App. 1925, holding approved).

In the present case, the record includes a citation and return showing service on the Secretary of State, the official designated by statute as eligible to receive it. Thus the question is squarely presented whether this is sufficient to confer jurisdiction, or whether, under the statute, the record must show compliance with the additional statutory requirement that the Secretary forward a copy of the process to defendant.

. . . .

We regard the statute as being ambiguous. It could be construed to mean that service is complete when the Secretary of State is served, whether he forwards the service or not; but that as the agent of the defendant, he ought to forward the service to the defendant. Or it could mean that the Legislature intended to require that in order for the Secretary of State to be conclusively presumed to be the attorney for the defendant in another state, he *must* forward the service; i.e., the Secretary of State is to be deemed the defendant's agent *if,* or *provided,* he forwards the service as required by the statute.

We regard the latter as being the intent of the statute. It achieves a result most consistent with justice and due process to both parties. Roberts v. Stockslager, 4 Tex. 307 (1849).

. . . .

The requirement of proof of forwarding of process which we construe the statute to impose will not cause any significant hardship to plaintiffs seeking judgments against non-residents. A certificate from the office of the Secretary of State, which the plaintiff could obtain for a trivial fee, would suffice. A contrary result would entail a much more serious hardship for defendants. &hellip

Furthermore, requiring proof of forwarding is consistent with our decisions which have insisted on compliance with statutes conferring personal jurisdiction. To support a default judgment, our decisions require particularity in pleading amenability to service, McKanna v. Edgar, 388 S.W.2d 927 (Tex. 1965), and in showing the fact of service, Roberts v. Stockslager, 4 Tex. 307 (1849). These decisions reflect a strong policy that defendants ought not to be cast in personal judgment without notice. See Roberts v. Stockslager, 4 Tex. at 309. As Justice Oliver Wendell Holmes said, speaking of statutes authorizing service by publication, ". . . great caution should be used not to let fiction deny the fair play that can be secured only by a pretty close adhesion to fact." McDonald v. Mabee, 243 U.S. 90, 91, 37 S. Ct. 343, 61 L. Ed. 608 (1917).

Our decision requires that the default judgments be set aside on the ground that the record fails to show that the district court acquired personal jurisdiction of the defendants. Accordingly, the judgments below are reversed, and the causes are remanded to the district court.

---

## NOTE

One court has held that if mailing is proper, proof of actual receipt of the certified mail by the nonresident is not required. *See Texas Real Estate Comm'n v. Howard*, 538 S.W.2d 429, 433 (Tex. Civ. App.—Houston [14th Dist.] 1976, writ ref'd n.r.e.).

### [6] Notice to Nonresidents

*Read Tex. R. Civ. P. 108.*

Civil Procedure Rule 108 provides that when the defendant is absent from the state, notice in the same form as citation to defendants served within the state "may be served by any disinterested person competent to make oath of the fact in the same manner as provided in Rule 106." The key questions concerning Rule 108's interpretation are as follows:

(1) Does Rule 108 incorporate all of Rule 106 or only 106(a) and not 106(b)? May a Dallas County officer mail notice to a nonresident of the state?

(2) Is Rule 108 a long-arm provision? See *U-Anchor* and accompanying notes in § 4.02[B].

---

**BUTLER v. BUTLER**, 577 S.W.2d 501 (Tex. Civ. App.—Texarkana 1978, writ dism'd). Issues pertinent to nonresident notice and waiver of the special appearance were addressed in this divorce and child custody case. In 1975 the husband left his wife, took with him a child born during the marriage, and moved to Louisiana where he filed divorce proceedings. The wife, after learning the location of her husband and child through notice of the Louisiana suit, regained custody of the child and filed divorce proceedings of her own in Texas in 1977. The husband filed a special appearance in the Texas action. At the hearing on the special appearance, however, the husband's attorney did not present evidence demonstrating a lack of amenability to process. Rather, he introduced evidence of the Louisiana divorce proceeding and attacked as defective the service of process, which had been made by substituted service on the husband's attorney rather than on the husband himself. The trial court ruled that the Texas Family Code authorized it to exercise jurisdiction over the husband. It also ruled that by arguing defective service, the husband's counsel waived the special appearance and converted it into a general appearance. The case went immediately to trial and the wife was granted a divorce and managing conservatorship of the children. The husband was ordered to pay child support and the wife's attorneys fees. The court of civil appeals affirmed the trial court's rulings. The court held that the substituted service, which the trial court had approved after motion and hearing, comported with the requirements of Civil Procedure Rules 108 and 106. On the issue of waiver of the special appearance, the court stated:

> The issue at a special appearance is jurisdiction, and nothing else. Thode, in his article on special appearance, explains:
>
> The words "not amenable to process issued by the courts of this state" can only be interpreted to mean that the special appearance is available solely to establish that the Texas court cannot, under the federal and state constitutions and the appropriate state statutes, validly obtain jurisdiction over the person or the property of the defendant with regard to the cause of action pled. Defective service or defective process, or even an attempt to bring the defendant before the court under the wrong statute does not authorize the use of the special appearance. 42 Texas L. Rev. 279, 312 (1964).
>
> The trial judge overruled the special appearance and found that it had jurisdiction based on . . . the Texas Family Code. Since the trial court had jurisdiction over the appellant under . . . the Texas Family Code, it was not error for the trial court to immediately proceed to trial in the absence of an answer having been filed by appellant.
>
> . . . .
>
> . . . The fact that appellant turned his special appearance into a general appearance in this case does not afford appellant additional time within which to file an answer. Appellant could have filed his answer along with his sworn special appearance motion under Rule 120a, *supra*, and have forestalled the default judgment which was taken by appellee. Since the court had jurisdiction under . . . the Texas Family Code through service of process under Tex. R. Civ. P. 108, the trial court was authorized to immediately proceed to judgment because no answer had been filed by appellant and the required time for answering had elapsed.

## § 4.05 Challenges to Jurisdiction by Nonresidents

### [A] The Special Appearance

In 1846, in the earliest days of Texas statehood, the First Legislature enacted a procedural statute that recognized a plea to the jurisdiction. The First Legislature also enacted another statute that provided that "[n]o judgment shall in any case be rendered against any defendant unless upon service, or acceptance, or waiver of process, or upon an appearance by the defendant, as prescribed in this chapter, except where otherwise expressly provided by law." Under these provisions, Texas courts apparently did allow nonresidents to appear specially to challenge the exercise of in personam jurisdiction.

Probably as a result of the Civil War, known in the South as the War Between the States, the legal landscape was changed radically by the inclusion of "general appearance" provisions in the Revised Statutes of 1879. First, Article 1242 stated, "The filing of an answer constitutes an appearance of the defendant so as to dispense with the necessity for the issuance or service citation upon him." Second, Article 1243 provided that if service were quashed on motion, the defendant was deemed to have entered his appearance at the next term of court. Third, Article 1244 added that if the judgment was reversed on appeal for want of service or defects in service, the defendant was deemed to have entered his appearance to the term of the trial court where he filed the mandate."

In 1889, these statutory provisions were interpreted by the Texas Supreme Court to mean that every appearance, even one made specially by a nonresident to challenge the exercise of jurisdiction, constituted a general appearance. In *York v. State,* the State of Texas brought suit against York, a resident of Missouri, to recover on a lease contract. York was served in Missouri. York appeared in the Texas court and made what he thought was a "special appearance" for the purpose of contesting personal jurisdiction. The court overruled his plea. When the case came to trial, York appeared, waived his demand for a jury, and relied solely on his plea to the jurisdiction for his defense. Judgment was rendered against York. On appeal, the Supreme Court of Texas held that Articles 1242, 1243, and 1244 had abolished the special appearance. The Court further held that every defense pleading was part of the answer, and by statute the answer was a general appearance that dispensed with the necessity of valid service on the defendant. Hence, as a result of York's appearance the Texas trial court had jurisdiction and the judgment was affirmed.

Thereafter, York appealed his case to the Supreme Court of the United States, contending that the denial of a special appearance was a denial of due process under the Constitution's Fourteenth Amendment. Somewhat surprisingly, the Supreme Court affirmed the judgment holding that "the state has full power over remedies and procedures in its own courts, and can make any order it pleases in respect thereto provided that substance of right is secured without unreasonable burden to parties and litigants. *York v. State,* 137 U.S. 15 (1890). As Professor E. Wayne Thode has explained, in many quarters, the Texas Supreme Court's decision was considered "the ultimate in jurisdictional provincialism until it was eliminated in 1962." *See* Thode, *In Personam Jurisdiction, Article 2031B, the Texas "Long-Arm" Jurisdiction Statute, and the Appearance to Challenge Jurisdiction in Texas and Elsewhere,* 42 Tex. L. Rev. 279 (1964).

Almost a century after the Civil War, by amendment of the rules of procedure nonresidents again became authorized to make special appearances in strict compliance with Civil Procedure Rule 120a. As *York* demonstrates, before the adoption of Civil Procedure Rule 120a in 1962, a nonresident defendant who appeared in a Texas judicial proceeding for the purpose of challenging the court's jurisdiction was deemed to have consented to its jurisdiction by making an appearance. This result occurred even when the nonresident was not otherwise amenable to process. Although an amicus curiae practice developed under which a local attorney exercised the pretense of being a true bystander, by the 1960s even this subterfuge had become unavailable., Professor Thode has suggested that the defendant appeared in the majority of the cases and contested on the merits rather than suffer a default judgment. Under this analysis, Texas attorneys representing defendants were undoubtedly employed by non-residents to contest more cases on merits than had been the experience of defendants' attorneys in other states.

*Read Tex. R. Civ. P. 120a, 122.*

The following Special Appearance is taken from Dorsaneo, *Texas Litigation Guide,* Chapter 60, *Special Appearance.*

**W. Dorsaneo, TEXAS LITIGATION GUIDE**

*§ 60.100[2] (1998)*[*]

NO. ______

| | | |
|---|---|---|
| ________ [*Plaintiff*]) | ) | IN THE ________ COURT |
| v. | ) | ________ COUNTY, TEXAS |
| ________ Defendant | ) | ______ JUDICIAL COURT |

SPECIAL APPEARANCE TO PRESENT MOTION OBJECTING TO JURISDICTION

TO THE HONORABLE COURT:

________ [*Name*], defendant in this cause, makes this special appearance under the authority of Texas Rule of Civil Procedure 120a for the purpose of objecting to the jurisdiction of the Court over the person and property of the defendant, and as grounds shows the following:

I.

This special appearance is made to ________ [the entire proceeding or the severable claim asserted by plaintiff wherein plaintiff seeks ________ (*specify such severable claim*)].

II.

This special appearance is filed prior to a motion to transfer or any other plea, pleading, or motion.

III.

This Court does not have jurisdiction over the defendant's ________ [person *or* property *or* person and property] for the reason that neither the party nor ________ [his *or* her *or* its] property is amenable to process issued by the courts of Texas. In this connection, defendant would further show that: ________ [*negate all theories of jurisdiction, e.g.*,

1. Defendant is not a resident of Texas, and neither is required to maintain nor maintains a registered agent for service in Texas.

2. Defendant does not now engage and has not engaged in business in Texas nor committed any tort, in whole or in part, within the state.

3. Defendant does not maintain a place of business in Texas, and has no employees, servants, or agents within the state.]

IV.

The assumption of jurisdiction by the Court over this defendant [and ________ (his *or* her) property] would offend traditional notions of fair play and substantial justice, depriving the defendant of due process as guaranteed by the Constitution of the United States.

WHEREFORE, defendant requests that this motion be set for hearing on notice to ________ [*name*], plaintiff, and upon such hearing, this motion be in all things sustained and

_________ [*the entire proceeding or specify severable claim*] be dismissed for want of jurisdiction.

Respectfully submitted,
_________ [*firm name, if any*]
_________ [*signature*]
_________ [*typed name*]
_________ [*address*]
_________ [*telephone number*]
_________ [*telecopier number, if any*]
_________ [*state bar i.d. number*]
Attorney for _________

VERIFICATION

STATE OF TEXAS
COUNTY OF _________

BEFORE ME, the undersigned Notary Public, on this day personally appeared _________ [*name*], who, being by me duly sworn on oath deposed and said that _________ [he *or* she] is the _________ [*insert appropriate party designation, e.g.,* defendant or duly authorized agent for _________ (*name*)] in the above-entitled and numbered cause; that _________ [he *or* she] has read the above SPECIAL APPEARANCE TO PRESENT MOTION OBJECTING TO JURISDICTION; and that every statement contained in the SPECIAL APPEARANCE is within _________ [his *or* her] personal knowledge and is true and correct. _________

[*signature of affiant*]

SUBSCRIBED AND SWORN TO BEFORE ME on the _________ day of _________, _________, to certify which witness my hand and official seal.

[*Seal*]

_________ [*signature*]
_________ [*typed name*]
Notary Public in and for the State of Texas
My commission expires _________

CERTIFICATE OF SERVICE

I hereby certify that a true and correct copy of the above SPECIAL APPEARANCE TO PRESENT MOTION OBJECTING TO JURISDICTION has this day been _________ [delivered in person *or* delivered in person by my agent *or* delivered by courier with receipted delivery *or* sent by certified mail by depositing it enclosed in a postpaid, properly addressed wrapper in a post office or official depository under the care and custody of the United States Postal Service *or* sent by telephonic document transfer] _________ [*if sent by telephonic document transfer, add if appropriate:* before 5:00 p.m. of the recipient's local time] to _________ [*name, address, and designation, including telecopier number if sent by telecopier, e.g.,* _________ (*name*), attorney of record for _________ (*name of party*), at _________ (*address*)].

SIGNED this _________ day of _________.

_________ [*signature*]
Attorney for Defendant

## KAWASAKI STEEL CORP. v. MIDDLETON

*699 S.W.2d 199 (Tex. 1985)*

PER CURIAM.

Oilworld Supply Company sued John Middleton for payment for oil well casing Middleton purchased from Oilworld. Middleton filed a counterclaim against Oilworld and third-party claims against Kawasaki Steel Corporation of Japan and Japan Cotton Company for defective casing. Kawasaki allegedly manufactured the casing, and Japan Cotton Company is the trading company that filled Oilworld's order for the casing. Kawasaki filed a special appearance under Tex. R. Civ. P. 120a contending: (1) that Kawasaki lacks minimum contacts with Texas so that the exercise of jurisdiction over its person by a Texas court would violate the Due Process Clause of the Fourteenth Amendment to the United States Constitution; (2) that Middleton has not alleged the facts required for service of process under the "Texas Long Arm Statute," Tex. Rev. Civ. Stat. Ann. art. 2031b (Vernon 1964); and (3) that Middleton did not properly effect service of process.

The trial court held that Kawasaki lacked minimum contacts with Texas and dismissed the cause against Kawasaki. The court of appeals reversed the judgment of the trial court and remanded the cause for trial. 687 S.W.2d 42. That court held Kawasaki did have minimum contacts with Texas and that a non-resident defendant may not contest defects in service of process in a special appearance. We refuse petitioner's application for writ of error with the notation "writ refused, no reversible error."

The facts are well stated in the opinion by the court of appeals and need not be repeated here. Personal jurisdiction is composed of two elements: (1) the defendant must be amenable to the jurisdiction of the court; and (2) if the defendant is amenable to the jurisdiction of the court, the plaintiff must validly invoke that jurisdiction by valid service of process on the defendant. Thode, *In Personam Jurisdiction: Article 2031(b), The Texas Longarm Statute; and the Appearance to Challenge Jurisdiction in Texas and Elsewhere*, 42 Tex. L. Rev. 279, 312–13 (1964).

The first issue is whether Kawasaki is amenable to the jurisdiction of Texas courts. We have held that article 2031b "reaches as far as the federal constitutional requirements of due process will permit." *U-Anchor Advertising, Inc. v. Burt*, 553 S.W.2d 760 (Tex. 1977). Thus, the issue is whether subjecting Kawasaki to the jurisdiction of Texas courts would violate the federal Due Process Clause.

. . . .

Kawasaki annually sells between 40 and 48 million dollars worth of steel that reaches Texas consumers and routinely confirms the content and destination of each order with the trading company that transports the steel to the Port of Houston. The inspection certificates for the Kawasaki casing sold to Middleton were prepared by Kawasaki and shown a Texas buyer. Moreover, at the time the cause of action arose, Kawasaki maintained an office in Houston that provided sales promotion, marketing research, and after-sales service to Kawasaki's customers in North America and Mexico.

Kawasaki argues there is some evidence that it did not "reasonably expect" its products to be sold in Texas because it did not retain the power to direct trading companies to sell or not sell its steel in Texas. "Reasonable expectation," not "right of control" is the controlling issue under the stream of commerce doctrine; therefore, Kawasaki is amenable to the jurisdiction of Texas courts.

The second issue is whether a non-resident defendant may challenge the plaintiff's failure to allege the facts required for service of process under article 2031b, defective service of process, or failure to properly effect service of process in a special appearance.

Before this court promulgated Rule 120a, any appearance by a non-resident defendant was a general appearance which subjected the defendant to the jurisdiction of the court. *York v. State*, 73 Tex. 651, 11 S.W. 869 (1889), *aff'd York v. Texas*, 137 U.S. 15, 11 S. Ct. 9, 34 L. Ed. 604 (1890). Thus, a non-resident defendant had only two options: he could either appear and consent to jurisdiction or allow a default judgment to be taken against him and attack the Texas judgment as being void if the plaintiff brought suit in the defendant's state to enforce the judgment.

Rule 120a altered the *York* rule by allowing a non-resident defendant to make a special appearance "for the purpose of objecting to the jurisdiction of the court over the person or property of the defendant, *on the ground that such party or property is not amenable to process issued by the courts of this state*." Tex. R. Civ. P. 120a. However, in all other respects the *York* rule is unchanged.

The key word is "amenable." Professor Thode, in a well-received article on Rule 120a, interprets this word in its context as follows:

> The words "not amenable to process issued by the courts of this state" can only be interpreted to mean that the special appearance is available solely to establish that the Texas court cannot, under the federal and state constitutions and the appropriate state statutes, validly obtain jurisdiction over the person or the property of the defendant with regard to the cause of action pled. Defective service or defective process, or even an attempt to bring the defendant before the court under the wrong statute does not authorize the use of the special appearance. If the defendant attempts to make a special appearance to raise any of these contentions, then his appearance is a general one and the rule of *York v. State* applies to him with full force.

Thode, *supra* at 312–13. Thode argues that the correct procedure to challenge a defect in *the manner* of obtaining jurisdiction (service or process) is by a Rule 122 motion to quash citation. *Id.* at 313. Rule 122 provides:

> If the citation or service thereof is quashed on motion of the defendant, such defendant shall be deemed to have entered his appearance at ten o'clock a.m. on the Monday next after the expiration of twenty (20) days after the day on which the citation or service is quashed, and such defendant shall be deemed to have been duly served so as to require him to appear and answer at that time, and if he fails to do so, judgment by default may be rendered against him.

Tex. R. Civ. P. 122. Thus, a non-resident defendant, like any other defendant, may move to quash the citation for defects in the process, but his only relief is additional time to answer rather than dismissal of the cause. A curable defect in service of process does not affect a non-resident defendant's amenability to service of process.

Under Professor Thode's analysis, contentions that (1) the allegations of the petition do not properly allege the jurisdictional facts required for service under the long-arm statute; (2) the plaintiff did not serve the defendant; (3) there are defects in the citation, etc., must be raised by amotion to quash, not a special appearance.

Several opinions by our courts of appeals have held that a non-resident defendant may challenge curable defects in a special appearance and that the proper disposition is dismissal of the cause. *TM Productions, Inc. v. Blue Mountain Broadcasting Co.*, 623 S.W.2d 427, 431–33 (Tex. Civ. App.—Dallas 1981), *writ ref'd n.r.e. per curiam*, 639 S.W.2d 450 (1982); *In Re D.N.S.*, 592 S.W.2d 35, 37 (Tex. Civ. App.—Beaumont 1979, no writ); *Mills v. Stinger Boats, Inc.*, 580 S.W.2d 106, 107–108 (Tex. Civ. App.—Eastland 1979, writ ref'd n.r.e.); *Menchaca v. Chrysler Life Insurance Co.*, 604 S.W.2d 287, 289 (Tex. Civ. App.—San Antonio 1980, no writ); *Gathers v. Walpace Co., Inc.*, 544 S.W.2d 169, 170 (Tex. Civ. App.—Beaumont 1976, writ ref'd n.r.e.); *Burgess v. Ancillary Acceptance Corp.*, 543 S.W.2d 738, 740 (Tex. Civ. App.—El Paso 1976, writ ref'd n.r.e.); *Curry v. Dell Publishing Co.*, 438 S.W.2d 887 (Tex. Civ. App.—El Paso 1969, writ ref'd n.r.e.). However, one court of appeals has followed Professor Thode's view. *Steve Tyrell Productions, Inc. v. Ray*, 674 S.W.2d 430, 434–35 (Tex. App.—Austin 1984, no writ).

The courts of appeals opinions which permit a non-resident defendant to contest curable defects misapply our opinion in *McKanna v. Edgar*, 388 S.W.2d 927 (Tex. 1965). *McKanna* involved an appeal by writ of error to the court of appeals of a default judgment. The defendant claimed that service of process was defective because the plaintiff failed to allege the jurisdictional facts under article 2031b. This court agreed and remanded the case for trial under Rule 123 which provides that when a judgment is reversed "because of defective service of process, no new citation shall be issued or served, but the defendant shall be presumed to have entered his appearance to the term of court at which mandate shall be filed." *Id.* at 930. We agree with Dean Newton that Professor Thode's interpretation is correct:

> But as the Dallas Court of Appeals noted in *TM Productions v. Blue Mountain*, decisions by the courts of civil appeals applying *McKanna* and *Whitney* [*Whitney v. L & L Realty Corporation*, 500 S.W.2d 94 (Tex. 1973)] have ignored the triggering requirements of those cases and applied their rule in ways which do not serve the rule's underlying rationale. Starting with the case of *Castle v. Berg* [415 S.W.2d 523 (Tex. Civ. App.)] in 1967, at least five of our courts of civil appeals have applied the rule to non-default cases. This application does not simply go beyond the holdings of the Supreme Court, it contradicts them. One of the bases for the *McKanna* and *Whitney* rule is that the issue of jurisdiction had not been litigated and therefore a failure to properly invoke jurisdiction by pleading could require reversal. Application of the *McKanna* and *Whitney* exception to a case where jurisdiction was actually litigated amounts to a negation of the very general rule to which *McKanna* and *Whitney* form an exception. *McKanna* and *Whitney* start with a recognition that res judicata applies to jurisdictional issues; the decisions of the courts of civil appeals functionally reject that recognition by misapplying the rule. The only basis offered is that the plaintiff did not properly plead jurisdictional facts. Such a narrow holding is inconsistent with the general rules of notice pleading. Indeed if the approach of the courts of appeals was applied to pleading generally, we would return to the thoroughly discounted English writ approach where a failure to dot an "i" or cross a "t" was fatal. Not even the legacy of *York v. State* can justify this result since in 1976, Rule 120a was changed to allow defendants to amend a special appearance "to cure defects." Further, *McKanna* and *Whitney*

> are cases where failure of notice to the defendant was a major factor. This cannot be a factor in non-default cases since the defendant appeared and participated. Finally, under *McKanna* and *Whitney*, the remedy was a reversal, not a dismissal. In the *Castle* case, the court held that the defendant was entitled to a dismissal for lack of jurisdiction. Not only are these decisions by the courts of civil appeals unjustified, where a dismissal occurs a plaintiff may lose a cause of action due to the statute of limitations. In such a case the error would be more than simple inconvenience and cost.

Newton, *Annual Survey of Texas Law; Conflict of Laws*, 36 Sw. L. J. 397, 406 (1982).

Thus, in a Rule 120a special appearance, the non-resident defendant has the burden of proof to negate all bases of personal jurisdiction. *Siskind v. Villa Foundation for Education, Inc.*, 642 S.W.2d 434, 438 (Tex. 1982). We hold that defective jurisdictional allegations in the petition, defective service of process, and defects in the citation must be challenged by a motion to quash, not a special appearance. We disapprove the opinions by our courts of appeals which hold that a non-resident defendant may contest curable defects in service of process in a special appearance.

Because Kawasaki is amenable to the jurisdiction of Texas courts, we refuse petitioner's application for writ of error with the notation "writ refused, no reversible error."

---

## NOTES AND QUESTIONS

(1) *Amenability to Process.* From the time of its first reported judicial construction, Civil Procedure Rule 120a has been interpreted to place the burden of showing a lack of amenability to process on the nonresident. *See* Guittard, *Appearance Under Rule 120a,* 27 Tex. B.J. 235 (1965). This is contrary to the federal practice. *See* Fed. R. Civ. P. 12(b)(2); *Product Promotions, Inc. v. Cousteau,* 495 F.2d 483 (5th Cir. 1974), *overruled on other grounds, Insurance Corp. of Ireland v. Compagnie des Bauxites de Guinee*, 456 U.S. 694, 702–703, 102 S. Ct. 2099, 72 L. Ed. 2d 492 (1982), as stated in *Burstein v. State Bar of Ca.*, 693 F.2d 511, 518 n.12 (5th Cir. 1982). Which approach is more sensible?

(2) *Affidavit Evidence.* As a result of 1990 amendments to Civil Procedure Rule 120a, affidavits can be used as evidence in a special appearance hearing in addition to or in lieu of live testimony. *See* Tex. R. Civ. P. 120a.

(3) *Serving a Nonresident Who Is Present to Contest Jurisdiction.* What if a nonresident comes to Texas to testify at a special appearance hearing? Can he or she be served with process and thereby be subjected to in personam jurisdiction? In *Oates v. Blackburn,* 430 S.W.2d 400, 403 (Tex. Civ. App.—Houston [14th Dist.] 1968, no writ), the court of civil appeals held that the presence is privileged because otherwise Civil Procedure Rule 120a would be rendered ineffective. The opinion is, however, less than crystal clear when the specially appearing nonresident is served in connection with unrelated litigation. What should the answer be?

(4) *The Nonresident's Burden.* In determining a special appearance motion, the relationship of the nonresident's "burden of proof to negate all bases of personal jurisdiction" to the plaintiff's jurisdictional allegations continues to trouble the bench and bar. *See Temperature Systems, Inc. v. Bill Pepper, Inc.*, 854 S.W.2d 669, 673–674 (Tex. App.—Dallas 1993, writ dism'd by agr.) (when there are no jurisdictional allegations in the plaintiff's petition, proof that defendant is

nonresident is sufficient to meet burden, but proof of nonresidency is not sufficient when plaintiff alleges jurisdictional facts).

(5) *Post-Judgment Special Appearances.* Despite the clear suggestion in the last sentence of Civil Procedure Rule 120a(1) that a special appearance motion cannot be made after judgment, several cases have authorized post-judgment special appearance motions as long as they are filed in due order. *See Koch Graphics, Inc. v. Avantech, Inc.*, 803 S.W.2d 432, 433 (Tex. App.—Dallas 1991, no writ).

(6) *The Effect of Improper Removal.* The filing of a notice of removal to federal court before a special appearance does not waive the right to thereafter challenge personal jurisdiction before a Texas court on remand. *Antonio v. Marino*, 910 S.W.2d 624, 629 (Tex. App.—Houston [14th Dist.] 1995, no writ).

---

## DAWSON-AUSTIN v. AUSTIN

*968 S.W.2d 319 (Tex. 1998)*

HECHT, Justice.

The issues we address in this divorce action are whether the district court had in personam jurisdiction over the wife, and if not, whether the court nevertheless had jurisdiction to divide the marital estate. The court of appeals upheld personal jurisdiction. 920 S.W.2d 776. We disagree.

### I

Since 1970, William Franklin Austin has been the president, chief executive officer, sole director, and sole stockholder of Starkey Laboratories, Inc., a Minnesota corporation in the business of manufacturing and distributing hearing aids. In 1977, Austin met Cynthia Lee Dawson at a seminar in Oregon, where she was living, and persuaded her to come to work for Starkey at its headquarters in Minnesota. Austin was 35 years old and divorced, and Dawson was 30 years old and separated from her husband. Dawson soon moved into Austin's Minnesota home and continued working for Starkey. On a business trip to China in 1980, Austin and Dawson recited marriage vows in a Beijing restaurant. Two years later they filed a marriage certificate in Minnesota. At some point Dawson assumed the surname, Dawson-Austin.

Dawson-Austin worked for Starkey until shortly after she and Austin separated in 1992. Over the years the business had grown. In 1980 Starkey was worth about $1.5 million with some $12 million in net revenues. By 1992 the company had become the second largest manufacturer of hearing aids in the world with sales totaling more than $200 million and a net worth of at least $40 million.

Throughout the marriage the couple's principal residence was in Minnesota, although they also owned homes elsewhere, including one they acquired in California in 1984. They never resided in Texas, and neither of them ever came to the state except on business, and then only a few times. When they separated in February 1992, Dawson-Austin was living in their California home, and she remained there. Austin moved to Texas on March 10. On April 10 Dawson-Austin filed for divorce in California but did not serve Austin until October 16. Austin filed for divorce in Texas on September 10, the first day he could do so under Texas law, Tex. Fam. Code § 6.301 (formerly Tex. Fam. Code § 3.21), and served Dawson-Austin four days later.

Dawson-Austin filed a special appearance and an amended special appearance, both of which the district court overruled. Dawson-Austin requested the court in dividing the couple's property to apply Minnesota law, under which she contends she would be entitled to a part of the increase in value of petitioner's Starkey stock attributable to the efforts of either spouse. The court refused and instead applied Texas law, holding that the stock was Austin's separate property subject only to any right of reimbursement of the community estate. The district court also struck Dawson-Austin's two expert witnesses retained to testify on the value of the community and its right of reimbursement, on the grounds that they were not timely identified in discovery. In a bench trial, Austin stipulated to Dawson-Austin's valuation of the community estate at $3,750,000. The court awarded Dawson-Austin 55.59% of the community—a little over $2 million.

Dawson-Austin appealed. The court of appeals in its initial opinion reversed the decree, holding that Minnesota law should have been applied in dividing the marital estate. On rehearing, however, a divided court of appeals affirmed the decree in all respects. 920 S.W.2d 776.

II

We first consider whether, as a matter of procedure, Dawson-Austin made a general appearance in the case.

Dawson-Austin filed *pro se* a single instrument including a special appearance, a motion to quash service of citation, a plea to the jurisdiction of the court, a plea in abatement, and subject to all of the above, an original answer. Only the answer was expressly made subject to the special appearance; the motion and pleas were not. The instrument contained a verification of the facts and allegations stated in each component of the instrument except the special appearance. Dawson-Austin contends that the failure to include the special appearance in the verification was a typographical error. The district court overruled Dawson-Austin's special appearance because it was not sworn as required by Rule 120a(1), Tex. R. Civ. P., and because a motion to quash service of citation, plea to the jurisdiction, and plea in abatement, all included in the same instrument with the special appearance, were not expressly made subject to the special appearance.

The day after the court's overruling of the special appearance, Dawson-Austin filed a motion for reconsideration and an amended special appearance. The court denied the amended special appearance "on the merits", in the court's words, and did not rule on the motion to reconsider.

The court of appeals held that Dawson-Austin's special appearance was properly overruled because it was unsworn. The court did not consider whether the other pleadings in the same instrument should have been expressly subjected to the special appearance. 920 S.W.2d at 782. The court also held that Dawson-Austin waived her amended special appearance because, before it was filed, Dawson-Austin argued her motion to quash and did not object to the district court's consideration of it. 920 S.W.2d at 782–783.

Austin argues that there are yet other reasons, in addition to those given by the lower courts, for concluding that Dawson-Austin made a general appearance in the proceeding. We address each of these arguments in turn.

A

As the lower courts both held, an unsworn special appearance does not comply with Rule 120a(1), Tex. R. Civ. P., and thus is ineffectual to challenge in personam jurisdiction. The lower courts also held, however, that the lack of verification can be cured by amendment. Austin argues that an unsworn special appearance cannot be cured and is itself a general appearance. Austin's argument is contrary to the express provision of Rule 120a(1) that a special appearance "may be amended to cure defects". By "cure", the rule means to restore the special appearance. The rule does not limit the kinds of defects that can be cured. The absence of a verification is such a defect, and an amendment that adds a verification cures the special appearance. Every court that has considered the issue agrees. *See Villalpando v. De La Garza,* 793 S.W.2d 274, 275–276 (Tex. App.—Corpus Christi 1990, no writ); *Carbonit Houston, Inc. v. Exchange Bank,* 628 S.W.2d 826, 828 (Tex. App.—Houston [14th Dist.] 1982, writ ref'd n.r.e.); *Stegall & Stegall v. Cohn,* 592 S.W.2d 427, 429 (Tex. App.—Fort Worth 1979, no writ); *Dennett v. First Continental Inv. Corp.,* 559 S.W.2d 384, 385–386 (Tex. App.—Dallas 1977, no writ).

Austin argues, alternatively, that even if an unsworn special appearance can be cured by amendment, the amendment must be filed before the special appearance is ruled on. This argument, too, finds no footing in Rule 120a(1). The rule simply does not require that an amendment be filed before a ruling on the special appearance, as long as the amendment is filed before there is a general appearance. *See Dennett,* 559 S.W.2d at 386 ("[T]he crucial focus is on the *allowance* of amendment, and the *timing* of the amendment is not determinative.") (emphasis in original).

Austin's arguments are not only contradicted by both the language and silence of Rule 120a, they misperceive what constitutes a general appearance. One court has explained:

> A party enters a general appearance whenever it invokes the judgment of the court on any question other than the court's jurisdiction; if a defendant's act recognizes that an action is properly pending or seeks affirmative action from the court, that is a general appearance.

*Moore v. Elektro-Mobil Technik GMBH,* 874 S.W.2d 324, 327 (Tex. App.—El Paso 1994, writ denied). Another court has stated the same proposition in the negative:

> "[A]lthough an act of defendant may have some relation to the cause, it does not constitute a general appearance, if it in no way recognizes that the cause is properly pending or that the court has jurisdiction, and no affirmative action is sought from the court."

*Investors Diversified Servs., Inc. v. Bruner,* 366 S.W.2d 810, 815 (Tex. Civ. App.—Houston 1963, writ ref'd n.r.e.) (quoting 6 C.J.S. *Appearances* § 13 (19—)); *see also Letersky v. Letersky,* 820 S.W.2d 12, 13 (Tex. App.—Eastland 1991, no writ); *United Nat'l Bank v. Travel Music, Inc.,* 737 S.W.2d 30, 32–33 (Tex. App.—San Antonio 1987, writ ref'd n.r.e.). These courts have accurately restated the principle underlying a general appearance. An unverified special appearance neither acknowledges the court's jurisdiction nor seeks affirmative action. While it cannot be used to disprove jurisdiction, it certainly does not concede it.

Thus, Dawson-Austin did not enter a general appearance by filing an unsworn special appearance or by amending it only after it was overruled.

B

Austin argues that Dawson-Austin made a general appearance by filing a motion to quash service, a plea to the jurisdiction, and a plea in abatement, all in the same instrument with the special appearance and all following the special appearance in the instrument, but none expressly made subject to the special appearance. The district court agreed with this argument; the court of appeals did not address it. The argument is contrary to Rule 120a, which states: "a motion to transfer venue and any other plea, pleading, or motion may be contained in the same instrument or filed subsequent thereto without waiver of such special appearance". The rule makes matters in the same instrument and subsequent matters subject to the special appearance without an express statement to that effect for each matter.

A few courts have referred to other matters being made subject to a special appearance but do not hold that "subject to" language is required to avoid waiver. *See International Turbine Serv., Inc. v. Lovitt,* 881 S.W.2d 805, 808 (Tex. App.—Fort Worth 1994, writ denied); *Koch Graphics, Inc. v. Avantech, Inc.,* 803 S.W.2d 432, 433 (Tex. App.—Dallas 1991, no writ); *Stegall & Stegall,* 592 S.W.2d at 429; *Frye v. Ross Aviation, Inc.,* 523 S.W.2d 500, 502 (Tex. Civ. App.—Amarillo 1975, no writ). Only two courts have addressed whether "subject to" language is required. In *Antonio v. Marino,* 910 S.W.2d 624, 629 (Tex. App.—Houston [14th Dist.] 1995, no writ), the court held that filing a stipulation without making it subject to the special appearance did not waive the special appearance. In *Portland Sav. & Loan Ass'n v. Bernstein,* 716 S.W.2d 532, 534–535 (Tex. App.—Corpus Christi 1985, writ ref'd n.r.e.), *cert. denied,* 475 U.S. 1016, 106 S. Ct. 1200, 89 L. Ed. 2d 313 (1986), the court held that motions for sanctions and to disqualify counsel that were not filed subject to the special appearance did not "comply with Rule 120a" and therefore constituted a general appearance. *Portland* is contrary to the plain language of Rule 120a and to that extent is overruled.

Because Dawson-Austin's motion and pleas fully complied with Rule 120a, they did not constitute a general appearance.

## C

The hearing on Dawson-Austin's special appearance, motion to quash service of process, plea to the jurisdiction, and plea in abatement was requested by Austin, not Dawson-Austin, because he wished the Texas court to proceed before the California court. As Austin's counsel told the district court, "we can't protect ourselves against the California lawsuit if we don't proceed today." Dawson-Austin did not ask the district court for a hearing on any of the matters she filed. On the contrary, Dawson-Austin filed a motion for continuance the day of the hearing on the grounds that she had not been given the requisite notice for the hearing, her counsel had just been hired to make an appearance and he was in a jury trial at the time of the hearing, discovery was needed on the special appearance, and discovery was needed on the motion to quash. Dawson-Austin's counsel reurged the motion for continuance throughout the hearing, and also requested a postponement because of Austin's and Dawson-Austin's unavailability to testify. The district court denied the continuance.

Austin argues that Dawson-Austin's motion for continuance was not made subject to the special appearance and was therefore a general appearance. The district court appears to have rejected this argument, and the court of appeals did not address it. Austin's argument is incorrect for several reasons. First, as already discussed, Rule 120a expressly states that pleadings and motions may be "filed subsequent [to a special appearance] without waiver of such special appearance". Dawson-Austin's motion for continuance was filed subsequent to her special appearance and thus, by the plain language of the rule, was not a general appearance. Second, the motion for continuance did not request affirmative relief inconsistent with Dawson-Austin's assertion that the district court lacked jurisdiction, which, as we have noted, is the test for a general appearance. Rather, the motion asked the court to defer action on all matters. Third, the motion was particularly appropriate, given that Austin, not Dawson-Austin, set the matters for hearing. Dawson-Austin was obliged to request that hearing of her motion and pleas be deferred until after the special appearance. Rule 120a(2) states: "Any motion to challenge the jurisdiction provided for herein shall be heard and determined before a motion to transfer venue or any other plea or pleading may be heard." She could not request a postponement of the special hearing without also requesting a postponement of her other matters on which Austin, not Dawson-Austin, had requested a hearing. Dawson-Austin was also entitled to seek a postponement of the special appearance hearing until she could complete discovery, as expressly permitted by Rule 120a, and she was entitled to ask for more time for discovery on her motion to quash, provided she did not attempt to take that discovery before the special appearance was decided.

Dawson-Austin was entitled to request more time to prepare for the special appearance hearing that Austin set. Her request to postpone consideration of her other matters was required if the special appearance hearing were to be delayed. Dawson-Austin's motion for continuance in no way constituted a general appearance.

D

Both Dawson-Austin's special appearance and her amended special appearance stated: "This special appearance is made to the severable claim asserted by BILL wherein BILL seeks a division of the parties' property." In other words, Dawson-Austin specially appeared only with respect to the claim for division of the marital estate, not the claim for divorce. (Since the couple had no children, these were the only two claims in the proceeding.) Rule 120a permits a special appearance to be made "as to an entire proceeding or as to any severable claim involved therein." It is well settled in this State that the division of a marital estate is not a claim severable from the rest of a divorce proceeding. Tex. Fam. Code § 7.001 ("In a decree of divorce or annulment, the court *shall* order a division of the estate of the parties . . ." (emphasis added)) (formerly Tex. Fam.Code § 3.63(a)). *See, e.g., Hollaway v. Hollaway,* 792 S.W.2d 168, 170 (Tex. App.—Houston [1st Dist.] 1990, writ denied); *Vautrain v. Vautrain,* 646 S.W.2d 309, 314 (Tex. App.—Fort Worth 1983, writ dism'd). Thus, Austin argues that Dawson-Austin's special appearance to a non-severable portion of the proceeding constituted a general appearance.

The cases that hold adjudication of divorce and division of the marital estate to be non-severable claims all do so in the context of Rules 41 ("Misjoinder and Non-Joinder of Parties"), 174 ("Consolidation; Separate Trials"), and 320 ("Motion [for New Trial] and Action of Court Thereon"), Tex. R. Civ. P. *See, e.g., Brown v. Brown,* 917 S.W.2d 358, 360–365 (Tex. App.—El Paso 1996, no writ) (McClure, J., concurring); *Biaza v. Simon,* 879 S.W.2d 349, 355 (Tex. App.—Houston [14th Dist.] 1994, writ denied); *Hollaway,* 792 S.W.2d at 170; *Seibert v. Seibert,* 759 S.W.2d 768, 769–770 (Tex. App.—El Paso 1988, writ denied); *Dewey v. Dewey,* 745 S.W.2d 514, 516 (Tex. App.—Corpus Christi 1988, writ denied); *Odom v. Odom,* 683 S.W.2d 135, 137 (Tex. App.—San Antonio 1984, writ ref'd n.r.e.); *Vautrain,* 646 S.W.2d at 313–317; *Underhill v. Underhill,* 614 S.W.2d 178, 181 (Tex. Civ. App.—Houston [14th Dist.] 1981, writ ref'd n.r.e.); *In re Marriage of Johnson,* 595 S.W.2d 900, 902–904 (Tex. Civ. App.—Amarillo 1980, writ dism'd w.o.j.); *Garrison v. Texas Commerce Bank,* 560 S.W.2d 451, 453–457 (Tex. Civ. App.—Houston [1st Dist.] 1977, writ ref'd n.r.e.); *Reed v. Williams,* 545 S.W.2d 33, 34 (Tex. Civ. App.—San Antonio 1976, no writ); *Angerstein v. Angerstein,* 389 S.W.2d 519, 520–521 (Tex. Civ. App.—Corpus Christi 1965, no writ).

No case holds that claims of divorce and division of property do not involve severable *jurisdictional* issues. The United States Supreme Court recognized long ago that a court could have jurisdiction to grant a divorce—an adjudication of parties' status—without having jurisdiction to divide their property—an adjudication of parties' rights. *Estin v. Estin,* 334 U.S. 541, 68 S. Ct. 1213, 92 L. Ed. 1561 (1948). The rule has been recognized in Texas, as one court has explained:

> Where the trial court in a divorce proceeding has no personal jurisdiction over the respondent, the trial court has the jurisdiction to grant the divorce, but not to determine the managing conservatorship of children or divide property outside the State of Texas. *Comisky v. Comisky,* 597 S.W.2d 6, 8 (Tex. Civ. App.—Beaumont 1980, no writ). It may also lack jurisdiction to divide property within the state. *See Shaffer v. Heitner,* 433 U.S. 186, 212, 97 S. Ct. 2569, 2584, 53 L. Ed. 2d 683 (1977).

*Hoffman v. Hoffman,* 821 S.W.2d 3, 5 (Tex. App.—Fort Worth 1992, no writ). The court in *Hoffman* held that a special appearance directed to an entire divorce proceeding should have been sustained only as to the claim for division of property:

> [T]he trial court erred in dismissing [the husband's] divorce petition for want of jurisdiction, even though it might not have jurisdiction to deal with the property of the parties. The special appearance should only have been granted to the extent of the trial court's recognition that it does not have personal jurisdiction over [the wife] and therefore may not divide the property of the parties located outside the State of Texas and possibly that located within the State of Texas.

*Id.* Section 6.308 of the Family Code now provides:

> (a) A court in which a suit for dissolution of a marriage is filed may exercise its jurisdiction over those portions of the suit for which it has authority.
>
> (b) The court's authority to resolve the issues in controversy between the parties may be restricted because the court lacks:
>
> > (1) the required personal jurisdiction over a nonresident party in a suit for dissolution of the marriage. . . .

Had Dawson-Austin specially appeared as to the entire proceeding, the district court could not have sustained it except as to the property division claim. The district court had jurisdiction to grant the divorce, and Dawson-Austin could not specially appear to that claim. If the court could sustain the special appearance as to only the one claim and not the other, directing the special appearance only to the claim for which it could be sustained could not be a general appearance.

E

Finally, Austin argues and the court of appeals held that Dawson-Austin, by asserting her motion to quash service of process at the conclusion of the hearing on her special appearance, made a general appearance before filing her amended special appearance the next day. The record does not support this argument.

Again, it must be recalled that Austin, not Dawson-Austin, requested the hearing on the motion to quash, along with the special appearance and Dawson-Austin's other matters, and insisted on going forward. Dawson-Austin did not raise any of the matters at the hearing; on the contrary,

Dawson-Austin, as has been noted, repeatedly requested a postponement as to all of them. As soon as the district court overruled Dawson-Austin's special appearance, the following colloquy occurred:

> [Austin's Attorney]: Your Honor, if I may, I would like to proceed on their—They have a motion before the Court to quash the process in this case, and I—
>
> THE COURT: Let me ask you this. We don't get that a lot, but I thought that under the rules if you filed a Motion to Quash the service of process and the Court quashes the service of process, then that day becomes the day you're served, and then you have the Monday next after the expiration of twenty days for service from that day to file your Answer.
>
> [Austin's Attorney]: Process is moot at this point.
>
> THE COURT: But they have already filed their Answer.
>
> [Austin's Attorney]: Process is moot at this point because they filed an Answer. So actually we don't need to approach that question.
>
> THE COURT: Okay, I agree. Do you disagree with that?
>
> [Dawson-Austin's Attorney]: Yes, Your Honor, because there's no—the construction of pleadings is that you can have it all contained in the same pleadings.
>
> THE COURT: No, I'm not talking about that. I'm talking—I'm only talking about the Motion to Quash the Citation. If you have a bad citation and you come into court and get the citation quashed, then the day the Court quashes your citation is the day you're served.
>
> [Dawson-Austin's Attorney]: That's right.
>
> THE COURT: Right?
>
> [Dawson-Austin's Attorney]: So we—
>
> THE COURT: Then you have until the Monday next to file an Answer.
>
> [Dawson-Austin's Attorney]: Plus twenty.
>
> THE COURT: Am I with you? Or are you with me?
>
> [Dawson-Austin's Attorney]: Yes, Your Honor.
>
> THE COURT: But she's already filed.
>
> [Dawson-Austin's Attorney]: Well, Your Honor, if it's bad service—if it's a bad service, then—and that's the way the motion is presented to the Court that it's a bad service, and if you were to quash it today, then she would have twenty days plus a Monday to enter the Answer, because—
>
> THE COURT: I wouldn't be quashing her general denial. She's already filed a general denial.
>
> [Dawson-Austin's Attorney]: She hasn't waived, Your Honor, unless the Court is ruling that she waived it, that by presenting it in a pleading to the Court.
>
> THE COURT: Oh, that the general denial is subject to the ruling?
>
> [Dawson-Austin's Attorney]: Yes, Your Honor.
>
> THE COURT: Well, I don't think that waived it, but I think the fact that—I think that the intrinsic deficiencies in her Special Appearance waives it. I think she does become here at that point.

> [Austin's Attorney]: Your Honor, then that being the case, that was the only other motion we wanted to urge today.

As the record shows, Dawson-Austin's counsel did not raise or argue the motion to quash or any other matter. Austin's counsel raised the motion to quash, and the court ruled it moot without a word from Dawson-Austin's counsel. Only then did the court ask Dawson-Austin's counsel whether he agreed, and he essentially conceded. Nothing else transpired before the filing and hearing of Dawson-Austin's amended special appearance. Thus, the district court properly considered the special appearance on the merits.

III

A

However, the district court erred in overruling Dawson-Austin's amended special appearance. Section 6.305(a) of the Family Code provides:

> If the petitioner in a suit for dissolution of a marriage is a resident or a domiciliary of this state at the time the suit for dissolution is filed, the court may exercise personal jurisdiction over the respondent or over the respondent's personal representative although the respondent is not a resident of this state if:
>
> (1) this state is the last marital residence of the petitioner and the respondent and the suit is filed before the second anniversary of the date on which marital residence ended; or
>
> (2) there is any basis consistent with the constitutions of this state and the United States for the exercise of the personal jurisdiction.

Tex. Fam. Code § 6.305(a) (formerly Tex. Fam. Code § 3.26(a)). Austin had been domiciled in Texas exactly six months to the day when he filed suit for divorce. *See id.* § 6.301 ("A suit for divorce may not be maintained in this state unless at the time the suit is filed either the petitioner or the respondent has been . . . a domiciliary of this state for the preceding six-month period. . .") (formerly Tex. Fam. Code § 3.21). Dawson-Austin, however, neither was nor ever had been a Texas resident. Thus the district court did not have in personam jurisdiction over Dawson-Austin unless it was under Section 6.305(a)(2).

The United States Constitution permits "a state court [to] take personal jurisdiction over a defendant only if it has some minimum, purposeful contacts with the state, and the exercise of jurisdiction will not offend traditional notions of fair play and substantial justice." *CMMC v. Salinas,* 929 S.W.2d 435, 437 (Tex. 1996) (citing cases); *International Shoe Co. v. Washington,* 326 U.S. 310, 66 S. Ct. 154, 90 L. Ed. 95 (1945). Dawson-Austin had no "minimum, purposeful contacts" with Texas. At the time Austin filed suit, Dawson-Austin resided in California, as Austin's petition itself alleged. She was served in California. At the hearing on her amended special appearance, she testified unequivocally and without contradiction from Austin that her only contact with the State of Texas had been to attend a business convention nine or ten years earlier. She had never lived in Texas, and Austin had not lived here before March 1992. There was no basis for the district court to exercise personal jurisdiction over Dawson-Austin, and Austin does not contend otherwise.

B

Even though the district court did not have in personam jurisdiction over Dawson-Austin, it is possible under the United States Constitution, and thus under Texas law, for the court to have had jurisdiction to divide the marital estate located in Texas. The property in Texas in which the parties claimed an interest was Austin's Dallas home and Texas bank accounts, which the parties agreed was community property, and the stock certificate evidencing Austin's shares in Starkey. As we have previously stated, Austin contends that his Starkey stock is separate property, while Dawson-Austin claims that she is entitled under Minnesota law to part of the increase in value of the stock attributable to her and Austin's efforts during marriage.

In *Pennoyer v. Neff,* 95 U.S. 714, 24 L. Ed. 565 (1877), the United States Supreme Court held that a state court could exercise jurisdiction over property within the state's borders and determine the rights and interests of non-residents. But in *Shaffer v. Heitner,* 433 U.S. 186, 97 S. Ct. 2569, 53 L. Ed. 2d 683 (1977), the Court abandoned this position and concluded instead that jurisdiction over property, like jurisdiction over persons, must be based on minimum, purposeful contacts and must not offend traditional notions of fair play and substantial justice.

> The fiction that an assertion of jurisdiction over property is anything but an assertion of jurisdiction over the owner of the property supports an ancient form without substantial modern justification. Its continued acceptance would serve only to allow state-court jurisdiction that is fundamentally unfair to the defendant.
>
> We therefore conclude that all assertions of state-court jurisdiction must be evaluated according to the standards set forth in *International Shoe* and its progeny.

*Id.* at 212, 97 S. Ct. at 2584. *Shaffer* was a shareholder derivative suit against officers and directors of two Delaware corporations. A Delaware court sequestered defendants' stock in the corporations, even though neither defendants nor their stock were physically present in Delaware, basing its jurisdiction to do so on a Delaware statute that deemed Delaware the situs of ownership of all stock in Delaware corporations. *Id.* at 192, 97 S. Ct. at 2573. The Supreme Court held that neither defendants nor their stock had sufficient contacts with Delaware to justify the state court's exercise of jurisdiction over them. *Id.* at 213–217, 97 S. Ct. at 2584–2587.

In the present case, the location in Texas of property that either is or is claimed to be part of the marital estate does not supply the minimum contacts required for the court to exercise jurisdiction over Dawson-Austin. Austin bought his Dallas home, opened his Texas bank accounts, and brought his Starkey stock certificate to Texas after he separated from Dawson-Austin. We do not believe that one spouse may leave the other, move to another state in which neither has ever lived, buy a home or open a bank account or store a stock certificate there, and by those unilateral actions, and nothing more, compel the other spouse to litigate their divorce in the new domicile consistent with due process. One spouse cannot, solely by actions in which the other spouse is not involved, create the contacts between a state and the other spouse necessary for jurisdiction over a divorce action. *See In the Interest of S.A.V.,* 837 S.W.2d 80, 83–84 (Tex. 1992) (holding that without personal jurisdiction over one parent, a court could still decide custody of a child living in the State, but could not determine support and visitation). Moreover, Dawson-Austin's claim to a part of the value of the Starkey stock is completely unrelated to the situs of the certificate; rather, it is based on the parties' efforts to increase the value of Starkey, most of which occurred in Minnesota. In no sense can it be said that Dawson-Austin ever "purposefully availed" herself of the privilege of owning property in this State. *See Burger King Corp. v.*

*Rudzewicz,* 471 U.S. 462, 475, 105 S. Ct. 2174, 85 L. Ed. 2d 528 (1985) (citing *Hanson v. Denckla,* 357 U.S. 235, 253, 78 S. Ct. 1228, 2 L. Ed. 2d 1283 (1958)).

Thus, the district court lacked jurisdiction to adjudicate Dawson-Austin's claim to part of the value of the Starkey stock or to divide the marital estate.

. . . .

The district court had jurisdiction only to grant a divorce and not to determine the parties' property claims. Accordingly, the judgment of the court of appeals is reversed and the case is remanded to the district court for rendition of judgment divorcing Austin and Dawson-Austin and dismissing all other claims for relief for want of jurisdiction.

BAKER, Justice, dissenting, joined by Justices Enoch and Abbott.

I respectfully dissent. After determining that it had jurisdiction, the trial court dissolved the parties' marriage, characterized Austin's Starkey Corporation stock as his separate property, and distributed about fifty-five percent of the community estate to Dawson-Austin and about forty-five percent to Austin. The court of appeals affirmed the trial court's judgment. [footnote omitted] I would affirm the court of appeals.

## I. BACKGROUND

Austin is the president of Starkey Laboratories, a Minnesota corporation. He owns sixty shares of Starkey stock, representing 100 per cent ownership. Austin owned the Starkey stock before he married Dawson-Austin. When Austin and Dawson-Austin married, they were domiciled in Minnesota. After continuing marital discord, they separated. There are no children of the marriage. Consequently, jurisdiction under Chapters 102, 152 or 159 of the Texas Family Code is not at issue.

The parties remained domiciled in Minnesota until just before this suit. In February 1992, Dawson-Austin moved to California. In March 1992, Austin moved to Texas. Dawson-Austin filed for divorce in California, but she did not obtain service on Austin for several months. After residing in Texas for six months, and before Dawson-Austin served him in the California divorce action, Austin filed for divorce in Texas. Austin had Dawson-Austin served four days later.

In response to Austin's petition, Dawson-Austin filed, in one instrument: (1) a special appearance; (2) a motion to quash service of citation; (3) a plea to the jurisdiction; (4) a plea in abatement; and (5) subject to all of these, a general denial. On the day of the hearing for these motions, Dawson-Austin filed a motion for continuance. The trial court denied the motion for continuance, denied the special appearance because it was not verified, and proceeded to hear Dawson-Austin's motion to quash, which it also denied. The next day, Dawson-Austin amended her special appearance and moved for reconsideration. After another hearing a few days later, the trial court denied Dawson-Austin's motion for reconsideration.

## II. SPECIAL APPEARANCE

The court of appeals held that the trial court properly overruled Dawson-Austin's original special appearance because it was unverified, and therefore defective. The court of appeals also held that because Dawson-Austin made a general appearance to argue other matters before filing her amended special appearance, the trial court properly overruled Dawson-Austin's amended special appearance and acquired jurisdiction. Dawson-Austin argues that the court of appeals erred when it held that she waived her special appearance by arguing her motion to quash after the trial court overruled her original special appearance.

A. Rule 120a

An objection to a Texas court's exercise of jurisdiction over a nonresident must be made by special appearance filed under Rule 120a of the Texas Rules of Civil Procedure. Rule 120a requires "strict compliance." *See Portland Sav. & Loan Ass'n v. Bernstein,* 716 S.W.2d 532, 534 (Tex. App.—Corpus Christi 1985, writ ref'd n.r.e.). A special appearance must be made and determined on sworn motion prior to any other plea, pleading, or motion that seeks affirmative relief. *See* Tex. R. Civ. P. 120a(1) and (2); *Liberty Enters., Inc. v. Moore Transp. Co.,* 690 S.W.2d 570, 571–72 (Tex. 1985). Any appearance not in compliance with Rule 120a is a general appearance. See Tex. R. Civ. P. 120a(1); *Portland Sav. & Loan Ass'n,* 716 S.W.2d at 534; *see also Burger King Corp. v. Rudzewicz,* 471 U.S. 462, 472 n.14, 105 S. Ct. 2174, 85 L. Ed. 2d 528 (1985) ("the personal jurisdiction requirement is a waivable right"). When a party generally appears, the trial court can exercise jurisdiction over the party without violating the party's due process rights. *See Kawasaki Steel Corp. v. Middleton,* 699 S.W.2d 199, 201 (Tex. 1985); *see also* Tex. Fam. Code § 6.305(a) (formerly Tex. Fam. Code § 3.26(a)). [footnote omitted]

A party may amend a special appearance. However, the party must not seek affirmative relief on any question other than that of the court's jurisdiction between the time it files its original special appearance and its amended special appearance. *See* Tex. R. Civ. P. 120a(2) (special appearance "shall be heard and determined before . . . any other plea or pleading may be heard."); *see also Liberty Enters.,* 690 S.W.2d at 571–72. Any intervening appearance to invoke the trial court's judgment about a "question other than the court's jurisdiction" is a general appearance. *See Moore v. Elektro-Mobil Technik GMBH,* 874 S.W.2d 324, 327 (Tex. App.—El Paso 1994, writ denied); *Investors Diversified Serv., Inc. v. Bruner,* 366 S.W.2d 810, 815 (Tex. Civ. App.—Houston 1963, writ ref'd n.r.e.).

B. Analysis

Because Dawson-Austin's original special appearance was not sworn, it was defective. *See* Tex. R. Civ. P. 120a(1). While Rule 120a allows for amendment, any amendment to cure a defective special appearance must be accomplished *before* arguing other matters. *See* Tex. R. Civ. P. 120a(2). Dawson-Austin did not amend her special appearance until *after* she argued other matters, namely her motion to quash and about discovery related to that motion. By doing so, Dawson-Austin invoked the trial court's jurisdiction and generally appeared. *See* Tex. R. Civ. P. 120a(1) and (2); *see also Elektro-Mobil Technik GMBH,* 874 S.W.2d at 327; *Portland Sav. & Loan Ass'n,* 716 S.W.2d at 535.

Dawson-Austin argues that because she sought a continuance before the hearing on her original special appearance, she could present her other motions before amending her special appearance. I would reject this argument. I generally agree that a motion for continuance is not a general appearance. A continuance would allow a party to amend its special appearance under Rule 120a. A continuance request for that purpose in no way invokes the trial court's judgment about anything other than the court's jurisdiction. *See Elektro-Mobil Technik GMBH,* 874 S.W.2d at 327. However, that is not what occurred in this case. Dawson-Austin did not seek a continuance to cure her defective special appearance, but instead contended that she needed time to take depositions to support *her motion to quash.* [footnote omitted] Regardless, Dawson-Austin did not provide the court of appeals with any briefing about whether the trial court improperly denied her a continuance. 920 S.W.2d at 782. She did not raise the issue in this Court.

Also, like the court of appeals, I reject Dawson-Austin's argument that she should be excused from arguing her motion to quash because Austin set the hearing. Dawson-Austin did not object to the trial court proceeding with her motion to quash or indicate to the trial court that she wanted to amend her special appearance before proceeding further. By arguing her motion to quash before amending her special appearance, Dawson-Austin committed a fatal procedural error and therefore generally appeared. *See Kawasaki Steel Corp.,* 699 S.W.2d at 201, 203. The Court should affirm the court of appeals.

III. DIVISIBLE DIVORCE

The Court compounds its error today by reversing the trial court's judgment except as to the grant of divorce. Where jurisdiction over the parties is established, Texas law does not allow a "divisible divorce." *See* Tex. Fam. Code § 7.001 (formerly Tex. Fam. Code § 3.63(a))("In a decree of divorce . . . the court shall order a division of the estate of the parties . . . ."); *see also Hollaway v. Hollaway,* 792 S.W.2d 168, 170 (Tex. App.—Houston [1st Dist.] 1990, writ denied); *Seibert v. Seibert,* 759 S.W.2d 768, 769–70 (Tex. App.—El Paso 1988, writ denied); *Vautrain v. Vautrain,* 646 S.W.2d 309, 314 (Tex. App.—Fort Worth 1983, writ dism'd). Here, because Dawson generally appeared, the trial court had jurisdiction over both parties. Therefore, it properly divided the marital estate.

Only recently, the Legislature codified the divisible divorce concept in cases where the court lacks jurisdiction over a nonresident party in a suit to dissolve a marriage. *See* Tex. Fam. Code § 6.308 (in a suit to dissolve a marriage, a court may exercise its jurisdiction "over those portions of the suit which it has authority.") (Added by Act of April 3, 1997, 75 th Leg., R.S., ch. 7, § 1 and 4 (eff. April 17, 1997), 1997 Tex. Gen. Laws 8, 27, 43). Because of its effective date, section 6.308 does not apply to this case. *See* Act of April 3, 1997, 75 th Leg., R.S., ch. 7, § 4, 1997 Tex. Gen. Laws 8, 43 ("The change in law made by this Act does not affect a proceeding under the Family Code pending on the effective date of this Act. A proceeding on the effective date of this Act is governed by the law in effect at the time the proceeding was commenced, and the former law is continued in effect for that purpose."). Because of the prior existing Texas law, and because the trial court had jurisdiction over both parties, it had to divide the marital estate.

The Court cites *Estin v. Estin,* 334 U.S. 541, 68 S. Ct. 1213, 92 L. Ed. 1561 (1948), for the proposition that the Supreme Court has recognized the concept of a "divisible divorce" and that it should apply here. *See Estin,* 334 U.S. at 549, 68 S. Ct. at 1218–19. In *Estin,* the wife initially sued for separation in New York. The husband answered, and the New York trial court granted a separation decree and awarded the wife permanent alimony. Two years later, after establishing residency in Nevada, the husband sued for divorce in Nevada. After constructive service (the wife was never personally served and never appeared), the Nevada court granted the husband a divorce. The Nevada divorce decree made no provision for alimony. The husband then stopped making alimony payments. When the wife tried to enforce the New York judgment, the husband argued that the Nevada divorce decree trumped the New York judgment. The New York court rejected his argument. The Supreme Court considered "whether Nevada could under any circumstances adjudicate rights of respondent [the wife] under the New York judgment when she was not personally served or did not appear in the [Nevada] proceeding." *Estin,* 334 U.S.

at 547, 68 S. Ct. at 1217–18. The Supreme Court held that under full faith and credit principles, the Nevada court could not adjudicate the wife's rights under the New York judgment, "mak[ing] the divorce divisible. . . ." *Estin,* 334 U.S. at 549, 68 S. Ct. at 1218–19. Thus *Estin* stands for the proposition that, in a case where an out-of-state respondent is not personally served and does not appear, and thus there is no personal jurisdiction, any part of an ex parte divorce decree that purports to affect the respondent's property interests is not enforceable under full faith and credit principles. *See Estin,* 334 U.S. at 542, 68 S. Ct. at 1215; *see also Conlon v. Heckler,* 719 F.2d 788, 794–96 (5th Cir. 1983); *Fox v. Fox,* 559 S.W.2d 407, 410 (Tex. Civ. App.—Austin 1977, no writ); *Risch v. Risch,* 395 S.W.2d 709, 711 (Tex. Civ. App.—Houston 1965, writ dism'd). *Estin's* holding does not override section 7.001's command that "the court shall order a division of the estate of the parties," whenever the court has jurisdiction over the respondent under section 6.305(a). *See* Tex. Fam. Code § 6.305(a) (formerly Tex. Fam. Code § 3.26(a)); *see also* Ismail v. Ismail, 702 S.W.2d 216, 221 (Tex. App.—Houston [1st Dist.] 1985, writ ref'd n.r.e.); *Comisky v. Comisky,* 597 S.W.2d 6, 9 (Tex. Civ. App.—Beaumont 1980, no writ); *Butler v. Butler,* 577 S.W.2d 501, 507 (Tex. Civ. App.—Texarkana 1978, writ dism'd).

I agree with the Court that "the district court did not have in personam jurisdiction over Dawson-Austin unless it was under Section 6.305(a)(2) [of the Texas Family Code]." 968 S.W.2d at 326. Indeed, but for her procedural errors, Dawson-Austin may have been able to establish that the trial court did not have in personam jurisdiction over her under section 6.305(a)(2). However, Dawson-Austin's procedural errors resulted in a general appearance which satisfied section 6.305(a)(2)'s requirements. *See Kawasaki Steel Corp.,* 699 S.W.2d at 201, 203; *see also Burnham v. Superior Court,* 495 U.S. 604, 110 S. Ct. 2105, 109 L. Ed. 2d 631 (1990) (holding that due process clause did not prevent California courts from exercising jurisdiction over nonresident husband served with divorce suit while in California on business trip). Dawson-Austin's general appearance gave the trial court jurisdiction to dissolve the marriage and to divide the marital estate, as it was required to do. *See* Tex. Fam. Code § 7.001.

Because the trial court's jurisdiction was founded on Dawson-Austin's general appearance, the "divisibility" of the divorce turns on Texas law, which, when the court has jurisdiction over the parties, requires the court to divide the marital estate. *See* Tex. Fam. Code § 7.001; *Hollaway,* 792 S.W.2d at 170; *Vautrain,* 646 S.W.2d at 314. This case should not be decided or "divided" on full faith and credit principles as in *Estin.*

## IV. CONCLUSION

Today the Court permits less than strict compliance with Rule 120a. I believe that Dawson-Austin's efforts to specially appear were flawed. Therefore, she made a general appearance and the trial court properly exercised its jurisdiction. I would affirm the courts below. Because the Court holds otherwise, I dissent.

---

## NOTES AND QUESTIONS

(1) *Amendments to Cure a Defective Special Appearance.* The last sentence of Civil Procedure Rule 120a(1) provides that: "Every appearance, prior to judgment, not in compliance with this rule is a general appearance." Under the rule, a special appearance must be made by sworn motion

but "may be amended to cure defects." After *Dawson-Austin,* it is clear that this means "unless amended" a defective special appearance can be "cured" and "restored." Moreover, the court states that "[t]he rule does not limit the kinds of defects that can be cured."

(2) *Due Order.* The concept of due order of pleadings has another nonobvious aspect. Due order pleas must be heard and determined in "due order," not merely filed in the right order. *See* Tex. R. Civ. P. 84. Based on Cynthia Dawson-Austin's experience, what procedures will you follow in making a special appearance?

(3) *Motions to Quash.* Because a motion to quash is a general appearance, it is generally not a good idea to file such a motion, especially because the types of defects asserted in such a motion can be asserted in other ways after judgment. *See* Tex. R. Civ. P. 320, 324; *see also* Tex. R. App. P. 25, 26, 30.

### [B] Postjudgment Challenges by Nonresidents

## KOCH GRAPHICS, INC. v. AVANTECH, INC.

*803 S.W.2d 432 (Tex. App.—Dallas 1991, no writ)*

ENOCH, Justice

Koch Graphics, Inc. appeals the overruling of its special appearance, the denials of its motion to quash process and motion for new trial, and the awarding of a default judgment in favor of Avantech, Inc. We reverse the trial court's judgment, render on Koch's special appearance, and order the cause dismissed for lack of personal jurisdiction over Koch.

FACTS

In September 1988, Avantech contacted Hudson Machinery Company, Inc., a New York corporation, concerning Avantech's prospective purchase of printing equipment then owned by Koch, also a New York corporation. Avantech and Hudson agreed on a selling price of $715,000, and Hudson received a $50,000 deposit. Koch was not involved in the negotiation of the agreement, but Avantech viewed the equipment at Koch's place of business in New York City. Koch agreed to sell the equipment to Hudson for $645,000 and received a $50,000 deposit from Hudson. Neither sale was completed. Koch kept Hudson's deposit and later sold the equipment to another party. Avantech demanded the return of its deposit from Hudson and Koch. When none was forthcoming, Avantech sued, claiming breach of contract, conversion, and unjust enrichment. [footnote omitted] In addition to the $50,000 in actual damages, Avantech requested punitive damages and attorney's fees.

Hudson filed a special appearance, which the trial court sustained. The court granted a partial default judgment against Koch on February 2, 1990. This judgment did not address Avantech's claim for punitive damages and attorney's fees. Koch filed a special appearance without supporting affidavits on March 5, 1990. Koch also filed a motion to quash service, a motion for new trial, and an original answer. All were made subject to its special appearance. Koch filed an amended special appearance which included a supporting affidavit and exhibits on March 14, 1990. On March 27, 1990, Avantech filed an amended petition in which it dropped its claim for punitive damages and attorney's fees, thus making the judgment final. The trial court held a hearing and overruled Koch's special appearance on March 30, 1990. The court denied Koch's motions to quash service and for new trial on April 12, 1990.

## SPECIAL APPEARANCE

Koch's first point of error challenges the overruling of its special appearance. Although the trial court held a hearing and allowed evidence, the trial court refused to reach the merits of the special appearance. The court stated that it did not have the power to entertain a special appearance after the entry of a default judgment. We disagree. At the time the Special Appearance and its amendment were filed, the trial court retained power since the judgment was interlocutory. *See Houston Health Clubs, Inc. v. First Court of Appeals,* 722 S.W.2d 692, 693–694 (Tex. 1987). Furthermore, it has been held that, within the period when the trial court has plenary power over its judgment, the court may address a special appearance. *Myers v. Emery,* 697 S.W.2d 26, 29 (Tex. App.—Dallas 1985, no writ). The trial court should have decided Koch's special appearance on the merits. Since the evidence which the parties presented at the special appearance hearing is in the record, we will address the merits of Koch's claim. *Lone Star Gas Co. v. Railroad Comm'n,* 767 S.W.2d 709, 710 (Tex. 1989); Tex. R. App. P. 81(c).

## WAIVER

As a starting point, we address the argument that Koch waived its claim by seeking affirmative relief from the trial court. Koch filed a special appearance and then filed motions to have the default judgment set aside and for new trial. The motions were expressly made subject to its special appearance. Rule 120a provides that "any other plea, pleading, or motion may be . . . filed subsequent thereto without waiver of such special appearance." Tex. R. Civ. P. 120a(1). The mere filing of the motions did not waive Koch's special appearance. Additionally, Koch's actions taken after the denial of its special appearance did not cause a waiver of its special appearance.

> If the objection to jurisdiction is overruled, the objecting party may thereafter appear generally for any purpose. Any such special appearance or such general appearance shall not be deemed a waiver of the objection to jurisdiction when the objecting party or subject matter is not amenable to process issued by the courts of this State.

Tex. R. Civ. P. 120a(3).

## PERSONAL JURISDICTION

A Texas court may exercise jurisdiction over a nonresident only if the Texas long-arm statute authorizes it and if the exercise is consistent with federal and state constitutional guarantees of due process. *Schlobohm v. Schapiro,* 784 S.W.2d 355, 356 (Tex. 1990). Avantech's pleadings assert that Koch was a third-party beneficiary to a contract Avantech had negotiated with Hudson and that Koch "had otherwise engaged in business in Texas." We note again that the trial court granted Hudson's special appearance and Avantech has not appealed that ruling. With those facts decided adversely to Avantech, we fail to see how a third-party beneficiary to a contract is amenable to suit in Texas when the prime negotiator of the contract is not, unless of course the third-party is otherwise subject to this state's jurisdiction. Thus, we come to the long-arm statute which allows jurisdiction over nonresidents who "do business" in Texas.

> In addition to other acts that may constitute doing business, a nonresident does business in this state if the nonresident:
>
> (1) contracts by mail or otherwise with a Texas resident and either party is to perform the contract in whole or in part in this state;

(2) commits a tort in whole or in part in this state; or

(3) recruits Texas residents, directly or through an intermediary located in this state, for employment inside or outside this state.

Tex. Civ. Prac. & Rem. Code Ann. § 17.042 (Vernon 1986).

Further, the Texas Supreme Court has set forth a test to determine whether the exercise of jurisdiction conforms with due process:

(1) The nonresident defendant or foreign corporation must purposefully do some act or consummate some transaction in the forum state;

(2) The cause of action must arise from, or be connected with, such act or transaction; even if the cause of action does not arise from a specific contact, jurisdiction may be exercised if the defendant's contacts with Texas are continuing and systematic; and

(3) The assumption of jurisdiction by the forum state must not offend traditional notions of fair play and substantial justice, consideration being given to the quality, nature, and extent of the activity in the forum state, the relative convenience of the parties, the benefits and protection of the laws of the forum state afforded the respective parties, and the basic equities of the situation.

*Schlobohm,* 784 S.W.2d at 358 (quoting, in part, *O'Brien v. Lanpar Co.,* 399 S.W.2d 340, 342 (Tex. 1966)). This test satisfies federal due process requirements. The first portion encapsulates the "minimum contacts" test requirement that a defendant purposefully avail himself of the benefits of the forum and reasonably expect to be called to court there. *See World-Wide Volkswagen v. Woodson,* 444 U.S. 286, 297, 100 S. Ct. 559, 567, 62 L. Ed. 2d 490 (1980); *Hanson v. Denckla,* 357 U.S. 235, 253, 78 S. Ct. 1228, 1239, 2 L. Ed. 2d 1283 (1958). The second portion reflects the changing standards of the "minimum contacts" test depending on whether the jurisdiction arises from contacts which are isolated (specific) or are continuing and systematic (general). See *Helicopteros Nacionales de Colombia v. Hall,* 466 U.S. 408, 413, 104 S. Ct. 1868, 1871, 80 L. Ed. 2d 404 (1984). The third portion provides the overriding concern that once the first two prongs are met, the courts of this state must still consider traditional notions of fair play and substantial justice. *International Shoe Co. v. Washington,* 326 U.S. 310, 316, 66 S. Ct. 154, 158, 90 L. Ed. 95 (1945).

At the special appearance hearing, Koch presented the deposition of its president. The deposition testimony showed that Koch is incorporated in New York, has had the same president since its inception, and that Koch has never been authorized to do business in Texas, maintained a place of business or an agent for service of process in Texas, done business in Texas, had any employees in Texas, solicited business in Texas, or owned any property in Texas. Specifically in connection with this transaction, the deposition showed that Koch never entered into a contract with Avantech, performed or agreed to perform duties in Texas, was present in Texas, or directed communications to Avantech. The deposition also showed that the printing equipment had always been located at Koch's place of business in New York and that Koch had only dealt with Hudson. Avantech did not controvert any of these statements.

In a special appearance under rule 120a, the defendant has the burden to prove that it is not amenable to the jurisdiction of a Texas court. *Minexa Ariz., Inc. v. Staubach,* 667 S.W.2d 563, 565 (Tex. App.—Dallas 1984, no writ); *Carbonit Houston, Inc. v. Exchange Bank,* 628 S.W.2d 826, 829 (Tex. App.—Houston [14th Dist.] 1982, writ ref'd n.r.e.). It is the duty of this Court to review all of the evidence before the trial court on the question of jurisdiction. *Hoppenfeld v. Crook,* 498 S.W.2d 52, 55 (Tex. Civ. App.—Austin 1973, writ ref'd n.r.e.).

The uncontroverted evidence before the trial court shows Koch has no connection with Texas and only an indirect connection with Avantech. There is no evidence that Koch has ever purposefully acted or consummated any transaction in Texas. We conclude that Koch was not doing business in Texas. We further conclude that Koch did not purposely avail itself of the privilege of conducting activities in Texas; Koch did not purposely invoke the benefits and protection of Texas laws, and Koch did not have sufficient minimum contacts with Texas. Consequently, we do not reach consideration of traditional notions of fair play and substantial justice. We sustain Koch's first point of error. In view of our disposition of this point of error, we do not reach Koch's remaining points of error.

. . . .

We . . . sustain Koch's special appearance. The trial court's judgment is reversed, and the cause is dismissed for lack of personal jurisdiction over Koch Graphics, Inc.

### [C] The Doctrine of Forum Non Conveniens

Under some due process tests, the factor of convenience figures into the determination of due process. But there is also a separate doctrine of forum non conveniens, which gives the court some discretion to dismiss—even though the court may have jurisdiction—if the forum is relatively inconvenient and another forum exists that is significantly more convenient.

The doctrine is mentioned in relatively few Texas cases. Probably the best known case discussing the doctrine is *Gulf Oil Co. v. Gilbert,* 330 U.S. 501 (1947), a decision by the United States Supreme Court. Forum non conveniens is not a doctrine frequently resorted to in the federal courts today because 28 U.S.C. Section 1404(a) gives the federal courts power to transfer cases among themselves for the convenience of the parties and witnesses or in the interest of justice. Still, the doctrine does appear occasionally, because the Section 1404(a) transfer provision does not apply if the more convenient forum is the court of another nation. The courts of the several States, lacking a nationwide court system, invoke the doctrine of forum non conveniens more frequently.

It is important to bear in mind that, even if the court finds jurisdiction, forum non conveniens enables it to dismiss in deference to another forum, if the doctrine is applicable. If a lawyer represents a nonresident defendant who wishes to assert lack of personal jurisdiction, but believes that the facts make the issue a close one, what does this doctrine indicate the lawyer might do in addition to making a conventional attack on the jurisdiction? Might forum non conveniens be a second arrow in the quiver? Consider the following case.

---

## DIRECT COLOR SERVICES, INC. v. EASTMAN KODAK CO.

*929 S.W.2d 558 (Tex. App.—Tyler 1996, no writ)*

HADDEN, Justice.

This is an appeal from an order dismissing a suit on the grounds of *forum non conveniens.* The plaintiffs in the suit are the following nine entities: Direct Color Services, Inc.,

Haff-Daugherty Graphics, Inc., Halftone, Inc., Hi-Tech Color, Inc., Arthur Carroll, d/b/a Color Media, Rally Graphics, Inc., Dot's Incredible, Inc., Kingswood Graphics, Inc., and Dynagraf, Inc. (collectively, the "Appellants"). Appellants sued Eastman Kodak Company, Electronic Pre-Press Systems, Inc., Kodak Electronic Printing Systems, Inc., and Imaging Financial Services, Inc., f/k/a Eastman Kodak Credit Corporation (collectively the "Appellees"), alleging that the Designmaster 8000 System, a computer graphics imaging system which each Appellant either leased or purchased from Appellees, was defective. Suit was filed in County Court at Law No. Two of Smith County, Texas. Appellants sought damages for breach of contract, fraud, negligence, breach of warranty, and for violation of the Texas Deceptive Trade Practices—Consumer Protection Act ("DTPA") and Massachusetts General Laws, Chapter 93A. Appellees filed a motion to dismiss based upon the doctrine of *forum non conveniens*. After several hearings, the trial court granted the motion and dismissed the case.

In their single point of error, the Appellants challenge the dismissal, alleging that the trial court abused its discretion in granting the motion on the grounds of *forum non conveniens*. We will affirm the order of the trial court.

Appellants are involved in the color electronic pre-press industry which is a part of the printing industry. One of the Appellants, Arthur Carroll, d/b/a Color Media, is a sole proprietorship doing business in California. The remaining eight Appellants are foreign corporations. Their states of incorporation are as follows:

Direct Color Services, Inc. — Oregon

Haff-Daugherty Graphics, Inc. — Florida

Dot's Incredible, Inc. — Florida

Kingswood Graphics, Inc. — New York

Halftone, Inc. — New Jersey

Hi-Tech Color, Inc. — Idaho

Rally Graphics, Inc. — New York

Dynagraf, Inc. — Massachusetts

No Appellant is a Texas corporation. None has its place of business in Texas, and none is authorized to do business in Texas. Similarly, no Appellee is a Texas corporation, and no Appellee has its principal place of business in Texas, although three Appellees are authorized to do business in Texas.

Each Appellant either leased a Designmaster 8000 System from Eastman Kodak Credit Corporation, or purchased a Designmaster 8000 System from Electronic Pre-Press Systems, Inc. or Kodak Electronic Printing Systems, Inc. Appellants alleged numerous causes of action and damages arising from the use of the Designmaster 8000 System, and sought both exemplary damages and attorneys fees. However, none of the transactions underlying Appellants' claims occurred in Texas or had any connection to the state of Texas or its citizens. The following is a summary of the Appellants' tort and contract claims:

. . . .

[The court here analyzes plaintiffs' tort claims, examining where plaintiffs' alleged injuries occurred, where the conduct causing such injuries occurred, and where the relationships between the various plaintiffs and defendant were centered, finding, in each case, no connection to Texas.]

Contract Claims

The Appellants also alleged several contract claims. The contracts that the Appellants signed with either Electronic Pre-Press Systems, Inc. or Kodak Electronic Printing Systems, Inc. provided that the law of the state of Massachusetts would apply to any disputes over the contract. Several Appellants signed one or more service agreements with Electronic Pre-Press Systems, Inc., Eastman Kodak Company, or Kodak Electronic Printing Systems, Inc. These service agreements likewise had a choice of law provision applying Massachusetts law. Each Appellant also leased at least one Designmaster System from Eastman Kodak Credit Corporation. These lease agreements contained a provision that New York law would apply to any dispute between the parties over the lease agreement.

. . . .

The trial court found that the application of the doctrine of *forum non conveniens* was appropriate in this action for several reasons, and included the following in its order of dismissal:

1. No Plaintiff is a Texas resident or has its principal place of business in Texas;

2. No Defendant is a Texas resident or has its principal place of business in Texas;

3. The contracts which are the subject of Plaintiffs' claims contain provisions that the laws of Massachusetts and New York shall govern any claims involving such contracts. None of the transactions between any Plaintiff and any Defendant giving rise to any Plaintiff's claims occurred in Texas. Accordingly, Texas law is not the substantive law governing any claims;

4. Alternative forums are adequate and available to resolve the claims including at least Massachusetts, Oregon, New York, Florida, New Jersey, Idaho and California;

5. The persons with knowledge of facts relevant to the claims are, with very limited exceptions, in states other than Texas, and no party can compel the attendance of any witnesses at trial;

6. None of Plaintiffs' claims or alleged damages arose or occurred in Texas;

7. The claims are complex and will require significant time and resources to resolve; it is unjust to impose on the citizens of Smith County as well as the Court the burden of resolving litigation that has no Texas connection.

The doctrine of *forum non conveniens* is an equitable doctrine exercised by courts to resist imposition of an inconvenient jurisdiction on a litigant, even if jurisdiction is supported by the long-arm statute and would not violate due process. *Sarieddine v. Moussa*, 820 S.W.2d 837, 839 (Tex. App.—Dallas 1991, writ denied). Although the Texas Supreme Court has neither enthusiastically embraced the doctrine of *forum non conveniens*, nor revealed fully its contours, it has acknowledged the existence of the doctrine as announced by the United States Supreme Court in *Gulf Oil Corp. v. Gilbert*, 330 U.S. 501, 67 S. Ct. 839, 91 L. Ed. 1055 (1947). *A.P. Keller Dev., Inc. v. One Jackson Place, Ltd.*, 890 S.W.2d 502, 505 (Tex. App.—El Paso 1994, no writ), *citing Flaiz v. Moore*, 359 S.W.2d 872, 874 (Tex. 1962). Texas recognizes the doctrine as a procedural rule which does not determine jurisdiction, but only determines that the jurisdiction which exists should not be exercised where another forum, also having jurisdiction, is better able to act. *McNutt v. Teledyne Indus., Inc.*, 693 S.W.2d 666, 668 (Tex. App.—Dallas 1985, writ dism'd). A Texas court will exercise the doctrine of *forum non conveniens* when it determines that, for the convenience of the litigants and witnesses, and in the interest of justice, the action should be instituted in another forum.[1] *Sarieddine*, 820 S.W.2d at 839; *Van Winkle-Hooker Co. v. Rice*, 448 S.W.2d 824, 826 (Tex. Civ. App.—Dallas 1969, no writ). . . .

. . . .

There are several steps in conducting *forum non conveniens* analysis. *Sarieddine*, 820 S.W.2d at 841. First, there must be a determination that an alternative forum exists, because the doctrine presumes that at least two forums are available to the plaintiff to pursue the claim. *Sarieddine*, 820 S.W.2d at 841; *Van Winkle-Hooker Co.*, 448 S.W.2d at 826. The alternative forum element has two components, that is, an alternative forum must be available and adequate. An exception to the general rule that the defendant bears the burden on all elements of *forum non conveniens* is that, once the defendant establishes that an "available" forum exists, the plaintiff must prove that the available forum is not adequate. *Vaz Borralho v. Keydril Co.*, 696 F.2d 379, 393–394 (5th Cir. 1983).

The second and third steps are to weigh the private and public interest factors to be considered by the court in determining whether the doctrine of *forum non conveniens* should be applied. These factors were articulated by the United States Supreme Court in *Gilbert*. The *Gilbert* factors are not exhaustive, however, and a trial court has the discretion to consider other relevant factors bearing on the issue. The important private interests of litigants that a trial court may consider are:

1. Relative ease of access to sources of proof;

2. Availability of compulsory process for attendance of unwilling, and the cost of obtaining attendance of willing, witnesses;

3. Possibility of view of premises, if view would be appropriate to the action; and

4. All other practical problems that make trial of a case easy, expeditious and inexpensive.

*Gilbert*, 330 U.S. at 508, 67 S. Ct. at 843.

The public interest concerns recognized by the *Gilbert* court include:

1. Administrative difficulties caused by litigation not handled at its origin;

2. Jury duty imposed upon people of a community which has no relation to the litigation;

3. Inability of people whose affairs may be touched by litigation to learn of it other than by way of report if held in remote part of the country;

4. Local interest in having localized controversies decided at home; and

5. Appropriateness of having a trial in a diversity case in a forum that is familiar with the state law that must govern the case, rather than having a court in some other forum untangle problems in conflict of laws and in law that is foreign.

*Id.* at 508–509, 67 S. Ct. at 843. The factors listed above have been recognized expressly in Texas. *See Sarieddine*, 820 S.W.2d at 840.

---

[1] Historically, there has been some question in Texas as to which causes of actions are subject to *forum non conveniens* analysis. In *Dow Chemical Co. v. Alfaro*, 786 S.W.2d 674 (Tex.), *cert. denied*, 498 U.S. 1024, 111 S. Ct. 671, 112 L. Ed. 2d 663 (1990), the Texas Supreme Court held that Section 71.031 of the Civil Practice and Remedies Code abolished *forum non conveniens* in cases involving personal injury and wrongful death. The Texas Legislature has since codified the doctrine of *forum non conveniens* for personal injury and wrongful death cases at Section 71.051 of the Texas Civil Practice and Remedies Code, but the new statute only applies to causes of action filed on or after September 1, 1993. However, *Alfaro* and its progeny are limited to personal injury and wrongful death suits under Section 71.031, and are not applicable to the instant case. *See Sarieddine*, 820 S.W.2d at 841.

## A. ALTERNATE FORUMS ANALYSIS

In order to invoke the doctrine of *forum non conveniens*, there must exist at least two forums which are available to Appellants. *Sarieddine*, 820 S.W.2d at 841. A forum is "available" when the entire case and all the parties can come within the jurisdiction of that forum. *Quintero v. Klaveness Ship Lines*, 914 F.2d 717, 727 (5th Cir. 1990), *cert. denied*, 499 U.S. 925, 111 S. Ct. 1322, 113 L. Ed. 2d 255 (1990). Once the moving party establishes that an available forum exists, the burden is on the plaintiff to prove that the available forum is not adequate. *Vaz Borralho*, 696 F.2d at 393–394. A forum is considered "adequate" when the parties will not be deprived of all remedies or treated unfairly. *In re Air Crash Near New Orleans, La.*, 821 F.2d 1147, 1165 (5th Cir. 1987), *vacated*, 490 U.S. 1032, 109 S. Ct. 1928, 104 L. Ed. 2d 400 (1988).

It appears from the record that Appellants have alternate forums in which to bring their claims. . . . .

[The court here analyzes other forums available to plaintiffs, concluding each plaintiff had at least two other forums in which the action could have been brought.]

## B. PRIVATE AND PUBLIC INTEREST FACTORS

We will next review the private and public interest factors which were before the trial court. No Appellant or Appellee has its principal place of business in Texas. The sources of proof available to Appellees to defend against Appellants' claims are in other states, primarily New York and Massachusetts. No one identified by Appellants as having knowledge of relevant facts is within subpoena range of the Smith County courthouse. Appellants argue that at least three witnesses reside in Texas. However, one of the three witnesses is Appellants' expert who resides in Houston. Experts are selected by the parties and are available virtually anywhere in the United States. To give controlling weight to this factor would allow any plaintiff to easily circumvent the *forum non conveniens* doctrine by choosing an expert in an inconvenient forum. *See Norman v. Norfolk & Western Railway Co.*, 228 Pa. Super. 319, 323 A.2d 850, 855 (1974). The other two witnesses are fact witnesses, and these two persons, Richard Crawford and Kay Crawford, moved to Texas after the lawsuit was filed. If the case were tried in Smith County, Texas, Appellees would be unable to compel the attendance of witnesses, including the few who reside in Texas. Continuation of this trial in Texas could cause Appellees to incur significant expense which could be avoided if the case is tried in an available jurisdiction.

Furthermore, the laws of potentially seven different states may apply to Appellants' claims. The relevant and appropriate choice of law rules which the trial court would have to apply in the instant case, along with the specific contractual provisions, dictate that the laws of several states would govern the claims asserted by Appellants. Texas is not one of those states. Thus, the application of a unique set of laws to each Appellant would be confusing and would be unduly burdensome for the Texas trial court.

Also, the trial court found that there would be administrative difficulties caused by trying the case in Smith County, Texas. It would impose jury duty upon citizens of Smith County to hear a cause of action that has no connection whatsoever to Smith County. It would also require the Smith County, Texas, court to devote its time to a complex, multi-party, commercial lawsuit involving non-Texas residents at the expense of the court's criminal, family, and general civil cases involving Texas citizens. Moreover, the citizens of Smith County, who will likely have their access to the judicial system delayed for six to eight weeks or more, are unable to have their day in court in Massachusetts, New York, or some other state whose courts would have jurisdiction over the instant claims. Smith County and Texas tax dollars would be used to resolve disputes that have no relation to Smith County or Texas. Also, local interest in the trial would be far greater in the areas where Appellees reside or in the areas where each Appellant has its principal place of business located.

Finally, Appellants contend that the ruling was improper because Appellees have sufficient connections to the state of Texas and Smith County which justify the retention of this case for trial in Smith County, Texas. In support of this argument, Appellants cite the numerous routine business activities of Eastman Kodak Company in Texas, including ownership of property, maintaining offices, conducting sales, and contracting for and servicing Designmaster 8000 Systems. However, none of these activities are shown by Appellants to have any relationship to the contracting for and servicing of the Designmaster 8000 Systems which were sold or leased to Appellants. Our conclusion is that the private and public interest factors support the trial court's dismissal for *forum non conveniens*.

## C. LATENESS OF MOTION

Appellants next assert that the lateness of the motion to dismiss for *forum non conveniens* was harmful to Appellants and denies substantial justice if allowed to stand. The motion to dismiss on the grounds of *forum non conveniens* was filed by Appellees nine months after the case was filed. . . .

The Texas Supreme Court has addressed the question of when *forum non conveniens* may be appropriately raised:

> If the court is to decline jurisdiction on that ground [forum non conveniens], the question must be raised at a time and in a manner that will give the parties an opportunity to present evidence regarding the circumstances that are relevant to a determination of whether jurisdiction should or should not be retained.

*Flaiz*, 359 S.W.2d at 875 (Tex. 1962). In its opinion, the *Flaiz* court specifically analyzed New York law on *forum non conveniens* and when it could be raised in that jurisdiction. The court noted that some authority existed in New York for raising *forum non conveniens* for the first time on appeal and also referenced authority that a defendant must raise *forum non conveniens* no later than the end of trial. The *Flaiz* court expressly stated its disagreement with the rule that *forum non conveniens* could be raised on appeal. The *Flaiz* court did not, however, express any disagreement with the rule that a defendant has until trial to raise *forum non conveniens*. *Id.* We conclude therefore, based on Flaiz, that the issue of *forum non conveniens* may be raised anytime before trial.[2]

Our examination of the record in light of the elements outlined above leads to the conclusion that dismissal based on *forum non conveniens* was appropriate. The trial court's dismissal based on *forum non conveniens* does not rise to the level of arbitrary and unreasonable action and was, therefore, not an abuse of discretion. Appellants' sole point of error is overruled.

The Order of the trial court is affirmed.

---

[2] The Texas Civil Practices and Remedies Code § 71.051 et seq. requires a motion to dismiss on the grounds of *forum non conveniens* to be filed not later than a motion to transfer venue. Tex. Civ. Prac. & Rem. Code Ann. § 71.05(e). However, this statute does not apply to actions other than personal injury or wrongful death.

---

**DOW CHEMICAL v. CASTRO ALFARO,** 786 S.W.2d 674 (Tex. 1990). Domingo Castro Alfaro, a Costa Rican resident, and 81 other Costa Ricans sued Dow Chemical Company and Shell Oil Company in Harris County alleging personal injury claims resulting from exposure to dibromochloropropane (DBCP), a pesticide used by the claimants' employer, Standard Fruit Company, on banana farms in Costa Rica. The employees exposed to DBCP allegedly suffered several medical problems, including sterility.

After unsuccessfully attempting to remove the case to federal court, the defendants sought dismissal of the case under the doctrine of forum non conveniens. Despite a finding of personal jurisdiction over the defendants, the trial court dismissed the case on the ground of forum non conveniens. The First Court of Appeals held that Texas courts lack the authority to dismiss on the grounds of forum non conveniens. 751 S.W.2d 208. In affirming the court of appeals, the Texas Supreme Court held that "the legislature has statutorily abolished the doctrine of forum non conveniens in suits brought under section 71.031 of the Texas Civil Practice and Remedies Code." The Court's interpretation of section 71.031 was based on the refusal of writ of error in *Allen v. Bass,* 47 S.W.2d 426 (Tex. Civ. App.—El Paso 1932, writ ref'd), in which the court of appeals held that former R.C.S. Article 4678, the statutory predecessor of section 71.031, conferred an "absolute right" of a citizen of a "neighboring state" to maintain a "transitory action" in Texas.

---

## NOTE

*Codification of Forum Non Conveniens.* In February 1993 the Texas Legislature amended Chapter 71 of the Civil Practice and Remedies Code to embrace the doctrine of forum non conveniens for personal injury and wrongful death cases. The statute applies to causes of action filed on or after September 1, 1993. In 1997, the Texas Legislature again amended the statute on forum non conveniens. Among the more significant changes was one providing that a request for stay or dismissal would be timely if filed not later than 180 days after the time required for filing a motion to transfer venue of the claim or action. *See* C.P.R.C. § 71.051(d). In addition, a new section was added addressed specifically to claims for injury due to exposure to asbestos. *See* C.P.R.C. § 71.052.

# CHAPTER 5

# PLEADINGS

## SCOPE

This chapter covers pleadings. Topics examined include the historical background of pleadings, basic pleading requirements, the requirement to state a "cause of action," the requirement to give "fair notice" of legal theories and factual elements, plaintiff's and defendant's pleadings including petitions, answers, and denials, and supplemental and amended pleadings. Illustrations of sample pleading forms are provided, and an appendix provides examples of a number of forms from a specific commercial litigation case.

## § 5.01 Historical Background

In 1840, the Fourth Congress of the Republic of Texas implemented the constitutional directive, contained in the Constitution of 1836, to adopt the common law of England "with such modifications as our circumstances . . . may require." (Section 13, Article IV, 1 *Laws of Texas* 1074 (Gammel 1898). Section 1 of the act of February 5, 1840 provided:

> . . . [T]he adoption of the common law shall not be construed to adopt the common law system of pleading, but the proceedings in all civil suits shall, as heretofore, be conducted by petition and answer; but neither petition nor answer shall be necessary in a cause to recover money before a justice of the peace.

2 H. Gammel, *Laws of Texas* 262–67 (1898).

As Professor Joseph McKnight has explained, "It is chiefly because the Spanish system of pleading was simple and direct that it was so well suited to the needs of frontier life. [footnote omitted] Unlike English common law pleading, no premium was placed on great formalities or the niceties of pleas that can be mastered only by the most exacting training. The Spanish system of pleading by simple petition and answer was ideally suited to frontier conditions—and the ignorance (or lack of training) of local judges. [footnote omitted] The willingness with which Anglo-Texas frontiersmen accepted this system was probably influenced by an impatience with the fine distinctions of common law pleading encountered in the United States, at least in matters involving any substantial amount of money or property." McKnight, *The Spanish Influence on the Texas Law of Civil Procedure,* 38 Tex. L. Rev. 24, 26 (1959).

The nature of the simplified system of pleading, or at least the attitude with which the pleading process was approached, is described in *Hamilton v. Black,* Dallam, 587 (1844), in which the Texas Supreme Court said: "The object of our statutes on the subject of pleading, is to simplify as much as possible that branch of the proceedings in courts which by the ingenuity and learning of both common and civil law lawyers and judges, has become so refined in its subtleties as to substitute in many instances the shadow for the substance. Our statutes require, at the hands of the petitioner to a court of justice only a statement of the names of the parties plaintiff and defendant, a full and fair exposition of his cause of action, and finally the relief which he seeks." This sensible attitude was gradually replaced by a mass of technicalities. *See* Franklin, *Simplicity in Procedure,* 4 Tex. L. Rev. 83 (1925). Former Article 1997 of the Revised Civil Statutes of 1925, originally enacted in the late 1870s, required a pleader to allege the "facts constituting the cause of action or the defendant's grounds of defense." *See* former R.C.S. Art. 1997.

A movement for procedural change that focused, in part, on a simplification of the pleading rules was made manifest in 1938 as a result of the adoption of the Federal Rules of Civil Procedure. The general federal pleading rule, Federal Civil Procedure Rule 8(a), requires "a short and plain statement of the claim showing that the pleader is entitled to relief." The value-laden terms "facts" and "cause of action" were not included because of the technical baggage that accompanied them. Although no definition was attempted in the federal rules of the meaning of the term "claim," the forms the federal drafters prepared as examples reflect a substantial departure from the detailed, long-form pleading required previously. *See* Clark, *The Texas and The Federal Rules of Civil Procedure,* 20 Tex. L. Rev. 4 (1941); Stayton, *The Scope and Function of Pleading Under the New Federal and Texas Rules: A Comparison,* 20 Tex. L. Rev. 16 (1941).

Effective May 15, 1939, the Supreme Court of Texas was vested with full rulemaking power in the "practice and procedure" in civil actions. Gov. C. § 22.004. Shortly thereafter, the Court appointed a committee of lawyers, judges, and law professors to suggest a set of rules for the control of civil actions, including rules to govern the pleading process. Although the Texas rules concerning pleadings were patterned in part on the Federal Rules of Civil Procedure, a conscious decision was made to avoid wholesale adoption of the federal short form of pleading on the theory that the federal form of pleading would be incompatible with Texas jury submission practice. Moreover, the general denial, which had been abolished between the years 1913 and 1915 in Texas, was retained because it had been in use for over a century. *See* Stayton, *The Scope and Function of Pleading Under the New Federal and Texas Rules: A Comparison,* 20 Tex. L. Rev. 16, 19, 20–21 (1941). *See also* Stayton, *The General Issue in Texas,* 9 Tex. L. Rev. 1, 12–18 (1930).

Under the Texas Rules of Civil Procedure as originally promulgated, the pleading rules were modified by the elimination of the requirement that the pleader plead the "facts constituting the plaintiff's cause of action or the defendant's ground of defense." *See* former R.C.S. Art. 1997. This requirement to plead "facts" as distinguished from "evidence" or "legal conclusions" was replaced by a requirement that pleadings "consist of a statement in plain and concise language of the plaintiff's cause of action or the defendant's grounds of defense." *See* Tex. R. Civ. P. 45 superseding former R.C.S. Art. 1997. Significantly, the concept of "fair notice" was added as the principal pleading requirement. *See* Tex. R. Civ. P. 45 ("That an allegation be evidentiary or be of legal conclusion shall not be grounds for objection when fair notice to the opponent is given by the allegations as a whole"). This odd mixture of old and new pleading concepts was accompanied by another major change. The "new rules" abolished the general demurrer as a procedural device and provided for the waiver of pleading defects, unless the defect is raised by an "exception in writing . . . brought to the attention of the judge in the trial court before the instruction or charge to the jury or, in a non-jury case, before the judgment is signed." *See* Tex. R. Civ. P. 90. Before the adoption of Civil Procedure Rule 90, pleading defects could be raised for the first time in a motion for new trial. *See, e.g., Gulf C. & S. Ry. Co. v. Vieno,* 26 S.W. 230, 231 (Tex. Civ. App. 1894, no writ); *but see Southwestern Life Ins. Co. v. Powers,* 122 S.W.2d 1056, 1057 (Comm. App. Sec. A 1939, opinion adopted) (objection to insufficiency of answer to join issue on contested facts "cannot be made for the first time in the appellate court").

## § 5.02 An Overview of Texas Pleadings and Their Functions

To understand Texas pleading, a new terminology must be mastered. The following pleadings are in current use in Texas and the following descriptions give a basic understanding of their functions:

### [A] Plaintiff's Pleadings

*Plaintiff's Original Petition.* In Texas, the plaintiff's pleading that commences the action is called an original petition (not a complaint). An original petition should contain certain formal elements, such as allegations of jurisdiction, venue, the pertinent discovery level and the names of the parties and their residences. It must also allege the cause or causes of action and include a prayer for relief.

*Plaintiff's Supplemental Petition.* For historical reasons, a plaintiff's reply to a defendant's answer is called a supplemental petition. It may include special exceptions and denials or avoidances of pleas included in the answer.

*Amendment and Supplementation.* A plaintiff may, within the bounds allowed by the rules, file an amended original petition ("Plaintiff's First Amended Original Petition") or an amended supplemental petition ("Plaintiff's First Amended Supplemental Petition"). The process of amendment and supplementation may also be used by a defendant.

### [B] Defendant's Pleadings

*The Special Appearance Motion.* We have already considered special appearance practice in Chapter 4 on jurisdiction over the person, but you should be aware that a special appearance motion contesting a nonresident's amenability to process is a defendant's plea that, if filed, must be filed first.

*Motion to Transfer Venue.* The motion to transfer venue because the county where the action is pending is not a proper county or because the venue selected by the claimant is inconvenient is covered in Chapter 6 on venue. It is mentioned here so that it can be placed in its proper place in the pleading scheme. An objection to improper or inconvenient venue is waived if the motion to transfer is not filed prior to or concurrently with any other plea except a special appearance motion.

*Motion to Quash Citation.* A defendant may attack the propriety of the service by this plea. As you learned in Chapter 4, it is seldom used, however, because even when citation is quashed, the only effect is to delay the appearance day. A motion to quash is a general appearance and should not be filed by a nonresident who contests personal jurisdiction.

*Plea in Abatement.* The plea in abatement is the method of raising a fundamental defect in the mode of bringing the action, other than on personal jurisdiction, citation, or venue grounds. It is thus a "catchall" type of plea. Its most frequent use is to raise such matters as the prior pendency of another action or the nonjoinder of a person needed for just adjudication.

*Plea to the Jurisdiction.* As you learned in Chapter 3, a challenge to the court's exercise of jurisdiction of the subject matter of the action is made by a plea to the jurisdiction. Customarily, the pleading is sworn, although no rule of procedure requires it.

*Special Exceptions.* This plea attacks the sufficiency of the opponent's pleadings, raising defects of either form or substance. In other words, if the pleading is vague, contains improper matter or fails to state grounds on which relief can legally be granted, the special exception is a proper vehicle for raising these defects. The special exception fulfills the function that the motion to dismiss for failure to state a claim and the motion for more definite statement fulfill in federal court.

*General Denial.* Texas allows the defendant to deny the petition generally, putting the plaintiff to proof on most issues.

*Specific Denials and Denials Under Oath.* A defendant may deny given facts specifically even when a general denial is permitted. However, in some instances, a defendant is required to deny allegations specifically, and a general denial is ineffective to require the plaintiff to prove these allegations.

*Affirmative Defenses.* An affirmative defense is one that sets up an independent ground defeating plaintiff's recovery, i.e., one that does not operate by denying elements of the claim. Affirmative defenses must be alleged affirmatively, as well as proved, by the defendant. A general denial is ineffective to raise them.

## § 5.03 Sample Pleadings

On the pages that follow, you will encounter a plaintiff's petition, a defendant's answer including special exceptions, a setting for a hearing on special exceptions, the court's order on the exceptions and plaintiff's amended pleading. The elements of the petition are alleged with varying degrees of specificity and care. The answer contains several different kinds of defensive theories. You should be conscious of the different functions of the different pleadings and of the strategy of the attorneys.

This material is taken from D. Crump, *The Anatomy of a Civil Suit: Obiedio v. J. Weingarten, Inc.* (1977)*

---

NO. 862,428

| | |
|---|---|
| DELFINA OBIEDIO | ) IN THE DISTRICT COURT |
| V. | ) HARRIS COUNTY, TEXAS |
| J. WEINGARTEN, INC. | ) 125th JUDICIAL DISTRICT |

PLAINTIFF'S ORIGINAL PETITION

To the Honorable Judge of Said Court:

NOW COMES DELFINA OBIEDIO, hereinafter called Plaintiff, complaining of J. WEINGARTEN, INC., hereinafter called Defendant, and for cause of action would respectfully show unto the Court as follows:

---

I.

The Defendant, J. WEINGARTEN, INC., is a corporation doing business in the State of Texas, who may be served with Citation by service upon their statutory agent, ABE WEINGARTEN, 600 Lockwood, Houston, Harris County, Texas.

II.

This suit is brought for the recovery of the damages to which your Plaintiff is legally entitled as the result of an accident which occurred on or about May 7, 1969, at the Weingarten Store No. 14, located at 1100 Quitman, Houston, Harris County, Texas. At this time, Plaintiff was getting a shopping cart from a stacked row when she slipped and fell due to the improper manner in which the carts were aligned and the unsafe condition of Defendant's floor. Plaintiff was not guilty of any negligence. On the contrary, Plaintiff's injuries were caused by the failure of J. WEINGARTEN, INC. and its agents to observe the applicable statutory laws and ordinances and their failure to exercise that degree of care in the maintenance of their premises as would have been exercised by a person of ordinary prudence under the same or similar circumstances.

[This petition further alleges that the plaintiff has incurred physical pain, mental anguish and charges for medical services; that she will in all probability incur further such damages in the future; and that her damages are in the sum of $10,000. The petition is signed by Stephen T. Elder as attorney for plaintiff.]

---

NO. 862,428

| | | |
|---|---|---|
| DELFINA OBIEDIO | ) | IN THE DISTRICT COURT OF |
| V. | ) | HARRIS COUNTY, TEXAS |
| J. WEINGARTEN, INC. | ) | 125TH JUDICIAL DISTRICT |

DEFENDANT'S ORIGINAL ANSWER

To the Honorable Judge of Said Court:

Comes now J. WEINGARTEN, INC., Defendant in the above styled and numbered cause, and for answer to Plaintiff's Petition would respectfully show unto the Court:

I.

Defendant specially excepts to the allegations contained in Plaintiff's original petition and more particularly those allegations which provide:

> At this time Plaintiff was getting a shopping cart from a stacked row when she slipped and fell due to the improper manner in which the carts were aligned and the unsafe condition of Defendant's floor;

such allegation being vague and general and does not apprise this Defendant of the manner in which the carts' alignment was improper or the manner in which the condition of Defendant's floor was unsafe or the manner in which J. Weingarten, Inc. was negligent, such allegation wholly failing to apprise your Defendant of the claim being made against it by Plaintiff of which exception Defendant prays judgment of the Court.

II.

Defendant specially excepts to the allegations of Plaintiff's petition and more particularly allegations contained in Paragraph II thereof which provide:

> On the contrary, Plaintiff's injuries were caused by the failure of J. Weingarten, Inc., and its agents to observe the applicable statutory laws and ordinances and their failure to exercise that degree of care in the maintenance of their premises as would have been exercised by a person of ordinary prudence under the same or similar circumstances";

in that such allegation is vague and general and does not apprise this Defendant of:

(a) which statutory laws Plaintiff alleges that J. Weingarten, Inc. has failed to observe;

(b) which ordinances Plaintiff contends J. Weingarten, Inc. failed to observe causing Plaintiff's injuries;

(c) in what manner Defendant, J. Weingarten, Inc., was negligent in failing to maintain their premises,

of which exception Defendant prays judgment of the Court.

III.

As authorized by Rule 92 of the Rules of Civil Procedure, this Defendant denies the allegations of Plaintiff's petition.

IV.

For further and special answer herein, if such be necessary, and in the alternative, this Defendant avers that such injuries and damages as Plaintiff may have sustained were proximately caused by the failure of Plaintiff to exercise that degree of care which would have been exercised by persons of ordinary prudence in the exercise of ordinary care under the same or similar circumstances.

V.

In the further alternative, if such be necessary, this Defendant avers that the sole proximate cause of the occurrence made the basis of Plaintiff's suit was the act or omission of some third person or the condition of some instrumentality over which this Defendant had or exercised no control and for which this Defendant is not in law responsible.

VI.

In the further alternative, if such be necessary, this Defendant avers that the occurrence made the basis of Plaintiff's suit was an unavoidable accident.

WHEREFORE, premises considered, Defendant prays that it go hence without day, with its costs and for general relief.

____________________________

ATTORNEYS FOR DEFENDANT

---

Having filed an answer containing several attacks on plaintiff's pleading, Mr. Thompson [defendant's attorney] next took the step of securing a hearing on those attacks (special exceptions), by calling the clerk of the court. On securing a date, he then notified plaintiff's counsel by the following LETTER GIVING NOTICE OF SETTING:

March 5, 1971

Mr. Stephen F. Elder
Attorney at Law
301 Houston First Savings Building
Houston, Texas 77002

Re: No. 862,428—*Delfina Obiedio vs. J. Weingarten, Inc.*—125th District Court

Dear Mr. Elder:

Hearing on special exceptions of Defendant, J. Weingarten Inc., will be at 9:00 A.M. on Monday, April 12, 1971 in the 125th Judicial District Court.

Very truly yours,

____________________________

---

NO. 862,428

DELFINA OBIEDIO ) IN THE DISTRICT COURT OF
V. ) HARRIS COUNTY, TEXAS
J. WEINGARTEN, INC. ) F-125TH JUDICIAL DISTRICT

ORDER

BE IT REMEMBERED on this day came on to be heard Defendant's Special Exceptions to Plaintiff's Original Petition and the Court after considering such exceptions is of the opinion that they should be sustained and it is therefore,

ORDERED, ADJUDGED and DECREED that Defendant's Special Exceptions to Plaintiff's Original Petition be sustained and that Plaintiff be given leave to amend.

SIGNED, RENDERED and ENTERED this ______ day of ______, 1971.

______________________________

JUDGE PRESIDING

APPROVED

______________________________

ATTORNEY FOR DEFENDANT

______________________________

ATTORNEY FOR PLAINTIFF

[The following instrument was filed by plaintiff's lawyer after plaintiff's deposition was taken and a trial setting was obtained:]

NO. 862,428

| | | |
|---|---|---|
| DELFINA OBIEDIO | ) | IN THE DISTRICT COURT OF |
| V. | ) | HARRIS COUNTY, TEXAS |
| J. WEINGARTEN, INC. | ) | 125TH JUDICIAL DISTRICT |

PLAINTIFF'S FIRST AMENDED ORIGINAL PETITION

TO THE JUDGE AND JURY OF THIS COURT:

This suit is brought by Delfina Obiedio, Plaintiff, against J. Weingarten, Inc., Defendant. The suit is for personal injuries sustained by Mrs. Obiedio.

I.

The Plaintiff has for many years been a resident of Harris County. The Defendant, J. Weingarten, Inc. is a corporation doing business in the State of Texas. Defendant is already before this Court on this matter, so service is not necessary.

II.

This suit is brought for the recovery of the damages to which Mrs. Obiedio is legally entitled as a result of an accident which occurred at the Weingarten's Store No. 14, located at 1100 Quitman, here in Houston, Harris County, Texas on or about the 7th of May, 1969. At that time, Mrs. Obiedio had just come into the store to shop for groceries. To carry her groceries, she sought to get a shopping cart from a row of carts stacked with the baskets inside each other as is customarily done in grocery stores. The carts were in a bad state of repair: the baskets were bent; some of the wheels would not turn and the tubular metal frames of some of the carts were bent. In spite of the state of repair of the carts, Mrs. Obiedio had previously been able to pull one cart away from the stack without difficulty. However, on the occasion in question three or four baskets stuck together and all started rolling toward Mrs. Obiedio. The baskets ran over Mrs. Obiedio, she was knocked off balance and fell to the floor. Mrs. Obiedio was not guilty of any negligence. On the contrary, it is alleged that her injuries were caused by the failure of J. Weingarten, Inc. and its agents to exercise that degree of care in their maintenance of their store as would have been exercised by a person of ordinary prudence under the same or similar circumstances. Specifically, it is alleged that J. Weingarten, Inc. and the company's employees at Store No. 14 ought not to have crammed the bent and broken carts together, or ought to have made sure that they were in sufficiently good repair that an elderly lady could pull a single cart away from a row.

III.

Mrs. Obiedio has required medical care and in reasonable probability will require additional medical care. Her injuries and their effect have caused her to suffer great physical pain and mental anguish. She will probably continue to suffer from such physical pain for a long time in the future, if not for the rest of her life.

Mrs. Obiedio has incurred, and will likely incur, in the future, charges for medical services. These charges represent the usual, reasonable and customary charges for like and similar services in the vicinity where they have been rendered.

By reason of all of the above and foregoing, Mrs. Obiedio has been caused to suffer damages in the reasonable and just sum of TWENTY-FIVE THOUSAND DOLLARS ($25,000) for which sum she now sues.

WHEREFORE, Mrs. Obiedio earnestly asks that upon final trial of this case, she have judgment against J. Weingarten, Inc., for her damages in the reasonable and just sum of TWENTY-FIVE THOUSAND DOLLARS ($25,000.00), that she have interest on the judgment at the legal rates, and that she recover her costs of Court in this behalf expended and that she have such other and further relief, general and special, at law and in equity to which she may show herself justly entitled.

Respectfully submitted,

____________________________

ATTORNEY FOR PLAINTIFF

---

## NOTES AND QUESTIONS

(1) *Analyze the Petition.* What cause or causes of action has plaintiff alleged? What relief and what kinds of damages has she requested, and why?

In the materials that follow, we will see that a plaintiff's original petition should allege proper causes of action and give "fair notice" of the legal theories and factual elements comprising them. Does the plaintiff's initial pleading meet this standard? Does the amended original petition meet this standard? What allegations or claims are problematic in each?

(2) *Analyze the Answer.* What kinds of defenses or defensive theories has defendant's lawyer pleaded in the answer? What is the function of each enumerated paragraph?

Why does the answer not simply end with the third paragraph (the one containing the statement that "Defendant denies the allegations" of plaintiff)? Why are the rest of the paragraphs included (for example, what would happen if defendant tried to rely on contributory negligence at trial without pleading paragraph IV of the answer)?

(3) *What Must Defendant Plead?* There is some question whether defendant is required to plead the matters in Paragraphs V and VI of the answer (because "sole proximate cause" and "unavoidable accident" are not affirmative defenses, but instead go to rebut the plaintiff's claim of causal negligence). If there is doubt about the need for pleading a particular claim or defense, what should the lawyer do? What is lost by pleading it?

(4) *Special Exceptions.* The special exception is the vehicle for challenging either form (such as vagueness) or content (such as failure to state a cause of action) of the petition. What are the special exceptions used for in the *Obiedio* case?

(5) *The Special Exception Hearing.* The hearing on these special exceptions is likely to have been short and informal. The court's docket probably contained 10 or 20 other matters for similar hearings, to be held within an hour or two, before the jury trial or other business of the court for the day. There would be no evidence at the hearing (why not?). The court would probably call both attorneys to come before the bench and inquire what the matter was about, to which defendant's lawyer would probably respond by stating what was contained in the exceptions, in summary form, arguing, perhaps, that "we can't tell whether they mean we're negligent in upkeep of the baskets, or in buying this kind of basket, or in having them stacked wrong, or what." Plaintiff might respond, "Well, Judge, we say in there that the negligence was in the way the carts were aligned and in the way the floor was kept, and I don't see how we could be much more specific." The case is unlikely to be controlled by law specifically on point (there are few cases about shopping cart pleading), and so the court would simply make its own judgment on the matter on the spot, directing the prevailing party to draw an order for the court to sign.

(6) *Strategic Considerations.* What strategy is behind the defendant's desire to make the plaintiff plead more specifically? It is probably not an effort to learn the facts because that can be done through discovery. To identify the strategy, ask yourself this question: What happens if a plaintiff pleads a specific, narrow act of negligence and then at trial, attempts to introduce evidence of a slightly different act of negligence? Incidentally, notice that the defendant's own pleading of contributory negligence is broad and general. Why? What could the plaintiff do to make the defendant be more specific?

Compare the plaintiff's amended original petition with the initial one. Has the plaintiff pleaded very specifically or kept the pleading general? What, if anything, has been gained by the defendant's exceptions? Were they worth the effort?

(7) *Unliquidated Damages.* Notice that the petition alleges a specific amount of unliquidated damages. Under current rules, this would be improper. Rather, if damages are unliquidated, the plaintiff should simply include a "statement that the damages sought are within the jurisdictional limits of the court." Tex. R. Civ. P. 47(b).

(8) *The Function of the Pleadings.* While we are talking about various kinds of pleadings, it might be worthwhile to ask: What functions do the pleadings fulfill, or what functions are they supposed to accomplish? Is it the function of the pleadings to dispose of the actions completely? Under what conditions *can* the pleadings dispose of the action completely, and how frequent an occurrence would you suppose this would be? What happens if the plaintiff's petition properly states jurisdiction, parties, venue, a cause of action and a prayer for relief, but it simply alleges facts that your client claims are untrue? What mechanisms exist for disposing of the action? If disposition of the action is not generally the function of pleadings, what do they accomplish?

## § 5.04 Plaintiff's Petition

### [A] General Considerations and Formal Elements

*Read Tex. R. Civ. P. 22, 28, 45, 47, 48, 50, 58, 79, 190.*

The immediate function of the petition is to commence a civil action. It should be noted, however, that a bona fide intention to prosecute the action and diligence in obtaining service are necessary to toll the statute of limitations. *See Reed v. Reed,* 158 Tex. 298, 311 S.W.2d 628, 631 (1958). The petition is required to state the names of the parties and their residences. A defendant that is doing business under an assumed name may sue and be sued in "its partnership, assumed or common name . . . , but on a motion by any party or on the court's own motion the true name may be substituted." Tex. R. Civ. P. 28. This rule tolls the statute of limitations when suit is filed against a business entity in its assumed or common name. *See L.L.M. v. Mayes,* 733 S.W.2d 642, 644 (Tex. App.—San Antonio 1987, no writ), holding that when the original petition named Lester L. Munson d/b/a/ Naco Brake & Alignment and limitations ran before amended petition was filed, naming L.L.M., Inc. d/b/a/ Naco Brake & Alignment, limitations was tolled as to L.L.M., Inc.; *see also Cockrell v. Estevez,* 737 S.W.2d 138, 140 (Tex. App.—San Antonio 1987, no writ) ("[w]hen an intended defendant is sued under an incorrect name, jurisdiction is proper after service on the defendant under the misnomer, but it must be clear that no one was misled"); *cf. Continental Southern Lines, Inc. v. Hilland,* 528 S.W.2d 828, 830 (Tex. 1975) (suit named wrong defendant). Civil Procedure Rule 28 does not apply if the plaintiff fails to join the proper party doing business under the assumed name. *Bailey v. Vanscot Concrete Co.,* 894 S.W.2d 757, 760 (Tex. 1995).

Although no specific rule requires it, the petition should contain allegations that demonstrate the basis for the court's subject matter jurisdiction, jurisdiction over the person or property of the defendant(s), and the propriety of the venue. The problem of pleading jurisdiction is exemplified by cases in Chapter 3 on subject matter jurisdiction, such as *Peek v. Equipment Service Co. of San Antonio,* 779 S.W.2d 802 (Tex. 1989). Jurisdictional allegations concerning nonresidents must also be drafted with care to avoid a motion to quash service of citation and to support a default judgment against a direct attack. *Kawasaki Steel Corp. v. Middleton,* 699 S.W.2d 199, 203 (Tex. 1985). Jurisdiction of a person who resides within the territory is usually shown by showing that fact and indicating where service can be effectuated.

As a result of the 1999 amendments to the Texas Rules of Civil Procedure, a plaintiff must allege in the first numbered paragraph of the original petition whether discovery is intended to be conducted under Level 1, 2, or 3 of Civil Procedure Rule 190. Tex. R. Civ. P. 190.1. As will be explained in detail in the discovery chapters of this text, Level 1 allows a party seeking recovery of no more than $50,000 to insist that discovery be minimal. Level 2 provides an intermediate amount of discovery that should be adequate in most cases, and Level 3 is available for cases that need special attention. *See* Tex. R. Civ. P. 190, Comment 1. The requirement of an affirmative pleading of limited relief binds the pleader to a maximum claim of no more than $50,000. Tex. R. Civ. P. 190, Comment 2 ("the rule in *Greenhalgh v. Service Lloyds Ins. Co.,* 787 S.W.2d 938 (Tex. 1990) does not apply").

The primary function of the petition is to provide the defendant or defendants "a short statement of the cause of action sufficient to give fair notice of the claim involved" and the relief requested. It is not grounds for objection that an allegation is "evidentiary" or is a "legal conclusion" when fair notice is given by the allegations of the petition as a whole. Specific rules of procedure supplement and clarify the method of giving fair notice. *See, e.g.,* Tex. R. Civ. P. 56. Civil Procedure Rule 47 requires that pleadings seeking unliquidated damages contain a statement that the damages sought are "within" the jurisdictional limits of the court, not that they exceed the court's minimum jurisdictional limits.

### [B] Pleading a "Cause of Action"

*Read Tex. R. Civ. P. 45, 47.*

The concept of cause of action—although downplayed in some procedural systems—is essential to a proper understanding of procedure. It is important in pleading because the Texas rules require a statement of a "cause of action." It is likewise important to an understanding of permissive and required joinder of claims and parties, res judicata (which prohibits the splitting of a cause of action), and jury submission (because the charge should contain all elements of the cause of action that are contested). Incidentally, understanding of the notion of a cause of action is important not only in Texas but in other procedural systems.

The concept of cause of action is embedded in its historical context. Hence, this section begins with attempts made to define it both recently and historically.

#### [1] Basic Pleading Requirements: Defining a "Cause of Action"

Consider the following excerpt from a treatise on common-law pleading: "The declaration must state distinctly and with certainty every fact that is essential to the plaintiff's prima facie case. No essential allegation can be imported into the declaration by inference or intendment. The principal points necessary to be shown in the statement of a cause of action are:

(a) the plaintiff's right;

(b) the defendant's wrongful act violating that right;

(c) the consequent damages."

Shipman, *Handbook on Common-Law Pleading*, 3d ed. (H.B. Ballantine, ed. 1923) at 196.

In light of this definition, reconsider the plaintiff's original petition in *Obiedio v. J. Weingarten, Inc.*, as amended, which is set forth in Section 5.03. Does it meet the requirements set forth above by identifying the source of the plaintiff's right, the wrongful act and damages so that every essential fact is set forth "distinctly and with certainty"? What should happen if, at the trial, plaintiff attempts to rely not on a negligence theory alone, but also on a strict products liability theory as well. Does the claim in the petition show sufficient elements for that claim, too? (Note that the facts, set forth in the Appendix to Chapter 1, might arguably support such a theory, and perhaps there are some factual allegations in the petition that give notice of the potential applicability of the theory.)

Consider the following treatment of the term "cause of action" from one of Dean Page Keeton's early articles, Keeton, *Action, Cause of Action, and Theory of the Action in Texas,* 11 Tex. L. Rev. 145, 146–149, 157, 158 (1933).*

> Since the rules with respect to joinder, amendments, pleading, and splitting of causes of action in Texas are quite similar to those in the code states, the use of the term "cause

of action" has been substantially the same here as in those jurisdictions. For that reason, a brief examination of the different views as to what meaning should be attributed to the term "cause of action" under the codes would not be amiss. The three views which in all probability are the most divergent and at the same time the most representative of the different ideas are stated below—

(1) Professor O. L. McCaskill contends that the meaning of the term as used in the codes consists of "that group of operative facts which, standing alone, would show a single right in the plaintiff and a single delict to that right giving cause for the state, through its courts, to afford relief to the party or parties whose right was invaded."[2] Moreover, by "right," as used here, is meant remedial right. Under this definition, which definitely ties up the concept "cause of action" with remedies, we would have causes limited according to the extent of rights as enforced under old common law forms of action. In other words, no distinction would be made between the cause of action and the *form of the action* as used at common law.

(2) It seems that most of the experts on procedure have insisted that the scope of the cause of action should be determined without reference to the remedy or remedies sought. Professor C. E. Clark contends that "the accepted definition of the code cause is one which makes the break from one cause to another depend not on the limits of some ancient writ, but upon some apparent break in sequence of a series of acts or events, which have actually taken place."[3] He asserts, therefore, that the code cause of action is a group of operative facts giving cause or ground for judicial interference. It is not necessary, of course, under the definition that there be an absolute identity of all the operative facts for the cause of action to remain the same in dealing with amendments or with pleading in subsequent or different suits. Only the general fact situation must be the same. Professor Clark would employ a process of matching up the operative facts stated in the two forms of pleading. It is very similar to the layman's conception of what his cause of action would be if asked to state the facts on which he relies for recovery.

(3) Pomeroy asserts that every judicial action involves the following elements: a primary right possessed by the plaintiff, and a corresponding duty devolving upon the defendant; a delict or wrong done by the defendant which consisted in a breach of such primary right and duty: a remedial right in favor of the plaintiff, and a remedial duty resting on the defendant springing from this delict, and finally the remedy itself.[4] Of these elements, the facts showing the primary right and duty and the delict or wrong, combined, constitute the cause of action. The remedy which is sought, under this definition, has no relation to the cause of action but constitutes the object of the suit. The difficulty here lies in determining just what Pomeroy meant by a primary right.

In all the definitions just given, it is the facts which constitute the cause of action, but in each case the extent of these facts varies. Moreover, all assume that in order to have a cause of action, it is necessary that the facts show a right of the plaintiff and a breach of that right, although it is not necessary in every instance that a single cause be so limited. In other words, although it is essential that there must be an infringement of a right, it does

---

[2] McCaskill, *Actions and Causes of Action,* (1925) 34 Yale L. Jour. 614.

[3] Clark, *The Code Cause of Action,* (1924) 33 Yale L. Jour. 817.

[4] Pomeroy, Remedies and Remedial Rights (2d ed. 1883) 494–500, §§ 452–458.

not follow that because there is a violation of a single right, there is only one cause of action. This will depend upon the meaning of both the cause of action and the right.

We turn now from the opinions of experts and textwriters as to the code cause of action and, looking to the decisions of the courts, primarily of Texas, attempt an analysis of such cases in an effort not only to determine what the courts have actually done but to evolve an accurate concept of the cause of action under the Texas pleading. Aside from those cases in which purely declaratory relief may be obtained, in passing on the sufficiency of a petition against which demurrer has been urged, the authorities have generally held that a cause of action at law consists of the existence of a right in the plaintiff and an invasion of that right by some act or omission on the part of the defendant,[5] and, when necessary for recovery according to the substantive law, the consequent damages.[6] Some of the cases have held that the facts alleged which establish the existence of the right and its violation constitute the cause of action;[7] on the other hand, it has also been said that the cause of action does not consist of the allegations of facts but of the unlawful violation of a right which these facts show. "These facts are merely the means, and not the end. They do not constitute the cause of action, but they show its existence by making the wrongs appear."[8]

. . . .

It is believed that the cause of action should not be regarded as synonymous with the remedy or with the theory of the action, which will be discussed hereafter; neither should it be considered as a group of operative facts giving rise to judicial recognition, although containing serveral rights; on the other hand, it is submitted that an entire cause of action should consist of of facts showing a single substantive right, together with a breach or threatened violation of that substantive right, and, where necessary for recovery according to the substantive law, the consequent damages. [footnote omitted] The term "right" is, of course, used here in a broad sense, perhaps not the equivalent of "right" in the Hohfeldian sense. For example, when fraud is practiced on a party in entering into a contract a substantive right has been violated; namely, a right to contract without being subjected to fraud. For a violation of this right, the defrauded party has at least two remedies: the equitable one of rescission of the contract, or the legal one of damages for deceit based on an affirmance.[37] The plaintiff may, moreover, state the facts constituting his cause of action so that either of the remedies would be proper, requiring no election until all the evidence has been introduced.

Subsequent to the adoption of the 1941 Rules of Civil Procedure, the Amarillo Court of Civil Appeals, in *Christy v. Hamilton,* 384 S. W. 2d 795, 796 (Tex. Civ. App.—Amarillo 1964, no writ), put the matter in the following terms:

---

[5] Hutchinson v. Ainsworth, 73 Cal. 452, 455, 15 Pac. 82, 84, 2 Am. St. Rep. 823, 825 (1887); Phoenix Lumber Co. v. Houston Water Co., 94 Tex. 456, 61 S.W. 707 (1901).

[6] Phillio v. Blythe, 12 Tex. 124, 127 (1854); Scanlon v. Galveston, H. & S. A. Ry., 86 S.W. 930 (Tex. Civ. App. 1905); Townes, Texas Pleading (2d ed. 1913) 479–506; 2 Freeman, Judgments (5th ed. 1925) 1433, § 678.

[7] "It frequently happens that different remedies arising out of the same facts are open to the plaintiff, any one of which he may pursue. It therefore follows that the facts and not the remedy, strictly speaking, constitute the cause of action." Elmo v. James, 282 S.W. 835 (Tex. Civ. App. 1926); *accord:* Hutchinson v. Ainsworth, 73 Cal. 452, 15 Pac. 82, 2 Am. St. Rep. 823 (1887).

[8] Baltimore S. S. Co. v. Phillips, 274 U.S. 316, 47 Sup. Ct. 600, 71 L. Ed. 1069 (1927); Chabman v. Washburn Wire Co., 33 R.I. 289, 302, 80 Atl. 394, 400 Ann. Cas. 1913D, 730, 735 (1911).

[37] Karlen v. El Jardin Immigration Co., 277 S.W. 173 (Tex. Civ. App. 1925).

It is elementary that a plaintiff's petition shall contain a statement in plain and concise language of the plaintiff's cause of action and shall give fair notice of the claim involved. Rule 47, Texas Rules of Civil Procedure. It must also appear from the face of a petition that a primary legal right rests in the plaintiff, that there is a primary legal duty connected with this right resting on the defendant, and that there has been a breach of this duty by the defendant.

---

## NOTES AND QUESTIONS

(1) *Sufficiency of Petition.* Based on the foregoing excerpts, would the following petitions satisfy basic pleading requirements? The first example (in (a), *below*) is taken from a suit brought by the owners of the surface estate against lessees under an oil and gas lease for alleged damages to the plaintiffs' land and cattle. The second example (in (b), *below*) is taken from the forms devised to aid in the interpretation of Fed. R. Civ. P. 8(a) ("short and plain statement of the claim showing that the pleader is entitled to relief").

> (a) That the defendants have heretofore during the last year, drilled several oil and gas [wells] upon the above tract of land, the surface of which belongs to these plaintiffs; and that during the process of drilling, operating and connecting the same to pipeline which crosses plaintiffs said land, the defendants, their agents, servants or employees have conducted such operations, drilling and connecting with the said pipeline across plaintiffs said property that they have damaged these plaintiffs in the following manner. . . .
>
> That the damages to these plaintiffs grassland over which defendants laid connecting lines from the pipeline to the wells, as well as the driving of the heavy machinery, trucks and numerous vehicles on and across said grassland to the reasonable damage of $50.00 per well of $200.00, plus the damage of $1.00 per rod for the damages due to the laying of 320 rods of pipeline across this land; that the oil and debris were allowed to polute [sic] the plaintiffs fish pond on this property in the sum of $200.00.

*Christy v. Hamilton,* 384 S.W.2d 795 (Tex. Civ. App.—Amarillo 1964, no writ).

> (b) On June 1, 1936, in a public highway called Boylston Street in Boston, Massachusetts, defendant negligently drove a motor vehicle against plaintiff who was then crossing said highway.
>
> As a result plaintiff was thrown down and had his leg broken and was otherwise injured, was prevented from transacting his business, suffered great pain of body and mind, and incurred expenses for medical attention and hospitalization in the sum of one thousand dollars." [demand for relief]

Appendix of Forms, Federal Rules of Civil Procedure Form 9.

(2) *What Constitutes Fair Notice of a Claim?* What additional information is added by the word "negligently?" Is there more than one way to drive "negligently"? Should it be necessary to identify the specific acts and omissions? Are the injury damage allegations in the federal form sufficient to apprise the defendant of the evidence plaintiff will introduce at trial?

### [2] "Fair Notice" of the Substantive Legal Theory

## CASTLEBERRY v. GOOLSBY BLDG. CORP.

*617 S.W.2d 665 (Tex. 1981)*

CAMPBELL, Justice.

This is a suit for actual and exemplary damages under Article 5525,[1] the Texas Survival Statute. The trial court rendered summary judgment that Plaintiff Clarence E. Castleberry take nothing as to Defendant Goolsby Building Corporation. The Court of Civil Appeals affirmed the judgment of the trial court. 608 S.W.2d 763. We affirm the judgment of the Court of Civil Appeals.

Richard Ernest Castleberry was employed by Goolsby Building Corporation. On June 5, 1978, he was killed in an industrial accident while in the course of his employment. Clarence E. Castleberry, Individually as surviving natural parent and as Administrator of the Estate of Richard Ernest Castleberry, Deceased, (Administrator) sued the City of Corpus Christi and Goolsby Building Corporation.[2]

The Administrator alleged Richard's death was caused by certain "acts and/or omissions to act, which . . . constitute gross, wanton, and willful negligence," "grossly negligent acts," "negligent, or grossly negligent, acts and omissions" and "ordinary or gross negligence." Goolsby Building Corporation alleged in its motion for summary judgment that the Administrator failed to state a cause of action. The trial court rendered summary judgment that the Administrator take nothing against Goolsby Building Corporation.

The Administrator argues the Workers' Compensation Act does not bar a deceased's cause of action for intentional injuries which survive to the estate under Article 5525, the Texas Survival Statute. We agree.

Article 5525 provides for the survival of a common law action for damages which could have been instituted by the deceased for injuries resulting in death. The action may be asserted by the heirs or administrator in behalf of the estate. Article 5525; *Mitchell v. Akers,* 401 S.W.2d 907 (Tex. Civ. App.—Dallas 1966, writ ref'd n.r.e.).

The Workers' Compensation Act exempts employers from common law liability based on negligence or gross negligence, except in [wrongful] death cases for exemplary damages as provided for in Artice 8306, § 5. *Paradissis v. Royal Indemnity Co.,* 507 S.W.2d 526 (Tex. 1974). The Act does not exempt employers from common law liability for intentional injuries. *Reed Tool Co. v. Copelin,* 610 S.W.2d 736 (Tex. 1980); *Middleton v. Texas Power & Light Co.,* 108 Tex. 96, 185 S.W. 556 (1916). This cause of action is guaranteed to the employee by the Texas Constitution and cannot be taken away by the Legislature. Tex. Const. art. I, § 13; *Reed Tool Co. v. Copelin, supra.* We hold the Workers' Compensation Act does not bar a deceased's cause of action for intentional injuries which survive to the estate under Article 5525.

The Administrator further argues the pleadings are sufficient to allege an "intentional injury" to Richard Castleberry by Goolsby Building Corporation.

---

[1] All statutory references are to Texas Revised Civil Statutes Annotated.

[2] The cause of action against Goolsby Building Corporation was severed from the cause of action against the City of Corpus Christi and a final judgment was rendered in favor of Goolsby Building Corporation. The City of Corpus Christi is not a party to this appeal.

Under Rules 45 and 47, pleadings are sufficient if they give the opposing attorney fair notice of the claim involved. Tex. R. Civ. P. 45 and 47; *Stone v. Lawyers Title Ins. Corp.*, 554 S.W.2d 183 (Tex. 1977). The object and purpose of pleading is to give fair and adequate notice to the party being sued of the nature of the cause of action asserted against him so he may adequately prepare his defense. *McCamey v. Kinnear,* 484 S.W.2d 150 (Tex. Civ. App.—Beaumont 1972, writ ref'd n.r.e.). The Administrator's allegations are insufficient to give the opposing attorney fair notice that this cause of action was for an "intentional injury."

The Administrator contends an allegation of willful negligence or willful gross negligence is sufficient to allege an "intentional injury." An allegation of willful negligence or willful gross negligence is an allegation based upon negligence and is insufficient to allege an "intentional injury." An injury caused by willful negligence or willful gross negligence is not an intentional injury necessary to avoid the effect of the Workers' Compensation Act.

The judgments of the courts below are affirmed.

---

## NOTES AND QUESTIONS

(1) *Remedies.* Lab. C. § 408.001(a)–(c) supplants former R.C.S. Art. 8306 § 5 and provides that recovery of compensation benefits is generally the exclusive remedy of an employee or a legal beneficiary but "does not prohibit the recovery of exemplary damages by the surviving spouse or heirs of the body of a deceased employee whose death was caused by an intentional act or omission of the employer or by the employer's gross negligence" as defined in Chapter 41 of the Civil Practice and Remedies Code.

(2) *Pleading Negligence Per Se. Castleberry* states that fair and adequate notice of the cause of action is required so that the defendant can adequately prepare a defense. *Murray v. O & A Express, Inc.*, 630 S.W.2d 633 (Tex. 1982), arising from the nighttime collision of an automobile with an improperly parked truck, elaborates on this notion. The driver of the automobile and the estate of a passenger killed in the wreck filed suit for negligence and wrongful death against the truck driver and the company for which he worked. The pleadings asserted that the truck driver was negligent in parking the truck so that it protruded into the plaintiffs' lane of traffic, in failing to put out warning signals or devices, and "in other acts of negligence." At trial, however, plaintiffs' attorney did not pursue a theory of common law negligence, but instead relied on negligence per se. Negligence per se, advanced in the opening statement, maintained throughout the trial, and addressed in the jury charge, was predicated on the idea that the truck's protrusion and the lack of warning signals violated statutory provisions, specifically R.C.S. Art. 6701d, §§ 93, 125. From a judgment for the plaintiffs, the defendants appealed, alleging error in the variance between the pleadings and the jury charge, which stated that the truck driver's violation of the statute constituted negligence as a matter of law.

In its opinion in *Murray,* the Texas Supreme Court, after noting that pleadings are required to provide fair and adequate notice on which to prepare a defense, stated:

> The unexcused violation of a penal statute constitutes negligence as a matter of law if such statute was designed to prevent injuries to a class of persons to which the injured party belongs. . . . When a defendant is alleged to be negligent as a matter of law because of

> the violation of a statute and a statutory violation is proven, the defendant's negligence is not at issue unless evidence of excuse is presented. . . . The defendant in such a suit must frame his defense in terms of the recognized excuses for violation of a statute. [footnote omitted] Since these excuses must be affirmatively raised by the evidence, it is important that the party alleged to be negligent as a matter of law be informed prior to trial that the opposing party relies upon the statutory violation. Thus, a party relying upon a statutory violation should plead this reliance on that basis. [citations omitted] Further, the pleader should reasonably identify the statute relied upon. [citation omitted]

630 S.W.2d at 636.

Notwithstanding the failure of the plaintiffs' pleadings to comply with these rules, the court affirmed the trial court's judgment for plaintiffs because such failure was never raised at trial:

> . . . O & A made no special exceptions to the pleadings of Murray even though those pleadings were general. Moreover, O & A did not object to the opening statement of Murray which made clear his reliance upon the statutes. Murray's evidence of statutory violations was likewise admitted without objection to the lack of pleadings. Finally, O & A never excepted to the lack of pleadings supporting the court's charge which instructed the jury that O & A and Young were negligent as a matter of law. Having failed to except to the lack of pleadings at any point during trial, O & A has waived any error in the pleadings of Murray.

630 S.W.2d at 636–637.

The following case, *Darr Equipment Co. v. Owens,* also considers this matter of waiver and the standards for assessing whether or not waiver has occurred.

(3) *Surplusage?* A number of cases state the principle that a general allegation that is accompanied by specific allegations should be considered as "mere surplusage." *See, e.g., Weingartens, Inc. v. Price*, 461 S.W.2d 260 (Tex. Civ. App.—Houston [14th Dist.] 1970, writ ref'd n.r.e.). Does this rule of construction make sense? Should an opposing party be required to specially except to the general allegation even when it is accompanied by specific allegations? Should an objection to evidence at variance with the pleadings be necessary to avoid trial by consent? Should an objection to the court's charge on the same basis be necessary to avoid trial by consent?

---

## DARR EQUIPMENT COMPANY v. OWENS

*408 S.W.2d 566 (Tex. Civ. App.—Texarkana 1966, no writ)*

CHADICK, Chief Justice.

. . . .

The action Owens pled against Baillio individually is stated in this language, to-wit:

> ". . . defendant, Dent Baillio, falsely and/or fraudulently and/or negligently represented to the plaintiff that he was defendant, Darr Equipment Company's, agent and had full and complete authority from said defendant company to contract on behalf of said defendant

company to sell and deliver the hereinabove described personal property to the plaintiff upon the terms and conditions heretofore described, which false and/or fraudulent and/or negligent representations were relied upon by the plaintiff."

Counsel for Darr Equipment Company now, as well as in the trial court construes the statement as an effort by Owens to plead deceit (actionable fraud), a tort action. On the basis of the proof offered in the trial court and the position taken in this court counsel for Owens interprets a part of the quoted pleading as the statement of an action for breach of implied warranty of agency, an action ex contractu. All elements of either of the actions the parties suggest are not set out in the quoted pleading, and such actions at best are imperfectly pled.

The rule applicable to the construction of the quoted pleading may be found in Gulf, Colorado and Santa Fe Railway Company v. Bliss, Tex., 368 S.W.2d 594, in this language, to-wit:

> "The petition will be construed as favorably as possible for the pleader. The court will look to the pleader's intendment and the pleading will be upheld even if some element of a cause of action has not been specifically alleged. Every fact will be supplied that can reasonably be inferred from what is specifically stated. . . ."

The appellee Owens' brief argues the pleading sufficiently states a breach of implied warranty action because:

> "Summarized, the appellee's pleading was that the agent falsely represented to the plaintiff that he was the appellant's agent and had full and complete authority from the appellant to contract on behalf of the appellant to sell and deliver the machinery to the appellee upon the described terms and conditions. Since the representation was false, it would seem fair to consider the allegation to be one that Baillio actually had no such authority.
>
> "It is correct that the appellee did not state in so many words that Baillio falsely represented his authority and thereby impliedly warranted he had such authority, but the legal consequences of a false representation as to authority would be a conclusion of law. . . ."

Although the construction Owens places on the language used is not inescapable, in the absence of objection the allegations appear sufficient to give Darr Equipment Company fair notice that Owens was suing Baillio individually for breach of an implied warranty of agency. Rule 45, Vernon's Ann. Rules of Civil Procedure.

Darr Equipment Company did not object to the imperfect pleadings and failure to object constituted waiver under Rule 90, V.A.T.R., and consent to a trial of the breach of implied warranty of agency action. . . .

. . . .

---

## NOTES AND QUESTIONS

(1) *Fair Notice and Special Exceptions.* If an "objection" (special exception) had been made in *Darr,* would it have been error not to sustain it? *See* Tex. R. Civ. P. 90, 91. What is necessary to give "fair notice" of the substantive legal theory relied on if a special exception is made?

Should the pleading be upheld "even if some element of a cause of action has not been specifically alleged" when an objection is leveled at the pleading imperfection?

(2) *Harmful vs. Harmless Errors.* Is the error always harmful? *See* Tex. R. App. P. 44, 61. An objection to testimony is required to preserve the error when the special exception has been improperly overruled, otherwise the error is treated as harmless. *Republic Bankers Life Ins. Co. v. McCool,* 441 S.W.2d 314, 317 (Tex. Civ. App.—Tyler 1969, no writ).

### [3] "Fair Notice" of Factual Theories

## WHITE v. JACKSON

*358 S.W.2d 174 (Tex. Civ. App.—Waco 1962, writ ref'd n.r.e.)*

TIREY, Justice.

This is an appeal by writ of error from a default judgment.

A statement is necessary. In May 1961, Willie Jackson filed his original petition in the District Court of Dallas County against Henry White, a resident of Dallas County, and caused citation to be issued and served on White, but he failed to answer. We quote the pertinent parts of the petition:

> "On or about the 7th day of June 1959, plaintiff sustained severe and extensive injuries and damages as a direct and proximate result of the negligence of defendant, all to the actual damage of plaintiff in an amount greatly in excess of One Thousand Dollars ($1000.00) and within the jurisdiction of the District Court.
>
> "Wherefore, premises considered, plaintiff prays that defendant be cited to appear and answer herein, and that upon final trial, plaintiff have judgment against defendant for all damages proved, costs of court, interest at the rate of 6% per annum from the date of the judgment until same is paid, and for such other and further relief as to which plaintiff may be justly entitled, whether at law or in equity."

On June 12, 1961, judgment was rendered against defendant in favor of plaintiff, and in the judgment we find this recital:

> "the matters of fact and things in controversy being submitted to the court in their due and regular order, and it appearing to the court upon good and sufficient evidence that plaintiff is entitled to recover of and from Henry White, defendant, the sum of $20,510."

. . . .

The judgment is assailed on 5 Points. They are substantially to the effect that the Trial Court erred in entering judgment: (1 and 2) Based upon appellee's petition for the reason that the petition is not sufficient to support a default judgment, because it failed to allege any facts or circumstances from which it could be found that appellant breached any duty whatsoever which he might have owed appellee in connection with whatever act or omission of the appellant is claimed as negligence; and failed to allege any act or omission whatsoever of appellant which could constitute negligence; (3 and 4) That the Court erred in entering judgment for any amount of money for the reason that appellee's petition failed to allege any injury, fact or act from which any damages could have resulted to appellee; and that the Court erred in entering judgment in the sum of $20,510.00 in favor of appellee for the reason that his petition could in no event support a judgment substantially in excess of $1,000.00; (5) That the judgment of $20,510.00

is erroneous, because such petition did not give appellant notice as to the nature of appellee's claim and the relief sought as required by the Fourteenth Amendment of the Constitution of the United States, and as also required by Article 1, Sec. 19 of the Constitution of the State of Texas, Vernon's Ann.St.

. . . .

Going back to appellee's petition, we find that it fails to allege any act or omission on the part of appellant which constituted negligence; we find no allegation of fact indicating that appellant owed appellee any duty whatsoever in connection with whatever might be the basis of appellee's claim against him. No facts are alleged in the petition. The only word contained in appellee's petition which might be considered any clue as to the nature of appellee's claim is the word "negligence." But, there can be no negligence unless a duty is present, and here none is alleged. The term "negligence" is not used to characterize any specific act or omission made by appellant, and there is no way of ascertaining from the pleading that appellant may or might have owed appellee a duty of any kind whatsoever. So the word "negligence," standing alone, provides the only starting point for determination of whether or not appellee's petition was sufficient to support a default judgment. . . . . In Missouri Pacific Ry. Co. v. Hennessey, 75 Tex. 155, 12 S.W. 608, we find this statement of the Rule:

> "A mere abstract proposition that defendant was guilty of negligence which resulted in injury to the plaintiff would not be sufficient. The act done or omitted constituting negligence must be averred and proved. Hence it follows that an act done or omitted which is relied on to establish negligence must be alleged, or proof of it will not be allowed. Where, from the nature of the case, the plaintiff would not be expected to know the exact cause, or the precise negligent act which becomes the cause, of an injury, and where the facts are peculiarly within the knowledge of the defendant, he would not be required to allege the particular cause, but it would be sufficient to allege the fact in a general way, as that there was a defect of machinery of structure, or want of skill in operating on the part of defendant or its servants, or some such fact as would give the defendant notice of the character of proof that would be offered to support the plaintiff's case. . . . If an injury occurs under such circumstances that a negligent act on the part of defendant cannot be alleged or proved, and where no relation exists between the parties that demands immunity from injury, there can be no recovery."

The foregoing rule is very broad and comprehensive and our Supreme Court has not seen fit to change it. It seems to us that appellee alleged no more than a legal conclusion to the effect that appellant was liable to him as a result of negligence; that appellee's pleading is and was fatally defective; that in effect it contained nothing more than the unsupported statement that appellant is liable to appellee because of some unknown act or omission of negligence resulting in some unknown injury or damage to appellee; such allegations are obviously a conclusion on the part of appellee and do not furnish any information whatsoever from which such conclusion could be drawn. The allegation of negligence is a mere conclusion of the pleader, and such allegation is not admitted by either a general demurrer or by default, and such allegation in the petition could in no event support a judgment by default under Rules 45, 47 and 90, T.R.C.P. See also Cragin v. Lovell, 109 U.S. 194, 197, 27 L. Ed. 903.

Needless to say that appellee's pleading was wholly insufficient to permit appellant to identify anything or to estimate the scope of the dispute, which is well illustrated by a judgment for $20,510.00 against him, based upon a petition alleging damages only "in excess of $1,000.00."

We think for the reasons stated that Points 1 and 2 must be sustained, and this will require that the cause be reversed and remanded.

Appellant's 3rd Point is substantially that the Court erred in entering judgment for any amount of money, for the reason that the petition failed to allege any injury, fact or act from which any damages could have resulted to appellee. We think it is obvious that this point must be sustained. For the rules prescribing the detail with which the damages must be alleged, see Vol. 2, McDonald, Texas Civ. Prac., Sec. 6.17, at p. 576. Going back to the appellee's petition in this cause, the defendant was not advised of the alleged damages and injuries to appellee, either to his person or to his property. We think that a pleading which wholly failed to state whether or not the alleged injuries or damages were personal or whether the damage was to property, is fatally defective and will certainly not support a judgment by default for any amount. The petition, as we have stated before, does not allege any act, circumstance or injury from which damages normally flow or can be remotely implied. Certainly none can be supplied by the court. It is the general rule of pleadings that fair notice is a guide for determining whether or not a petition contains sufficient allegations on which to base an award of damages in any amount. See Rules 45 and 47 T.R.C.P. See also 17 Tex. Jur. 2d, Damages, Sec. 192. The petition here does not allege any facts from which the court can supply any measure of damages whatsoever, and we think such failure requires the judgment to be reversed and remanded. See Caswell v. J. S. McCall & Sons, Tex. Civ. App., 163 S.W. 1001, n.w.h.

We have carefully considered Points 4 and 5, and we think each should be sustained. Since we are of the view that the cause must be reversed and remanded, it will unduly extend this opinion to make further comment on Points 4 and 5, and for that reason we do not do so. Accordingly, this cause is reversed and remanded.

McDONALD, C. J., and WILSON, J., concur in the result.

---

## WILLOCK v. BUI

*734 S.W.2d 390 (Tex. App.—Houston [1st Dist.] 1987, no writ)*

WARREN, Justice.

By writ of error, appellant contends that a default judgment entered against him should be set aside because:

(1) the pleadings were inadequate to support a default judgment;

(2) the trial court erroneously awarded damages for past, present, and future medical expenses, without receiving expert testimony; and

(3) the evidence was insufficient to support the default judgment.

As appellant has not furnished us with a statement of facts, we may not review his second and third points of error, which complain of the quality and sufficiency of the evidence. Tex. R. App. P. 54(a). We will consider appellant's first point of error claiming that appellee's petition was inadequate to support a default judgment.

The pertinent part of appellee's petition reads as follows:

II.

Defendant, George Michael Willock, is a resident of Houston, Harris County, Texas and may be served with process at his address at 1247 S. Kirkwood, Houston, Texas 77077.

III.

On January 9, 1985 at approximately 8:00 a.m., Toan Viet Bui sustained serious personal injuries while driving a 1985 Toyota pickup truck which was involved in a rear-end collision, which forced his vehicle into the car in front of him. The automobile which Toan Viet Bui was operating was struck from behind during the collision which involved a Pontiac, Texas license plate number 323-ADH, driven by George Michael Willock. The collision occurred at 1300 Hays Road, Houston, Texas.

IV.

The collision described in paragraph III above and made the basis of this suit was directly and proximately caused by the negligence of George Michael Willock. On the occasion in question, George Michael Willock was guilty of acts of negligence each of which were a proximate cause of the collision made the basis of this suit.

V.

Plaintiff alleges that the damages sustained will greatly exceed the minimum jurisdictional limit of this Court.

WHEREFORE, PREMISES CONSIDERED, Plaintiff prays that Defendants be cited to appear herein and that upon hearing, Plaintiff have judgment against Defendant for his damages, plus interest and costs and such other and further relief, both general and special, at law or in equity, to which Plaintiff may show himself justly entitled.

Though a part of the petition is inartfully drawn, it nevertheless informs the appellant of the time and the place of the automobile collision, that appellee sustained personal injuries in the collision, and that appellee is contending the collision and the appellee's injuries were proximately caused by the appellant's negligence. Tex. R. Civ. P. 45(b) only requires that the petition "[c]onsist of a statement in plain and concise language of the plaintiff's cause of action. &hellip" Tex. R. Civ. P. 47 requires that the petition shall contain "(a) a short statement of the cause of action sufficient to give fair notice of the claim involved . . .," and "(c) a demand for judgment for all the other relief to which the party deems himself entitled."

Pleadings are sufficient if they give the opposing party fair notice of the claim involved. *Castleberry v. Goolsby Bldg. Corp.,* 617 S.W.2d 665 (Tex.1981).

In order to support a default judgment, it is not necessary that the plaintiff set out in his pleadings, evidence on which he relies to establish his asserted cause of action. *Edwards Feed Mill v. Johnson,* 158 Tex. 313, 311 S.W.2d 232 (1958). Nor is it a requisite that a petition be technically sufficient to state a cause of action in order to sustain a default judgment. it;Id.

A fair interpretation of the petition is that the appellee claims that he and the appellant were involved in an automobile collision, and that he was injured as a result of the appellant's negligence. The petition adequately informed appellant of the nature of the claim against him in compliance with Tex. R. Civ. P. 45 and 47.

Affirmed.

. . . .

HOYT, Justice, dissenting.

I respectfully dissent and would sustain the appellant's first point of error, because the appellee's pleadings fail to allege a legal duty owed by the appellant to the appellee.

. . . ..

This pleading is insufficient as a matter of law to charge the appellant with a duty of any kind. In fact, the pleading fails to apprise the appellant of what his specific involvement was in the collision. Appellee's assertion that the appellant's vehicle was "involved" in a collision with him, that also involved several other vehicles, does not assert a violation of any duty or responsibility owed by the appellant to the appellee. I would sustain the first point of error, reverse the judgment, and remand this cause to the trial court.

---

## NOTES AND QUESTIONS

(1) *Comparative Analysis.* Compare the pleadings in *White v. Jackson* and *Willock v. Bui* with Federal Form 9 in [1], *above.* If the federal form is used as a drafting guide, can the *White v. Jackson* petition be revised to comply with Civil Procedure Rules 45 and 47? Is the petition in *Willock v. Bui* in Compliance with the specific "act or omission" requirements set forth in *White v. Jackson*? Is it as factually detailed as the federal form?

A proposal to amend the Texas pleading rules made in September 1997 by the Advisory Committee to the Texas Supreme Court would require a pleader to allege "a short statement of the claims, stating the legal theories and in general the factual bases of the claims sufficient to give fair notice." *See* proposed Tex. R. Civ. P. 21(a) of the Recodification Draft; *cf.* Tex. R. Civ. P. 194, 196. How does the federal form advise the defendant of the nature of the duty breached?

(2) *The Standard for Sufficiency.* One court of appeals has stated that the test for determining the sufficiency of a pleading is whether an opposing attorney of reasonable competence could, with the pleading before him or her, ascertain the nature and the basic issues of the controversy and the testimony that will probably be relevant. *Daniels v. Conrad,* 331 S.W.2d 411, 415 (Tex. Civ. App.—Dallas 1959, writ ref'd n.r.e.).

(3) *"Magic Words" Are Not Required.* Recently the Texas Supreme Court cited and quoted with approval the *Gulf* principle articulated in *Darr.* In *Roark v. Allen,* 633 S.W.2d 804 (Tex. 1982), the Roarks sued two physicians for malpractice in the delivery of their son. The child required surgery for skull fractures caused by the use of forceps. The physicians appealed from a judgment for the Roarks. As one point of error they argued that the plaintiffs' petition was insufficient to raise the issue of negligent delivery against one of the doctors inasmuch as the pleading did not state expressly that the doctor was "negligent," that the doctor did not use ordinary care, or that the doctor's negligence during the delivery was the proximate cause of the child's injuries. The Court of Civil Appeals agreed and reversed. The Supreme Court reversed the Court of Civil Appeals on that point and affirmed the trial court's judgment against the doctor.

After noting that there had been no special exception to the plaintiff's petition and after citing the *Gulf* principle and the fair-and-adequate-notice rule as applied in *Castleberry* and *Murray* in [2], *above*, and in *Stone v. Lawyers Title Ins. Corp.*, 554 S.W.2d 183 (Tex. 1977), the court concluded:

> The Roarks alleged that Dr. Matthews delivered the child and, as a result of the delivery, the child sustained a fractured skull; the fractures caused the child intense physical pain and mental anguish and caused the parents to incur additional medical expense. [footnote omitted] We hold this was sufficient to give Dr. Matthews fair notice that he would have to defend against a claim involving the manner in which he delivered the child. We do not consider it fatal that the Roarks did not use the word "negligent" in connection with the delivery or otherwise specifically indicate that Dr. Matthews failed to exercise ordinary care. This can be inferred from the petition as a whole and from the following specific language: "As a result of the delivery, or attempts at delivery, by the Defendants, *jointly and severally,* the infant sustained bilateral depressed skull fractures." (Emphasis added). The phrase "jointly and severally" usually refers to liability; if two defendants are jointly and severally liable, the plaintiff may sue one or the other or both of them for the entire amount of the damages. . . . Such legal terminology, although used vaguely, was sufficient to alert Dr. Matthews that the Roarks intended to hold him liable for some act connected with his delivery of the child. If Dr. Mathews considered the petition obscure, he should have specially excepted to it and he has waived any defect by his failure to do so.

### [4] Pleading Injuries and Damages

*Read Tex. R. Civ. P. 56.*

## WEINGARTENS, INC. v. PRICE

*461 S.W.2d 260 (Tex. Civ. App.—Houston [14th Dist.] 1970, writ ref'd n.r.e.)*

SAM D. JOHNSON, Justice.

Suit for personal injuries alleged to be in the sum of $17,500 brought by Rosie Price, joined by her husband, James Price, against Weingarten's, Inc. Based on answers to special issues found by the jury judgment was entered for the plaintiffs in the sum of $5,000. Appellant Weingartens duly effects appeal to this Court.

In their petition plaintiffs alleged that Mrs. Price had gone to the Weingartens supermarket to purchase groceries; that while shopping inside the store she tripped and fell over the end of an unattended dolly which was protruding into the aisle way; and that Weingartens had negligently left the dolly in the aisle was proximately causing the injuries made the basis of the suit. The petition then continued as follows:

> ". . . As a result of such negligence, your Plaintiff, Rosie Price, has been damaged in the just and reasonable sum of SEVENTEEN THOUSAND FIVE HUNDRED DOLLARS ($17,500.00) for which sum your Plaintiff, James Price here now sues in her behalf; such damages to your Plaintiffs, consisting of damages for reasonable and necessary medical expenses incurred and to be incurred in the future, past and future physical pain and mental anguish, and loss of services as a wife.
>
> "WHEREFORE, PREMISES CONSIDERED, Plaintiffs pray that the Defendant be cited to appear and answer herein, and that upon final trial hereof, Plaintiff James Price have

judgment against the Defendant in the just and reasonable sum of SEVENTEEN THOUSAND FIVE HUNDRED DOLLARS ($17,500.00), as to and for injuries sustained by his wife, Rosie Price; that they have interest on the judgments at the legal rate; that they have all costs of Court herein expended, and that they have such other and further relief, both general and special, at law and in equity, to which they may show themselves to be justly entitled, and in duty bound will ever pray."

In the trial before the jury Mrs. Price testified that prior to her fall she had taken in sewing. She was then asked how much income per month she made from such sewing. Specific objection was then interposed by counsel for the defendant because loss of income had not been pled by the plaintiffs. The court overruled the objection and the witness proceeded to testify that she earned $20 to $25 per month before the accident and that after the accident she had been unable to earn anything.

The court's charge to the jury contained a single damage issue consisting of six elements. The third and fourth of these were as follows:

"c. Loss of earnings in the past."

"d. Loss of earning capacity which, in reasonable probability, she will sustain in the future."

Specific objection was made by the defendant to the inclusion of these two elements in the court's charge for the reason that loss of income and loss of earning capacity had not been pled. This objection was likewise overruled. The above two elements were included in the damage issue submitted to the jury, and the jury's finding in answer to such issue ($5,000) therefore included consideration of loss of earnings and loss of earning capacity in the future.

Appellant here presents only two points of error. These points are directed to the admission of testimony and the inclusion in the damage issue of the elements of loss of earnings and loss of earning capacity. Weingartens, the appellant, contends here, as it did in the trial court, that there were no pleadings to support the admission of the testimony or the submission of these elements in the damage issue. Appellants contend that the trial court therefore erred and pray that the cause be reversed and remanded. We conclude that appellant's points of error must be sustained.

. . . .

At the outset in the case at bar it is to be noted that no special exception to the plaintiff's quoted pleading was made by the defendant. It is also to be noted that the plaintiffs made no request at any time for permission to file a trial amendment and none was made. Lastly, we believe it quite clear from the record that the questioned areas of loss of earnings and loss of earning capacity were not tried by consent. See Matthews v. General Accident Fire & Life Assur. Corp., 161 Tex. 622, 343 S.W.2d 251 (1961).

. . . .

. . . . Loss of earnings and loss of earning capacity are items of "special damages." McCormick, Damages, p. 37; Texas & P. Ry. Co. v. Bowlin, 32 S.W. 918 (Tex. Civ. App., err. ref.); Missouri, K. & T. Ry. Co. of Texas v. Johnson, 37 S.W. 771 (Tex. Civ. App., no writ hist.); St. Louis Southwestern Ry. Co. of Texas v. Niblack, 53 Tex. Civ. App. 619, 117 S.W. 188, err. ref., and are not implied from the itemization of other dissimilar "special damages."

Loss of earnings and loss of earning capacity are without support in the petition of the plaintiff. Appellant's points of error are sustained. The judgment of the trial court is reversed and remanded.

---

## NOTES AND QUESTIONS

(1) *General and Special Damages.* General damages are damages that "naturally and necessarily" attend a particular injury. An example of general damages is pretrial pain and suffering, which is presumed to accompany a serious injury. *Pecos & N.T. Ry. Co. v. Huskey,* 166 S.W. 493, 494 (Tex. Civ. App.—Amarillo 1914, writ ref'd). Special damages are damages that tend to vary from person to person. They must be specifically pleaded. Examples of special damages are future pain and suffering and medical expenses. *Young v. Howell,* 236 S.W.2d 247, 248 (Tex. Civ. App.—Texarkana 1951, no writ); *Merchants Bldg. Corp. v. Adler,* 110 S.W.2d 978, 984 (Tex. Civ. App.—Dallas 1937, dis.).

(2) *Loss of Inheritance Damages in Wrongful Death Cases.* In *Yowell v. Piper Aircraft Corp.,* 703 S.W.2d 630 (Tex. 1986), a wrongful death case, defendant Piper argued that the Yowells should not recover loss of inheritance damages because they failed to plead loss of inheritance, a type of special damages that must be specially pleaded. However, the Yowells did allege lost future earnings, indicating that the figures did not include loss of companionship, guidance, and service. Furthermore, the lost earnings figures were supported by allegations of the decedents' life expectancy, work expectancy, salaries, benefits, and other relevant data. Although the court stated that the better pleading practice would have been to use phrases such as "loss of inheritance" or "loss of pecuniary benefit," it concluded such phrases are not required. In effect, the Yowells asked for compensation for their fair share of the decedents' lost earnings. Thus, the pleadings gave fair notice that plaintiffs were seeking lost pecuniary benefits. The court concluded: "Because lost inheritance is a lost pecuniary benefit, we find that the Yowells have pleaded loss of inheritance damages sufficiently to satisfy our liberal rule of pleading."

(3) *Pleading Damage Measures.* Although a measure of damage need not be pleaded specifically, the pleading must be sufficiently detailed to support submission of an appropriate measure. For example, when the action involves damage to personalty, the petition should provide information concerning the value before and after the event if the market-value rule is to be employed. "It is not permissible . . . for the plaintiff to allege his damages under the market value rule and then establish them under the rule which allows a recovery of the reasonable cost of repair." *Tinney v. Williams,* 144 S.W.2d 344, 346 (Tex. Civ. App.—Amarillo 1940, no writ). Review *White v. Jackson,* in [3], *above.*

### [5] Alternative or Hypothetical Claims

*Read Tex. R. Civ. P. 48.*

## BIRCHFIELD v. TEXARKANA MEMORIAL HOSP.

*747 S.W.2d 361 (Tex. 1987)*

WALLACE, Justice.

Kellie Birchfield was born prematurely with a congenitally functionless right eye. Shortly after her release from the hospital, she was diagnosed as having retrolental fibroplasia (RLF) in her left eye and is now totally blind. Her parents, Phillip and Mary Jo Birchfield, individually and as next friends of Kellie, sued Texarkana Memorial Hospital (Wadley) and her three treating physicians, Dr. Jon Hall, Dr. Noel Cowan, and Dr. Betty Lowe. The petition alleged negligence on the part of all four defendants plus a D.T.P.A. action against Wadley under the 1973 version of the Act. Deceptive Trade Practices Act, ch. 143, 1973 Tex. Gen. Laws at 322–43. The jury answered all issues favorably to the Birchfields. The trial court rendered judgment for actual damages against all defendants and exemplary damages against Wadley, but refused to render judgment on the D.T.P.A. action. The Court of Appeals initially affirmed the judgment, 718 S.W.2d 313, but on rehearing, reversed and remanded for trial. 718 S.W.2d 345. We reverse the judgment of the court of appeals and render judgment for the Birchfields.

As a premature infant, Kellie was administered approximately 400 hours of supplemental oxygen without adequate monitoring of arterial blood gases. This occurred even though a 1971 report published by the American Academy of Pediatrics cautioned the medical community about the danger of RLF in premature infants receiving supplemental oxygen, and advised practitioners to closely monitor arterial blood gases of such infants. In the wake of the report Dr. Lowe predicted at a pediatrics section meeting, attended by a Wadley administrator, that the hospital was "going to have blind babies" unless it acquired the facilities to adequately monitor blood gases. However, during the period from 1971 through 1973 Wadley expended approximately $200 per year for nursery improvements. Kellie was born in August of 1974.

The jury found the individual doctors negligent and Wadley both negligent and grossly negligent in failing to properly treat Kellie. It also found that Wadley had violated the D.T.P.A. by holding out to the Birchfields that the hospital was adequately equipped to handle premature babies when it was not. The damage award was $2,111,500 actual damages against all defendants, jointly and severally, plus $1,200,000 exemplary damages against Wadley.

. . . .

## DAMAGES

D.T.P.A. Damages

The Birchfields challenge the rulings of both the trial court and the court of appeals concerning questions of damages. At trial, the Birchfields secured jury findings that Wadley violated the Deceptive Trade Practices Act, that the Birchfields were adversely affected by that violation, and that Wadley was negligent and grossly negligent. The Birchfields argue that the courts below erred in failing to award *both* exemplary damages as found by the jury and treble damages under the D.T.P.A. We disagree. This argument overlooks the fact that the jury found that Wadley's deceptive act or practice, as well as each defendants' acts of negligence, were the proximate or producing cause of the *same damages. See, Allstate Ins. Co. v. Kelly,* 680 S.W.2d 595, 606 (Tex. App.—Tyler 1984, writ ref'd n.r.e.). The Birchfields' special issues on damages merely requested the jury to fix a sum of money which would compensate Kellie and her parents, "for the damages proximately resulting from the occurrence in question." In the absence of separate and distinct findings of actual damages on both the acts of negligence and the deceptive acts or practices, an award of exemplary damages *and* statutory treble damages would be necessarily predicated upon the same findings of actual damages and would amount to a double recovery of punitive damages. *Id.*

In the alternative, the Birchfields claim that they were entitled to elect whether to recover the exemplary damages as found by the jury or statutory treble damages. In light of our holding that the Birchfields were not entitled to both treble and exemplary damages, they were confronted with a situation where an election would be required. *Kish v. Van Note,* 692 S.W.2d 463, 466–67 (Tex. 1985). The court of appeals held that since the Birchfields, before entry of judgment, failed to unequivocally waive the findings on exemplary damages, they had waived their right to complain on appeal that the trial court erred in failing to award treble damages. 718 S.W.2d at 339. We find no support for that proposition. The judgment of the court should be "so framed as to give the party *all the relief* to which he may be entitled." Tex. R. Civ. P. 301, (emphasis added). While a formal waiver by the Birchfields would have been in order, it was not a prerequisite to the recovery of all of the damages to which they were lawfully entitled. *Hargrove v. Trinity Universal Insurance Co.*, 152 Tex. 243, 256 S.W.2d 73, 75 (1953). We hold that where the prevailing party fails to elect between alternative measures of damages, the court should utilize the findings affording the greater recovery and render judgment accordingly.

. . . .

[In accordance with this holding, the court awarded the Birchfields treble damages under the D.T.P.A. claim.]

### [6] The "Demand for Relief"; Prayer

*Read Tex. R. Civ. P. 47.*

*Dollar Amount Claimed.* Civil Procedure Rule 47 was amended in 1977 to provide that an original petition seeking unliquidated damages should contain only the allegation that the damages sought exceed the minimum jurisdictional limits of the court. *See also* R.C.S. Art. 4590i, § 5.01 ("Pleadings in a suit based on a health care liability claim shall not specify an amount of money claimed as damages"). The purpose of the amendments was to limit newspaper publicity based on inflated damage claims in personal injury litigation. In 1990, Rule 47 was amended again to require that pleadings seeking unliquidated damages contain a statement that the damages sought are within the jurisdictional limits of the court, not that they exceed the court's minimum jurisdictional limits.

Before the amendments, a pleading seeking damages "in excess of the minimum jurisdictional limits of the court" would not support a default judgment. *White Motor Co. v. Loden,* 373 S.W.2d 863, 866 (Tex. Civ. App.—Dallas 1964, no writ).

It is not entirely clear what is meant by a claim for "unliquidated damages." In the context of default judgment, a claim is liquidated only if the amount of damages can be calculated accurately by the court from the allegations contained in the petition and an instrument in writing on which the claim is based. *Freeman v. Leasing Assocs., Inc.,* 503 S.W.2d 406, 408 (Tex. Civ. App.—Houston [14th Dist.] 1973, no writ). Would you consider an action on an oral contract to recover a specific agreed dollar sum a liquidated claim? What about a claim for exemplary damages? What about a conversion claim involving a finding of the fair value of a chattel as of a specified date?

*Use of the General Prayer and Special Prayer.* In a general prayer, the pleader requests all relief, legal or equitable, to which the pleader is entitled. The general prayer is ordinarily sufficient to authorize a judgment for any relief, consistent with the cause of action pleaded, that is within the jurisdiction of the court. *Goldberg v. Goldberg,* 392 S.W.2d 168, 171 (Tex. Civ. App.—Fort Worth 1965, no writ). At times, usually when the relief sought is of a non-monetary character, a special (specific) prayer is required. Claims for injunctive relief, rescission, and removal of a cloud on the title to property are examples of when a specific prayer is required. *See, e.g., Fant v. Massie,* 451 S.W.2d 774, 776 (Tex. Civ. App.—Austin 1970, writ ref'd n.r.e.) (injunction); *Burnett v. James,* 564 S.W.2d 407, 409 (Tex. Civ. App.—Dallas 1978, writ dism'd) (rescission); *West Texas Dist. Baptist Ass'n v. Pilgrim Rest Bapt. Ch.,* 368 S.W.2d 814, 817 (Tex. Civ. App.—Fort Worth 1963, writ ref'd n.r.e.) (title to real property).

A pleader must take great care in making sure that the special prayer is not "inconsistent" with the relief sought under the general prayer. *See Tennessee Life Ins. Co. v. Nelson,* 459 S.W.2d 450, 454–455 (Tex. Civ. App.—Houston [14th Dist.] 1970, no writ).

*Prejudgment Interest and the Prayer.* The subject of prejudgment interest has created other difficulties. In *Republic Nat. Bank v. Northwest Nat. Bank of Fort Worth,* 578 S.W.2d 109, 116–117 (Tex. 1978), the Texas Supreme Court ruled that "[w]here prejudgment interest is sought at common law as an element of damages, the plaintiff must plead for it. Such is not the case where prejudgment interest is sought on the basis of a written contract fitting the description of article 5069—1.03. An award of this statutory interest, or interest *eo nomine* as it is known, may be supported by a prayer for general relief."

### [7] Certification and Sanctions for Frivolous Pleadings and Motions

The following excerpt from Dorsaneo, *Texas Litigation Guide,* Ch. 3, *Professional Responsibility,* discusses the attorney's duty to pursue only legitimate, "nonfrivolous" claims and defenses.

## W. Dorsaneo, TEXAS LITIGATION GUIDE

*§ 3.07[1] (1998)*[*]

§ 3.07 Obligations of Attorneys Acting as Advocates

. . .

[b] Sanctions Under Statute

[i] Relationship of Sanction Provisions

Several Texas rules and statutes, in addition to the Disciplinary Rules of Professional Conduct [*see* State Bar Rules, Art. 10 § 9, Rule 3.01], forbid the filing of frivolous actions and provide for sanctions. Sanctions for filing frivolous pleadings and motions are available under Chapter 10 of the Civil Practice and Remedies Code [*see* C.P.R.C. § 10.001 *et seq.*] and have often been imposed under Civil Procedure Rule 13 [*see* T.R.C.P. 13; *cf.* Fed. R. Civ. P. 11; *see also* [c], *below*].

Chapter 10 was enacted in 1995 and applies to pleadings and motions in suits commenced on or after September 1, 1995 [Acts 1995, 74th Leg., ch. 137 § 2]. Chapter 10 provides that, notwithstanding the Supreme Court's rulemaking authority under the Government Code [*see* Gov. C. § 22.004(c)], the Supreme Court may not amend or adopt rules in conflict with Chapter 10. However, Chapter 10 does not explicitly repeal or alter current Civil Procedure Rule 13.

In addition, Chapter 9 of the Civil Practice and Remedies Code deals with frivolous pleadings [*see* C.P.R.C. § 9.001 *et seq.*]. This chapter was enacted in 1987. In the same year the Texas Supreme Court amended Civil Procedure Rule 13 and added language, pursuant to the Court's rulemaking authority, repealing Chapter 9 to the extent it conflicts with Rule 13 [*see* Gov. C.

§ 22.004(c)—adoption of rule by Supreme Court repeals conflicting procedural laws]. When Rule 13 was amended again in 1990, the repealing language was omitted. Nevertheless, it is clear that the statute has been superseded to the extent of any conflict. The two provisions are in fact quite similar in the standards set out and the sanctions allowed [see C.P.R.C. § 9.012; *see* [c], *below*]. However, Chapter 9 contains a provision under which the court must report an attorney's conduct to an appropriate State Bar grievance committee if the court imposes sanctions and finds that the attorney has consistently engaged in activity that results in sanctions. The report must contain (1) the name of the attorney, (2) the court's finding that the pleading was signed in violation of the statutory standards, (3) a description of the sanctions imposed against the attorney and the represented party, and (4) the finding that the attorney has consistently engaged in activity that results in sanctions [*see* C.P.R.C. § 9.013]. Civil Procedure Rule 13 does not contain a similar provision. Because the provision is not inconsistent with Rule 13, presumably it continues in effect.

The power to sanction may also be implicit in a particular statute or rule or found in the court's inherent power to administer justice [*see* Metzger v. Sebek, 892 S.W.2d 20, 51 (Tex. App.—Houston [1st Dist.] 1994, den.)]. When a trial court's order of sanctions refers to a specific rule, either by citing the rule, tracking its language, or both, the reviewing court need not consider whether the sanctions might have been proper under the court's inherent power or some other authority. The reviewing court's role is to determine whether the trial court properly applied the specific rule [*see* Metzger v. Sebek, 892 S.W.2d 20, 51 (Tex. App.—Houston [1st Dist.] 1994, den.); Aldine Independent School Dist. v. Baty, 946 S.W.2d 851, 852 (Tex. App.—Houston [14th Dist.] 1997, no writ)—when trial court tracked Rule 13 language, although it did not cite to rule, appellate court limited review to whether sanctions met Rule 13 requirements].

Sanctions may be imposed at other stages of an action based on the frivolous or groundless filing of papers or other proscribed activities. Abuse of the discovery process is the subject of extensive and detailed sanction rules that are discussed in Ch. 95, Discovery Sanctions. Groundless or frivolous appeals are also subject to special rules [*see* T.R.A.P. 45, 62]. A wide variety of conduct may result in charges of contempt of court [*see* Ch. 133, *Contempt*].

[ii] C.P.R.C. Chapter 10

Under Chapter 10 of the Civil Practice and Remedies Code, the signing of a pleading or motion as required by the Texas Rules of Civil Procedure constitutes a certificate by the signatory that to the signatory's best knowledge, information, and belief, formed after reasonable inquiry, all of the following are true [C.P.R.C. § 10.001—applies to pleadings and motions in suits commenced on or after September 1, 1995]:

1. The pleading or motion is not being presented for any improper purpose, including to harass or to cause unnecessary delay or needless increase in the cost of litigation.

2. Each claim, defense, or other legal contention in the pleading or motion is warranted by existing law or by a nonfrivolous argument for the extension, modification, or reversal of existing law or the establishment of new law.

3. Each allegation or other factual contention in the pleading or motion has evidentiary support or, for a specifically identified allegation or factual contention, is likely to have evidentiary support after a reasonable opportunity for further investigation or discovery.

4. Each denial in the pleading or motion of a factual contention is warranted on the evidence or, for a specifically identified denial, is reasonably based on a lack of information or belief.

However, a general denial under the Rules of Civil Procedure may be made without violating this provision [*see* C.P.R.C. § 10.004(f); *see also* T.R.C.P. 92].

If an attorney or party signs a paper in violation of this provision, any party may file a motion for sanctions, describing the specific conduct involved, or the court on its own initiative may enter an order describing the specific conduct and directing the alleged violator to show cause why the conduct has not violated the statute [C.P.R.C. § 10.002(a), (b)]. The court may award to a party prevailing on a motion the reasonable expenses and attorney's fees incurred in presenting or opposing the motion, and if no due diligence is shown the court may award to the prevailing party all costs for inconvenience, harassment, and out-of-pocket expenses incurred or caused by the litigation [C.P.R.C. § 10.002(c)].

The court must provide the party who is the subject of the motion for sanctions notice of the allegations and a reasonable opportunity to respond [C.P.R.C. § 10.003]. If the court determines that a person has signed a pleading or motion in violation of these statutes, the court may impose a sanction on the person, a party represented by the person, or both [C.P.R.C. § 10.004(a)]. The sanction must be limited to what is sufficient to deter repetition of the conduct or comparable conduct by others similarly situated [C.P.R.C. § 10.004(b)]. A sanction may include one or more of the following [C.P.R.C. § 10.004(c)]:

1. A directive to the violator to perform, or refrain from performing, an act.

2. An order to pay a penalty into court.

3. An order to pay to the other party the amount of the reasonable expenses incurred by the other party because of the filing of the pleading or motion, including reasonable attorney's fees.

The court may not award monetary sanctions against a represented party (as opposed to an attorney) for a violation of the provision that requires claims and defenses to be warranted by existing law or a nonfrivolous argument for the extension, modification, or reversal of existing law [C.P.R.C. § 10.004(d); *see* C.P.R.C. § 10.001(2)]. Also, the court may not award monetary sanctions on its own initiative if, before the court issues its order to show cause, there is a voluntary dismissal or settlement of the claims made by or against the party or the party's attorney who is to be sanctioned [C.P.R.C. § 10.004(e)].

In its order imposing sanctions, the court must describe the conduct the court has determined violated Chapter 10 and explain the basis for the sanctions [C.P.R.C. § 10.005].

### [c] Sanctions Under Rule 13

#### [i] Basis for Sanctions

Under Civil Procedure Rule 13, the signature of an attorney or party constitutes a certificate that the attorney has read the pleading, motion, or other paper and that, to the best of the lawyer's knowledge, information, and belief formed after reasonable inquiry, the instrument is neither (1) groundless and brought in bad faith, nor (2) groundless and brought for the purpose of harassment [T.R.C.P. 13]. Additionally, Rule 13 states that an attorney or party may be held in contempt of court for bringing a fictitious suit as an experiment to get an opinion of the court, for filing any fictitious pleading in a cause for the purposes of securing an advisory opinion, or for making statements in a pleading that the attorney knows to be groundless and false if the statements are made for the purposes of securing a delay of the trial of the cause [T.R.C.P. 13].

The term "bad faith" under Civil Procedure Rule 13 has been held to mean not simply bad judgment or negligence, but the conscious doing of a wrong for a dishonest, discriminatory, or malicious purpose [Stites v. Gillum, 872 S.W.2d 786, 794–796 (Tex. App.—Fort Worth 1994, den.); *cf.* Campos v. Ysleta General Hosp., Inc., 879 S.W.2d 67, 71 (Tex. App.—El Paso 1994, den.)]. There is a presumption under Rule 13 that papers are filed in good faith [T.R.C.P. 13]. Therefore, the burden is on the party moving for sanctions to overcome this presumption [GTE Communications v. Tanner, 856 S.W.2d 725, 731 (Tex. 1993)].

Groundless under Civil Procedure Rule 13 means that there is no basis in law or fact for the pleading and it is not warranted by a good-faith argument for the extension, modification, or reversal of existing law [T.R.C.P. 13; *see also* Donwerth v. Preston II Chrysler-Dodge, 775 S.W.2d 634, 637 (Tex. 1989)—term "groundless" under Rule 13 has same meaning as "groundless" under DTPA; *see also* Bus. & Com. C. § 17.50(c)]. However, the otherwise identical language of Chapter 10 of the Civil Practice and Remedies Code substitutes the phrase "non-frivolous argument" for "good-faith argument" [*see* C.P.R.C. § 10.001(2); *see also* [b][ii], *above*].

A general denial under the Civil Procedure Rules does not constitute a groundless pleading in violation of the rule, nor does the amount claimed for damages constitute a groundless claim in violation of the rule [T.R.C.P. 13].

---

Consider the following case.

## GTE COMMUNICATIONS v. TANNER

*856 S.W.2d 725 (Tex. 1993)*

HECHT, Justice.

In this original mandamus procceding, relator GTE Communication Systems Corporation, a defendant in pending litigation, seeks review of sanctions imposed against it by the respondent district court. The district court concluded that four of GCSC's amended answers, its motion for summary judgment, and two affidavits in support of the motion were groundless and filed in bad faith, in violation of Rule 13, Tex. R. Civ. P. The district court also concluded that GCSC failed to produce a certain document in response to a discovery request, in violation of Rule 215, Tex. R. Civ. P. As sanctions, the district court struck GCSC's pleadings and ordered it to pay plaintiffs $150,000 in attorney fees. We granted leave to file application for writ of mandamus to review these rulings. For reasons that follow, we conditionally grant the writ.

### I

The litigation pending in the district court arises out of the following circumstances. Rene Duran and Jesse Ramirez, Jr. were riding bicycles along the sidewalk outside a grocery store when Duran struck a sharp-edged metal cable which had been stretched across the sidewalk at the level of his neck. Duran was nearly decapitated by the cable and died of his injuries. At the shock of this accident, Ramirez fell from his bicycle and sustained injuries. The cable, which was several feet long, had been made by unwinding the 18" flexible sheath that protected the cord of electric wires connecting a telephone handset to the body of a pay telephone mounted on the wall outside the grocery store. Police investigating Duran's death obtained information that a young man, the grandson of the proprietor of the grocery store, had stretched the cable across the sidewalk as a prank. Before the young man could be arrested and charged with murder, he committed suicide.

Duran's estate and survivors, along with Ramirez and his next friends, filed suit claiming that the telephone was unreasonably dangerous as designed, manufactured and distributed, because the metal sheath covering the telephone handset cord could easily be disassembled and stretched into a cable. In their original petition, plaintiffs alleged that defendant ATS Pay Phone Supply, Inc., had manufactured the telephone, and did not name GTE Communication Systems Corporation as a defendant. Subsequently, plaintiffs amended their petition to add GCSC as a defendant, alleging that it was the manufacturer of the telephone. In answer to plaintiffs' allegations, GCSC denied that it had designed, manufactured, marketed, sold or distributed the sheathed cord.

After some discovery had been conducted, GCSC moved for summary judgment on several grounds, including: that it had not designed, manufactured, or marketed the sheathed cord that caused Duran's injuries; that the sheath was not defective; that if the sheath was unreasonably dangerous, it was solely because it had been altered; that the alteration of the sheathed cord which led to plaintiffs' injuries was unforeseeable; and that the criminal conduct involved in stretching the cable across the sidewalk was a new, independent, superseding or intervening cause of plaintiffs' injuries. The first of these grounds was supported by the affidavits of Robert Zimmerman, a long-time employee of GCSC, and Oscar Jiminez, an employee of General Cable Company, a manufacturer of telephone handset cables. Zimmerman's affidavit stated that in manufacturing telephone handsets GCSC had used only sheathed cords made by General Cable, and that if the sheath that injured Duran was not General Cable's, then the handset was not GCSC's. Jiminez' affidavit stated that he had examined the remnants of the sheath that injured Duran and found six distinct differences between those remnants and sheaths manufactured by General Cable. Thus, Jiminez concluded that General Cable had not designed, assembled or distributed the cord involved in the accident.

In response to GCSC's motion for summary judgment, plaintiffs asserted that the identity of the manufacturer of the cord had not been established but was much in dispute. Plaintiffs argued that even if GCSC had not made the cord, it had certainly made the telephone, and that the telephone was defective because the cord was part of it. The trial court denied summary judgment without indicating a specific reason.

Several months later, plaintiffs filed a motion for sanctions requesting that the district court strike GCSC's pleadings and award plaintiffs $150,000 in attorney fees. This motion complained that GCSC's assertions that it was not involved in making and distributing the sheathed cord which injured the plaintiffs had been interposed in bad faith and with knowledge that the assertions were false. The motion also complained that GCSC had failed to produce unspecified documents (actually, as it later developed, a single document) which showed that it knew of the dangers inherent in the cord and could have foreseen the type of accident in which plaintiffs were injured. The motion requested sanctions for discovery abuse and under Rule 13, Tex. R. Civ. P. After an evidentiary hearing the district court granted plaintiffs' motion without indicating the reasons for its ruling.

GCSC petitioned the court of appeals for a writ of mandamus directing the district court to vacate its order. The appeals court conditionally granted its writ, holding that the order did not state "the particulars" of good cause warranting the imposition of sanctions, as required by Rule 13. *GTE Communication Systems Corp. v. Curry,* 819 S.W.2d 652, 653 (Tex. App.—San Antonio 1991, orig. proc.). Immediately after the court of appeals issued its opinion, the district court vacated its original order and, without notice to GCSC, signed a new order prepared by plaintiffs, setting out in 24 paragraphs three reasons for sanctioning GCSC by dismissing its pleadings and assessing $150,000 attorney fees against it.

One reason the district court gave for imposing sanctions was that GCSC had abused the discovery process by failing to produce a certain memorandum prepared by employees of a corporation, GTE of Florida, Inc., for circulation to several departments within that corporation. GTFL, as it is referred to, and GCSC are separate corporations. It is unclear from the record before us how or even whether they are related. The relevant portion of the memorandum states: "Presently GTFL is using over 5,000 handsets per year for maintenance change out because the armored handset cord has been uncoiled by an excessive pull by the end user. Several of these handset failures have resulted in litigation against GTFL." Plaintiffs obtained this memo from another party in the litigation. To show that GCSC was aware of the memo and had failed to produce it, plaintiffs offered as their only evidence the testimony of Charles James, president of ATS, the corporation plaintiffs once alleged was the manufacturer of the sheath. James stated that, based upon his experience in the pay telephone industry, it was "totally inconceivable" that GCSC did not have the memo, and GCSC could compel its production from GTFL because the two corporations were affiliated. The district court "credited" James' testimony and "discredited" GCSC's evidence that it was unaware of the memo and that it had no control over GTFL to compel that entity to produce the memo. James also admitted, however, that he had never worked for GCSC or GTFL and did not actually know whether GCSC had ever been in possession of the GTFL memo.

A second reason the district court gave for imposing sanctions was that GCSC had acted in bad faith in asserting in its summary judgment motion that, as a matter of law, plaintiffs' accident was unforeseeable. The court assumed that GCSC knew of the GTFL memo when it filed its motion for summary judgment, and therefore knew of the problems with the sheathed cord. Possessed of this knowledge, the court reasoned, GCSC's assertion that plaintiffs' accident was unforeseeable as a matter of law was groundless and could only have been made in bad faith. Based upon this analysis, the district court concluded that GCSC's summary judgment motion violated Rule 13.

The district court also concluded, as its third reason for sanctions, that GCSC's amended answers, motion for summary judgment and supporting affidavits in which it denied that it had manufactured the sheathed cord were groundless and brought in bad faith, in violation of Rule 13. The court based this conclusion upon the testimony of two experts, one of whom was James. Plaintiffs first developed this testimony after GCSC's motion for summary judgment was denied and offered it at the hearing on the motion for sanctions. Both witnesses testified that they had concluded from examining the sheath that GCSC had manufactured it. At the hearing, GCSC introduced the affidavits that it had filed in support of its motion for summary judgment, in addition to other evidence that it had not manufactured the sheath.

GCSC again sought a writ of mandamus from the court of appeals, but this time the court denied leave to file the petition. GCSC then moved for leave to file its petition in this Court, which we granted. 36 Tex. Sup. Ct. J. 686 (April 3, 1993).

## II

We first consider whether the district court abused its discretion in sanctioning GCSC for abuse of the discovery process under Rule 215, Tex. R. Civ. P. To answer this question we must answer two others: did the district court properly find that GCSC had "possession, custody or control" of the GTFL memo within the meaning of Rule 166b(2)(b), Tex. R. Civ. P., such that GCSC should have produced it; and if so, were the sanctions imposed for the failure to produce the memo just. We conclude that both these questions must be answered negatively.

Rule 166b(2)(b), Tex. R. Civ. P., provides in pertinent part:

> A person is not required to produce a document or tangible thing unless it is within the person's possession, custody or control. Possession, custody or control includes constructive possession such that the person need not have actual physical possession. As long as the person has a superior right to compel the production from a third party (including an agency, authority or representative), the person has possession, custody or control.

The phrase, "possession, custody or control", within the meaning of this rule, includes not only actual physical possession, but constructive possession, and the right to obtain possession from a third party, such as an agent or representative. The right to obtain possession is a legal right based upon the relationship between the party from whom a document is sought and the person who has actual possession of it. For example, in *State v. Lowry,* 802 S.W.2d 669, 673–674 (Tex. 1991), we held that a request for production directed to the Attorney General required production of documents held by all divisions of that office.

A party seeking sanctions has the burden of establishing his right to relief. Thus, when a motion for sanctions asserts that a respondent to a discovery request has failed to produce a document within its possession, custody or control, the movant has the burden to prove the assertion. In this case, plaintiffs failed to meet that burden.

The only evidence plaintiffs offered to show that GCSC had actual possession of the memo was the testimony of Charles James that it was "totally inconceivable" to him that GCSC did not have the memo. James admitted, however, that he had never worked for GCSC and had no personal knowledge of whether GCSC had ever had the GTFL memo. The memo has not been located in GCSC's files, no GCSC employee has acknowledged ever seeing it, and there is no circumstantial evidence that would indicate that GCSC ever had the memo. Under these circumstances, James' testimony is no more than mere surmise.

Likewise, there is no evidence that GCSC had constructive possession of the document or a right to compel its production. Plaintiffs adduced no evidence regarding the corporate relationship between GTFL and GCSC, or any right of the latter to control the former. In fact, the only testimony regarding control was James' speculation regarding the ability of GCSC's parent to control its subsidiaries, assuming both GCSC and GTFL were subsidiaries of the same parent. There is no evidence that GCSC ever actually did exercise control of any type over GTFL.

As a rule, the district court's resolution of a factual issue is entitled to deference in a mandamus proceeding and should not be set aside unless it is clear from the record that only one decision could have been reached. *Walker v. Packer,* 827 S.W.2d 833, 839–40 (Tex. 1992). Here, it is quite clear that from the record before it the district court could not have found that GCSC had possession, custody or control over the GTFL memo within the meaning of Rule 166b(2)(b) such that GCSC should have produced it.

Furthermore, even if GCSC had failed to produce the GTFL memo, the district court's sanction of striking GCSC's pleadings would not have been just, as required by Rule 215, Tex. R. Civ. P. "[J]ust sanctions must not be excessive. . . . [C]ourts must consider the availability of less stringent sanctions and whether such lesser sanctions would fully promote compliance."

*TransAmerican Natural Gas Corporation v. Powell,* 811 S.W.2d 913, 917 (Tex. 1991). The record must reflect that the court considered the availability of lesser sanctions. *Otis Elevator Co. v. Parmelee,* 850 S.W.2d 179, 181 (Tex. 1993). Case determinative sanctions may be imposed in the first instance only in exceptional cases when they are clearly justified and it is fully apparent that no lesser sanctions would promote compliance with the rules. Here, the order which the district court signed stated that lesser sanctions would have been ineffective, but the court did not explain why, and the record does not indicate why. We give no deference to such unsupported conclusions. *Chrysler Corp. v. Blackmon,* 841 S.W.2d 844, 853 (Tex. 1992). We fail to see why any number of lesser sanctions, from fines to contempt, would not have promoted compliance with discovery, if there had been abuse here.

The sanctions imposed by the district court precluded GCSC from presenting the merits of its position at trial. Before a court may deprive a party of its right to present the merits of its case because of discovery abuse, it must determine that "a party's hindrance of the discovery process justifies a presumption that its claims or defenses lack merit." *TransAmerican,* 811 S.W.2d at 918. No such presumption is warranted here. We have concluded that GCSC did not fail to comply with discovery. Even in the district court's view, GCSC only failure was to produce a single document which states that "several . . . handset failures have resulted in litigation" without any indication of the nature of such litigation or whether personal injuries had occurred. Even if GCSC had failed to comply with discovery, there is nothing in the record to justify striking GCSC's pleadings as a consequence.

Accordingly, we conclude that the district court clearly abused its discretion in sanctioning GCSC for an abuse of the discovery process under Rule 215.

III

We next consider whether the district court abused its discretion in imposing sanctions under Rule 13, Tex. R. Civ. P. Rule 13 states in pertinent part:

> The signatures of attorneys or parties constitute a certificate by them that they have read the pleading, motion, or other paper; that to the best of their knowledge, information, and belief formed after reasonable inquiry the instrument is not groundless and brought in bad faith or groundless and brought for the purpose of harassment. . . . If a pleading, motion or other paper is signed in violation of this rule, the court, upon motion or upon its own initiative, after notice and hearing, shall impose an appropriate sanction available under Rule 215-2b, upon the person who signed it, a represented party, or both.

Courts shall presume that pleadings, motions, and other papers are filed in good faith. No sanctions under this rule may be imposed except for good cause, the particulars of which must be stated in the sanction order. "Groundless" for purposes of this rule means no basis in law or fact and not warranted by good faith argument for the extension, modification, or reversal of existing law.

The district court sanctioned GCSC for filing amended answers, a motion for summary judgment and the supporting affidavits of Zimmerman and Jiminez, which deny that GCSC was involved in making or distributing the sheathed cord which caused plaintiffs' injuries. By its express language, Rule 13 applies only to pleadings, motions and other papers signed by attorneys. Since the Zimmerman and Jiminez affidavits were not signed by GCSC's attorneys, it was a clear abuse of discretion for the district court to base an imposition of sanctions under Rule 13 on them. The issues, then, are whether the district court abused its discretion GCSC's in concluding that GCSC's amended answers and motion for summary judgment are sanctionable, and in striking GCSC's pleadings.

Such papers cannot serve as a basis for sanctions under that portion of Rule 13 quoted above, and on which the district court relied, unless the papers are "groundless" as defined by the rule. Plaintiffs contend, and the district court concluded, that GCSC's amended answers and summary judgment motion are groundless because there is no basis in fact for GCSC's denial that it was involved in the manufacture or distribution of the sheathed cord which caused plaintiffs' injuries. Plaintiffs make two arguments in support of their contention.

Plaintiffs' first argument is that the evidence establishes as a matter of law that GCSC manufactured the sheathed cord, and that GCSC's denial of this fact was therefore groundless. The evidence in the record before us demonstrates that the identity of the manufacturer of the cord is vigorously disputed, and certainly not established as a matter of law. GCSC's effort to establish that it was not the manufacturer of the cord was not groundless.

Plaintiffs' second argument is that because, at the very least, a fact question existed regarding GCSC's involvement in the manufacture and distribution of the sheathed cord, GCSC's assertion in its motion for summary judgment that no such fact question existed was groundless. In other words, plaintiffs argue that a party who knows that material facts are in dispute may be sanctioned for moving for summary judgment. While we do not disagree that the filing of a motion for summary judgment may give rise to sanctions under Rule 13, just as the filing of any other pleading or motion, this is not such a case. At the time GCSC filed its motion, the only evidence adduced by the parties indicated that GCSC had not made or distributed the sheathed cord. Indeed, plaintiffs themselves originally pleaded that ATS manufactured the cord, not GCSC. By their own admission, plaintiffs did not develop any evidence to contradict GCSC's assertions until after GCSC's motion was denied. Even if GCSC was not entitled to summary judgment, it cannot be said that its motion had no basis in law or fact.

Thus, the district court clearly abused its discretion in determining that GCSC's assertions were groundless. To impose sanctions under Rule 13, the district court was also required to find that GCSC's assertions were made in bad faith or for the purpose of harassment. Since plaintiffs do not contend, and the district court did not find, that GCSC's assertions were harassing, a finding of bad faith was a prerequisite to sanctions. Rule 13 prescribes that courts presume that papers are filed in good faith. Thus, the burden is on the party moving for sanctions to overcome this presumption. Plaintiffs failed to carry this burden. The only basis the district court gave for finding that GCSC had acted in bad faith was that GCSC had ignored or concealed evidence that it had been involved in making and distributing the sheathed cord that injured the plaintiffs. As we have seen, however, there is no proof that GCSC, before it moved for summary judgment, was aware of any evidence that it was involved in the manufacture or distribution of the sheathed cord.

Furthermore, a motion for summary judgment asserting that no genuine issue of material fact exists is not proved groundless or in bad faith merely by the filing of a response which raises an issue of fact, even if the response was or could have been anticipated by the movant. Nor is denial of a motion for summary judgment alone grounds for sanctions. Rule 13 does not permit sanctions for every pleading or motion that requests relief which is denied. In this case, the district court abused its discretion in finding that GCSC had acted in bad faith.

The district court also sanctioned GCSC for asserting in its motion for summary judgment that it did not know of any defects in the sheathed cord and could not have foreseen an accident like plaintiffs', when it was aware of the GTFL memo. Since we have determined that there is no evidence that GCSC was aware of the GTFL memo when it filed its motion for summary judgment, and plaintiffs have offered no other evidence of GCSC's knowledge of any defects in the cord, we conclude that such assertions were not groundless or made in bad faith.

Even if GCSC's assertions in its amended answers and motion for summary judgment had been sanctionable, they would not have warranted striking GCSC's pleadings. Rule 13 requires that sanctions imposed be "appropriate", which is the equivalent of "just" under Rule 215. *TransAmerican,* 811 S.W.2d at 916–17 n. 4. Neither standard allows imposition of excessive sanctions. Moreover, while the due process concerns under the two rules are not completely congruent, case determinative sanctions may not be imposed under either rule unless the violation warrants adjudication of the merits. Even if GCSC had violated Rule 13, there is nothing in the record to suggest that the violation could not have been fully redressed far short of striking GCSC's pleadings.

Thus, we hold that the district court clearly abused its discretion in imposing sanctions under Rule 13.

IV

Finally, we consider whether GCSC has an adequate remedy by appeal. We have previously held that appeal from the imposition of case determinative, or "death penalty", sanctions is inadequate, unless the sanctions are imposed simultaneously with a final, appealable judgment. *TransAmerican,* 811 S.W.2d at 920; *Chrysler,* 841 S.W.2d at 845 n. 2. For the same reasons expressed in those cases, GCSC has no adequate remedy by appeal in this case, and we exercise our discretion to issue the extraordinary writ.

We have held that an assessment of attorney fees which is not to be paid until final judgment is rendered may be adequately challenged by appeal. *Braden v. Downey,* 811 S.W.2d 922 (Tex. 1991). Here, however, where we have concluded in considering case determinative sanctions that the district court clearly abused its discretion in awarding any sanctions at all, there remains no basis for the award of attorney fees.

Accordingly, we conclude that GCSC is entitled to have the district court's sanction order set aside.

* * * * * *

We therefore direct the district court to vacate its orders of November 14, 1991, and June 12, 1992, assessing sanctions and attorney fees. We assume the district court will promptly comply. The writ of mandamus will issue only if it does not.

### [8] Standard Negligence Petition

Negligence Petition: Traditional Form

| | | |
|---|---|---|
| JASON PINKTON, and | ) | |
| MARCY PINKTON, Plaintiffs | ) | IN THE DISTRICT COURT OF |
| vs. | ) | DALLAS COUNTY, TEXAS |
| ACE CONSTRUCTION, | ) | 192nd JUDICIAL DISTRICT |

TERRY ACE, and LARRY )
ACE, jointly and severally )

PLAINTIFFS' FIRST AMENDED ORIGINAL PETITION

TO THE HONORABLE JUDGE OF SAID COURT:

NOW COME Marcy Pinkton and her husband, Jason Pinkton, hereinafter called Plaintiffs, complaining of Ace Construction, a partnership composed of Jerry Ace and Larry Ace, individually and doing business as Ace Construction, hereinafter called Defendants, and by way of Amended Petition and for cause of action your Plaintiffs would respectfully show unto the Court the following:

I.

Your Plaintiffs are resident citizens of Dallas County, Texas. The Defendant, Ace Construction, maintains an office and place of business in the City of Dallas, Dallas County, Texas, and has in said Dallas County, Texas, an agent or representative upon whom service of citation may be had in this cause. Larry Ace resides in the County of Dallas, State of Texas, where he may be found for purpose of service of citation herein. The Defendant, Jerry Ace, individually and doing business as Ace Construction, resides in the County of Dallas, State of Texas, where he has heretofore been served with citation in this cause.

II.

Your Plaintiffs would show that at all times material to this cause of action, Ace Construction was engaged in the business of erecting houses and other structures. In connection with its business operations it used, owned and maintained various motor vehicles, the basis of this suit. On the afternoon of January 31, 1949, Marcy Pinkton was riding as a passenger in a Mercury automobile which was being operated in a northerly direction along Swanee Street in the City of Dallas, Dallas County, Texas. Such Mercury automobile was being operated by Jason Pinkton, who was in all things conducting himself in a careful, lawful and prudent manner and who was exercising due care for his own safety and that of his passenger. At or about the hour of 1 o'clock P.M. on January 31, 1949, the vehicle in which Marcy Pinkton was riding as a passenger approached the intersection of Swanee Street and Maple Glen Road. At such intersection, traffic is controlled by signal lights. There was displayed a red traffic signal light and Jason Pinkton brought the Mercury automobile to a stop behind another car, which was also proceeding in a northerly direction along Swanee Street. When the light changed to green for northbound traffic on Swanee Street, the first automobile proceeded forward and Jason Pinkton started his car forward. After the Mercury automobile in which Marcy Pinkton was riding as a passenger had crossed Maple Glen Road, the vehicle proceeding ahead of it was brought to a stop for the purpose of making a left turn, which could not be made immediately because of the approach of southbound traffic. Jason Pinkton brought the Mercury automobile to a stop and then suddenly and without warning the pick-up truck of Jerry Ace crashed into the rear of the Mercury automobile. This pick-up truck was on such occasion being operated by Jerry Ace, who was then and there acting in the course and scope of his representation of Ace Construction, a partnership composed of the said Jerry Ace and Larry Ace. As a result thereof, Marcy Pinkton was caused to suffer serious bodily injuries, which will be described hereinafter with particularity.

III.

The collision of January 31, 1949, out of which this suit arises, resulted from the negligence of Jerry Ace, while acting as the representative of Ace Construction, a partnership composed of Jerry Ace and Larry Ace, in some one or more of the following particulars:

1. In failing to maintain a proper lookout.
2. In failing to make proper application of the brakes on the pick-up truck.
3. In failing to make timely application of the brakes on the pick-up truck.
4. In failing to bring the pick-up truck to a stop before it struck the rear of the Mercury automobile in which Marcy Pinkton was riding as a passenger.
5. In failing to maintain proper stopping distance behind the Mercury automobile.
6. In following the Mercury automobile more closely than was reasonable and prudent under the existing circumstances, having due regard for the condition of and traffic upon Swanee Street, in violation of law.
7. In failing to turn the pick-up truck to the right to avoid striking the rear of the Mercury automobile.
8. In operating the pick-up truck at a rate of speed in excess of that at which it would have been operated by a person of ordinary prudence in the exercise of ordinary care under the same or similar circumstances.
9. In failing to maintain proper control of the pick-up truck.

Each and all of the above and foregoing acts, both of omission and commission, were negligent and constituted negligence and were each and all a proximate cause of the collision made the basis of this suit, of the injuries suffered by Marcy Pinkton, and of the damages sustained by your Plaintiffs as a result thereof.

IV.

In the collision of January 31, 1949, which is made the basis of this suit, Marcy Pinkton was caused to be thrown about violently in the car in which she was riding as a passenger. She suffered a severe whiplash injury to her neck and cervical spine. Her shoulders and upper back were injured and damaged. She has been caused to experience frequent severe headaches and spells of dizziness. She suffered a severe traumatic nervous shock, which has produced great nervousness. It was necessary for her attending physician to apply traction to her neck and head and to use diathermy treatments. Her injuries and the effects thereof have caused Marcy Pinkton to suffer from great and excruciating physical pain and mental anguish and she will in all reasonable probability continue to suffer from such physical pain and mental anguish, as well as from great nervousness, for a long time in the future, if not for the balance of her natural life. On January 31, 1949, Marcy Pinkton was a woman of the age of twenty-eight years, who had a life expectancy of seventy-two years according to the Standard Ordinary Tables of Mortality. She was a housewife, who customarily maintained her home for her husband and family. She has been handicapped in the discharge of her household duties and has required the assistance of others. It is reasonably probable that she will continue to be handicapped in the discharge of her household duties in the future and that she will continue to require assistance from others. Her activities since January 31, 1949, have been and it is reasonably probable that her future activities will be engaged in under the handicaps of pain and suffering. Marcy Pinkton has required medical care and will in the future in reasonable probability require additional medical care. Your Plaintiffs have been required to pay and incur liability to pay and will in the future in reasonable probability be required to pay and incur liability to pay the charges which have been made and which will be made for the services rendered and to be rendered unto Marcy Pinkton. The charges which have been made and which will be made have represented and will represent the usual, reasonable and customary charges for like and similar services in the vicinity where they have been and will be made necessary in connection with the proper treatment of the injuries suffered by Marcy Pinkton in the collision of January 31, 1949, which is made the basis of this suit. By reason of all of the above and foregoing, your Plaintiffs have been caused to suffer damages far in excess of the minimum jurisdictional limits of the court.

WHEREFORE, Premises Considered, the Defendant, Jerry Ace, individually and doing business as Ace Construction, having heretofore appeared and answered herein, your Plaintiffs pray that the Defendants, Ace Construction, a partnership composed of Jerry Ace and Larry Ace, be served in terms of the law to appear and answer herein and that upon final trial of this cause, your Plaintiffs have judgment against the Defendants, jointly and severally, for $50,000 damages; that they have interest on the judgment at the legal rate; that they recover their costs of Court in this behalf incurred, and that they have such other and further relief, general and special at law and in equity, to which they may show themselves justly entitled and in duty bound will ever pray.

Respectfully submitted,

______________________________

---

### NOTE

(1) *Sufficiency.* Be prepared to discuss the preceding negligence petition in light of the technical requirements of the Rules of Civil Procedure discussed above.

## § 5.05 Defendant's Answer

### [A] Contents and Primary Function of the Answer

The immediate function of the answer is to avoid judgment by default. Civil Procedure Rule 99 requires the citation to command the defendant to appear by filing a written answer to the plaintiff's petition at or before 10:00 A.M. on the Monday next after the expiration of 20 days after the date of service of. *See* Tex. R. Civ. P. 99. The primary function of the answer is to set forth the defendant's grounds of defense in plain and concise language. *See* Tex. R. Civ. P. 45. A general denial of matters pleaded by the adverse party that are not required to be denied under oath is sufficient to put the adverse party's allegations in controversy. *See* Tex. R. Civ. P. 92. The original answer may include the following:

(1) A special appearance. *See* Tex. R. Civ. P. 120a.

(2) A motion to transfer. *See* Tex. R. Civ. P. 86.

(3) A special exception. *See* Tex. R. Civ. P. 90, 91.

(4) A plea in abatement or to the jurisdiction. *See* Tex. R. Civ. P. 85.

(5) A general denial. *See* Tex. R. Civ. P. 92.

(6) Special denials. *See* Tex. R. Civ. P. 93.

(7) Any matter in avoidance or estoppel (*i.e.,* affirmative defenses). *See* Tex. R. Civ. P. 85, 94.

(8) Inferential rebuttal defenses. *See* Tex. R. Civ. P. 278.

You have already learned the form and function of the special appearance. The motion to transfer will be considered in the next chapter. The cases in the textual material in this section deal with other matters that may be contained in the defendant's answer.

### [B] Use of Defensive Pleas

Which plea or pleas can be used to raise each of the following kinds of defenses or defensive theories?

(1) In a negligence action, defendant disputes plaintiff's claim as to how the accident happened.

(2) In a negligence action, defendant wants to assert the defense of contributory negligence as a total or partial bar.

(3) In a negligence action, defendant wants to complain that plaintiff's allegation of the negligence element in the cause of action is vague and confusing as it is alleged.

(4) In a suit on a written instrument purporting to be a contract, defendant wants to deny execution of the instrument, among other denials. (Note: a denial of execution of a written instrument is one of the pleadings that Texas requires be made under oath.)

(5) A claim that venue in the case is improper and the action should be transferred to a place of proper venue.

(6) A claim that the defendant, a corporation incorporated and having its principal place of business in Ohio, does not do business in Texas.

(7) A claim that a person needed for just adjudication has not been joined in the suit.

(8) In a suit on a contract for the sale of land, defendant wants to raise the fact that the petition expressly shows that the alleged contract was oral only and thus seems to violate the statute of frauds.

The plaintiff's petition, as is suggested above, must meet certain criteria with respect to specificity and legal sufficiency. However, if a defendant does not enforce the right to a sufficient pleading by plaintiff, the defendant waives that right. At the pretrial stage, this enforcement is done by one of the pleading types denominated above. Which one is it? And why would a defendant want to insist on specific pleading by plaintiff? Why might plaintiff wish to avoid it?

### [C] Special Exceptions

*Read Tex. R. Civ. P. 90, 91.*

## McCAMEY v. KINNEAR 4

*484 S.W.2d 150 (Tex. Civ. App.—Beaumont 1972, writ ref'd n.r.e.)*

KEITH, Justice.

Plaintiff appeals from a judgment of dismissal of his suit wherein he sought to recover of the defendant attorney's fees paid to defendant in connection with a patent application. Plaintiff also sought recovery of certain expenses incurred by reason of the alleged inaction of defendant. At the outset we note affirmatively that while plaintiff has prosecuted the appeal with diligence, such comment does not apply to his trial court actions.

On the day the case was specially set for trial upon the "try or dismiss" docket, defendant filed a motion to dismiss plaintiff's cause of action, the allegations being set out in the margin.[1]

The court's order, entered on January 31, 1972, recited that the defendant's motion to dismiss having been heard, and "it appearing to the Court that said motion should be in all things granted; it is therefore ordered, adjudged and decreed that defendant's motion to dismiss be in all things granted."

This order of dismissal was preceded by some unusual maneuvers which require mention at this point. Defendant leveled many exceptions to plaintiff's original petition, some of which were sustained by an order entered May 4, 1970, defendant's exceptions to such action being duly noted. Although plaintiff did not file amended pleadings until the very day of the dismissal (a matter which will be mentioned later), the docket sheet in our record shows that defendant procured three continuances, the last being on October 7, 1971. Upon this latter date, the trial court entered a specific and detailed order setting the case for trial on January 31, 1972, and advised counsel that it would be tried or dismissed upon said date "depending upon any announcements which may or may not be made by counsel at such time."

On January 31, 1972, the date set for trial, plaintiff filed what he denominated a "Trial Amendment" but which was in fact an amended original petition. *See Rule 71*, Texas Rules of Civil Procedure. Our record does not reveal that leave was granted to file the instrument, whatever it might have been, under either *Rule 63* or *Rule 66*, nor does the record show that such instrument ever came to the attention of the trial court before the order of dismissal was entered. On the other hand, the record is equally silent as to any motion to strike the pleading filed in violation of the rules just mentioned. See in this connection 2 McDonald, Texas Civil Practice (1970 Rev. Vol.), § 8.06, pp. 323, et seq.;

Plaintiff timely gave notice of appeal from the order of dismissal, duly perfected his appeal, and now assigns many points of error. We do not find it necessary to discuss all of such points of error under our view of the record.

Plaintiff devotes much of his brief to the proposition that the trial court erred in granting the defendant's motion to dismiss (Footnote 1), contending that such motion was a general demurrer

---

[1] "Defendant would show the Court that it is useless to pick a jury in this cause or to take up the Court's time because said Plaintiff does not state a cause of action in this suit, and it would be a waste of the Court's time and a waste of the Jury's time to pick a jury in this cause, and said suit should be in all things dismissed."

in legal disguise which is forbidden by *Rule 90*. Under our view of the record, we do not reach the point. Instead, we turn to the controlling issue in the appeal, the action of the trial court upon the exceptions.

When special exceptions addressed to a pleading are sustained, the party has two options available to him: (a) he may amend to meet the exceptions and this he may do as a matter of right; or, (b) he may stand upon his pleadings, refuse to amend, and test the validity of the ruling upon appeal. Harold v. Houston Yacht Club, 380 S.W.2d 184, 186 (Tex. Civ. App., Houston, 1964, no writ); M.C. Winters, Inc. v. Lawless, 407 S.W.2d 275, 277 (Tex. Civ. App., Dallas, 1966, error dism.); and Farris v. Nortex Oil & Gas Corporation, 393 S.W.2d 684, 690 (Tex. Civ. App., Texarkana, 1965, error ref. n.r.e.).

A reasonable time should be allowed a party desiring to amend to conform to the ruling upon the special exceptions; but this is a matter within the sound discretion of the court not to be overthrown except for an abuse of discretion. Farias v. Besteiro, 453 S.W.2d 314, 317 (Tex. Civ. App., Corpus Christi, 1970, error ref. n.r.e.), and cases therein cited. The plaintiff, being ever under the duty of prosecuting his suit with diligence under the penalty of having it dismissed for want of prosecution, must also use diligence in amending his pleadings after an order sustaining exceptions. 4 McDonald, Texas Civil Practice (1971 Rev.Vol.), § 17.18, pp. 101–102. In our case, the plaintiff waited nearly twenty months—and through three trial settings—before filing his amended pleading upon the very day the case was set upon the "try or dismiss" docket.

Under the circumstances of this case, we hold that the long unexplained delay in filing the amended pleadings amounted in law to a refusal to amend. When a party stands firm on his pleadings, as we have held the plaintiff did in this case, the trial court may dismiss the cause if the remaining allegations fail to state a cause of action. Rutledge v. Valley Evening Monitor, 289 S.W.2d 952, 953 (Tex. Civ. App., San Antonio, 1956, no writ) and City of Roma v. Starr County, 428 S.W.2d 851, 853 (Tex. Civ. App., San Antonio, 1968, error ref. n.r.e.).

Having reviewed the remnants of the original petition, after the exceptions had been sustained, we are of the opinion that the remaining allegations of the petition failed to state a cause of action. The trial court was authorized, under these circumstances, to dismiss the case. Rutledge v. Valley Evening Monitor, supra; Wiseman v. Zorn, 309 S.W.2d 253, 259 (Tex. Civ. App., Houston, 1958, no writ).

The order sustaining the special exceptions was interlocutory in nature and plaintiff had no right of appeal therefrom. *Mueller v. Banks*, 317 S.W.2d 254, 255 (Tex. Civ. App., San Antonio. 1958, no writ). However, when the court entered the order of dismissal on January 31, 1972, following plaintiff's failure to amend within a reasonable time, plaintiff's right to appeal was then exercised. We now turn to the validity of the special exceptions and review the action of the trial court in entering the order sustaining such exceptions.[2]

Special Exceptions 5, 8, 9 and 10 were worded identically and challenged different parts of plaintiff's pleading. We quote the exception:

> "Plaintiff [sic, *Defendant*] excepts . . . [naming the particular paragraph of the petition] because said allegations are too general; because said allegations are a mere conclusion of the pleader; because no facts are alleged on which said conclusions are based; because said allegations do not inform this defendant of the facts on which the plaintiff intends to rely;

[2] In fairness to the trial judge who entered the order of dismissal, we note in our record that the order upon special exceptions was entered by his predecessor upon the bench.

> because said allegations do not inform this defendant of the proof that he will be required to meet on the trial of this cause and because said allegations are calculated to surprise and prejudice the defendant on the trial of this cause; because said allegations are calculated to cause a mistrial; said allegations should be in all things stricken and of this exception the defendant prays judgment of the Court."

It is obvious that this "special exception" did not comply with the provisions of *Rule 91* and even a cursory examination of the allegations attacked shows that in each instance the exception was without merit. The exception quoted was simply a broadside attack and did not "point out intelligibly and with particularity the defect, omission, obscurity, duplicity, generality, or other insufficiency in the allegations in the pleading excepted to" as required by *Rule 91*. There were other exceptions sustained which are subject to the same criticism and the result of the court's action was to eliminate from plaintiff's pleading the necessary allegations upon which his cause of action was predicated. In effect, such exceptions were "nothing more than the old general demurrer" which was abolished in 1941 when *Rule 90* was adopted. Huff v. Fidelity Union Life Insurance Company, 158 Tex. 433, 312 S.W.2d 493, 499 (1958).

These particular exceptions also lacked merit for the reasons pointed out in Kelly v. Wright, 144 Tex. 114, 188 S.W.2d 983, 985 (1945):

> "Rule 91 provides that a special exception shall not only point out the particular pleading excepted to, but shall also point out intelligibly and with particularity the defect, omission, obscurity, duplicity, generality, or other insufficiency in the allegation in the pleading excepted to.
>
> "The exceptions in question merely assert that the petition failed to show any grounds for equitable relief or state a cause of action. They do not point out intelligibly and with particularity the reasons for such conclusions. Therefore, the trial court erred in sustaining them."

See also, Pargas of Canton, Inc. v. Clower, 434 S.W.2d 192, 196 (Tex. Civ. App., Tyler, 1968, no writ); Chakur v. Zena, 233 S.W.2d 200, 201 (Tex. Civ. App., San Antonio, 1950, no writ).

The object and purpose of pleading is to give fair and adequate notice to the party being sued of the nature of the cause of action asserted against him so that he may adequately prepare his defense thereto. Plaintiff's original petition in this case fairly and adequately advised defendant of the nature of the cause of action being asserted against him. The plaintiff was not required to plead his evidence in detail and if the defendant desired more factual detail as to the basis of the claim, he had but to invoke the discovery processes authorized by the rules.

It follows, therefore, that the trial court having erred in sustaining the special exceptions, likewise erred in dismissing the case. The judgment below must be reversed and the cause remanded. We note, however, that plaintiff, by his inaction below, has delayed a disposition of his case and has contributed to the clogging of the dockets of both the trial and appellate courts. Such action is not to be commended and it is suggested that a repetition of this spectacle could be avoided by utilizing the provisions of *Rule 166*.

Reversed and remanded.

---

## NOTES AND QUESTIONS

(1) *Formal Defects.* A general allegation of negligence has long been held to be subject to special exception. "The usual reason for excepting to general pleadings is to obtain further information about and narrow the claims or defenses asserted by the adverse party. One who does not need such information to prepare for trial will probably permit the pleading to go unchallenged. . . ." *Kainer v. Walker*, 377 S.W.2d 613, 615 (Tex. 1964), *overruled and disapproved on other grounds, Burk Royalty Co. v. Walls*, 616 S.W.2d 911, 925 (Tex. 1981). The same logic applies to other general allegations, e.g., "breach," "default," etc. Would you permit the pleading to go unchallenged if there was a general allegation?

(2) *Substantive Defects.* Failure to plead a component or constituent element of a "cause of action" is considered a substantive pleading defect. As noted above, however, the defect can be waived. Moreover, waiver of the pleading defect does not obviate the requirement of proof of all component elements of a ground of recovery or defense at trial. In short, waiver of the pleading defect does not constitute an admission of an unpleaded element. *See* Tex. R. Civ. P. 301. What then is waived by failure to except? *See* Deffebach & Brown, *Waiver of Pleading Defects and Insufficiencies in Texas*, 36 Tex. L. Rev. 459 (1958).

(3) *Flawed Exceptions—Insufficient Specificity.* In interpreting the specificity requirement of Civil Procedure Rule 91, one court has stated that: "An objection should be sufficiently specific so that the opposing party may be informed of the defect and amend his pleadings accordingly, provided the defect be of such a nature that may be cured by an amendment. An objection to pleading made in compliance with the requirements of Rule 91 . . . is similar to a valid objection to the introduction of evidence. It must be informative so that it may be obviated if possible." *Ragsdale v. Ragsdale*, 520 S.W.2d 839, 842 (Tex. Civ. App.—Fort Worth 1975, no writ). Will it always be harmful (reversible) error for the trial court to sustain a general demurrer? See *Kelly v. Wright*, 144 Tex. 114, 188 S.W.2d 983, 986 (1945), in which the Texas Supreme Court held that even though error was committed in sustaining the demurrer, since it ". . . affirmatively appears from the sworn pleadings of petitioners that they cannot in good faith allege a cause of action . . . it would be a futile and useless procedure to reverse the judgment."

(4) *Improper Use of the Special Exception—the "Speaking Demurrer."* Traditionally, a demurrer, whether of the general or special variety, could not be used to set forth factual propositions not appearing in the pleading under attack in order to challenge the validity of the ground of recovery or defense. "Speaking demurrers were not permitted under the former nor is it permitted by present practice." *Ragsdale v. Ragsdale*, 520 S.W.2d 839, 843 (Tex. Civ. App.—Fort Worth 1975, no writ). On the hearing of the special exception, the allegations of the pleading under attack must be taken as true. *McFarland v. Reynolds*, 513 S.W.2d 620, 626 (Tex. Civ. App.—Corpus Christi 1974, no writ). An example of a "speaking" demurrer appears in *Travelers Indem. Co. v. Holt Mach. Co.*, 554 S.W.2d 12, (Tex. Civ. App.—El Paso 1977, no writ), a case involving an action on a fidelity bond. The bonding company denied coverage in its answer by a general denial and special pleas concerning exclusions from coverage under the provisions of the bond. On the date of trial, plaintiff's counsel filed an instrument, styled a "Motion to Strike" the special pleas, which stated:

> Defendant has never raised this asserted reason heretofore with its insured, the Plaintiff, as a reason why Defendant's liability to Plaintiff was denied under the policy, and Defendant now attempts to assert a new reason of its alleged non-liability. The law provides that where an insurance company states to an insured its grounds for denial of coverage or liability, that under the circumstances here, the insurance company waives its rights to assert new and additional grounds at trial. Because the new grounds now attempted to be asserted have never heretofore been given by the Defendant insurance company as grounds for refusing to defend or assume liability for Plaintiff's claim, the new grounds must be deemed waived and stricken. . .

What new "facts" are set forth in the so-called motion? Suppose all of the facts were set forth in the special pleas of the defendant; would the motion still speak? Could the new fact be set forth in an affidavit in support of a motion for summary judgment?

"If defendant must rely upon . . . extrinsic facts, he should plead those facts by a plea in bar, a plea in abatement or by a motion for summary judgment." *Ragsdale v. Ragsdale*, 520 S.W.2d 839, 843 (Tex. Civ. App.—Fort Worth 1975, no writ). Isn't a motion for summary judgment that is supported by summary judgment proof (e.g., affidavits) similar to a "speaking demurrer"?

Consider the following answer, which contains special exceptions, with a view toward determining whether or not they are in conformity with the Rules of Civil Procedure:

DEFENDANT'S ORIGINAL ANSWER

I.

Defendants specially except to said Petition in its entirety because nowhere in said Petition is it alleged that Defendants, or either of them, made any misrepresentations as to presently existing facts, and that in the absence of such allegations said Petition fails to state a ground of recovery upon which relief may be granted. And of this their special exception Defendants pray judgment of the court.

II.

Defendants specially except to Paragraph V of said Petition, wherein it is alleged that certain personal property of the Plaintiffs became damaged in the sum of Fifty Dollars ($50.00) from being mildewed, for the reason that said allegation is too vague, general and indefinite in that it does not specify the particular items of property which allegedly became damaged, and that therefore Defendants are not given fair notice of what Plaintiffs expect to prove under said allegation and are not enabled properly to prepare any defense thereto. And of this their special exception Defendants pray judgment of the court.

III.

Defendants specially except to Paragraph VI of said Petition, wherein it is alleged that Plaintiffs have undergone physical and mental suffering, for the following reasons:

(1) Any promises or representations (if any were made) that Defendants would repair or alter the construction of the floor of Plaintiffs' garage were made after the property had been sold and possession thereof had been delivered to Plaintiffs. Since said promises or

representations, if any, were made after the consummation of the sale of the property, Plaintiffs could not have relied upon the representations or promises as an inducement to enter into the contract and, therefore, any damages arising from the failure to perform said representations and promises cannot be recovered in a suit for breach of warranty. And of this their special exception Defendants pray judgment of the court.

(2) The only cause of action alleged by Plaintiffs in their Petition is one of breach of warranty in the sale of real estate, and damages for physical and mental suffering are not recoverable in an action for breach of warranty, the proper measure of damages being the difference between the value of the property as warranted and its value as actually conveyed. Therefore, said allegations as to physical and mental sufferings are immaterial and would be prejudicial to Defendants if read to the jury trying this cause, and said allegation should, therefore, be stricken from the Plaintiffs' Petition. And of this their special exception Defendants pray judgment of the court.

(5) *Presentation of the Special Exception.* The burden is on the party making the special exception to bring it to the attention of the court. *Castilleja v. Camero*, 402 S.W.2d 265, 268 (Tex. Civ. App.—Corpus Christi 1966), *aff'd on other grounds*, 414 S.W.2d 424, 425–428 (Tex. 1967). Despite the literal language of Rule 90, the exception should be presented before trial in order to avoid waiver. *See, e.g.,* Dallas Civ. Dist. Ct. R. 1.10 (requiring presentation of dilatory pleas and exceptions before trial).

(6) *Relationship to Summary Judgment Practice.* The summary judgment rule (Civil Procedure Rule 166a) provides that the movant may proceed "with or without supporting affidavits." On the one hand, the Supreme Court of Texas has indicated that summary judgment may be rendered on the pleadings when the petition does not state a legal claim or cause of action. *See Castleberry v. Goolsby* in § 5.04[B][2]. On the other hand, the Supreme Court has rejected the idea that a summary judgment is proper merely because the petition fails to adequately state a cause of action. In *Texas Dept. of Corrections v. Herring*, 513 S.W.2d 6, 9–10 (Tex. 1974), the petitioner had been granted summary judgment on the basis that the plaintiff failed to state a cause of action under the Texas Tort Claims Act "since no 'use of tangible property' was alleged as required. . . ." The Supreme Court affirmed the reversal of the summary judgement in the following terms:

> However, the question to be resolved is whether Herring, under the instant circumstances, may be denied the opportunity to amend his pleadings because they were attacked via a summary judgment motion instead of a special exception. It is recognized that a party may plead himself out of court; *E.g.*, the plaintiff may plead facts which affirmatively negate his cause of action. See for example Morris v. Hargrove, 351 S.W.2d 666 (Tex. Civ. App.—Austin 1961, writ ref'd n.r.e.), and Schroeder v. Texas & Pacific Ry. Co., 243 S.W.2d 261 (Tex. Civ. App.—Dallas 1951, no writ). In such instance it is proper to grant the defendant's motion for summary judgment. The instant case is clearly distinguishable however. Here, as we have held, Herring's pleadings were insufficient; that is, they failed to state a cause of action. The Department of Corrections leveled no special exceptions to Herring's pleadings and thus no opportunity to amend his pleadings to state a cause of action was afforded.
>
> Had the Department of Corrections filed special exceptions which were sustained by the court, Herring would have had an opportunity to amend as a matter of right. McCamey v. Kinnear, 484 S.W.2d 150 (Tex. Civ. App.—Beaumont 1972, writ ref'd n.r.e.). But only

after a party has been given an opportunity to amend after special exceptions have been sustained may the case be dismissed for failure to state a cause of action.

In the instant case Herring was precluded opportunity to amend his pleadings once the trial court had granted the motion for summary judgment. This court believes that the protective features of special exception procedure should not be circumvented by a motion for summary judgment on the pleadings where plaintiff's pleadings, as here, fail to state a cause of action. To do so would revive the general demurrer discarded by Rule 90, Texas Rules of Civil Procedure. McDonald, Summary Judgments, 30 Tex. L. Rev. 285, 297 (1951); Suggs and Stumberg, Summary Judgment Procedure, 22 Tex. L. Rev. 433, 439–40 (1944); 2 McDonald, Texas Civil Practice, § 7.18 at 205.

We agree with the court of civil appeals that the instant motion for summary judgment alleging that the plaintiff's pleadings fail to state a cause of action cannot take the place of a special exception. Accordingly, this case must be returned to the trial court. If the Department of Corrections files a special exception which is sustained and Herring still fails to state a cause of action, [footnote omitted] then the case may properly be dismissed.

*The judgment of the court of civil appeals is affirmed.*

Can you distinguish *Castleberry* from *Herring*? What was the substantive defect in *Castleberry*? Was the defect in *Castleberry* of more magnitude?

### [D] The Plea in Abatement

Although the plea is referred to in Civil Procedure Rule 85, its function is not explained by the rules of civil procedure. A plea in abatement does not challenge the merits of the plaintiff's cause of action.

## CURTIS v. GIBBS

*511 S.W.2d 263 (Tex. 1974)*

GREENHILL, Chief Justice.

In this original mandamus proceeding, we are called upon to settle a jurisdictional conflict between the 202nd District Court of Bowie County and the Third Domestic Relations Court of Dallas County. The conflict arises from a child custody dispute between the parents of Shawn Danelle Curtis and Shanna Michelle Curtis, ages 8 and 7, respectively. For simplification, the Relator Daniel Curtis, the children's father, will be referred to as "the father," and the respondent, Jerri Curtis Spencer, as "the mother." The 202nd District Court of Bowie County will be called "the Bowie court," and the Third Domestic Relations Court of Dallas County will be called "the Dallas court." The judge of the Dallas court, the Honorable Dan Gibbs, is the principal respondent herein.

The background of the case will be set out later herein. The immediate reasons for the mandamus proceedings are these:

The father and mother were divorced by a judgment of the Bowie court in 1971, and the mother was awarded custody of the children; but she was not to remove the children from Bowie and an adjacent county without permission. The parents and the children all lived in Bowie County at that time.

On January 18, 1974, the father filed a petition for change of custody in the Bowie court. Subsequently, on February 15, 1974, the mother filed a petition in the Dallas court to remove restrictions on her custody of the children and to increase the father's child support payments.

Judge Guy Jones, Judge of the Bowie court, issued a writ of attachment ordering that the children, who were in Dallas with their mother, be returned to Bowie County. Judge Dan Gibbs of the Dallas court issued an order suspending the writ of attachment and forbidding the sheriff of Dallas County from executing it. The father thereupon filed his original petition in this court seeking writs of mandamus and prohibition directing Judge Gibbs to abate the mother's suit in Dallas County and to vacate orders interfering with the Bowie County proceeding. After the filing of the petition in this court, the father has presented his plea in abatement in the Dallas court, and Judge Gibbs has overruled it.

We conclude that the Bowie court first acquired jurisdiction of the controversy between the parties and therefore retained dominant jurisdiction to the exclusion of other courts. Judge Gibbs had no right to interfere with the actions or orders of Judge Jones, or to take any other action with respect to the suit filed in Dallas except to sustain the plea in abatement and to dismiss the suit.

In order to discuss adequately the contentions raised by the parties in this court, it will be necessary to set out the history of this litigation in some detail. As noted, the father and the mother were divorced in Bowie County in 1971. The decree gave the mother custody of the children, subject to the restriction that she must not remove them from Bowie County, Texas, or Miller County, Arkansas, for a period longer than ten days without permission. In 1973, the mother filed a petition in the Bowie court seeking to expunge this restriction, but the petition was denied. No appeal was taken from that order.

In December of 1973, the mother, now remarried, determined to move to Dallas with her present husband. For reasons concerning which there is conflicting testimony, she left the children with the father in Bowie County. The father apparently believed that the mother intended to leave the children with him indefinitely.

On January 18, 1974, the father filed in Bowie County a suit to change custody, i.e., to obtain custody of the children. He did not immediately procure a citation in that suit; but on February 4, his counsel wrote to the mother requesting that she sign a waiver of citation.

On February 12, 1974, the mother took the children from the home of the father in Bowie County upon the representation that she was taking them for an overnight visit. In fact, she took them with her to Dallas and put them in school there. She has not since returned the children to the father, nor does she intend to do so.

This act precipitated a series of legal moves which has culminated in the present mandamus action. On February 13, 1974, the father procured a citation to the mother in his pending Bowie County suit. The following day, February 14, 1974, Judge Jones of the Bowie court issued his writ of attachment commanding the return of the children to Bowie County.

On February 15, 1974, the mother filed a new suit in Dallas County, asking for unrestricted custody and for increased child support. Judge Gibbs of the Dallas court issued a temporary restraining order forbidding the father from removing the children from Dallas County, and setting a hearing on a temporary injunction for February 22.

On February 22, the father appeared in the Dallas court and filed a Motion to Transfer, a Motion to Change Venue, and a Motion to Dismiss. The last of these motions alleged pendency of the prior action in Bowie County, but it was not sworn to as required by Rule 93, Texas Rules of Civil Procedure.

After a hearing, Judge Gibbs issued a temporary injunction forbidding removal of the children from Dallas County and "suspending" the Bowie County writ of attachment "until this court can determine the status of this matter in relation to the case pending in Bowie County."

On March 12, Judge Jones in Bowie County issued another writ of attachment for the children. Judge Tate McCain, sitting in Judge Gibbs's court in Dallas, issued an order directing the sheriff of Dallas County to suspend any Bowie County writ of attachment pending further orders of Judge Gibbs.

On March 18, the father filed a proper plea in abatement in the Dallas court, setting up the pendency of the Bowie County proceeding. On March 19, he filed his petition for writs of prohibition and mandamus in this court. When the petition came on for submission, on March 27, it appeared that the plea in abatement was pending in Judge Gibbs's court. Accordingly, we directed Judge Gibbs to pass upon the plea in abatement. Judge Gibbs held a hearing on the plea in abatement; and, on April 2, he overruled it.

. . . .

The general common law rule in Texas is that the court in which suit is first filed acquires dominant jurisdiction to the exclusion of other coordinate courts. Cleveland v. Ward, 116 Tex. 1, 285 S.W. 1063 (1926), Ex parte Lillard, 159 Tex. 18, 314 S.W.2d 800 (1958). Any subsequent suit involving the same parties and the same controversy must be dismissed if a party to that suit calls the second court's attention to the pendency of the prior suit by a plea in abatement. If the second court refuses to sustain a proper plea in abatement, or attempts to interfere with the prior action, this court has the power to act by mandamus or other appropriate writ to settle the conflict of jurisdictions. Cleveland v. Ward, *supra*; Wheeler v. Williams, 158 Tex. 383, 312 S.W.2d 221 (1958); Way & Way v. Coca-Cola Bottling Co., 119 Tex. 419, 29 S.W.2d 1067 (1930); Conn v. Campbell, 119 Tex. 82, 24 S.W.2d 813 (1930).

There is an exception to the rule of *Cleveland v. Ward* which the mother seeks to invoke in this case. It has been held that the plaintiff in the first suit may be guilty of such inequitable conduct as will estop him from relying on that suit to abate a subsequent proceeding brought by his adversary. V.D. Anderson Co. v. Young, 128 Tex. 631, 101 S.W.2d 798 (1937); Russell v. Taylor, 121 Tex. 450, 49 S.W.2d 733 (1932); Johnson v. Avery, 414 S.W.2d 441 (Tex. 1966).

In those cases, answers were filed to the pleas in abatement in the subsequent proceedings alleging that the plaintiffs in the prior suits (1) had filed suit merely to obtain priority, without a bona fide intention to prosecute the suit, and (2) had prevented their adversaries from filing the subsequent suits more promptly by fraudulently representing that they would settle. This court held that those contentions alleged facts which, if established, would estop the plaintiff in the prior action from asserting his plea in abatement. The court in which subsequent suit was filed, having jurisdiction to pass on the plea in abatement addressed to it, had jurisdiction to determine the fact issues raised by the allegations of fraud. If that court overruled the plea in abatement, then it, the subsequent court, had dominant jurisdiction of the controversy unless and until its action in overruling the plea in abatement was reversed upon appeal.

The mother contends that V.D. Anderson Co. v. Young controls the present case. She argues that relator's delay of twenty-six days, from January 18 to February 13, between filing suit in Bowie County and procuring issuance of citation indicated bad faith which should estop the father from relying on that suit to abate the mother's subsequent suit in Dallas County. We disagree. It is true that this court has held that a plea in abatement might properly be overruled where the party asserting it had delayed unreasonably in procuring a citation. Reed v. Reed, 158 Tex. 298, 311 S.W.2d 628 (1958). There, however, the period of delay was nearly fifteen months, and the second suit was filed and citation served therein before citation issued in the first suit. In the present case, the father waited only twenty-six days before procuring citation; and the evidence shows that, during that time, he attempted to obtain a waiver of service. Significantly, also, the mother did not file her suit during the period of delay. Even if the father had not filed the Bowie County suit until February 13, when he took out a citation, it would still have had priority over the mother's suit which was not filed until February 15.

V.D. Anderson Co. v. Young and its progeny depend upon the existence of an issue of fact in connection with the plea in abatement. We hold here, as a matter of law, that there was no want of diligence shown on the part of the father sufficient to raise an issue of estoppel so as to defeat his plea in abatement.

The mother further contends that the father waived his plea in abatement by the motions he filed in the Dallas court on February 22. We overrule this contention. The only issue raised in the father's motions, other than the pendency of a prior action, was that of venue. A plea of privilege contesting the venue did not waive a subsequent plea of prior action pending even when our rules required due order of pleading. Royal Petroleum Co. v. McCallum, 134 Tex. 543, 135 S.W.2d 958 (1940); Benson v. Fulmore, 269 S.W. 71 (Tex. Comm. App. 1925, judgm't adopted).

The mother points out that the father's original petition in the Bowie County suit was filed under the docket number of the 1971 divorce action. We hold that the docket number is irrelevant. Under the pre-Family Code law, the courts had continuing jurisdiction after final judgment to modify child support orders, but not child custody orders. Mistakes in filing under the wrong docket number were frequent. In that context, we have treated a petition which sets forth a cause of action within the jurisdiction of the court in which it is filed as effective to commence a new suit even though it was erroneously filed as a motion to modify judgment in a previous cause. Boney v. Boney, 458 S.W.2d 907 (Tex. 1970); Ex parte Lillard, 159 Tex. 18, 314 S.W.2d 800 (1958). We apply the same rule here.

The mother further asserts that venue properly lies in Dallas County under Texas Family Code § 11.04 because the legal residence of the children is in Dallas County where she now resides. This is also irrelevant. The Dallas court did not have jurisdiction to pass on the venue question in connection with a plea of prior action pending. The court which has dominant jurisdiction of the controversy, in this case the Bowie court, has exclusive jurisdiction to determine the venue question. Neal v. Texas Employers' Insurance Ass'n, 118 Tex. 236, 14 S.W.2d 793 (1929); Wheelis v. Wheelis, 226 S.W.2d 224 (Tex. Civ. App. 1950, no writ history). If the mother objects to the venue, her remedy is to file a motion to transfer in the Bowie court. Texas Family Code § 11.06(a).

We hold that the Bowie court has dominant jurisdiction of the parent-child relationship with respect to the children involved in this suit. It was the clear duty of Judge Gibbs to sustain the plea in abatement and to dismiss the mother's suit.

Accordingly, the following writs shall issue:

(1) A writ of prohibition directing Judge Gibbs to take no further action with respect to Cause No. 74-2063-DR/3, styled "In the Interest of Shawn Danelle Curtis and Shanna Michelle Curtis," pending in his court, except to dismiss the same, and

(2) a writ of mandamus directing Judge Gibbs to vacate any and all orders of his court which interfere with the exercise of the jurisdiction of the 202nd District Court of Bowie County in this matter.

---

**WYATT v. SHAW PLUMBING CO.**, 760 S.W.2d 245 (Tex. 1988). Wyatt sued Shaw Plumbing in Duval County, alleging fraud and violation of the Deceptive Trade Practices Act, in connection with Shaw's work on Wyatt's Duval County residence. Shaw promptly responded by suing Wyatt in Nueces County for the contract price, adding as a defendant an individual named Spear, who it claimed was Wyatt's agent. The Nueces County suit was tried first, even though later filed, and even though Wyatt filed two pleas in abatement. The Texas Supreme Court, per Justice Ray, reversed a judgment for Shaw Plumbing, holding that the pleas in abatement must be granted:

> When an inherent interrelation of the subject matter exists in two pending lawsuits, a plea in abatement in the second action must be granted. It is not required that the exact issues and all the parties be included in the first action before the second is filed, provided that the claim in the first suit may be amended to bring in all necessary and proper parties and issues. *See* 2 R. McDonald, *supra* p. 3, § 7.10, at 165. In determining whether an inherent interrelationship exists, courts should be guided by the rule governing persons to be joined if feasible and the compulsory counter-claim rule. *See* Tex. R. Civ. P. 39, 97(a).
>
> Shaw Plumbing should have brought its compulsory counter-claim on the contract in Wyatt's tort and DTPA suit in Duval County. If Shaw Plumbing had joined Morgan Spear, venue would have been proper in the Duval County suit filed by Wyatt, where the cause of action arose. [footnote omitted] If Wyatt had sued Shaw Plumbing in Nueces County, venue would have also been proper because Shaw's principal office was situated in Nueces County. However, since Wyatt filed suit first, he chose Duval County.
>
> It is well settled that when suit would be proper in more than one county, the court in which suit is first filed acquires dominant jurisdiction to the exclusion of other courts. *Curtis v. Gibbs*, 511 S.W.2d 263, 267 (Tex. 1974). . . .
>
> . . . .
>
> There are three exceptions to the rule . . . that the court where suit is first filed acquires dominant jurisdiction: 1) Conduct by a party that estops him from asserting prior active jurisdiction; 2) lack of persons to be joined if feasible, [footnote omitted] or the power to bring them before the court; and 3) lack of intent to prosecute the first lawsuit. *Young*, 128 Tex. at 636-37, 101 S.W.2d at 800–01; *see also Curtis*, 511 S.W.2d at 267. None of these exceptions applies in this case.
>
> . . . .

Justice Gonzalez, joined by Chief Justice Phillips and Justice Mauzy, dissented. The dissenters concluded, first, that venue would not have been proper in Duval County as to the additional defendant, Spear, under then-controlling venue laws. Thus, the suit in Duval County could not accommodate all "necessary and proper parties," and the ruling on the Nueces plea in abatement should have been discretionary with the trial judge. The dissenters also argued that an exception recognized in *Curtis v. Gibbs* should apply:

There is still another reason for why the Nueces County trial judge acted properly in refusing to abate the second suit. *Curtis v. Gibbs*, 511 S.W.2d at 267, stated the following exception to the general rule of dominant jurisdiction:

> [T]he plaintiff in the first suit may be guilty of such inequitable conduct as will estop him from relying on that suit to abate a subsequent proceeding brought by his adversary.

In this case, Wyatt filed this DTPA suit against Shaw Plumbing after having already received Shaw Plumbing's thirty day demand letter, and he did so without giving the thirty day notice required of him under the Deceptive Trade Practices-Consumer Protection Act. Tex. Bus. & Com. Code Ann. § 17.505 (Vernon 1987).

Wyatt's failure to give the required statutory notice enabled him to beat Shaw Plumbing to the courthouse and fix venue in Duval County. The proper remedy for a party's failure to give the required DTPA notice is ordinarily abatement rather than dismissal. *The Moving Company v. Whitten*, 717 S.W.2d 117 (Tex. App.—Houston [14th Dist.] 1986, writ ref'd n.r.e.); *see also Schepps v. Presbyterian Hospital*, 652 S.W.2d 934 (Tex. 1983). Under the circumstances of this case, I would hold that although a party's failure to comply with the statutory notice requirement will not result in dismissal, it is nevertheless a type of "inequitable conduct" that cannot be used as a vehicle for fixing venue. Thus, I would further hold that Wyatt's failure to give the required DTPA notice estops him from relying on his first-filed suit to abate the subsequent suit.

---

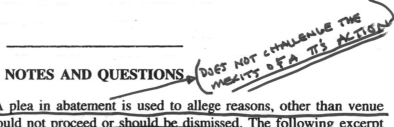

## NOTES AND QUESTIONS

(1) *The Plea in Abatement.* A plea in abatement is used to allege reasons, other than venue or jurisdiction, why the case should not proceed or should be dismissed. The following excerpt from Dorsaneo, *Texas Litigation Guide*, Ch. 70, *Answer*, discusses the use of the plea in abatement.

### W. Dorsaneo, TEXAS LITIGATION GUIDE

*§ 70.03[7] (1998)**

§ 70.03[7][a] Nature and Purpose

A plea in abatement may be directed to a wide range of issues; it may be based on any fact that is not in the petition and does not challenge venue or jurisdiction but that presents a reason to suspend or dismiss the case [*see* Austin Neighborhoods Coun. v. Bd. of Adjust., 644 S.W.2d 560, 565 n.17 (Tex. App.—Austin 1982, ref. n.r.e.)]. For example, a plea may be used to attack the petition based on matters such as the following:

1. The capacity of the parties [*see* Bluebonnet Farms v. Gibraltar Sav. Ass'n, 618 S.W.2d 81, 83 (Civ. App.—Houston [1st Dist.] 1981, ref. n.r.e.); *see also* Develo-Cepts, Inc. v. City of Galveston, 668 S.W.2d 790, 793 (Tex. App.—Houston [14th Dist.] 1984, no writ)—plea in abatement may be used to challenge standing to sue].

---

(2) A defect in the parties, such as a failure to join parties who should be joined if feasible [*see* T.R.C.P. 39; Spruill v. Spruill, 624 S.W.2d 694, 697 (Tex. App.—El Paso 1981, dis.); Good v. Stansberry, 240 S.W. 958, 960 (Civ. App.—Amarillo 1922, dis. w.o.j.)].

(3). The pendency of administrative proceedings [*see, e.g.,* Day v. State, 489 S.W.2d 368, 371 (Civ. App.—Austin 1972, ref. n.r.e.)].

(4) The pendency of another action involving the same parties and controversy [*see* Wyatt v. Shaw Plumbing Co., 760 S.W.2d 245, 247–248 (Tex. 1988); Curtis v. Gibbs, 511 S.W.2d 263, 267 (Tex. 1974); Schulz v. Schulz, 726 S.W.2d 256, 257 (Tex. App.—Austin 1987, no writ)].

A common use of the plea in abatement is to allege the action is premature—in other words, to assert that there is a condition precedent to bringing suit that has not yet occurred. For example, in a DTPA action, the complaining party must give written notice to the party complained of as a "prerequisite" to filing suit. *See* Tex. Bus. & Com. C. § 17.505(a). Similarly, written notice of a health care liability claim must be given prior to filing suit. *See* R.C.S. Art. 4590i, § 4.01(a). If such notices are not given before suit is filed, the defendant's response should be to file a plea in abatement.

(2) *Mechanics of the Plea.* The following excerpt from *Bryce v. Corpus Christi Area, Etc.*, 569 S.W.2d 496 (Tex. Civ. App.—Corpus Christi 1978, writ ref'd n.r.e), contains the discussion of the mechanics of the plea:

> A plea in abatement should not only show the grounds upon which the suit is improperly brought, but should also show how it should have been brought, and should always state facts, not conclusions of law. *State v. Goodnight*, 70 Tex. 682, 11 S.W. 119 (1888). When such a plea is sustained, the suit should not be dismissed until the plaintiff has been given a reasonable opportunity to amend, if it is possible to do so, and thereby remove the obstacle which defeated the suit initially filed.
>
> Even if the case is dismissed, it is revived upon the removal of such obstacle which prevented its further prosecution in the first instance. *Life Ass'n of America v. Goode*, 71 Tex. 90, 8 S.W. 639 (1888); *Humphrey v. National Fire Ins. Co.*, 231 S.W. 750 (Tex. Com. App. 1921, opinion adopted). The sufficiency of the plea must be tested by its own allegations, and cannot be assisted by allegations in any other plea. *Breen v. Texas and Pacific Railway Company*, 44 Tex. 302 (1875); 1 Tex. Jur. 2d, Abatement and Revival, § 71.

(3) *Verify It.* Many of the matters that would support abatement are matters which must be verified by affidavit pursuant to Civil Procedure Rule 93. *See, e.g.*, Tex. R. Civ. P. 93(4). Even if no provision of a rule of procedure or statute requires sworn pleadings, the plea is customarily verified. *See Sparks v. Bolton*, 335 S.W.2d 780, 785 (Tex. Civ. App.—Dallas, 1960, no writ). The sworn pleading or supporting affidavit is not evidence. The party presenting the plea must be prepared to introduce evidence at the hearing. *Continental Oil Co. v. P. P. G. Industries*, 504 S.W.2d 616, 621 (Tex. Civ. App.—Houston [1st Dist.] 1974, writ ref'd n.r.e.), *disapproved on other grounds, In re Smith Barney, Inc.*, 975 S.W.2d 593, 598 (Tex. 1998).

(4) *Plea to the Jurisdiction Distinguished.* Although both a plea in abatement and a plea to the jurisdiction are dilatory pleas, a plea to the jurisdiction is properly used to urge that the court lacks subject matter jurisdiction over the controversy, whereas a plea in abatement, if sustained, might merely require an abatement (temporary suspension) of the action until the obstacle to its further prosecution is removed or satisfied. *See Schulz v. Schulz*, 726 S.W.2d 256, 257 (Tex. App.—Austin 1987, no writ).

(5) *Comity.* What happens when the suits are filed in different states? "The mere pendency of an action in one state does not require the abatement of a suit in another state between the same parties and involving the same subject matter; however, as a matter of comity, it is customary for the court in which the later action is instituted to stay proceedings for a reasonable time." *Project Engineering USA Corp. v. Gator Hawk, Inc.*, 833 S.W.2d 716, 724 (Tex. App.—Houston [1st Dist.] 1992, no writ).

(6) *Time for Making a Plea in Abatement.* The rules are silent as to the time for making a plea in abatement. Although the plea is not subject to "due order" rules like special appearance motions and motions to transfer venue, case law supports a requirement that the plea must be urged within a reasonable amount of time after the grounds are apparent. The failure to timely urge a plea in abatement may result in waiver. *Howell v. Mauzy*, 899 S.W.2d 690, 698 (Tex. App.—Austin 1994, writ denied).

### [E] The General Denial

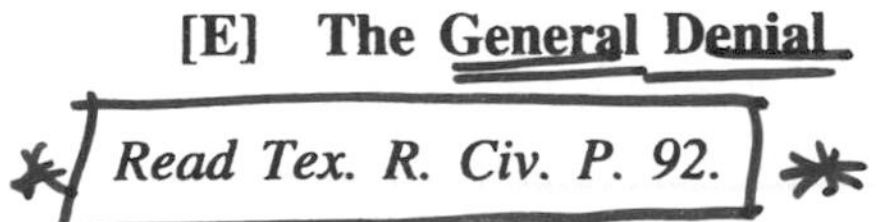

*Read Tex. R. Civ. P. 92.*

**BAHR v. KOHR**

*980 S.W.2d 723 (Tex. App.—San Antonio 1998, no pet. h.)*

ANGELINI, Justice.

Nature of the Case

Raymond D. Bahr, M.D. and his wife, Patricia Bahr (the "Bahrs") appeal a judgment entered in favor of Bradley D. Kohr and his wife, Vivian E.S. Kohr (the "Kohrs"). The Bahrs filed suit against the Kohrs under the Uniform Fraudulent Transfer Act. *See* Tex. Bus. & Com. Code Ann. § 24.001 *et seq.* (Vernon 1987). After a trial to the bench, the court entered a take-nothing judgment in favor of the Kohrs. In their issues presented, the Bahrs argue that the court erred in admitting parol evidence and evidence regarding separate property when only a general denial was filed. . . .

Factual Background

On or about March 7, 1987, the Bahrs obtained an agreed judgment in Maryland against Dutchman Hereford Co., and Mr. Kohr in the amount of $200,000. Mrs. Kohr was not a party to that suit. The agreed judgment provided for periodic payments and was secured by a ranch in Montana. On or about June 9, 1988, the Kohrs purchased 268 acres of real property in Gillespie County. The 268 acres was conveyed by a general warranty deed which stated that ten dollars and other good and valuable consideration was paid by grantees, Bradley D. Kohr and wife, Vivian E.S. Kohr. On January 31, 1994 the Bahrs recorded the Maryland judgment with the district clerk of Kerr County. Mr. Kohr executed a deed to Mrs. Kohr on February 10, conveying to her as her separate property, 68 acres of the Gillespie County property. The remaining 200 acres were claimed as a homestead by the Kohrs. The Bahrs then instituted this lawsuit, contending that the transfer of the 68 acres was a fraudulent conveyance because Mr. Kohr had no other assets to satisfy the Maryland judgment.

The only witnesses at trial were Mr. and Mrs. Kohr. The Kohrs testified that the money used to purchase the 268 acres came from Mrs. Kohr's separate property money market account. The trial court made the following relevant findings of fact and conclusions of law:

4. The Kohrs sold the New Jersey farm in 1987 for a considerable profit. The Kohrs partitioned the proceeds of the sale of the New Jersey farm between themselves as each other's separate property. Thereafter, the Kohrs kept their separate proceeds segregated from each other's accounts.

5. Brad Kohr used his proceeds from the sale of the New Jersey farm to pay separate business debts he had incurred.

6. Vivian Kohr deposited her share of the proceeds from the sale of the New Jersey farm into account number 0006421 at Flemington National Bank and Trust Company, in Flemington, New Jersey. The account was in Vivian Kohr's name only and was her separate property or her sole management community property.

The court found that the Gillespie County property was purchased from money deposited in Mrs. Kohr's separate account at Flemington National Bank. Thus, the 268 acres were Mrs. Kohr's separate property and a resulting trust was created in favor of Mrs. Kohr. The court found that the conveyance of the 68 acres to Mrs. Kohr from Mr. Kohr clarified the title to the property and was not a fraudulent conveyance.

. . . . In their second issue presented, the Bahrs allege that the court erred in admitting the Kohrs' evidence of separate property when only a general denial was filed and an affirmative defense of separate property or separate funds was not pled. . . .

. . . .

Affirmative Defense

In their second issue presented, the Bahrs allege that the trial court erred by admitting evidence regarding separate funds or separate property because the Kohrs filed only a general denial and failed to plead an affirmative defense of separate property or separate funds. Rule 94 of the Rules of Civil Procedure sets forth a list of specific affirmative defenses, which does not include separate property or separate funds. Tex. R. Civ. P. 94. However, Rule 94 also provides that any other matter constituting an avoidance or an affirmative defense must be specifically pled. An affirmative defense does not tend to rebut the factual propositions asserted in the plaintiff's case, but rather seeks to establish an independent reason why the plaintiff should not recover. *Gorman v. Life Ins. Co. of North America,* 811 S.W.2d 542, 546 (Tex. 1991), *cert. denied,* 502 U.S. 824, 112 S. Ct. 88, 116 L. Ed. 2d 60 (1991). "An affirmative defense is one of avoidance, rather than a defense in denial." *Id.* The Kohrs argue that separate property or separate funds are not affirmative defenses and their general denial put in issue the ownership of the Gillespie County property. "A general denial of matters pleaded by the adverse party which are not required to be denied under oath, shall be sufficient to put the same in issue." Tex. R. Civ. P. 92.

The Bahrs point to two cases for the proposition that separate property or separate funds are affirmative defenses. *See Weatherall v. Weatherall,* 403 S.W.2d 524 (Tex. Civ. App.—Houston 1966, no writ); *Grogan v. Henderson,* 313 S.W.2d 315 (Tex. Civ. App.—Texarkana 1958, writ ref'd n.r.e.). In *Weatherall,* the trial court awarded damages to a spouse who had contributed community funds to the other spouse's separate property. *Weatherall,* 403 S.W.2d at 525.The court found that the trial court erred in awarding the damages because the pleadings did not assert separate property or more importantly reimbursement. *Id.* at 526. The *Weatherall* case seems to focus more on reimbursement as the affirmative defense that must be plead in order to recover damages. In the *Grogan* case, the court acknowledged that the appellees did not plead separate property as an affirmative defense. *Grogan,* 313 S.W.2d at 320. However, the court found that evidence of separate funds was submitted to the jury without objection and therefore the issue was waived. *Id.* The case does not hold that separate property must be plead as an affirmative defense.

In this case, we do not find that separate property or separate funds are affirmative defenses. In order to prove that Mr. Kohr fraudulently conveyed the Gillespie County property, the Bahrs must necessarily prove the ownership of the property. An affirmative defense must be capable of defeating the plaintiff's cause of action even though the plaintiff proves its case. Without proving that Mr. Kohr owns the property, the Bahrs cannot prevail on their claim. The Kohrs' general denial properly raised the issue of ownership of the Gillespie County property. Thus, the court did not err in admitting evidence regarding separate funds or separate property. We overrule the second issue presented.

. . . .

---

## NOTES AND QUESTIONS

*See Tex. R. Civ. P. 93, 94, 95.*

(1) *General Denial.* No particular form of general denial is required. One traditional form is as follows:

> Defendant ______ [*name*], denies each and every, all and singular, the allegations in Plaintiff's Original Petition, and demands strict proof thereof.

(2) *Argumentative Denials, Alibis, and Converse Theories.* Would evidence that the event was the result of an "Act of God" or an "unavoidable accident" be admissible under a general denial?

(3) *Relationship to Other Defenses.* Suppose A sues B, who, according to A's allegations, guaranteed C's note to A under the terms of a written guaranty agreement. If B files a general denial, will B be able to introduce evidence that:

(a) The guaranty is without consideration;

(b) B did not sign the guaranty;

(c) C had paid the note?

### [F] Special Denials

#### [1] Conditions Precedent

*Read Tex. R. Civ. P. 54, 93.*

### DAIRYLAND COUNTY MUTUAL INS. CO. OF TEXAS v. ROMAN

*498 S.W.2d 154 (Tex. 1973)*

WALKER, Justice.

This is a suit to recover under the uninsured motorist provisions of an automobile liability insurance policy. On the controlling questions presented for decision, we hold: (1) that a minor insured is not necessarily excused from complying with the notice requirements of the policy throughout the time he is under the disability of minority; (2) that where the plaintiff avers generally that all conditions precedent have been performed and no attempt is made to raise an issue of notice except by a sham pleading, the defendant is not entitled to a reversal on the ground that the plaintiff failed to establish that a written notice condition was performed; and (3) that a release given without consideration does not constitute a "settlement" within the meaning of Exclusion (b) in Part IV of the policy.

The suit was brought by George Cruz Roman, Jr., against his insurer, Dairyland County Mutual Insurance Company of Texas, to recover damages for personal injuries sustained by him in an accident that occurred shortly after midnight on July 4, 1970, a few miles north of San Antonio on Interstate Highway 35. Plaintiff, who was accompanied by Mary Lou Valdez, was driving in a northerly direction on the highway when the muffler on his 1956 Chevrolet automobile became dislodged and began dragging on the pavement. He stopped his vehicle on the left side of the roadway and crawled under the car to remove the muffler. After he had completed his work and while he was emerging from under the car, it was struck in the rear by a vehicle driven by Ethan Odoms, an uninsured motorist. Immediately following this collision, an automobile driven by Charlene Hayes in a northerly direction in the right-hand lane of the highway was struck either by Odoms' car or by a piece of debris from the collision. Neither Miss Valdez nor Mrs. Hayes was injured, but plaintiff sustained personal injuries consisting primarily of a large laceration of the face and forehead.

At the time of the accident plaintiff was 19 years of age[1] and was the named insured in an automobile liability insurance policy issued by defendant. He is the only person named as an insured, and his automobile is the only vehicle described in the policy. The policy contained the standard uninsured motorist coverage and the usual general condition requiring written notice of an accident, occurrence or loss to be given by the insured to the company as soon as practicable. Five days after the accident, plaintiff's mother talked with the insurance agent in Uvalde through whom the policy had been acquired and informed him of the details of the accident and that Odoms was uninsured. Neither defendant nor any of its agents received written notice of the accident, however, until August 5, 1970, when defendant was served with the citation and the accompanying petition in this suit.

. . . .

The provision of the present policy requiring that notice of the accident be given the insurer as soon as practicable is a condition precedent to liability. In the absence of waiver or other special circumstances, failure to perform the condition constitutes an absolute defense to liability on the policy. Klein v. Century Lloyds, 154 Tex. 160, 275 S.W.2d 95; New Amsterdam Cas. Co. v. Hamblen, 144 Tex. 306, 190 S.W.2d 56. . . .

. . . .

This does not mean that defendant is entitled to a reversal of the trial court's judgment because of plaintiff's failure to obtain a finding that proper written notice was given within the time

[1] A statute adopted by the 63rd legislature and effective August 27, 1973, provides that, subject to one exception with respect to property held by a custodian under the Texas Uniform Gifts to Minors Act, Art. 5923—101, Vernon's Ann. Tex. Civ. St., a person who is at least 18 years of age shall have all the rights, privileges and obligations of a person who is 21 years of age. Acts 1973, 63rd Leg., p. —, ch.—.

provided in the policy. Plaintiff alleged generally that he had complied with all conditions precedent under the policy. Rule 54, Texas Rules of Civil Procedure, provides that a party who so avers performance of conditions precedent "shall be required to prove only such of them as are specifically denied by the opposite party." Defendant did not specifically deny performance by plaintiff of any condition precedent, but alleged that

> "Plaintiff has solely [sic] failed to comply with the conditions of said policy, to wit:" followed by a xerographic reproduction of the entire "Conditions" section of the policy. One of the seventeen numbered divisions of the section contains the notice requirement now urged by defendant, but many provisions in the section obviously have no bearing on the present case.

The Court of Civil Appeals recognized that defendant's pleading was not in compliance with Rule 54. It reasoned that while the trial court might have been authorized to disregard the pleading or require a repleader, this had not been done since evidence concerning notice was freely introduced and an issue relating to notice was submitted. There is also a footnote to the opinion suggesting that the deficiency in the pleading may have been waived by plaintiff's failure to except. We do not agree.

In Sherman v. Provident Am. Ins. Co., Tex. Sup., 421 S.W.2d 652, the insurance company had a somewhat similar pleading that set up all the policy exclusions. Until the case reached this Court, all parties proceeded on the assumption that the exclusions were properly raised by the pleadings. The Shermans, who were plaintiffs there, introduced no evidence to negative the exclusions, because it was their position that the company had the burden of proving that the loss fell within one or more of the exceptions. The trial court instructed a verdict for the company, and the Court of Civil Appeals affirmed. These judgments were affirmed by this Court with two members dissenting. The majority recognized that the company's pleading was in violation of Rule 94, T.R.C.P., but concluded that the trial court's judgment for the company could not be reversed on that ground since no question as to sufficiency of the pleading had been raised in the trial court or preserved on appeal. This holding was based, in some measure at least, on the provisions of Rule 90, T.R.C.P., which is quoted in the margin.[3]

Our situation here is the converse of that in *Sherman.* The trial court rendered judgment for plaintiff, and it is the defendant that seeks a reversal. Although evidence concerning notice was admitted and an issue concerning notice was submitted, the trial court overruled defendant's objections and requests that sought submission of an issue inquiring whether written notice containing the information required by the policy was given as soon as practicable. As the case reaches us then, and there being nothing to the contrary in the record, it may fairly be assumed that the trial court chose to disregard defendant's pleading that all policy conditions were breached. Be that as it may, there is no pleading specifically raising the written notice condition as required by Rule 54. In these circumstances defendant will not be heard to complain of the trial court's refusal to submit an issue thereon or of plaintiff's failure to obtain a finding or otherwise establish that the condition was performed. See International Sec. Life Ins. Co. v. Maas, Tex. Civ. App., 458 S.W.2d 484 (wr. ref. n.r.e.).

---

[3] Rule 90. Waiver of Defects in Pleading. General demurrers shall not be used. Every defect, omission or fault in a pleading either of form or of substance, which is not specifically pointed out by motion or exception in writing and brought to the attention of the Judge in the trial court before the instruction or charge to the jury or, in a non-jury case, before the rendition of judgment, shall be deemed to have been waived by the party seeking reversal on such account; provided that this rule shall not apply as to any party against whom default judgment is rendered.

. . . .

Defendant's other points of error have been considered, and in our opinion they do not warrant a reversal of the judgments below. The judgment of the Court of Civil Appeals is accordingly affirmed.

---

## NOTES AND QUESTIONS

(1) *Application of the Waiver Rule.* As the principal case points out, the literal language of Civil Procedure Rule 90 provides that a waiver of pleading defects resulting from the failure to point them out applies only to the party seeking reversal "on such account." Tex. R. Civ. P. 90. Under this wording, "the anomalous result is that waiver does not depend [entirely] upon the action of the parties, but upon the entry of judgment in the trial court." Deffebach & Brown, *Waiver of Pleading Defects and Insufficiencies in Texas*, 36 Tex. L. Rev. 459, 471 (1958). One court of appeals has held that this means that the plaintiff's failure to except to an improper verification for a denial was not a waiver of the defect when the defendant sought reversal after the trial court disregarded the defendant's defective pleading. *Davis v. Young Californian Shoes, Inc.*, 612 S.W.2d 703, 704 (Tex. Civ. App.—Dallas 1981, no writ); *cf. Federal Parts v. Robert Bosch Corp.*, 604 S.W.2d 367, 369–370 (Tex. Civ. App.—Fort Worth 1980, writ ref'd n.r.e.).

(2) *Special Exception Not Required in Response to a Defective Denial.* Another possible rationale for the conclusion that Roman was not required to specially except to the insurance company's defective pleading is the rule that complaint regarding a defective denial is not waived by a failure to specially except. *See Heusinger Hardware Co. v. Frost National Bank*, 364 S.W.2d 851, 856 (Tex. Civ. App.—Eastland 1963, no writ) ("As stated in Volume 2 McDonald, *Tex. Civil Practice*, pages 657, 658, 'Where the defective plea is in the nature of a denial, and if effective would impose on the pleader's opponent an additional onus of proof, the opponent is not required to except specially. The defective plea is insufficient to require him to make proof and he avoids a waiver of the pleading defect by objecting to any evidence tendered by the pleader or any questions on cross-examination, tending to raise the issue.' ")

(3) *Relevance of Rule 93.* Do the provisions of Civil Procedure Rule 93(12) have any relevance or application to the principal case?

(4) *Relationship to Rule 94.* Read the last sentence of Civil Procedure Rule 94. What function does it perform? How does it differ in application from Rule 54? Who does have the burden of proof on exceptions specified in an insurance contract? *See* Ins. C. § 21.58.

(5) *Statutory Notice as a Condition Precedent.* It should also be noted that a specific pleading of notice in satisfaction of a particular statutory prerequisite to recovery has been held subject to Civil Procedure Rule 54's imposition of a specific denial requirement. *Investors, Inc. v. Hadley*, 738 S.W.2d 737, 741 (Tex. App.—Austin 1987, no writ) (interpreting second sentence of Rule 54 as requiring specific denial of statutorily required notice of claim under Deceptive Trade Practices Act when plaintiffs specifically pleaded notice even though plaintiffs did not "generally aver" performance of all conditions precedent to recovery.)

### [2] Verified Denials

*Read Tex. R. Civ. P. 93.*

## BAUER v. VALLEY BANK OF EL PASO

*560 S.W.2d 520 (Tex. Civ. App.—El Paso 1977, no writ)*

OSBORN, Justice.

This is an appeal from a judgment based upon a promissory note and a guaranty agreement. We affirm.

The Valley Bank of El Paso brought suit upon a promissory note of Gateway Investment Company and a written guaranty agreement signed on the same date as the note by Carlton C. Freed and L. F. Bauer, officers of Gateway. Only Mr. Bauer appeals from the judgment in favor of the Bank. In his answer, Mr. Bauer pled a general denial, and also affirmatively alleged that at the time the guaranty was signed, the President of the Bank represented that no reliance would be placed on the guaranty agreement. The note and guaranty agreement were received into evidence with proof that no payment had ever been made on the note. Mr. Bauer testified that he was told he would never be called upon to honor the guaranty. That testimony was contradicted by witnesses for the Bank. In the only issue answered by the jury, they found that the Bank did not make a representation to Mr. Bauer that he would not be guarantying the debt of Gateway.

The Appellant presents six points of error. The first three complain of the entry of judgment for Appellee when there was no special issue requested or answered favorably to the Bank, other than on the defensive issue of misrepresentation. The contention is presented that there should have been issues submitted to the jury as to whether or not there was a meeting of the minds on the guaranty agreement, whether or not there was a binding contract, and whether or not there was any consideration for the agreement.

Appellant did not deny the execution of the guaranty agreement, nor did he assert that the agreement was without consideration. Without a sworn plea under Rules 93(h) and (j), Tex. R. Civ. P.,* those issues were not before the trial Court. Since execution of the guaranty agreement was not an issue, it was only necessary that the agreement be introduced into evidence to prove up its terms. *American Fiber Glass, Inc. v. General Electric Credit Corporation*, 529 S.W.2d 298 (Tex. Civ. App.—Fort Worth 1975, writ ref'd n.r.e.); *American Petrofina Company of Texas v. Bryan*, 519 S.W.2d 484 (Tex. Civ. App.—El Paso 1975, no writ); *VanHuss v. Buchannan*, 508 S.W.2d 412 (Tex. Civ. App.—Fort Worth 1974, writ dism'd). In *Safway Scaffolds Company of Houston v. Sharpstown Realty Company*, 409 S.W.2d 883 (Tex. Civ. App.—Waco 1966, no writ), the court said:

> ". . . In the absence of a verified denial of the execution by defendants or by their authority of the written instruments upon which the pleading is founded, under Rule 93(h), Texas Rules of Civil Procedure, the instruments were received in evidence as fully proved. *Newborn v. Spiro*, Tex. Civ. App., 387 S.W.2d 769; *Ship Ahoy v. Whalen*, Tex. Civ. App., 347 S.W.2d 662; *Butler v. Merchants Nat. Bank of Mobile*, Tex. Civ. App., 325 S.W.2d 229; *Manning v. Barnard*, Tex. Civ. App., 277 S.W.2d 160, writ ref. n.r.e. *See Collins v. F. M. Equipment Co.*, 162 Tex. 423, 347 S.W.2d 575."

* Rules 93(h) and (j) are now embodied in Rules 93(7) and (9).

The agreement as received into evidence fully proved the indemnity obligation of Mr. Bauer. There being no issue raised on execution, consideration, or ambiguity, there was no issue to present to the jury, other than the defensive issue of misrepresentation and that issue was decided adversely to Appellant. The first three points of error are overruled.

Appellant next asserts that since only a defensive issue was submitted to the jury, the trial Court thereby placed the burden of proof for the entire case on the Appellant, who was a Defendant in the trial Court. This is not so at all. The guaranty agreement, when received into evidence, established the Appellant's liability, subject to defensive issues, and Appellee thereby met its burden of proof. Appellant's argument with regard to the right to open and close where it had the burden on the only issue submitted has not been preserved by proper assignment in the amended motion for new trial and may not be considered. *Wagner v. Foster*, 161 Tex. 333, 341 S.W.2d 887 (1960). Point of Error No. IV is overruled.

The Appellant next contends that the net effect of the trial Court's charge was to grant Appellee an instructed verdict and that such was error. The Appellee did, in fact, make a motion for instructed verdict at the close of the evidence, which the trial Court overruled. The Court correctly overruled such motion because there was a defensive issue to be submitted to the jury. But there was no fact issue as to the Bank's case as pled and proved on the guaranty agreement and the Court was not required to submit any issue on a fact which was not in dispute. Rule 277, Tex. R. Civ. P.; *Wright v. Vernon Compress Company*, 156 Tex. 474, 296 S.W.2d 517 (1956); *Burbridge v. Rich Properties Inc.*, 365 S.W.2d 657 (Tex. Civ. App.—Houston 1963, no writ); *Hall v. Texas State Bank*, 298 S.W.2d 188 (Tex. Civ. App.—Austin 1957, writ ref'd n.r.e.). Point of Error No. V is overruled.

. . . .

*The judgment of the trial Court is affirmed.*

---

## NOTES AND QUESTIONS

(1) *Sworn Denial of Execution of an Instrument.* What is the effect of a proper sworn denial of execution? The denial increases the onus of proof that is placed on the pleader's opponent. *See* Tex. R. Civ. P. 93(7) ("In the absence of such a sworn plea, the instrument shall be received in evidence as fully proved"). What if the denial is defective? *See Heusinger Hardware Co. v. Frost National Bank*, 364 S.W.2d 851 (Tex. Civ. App.—Eastland 1963, no writ).

(2) *Authentication of Documents.* What is the usual way for authenticating documents? The easiest way is through the request for admissions. Read Tex. R. Civ. P. 198. In *Bauer*, if Bauer had made a sworn denial, Valley Bank would have sent a request for admissions asking him to admit the genuineness of the guaranty agreement. If Bauer had denied the genuineness or had sent a response detailing the reasons why he could neither admit nor deny it, Valley Bank then would have had to produce evidence in accordance with Tex. R. Evid. 901.

(3) *Strict Compliance Required.* Civil Procedure Rule 93(7) requires a sworn denial of an allegation that an instrument was signed by the authority of the party who is being sued on the instrument. Consider the following excerpt from *Baylor University Medical Center v. Van Zandt*,

620 S.W.2d 707 (Tex. Civ. App.—Dallas 1981, no writ) (discussing former Rule 93(h), now Rule 93(7)):

> [A]ppellant pleaded that its suit was on a written contract executed by appellee or an authorized agent of appellee. Appellee did not deny the execution of the contract or the allegation that he or his authorized agent signed it, as required by Tex. R. Civ. P. 93(h). Consequently, appellee has admitted that the contract was signed by him or by his authority. *Public Service Life Ins. Co. v. Copus*, 494 S.W.2d 200 (Tex. Civ. App.—Tyler 1973, no writ). Appellee contends, however, that since it is apparent from the face of the record that neither he nor his authorized agent signed the contract, it was not necessary to deny appellant's allegation under oath as required by rule 93(h). We do not agree. It is not apparent from the face of the record that neither appellee nor *his authorized agent* signed the contract sued upon. Therefore, rule 93(h) applies to this case and, because it was not complied with, appellant established all the requirements . . . [for venue] . . . by its pleadings and its tender into evidence of the contract.

If a sworn denial is properly made, the burden is on the opposing party to show that there was the requisite authority to sign; it is not enough to show the authenticity of the instrument. A brief review of the law of agency will demonstrate that proving authority is generally a more difficult task than proving authenticity.

---

## NOTE ON DENIALS OF "CAPACITY"

One of the most baffling provisions in Civil Procedure Rule 93 is the subsection requiring a verified denial of liability in the "capacity" in which a defendant is sued. One court of appeals has said that "capacity" as used in subsections (1) and (2) of the rule does not relate to the merits of the cause of action or defense but only to the standing of a party to assert or defend the action before the court. *Conrad v. Artha Garza Co.*, 615 S.W.2d 238, 240 (Tex. Civ. App.—Dallas 1981, no writ). While this approach makes some sense, other courts required defendants to deny individual or personal liability. *See Lee v. O'Leary*, 742 S.W.2d 28, 33 (Tex. App.—Amarillo 1987, no writ); *see also McCoy v. Nelson Utilities Services, Inc.*, 736 S.W.2d 160, 165 (Tex. App.—Tyler 1987, writ ref'd n.r.e.) ("Neither Johnny McCoy nor George McCoy verified that portion of his pleading denying liability in his individual capacity. Therefore, the defense of limited individual liability as provided [by statute] was not properly raised in the trial court and therefore [is] not before us on appeal."). *Cf. John Chezik Buick v. Friendly Chevrolet Co.*, 749 S.W.2d 591 (Tex. App.—Dallas 1981, writ denied) ("Rule 93(2) refers to mistaken legal capacity and does not require a party to allege in a verified pleading that he is not a party to the contract"). The Texas Supreme Court has held that Civil Procedure Rule 93(2) "requires that a verified plea be filed anytime there is a question concerning a plaintiff's or defendant's right to bring suit or be sued in *whatever* capacity he is suing. . . . Its application is not limited to cases of representative capacity only. The rule means just what it says." Pledger v. Schoellkopf, 762 S.W.2d 145, 146 (Tex. 1988).

---

## NOOTSIE v. WILLIAMSON COUNTY APPRAISAL

*925 S.W.2d 659 (Tex. 1996)*

SPECTOR, Justice.

Following the voters' passage of a constitutional amendment calling upon the Legislature "[t]o promote the preservation of open-space land," the Legislature defined ecological laboratories as property promoting "farm and ranch purposes." The question here is whether the Legislature acted constitutionally. The trial court ruled that the ecological laboratory provision is constitutional. The court of appeals reversed. 905 S.W.2d 289, 292. We hold that the statute is constitutional and therefore reverse the judgment of the court of appeals.

### I

The Texas Constitution commands that "[t]axation shall be equal and uniform" and that real property "shall be taxed in proportion to its value." Tex. Const. art. VIII, §§ 1(a), 1(b). This Court has long interpreted "value" as "market value." *See Lively v. Missouri, K. & T. Ry. Co.,* 102 Tex. 545, 120 S.W. 852, 856 (1909). In 1978, the voters added the following amendment to the Constitution:

> To promote the preservation of open-space land, the legislature shall provide by general law for taxation of open-space land devoted to farm or ranch purposes on the basis of its productive capacity and may provide by general law for taxation of open-space land devoted to timber production on the basis of its productive capacity. The legislature by general law may provide eligibility limitations under this section and may impose sanctions in furtherance of the taxation.

Tex. Const. art. VIII, section 1-d-1(a). The Legislature then defined "open-space land" subject to productive capacity taxation as

> land currently devoted principally to agricultural use to the degree of intensity generally accepted in the area and that has been devoted principally to agricultural use or to production of timber or forest products for five of the preceding seven years or *land that is used principally as an ecological laboratory by a public or private college or university.*

Tex. Tax Code § 23.51(1) (emphasis added).

Nootsie, Limited, owns land subject to ad valorem taxation by both the Travis County and Williamson County Appraisal Districts. As stipulated at trial, the property qualifies under section 23.51(1) because the University of Texas, Baylor University, the University of Houston, and St. Edward's University have used the land as an ecological laboratory since 1967. The Travis County Appraisal District has granted Nootsie's application for productive capacity taxation as an ecological laboratory every tax year since 1979, and the Williamson County Appraisal District granted Nootsie's application from 1979 until 1989. In 1990, however, the Williamson County Appraisal District ("district") denied Nootsie's application, claiming that the ecological laboratory provision exceeds the legislative mandate contained in article VIII, section 1-d-1(a) of the Texas Constitution. The district's appraisal review board agreed.

Nootsie then filed an appeal for judicial review. The district answered and filed a counterclaim and third-party petition naming the Attorney General of Texas as a third-party defendant. The district sought a declaratory judgment that section 23.51(1) violates the Constitution because of the inclusion of ecological laboratories as open-space land.

The trial court ruled that section 23.51(1) is constitutional. After raising the issue of the district's capacity to file its counterclaim *sua sponte*, the court of appeals held that the district could bring its challenge and that section 23.51(1) violates the Constitution. *See* 905 S.W.2d at 291–93.

II

A plaintiff has *standing* when it is personally aggrieved, regardless of whether it is acting with legal authority; a party has *capacity* when it has the legal authority to act, regardless of whether it has a justiciable interest in the controversy. *See Hunt v. Bass,* 664 S.W.2d 323, 324 (Tex. 1984); *Pledger v. Schoellkopf,* 762 S.W.2d 145, 146 (Tex. 1988). Nootsie argues that the district had neither standing nor capacity to file its counterclaim. We disagree with Nootsie's standing argument and do not reach its capacity argument.

Although Nootsie never raised standing at trial, it may raise the issue on appeal for the first time because standing implicates the trial court's subject matter jurisdiction. *See Texas Ass'n of Bus. v. Texas Air Control Bd.,* 852 S.W.2d 440, 443–44 (Tex. 1993). We have noted that "[t]he general test for standing in Texas requires that there '(a) shall be a real controversy between the parties, which (b) will be actually determined by the judicial declaration sought.' " *Id.* at 446 (quoting *Board of Water Engineers v. City of San Antonio,* 155 Tex. 111, 283 S.W.2d 722, 724 (1955)).

Nootsie argues that as a political subdivision of the State, the district has no inherent vested rights protected by the Constitutions of Texas and the United States. *See Deacon v. City of Euless,* 405 S.W.2d 59, 62 (Tex. 1966). This argument misses the mark because the district does not contend that the statute violates constitutional rights belonging to the district. Instead, the district asserts an interest because it is charged with implementing a statute that it believes violates the Texas Constitution. This interest provides the district with a sufficient stake in this controversy to assure the presence of an actual controversy that the declaration sought will resolve. *See Nueces County Appraisal Dist. v. Corpus Christi People's Baptist Church, Inc.,* 860 S.W.2d 627, 630 (Tex. App.—Corpus Christi 1993) (holding that an appraisal district is the proper party to challenge the constitutionality of a tax statute), rev'd on other grounds, 904 S.W.2d 621 (Tex. 1995); *cf. Robbins v. Limestone County,* 114 Tex. 345, 268 S.W. 915, 917 (1925) (holding that county and road districts can sue the state highway commission on the ground of the invalidity of statutes).

We do not reach the merits of Nootsie's argument that the district acted without legal authority when it contested the constitutionality of the statute. After the district filed its counterclaim and third-party petition against the state, neither Nootsie nor the Attorney General raised the capacity issue. Unlike standing, an argument that an opposing party does not have the capacity to participate in a suit can be waived. Texas Rule of Civil Procedure 93(1) requires a party to file a verified pleading if it argues that "the plaintiff has not legal capacity to sue or that the defendant has not legal capacity to be sued." We have not hesitated in previous cases to hold that parties who do not follow rule 93's mandate waive any right to complain about the matter on appeal. *See, e.g., Roark v. Stallworth Oil & Gas, Inc.,* 813 S.W.2d 492, 494 (Tex. 1991); *Pledger,* 762

S.W.2d at 146. Here, Nootsie first questioned the district's capacity in its briefing before this Court. Therefore, Nootsie has waived its complaint about capacity.

III

Nootsie argues next that section 23.51(1) does not violate the Texas Constitution and that the court of appeals erred by finding otherwise. We agree.

. . . .

[The opinion of Justice Gonzalez, concurring and dissenting, is omitted.]

### [G] Affirmative Defenses

*Read Tex. R. Civ. P. 94.*

## ECKMAN v. CENTENNIAL SAV. BANK

*784 S.W.2d 672 (Tex. 1990)*

HIGHTOWER, Justice.

Respondent's motion for rehearing is overruled. The opinion of October 26, 1988 is withdrawn and the following is substituted.

This case under the Deceptive Trade Practices—Consumer Protection Act (DTPA), Tex. Bus. & Com. Code Ann. § 17.41 *et seq.* (Vernon 1987), involves the issues of whether the plaintiff has the burden to plead and prove the inapplicability of the $25,000,000 exception to business consumer status under section 17.45(4) of the DTPA. A jury returned a verdict in favor of the petitioners, Carl E. Eckman, Jr., James E. Nicholson, M.D., and Gary Hutchinson, M.D. (hereinafter "the Eckman group") on their DTPA claim. The trial court, however, rendered judgment non obstante veredicto favoring respondent Centennial Savings Bank (hereinafter "Centennial"). The court of appeals affirmed. 742 S.W.2d 826. We reverse and remand this cause to the court of appeals.

. . . .

. . . Centennial filed special exceptions, generally asserting that the Eckman group had "failed to plead that they are consumers within the meaning of the DTPA." However, Centennial's special exceptions did not mention the exclusion concerning business consumers that have assets of $25,000,000 or more. In their amended pleadings, the Eckman group specifically alleged that "they are business consumers within the meaning of section 17.45(4)(10), Texas Deceptive Trade Practices—Consumer Protection Act, and sought to acquire goods or services during the course of the transaction."

After a jury verdict in favor of the Eckman group on their DTPA claim,[3] the trial court rendered judgment *non obstante veredicto* in favor of Centennial. The trial court apparently reasoned that

[3] At trial, Centennial introduced financial statements of the Eckman group and Mr. Jackson indicating their gross assets as follows:

| | | |
|---|---|---|
| Eckman | — | $10,146,036 as of 10/84 |
| Nicholson | — | $6,891,185 as of 10/84 |
| | — | $7,302,645 as of 8/85 |
| Hutchison | — | $5,174,935 as of 10/84 |
| | — | $6,368,698 as of 9/85 |

since the joint venture claimed gross assets in excess of $25,000,000, the Eckman group lacked standing as consumers under the DTPA. [footnote omitted] The court of appeals affirmed, holding that Centennial was entitled to judgment n.o.v. because the Eckman group failed to prove that their assets were less than $25,000,000 [footnote omitted] and therefore did not qualify as a "business consumer" under the DTPA.

A Plaintiff must be a "consumer" to maintain a private action under the DTPA. *Knight v. International Harvester Credit Corp.*, 627 S.W.2d 382, 388 (Tex. 1982). The DTPA defines a consumer as:

> . . . an individual, partnership, corporation, this state, or a subdivision or agency of this state who seeks or acquires by purchase or lease, any goods or services, *except* that the term does not include a business consumer that has assets of $25 million or more, or that is owned or controlled by a corporation or entity with assets of $25 million or more.

Tex. Bus. & Com. Code Ann. § 17.45(4) (Vernon 1987) (emphasis added). "Business consumers" are defined to include individuals, partnerships, or corporations who seek or acquire by purchase or lease, any goods or services for commercial or business use. Tex. Bus. & Com. Code Ann. § 17.45(10) (Vernon 1987). Thus, business consumers, whether individuals or businesses, with assets of $25,000,000 or more are excluded from DTPA coverage. This case raises the narrow issue of whether the plaintiff must plead and prove the inapplicability of the $25,000,000 exception or whether the defendant has the burden to plead and prove the applicability of the $25,000,000 exception as an affirmative defense.

. . . .

Treating the $25,000,000 exception as an affirmative defense promotes efficiency in DTPA litigation. The comparative likelihood that a certain situation may occur in a reasonable percentage of cases should be considered when determining whether a fact should be allocated as an element of the plaintiff's case or to the defendant as an affirmative defense. *See* 2 R. McDonald, *Texas Civil Practice in District and County Courts,* § 7.34.1 (rev. 1982). Obviously, most litigants do not have assets of $25,000,000 or more. Requiring every DTPA plaintiff to prove that he is not a multimillionaire would be an inefficient and uneconomical use of judicial resources. Section 17.44 requires that the DTPA "shall be liberally construed and applied to promote its underlying purposes, which are to protect consumers . . . and to provide efficient and economical procedures to secure such protection." Tex. Bus. & Com. Code Ann. § 17.44 (Vernon 1987). *See Jim Walter Homes, Inc. v. Valencia,* 690 S.W.2d 239, 242 (Tex. 1985); *Joseph v. PPG Industries, Inc.*, 674 S.W.2d 862, 865 (Tex. App.—Austin 1984, writ ref'd n.r.e.). Requiring the defendant to plead and prove the $25,000,000 exception as an affirmative defense is consistent with the statutory mandate "to provide efficient and economical procedures" to protect consumers. Adopting this procedure best serves the interests of judicial efficiency and economy.

Since in most cases the claimant does not have assets of $25,000,000 or more, the burden of raising and negating the applicability of the $25,000,000 exception to business consumer status

---

Jackson — $6,345,740 as of 5/84

Based upon the financial statements, the total gross assets of Mr. Eckman, Dr. Nicholson and Dr. Hutchison ranged from $22,212,156 to $23,817,379 and the total gross assets of Mr. Eckman, Dr. Nicholson, Dr. Hutchison and Mr. Jackson ranged from $28,557,896 to $30,163,119. However, since the joint venture and Mr. Jackson are not parties in this case and the total gross assets of Mr. Eckman, Dr. Nicholson and Dr. Hutchison are less than $25,000,000, we reserve the question of whether Mr. Eckman, Dr. Nicholson and Dr. Hutchison are individual "business consumers" who are subject to the $25,000,000 DTPA limitation individually and not as a group.

should not be cast upon the plaintiff. The result reached by the court of appeals in this case is unduly prejudicial toward a business consumer in a DTPA suit because the claimant would be required to plead and prove both that he is a consumer under section 17.45(10) and that he does not fall within the $25,000,000 exception to business consumer status under section 17.45(4). If the plaintiff should fail to plead specifically the inapplicability of the exception and fail to produce evidence that he falls outside the exception, the defendant would be entitled to a directed verdict. Barring a plaintiff's recovery because he did not raise and prove the inapplicability of an exception to standing would be unfair, especially if the plaintiff had succeeded in pleading and proving all other elements necessary for recovery under the DTPA.

Under our present holding—treating the $25,000,000 exception as an affirmative defense—evidence concerning the plaintiff's financial status is irrelevant unless the issue is raised by the defendant. However, once the issue is raised, information concerning the plaintiff's assets and financial status will be discoverable to determine the applicability of the $25,000,000 exception.[6] This court has long recognized the danger that a jury will be prejudiced by evidence of a party's financial status. *See Texas Co. v. Gibson,* 131 Tex. 598, 116 S.W.2d 686, 687 (1938). As a result, Texas courts have been cautious concerning evidence of a party's wealth. *See Coca Cola Bottling Co. v. Tannahill,* 235 S.W.2d 224, 226 Tex. Civ. App.—Fort Worth 1950, writ dism'd); *Wilmoth v. Limestone Products Co.*, 255 S.W.2d 532, 534 (Tex. Civ. App.—Waco 1953, writ ref'd n.r.e.); *Upjohn Co. v. Petro Chemicals Suppliers, Inc.*, 537 S.W.2d 337, 340 (Tex. Civ. App.—Beaumont 1976, writ ref'd n.r.e.); *First National Bank of Marshall v. Beavers,* 619 S.W.2d 288, 289 (Tex. Civ. App.—Texarkana 1981, writ ref'd n.r.e.); *First National Bank of Amarillo v. Bauert,* 622 S.W.2d 464, 469 (Tex. App.—Amarillo 1981, no writ); *Murphy v. Waldrip,* 692 S.W.2d 584, 588 (Tex. App.—Fort Worth 1985, writ ref'd n.r.e.). Consequently, whenever possible, trial courts and parties should attempt to resolve the applicability of the $25,000,000 exception prior to trial. For the reasons explained herein, we hold that the defendant has the burden to plead and prove the applicability of the $25,000,000 exception to business consumer status as an affirmative defense.

. . . .

Accordingly, we reverse and remand the cause to the court of appeals.

---

## ECHOLS v. BLOOM

*485 S.W.2d 798 (Tex. Civ. App.—Houston [14th Dist.] 1972, writ ref'd n.r.e.)*

BARRON, Justice.

This suit was brought by appellant Robert Echols for specific performance of an alleged earnest money contract for the sale of a tract of realty. In a trial before the court judgment was rendered in favor of appellees denying the relief sought. The trial court filed requested findings of fact and conclusions of law. In these the court characterized the instrument in question as a contract containing an "option offer" and it found that (1) the option offer was without valuable

[6] Litigants subjected to overly intrusive or frivolous discovery requests are adequately protected by the rules of civil procedure.

consideration and was therefore unenforceable, (2) that the offer of sale was withdrawn prior to acceptance, (3) that the entire instrument was procured by fraudulent representations, (4) that the parties contracted while operating under a mutual mistake of fact as to the time for execution of the instrument and (5) that the description of the realty to be conveyed was impermissibly vague.

Appellant's recourse to this Court seeks to reverse the judgment adverse to him by attacking each of the findings recounted above. We think that the issues of consideration for the option and withdrawal of the offer prior to acceptance are dispositive.

The contract of sale included the following paragraph:

> (2) Sellers are to execute this contract as an offer to Buyer and Buyer is to have the right to accept or reject such offer for fourteen (14) days from the date hereof and Seller agrees that such offer shall be irrevocable and shall be binding upon Sellers. If Buyer notifies Sellers within said fourteen (14) day period of Buyer's intention to accept such offer this contract shall be placed with the American Title Company with instructions to proceed forthwith.

This provision embodies a formal offer to sell real estate to appellant, with a concurrent promise by appellees to keep the offer open for two weeks. In other words, two transactions appear—an ordinary offer to sell and a contract not to revoke that offer or to impede performance by conveyance to a third person.

It is axiomatic that to be valid and enforceable a contract establishing an option must be supported by consideration. 13 Tex. Jur. 2d Contracts Sec. 38 (1960).[1] Often the consideration is, as here, a sum of money to be regarded as a parcel of the total purchase price in the event the option-holder elects to buy. If an option is contained in a contract which itself is supported by a sufficient consideration, no independent consideration for the option itself need appear. Colligan v. Smith, 366 S.W.2d 816 (Tex. Civ. App.—Fort Worth 1963, writ ref'd n.r.e.). However, if no consideration in fact passes, the option giver has power of revocation just as in the case of other revocable offers. Granger Real Estate Exch. v. Anderson, 145 S.W. 262, 264 (Tex. Civ. App.—Austin 1912, no writ), and cases cited; 13 Tex. Jur. 2d Contracts Sec. 39 (1960); 1A Corbin, Corbin on Contracts Sec. 263 (1963); 58 Tex. Jur. 2d Vendor and Purchaser Sec. 61 (1964).

The instrument presently before us was signed and dated July 11, 1969. By its terms appellant was given the power of accepting appellees' offer for fourteen days thereafter, that is, up to and including July 25, 1969. The only possible consideration for such option is the sum of $500 earnest money recited as deposited with a title company as escrow agent "upon the execution hereof." The record conclusively demonstrates that the $500 was not tendered and accepted until July 25, 1969, the last day of the option period. Thus, for the preceding thirteen days of that period no consideration passed in support of the option agreement. As documented above, the absence of consideration rendered the option unenforceable by appellant during that time period. Although consideration for a contract of sale can serve as consideration for an included option agreement as well, we have found no case involving options within sales contracts which enforced the option and held the offer of sale irrevocable from its inception where the contract consideration did not pass until the option period was virtually extinguished.

Appellant contends that, despite the above, appellees failed to file a verified plea of failure of consideration as required by Tex. R. Civ. P. 93(j).* However, appellant failed to except to

---

[1] Cf. Tex. Bus. & Comm. Code Ann. sec. 2.205 (Tex. UCC 1967), V.T.C.A., dealing with personalty.

* Rule 93(j) is now embodied in Rule 93(9).

the nonverification of appellees' pleadings and thus waived his objection. Tex. R. Civ. P. 90; Smith v. Walters, 468 S.W.2d 889 (Tex. Civ. App.—Dallas 1971, no writ). It is true that, under Tex. R. Civ. P. 94, failure of consideration must be affirmatively pleaded. We think appellees' first amended answer probably contains a sufficient affirmative plea of failure of consideration. In paragraph I appellees alleged that appellants "in fact, had not deposited such sum ($500)," and in the succeeding paragraph they alleged that, because of false representations that $500 had been paid, appellees "were under the impression that there was consideration for the Contract. . . ." Even so, appellant has waived any complaint under Rule 94 by failing to object. Rather, the issue of failure of consideration appears to have been tried by consent. Tex. R. Civ. P. 67.

. . . .

Inasmuch as no enforceable option agreement was consummated, appellees were empowered to revoke their offer of sale prior to appellant's acceptance. Because we are not disposed to disturb the trial court's finding that no acceptance preceded revocation by Dr. Bloom, the trial court's judgment is affirmed.

---

### NOTES AND QUESTIONS

(1) *Affirmative Defenses.* Who has the burden of persuasion on an affirmative defense? Isn't the essential quality of an affirmative defense that even if all that the opposing pleader says is true, there is an independent reason why the ground of recovery (or defense) is defeated?

(2) *Verified Affirmative Defenses.* What is the logic behind requiring a verification of some affirmative defenses? Is the "onus of proof" shifted by a verified avoidance? Is the failure to verify waivable at the pleading stage?

(3) *Failure vs. Want of Consideration.* Do you think that the option was initially supported by consideration? What was it? Why did it fail?

## § 5.06 Amended and Supplemental Pleadings

### [A] Amended Pleadings

*Read Tex. R. Civ. P. 62–67.*

Amended pleadings are liberally permitted to be filed "at such times as not to operate as a surprise to the opposite party; provided, that any pleadings, responses or pleas offered for filing within seven days of the date of trial or thereafter . . . shall be filed only after leave of the judge is obtained." *See* Tex. R. Civ. P. 63. *See also Lee v. Key West Towers, Inc.* 783 S.W.2d 586, 588 (Tex. 1989). The judge may alter the time period in a pretrial order. *See* Tex. R. Civ. P. 63, 66. In several counties, the period has been modified by local rules of procedure.

The function of an amended pleading, as distinguished from a supplemental petition or answer, is to add something to or withdraw something from what had been previously pleaded to correct what had been incorrectly stated by the party making the amendment, or to plead new matter that constitutes an additional claim or defense permissible to the action. *See* Tex. R. Civ. P. 62.

An amended pleading supersedes its predecessor. When a party seeks to amend a pleading within seven days of the date of trial or during the trial (*See* Tex. R. Civ. P. 66) the objecting party must make a complaint to the effect that the new matter constitutes a "surprise" (*See* Tex. R. Civ. P. 63) or otherwise "satisfy the court that the allowance of such amendment would prejudice him in maintaining his action of defense upon the merits." *See* Tex. R. Civ. P. 66. Apparently, in order to test the sincerity of the objecting party, case law requires that party to seek a continuance to complain on appeal that the trial court erred in permitting the amendment. *Myers v. King,* 506 S.W.2d 705 (Tex. Civ. App.—Houston [1st Dist.] 1974, writ ref'd n.r.e.).

A rule of procedure provides that written pleadings, before the time of submission, are necessary to the submission of jury questions, as is provided in Civil Procedure Rules 277 and 279. *See* Tex. R. Civ. P. 67. Rule 67 has been construed to mean that in a case tried to a jury, an opposing party need not have objected to the introduction of testimony as a prerequisite to making a complaint concerning the absence of an "issue" from the opposing party's pleadings. In other words, an issue is not tried by implied consent of the parties in a jury case merely because no objection to the admissibility of the testimony concerning the issue was made at the proper time. *See* Tex. R. Civ. P. 67. On the other hand, if no objection is made to the testimony at the proper time, the party who introduced it would ordinarily be entitled to a trial amendment pursuant to Civil Procedure Rule 66 because the "objecting party" would ordinarily be unable to "satisfy the court that the allowance of such amendment would prejudice him. . . ." Tex. R. Civ. P. 66.

In a non-jury case, because there is no submission of jury questions, it appears that "trial by implied consent" may occur merely by virtue of the failure to object at the time the testimony, not otherwise raised by the pleadings of the offering party, introduced without objection. *See Gadd v. Lynch,* 258 S.W.2d 168 (Tex. Civ. App.—San Antonio 1953, writ ref'd). For an excellent discussion of the relationship of the trial amendment rule (Tex. R. Civ. P. 66) to the rule governing amendments to conform issues tried without objection (Tex. R. Civ. P. 67), *see* Deffebach & Brown, *Waiver of Pleading Defects,* 36 Tex. L. Rev. 459 (1958).

---

## BURNETT v. FILE

*552 S.W.2d 955 (Tex. Civ. App.—Waco 1977, writ ref'd n.r.e.)*

JAMES, Justice.

This is an appeal by Plaintiff Burnett from a take nothing judgment rendered against him on a jury verdict, in a suit for personal injuries resulting from an automobile rear-end collision. We affirm the judgment of the trial court.

Plaintiff-Appellant O. J. Burnett sued Defendant-Appellee Virgil E. File for personal injuries allegedly sustained by Plaintiff-Appellant growing out of an automobile accident wherein Defendant-Appellee File allegedly rearended Plaintiff-Appellant Burnett.

Trial was to a jury, which found that Plaintiff-Appellant Burnett was not injured as a result of the collision, in Answer to Special Issue No. 1. Pursuant to said verdict, the trial court entered judgment that Plaintiff-Appellant take nothing.

Plaintiff-Appellant asserts error on the part of the trial court (1) in refusing Plaintiff leave to file a trial amendment, (2) in refusing to submit the definition of "injury" as submitted by Plaintiff, (3) in submitting an erroneous definition of "injury" to the jury, (4) in conditionally submitting Special Issues Nos. 2 through 14 on a positive finding of Special Issue No. 1, and (5) that the jury's answer to Special Issue No. 1 is factually insufficient. We overrule all of Plaintiff's points of error and affirm.

The basis of this suit is an alleged rearend collision that occurred on March 9, 1974, near the intersection of Irving and Hampton Boulevards in Dallas County. Plaintiff was stopped for traffic in front of him at that intersection when he was allegedly hit from the rear by the automobile driven by the Defendant. Plaintiff's Original Petition in this case was filed on July 31, 1974. In October 1974, Defendant filed its answer in the case. Plaintiff filed his Second Amended Original Petition on March 20, 1976, which is the pleading he went to trial upon. In none of said pleadings did Plaintiff allege any aggravation of any pre-existing condition. In other words, in said pleadings Plaintiff alleged personal injuries growing out of the accident of March 9, 1974.

The case proceeded to trial on April 12, 1976, and the jury returned a verdict on April 13, 1976, finding that Plaintiff sustained no injury in the accident. After Plaintiff had rested his case and near the end of the trial, Plaintiff's counsel "served notice" that he intended to file a Trial Amendment of some sort. Plaintiff did tender a Trial Amendment some time after both parties had closed and prior to the submission of the court's charge to the jury. By said Trial Amendment the Plaintiff alleged for the first time that on the occasion of the March 9, 1974, accident in question, he was suffering from a "pre-existing disease or condition" which was "incited, accelerated, and/or aggravated" by the accident in question. Defendant objected to the filing of said Trial Amendment alleging surprise, and because the case was tried on the theory of an original injury, whereupon the trial court denied Plaintiff leave to file such Trial Amendment.

Plaintiff-Appellant contends the trial court abused its discretion in denying him leave to file such Trial Amendment. We do not agree.

The filing of a Trial Amendment is within the sound discretion of the trial court and unless the trial court clearly abuses that discretion no reversible error is shown. Rule 66, Texas Rules of Civil Procedure; *Victory v. State* (Tex. 1942) 138 Tex. 285, 158 S.W.2d 760, 763.

The instant case was pleaded by Plaintiff and tried upon the theory that Plaintiff sustained an original injury as the result of the accident of March 9, 1974. It was after both sides had closed and before the court's charge was submitted to the jury that Plaintiff sought leave from the trial court to file the Trial Amendment in question. Had same been granted, it would have changed the entire nature and complexion of the lawsuit. Moreover, there was no explanation by the Plaintiff as to why he was not aware of the "aggravation" basis of his Trial Amendment sooner. In the language of our Supreme Court: "to require the trial court to permit amendments such as the one filed in this case would disrupt orderly procedure and lead to frequent interruptions and interminable delay in concluding expensive jury trials. McDonald's Texas Civil Practice; vol. 2, page 737." *Westinghouse Electric Corp. v. Pierce* (Tex. 1954) 153 Tex. 527, 271 S.W.2d 422; *King v. Skelly* (Tex. 1970) 452 S.W.2d 691. Here, the Defendant had the right to assume that the case made by the pleadings and testimony was the case and the only case he was called upon to defend and to prepare his defense accordingly. See *Westinghouse, supra,* and the cases cited in support of this proposition, 271 S.W.2d on page 424; *Erisman v. Thompson* (Tex. 1943)

140 Tex. 361, 167 S.W.2d 731; *Safety Casualty Co. v. Wright* (Tex. 1942) 138 Tex. 492, 160 S.W.2d 238.

Under the record before us, we cannot say the trial court abused its discretion in denying leave to Plaintiff to file the Trial Amendment.

Special Issue No. 1 as submitted to the jury inquired:

"Do you find from a preponderance of the evidence that O. J. Burnett was injured as a result of the occurrence on March 9, 1974?

"You are instructed that a person is "injured" if he receives damage or harm to the physical structure of the body.

"Answer 'we do' or 'we do not.' To this issue the jury answered 'we do not.' "

Then the court instructed the jury that "if you have answered the above issue 'we do' then you will answer Issues Numbers 2, 4, 6, 8, 10, 12, and 14; otherwise, do not answer them." In this connection, Issues Nos. 2 through 14 were issues inquiring into primary negligence (and proximate cause) of Defendant together with a damage issue.

Plaintiff requested that the trial court define "injury" to the jury as follows:

"You are instructed that a person is 'injured' if he receives damage or harm to the physical structure of the body. Such damage or harm includes such diseases and infections as naturally result therefrom, and the incitement, acceleration, or aggravation of any previously existing disease or condition by reason of such damage or harm to the physical structure of the body."

The trial court refused to submit Plaintiff's proffered definition of "injury," which refusal Plaintiff asserts as error. As stated above, Plaintiff had no pleadings to support such a definition.

However, Plaintiff strongly urges that the issue of "aggravation" was tried by implied consent on the part of the Defendant, under the provisions of Rule 67, Texas Rules of Civil Procedure. We do not agree. The record clearly establishes the Defendant's objection to the Trial Amendment and requested instructions on aggravation as hereinabove set out. In *Harkey v. Texas Employers Ins. Assn.* (Tex. 1948) 146 Tex. 504, 208 S.W.2d 919, our Supreme Court held that although the Defendant did not object to the testimony relative to an issue but did object to its submission because it was not pleaded, it could not be held that the issue was tried by consent. In that case the Defendant offered no objection to testimony on an essential issue, but it did object to its submission because it was not pleaded. The Supreme Court held that the issue could not be presumed to have been tried by consent and that submission of such unpleaded essential issue over proper objection constituted reversible error. Also see *Missouri-Kansas-Texas Railroad Co. v. Franks* (Tex. Civ. App. Eastland CA 1964) 379 S.W.2d 415, NRE.

In the case at bar, under the record before us, the rule enunciated in *Harkey* applies, and it cannot be said that the issue of aggravation was tried by implied consent.

. . . .

Finding no reversible error in the record we affirm the trial court's judgment.

AFFIRMED.

---

## GREENHALGH v. SERVICE LLOYDS INS. CO.

*787 S.W.2d 938 (Tex. 1990)*

MAUZY, Justice.

The issue in this case is whether a trial court abuses its discretion by allowing a post-verdict amendment increasing the amount of damages in Plaintiff's pleadings to conform to the amount awarded by the jury when Defendant presents no evidence of surprise or prejudice. We hold that under Texas Rules of Civil Procedure 63 and 66, a trial court must allow a trial amendment that increases the amount of damages sought in the pleadings to that found by the jury unless the opposing party presents evidence of prejudice or surprise.

Plaintiff Greenhalgh and Service Lloyds Insurance Company (Service Lloyds), his workers' compensation carrier, agreed to a settlement of Greenhalgh's workers' compensation claim. However, Service Lloyds refused to pay Greenhalgh's medical expenses as required by the settlement. Greenhalgh subsequently filed this bad-faith insurance claim against Service Lloyds. The jury found in favor of Greenhalgh on each of his theories of recovery: breach of the duty of good faith and fair dealing, bad-faith insurance practices, gross negligence, negligence, and intentional infliction of emotional distress. Greenhalgh pleaded for $10,000 in actual damages and $100,000 in punitive damages; the jury awarded $8,000 in actual damages and $128,000 in punitive damages.

Because Greenhalgh had pleaded for only $100,000 in punitive damages, he requested leave to amend his pleadings to conform the amount of damages to that found by the jury and supported by the evidence. In its responsive motion, Service Lloyds alleged that the amendment was prejudicial because Service Lloyds had relied on the $100,000 amount in Plaintiff's pleadings in preparing for trial and in deciding whether to settle the case. The trial court allowed the post-verdict amendment. The court of appeals held that the trial court abused its discretion in allowing the amendment and reduced the punitive damages to $100,000.

The court of appeals reasoned that "because a defendant receives notice of the upper limit of punitive damages only by way of pleadings, it is an abuse of discretion to allow a post-verdict trial amendment increasing punitive damages when proper objections are made." 771 S.W.2d 688, 697. We disagree. The holding of the court of appeals ignores the mandates of the procedural rules regarding amendment of pleadings during trial. *See* Tex. R. Civ. P. 63 and 66.

Not only did the trial court not abuse its discretion in granting the amendment, it would have been an abuse of discretion if the trial court had refused the amendment. Under Rules 63 and 66 a trial court has no discretion to refuse an amendment unless: 1) the opposing party presents evidence of surprise or prejudice, Tex. R. Civ. P. 63 and 66; *Hardin v. Hardin,* 597 S.W.2d 347, 350–51 (Tex. 1980) (Campbell, J., concurring); *see Food Source, Inc. v. Zurich Ins. Co.,* 751 S.W.2d 596, 599 (Tex. App.—Dallas 1988, writ denied); or 2) the amendment asserts a new cause of action or defense, and thus is prejudicial on its face, and the opposing party objects to the amendment. *Hardin v. Hardin,* 597 S.W.2d 347 (Tex. 1980). The burden of showing prejudice or surprise rests on the party resisting the amendment. *Patino v. Texas Employers Insurance Association,* 491 S.W.2d 754, 756 (Tex. Civ. App.—Austin 1973, writ ref'd n.r.e.).

Because Greenhalgh's amendment raised no new substantive matters and because there was no showing of surprise or prejudice by Service Lloyds, the trial court properly granted leave to file the amendment. [footnote omitted]

Service Lloyds relies on appellate court holdings that a trial court abuses its discretion in allowing a post-verdict amendment increasing damages to conform to the verdict. *Burk Royalty Co. v. Walls,* 596 S.W.2d 932, 938 (Tex. Civ. App.—Fort Worth 1980, *aff'd on other grounds,* 616 S.W.2d 911 (Tex. 1981); *Winn-Dixie Texas, Inc. v. Buck,* 719 S.W.2d 251, 255 (Tex. App.—Fort Worth 1986, no writ). [footnote omitted] We disapprove these holdings because they directly conflict with Rules 63 and 66.

TEXAS RULES OF CIVIL PROCEDURE 63 and 66

It is well established that a party may amend its pleading after verdict but before judgment, *American Produce & Vegetable Co. v. J.D. Campisi's Italian Restaurant,* 533 S.W.2d 380, 386 (Tex. Civ. App.—Tyler 1975, writ ref'd n.r.e.). Rule 63 states:

> Parties may amend their pleadings, . . . as they may desire by filing such pleas with the clerk at such time as not to operate as a surprise to the opposite party; provided, that any amendment offered for filing within seven days of the date of trial *or thereafter,* . . . shall be filed only after leave of the judge is obtained, *which leave shall be granted by the judge unless there is a showing that such amendment will operate as a surprise* of the opposite party.

(Emphasis added).

The language of Rule 63 makes it clear that without a showing of surprise the trial court must grant leave for a party to file the amendment when requested within seven days of trial or thereafter. Thus, a party's right to amend under Rule 63 is subject only to the opposing party's right to show surprise. *Hardin v. Hardin,* 597 S.W.2d 347, 349 (Tex. 1980). However, the trial court may conclude that the amendment is on its face calculated to surprise or that the amendment would reshape the cause of action, prejudicing the opposing party and unnecessarily delaying the trial. *Id.* [footnote omitted]

An amended pleading that changes only the amount of damages sought does not automatically operate as surprise within the contemplation of Rule 63. *See Drury v. Reeves,* 539 S.W.2d 390, 394 (Tex. Civ. App.—Austin 1976, no writ). A party opposing an amendment increasing damages must present evidence to show that the increase resulted in surprise. Because Service Lloyds presented no evidence of surprise, the trial court properly allowed the amendment as required under Rule 63.

Rule 66 further confirms the propriety of the trial court's granting leave for Greenhalgh to file his amendment. Rule 66 provides in part:

> If during the trial any defect, fault or omission in a pleading, either of form or substance, is called to the attention of the court, the court may allow the pleadings to be amended and *shall do so freely* when the presentation of the merits of the action will be subserved thereby and the objecting party fails to satisfy the court that the allowance of such amendment would prejudice him in maintaining his action or defense upon the merits.

(Emphasis added). In *Vermillion v. Haynes,* 147 Tex. 359, 215 S.W.2d 605, 609 (Tex. 1948), this Court held that the trial court abused its discretion in denying a trial amendment filed after the close of evidence in a nonjury trial. Rule 66 "directs that the court shall 'freely' allow an amendment" when it subserves the merits of the case and the opposing party fails to show prejudice. *Id.*

The "defect" that Greenhalgh sought to cure in his amendment was to conform his pleadings to the evidence and jury findings on punitive damages. Service Lloyds failed to complain in the trial court that the evidence did not support the jury's finding on punitive damages—nor has it made this argument on appeal. We have held that when objections carry neither suggestion nor hint that the opposing party was in any manner surprised or prejudiced, both the spirit and the intent of Rule 66 require that the amendment be permitted. *Id.* Thus the trial court properly allowed the amendment under Rules 63 and 66.

We hold that in the absence of a showing of surprise or prejudice by an opposing party, a trial court must grant leave to a party to amend his or her pleadings to conform the amount of damages requested to that awarded by the jury. We reverse the judgment of the court of appeals and affirm the judgment of the trial court.

[The concurring opinion of Justice Hecht is omitted.]

---

## NOTES AND QUESTIONS

(1) *The Basis for the Amendment.* Consider the following excerpt from *Westinghouse Electric Corp. v. Pierce,* 271 S.W.2d 422, 424–425 (Tex. 1954):

> We do not regard Vermillion v. Haynes, 147 Tex. 359, 215 S.W.2d 605, as controlling here. In that case, trial was before the court without a jury. It involved a claim for rents. After the close of the testimony and before judgment, the defendant tendered a trial amendment setting up for the first time the defense of limitations. This court held that the trial judge abused his discretion in refusing to allow the amendment. There the amendment sought only to assert a defense in law to facts already established, while here the effort was to change the fact basis of the suit; there the trial was before the court, the new defense offered requiring only a judicial decision of a new law question not theretofore in the suit, while here trial was to a jury, the new matter being entirely factual and requiring an entire reshaping of the defense on the new facts.

Similarly, the recovery of prejudgment interest does not require any evidentiary proof at trial. It simply requires a mechanical application of the proper formula by the trial court after the verdict has been returned. "This being the case, [the] trial amendment could not have caused any surprise or prejudice. . . . We hold the trial court's refusal of the amendment was arbitrary and unreasonable and therefore an abuse of discretion." *Benavidez v. Isles Constr. Co.,* 726 S.W.2d 23, 26 (Tex. 1987).

(2) *Need for Post-Verdict Amendments.* A post-verdict amendment must be made when damages awarded by the jury exceed the amount alleged by the plaintiff. In the absence of such a request, the judgment must conform to the pleadings. *Picon Transp., Inc. v. Pomerantz,* 814 S.W.2d 489, 490 (Tex. App.—Dallas 1991, writ denied).

(3) *Amending Defective Denials.* A party is entitled to amend its answer to verify its denial less than seven days before trial. The Texas Supreme Court discussed this situation in *Chapin & Chapin v. Texas Sand & Gravel*, 844 S.W.2d 664, 665 (Tex. 1992):

By adding a verified denial in this case, Chapin did not change a single substantive issue for trial. Chapin's position throughout had been that it has already paid for all it got. The only change was procedural: Texas Sand would have been obliged to rebut Chapin's substantive defense and could not simply insist [on] judgment on the pleadings. If Texas Sand had relied upon the absence of a verified denial to the extent that it was unprepared to proceed to trial and would thus have been prejudiced by Chapin's amendment, it would have been entitled to a continuance. However, Texas Sand's counsel stated that he was prepared to prove that all deliveries had been made or accounted for and that the amount claimed was owed. In these circumstances . . . we conclude that the trial court's refusal to allow Chapin to verify its denial was an abuse of discretion.

### [B] Supplemental Petitions and Answers

*Read Tex. R. Civ. P. 69, 78, 82, 83.*

The function of supplemental petitions and answers is limited. They are used to respond to "new matter" contained in the last preceding pleading of the adverse party. *See* Tex. R. Civ. P. 69.

---

## ROYAL TYPEWRITER CO. v. VESTAL

*572 S.W.2d 377 (Tex. Civ. App.—Houston [14th Dist.] 1978, no writ)*

COULSON, Justice.

Appellant, Royal Typewriter Company, plaintiff below, appeals from a take nothing judgment following a nonjury trial in a suit on a contract against appellees Vestal, Middlebrook, and U. S. Land Development Company, defendants below. Appellant conceded at argument that Middlebrook is not a party to this appeal. We affirm.

On December 5, 1972, a contract was executed by Royal, purportedly with U. S. Land Development Company, for the rental of a copying machine. The agreement was signed by one "Julian Holsten" whose title, as written on the agreement, was "Sales Mgr." The copier was installed on December 8, 1972. On February 21, 1975, Royal filed suit against Vestal, Middlebrook, and U. S. Land Development, alleging that "the Defendants did . . . make and execute" the rental agreement, and that payments totaling $1,254.20 were due and not paid. Royal thus asserted damages resulting from breach of a contract with defendants.

Defendants, in addition to a general denial, pled that they did not execute the contract in question and were not indebted to Royal. Royal filed no additional pleadings. At argument Royal conceded that the actual contract had not been proved and that ratification was the only issue upon which they rely in their appeal to bind defendants. Royal had requested additional findings of fact and conclusions of law on the issue of ratification. The trial judge refused to make any additional findings or conclusions on that issue. We conclude that Royal was not entitled to such additional findings, and cannot prevail upon the theory of ratification in this appeal because ratification was not pled.

The Supreme Court of Texas has held that ratification is a plea in avoidance and thus is an affirmative defense which, in the absence of trial by consent, is waived if not affirmatively pled under Rule 94, Texas Rules of Civil Procedure. *Petroleum Anchor Equipment, Inc. v. Tyra,* 419 S.W.2d 829, 835 (Tex. Sup. 1967). The record before this court does not indicate that the issue of ratification was tried by consent. Rule 94 requires that "[i]n pleading to a preceding pleading, a party shall set forth affirmatively . . . any . . . matter constituting an avoidance or affirmative defense." The rule itself is not limited to "defendants" but applies to all parties. When a plaintiff desires to rely on an affirmative matter in avoidance of a defense pled in the defendant's answer, he must allege it in a supplemental petition, unless it is already put in issue by the petition. Rule 94 thus imposes on the plaintiff the requirement that he plead any matter in avoidance on which he intends to rely. *Sustala v. North Side Ready-Mix Concrete Co.,* 317 S.W.2d 64 (Tex. Civ. App.—Houston 1958, no writ); *LoBue v. United Services Planning Association,* 467 S.W.2d 574 (Tex. Civ. App.—Fort Worth 1971, writ dism'd); McDonald, Texas Civil Practice, Vol 2, 1970, § 8.02 p. 319.

In the case before us, under these principles, once the defendants pled that they did not execute the contract, it then became incumbent upon Royal to file a supplemental pleading asserting ratification if it intended to rely upon that as a defense to defendants' denial of the contract. The purpose of requiring the pleading of affirmative defense is to put the other party on notice of the matters to be relied on and to enable him to ascertain what proof he may need to meet such defenses. In this case defendants asserted, and the evidence supported the conclusion, that they did not make the contract. The contract was signed by a person not a party to the suit. Royal did not establish any actual or apparent authority of Holsten to execute the contract. Thus the contract itself did not bind defendants. After the trial was concluded, and judgment handed down, Royal attempted to obtain a finding on ratification. The trial judge properly refused to make such a finding, and Royal has no basis on which to persuade this court to make a finding on the affirmative defense of ratification which it neglected to plead. The judgment of the trial court is affirmed.

Affirmed.

---

## NOTES AND QUESTIONS

(1) *Need for Supplemental Petitions.* Civil Procedure Rule 94 is entitled "Affirmative Defenses." When is it necessary for a plaintiff to assert a "matter constituting an avoidance or affirmative defense?" Read Tex. R. Civ. P. 82. Suppose A sues B on a promissory note. B files a general denial and alleges that A executed a written release and attaches it to her answer. If A contends that she did not sign the release, must A file a supplemental petition? If A contends that the release was without consideration, must A file a supplemental petition? If A contends the release was procured by fraud, must A file a supplemental petition?

(2) *Comparison to Federal Rule.* It is worth noting that the federal rules take a different approach. Federal Rule of Civil Procedure 8(d) expressly provides that "[a]verments in a pleading to which no responsive pleading is required or permitted shall be taken as denied or avoided." Federal Rule 7 requires a "reply to a counterclaim denominated as such" but otherwise disallows a reply to an answer.

## § 5.07 Specialized Pleading Forms

### [A] The Sworn Account Petition

*Read Tex. R. Civ. P. 185.*

### AIRBORNE FREIGHT CORP. v. CRB MARKETING, INC.

*566 S.W.2d 573 (Tex. 1978)*

PER CURIAM.

This is a suit on a sworn account brought by Airborne Freight Corporation against CRB Marketing pursuant to Tex. R. Civ. P. 185. Attached to the plaintiff's petition were copies of invoices for services rendered and an affidavit from plaintiff's collection manager that the claim was just and true, that it was due, and that all just and lawful credits had been allowed. The defendant CRB answered only by an unsworn denial. At trial, Airborne Freight introduced evidence bearing only on the issue of reasonable attorney's fees. After a nonjury hearing, the county court at law rendered judgment in favor of Airborne Freight for $1,063.12, representing the principal debt, attorney's fees, and interest. Upon CRB's appeal, the court of civil appeals reversed and rendered judgment that Airborne Freight take nothing. 561 S.W.2d 37. It held that no evidence supported the judgment because the sworn account was not formally offered in evidence. Airborne Freight now contends that the sworn account filed in accordance with Rule 185 is itself evidence to support the trial court's judgment without the necessity of introducing it into evidence.

Rule 185 provides in part:

> When any action or defense is founded upon an open account or other claim for goods, wares and merchandise, including any claim for a liquidated money demand based upon written contract or founded on business dealings between the parties, or is for personal service rendered, or labor done or labor or materials furnished, on which a systematic record has been kept, and is supported by the affidavit of the party, his agent or attorney taken before some officer authorized to administer oaths, to the effect that such claim is, within the knowledge of affiant, just and true, that it is due, and that all just and lawful offsets, payments and credits have been allowed, *the same shall be taken as prima facie evidence thereof,* unless the party resisting such claim shall, before an announcement of ready for trial in said cause, file a written denial, under oath, stating that each and every item is not just or true, or that some specified item or items are not just and true; . . . . *When the opposite party fails to file such affidavit, he shall not be permitted to deny the claim,* or any item therein, as the case may be. [Emphasis added].

It is settled that if the defendant fails to file a written denial under oath and in the form provided, he will not be permitted to dispute receipt of the items or services or the correctness of the stated charges. *Wilson v. Browning Arms Co.*, 501 S.W.2d 705 (Tex. Civ. App.—Houston [14th Dist.] 1973, writ ref'd). The defendant may, however, assert defenses in the nature of confession and avoidance without filing a sworn denial if they are properly pleaded. *Jorrie Furniture Co. v. Rohm*, 442 S.W.2d 476 (Tex. Civ. App.—San Antonio 1969, no writ). Of course, a sworn account is not *prima facie* evidence of the debt as against a stranger to the transaction. *Hilton v. Musebeck Shoe Co.*, 505 S.W.2d 341 (Tex. Civ. App.—Austin 1974, writ ref'd n.r.e.).

The answer filed by CRB did not plead any affirmative defenses or raise the issue that CRB was not a party to the transaction. It merely stated that CRB had no record of contracting for the services and demanded strict proof that it had authorized such services. The invoices attached to plaintiff's sworn account affidavit named CRB as the party to be billed for the services. Under these circumstances, CRB's unsworn denial did not place in issue any element of the plaintiff's cause of action. The sworn account therefore constituted *prima facie* evidence of the debt, without the necessity of formally introducing the account into evidence. Since the defendant failed to file a sworn denial of the account, no further evidence was required. Tex. R. Civ. P. 185; *Wilson v. Browning Arms Co., supra; O'Brien v. Cole*, 532 S.W.2d 151, 152 (Tex. Civ. App.—Dallas 1976, no writ); *Alton R. Fairchild Inc. v. M-P Cotton Felt Co.*, 403 S.W.2d 527 (Tex. Civ. App.—Fort Worth 1966, no writ); *cf. Meaders v. Biskamp* 159 Tex. 79, 316 S.W.2d 75, 78 (1958).

The court of civil appeals cited *Hilton v. Musebeck Shoe Co.*, 505 S.W.2d 341 (Tex. Civ. App.—Austin 1974, writ ref'd n.r.e.); *Johnson v. Walker*, 330 S.W.2d 508 (Tex. Civ. App.—San Antonio 1959, no writ); and *Chisos Mining Co. v. Chicago Pneumatic Tool Co.*, 142 S.W.2d 549 (Tex. Civ. App.—El Paso 1940, writ dism'd judgmt cor.), in support of its holding that the sworn account must be offered in evidence even when no sworn denial has been filed. *Hilton* involved a stranger to the transaction, while *Johnson* was a case in which the plaintiff failed to properly plead a sworn account. Those cases are therefore inapposite. *Chisos Mining* states that the account must be offered in evidence in a case such as this, but that statement was unnecessary to the holding of the case, and such language is hereby expressly disapproved.

The holding of the court of civil appeals is in conflict with Rule 185. Accordingly, the application for writ of error is granted, and without hearing oral argument, the judgment of the court of civil appeals is reversed and that of the trial court affirmed. Tex. R. Civ. P. 483.

### [B] Types of Claims

What types of claims are encompassed within the literal language of Rule 185? Consider the following excerpt from Dorsaneo, *Texas Litigation Guide*, Ch. 11, *Plaintiff's Original Petition*.

## W. Dorsaneo, TEXAS LITIGATION GUIDE

*§ 11.05 (1998)**

§ 11.05 Suit on Sworn Account

[1] In General

Rule 185 of the Texas Rules of Civil Procedure provides a method by which a plaintiff may present a prima facie case of the validity of certain claims by satisfying particular pleading requirements. If the claim is within the scope of Rule 185 and if these particular pleading requirements are satisfied, the opposing party may be precluded from challenging the claim or any item included in it [Leyendecker v. Santa Rosa Medical Center, 533 S.W.2d 868, 869–870 (Civ. App.—Tyler 1976, no writ)]. Unless the defendant properly denies the account under oath, there can be no dispute as to the receipt of the items or services or the correctness of the stated charges [Airborne Freight Corp. v. CRB Marketing, Inc., 566 S.W.2d 573, 575 (Tex. 1978)]. The rule making a verified account prima facie evidence in the absence of a sworn written denial applies only to the parties to the original transaction. For example, a successor in interest to one of the original parties may controvert or disprove the account despite the failure to file a written denial under oath [Volvo Petroleum, Inc., v. Getty Oil Co., 717 S.W.2d 134, 138 (Tex. App.—Houston [14th Dist.] 1986, no writ)].

[2] Scope of Rule 185

Rule 185 provides that the following claims are within its scope [T.R.C.P. 185]:

1. An action founded upon an open account or other claim for goods, wares, and merchandise "including any claim for a liquidated money demand based upon written contract or founded on business dealings between the parties."

2. An action for personal services rendered.

3. An action for labor done.

4. An action for labor furnished.

5. An action for material furnished.

Rule 185 was taken from Article 3736 of the Revised Civil Statutes, which originally encompassed only an action on an open account. In 1931, the statute was amended to include liquidated demands based on written contract or business dealings between the parties and claims for personal services rendered on which a systematic record of accounts has been kept. One purpose of the amendment was to include "accounts stated" as well as "open accounts" in the actions contemplated by the rule [Hollingsworth v. Northwestern National Ins. Co., 522 S.W.2d 242, 245 (Civ. App.—Texarkana 1975, no writ); *cf.* Unit, Inc. v. Ten Eyck-Shaw, Inc., 524 S.W.2d 330, 334 (Civ. App.—Dallas 1975, ref. n.r.e.)]. A second purpose of the amendment was to include claims for personal services rendered [*see* Juarez v. Dunn, 567 S.W.2d 223, 226 (Civ. App.—El Paso 1978, ref. n.r.e.)]. Subsequently, in 1950, a second amendment added suits for "labor done or labor or material furnished" to the sworn account rule [*see* Tomasic & Kieval, *Sworn Accounts and Summary Judgment Proceedings in Texas: A Proposed Change*, 17 S. Tex. L.J. 147, 150 (1976)].

Hence, the scope of Rule 185 has been expanded by amendment beyond the contours of the common law "sworn account" [*see, e.g.*, Meaders v. Biscamp, 159 Tex. 79, 316 S.W.2d 75, 78 (1958)—"[i]t has been held that a sworn account is defined according to its popular sense and applies only to transactions between persons, in which there is a sale upon one side and a purchase upon the other, whereby title to *personal* property passes from one to the other, and the relation of debtor and creditor is created by general course of dealing (which may include only one transaction between the parties). It does not mean transactions between parties resting upon special contract"]. Unfortunately, until 1984, Rule 185 was entitled "Suit on Sworn Account," even though the body of the rule never has included that term [*see* Seisdata v. Compagnie General De Geophysique, 598 S.W.2d 690, 691 (Civ. App.—Houston [14th Dist.] 1980, ref. n.r.e.)—holding that Rule 185 is not restricted to types of claims described in *Meaders,* which dealt only with the recovery of attorney's fees under former R.C.S. Art. 2226; Larcon Petroleum, Inc. v. Autotronic Systems, 576 S.W.2d 873, 875 (Civ. App.—Houston [14th dist.] 1979, no writ); *see also* Schorer v. Box Service Co., 927 S.W.2d 132, 135 (Tex. App.—Houston [1st Dist.] 1996, den.)—concurring opinion, citing Texas Litigation Guide for proposition that scope of Rule 185 has been expanded beyond contours of common-law sworn account rules as discussed in *Meaders v. Biscamp*].

The courts have had difficulty in arriving at a consistent interpretation of the scope of Rule 185. The most common problem relates to a supposed distinction between "sworn accounts" and "special contracts." A special contract has been defined as "one with peculiar provisions or stipulations not found in the ordinary contract relating to the same subject matter and [which] provisions . . . if omitted from the ordinary contract, the law will never supply" [Eisenbeck v. Buttgen, 450 S.W.2d 696, 702 (Civ. App.—Dallas 1970, no writ)—alleged oral employment contract providing for percentage of gross receipts in addition to set salary as special contract; Brown v. Starrett, 684 S.W.2d 145, 146 (Tex. App.—Corpus Christi 1984, no writ)]. There is caselaw to the effect that a special contract may not be the subject of an action under Rule 185 because "[i]t does not apply to transactions between parties resting upon special contracts other than those giving rise to the transactions mentioned in the rule" [Hollingsworth v. Northwestern National Ins. Co., 522 S.W.2d 242, 244 (Civ. App.—Texarkana 1975, no writ); *cf.* Robinson v. Faulkner, 422 S.W.2d 209, 212–213 (Civ. App.—Dallas 1967, ref. n.r.e.)—oral contract for services rendered not qualifying as "sworn account" under T.R.C.P. 185]. Finally, it has also been suggested that the benefits of Rule 185 specifically include an action founded on "any claim for a liquidated money demand based upon a written contract or founded on business dealings between the parties" [Brown v. Starrett, 684 S.W.2d 145, 146 (Tex. App.—Corpus Christi 1984, no writ),—"special contract" exception did not apply to oral contract to remodel house; *cf.* DeWees v. Alsip, 546 S.W.2d 692, 694 (Civ. App.—El Paso 1977, no writ)—suit on promissory note for sale of partnership is not within Rule 185]. It has also ben held that Rule 185 is inapplicable to suits on lease agreements [*see* Schorer v. Box Service Co., 927 S.W.2d 132, 134 (Tex. App.—Houston [1st Dist.] 1996, den.); Meinke Discount Muffler v. Coldwell Banker, 635 S.W.2d 135, 138 (Tex. App.—Houston [1st Dist.] 1982, ref. n.r.e.)]. The so-called special contract exception no longer appears to be a problem in the context of awarding attorney's fees pursuant to the general attorney's fees statute [*see* C.P.R.C. §§ 38.001–38.006]. An amendment to that statute authorizes recovery of attorney's fees "if the claim is for: . . . (8) an oral or written contract" [C.P.R.C. § 38.001(8)].

### [C] Standard "Sworn Account" Petition

PLAINTIFF'S ORIGINAL PETITION

TO THE HONORABLE COURT:

__________ [*Name*], plaintiff, complains of __________ [*name*], defendant, and for cause of action shows:

I.

Plaintiff is a corporation, with its principal office and place of business in the City of Houston, Travis County, Texas. Defendant is an individual whose residence is located in Dallas County, Texas. Service of citation may be had on defendant by serving __________ [him *or* her] at defendant's residence at 1234 Elm Street, Dallas, Texas. Plaintiff __________ [affirmatively pleads that __________ (he *or* she) seeks only monetary relief aggregating $50,000 or less, excluding costs, prejudgment interest, and attorney's fees under Civil Procedure Rule 190.2 *or* pleads that discovery should be conducted in accordance with a discovery control plan under Civil Procedure Rule 190.3 *or* pleads that discovery should be conducted in accordance with a tailored discovery control plan under Civil Procedure Rule 190.4].

II.

On the several occasions from March 15, 1996, to August 25, 1996, as more particularly shown on the attached Exhibit A, a verified account representing a liquidated money demand, which is incorporated by reference, plaintiff sold and delivered to defendant goods, wares, and merchandise consisting of paints, solvents, brushes, and tapes, as more specifically itemized on Exhibit A. The sales were made at the special instance and request of defendant, and the goods were sold and delivered in the regular course of business. In consideration of the sales, on which a systematic record has been kept, defendant promised and became bound and liable to pay plaintiff the prices charged for the goods in the total amount of $________ [*specify*], being a reasonable charge for such items, as further shown on the attached Exhibit A. Despite numerous demands by plaintiff upon defendant for payment, defendant has refused and failed to pay the account, to plaintiff's damage in the sum of $________ [*specify*], plus interest as alleged below.

[*Add if attorney's fees are sought*]

III.

On January 16, 1997, plaintiff presented defendant with the account. In this connection, plaintiff employed the undersigned attorneys to represent plaintiff and agreed to pay them a reasonable attorney's fee for their service, which plaintiff alleges to be the sum of $________ [*specify*].

IV.

Plaintiff further shows that under Finance Code § 302.002, interest on open accounts accrues at the rate of 6 percent per annum, commencing on the 30th day after the day on which the sum is due and payable. Plaintiff is, therefore, entitled to prejudgment interest from the 30th day after each unpaid item of the account became due and payable, which was ________ days after the delivery date set forth in the attached Exhibit A, until the date of judgment.

WHEREFORE, plaintiff requests that defendant be cited to appear and answer and that upon final hearing, plaintiff have judgment against defendant for $________ [*specify*], plus interest before and after judgment as provided by law, attorney's fees in the sum of $________ [*specify*], and such other and further relief to which plaintiff is justly entitled.

Respectfully submitted,

____________________ [*firm name, if any*]
By: ____________________ [*signature*]
____________________ [*typed name*]
____________________ [*address*]
____________________ [*telephone number*]
____________________ [*telecopier number, if any*]
____________________ [*state bar i.d. number*]
Attorney for ____________________

## EXHIBIT "A"

[*Set out verified account, e.g.*]

**ABC CORPORATION**

John Doe
1234 Elm Street
Dallas, Texas

**Statement of Account**

| Shipment Date | Item | No. | Price/Unit | Total Price |
|---|---|---|---|---|
| 3-15-95 | R-25 | 250 Gls. | $ 5.73 | $ 1,432.50 |
| 4-12-95 | S-1 | 10 Gls. | $ 3.15 | $ 31.50 |
| 8-25-95 | Misc. | 15 units | $ 1.57 | $ 23.55 |
| | | | | $ 1,487.55 |

[*Affidavit to the Account*]

THE STATE OF TEXAS, }
COUNTY OF HARRIS }

BEFORE ME, the undersigned Notary Public in and for said County and State, on this day personally appeared John Doe, known to me, and, after being duly sworn, stated on oath that the foregoing and annexed account in favor of John Doe and against Richard Roe for the sum of $1,487.55 is within the knowledge of affiant, just and true, that it is due and unpaid, and that all just and lawful offsets, payments and credits have been allowed.

__________________ [*signature of affiant*]

SWORN AND SUBSCRIBED TO BEFORE ME, on ________.

[*Seal*]

__________________________ [*signature*]
__________________ [*typed or stamped name*]
Notary Public in and for Harris County, Texas
My commission expires ____________ [*date*].

## NOTES AND QUESTIONS

(1) *Types of Claims*. Review the sample petition and then ask yourself if the pleading would satisfy Rule 185:

(a) Does the petition allege or identify the type of claim involved?

(b) Does it show with reasonable certainty the nature of the items sold?

(c) If the transaction had involved services, how would they be properly identified?

(d) Does the petition show that a systematic record has been kept?

(e) Is the claim "supported by the affidavit of the party, or his agent or attorney taken before some officer authorized to administer oaths, to the effect that such claim is, within the knowledge of the affiant, just and true, that it is due, and that all just and lawful offsets, payments and credits have been allowed"?

(2) *Defensive Considerations.* How would a person defend against the allegations contained in the sample petition? Until recently, technical precision has been required of a person wishing to deny a claimant's allegations when made in accordance with Civil Procedure Rule 185. That is, it was required to "file a written denial, under oath, stating that each and every item is not just or true, or that some specified item or items are not just and true." Failure to word the denial in the exact language of the rules invalidated the denial as an effective defense to the plaintiff's claim. *See Crystal Investments v. Manges*, 596 S.W.2d 853 (Tex. 1980); *Oliver Bass Lumber Co. v. Kay and Herring Butane Gas Co.*, 524 S.W.2d 600 (Tex. Civ. App.—Tyler 1975, no writ). In 1983, however, there were signs that the particularistic requirements for the defendant's answer were being relaxed. In *Stevens Foods, Inc. v. Loggins Meat Co.*, 644 S.W.2d 908 (Tex. Civ. App.—Tyler 1983, no writ), the Tyler Court of Appeals, distinguishing the facts of *Manges*, expressly overruled its earlier decision in *Oliver Bass*, noting the objective specified in Tex. R. Civ. P. 1 that the rules be liberally construed. Of course, as indicated in *Airborne Freight Corp. v. CRB Marketing, Inc.*, in [A], *above*, the stringent Rule 185 requirements for the defendant's answer have never existed for the defendant who was a "stranger to the account" (e.g., one who did not sign the contract underlying the sworn account). For pleading purposes, the stranger has only to worry about filing a sworn denial under Rule 93 to support his assertion that he was indeed a stranger. *See, e.g., Hilton v. Musebeck Shoe Co., Inc.*, 505 S.W.2d 341 (Tex. Civ. App.—Austin 1974, writ ref'd n.r.e.); *Booher v. Criswell*, 531 S.W.2d 844 (Tex. Civ. App.—Dallas 1975, no writ) (denial of liability in capacity sued); *Juarez v. Dunn*, 567 S.W.2d 223 (Tex. Civ. App.—El Paso 1978, writ ref'd n.r.e.) (denial of partnership).

(3) *Special Exceptions and Rule 185.* The particularized pleading requirements of Rule 185 were liberalized by the Texas Supreme Court when the rule was amended in 1984. From the standpoint of the particularity required of a claimant, the last sentence of the amended rule appears to require the defendant to specially except to a petition that either contains or incorporates a claim or an account that is not detailed or particularized (*i.e.*, "$5,000 for legal services"). After obtaining more specific information, a party who is resisting a claim can "file a written denial, under oath." How specific or particularized must the denial be? Does a sworn general denial satisfy the literal requirements of the procedural rule? It is still clear that an unverified general

denial does not. *Vance v. Holloway*, 689 S.W.2d 403, 404 (Tex. 1985). Is there any penalty for false swearing? For a comprehensive review of the special pleading requirements of Rule 185, see *Requipco, Inc. v. Am-Tex Tank & Equipment*, 738 S.W.2d 299 (Tex. App.—Houston [14th Dist.] 1987, no writ).

### [D] Trespass to Try Title

*Read Tex. R. Civ. P. 783 through 813.*

## HUNT v. HEATON

*643 S.W.2d 677 (Tex. 1983)*

CAMPBELL, Justice.

This suit was brought as a trespass to try title action. The trial court held Hunt could not offer evidence of his title because he did not file his abstract of title within 20 days of demand. The court rendered judgment that Hunt take nothing. The court of appeals affirmed the trial court judgment. 631 S.W.2d 549. We affirm the judgment of the court of appeals.

Heaton answered Hunt's petition by pleading "not guilty" and demanded that Hunt furnish an abstract of the title he would rely on at trial. Tex. R. Civ. P. 791.[1] Hunt did not request an extension of time to file the abstract as authorized by Rule 792 of the Texas Rules of Civil Procedure..[2] Five years after the demand was made, and 39 days prior to the trial, Hunt filed the abstract. Five days later, Hunt filed a document styled "Notice of Intention to Submit Certified Copies of Recorded Instruments." Certified copies of the deeds relied on by Hunt were attached.

The trial court refused to allow Hunt's evidence of his title. The court relied on that portion of Rule 792 which provides that if no abstract is filed within the time period allowed by the Rule, "no evidence of the claim or title of such opposite party shall be given on trial." Hunt complains that Rule 792 should not be read so strictly. He argues the purpose of the Rule is to provide the opposing party with adequate notice of a claim and Heaton had adequate notice because the abstract was filed 39 days before trial.

Rule 792 states the abstract of title *shall*, be filed with the court within 20 days of the demand, or within such further time as the court should grant for good cause. The courts freely grant extensions of time if the extension will not prejudice the other parties. *Corder v. Foster*, 505 S.W.2d 645 (Tex. Civ. App.—Houston [1st Dist.] 1973, writ ref'd n.r.e.). In this case, Hunt made no effort to secure an extension of time to file his abstract. There is no evidence showing good cause for filing the abstract five years late. Therefore, the trial court correctly refused to admit Hunt's evidence of title.

Hunt relies upon *Corder v. Foster, supra; McCraw v. City of Dallas*, 420 S.W.2d 793 (Tex. Civ. App.—Dallas 1967, writ ref'd n.r.e.); and *Davis v. Dowlen*, 136 S.W.2d 900 (Tex. Civ.

---

[1] Rule 791. May Demand Abstract of Title.

After answer filed, either party may, by notice in writing, duly served on the opposite party or his attorney of record, not less than ten days before the trial of the cause, demand an abstract in writing of the claim or title to the premises in question upon which he relies.

[2] Tex. R. Civ. P. 792. Time to File Abstract.

Such abstract of title shall be filed with the papers of the cause within twenty days after the service of the notice, or within such further time as the court on good cause shown may grant; and, in default thereof, no evidence of the claim or title of such opposite party shall be given on trial.

App.—Beaumont 1939, writ dism'd judgm't cor.), to support his position that Rule 792 should not be applied strictly when adequate notice is given. The *McCraw* case is distinguishable because the documents were not offered to prove the City's superior title. Rule 792 states, "no evidence of the *claim or title* of such opposite party shall be given on trial." (Emphasis added). The Rule applies only when the documents demanded are offered to prove the opposite party's superior title. *Corder v. Foster, supra*, is distinguishable because no objection was made at trial to the introduction of the title documents. *Davis v. Dowlen, supra,* is distinguishable because good cause for an extension of time was shown in that case.

This Court will not disregard a rule of procedure which has been in existence for over 100 years. Although the sanction available for failure to comply with a demand can be considered harsh, extensions of time are freely given when requested. Hunt did nothing to comply with the demand or the rules for almost five years. "Abstract justice achieved by a complete disregard of the rules governing trials in our courts may appeal to some as a means of arriving at an end thought to be desirable. It is not a proper philosophy to use in affirming or reversing judgments." *Scheffer v. Chron*, 560 S.W.2d 419 (Tex. Civ. App.—Beaumont 1977, writ ref'd n.r.e.).

Hunt next contends the certified copies of title documents which were filed 34 days before trial were admissible under art. 3726,[3] despite his failure to comply with Rule 792. Art. 3726 states:

> Every instrument of writing which is permitted or required by law to be recorded in the office of the Clerk of the County Court, and which has been . . . so recorded . . . for a period of ten (10) years in the book used by said Clerk for the recording of such instruments . . . shall be admitted as evidence in any suit in this State, without the necessity of proving its execution; . . . provided, that the party to give such instrument in evidence shall file the same among the papers of the suit in which he proposes to use it, at least three (3) days before the commencement of the trial . . . and give notice . . . to the opposite party or his attorney. . . .

Hunt argues the provisions of Rule 792 conflict with the provisions of art. 3726, and that art. 3726, a statute, should control over Rule 792, a rule of procedure. We disagree.

The purpose of art. 3726 is to authenticate an "ancient document" without the necessity of proving its execution. *Beaumont Pasture Co. v. Preston & Smith*, 65 Tex. 448 (1886); *Hancock v. Tram Lumber Co.*, 65 Tex. 225, 232 (1885). The statute is not designed to eliminate all objections to an ancient document, only objections based on its authenticity. There is no contention that Hunt's documents were not authentic or not executed with the proper formalities. The objection here is that the documents were not produced after a timely demand was made for them. There is no conflict between art. 3726 and Rule 792 because they serve different purposes. Art. 3726 authenticates ancient documents; Rule 792 compels discovery.

The cases relied on by Hunt are not applicable. No abstract was demanded in *Fenley v. Ogletree*, 277 S.W.2d 135 (Tex. Civ. App.—Beaumont 1955, writ ref'd n.r.e.). The court in *Semmes v. Olivarez*, 368 S.W.2d 46 (Tex. Civ. App.—Austin 1963, no writ), held that, although the title documents in question were admissible in evidence under art. 3726, whether they could be used to prove superior title need not be determined under the facts of that case. 368 S.W.2d at 49. In *Farhart v. Blackshear*, 434 S.W.2d 395 (Tex. Civ. App.—Houston [1st Dist.] 1968,

[3] Tex. Rev. Civ. Stat. Ann. art. 3726.

writ ref'd n.r.e.), the complaining party failed to preserve his error by objecting to the admission of the title documents at trial.

Hunt's last contention is that the case was tried by consent as a boundary suit, rather than a trespass to try title action. He argues the trial court erred in rendering a take nothing judgment against him on the basis of his failure to introduce title documents because he is not required to establish superior title in a boundary suit.

Boundary disputes may be tried by a statutory trespass to try title action. *Plumb v. Stuessy*, 617 S.W.2d 667, 669 (Tex. 1981); *Stanolind Oil & Gas Co.*, 136 Tex. 5, 133 S.W.2d 767, 770 (1939). Hunt's pleadings are in the form prescribed by the Rule for pleading a trespass to try title action. Tex. R. Civ. P. 783. The pleadings cannot be construed as doing more than alleging a suit for trespass. A petition alleging trespass to try title always puts title and possession in issue. *Poth v. Roosth*, 146 Tex. 7, 202 S.W.2d 442, 445 (1947). In the absence of a special pleading alleging a boundary dispute, as in *Plumb v. Stuessy*, Hunt's title to the disputed land was in issue.

Any one of a number of facts may determine title or possession, but the cause of action remains the same—trespass to try title. That the case may have turned factually on the question of boundary does not alter the cause of action pleaded and disposed of by the judgment. *Permian Oil Co. v. Smith*, 129 Tex. 413, 107 S.W.2d 564, 570 (1937). *Freeman v. McAninch*, 87 Tex. 132, 27 S.W. 97, 98 (1894).

To recover in trespass to try title, the plaintiff must rely upon the strength on his own title and not upon the weakness of the defendant's. *Plumb v. Stuessy, supra* 617 S.W.2d at 668; *Land v. Turner*, 377 S.W.2d 181 (Tex. 1964).Hunt sought to prove his title by a chain of instruments beginning with a patent from the State, and ending with a deed conveying the land to him. This is a proper means of proving a superior title in a trespass to try title action. *Land v. Turner, supra* at 183. Because of the failure to file an abstract of the chain of title, the trial court properly excluded any offer of proof by Hunt relating to his claim or title. Hunt failed to prove his superior title and therefore, the correct judgment is that he take nothing. *Poth v. Roosth, supra* 202 S.W.2d at 444.

The judgment of the court of appeals is affirmed.

SONDOCK, J., concurs with opinion.

BARROW, J., dissents with opinion, in which SPEARS, J., joins.

SONDOCK, Justice, concurring.

I concur in the result because of the present wording of Tex. R. Civ. Pro. Rule 792. This case magnifies the need to streamline the unnecessary formalities of trespass to try title actions. Fictitious proceedings in the action of ejectment were abolished in this state in 1840. Tex. Rev. Civ. Stat. Ann. (Art. 7364). Trespass to try title has remained a sacred cow that should not be permitted to continue to feed on unnecessary technicalities.

BARROW, Justice, dissenting.

I respectfully dissent.

This suit, although brought in the form of a trespass to try title action, involves only the location of the correct boundary line between petitioner Harold L. Hunt and respondent Dan Heaton. Since this was a boundary dispute, Hunt's failure to timely file the requested abstract of title did not foreclose his right to establish proper boundary. Therefore, the court of appeals erred in affirming the instructed verdict granted against Hunt by the trial court at the close of his evidence.

It is established that boundary disputes may be tried by a statutory action of trespass to try title. *Plumb v. Stuessy*, 617 S.W.2d 667 (Tex. 1981); *Standolind Oil & Gas Co. v. State*, 136 Tex. 5, 133 S.W.2d 767 (1939); *Schiele v. Kimball*, 113 Tex. 1, 194 S.W. 944 (1917). In such an action the plaintiff is not required to establish superior title to the property in question in the manner required in a formal trespass to try title action. *Plumb v. Stuessy, supra* 617 S.W.2d at 669; *Rocha v. Campos*, 574 S.W.2d 233, 235 (Tex. Civ. App.—Corpus Christi 1978, no writ); *see Poth v. Roosth*, 146 Tex. 7, 202 S.W.2d 442 (1947); *Brown v. Eubank*, 378 S.W.2d 707 (Tex. Civ. App.—Tyler 1964, writ ref'd n.r.e.).

The crucial question in this case is the nature of Hunt's suit. The proper test for determining whether the case is one of boundary is as follows: If there would have been no case but for the question of boundary, then the case is necessarily a boundary case even though it might incidentally involve a question of title. *Plumb v. Stuessy, supra.*

All the parties involved have continually treated this case as a boundary dispute. At the outset of the trial, counsel for Hunt stated:

> In any event, Your Honor, the dispute, the issue here is precisely where the boundary line between Mr. Heaton's property and Mr. Hunt's property lies. And that has become disputed through the years which some ancient surveys of the property and some documents which really don't reflect the precise location of a railroad right of way. Mr. Heaton claims the railroad right of way, Mr. Hunt claims the property immediately adjacent to the north thereof. And that is the sole issue in the Plaintiff's view which is before the Court here today. . . .

Heaton's attorney replied in part as follows:

As counsel said, this is a boundary question. And it involves a right of way of the old Santa Fe spur east of 149 into the town of Montgomery just east of where the depot was.

The testimony of both Hunt and Heaton demonstrates the dispute was over the location of the boundary between Hunt's property and the abandoned railroad right-of-way owned by Heaton. Hunt testified that his southern boundary line was pointed out to him by F.G. Huffman who had surveyed the property. Heaton testified that after he bought the abandoned railroad right-of-way, the Hunts complained when he started to clean it up. At this time, a dispute arose over the boundary which resulted in this court action.

Heaton did not dispute that Hunt is the owner of the property north of Heaton's property. Heaton testified in part:

Q: And do you dispute today that Mr. Hunt is the owner of the property north of yours?

A: I do not.

Q: Alright. And the question that we're really here to determine today is not whether Mr. Hunt owns any property but really what property he owns; isn't that correct?

A: Well, I understand that it's the north boundary of the railroad track, railroad right of way.

Q: I do not. That we're trying to locate here?

A: Right.

Q: That's right. Okay. So you don't have any dispute of Mr. Hunt owning property there, do you?

A: North of that.

Q: Right. But whether or not we can find out what that property line is really what we're here to do today, isn't it?

A: The north boundary of the railroad right of way.

The record clearly demonstrates that this case involves only a dispute over the proper boundary line and the parties have acknowledged the case as a boundary dispute. Therefore, Hunt was not required to establish his superior title to the property in question in the manner required by a formal trespass to try title action. *Plumb v. Stuessy, supra.* Consequently, his failure to timely file his abstract is not fatal to his suit to establish the correct boundary line.

The trial court erred in granting the instructed verdict for Heaton at the close of Hunt's case. This error would require a reversal of the judgment and a remand of the cause for a new trial. In any event, the abstract was filed by Hunt some thirty-nine days before the trial. Since Hunt's title was not in dispute, the delay in filing the abstract could not have prejudiced Heaton in any manner. Any error in not timely filing the abstract was therefore harmless. Rule 434, Rule 504, Tex. R. Civ. Pro. *McGraw v. City of Dallas,* 420 S.W.2d 793 (Tex. Civ. App.—Dallas 1967, writ ref'd n.r.e.).

I would reverse the judgments of the lower courts and remand the cause to the trial court for trial on the merits.

SPEARS, J., joins in this dissent.

---

## NOTES AND QUESTIONS

(1) *Harsh Result.* Civil Procedure Rule 792 was amended in 1987 in an attempt to moderate the harsh result in the principal case. Compare the rule as quoted by the court in footnote 2 and the current rule. Do you think that the amendment accomplishes this objective?

(2) How harsh is the result in the *Heaton* case? Consider the following brief excerpts from *Jordan v. Bacon*, 739 S.W.2d 629, 631–632 (Tex. Civ. App.—Beaumont 1987, no writ):

> We acknowledge that a plaintiff, in a trespass to try title suit, has the initial burden of proving that said plaintiff has title to the land in litigation by at least one of four methods:
>
> > (1) record title from the sovereignty of the soil down to himself; (2) title from a common source, *i.e.*, a source from which the defendant also claims title; (3) title by limitation; or (4) a presumptive title arising from possession of the property at a time antedating the defendant's possession. *Land v. Turner*, 377 S.W.2d 181, 183 (Tex. 1964); *Walters v. Pete*, 546 S.W.2d 871, 875 (Tex. Civ. App.—Texarkana 1977, writ ref'd n.r.e.). . . .
>
> . . . .
>
> In *Hejl v. Wirth*, 161 Tex. 609, 343 S.W.2d 226 (1961), the Supreme Court wrote that, in a trespass to try title suit, the plaintiff must recover upon the strength of his own title. If the plaintiff fails to establish his title, the effect of a take nothing judgment against plaintiff

is to vest title in the defendant. But the Supreme Court also acknowledged that this rule is a very harsh rule. We agree. And we respectfully ask the Supreme Court to reexamine and rethink the same in a procedurally correct manner.

## APPENDIX, CHAPTER 5

## PLEADINGS FROM A SUIT INVOLVING COMMERCIAL LITIGATION

### PLEADINGS IN *WILSON v. PRAIRIE AT GARWOOD CENTER, INC.*

The following set of pleadings is adapted from a commercial litigation case. In these pleadings, you will see examples of most of the different kinds of defensive pleadings, examples of verified pleading requirements, different causes of action pleaded with varying degrees of care in the plaintiff's petition and other matters you have studied in this chapter. As you read them, you should consider their effects on discovery, as reflected in Appendix B to Chapter 10.

NO. 79-3989

| | | |
|---|---|---|
| JAMES R. WILSON | ) | |
| V. | ) | |
| PRAIRIE AT GARWOOD | ) | |
| CENTER, INC., D. VINCENT | ) | IN THE DISTRICT COURT OF |
| NIHAUSER, A.J. | ) | MANERO COUNTY, TEXAS |
| STONE, JOHN BLASKI | ) | 638TH JUDICIAL DISTRICT |
| THOMAS A. BAIN | ) | |
| AND BENNO R. | ) | |
| JOHNSTON | ) | |

PLAINTIFF'S ORIGINAL PETITION

TO THE HONORABLE JUDGE OF SAID COURT:

Comes now, James R. Wilson, and would show the court as follows:

I.

Plaintiff, James R. Wilson, is a resident of Manero County, Texas. Defendant, Prairie at Garwood Center, Inc., is a corporation incorporated in Texas and having its registered office in Manero County, Texas, and may be served with process by serving its registered agent and President, D. Vincent Nihauser, at 5700 Crockett Street, London, Texas. D. Vincent Nihauser is an individual residing in Manero County, Texas, and may be served with process at 5700 Crockett Street, London, Texas. . . . [Residence and service information on other defendants would appear in the petition but is here omitted.]

II.

On or about October 10, 1985, Defendants, individually and through the Prairie at Garwood Center, Inc. ("Center") purchased a shopping center known as:

> Lot 10, Block 18, Glendale Hills Subdivision, a subdivision of Manero County, Texas, according to the map or plat thereof recorded in volume 63, page 218, of the Manero County Map Records.

Contemporaneously with such purchase, Defendants, acting through Prairie at Garwood Center, Inc., and D. Vincent Nihauser, agreed that in consideration of the brokerage services rendered by James R. Wilson, James R. Wilson would and did receive an eight (8) percent cost-free interest in and to the gross profits of the said Center (the "cost-free interest"). The said agreement was subsequently reduced to writing and is attached hereto as exhibit A, which is incorporated herein for all purposes.

III.

Commencing with the year 1988, and continuing to the date of filing hereof, Defendants failed to pay Plaintiff any portion of the said cost-free interest. Thereafter, Plaintiff has made repeated demand upon Defendants, but Defendants have failed and refused, and do fail and refuse, to make further payment thereon, which conduct constitutes a breach of the said agreement.

IV.

Plaintiff has made demand upon Defendants for an accounting of the gross profits of the said Center and for the books and records thereof, but Defendants have failed and refused, and do fail and refuse, to render such accounting or such books and records. Plaintiff has no knowledge of the amount that could constitute his said cost-free interest, but has suffered actual damages in an amount exceeding the minimum jurisdictional limits of the court.

V.

Defendants, and each of them, have entered into a conspiracy to defraud Plaintiff of his cost-free interest and have diverted sums of money representing his interest to their own use and benefit. Defendants supplied all funds to purchase the Center and at all times material hereto have maintained same by contributions proportionate to their fractional ownership. They have entered into an agreement of joint venture. Although the alleged corporate defendant here, Prairie at Garwood Center, Inc., was chartered by the Secretary of State of the State of Texas, no organizational meeting therefor was held, no directors were elected and no stock was issued. The de facto owners of the said Center are the individual Defendants named herein.

VI.

Because Defendants have denied Plaintiff's interest in the said Center and have entered upon a course of conduct calculated to defeat his said interest, Plaintiff requests that the court enter a declaratory judgment declaring his cost free interest in and to the Center, and decreeing a constructive trust upon such amounts as are equal to funds of Plaintiff that have been diverted by Defendants.

VII.

As a result of the breaches of agreements herein, Plaintiff has been compelled to retain legal counsel and has retained the services of the firm of Jacob Green & Associates, Inc., and Jacob Green, and has agreed to pay him a reasonable attorney's fee. Plaintiff would show that the amount of such fee would exceed the sum of $5000, for recovery of which Plaintiff sues all Defendants pursuant to Tex. Rev. Civ. Stat. Ann. art. 2226.

WHEREFORE, Plaintiff prays that he have judgment for all sums owed him hereunder, that Defendants be ordered to render a full and true accounting, that he have a declaratory judgment declaring his interest in and to the Center, that he have a judgment imposing the constructive trust prayed for herein, that he recover his attorney's fees as prayed for and that he have such other and further relief, in law and in equity, general and special, to which he may show himself entitled.

RESPECTFULLY SUBMITTED,
Jacob Green & Associates, Inc.
by ______________________________
Attorneys for Plaintiff
2318 Vernon Ave.
London, Tx. 66016
666-639-7489

---

**Exhibit A**

James R. Wilson
Real Estate Investments
Mr. D. Vince Nihauser
5700 Crockett Street
London, Tx. 66016

Re: *Prairie at Garwood Center, Inc.*

Dear sir:

This will confirm our agreement that I am to receive an eight percent (8%) cost-free interest in and to the above-referenced property.

If this represents your understanding, please so signify by signing below.

Very truly yours,

/S/ James R. Wilson
James R Wilson

/S/ Vincent Nihauser
Vincent Nihauser, individually and as President of Prairie at Garwood Center, Inc.

NO. 79-3989

JAMES R. WILSON )
V. )
PRAIRIE AT GARWOOD ) IN THE DISTRICT COURT OF
CENTER, INC., D. VINCENT ) MANERO COUNTY, TEXAS
NIHAUSER, A.J. STONE, ) 638TH JUDICIAL DISTRICT
JOHN BLASKI, )
THOMAS A. BAIN )

AND BENNO R. )
JOHNSTON )

## DEFENDANTS' ORIGINAL ANSWER AND COUNTERCLAIM

TO THE HONORABLE JUDGE AND JURY OF SAID COURT:

Come now, Prairie at Garwood Center, Inc., D. Vincent Nihauser, A.J. Stone, John Blaski, Thomas A. Bain and Benno R. Johnston, and file this their answer and counterclaim, and would show as follows:

I.

As authorized by Rule 92 of the Texas Rules of Civil Procedure, Defendants assert a general denial herein.

II.

For further answer, if such be necessary, Defendants would show that there has been a failure of consideration and a lack of consideration in that Plaintiff failed to perform services in accordance with the agreement asserted by him.

III.

Defendants would further answer and defend, if such be necessary, by showing that the agreement alleged by Plaintiff is not expressed in a writing complying with the Texas Real Estate Licensing Act or the Statute of Frauds.

IV.

Defendants would further answer and defend, if such be necessary, by showing that Plaintiff's claim has been the subject of an accord and satisfaction or release.

V.

Defendants would further answer and defend by showing that Plaintiff was in a position of trust and confidential relationship with Defendants, and that he breached his fiduciary obligation by creating and causing Defendants to sign documents which he has now chosen to interpret to provide him with moneys far in excess of any services.

VI.

Defendants would further answer and defend, if such be necessary, by showing that the amounts claimed by Plaintiff and paid to him are grossly disproportional to the consideration and to the value and to services performed by Plaintiff, are unconscionable and are in violation of Tex. Bus. & Comm. Code §§ 17.45, 17.46 and 17.50 (the Texas Deceptive Trade Practices Act).

## COUNTERCLAIM

VII.

Defendants reallege paragraphs II through VI as though fully set out herein.

VIII.

Defendants have in connection with the transaction herein paid Plaintiff amounts in excess of $21,000 to which, owing to the facts and law hereinbefore set forth, Plaintiff was not entitled. Plaintiffs pray for the relief accorded by Tex. Bus. & Comm. Code § 17.50(b), including three times actual damages and attorney's fees.

WHEREFORE, Defendants pray that Plaintiff take nothing by his suit, that Defendants have judgment on their Counterclaim, and that the court grant such other and further relief as to which Defendants may show themselves justly entitled.

RESPECTFULLY SUBMITTED,

ARP, GIPFELS, GRAHAM &<br>
RYE<br>
by ____________________<br>
Attorneys for Defendants<br>
5701 Crockett St.<br>
London, Tx. 66016

STATE OF TEXAS<br>
COUNTY OF MANERO

Before me, the undersigned authority, personally appeared on this day D. Vincent Nihauser, and, being by me duly sworn, stated upon his oath that he has read paragraph II hereof and that the matters of fact stated therein are within his personal knowledge and are true and correct.

____________________<br>
D. Vincent Nihauser

SUBSCRIBED and SWORN TO BEFORE ME this ______ day of ______, 1989.

[*Seal*]

____________________<br>
Notary Public in and for Manero County,<br>
Texas

NO. 79-3989

| | | |
|---|---|---|
| JAMES R. WILSON | ) | IN THE DISTRICT COURT OF |
| V. | ) | MANERO COUNTY, TEXAS |
| PRAIRIE AT GARWOOD CEN- | ) | 638TH JUDICIAL DISTRICT |
| TER, INC. ET AL. | ) | |

DEFENDANTS' SPECIAL EXCEPTIONS

TO THE HONORABLE JUDGE OF SAID COURT:

Come now Defendants, Prairie at Garwood Center, Inc., et al., and would show the court as follows:

I.

Defendants specially except to Plaintiff's Petition in its entirety in that it fails to allege or to prove any facts with respect to whether Plaintiff is a licensed real estate broker, or is qualified to maintain this suit, which allegation is required by the Texas Real Estate Licensing Act for recovery of any fee based upon real estate brokerage. The said Act, Defendants would show, specifically states that a claimant must "allege" and "prove" such facts.

II.

Defendants specially except to Paragraph II of Plaintiff's Petition in that it alleges an agreement for real estate brokerage services but affirmatively shows that the writing upon which the alleged agreement is purportedly based does not comply with Section 20 of the Real Estate Licensing Act or cases decided thereunder. Specifically, Exhibit A, attached to the Petition and alleged to be the writing evidencing the purported agreement, does not contain a specific description of the land to be conveyed or of the fee to be paid the alleged broker as required by the said Act and cases.

III.

Defendants specially except to Paragraph II of Plaintiff's Petition in that it alleges an agreement for transfer of an interest in realty but affirmatively shows that the writing upon which the alleged agreement purports to be based fails to comply with the Statute of Frauds in that it contains no sufficient description of the land or interest therein purportedly conveyed.

IV.

Defendants specially except to that portion of Paragraph V wherein Plaintiff alleges that "Defendants, and each of them, have entered into a conspiracy to defraud Plaintiff," in that it is conclusionary and not supported by pled facts showing what any individual defendant allegedly did that gives rise to any cause of action, to any conspiracy or to any fraud.

Defendants further specially except to the entirety of the said Paragraph V in that, without the said conclusionary allegation that they "conspired" to "defraud," the allegations state no claim against any Defendant.

WHEREFORE, Defendants pray judgment of the court for a setting of a date by which Plaintiff may amend, and for such other relief to which they may show themselves entitled.

RESPECTFULLY SUBMITTED,

ARP, GIPFELS, GRAHAM & RYE
by ______________________
Attorneys for Defendants
5701 Crockett St.
London, Tx. 56016

---

ARP, GIPFELS, GRAHAM & RYE

Attorneys & Counselors

Mr. Jacob Green
2318 Vernon Ave.
London, Tx. 66016

CERTIFIED MAIL—RETURN
RECEIPT REQUESTED

Re: Wilson v. Prairie at Garwood Center, et al.

Dear sir:

A hearing on Defendants' Special Exceptions has been set for Monday, May 21, 1989, at 9:00 a.m., in the 638th District Court of Manero County, Texas, by telephone conversation between the undersigned and the clerk of the said court.

Very truly yours,

Grant Riley
ARP, GIPFELS, GRAHAM &
RYE

cc: clerk, 638th District Court, Manero County Courthouse, London Tx.

NO. 79-3989

| | | |
|---|---|---|
| JAMES R. WILSON | ) | IN THE DISTRICT COURT OF |
| V. | ) | MANERO COUNTY, TEXAS |
| PRAIRIE AT GARWOOD CEN- | ) | 638TH JUDICIAL DISTRICT |
| TER, INC. ET AL. | ) | |

ORDER ON SPECIAL EXCEPTIONS

Came on to be heard this day Defendant's Special Exceptions numbered I through IV, and the Court being of the opinion that some of such exceptions are meritorious and should be granted, as herein set forth, it is

ORDERED, ADJUDGED AND DECREED that the following special exceptions are granted or denied as indicated:

I GRANTED / DENIED
II GRANTED / DENIED
III GRANTED / DENIED
IV GRANTED / DENIED

It is further ordered that Plaintiff shall have leave to amend, such amendment to be filed on or before ______, 1989.

Signed this ______ day of ______, 1989.

______________________
Judge Presiding

## NOTES AND QUESTIONS

(1) *Analyzing Plaintiff's Pleadings.* What causes of action has Plaintiff alleged? What kinds of relief has he requested, and why? Do the factual allegations of Plaintiff seem to support the requests for relief, if true? The causes of action?

As you have seen from this chapter, the Plaintiff's petition must allege proper causes of action and must give "fair notice" of the legal and factual theories comprising them. Does the petition measure up to this standard? What claims or allegations are problematic?

(2) *Analyzing Defendant's Pleadings.* What kinds of defenses or defensive theories has defendant's lawyer alleged in the answer? Why does the answer not simply end with the first paragraph (the one asserting the general denial)? Notice that paragraph II of the answer is verified (that is, sworn) at the end of the answer; why do you suppose this is done? Why are the other paragraphs specifically included? What would happen at trial if, for example, defendants tried to rely on a defense of accord and satisfaction without having pled anything other than a general denial?

(3) *Use of Special Exceptions.* Special exceptions can be used to attack either the form of a pleading (such as for vagueness) or its failure to state a lawful claim or defense. What functions do the various special exceptions asserted by defendants fulfill here? Why does the defense want the statute-of-frauds special exception granted? What effect could that have? Why does the defense want plaintiff ordered to be more specific about the "conspiracy" to defraud? Why might plaintiff desire to be vague about it? What, if anything, has the defense gained by obtaining the order that the judge entered at the pretrial stage?

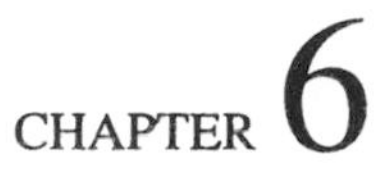

# VENUE

## SCOPE

This chapter covers venue. Topics examined include venue based in the county of the defendant's residence or principal office, venue based in the county where the events or omissions giving rise to the claim occurred, transfer of venue, exceptions to the venue rules, litigating venue rights, waiver of venue, change of venue, and multi-district litigation.

## § 6.01 The Basic Venue Scheme

From 1836 until 1983, under Texas venue law, the basic principle was that, in the absence of an exception, venue was fixed in the county of the defendant's "domicile." As noted by Professor Joseph McKnight in *The Spanish Influence on the Texas Law of Civil Procedure,* 38 Tex. L. Rev. 24, 36 (1959), "Spanish law greatly insisted on fixing venue at the defendant's domicile. Texas, in turn, drew its venue statute from the Spanish model and has always adhered to the basic Spanish principle, though statutory exceptions are ever increasing."

During the final days of the 68th legislative session in May 1983, the Texas Legislature adopted an amended version of Article 1995, Venue (now superseded by chapter 15 of the Civil Practice and Remedies Code), and repealed another statute (R.C.S. Art. 2008), which granted an interlocutory appeal of venue orders before final judgment. Shortly thereafter, the Texas Supreme Court promulgated new procedural rules to set forth the procedural application of the new venue law. *See* Tex. R. Civ. P. 86–89. These complementary developments marked a major departure from prior Texas venue practice, which had been criticized on numerous occasions by numerous jurists and commentators. For criticisms of the excessive complexity and wastefulness of the prior law, see Greenhill, *State of the Judiciary,* 42 Tex. B.J. 379, 383 (1979); Guittard & Tyler, *Revision of the Texas Venue Statute: A Reform Long Overdue,* 32 Baylor L. Rev. 561 (1980) and Spradley, *Texas Venue: The Pathology of the Law,* 36 Sw. L.J. 645 (1982).

In August 1995, the 74th Texas Legislature again made wholesale revisions in the general venue statute. The 1995 venue amendments apply only to a suit commenced on or after September 1, 1995, except that C.P.R.C. § 15.018 (mandatory venue exception for FELA and Jones Act claims) applies only to suits filed after January 1, 1996. The 1995 amendments to Chapter 15 of the Civil Practice and Remedies Code generally restrict the venue choices that were made available to plaintiffs by the 1983 amendments. The amendments change the general venue rule by limiting venue choices available to claimants in actions against corporations, unincorporated associations and partnerships, and by providing for a venue transfer on the defendant's motion from a county of proper venue to another county for "the convenience of the parties and witnesses and in the interest of justice." C.P.R.C. § 15.002(b). The amendments require each plaintiff to establish proper venue, independently of any other plaintiff, and provide special rules for intervening plaintiffs. C.P.R.C. § 15.003. The amendments also make a number of adjustments to the mandatory venue exceptions contained in Subchapter B and to the permissive venue exceptions contained in Subchapter C.

Section 15.002 of the Civil Practice and Remedies Code contains a new general rule:

CIVIL PRACTICE AND REMEDIES CODE

CHAPTER 15. VENUE

SUBCHAPTER A. DEFINITIONS; GENERAL RULES

C.P.R.C. § 15.002. *Venue: General Rule.* (a) Except as otherwise provided by this subchapter or Subchapter B or C, all lawsuits shall be brought:

(1) in the county in which all or a substantial part of the events or omissions giving rise to the claim occurred;

(2) in the county of defendant's residence at the time the cause of action accrued if defendant is a natural person;

(3) in the county of the defendant's principal office in this state, if the defendant is not a natural person; or

(4) if Subdivisions (1), (2), and (3) do not apply, in the county in which the plaintiff resided at the time of the accrual of the cause of action.

C.P.R.C. § 15.001. *Definitions.* (b) "Proper venue" means:

(1) the venue required by the mandatory provisions of Subchapter B or another statute prescribing mandatory venue; or

(2) if Subdivision (1) does not apply, the venue provided by this subchapter [the general rule] or Subchapter C [permissive venue provisions].

### [A] Defendant's Residence (Natural Persons)

## MIJARES v. PAEZ

*534 S.W.2d 435 (Tex. Civ. App.—Amarillo 1976, no writ)*

ROBINSON, Justice.

Plaintiff Maria Rosario Paez brought a paternity suit against Carlos Javier Mijares in Lubbock County. Defendant Mijares [sought to have the venue of the action transferred to El Paso County and contended] . . . that the trial court "erred in finding" that appellant resided in Lubbock County for venue purposes. . . . Affirmed.

Defendant was not a minor at any time pertinent to this suit. He testified that he enrolled in Texas Tech University in Lubbock County, Texas, in January, 1974, and was still enrolled there in the fall semester of 1975. During the spring and fall semesters of 1974 he resided in university housing. He returned to El Paso during the summer of 1974 and at Christmas. He was enrolled in Texas Tech University during both the spring and summer semesters of 1975, as well as during the fall semester of 1975 when the hearing was held.

The defendant registered to vote in Lubbock County, listing his dormitory address in Lubbock County as his home address. At the time of the hearing, he was maintaining an apartment in Lubbock where he took his meals. He was served with citation in Lubbock County.

The defendant testified that he intended to complete a bachelor's degree at Texas Tech, but that he was only in Lubbock County to go to school, that he did not like Lubbock, and that it would never be his home.

When the defendant registered to vote in Lubbock County, giving his dormitory address as his residence, he represented that Lubbock County was his "current permanent residence address." V.A.T.S. Election Code, Art. 5.13b, subd.1(8).

Furthermore, the defendant could be a resident of Lubbock County for venue purposes even if his domicile were elsewhere. Although a person may have only one domicile, he may establish more than one residence for venue purposes. Even a rented room may qualify and the intent to make a permanent home is not necessary to the establishment of a second residence away from the domicile. *Snyder v. Pitts,* 150 Tex. 407, 241 S.W.2d 136 (1951). In *Snyder,* the Supreme Court announced a three element test to determine whether a second residence away from a domicile has been established. The proof must show that (1) the defendant possesses a fixed place of abode, (2) occupied or intended to be occupied consistently over a substantial period of time, (3) which is permanent rather than temporary.

The court in *Ward v. Lavy,* 314 S.W.2d 381 (Tex. Civ. App.—Eastland 1958, no writ) applied the *Snyder* test to facts similar to those before us. It held that a student at Hardin-Simmons University located in Taylor County had established residence in Taylor County for venue purposes by virtue of his enrollment in that university with the intention of remaining one or two years together with his rental of an apartment there.

We conclude that the trial court did not err in finding that the defendant was a resident of Lubbock County for venue purposes.

The order of the trial court overruling defendant's plea of privilege and retaining venue in Lubbock County is affirmed.

---

## NOTES AND QUESTIONS

(1) *Applying the Venue Residence Test.* The most troublesome part of the *Snyder v. Pitts* test quoted in the principal case is the requirement that the second residence be "permanent rather than temporary." What does "permanent" mean in light of the result reached in *Mijares?* What is a "substantial period of time"? Would six months qualify? The "general rule" (*See* C.P.R.C. § 15.002, *above*) and the exceptions identified in this note focus on the residence of natural persons at the time the cause of action accrued rather than on residence at the time suit was filed.

(2) *Venue at Plaintiff's Residence.* Suit can be brought in the county in which the plaintiff resides at the time the cause of action accrued only if C.P.R.C. § 15.002(1)–(3) do not apply. C.P.R.C. § 15.002(4). As a result, venue is ordinarily not proper in the county of plaintiff's residence. In fact, only two mandatory exceptions (*See* C.P.R.C. §§ 15.017, 15.018) and two

permissive exceptions (*See* C.P.R.C. §§ 15.032, 15.033) provide the plaintiff's residence (at the time when the cause of action accrued) as a venue choice.

### [B] Defendant's Principal Office (Legal Persons)

The amended venue statute defines principal office as follows:

CIVIL PRACTICE AND REMEDIES CODE

CHAPTER 15. VENUE

SUBCHAPTER A. DEFINITIONS; GENERAL RULES

C.P.R.C. § 15.001. *Definitions.* In this chapter:

(a) "Principal office" means a principal office of the corporation, unincorporated association, or partnership in this state in which the decision makers for the organization within this state conduct the daily affairs of the organization. The mere presence of an agency or representative does not establish a principal office.

By providing a localized "nerve center" approach in the statutory definition of the term "principal office," this statute means that business litigation against many companies is generally conducted in major metropolitan areas where the "decision makers" conduct the daily affairs of the organization unless the action is commenced in "the county in which all or a substantial part of the events or omissions giving rise to the claim occurred." Thus, for actions commenced on or after September 1, 1995, corporations and other legal persons can no longer be properly sued in a county solely on the basis that they have an "agency or representative" in that county. *See* former C.P.R.C. §§ 15.036, 15.037; *see also Ruiz v. Conoco, Inc.,* 868 S.W.2d 752 (Tex. 1993).

### [C] County in Which All or a Substantial Part of the Events or Omissions Giving Rise to the Claim Occurred

The Texas general rule for venue has adopted the federal standard, which focuses on where "all or a substantial part of the events or omissions giving rise to the claim occurred" and abandons the test of where "all or part" of the cause of action accrued. *See* 18 U.S.C. § 1391. *Cottman Transmission Sys. v. Martino,* 36 F.3d 291 (3d Cir. 1994), discusses this shift in the federal rules, pointing out that the intent of the change was to make venue determinations simpler. Under the former rule, whenever multiple forums were involved in the dispute, litigation proliferated regarding which district was the one in which the claim arose. The new language is purportedly more accommodating, although it is debatable whether determining what constitutes a "substantial part" will involve less litigation than the prior standard. In any event, the current rule maintains fairness considerations, because the substantiality requirement assures the defendant will not be required to litigate in a remote venue having no genuine relationship to the dispute.

---

## NOTES

(1) *The "Substantial Part" Test. Cottman Transmission Sys. v. Martino,* 36 F.3d 291 (3d Cir. 1994); indicates the federal standard is no masterpiece of clarity. Other federal cases interpreting

the "substantial part" formulation include *American Heart Disease Prevention Foundation, Inc. v. Hughey,* 905 F. Supp. 893 (D. Kan. 1995); *Robertson v. Merola,* 895 F. Supp. 1 (D.D.C. 1995) and *Kondrath v. Arum,* 881 F. Supp. 925 (D. Del. 1995).

(2) *Comparison With Prior Standard.* Under the predecessor statute, venue was proper where all or part of the "cause of action accrued." *See* former C.P.R.C. § 15.001. Furthermore, it was reasonably clear that given a tort action, in which damage or injury was alleged, venue was proper in the county where the injury occurred as well as where the defendant's conduct breached the applicable standard of care. *See, e.g., Lubbock Mfg. Co. v. Sames,* 598 S.W.2d 234, 236 (Tex. 1980). Shifting the analysis to where the claim occurred makes this unclear. The current general venue rule appears to restrict the plaintiff's venue choice to "the" county in which a substantial part of the matters giving rise to the claim occurred. C.P.R.C. § 15.002(a)(1). One possible interpretation would have the unfortunate effect of forcing parties and courts to choose a single county as the one in which a "substantial part" of the events occurred.

### [D] Transfer Based on Convenience

A motion to transfer, under the general venue rule may be based on convenience. Specifically, C.P.R.C. § 15.002(b) provides:

> (b) For the convenience of the parties and witnesses and in the interest of justice, a court may transfer an action from a county of proper venue under this subchapter or Subchapter C to any other county of proper venue on motion of a defendant filed and served concurrently with or before the filing of the answer, where the court finds:
>
> (1) maintenance of the action in the county of suit would work an injustice to the movant considering the movant's economic and personal hardship;
>
> (2) the balance of interests of all the parties predominates in favor of the action being brought in the other county; and
>
> (3) the transfer of the action would not work an injustice to any other party.

Although facially similar to federal statutory provisions enacted in 1948 (28 U.S.C. § 1404(a)), a number of differences exist. Under the Texas version, only the defendant may seek a transfer urging a more convenient county. In addition, the Texas statute authorizes a transfer to "another county of proper venue" as compared to the federal counterpart to a "district or division where it might have been brought." The Texas statute also requires a due order approach for urging a convenience transfer by a motion "served concurrently with or before the filing of the answer." Finally, while both statutes speak of transfer "for the convenience of the parties and witnesses and in the interest of justice," the Texas statute lists three additional factors (*See* (b)(1)–(3), *above*) to support a transfer. Federal caselaw governing convenience transfers provides little insight. Federal jurisprudence on this matter has been described as an "ad hoc balancing test applied by trial courts with appellate courts seldom determining an abuse of discretion." *See* Steinberg, *The Motion to Transfer and the Interests of Justice,* 66 Notre Dame L. Rev. 443 (1990) (describing Section 1404 motions as "vehicles for defendant delay," resulting in an increasing burden on the already backlogged federal courts). Federal courts are not in agreement as to the relevant factors, nor the importance of particular factors, in ruling on a motion to transfer based on convenience. *See Easter Scientific Marketing, Inc. v. Tekna-Seal, Inc.,* 695 F. Supp. 173, 180 n.13 (E.D. Va. 1988) (discussing 20 distinctive factors).

The new provision raises a number of interesting questions.

- Who bears the burden of proof on a motion to transfer based on convenience? Presumptively, the defendant, as movant, bears the burden.
- What is appropriate proof that the "convenience of the parties and witnesses and the interest of justice" support a transfer, that the "balance of interests of all the parties predominates" in favor of a transfer, and the transfer "would not work an injustice to any other party"?
- What is the interplay between a motion to transfer based on convenience and a plea of forum non conveniens? If the more convenient forum is outside Texas, the latter doctrine should be urged.
- Although the Texas legislature considered a multi-district venue provision for related litigation, it is not a part of the final venue statute passed. Is the pendency of related cases an appropriate factor? *See* § 6.06. (No longer good)
- May a transferee court "reconsider" a motion to transfer based on convenience? Could the case be transferred a second time? In a number of federal cases, multiple motions to transfer have been granted giving rise to "the appearance of judicial ping-pong." Steinberg, *The Motion to Transfer and the Interests of Justice,* 66 Notre Dame L. Rev. 443, 482 (1990). Do the time limits mandated in the Texas statute for raising venue complaints solve this problem? Y
- Paramount consideration should be given to the ability to compel witnesses' trial testimony as well as the attendant costs of litigating in a distant county.

## § 6.02 Exceptions to the General Rule

### [A] Types of Exceptions

There are a number of exceptions to the general venue rule. Several of the exceptions pertain to the substantive nature of the plaintiff's cause of action. For example, the amended venue statute includes exceptions which pertain to actions sounding in contract (*See* C.P.R.C. §§ 15.033, 15.035), actions sounding in tort (*See* C.P.R.C. §§ 15.017, 15.033), actions involving real property (*See* C.P.R.C. § 15.011), suits for specialized types of injunctive relief (*See* C.P.R.C. §§ 15.012, 15.013), and actions for mandamus against the State of Texas or the head of a department of the State government (*See* C.P.R.C. § 15.014). As a result of the 1995 amendments, mandatory exceptions have been added for landlord-tenant litigation (*See* C.P.R.C. § 15.0115), FELA and Jones Act cases (*See* C.P.R.C. § 15.018) as well as inmate litigation (*See* C.P.R.C. § 15.019).

Other exceptions depend on the type of defendant. For example, particular exceptions apply to counties (*See* C.P.R.C. § 15.015), certain other political subdivisions (*See* C.P.R.C. § 15.0151), insurance companies (*See* C.P.R.C. § 15.032), manufacturers of consumer goods (*See* C.P.R.C. § 15.033), and transient persons (*See* C.P.R.C. § 15.039).

There are many venue provisions contained in other statutes. For example, Chapter 65 of the Civil Practice and Remedies Code contains a section concerning the venue of suits for injunctive relief. *See* C.P.R.C. § 65.023. Under this provision, venue for injunction suits is mandatory in the county of the defendant's "domicile." But the injunction venue statute applies only to suits in which the relief sought is purely or primarily injunctive. *See In re Continental Airlines,* — S.W.2d —, —, 42 Sup. Ct. J. 147 (Tex. 1998) (suit for declaratory relief coupled with request for temporary, but not permanent injunction, was not purely or primarily injunctive). In addition, the Texas Tort Claims Act provides that "[a] suit under this chapter shall be brought in the county in which the cause of action or a part of the cause of action arises." *See* C.P.R.C. § 101.102. This language has been construed to be a venue provision rather than a jurisdictional provision. *Brown v. Owens*, 674 S.W.2d 748, 750 (Tex. 1984) (construing caption of previous statute containing same language). Specific sections of the basic venue statute set forth in Chapter 15 of the Civil Practice and Remedies Code make it clear that when venue is dealt with in another statute, there is no conflict because the other statute takes precedence. *See* C.P.R.C. § 15.016 (other mandatory venue), C.P.R.C. § 15.038 (other permissive venue).

### [B] Mandatory and Permissive Exceptions

When an exception provides that an action "shall be brought" in a particular county, the requirement is mandatory in the sense that it controls over other permissive exceptions as well as the general rule. Subchapter B of Chapter 15 of the Civil Practice and Remedies Code contains mandatory exceptions. Subchapter C of Chapter 15 contains permissive exceptions to the general rule contained in C.P.R.C. § 15.002. An exception to the general rule may be relied on by either the plaintiff or by the defendant under the amended venue statute. However, permissive exceptions cannot be relied on by a defendant to transfer an action to another county, unless the county of suit is not a county of proper venue. *See* C.P.R.C. § 15.063; Tex. R. Civ. P. 86, 87.

On the other hand, because mandatory exceptions override permissive exceptions as well as the general rule, a defendant may be able to achieve a transfer of venue to a county of mandatory venue. *See* Tex. R. Civ. P. 86, 87.

Finally, if more than one mandatory provision applies so that an apparent conflict between two provisions of equal rank occurs, the principal relief sought is said to determine venue. This tie-breaker is easy to articulate but difficult to apply. *See Brown v. Gulf Television Co.*, 157 Tex. 607, 306 S.W.2d 706, 709 (1957); *cf. Gonzalez v. Texaco, Inc.* 645 S.W.2d 324 (Tex. App.—Corpus Christi 1982, no writ).

CIVIL PRACTICE AND REMEDIES CODE

CHAPTER 15. VENUE

SUBCHAPTER B. MANDATORY VENUE

C.P.R.C. § 15.011. *Land.* Actions for recovery of real property or an estate or interest in real property, for partition of real property, to remove encumbrances from the title to real property, for recovery of damages to real property, or to quiet title to real property shall be brought in the county in which all or a part of the property is located.

C.P.R.C. § 15.0115. *Landlord-Tenant.* (a) Except as provided by another statute prescribing mandatory venue, a suit between a landlord and a tenant arising under a lease shall be brought in the county in which all or a part of the real property is located.

(b) In this section, "lease" means any written or oral agreement between a landlord and a tenant that establishes or modifies the terms, conditions, or other provisions relating to the use and occupancy of the real property that is the subject of the agreement.

C.P.R.C. § 15.012. *Injunction Against Suit.* Actions to stay proceedings in a suit shall be brought in the county in which the suit is pending.

C.P.R.C. § 15.013. *Injunction Against Execution of Judgment.* Actions to restrain execution of a judgment based on invalidity of the judgment or of the writ shall be brought in the county in which the judgment was rendered.

C.P.R.C. § 15.014. *Head of State Department.* An action for mandamus against the head of a department of the state government shall be brought in Travis County.

C.P.R.C. § 15.015. *Counties.* An action against a county shall be brought in that county.

C.P.R.C. § 15.0151. *Certain Political Subdivisions.* (a) Except as provided by a law not contained in this chapter, an action against a political subdivision that is located in a county with a population of 100,000 or less shall be brought in the county in which the political subdivision is located. If the political subdivision is located in more than one county and the population of each county is 100,000 or less, the action shall be brought in any county in which the political subdivision is located.

(b) In this section, "political subdivision" means a governmental entity in this state, other than a county, that is not a state agency. The term includes a municipality, school or junior college district, hospital district, or any other special purpose district or authority.

C.P.R.C. § 15.016. *Other Mandatory Venue.* An action governed by any other statute prescribing mandatory venue shall be brought in the county required by that statute.

C.P.R.C. § 15.017. *Libel, Slander, or Invasion of Privacy.* A suit for damages for libel, slander, or invasion of privacy shall be brought and can only be maintained in the county in which the plaintiff resided at the time of the accrual of the cause of action, or in the county in which the defendant resided at the time of filing suit, or in the county of the residence of defendants, or any of them, or the domicile of any corporate defendant, at the election of the plaintiff.

C.P.R.C. § 15.018. *Federal Employers' Liability Act and Jones Act.* (a) This section only applies to suits brought under the federal Employers' Liability Act (45 U.S.C. Section 51 et seq.) or the Jones Act (46 U.S.C. Section 688).

(b) All suits brought under the federal Employers' Liability Act or the Jones Act shall be brought:

(1) in the county in which all or a substantial part of the events or omissions giving rise to the claim occurred;

(2) in the county where the defendant's principal office in this state is located; or

(3) in the county where the plaintiff resided at the time the cause of action accrued.

C.P.R.C. § 15.019. *Inmate Litigation.* (a) Except as provided by Section 15.014, an action that accrued while the plaintiff was housed in a facility operated by or under contract with the Texas Department of Criminal Justice shall be brought in the county in which the facility is located.

(b) An action brought by two or more plaintiffs that accrued while the plaintiffs were housed in a facility operated by or under contract with the Texas Department of Criminal Justice shall be brought in a county in which a facility that housed one of the plaintiffs is located.

(c) This section does not apply to an action brought under the Family Code.

## SUBCHAPTER C. PERMISSIVE VENUE

C.P.R.C. § 15.031. *Executor; Administrator; Guardian.* If the suit is against an executor, administrator, or guardian, as such, to establish a money demand against the estate which he represents, the suit may be brought in the county in which the estate is administered, or if the suit is against an executor, administrator, or guardian growing out of a negligent act or omission of the person whose estate the executor, administrator, or guardian represents, the suit may be brought in the county in which the negligent act or omission of the person whose estate the executor, administrator, or guardian represents occurred.

C.P.R.C. § 15.032. *Insurance.* Suit against fire, marine, or inland insurance companies may also be commenced in any county in which the insured property was situated. A suit on a policy may be brought against any life insurance company, or accident insurance company, or life and accident, or health and accident, or life, health, and accident insurance company in the county in which the company's principal office in this state is located or in the county in which the loss has occurred or in which the policyholder or beneficiary instituting the suit resided at the time the cause of action accrued.

C.P.R.C. § 15.033. *Breach of Warranty by Manufacturer.* A suit for breach of warranty by a manufacturer of consumer goods may be brought in any county in which all or a substantial part of the events or omissions giving rise to the claim occurred, in the county in which the manufacturer has its principal office in this state, or in the county in which the plaintiff resided at the time the cause of action accrued.

C.P.R.C. § 15.035. *Contract in Writing.* (a) Except as provided by Subsection (b), if a person has contracted in writing to perform an obligation in a particular county, expressly naming the county or a definite place in that county by that writing, suit on or by reason of the obligation may be brought against him either in that county or in the county in which the defendant has his domicile.

(b) In an action founded on a contractual obligation of the defendant to pay money arising out of or based on a consumer transaction for goods, services, loans, or extensions of credit intended primarily for personal, family, household, or agricultural use, suit by a creditor on or by reason of the obligation may be brought against the defendant either in the county in which the defendant in fact signed the contract or in the county in which the defendant resides when the action is commenced. No term or statement contained in an obligation described in this section shall constitute a waiver of these provisions.

C.P.R.C. § 15.038. *Other Permissive Venue.* An action governed by any other statute prescribing permissive venue may be brought in the county allowed by that statute.

C.P.R.C. § 15.039. *Transient Person.* A transient person may be sued in any county in which he may be found.

### [C] Exceptions Based on the Type of Cause of Action

*Contract Actions*

*Read C.P.R.C. § 15.035.*

To maintain venue under the exception applicable to actions on written contracts, the following venue facts must be established:

(1) The defendant is a person reached by the statute;

(2) The claim is based on a written contract;

(3) The contract was entered into by the defendant or by a person authorized to bind the defendant, or was assumed or ratified by the defendant; and

(4) The contract's terms provide for performance of the obligation sued on by identifying a particular county or a definite place therein.

*See McGregor v. Properties Inv. of Huntsville*, 527 S.W.2d 502, 504–505 (Tex. Civ. App.—Houston [14th Dist.] 1975, writ dism'd).

Suppose the contract in writing provides for performance of the obligation sued on by "making payment in Amarillo"? *See Southwestern Inv. Co. v. Shipley*, 400 S.W.2d 304 (Tex. 1966) ("payable in Amarillo, Texas" was insufficient because Amarillo lies within two counties). What about "payable in Dallas, Texas"? What about "payable in Amarillo, Potter County, Texas"?

Several cases make it clear that the contractual provision providing for performance in a particular county must be at least one of the obligations sued on. The fact that one obligation under a contract is to be performed under the contractual terms at a specific place does not mean that another distinct contractual undertaking (obligation) is also to be performed there. *See Rorschach v. Pitts*, 248 S.W.2d 120 (Tex. 1952), in which the court would not imply that a provision that required a gas processing plant to *take delivery of gas* in Hutchinson County also required that the place of payment for the gas was in Hutchinson County. *See also Blakely v. Craig*, 505 S.W.2d 359, 361 (Tex. Civ. App.—Dallas 1974, no writ).

Special rules apply if the action involves a breach of a contractual obligation to pay money arising out of most types of consumer transactions. In these cases, suit may only be brought in either the county where the contract was signed or the county where the defendant resides when the action is commenced. *See* C.P.R.C. § 15.035(b); *see also Amaya v. Texas Securities Corp.*, 527 S.W.2d 218, 221–222 (Tex. Civ. App.—San Antonio 1975, writ ref'd n.r.e.); John J. Sampson, *Distant Forum Abuse in Consumer Transactions: A Proposed Solution*, 51 Tex. L. Rev. 269 (1973). It is also worth noting that filing suit in any county other than the county in which the defendant resides at the time of the commencement of the action, or in which the defendant in fact signed the contract, may be a deceptive trade practice. *See* Bus. & Com. C. § 17.46(b)(22).

### *Actions for Breach of Warranty*

*Read C.P.R.C. § 15.033.*

Suits for breach of warranty by a manufacturer of consumer goods may be brought in any county:

(1) Where all or a substantial part of the events or omissions giving rise to the claim occurred;

(2) Where the manufacturer's principal office is located; or

(3) Where the plaintiff or plaintiffs resided at the time the cause of action accrued.

C.P.R.C. § 15.033.

The exception applies only to manufacturers, not retailers. *Rogers v. Searle*, 533 S.W.2d 431, 433 (Tex. Civ. App.—Corpus Christi 1976, no writ).

### *Actions for Defamation and Invasion of Privacy*

*Read C.P.R.C. § 15.017.*

Actions for libel, slander, or invasions of privacy "shall be brought and can only be maintained" in the county where the plaintiff resided at the time the cause of action accrued or in the county where the defendants, or any of them, reside, or the domicile of any corporate defendant, at the election of the plaintiff. C.P.R.C. § 15.017. It is no longer necessary to prove at a venue hearing that a cause of action exists. Tex. R. Civ. P. 87(3)(a); *see Acker v. Denton Pub. Co.*, 937 S.W.2d 111, 116 (Tex. App.—Fort Worth 1996, writ denied).

*Actions for Deceptive Trade Practices*

*Read Bus. & Com. C. § 17.56.*

Actions brought under the Deceptive Trade Practices Act may be brought in any county in which venue is proper under Chapter 15 of the Civil Practice and Remedies Code or in a county in which the defendant or an authorized agent of the defendant solicited the transaction made the subject of the action at bar. Bus. & Com. C. § 17.56. *See Dairyland County Mutual Ins. Co. v. Harrison*, 578 S.W.2d 186, 191 (Tex. Civ. App.—Houston [14th Dist.] 1979, no writ) (telephone directory advertisement was sufficient proof of business solicitation in particular county); *see also Jim Walter Homes, Inc. v. Altreche*, 605 S.W.2d 733 (Tex. Civ. App.—Corpus Christi 1980, no writ).

*Actions Involving Land*

*Read C.P.R.C. § 15.011.*

The mandatory venue statute for certain real property actions requires actions to which it applies to be brought in the county where all or part of the realty is located. This statute governs venue in the following actions. (C.P.R.C. § 15.011):

(1) For the recovery of real property or an estate or interest in real property.

(2) For partition of real property.

(3) To remove encumbrances from the title to real property.

(4) For the recovery of damages to real property.

(5) To quiet title to real property.

This statute is strictly construed by the courts, and is triggered only if an action clearly falls within one of the enumerated types of causes of action. It will not apply merely because a lawsuit involves land in some manner. For example, in a suit for breach of an oil and gas lease, the ultimate purpose of the suit is to recover damages for breach of contract. Therefore, the suit is not an action to recover land or quiet title and venue is not mandatory in the county where the land is located. *Trafalgar House Oil & Gas v. De Hinojosa*, 773 S.W.2d 797, 798 (Tex. App.—San Antonio 1989, no writ); *see also Scarth v. First Bank & Trust Co.*, 711 S.W.2d 140, 142–143 (Tex. App.—Amarillo 1986, no writ) (when ultimate purpose of suit is to obtain declaration regarding validity of deed of trust lien, mandatory venue provision is inapplicable).

When suit is brought in a county under Section 15.011 and the defendant moves to transfer venue to another county, the plaintiff has the burden of proving that venue is maintainable in the county in which the land is located by showing that (1) the nature of the suit comes within the terms of Section 15.011, and (2) the land is situated in the county of the suit. *Caldwell Nat. Bank v. O'Neil*, 785 S.W.2d 840, 843 (Tex. App.—El Paso 1990, writ denied); *see* C.P.R.C. § 15.011.

Most of the cases interpreting the pre-1983 venue statute governing real property cases retain precedential value under the current statute, to the extent that the statutory language has not been modified. *See Scarth v. First Bank & Trust Co.*, 711 S.W.2d 140, 142 (Tex. App.—Amarillo 1986, no writ). Like the current statute (*See* C.P.R.C. § 15.011), the former statute mandated venue in the county where the land was located in suits for the recovery of lands, to remove encumbrances on the title of land, or to quiet title to land. former R.C.S. Art. 1995(14) (repealed 1983). Under prior law, however, venue was permitted, not required, in the county where the land was located in actions for the partition of land. former R.C.S. Art. 1995(13). Moreover, in 1983, actions for damage to real property and to prevent or stay waste on lands were removed from the mandatory venue statute for real property actions (*See Maranatha Temple, Inc. v. Enterprise Products Co.*, 833 S.W.2d 736, 739 (Tex. App.—Houston [1st Dist.] 1992, writ denied)), although these types of action for damages to real property were added back into the statute in 1995. C.P.R.C. § 15.011.

## [D] Multiple Claims and Parties

### [1] Multiple Claims

Before the 1983 revision of the general venue statute, under well-recognized principles of long standing, if venue was proper as to one of several claims against the same defendant, other claims against the same defendant that were properly joined (*See* Tex. R. Civ. P. 51) could be tried in the same county to avoid a multiplicity of suits. *Middlebrook v. David Bradley Mfg. Co.*, 86 Tex. 706, 26 S.W. 935 (1894). This principle, traditionally referred to as the *Middlebrook* doctrine, does not require the claims to arise from the same transaction or occurrence. *Middlebrook v. David Bradley Mfg. Co.,* 86 Tex. 706, 26 S.W. 935 (1894). Under the traditional rule, however, the claim on which venue was based had to be asserted in good faith. *Noel v. Griffin & Brand of McAllen, Inc.*, 478 S.W.2d 633, 635 (Tex. Civ. App.—Corpus Christi 1971, no writ). Another limitation on the application of the *Middlebrook* doctrine was that it did not override a mandatory venue exception. *See Pinkston v. Farmers State Bank of Center*, 201 S.W.2d 595, 601–603 (Tex. Civ. App.—Beaumont 1947, no writ). Moreover, although the cases are somewhat confusing on this point, the doctrine could not be used to sustain venue against a defendant who was not a party to the in-county claim or cause of action. *See Gilmer v. Texas*, 281 S.W.2d 109, 113 (Tex. Civ. App.—Austin 1955, no writ). *Cf. Van Scheele v. Kugler-Morris Gen. Contractors, Inc.*, 532 S.W.2d 375, 381–382 (Tex. Civ. App.—Dallas 1975, dis.).

The 1983 amendments both codified the *Middlebrook* doctrine and extended it to cases involving multiple plaintiffs and multiple defendants. Under former C.P.R.C. § 15.061, if the court had venue on one claim, other properly joined claims made by other plaintiffs and claims against other defendants could be joined as additional claims in the same county, unless a mandatory exception applied to the joined claims. The 1995 amendments repealed this broad provision because it was subject to abuse. *See Polaris Investment Management Corp. v. Abascal*, 890 S.W.2d 486 (Tex. App.—San Antonio 1994, orig. proceeding). Although the current statute does not expressly embrace the *Middlebrook* doctrine, it appears to have been reinstated by the repeal of C.P.R.C. § 15.061. In addition, the following section of the current venue statute concerns multiple claims in cases involving a mandatory exception.

CIVIL PRACTICE AND REMEDIES CODE

CHAPTER 15. VENUE

SUBCHAPTER A. DEFINITIONS; GENERAL RULES

C.P.R.C. § 15.004. *Mandatory Venue Provision Governs Multiple Claims.* In a suit in which a plaintiff properly joins two or more claims or causes of action arising from the same transaction, occurrence, or series of transactions or occurrences, and one of the claims or causes of action is governed by the mandatory venue provisions of Subchapter B, the suit shall be brought in the county required by the mandatory venue provision.

*Venue Problems*

(1) Assume that a resident of Travis County executed three promissory notes in favor of a corporation having its principal office in Harris County. Assume that only one of the notes provides that it is payable in Harris County, Texas. Can venue be sustained there under the *Middlebrook* doctrine on the remaining notes? What if the *Middlebrook* doctrine had not been reinstated?

(2) Assume that a resident of Wise County brings a wrongful termination case against her employer, a Texas corporation having its principal place of business in Dallas County. Assume that the plaintiff's petition is filed in Tarrant County and alleges a breach of contract, bad faith, defamation, and intentional infliction of emotional distress. If the defendant establishes mandatory venue in Wise County as to the defamation claim, what part of the case will be transferred to Wise County?

### [2] Multiple Defendants

The following sections of Chapter 15 of the Civil Practice and Remedies Code contain a familiar transactional test concerning the joinder of multiple defendants (*see* Tex. R. Civ. P. 40) as well as an antiwaiver provision.

CIVIL PRACTICE AND REMEDIES CODE

CHAPTER 15. VENUE

SUBCHAPTER A. DEFINITIONS; GENERAL RULES

C.P.R.C. § 15.005. *Multiple Defendants.* In a suit in which the plaintiff has established proper venue against a defendant, the court also has venue of all the defendants in all claims or actions arising out of the same transaction, occurrence, or series of transactions or occurrences.

SUBCHAPTER D. GENERAL PROVISIONS

C.P.R.C. § 15.0641. *Venue Rights of Multiple Defendants.* In a suit in which two or more defendants are joined, any action or omission by one defendant in relation to venue, including a waiver of venue by one defendant, does not operate to impair or diminish the right of any other defendant to properly challenge venue.

*Venue Problems*

(1) Assume that an automobile collision occurs in Dallas County. Assume further that the injured claimant resides in Harris County, that the driver of the truck that collided with the claimant's vehicle resides in Travis County and that his employer, the owner of the truck, is a Texas corporation with its principal office in Collin County. What venue choices are open to the claimant? Can venue be maintained in Dallas County as to both the driver and his employer? Can venue be maintained in Collin County as to both the employer and the driver? Can venue be maintained in Travis County as to both the driver and employer?

(2) Assume the same facts as in (1) above. Also assume that the claimant brings suit in Harris County against all of the parties mentioned above and against the manufacturer of the truck. What effect does joinder of the manufacturer have?

(3) Assume the same facts as in (1) above. Further assume that the claimant brings suit in Harris County against all of the parties mentioned in (1) and against his spouse, who also resides in Harris County, on the theory that she negligently operated the vehicle in which the claimant was riding. Can venue be maintained in Harris County under these circumstances? Suppose a claim for intentional or negligent infliction of emotional distress is alleged against the spouse based on conduct unrelated to the car wreck?

### [3] Multiple Plaintiffs; Intervention

CIVIL PRACTICE AND REMEDIES CODE

CHAPTER 15. VENUE

SUBCHAPTER A. DEFINITIONS; GENERAL RULES

C.P.R.C. § 15.003. *Multiple Plaintiffs and Intervening Plaintiffs.* (a) In a suit where more than one plaintiff is joined each plaintiff must, independently of any other plaintiff, establish proper venue. Any person who is unable to establish proper venue may not join or maintain venue for the suit as a plaintiff unless the person, independently of any other plaintiff, establishes that:

(1) joinder or intervention in the suit is proper under the Texas Rules of Civil Procedure;

(2) maintaining venue in the county of suit does not unfairly prejudice another party to the suit;

(3) there is an essential need to have the person's claim tried in the county in which the suit is pending; and

(4) the county in which the suit is pending is a fair and convenient venue for the person seeking to join in or maintain venue for the suit and the persons against whom the suit is brought.

(b) A person may not intervene or join in a pending suit as a plaintiff unless the person, independently of any other plaintiff:

(1) establishes proper venue for the county in which the suit is pending; or

(2) satisfies the requirements of Subdivisions (1) through (4) of Subsection (a).

(c) Any person seeking intervention or joinder, who is unable to independently establish proper venue, or a party opposing intervention or joinder of such a person may contest the decision of the trial court allowing or denying intervention or joinder by taking an interlocutory appeal to the court of appeals district in which the trial court is located under the procedures established for interlocutory appeals. The appeal must be perfected not later than the 20th day after the date the trial court signs the order denying or allowing the intervention or joinder. The court of appeals shall:

(1) determine whether the joinder or intervention is proper based on an independent determination from the record and not under either an abuse of discretion or substantial evidence standard; and

(2) render its decision not later than the 120th day after the date the appeal is perfected by the complaining party.

*Venue Problems*

(1) Assume that a person who resides in Matagorda County purchased a Ford truck from a dealership in Nueces County, Texas, and believes that the truck is defective and unmerchantable in breach of implied warranties. What venue choices are available to the purchaser? If suit is brought in Matagorda County, can other plaintiffs who purchased other trucks from Ford in other places and who do not reside in Matagorda County join as parties plaintiff? What type of showing will be needed if Ford contests venue?

(2) Assume the same facts as in (1), above. Can other plaintiffs intervene after the original plaintiff's venue rights have been determined?

---

## BRISTOL-MYERS SQUIBB CO. v. GOLDSTON

*983 S.W.2d 369 (Tex. App—Fort Worth 1998, pet. dism'd by agr.)*

DAUPHINOT, Justice.

### INTRODUCTION

This is an interlocutory appeal from the trial court's order denying Appellants Bristol-Myers Squibb Co., Surgitek, Inc., Medical Engineering Corporation, CBI Medical, Inc., and Natural Y/Aesthetech's ("Defendants") [footnote omitted] motions to transfer venue and motions to strike joinders and interventions. We are asked to decide whether breast implants are consumer goods under the Texas Civil Practice and Remedies Code and whether the joining plaintiffs [footnote omitted] have established an essential need to try their claims in Wichita County. We affirm in part and reverse and remand in part.

### FACTUAL AND PROCEDURAL BACKGROUND

This is a products liability case in which Tonya Lynne Goldston and Foy Goldston and the joining plaintiffs ("Plaintiffs") sued Defendants for injuries received as the result of allegedly defective breast implants. The female plaintiffs were members of a nationwide class-action suit, but they opted out of the settlement agreement reached in that suit and chose to pursue their own lawsuits. Tonya Lynne Goldston and her husband, Foy Goldston, filed suit in Wichita County on July 23, 1996. Over one hundred plaintiffs, women with breast implants and their husbands, attempted to join the Goldstons' suit.

Defendants filed numerous motions to transfer venue to Dallas County and a motion to strike joinders and interventions. The trial court denied the motions to transfer venue and, applying pre-1995 venue law, denied the motion to strike joinders and interventions. Defendants then filed their first interlocutory appeal. Holding that the post-1995 venue laws applied, this court reversed the order of the trial court and remanded the case for further proceedings under the post-1995 venue laws. [footnote omitted] On remand, the trial court, applying post-1995 venue law, again denied Defendants' motions to transfer venue to Dallas County and to strike the joinders and interventions. This second interlocutory appeal followed.

VENUE REQUIREMENTS FOR INTERVENING PLAINTIFFS

The Texas Civil Practice and Remedies Code provides that "[i]n a suit where more than one plaintiff is joined each plaintiff must, independently of any other plaintiff, establish proper venue."[5]

Any person who is unable to establish proper venue may not join or maintain venue for the suit as a plaintiff unless the person, independently of any other plaintiff, establishes that:

(1) joinder or intervention in the suit is proper under the Texas Rules of Civil Procedure;

(2) maintaining venue in the county of suit does not unfairly prejudice another party to the suit;

(3) there is an essential need to have the person's claim tried in the county in which the suit is pending; and

(4) the county in which the suit is pending is a fair and convenient venue for the person seeking to join in or maintain venue for the suit and the persons against whom the suit is brought.[6]

Therefore, a person may not intervene or join in a pending suit as a plaintiff unless the person, independently of any other plaintiff, either (a) establishes proper venue for the county in which the suit is pending or (b) satisfies the four requirements listed above.[7]

CATEGORIES OF PLAINTIFFS

There are ninety-two Plaintiffs remaining in this case, fifty-five women who received breast implants and the thirty-seven spouses of these women. [footnote omitted] Plaintiffs can be categorized into four groups:

Group A: Women who were residents of Wichita County at the time they were implanted and who were implanted in Wichita County and their spouses. There are thirteen Plaintiffs, eight women and five spouses, in this group. [footnote omitted]

Group B: Women who were residents of Wichita County at the time they were implanted but who were not implanted in Wichita County and their spouses. There are twenty-one Plaintiffs, thirteen women and eight spouses, in this group. [footnote omitted]

---

[5] Tex. Civ. Prac. & Rem. Code Ann. § 15.003(a) (Vernon Supp. 1999).

[6] Id.

[7] See id. § 15.003(b).

Group C: Women who were not residents of Wichita County at the time they were implanted and who were not implanted in Wichita County and their spouses. There are thirty-seven Plaintiffs, twenty-one women and sixteen spouses, in this group. [footnote omitted]

Group D: There are twenty-one Plaintiffs, thirteen women and eight spouses, in this group. [footnote omitted] Plaintiffs' attorney has indicated that there are not any affidavits or other proof as to where these women were implanted or where they resided at the time they were implanted.

WHETHER BREAST IMPLANTS ARE CONSUMER GOODS

In their first issue on appeal, Defendants ask this court to decide whether breast implants are "consumer goods" under the Texas Civil Practice and Remedies Code. Section 15.033 allows a suit for breach of warranty by a manufacturer of consumer goods to be brought in the county in which the plaintiff resided at the time the cause of action accrued.[13]

If breast implants are consumer goods, then Plaintiffs in groups A and B, those who resided in Wichita County when they were implanted, could rely on section 15.033 to independently establish proper venue in Wichita County. If breast implants are not consumer goods, Plaintiffs in groups A and B must either establish proper venue some other way or satisfy the four factors of section 15.003(a).[14]

Defendants contend that this issue is properly before this court on interlocutory appeal pursuant to section 15.003(c), which provides that [a]ny person seeking intervention or joinder, who is unable to independently establish proper venue, or a party opposing intervention or joinder of such a person may contest the decision of the trial court allowing or denying intervention or joinder by taking an interlocutory appeal to the court of appeals district in which the trial court is located under the procedures established for interlocutory appeals.[15]

This statute does not state that a party opposing intervention or joinder of any person may immediately appeal. It only permits a party opposing intervention or joinder of such a person, meaning a person who is unable to independently establish proper venue, to file an interlocutory appeal.[16] Section 15.003(c) does not provide for an interlocutory appeal from the trial court's determination that a person seeking intervention or joinder has independently established proper venue.[17] Furthermore, section 15.064 states that the trial court shall determine venue questions from the pleadings and affidavits and that no interlocutory appeal shall lie from that determination.[18]

Plaintiffs in groups A and B, those who resided in Wichita County when they were implanted, are relying on section 15.033 to independently establish proper venue in Wichita County. They

[13] Tex. Civ. Prac. & Rem. Code Ann. § 15.033 (Vernon Supp. 1999).

[14] Id. § 15.003(a)(1)–(4).

[15] Id. § 15.003(c) (emphasis added).

[16] *See* Surgitek, Inc. v. Adams, 955 S.W.2d 884, 888 (Tex. App.—Corpus Christi 1997, pet. requested) (holding that the phrase "of such a person" relates back to "person seeking intervention or joinder, who is unable to independently establish proper venue").

[17] *See* Abel v. Surgitek, 975 S.W.2d 30, 36 (Tex. App.—San Antonio 1998, pet. granted) (holding that no interlocutory appeal is available from a general venue determination); Surgitek, 955 S.W.2d at 887 (holding that section 15.003(c) "allows an interlocutory appeal for one specific purpose: to 'contest the decision of the trial court allowing or denying intervention or joinder' " and that appellate court's inquiry is limited to whether joinder or intervention is proper).

[18] Tex. Civ. Prac. & Rem. Code Ann. § 15.064(a) (Vernon 1986).

are not trying to satisfy the four requirements of section 15.003(a)[19] We hold that the trial court's determination that Plaintiffs in groups A and B have independently established proper venue is not appealable until after the trial on the merits. We therefore do not have jurisdiction during this interlocutory appeal to decide whether Plaintiffs in groups A and B have independently established proper venue.[20] Accordingly, we do not address whether or not breast implants are consumer goods.

TONYA LYNNE GOLDSTON AND FOY GOLDSTON

Tonya Lynne Goldston and Foy Goldston are the original plaintiffs in this lawsuit. Although categorized in group C, they are not joining plaintiffs. Therefore, the only part of the trial court's order that is applicable to them is the denial of Defendants' motions to transfer venue. The Goldstons must meet the requirements of the general venue rule.[21]

As previously stated, the trial court determines venue based on the pleadings and affidavits, and there is no provision for an interlocutory appeal from this determination.[22] We therefore do not have jurisdiction to determine whether venue is proper for Tonya Lynne Goldston and Foy Goldston.

ESSENTIAL NEED

In their second issue on appeal, Defendants argue that the joining plaintiffs have not established an "essential need" to try their claims in Wichita County. This issue applies to the remaining thirty-five Plaintiffs in group C, those women who were not residents of Wichita County at the time they were implanted and who were not implanted in Wichita County. These women cannot independently establish proper venue in Wichita County and therefore must satisfy the four requirements of section 15.003(a):

(1) joinder or intervention in the suit is proper under the Texas Rules of Civil Procedure;

(2) maintaining venue in the county of suit does not unfairly prejudice another party to the suit;

(3) there is an essential need to have the person's claim tried in the county in which the suit is pending; and

(4) the county in which the suit is pending is a fair and convenient venue for the person seeking to join in or maintain venue for the suit and the persons against whom the suit is brought.[23]

---

[19] Tex. Civ. Prac. & Rem. Code Ann. §§ 15.003(a)(1)–(4), 15.033 (Vernon Supp. 1999). Plaintiffs in group A contend that they can also independently establish proper venue in Wichita County pursuant to section 15.002(a)(1), as they were implanted in Wichita County. Id. § 15.002(a)(1) (general venue rule allowing suit to be brought in the county in which all or a substantial part of the events or omissions giving rise to the claim occurred).

[20] *See* Surgitek, 955 S.W.2d at 887 (holding that because section 15.003(c) does not authorize interlocutory appeal of trial court's denial of motion to transfer venue, appellate court was without jurisdiction to consider appellants' point of error).

[21] See Tex. Civ. Prac. & Rem. Code Ann. § 15.002 (Vernon Supp. 1999).

[22] See Tex. Civ. Prac. & Rem. Code Ann § 15.064(a) (Vernon 1986); Bristol-Myers Squibb Co. v. Barner, 964 S.W.2d 299, 301 (Tex. App.—Corpus Christi 1998, no pet.) (holding that decision regarding transfer of venue is not subject to interlocutory appeal).

[23] Tex. Civ. Prac. & Rem. Code Ann. § 15.003(a)(1)–(4) (Vernon Supp. 1999).

Although Defendants state in their brief that they do not concede that any of the four requirements have been satisfied, their brief does not contain any arguments, authorities, or record citations to show that Plaintiffs have not satisfied requirements one, two, and four.[24] Our discussion therefore will focus on the essential need requirement.

### Standard of Review

We are to review the trial court's order to determine whether the joinder or intervention is proper based on an independent determination from the record, and we do not apply either an abuse of discretion or substantial evidence standard of review.[25] "We must independently review the pleadings and affidavits to determine whether [Plaintiffs] made prima facie proof of the joinder requirements and, if so, whether the prima facie proof was'destroyed' by conclusive evidence to the contrary."[26]

The determination of whether joinder or intervention is proper is based upon (1) factual determinations concerning the nature of the underlying lawsuit and the situation of the various parties before the trial court and (2) the application of the four requirements of section 15.003(a) to those facts.[27]

With regard to the underlying factual determinations, "[w]e must still defer to the trial court's determination of these matters and may not substitute our findings for those of the trial court on controverted questions of fact."[28] (noting that there is no indication in section 15.003 that the legislature intended for appellate courts to make independent fact findings about the nature of the underlying lawsuit and the situation of the parties). However, we independently, or de novo, interpret and apply the legal requirements of section 15.003(a) to the facts of the case as found by the trial court, independent of any deference to the conclusions of the trial court.[29]

### Definition of Essential Need

The legislature did not define "essential need" in the venue statutes, and the parties are in disagreement as to its meaning. In interpreting a statute, we are to give words their ordinary meaning.[30]

Defendants contend that it means "indispensably necessary" and that Plaintiffs must prove that Wichita County is the only possible venue. Plaintiffs argue that "of the utmost importance" is the proper definition.

Black's Law Dictionary defines essential as "[i]ndispensably necessary; important in the highest degree; requisite. That which is required for the continued existence of a thing."[31]

And it defines need as "[a] relative term, the conception of which must, within reasonable limits, vary with the personal situation of the individual employing it. Term means to have an urgent or essential use for (something lacking); to want, require."[32]

---

[24] See Tex. R. App. P. 38.1(h).

[25] See Tex. Civ. Prac. & Rem. Code Ann. § 15.003(c)(1) (Vernon Supp.1999); Abel, 975 S.W.2d at 36–37.

[26] Abel, 975 S.W.2d at 38.

[27] *See* Surgitek, 955 S.W.2d at 888.

[28] Id.

[29] See id.

[30] *See* Tex. Gov't Code Ann. § 312.002 (Vernon 1998).

[31] Black's Law Dictionary 546 (6th ed. 1990).

[32] Id. at 1031.

As this definition indicates, a determination of whether there is an essential need must be made on a case-by-case basis based on the specific facts as they relate to the individual Plaintiffs.

## APPLICATION OF LAW TO FACTS

Plaintiffs have provided prima facie evidence in the form of pleadings and affidavits to establish that there is an essential need to have the suit tried in Wichita County. First, all of the female plaintiffs in group C have the same treating physician, Dr. Danny Bartel, who offices in Wichita County. In his affidavit, Dr. Bartel states that he has examined, treated, and cared for these Plaintiffs, including conducting an initial interview, reviewing each patient's history and medical records, and performing a physical examination and laboratory tests. Dr. Bartel is an expert witness for each female Plaintiff.

Second, Plaintiffs' fact and expert witnesses are located in and around Wichita County. Each female Plaintiff recites in her affidavit that "[m]y fact witnesses, expert witnesses and treating physicians are residents in and around Wichita County, Texas. It would be unduly burdensome and an extreme hardship on myself and individuals involved in my lawsuit if my case were to be transferred from Wichita County, Texas."

Furthermore, all of the group C Plaintiffs are represented by Hank Anderson, who also offices in Wichita County. Mr. Anderson stated in his affidavit that, if the cases were transferred to Dallas County, it would be two to three years before the cases could go to trial. There are also affidavits from two Dallas attorneys noting that it would be several years before the cases could be tried in Dallas County. Mr. Anderson states in his affidavit that "[s]uch a period of delay would be highly detrimental to the interests of my clients, as many are experiencing ongoing and deteriorating disease problems." Mr. Anderson also notes in his affidavit that the expenses of litigation would be increased by having to try suits in Wichita County and in Dallas County and that procedures for informal discovery are already in place in Wichita County.

We have independently reviewed the pleadings and affidavits and have determined that the group C Plaintiffs have made prima facie proof of the joinder requirements and that this prima facie proof was not destroyed by conclusive evidence to the contrary. We therefore affirm the trial court's denial of the motions to strike joinders and interventions as to Plaintiffs in group C.

## PLAINTIFFS IN GROUP D

As previously stated, Plaintiffs' attorney has indicated that there are not any affidavits or other proof as to where these women were implanted or where they resided at the time they were implanted. We must therefore conclude that these Plaintiffs cannot independently establish proper venue and are trying to satisfy the four requirements of section 15.003. They have not, however, presented prima facie evidence in the form of pleadings and affidavits that they have satisfied the four requirements. These Plaintiffs have not met their burden. We therefore reverse the trial court's denial of the motions to strike joinders and interventions as to Plaintiffs in group D and remand this case to the trial court for further proceedings consistent with this opinion.

## HOLDING

We do not have jurisdiction to decide whether venue is proper for Tonya Lynne Goldston and Foy Goldston or for Plaintiffs in groups A and B. We affirm the trial court's denial of the motions to strike joinders and interventions as to Plaintiffs in group C. We reverse the trial court's denial of the motions to strike joinders and interventions as to Plaintiffs in group D and remand this case to the trial court for further proceedings consistent with this opinion.

### [E] Counterclaims, Cross-Claims, and Third Party Actions

The manner in which counterclaims (*See* Tex. R. Civ. P. 97(a), (b) (defined as "a claim as one made in a pleading to a claim made by an opposing party")), cross-claims (*See* Tex. R. Civ. P. 97(c) (defined as "a claim made against a co-party")), and third-party claims (*See* Tex. R. Civ. P. 38 (providing for a cross-action by a defendant against a person "not a party to the action who is or may be liable" to the defendant or to the plaintiff for all or part of the plaintiff's claim against the defendant)) affect venue has also been addressed in the Civil Practice and Remedies Code at Section 15.062 as follows:

CIVIL PRACTICE AND REMEDIES CODE

CHAPTER 15. VENUE

SUBCHAPTER D. GENERAL PROVISIONS

C.P.R.C. § 15.062. *Counterclaims, Cross Claims, and Third-Party Claims.* (a) Venue of the main action shall establish venue of a counterclaim, cross claim, or third-party claim properly joined under the Texas Rules of Civil Procedure or any applicable statute.

(b) If an original defendant properly joins a third-party defendant, venue shall be proper for a claim arising out of the same transaction, occurrence, or series of transactions or occurrences by the plaintiff against the third-party defendant if the claim arises out of the subject matter of the plaintiff's claim against the original defendant.

## § 6.03 Litigating Venue Rights

*Read Tex. R. Civ. P. 86 through 89.*

### [A] Venue Pleadings

Before September 1, 1983, the manner in which a defendant sought to obtain a transfer of the action to another county was by filing a sworn plea of privilege. Ordinarily, the "privilege" asserted was the basic privilege of being sued in the county where the pleader resided. The plea was also required to contain a formal allegation that "no exception to exclusive venue in the county of one's residence provided by law exists in said cause." In order to maintain venue of the action in the county of suit, the plaintiff was required to controvert the plea of privilege by filing a controverting plea, under oath, setting out specifically the grounds relied on to confer venue of the cause on the court where the cause was pending. When the plea of privilege was controverted, the venue issues were determined by a trial of the venue facts, with the general rule being that the plaintiff had to establish, by a preponderance of the evidence, the application of one or more of the exceptions relied on.

Virtually all aspects of the pre-September 1, 1983, procedures summarized in the preceding paragraph have been modified by the amendment of R.C.S. Art. 1995 (now codified in Chapter 15 of the Civil Practice and Remedies Code) and its companion procedural rules. Under modern venue practice a motion to transfer venue is required; the primary basis for transfer (other than on grounds of inconvenience or inability to obtain a fair trial) is that venue is not proper in the county of suit and is proper in the county to which transfer is sought (or that venue is mandatory in a particular county despite the fact that venue is otherwise proper where the action was filed); no response is necessary except as required by Civil Procedure Rule 87(3)(a).

### [B] Venue Hearings

Before September 1, 1983, it was often necessary for the plaintiff to prove a cause of action as one of the venue facts. At the venue hearing, live testimony was required to establish the venue facts. Affidavits were not a permissible substitute.

Each of these aspects of former venue practice was eliminated by the 1983 amendments. First, to eliminate the former requirement that the plaintiff prove on the merits that a cause of action existed against a defendant to establish proper venue as to that cause of action and that defendant, the statute was amended to provide "[i]n all venue hearings, no factual proof concerning the merits of the case shall be required to establish venue." *See* C.P.R.C. § 15.064(a); *see also* Tex. R. Civ. P. 87(2)(b). Second, to eliminate "minitrials" on venue issues altogether, the statute was amended to provide that "[t]he court shall determine venue on the basis of the pleadings and affidavits." C.P.R.C. § 15.064(a). Finally, to resolve venue controversies involving conflicting affidavits, Rule 87 was amended to provide that a claimant's prima facie proof that venue is proper could not be controverted by a defending party to obtain a venue transfer unless the motion to transfer is based on the grounds that an impartial trial cannot be held in the county of suit or "on an established ground of mandatory venue" as reflected in the movant's "prima facie proof." Tex. R. Civ. P. 87(3)(a)–(c). But, as explained in the next subsection, "[o]n appeal from the trial on the merits, if venue was improper, it shall in no event be harmless error and shall be reversible error" and "[i]n determining whether venue was or was not proper, the appellate court shall consider the entire record, including the trial on the merits." C.P.R.C. § 15.064(b). Thus, plaintiffs were provided ample statutory encouragement to avoid unfounded venue claims.

---

## ACKER v. DENTON PUB. CO.

*937 S.W.2d 111 (Tex. App.—Fort Worth 1996, writ denied)*

HOLMAN, Justice.

Gary Lewis Acker, pro se, appeals the summary judgment of a district court in Denton County that he take nothing on claims by which he sought $9.6 million in damages for alleged injury from newspaper articles written about him. Acker asserted causes of action for defamation, invasion of privacy, and deceptive trade practices. One defendant, Denton Publishing Company, publishes three newspapers, the *Lewisville News*, the *Denton Record-Chronicle*, and the *Grapevine Sun*. Other defendants were Fred W. Patterson, an officer of the publishing company, Fred W. Patterson, Jr., general manager of the publishing company, Tom Bateman, a vice president, Roy Appleton, a director, Cynthia Baker and James Florez, staff writers, and Dawn Cobb, managing editor of the *Lewisville News*. Finding no reversible error, we affirm.

Although there are seven points of error, we will not address them in numerical order. Instead, we will consider them in the chronological order in which the issues arose.

FIRST MOTION TO TRANSFER VENUE

We begin with the complaint of the third point, that venue was erroneously transferred from Tarrant County to Denton County. This suit originated on August 7, 1995 in the 96th Judicial District Court, Tarrant County, where the defendants answered subject to their motion to transfer venue to Denton County. Mr. Acker is a resident of Denton County.

In the motion to transfer, the defendants asserted that venue in Denton County was mandated by Tex. Civ. Prac. & Rem. Code Ann. § 15.017 (Vernon 1986). The motion recited that Denton Publishing Company is a corporation domiciled in Denton County, where its registered office and registered agent are located. The motion stated that all the defendant individuals except Tom Bateman reside in Denton County, where causes of action asserted by Mr. Acker allegedly arose. Although Tom Bateman works in Denton County, the motion concedes that he resides in Tarrant County where Mr. Acker filed suit. The portion of Section 15.017 that applies to the facts of this case is:

> A suit for damages for libel, slander, or invasion of privacy shall be brought and can only be maintained in the county in which the plaintiff resided at the time of the accrual of the cause of action . . . or in the county of the residence of defendants, or any of them, . . . at the election of the plaintiff.

Tex. Civ. Prac. & Rem. Code Ann. § 15.017 (Vernon 1986). Section 15.017 is a "mandatory" venue provision. *See* Tex. R. Civ. P. 87.2(a).

The defendants supported their motion with affidavits of Fred W. Patterson, Jr. and Tom Bateman, and because they sought to transfer venue to Denton County, the defendants had the burden to prove venue facts showing that venue was maintainable in Denton. *Id.* Venue facts for defendants to prove under Section 15.017 were:

(1) that the causes of action alleged include libel, slander, or invasions of privacy;

(2) that Mr. Acker resided in Denton County at the time the alleged causes accrued;

(3) that all defendants reside in Denton, not Tarrant; and

(4) that Tom Bateman, a resident of Tarrant, is not a proper defendant in this suit.

On the other hand, Mr. Acker had the burden to prove venue facts showing that venue was maintainable in Tarrant. Tex. R. Civ. P. 87.2(a). To meet his burden of proof and maintain the venue of this suit in the 96th District Court in Tarrant County under Section 15.017, Mr. Acker had to prove only two venue facts:

(1) the causes of action alleged include libel, slander, or invasion of privacy; and

(2) a defendant resides in Tarrant County.

Here, the 96th District Court in Tarrant County was required to resolve the defendants' venue challenge from the plaintiff's pleadings, the defendants' pleadings, and the affidavits filed by two of the defendants. Tex. Civ. Prac. & Rem. Code Ann. § 15.064(a) (Vernon 1986); Tex. R. Civ. P. 87.3(b). From the pleadings, that court could reasonably conclude that two of Mr. Acker's causes of action were libel and invasion of privacy. From the defendants' motion to transfer, that court could reasonably conclude that the motion was grounded upon the mandatory provision of Section 15.017.

Other than his pleadings, Mr. Acker did not offer the 96th District Court any proof that would support venue in Tarrant County. He did not file any affidavit, and his reply to the defendants' affidavits and motion to transfer venue consisted of bare conclusions that the motion was "premature and inappropriate" and that venue in Tarrant County could be established once discovery was completed. When a defendant pleads a venue fact and the plaintiff fails to specifically deny it, the trial court is required to consider that venue fact true. Tex. R. Civ. P. 87.3(a).

Nevertheless, the first venue fact that Mr. Acker had to prove—that some of his causes of action were within the scope of Section 15.017—was established by the allegations of his pleadings that were on file in the 96th District Court. Mr. Acker was relieved of the burden of proving his second venue fact, but only because it was judicially admitted, both by the defendants' motion to transfer (conceding that defendant Tom Bateman resides in Tarrant County) and Tom Bateman's own affidavit verifying that he resides in Tarrant. Thus, Mr. Acker's pleadings proved one of the venue facts necessary to maintain venue in Tarrant County, and the defendants proved the second venue fact for him.

From the 96th District Court's order transferring venue, it appears that the transfer was made because the venue facts alleged in the defendants' motion to transfer were supported with the Patterson and Bateman affidavits as prima facie proof that the defendants were entitled to the transfer, and because Mr. Acker failed to controvert with sworn proof of his own. If venue is not proper in the county where suit is filed, a trial court must transfer the case to a county where venue is proper. Tex. Civ. Prac. & Rem. Code Ann. § 15.063(1) (Vernon 1986). But if a plaintiff files suit in a county of proper venue, it is reversible error to transfer venue under section 15.063(1) even if the county of transfer would have been proper if originally chosen by the plaintiff. *Wilson v. Texas Parks & Wildlife Dept.*, 886 S.W.2d 259, 261 (Tex. 1994). . . .

. . . .

For years, libel plaintiffs at venue hearings were required to offer prima facie proof of the existence of a cause of action against the defendant. *See General Motors Acceptance Corp. v. Howard*, 487 S.W.2d 708, 710 (Tex. 1972); *A.H. Belo Corp. v. Blanton*, 133 Tex. 391, 129 S.W.2d 619, 621–22 (Tex. 1939); *Betancourt v. Whittle*, 659 S.W.2d 895, 897 (Tex. App.—San Antonio 1983, no writ). It is no longer necessary to prove at a venue hearing that a cause of action exists. Tex. R. Civ. P. 87.3.(a). From the evidence in this case, the trial court was aware that all of the litigants except Tom Bateman reside or are domiciled in Denton County and Mr. Acker's claims had their origin in Denton County, not Tarrant County.

Facially, Mr. Acker's basis for claiming venue in Tarrant County was that he had joined Tom Bateman, a Tarrant County resident, as a defendant. The record, however, does not substantiate any claim by Mr. Acker against Tom Bateman for acts done by him in his individual capacity. Although Mr. Acker's petition names Mr. Bateman as one of the defendants, it does not allege that Bateman personally committed any wrongs. Tom Bateman's affidavit in support of the motion to transfer venue from Tarrant County was not controverted by Mr. Acker and is competent evidence that Mr. Bateman did not personally perform, assist, or supervise the alleged libel. Mr. Bateman's only relation to the matters alleged by Mr. Acker is that Mr. Bateman is a corporate officer of the publishing company.

After bathing Mr. Acker's Tarrant County venue claim in the light of the entire record, we must conclude that Mr. Bateman was not a proper defendant in the suit. *See ACF Indus., Inc. v. Carter*, 903 S.W.2d 423, 424 (Tex. App.—Texarkana 1995, writ dism'd by agr.). The record as a whole reveals no genuine issue of material fact that would support a cause of action by Mr. Acker against Mr. Bateman individually. Because our review of the entire record shows that the prima facie venue proof in the Tarrant County court was misleading, we conclude that Tarrant County was not a county of proper venue, and the 96th District Court's order to transfer venue to the proper county, Denton, was not reversible error. The third point of error is overruled.

. . . .

MOTION TO TRANSFER VENUE FROM DENTON

In the fourth point of error, Mr. Acker complains about the 362nd District Court's denial of his motion to transfer venue from the 362nd District Court to either Dallas or Travis Counties. That motion appears to be grounded on Mr. Acker's concern that the case would not be tried fairly in Denton because the defendant publishing company owns and operates the only daily newspaper in the county. The inability to obtain a fair and impartial trial of a civil case may be grounds for a change of venue. Tex. R. Civ. P. 257. A motion on those grounds must be supported by competent affidavits of the party seeking the transfer and three credible residents of the county where the suit is pending. *Id.*

Mr. Acker did not furnish the required number of affidavits, and because he did not comply with Rule 257, we find no error in the denial of his motion to transfer venue from Denton County. We overrule point of error number four.

. . . .

[Affirmed.]

---

## NOTES AND QUESTIONS

(1) *Timing Considerations.* Civil Procedure Rule 86 provides that an objection to improper venue is waived if not made by written motion filed before or concurrently with any other plea, pleading or motion. *See also* C.P.R.C. § 15.063. It should be noted that: "A motion to transfer venue because an impartial trial cannot be had in the county where the action is pending is governed by the provisions of Rule 257." Tex. R. Civ. P. 86. A defendant may subpoena witnesses and use the various discovery devices without waiving the venue challenge. *See* Tex. R. Civ. P. 88. Before taking other actions that could be construed as being inconsistent with the venue challenge, care must be exercised. In *Nacol v. Williams,* 554 S.W.2d 286, 288 (Tex. Civ. App.—Eastland 1977, writ dism'd), the defendant was held to have waived the basic venue privilege existing under prior law by *presenting* a motion to require the plaintiff to post security for costs even though the motion was filed after the venue challenge! Consider the following excerpt:

> This case is distinguishable from *Talbert v. Miles,* 477 S.W.2d 710 (Tex. Civ. App.—Waco 1972, no writ) relied on by appellant in that in *Talbert* there was no evidence the motion to rule for costs was submitted to the court for determination or that any action of any nature was taken on the motion by anyone after it was filed.
>
> In the case at bar, when the appellant filed his motion with an order attached for the judge to sign, the court had a duty to act on the motion.

(2) *Follow the Motion With a Request for a Hearing.* As reflected in the following excerpt from *Whitworth v. Kuhn,* 734 S.W.2d 108, 111 (Tex. App.—Austin 1987, no writ), a movant must take the initiative to present a motion to transfer to the trial court:

Texas R. Civ. P. Ann. 87(1) (Supp. 1987) provides in part:

> The determination of a motion to transfer venue shall be made promptly by the court and such determination must be made in a reasonable time prior to commencement of the trial on the merits. The movant has the duty to request a setting on the motion to transfer.

It is apparent that this language contemplates a speedy determination of a venue question. Indeed, we find it implicit in the language and purpose of this rule that a movant may not sit on his rights indefinitely without incurring waiver. *See* 3 W. Dorsaneo, *Texas Litigation Guide* § 61.05[4] (1987). Thus, while a trial court may rule on a venue motion without a hearing, the movant is under a duty to request a hearing to urge his motion within a reasonable time. Here, Whitworth waited more than a year after filing his motion to transfer venue before requesting a hearing on that motion. His complete lack of diligence is inconsistent with the purpose of Rule 87(1), and the trial court could have refused his motion on that basis.

(3) *The Scope of Waiver.* C.P.R.C. § 15.0641 resolves a split among Texas intermediate courts and clarifies that waiver by one defendant of its right to contest venue does not operate as a waiver to a co-defendant's right to timely challenge venue.

(4) *The Effect of a Nonsuit on Venue Determination.* Under pre-1983 venue practice, if a plaintiff took a nonsuit while the defendant's plea of privilege was pending, venue was fixed in the county to which transfer was sought. *See Tempelmeyer v. Blackburn,* 175 S.W.2d 222, 224 (Tex. 1943); *see also Ruiz v. Conoco, Inc.,* 868 S.W.2d 752, 756–757 (Tex. 1993). Under post-1983 practice, when a nonsuit is filed, the trial court and any reviewing court "must consider the state of the record at that point." *GeoChem Tech Corporation v. Verseckes,* 962 S.W.2d 541, 543 (Tex. 1998). Thus, if an objection to venue has been filed and the plaintiff then takes a nonsuit and has not specifically denied the venue facts alleged by the party seeking transfer, the venue facts are taken as true. But a plaintiff does not lose the right to choose between two counties in which venue is proper as shown in the defendant's motion to transfer "by filing its first suit in a county in which venue is improper." *GeoChem Tech Corporation v. Verseckes,* 962 S.W.2d 541, 544 (Tex. 1998). In other words, it appears that a nonsuit waives the right to contest venue facts alleged in the movant's motion to transfer but not the right to choose a proper venue in that context.

### [C] Appellate Review of Venue Rulings

Because of the importance of a party's venue rights, as well as the elimination of interlocutory appeals for "venue determinations," the 68th Texas Legislature developed an unusual rule for the appeal of venue rulings. Section 15.064(b) of the Civil Practice and Remedies Code provides: "On appeal from the trial on the merits, if venue was improper it shall in no event be harmless error and shall be reversible error. In determining whether venue was or was not proper, the appellate court shall consider the entire record, including the trial on the merits."

---

**RUIZ v. CONOCO, INC.** 868 S.W.2d 752 (Tex. 1993). Javier Ruiz, a resident of Hidalgo County, suffered severe head injuries in Webb County while working for Cameron Iron Works,

Inc. on a well owned by Conoco, Inc. Ruiz ultimately sued Conoco in Starr County through his wife who had been appointed his guardian. Ruiz claimed that venue was proper in Starr County under a former permissive venue exception that was repealed in 1995 under which: "Foreign corporations . . . not incorporated by the laws of this state, and doing business in this state, may be sued in any county in which . . . the company may have an agency or representative." Conoco sought to have the action transferred to Harris County. Despite the fact that it ruled as a matter of law that Conoco had no agency or representative in Starr County, the Texas Supreme Court interpreted Civil Practice and Remedies Code Section 15.064(b) by devising the following deferential standard of review:

> . . . . The procedure mandated by this statute is fundamentally flawed because it allows appellate review of venue on a basis different from that on which it was decided. In deciding a motion to transfer venue, the trial court is required by Rule 87, Tex. R. Civ. P., to take as true those facts of which prima facie proof is made by the party with the burden of such proof; yet in reviewing the trial court's decision, an appellate court must reverse (there cannot be harmless error) if other evidence in the record, even evidence adduced after venue was determined, destroys the prima facie proof on which the trial court relied. Prima facie proof is not subject to rebuttal, cross-examination, impeachment or even disproof. The evidence as a whole may well show that prima facie proof was misleading or wrong. But while the wisdom of the statute may be challenged, there is no misunderstanding its plain language: an appellate court is obliged to conduct an independent review of the entire record to determine whether venue was proper in the ultimate county of suit. *See* Price, *supra,* at 878–79.
>
> This review should be conducted like any other review of a trial court's fact findings and legal rulings, except that the evidence need not be reviewed for factual sufficiency. If there is probative evidence to support the trial court's determination, even if the preponderance of the evidence is to the contrary, we believe the appellate court should defer to the trial court. A remand to reconsider the issue, which is the relief ordinarily afforded for factual insufficiency of the evidence, would only increase the expense and delay of litigation in order to resolve an issue which, though important, is unrelated to the merits. Moreover, it exacerbates the difficulties already present in the rule if the appellate court decides, based on all the evidence, that the case should be remanded for a redetermination of venue, based on prima facie proof. (Would a second trial be required?) The statute does not mandate factual sufficiency review, and we believe it is neither necessary nor wise.
>
> Therefore, if there is any probative evidence in the entire record, including trial on the merits, that venue was proper in the county where judgment was rendered, the appellate court must uphold the trial court's determination. If there is no such evidence, the judgment must be reversed and the case remanded to the trial court. The error cannot be harmless, according to the statute. If there is any probative evidence that venue was proper in the county to which transfer was sought, the appellate court should instruct the trial court to transfer the case to that county. Only if there is no probative evidence that venue was proper either in the county of suit or in the county to which transfer was sought should the appellate court remand the case to the trial court to conduct further proceedings on the issue of venue. This is one instance in which remand cannot be avoided. Rule 87(3)(d), Tex. R. Civ. P., contemplates that additional proof may be ordered in connection with a motion to transfer if neither party makes the required showing at first. In the unusual instance where there

is no probative evidence in the record that venue is proper anywhere, a remand is unavoidable.

The issue for us, then, is whether there is any probative evidence in the record to support the trial court's determination that venue was proper in Starr County. As in any other situation, we view the record in the light most favorable to the trial court's ruling. We do not defer, however, to the trial court's application of the law.

868 S.W.2d 752, 757–758 (Tex. 1993).

---

## WILSON v. TEXAS PARKS AND WILDLIFE DEPT.

*886 S.W.2d 259 (Tex. 1994)*

HIGHTOWER, Justice.

This cause requires that we determine whether a trial court commits reversible error by transferring a civil lawsuit filed in a Texas county that qualifies as a proper venue to another county that originally might have been considered a proper venue. Lydia Wilson, Curtis Wilson, Angela Wilson Kramm, and Lila Wilson (collectively "Plaintiffs") sued the Texas Parks and Wildlife Department ("Department") in district court in Travis County, alleging that the Department's negligence caused the drowning deaths of Wilford and Wilton Wilson. The Department filed a motion to transfer venue of Plaintiffs' action to Blanco County. The motion was granted and the case was transferred to Blanco County where, after a jury trial, a take-nothing judgment was rendered in favor of the Department. The court of appeals affirmed, holding that the transfer of a lawsuit from one county of proper venue to another county of proper venue is not reversible error. 853 S.W.2d 825. For the reasons explained herein, we reverse the judgment of the court of appeals, remand this cause to the trial court in Blanco County, and order that the cause be transferred to Travis County for a new trial.

### I.

On the afternoon of May 16, 1987, the Wilson fishing party, including Wilford and Wilton Wilson, arrived at Pedernales Falls State Park ("the Park") to go fishing. The Park is located in Blanco County and is owned and operated by the Department. The fishing party walked and waded across one-hundred yards of river bed to get to their fishing spot. By 4:00 p.m., the party was fishing from atop a rock surrounded by water. At 8:00 p.m., the party was joined by two additional members of the Wilson family. Shortly thereafter, the party noticed rising water and attempted to retrace their steps across the river bed. Wilford and Wilton Wilson were unable to cross the river and drowned.

Plaintiffs sued the Department in Travis County, alleging that the Department's negligence caused the drowning deaths of Wilford and Wilton Wilson. Specifically, Plaintiffs alleged that the Department was negligent in the design, implementation, and maintenance of the Park's flood early warning system and in the training of Park personnel. The Department filed a motion to transfer venue of the suit to Blanco County, the site of the drownings. The motion was granted and the suit was transferred. Trial was to a jury who found that the Department was negligent, but failed to find that this negligence was a proximate cause of the deaths. Additionally, the jury found that Wilford and Wilton Wilson's negligent conduct was a proximate cause of their deaths. Finally, the jury found that the Wilson fishing party was not fishing within the park boundaries. Based on the jury's verdict, the trial court rendered a take-nothing judgment in favor of the Department. The court of appeals affirmed, holding that the transfer of a lawsuit from a county of proper venue to another county of proper venue is not reversible error.

II.

The Department contends that the transfer of a civil lawsuit from a county that qualifies as a proper venue to another county that might originally have been considered a proper venue is not reversible error as a matter of law. We disagree.

Venue selection presupposes that the parties to the lawsuit have choices and preferences about where their case will be tried. *See* Tex. Civ. Prac. & Rem. Code Ann. 15.001–15.040 (Vernon 1986 & Supp. 1994); *Maranatha Temple, Inc. v. Enterprise Prod. Co.,* 833 S.W.2d 736, 741 (Tex. App.—Houston [1st Dist.] 1992, writ denied) (recognizing that the plaintiff has the right to file suit in any permissible county). Venue may be proper in many counties under general, mandatory, or permissive venue rules. *See* Tex. Civ. Prac. & Rem. Code Ann. 15.001–15.040. The plaintiff is given the first choice in the filing of the lawsuit. *See Tieuel v. Southern Pac. Transp. Co.* 654 S.W.2d 71, 775 (Tex. App.—Houston [14th Dist.] 1983, no writ). If the plaintiff's venue choice is not properly challenged through a motion to transfer venue, the propriety of venue is fixed in the county chosen by the plaintiff. Tex. Civ. Prac. & Rem. Code Ann. 15.063 (Vernon 1986); Tex. R. Civ. P. 86—1. If a defendant objects to the plaintiff's venue choice and properly challenges that choice through a motion to transfer venue, the question of proper venue is raised. Tex. R. Civ. P. 86. The burden is on the plaintiff to prove that venue is maintainable in the county of suit. *Id.* 87—2(a). If the plaintiff fails to meet this burden, the trial court must transfer the lawsuit to another specified county of proper venue.[1] Tex. Civ. Prac. & Rem. Code Ann. 15.063(1) ("The court . . . shall transfer an action to another county of proper venue if . . . the county in which the action is pending is not a proper county. . ."); *Tieuel,* 654 S.W.2d at 775 (recognizing that if the plaintiff files suit in a county where venue does not lie, the plaintiff waives the right to choose and the defendant may have the suit transferred to a proper venue). If the plaintiff meets the burden, the trial court must maintain the lawsuit in the county where it was filed. Tex. R. Civ. P. 87–3(c) ("If a claimant has adequately pleaded and made prima facie proof that venue is proper in the county of suit . . . then the cause shall not be transferred but shall be retained in the county of suit. . .").

Together, Rule 87—3(c) and section 15.063(1) require that a lawsuit pleaded and proved to be filed in a county of proper venue may not be transferred. Therefore, if the plaintiff chooses a county of proper venue, and this is supported by proof as required by Rule 87, no other county can be a proper venue in that case.[2] This rule gives effect to the plaintiff's right to select a proper venue. *Maranatha Temple, Inc.,* 833 S.W.2d at 741.

The Department urges that reversible error exists only if the county of trial was one where permissive or mandatory venue never could have been sustained. Such a rule would eviscerate

---

[1] In such a case, the right to chose [sic] a proper venue passes to the defendant who must prove that venue is maintainable in the county to which transfer is sought.

[2] This opinion only addresses transfer of venue pursuant to section 15.063(1) of the Texas Civil Practice and Remedies Code and expresses no opinion regarding transfer of venue pursuant to sections 15.063(2) and (3). We recognize that these section may apply to make transfer of venue appropriate.

the plaintiff's right to select venue. *Id.* The First Court of Appeals correctly understood the harsh effect of such a rule:

> [W]hen the plaintiff files suit in a permissible county, and the trial court wrongly transfers venue to another county, even a permissible one, the plaintiff has lost his right to choose where to bring his suit. He has neither waived his option by filing in an impermissible county nor had his suit transferred because the defendant has properly shown that it should be. Yet, he lost the right to bring suit in the permissible county of his choice. He has lost a right which he neither waived nor was rightfully divested of. The harmless error rule should not apply to such a circumstance.

*Id.*[3] Furthermore, the Department asks us to fashion a rule that runs contrary to the mandatory admonishment of Rule 87–3(c) and that renders section 15.063(1) meaningless. This we cannot do. Tex. Gov't Code Ann. 311.021(2) (Vernon 1988) ("In enacting a statute, it is presumed that . . . the entire statute is intended to be effective."); *Monsanto Co. v. Cornerstone Mun. Util. Dist.*, 865 S.W.2d 937, 939 (Tex. 1993) (stating that this court seeks the intent of the legislature as found in the plain and common meaning of the words and terms used).

Accordingly, we hold that if a plaintiff files suit in a county of proper venue, it is reversible error to transfer venue under section 15.063(1) even if the county of transfer would have been proper if originally chosen by the plaintiff. We now consider whether venue was proper in the county where suit was initially brought in this case.

III.

The standard of appellate review is governed by section 15.064(b) of the Texas Civil Practice and remedies Code which provides:

> On appeal from the trial on the merits, if venue was improper it shall in no event be harmless error and shall be reversible error. In determining whether venue was or was not proper, the appellate court shall consider the entire record, including the trial on the merits.

Tex. Civ. Prac. & Rem. Code Ann. 15.064(b) (Vernon 1986); *Ruiz v. Conoco, Inc.*, 868 S.W.2d 752, 757 (Tex. 1993). The "appellate court is obligated to conduct an independent review of the entire record to determine whether venue was proper in the ultimate county of suit." *Ruiz,* 868 S.W.2d at 758; *see also* Dan R. Price, *New Texas Venue Statute: Legislative History,* 15 St. Mary's L.J. 855, 878–879 (1984). Under the rule announced today, if Travis County, the venue chosen by Plaintiffs, was a county of proper venue, then Blanco County cannot be a county of proper venue as a matter of law.[4] We review the entire record, including the trial on the merits, to determine whether there is any probative evidence that venue was proper in Travis County. *Ruiz,* 868 S.W.2d at 758. This review strikes a balance between the competing interests of the plaintiff and the defendant. It preserves the plaintiff's right to select and maintain suit in a county

---

[3] The court in *Maranatha Temple, Inc.* recognized additional beneficial effects of the rule we announce today:

> Parties who would otherwise be likely to knowingly assert faulty grounds for a transfer of venue will be less likely to do so if they face automatic reversal once it is determined on appeal that the transfer was erroneous . . . [and such a rule] . . . will guard against the forum shopping that occurs when a party intentionally asserts faulty, invalid grounds for a change of venue from one permissible county to another permissible county which he perceives is more favorable.

883 S.W.2d at 741.

[4] The parties agree that Blanco County would have been a proper venue had the Plaintiffs originally filed suit there.

of proper venue. And, it protects the defendant from fraud or inaccuracy at the pleading stage. *See* Dan R. Price, *New Texas Venue Statute: Legislative History,* 15 St. Mary's L.J. 855, 877–78 (1984) (recognizing that the appellate court's review of the entire record protects against fraud or inaccuracy that might not be discoverable at the motion to transfer venue stage).

Because the Plaintiffs have sued a governmental entity, venue in this case is governed by section 101.102 of the Texas Civil Practice and Remedies Code, which provides that "suit under this chapter shall be brought in state court in the county in which the cause of action or a part of the cause of action arises." Tex. Civ. Prac. & Rem. Code Ann. 101.102 (Vernon Supp. 1994). Plaintiffs assert that their cause of action for negligence arose, in part, from the acts which occurred at the Department's headquarters in Travis County: (1) deciding not to arm the Johnson City River Bridge sensor to trigger the sirens; (2) negligently designing the flood early warning system which is not audible in certain areas of the flood danger zone; (3) advising park patrons, through the use of signs, articles, and maps prepared in Travis County, to rely on the sirens to warn them of oncoming flood or rising waters while failing to warn them that the sirens may not be audible in certain areas of the river bed; and (4) failing to oversee the proper arming and rearming of the flood early warning system and to maintain in a ready state the sirens, towers, computer console, and radios.

Tom McGlathery, Regional Park Director for the Department, testified that the decision not to arm the Johnson City River Bridge sensor was made, in part, by Barry Bennett at the Department's headquarters in Travis County. Mr. McGlathery also testified that the individuals responsible for the content of the signs and map handouts detailing the Park's flood early warning system were employed at the Department's headquarters in Travis County. Wilbur Mengers, superintendent of the Park, testified that the signs and maps concerning the flood early warning system came from Travis County. Together, this testimony constitutes probative evidence that acts giving rise to the Plaintiffs' cause of action occurred in Travis County. Accordingly, venue was proper in Travis County under section 101.102 of the Texas Civil Practice and Remedies Code.

Because we find that Travis County, the venue chosen by Plaintiffs, was a county of proper venue, we hold that Blanco County was an improper venue as a matter of law. The trial of this lawsuit in Blanco County constitutes reversible error. *See* Tex. Civ. Prac. & Rem. Code Ann. § 15.064(b).

For the reasons explained herein, we reverse the judgment of the court of appeals, remand this cause to the trial court in Blanco County, and order that the cause be transferred to Travis County for a new trial.

---

## NOTE

*Review of Venue Rulings.* The 1995 changes to the Texas venue scheme in the Civil Practice and Remedies Code contain a number of provisions addressed to the review of venue ruling. The method of review is dependent on the basis of the ruling:

C.P.R.C. § 15.002(c). A court's ruling or decision to grant or deny a transfer under Subsection (b) [based on convenience] is not grounds for appeal or mandamus and is not reversible error.

C.P.R.C. § 15.003(c). Any person seeking intervention or joinder, who is unable to independently establish proper venue, or a party opposing intervention or joinder of such a person may contest the decision of the trial court allowing or denying intervention or joinder by taking an interlocutory appeal to the court of appeals district in which the trial court is located under the procedures established for interlocutory appeals. The appeal must be perfected not later than the 20th day after the date the trial court signs the order denying or allowing the intervention or joinder. The court of appeals shall:

(1) determine whether the joinder or intervention is proper based on an independent determination from the record and not under either an abuse of discretion or substantial evidence standard; and

(2) render its decision not later than the 120th day after the date the appeal is perfected by the complaining party.

C.P.R.C. § 15.0642. A party may apply for a writ of mandamus with an appellate court to enforce the mandatory venue provisions of this chapter. An application for the writ of mandamus must be filed before the later of:

(1) the 90th day before the date the trial starts; or

(2) the 10th day after the date the party receives notice of the trial setting.

### [D] The Disposition of the Action

## GEOPHYSICAL DATA PROCESSING CENTER v. CRUZ

*576 S.W.2d 666 (Tex. Civ. App.—Beaumont 1978, no writ)*

CLAYTON, Justice.

This cause was filed by Rafael B. Cruz, appellee, against three defendants—Lee Webster, Whitehall Corporation, and Geophysical Data Processing Center, Inc. (GDPC), appellant. Defendants Webster and Whitehall filed a plea of privilege to be sued in Dallas County. Appellant did not file a plea of privilege. The trial court sustained the plea of privilege filed by defendants Webster and Whitehall and transferred the cause as to these defendants to Dallas County. The trial court further held that all parties were indispensable, and the causes of action were not severable. Accordingly, the entire cause of action, including the action against Geophysical Data Processing Center, Inc., was transferred to Dallas County, from which order appellant has appealed.

The sole question to be decided by this court is whether or not the trial court erred in transferring the entire cause to Dallas County.

Appellant urges error of the trial court in transferring the cause against it "because the causes of action asserted against GDPC, Whitehall and Webster are severable" and that "the causes of action asserted against [the three defendants] are joint and several."

To determine whether or not this cause is severable as to appellant and whether or not appellant is a necessary party to the cause of action asserted against Webster and Whitehall, resulting in the proper transfer of the cause of action in its entirety, we must first determine what causes of action have been pleaded by appellee and what relief has been sought. *Cogdell v. Fort Worth National Bank,* 537 S.W.2d 304 (Tex. Civ. App.—Fort Worth 1976, writ dism'd); *Whitley v. King,* 227 S.W.2d 241 (Tex. Civ. App.—Waco 1950, no writ). As the court states in *Whitley v. King, supra*: "The nature and objects of an action can be determined only from a consideration of all the material averments contained in the petition or complaint upon which the suit is based and the character of relief therein sought [citing cases]. Hence, the propriety of joining and severing parties and actions in any legal proceeding is dependent primarily, although not always exclusively, upon the state of the pleadings relevant to such proceeding."

Plaintiff's cause of action against the three defendants is based upon fraud for the actions of defendants, including appellant, in connection with a certain Software Licensing Agreement between appellee and appellant. Under the terms of this agreement, appellant, a wholly owned subsidiary of Whitehall, was to pay $15,000 for a temporary license for 180 days for the use of an "Explorer System" which consists of various computer programs used for the processing of geophysical data, such system to be used in its installation in Houston, Harris County, Texas. Plaintiff further contended that Webster was in absolute control of Whitehall and appellant during the entire time concerned in this suit. Appellant is a wholly owned subsidiary of Whitehall. All the actions by the defendant corporations (Whitehall and appellant) have been done at the instance and direction of Webster and "he has used the Defendant corporations to further his intention with regard to the defrauding of the Plaintiff or his rights in and to the Explorer System."

At the conclusion of the 180-day period, appellant was to pay balance due for such temporary license, but refused to do so and retained the system.

There are other contentions, stated in the petition, that at the end of the temporary license period appellant had a right to purchase a permanent license for the use of the system by paying an additional $35,000 during the term of the temporary license. The agreement further provided for licenses to appellant for other installations at locations outside its Houston office upon payment of $30,000 for the second installation and $15,000 for third and subsequent installations. Appellant, at the end of the temporary license period, retained the system although it failed to make payment for the permanent license. In addition, appellant made or caused to be made in conjunction with the other defendants, and expressly at the direction of Webster, another installation in Africa without paying the $30,000 as required by the agreement. Plaintiff further pleads that appellant represented to the geophysical industry that it had an exclusive system capable of performing the computer technology that in fact was being performed by appellant utilizing plaintiff's Explorer System and that by reason thereof the value of plaintiff's system was diminished; and further that appellant has represented to users of the system that appellant owns the rights in and to the system with authority to make installations, such representations being false, resulting in the diminished value of the system in the market place. Plaintiff further contends that appellant has been a "shell corporation operated for the use and benefit of the Defendant Whitehall and [appellant] has no assets other than the Explorer System and appellant is in fact an alter-ego of the Defendant Whitehall."

In *Commonwealth Bank & Trust Company v. Heid Bros., Inc.,* 122 Tex. 56, 52 S.W.2d 74 (Tex. Comm'n. App. 1932, jdgmt. adopted), it is stated:

> "A 'necessary party' to a suit, according to the general understanding of that term, is one who is so vitally interested in the subject-matter of the litigation that a valid decree cannot be rendered without his presence as a party."

In *Orange Associates v. Albright,* 548 S.W.2d 806 (Tex. Civ. App.—Austin 1977, writ dism'd), the court said:

> "A necessary party is one whose joinder is required in order to afford the plaintiff the complete relief to which he is entitled against the defendant who is properly suable in that county."

In *International Harvester Co. v. Stedman,* 59 Tex. 593, 324 S.W.2d 543 (1959), the Supreme Court states the well established rules as to the transferring of the entire cause when the plea of privilege of one of several defendants is sustained. The Supreme Court quotes from *Johnson v. First National Bank,* 42 S.W.2d 870 (Tex. Civ. App.—Waco 1931, no writ), as follows:

> "The rule seems to be that, where one of several defendants files a plea of privilege to be sued in the county of his residence, and the plea is sustained, if the cause of action is a joint action growing out of joint liability of all of the defendants, the suit must be transferred in its entirety to the county of the residence of the defendant whose plea is sustained. On the other hand, if the cause of action against several defendants is severable, or joint and several, the court should retain jurisdiction over the action in so far as it concerns the defendants whose pleas of privilege have not been sustained, and should transfer the suit in so far as it concerns the defendant whose plea is sustained."

In the pleadings of plaintiff, as pointed out above, the relief sought against the three defendants in this cause of action is so interwoven that to obtain the relief sought by the plaintiff necessitates the presence of all of the defendants. The pleadings concerning the express direction of the actions of the corporate defendants by Webster and the allegation of the alter-ego status of Whitehall and appellant require the presence of each and all the defendants for an adequate judgment to be rendered in this cause.

The cause of action asserted by plaintiff is such that he could not obtain the full relief to which he may be entitled, that is, a joint as well as several judgment against all defendants unless all were sued in the same action. *See Commonwealth Bank & Trust v. Heid Bros., Inc., supra*; *Orange Associates v. Albright, supra.*

The trial court properly transferred this entire cause to Dallas County, and the judgment is affirmed.

Affirmed.

---

## NOTES AND QUESTIONS

(1) *Statutory Reanalysis.* How would the same case be analyzed under the current venue statute? *See* C.P.R.C §§ 15.004, 15.005. Under the current statute, can one defendant's failure to assert venue complaints prejudice a codefendant? *See* C.P.R.C. § 15.0641.

(2) *Reconsideration of Prior Ruling.* Another procedural problem concerns the ability of a judge to reconsider a prior ruling on a motion to transfer. One court of appeals has held that the language of Tex. R. Civ. P. 87(5) prohibits reconsideration and that mandamus is available to correct the "void" order. *Dorchester M. L. P. v. Anthony*, 734 S.W.2d 151, 152 (Tex. App.—Houston [1st Dist.] 1987, no writ):

> Relator's predecessor in interest, Dorchester Gas Producing Company, filed the underlying suit in December, 1983, seeking to recover money damages against Cabot Pipeline

Corporation and other defendants for the alleged conversion of gas from producing wells located in the Panhandle Field in Gray and Carson Counties. On May 23, 1984, Judge Ken Harrison, then Presiding Judge of the 334th District Court, entered an order denying the defendants' motion to transfer venue. On February 27, 1987, the defendants filed a second motion to transfer venue, and on May 18, 1987, Judge Anthony, on her own motion, entered a purported order of transfer, stating that she had considered, *sua sponte*, the correctness of venue of the case and determined that proper venue was in Gray County. Judge Anthony's order also purported to vacate, sua sponte, "any previous orders relating to venue" in the case.

. . . . Here, the court *sustained* venue in the county of suit and denied the defendants' motion to transfer. Under such a circumstance, the express provisions of Rule 87(5) mandate that "no further motions to transfer shall be considered. . . ." We accordingly hold that Judge Anthony's venue order dated May 18, 1987, is void in that it purports to reconsider and vacate Judge Harrison's prior order that sustained venue in Harris County. Because the order is void, mandamus is an appropriate action to compel that the order be vacated, that the transmitted papers be returned to the 334th Judicial District Court, and that Judge Anthony proceed to trial. *See Brown v. Brown*, 566 S.W.2d 378, 380 (Tex. Civ. App.—Corpus Christi 1978, no writ).

As *Anthony* demonstrates, a civil trial court is without authority to change venue on its own motion. *City of La Grange v. McBee,* 923 S.W.2d 89, 90 (Tex. App.—Houston [1st Dist.] 1996, writ denied). A sua sponte order is void and of no effect. A case transferred pursuant to a void order remains on the docket of the court from which the transfer is attempted, and the transferee court obtains no jurisdiction. Accordingly, any judgment entered by the transferee court under those circumstances is fundamental error and may be attacked for the first time on appeal.

## § 6.04 Waiver of Venue Rights

### BRISTOL-MYERS SQUIBB CO. v. GOLDSTON

*957 S.W.2d 671 (Tex. App.—Fort Worth 1997, writ denied)*

DAY, Justice.

INTRODUCTION AND HOLDING

This is an interlocutory appeal from the trial court's order denying appellants Bristol-Myers Squibb and CBI Medical's [footnote omitted] challenge to venue based on the joinder of multiple plaintiffs. [footnote omitted] We are asked to decide whether, under a settlement opt-out agreement that allowed plaintiffs to opt-out and "retain all rights . . . that existed prior to the . . . agreement," pre-1995 or post-1995 venue law applies to the joinder of multiple plaintiffs. Because we find that the agreement did not prevent post-1995 venue law from applying, we reverse the trial court's order.

BACKGROUND FACTS

In a nationwide class action based on breast-implant, products-liability claims, a settlement agreement was reached. Goldston and the joining plaintiffs were class members. The settlement agreement contained a post-settlement, opt-out procedure that allowed class members to withdraw from the class and pursue their own lawsuits:

> Any Settlement Class Member who elects to opt out of the Agreement during the Second Opt Out Period . . . *shall retain all rights under applicable law that existed prior to the execution and approval of this agreement.*

Goldston and the joining plaintiffs opted out.

Goldston filed suit in Wichita County on July 23, 1996. The joining plaintiffs then joined the suit. Relying on section 15.003, Bristol-Myers filed a motion to transfer venue to Dallas County, challenged the legality of joining the joining plaintiffs, and moved to strike the joinders. *See* Tex. Civ. Prac. & Rem. Code Ann. § 15.003 (Vernon Supp. 1998). The joining plaintiffs asserted that pre-1995 venue law applied because of the language in the opt-out settlement agreement. The trial court agreed and refused to strike the joinders, specifically stating that its ruling was based on the application of pre-1995 venue law. Bristol-Myers filed an accelerated, interlocutory appeal. *See id.* § 15.003(c).

## THE PARTIES' CONTENTIONS ON APPEAL

On appeal, Bristol-Myers argues that post-1995 venue law applies because suit was filed after September 1, 1995, the effective date of the new venue law. Bristol-Myers asserts that the settlement agreement does not prevent the application of post-1995 law even in the face of the "all rights" language.

The joining plaintiffs counter that "all rights" includes venue; thus, the strict joinder requirements for multiple plaintiffs in the new venue statute do not apply, and Bristol-Myers has no right to an interlocutory appeal.

## THE LAW ON VENUE AND JOINDER

Before September 1, 1995, proper joinder for multiple plaintiffs was not addressed explicitly. However, joinder of multiple claims was regulated; thus, the old law provided for joinder of plaintiffs in one suit based on proper joinder of their claims:

> When two or more parties are joined as defendants in the same action or two or more claims or causes of action are properly joined in one action and the court has venue of an action or claim against any one defendant, the court also has venue of all claims or actions against all defendants unless one or more of the claims or causes of action is governed by one of the provisions of Subchapter B requiring transfer of the claim or cause of action, on proper objection, to the mandatory county.

Act of May 17, 1985, 69th Leg., R.S., ch. 959, § 1, 1985 Tex. Gen. Laws 3242, 3249, *repealed* by Act of May 8, 1995, 74th Leg., R.S., ch. 138, § 10, 1995 Tex. Gen. Laws 978, 981.

In 1995, the Legislature restricted the joinder of multiple plaintiffs by passing current section 15.003:

> (a) In a suit where more than one plaintiff is joined each plaintiff must, independently of any other plaintiff, establish proper venue. Any person who is unable to establish proper venue may not join or maintain venue for the suit as a plaintiff unless the person, independently of any other plaintiff, establishes that:
>
> (1) joinder or intervention in the suit is proper under the Texas Rules of Civil Procedure;

(2) maintaining venue in the county of suit does not unfairly prejudice another party to the suit;

(3) there is an essential need to have the person's claim tried in the county in which the suit is pending; and

(4) the county in which the suit is pending is a fair and convenient venue for the person seeking to join in or maintain venue for the suit and the persons against whom the suit is brought.

(b) A person may not intervene or join in a pending suit as a plaintiff unless the person, independently of any other plaintiff:

(1) establishes proper venue for the county in which the suit is pending; or

(2) satisfies the requirements of Subdivisions (1) through (4) of Subsection (a).

Tex. Civ. Prac. & Rem. Code Ann. § 15.003(a)–(b); *see also Masonite Corp. v. Garcia,* 951 S.W.2d 812, 818 (Tex. App.—San Antonio 1997, orig. proceeding & pet. requested) (noting that purpose of new venue law was to prevent forum shopping by multiple plaintiffs and allow an interlocutory appeal of a trial court's joinder determination). Under this new law, any party who is dissatisfied with the trial court ruling on intervention or joinder can file an interlocutory appeal. *See* Tex. Civ. Prac. & Rem. Code Ann. § 15.003(c).

Thus, our main issue becomes whether pre-1995 or post-1995 law applies. If pre-1995 law applies, we have no jurisdiction over this appeal because that is not a proper remedy under the old law. But if post-1995 law applies, we have jurisdiction, and the joining plaintiffs must have independently established either proper venue or the four requirements of section 15.003(a), including essential need. *See* J. Patrick Hazel, Texas Venue 62 (1996).

DISCUSSION

The joining plaintiffs assert that the opt-out settlement agreement effectively froze their venue "rights" as of the date of the agreement, which was before 1995. The joining plaintiffs do not dispute that they filed their suit against Bristol-Myers in Wichita County after September 1, 1995. But they argue that venue is a "right" that is protected by the settlement agreement. We disagree.

First, venue is a procedural rule and not a substantive right. *See Snyder v. Pitts,* 150 Tex. 407, 241 S.W.2d 136, 142 (1951) (orig. proceeding) (stating venue statues are merely for the parties' convenience); *Bristow v. Nesbitt,* 280 S.W.2d 957, 959 (Tex. Civ. App.—Eastland 1955, no writ). Thus, venue would not be included under the settlement agreement's "rights" language.

Second, venue for the trial of a lawsuit depends upon the nature of the suit and parties; it is a matter of public concern, and the venue statutes are structured in accord with many public policy principles. *See Bonner v. Hearne,* 75 Tex. 242, 12 S.W. 38, 39 (1889). Because venue is fixed by law, any agreement or contract whereby the parties try to extend or restrict venue is void as against public policy. *See Fidelity Union Life Ins. Co. v. Evans,* 477 S.W.2d 535, 537 (Tex. 1972); *International Travelers' Ass'n v. Branum,* 109 Tex. 543, 212 S.W. 630, 631 (1919); *cf. Accelerated Christian Educ., Inc. v. Oracle Corp.,* 925 S.W.2d 66, 70 (Tex. App.—Dallas 1996, no writ) (holding forum-selection clause dictating venue in another state valid unless enforcement unreasonable or public interest favors jurisdiction in another, noncontracted-for forum). In other words, an advance agreement regarding venue may not encroach on the statutory scheme for fixing mandatory venue. *See Evans,* 477 S.W.2d at 536.

We doubt that the opt-out settlement agreement was intended to affect Texas venue. In fact, the joining plaintiffs stated at oral argument that the court probably had "no earthly idea" about Texas venue laws. However, even if the agreement was meant to apply to venue, it would be void as against public policy. To not apply the law in effect at the time Goldston filed her suit against Bristol-Myers would be applying a more permissive joinder law to the joining plaintiffs, which is prohibited.

Finally, were we to apply pre-1995 venue law to Goldston's suit, the doors would be open for Goldston to successfully claim that pre-1995 procedural rules, such as discovery and the rules of civil procedure, apply. This result would be untenable and would allow parties to circumvent the procedural rules by agreement.

## CONCLUSION

Because the settlement agreement does not affect which venue law applies, current section 15.003 applies to Goldston's suit. Bristol-Myers correctly filed an interlocutory appeal under that section to challenge the trial court's ruling applying pre-1995 venue law to the joining plaintiffs. Accordingly, the joining plaintiffs had to meet the requirements of section 15.003 to prove proper venue.

We reverse the order of the trial court applying pre-1995 venue law to the joining plaintiffs and remand for further proceedings under post-1995 venue laws.

---

## NOTE

*Written Consent of the Parties.* Although parties may not contract out of the basic venue scheme, a contract that provides for performance in a particular county of the obligation sought to be enforced may provide the basis for venue in the county of performance. *See* C.P.R.C. § 15.035. Section 15.063 of the Civil Practice and Remedies Code provides the following in relevant part:

> The court, *on motion filed and served concurrently with or before the filing of the answer,* shall transfer an action to another county of proper venue where:
>
> . . . .
>
> (3) *written consent* of the parties to transfer to any other county *is filed at any time* (emphasis supplied).

How should the italicized language in the statute be construed? *See* Tex. R. Civ. P. 86: "A written consent of the parties to transfer the case to another county may be filed with the clerk of the court at any time." *See also* Tex. R. Civ. P. 255. Does the language quoted from new Rule 86 help you to answer this question? Does it affect the holding of the principal case?

## § 6.05 Change of Venue Because Impartial Trial Cannot be Had

*Read C.P.R.C. § 15.063; Tex. R. Civ. P. 86(1), 87(2)(c), (5), 257, 258, 259.*

## UNION CARBIDE CORP. v. MOYE

*798 S.W.2d 792 (Tex. 1990)*

SPEARS, Justice.

This mandamus proceeding arises out of a suit in which over two thousand plaintiffs are alleging harm from exposure to toxic chemicals around the Lone Star steel plant in Morris County. Relators here are Union Carbide Corporation and most of the four hundred defendants in the underlying suit (hereinafter referred to as Union Carbide). Union Carbide filed in the trial court a motion to transfer venue on the ground that an impartial trial could not be had in Morris County. Tex. R. Civ. P. 257. The Trial judge conducted a hearing based on a written record only and refused to allow live testimony. The trial judge *overruled* the motion to transfer venue.

Union Carbide contends that, under Texas Rule of Civil Procedures 258, it was entitled to a full evidentiary hearing with the presentation of live testimony in support of its motion to transfer venue. Alternatively, Union Carbide contends it was entitled to a continuance in order to better prepare for the written submission of its venue motion. We address only the second contention.

After the motion to transfer venue was filed in September 1988, the parties engaged in discovery relevant to the motion. Interrogatories were sent to the plaintiffs in order to identify their relatives in Morris County. Depositions of corporate representatives were noticed. Expert witnesses were designated and deposed.

On January 13, 1989, the trial court handed down an order reciting the parties' agreement "regarding the designating of expert witnesses and persons having knowledge of relevant facts to be called to testify at the venue hearing. . . ." The order further stated that it applied "only to potential witnesses who may testify at the hearing on Defendants' Motion to Transfer Venue. . . ." The record also reflects that, when the trial judge was scheduling the venue hearing, he stated his expectation that the hearing might last as long as eight weeks. All of the above circumstances led Union Carbide to believe that the court would conduct an evidentiary hearing at which witnesses would be allowed to testify.

On the day the venue hearing was scheduled to begin, plaintiffs filed a motion opposing oral testimony. After allowing Union carbide less than twenty-four hours to respond, the trial court sustained the plaintiffs' motion and ruled that no oral testimony would be permitted at the venue hearing.

Union Carbide was taken by surprise. Because it had anticipated an eight-week venue hearing, Union Carbide had not arranged to have all of its evidence immediately available at the start of the hearing. Many of the witnesses Union Carbide had expected to call were not in Morris County at that time. Numerous deposition transcripts were not yet available. And, because the trial court had previously extended plaintiffs' deadline for responding to interrogatories to a date after the hearing would be concluded, the defendants had intended to call certain plaintiffs as live witnesses. Thus, Union Carbide had made preparations to assemble its proof in format for a lengthy evidentiary hearing, and its plans were effectively blocked by the trial court's sudden change.

Union Carbide moved for a continuance and requested additional time in order to supplement the record with more affidavits and discovery products. The trial judge denied the continuance and instructed Union Carbide to "present what you have now." Thus, Union Carbide was left unprepared and was unable to present for consideration numerous affidavits and depositions that it might otherwise have had ready.

Given these circumstances, we conclude that the trial court abused its discretion in denying a continuance. Texas Rule of Civil Procedure 258 provides that "reasonable discovery" in support of a motion to change venue "shall be permitted" and expressly provides that deposition testimony and other discovery products may be attached to affidavits on the motion. Since the trial court ruled before most of Union Carbide's discovery products were even available, it effectively denied Union Carbide this right to reasonable discovery set forth in Rule 258.[1] Moreover, because the trial court implicated itself in misleading Union Carbide as to the format for proof, we conclude that the court effectively deprived Union Carbide of its fundamental due process right to notice and a hearing. Having been misled as to the form of proof that would be acceptable, Union Carbide was placed in the untenable position of being allowed to attend the hearing without being able to submit its proof. Union Carbide cannot be penalized for relying on the court's own order as to the form of proof that would be acceptable. Justice requires that Union Carbide be afforded a reasonable opportunity to supplement the venue record with appropriate affidavits and discovery products prior to the trial court's ruling on the venue motion. *Powell v. United States,* 849 F.2d 1576 (5th Cir. 1988) (holding that trial court's failure to give adequate notice that case would be decided on a written summary judgment record constituted harmful error).

We conditionally grant the writ of mandamus. The trial judge must vacate his order overruling defendants' motion to change venue and, prior to ruling on the venue motion, must permit a reasonable period of time for supplementation of the record. The writ will issue only if the trial judge fails to act in accordance with this opinion.

HECHT, Justice, concurring.

I join the Court in holding that the trial court clearly abused its discretion by denying relators a fair opportunity to present written evidence—affidavits, depositions and discovery responses—on their motion to transfer venue of the underlying litigation on the ground that an impartial trial cannot be had in Morris County. Thus, I agree that the trial court must vacate its order denying relators' motion and must afford them a reasonable opportunity to present evidence in support of their motion. On this score the Court is unanimous.

Whether the trial court can, should or must hear live testimony in connection with relators' motion remains unclear. The Court says only: "While it is clear that Texas Rule of Civil Procedure 258 [footnote omitted] requires a trial judge to allow deposition testimony [on a motion made under Rule 257], we do not at this time address the question of whether or in what circumstances Rule 258 also *requires* that a trial judge allow live testimony on [such motion]." *Supra* at 793 n.1 (emphasis added). Significantly, the Court expresses no similar reservation regarding the trial court's power to hear live testimony, as distinguished from its duty to do so. Nor does the Court respond to Justice Gonzalezes' compelling arguments for allowing the trial court to hear live testimony in at least some cases. On these issues, which have been fully briefed and argued and are ripe for decision, the Court sends the participants away in the same uncertainty in which they came to us, leaving them to read between the lines.

I agree with Justice Gonzalez that the trial court is authorized and even obliged by Rule 258 to hear live testimony when it is necessary to resolve issues that cannot be determined on a written

[1] While it is clear that Texas Rule of Civil Procedure 258 requires a trial judge to allow deposition testimony, we do not at this time address the question of whether or in what circumstances Rule 258 also requires that a trial judge allow live testimony or an application to transfer venue.

record. A witness' credibility, for example, may be an important consideration in deciding a motion under rule 257 that is difficult to ascertain from affidavits or transcribed deposition testimony. Other issues, however, may readily be resolved upon written evidence. Again as an example, the strengths and weaknesses of surveys or demographic data, often evidence material to the possibility of an impartial trial in the forum, are sometimes, although not always, of course, apparent from entirely written evidence. I do not agree with Justice Gonzalez, therefore, that live testimony is necessary whenever the availability of an impartial trial in the forum is disputed. I would hold that under 258 a trial court may hear live testimony and must do so if, but only if, the issues cannot fairly be tried on a written record.

. . . .

I therefore concur in the Court's opinion as far as it goes, and in its judgment.

GONZALEZ, Justice, concurring.

. . . . I would hold that when there is a controversy over whether an impartial trial can be had in the county where the action is pending, the parties have a right to an oral hearing under rule 258 of the Texas Rules of Civil Procedure.

. . . .

The facts in a statutory venue hearing are relatively objective. On the other hand, the existence of prejudice, favoritism and partiality so great that a fair trial cannot be had in the county where suit is pending is more subjective, with proof resting ultimately on opinion. Affidavits, depositions, and other documentary proof may shed some light on the scope of the alleged problem, but they are a poor substitute for an oral hearing. With an oral hearing, the trial judge can listen and observe the testimony of the witnesses in full view of the interested parties.

It is difficult, if not impossible, for the trial judge to evaluate the credibility of the witnesses and the weight to be given their testimony from reading the cold record. The importance of the issues at stake and the difficulty of adjudication by reading the record, require that the parties have the right to a hearing in open court. This procedure is not only superior to that advocated by the respondents but it is the procedure mandated by Texas Rule of Civil Procedure 258.

For these reasons, I concur that the trial judge must vacate the order overruling the defendants' change of venue and I would order that he conduct an evidentiary hearing before ruling on the motion to transfer.

---

## NOTES AND QUESTIONS

(1) *Timing Considerations.* When must a motion to transfer because an impartial trial cannot be had be filed? Under former Civil Procedure Rules 257–259, there had been no due order rule, that is, application on any of the grounds listed in Rule 257 has been possible at any time before or after answer or immediately before trial. *See City of Abilene v. Downs*, 367 S.W.2d 153, 155–156 (Tex. 1963); *Atchison, Topeka & Santa Fe Ry. Co. v. Holloway*, 479 S.W.2d 700, 706 (Tex. Civ. App.—Beaumont 1972, writ ref'd n.r.e.). Has the prior law changed? When must an application on the ground of written consent be filed?

(2) *Deciding the Rule 257 Motion.* Civil Procedure Rule 258 sets out the basic procedure for deciding whether or not the Rule 257 motion (motion to transfer because impartial trial cannot

be had) should be granted. Given that the language of Rule 258 is taken (except for the last sentence) verbatim from former Rule 258, prior case law is instructive for interpreting its meaning. Assuming the movant complies with the requirements of Rule 257, i.e., submits his or her own affidavit as well as those of three credible persons residing in the county of suit showing inability to obtain an impartial trial (*See Carrasco v. Goatcher*, 623 S.W.2d 769, 771 (Tex. App.—El Paso 1981, no writ), transfer is mandatory unless the adverse party attacks the credibility of the movant by submitting the affidavit of a credible person. *See City of Abilene v. Downs*, 367 S.W.2d 153, 155–156 (Tex. 1963). Once the adverse party joins issue by submitting the controverting affidavit, the burden of proof is on the movant to show that an impartial trial cannot be had in the county where the suit is pending. *See Carrasco*, 623 S.W.2d at 769; *Henson v. Tom*, 473 S.W.2d 258, 260 (Tex. Civ. App.—Texarkana 1971, writ ref'd n.r.e.). If the issue is joined, the procedure for adjudicating the matter differs significantly from that for the motion governed by Civil Procedure Rules 87–89 to accomplish transfer on the ground that the county where the action is pending is not a proper county. Unlike motions decided under Rules 86–89, if an issue is joined regarding the ability to obtain a fair trial in the county where suit is filed, it must be tried by the judge; the issue is not resolved solely on the basis of affidavits and discovery products. In *City of Irving v. Luttrell*, 351 S.W.2d 941, 942–943 (Tex. Civ. App.—Amarillo 1961, no writ), the trial court made the decision regarding a Rule 257 motion without a hearing and only on the basis of affidavits:

> [The language of Rule 258] implies that there shall be a hearing before the court for the purpose of presenting evidence in support of the opposing affidavits. . . . It is apparent the trial court sustained the application for change of venue without hearing any evidence, but did so after considering the respective affidavits only. . . . It is thus apparent appellees failed to sustain their burden of proof. . . . *Id.*

*See also Galveston, H. & S.A. Ry. Co. v. Nicholson*, 57 S.W. 693, 695 (Civ. App. 1900, writ ref'd); *Robertson v. Robertson*, 382 S.W.2d 945, 946–947 (Civ. App.—Amarillo 1964, writ ref'd n.r.e.); *Governing Bd. v. Pannill*, 659 S.W.2d 670, 689 (Tex. App.—Beaumont 1983, writ ref'd n.r.e.) (holding affidavits are not evidence but merely pleadings). But what is the relevance of the last sentence of Tex. R. Civ. P. 258?

(3) *To What County?* If the motion to transfer is sustained, the judge must transfer the case as specified in Civil Procedure Rule 259. In line with the language of Section 15.063 of the Civil Practice and Remedies Code, Rule 259 states that the court must transfer the case to a county of proper venue if one is available. Under this rule, the court must first try to find an adjoining county of proper venue. If there is no proper adjoining county, transfer must be made to *any* county of proper venue. Only if there is no county of proper venue other than the county of suit may the court transfer the case to an adjoining county without regard to its being a proper one, but because an impartial trial can be had there. As before, if the motion to transfer is sustained, the parties may agree on a transferee county and the court must transfer the case to that county.

(4) *The Collision Between Appellate Rule 44 and C.P.R.C. § 15.064.* Appellate Rule 44, the harmless error rule, applies to all procedural errors including the violation of apparently mandatory rules such as Civil Procedure Rule 258. A judgment is not to be reversed for an error of law unless the error amounts to a denial of the appellant's rights that was reasonably calculated to cause the rendition of an improper judgment. *See Lone Star Steel Co. v. Scott,* 759 S.W.2d 144, 147 (Tex. App.—Texarkana 1988, writ denied) (holding that error in not transferring case

was harmless). Does this holding conflict with the language in Section 15.064(b) that "if venue was improper it shall in no event be harmless error and shall be reversible error"? Does Section 15.064 have anything to do with Rules 257–259? What would the majority in *Moye* say about this issue? What about Justice Gonzalez?

## § 6.06 Multidistrict Litigation

### W. Dorsaneo, TEXAS LITIGATION GUIDE

*§ 61.40 (1998)**

§ 61.40 Pretrial Consolidation of Cases Pending in the Same or Different Counties

[1] Adoption of Rule of Court Administration

Effective October 1, 1997, the Texas Supreme Court added Rule 11 to the Texas Rules of Judicial Administration. The rule is applied to any case that involves material questions of fact and law in common with another case pending in another court on or after October 1, 1997, regardless of venue rights [Tex. R. Jud. Admin. 11.1]. The constitutionality of Rule 11 has been placed in question because Article 5, § 7 of the Texas Constitution requires district court to conduct proceedings "at the county seat of the county in which the case is pending, except as otherwise provided by law" [Tex. Const. Art. 5, § 7; *see* Howell v. Mauzy, 899 S.W.2d 690, 699 (Tex. App.—Austin 1994, den.)—in interpreting the constitutional provision, court stated the phrase "as otherwise provided by law" was added "to permit greater flexibility in cases pending in districts embracing two or more counties"; *see* Critics Claim Rule Erodes Venue Rights, Tex. Lawyer, Sept. 19, 1997, at 1, col. 4]. Moreover, because the appointment of a pretrial judge may oust the presiding judge of a district court from jurisdiction, a similar problem may involve Article 5, Section 8, of the Texas Constitution [Tex. Const. Art. 5, § 8; *see* Lord v. Clayton, 163 Tex. 62, 352 S.W.2d 718, 721–722 (1961)—regular district court cannot be deprived of jurisdiction conferred by Constitution].

[2] Appointment of Pretrial Judges

[a] General Principles

On a party's motion, a presiding judge of an administrative judicial region in which a case is pending may assign an active district judge, including himself or herself, to a case to conduct all pretrial proceedings and decide all pretrial matters [Tex. R. Jud. Admin. 11.3(a)]. Significantly, the rule provides that the Chief Justice of the Texas Supreme Court may assign an active district judge to other administrative regions to be assigned as a pretrial judge [Tex. R. Jud. Admin. 11.2(d)]. The judge who is assigned will be a pretrial judge [Tex. R. Jud. Admin. 11.2(c)—definition]. The pretrial judge will preside over all pretrial proceedings in the case in place of the regular judge. The pretrial judge will decide all pretrial motions, including motions to transfer venue and motions for summary judgment. The pretrial judge and the regular judge of a court in which the case is pending must consult on setting a trial date [Tex. R. Jud. Admin. 11.3(b)]. The same pretrial judge need not be assigned in all related cases. If more than one pretrial judge is assigned in related cases, either in the same region or in different regions, the pretrial judges must consult with each other in conducting pretrial proceedings and deciding pretrial matters [Tex. R. Jud. Admin. 11.3(c)]. A pretrial judge assignment terminates when all pretrial proceedings in a case have been completed, the pretrial judge ceases to be an active district judge, or the presiding judge in the exercise of discretion terminates the assignment [Tex. R. Jud. Admin. 11.3(f)].

[b] Objections to Pretrial Judge

An assignment under Rule 11 of the Texas Rules of Judicial Administration is not made pursuant to section 74.054 of the Government Code, and therefore a pretrial judge is not subject to an objection under section 74.053 of the Government Code [Tex. R. Jud. Admin. 11.3(e)].

[c] Motion for Assignment of a Pretrial Judge

A pretrial judge may be assigned only on the motion of a party to a case or at the request of the regular judge of a court in which a case is pending [Tex. R. Jud. Admin. 11.4]. The motion may be accompanied by a brief [Tex. R. Jud. Admin. 11.4(e)]. Also, the presiding judge of the administrative region may request briefs. The motion for obtaining assignment of pretrial judge must be filed in all related cases and must state [Tex. R. Jud. Admin. 11.4(b)]:

1. The number and style of the case;
2. The number and style of the related case, and the court and county in which it is pending;
3. The material questions of fact and law common to the cases;
4. The reasons why the assignment would promote the just and efficient conduct of the action; and
5. Whether all parties agree to the motion.

Although the administrative rule is silent on this point, the movant will also probably want to include a request for the appointment of a particular judge in the same administrative region, including the presiding judge himself or herself, or a request that the presiding judge request the Chief Justice of the Texas Supreme Court to assign an active district judge from another region to allow for his or her assignment as a pretrial judge [Tex. R. Jud. Admin. 11.3].

A party must serve any papers filed under this rule on all parties in the related cases and the presiding judge or judges for the administrative judicial region or regions in which the original cases are pending [Tex. R. Jud. Admin. 11.4(j)]. If a judge files any paper under this rule, the clerk of the court in which the paper is filed must send a copy to all parties in the cases and the presiding judge or judges for those cases. The clerk of the court where a case is pending in which assignment of a pretrial judge is sought shall serve as the clerk for the presiding judge under this rule [Tex. R. Jud. Admin. 11.4(j)].

[d] Response to Motion for Assignment of a Pretrial Judge

A response to the motion for assignment of a pretrial judge may be filed by any party to the case [Tex. R. Jud. Admin. 11.4(d)]. A response may also be filed by the regular judge of the court in which the case is pending, the regular judge of the court in which the related case is pending (if no pretrial judge has already been assigned in that case), the pretrial judge assigned to the related case if a pretrial judge has been assigned, and any party to the case or cases which involve common material questions of fact and law.

[e] Hearing on the Motion for Assignment of a Pretrial Judge

Absent agreement of all parties, the presiding judge of an administrative judicial region must conduct an oral hearing on a motion to assign a pretrial judge. Despite Article 5, Section 7, of the Texas Constitution, the Administrative Rule also provides that the hearing may be held in any county within the region or in Travis County. The presiding judge of an administrative region must give notice of the time and place for the hearing to all parties and the regular or pretrial judges in all cases which involve common material issues of fact and law [Tex. R. Jud. Admin. 11.4(f)].

The presiding judge may consider all documents filed in all the related cases, all discovery conducted in the related cases, affidavits filed with the motion, and oral testimony [Tex. R. Jud. Admin. 11.4(g)].

The presiding judge must grant the motion if the judge determines that the case involves material questions of fact and law common to a case in another court or county, and assignment of a pretrial judge would promote the just and efficient conduct of the case [Tex. R. Jud. Admin. 11.4(h)]. If the judge does not find both that the case involves material questions of fact and law common to a case in another court or county, and assignment of a pretrial judge would promote the just and efficient conduct of the case, the judge must deny the motion. The presiding judge must issue an order deciding the motion. The order must be filed in the case in which assignment of a pretrial judge was sought [Tex. R. Jud. Admin. 11.4(i)].

### [f] Review of an Order Assigning a Pretrial Judge

A presiding judge's order granting or denying a motion for appointment of a pretrial judge may be reviewed only by the Texas Supreme Court in an original mandamus proceeding [Tex. R. Jud. Admin. 11.5].

# CHAPTER 7

## PARTIES

### SCOPE

This chapter covers issues related to parties. The chapter addresses such topics as joinder of claims and parties by both the plaintiff and the defendant, intervention and voluntary joinder of new parties, interpleader, compulsory joinder, and class actions.

## § 7.01 Permissive Joinder of Claims

*Read Tex. R. Civ. P. 51.*

### JAMESON v. ZUEHLKE

*218 S.W.2d 326 (Tex. Civ. App.—Waco 1948, writ ref'd n.r.e.)*

TIREY, Justice.

This is a suit for damages for malicious prosecution and assault. The jury's verdict was favorable to plaintiff, and defendant has appealed.

The jury found in its verdict (1) that defendant Jameson acted without probable cause in filing a complaint against plaintiff for the theft of his cow; (2) that he acted with malice; (3) that plaintiff sustained actual damages by being named in the criminal complaint; (4) that such damages amounted to the sum of $100.00; (5) that exemplary damages should be assessed against defendant and they fixed the exemplary damages in the sum of $2000.00; (6) that defendant committed an assault and battery on the plaintiff on the 22nd of October, 1947, and that said assault was not committed in self-defense; (7) that in committing the assault and battery the defendant acted with malice, and that plaintiff sustained actual damages in the sum of $200.00. The jury further found that exemplary damages should be assessed against defendant for said assault and battery and fixed said sum at $200.00.

Point 1 is: "The error of the court in overruling defendant's plea in abatement and of misjoinder of causes of action." We think this point is without merit.

Appellant and appellee lived on adjoining farms and the fence between them was in bad repair. Appellant's stock had been making some depredations on appellee's crops and appellee, acting upon the advice given him by the County Attorney, impounded one of appellant's cows on December 3, 1946. Appellant instituted a search for the cow and shortly found her on appellee's property. Appellant then went to the Justice of the Peace of his precinct for the purpose of filing a complaint for cattle theft against appellee, but failing to find said Justice of the Peace he went into an adjoining precinct where he found the Justice of the Peace of such precinct and filed a complaint for cattle theft and caused appellee to be placed under arrest. Appellee was arrested about seven or eight o'clock in the evening on December 4, 1946 and carried to the jail at Meridian, but was not actually confined in the jail, and was released on an appearance bond about four or five hours after his arrest. Appellee was not indicted by the Grand Jury and the charge filed against him was dismissed. Appellee later filed suit against appellant for malicious prosecution and appellant was served with citation. Shortly after this, appellant and appellee were both attending a public auction for the sale of livestock at Clifton. Appellee took a seat provided for the general public and was sitting down at the time appellant approached him and struck him on the arm with some object and invited him to come outside of the building and fight. Evidence was tendered to the effect that appellant cursed appellee and applied vile epithets to him, also that appellee cursed appellant and applied vile epithets to him. Appellee followed appellant outside and his excuse for doing so was that he thought he would have to fight the appellant sometime. After they got outside appellant struck appellee two blows before appellee started fighting. After the fight was over appellee required the services of a physician, it being necessary to take six stitches to close one of the facial wounds. Evidence was also tendered to the effect that appellant's nose was broken in the fight. Both parties pleaded guilty to fighting and paid fines in the Justice Court. A few days after the fight the appellee filed an amended pleading in which he asked for damages for malicious prosecution and for the assault and battery committed upon him by the appellant. We think the record is without dispute that both alleged causes of action grew out of a related transaction.

Rule 51, Texas Rules of Civil Procedure, provides in part: "(a) The plaintiff in his petition or in a reply setting forth a counterclaim and the defendant in an answer setting forth a counterclaim may join either as independent or as alternate claims as many claims either legal or equitable or both as he may have against an opposing party."

Our view is that where the parties are the same, there are no restrictions except as stated with reference to the requirements of Rules 39, 40 and 43, referred to in Rule 51, supra, which are not pertinent here. Moreover, where the parties are different, full freedom of joinder is permitted subject to the rules of joinder of the parties. . . .

. . . .

---

## NOTES AND QUESTIONS

(1) *Comparison With Federal Rule.* The Texas joinder of claims rule (Tex. R. Civ. P. 51) was taken without modification from the 1937 version of its federal counterpart, Fed. R. Civ. P. 18(a). Under the Texas rule, it is clear that in a case involving only one plaintiff and one defendant, there can be no misjoinder of claims, because the claims need not arise from the same transaction or occurrence or series of transactions, etc. *Cf.* Tex. R. Civ. P. 40. The opinion in *Jameson* mentions "restrictions" imposed by Rules 39, 40 and 43. We will discuss this point later in the chapter.

(2) *Relationship to Res Judicata.* Does Civil Procedure Rule 51 require joinder of claims? Suppose the claims arise from the same transaction or occurrence. Would it be sensible to compel their joinder in order to facilitate the economical functioning of our judicial system? Traditionally, this question has been considered a part of the law of res judicata. A cause of action may not

be split. The problem is in identifying the breadth of the term "cause of action." For example, what claims comprise a tort cause of action for damages? Must a property damage claim be joined with a personal injury claim? *See Garrett v. Matthews,* 343 S.W.2d 289 (Tex. Civ. App.—Amarillo 1961, no writ). Suppose the property damage claim has been assigned to an insurance company? *See Traders & Gen. Life Ins. Co. v. Richardson,* 387 S.W.2d 478 (Tex. Civ. App.—Beaumont 1965, writ ref'd).

## § 7.02 Permissive Joinder of Parties by the Plaintiff

*Read Tex. R. Civ. P. 40, 51.*

### RUSSELL v. HARTFORD CASUALTY INS. CO.

*548 S.W.2d 737 (Tex. Civ. App.—Austin 1977, writ ref'd n.r.e.)*

SHANNON, Justice.

The opinion of this Court filed on February 2, 1977, is withdrawn, and the following opinion replaces it.

This is an appeal from a summary judgment entered by the district court of Travis County. Appellants, John L. Russell and wife, Linda L. Russell, filed suit against Wendland Farm Products, Inc., Hartford Casualty Insurance Company, Airways Rent-A-Car System, Inc., and Warren Cowley, doing business as Airways Rent-A-Car of Austin, Texas. The district court severed appellants' causes of action asserted against Hartford, Airways Rent-A-Car System, and Cowley from the negligence cause of action asserted by appellants against Wendland. The district court then entered a summary judgment in favor of Hartford, Airways Rent-A-Car System, and Cowley that appellants take nothing. We will affirm that judgment.

On September 11, 1974, a truck owned by Wendland Farm Products, Inc., and operated by its employee, collided with an automobile driven by Mrs. Russell. As a result of the collision Mrs. Russell was injured and her automobile was wrecked.

On the same day an adjuster for Hartford called upon the Russells. The adjuster arranged, at Hartford's cost, to provide a temporary rent car for the Russells' use from Airways Rent-A-Car System, Inc., and Warren Cowley, doing business as Airways Rent-A-Car of Austin, Texas.

Seven days later Hartford canceled the rental car arrangement. On the same day an employee of Airways requested the Russells to return the rent car. They returned the car on the following day. Airways did not charge the Russells for the use of the car.

Because the entry of the summary judgment was grounded upon appellees' theory that appellants failed to state a cause of action, the petition will be examined.

As against Wendland, appellants alleged that their damages were caused proximately by the negligence of Wendland's driver. Appellants sought to recover $264,200 for personal injuries, past and future medical expenses, an unwanted pregnancy, loss of wages, loss of Mrs. Russell's services, and loss of their car. They also sought $900,000 in exemplary damages from Wendland for alleged gross negligence.

The Russells also joined Hartford as a defendant in their negligence suit against Wendland. The Russells pleaded that one basis for Hartford's joinder was that it was the liability carrier for Wendland and, as such, Hartford was bound to pay any judgment obtained against Wendland.

As another basis for joinder, the Russells alleged that Hartford was "directly liable" to them by virtue of Tex. Ins. Code Ann. art. 21.21 § 16 (1973).

In the second "count" of the petition, appellants enumerated a litany of wrongs allegedly committed by Wendland, Hartford, Airways and Cowley, and all flowing in some manner from Hartford's cancellation of the rent-car arrangement. For purposes of convenience, these complaints will be termed the "unfair settlement practices" and the "conspiracy" theories.

Under their "unfair settlement practices" theory, the Russells pleaded that Hartford was guilty of engaging in false, misleading, or deceptive acts or practices in violation of Tex. Bus. and Comm. Code Ann. § 17.46(b) (1973) by causing confusion or misunderstanding on the part of the Russells as to the "sponsorship and approval" of a rent car by them until Hartford could obtain a comparable replacement vehicle for them; by representing that the Russells had unlimited use of the rent car with respect to time and mileage until Hartford obtained for them a replacement vehicle, and by making false or misleading statements concerning the need for a replacement vehicle or the need for and expense of repair of the Russells' car.

Also, under their "unfair settlement practices" theory, the Russells alleged that Hartford violated Tex. Ins. Code Ann. art. 21.21 § 4(4) (1957) in attempting "to coerce and intimidate" them by canceling the rent-car arrangement.

Finally, the Russells pleaded that Hartford violated Tex. Ins. Code Ann. art. 21.21-2 (1973) by knowingly misrepresenting to them pertinent facts or policy provisions relating to Wendland's coverage; by not attempting in good faith to effectuate prompt, fair, and equitable settlement of their claim; and by not attempting in good faith to settle promptly their claim where liability had become reasonably clear under one part of the policy in order to influence settlement under other parts of the policy.

The Russells sought to obtain a recovery from Hartford in the total sum of $45,000 for engaging in such unfair practices.

As another basis for joinder of Hartford, appellants alleged that Wendland "ratified Hartford's wrongful acts." In this connection appellants alleged that their attorney wrote to Hartford offering to settle the property damage aspect of the case for $3200 and advising Hartford of the "damaging effects of their [Hartford's] unfair, and deceptive settlement practices upon the Plaintiffs [the Russells] . . ." Hartford was requested to send a copy of that letter to its insured, Wendland. The Russells pleaded further that Hartford advised Wendland, and because Wendland unreasonably failed to request Hartford to accept the settlement offer, *Wendland* "ratified" Hartford's unfair settlement practices, and that this somehow furnished a further ground for joinder of *Hartford.*

The Russells' "conspiracy" theory is difficult to summarize. The appellants pleaded that Hartford and Wendland as "First Conspirator" and Airways Rent-A-Car System, Inc., and Cowley as "Second Conspirator" entered into a conspiracy "to injure" the Russells. The conspirators allegedly arranged to furnish a rent car to the Russells without informing them about any limitations on the number of days permitted by the arrangement or by the number of miles allowed to be driven each day and without informing the Russells as to the terms of the cancellation of the rent-car arrangement. Thereafter, the "First Conspirator" directed the "Second Conspirator" to advise the Russells of the cancellation of the arrangement and of the mileage limitations in the arrangement. As a result of such alleged conspiracy Mr. Russell had to arrange for a ride to work and arrangements had to be made with friends, relatives, and neighbors to take Mrs. Russell to the physician and other places. For such damages allegedly flowing from the conspiracy, the Russells sought as their due $540,000.

Under their first point of error, appellants claim that joinder of the liability insurance company was permitted by the exception in Tex. R. Civ. P. 51(b).

In Texas, and in most states, the liability insurance company, in absence of a statute or an express provision of the insurance contract, cannot be sued directly in a tort suit with or without the joinder of the insured. Green, *Blindfolding the Jury,* 33 Texas L. Rev. 157, 158 (1954). That rule is expressed in Tex. R. Civ. P. 51(b) and other rules.[1] Rule 51(b) prohibits the joinder of a liability or indemnity insurance company in a tort case unless the insurance company is ". . . by statute or contract directly liable to the person injured or damaged."

Appellants say that any one of the several statutory causes of action asserted by them against the liability insurance company for alleged violations of the Texas Insurance Code and the Texas Business and Commerce Code permits them to join the insurer under the exception in Rule 51(b). Appellants say that the insurer is by those statutes "directly liable to the person injured or damaged."

Appellants' argument ignores the fact that the exception in Rule 51(b) permits the joinder of the liability insurer in tort cases in which a statute has made the insurer directly liable for the injuries or damages resulting from the tortious act of its insured. Appellants' statutory causes of action have nothing to do with the insured's tortious conduct or with injuries or damages flowing from that conduct. The alleged violations of the Texas Insurance Code and the Texas Business and Commerce Code asserted by appellants refer to alleged conduct of the insurer or its adjuster which occurred days or weeks after the tort of its insured, and which, of course, had nothing to do with the tort.

The Rules of Civil Procedure should be construed so as to produce harmony rather than discord. *Ex parte Godeke,* 163 Tex. 387, 355 S.W.2d 701 (1962). Rule 51(b) should be read in conjunction with Rule 40. Rule 40 limits the joinder of defendants to situations in which the right to relief asserted against the defendants arises out of the same transaction or occurrence or series of occurrences and if any question of law or fact common to all of them will arise in the action.

In the case at bar, appellants' allegations concerning violations of the Texas Insurance Code and the Texas Business and Commerce Code do not arise out of the truck-automobile collision, nor do the allegations present questions of law or fact common to those presented in the negligence suit. It follows that if there were a legal basis for appellants' suit for violations of the Texas Insurance Code and the Texas Business and Commerce Code against Hartford, still that would not be a basis for the joinder of Hartford in the negligence suit against Hartford's insured.

Contrary to assertions in their brief and in oral argument, appellants did not plead that Hartford was directly liable to them by virtue of some "direct action" provision in the insurance policy issued to Wendland.

We have concluded that Rule 51(b) afforded no basis for the joinder of the liability insurer in appellants' suit for negligence against the insured, Wendland.

. . . .

---

[1] Similar prohibitions appear in the rules governing third-party practice and counterclaims and cross-claims. Tex. R. Civ. P. 38(b) and 97(f).

## NOTES AND QUESTIONS

(1) *Rule 40's First Prong.* If a plaintiff sues two or more defendants, can you think of a situation in which relief is not sought "jointly, severally, or in the alternative"?

(2) *Misinterpretation of Rule 40's Three Independent Requirements.* Despite the clear language of Civil Procedure Rule 40, a number of intermediate appellate courts have read the procedural rule as if each requirement constituted a separate alternative basis for permissive joinder. For example, in *Lambert v. H. Molsen & Co., Inc.,* 551 S.W.2d 151 (Tex. Civ. App.—Waco 1977, writ ref'd n.r.e.), a buyer brought an action against three sellers of cotton who had each separately agreed to sell cotton to the buyer. Because the contracts were executed individually and without joint obligations, the defendants moved to sever. The motions were overruled. The Waco Court said the following:

> Defendants say that Rule 40 requires more than common fact and law questions for joinder of separate causes against several defendants, and that it also requires as a mandatory predicate for the joinder that plaintiff's case against the defendants must arise out of the same transaction or same series of transactions. Thus, they say, they were entitled to the severances as a matter of law. We disagree. Defendants' construction of Rule 40 is too restrictive. It is settled that questions of joinder of parties and causes of action, consolidation, and severance, are addressed to a broad discretion bestowed upon the trial courts in such procedural matters by our rules of civil procedure. Rules 37 to 43, 97, and 174; *Hamilton v. Hamilton,* 154 Tex. 511, 280 S.W.2d 588, 591 (1955). Absent a showing of an abuse of the discretion, prejudicial to the complainant, the court's rulings in those matters will not be disturbed on appeal. *Parker v. Potts,* 342 S.W.2d 634, 636 (Tex. Civ. App.—Fort Worth, 1961, writ ref'd n.r.e.).
>
> . . . In our case the contracts sued upon are identically worded in every material respect; each was solicited and executed on behalf of Molsen by the same agent; and, as we have said, all raise the same questions of law and fact which are crucial to this dispute. On the trial, the same testimony on trade customs and practices, technical terms and their meaning, expenses saved by Molsen, and micronaire range production statistics dealing with the major factual disputes in the case, was relevant to all defendants. The only fact question not common to all was the landlord's share issue. Jackson conceded during his testimony that the contracts were intended to include the shares of his landlord. Struve and Lambert did not. However, the jury found in favor of Struve and Lambert, so no harm resulted to any defendant on this issue.
>
> Our review of the record has failed to reveal the prejudice to defendants they claim was generated by trying their cases together. We find no abuse of discretion in the court's rulings on the motions for severance. *See Texas Employment Commission v. International Union of Electrical, Radio And Machine Workers,* 163 Tex. 135, 352 S.W.2d 252, 253 (1962); *Hindman v. Texas Lime Co.,* 157 Tex. 592, 305 S.W.2d 947, 954 (1957).

Is this a proper construction of the rule? Are the claims logically related?

(3) *Relationship of Rules 40 and 51.* Civil Procedure Rules 40 and 51 must be read together. There is some ambiguity in the Texas rules on permissive joinder of claims (Rule 51) and

permissive joinder of parties (Rule 40) in certain multiple party/multiple claims hypotheticals. Consider the following excerpt from Frumer, *Multiple Parties and Claims in Texas,* 6 Sw. L.J. 135, 144 (1952)* for an analysis of the interrelationship of Civil Procedure Rules 40, 41, and 51.

> (c) *A* has a cause of action against *B* and *C* on a note executed jointly by them, and another cause of action upon a separate and entirely unrelated note executed jointly by *B, C,* and *D.* May *A* join both of these causes of action in one action against *B, C,* and *D? D* is not concerned with the cause of action solely against *B* and *C,* there are no common questions of law or fact, and the joinder of both causes of action in one petition would be improper. However, if the causes of action are joined, the court should sever the cause of action against *B* and *C* from the cause of action against *B, C,* and *D,* ordering that each be docketed as a separate suit. Of course, if the two causes of action were so related as to be within the scope of Rule 40(a), it would be immaterial that *D* is not concerned with the cause of action against *B* and *C.* Note that under that rule a "defendant need not be interested in . . . defending against all the relief demanded. Judgment may be given . . . against one or more defendants according to their respective liabilities."

Do you agree with the foregoing interpretation? If you do agree, you must also agree that a misjoinder of parties can create a misjoinder of claims. How is the misjoinder problem handled under Rule 40? Does the court have discretion in how it is handled? Why should there be any limitation? Can't the problem be handled by giving the trial judge discretion to grant separate trials when this would be appropriate, economical, and nonprejudicial?

The foregoing hypothetical is similar to *Federal Housing Administrator v. Christianson,* 26 F. Supp. 419 (D. Conn. 1939). The federal rule was amended to deal with interpretive problems involving the last two sentences of the counterpart Rule 18(a). The federal rule now provides "A party asserting a claim to relief as an original claim, counterclaim, cross-claim, or third party claim, may join, either as independent or as alternate claims, as many claims, legal, equitable, or maritime, as he has against an opposing party." There is no reference to limitations on claim joinder by the joinder of parties rules. The apparent effect of the amendment is to permit joinder of unrelated claims so long as there is one common claim linking the defendants together. In response to the question of why there must be one common claim, Professor Kaplan states "rulemakers must not march too far ahead of the parade." Kaplan, *1966 Amendments of the Federal Rules of Civil Procedure* (II), 81 Harv. L. Rev. 591, 597 (1968).

(4) *Proper Analysis of Rules 40 and 51.* Professor Kaplan indicates that the following hypotheticals would involve proper joinder of claims and parties under the revised federal rule.

> *Case I.* Plaintiff sues *A* and *B* in one action for breaches of contracts made with them respectively: the two contracts arose out of the same transaction and a common question of law or fact will arise. Suppose plaintiff wants to join in the action claims for libel against *A* and *B* respectively; the libels both arose out of the same transaction but one unconnected with the contract transaction, and a common question of law or fact will arise unconnected with any contract question.
>
> *Case II.* Contract claims against *A* and *B* as in Case I. Plaintiff wants to join in the action a libel claim against *A;* this claim arose out of the same transaction as the contract claims

* Reprinted with permission of the Southwestern Law Journal, copyright © 1952.

and there is a question of law or fact with respect to the libel that will also arise with respect to the contracts.

*Case III.* Contract claims against *A* and *B* as in Case I. Plaintiff wants to join in the action a libel claim against *A;* this claim did not arise out of the same transaction as the contract claims and there is no question of law or fact regarding the libel that will also arise with respect to the contracts.

Is this consistent with the Frumer article excerpt above? Obviously, it is not. Kaplan's case III is a simplified version of the case posed by Frumer. Is the difference compelled by the second sentence of Rule 51? Must the second sentence of Rule 51 be construed as itself imposing limits on joinder of claims against properly joined multiple parties?

(5) *Relationship to Limitations Statutes.* Sections 16.068 and 16.069 of the Civil Practice and Remedies Code allow, under limited circumstances, all parties to amend and add additional grounds of recovery/defense that otherwise might have been time-barred. If a plaintiff's later added claim could have been asserted at the time that the original action was filed (i.e., was not time-barred), it is not time-barred if subsequently added in an amended pleading unless it is wholly based on a new, distinct or different transaction or occurrence. C.P.R.C. § 16.068; *Milestone Properties, Inc. v. Federated Metals Corporation,* 867 S.W.2d 113, 114–118 (Tex. App.—Austin 1993, no writ) (construing C.P.R.C. § 16.068). The same concept applies to a counterclaim or cross-claim if it is filed not later than the 30th day after the defendant's answer day. *See, e.g., Oliver v. Oliver,* 889 S.W.2d 271, 272–274 (Tex. 1994) (wife's counterclaim for fraud arose out of same transaction as husband's divorce action).

(6) *Inadvertent Omission of Parties; Rejoinder.* The Texas Supreme Court has held that the inadvertent omission of a party-plaintiff from an amended petition did not result in the claim being barred when the omission was corrected by another amendment and the defendants were not otherwise prejudiced. *American Petrofina, Inc. v. Allen,* 887 S.W.2d 829, 830–831 (Tex. 1993).

## § 7.03 Joinder of Claims by the Defendant

### [A] Counterclaims

*Read Tex. R. Civ. P. 97.*

#### JACK H. BROWN & CO. v. NORTHWEST SIGN CO.

*718 S.W.2d 397 (Tex. App.—Dallas 1986, writ ref'd n.r.e.)*

GUITTARD, Chief Justice.

The question on this appeal is whether the present suit is barred by a prior default judgment and the compulsory counterclaim rule embodied in rule 97(a) of the Texas Rules of Civil Procedure. The present suit was brought by "Signgraphics," an assumed name of Jack H. Brown & Company, Inc., a Texas corporation, against Northwest Sign Company, an Idaho corporation, for the price of steel pipe furnished for the erection of a Holiday Inn sign in Idaho. Northwest filed a special appearance challenging the personal jurisdiction of the Texas court. Northwest also filed a motion for summary judgment asserting that Signgraphics's claim in the present suit is barred by the failure of Signgraphics to present it as a counterclaim in an Idaho suit by

Northwest against Signgraphics on a contract for erection of the sign. Although the trial court overruled Northwest's special appearance, it awarded a summary judgment to Northwest based upon the compulsory counterclaim rule and also upon the ground of *res judicata*. Since we agree that the compulsory counterclaim rule applies, we affirm the summary judgment without reaching the *res judicata* question. Also, we do not reach Northwest's cross-point complaining of the court's overruling its special appearance because it is presented only in the alternative.

The summary judgment proof discloses the following facts. Signgraphics made a written contract with Weston, the operator of a Holiday Inn in Idaho, to fabricate and install a Holiday Inn sign on supporting steel pipe to be provided by Weston. Signgraphics then made a written subcontract with Northwest for installation of the sign. In accordance with the subcontract, Signgraphics made the sign, but Weston had difficulty obtaining the steel pipe. Northwest then asked Signgraphics to supply the pipe. Signgraphics obtained the pipe, shipped it along with the sign to Northwest, and billed Northwest for the pipe. Northwest erected the pipe and installed the sign. Signgraphics refused to pay for the installation, and Northwest refused to pay for the pipe.

In the earlier suit, Northwest sued Signgraphics in Idaho and obtained a default judgment. Northwest brought the Idaho judgment to Texas, obtained an order giving the judgment full faith and credit, and garnished Signgraphics's bank account. *See Northwest Sign Co. v. Jack H. Brown & Co.*, 680 S.W.2d 808 (Tex. 1984), *cert. denied*, 471 U.S. 1113, 105 S. Ct. 2353, 86 L. Ed. 2d 255 (1985). Signgraphics then brought the present suit in Texas for the price of the pipe.

Signgraphics contends that its claim was not a compulsory counterclaim in the Idaho suit because the sale of the pipe was an oral transaction subsequent to and separate from the written subcontract for installation of the sign, on which Northwest brought its suit in Idaho. Since the law of Idaho has not been proved or cited, we assume it is the same as the law of Texas, and apply rule 97(a) of the Texas Rules of Civil Procedure. This rule requires a pleading to assert as a counterclaim any claim against the opposing party "if it arises out of the transaction or occurrence that is the subject matter of the opposing party's claim. . . ."

Decisions under this rule throw little light on the problem of determining what is "the transaction or occurrence that is the subject matter of the opposing party's claim." The only pertinent decision of the Supreme Court of Texas is *Griffin v. Holiday Inns of America*, 496 S.W.2d 535, 539 (Tex. 1973), which indicates that the compulsory counterclaim rule is broader than the rule of *res judicata.* There the plaintiff had filed a previous suit for the balance claimed on a contract to pave a parking lot and the defendant had counterclaimed for breach of the same contract. Recovery was denied to both parties in the first suit. In the second suit, the plaintiff sued for the same work in *quantum meruit.* The supreme court held that the *quantum meruit* claim was not barred by res judicata because it was not considered a "different cause of action," but it was barred by rule 97(a) because it arose out of the same transaction—the paving of the parking lot—that was the subject matter of the defendant's counterclaim for damages in the first suit.

Other Texas courts have given rule 97(a) a similarly broad interpretation. The rule has been held to apply in the following cases. *Bailey v. Travis*, 622 S.W.2d 143, 144 (Tex. Civ. App.—Eastland 1981, writ ref'd n.r.e.), held that a legal malpractice claim was barred by failure to assert it in a previous suit for attorney's fees. *Corpus Christi Bank & Trust v. Cross*, 586 S.W.2d 664, 666–67 (Tex. Civ. App.—Corpus Christi 1979, writ ref'd n.r.e.), held similarly in a suit against an accountant. *Upjohn Co. v. Petro Chemicals Suppliers, Inc.*, 537 S.W.2d 337, 340 (Tex.

Civ. App.—Beaumont 1979, writ ref'd n.r.e.), held that a seller's claim for unpaid invoices was a compulsory counterclaim in a suit against the seller for fraud in bribing the buyer's agent. *Burris v. Kurtz*, 462 S.W.2d 347, 348 (Tex. Civ. App.—Corpus Christi 1971, writ ref'd n.r.e.), held that a suit for alleged impropriety in handling a retail installment contract was barred by failure to assert the claim in a previous suit against the plaintiff on the contract. *Powell v. Short*, 308 S.W.2d 532, 534 (Tex. Civ. App.—Amarillo 1958, no writ), held that a claim of malicious prosecution for giving a worthless check was a compulsory counterclaim in a suit by the payee to collect on the check. *Connell v. Spivey*, 264 S.W.2d 458, 459 (Tex. Civ. App.—El Paso 1954, no writ), held that a claim for breach of contract for pasturing cattle was a compulsory counterclaim in a suit to recover the balance due on the contract.

On the other hand, rule 97(a) has been held not to bar a later suit in the following cases. *Reliance Universal, Inc. v. Sparks Industrial Services*, 688 S.W.2d 890, 891 (Tex. App.—Beaumont 1985, writ ref'd n.r.e.), held that a claim by the buyer of material for the sellers' negligence, after delivery, in directing use of materials was not a compulsory counterclaim in a suit by the seller for the price of the materials. *Astro Sign Co. v. Sullivan*, 518 S.W.2d 420, 426 (Tex. Civ. App.—Corpus Christi 1974, writ ref'd n.r.e.), held that a suit by a former employee for his commissions did not arise out of the same transaction as an earlier suit by the employer for conversion of property by the employee after his discharge. *Gulf States Abrasive Manufacturing, Inc. v. Oertel*, 489 S.W.2d 184, 188 (Tex. Civ. App.—Houston [1st Dist.] 1972, writ ref'd n.r.e.), held that claims against a corporation for personal services and conversion of stock were not compulsory counterclaims in a suit by the corporation for breach of fiduciary duties in setting up a competing corporation.

These cases reveal no consistent test of what is the same "transaction or occurrence." We look, therefore, to the decisions and commentaries interpreting rule 13(a) of the Federal Rules of Civil Procedure, from which Texas Rule 97(a) is taken. The leading case on compulsory counterclaims is *Moore v. New York Cotton Exchange*, 270 U.S. 593, 46 S. Ct. 367, 70 L. Ed. 750 (1926), in which the Supreme Court construed the former equity rule that preceded federal rule 13. The Court adopted a broad interpretation of the rule, holding that a claim that the plaintiff was purloining quotations from the defendant's exchange was a compulsory counterclaim to the plaintiff's suit alleging that the defendant was violating the antitrust laws by refusing to furnish him ticker service. The Court said that "transaction" has a flexible meaning that "may comprehend a series of many occurrences, depending not so much upon the immediateness of their occurrence as upon their logical relationship." *Moore*, 270 U.S. at 610, 46 S. Ct. at 371.

Professor Charles Alan Wright has written that this "logical relationship" test is the only satisfactory method of determining whether a counterclaim is compulsory. He analyzes and discards other suggested tests, including whether substantially the same evidence will support or refute both the plaintiff's claim and the counterclaim, whether the issues of fact and law are largely the same, and whether *res judicata* would bar the subsequent suit in the absence of a compulsory counterclaim rule. Wright, *Estoppel by Rule: The Compulsory Counterclaim Under Modern Pleading*, 39 Iowa L. Rev. 255, 270–73 (1954); C. Wright, *Federal Courts* § 79, at 527–29 (4th ed. 1983). Professor Wright points out that if a counterclaim would be compulsory under any of these three tests it would be so likewise under the "logical relationship" test, but that the converse is not true because some claims that come within the purpose of the compulsory counterclaim rule would not be compulsory under these other tests. 39 Iowa L. Rev. at 271, 272. Professor Wright suggests that the purpose of compelling counterclaims is to reduce the volume of litigation and promote the just, speedy, and inexpensive determination of controversies by barring relitigation of the same sets of facts. 39 Iowa L. Rev. at 263. Thus, we conclude that application of the rule requires that both claims concern at least some of the same facts. *Plant v. Blazer Financial Services, Inc.*, 598 F.2d 1357, 1360–61 (5th Cir. 1979).

We recognize that the "logical relationship" test does not provide an easy solution in every case, although it does give a broader scope to the rule than any of the other tests. There is no logical relationship when none of the same facts are relevant to both claims. However, whenever the same facts, which may or may not be disputed, are significant and logically relevant to both claims, the "logical relationship" test is satisfied. This test is consistent with the decision of the Supreme Court of Texas in *Griffin*, as well as most, if not all, of the other Texas decisions cited.

In the present case we conclude that the "logical relationship" test is satisfied. Signgraphics's contract with Weston to fabricate and install the sign was the basic transaction out of which arose both the subcontract on which Northwest sued in Idaho and the later oral contract on which Signgraphics sued in the present suit. Performance of both of these contracts was necessary to enable Signgraphics to perform its contract with Weston. Moreover, performance by Signgraphics of its contract to furnish the pipe was necessary to enable Northwest to perform its subcontract with Signgraphics. Evidence of both of the earlier contracts is relevant to the present suit. Thus, although three distinct contracts are involved, there is a logical relationship between them. We hold that Signgraphics's claim arose out of the transaction or occurrence that was the subject of Northwest's claim, and, therefore, that the present suit is barred by Rule 97(a).

Signgraphics contends further that its claim should not be barred because the Idaho judgment was based on a default after service on Signgraphics of a nonresident notice that this Court held to be insufficient in *Northwest Sign Co. v. Jack H. Brown & Co.*, 677 S.W.2d 135 (Tex. Civ. App.—Dallas 1984), *rev'd*, 680 S.W.2d 808 (Tex. 1984). However, the sufficiency of the service and the jurisdiction of the Idaho court were upheld by the Supreme Court of Texas in *Northwest Sign Co. v. Jack H. Brown & Co.*, 680 S.W.2d 808 (Tex. 1984), *cert. denied*, 471 U.S. 1113, 105 S. Ct. 2353, 86 L. Ed. 2d 255 (1985). Signgraphics cites no authority supporting the view that the compulsory counterclaim rule does not apply to a default judgment. Nothing in rule 97(a) indicates that it does not apply to default judgment cases. The rule has been applied to cases where the former defendant did not file an answer because his insurer made a settlement with the plaintiff. *Harris v. Jones*, 404 S.W.2d 349, 351-52 (Tex. Civ. App.—Eastland 1966, writ ref'd); *Fireman's Ins. Co. v. L. P. Stewart & Bros.*, 158 A.2d 675, 677 (D.C. 1960). We conclude that a party has no right to let an adverse claim go by default and reserve his counterclaim for a time and place of his own choice. The same policy reasons apply as if he had appeared and defended the opposing claim. Consequently, we hold that Signgraphics's present claim is barred by its failure to present its present claim as a counterclaim in the Idaho suit.

Accordingly, we overrule Signgraphics's points of error. Northwest's cross-point complaining of the trial court's overruling of its special appearance is presented only in the alternative. Consequently, we do not reach the cross-point.

Affirmed.

HOWELL, J., dissenting with opinion.

HOWELL, Justice, dissenting.

I dissent. In stating that a party "has no right" to default his opponent's action and thereafter litigate his counterclaim at "a time and place of his own choice," the majority infers that the

Idaho default was a conscious and deliberate strategic manuever of Signgraphics, the Texas signmaker. The trial court made no such finding, the Idaho signmaker makes no such claim, and the record does not warrant this court to so hold *sua sponte*.

Likewise, the majority holds by inference that the failure of the Texas signmaker to cite authority "supporting the rule that the compulsory counterclaim rule does not apply to a default judgment" is a sufficient ground for an affirmance. The decision harkens back to the medieval rule that if there be no writ, there be no right. Where the law upon a point has not been decided, it is our obligation to declare the law, not to simply affirm because the appellant has no case directly in point.

Sound legal analysis leads to the conclusion that neither the compulsory counterclaim rule, nor any theory of *res judicata* should be applied to default judgment situations. The courts of our nation enter a myriad of defaults against the impecunious. The most frequent reason, by far, that a defaulting defendant fails to meet his underlying obligation is that he has no money; the reason that he defaults is that he has neither a defense, nor funds to retain counsel to present a defense. That class of default is easily distinguishable and is of little present concern because, once a default of that class is entered, it is rarely contested and, more often than not, the plaintiff ultimately realizes little or nothing upon his judgment.

The class of default which is subsequently contested almost always involves mistake, oversight, misunderstanding, and other human failing. In the majority of instances, the failing which leads to the default is not the personal failing of the defaulting defendant but is the failing of the defendant's agent, generally a member of the bar certified as competent to protect the rights of the public by the very court system which has exacted the default.

Defaults are necessarily punitive. In every instance, they represent the forfeiture of the right to present evidence and to be heard as to the merits of the opposing party's claim. Of course, every system for the regulation of human conduct must have its sanctions; experience demonstrates that without *reasonable* sanctions and the *reasonable* application thereof, our judicial system would collapse. This case squarely presents the question of what is a reasonable sanction for the Texas signmaker's Idaho default. Regrettably the majority has avoided rather than answered the core question presented by this record.

The question, having been properly outlined and placed in its proper context is easily answered: The compulsory counterclaim rule is not applicable to default judgments. Neither should a default judgment be granted res judicata effect over and beyond the actual res awarded to the plaintiff who prevails upon default.

The law has long recognized the harsh and punitive effect of defaults. Upon default, the plaintiff may not amend; he may not make additional claims, not unless he serves those claims upon the defaulting defendant and obtains subsequent default thereon; he may not recover more than that for which he has sued; the may not state additional grounds for recovery; and if his evidence will not support all relief granted, the default will not as a rule be modified—it will be set aside in its entirety.

These rules have been fashioned by the courts to ameliorate the punitive effect of defaults. The within majority decision violates them. The Idaho signmaker is being given relief that it did not plead; relief to a dollar value in excess of the defaulted Idaho petition is being awarded; relief different in kind is being granted; relief not supported by evidence received at the default hearing is being assessed. The well established law of Texas pertaining to defaults has been traversed *sub silentio*.

The only theoretical justification advanced by the majority is that which it has gleaned from Professor Wright's statement that the law of compulsory counterclaim reduces the volume of litigation and promotes "the *just*, speedy and inexpensive determination of controversies. . . . (emphasis added)." Texas has long held that it is not "just" to assess against a defaulting defendant anything over and beyond that which was precisely claimed and precisely put in evidence in the case wherein the default occurred. Professor Wright's analysis, while persuasive as a general proposition, must yield to the Texas concept of proper sanctions against a defaulting defendant. It is to be further noted that the Professor's stated goal of an inexpensive determination is largely inapplicable to defaults. Default hearings are short and summary proceedings; defaults are often granted upon the pleadings or upon affidavit. To exempt defaults from the compulsory counterclaim rule and from the rule of res judicata still only requires but one full blown trial upon the merits. The judgment below should be reversed.

Finally, the majority has neither reached nor ruled upon the Idaho signmaker's conditional cross-point urging that its special appearance was improperly overruled. The cross-point should be sustained and this action should be dismissed. *U-Anchor Advertising, Inc. v. Burt*, 553 S.W.2d 760 (Tex. 1977).

---

## NOTES AND QUESTIONS

(1) *Opposing Parties*. Who is an "opposing party" within the meaning of Tex. R. Civ. P. 97(a), (b)? If A sues B and C claiming personal injury damages from them on a theory of negligence, are B and C "opposing parties"? Would your answer differ if B made a claim for contribution against C? Would B be required to join with the claim for contribution against C a claim for damage to his or her truck arising from the same accident? Would C be required to make a claim for contribution to counter B's claim? Would C be required to join a claim for personal injury against A? Against B?

(2) *Prohibited Counterclaims*. Are any counterclaims prohibited under Rule 97? *See* Kennedy, *Counterclaims Under Federal Rule 13,* 11 Hous. L. Rev. 255 (1974). Suppose the counterclaim is above the maximum jurisdictional limits of the court? Below the minimum? *See* Tex. R. Civ. P. 97(c). Consider the following excerpt from a student note, 24 Tex. L. Rev. 100 (1945).*

> PROCEDURE—COUNTERCLAIM—JOINDER.—Plaintiff sued in the district court on two promissory notes in the amount of $250 each plus attorney's fees. Two items were pleaded by way of set-off, neither of which was in any way connected with the promissory notes, the total being less than the minimum jurisdictional amount. *Held,* that the court had jurisdiction of the counterclaim, although less than the minimum jurisdictional amount, since the claim was of such a character as to be available as a set-off and was pleaded only defensively, no affirmative relief being sought, *Moritz v. Byerly,* 185 S.W.(2d) 589 (Austin Civ. App. 1945).
>
> When defendant's cross-action, counterclaim, or set-off is connected with the subject matter of the suit, a court has power to render judgment on it even though it may be a claim for less than the minimum amount of which the court has jurisdiction. *Kirby v.*

> *American Soda Fountain Co.*, 194 U.S. 141 (1904); *Chambers v. Cannon*, 62 Tex. 293 (1884); *Baker v. Black*, 83 S.W.(2d) 811 (Tex. Civ. App. 1935) *rev'd on other grounds*, 111 S.W.(2d) 706; *Sachs v. Goldberg*, 159 S.W. 92 (Tex. Civ. App. 1913, error ref'd). Liberality in the allowance of set-off and counterclaim is to be expected in the interest of avoiding a multiplicity of suits. *Thomas v. Hill*, 3 Tex. 270 (1843); *Watts v. Gibson*, 33 S.W.(2d) 777 (Tex. Civ. App. 1930); *see Gulf, C. & S. F. Ry. v. Pearlstone*, 53 S.W.(2d) 1001 (Tex. Civ. App. 1932). It seems that there is no jurisdiction of a cross-action filed by one defendant against another defendant if the amount is less than the minimum jurisdictional amount and if the court considers the cross-action to be independent of the main suit. *Hull v. First Guaranty State Bank*, 199 S.W. 1148 (Tex. Civ. App. 1918); *Dallas v. Rutledge*, 258 S.W. 534 (Tex. Civ. App. 1924). A court has no jurisdiction of a cross-action which exceeds its maximum jurisdictional amount. *Gimbel v. Gomprecht*, 89 Tex. 497, 35 S.W. 470 (1896); *Turner v. Larson*, 72 S.W.(2d) 397 (Tex. Civ. App. 1934, error dism'd).
>
> A permissive counterclaim, Fed. Rules Civ. Proc. (1939) Rule 13b, Tex. Rules Civ. Proc. (1941) Rule 97b, may be litigated in an independent action, and therefore will ordinarily require independent jurisdictional grounds. *Utah Radio Products v. Boudette*, 78 F.(2d) 793 (C.C.A. 1st, 1935); *U.S. Expansion Bolt Co. v. Krontke Hardware Co.*, 234 Fed. 868 (C.C.A. 7th, 1916); *Weisz v. Horton*, 148 S.W.(2d) 219 (Tex. Civ. App. 1941, error dism'd, judg. correct). But if limited solely to set-off, *i.e.*, matter to reduce plaintiff's recovery, there seems to be an exception to the general rule and no independent jurisdictional amount is required. 1 Moore, *Federal Practice* (1938) § 13.03, p. 696; Shulman and Jaegerman, *Some Jurisdictional Limitations on Federal Procedure* (1936) 45 Yale L. J. 393, 415. Jurisdictional requirements can be met by aggregating two or more permissive counterclaims. 1 Moore, *Federal Practice* 698.

*See also Tex. R. Civ. P. 97(g). Review Tex. R. Civ. P. 97(a).*

(3) *Procedural Penalty*. What are the consequences of failing to make a counterclaim that is compulsory? Are they too harsh? *See* Wright, *Estoppel by Rule: The Compulsory Counterclaim Under Modern Pleading*, 38 Minn. L. Rev. 423 (1954). Consider the following from Kennedy, *Counterclaims Under Federal Rule 13*, 11 Hous. L. Rev. 255 (1974).*

> It can be persuasively argued that the traditional *res judicata* consequence of totally barring relitigation is too harsh. A more rational consequence than total bar, in this view, would be to make the relitigator pay court costs and attorneys' fees for not raising the claim in the first litigation. This approach minimizes the supposed success of the traditional approach in granting repose to the plaintiff, and in protecting the courts from relitigation.
>
> Another approach, specifically focusing on the compulsion aspect of rule 13(a), takes a different but related tack. It is argued that the consequence of total preclusion ought to be based on a theory of estoppel, when the party has knowingly waived his right to counterclaim, and should not be applied automatically whenever it appears that the defendant had a claim that arose out of the same transaction or occurrence. Although the traditional *res judicata* concept is often recited, the estoppel theory is gaining ground, especially in cases where reasonable grounds can be shown why the attorney did not raise a counterclaim in the previous litigation. For example, when the defense in the first suit was handled by

an insurance company attorney, or the case was settled, it is now being recognized that it is more appropriate to apply rule 13(a) on an estoppel or waiver basis.

(4) *Interpretation of the Compulsory Counterclaim Proviso.* Assume that a case is settled by an injured party's insurance agent who obtains a dismissal of a suit filed against the insured who has filed no counterclaim in the dismissed action. Is the insured a "pleader" as described in Tex. R. Civ. P. 97(a)? What is the proper interpretation of the proviso at the end of subdivision (a)? Isn't this the same type of problem discussed by Professor Kennedy? It appears that Texas courts currently view the matter in res judicata terms. *Griffin v. Holiday Inns of America,* 496 S.W.2d 535, 539 (Tex. 1973).

(5) *Default Judgments.* Does the compulsory counterclaim rule apply in default judgment cases? Several appellate courts have held that it does. *See Jones v. First Nat'l Bank of Anson,* 846 S.W.2d 107, 109 (Tex. App.—Eastland 1992, no writ); *see also Jack H. Brown v. Northwest Sign Co.,* 718 S.W.2d 397 (Tex. App.—Dallas 1986, writ ref'd n.r.e.) (holding in the affirmative).

### [B] Cross-Claims

*Reread Tex. R. Civ. P. 97(e).*

### NOTES AND QUESTIONS

(1) Are any cross-claims compulsory? *See* former C.P.R.C. § 33.017 (Claims Determined in Primary Suit), which provided: "All claims for contribution between named defendants must be determined in the primary suit, but a named defendant may sue a person who is not a party to the primary suit and who has not settled with the claimant." As a result of the repeal of the statute and the permissive language of subdivision (e) of Civil Procedure Rule 97, it appears that cross-claims are permissive.

(2) Can a cross-claim also be a counterclaim? When are co-parties also opposing parties? If A sues B and C, and B sues C for damage to B's car resulting from the same collision by cross-claim, is B an opposing party vis-a-vis C? Is C an opposing party vis-a-vis B?

## § 7.04 Permissive Joinder of Parties by the Defendant

*Read Tex. R. Civ. P. 38, 97(f).*

### HEISEY v. BOOTH

*476 S.W.2d 782 (Tex. Civ. App.—Fort Worth 1972, writ dism'd)*

MASSEY, Chief Justice.

One Reece sued J. E. Booth for $329.60 and attorney's fees under the provisions of Texas Rules of Civil Procedure 185, "Suit on Sworn Account." Booth filed the sworn denial contemplated by the rule.

Under the provisions of T.R.C.P. 38, "Third-Party Practice," Booth proceeded to bring Leroy Heisey into the same case, as a third-party defendant. Booth alleged—alternative to his defensive position as applied to Reece's suit—that if he was liable to Reece then Heisey was liable to him (Booth) because their relationship was that of principal and agent as applied to his own transaction with Reece; that in consequence Heisey owed him the duty of indemnity or reimbursement. See generally 3 Am. Jur. 2d, p. 612, "Agency," Sec. 243, "(Reimbursement and Indemnification of Agent)—Generally." Reece never at any time made Heisey a defendant of whom any relief was sought, contenting himself with his claim against Booth.

At the date the case was set for trial Reece and Booth appeared and announced ready. Heisey, though having filed an unsworn general denial to Booth's third-party petition, failed to appear. Thereupon, without any evidence introduced, Reece and Booth represented to the court that in so far as the lawsuit obtained between themselves they had agreed to settle and dispose of the same by Booth's stipulation and agreement that judgment be rendered against him for the sum of $329.60, plus court costs. In other words, the agreement was for judgment to be rendered against Booth for plaintiff Reece on Reece's suit on sworn account—except for attorney's fees. Such was the judgment entered. Support therefor consisted of merely the stipulation mentioned, not by any evidence.

In this connection Heisey is bound by the judgment; i.e., he is estopped to deny that Booth is liable to Reece for $329.60 perforce the judgment. Of course this does not mean that upon trial of the case against Heisey that the justness of the account upon which Reece sued Booth would not be necessary to be proved by evidence. Reece never sought any relief against Heisey nor was any obtained in the judgment. Booth alone sought relief, and he was granted as a judgment-over, against Heisey, in the amount of $329.60, following a trial in which there was no evidence establishing either that Reece's account was just or that the transaction out of which it arose was one as to which Booth was the agent of Heisey.

T.R.C.P. 38, "Third-Party Practice," provides, in part: "If . . . service is completed upon the cross-action, the person so served, hereinafter called the third-party defendant, *shall make his defenses under the rules applicable to the defendant,* (emphasis supplied). . . . The third-party defendant may assert any defenses which the third-party plaintiff has to the plaintiff's claim. . . ." Booth insists that it was the obligation of Heisey to make the Booth defenses to the suit against him by Reece; i.e., to deny the entitlement of Reece because of his suit against him upon sworn account by that sworn denial contemplated by T.R.C.P. 185 (despite the fact that Heisey had not been made a party defendant by Reece) or forfeit the right to insist that evidence be produced on trial in proof of the matters sued upon, as establishing a *prima facie* case as applied to the indebtedness. Since Heisey filed no such sworn denial of the sworn account he is according to Booth, liable to him. The trial court agreed and rendered judgment for Booth decreeing that Heisey was liable in the amount of $329.60.

The trouble with the Booth theory is that Reece never at any time had any pleadings seeking relief against Heisey. It is to the allegations against him, as Booth's defendant, to which Heisey is obliged by the rule to "make his defenses" as contemplated by T.R.C.P. 38. Heisey is not obliged to make the defenses of Booth. He is not punished for failure to do so; neither is there any easing of the burden of proof of either Reece or Booth, as against Heisey, in consequence of such failure. Heisey is not obligated to verify pleadings in denial of Reece's account merely because Booth is required by rule to do so if he, Booth, wishes to require that Reece prove his case by evidence. Reece's suit on sworn account was against Booth alone. Heisey was a stranger to the transaction sued upon by Reece; i.e., a stranger to the transaction because of which Reece sued Booth. Robertson v. Rexall Drug & Chemical Company, 410 S.W.2d 200 (Fort Worth Civ. App., 1966, no writ hist.).

As a stranger Heisey could controvert and disprove the account of Reece without having filed a written denial under oath, and by his general denial—in so far as his own liability be involved,—he put the burden on any who would prove the account the necessity to establish it by evidence. 1 *Tex. Jur. 2d* 321, "Accounts and Accounting," Sec. 71, "Necessity that account exist by virtue of contract between parties to action." Heisey did not appear upon the hearing where Reece and Booth settled the controversy theretofore existent. Had he done so, yet stood mute, no judgment could have been rendered against him on pleadings alone, without evidence, though Reece would have been entitled to judgment against Booth without proof had Booth failed to deny Reece's account under oath. Of course Booth had so pled—but the judgment against him was by settlement. His pleading was never stricken.

It should also be remembered that Booth alleged that Heisey was his principal. Heisey filed a general denial and such obliged Booth to prove agency. 2 Tex. Jur. 2d, p. 679, "Agency," Sec. 224, "Denial of authority in answer—Requirements as to verification." Any supportable judgment for Booth against Heisey necessarily depended upon proof of his agency for Heisey as applied to the material transaction giving rise to the claim of Reece upon which he was sued. There was no such proof. The evidence does not support Booth's judgment against Heisey, even assuming the account of Reece to have been proved by evidence. As already noted, there was none.

Judgment is reversed and the cause remanded for another trial.

---

## NOTES AND QUESTIONS

(1) *Interpretation of Civil Procedure Rule 38.* In *Heisey,* Justice Massey, in assessing the circumstances under which a third-party defendant would be bound by a judgment for the plaintiff against a third-party plaintiff, struggled with interpretation of language in Civil Procedure Rule 38: "The third-party defendant is bound by the adjudication of the third-party plaintiff's liability to the plaintiff. . . ." This language was adopted by the Texas Supreme Court from the 1937 version of Fed. R. Civ. P. 14. With the 1946 amendments to the rule, the language was removed from the federal rule. The Advisory Committee for the 1946 amendments wrote that the sentence was stricken, "not to change the law, but because the sentence states a rule of substantive law which is not within the scope of a procedural rule. It is not the purpose of the rules to state the effect of a judgment." Effective April 1, 1984, Civil Procedure Rule 38 was also amended by eliminating the same language from the Texas rule. Does this mean that the third party defendant is not "bound" by an adjudication of the primary defendant's liability?

(2) *Answering the Plaintiff's Petition.* Does Civil Procedure Rule 38 ever require the third-party defendant to file an answer to the plaintiff's petition? Suppose the third-party plaintiff fails to plead an available affirmative defense. Must the third-party defendant plead it affirmatively? How may the third-party defendant "assert" such a defense?

(3) *Purpose of Third-Party Practice.* What persons are eligible to be third-party defendants? The rule provides for the bringing of such actions "against a person not a party to the action who is or may be liable to him [i.e., the defendant] or to the plaintiff for all or part of the plaintiff's claim against him [i.e., the defendant]." Assume A, B and C become involved in an open intersectional collision. As a result of the collision all sustain serious bodily injuries. A sues B. May B bring a third-party action against C for B's personal injuries? May B bring a third-party

action against C for contribution or indemnity? What is the significance, if any, of the phrase "or to the plaintiff"? *Compare* Fed. R. Civ. P. 14(a). Suppose plaintiff does not desire to assert a claim against the person alleged to be liable "to the plaintiff." Can plaintiff be forced to do so? *See* Tex. R. Civ. P. 39. Although these questions are relevant to jury submission, they are especially important to the apportionment of·damages in negligence cases. *Cf. Haney Electric Co. v. Hurst,* 624 S.W.2d 602 (Tex. Civ. App.—Dallas 1981, writ dism'd) (explores apportionment of damages under comparative negligence when third-party defendant is not sued by plaintiff).

(4) *Contribution Defendants.* The primary purpose of impleader under modern practice is to provide for the assertion of contribution claims against tortfeasors who have not been named as defendants by the plaintiff. Subchapter B of Chapter 33 of the Civil Practice and Remedies Code provides contribution rights to defendants who are "jointly and severally liable" to plaintiffs such that they are legally accountable for all damages recoverable by the plaintiff. *See* C.P.R.C. §§ 33.015, 33.016. The joinder of a "contribution defendant" allows the defendant to assert a claim for contribution and to obtain a judgment against the contribution defendant based on an assessment of the contribution shares of each defendant and each contribution defendant. *See* C.P.R.C. § 33.016. It appears that the same tortfeasor can be joined as a "responsible third party" and as a "contribution defendant." *See* C.P.R.C. § 33.004(b).

(5) *Responsible Third Parties.* As a result of the 1995 amendments to Chapter 33 of the Civil Practice and Remedies Code, "a defendant may seek to join a responsible third party who has not been sued by the claimant." *See* C.P.R.C. § 33.004. The term "responsible third party" means a person who is or may be liable to the plaintiff for all or part of the damages claimed against the named defendant or defendants, but who was not sued by the claimant. C.P.R.C. § 33.011(b). The purpose of joining such a responsible third party is to affect the trier of facts' apportionment of responsibility as a result of the inclusion of "each responsible third party who has been joined under Section 33.004" in the primary comparative apportionment question. *See* C.P.R.C. § 33.003. This may affect the amount of liability incurred by the defendant by influencing the trier of fact to assign a lower percentage of responsibility to the defendant. *See* C.P.R.C. § 33.013.

(6) *The Need for Leave of Court.* Civil Procedure Rule 38 provides that leave of court to prosecute a third-party action must be obtained unless the third-party petition is filed "not later than thirty (30) days after he [the defendant] serves his original answer." Tex. R. Civ. P. 38(a). Does this mean the defendant's initial original answer or any original answer? What if leave of court is not obtained? *See Trueheart v. Braselton*, 875 S.W.2d 412, 414 (Tex. App.—Corpus Christi 1994, no writ)—trial court did not abuse discretion in refusing to strike third-party petition filed without obtaining leave of court.

(7) *Venue of Cross-Actions.* For venue purposes, a third-party action was formerly viewed as a "distinct and severable" controversy or cause of action. *Union Bus Lines v. Byrd,* 142 Tex. 257, 177 S.W.2d 774, 776 (1944). This traditional view was altered for negligence cases by the decision in *Arthur Brothers, Inc. v. U.M.C., Inc.*, 647 S.W.2d 244 (Tex. 1982). Section 15.062(a) of the Civil Practice and Remedies Code now provides that venue of the main action governs venue of cross-claims, counterclaims and third-party actions. C.P.R.C. § 15.062(a). Furthermore, if an original defendant properly joins a third-party defendant, venue is proper for a claim arising out of the same transaction, occurrence, or series of transactions or occurrences by the plaintiff against the third-party defendant if the claim arises out of the subject matter of the plaintiff's claim against the original defendant. C.P.R.C. § 15.062(b).

(8) *Relationship to Civil Procedure Rule 97(f).* If A, B, and C are involved in a three-car collision and A sues B for damages, can B join C in connection with a counterclaim against A? *See* Tex. R. Civ. P. 97(f). Suppose B joins C as a third-party defendant. *See* Tex. R. Civ. P. 97(e). If B joins C as a third-party defendant, must C assert a counterclaim against A even though A has not asserted a claim against C? Is A an opposing party as to C? *See* Tex. R. Civ. P. 97(a). What is the difference between Civil Procedure Rules 38 and 97?

## § 7.05 Intervention; Voluntary Joinder of New Parties

*Read Tex. R. Civ. P. 60.*

### MULCAHY v. HOUSTON STEEL DRUM COMPANY

*402 S.W.2d 817 (Tex. Civ. App.—Austin 1966, no writ)*

PHILLIPS, Justice.

This case involves the right of appellant Mulcahy to intervene in a Bill of Review proceeding brought by the appellee Houston Steel Drum Company against the Secretary of State and Attorney General of Texas seeking to reinstate its corporate charter previously forfeited for failure to pay franchise taxes to the State of Texas.

After the court heard appellee's motion to strike appellant's pleadings in intervention, the court ruled as a matter of law that appellant had not alleged sufficient facts to entitle him to intervene. The parties had stipulated that the facts alleged in appellant's pleadings were true for the purposes of the hearing.

We affirm the judgment of the trial court.

In January of 1965 appellee filed its Bill of Review in the District Court of Travis County naming the Secretary of State and the Attorney General as respondents alleging that it was granted a corporate charter by the State of Texas in 1954; that in November of 1964 a default judgment had been entered against appellee for forfeiting its corporate charter for nonpayment of its franchise taxes to the State for the years 1960–64; that such failure of appellee to pay the taxes was due to its internal reorganization during the period, with a resulting confusion and lack of receipt of notices by the past and present shareholders, officers and directors of appellee; that contrary to the allegation of the State's petition in the forfeiture proceeding, appellee had assets with which to satisfy a tax judgment; that appellee had since filed all necessary tax returns and paid all franchise taxes, interest and penalties due the State; and prayed that it have judgment setting aside the forfeiture and reinstating the charter.

The Secretary of State and the Attorney General filed a general denial.

Appellant filed his petition in intervention, and later an amendment thereto, opposing the reinstatement of appellee's charter, alleging a justiciable interest in the suit based on the fact that he was an officer, stockholder and director of appellee prior to February, 1961 and that he did accounting work for appellee prior to February 1961. Appellant further alleged that he would be prejudiced should he be denied intervention on the side of the State because the allegations in appellee's Bill of Review implied criticism of his accounting work for appellee prior to February, 1961, which constituted an adverse reflection on his professional reputation as a certified public accountant. That the recitals in the Bill of Review to the effect that appellee's books and records were not maintained so as to reflect its franchise tax liability constitute a serious reflection upon appellant's professional reputation as a certified public accountant charged with the duty and responsibility of maintaining appellee's books and records, all of which duties and responsibilities were performed properly and effectively by appellant with the full knowledge of appellee.

Appellee filed a motion to strike the intervention on the grounds that as a matter of law appellant had not alleged facts sufficient to entitle him to intervene in the suit.

Without hearing evidence, and on the stipuation of the parties that for purposes of the hearing, the facts alleged by appellant would be taken as true, the trial court heard argument of counsel and entered its order striking appellant's intervention.

Subsequent to this order, the trial court entered judgment for appellee setting aside the prior judicial forfeiture and reinstating appellee's charter.

At no point in its Bill of Review or in the judgment entered in this case did appellee name appellant or accuse him of any fault in the delinquencies in appellee's payment of its taxes. Nor is any stockholder, officer or director named or identified in the Bill of Review.

The Texas Rules of Civil Procedure provide that any party may intervene in an action subject to being stricken out for sufficient reason at the motion of one of the parties. Rule 60, T.R.C.P.

The right to intervene is given in furtherance of a speedy disposition of suits and to prevent multiplicity of actions. However, since the original parties to the pending suit must be protected from the disadvantages of intervention, trial courts have a wide discretion in judging the sufficiency of an opposing party's motion to dismiss the intervenor. 44 Tex. Jur. 2d, Sec. 41, and Sec. 63.

The litigation in the trial court involved in this appeal was, first, a suit by the State to forfeit a corporate charter which it had granted to appellee and, second, a Bill of Review to set aside the default judgment granted in the prior suit and to reinstate the corporate charter of appellee. The grounds for such forfeiture were nonpayment of franchise taxes imposed by the State on corporations as one condition for retaining their corporate charter privileges previously granted by the State.

Appellant's attempt to intervene in this litigation based on his capacity as a former stockholder, officer and director, in order to take a position as party defendant in the Bill of Review constituted an attempt by appellant to question the legality of the existence of the corporation.

The litigation in both cases is in the nature of a quo warranto proceeding. The Supreme Court defined such action in *Miller v. Davis*, 136 Tex. 299, 150 S.W.2d 973, 978, 136 A.L.R. 177, as follows:

> "It is the rule that where a corporation has been formed under color of law, only the State can question its corporate existence, and that in a direct proceeding wherein the State is a party, and the action is in the nature of a quo warranto proceeding."

To entitle a party to intervene in a suit, he must be at least a proper party to the suit. 44 Tex. Jur. 2d, Parties, Sec. 44. Appellant is not a proper party to a quo warranto action.

. . . .

In this litigation whereby the State has contested the existence of one of its corporations, appellant has attempted to assume a co-party status, along with the State, in order to exert a measure of control over the way the litigation is handled. While such authority is clearly contrary to the basic rules of quo warranto actions, appellant is attempting to accomplish it by resort to the rules governing intervention and citation of general rules relating to intervention.

The rule applicable here is stated in King v. Olds, 71 Tex. 729, 12 S.W. 65 (1888) as follows:

> "The intervenor's interest must be such that if the original action had never been commenced, and he had first brought it as the sole plaintiff, he would have been entitled to recover in his own name to the extent at least of a part of the relief sought; or, if the action had first been brought against him as the defendant, he would have been able to defeat the recovery, in part at least. His interest may be either legal or equitable."

To apply the foregoing general rule to the instant litigation, it is apparent that the appellant would have had no standing, on either legal or equitable grounds, to have brought the original suit against appellee seeking forfeiture of its charter for nonpayment of franchise taxes. Filing such action was within the sole discretion and power of the Attorney General. The subsequent Bill of Review suit filed by appellee involves the same original parties and the sole subject matter is the question of whether the default judgment in the State's former action should be set aside. The Bill of Review could not have been filed naming appellant as co-defendant along with the State because appellant has no interest or standing in the matter from which appellee could pray for either recovery or relief. The Bill of Review suit was part and parcel of the prior quo warranto action and its filing gave appellant no standing to attempt to defeat it either in whole or in part.

The sufficiency of a petition in intervention is tested by its allegations of fact on which the right to intervene depends. A petition will fail if no right to intervene is shown because no sufficient interest is alleged. *Watkins v. Citizens National Bank*, 1909, 53 Tex. Civ. App. 437, 115 S.W. 304, no writ hist.

A remote or contingent interest in a suit does not entitle a party to intervene. 44 Tex. Jur. 2d, Sec. 44.

We affirm the judgment of the trial court.

---

## NOTES AND QUESTIONS

(1) *Proper Parties*. Who is a "proper" party? *See* Tex. R. Civ. P. 40. Doesn't Mulcahy have an interest in the litigation? What kind of interest does he have? Will it be impaired or impeded if he is not permitted to be a party? Is it adequately protected? *See* Fed. R. Civ. P. 24(a).

*Guaranty Federal v. Horseshoe Operating*, 793 S.W.2d 652 (Tex. 1990), demonstrates another application of the analysis used to scrutinize a challenged intervention. At the request of its borrower, Petrolife, Inc., University Savings had a teller's check issued to Intercontinental as payment for gasoline under a contract. Later, also at Petrolife's request, University Savings stopped payment on the teller's check. When Intercontinental sued University Savings, Petrolife intervened as a defendant. The trial court struck the intervention, but the court of appeals reversed. The Texas Supreme Court agreed that the trial court had abused its discretion and held:

> Rule 60 of the Texas Rules of Civil Procedure provides that "[a]ny party may intervene, subject to being stricken out by the court for sufficient cause on the motion of the opposite party. . . ." Tex. R. Civ. P. 60. An intervenor is not required to secure the court's permission

> to intervene; the party who opposed the intervention has the burden to challenge it by a motion to strike. *See In re Nation,* 694 S.W.2d 588 (Tex. App.—Texarkana 1985, no writ); *Jones v. Springs Ranch Co.*, 642 S.W.2d 551 (Tex. App.—Amarillo 1982, no writ). Without a motion to strike, the trial court abused its discretion in striking Petrolife's plea in intervention.
>
> Furthermore, under Rule 60, a person or entity has the right to intervene if the intervenor could have brought the same action, or any part thereof, in his own name, or, if the action had been brought against him, he would be able to defeat recovery, or some part thereof. *Inter-Continental Corp. v. Moody,* 411 S.W.2d 578, 589 (Tex. Civ. App.—Houston [1st Dist.] 1966, writ ref'd n.r.e.); *Texas Supply Center, Inc. v. Daon Corp.* 641 S.W.2d 335, 337 (Tex. App.—Dallas 1982, writ ref'd n.r.e.). The interest asserted by the intervenor may be legal or equitable. *Moody,* 411 S.W.2d at 589. Although the trial court has broad discretion in determining whether an intervention should be stricken, it is an abuse of discretion to strike a plea in intervention if (1) the intervenor meets the above test, (2) the intervention will not complicate the case by an excessive multiplication of the issues, and (3) the intervention is almost essential to effectively protect the intervenor's interest. *Moody,* 411 S.W.2d at 589; *Daon Corp.*, 641 S.W.2d at 337.
>
> Under the facts alleged in Petrolife's plea in intervention and counterclaim and University Savings' response to ICC's motions for partial summary judgment, Petrolife meets the above test. Furthermore, the intervention will not complicate the case by an excessive multiplication of the issues and is almost essential to effectively protect Petrolife's interests. Judicial economy requires that Petrolife intervene and participate in the trial in order to avoid a multiplicity of lengthy lawsuits. It is undisputed that Petrolife's rights and interests will be affected by the judgment in this case. Therefore, we hold that the trial court abused its discretion in striking Petrolife's plea in intervention.

793 S.W.2d at 657–658.

(2) *Avoidance of Multiplicity of Suits.* Intervention is ordinarily favored because it avoids a multiplicity of suits. If A sued B for breach of contract, should C be permitted to intervene to sue B on an entirely unrelated contract concerning different subject matter? Could C and A have originally joined together as plaintiffs? *See* Tex. R. Civ. P. 40.

(3) *Prudential Limits on Permissive Intervention.* In *Roberson v. Roberson,* 420 S.W.2d 495 (Tex. Civ. App.—Houston [14th Dist.] 1967, writ ref'd n.r.e.), a plea in intervention was filed by a putative wife in a divorce proceeding. The putative wife claimed that Dr. Roberson acquired properties during the time that she lived with him. She asserted a claim to the properties. Her intervention was stricken. Consider the following excerpt from the opinion:

> Appellants first attack the order of the trial court in striking the plea of intervention of Marinelle Pullen. Marinelle makes claim to a portion of the property acquired by Dr. Roberson while she was claiming to be his putative wife. See 1 Speer's Marital Rights in Texas (4th Ed.), Sec. 56, p. 62. While the striking of a plea in intervention is ordinarily a discretionary matter with the trial court, there are limits to this rule. See Inter-Continental Corp. v. Moody, 411 S.W.2d 578 (Tex. Civ. App.), writ ref., n.r.e.; McAdow Motor Co. v. Luckett, 131 S.W.2d 267 (Tex. Civ. App.), no writ; Gullo v. City of West University Place, 214 S.W.2d 851 (Tex. Civ. App.), writ dism'd, w.o.j.; 1 McDonald, Texas Civil Practice, Sec. 3.47. However, in the case, an alleged putative wife seeks to intervene in a suit between husband and wife for divorce where a division of an abundance of community

property is required. The burdens on the court were already heavy before the attempted intervention. The master in chancery had held hearings on several occasions attempting to determine values and the extent of community property before the filing of the intervention. Suit for divorce was filed on April 1, 1964 and the master was appointed on October 13, 1965. After extensive and complicated hearings the master filed his report on September 20, 1966. Depositions were taken and the master held at least five hearings before the plea of intervention was filed on May 25, 1966, more than two years after the suit was filed. Moreover, the issues required to determine the lack of knowledge and innocence of the intervenor and the putative nature of the alleged marriage were entirely distinct transactions involving issues materially different from those already before the court. Marinelle Pullen could have and now can, in a separate suit against one or both parties to this action, protect the interest, if any, she might have in the property involved. Had the trial court allowed such intervention, this suit for divorce between husband and wife and division of community property probably would have been confused and clouded by a new and complicated set of issues. We believe that interminable trouble, confusion and delay would have resulted by the intervention. The trial court was well within his discretion and was correct in striking the intervention under all the circumstances. O'Brien v. First State Bank & Trust Co. of Taylor, 239 S.W. 715 (Tex. Civ. App.), no writ; Jones v. English, 235 S.W.2d 238 (Tex. Civ. App.), writ dism'd.; 44 Tex. Jur. 2d, pp. 195, 196, Sec. 44; Rules 40 and 60, Texas Rules of Civil Procedure. We hold that intervenor is not a necessary and indispensable party to this action. See 1 McDonald, Texas Civil Practice, Sec. 3.16. Broad discretion is accorded the trial judge in the matter of intervention.

Moreover, the apparently tenuous position of intervenor as being an innocent putative wife of Dr. Roberson, and her consequent claim to a part of the property as against the rights of Mrs. Elsie Roberson, adds force to the decision of the trial court in striking the intervention. We overrule appellants' points of error.

Was her intervention stricken because she filed it too late? What does the court mean about complications? What about the nature of her interest?

(4) *Compulsory Intervention?* Is intervention ever mandatory? *See Traders & General Insurance Co. v. Richardson,* 387 S.W.2d 478 (Tex. Civ. App.—Beaumont 1965, writ ref'd). The court held that an insurance company that had received an assignment of a property damage claim from its insured was barred from asserting that claim because it did not intervene in an action for personal injuries brought by its insured against the party to the accident that gave rise to the claim. The court based its decision on the doctrine of splitting a cause of action. The court would probably not have come to the same result if the company had not had notice of the first suit.

(5) *Venue Requirements.* Does an intervening plaintiff need to establish an independent basis for venue? Reconsider Section 15.003 of the Civil Practice and Remedies Code.

## § 7.06 Interpleader

*Read Tex. R. Civ. P. 43.*

### DOWNING v. LAWS

*419 S.W.2d 217 (Tex. Civ. App.—Austin 1967, writ ref'd n.r.e.)*

PHILLIPS, Chief Justice.

. . . .

The original suit filed by appellee Laws was for the purpose of obtaining a judicial resolution of competing claims to earnest money deposited with him as an escrow agent under the terms of a realty sales contract. Laws filed his suit against appellant Downing who had signed the contract as purchaser. At this time Downing, who had delivered the abovementioned earnest money to Laws, was demanding the return of the money.

In this same suit against Downing, Laws also sued Natalie M. Collins and the abovementioned defendants as owners and sellers of the land described in the contract who also were asserting a right to the earnest money Downing had placed with Laws.

Consequently, the abovementioned suit was filed against all such parties in the District Court of Travis County where several of the defendants then resided.

. . . .

Appellee Laws is not a wholly disinterested stakeholder with respect to the earnest money deposited with him under the terms of the realty sales contract as under certain conditions of the contract he is entitled to a portion thereof. Consequently, this suit might better be described as a suit in the nature of interpleader. At the same time however he has been beset by two wholly opposing and conflicting claims concerning the ownership and proper disposition of the earnest money. It might also be pointed out here that at the time of filing of appellees' suit, the sellers, before electing to sue for damages for the breach of the contract, had the option of suing for specific performance thereof.

A summary of the positions of the parties hereto at the time Laws filed his suit is as follows: he was holding earnest money as an escrow agent about which opposing parties were making competing and conflicting claims; the claimants competing for the earnest money were all represented by counsel; the realty sales contract governing the disposition of the earnest money expressly calls for the forfeiture of the earnest money as liquidated damages in the event of the purchaser's default; the purchaser's attorneys were asserting a defective title; the purchaser's attorneys were also, as indicated in their title opinion, asserting a misrepresentation about irrigation rights to the land; in addition, the purchaser claimed that the contract was unenforceable under the Statute of Frauds.

Tex. R. Civ. P. 43[2] which governs interpleader was not intended to limit an action in interpleader to one wholly disinterested in the suit: "It is not ground for objection . . . that the plaintiff avers that he is not liable in whole or in part to any or all of the claimants." Citizens National Bank of Emporia v. Socony Mobil Oil Co., 372 S.W.2d 718 (Tex. Civ. App. Amarillo 1963, writ ref'd n.r.e.); Franklin Life Insurance Co. v. Greer, 219 S.W.2d 137 (Tex. Civ. App. Texarkana 1949, aff'd in part rev. in part; 148 Tex. 166, 221 S.W.2d 857, 1949).

Rule 43 was taken from Federal Rule 22 with minor textual changes. There can be little doubt that Federal Rule 22 was intended to dispense with many of the crippling restraints on interpleader

---

[2] "Rule 43. Interpleader

Persons having claims against the plaintiff may be joined as defendants and required to interplead when their claims are such that the plaintiff is or may be exposed to double or multiple liability. It is not ground for objection to the joinder that the claims of the several claimants or the titles on which their claims depend do not have a common origin or are not identical but are adverse to and independent of one another, or that the plaintiff avers that he is not liable in whole or in part to any or all of the claimants. A defendant exposed to similar liability may obtain such interpleader by way of cross-claim or counterclaim. The provisions of this rule supplement and do not in any way limit the joinder of parties permitted in any other rules."

that had developed in equity and to liberalize the practice that, among other things, an interested and hostile party could file an action in interpleader and avoid a multiplicity of lawsuits. John Hancock Mutual Life Insurance Company v. Kegan, 22 F.Supp. 326 (D.C. Md. 1938); Barron and Holtzoff, Federal Practice § 551.

The adoption of Rule 43 in Texas also extended and liberalized the equitable remedy of interpleader. Security State Bank v. Shanley, 182 S.W.2d 136 (Tex. Civ. App. San Antonio, 1944, no writ).

. . . .

At the time appellee filed his suit in the case at bar there is no doubt but that he was beset with conflicting claims on the part of all the defendants which, to concede to the demands of either, he must have acted at his peril.

Likewise we hold that the cross-action brought against Laws and Downing is properly maintainable in Travis County, Texas because it arises out of the same transaction and involves the same issues of fact and law as the original suit. Luse v. Union City Transfer, 324 S.W.2d 935 (Tex. Civ. App. Waco 1959, writ dism'd); Service Drilling Co. v. Woods, 120 S.W.2d 608 (Tex. Civ. App. Austin 1938, no writ).

. . . .

The judgment of the trial court is affirmed.

[The dissent of Justice Hughes is ommitted.]

---

## NOTES AND QUESTIONS

(1) *Purpose of Interpleader*. As the *Downing* case illustrates, the device of interpleader permits an innocent stakeholder to require rival claimants to fight it out. It supplements the other joinder devices. As the rule indicates, it may be asserted by way of cross-claim or counterclaim. Is the device necessary when the stakeholder is not disinterested?

(2) *Recovery of Attorney's Fees*. Texas follows the rule that a disinterested stakeholder who has reasonable doubts as to the party entitled to the funds or property in his or her possession, and who in good faith interpleads the claimants, is entitled to an allowance of attorney's fees. *United States v. Ray Thomas Gravel Co.*, 380 S.W.2d 576, 580 (Tex. 1964). The allowance is usually from the "fund" in controversy. *Vassiliades v. Theophiles*, 115 S.W.2d 1220 (Tex. Civ. App.—Beaumont 1938, writ dism'd).

(3) *Venue Requirements*. Under the present venue statute that is dealt with in Chapter 6, C.P.R.C § 15.005 would be applicable to interpleader defendants. The issue would be whether the claims arose out of the same transaction, occurrence, or series of transactions or occurrences.

(4) *Subject Matter Jurisdiction*. The value or amount of the fund or property in the possession of the stakeholder appears to control the question of subject matter jurisdiction. *See Vassiliades v. Theophiles*, 115 S.W.2d 1220 (Tex. Civ. App.—Beaumont 1938; writ dism'd).

(5) *Possible Due Process Limits: Nonresident Claimants*. A limitation on the availability of interpleader in state court exists when one of the claimants is a nonresident over whom personal

jurisdiction cannot be obtained. Presence of the property or fund in question is not sufficient. *New York Life Insurance Company v. Dunlevy,* 241 U.S. 518 (1916); *cf. Shaffer v. Heitner*, 433 U.S. 186, 97 S. Ct. 2569, 53 L. Ed. 2d 683 (1977), noted in Chapter 4. The Federal Interpleader Act was passed in 1917 in response to *Dunlevy.* The Act obviates the problem by providing for nationwide service of process. 28 U.S.C. §§ 1335, 1397, 2361. *See* Chafee, *Interstate Interpleader,* 33 Yale L.J. 685 (1924); Chafee, *Federal Interpleader Since the Act of 1936,* 49 Yale L.J. 377 (1940).

## § 7.07 Compulsory Joinder of Parties

*Read Tex. R. Civ. P. 30–32.*

### YANDELL v. TARRANT STATE BANK

*538 S.W.2d 684 (Tex. Civ. App.—Fort Worth 1976, writ ref'd n.r.e.)*

BREWSTER, Justice.

The Tarrant State Bank, appellee, filed this suit against Olen W. Yandell, appellant, as guarantor of a note made by Circle Y Farms, Inc., payable to the order of appellee, and did not join the maker of the note as a party defendant in the case.

The appellant filed a plea in abatement alleging that the maker of the note was a necessary party in view of Rule 31, T.R.C.P., and asked that the case either be dismissed or abated until the maker was made a party to the suit. The appellee had in its trial petition alleged two reasons why it says it was not required by law to make the maker of the note a party to the suit against appellant, those reasons being: (1) Circle Y Farms, Inc., was actually or notoriously insolvent and has instituted a bankruptcy proceeding that is still pending, and (2) in the alternative, the joinder of Circle Y Farms, Inc., is unnecessary because in the guaranty agreement it specifically waived its right to require the joinder of the maker of the note as a party to the suit.

The note involved was executed by Circle Y Farms, Inc., by Olen Yandell, on February 9, 1975. It was for the principal sum of $12,000.00. The guaranty involved was in writing and was executed by appellant, Olen Yandell, on November 9, 1974. The guaranty agreement, among others, contained the following provisions:

". . . In particular, and without in any way limiting the foregoing, Guarantor waives any right to have Customer joined with Guarantor in any suit brought against Guarantor on this guaranty, and further waives any right to require Bank to forthwith sue Customer to collect the Obligations as a prerequisite to Bank's taking action against Guarantor under this guaranty. . . ."

The appellee filed a motion for summary judgment wherein it again alleged that it was not necessary for it to make Circle Y Farms, Inc., the maker of the note, a party to the suit for the two reasons set out above.

The trial court overruled appellant's plea in abatement and granted a summary judgment in appellee's favor for $12,000.00 plus $1,200.00 attorney's fee, with interest on the entire amount from date of judgment at the rate of 9% per annum.

This appeal is brought by appellant, Yandell, from that summary judgment.

We reverse the part of the judgment that awards a recovery of attorney's fees and remand that part of the case for a new trial. The rest of the judgment is affirmed.

Rule 31, T.R.C.P., provides: "No surety shall be sued unless his principal is joined with him, or unless a judgment has previously been rendered against his principal, except in cases otherwise provided for in the law and these rules."

Article 1986, V.A.T.S., provides:

"The acceptor of a bill of exchange, or a principal obligor in a contract, may be sued either alone or jointly with any other party who may be liable thereon; but no judgment shall be rendered against a party not primarily liable on such bill or other contract, unless judgment be also rendered against such acceptor or other principal obligor, except where the plaintiff may discontinue his suit against such principal obligor as hereinafter provided."

Article 1987, V.A.T.S., provides:

"The assignor, indorser, guarantor and surety upon a contract, and the drawer of a bill which has been accepted, may be sued without suing the maker, acceptor or other principal obligor, when the principal obligor resides beyond the limits of the State, or where he cannot be reached by the ordinary process of law, or when his residence is unknown and cannot be ascertained by the use of reasonable diligence, or when he is dead, or actually or notoriously insolvent."

The rule and statutes just referred to relating to parties in cases such as this apply to guarantors, both in instances where the guaranty is absolute, and also where it is conditional. *Wood v. Canfield Paper Co.,* 117 Tex. 399, 5 S.W.2d 748 (1928, op. ad.).

The summary judgment appealed from does not show which of the two reasons urged by appellee was considered by the trial court as being the one that authorized the appellee to bring this suit against the appellant guarantor without joining the maker of the note as a party to the suit. Because of that fact the appellant has undertaken to show in his brief, as it had to do in order to get a reversal, that the maker of the note was not actually or notoriously insolvent, and also that the rule and statutes above referred to providing that the maker should be a party to the suit could not be waived. *See McKelvy v. Barber,* 381 S.W.2d 59 (Tex. Sup., 1964); *Hudson v. Buddie's Super Markets, Inc.,* 488 S.W.2d 143 (Tex. Civ. App., Fort Worth, 1972, no writ hist.); and *LeJeune v. Gulf States Utilities Company,* 410 S.W.2d 44 (Tex. Civ. App., Beaumont, 1966, ref., n.r.e.).

In appellant's 5th and 6th points of error he contends that the trial court erred in holding that the maker of the note, Circle Y Farms, Inc., was either actually or notoriously insolvent. If the maker of the note had been actually or notoriously insolvent then an exception to Rule 31 would have existed. *See* Art. 1987, V.A.T.S.

The rule relied on by appellant in this case as entitling him to a reversal is stated in 53 Tex. Jur. 2d 655, Suretyship, Sec. 89, as follows: "But where on the face of the record the relationship of the parties appears to be principal and surety, and no excuse is pleaded and proved for nonjoinder of the principal, a judgment against the surety alone is erroneous, irrespective of whether objection was raised in the lower court."

The only references in the transcript to this insolvency issue are contained in the plaintiff's petition, the motion for summary judgment, and in the affidavit of Ted Hughes, the president of appellee bank, which affidavit was submitted in support of appellee's motion for summary judgment.

Appellee's unsworn petition contained the following allegations: "The maker and principal of the aforesaid promissory note, Circle Y Farms, Inc., is now and was, at the time this suit was instituted, actually or notoriously insolvent in that said corporation has filed a petition in bankruptcy and said bankruptcy proceedings are now pending. Consequently, said corporation is not, and need not be, joined as a defendant herein."

These allegations were repeated in appellee's unsworn motion for a summary judgment.

The allegations in those pleadings as to insolvency did not constitute any summary judgment evidence that the trial court could consider in determining at the summary judgment hearing that Circle Y Farms, Inc., was actually or notoriously insolvent. *Humphreys v. Texas Power & Light Company*, 427 S.W.2d 324 (Tex. Civ. App., Dallas, 1968, ref., n.r.e.) and *Richardson v. Thompson,* 390 S.W.2d 830 (Tex. Civ. App., Dallas, 1965, ref. n.r.e.).

The affidavit of Ted Hughes, president of appellee bank, contained the following statement: "Tarrant State Bank has heretofore received a notice of bankruptcy proceedings concerning Circle Y Farms, Inc., a true and correct copy of which is attached to this affidavit. Tarrant State Bank has not received any notification that said proceedings have been dismissed and said proceedings are believed by affiant to be still pending."

And attached to that affidavit was a copy of the notice that Hughes swore had been served on Tarrant State Bank advising it that bankruptcy proceedings had been instituted involving Circle Y Farms, Inc.

The statement in the Hughes' affidavit is the only summary judgment evidence in the record on the insolvency issue. That evidence did not establish as a matter of law that Circle Y Farms, Inc., the maker of the note, was actually or notoriously insolvent.

We therefore hold that appellant is correct in his contentions in points of error Nos. 5 and 6 that appellee did not prove as a matter of law at the summary judgment hearing that the maker of the note was actually or notoriously insolvent. This alone, however, does not entitle the appellant to a reversal of the case. Appellee had alleged that there was another reason why it was entitled to sue the guarantor without joining the maker of the note, said reason being that the guarantor had waived its right to have the maker of the note made a party to the suit.

In appellant's second, third and fourth points of error he contends that the trial court erred in permitting appellant as guarantor of the note, to be sued without joining the maker as a party defendant, and in holding that the guarantor of the note could legally waive the right given to him by Rule 31 and Articles 1986 and 1987 to have the maker of the note joined in this suit as a party defendant.

We overrule those points of error.

By the paragraph that we have hereinabove quoted out of the guaranty agreement the appellant, guarantor, did expressly waive the right given him by Rule 31 and the statutes referred to, to have the maker of the note joined in this suit as a party defendant. It would be hard to think of language that would more clearly express an agreement to waive that right.

The real question presented here is: assuming that appellant did for a valuable consideration expressly agree to waive his statutory right to have the maker of the note joined in the suit as a party defendant, is the agreement valid and enforceable?

A surety is a favorite in the law. *Jarecki Mfg. Co. v. Hinds,* 295 S.W. 274 (Tex. Civ. App., Eastland, 1927, writ. dism. in 6 S.W.2d 343).

Rule 31, T.R.C.P., and the above mentioned statutes give the surety the right or privilege of having his principal made a party defendant to any suit brought against the surety. The rights or privileges bestowed by that rule and by those statutes are solely for the benefit of the surety.

The following is from *United Benefit F. Ins. Co. v. Metropolitan Plumbing Co.,* 363 S.W.2d 843 (Tex. Civ. App., El Paso, 1962, no writ hist.), at page 847: "It is well settled that a right or privilege given by statute may be waived or surrendered, in whole or in part, by the party to whom or for whose benefit it is given, if he does not thereby destroy the rights and benefits conferred upon or flowing to another in or from the statute or other legal or equitable source."

In *Zurich General Accident & Liability Ins. Co. v. Fort Worth Laundry Co.,* 63 S.W.2d 236 (Tex. Civ. App., Fort Worth, 1933, no writ hist.), the Court said: " 'The doctrine of waiver from its nature, is applicable, generally speaking, to all rights or privileges to which a person is legally entitled, whether secured by contract, conferred by statute, or guaranteed by the constitution. . . .' "

A person can even waive rights given to him by the constitution. *Young v. City of Colorado,* 174 S.W. 986 (Tex. Civ. App., Fort Worth, 1915, writ ref.), *and see* 60 Tex. Jur. 2d 194, Waiver, Sec. 10.

A case that is directly in point on the issue of whether or not an agreement to waive the joinder rule is valid and enforceable, is *Moore v. Downie Bros. Circus,* 164 S.W.2d 420 (Tex. Civ. App., Fort Worth, 1942, no writ hist.). In that case suit was brought on a guaranty agreement in which the guarantor had agreed to waive the joinder of the principal obligor in a suit. Plaintiff's right to sue the guarantor without making the principal obligor a party was challenged by special exception. The trial court overruled the special exception and it was contended that this ruling was erroneous. The court there said on this point: "Sufficient answer to this contention is that the written obligation sued on, with all its provisions, was specifically pleaded; by its terms defendant agreed that he would perform without involving W. M. Moore (the principal obligor)." Our analysis of that opinion is that the point referred to was one of two grounds on which the case was affirmed. We do not consider the holding to be dicta.

Other opinions wherein the language used indicates that the courts involved believed that rights such as those involved here can be waived are: *Universal Metals & Machinery, Inc. v. Bohart,* 539 S.W.2d 874, 19 Tex. Sup. Ct. J. 212 (Tex. Sup., 1976), and *Zimmerman v. Bond,* 392 S.W.2d 149 (Tex. Civ. App., Dallas, 1965, no writ hist.). See also 28 Am. Jur. 2d 850, 851, Estoppel and Waiver, Sec. 164; and 60 Tex. Jur. 2d 193, Waiver, Sec. 10.

In this case the rights waived were rights created by the rule and statutes involved solely for the benefit of the guarantor (appellant). By waiving his right to have the maker made a party defendant he did not destroy rights and benefits conferred on anyone else by the rule or by the statutes or by any other legal or equitable sources.

We hold that the appellant's agreement to waive his right to have the maker of the note made a party defendant is valid and enforceable and that the trial court did not err in overruling appellant's plea in abatement.

In appellee's petition it pleaded this waiver as entitling it to bring the action without joining the Circle Y Farms, Inc., as a party, and at the summary judgment hearing appellee proved by affidavit the execution of the guaranty agreement by Yandell and its contents. We are convinced that appellee established its right to the summary judgment for the $12,000.00.

After we had prepared the opinion in this case, but before it had been handed down, we have received a copy of the opinion of the Beaumont Court of Civil Appeals in the case of *Walter Cook v. Citizens National Bank of Beaumont,* 538 S.W.2d 460 which opinion was handed down on June 10, 1976.

In the *Cook* case the principal question before the court was whether Rule 31 and the related statutes apply in instances where the guarantor has become primarily liable by contract on the debt. Up until the decision in the case of *Wood v. Canfield Paper Co.,* supra, there had been a conflict in the decisions on that point. That case held that the statute which is now set out in Rule 31 and its related statutes apply even if the guarantor is primarily liable. They apply to both absolute and conditional guarantors. Since the Supreme Court adopted the opinion of the Commission of Appeals in the *Wood* case, and has not overruled it as far as we can find, we agree with the Beaumont Court in its conclusion that the holding in the *Wood v. Canfield* case is still the law.

The holding in the *Cook* case has not changed our opinion hereinabove announced, that the requirement of Rule 31 and its related statutes that the maker of a note be made a party in a suit against a guarantor of said note can be waived by the guarantor.

. . . .

## NOTES AND QUESTIONS

(1) *Primary vs. Secondary Liability of Guarantors.* What does it mean that a guarantor is "primarily liable"? In *Ferguson v. McCarrell,* 582 S.W.2d 539 (Tex. Civ. App.—Austin 1979), *aff'd per curiam* 588 S.W.2d 895 (Tex. 1979), the question arose of whether endorsers and guarantors of payment on promissory notes could be sued without resort to and the joinder of the original maker of the note by virtue of their status as guarantors of payment. The defendant guarantors contended that it was improper for the trial court to sever the corporate maker of the notes and to proceed to judgment against them in the absence of pleading and proof that the corporate maker was "actually or notoriously insolvent." In rejecting this contention the Court of Civil Appeals held that the guarantors became "primary obligors" who could be sued without the joinder of the original maker of the instruments. In refusing the writ, the Supreme Court expressly disapproved of the decision of the Court of Civil Appeals in *Cook v. Citizens National Bank of Beaumont,* 538 S.W.2d 460 (Tex. Civ. App.—Beaumont 1976, no writ). In *Cook,* apparently a separate "Guaranty Agreement" was executed. Nonetheless, the per curiam opinion indicates: "We conclude that Section 3.416(a) . . . controls this case." *See* Bus. & Com. C. § 3.416(a) (A guarantor on an instrument who places the words "payment guaranteed" or their equivalent on an instrument agrees that if the instrument is not paid when due, the guarantor will pay it without resort by the holder to any other party). Moreover, "[w]ords of guaranty which do not otherwise specify guarantee payment." Bus. & Com. C. § 3.416(c). *See also Universal Metals and Machinery, Inc. v. Bohart,* 539 S.W.2d 874 (Tex. 1976), discussed in Dorsaneo, *Creditor's Rights: Annual Survey of Texas Law,* 31 Sw. L.J. 213, 232–234 (1977). *See also* Winship, *Annual Survey of Texas Law: Commercial Transactions,* 31 Sw. L.J. 165, 201–203 (1977) for a discussion of this problem. Former section 3.416 has been superseded by Sections 3.419 and 3.605 of the Business and Commerce Code. *See* Bus. & Com. C. §§ 3.419, 3.605.

(2) *Recodification of 1840 Statutes.* The 69th Legislature repealed Articles 1986 and 1987 of the Revised Civil Statutes and replaced them with Section 17.001 of the Civil Practice and Remedies Code:

## CIVIL PRACTICE AND REMEDIES CODE

### CHAPTER 17. PARTIES; CITATION; LONG-ARM JURISDICTION

### SUBCHAPTER A. PARTIES TO SUIT

C.P.R.C. § 17.001. *Suit on Contract With Several Obligors or Parties Conditionally Liable.* (a) Except as provided by this section, the acceptor of a bill of exchange or a principal obligor on a contract may be sued alone or jointly with another liable party, but a judgment may not be rendered against a party not primarily liable unless judgment is also rendered against the principal obligor.

(b) The assignor, endorser, guarantor, or surety on a contract or the drawer of an accepted bill may be sued without suing the maker, acceptor, or other principal obligor, or a suit against the principal obligor may be discontinued, if the principal obligor:

(1) is a nonresident or resides in a place where he cannot be reached by the ordinary process of law;

(2) resides in a place that is unknown and cannot be ascertained by the use of reasonable diligence;

(3) is dead; or

(4) is actually or notoriously insolvent.

*Read Tex. R. Civ. P. 39.*

---

## COOPER v. TEXAS GULF INDUSTRIES, INC.

*513 S.W.2d 200 (Tex. 1972)*

SAM D. JOHNSON, Justice.

Petitioners Dr. Griffin Cooper and his wife, Dolores, appeal from summary judgment that they take nothing in a suit for cancellation and rescission of a sale of real estate to them by Texas Gulf Industries, Inc. (T.G.I.). Cooper and his wife sued T.G.I. on September 28, 1971 alleging fraud as ground for rescission and cancellation of the sale. T.G.I. moved for summary judgment asserting Dr. Cooper previously filed a suit on December 29, 1970, which suit was dismissed with prejudice on January 29, 1971, and that such dismissal with prejudice was *res judicata* of the instant action. The trial court granted T.G.I.'s motion for summary judgment that plaintiffs take nothing and the court of civil appeals affirmed. 495 S.W.2d 273. We reverse and remand.

In the prior suit filed December 29, 1970 Dr. Cooper was the sole plaintiff. He sought to terminate a management contract on the property at issue and alternatively sought to rescind the sale of the property. The trial court dismissed the first suit "with prejudice."

The Coopers argue that dismissal of the prior suit with prejudice is not *res judicata* of the instant suit because Dolores Cooper, being a grantee along with her husband in the deed to the real estate at issue, was a necessary party to a suit to cancel and rescind the sale. Accordingly, the Coopers assert, the trial court had no jurisdiction in the prior case and the judgment of dismissal with prejudice is invalid.

A decision on whether a wife is an indispensable party in an action which concerns her joint community property necessitates (1) a study of the Texas Family Code, Section 5.22 (1971),[1] to determine the nature of the community property, (2) a reexamination of the rule that a husband can act for and represent his wife in an action concerning their joint community property under the doctrine of virtual representation, and (3) a discussion of the application of Rule 39, as amended, Texas Rules of Civil Procedure (1971), concerning the joinder of parties.

## THE NATURE OF THE COMMUNITY PROPERTY

T.G.I. says in its brief that the property in question is community property and the record bears this out. Both Coopers were named in the deed to the property in question and both signed a deed of trust executed in favor of T.G.I. Insofar as can be ascertained, both Coopers were obligated also on the notes given as consideration. Part of the consideration was payment of $45,000 in cash; the record does not reveal the source of these funds. Under Section 5.02, Texas Family Code (Supp.1971), property possessed by either spouse during marriage is presumed to be community property. In light of this presumption, and the absence of contrary evidence in the record, the court adopts T.G.I.'s statement that the property involved is community.

Under Section 5.22 community property falls into two categories with respect to management: *sole* management community property and *joint* management community property. On the basis of the record before us, the court must assume that the property is subject to joint management. Section 5.24 says, "[d]uring marriage, property is presumed to be subject to the sole management, control, and disposition of a spouse *if* it is held in his or her name. . . ." [Emphasis added.] All of the evidence, as noted above, indicates joint ownership of and joint liability for the property in question.

## THE DOCTRINE OF VIRTUAL REPRESENTATION

One of the basic questions in this case is whether Dr. Cooper, in bringing the first suit without the joinder of his wife, acted as a representative of the community; whether he "virtually

[1] Section 5.22 recites:

"§ 5.22. Community Property: General Rules

"(a) During marriage, each spouse has the sole management, control, and disposition of the community property that he or she would have owned if single, including but not limited to:

(1) personal earnings;

(2) revenue from separate property;

(3) recoveries for personal injuries; and

(4) the increase and mutations of, and the revenue from, all property subject to his or her sole management, control, and disposition.

"(b) If community property subject to the sole management, control, and disposition of one spouse is mixed or combined with community property subject to the sole management, control, and disposition of the other spouse, then the mixed or combined community property is subject to the joint management, control, and disposition of the spouses, unless the spouses provide otherwise by power of attorney or other agreement in writing.

"(c) Except as provided in Subsection (a) of this section, the community property is subject to the joint management, control, and disposition of the husband and wife, unless the spouses provide otherwise by power of attorney or other agreement in writing."

represented" his wife in that action. If the doctrine has vitality, the dismissal with prejudice of that first suit would be binding upon the wife, Mrs. Dolores Cooper, and *res judicata* as to the second and instant suit.

Under the doctrine of virtual representation, a suit naming only the husband as a party is nonetheless binding on the wife. Starr v. Schoellkopf Co. 131 Tex. 263, 113 S.W.2d 1227 (1938); Gabb v. Boston, 109 Tex. 26, 193 S.W. 137 (1917); Jergens v. Schiele, 61 Tex. 255 (1884); Cooley v. Miller, 228 S.W. 1085 (Tex. Comm'n App. 1921, judgmt adopted); Hall v. Aloco Oil Co., 164 S.W.2d 861 (Tex. Civ. App.—Amarillo 1942, writ ref'd); 30 Tex. Jur. 2d Husband and Wife § 167. The basis for virtual representation is the husband's power of sole management of the entire community.

Section 5.22 of the Family Code takes away the husband's sole right to manage all of the couple's community property. When joint management community property is involved, the husband and wife are now joint managers. The wife is her husband's equal with respect to management; she stands in the same position as any other joint owner of property. While another section[2] provides that a spouse may sue and be sued without the joinder of the other, neither spouse may virtually represent the other. The rights of the wife, like the rights of the husband and the rights of any other joint owner, may be affected only by a suit in which the wife is called to answer. If one of the spouses wishes the other to represent him or her, Section 5.22(c) of the Family Code permits that arrangement provided the consenting spouse authorizes that representation by a power of attorney or other agreement in writing. No such writing is in evidence here.

Dolores Cooper was not a party to the first suit; the doctrine of virtual representation was abolished by the new Family Code; there was no writing authorizing her husband to represent her. Accordingly, her interest in the Coopers' joint management community property is untouched by the judgment of dismissal with prejudice of the first suit.

## THE JOINDER OF PARTIES

Having determined that the wife was not virtually represented by her husband, a second question is urged for consideration: was Dolores Cooper an indispensable party in the first suit? Under the traditional view, if she *was* an indispensable party, the judgment in the first suit would be invalid and not *res judicata* as to either of the Coopers; if she was *not* an indispensable party, then the judgment would be binding on Dr. Cooper since he was a party, although still not binding on Mrs. Cooper. Petroleum Anchor Equipment, Inc. v. Tyra, 406 S.W.2d 891 (Tex. 1966).

Amended Rule 39,[3] however, initiated an entirely new method for resolving the question of joinder of parties. Amended Rule 39, effective January 1, 1971, is almost an exact copy by Texas

---

[2] "§ 4.04. Joinder in Civil Suits

"(a) A spouse may sue and be sued without the joinder of the other spouse.

"(b) When claims or liabilities are joint and several, the spouses may be joined under the rules relating to joinder of parties generally."

[3] "Rule 39. Joinder of Persons Needed for Just Adjudication

"(a) Persons to be Joined if Feasible. A person who is subject to service of process shall be joined as a party in the action if (1) in his absence complete relief cannot be accorded among those already parties, or (2) he claims an interest relating to the subject of the action and is so situated that the disposition of the action in his absence may (i) as a practical matter impair or impede his ability to protect that interest or (ii) leave any of the persons already parties subject to a substantial risk of incurring double, multiple, or otherwise inconsistent obligations by

of Federal Rule 19, Federal Rules of Civil Procedure, which is also of recent origin, having been adopted in 1966.

Prior to the amendment to Rule 39, Texas resolved questions of joinder of parties by efforts to catalogue parties as "proper," "necessary," "indispensable," "conditionally necessary," or "insistible." Typical of that approach is this court's preamendment opinion in Petroleum Anchor Equipment, Inc. v. Tyra, *supra,* where it is stated:

> "It is at once apparent that the 'necessary' parties of which the rule speaks fall into two categories: (1) those who under the paragraph (a) '*shall* be made parties,' and (2) those who under paragraph (b) 'ought to be parties if complete relief is to be accorded between those already parties.' It is also at once apparent that 'persons having a joint interest' within the meaning of paragraph (a), properly interpreted, are *indispensable* parties, but that those who simply ought to be joined if complete relief is to be accorded between those already parties are not *indispensable.* The rule expressly confers discretion upon trial courts to proceed without joinder of persons in the second category if jurisdiction over them can be acquired only by their consent or voluntary appearance. If joinder of such persons is discretionary, their joinder cannot be essential to jurisdiction of a court to proceed to judgment." 406 S.W.2d 891 at 893.

That historical and classical approach to the joinder of parties has now been wholly replaced. The reasons and legal literature which impelled the adoption of the new approach are well summarized in 7 C. Wright & A. Miller, Federal Practice and Procedure § 1601 (1972). One of the aims of the revised rule was to avoid questions of jurisdiction. The text states:

> "In addition to the failure of many courts to articulate satisfactory bases of decision prior to 1966, the Advisory Committee referred to other defects in the original version of Rule 19. Paramount among these was a problem of "jurisdiction" that arose in connection with the concept of indispensable parties. The Committee felt that the rule's [original] wording suggested that the absence of an indispensable party 'itself deprived the court of the power to adjudicate as between the parties already joined.' As is discussed in another section, failure to join a party under Rule 19 is not really a jurisdictional matter inasmuch as the court does have subject matter jurisdiction over the action before it; what is involved is a question of whether the court should decline to adjudicate the dispute because certain persons are

---

reason of his claimed interest. If he has not been so joined, the court shall order that he be made a party. If he should join as a plaintiff but refuses to do so, he may be made a defendant, or, in a proper case, an involuntary plaintiff.

"(b) Determination by Court Whenever Joinder Not Feasible. If a person as described in subdivision (a)(1)-(2) hereof cannot be made a party, the court shall determine whether in equity and good conscience the action should proceed among the parties before it, or should be dismissed, the absent person being thus regarded as indispensable. The factors to be considered by the court include: first, to what extent a judgment rendered in the person's absence might be prejudicial to him or those already parties; second, the extent to which, by protective provisions in the judgment, by the shaping of relief, or other measures, the prejudice can be lessened or avoided; third, whether a judgment rendered in the person's absence will be adequate; fourth, whether the plaintiff will have an adequate remedy if the action is dismissed for non-joinder.

"(c) Pleading Reasons for Nonjoinder. A pleading asserting a claim for relief shall state the names, if known to the pleader, of any persons as described in subdivision (a)(1)–(2) hereof who are not joined, and the reasons why they are not joined.

"(d) Exception of Class Actions. This rule is subject to the provisions of Rule 42. Amended by order of July 21, 1970, effective January 1, 1971."

absent. The present language of Rule 19(a) and Rule 19(b) should help eliminate this confusion."

*And see* C. Wright, Law of Federal Courts § 70 at 298–99 (2d ed. 1970).

Contrary to our emphasis under Rule 39 before it was amended, today's concern is less that of the jurisdiction of a court to proceed and is more a question of whether the court ought to proceed with those who are present. Rippey v. Denver United States National Bank, 42 F.R.D. 316 (D. Colo. 1967). The United States Supreme Court provides a helpful discussion of the objectives sought by its amended Rule 19 in Provident Tradesmens Bank & Trust v. Patterson, 390 U.S. 102, 88 S. Ct. 733, 19 L. Ed. 2d 936 (1968). One of the practical factors the court took into consideration in holding that an absent party was not jurisdictionally indispensable was the fact that the case had actually been tried as to those parties who were present and there was no objection at the trial level concerning the nonjoinder of a party. As expressed in Continental Insurance Co. of New York v. Cotten, 427 F.2d 48, 51 (9th Cir. 1970), "at the appellate stage there is reason not to throw away a judgment just because it did not theoretically settle the whole controversy."

The amended rule includes practical considerations within the rule itself, including the extent to which an absent party may be prejudiced, the extent to which protective provisions may be made in the judgment, and whether in equity and good conscience the action should proceed or be dismissed. The factors mentioned in the rule which a judge may consider are not exclusive. Provident Tradesmens Bank & Trust Company v. Patterson, supra; Bixby v. Bixby, 50 F.R.D. 277 (S.D. Ill. 1970); 7 C. Wright & A. Miller, Federal Practice and Procedure, *supra*, at 14. As expressed in Schutten v. Shell Oil Co., 421 F.2d 869, 874 (5th Cir. 1970), "[t]he watchwords of Rule 19 are 'pragmatism' and 'practicality.' The court must, however, always consider the possibility of shaping a decree in order to adjudicate between the parties who have been joined."

Under the provisions of our present Rule 39 it would be rare indeed if there were a person whose presence was so indispensable in the sense that his absence deprives the court of jurisdiction to adjudicate between the parties already joined. Although not of controlling importance, the very title of the rule has been changed from "Necessary Joinder of Parties" to "Joinder of Persons Needed for Just Adjudication." Subdivision (a) provides that certain persons "shall be joined," but there is no arbitrary standard or precise formula for determining whether a particular person falls within its provisions. It is clear, moreover, that the persons described in the subdivision are to be joined only if subject to service of process. When such a person cannot be made a party, the court is required to determine "whether in equity and good conscience the action should proceed among the parties before it, or should be dismissed."

Under the foregoing analysis of Rule 39 we determine that the named parties in the first suit, Dr. Cooper and T.G.I., were properly before the court for the resolution of the issues between them; that the judgment of dismissal with prejudice resolved those issues and is necessarily *res judicata* as to the claims of Dr. Cooper in the second and instant suit; that the judgment of dismissal is not *res judicata*, however, with respect to the rights and claims of Mrs. Dolores Cooper; and finally, that the judgment of dismissal is conclusive as to Dr. Cooper except to the extent that it might have to be disregarded in giving Mrs. Cooper all the relief to which she may show herself entitled.

The judgments of the courts below are reversed and the cause remanded to the trial court for further proceedings consistent with this opinion.

Concurring opinion by WALKER, J., in which GREENHILL, C. J., joins.

WALKER, Justice (concurring).

I am in general agreement with the opinion and concur in the judgment of the Court. It should be pointed out, however, that there has been no showing that Mrs. Dolores Cooper participated in the prior litigation. See 46 Am. Jur. 2d, Judgments § 535; Restatement, Judgments § 84.

GREENHILL, C. J., joins in this concurring opinion.

---

## NOTES AND QUESTIONS

(1) *Virtual Representation and Compulsory Joinder.* What is the relationship of the doctrine of virtual representation to the question of compulsory joinder? When may a trustee represent a beneficiary? In *Mason v. Mason,* 366 S.W.2d 552 (Tex. 1963), the Texas Supreme Court stated that the cestui que trust may be represented by the trustee in all actions relating to the trust, if the rights of the cestui que trust as against the trustee, or the rights of the cestuis que trust between themselves are not in conflict. The question is one of the adequacy of representation. Another example of virtual representation is the class action. *See* Tex. R. Civ. P. 42. *See* § 7.08.

(2) *Understanding Cooper's Philosophy.* How much of the judgment against Dr. Cooper would have to be disregarded "in giving Mrs. Cooper all the relief to which she may show herself entitled"? Can a sale be rescinded by halves? What about the release of a joint note? In *Dulak v. Dulak,* 513 S.W.2d 205 (Tex. 1974), a companion case to *Cooper,* eight brothers and sisters sued a ninth brother over matters pertaining to their father's estate. The plaintiffs alleged that prior to the father's death, the defendant brother had converted funds belonging to the father and through undue influence had secured the father's release of a promissory note executed by the defendant and his wife for the purchase of the father's farm. The jury agreed with the plaintiffs' allegations and the trial court rendered a judgment awarding actual and exemplary damages and cancelling the release. The Court of Civil Appeals affirmed the judgment. Although the Texas Supreme Court ultimately affirmed the award of actual damages, it reversed the part of the judgment ordering exemplary damages and cancellation of the release. On appeal, the defendant had argued two points regarding the release. First, he asserted that, because his wife had signed the note, she was an indispensable party and the plaintiffs' failure to join her in the suit rendered void the court's order cancelling release of the note. Second, he argued that no evidence of undue influence existed to justify cancellation. On the first point, the court, citing *Cooper,* held that failure to join the wife was not a jurisdictional defect, that the judgment was not rendered void by her nonjoinder, and that the judgment, unless otherwise erroneous, was binding on all parties to the suit. In assessing the second point, however, the court found the judgment was indeed erroneous. There was no evidence of undue influence to support cancellation of the release.

(3) *Modern Compulsory Joinder Analysis.* In *Provident Tradesmens Bank & Trust Co. v. Patterson,* 390 U.S. 102, 118–119 (1968), the United States Supreme Court per Harlan, J. rejected in the following terms the contention that there is a predetermined class of persons without whose joinder the action cannot proceed:

> To say that a court "must" dismiss in the absence of an indispensable party and that it "cannot proceed" without him, puts the matter the wrong way around: A court does not know whether a particular person is "indispensable" until it has examined the situation to determine whether it can proceed without him.

Justice Harlan also appears to have rejected the following argument:

> (1) there is a category of persons called "indispensable parties"; (2) that category is defined by substantive law and the definition cannot be modified by rules; (3) the right of a person falling within that category to participate in the lawsuit in question is also a substantive matter, and is absolute.

(4) *Method for Raising Nonjoinder.* Doesn't Civil Procedure Rule 39 contemplate that the absence of the nonjoined person will be raised by plea in abatement before trial? Should a party who lost in the trial court be able to raise the absence of a non-joined person insofar as the judgment affects parties who participated in the trial? *See* Dorsaneo, *Compulsory Joinder of Parties in Texas,* 14 Hous. L. Rev. 345, 369 (1977) and *Pirtle v. Gregory, below.*

(5) *Fundamental Error.* Under prior law, the absence of an indispensable party was viewed as "fundamental" (jurisdictional) error, which abrogated the court's power to adjudicate the dispute between the parties before it. *See Petroleum Anchor Equipment, Inc. v. Tyra,* 406 S.W.2d 891 (Tex. 1966). Persons having a "joint," "common" or "united" interest under substantive law were viewed as indispensable. The quoted phrases were difficult to interpret properly. Hence, the older method of analysis was abandoned. *See* Reed, *Compulsory Joinder of Parties in Civil Actions,* 55 Mich. L. Rev. 327, 340 (1957).

(6) *Persons Who Should be Regarded as Indispensable.* Consider Civil Procedure Rule 39(b). When should a person be "regarded as indispensable"? If A sues B for partition of Blackacre and neither A nor B raises at trial the absence of C (who also claims an interest in Blackacre), is the judgment of the trial court which divided the tract void? Can A or B attack it on appeal on the basis that they were prejudiced by C's absence? What about C's interest? If C knew of the litigation but purposely bypassed it, should we protect C?

---

## PIRTLE v. GREGORY

*629 S.W.2d 919 (Tex. 1982)*

PER CURIAM.

Stanley Pirtle brought suit for specific performance and for removal of cloud on 512 acres of land. Pirtle sued Layne Gregory, Grady Gregory, and Kathy Coker because they had contracted in writing but failed to execute an oil and gas lease to Pirtle, as lessee. Layne and Grady Gregory later executed an oil and gas lease on the property to James P. Flanagan. Plaintiff Pirtle originally sued Flanagan as one of the defendants, but took a nonsuit as to him. The trial court rendered judgment for Pirtle commanding the Gregorys and Coker to execute the oil and gas lease, but the court of appeals reversed that judgment, believing that the absence of Flanagan from the suit constituted fundamental error. 623 S.W.2d 955 (Tex. App.).

"Fundamental error" in civil actions arose in Texas under old statutes that stated that cases on appeal could be reviewed "on an error in law either assigned or apparent on the face of the record." 2 Gammel, Laws of Texas 1562 (1898); 3 Gammel, Laws of Texas 393 (1898). The practice of appellate courts in considering unassigned errors was the source of much mischief, and when the Texas Supreme Court promulgated its Rules of Civil Procedure in 1941, old article 1837 was repealed. Since that time, there has been no rule or statute that authorizes appellate consideration of errors for which there was no trial predicate that complained of the error. *McCauley v. Consolidated Underwriters,* 157 Tex. 475, 304 S.W.2d 265, 266 (1957); *Ramsey v. Dunlop,* 146 Tex. 196, 205 S.W.2d 979, 984 (1947) (Alexander, J., concurring). Fundamental error survives today in those rare instances in which the record shows the court lacked jurisdiction or that the public interest is directly and adversely affected as that interest is declared in the statutes or the Constitution of Texas. State Bar of Texas, Appellate Procedure in Texas § 11.5 (2d ed. 1979).

The reason for the requirement that a litigant preserve a trial predicate for complaint on appeal is that one should not be permitted to waive, consent to, or neglect to complain about an error at trial and then surprise his opponent on appeal by stating his complaint for the first time.

Flanagan is said to be an indispensable party to this cause, because the defendants gave him an oil and gas lease and the validity of that lease has not been adjudicated. The defendants should not be heard to complain for the first time on appeal, however, because they did not complain at the trial level by exception, plea in abatement, motion to join other parties or otherwise.

We reaffirm the views we expressed in *Cooper v. Texas Gulf Industries, Inc.,* 513 S.W.2d 200 (Tex. 1974). We there stated:

> Under the provisions of our present Rule 39 it would be rare indeed if there were a person whose presence was so indispensable in the sense that his absence deprives the court of jurisdiction to adjudicate between the parties already joined.

*Id.* at 204.

In a case such as this, parties who participate in the trial without complaint will not be heard to complain at the appellate stage when "there is reason not to throw away a judgment just because it did not theoretically settle the whole controversy." *Continental Insurance Co. of New York v. Cotten,* 427 F.2d 48, 51 (9th Cir. 1970) [citing *Provident Tradesmens Bank & Trust Co. v. Patterson,* 390 U.S. 102, 88 S. Ct. 733, 19 L. Ed. 2d 936 (1967)].

Pursuant to Texas Rules of Civil Procedure, Rule 483, we grant the writ of error and, without hearing oral argument, reverse the judgment of the court of appeals and remand this cause to that court for disposition of the other points not reached.

---

## NOTES AND QUESTIONS

(1) *Subsequent Case Developments. Pirtle* followed a whole set of cases limiting the "fundamental error" concept as applied to nonjoinder of allegedly indispensable persons. In *Vondy v. Commissioners Court,* 620 S.W.2d 104 (Tex. 1981), a constable sought a writ of mandamus against the Commissioner's Court and four of its five members to compel them to set a reasonable

salary for the office of constable. One commissioner was not named as a party, but no objection was made in the trial court concerning his absence, and judgment was rendered denying relief to the constable. On the theory that failure to join the fifth commissioner was "fundamental error," the Eastland Court of Civil Appeals vacated the trial court's order on its own motion and dismissed the action. The Texas Supreme Court, citing *Cooper's* "rare indeed" language, reversed:

> To determine whether a party is jurisdictionally indispensable under Rule 39, the surrounding facts and circumstances of each case must be examined. In the present case, the facts fail to warrant a finding that Commissioner Head was truly an indispensable party under our interpretation of Rule 39 Tex. R. Civ. P. This is not a situation where a judgment would adversely affect the interests of absent parties who had no opportunity to assert their rights in the trial court. *See Provident Tradesmens Bank & Trust Co. v. Patterson,* 390 U.S. 102, 110, 126, 88 S. Ct. 733, 746, 19 L. Ed. 2d 936 (1968). Here, the interests of all the parties could be adjudicated and complete relief given. Further, the remaining commissioners would not be subject to a substantial risk of incurring double, multiple, or otherwise inconsistent obligations due to the absence of Commissioner Head. We conclude, therefore, that because Head was not an indispensable party to the proceeding, the nonjoinder of Head was not fundamental error.

A similar approach was taken in *McCarthy v. George,* 618 S.W.2d 762 (Tex. 1981). In that case a decedent's heirs sued in trespass to try title for an undivided one-half interest in certain acreage. The heirs claimed that they were co-tenants with the defendants, i.e., that their share consisted of an undivided one-half interest and the defendants' share consisted of a like one-half interest. One of the heirs, Charles Gooch, was found by the trial court not to have given the plaintiffs' counsel the authority to represent him. Because the trial court considered Gooch to be a "necessary party," he was joined as an "involuntary plaintiff." Thereafter, the plaintiffs, including Gooch, recovered an undivided one-half interest in the tract. The Court of Civil Appeals reversed. The appellate court concluded that Rule 39's provision for the joinder of a person as an "involuntary plaintiff" in "proper cases" applies only when some substantive relation between the parties (e.g., trustee-beneficiary) permits one to sue for the other. Consequently, the appellate court held that it was improper for the trial court to join Gooch as involuntary plaintiff. The court found no indication of a right on the part of the plaintiffs to bring the action as trustees for Gooch. The court concluded as well that one co-tenant could not proceed against another co-tenant without the joinder of an omitted co-tenant, the Court of Civil Appeals reasoning that the allegations of the petition necessarily put Gooch's title in issue.

The Texas Supreme Court reversed the decision of the Court of Civil Appeals without hearing oral argument. In reaching its decision, the court relied on the statement in *Cooper* that, "At the appellate stage there is a reason not to throw away a judgment just because it did not theoretically settle the whole controversy." The case was remanded to the Court of Civil Appeals for a determination of certain points which, if sustained, would have required rendition of the judgment for the defendants. On remand, the Court of Civil Appeals again considered the propriety of joining Gooch as an "involuntary plaintiff." After reaffirming its prior holding that "this is not a 'proper case' for the utilization of the involuntary plaintiff device," the intermediate appellate dismissed that part of the action insofar as it concerned Gooch. It then affirmed the rest of the trial court's judgment.

*Pirtle* says in dictum, "Fundamental error survives today in those rare instances in which the record shows the court lacked jurisdiction or that the public interest is directly and adversely affected as that interest is declared in the statutes or the Constitution of Texas." *Pirtle*, 629 S.W.2d at 920. What do the "rare instances" now include? The next case sheds light on the interaction of Civil Procedure Rule 39 with statutory provisions and rules of procedure which literally require the plaintiff to include or account for all designated persons.

---

## MINGA v. PERALES

*603 S.W.2d 240 (Tex. Civ. App.—Corpus Christi 1980, no writ)*

BISSETT, Justice.

This case, which all parties treat as a trespass to try title action, involves an appeal by W.A. Minga, in his capacity as the foreign administrator of the Estate of T.F. Minga, from a judgment awarding title to, and possession of a fifteen acre tract of land located in Hidalgo County, Texas, to Mr. and Mrs. Gilberto Perales, Manuela Hidalgo and Gertrudes Hidalgo, plaintiffs. We reverse and remand.

Plaintiffs claim that they acquired title to the land in question by adverse possession. W.A. Minga was sued in his capacity of "Administrator of the Estate of T.F. Minga." The case was tried to a jury, which answered the special issues which were submitted favorably to plaintiffs. The judgment decreed that "Plaintiffs recover from Defendant the title and possession" of the fifteen acre tract.

As disclosed by the pleadings and the judgment, none of the heirs at law of T.F. Minga, Deceased, were made parties to the suit. The first issue to be resolved is whether the trial court committed fundamental error in proceeding to trial and rendering judgment for plaintiffs in the absence of joinder of the heirs at law of T.F. Minga, Deceased. We hold that it did.

Tex. Rev. Civ. Stat. Ann. art. 1982 (1964) provides:

> In every suit against the estate of a decedent involving the title to real estate, the executor or administrator, if any, and the heirs shall be made parties defendant.

The provisions of Article 1982 are mandatory. The heirs at law of a decedent are jurisdictionally indispensable parties when the suit against the estate involves the title to real estate. *Jones v. Gibbs,* 130 S.W.2d 274 (Tex. Comm. App. 1939, opinion adopted).

Failure to join jurisdictionally indispensable parties constitutes fundamental error which an appellate court must recognize when it becomes apparent in the record. *Petroleum Anchor Equipment, Inc. v. Tyra,* 406 S.W.2d 891 (Tex. Sup. 1966); *In Re Estate of Bourland v. Hanes,* 526 S.W.2d 156 (Tex. Civ. App.—Corpus Christi 1975, writ ref'd n.r.e.); *Airport Coach Service, Inc. v. City of Fort Worth,* 518 S.W.2d 566 (Tex. Civ. App.—Tyler 1974, writ ref'd n.r.e.). It has been held that failure to join jurisdictionally indispensable parties renders the judgment void. *Allen v. Matthews,* 210 S.W.2d 849 (Tex. Civ. App.—Austin 1948, writ ref'd n.r.e.); *Crickmer v. King,* 507 S.W.2d 314 (Tex. Civ. App.—Texarkana 1974, no writ).

Rule 39, T.R.C.P., requires that persons having a joint interest in the subject matter of a suit shall be made parties, either as plaintiffs or defendants. When a person's interest in a subject matter of a suit is directly involved and must be considered and decided in the process of adjudicating the issues presented by the pleadings, that person has a joint interest in the subject matter of the suit and is an indispensable party to the action. *Jennings v. Srp,* 521 S.W.2d 326 (Tex. Civ. App.—Corpus Christi 1975, no writ).

Under Texas law, when a person dies intestate, the title to all property owned by the decedent vests immediately and directly in his heirs, subject, however, to administration if the same be necessary, Tex. Prob. Code Ann. § 37 (Supp. 1980). Title to such land is not in the administrator of the estate. He is not the equivalent of a trustee. *Jennings v. Srp, supra*, at page 330 of the published opinion. The judgment of the trial court must be reversed and the cause remanded in order that the heirs at law of T.F. Minga, Deceased, may be made parties defendant.

There is another reason why the judgment of the trial court must be reversed and the cause remanded. According to the evidence, T.F. Minga died intestate in the State of Tennessee during the year 1952. W.A. Minga, defendant herein, a son of the decedent, qualified in a proper probate court in Tennessee as administrator of his father's estate shortly after his father's death. He was acting in that capacity at the time of trial. There is no evidence that he was ever appointed by a Texas probate court as ancillary administrator of the Estate of T.F. Minga, Deceased. Therefore, while plaintiffs' suit assumes an ongoing administration, the record reveals that defendant is administrator of the T.F. Minga Estate only with respect to its assets which are located in Tennessee. The land involved in this case is situated in Texas.

The general rule is that a foreign representative cannot sue or be sued in the courts of this State. *Faulkner v. Reed,* 241 S.W. 1002 (Tex. Com. App. 1922, judgmt. adopted); *Eikel v. Bristow Corp.,* 529 S.W.2d 795 (Tex. Civ. App.—Houston [1st Dist.] 1975, no writ). The basis for the rule is that no judgment can be rendered against an estate unless it has a legal representative before the court. A foreign representative has no extraterritorial authority; he can only administer such assets as are within the jurisdiction of the court which appointed him. Thus, a valid administration of assets in Texas must be through a representative duly appointed in Texas. *Faulkner v. Reed, supra.*

Plaintiffs contend that defendant consented to the jurisdiction of the trial court. We disagree. Parties cannot confer jurisdiction over the estate by agreement or waiver when no person is authorized to represent said estate in the state where the lawsuit is pending. *Eikel v. Burton,* 530 S.W.2d 907 (Tex. Civ. App.—Houston [1st Dist.] 1975, writ ref'd n.r.e.). This follows from the fact that power of a Texas court over an estate which is represented only by a foreign administrator concerns much more than mere jurisdiction over the person of the administrator; it concerns jurisdiction over the assets of the estate itself. See *Eikel v. Burton*, supra, and *Jennings v. Srp,* supra.

W.A. Minga, in his capacity as administrator of his father's estate by virtue of such appointment in the State of Tennessee, had no interest in the land in question. The trial court erred in proceeding to trial in this case where plaintiffs were suing only a foreign representative of the estate of a decedent in a suit involving title to land and in rendering judgment against the foreign administrator in his representative capacity.

The judgment of the trial court is REVERSED and the cause is REMANDED to the trial court for further proceedings.

## NOTES AND QUESTIONS

(1) *Criticism of Minga's Analysis. Minga* was decided after *Cooper.* Note, however, that it appears to be based on a "joint interest" analysis or what is referred to in *Cooper* as the "historical and classical" approach. Based on the reasoning in *Cooper*, is *Minga* analytically correct? If the assets of the estate do not pass to the administrator, why did the plaintiffs select him as a defendant? What do you think of the other reason for the reversal of the trial court's judgment?

(2) *Relationship of Rule 39 to Other Rules and Statutes.* What happens when another rule of civil procedure appears to require joinder? Tex. R. Civ. P. 757 requires that all joint owners be served with citation in an action for partition. The Tyler Court of Civil Appeals has held that all joint owners be made parties. *See Carper v. Halamicek,* 610 S.W.2d 556, 558 (Tex. Civ. App.—Tyler 1980, no writ).

*Minga* and *Carper* were decided before *Pirtle.* Are they still good law after *Pirtle?* Consider the authorities cited in that case. Involved in *Ramsey v. Dunlop,* 205 S.W.2d 979 (Tex. 1947) was an election contest, with the loser asserting that the winner did not meet the residence requirements to hold office. The winner had received twelve votes; the loser, two. The trial court agreed with the loser's contention and held that the loser should take office; the winner appealed. The Court of Civil Appeals held the trial court had erred by awarding office to one who had not received a plurality of the votes, notwithstanding that the election winner did not meet residence requirements. This point regarding plurality had not been assigned as error, and the loser of the election contended it was wrong for the appellate court to consider it. The Supreme Court held that the Court of Civil Appeals did not wrongfully consider the plurality issue. It noted that the procedural rules generally precluded assessment of unassigned error, but that such points could be considered if they involved fundamental public policy as reflected in statutory and constitutional provisions. The court then found such provisions existed to conclude that the plurality requirement did involve a matter of fundamental public policy. The Supreme Court extended the *Ramsey* approach in *McCauley v. Consolidated Underwriters,* 304 S.W.2d 265 (Tex. 1957). The court stated that the concept of fundamental error applied to situations involving questions of public policy like the one in *Ramsey.* The concept applied as well to situations in which the court rendering judgment lacked subject matter jurisdiction, e.g., when a county court awarded a divorce. The court also stated, however, that "fundamental error" was to be narrowly construed. Is that what the *Pirtle* court meant by its "rare instances" language? Using narrow construction, do the statutory and regulatory provisions at issue in *Minga* and *Carper* fall within the *Pirtle* exception? Are these provisions jurisdictional or do normal waiver principles apply?

The continued viability of the *Minga* and *Carper* view of statutory provisions and rules indicating joinder is necessary is placed in even greater doubt by *Cox v. Johnson,* 638 S.W.2d 867 (Tex. 1982). In that case there was failure to join a joint payee of a promissory note. Tex. Bus. & Com. Code § 3.110(d) provides that when an instrument is payable to two or more persons, it may be enforced *only* by all of them. In spite of the statute and in express disapproval of an earlier holding to the contrary in *Hinojosa v. Love,* 496 S.W.2d 224 (Tex. Civ. App.—Corpus Christi 1973, no writ), the court held that the failure to join the other payee was not fundamental error. The court relied on the pragmatic approach of *Cooper* and *Cooper*'s "rare indeed" language. In other words, normal principles of waiver did apply because the statutory requirement could not be raised for the first time on appeal.

(3) The 69th Legislature repealed Article 1982 of the Revised Civil Statutes and replaced it with Section 17.002 of the Civil Practice and Remedies Code.

CIVIL PRACTICE AND REMEDIES CODE

CHAPTER 17. PARTIES; CITATION; LONG-ARM JURISDICTION

SUBCHAPTER A. PARTIES TO SUIT

C.P.R.C. § 17.002. *Suit Against Estate for Land Title*. In a suit against the estate of a decedent involving the title to real property, the executor or administrator, if any, and the heirs must be made parties defendant.)

## § 7.08 Class Actions

*Read Tex. R. Civ. P. 42.*

### WEATHERLY v. DELOITTE & TOUCHE

*905 S.W.2d 642 (Tex. App.—Houston [14th Dist.] 1995, writ dism'd w.o.j.)*

DRAUGHN, Justice.

This is an interlocutory appeal from an order denying class certification. *See* Tex. Civ. Prac. & Rem. Code Ann. § 51.014(3) (Vernon 1986). Appellants, J.D. Weatherly and Elliott Horwitch, bring two points of error complaining the trial court abused its discretion in denying class certification. Because we find the trial court abused its discretion, we reverse and remand.

Entertainment Marketing, Inc. (EMI) is a wholesale distributor of consumer electronics and computer products. On April 16, 1987, EMI sold convertible subordinated debentures and common stock to the public. Appellants purchased debentures as part of EMI's public offering. On April 15, 1992, appellants filed suit alleging that EMI's management and accountants conspired to misrepresent EMI's net income in separate, but identical, prospectuses circulated to investors in connection with the public offering. Specifically, appellants alleged that EMI's top management (the EMI defendants) overstated EMI's sales and net income by reporting fictitious sales of EMI inventory in prior fiscal years. [footnote omitted] Appellants also alleged that EMI's accountants (the accountant defendants): (1) knew at the time they audited EMI's financial statements that EMI was planning the April 1987 public offering of debentures and common stock; (2) participated in reporting EMI's overstated financial performance; and (3) were reckless or negligent in audits of EMI. [footnote omitted] Appellants alleged that EMI could not have made the securities offering if its true financial performance had been disclosed to the public.

In each year following the April 1987 offering, EMI reported a loss. In 1992, EMI declared bankruptcy. The undisputed evidence shows that neither the debentures nor the stocks were ever traded at a price as high as the price at which they were offered in April 1987. Thus, all investors who purchased EMI debentures and/or stock in April 1987, suffered losses on their investment.

In their petition, appellants alleged multiple causes of action and sought certification of the class of plaintiffs who: (1) purchased EMI debentures and stocks between April 16, 1987, and

April 30, 1987; and (2) lost all or part of their investments. Appellants subsequently filed a separate Motion for Class Certification. On November 5, 1993, the trial court held a hearing at which appellants offered only certain exhibits. On November 24, 1993, the trial court, without entering an order, denied appellants' motion. Appellants filed a motion seeking a rehearing on their earlier Motion for Class Certification and alternatively, seeking certification of the class of plaintiffs who purchased only debentures. On April 14, 1994, the trial court denied appellants' motions and appellants perfected this appeal. The trial court's order does not state the reason for denial of class certification and the record does not contain findings of fact or conclusions of law, despite appellants' timely request. On appeal, appellants request only that their claim under the Texas Securities Act, Tex. Rev. Civ. Stat. Ann. art. 581-33 (Vernon Supp. 1995) (the Act), be certified as a class action.

In two points of error, appellants contend the trial court abused its discretion in denying their motions for class certification under Tex. R. Civ. P. 42.

In order to gain certification of a class action, a party must meet all the requirements of Tex. R. Civ. P. 42(a) and satisfy one of the subsections of Tex. R. Civ. P. 42(b)(4). Under Rule 42(a), appellants must show:

(1) numerosity—the number of plaintiffs is so numerous that joinder of all class members is impracticable;

(2) commonality—there are questions of law or fact common to the class;

(3) typicality—the claims of the proposed representatives are typical of those of the class; and

(4) adequacy—the proposed representatives will fairly and adequately protect the interest of the class.

Tex. R. Civ. P. 42(a)(1)–(4).

Appellants claim they satisfied Rule 42(b)(4), because they showed that:

(1) questions of law or fact common to the members of the class predominate over questions affecting individual members; and

(2) a class action is superior to other available methods for the fair and efficient adjudication of their claim.

Tex. R. Civ. P. 42(b)(4).

There is no right to bring a lawsuit as a class action. *Vinson v. Texas Commerce Bank*, 880 S.W.2d 820, 824 (Tex. App.—Dallas 1994, no writ). Rather, rule 42 provides only that the trial court *may* certify a class action if the plaintiff satisfies the requirements of the rule. *Id.* (emphasis in original). However, when the trial court makes a decision of class status at an early stage of the proceeding before supporting facts are fully developed, it should err in favor of, and not against, maintenance of the class action. *National Gypsum Co. v. Kirbyville Indep. School Dist.*, 770 S.W.2d 621, 627 (Tex. App.—Beaumont 1989, writ dism'd w.o.j.); *Life Ins. Co. of Southwest v. Brister*, 722 S.W.2d 764, 774–75 (Tex. App.—Fort Worth 1986, no writ). This is so because the class certification order is always subject to modification should later developments during the course of the trial so require. *Id.*; *see* Tex. R. Civ. P. 42(c)(1).

Trial courts enjoy broad discretion in determining whether a lawsuit should be maintained as a class action. *Dresser Indus., Inc. v. Snell*, 847 S.W.2d 367, 371 (Tex. App.—El Paso 1993, no writ). At the certification stage, the burden of proof is on the plaintiffs to establish their right to maintain an action as a class action. *Life Ins. Co. of Southwest v. Brister*, 722 S.W.2d 764, 773 (Tex. App.—Fort Worth 1986, no writ). Though they must do more than merely allege that the requirements have been met and must at least show some facts to support certification, class proponents generally are not required to prove a prima facie case or make an extensive evidentiary showing in support of a motion for class certification. *Clements v. League of United Latin American Citizens*, 800 S.W.2d 948, 952 (Tex. App.—Corpus Christi 1990, no writ); *Brister*, 722 S.W.2d at 773. The trial court may base its decision on pleadings or other material in the record. *Clements*, 800 S.W.2d at 952; *National Gypsum Co.*, 770 S.W.2d at 626–27.

On appeal, review of trial court's decision granting or denying certification is limited to determining whether the court abused its discretion. *Morgan v. Deere Credit, Inc.*, 889 S.W.2d 360, 365 (Tex. App.— Houston [14th Dist.] 1994, no writ); *Amoco Prod. Co. v. Hardy*, 628 S.W.2d 813, 816 (Tex. App.—Corpus Christi 1981, writ dism'd). In reviewing the trial court's ruling on certification, the appellate court is required to view the evidence in a light most favorable to the trial court's action, and indulge every presumption in favor of the trial court's action. *Dresser*, 847 S.W.2d at 372; *Angeles/Quinoco Securities Corp. v. Collison*, 841 S.W.2d 511, 513 (Tex. App.—Houston [14th Dist.] 1992, no writ). A trial court does not abuse its discretion when it bases its decision on conflicting evidence. *Wiggins v. Enserch Exploration, Inc.*, 743 S.W.2d 332, 334 (Tex. App.—Dallas 1987, writ dism'd w.o.j.); *RSR Corp. v. Hayes*, 673 S.W.2d 928, 930 (Tex. App.—Dallas 1984, writ dism'd). That the trial court, in the opinion of the appellate court, made an error in judgment, does not alone demonstrate an abuse of discretion. *Morgan*, 889 S.W.2d at 365; *Dresser*, 847 S.W.2d at 371. Rather, a trial court abuses its discretion when it: (1) does not properly apply the law to the undisputed facts; (2) acts arbitrarily or unreasonably; or (3) rules upon factual assertions not supported by material in the record. *See Angeles/Quinoco*, 841 S.W.2d at 513; *Wiggins*, 743 S.W.2d at 334; *RSR*, 673 S.W.2d at 930; *Mahoney v. Cupp*, 638 S.W.2d 257, 261 (Tex. App.—Waco 1982, no writ).

In this case, the trial court abused its discretion on all three counts. There was simply no basis in law or fact for the trial court to have denied class certification in this case. . . . Based on the law of this state and this circuit, we conclude that appellants met all the requirements of subsection (a) and satisfied subsection (b)(4) of Tex. R. Civ. P. 42. Because appellees brief extensively the issues of commonality and adequacy of representation, we address those issues first.

Commonality of Issues and Predominance of Common Issues and Facts

The factual or legal basis for suit must be common to all members in a class action. *Dresser*, 847 S.W.2d at 372. Questions common to the class are those questions which, when answered as to one class member, are answered as to all class members. *Brister*, 722 S.W.2d at 772; *RSR*, 673 S.W.2d at 930. The commonality requirement does not mean that all questions of law and fact must be identical, but that an issue of law or fact exists that inheres in the complaints of all the class members. *Dresser*, 847 S.W.2d at 372.

Common issues of law or fact must also predominate over the issues requiring individual adjudication for each class member. *Brister*, 722 S.W.2d at 772. The test to be used in evaluating the predominance issue is not whether the common issues outnumber the individual issues, but whether common or individual issues will be the object of most of the efforts of the litigants and the court. *National Gypsum*, 770 S.W.2d at 625; *Brister*, 722 S.W.2d at 772. If common issues predominate, then a judgment in favor of the class members should decisively settle the entire controversy and all that should remain is for other members of the class to file proof of their claim. *Id.* In order to decide whether the common issues predominate, the court must initially identify the substantive law issues that will control the outcome of the litigation. *Id.* The purpose of the court's inquiry into the substantive law issues is to determine whether the character and nature of the case satisfies the requirements of the class action procedural rules, not to weigh the substantive merits of each class member's claim. *Id.*

Appellees argue that reliance and individual choice of law issues predominate in this litigation and defeat appellants' assertion of commonality. [footnote omitted] We disagree. Article 581-33 of the Texas Securities Act does not require the buyer to prove reliance on the seller's misrepresentation or omission. *Granader v. McBee*, 23 F.3d 120, 123 (5th Cir. 1994); *Anheuser-Busch Companies, Inc. v. Summit Coffee Co.*, 858 S.W.2d 928, 936 (Tex. App.—Dallas 1993, writ denied). An omission or misrepresentation is material if there is a substantial likelihood that a *reasonable* investor would consider it important in deciding to invest. *See id.* (emphasis added). An investor is not required to prove that he would have acted differently but for the omission or misrepresentation. *Id.* Thus, in the instant case, the focus under the Texas Securities Act is on the conduct of the seller or issuer of securities, i.e., whether they made a material misrepresentation, not on the conduct of individual buyers. A misrepresentation that is material to one class member as a reasonable investor will be material as to all class members. *See id.*; *Brister*, 722 S.W.2d at 772.

The accountant defendants point out that the only allegation against them is that they materially aided the seller or issuer of EMI securities. *See* Tex. Rev. Civ. Stat. Ann. art. 581-33(F)(2). They argue that "aider" liability requires each individual investor to prove causation. In support of their argument, the accountant defendants rely primarily on *In re Gas Reclamation Inc. Securities Litigation*, 733 F. Supp. 713 (S.D.N.Y. 1990). In *Gas Reclamation*, the court recognized a causation requirement for proving aider liability under federal securities law. *See id.* at 721–22. While that case also involved a pendent Texas Securities Act claim under section 33(F)(2), the court never held that a buyer is required to prove causation under section 33(F)(2). Indeed, there is nothing in the Act, the Comment, or any case interpreting the Act to suggest that section 33(F)(2) imposes an additional causation requirement on the buyer to establish the aider's liability.

Even if we were to recognize a causation requirement, . . . [a]ccording to appellants, "but for" the fraud, the value of EMI securities would not have been inflated and appellants and other investors/proposed class members would not have incurred the loss. Thus, the focus of the causation issue in this case would not be on the individual class members' reliance, but on the accountant defendants' participation in the fraud and whether that conduct caused the investment to lose its value. *See id.* Further, because appellants seek class certification only on behalf of those investors who purchased securities during the public offering and who "lost all or part of their investment," the only individual questions in this class action will be the amount of the loss for each investor. Clearly, individual reliance or causation issues do not defeat commonality in this case.

As we noted, appellees also contend individual choice of law issues are predominant and defeat commonality. Many of the securities offered by EMI were allocated to national brokerage houses. As a result, of the fifty-five EMI debentureholders identified by appellants, only Weatherly is from Texas. In addition, appellants identified more than one hundred and forty EMI stockholders from twenty-two states, Bermuda and Canada.

Although the trial court did not have evidence of the laws of other states before it, appellees assert that the Texas Securities Act differs from the Uniform Securities Act adopted by the majority of states. Tex. Rev. Civ. Stat. Ann. art. 581-33 (Vernon 1964 & Supp. 1994), Comment On Specific Sections; 1 Blue Sky L. Rep. (CCH) 5500. In particular, appellees maintain that the Uniform Act does not contain a section on "aider" liability. *See* Tex. Rev. Civ. Stat. Ann. art. 581-33, Comment § 33(F); 1 Blue Sky Rep. 5550, Uniform Securities Act § 410. Relying primarily on federal district court cases from Massachusetts, appellees further argue the burden is on appellants, as class proponents, to show that the law of the forum state is the same as the laws of the other states. *Gorsey v. I.M. Simon & Co., Inc.*, 121 F.R.D. 135, 140 (D. Mass. 1988); *Priest v. Zayre Corp.*, 118 F.R.D. 552, 558 (D. Mass. 1988).

Appellees' arguments are without merit. First, by pointing out that the Texas Securities Act differs from the Uniform Securities Act, appellees are implying that the laws of the states where class members purchased EMI securities and which have adopted the Uniform Act apply. However, it is improper at the certification stage for this court to determine which law applies. *See Angeles/Quinoco*, 841 S.W.2d at 516–17. Second, even if we could consider the application of foreign law to this dispute, the burden is on appellees, not appellants, to demonstrate the application of that law. Under Texas law the burden is on the party asserting the application of foreign law to first show the existence of a true conflict of laws and then to demonstrate which law should apply based on state contacts to the asserted claims. . . .

In this case, appellants allege securities fraud and conspiracy to commit securities fraud. Proof of liability will focus solely on appellees' conduct and core documents (identical prospectuses and financial statements contained therein) disseminated to all members of the proposed class. In other words, proof of liability will be based on the same evidence and involve the same issues for all proposed class members. Those common issues include: (1) the existence of misrepresentations in those core documents; (2) the materiality of those misrepresentations; (3) the role of appellees as either "sellers," "controlling persons," or "aiders;" and (4) damages.

"Many courts have held that where members of the class are subject to the same misrepresentations or omissions by reason of common documents, or where the defendant is alleged to have engaged in a common course of conduct, the commonality requirement is met and class certification is appropriate." *Adams,* 791 S.W.2d at 291 (citations omitted). As noted by the court in *Adams*, a class action is a particularly well-suited method of adjudicating a securities fraud actions because such litigation, more often than not, involves large numbers of plaintiffs whose core complaints are closely similar if not identical. *Id.* at 292.

Adequacy of Representation

The named parties in a class action must fairly and adequately protect the interests of the class. *Dresser*, 847 S.W.2d at 373. This requirement consists of two requirements: (1) it must appear that the representative parties, through their attorneys, will vigorously prosecute the class claims; and (2) there must be an absence of conflict or antagonism between the interests of the named plaintiffs and those of other members of the proposed class. *Reserve Life*, slip op. at 12, — S.W.2d at — *Adams*, 791 S.W.2d at 291.

Adequacy of representation is a question of fact and must be determined based on the individual circumstances of each case. *Forsyth v. Lake LBJ Inv. Corp.*, 903 S.W.2d 146, 150 (Tex. App.—Austin 1995, n.w.h.); *Dresser*, 847 S.W.2d at 373. It is addressed to the sound discretion of the court. *Id.* Factors affecting this determination include: (1) adequacy of counsel; (2) potential for conflicts of interest; (3) the personal integrity of the plaintiffs; (4) the representative's familiarity with the litigation, and their belief in the legitimacy of the grievance; (5) whether the class is unmanageable because of geographical limitations; and (6) whether the plaintiffs can afford to finance the class action. *Id.*

The only antagonism or conflict suggested by appellees is the fact that appellants are debentureholders and other proposed class members are stockholders. Citing several federal district court cases, appellees suggest that because appellants are debentureholders, their interests in this litigation are antagonistic to those of stockholder class members. *See Model Associates, Inc. v. U.S. Steel Corp.*, 88 F.R.D. 338, 339–40 (S.D. Oh. W.D. 1980); *Blumenthal v. Great Am. Mortgage Investors*, 74 F.R.D. 508, 516 (N.D. Ga. 1976); *Carlisle v. LTV Electrosystems, Inc.*, 54 F.R.D. 237, 239 (N.D. Tex. 1972). It is true that considerations motivating the purchase of debentures are very different from those motivating the purchase of equity shares of stock. *See id.* In particular, appellees observe that debentureholders are creditors of the corporation and entitled to payment before shareholders upon dissolution. *See* Black's Law Dictionary 401 (6th ed. 1990). However, that fact is irrelevant for purposes of our inquiry because appellants' claim is not against the corporate issuer of securities, EMI, and does not involve liquidation. Appellants do not seek class representation in a bankruptcy proceeding. Further, appellants' considerations or motivations in purchasing debentures rather than stocks are inconsequential because their Texas Securities Act claim does not require them to prove reliance. Rather, the issue is whether a reasonable investor would have considered the information in the prospectuses important in deciding to invest. *See Anheuser-Busch*, 858 S.W.2d at 936. In any event, there is no antagonism such as existed in *Forsyth* where a number of class members actually intervened to oppose the class action. *See Forsyth*, 903 S.W.2d at 148.

Nevertheless, appellees, again relying on various federal district court cases, insist that the trial court did not abuse its discretion by denying class certification under the first prong of the adequacy of representation test based on appellants lack of personal knowledge of the underlying claim. The law in Texas is to the contrary. As stated by this court in *Reserve Life*, the question is whether class representatives, *through their attorneys*, will vigorously prosecute the class claims. *Reserve Life*, slip op. at 9, — S.W.2d at — (emphasis added). In other words, the qualifications and experience of class counsel is of greater consequence than the knowledge of class representatives. *Longden*, 123 F.R.D. at 558.

Here, appellees do not question the competence or zeal of appellants' counsel in pursuing this litigation. Rather, they point to the fact that appellants' knowledge of the facts giving rise to their claims originates from their attorneys, not from their personal knowledge. As noted by the *Longden* court, in light of conspiracy and concerted scheme allegations and the complex nature of securities law, it is unreasonable to expect class representatives to possess detailed knowledge of the facts surrounding the potential fraud. *Id.*

The record in the instant case demonstrates that appellants have sufficient knowledge of the nature of their claims as well as their duties as class representatives. Appellants reviewed the petition in this case before it was filed. They know that EMI allegedly recorded sales that did not occur. They also know that the accountant defendants were allegedly negligent in their year-end audits of EMI sales transactions and may have conspired with EMI with regard to those fraudulent sales. More importantly, they have personal knowledge of the only relevant facts to which they and other class members will be called upon to testify at trial; namely, that they purchased EMI securities based on the prospectuses circulated during the public offering on April 16, 1987, and that their securities are now worthless.

Furthermore, appellants understand that as class representatives they represent other purchasers of EMI stocks and debentures. Specifically, they know that class members include "people that did the initial purchase on 6 and 1/2 percent subordinated . . . debentures and . . . the stock purchasers of the same date." They are aware that their duties include participating in the decision process as required, appearing at hearings, depositions and at trial, and monitoring the progress of the litigation. Few persons, other than attorneys involved in class litigation, can accurately articulate the full extent of the fiduciary responsibilities and other efforts required of a class plaintiff. *Id.*

Appellees point out that appellants have not attended any hearings in this case, have not been involved in the discovery process, and have left management of this litigation to their attorneys, who initially advised them to pursue this action and who are now financing this lawsuit. However, class certification does not require a higher standard of involvement from a proposed class representative than from an individual plaintiff. *Gibb v. Delta Drilling Co.*, 104 F.R.D. 59, 77 (N.D. Tex. 1984). Further, rule 42 does "not require as a condition of certification that there be a preliminary showing of willingness and ability to bear costs of representation." *Salvaggio v. Houston Indep. School Dist.*, 709 S.W.2d 306, 310 (Tex. App.—Houston [14th Dist.] 1986, writ dism'd). Rather, the rule requires only that the class representatives fairly and adequately protect the interest of the class. *Id.* If other class members or the trial court later conclude that appellants or counsel cannot adequately protect the interests of the class, the court can decertify the class. Tex. R. Civ. P. 42(c).

Finally, appellees complain that appellants did not diligently pursue certification in this case. *See Forsyth*, 903 S.W.2d at 149. Where there is such a complaint, this court has held there must be a showing of prejudice to the class or the opposing party. *Angeles/Quinoco*, 841 S.W.2d at 515. In this case, appellees failed to preserve error on this issue because they did not bring their complaint about delay to the trial court's attention. *Id.*; *see* Tex. R. Civ. P. 42(a). Even if error had been preserved, the undisputed evidence in the record shows that appellants moved for class certification "as soon as practicable" and that appellees were not prejudiced by any alleged delay. *See* Tex. R. Civ. P. 42(c)(1). Appellants satisfied the adequacy of representation requirement.

Named Plaintiffs' Claims Are Typical of the Class

The claims of the class representatives must be typical of the class as a whole. *Dresser,* 847 S.W.2d at 372. That is, the representatives must "possess the same interest and suffer the same injury." *Id.* (quoting *East Texas Motor Freight v. Rodriguez*, 431 U.S. 395, 403, 97 S. Ct. 1891, 1896–97, 52 L. Ed. 2d 453, 462 (1977)). Although it is not necessary that the named representative suffer precisely the same injury as the other class members, there must be a nexus between the injury suffered by the representative and the injuries suffered by other members of the class. *Dresser*, 847 S.W.2d at 372. To be typical, the named plaintiffs' claims must arise from the same event or course of conduct giving rise to the claims of other class members. *Adams*, 791 S.W.2d at 290. These claims must also be based on the same legal theory. *Id.* Ordinarily, the presence of even an arguable defense peculiar to the named plaintiff or a small subset of the plaintiff destroys the typicality of the class. *Id.* However, factual differences have not defeated class certification in other securities actions where the claims arose from the same legal theory. *Id.*

. . . .

Clearly, there is a nexus between appellants' injury and other class members' injury because appellees allegedly made the same misrepresentations in the same documents circulated to all investors, each of whom lost money on their investment. *See Dresser*, 847 S.W.2d at 372. Furthermore, appellants and other class members rely on the same theory of liability under the Texas Securities Act. *See Adams*, 791 S.W.2d at 290. Appellants therefore met the typicality requirement.

Numerosity

This determination is not based on numbers alone. *National Gypsum*, 770 S.W.2d at 624. Rather, the test is whether joinder of all members is practicable in view of the size of the class and such factors as judicial economy, the nature of the action, geographical locations of class members, and the likelihood that class members would be unable to prosecute individual lawsuits. *Id.* As previously described, appellants have identified at least fifty-five individuals and entities who purchased EMI debentures and at least one hundred and forty-four individuals and entities who purchased EMI stock on or about April 16, 1987 through April 30, 1987. Appellees contend that appellants did not satisfy this requirement because appellants did not adequately identify those "purchasers who lost all or part of their investments" as alleged in their petition. This argument is without merit. As we have stated, the undisputed evidence shows that the price of EMI securities never rose as high as the April 1987 purchase price. Thus, all purchasers of securities during the public offering and therefore, all proposed class members lost money on their investments. We cannot say that appellants failed to identify the proposed class merely because they do not distinguish those class members who lost all their investment from those who lost only part of their investment as a result of selling out before the price dropped further. Thus, appellants have adequately identified the members of the proposed class.

Appellees also argue that appellants can only represent the fifty-five debentureholders and that joinder of that many parties is not impracticable. Appellees' argument presumes that appellants' interests as debentureholders are antagonistic to those of other proposed class members who are only stockholders. As we have noted, there is no reason why appellants cannot represent both debentureholders and stockholders. Clearly, joinder of some two hundred parties dispersed throughout the United States, Bermuda, and Canada is impracticable.

Appellees further argue that the trial court could reasonably have concluded that joinder was not impracticable because the record shows that only three plaintiffs have so far sought to litigate their claim and that appellants filed this suit only after learning about their claims from their attorney. Considering appellants' circumstances in bringing suit, it is possible that other proposed class members have not pursued litigation of their claims because they are unaware of such claims. In any event, there is no presumption, as appellees suggest, that other class members have chosen not to pursue their claims simply because they have not filed suit or intervened in the proposed class action. Indeed, class certification will enable appellants to provide the necessary notice. *See* Tex. R. Civ. P. 42(c). If after receiving notice other class members express a desire not to pursue this litigation, the trial court can decertify the class. *See id.*

Finally, appellants point out that if the denial of class certification is upheld, other members of the proposed class will be barred by limitations from prosecuting their claims. *See* 15 U.S.C. § 77m (1981); 1 Blue Sky L. Rep. (CCH) 5550, Uniform Securities Act § 410(e); Tex. Rev. Civ. Stat. Ann. art. 581-33(H)(2)(b); *see also Grant v. Austin Bridge Constr. Co.*, 725 S.W.2d 366, 370 (Tex. App.—Houston [14th Dist.] 1987, no writ) (holding that limitations are tolled by the filing of a class action suit and begin to run again when certification is denied). Appellees assert that we cannot consider appellants' limitations argument at the certification stage because it goes to the substantive merits of their claim. We disagree. Appellants do not ask us to determine whether the individual claims of other proposed class members are barred by limitations; they concede that fact. Instead, they argue that the only vehicle by which those proposed class members can pursue their claims is by this class action, which the parties agree was timely filed. One factor to consider in determining the propriety of class certification is whether members of the proposed class will be unable to prosecute individual lawsuits. *See National Gypsum*, 770 S.W.2d at 624. If class certification in this case is denied, other members of the proposed class will be unable to prosecute individual lawsuits due to limitations. That fact favors certification.

Because of the size of the proposed class, the dispersal of class members and the fact that individual claims will be barred by limitations, practicability and judicial economy are best served by prosecuting appellants' claims as a class action. Thus, appellants met the numerosity requirement.

Superiority of Class Action

A class action is superior to other methods of adjudication where any difficulties which might arise in the management of the class are outweighed by the benefits of classwide resolution of common issues. *Dresser*, 847 S.W.2d at 375; *National Gypsum*, 770 S.W.2d at 626. In assessing whether a class action is superior, the court may consider whether: (1) class members have an interest in resolving the common issues by class action; (2) class members will benefit from discovery already commenced; and (3) the court has invested time and effort in familiarizing itself with the issues in dispute. *Id.* This case was set for trial. The record reflects that significant discovery has been completed and that the court has invested considerable time in familiarizing itself with this dispute. Other class members who wish to join the class will benefit from the time and effort invested by the parties and the court to date. Given the commonality of issues and the discovery already completed, the potential filing of some two hundred individual lawsuits would be repetitive and a waste of judicial resources. Thus, we conclude that appellants met this requirement.

Accordingly, we hold that the denial of class certification is not supported by the law or the undisputed facts in the record and, therefore, constituted an abuse of discretion. We sustain appellants' points of error, reverse the trial court's order and remand to that court for proceedings consistent with this opinion.

---

**GENERAL MOTORS CORP. v. BLOYED**, 916 S.W.2d 949 (Tex. 1995). Plaintiffs were truck owners who filed a class action suit for damages related to "side-saddle" gas tanks that rendered their vehicles susceptible to explosion on side impact. The parties announced a settlement eight months into litigation. Bloyed and a subgroup of class members objected, unsuccessfully, to the settlement and appealed the unfavorable ruling. The Texas Supreme Court held the trial court correctly analyzed the fairness of the settlement according to whether the terms were fair, adequate, and reasonable and whether the agreement was the product of honest negotiations or of collusion. Although the terms were of uncertain value to the plaintiffs, they were found to be reasonable, as the plaintiffs faced serious difficulties in prevailing on the merits had the case gone to trial. However, the settlement was set aside because notice to class members of the terms of the proposed settlement, particularly the projected attorney's fees and expenses, was held to be inadequate. Although attorney's fees were to be paid outright by the defendant (not subtracted from the class members' awards), the court found that plaintiffs nevertheless had a right to know the amount, as it represented an integral part of the overall amount the defendant was willing to pay to avoid litigation. Specifically, the court held that class action settlement notices must contain the maximum amount of attorney's fees sought and must specify the proposed method of calculating the award, regardless of whether the fees are to be deducted from plaintiffs' awards.

---

## NOTES AND QUESTIONS

(1) *Burden to Obtain Class Certification.* Consider the following excerpt from *Smith v. Lewis,* 578 S.W.2d 169, 172 (Tex. Civ. App.—Houston [14th Dist.] 1979, writ ref'd n.r.e.) concerning the burden to secure class certification:

> The 1977 amendment to Tex. R. Civ. P. 42 was patterned after Fed. R. Civ. P. 23 with little change. No Texas courts have decided the construction to be given to the amendment; thus we have looked to the Federal courts for guidance. Even though a number of Federal courts have held that a district judge has an obligation on his own motion to determine whether an action shall proceed as a class action, *Senter v. General Motors Corp.,* 532 F.2d 511 (6th Cir. 1976), *cert. denied,* 429 U.S. 870, 97 S. Ct. 182, 50 L. Ed. 2d 150 (1976), the failure to do so has not been held to violate a substantive right so as to be harmful per se. The Federal courts, including the U.S. Supreme Court, have placed the burden directly on the plaintiff to present his motion for "class certification" in a timely manner. *East Texas Motor Freight System, Inc., v. Rodriguez,* 434 U.S. 810, 98 S. Ct. 45, 54 L. Ed. 2d 67 (1977); *Adise v. Mather,* 56 F.R.D. 492 (D. Colo. 1972); *Carracter v. Morgan,* 491 F.2d 458 (4th Cir. 1973), as well as to produce facts, if necessary, to demonstrate that the case meets the prerequisites of a class action. *Carracter v. Morgan, supra.* It is to be noted that the standard for determining whether a plaintiff may maintain a class action is not whether he will ultimately prevail on his claim, but rather, whether he meets the demands of Fed. R. Civ. P. 23(a) and (b), *Huff v. N. D. Cass Company of Alabama,* 485 F.2d 710 (5th Cir. 1973).

(2) *Notice to Class Members.* Is "individual" notice required in all types of class actions under Civil Procedure Rule 42? What is "individual" notice? Who bears the cost of the notice under the rule?

(3) *Shareholder's Derivative Actions.* When Civil Procedure Rule 42 was originally drafted in 1941, it expressly governed both class actions and shareholders' derivative suits. With the substantial revision of Rule 42 in 1977 so that it generally paralleled Fed. R. Civ. P. 23, reference to derivative suits was dropped. There was no concomitant adoption of a rule comparable to Fed. R. Civ. P. 23.1. In *Zauber v. Murray Savings Ass'n,* 591 S.W.2d 932 (Tex. Civ. App.—Dallas 1979), *writ ref'd n.r.e. per curiam,* 601 S.W.2d 940 (Tex. 1980), the court held: "In light of the [1977 revision of the rule], the supreme court clearly intended rule 42 to govern only class

actions; derivative actions brought in the right of a corporation are governed solely by article 5.14 of the Texas Business Corporation Act." Civil Procedure Rule 42 was amended in 1984 to correlate the procedural rules with Article 5.14 of the Business Corporation Act. Article 5.14 was completely rewritten in 1997.

(4) *Interpretation of Rule 42(a).* Despite the literal language of Civil Procedure Rule 42(a), the Texas Supreme Court has concluded that a sole minority shareholder may bring a derivative action against the corporation's other shareholders even though he or she is only "similarly situated" with himself or herself. *Eye Site, Inc. v. Blackburn*, 796 S.W.2d 160, 162–63 (Tex. 1990) ("The rule does not place any minimum numerical limits on the number of shareholders who must be 'similarly situated.' It follows that if the plaintiff is the only shareholder 'similarly situated,' he is in compliance with both the letter and purpose of the rule.").

# CHAPTER 8

## THE EFFECTS OF PRIOR ADJUDICATION (RES JUDICATA)

### SCOPE

This chapter focues on the effects of prior adjudication, chiefly res judicata. The chapter also covers the binding effect of prior litigation on the parties, merger and bar (claim preclusion), collateral estoppel (issue preclusion), election of remedies, and the law of the case doctrine.

## § 8.01 Res Judicata

The doctrine of res judicata deals generally with the conclusive effects of judgments. The term "res judicata" has been used to encompass the separate doctrines of merger and bar (precluding relitigation of a claim when a subsequent suit is brought on the same cause of action) and collateral estoppel or estoppel by judgment (precluding relitigation of an issue or issues common to separate causes of action). *See Puga v. Donna Fruits Co.,* 634 S.W.2d 677, 679 (Tex. 1982); *Houston Terminal Land Co. v. Westergreen,* 119 Tex. 204, 27 S.W.2d 526 (1930), adopting analysis from *Cromwell v. County of Sac,* 94 U.S. 351, 353, 24 L. Ed. 195 (1876). As will become clear in the sections below, the distinction between the doctrine of res judicata as a plea of bar (claim preclusion) and as a plea of collateral estoppel (issue preclusion) is important in determining the breadth of the estoppel worked by the prior judgment. *Puga v. Donna Fruits Co.*, 634 S.W.2d at 679.

### [A] The Doctrine of Merger and Bar (Claim Preclusion)

Traditionally it has been considered a great evil to split a cause of action. A major justification for the rule is the avoidance of a multiplicity of suits and, therefore, vexatious litigation and the unnecessary consumption of judicial resources. *See* Cleary, *Res Judicata Reexamined,* 57 Yale L.J. 339, 344–349 (1948).

The basic rules are as follows: If a plaintiff recovered in the first action instituted on a particular "cause of action," that cause of action is viewed as having merged into the judgment such that it cannot be reasserted. Moreover, because the parameters of a cause of action are analytically distinct from the claim actually litigated (i.e., the claimant could have asserted only one part of the cause of action), even unadjudicated claims are barred when they constitute a part of the same cause of action. They should have been litigated because a cause of action may not be split. On the other hand, if the plaintiff lost in the first law suit on the cause of action, the cause of action and all claims comprising it are said to be barred by the judgment. While these rules are relatively clearcut, courts have had great difficulty in defining the boundaries of particular causes of action, and various methods have been employed to try to do so. Justice Zollie Steakley and Weldon U. Howell, Jr. set forth three methods for deciding what constitutes a cause of action for the purpose of res judicata (merger and bar) in *Ruminations on Res Judicata,* 28 Sw. L.J.

355 (1974). *See also* Keeton, *Action, Cause of Action, and Theory of the Action in Texas,* 11 Tex. L. Rev. 145 (1933). In the context of the doctrine of res judicata, at least the following approaches have been considered and used in Texas at one time or another.

1. *Individualized/Same Evidence Approach.* Early Texas authority indicated that if a claim asserted in a second action was technically different from the claim asserted in an earlier lawsuit, the latter action was not barred. *See Moore v. Snowball,* 98 Tex. 16, 81 S.W. 5, 7–10 (1904). Under this approach to the problem, a single cause of action exists when a particular set of facts is sufficient to individualize a specific rule of law such that it can be distinguished from any other claim against the same party:

> Even a minimal alteration of material facts may constitute a new cause of action, if the alteration makes available a new rule of substantive law. . . . This "small-sized" cause of action generally restricts the operation of *res judicata*; much like the ancient common law forms of action, this concept strictly limits an action according to the rights enforced under it. While acclaimed as a simple and consistent criterion for defining cause of action, this concept has also been criticized as being too narrow for practical application and oblivious to important policy considerations.

Steakley & Howell, *Ruminations on Res Judicata,* 28 Sw. L.J. 355, 361–362 (1974).

2. *Pragmatic Approach.* The doctrine of merger and bar has been said to preclude relitigation of matters a party could have interposed, but that the party failed to interpose, in an action between the same parties or their privies in reference to the same subject matter. *Freeman v. McAninch,* 87 Tex. 132, 27 S.W. 97 (1894); *Ogletree v. Crates,* 363 S.W.2d 431, 435–436 (Tex. 1963). Under this method, termed the "pragmatic approach," a matter that could have been litigated in the first action should have been litigated then, rather than in a subsequent action. In using the approach, the court considers matters of practicality (e.g., trial convenience, judicial economy, and common usage) and whether the additional facts involved in the second action are so closely related to those litigated in the prior action that it makes sense to consider the two situations as one "cause of action." The main difficulty with the pragmatic approach is that it is inherently unpredictable, owing to heavy reliance on policy factors and judicial discretion, which, in turn, hinder the development of precedent. Steakley & Howell, *Ruminations on Res Judicata*, 28 Sw. L.J. 355, 362–363 (1974).

3. *Procedural Duty Approach.* This approach bears a strong resemblance to and suffers from the same problems as the pragmatic approach. Under the procedural duty approach, however, the focus appears not to be on an abstruse analysis of whether a particular "cause of action" has been split, but rather on whether a procedural duty has been violated in failing to set up in the first suit another claim that bears a relationship to it.

4. *Transactional Approach.* The Restatement (Second) of Judgments adopts a transactional analysis approach to claim preclusion. Under this approach, all claims arising out of the same transaction or series of transactions are barred, even if based on different theories or involving different remedies. Restatement (Second) of Judgments § 24. As shown by the following cases, the Texas Supreme Court has embraced the transactional approach and expressly overruled other tests of what constitutes a cause of action for res judicata purposes.

---

## BARR v. RESOLUTION TRUST CORP.

*837 S.W.2d 627 (Tex. 1992)*

GONZALEZ, Justice.

The issue in this case is whether a claim by Sunbelt Federal Savings against George Barr based on a partnership promissory note and guarantee agreement is barred by the doctrine of res judicata. The trial court granted Barr's motion for summary judgment based on res judicata. The court of appeals, with one Justice dissenting, reversed the trial court's judgment, holding that the doctrine did not apply. 824 S.W.2d 600. We reverse the judgment of the court of appeals and affirm the trial court's judgment.

In 1985, Barr and Ron Knott were partners in the Bar III Venture. On March 14, 1985 Barr III executed a promissory note for $369,750 in favor of Sunbelt's predecessor in interest. The same day, Barr and Knott executed a personal guarantee of the note. In March 1987, Bar III defaulted on the note.

On May 24, 1988, Sunbelt filed two separate lawsuits on the note. In one suit, Sunbelt alleged liability against the partnership as maker of the note and against Knott as guarantor of the note. In the other, Sunbelt alleged that Barr was personally liable because of his unconditional guarantee of the note.

Barr moved for summary judgment in the latter lawsuit on the grounds that the terms of the guaranty agreement were too uncertain to be enforceable. Barr argued that the agreement, a standard form containing a number of options to choose and blanks to complete, was not sufficiently completed to ascertain his liability. The trial court granted the motion, and rendered a final take-nothing judgment. Sunbelt did not appeal the judgment.

Thereafter, Sunbelt amended its pleadings in the suit against the partnership and Knott by adding Barr as a defendant, alleging that his status as a partner created liability for the note. Barr's answer asserted res judicata, among other defenses.

Barr moved for summary judgment on the grounds that the take-nothing judgment in the first lawsuit barred litigation of the claims against him in the second lawsuit. Sunbelt also moved for summary judgment, requesting a judgment on the note. The trial court granted Barr's motion and denied Sunbelt's. This interlocutory judgment became final when the court rendered judgment for Sunbelt on its claims against the partnership and Knott to the full amount of the note.

Sunbelt appealed, arguing that the trial court should have granted its summary judgment instead of Barr's. The court of appeals, with one justice dissenting, determined that the first suit did not bar the second. However, the court concluded that questions of fact prevented rendition in Sunbelt's favor, and thus remanded the case to the trial court. Both Barr and Sunbelt sought review in our court.

Much of the difficulty associated with the doctrine of res judicata is due to the confusion of several related theories. Broadly speaking, res judicata is the generic term for a group of related concepts concerning the conclusive effects given final judgments. *Puga v. Donna Fruit Co.*, 634 S.W.2d 677, 679 (Tex. 1982). Within this general doctrine, there are two principal categories:

(1) claim preclusion (also known as res judicata); and (2) issue preclusion (also known as collateral estoppel.) [footnote omitted] Res judicata, or claims preclusion, prevents the relitigation of a claim or cause of action that has been finally adjudicated, as well as related matters that, with the use of diligence, should have been litigated in the prior suit. *Gracia v. RC Cola-7-Up Bottling Co.*, 667 S.W.2d 517, 519 (Tex. 1984); *Bonniwell v. Beech Aircraft Corp.*, 663 S.W.2d 816, 181 (Tex. 1984). Issue preclusion, or collateral estoppel, prevents relitigation of particular issues already resolved in a prior suit. [footnote omitted] *Bonniwell,* 663 S.W.2d at 818. Barr's argument, that Sunbelt should have brought all theories of liability in one suit, is the defense of claim preclusion.

Claim preclusion prevents splitting a cause of action. *Jeanes v. Henderson,* 688 S.W.2d 100, 103 (Tex. 1985). The policies behind the doctrine reflect the need to bring all litigation to an end, prevent vexatious litigation, maintain stability of court decisions, promote judicial economy, and prevent double recovery. Zollie Steakley & Weldon U. Howell, Jr., *Ruminations on Res Judicata,* 28 Sw. L.J. 355, 358–59 (1974).

The question that has given courts the most difficulty is determining what claims should have been litigated in the prior suit. Early on, this Court held that res judicata "is not only final as to the matter actually determined, but as to every other matter which the parties might litigate in the cause, and which they might have decided." *Foster v. Wells,* 4 Tex. 101, 104 (1849). We have never repudiated this definition of claim preclusion, and it appears in some form in most definitions of res judicata. *See, e.g., Jeanes v. Henderson,* 688 S.W.2d 100, 103 (Tex. 1985) (res judicata bars not only what was actually litigated but also claims that could have been litigated in the original cause of action). If taken literally, this definition of the rule would require that all disputes existing between parties be joined regardless of whether the disputes have anything in common. This court has resorted to a wide variety of theories and tests to give res judicata a more restrictive application. [footnote omitted] *See generally* 5 William V. Dorsaneo III, *Texas Litigation Guide* § 131.06[4][b][ii] (1991); Steakley, 28 Sw. L.J. 355.

Even if only cases from more recent times are considered, our holdings with respect to res judicata are difficult to reconcile. In *Griffin v. Holiday Inns of America*, 496 S.W.2d 535 (Tex. 1973), the court determined that a take-nothing judgment in a suit to recover in contract for services and materials did not preclude a subsequent suit to be compensated in quantum meruit. The court rejected the view that a judgment as to one claim is res judicata of all claims or causes of action arising out of the same transaction, and stated that, "[a]s a general rule a judgment on the merits in a suit on one cause of action is not conclusive of a subsequent suit on a different cause of action except as to issues of fact actually litigated and determined in the first suit." *Id.* at 538. The court acknowledged, however, that alternative theories of recovery for the same "claim" may not be brought in different lawsuits. [footnote omitted]

Thus, in *Griffin*, the court determined that a "cause of action" for res judicata purposes is something more than the set of facts necessary to establish a single theory of recovery but not necessarily the entire transaction between the parties. *Id.* at 537–38. The court gave no guidance on the question of how to make this fine distinction between a mere alternative theory of recovery and a different cause of action. Every theory of recovery has its unique elements of proof. As the *Griffin* case illustrates, only slight variations of the facts to support different theories of the same incident can result in a court finding different causes of action, thus thwarting the purposes of res judicata. *See* Steakley, 28 Sw. L.J. at 361–62.

The court took an entirely different approach in *Westinghouse Credit Corp. v. Kownslar,* 496 S.W.2d 531 (Tex. 1973). In that case Kownslar had guaranteed all promissory notes by the maker.

The issue was whether res judicata required that Westinghouse bring in one suit its claims for all notes guaranteed by Kownslar that were then in default. Rather than decide whether there was more than one cause of action involved, the court decided the case solely on whether it appeared that the policies of res judicata required such a result. [footnote omitted]

This pure policy approach as exemplified by *Westinghouse* makes it virtually impossible to determine in advance what policy will win out in any given case. Without any objective standards, each case is decided ad hoc, and therefore the doctrine is "inherently unpredictable" and "affords little basis for consistency and formulation of precedent." Steakley, 28 Sw. L.J. at 362–63. *Westinghouse* is the only case we have decided solely on policy grounds.

Then, in *Texas Water Rights Comm. v. Crow Iron Works,* 582 S.W.2d 768 (Tex. 1979), the court shifted the focus from the cause of action to the subject matter of the litigation. The question was whether a major lawsuit instigated to sort out water rights to the lower Rio Grande river precluded a subsequent suit based on the claim that during the pendency of that suit the plaintiff had purchased additional rights. The court concluded that the subsequent claim was barred, noting that:

> The scope of res judicata is not limited to matters actually litigated; the judgment in the first suit precludes a second action by the parties of their privies not only on matters actually litigated, but also on causes of action or defenses which arise out of the same subject matter and which might have been litigated in the first suit.

*Id.* at 771–72. *Accord, Gracia,* 667 S.W.2d at 519. Thus this definition is not consistent with earlier formulations of the rule, such as in *Griffin,* that only issues related to a single cause of action are barred in a subsequent suit. While we did not expressly overrule the *Griffin* test in either *Crow Iron Works* or *Gracia* we do so now.

A determination of what constitutes the subject matter of a suit necessarily requires an examination of the factual basis of the claim or claims in the prior litigation. It requires an analysis of the factual matters that make up the gist of the complaint, without regard to the form of action. Any cause of action which arises out of those same facts should, if practicable, be litigated in the same lawsuit. *Garcia,* 667 S.W.2d at 519; *Crow Iron Works,* 582 S.W.2d at 772.

The definition of res judicata in *Garcia* and *Crow Iron Works* is substantially similar to the rule of compulsory counterclaims embodied in the rules of civil procedure. A party defending a claim must bring as a counterclaim any claim that "arises out of the transaction or occurrence that is the subject matter of the opposing party's claim. . . ." Tex. R. Civ. P. 97.

The Restatement of Judgments also takes the transactional approach to claims preclusion. It provides that a final judgment on an action extinguishes the right to bring suit on the transaction, or series of connected transactions, out of which the action arose. Restatement of Judgments 24(1). A "transaction" under the Restatement is not equivalent to a sequence of events, however, the determination is to be made pragmatically, "giving weight to such considerations as whether the facts are related in time, space, origin, or motivation, whether they form a convenient trial unit, and whether their treatment as a trial unit conforms to the parties' expectations or business understanding or usage." [footnote omitted] *Id.* 24(2).

We conclude that the transactional approach to claims preclusion of the Restatement effectuates the policy of res judicata with no more hardship than encountered under rule 97(a) of the rules of civil procedure. Modern rules of procedure obviate the need to give parties two bites at the apple, as was done in *Griffin,* to ensure that a claim receives full adjudication. Discovery should put a claimant on notice of any need for alternative pleading. Moreover, if success on one theory becomes doubtful because of developments during trial, a party is free to seek a trial amendment.

In the case now before us, there is no valid reason to subject Barr to two different lawsuits. In the suit brought previously against Barr, the bank alleged that he executed the guarantee on the same day and as part of the "same transaction" as the promissory note. In both suits Sunbelt seeks to hold Barr primarily liable for payment of the note and seeks the same amount of damages. Both suits require proof establishing the notes of the partnership, that the notes are due, and that the partnership has defaulted. The only factual allegation that Sunbelt pleaded in the second suit that was not in the first is that Barr is a general partner of Bar III Venture.

It is clear that in this case the execution of the partnership note and Barr's guarantee of it were related in time and space and motivation, and the parties considered it as a single transaction. The issues of both claims form a convenient trial unit, whereas separate lawsuits would require significant duplication of effort of the court and the parties involved. With due diligence, the claim that Barr was liable because he is a partner could have been joined in the suit on his guarantee of the partnership note.

We reaffirm the "transactional" approach to res judicata. A subsequent suit will be barred if it arises out of the same subject matter of a previous suit and which through the exercise of diligence, could have been litigated in a prior suit. For these reasons, the judgment of the court of appeals is reversed and that of the trial court is affirmed.

---

## GETTY OIL CO. v. INSURANCE CO. OF N. AMERICA

*845 S.W.2d 794 (Tex. 1992)*

PHILLIPS, Chief Justice.

The purchaser of certain chemicals brought suit against the seller and its insurers, claiming that they were contractually obligated to provide insurance to cover a judgment against the purchaser in a wrongful death action precipitated by the explosion of the chemicals. The trial court granted summary judgment for the defendants on four grounds. . . . The court of appeals affirmed on the theory of res judicata. 819 S.W.2d 908 (Tex. App.—Houston 1991). We affirm the judgment of the court of appeals in part, reverse in part, and remand the cause to the trial court or further proceedings.

### I. Facts and Procedural Background

Getty Oil Company ("Getty") purchased various chemicals for NL Industries, Inc. ("NL") for Getty's oil production and exploration operations in the Midland, Texas, area. . . .

On November 22, 1983, a barrel of chemical emulsifier delivered by NL under Order No. HB-5357 exploded in the vicinity of a Getty well, killing Carl Duncan, an independent contractor working for Getty.

Duncan's estate and survivors brought wrongful death and survival actions in the 130th Judicial Court of Matagorda County against Getty, NL and its subsidiaries, and others. [footnote omitted]

Getty filed a cross-claim against NL, alleging that NL's negligence proximately caused the injury to Duncan, that the chemicals manufactured by NL were defective, and that NL breached warranties in connection with the sale of the chemicals. Getty also asserted a contractual right of indemnity against NL under the terms of HB-5357 (quoted above), and a contribution claim because of NL's negligence. The jury found Getty 100% negligent and grossly negligent in causing the accident. The trial court rendered judgment on the jury verdict for $3,757,000 actual damages and $25,000,000 punitive damages. The trial court also rendered judgment that "all Cross-Actions for contributions and or indemnity based upon the contracts are denied." Getty appealed the portion of the judgment denying it contribution and indemnity, and the court of appeals affirmed the judgment of the trial court. *Getty Oil Corp. v. Duncan,* 721 S.W.2d 475 (Tex. App.—Corpus Christi 1986, ref. n.r.e.). Getty's insurers, Travellers Insurance Company, Travellers Indemnity Company, and English & American Insurance Company, settled the claim for $14 million.

Getty then filed an insurance claim with NL's insurers. After they refused to honor the claim, Getty sued NL and its primary and excess insurance carriers, Insurance Company of North ("INA") and Youell and Companies [footnote omitted] ("Youell"), respectively. [footnote omitted] . . . NL, INA and Youell jointly moved for summary judgment, . . . [and] on May 3, 1990, the trial court granted the defendants' motions for summary judgment. . . . Getty appealed the summary judgment for defendants, and the court of appeals affirmed on res judicata grounds, holding that Getty's claims were barred because it was seeking the same relief under a different theory that it unsuccessfully sought in the first suit. 819 S.W.2d at 915. Getty now seeks a reversal of the court of appeals' judgment and the trial court's summary judgment. [footnote omitted]

II. Res Judicata

. . . .

We recently clarified that Texas follows the "transactional" approach to res judicata. *See Barr v. Resolution Trust Corp.*, 837 S.W.2d 627 (Tex. 1992). Under this approach, a judgment in an earlier suit "precludes a second action by the parties and their privies not only on matters actually litigated, but also on causes of action or defenses which arise out of the same subject matter and which might have been litigated in the first suit." *Id.* at 630; *Texas Water Rights Comm. v. Crow Iron Works*, 582 S.W.2d 768, 771–72 (Tex. 1979).

We conclude that Getty's present suit arises out of the same subject matter as its earlier cross-claim against NL asserted in the Duncan suit. The Restatement (Second) of Judgments, which recognizes the transactional test, suggests that factors to consider in determining whether facts constitute a single "transaction" are "their relatedness in time, space, origin, or motivation, and whether, taken together, they form a convenient unit for trial purposes." Restatement (Second) of Judgments 24 cmt. b (1980). Getty's present action against NL arose from the same accident that was adjudicated in the Duncan suit. The present suit also concerns the same contract, HB-5357, and the same section of that contract, the "Insurance and Indemnity" section. Finally, Getty seeks the same relief against NL here as in its earlier cross-claim: reimbursement for Getty's liability to Duncan's estate and beneficiaries. Thus, both Getty's actions against NL derived from the same transaction. [footnote omitted]

Getty argues that res judicata cannot bar its present claims against NL because these claims did not accrue until judgment was rendered in the Duncan suit. That is, Getty had no liability and hence no need for insurance coverage until liability was assigned. The contingent nature of these claims, however, does not preclude the operation of res judicata. We held in Barr that "[a] subsequent suit will be barred if it arises out of the same subject matter of a previous suit and which, through the exercise of diligence, could have been litigated in a prior suit." 837 S.W.2d at 631. Getty could have asserted its present claims in the Duncan suit, with their resolution being contingent on the plaintiffs' claim. Texas Rule of Civil Procedure 51(b) provides:

> Joinder of Remedies. Whenever a claim is one heretofore cognizable only after another claim has been prosecuted to conclusion, the two claims may be joined in a single action; but the court shall grant relief in that action only in accordance with the relative substantive rights of the parties.

*See Parkhill Produce Co. v. Pecos Valley Southern Ry. Co.*, 348 S.W.2d 208 (Tex. Civ. App. San Antonio 1961, ref. n.r.e.). For example, we have held that an indemnitee may bring a claim against an indemnitor before judgment is assigned against the indemnitee. *See Gulf, Colorado & Santa Fe Ry. Co. v. McBride,* 159 Tex. 442, 322 S.W.2d 492, 495 (Tex. 1958); *Mitchell's, Inc. v. Friedman*, 157 Tex. 424, 431, 303 S.W.2d 775, 779 (Tex. 1957); *K & S Oil Well Service, Inc. v. Cabot Corp.*, 491 S.W.2d 733, 739 (Tex. Civ. App.—Corpus Christi 1973, ref. n.r.e.). Forcing the indemnity suit to wait for judgment in the liability suit "would contravene the policy of the courts to encourage settlements and to minimize litigation." *Id.*

Getty itself took advantage of this rule in its initial cross-action against NL, in which Getty asserted its claim under the indemnity provision of HB-5357. The fact that Getty had no claim for indemnity against NL until the trial court rendered judgment did not preclude this cross-claim. Likewise, Getty could have brought its other contingent cross-claims against NL in the Duncan action. The fact that Getty's claims against NL were contingent on Getty incurring liability in the Duncan suit does not in and of itself preclude operation of res judicata. [footnote omitted]

. . . .

Getty replies that even if INA and Youell were in privity with NL, res judicata would not bar Getty's present claims against them because Getty could not have asserted those claims in the Duncan suit. The insurance policies themselves specifically prohibited any claim from being brought against INA or Youell before the insured's liability was reduced to judgment or compromised. [footnote omitted] We have held that when such "no action" policy provision exists, "a third party's right of action against the insurer does not arise until he has secured such an agreement or a judgment against the insured." *Great American Ins. Co. v. Murray,* 437 S.W.2d 264, 265–66 (Tex. 1969); *see also State Farm County Mut. Ins. Co. of Texas v. Ollis,* 768 S.W.2d 722, 723 (Tex. 1989).

Moreover, Tex. R. Civ. P. 38(c) prohibited Getty from joining INA and Youell in the Duncan suit. This rule provides, with respect to the joinder of third parties:

> (c) This rule shall not be applied, in tort cases, so as to permit the joinder of a liability or indemnity insurance company, unless such company is by statute or contract liable to the person injured or damaged.
>
> Rule 38(c) has been held to prohibit the joinder of insurers in situations resembling this case. *See Langdeau v. Pittman,* 337 S.W.2d 343, 355 (Tex. Civ. App.—Austin 1960, ref. n.r.e.).

Since Getty could not have asserted its present claims against INA or Youell in the Duncan suit, it is not now precluded by res judicata from bringing these claims. We accordingly reverse the judgment of the court of appeals affirming the trial court's summary judgment against INA and Youell on the grounds of res judicata, and we remand this portion of the cause to the trial court for further proceedings.

. . . .

---

## NOTES

(1) *Final Judgment Requirement.* A final judgment has res judicata effect despite the pendency of an appeal unless the appeal is by trial de novo. *Scurlock Oil Co. v. Smithwick*, 724 S.W.2d 1, 6 (Tex. 1986); *see also* Restatement (Second) of Judgments § 13, comment f, providing that "[t]he better view is that judgment otherwise final remains so despite the taking of an appeal."

(2) *Relationship to Federal Law.* When the first lawsuit is decided in federal court, the federal law of res judicata (claim preclusion) controls the determination of whether a later state court action is barred, unless the federal court did not possess jurisdiction over the omitted state claims or, even if the federal court had jurisdiction, it would clearly have declined to exercise it as a matter of discretion. *Eagle Properties, Ltd. v. Scharbauer,* 807 S.W.2d 714, 718–21 (Tex. 1990) (not deciding whether federal law of collateral estoppel (issue preclusion) would control in same case); *Jeanes v. Henderson,* 688 S.W.2d 100, 103 (Tex. 1985). The critical focus is not on the relief requested in the federal action, but whether the plaintiff bases both the federal and state actions on the same nucleus of operative facts. *Fernandez v. Memorial Health Care Systems, Inc.*, 896 S.W.2d 227, 231 (Tex. App.—Houston [1st Dist.] 1995, no writ). In this connection, the Fifth Circuit Court of Appeals has also adopted the "transactional" analysis discussed in *Barr. See Ocean Drilling & Explo. v. Mont Boat Rental Serv.*, 799 F.2d 213, 217 (5th Cir. 1986).

(3) *Withdrawn Claims.* Voluntarily withdrawn claims are subject to the doctrine of res judicata. *Jones v. Nightingale*, 900 S.W.2d 87, 88–90 (Tex. App.—San Antonio 1995, writ ref'd). However, the doctrine of res judicata does not bar a cause of action created after the entry of judgment in a prior suit when a change in the law or facts subsequent to the first adjudication changes or creates substantive rights not existing until after the first judgment. *See Besing v. Vanden Eykel*, 878 S.W.2d 182, 184 (Tex. App.—Dallas, 1994, writ denied).

### [B] Collateral Estoppel (Issue Preclusion)

#### [1] Basic Elements

Collateral estoppel (also known as estoppel by judgment) involves factual determinations actually litigated in a prior suit rather than matters that should have been but were not litigated. It does not matter whether the matter litigated was part of the same cause of action litigated in the first action. *See generally* McGlinchey, *Collateral Estoppel,* 4 Hous. L. Rev. 73 (1966).

## RIOS v. DAVIS

*373 S.W.2d 386 (Tex. Civ. App.—Eastland 1963, writ ref'd)*

COLLINGS, Justice.

Juan C. Rios brought this suit against Jessie Hubert Davis in the District Court to recover damages in the sum of $17,500.00, alleged to have been sustained as a result of personal injuries received on December 24, 1960, in an automobile collision. Plaintiff alleged that his injuries were proximately caused by negligence on the part of the defendant. The defendant answered alleging that Rios was guilty of contributory negligence. Also, among other defenses, the defendant urged a plea of res judicata and collateral estoppel based upon the findings and the judgment entered on December 17, 1962, in a suit between the same parties in the County Court at Law of El Paso County. The plea of res judicata was sustained and judgment was entered in favor of the defendant Jessie Hubert Davis. Juan C. Rios has appealed.

It is shown by the record that on April 11, 1961, Popular Dry Goods Company brought suit against appellee Davis in the El Paso County Court at Law, seeking to recover for damages to its truck in the sum of $443.97, alleged to have been sustained in the same collision here involved. Davis answered alleging contributory negligence on the part of Popular and joined appellant Juan C. Rios as a third party defendant and sought to recover from Rios $248.50, the alleged amount of damages to his automobile. The jury in the County Court at Law found that Popular Dry Goods Company and Rios were guilty of negligence proximately causing the collision. However, the jury also found that Davis was guilty of negligence proximately causing the collision, and judgment was entered in the County Court at Law denying Popular Dry Goods any recovery against Davis and denying Davis any recovery against Rios.

Appellant Rios in his third point contends that the District Court erred in sustaining appellee's plea of *res judicata* based upon the judgment of the County Court at Law because the findings on the issues regarding appellant's negligence and liability in the County Court at Law case were immaterial because the judgment entered in that case was in favor of appellant. We sustain this point. We are unable to agree with appellee's contention that the findings in the County Court at Law case that Rios was guilty of negligence in failing to keep a proper lookout and in driving on the left side of the roadway, and that such negligent acts were proximate causes of the accident were essential to the judgment entered therein. The sole basis for the judgment in the County Court at Law as between Rios and Davis was the findings concerning the negligence of Davis. The finding that Rios was negligent was not essential or material to the judgment and the judgment was not based thereon. On the contrary, the finding in the County Court at Law case that Rios was negligent proximately causing the accident would, if it had been controlling, led to a different result. Since the judgment was in favor of Rios he had no right or opportunity to complain of or to appeal from the finding that he was guilty of such negligence even if such finding had been without any support whatever in the evidence. The right of appeal is from a judgment and not from a finding. The principles controlling the fact situation here involved are, in our opinion, stated in the following quoted authorities and cases. The annotation in 133 A.L.R. 840, page 850 states:

> "According to the weight of authority, a finding of a particular fact is not *res judicata* in a subsequent action, where the finding not only was not essential to support the judgment, but was found in favor of the party against whom the judgment was rendered, and, if allowed to control, would have led to a result different from that actually reached."

In the case of Word v. Colley, Tex. Civ. App., 173 S.W. 629, at page 634 of its opinion (Error Ref.), the court stated as follows:

> "It is the judgment, and not the verdict or the conclusions of fact, filed by a trial court which constitutes the estoppel, and a finding of fact by a jury or a court which does not become the basis or one of the grounds of the judgment rendered is not conclusive against either party to the suit."

In 2 Black on Judgments, p. 609, the author states the rule of estoppel by judgment as follows:

> " 'The force of the estoppel resides in the judgment. It is not the finding of the court or the verdict of the jury rendered in an action which concludes the parties in subsequent litigation, but the judgment entered thereon.'
>
> "The fact that the judgment in the suit in Cherokee county was in favor of defendants precluded them from bringing in review the findings of the judge, and we cannot believe that a party can be estopped by a judgment in his favor from denying findings of the court rendering said judgment the decision of which was not essential or material to the rendition of the judgment. Philipowski v. Spencer, 63 Tex. 607; Sheffield v. Goff, 65 Tex. 358; Manning v. Green, 56 Tex. Civ. App. 579, 121 S.W. 725; Whitney v. Bayer, 101 Mich. 151, 59 N.W. 415; Cauhape v. Parke, Davis & Co., 121 N.Y. 152, 24 N.E. 186; 23 Cyc. 1227, 1228."

The above quotation is quoted with approval by the Supreme Court of Texas in Permian Oil Company v. Smith, 129 Tex. 413, 73 S.W.2d 490 at page 500. See also Rushing v. Mayfield Company, Tex. Civ. App., 104 S.W.2d 619; Cambria v. Jeffery, 307 Mass. 49, 29 N.E.2d 555; Karameros v. Luther, 279 N.Y. 87, 17 N.E.2d 779.

We cannot agree with appellee's contention that *Rio Bravo Oil Company v. Hebert*, 130 Tex. 1, 106 S.W.2d 242, is contrary to and requires an adverse determination of appellant's third point. The language particularly relied upon by appellant in that case was as follows:

> "Although the judgment of the court was, as we formerly held, only a denial of the right to recover the particular land there in controversy, its estoppel is much broader, and concludes the parties upon every question which was directly in issue, and was passed upon by the court in arriving at its judgment. . . ."
>
> ". . . But, where the second action between the same parties is upon a different claim or demand, the judgment in the prior action operates as an estoppel only as to those matters in issue or points controverted, upon the determination of which the finding or verdict was rendered."

For the reasons stated the court erred in entering judgment for Jessie Hubert Davis based upon his plea of *res judicata* and collateral estoppel. The judgment is, therefore, reversed and the cause is remanded.

## NOTES AND QUESTIONS

(1) *Relationship to Counterclaim Rule.* Why wasn't Rios required to file a counterclaim in the prior suit?

(2) *Offensive Use of Findings.* Is Davis estopped to deny his negligence in the action brought by Rios? The doctrine of collateral estoppel is usually asserted defensively. If, however, in the second action Rios had argued as a basis for a judgment in his favor the prior adjudication of Davis's negligence, his argument would have constituted an offensive use of the doctrine. Some jurisdictions have prohibited such offensive use, but in *Bonniwell v. Beech Aircraft Corp.*, 633 S.W.2d 653 (Tex. 1983), the Texas Supreme Court, assessing two law suits stemming from the same plane crash, referred approvingly to the use. The plaintiffs in the first suit sued three defendants on a mixture of negligence and strict liability grounds. The defendants cross-claimed against each other for indemnity and contribution. The jury returned findings regarding the comparative fault of the various defendants that, in turn, determined the cross-claims. The second suit then proceeded to trial, that suit involving different plaintiffs but the same defendants sued on the same grounds as in the first suit. Again, the defendants cross-claimed for indemnity and contribution. Defendant Beech asserted that the issues regarding the cross-claims were identical to those decided in the earlier suit. Thus, Beech argued, relitigation of the issues at the heart of the cross-claims should be barred. Essentially, Beech was asserting the doctrine of collateral estoppel both defensively (as the "defendant" of the cross-claims against it) and offensively (as the "plaintiff" in its cross-claims against the other defendants). The Supreme Court agreed with Beech that relitigation of the issues surrounding the cross-claims was barred and said regarding offensive use of the doctrine:

> We recognize that the estoppel applied here is essentially offensive collateral estoppel. Application of the doctrine in this fashion is appropriate where the derivative claims of identical parties are based upon issues identical to those litigated in a prior suit. *Southern Pacific Transportation Co. v. Smith Material Corp.*, 616 F.2d 111, 114–15 (5th Cir. 1980). To hold those same issues may again be litigated between these defendants to establish mutual liabilities in a subsequent contoversy, would invite inconsistent adjudication contrary to the spirit and purpose of the doctrine of collateral estoppel.

The *Bonniwell* court, in reaching its decision, noted, "Texas courts have adopted the position that mutuality is required only as to the party against whom the plea of collateral estoppel is asserted" [citing *Windmill Dinner Theatre of Dallas v. Hagler,* 582 S.W.2d 585 (Tex. Civ. App.—Dallas 1979, writ dism'd); *Olivarez v. Broadway Hardware Co.,* 564 S.W.2d 195 (Tex. Civ. App.—Corpus Christi 1978, writ ref'd n.r.e.); *Hardy v. Fleming, below; Benson v. Wanda Petroleum Co., below* ("When persons against whom collateral estoppel operates have had their day in court, either as parties, privies, or through actual and adequate representation, application of the doctrine meets the requirements of due process")]. The abolition of the mutuality requirement was essential in the landmark federal case allowing offensive use of collateral estoppel by plaintiffs not parties to an earlier action. *See Parklane Hosiery v. Shore,* 439 U.S. 322 (1979) (offensive use was permissible when defendant had full and fair opportunity and stong incentive to litigate issue in earlier action, when plaintiff could not have joined in the earlier suit, and when judicial economy and efficiency would be served). For an analysis of the evolution of and limitations upon the use of the doctrine, see Kennedy, *Non-Party Offensive Collateral Estoppel in Products Liability Litigation,* in 1983 SMU Products Liability Institute (V. Walkowiak ed. 1983).

After handing down its original opinion in *Bonniwell,* on motion for rehearing, the Texas Supreme Court withdrew the opinion and substituted a new opinion in which it concluded that Beech could not use the collateral estoppel doctrine to support its claim because the issue that was litigated in the first suit and that Beech was using as an estoppel in the second suit "was not essential to the judgment" in the first action. *Bonniwell v. Beech Aircraft Corp.*, 663 S.W.2d 816, 818–819 (Tex. 1984). Hence, the "offensive use" of collateral estoppel issue that is discussed in the original opinion dropped from the case on rehearing.

Several Texas intermediate courts have approved the offensive use of collateral estoppel. *Dover v. Baker, Brown, Sharman & Parker*, 859 S.W.2d 441, 449 (Tex. App.—Houston [1st Dist.] 1993, no writ); *Tankersley v. Durish*, 855 S.W.2d 241, 244 (Tex. App.—Austin 1993, writ denied); *Phillips v. Allums,* 882 S.W. 2d 71, 75 (Tex. App.—Houston [14th Dist.] 1994, writ denied) (acknowledging trial court's discretion to apply offensive use doctrine considering fairness factors set forth in *Parkland Hosiery Co., Inc. v. Shore,* 439 U.S. 322, 332, 99 S. Ct. 645, 651–652, 58 L. Ed. 2d 552 (1979)).

(3) *The Meaning of "Essential and Material."* If Rios was the driver of the laundry truck, wasn't the finding of his negligence "essential and material" to the determination that Popular take nothing?

Is the reason why Rios's negligence was not "essential and material" that it was inconsistent with the judgment in his favor? Can a finding be "material" but not "essential"? Assume a "finding" of "no negligence" on the part of a defendant in Rios's position and a finding of "negligence" on the part of the plaintiff. Are both findings "material" to the take nothing judgment? Are they both essential or are alternative grounds nonessential? Does the losing party have any opportunity to appeal the findings? See *Providence Wash. Ins. Co. v. Owens,* 210 S.W. 558 (1919). Under principles of comparative apportionment (i.e., comparative negligence and comparative causation), are all of the percentages "essential and material"? *See Bonniwell v. Beech Aircraft Corp.*, 663 S.W.2d 816, 818–819 (Tex. 1984). Doesn't the judgment rest on them jointly?

It is not clear whether the Texas Supreme Court has fully embraced the concept that is set forth in comment (i) to Section 27 of the Restatement (Second) of Judgments that "[i]f a judgment of a court of first instance is based on determinations of two issues, either of which standing independently would be sufficient to support the result, the judgment is not conclusive with respect to either issue standing alone." *See Eagle Properties, Ltd. v. Scharbauer,* 807 S.W.2d 714, 721–722 (Tex. 1990). After quoting the Restatement, the court declined to follow it:

> While this alternative reasoning may have had some adverse effect on defendants' desire to appeal the judgment, it is clear that the federal court "rigorously considered" defendants' claims of fraudulent inducement, carefully reviewing each contention. Therefore, applying state law to the circumstances of this case, we hold that the defendants' claims of fraudulent inducement were "actually tried" in the federal court and that the court's findings on fraudulent inducement were "essential" to its judgment for the purposes of preclusion by collateral estoppel. . . . [E]xcept in very unusual cases, the abandonment of estoppel for the reason that a prior judgment rests on multiple grounds is inconsistent with the general rule in federal courts that a party is only entitled to one full and fair opportunity to litigate an issue.

(4) *Lower Court Judgments.* What is the impact of the following sections of the Civil Practice and Remedies Code on cases like *Rios v. Davis*?

CIVIL PRACTICE AND REMEDIES CODE

CHAPTER 31. JUDGMENTS

C.P.R.C. § 31.004. *Effect of Adjudicatino in Lower Trial Court.* (a) A judgment or a determination of fact or law in a proceeding in a lower trial court is not res judicata and is not a basis for estoppel by judgment in a proceeding in a district court, except that a judgment rendered in a lower trial court is binding on the parties thereto as to recovery or denial of recovery.

(b) This section does not apply to a judgment in probate, guardianship, lunacy, or other matter in which a lower trial court has exclusive subject matter jurisdiction on a basis other than the amount in controversy.

(c) For the purposes of this section, a "lower trial court" is a small claims court, a justice of the peace court, a county court, or a statutory county court.

C.P.R.C. § 31.005. *Effect of Adjudication in Small Claims or Justice of the Peace Court.* A judgment or a determination of fact or law in a proceeding in small claims court or justice of the peace court is not *res judicata* and does not constitute a basis for estoppel by judgment in a proceeding in a county court or statutory county court, except that the judgment rendered is binding on the parties thereto as to recovery or denial of recovery.

These statutory provisions modify the common law so that res judicata bars only those claims that were actually litigated in a limited jurisdiction court. *Webb v. Persyn*, 866 S.W.2d 106, 107 (Tex. App.—San Antonio 1993, no writ).

### [2] The Doctrine of Mutuality

## HARDY v. FLEMING

*553 S.W.2d 790 (Tex. Civ. App.—El Paso 1977, writ ref'd n.r.e.)*

WARD, Justice.

This is a medical malpractice case where summary judgment was rendered for the Defendant Doctor. Prior to the present suit, the Plaintiff had lost a workmen's compensation suit which was based on the same heart attack which he now claims was caused by the Doctor's negligence. The principal question concerns the correctness of the trial Court's action in sustaining the Defendant's plea of collateral estoppel where the Defendant asserting the plea was not a party or in privity with a party to the earlier litigation. We affirm.

On August 6, 1971, the Plaintiff, Karl Hardy, while at home suffered an apparent heart attack. He immediately placed himself under the care of the Defendant, Dr. B. K. Fleming, and was thereafter treated by that Doctor for about a month. On September 10th, the Defendant advised the Plaintiff that he could return to full duty work at the Columbian Carbon Black Company at Seminole. The Plaintiff's employment was physically strenuous and required that the Plaintiff sack carbon black, put the sacks on pallets, and move them to a cooler. On September 12th, the Plaintiff returned to his employment on a full duty basis, but, after only a few hours of work, he experienced additional heart problems and, according to him, suffered another heart attack.

Hardy then filed his claim for compensation based on this latter attack, and thereafter instituted suit to recover his benefits under the Texas Workmen's Compensation Act by cause entitled "*Karl Hardy v. Insurance Company of North America* ," Cause No. 6463 in the District Court of Gaines County, Texas. Upon trial before a jury, the Court submitted Special Issue No. 1 to the jury inquiring whether Mr. Hardy had sustained a heart attack on September 12, 1971. According to the judgment rendered, the finding to this issue was that the Plaintiff, Karl Hardy, did not sustain a heart attack on September 12, 1971. Based upon that finding, judgment was entered that Hardy take nothing from the Insurance Company of North America. That judgment, which was in July, 1973, has become final.

Hardy next filed this present suit in the District Court of Gaines County to recover his alleged damages sustained from being under the care of Dr. Fleming during August and September, 1971. This malpractice suit was based upon the alleged negligence of the Doctor in: (a) advising Mr. Hardy that he could return to work on a full-time basis when it was not safe to do so; (b) failing to advise Hardy of the nature and extent of the damage done to his heart and of his physical condition; (c) failing to perform such tests and procedures to determine the nature of the damage and injuries done to Hardy's heart as would have been done by a competent and ordinary prudent physician; and (d) failing to refer Hardy to an appropriate medical specialist. The Plaintiff further alleged that he returned to work on the date authorized by Dr. Fleming and, "within four hours, suffered a massive heart attack brought on by the work and exertion associated with his employment."

By way of answer, the Doctor has pled the above matters regarding Cause No. 6463, the submission of the special issue regarding the heart attack on September 12, 1971, the finding by the jury that Hardy did not sustain the heart attack, the final judgment, and that because of the principle of estoppel by judgment, Hardy is now prohibited in the present case from contending that he sustained a heart attack on September 12, 1971. The Doctor filed his first amended motion for summary judgment setting forth two points of law: (1) the doctrine of collateral estoppel bars the present action; and (2) there is no genuine issue of proximate causation in the case. The summary judgment proof consisted of the depositions of the two parties, certified copy of the judgment in Cause No. 6463, the Defendant's answers to the Plaintiff's interrogatories, and the depositions of Dr. William Gordon, Dr. J. B. Jensen, and Dr. Moses Muzquiz, Jr. As stated, the trial Court entered summary judgment for the Defendant on his motion which advanced the two grounds.

The Defendant's first point attacks the summary judgment on the ground that the doctrine of collateral estoppel is not applicable in this case. The Plaintiff points out that Dr. Fleming had no relationship with the Columbian Carbon Black Company, nor with the Insurance Company of North America. Thus, the issue to be determined is whether Dr. Fleming, who is a stranger to the prior suit, may assert the doctrine of collateral estoppel in this subsequent independent suit brought by the same Plaintiff.

The parties recognize the authorities and agree as to the principles. They agree that the tendency of the Courts has been toward an abandonment of the requirement of mutuality and the retention of the requirement of privity only to the party against whom the plea of collateral estoppel is made in the second case. They disagree as to the present rule in this State. The problem is ably discussed in Stephenson, "The Doctrine of Equitable Estoppel under Texas Law," 36 Tex. B.J. 45 (1973). *See* "Estoppel by Judgment—Mutuality Need, 31 A.L.R.3d 1044 (1970).

Originally, mutuality was essential to the invocation of collateral estoppel. *Kirby Lumber Corporation v. Southern Lumber Co.,* 145 Tex. 151, 196 S.W.2d 387 (1946). However, the requirement of mutuality is nowhere mentioned in the last definition of collateral estoppel made by the Supreme Court where it was stated:

> "The rule of collateral estoppel, or as sometimes phrased, estoppel by judgment, bars relitigation in a subsequent action upon a different cause of action of fact issues actually litigated and essential to a prior judgment. It has been said that the rule rests upon equitable principles and upon the broad principles of justice. . . . The rule is generally stated as binding a party and those in privity with him. . . ."

*Benson v. Wanda Petroleum Company,* 468 S.W.2d 361 (Tex. 1971). There, Wanda Petroleum Company had successfully defended a negligence case brought by the Porters. Mrs. Benson then brought her suit for damages for her injuries and those of her deceased husband who owned the automobile and which had been driven by the Porters. The plea of collateral estoppel was held inapplicable to Mrs. Benson's suit as Mrs. Benson was not a party to the former action, had not participated in or exercised any control over the other trial, nor did she have any right to do so, and was not shown to have any beneficial interest in recovery of damages for personal injuries on behalf of the plaintiffs in the other trial. The Supreme Court did not apply the doctrine of mutuality, which would have ended it, but relied instead on the due process test as was originally done in the leading case of *Bernhard v. Bank of America Nat. Trust & Savings Ass.'n.,* 19 Cal. 2d 807, 122 P.2d 892 (1942). That case was cited by Justice Steakley in his opinion. *See also Seguros Tepeyac, S. A., Compania Mexicana v. Jernigan,* 410 F.2d 718 (1969), cert. denied, 396 U.S. 905, 90 S. Ct. 219, 24 L. Ed. 2d 181. There, the Fifth Circuit, in passing on Texas law and in ignoring any requirement of mutuality, refers to a suggestion that mutuality as an element of collateral estoppel is "a dead letter."

The Plaintiff, Karl Hardy, the one against whom the plea of collateral estoppel is asserted, was the party Plaintiff to the prior adjudication and he lost on his claim that he sustained a heart attack on September 12, 1971. No useful public policy is served by permitting him to relitigate that identical issue in the present suit. *Seguros Tepeyac, S. A., Compania Mexicana v. Jernigan,* supra, 90 S. Ct. at 727. Dr. Fleming, the one now asserting the plea, was not a party or in privity with a party to the prior litigation. There is no compelling reason that such be required and, in this fact situation, no satisfactory reason for any requirement of mutuality. *Bernhard v. Bank of America Nat. Trust & Savings Ass'n, supra.* The Plaintiff's first point is overruled.

. . . .

The judgment of the trial Court is affirmed.

---

## NOTES AND QUESTIONS

(1) *Due Process Rights.* Why is there a requirement that the party to be bound by the determination of the issue must have been a party or in privity with a party in the prior case?

(2) *Adverse Consequences of Eliminating Matuality.* The elimination of the mutuality doctrine can arguably lead to harsh results when the effect of the finding made in the first case on subsequent litigation involving a different party is difficult to foresee. *See* Currie, *Mutuality of Collateral Estoppel—Limits of the Bernhard Doctrine,* 9 Stan. L. Rev. 281 (1957). Is *Hardy v.*

*Fleming, above,* a case in which the plaintiff would likely have foreseen the consequences of the prior adjudication?

## § 8.02 Parties Bound by Prior Adjudications

### BENSON v. WANDA PETROLEUM COMPANY

*468 S.W.2d 361 (Tex. 1971)*

STEAKLEY, Justice.

The source of the problem here is a collision which occurred on October 29, 1967 in Eastland County, Texas, involving a tractor and trailer owned by Wanda Petroleum Company, respondent, and an automobile owned by Merrel Benson, now deceased, and his wife, Mrs. Lily Benson, which was being driven by Thurman C. Porter. A third party identified as Donald Chalk collided with the Benson vehicle following the initial collision. Separate suits for damages for personal injuries were filed against Wanda in the District Court of Eastland County by Mrs. Benson and by Mr. and Mrs. Porter. The suits were consolidated by the trial court and when called for trial Mrs. Benson took a voluntary non-suit. The trial jury in the Porter suit found Wanda and its driver free of negligence and found Porter guilty of acts of negligence which proximately caused the collision. A take nothing judgment was entered in favor of Wanda.

This suit for damages for personal injuries suffered by her and by her deceased husband was subsequently filed by Mrs. Benson in the District Court of Harris County against Wanda and Chalk. The trial court severed the suit against Chalk and rendered summary judgment in favor of Wanda upon the theory that the fact findings and judgment in the Porter suit were binding on Mrs. Benson. The Court of Civil Appeals affirmed in the stated opinion that the Bensons and Porters were engaged in a joint enterprise as a matter of law, and hence were in privity; and that the Bensons rested under a secondary or derivative liability which must have been considered and determined in the Porter suit. 460 S.W.2d 453. We disagree and so reverse and remand.

The rule of collateral estoppel, or as sometimes phrased, estoppel by judgment, bars relitigation in a subsequent action upon a different cause of action of fact issues actually litigated and essential to a prior judgment. It has been said that the rule rests upon equitable principles and upon the broad principles of justice. Cauble v. Cauble, 2 S.W.2d 967 (Tex. Civ. App. 1927, writ dism'd). The rule is generally stated as binding a party and those in privity with him. See Kirby Lumber Corp. v. Southern Lumber Co., 145 Tex. 151, 196 S.W.2d 387 (1946); Cauble v. Cauble, supra; Evans v. McKay, 212 S.W. 680 (Tex. Civ. App. 1919, writ dism'd); Smith v. Wood, 115 Ga. App. 265, 154 S.E.2d 646 (1967); 46 Am. Jur. 2d, Judgments, § 394 (1969). Section 83 of the Restatement of Judgments (1942) states that a person who is not a party but who is in privity with the parties in an action terminating in a valid judgment is bound by the rules of res judicata. A comment to this section says in part: "Privity is a word which expresses the idea that as to certain matters and in certain circumstances persons who are not parties to an action but who are connected with it in their interests are affected by the judgment with reference to interests involved in the action, as if they were parties. . . . The statement that a person is bound by . . . a judgment as a privy is a short method of stating that under the circumstances and for the purpose of the case at hand he is bound by . . . all or some of the rules of res judicata by way of merger, bar or collateral estoppel." It has been emphasized that privity is not established by the mere fact that persons may happen to be interested in the same question or in proving the same state of facts. Coleman v. Bosworth, 180 Iowa 975, 164 N.W. 238 (1917); Smith v. Wood, supra. Also, that privity connotes those who are in law so connected with a party to the judgment as to have such an identity of interest that the party to the judgment represented the same legal right. Hixson v. Kansas City, 361 Mo. 1211, 239 S.W.2d 341 (1951); 46 Am. Jur. 2d, Judgments, § 532 (1969). But it is also recognized that there is no generally prevailing definition of privity which can be automatically applied to all cases involving the doctrine of res judicata and the determination of who are privies requires careful examination into the circumstances of each case as it arises. 50 C.J.S. Judgments § 788 (1947); 46 Am. Jur. 2d Judgments, § 532 (1969). In Kirby Lumber Corp. v. Southern Lumber Co., supra, privity was defined as meaning the mutual or successive relationship to the same rights of property; and it was said that persons are privy to a judgment whose succession to the rights of property therein adjudicated are derived through or under one or the other of the parties to the action, and which rights accrued subsequent to the commencement of the action. It has also been said that the Restatement definition corresponds to results generally reached by the courts, the elements of which are summarized in these words: "[t]he word 'privy' includes those who control an action although not parties to it . . .; those whose interests are represented by a party to the action . . .; successors in interests. . . ." Developments in the Law—Res Judicata, 65 Harv. L. Rev. 818, 856 (1952).

The rules of res judicata rest upon the policy of protecting a party from being twice vexed for the same cause, together with that of achieving judicial economy in precluding a party who has had a fair trial from relitigating the same issue. Bernhard v. Bank of America National Trust & Savings Ass'n, 19 Cal. 2d 807, 122 P.2d 892 (1942); and see Semmel, Collateral Estoppel, Mutuality and Joinder of Parties, 68 Colum. L. Rev. 1457 (1968). Due process requires that the rule of collateral estoppel operate only against persons who have had their day in court either as a party to the prior suit or as a privy, and, where not so, that, at the least, the presently asserted interest was actually and adequately represented in the prior trial. As to the latter, § 84 of the Restatement of Judgments (1942) states that a person who is not a party but who controls an action is bound by the adjudications of litigated matters as if he were a party where he has a proprietary or financial interest in the judgment or in the determination of a question of fact or of law with reference to the same subject matter or transaction.

The rationale of decisions in other jurisdictions that have considered the problem at hand in the context of the employer-employee relationship is instructive. This is illustrated by Makariw v. Rinard, 336 F.2d 333 (3rd Cir. 1964). Rinard took his automobile to YBH Sales and Service, Inc. for servicing, and accompanied YBH's mechanic, Makariw, on a road test. While Makariw was driving, the car hit a "pothole" and skidded into another car and an embankment. Makariw was killed and Rinard was injured. Rinard sued YBH for personal injuries and contended that Makariw's negligence caused the accident. Judgment was in his favor based on findings of negligence against Makariw. Makariw's Administratrix thereafter brought a suit against Rinard under the Pennsylvania Wrongful Death and Survival Acts. The federal district court granted Rinard's motion to dismiss the action on the grounds that any recovery would be barred by the prior finding in the Rinard suit that Makariw had been guilty of negligence, which was conclusive under the doctrine of collateral estoppel; it was reasoned that the derivative liability of the employer for the employee's negligence established the employee's privity with the employer and bound him to the previous fact findings. The court of appeals for the Third Circuit reversed for the stated reason that the legal representative of the employee had not had her day in court on the critical issues which premised her suit and was not bound by a final determination in the prior suit against the employer. Reliance was placed on decisions giving particular emphasis to considerations here present: the plaintiff in the later suit was neither a party to the former action nor in privity with any party in the sense that his rights were derived from one who was a party; and the cause of action always had been that of the present plaintiff who had no voice in the conduct of the prior suit, with no right to examine witnesses or to take other action to protect his interests. See Rice v. Ringsby Truck Lines, 302 F.2d 550 (7th Cir. 1962); Pesce v. Brecher, 302 Mass. 211, 19 N.E.2d 36 (1939); see also in accord, Adams v. Woodfin, 243 Ark. 348, 419 S.W.2d 796 (1967), and Shelley v. Gipson, 218 Tenn. 1, 400 S.W.2d 709 (1966). A like position was taken in Bolstad v. Egleson, 326 S.W.2d 506 (Tex. Civ. App. 1959, writ ref'd n.r.e.), without discussion.

The suit at bar is a separate and distinct action for redress for personal injuries. Mrs. Benson was not a party to the former action instituted by the Porters following her non-suit and they did not represent her in her claims against Wanda, respondent here. It was not shown that Mrs. Benson participated in, or exercised any control over, the trial in the Porter suit, or that she had any right to do so. She was not shown to have any beneficial interest in the recovery of damages for personal injuries on behalf of the Porters. In our view, the requirements of due process compel the conclusion that a privity relationship which will support application of the rules of res judicata does not exist under these circumstances. Accordingly, we hold that the fact findings and judgment in the Porter suit do not bar Mrs. Benson, and that she is entitled to her day in court in prosecuting this action in her own right.

The judgments below are reversed and the cause is remanded for trial.

---

## NOTES AND QUESTIONS

(1) *Other Applications of Privity Concept. Benson* sets forth the general principles by which a person not a party, but in privity with a party, may be bound by a valid judgment. The principal case also presents conditions under which a person would be held *not* to be in privity. What factual situation would adequately demonstrate privity to justify the application of the doctrine of res judicata? Consider *Lemon v. Spann,* 633 S.W.2d 568 (Tex. Civ. App.—Texarkana 1982, writ ref'd n.r.e.), demonstrating the application of the concept of privity to individuals on both sides of the versus. In Action 1, Blundell sued George Lemon, Sr., a real estate agent, to impose an equitable lien or enforce specific performance of a contract for the sale of certain land to Blundell and another, Spann. Alternatively, Blundell sought damages for fraudulent conduct on the part of Lemon, Sr. The conveyance to Blundell and Spann had been stopped by the sale of the land to George Lemon, Jr. The sale to Lemon, Jr., had been arranged by Lemon, Sr. In Action 1, Lemon, Sr., obtained a partial summary judgment on the lien and specific performance dimensions of the case and then obtained a severance of those issues from the remaining fraud allegations so that Lemon, Jr., could deal freely with the property. Blundell appealed on the ground that the fiduciary relationship with Lemon, Sr., as real estate agent entitled him to a constructive trust. The Court of Civil Appeals affirmed the lower court's judgment, holding that the matter of fiduciary relationship had not been presented as a fact issue in opposition to Lemon, Sr.'s motion for summary judgment and therefore could not be presented on appeal. Action 2

was filed before the appellate court decided the appeal of Action 1. In Action 2, Spann and Blundell sued Lemon, Jr., and the estate of Lemon, Sr., who had died in the meantime. They alleged fraud against both Lemons, breach of confidential relationship between Lemon, Sr., and Blundell, and authorization or ratification by Lemon, Jr., of his father's actions. The plaintiffs sought a constructive trust on the land and actual and punitive damages. The case went to trial with Lemon, Jr., as the only defendant. The trial court, based on a jury verdict, imposed a constructive trust on the property. Lemon, Jr. appealed, and the Court of Civil Appeals reversed on the basis of the doctrine of res judicata. The plaintiffs contended on appeal that the doctrine did not apply in that there were different parties (Spann as a new plaintiff and Lemon, Jr., as a new defendant) and different issues in the second suit (e.g., pursuit of a constructive trust, which was not sought at the trial court level in the first action). After reviewing the concept of privity in a manner similar to *Benson,* the court responded to the different-parties argument:

> The rights of Harlin Spann and George Lemon, Jr. in the tract of land were mutual to those of Blundell and George Lemon, Sr., respectively. Further, they were derivative. Spann conceded that any interest he had in the property was to be through Blundell. Any judgment against George Lemon, Jr. is dependent on first establishing a cause of action against George Lemon, Sr., for fraud or breach of a fiduciary relationship. On these bases we determine that Spann and George Lemon, Jr. were privies to the parties in the first suit.

Regarding the different-issues argument, the court stated:

> [A]ppellees say that, as we recognized in our earlier opinion, they did not litigate the merits of imposing a constructive trust in the prior suit. However, this was an equitable matter which might have been litigated in the first suit seeking to enforce an equitable lien or specific performance. Even appellees recognized this when they asserted it on their earlier appeal as the basis to bar the granting of the partial summary judgment in the first suit. That judgment barred the equitable proceedings seeking a claim against the land and severed the fraud claims seeking damages. The instant judgment imposing a constructive trust is barred because that matter might have been litigated by the parties or their privies in the first suit.

(2) *Types of Claims.* Did *Benson* raise a plea of merger and bar or a plea of collateral estoppel? What about *Lemon?*

## § 8.03 Election of Remedies

### BOCANEGRA v. AETNA LIFE INS. CO.

*605 S.W.2d 848 (Tex. 1980)*

POPE, Justice.

Plaintiff, Janie Bocanegra, sued Aetna Life Insurance Company on a group medical and hospital policy and recovered judgment upon a jury finding that certain medical and hospital services she needed resulted from a non-occupational disease.[1] Previously Mrs. Bocanegra had filed with

[1] The court instructed the jury by using a part of the definition in the group policy:

You are instructed that the term "NON-OCCUPATIONAL DISEASE" means a disease which does not arise, and which is not caused or contributed to by, or as a consequence of, any disease which arises, out of or in the course of any employment or occupation for compensation or profit.

the Industrial Accident Board a claim, which she settled, for an occupational injury. The court of civil appeals held the settlement was an election which barred her later suit. That court reversed the judgment of the trial court and rendered judgment for Aetna. 572 S.W.2d 355. We hold that Mrs. Bocanegra did not make an informed election that barred her in this action. We reverse the judgment of the court of civil appeals and affirm the judgment of the trial court.

Mrs. Bocanegra began working for Clegg Company in 1965 as a book binder. Her work required her to lift and handle books. As she got out of bed one morning in April of 1975, she experienced a sharp pain in her lower back. She reported for work but did not tell her employer about her pain. On June 3, 1975, again on arising from bed, she had another severe pain, but still did not report any job-related injury. On June 29 the pain became so severe that she went to the emergency room of the Baptist Hospital. Her physician, Dr. Larry Miller, prescribed conservative treatment including two weeks in traction. He told Mrs. Bocanegra that she might have hurt her back at work. Failing to get any relief and after extensive tests, on August 11, she underwent surgery for a slipped disc. Dr. William Dossman performed the surgery. Mrs. Bocanegra never gave notice to her employer that she had sustained an occupational injury, but on August 18, after her operation, she filed with the Texas Industrial Accident Board her Notice of Injury or Occupational Disease and Claim for Compensation. In that notice she wrote, "I was lifting telephone books in the course and scope of my employment and injured my back and body generally." In her accompanying hardship affidavit, she swore, "I was hurt on the job on the above date while working for the above employer." On July 21, she filed a claim under the Aetna group policy on which she checked the box which asked if the claim was based on an accident. She also wrote on that claim form that the accident occurred "At work by lifting and bending." On July 29, she filed a second claim with Aetna on which she checked "No" to the question whether her claim was based on an accident. She also filed a claim with American Security Life Insurance Company on September 13 in which she stated that the accident occurred at work while lifting and bending. On September 17, she filed a similar claim with Presidential Life Insurance Company which gave the same information.

On October 27, Mrs. Bocanegra settled her worker's compensation claim for a general injury for $12,000 which the compensation carrier paid. The settlement agreement was "solely for lost wages and future impaired earning capacity," and it expressly excluded any payment for past or future medical or hospital expenses, the items that are here in question.

Mrs. Bocanegra, after her surgery and the settlement of her claim for an occupational injury, commenced these proceedings against Aetna to recover the amount of her medical and hospital bills. She asserted, and the jury found, that the medical and hospital services resulted from a non-occupational injury. She supported this claim by her own testimony that she was not injured on the job but that she did not know that fact until after her operation. At that time Dr. Dossman, her surgeon, told her that her back problem was the result of a degenerative disc disease that pre-dated but lingered after the onset of the initial back pain. She denied that she at any time ever told her doctors that she had sustained an injury on the job. Dr. Dossman confirmed Mrs. Bocanegra's testimony and testified that, in his opinion, her disc trouble was not related to her occupation. He testified: "About half of the time in this problem there is no known injury or cause of the problem, it just happens. About half of the time there is a history of some specific injury producing the problem." The court of civil appeals concluded that Mrs. Bocanegra's claim for an occupational injury was, as a matter of law, inconsistent with the state of facts upon which she later relied to obtain a judgment in her suit on the health policy that she had a non-occupational injury. The court rendered judgment that she take nothing.

The doctrine of election, although widely criticized,[2] survives in wide-ranging branches of the law that stretch from the widow's election in probate law to the choice in contract law between a suit for damages and one for rescission. *See* 5 Williston on Contracts §§ 683–688 (3d ed. Jaeger 1961). Election, an affirmative defense, has been held to bar remedies, rights, and inconsistent positions arising out of the same state of facts. 25 Am. Jur. 2d *Election of Remedies* § 7 (1966); Annot., 116 A.L.R. 601, 602 (1938). The situations in which an election might arise are so variable that an all-inclusive definition has been elusive, and discussions of the doctrine often borrow terms that may also appropriately relate to other affirmative defenses. For that reason, election is often confused with or likened to judicial estoppel, equitable estoppel, ratification, waiver or satisfaction. Those doctrines sometimes do not reach a situation that equity and good conscience need to reach through the doctrine of election.

A judicial estoppel may arise when a question necessary for the determination of a prior adjudication is decided. It constitutes a bar to a redetermination of that issue in a different cause. *Benson v. Wanda Petroleum Co.,* 468 S.W.2d 361 (Tex. 1971); *Long v. Knox,* 155 Tex. 581, 291 S.W.2d 292 (1956); *Houston Terminal Land Co. v. Westergreen,* 119 Tex. 204, 27 S.W.2d 526 (1930). Equitable estoppel differs from each of the above defenses, because it requires some deception that is practiced upon a party who relies upon it to his prejudice. *Barfield v. Howard M. Smith Co. of Amarillo,* 426 S.W.2d 834 (Tex. 1968); *Concord Oil Co. v. Alco Oil and Gas Corp.,* 387 S.W.2d 635 (Tex. 1965); *Gulbenkian v. Penn,* 151 Tex. 412, 252 S.W.2d 929 (1952). A ratification rests upon a manifestation of assent to confirm one's prior act or that of another. It may occur without any prior litigation and in the absence of any change of position by or prejudice to the other party. *Texas & Pac. Coal & Oil Co. v. Kirtley,* 288 S.W. 619 (Tex. Civ. App.—Eastland 1926, writ ref'd). Waiver, the voluntary relinquishment of a known right, is sometimes spoken of as intentional conduct inconsistent with the assertion of a known right. *Ford v. State Farm Mut. Auto. Ins. Co.,* 550 S.W.2d 663, 667 (Tex. 1977). Full satisfaction will bar a claim because the law will not permit double redress. *James and Company, Inc. v. Statham,* 558 S.W.2d 865 (Tex. 1977); *McMillen v. Klingensmith,* 467 S.W.2d 193 (Tex.1971); *Bradshaw v. Baylor University,* 126 Tex. 99, 84 S.W.2d 703 (1935).

The single underlying principle of the election doctrine has not been found. Estoppel in some form, ratification and unjust enrichment have been suggested as the basic reasons for an election, and in many instances they suffice. *Schenck v. State Line Telephone Co.,* 238 N.Y. 308, 144 N.E. 592 (1924); *Metroflight, Inc. v. Shaffer,* 581 S.W.2d 704 (Tex. Civ. App.—Dallas 1979, writ ref'd n.r.e.). The court of civil appeals in this case has, perhaps more soundly, held that inconsistency will bar an action in instances of manifest injustice. Even though the inconsistent position may not fit the mold of a better defined principle, an election will bar recovery when the inconsistency in the assertion of a remedy, right, or state of facts is so unconscionable, dishonest, contrary to fair dealing, or so stultifies the legal process or trifles with justice or the courts as to be manifestly unjust.

A similar loosely defined but useful equitable doctrine is the constructive trust. It is unlike other trusts, but equity raised it up in the name of good conscience, fair dealing, honesty, and

---

[2] It has been criticized because of its lack of any fixed legal underpinnings and called the following: a legal weed that judicial gardeners should root out, Hine, *Election of Remedies: A Criticism,* 26 Harv. L. Rev. 707, 719 (1913); a legal delusion, Note, *Election of Remedies: A Delusion?* 38 Colum. L. Rev. 292, 293 (1938); an anachronism, Fraser, *Election of Remedies: An Anachronism,* 29 Okla. L. Rev. 1 (1976); a problem child of the law, Merrem, *Election of Remedies,* 8 Sw. L.J. 109 (1954); and a remedy that has no independent viability, LaBay, *Election of Remedies: The California Basis,* 19 Hastings L. Rev. 1233, 1246 (1968).

good morals. *Omohundro v. Matthews,* 161 Tex. 367, 341 S.W.2d 401, 405 (1960). "A constructive trust is the formula through which the conscience of equity finds expression." *Beatty v. Guggenheim Exploration Co.,* 225 N.Y. 380, 386, 122 N.E. 378, 380 (1919). Equity provides the idea of constructive trusts as a tool to "frustrate skullduggery," 4 R. Powell, *Real Property* § 593 (1949), even though that kind of a trust is also grounded upon elusive principles.[3] Such a trust is purely a creature of equity. Its form is practically without limit, and its existence depends upon the circumstances. *Simmons v. Wilson,* 216 S.W.2d 847, 849 (Tex. Civ. App.—Waco 1949, no writ).

The election doctrine, therefore, may constitute a bar to relief when (1) one successfully exercises an informed choice (2) between two or more remedies, rights, or states of facts (3) which are so inconsistent as to (4) constitute manifest injustice. *See Custom Leasing, Inc. v. Texas Bank & Trust Co. of Dallas,* 491 S.W.2d 869 (Tex. 1973).

A number of seemingly inconsistent positions do not rise to the level of an election which will bar recovery. One may, for example, plead alternative and inconsistent facts without being barred. Rules 48 and 51, Texas Rules of Civil Procedure, authorize such procedures. One who pleads alternative or inconsistent facts or remedies against two or more parties may settle with one of them on the basis of one remedy or state of facts and still recover a judgment against the others based on the pleaded alternative or inconsistent remedies or facts. By analogy, an insurer's voluntary payment to a worker of weekly compensation benefits will not bar the defense that there was no accidental injury. *Lopez v. Associated Employers Ins. Co.,* 330 S.W.2d 522 (Tex. Civ. App.—San Antonio 1959, writ ref'd). *See also Southern Underwriters v. Schoolcraft,* 138 Tex. 323, 158 S.W.2d 991 (1942). The basis for the holding was to encourage prompt payments of compensation following injury. A holding that the payments were inconsistent with a denial of an accidental injury or that they constituted an admission of an injury would discourage prompt payment of weekly benefits. *Hartford Accident and Indemnity Co. v. Hale,* 400 S.W.2d 310, 312–13 (Tex.1966).

There is no election, that is, no inconsistency in choices, when one first unsuccessfully pursues a right or remedy which proves unfounded and then pursues the one that is allowed. *Poe v. Continental Oil & Cotton Co.,* 231 S.W. 717 (Tex. Com. App. 1921, holding approved); *Schwartz v. National Loan & Investment Co.,* 133 S.W.2d 133 (Tex. Civ. App.—Dallas 1939, writ ref'd); *Breland v. Guaranty Building & Loan Co.,* 119 S.W.2d 690 (Tex. Civ. App.—Fort Worth 1938, writ ref'd); 25 Am. Jur. 2d, *Election of Remedies* § 9. One may assert concurrent but inconsistent remedies or distinct causes of action against different persons arising out of independent transactions. *Shriro Corp. v. Ward,* 570 S.W.2d 395 (Tex. 1978); *American Savings & Loan Ass'n of Houston v. Musick,* 531 S.W.2d 581, 588–89 (Tex. 1975); *Custom Leasing, Inc. v. Texas Bank & Trust Co. of Dallas,* 491 S.W.2d 869, 871 (Tex. 1973); *Liberty Mutual Ins. Co. v. First National Bank in Dallas,* 151 Tex. 12, 245 S.W.2d 237 (1951).

One's choice between inconsistent remedies, rights or states of facts does not amount to an election which will bar further action unless the choice is made with a full and clear understanding of the problem, facts, and remedies essential to the exercise of an intelligent choice. *Leonard v. Hare,* 161 Tex. 28, 336 S.W.2d 619 (1960); *Slay v. Burnett Trust,* 143 Tex. 621, 187 S.W.2d

---

[3] "Without much conscious purpose or plan we have created this shambling creature. It is time to fence it in." J. Dawson, Unjust Enrichment 26 (1951). "It thus constitutes a fenceless field with hazy boundaries." 4 R. Powell, Real Property § 593, 565 (1949).

377, 379 (1945); *Loveless v. Texas Employers Ins. Ass'n,* 269 S.W.2d 454 (Tex. Civ. App.—Austin 1954, writ ref'd); 5 Williston on Contracts § 685 (3d ed. Jaeger 1961); Merrem, *Election of Remedies in Texas,* 8 Sw. L.J. 109, 110 (1954); 25 Am. Jur. 2d, *Election of Remedies* § 21 (1966). An exception to that rule exists when the choice of a course of action, though made in ignorance of the facts, will cause harm to an innocent party. *Slay v. Burnett Trust, supra* at 394; *Employers' Indemnity Corp. v. Felter,* 277 S.W. 376 (Tex. Com. App. 1925).

This present case aptly illustrates the reason that election should not bar a suit when a previous course of action or a settlement for less than the claim was grounded upon uncertain and undetermined facts. The definition of an occupational disease contained in section 20 of article 8306 is itself complex and difficult:

> Whenever the term "Occupational Disease" is used in the Workmen's Compensation Laws of this State, such term shall be construed to mean any disease arising out of and in the course of employment which causes damage or harm to the physical structure of the body and such other diseases or infections as naturally result therefrom. An "Occupational Disease" shall also include damage or harm to the physical structure of the body occurring as the result of repetitious physical traumatic activities extending over a period of time and arising in the course of employment; provided, that the date of the cumulative injury shall be the date disability was caused thereby. Ordinary diseases of life to which the general public is exposed outside of the employment shall not be compensable, except where such diseases follow as an incident to an "Occupational Disease" or "Injury" as defined in this section.

Under that definition, Mrs. Bocanegra's injury may have been an occupational one which was compensable, it may have been an "ordinary disease of life" which was not, or it may have been both. Tex. Rev. Civ. Stat. Ann. art. 8306, § 22. Many diseases, do not fit neatly within an either/or distribution, and the dispute whether such a condition is compensable or not is an ongoing one. Uncertainty in many complex areas of medicine and law is more the rule than the exception. It would be a harsh rule that charges a layman with knowledge of medical causes when, as in this case, physicians and lawyers do not know them. Mrs. Bocanegra's first physician, Dr. Miller, was of the opinion that the lifting and bending at the work bench was the cause of an occupational injury. Dr. Dossman advised her to the contrary after the surgery. The settlement agreement that Mrs. Bocanegra made with her compensation carrier showed that the carrier disputed liability, the period of time lost for the claimed occupational disease, and past and future medical expenses for which the carrier paid nothing. Mrs. Bocanegra lacked the requisite knowledge to bind her to an informed election.

Some of the Texas decisions cannot be harmonized, and they need discussion. *Seamans Oil Co. v. Guy,* 115 Tex. 93, 276 S.W. 424 (1925), while reaching a correct result, intermingles the doctrines of election, estoppel, and satisfaction. J. H. Guy and wife, lessors of an oil and mineral lease instituted suit against Seamans Oil Company and Empire Gas & Fuel Company for the cancellation of the lease. During the pendency of the suit against them, Seamans and Empire Gas could exercise none of the rights accorded by the lease, but they kept the lease alive by tendering timely delay rental payments which the Guys refused to accept. Just before the lease expired by its own terms, the Guys adopted an inconsistent posture, dismissed their suit for cancellation and drew a check on the bank for the delay rentals that they had previously rejected. By that time, the Guys' suit had fully accomplished its purpose to defeat any drilling or other operations. The court held that "[i]t would be shocking to a sense of justice to hold that the Guys could destroy the value of the leasehold by the claim that it did not exist and at the same time collect delay rentals upon the basis that it was a valid lease." The opinion, though primarily grounded upon an election, is an instance of full satisfaction which the Guys had already achieved through their lawsuit. Even though it was dismissed, the suit had fully accomplished the same purpose that a favorable judgment would have achieved. *Seamans* quotes from 10 Ruling Case Law 703, 704:

> If one having a right to pursue one of several inconsistent remedies makes his election, institutes suit, and prosecutes it to final judgment or receives anything of value under the claim thus asserted, or if the other party has been affected adversely, such election constitutes an estoppel thereafter to pursue another and inconsistent remedy. And where the right in the subsequent suit is inconsistent with that set up in the former suit, as distinguished from a merely inconsistent remedy, the party is estopped though the former suit may not have proceeded to judgment. But where the inconsistency is in the remedies it is generally considered that there is no estoppel where the former suit was dismissed without trial or before judgment.

The quotation is an early statement of the election doctrine and contains errors. An election may arise short of one's prosecution of a claim to final judgment. One may also receive something by way of settlement, even of substantial value, under an uncertain claim without making an election which bars recovery against another person. The quotation may be illustrative of some situations which might rise to the level of an election, but it is an unreliable statement of a general rule, and we reject it.

*Lomas and Nettleton Co. v. Huckabee,* 58 S.W.2d 863 (Tex. 1977) relied upon *Seamans, supra,* in holding there was an election. The Huckabees first asserted in their lawsuit that two insurance companies had insured the Huckabees' real and personal property that was destroyed in a fire. The Huckabees, upon the strength of that state of facts, recovered in a settlement one hundred percent of their claim for the destroyed realty and eighty percent of their claim for the destroyed personalty. Their lawsuit was then dismissed with prejudice. After succeeding with their claim that their property was insured, they adopted the inconsistent position that it was not insured and sued their agent for his neglect. We held that the Huckabees, after successfully asserting their claim on one state of facts and receiving almost the whole of their claim, would not be permitted a second recovery against another party by denying the truth of that state of facts. The case was correctly decided, but the quotation from *Seamans,* as discussed above, includes errors concerning the election doctrine. *Cf. Shriro Corp. v. Ward,* 570 S.W.2d 395 (Tex. 1978).

The court of civil appeals in *Metroflight, Inc. v. Shaffer,* 581 S.W.2d 704 (Tex. Civ. App.—Dallas 1979, writ ref'd n.r.e.), followed but criticized *Huckabee.* As is characteristic of this whole area of law, the opinion mixes equitable estoppel, ratification, satisfaction, judicial estoppel, unjust enrichment and other matters. Perhaps the underlying flaw in the analysis of the court of civil appeals in *Metroflight* is its basic assumption. Metroflight had sued in federal court claiming that it had insurance coverage for losses arising out of a plane crash. The defendant insurer denied coverage but later paid Metroflight eighty percent of the total claim. Metroflight, after dismissing its action in which it asserted insurance coverage, proceeded with a suit against its agent for damages on the basis of the inconsistent fact that the plane was not insured. The trial court held that Metroflight was barred by election. The court of civil appeals affirmed but criticized the *Huckabee* case, which it felt bound to follow. The *Metroflight* court assumed that Metroflight had dismissed its federal court claim asserting insurance coverage because pre-trial discovery had shown that claim to be groundless and certain to fail. This assumption, twice stated, is wrong. The insurer's settlement for eighty percent of the very large coverage-based claim shows the validity and strength of the claim that insurance actually existed.

In *Seamans, Huckabee,* and *Metroflight,* the respective plaintiffs realized most or all of what they claimed by asserting facts about which they were certain. By contrast, however, the fact upon which Mrs. Bocanegra relied in settling with her compensation carrier, the nature of her complex disease, was highly uncertain which was evidenced by the small settlement which included none of her hospital and medical bills.

The judgment of the court of civil appeals is reversed and the judgment of the trial court is affirmed.

CAMPBELL, J., concurring.

GARWOOD, J., not sitting.

CAMPBELL, Justice, concurring.

We should not attempt to draw an artificial distinction between this case and the decisions in *Huckabee* and *Metroflight* merely to avoid an admission that those decisions were erroneous. The claims in those cases were as uncertain as the claims in this case. Except for uncertainty there would obviously have been no compromise and settlement. This decision establishes a rule of law that whether a settlement with a defendant will be deemed an election barring suit against another defendant, upon facts inconsistent with those asserted to obtain the settlement, will be ultimately determined by this Court's opinion as to the degree of uncertainty as to the facts inconsistently asserted.

*Seamans Oil Co. v. Guy* was not decided upon the law of elections but was decided upon a clear-cut equitable estoppel. This Court in *Huckabee* followed a dictum quotation from Ruling Case Law which is incompatible with recognized principles of Texas procedure and policy. A party may plead and prove totally inconsistent claims and defenses in Texas. *Deal v. Madison,* 576 S.W.2d 409 (Tex. Civ. App.—Dallas 1978, writ ref'd n.r.e.); Rule 48, T.R.C.P.

Settlement agreements are highly favored in the law because they are a means of amicably resolving doubts and preventing lawsuits. *Miller v. Republic National Life Insurance Company,* 559 F.2d 426 (5th Cir. 1977); *Republic National Life Insurance Company v. Sussman,* 564 F.2d 98 (5th Cir. 1977); *Alvarez v. Employers' Fire Insurance Company,* 531 S.W.2d 218 (Tex. Civ. App.—Amarillo 1975, no writ); *Coastal States Gas Producing Company v. Apollo Industrial X-ray, Inc.,* 467 S.W.2d 239 (Tex. Civ. App.—Corpus Christi 1971, no writ); *Fidelity-Southern Fire Insurance Company v. Whitman,* 422 S.W.2d 552 (Tex. Civ. App.—Houston [14th Dist.] 1967, writ ref'd n.r.e.); *State v. Cook,* 407 S.W.2d 876 (Tex. Civ. App.—Waco 1966, writ ref'd n.r.e.); *Pearce v. Texas Employers Insurance Association,* 403 S.W.2d 493 (Tex. Civ. App.—Dallas 1966, writ ref'd n.r.e.) motion for rehearing overruled per curiam, 412 S.W.2d 647 (Tex. 1967).

Proper regard for these principles compels a conclusion that a mere compromise and settlement of a claim asserting facts inconsistent to those asserted in a claim against a different defendant should not bar the latter claim. The contrary conclusion, in effect, compels a party to proceed to final judgment against two or more defendants instead of settling with a defendant who is desirous of settlement. This would not diminish assertion of inconsistent claims but would merely diminish settlements.

We should concede our error and expressly overrule *Huckabee* and hold there is no election until final judgment on the merits.

---

## HANKS v. GAB BUSINESS SERVICES, INC.

*644 S.W.2d 707 (Tex. 1982)*

SONDOCK, Justice.

This suit arose from an alleged breach of a contract between Petitioner, Don K. Hanks, d/b/a Hanks Claims Service ("Hanks") and GAB Business Services, Inc. ("GAB") for the sale of an insurance adjusting business. The trial court rendered judgment for GAB. The court of appeals affirmed. 626 S.W.2d 564. We reverse the judgments of the courts below and render judgment for Hanks.

In May of 1977, Hanks contracted with GAB for the sale of his insurance adjustment business. The contract specifically included accounts receivable, ninety-five items of office furniture, goodwill, and a five-year covenant not to compete. The contract price of $95,000 provided for payments of $28,000 at closing, $33,500 due one year from the date of closing, and the balance due two years from closing. In connection with the sales contract, Hanks signed an employment contract with GAB, which also contained a covenant not to compete.

Approximately one year later, after GAB had paid the $33,500 installment, a dispute between the parties arose and Hanks resigned his position with GAB. Hanks commenced competing with GAB in violation of the non-competition agreement. Hanks continued to compete until March of 1979, when he voluntarily ceased competition.

During the time that Hanks was competing, GAB filed suit seeking injunctive relief and attorney's fees for Hanks' violation of the covenant not to compete. In July of 1979, after GAB failed to tender the last installment, which was then overdue, Hanks filed an amended answer and counterclaim for the final payment, exemplary damages, and attorneys fees. Later, GAB filed an amended petition seeking damages in addition to injunctive relief and asking to be excused from the final installment.

In response to the special issues submitted at trial, the jury found that GAB had been damaged in the amount of $1,200 for the eight month period in which Hanks actively competed in violation of the non-competition agreement and $5,850 future damages for the remainder of the five-year covenant period. GAB moved for judgment, requesting the permanent injunction and excuse from paying the final installment, in addition to the award of damages and $6,000 stipulated attorney's fees. At that time, the trial court required GAB to make an election between the jury award and the excuse remedy, whereupon GAB elected to be excused from making the final $33,500 payment. The trial court then entered judgment, excusing GAB from making the final installment, and awarding attorneys' fees on the contract.

The question presented by this case is: Did Hanks' breach of the covenant not to compete excuse GAB's obligation to pay the final installment due for the business purchased? The court of appeals applied the rule of Morgan v. Singley, 560 S.W.2d 746 (Tex. Civ. App.—Texarkana 1977, no writ) and held that GAB was excused from making the final payment. We do not agree.

A prerequisite to the remedy of excuse of performance is that covenants in a contract must be mutually dependent promises. Morgan v. Singley, *supra.* In the instant case, this rule does not apply because the covenant not to compete should properly be classified as an independent promise. "The rule is that 'when a covenant goes only to part of the consideration on both sides and a breach may be compensated for in damages, it is to be regarded as an independent covenant, unless this is contrary to the expressed intent of the parties.' " World Broadcasting System, Inc. v. Eagle Broadcasting Co., 162 S.W.2d 463, 465 (Tex. Civ. App.—San Antonio 1942, writ dism'd) citing 17 C.J.S., Contracts, § 344, at 800. The covenant not to compete in the Hanks/GAB contract only goes to part of the contract. The contract covers numerous items and the parties had bargained for a value of $5,000 to be assigned to the covenant not to compete, although the value assigned was admittedly for tax reasons. Further, there is no express language in the contract that indicates the parties intended the covenants to be mutually dependent. As explained in Landscape Design & Construction, Inc. v. Harold Thomas Excavating, Inc., 604 S.W.2d 374, 376 (Tex. Civ. App.—Dallas, 1980, writ ref'd n.r.e.), "A breach of a covenant which is part of a legally enforceable contract gives rise to a cause of action for damages rather than affecting the enforceability of the provisions of the agreement." See Reinert v. Lawson, 113 S.W.2d 293, 295 (Tex. Civ. App.—Waco 1938, no writ). In this case, Hanks' breach may be adequately compensated by damages.

Any right GAB had to partially rescind the contract when Hanks breached the covenant not to compete has been waived. A party who elects to treat a contract as continuing deprives himself of any excuse for ceasing performance on his own part. See Board of Regents, University of Texas v. S & G Construction Co., 529 S.W.2d 90 (Tex. Civ. App.—Austin 1975, writ ref'd n.r.e.); Houston Belt & Terminal Ry. Co. v. J. Weingarten, Inc., 421 S.W.2d 431 (Tex. Civ. App.—Houston [1st Dist.] 1967, writ ref'd n.r.e.). At all times during the dispute and subsequent litigation, GAB chose to treat the contract as continuing. GAB retained all the assets of the business and continued its operation. Moreover, GAB did not pursue its excuse remedy until it had already instituted action to enforce the contract, well over a year after Hanks' breach of the covenant not to compete.

In holding that GAB had not elected its remedy prior to judgment, the court of appeals relied on this Court's decision in Bocanegra v. Aetna Life Ins. Co., 605 S.W.2d 848 (Tex. 1980). The court reasoned that neither GAB's filing of the lawsuit nor its retention of the business operated as a "conclusive choice" that would create a "manifest injustice" within the meaning of the Bocanegra test. Similarly, the court held that GAB's actions did not waive its excuse remedy, reasoning that GAB's actions were only consistent with the closing of the contract and did not constitute "intentional inconsistent conduct." We disagree. At the time of Hanks' breach, GAB could have elected to partially rescind the contract. Because GAB retained the assets of the business and chose to treat the contract as continuing, it could not elect the excuse remedy prior to judgment.

Finally, Hanks argues that there is no evidence to support the jury's finding of $5,850 future damages for the remaining period of the five year covenant. The court of appeals did not reach this question because it held that GAB was excused from performance. We disagree with the trial court's judgment on this point. The bulk of GAB's evidence on future damages was excluded by the trial court. The remaining testimony consisted of speculation as to future losses. GAB only introduced records of claims and gross amounts rather than completed work or overhead figures necessary to compute future profits.

The judgments of the courts below are reversed and judgment is here rendered that Hanks recover the final installment with an offset for the $1,200 damages found by the jury in favor of GAB plus prejudgment interest from June 1, 1979, to date of judgment. In light of the fact that both parties prevailed on their respective actions under the contract, we render judgment that neither party recover attorneys' fees.

---

## NOTES AND QUESTIONS

(1) *Contours of Election Doctrine.* Do you find it strange that Mrs. Bocanegra could collect under one theory, then turn around and collect under the exact opposite theory? What factors were critical to the court's reasoning? Did it make a difference that the kinds of damages sought by Mrs. Bocanegra across the two actions were different and thus she could not be considered to have obtained a double recovery, prevention of which is one objective of the doctrine of election of remedies? Mrs. Bocanegra could have obtained an award of past and future medical expenses under workers' compensation (*See Hedgeman v. Berwind Railway Service Co.,* 512 S.W.2d 827 (Tex. Civ. App.—Houston [14th Dist.] 1974, writ ref'd n.r.e.)), but the settlement struck expressly excluded them. What if she had received such medical expenses in the settlement? Did the amount of money involved affect the court's judgment? The medical expenses in question amounted to $4,500. Was it that Mrs. Bocanegra "honestly" asserted inconsistent theories that prompted the court to hold she had not made an election? What if the first action in the *Bocanegra* case had gone to trial rather than settlement? Would the outcome have been different if the issue of whether Mrs. Bocanegra suffered from an occupational or nonoccupational disease had been litigated and a judgment rendered based on the way the issue was decided? (The settlement agreement between Mrs. Bocanegra and the workers' compensation insurance carrier stated specifically that, notwithstanding the settlement, liability was disputed.) Would litigation and adjudication have converted the case from an election-of-remedies case into a collateral-estoppel case? *Cf. Hardy v. Fleming,* in § 8.01[B][2].

(2) *Consequences of Successful Prosecution of Claim.* A number of workers' compensation cases have held that the prosecution of a claim in proceedings before the Texas Industrial Accident Board (now the Workers' Compensation Commission (WCC)) on one theory and resulting in an award of benefits accepted by the claimant constitutes an election of remedies and bars relitigation on a different theory or for a different measure of damages. *See Hedgeman v. Berwind Railway Service Co.,* 512 S.W.2d 827 (Tex. Civ. App.—Houston [14th Dist.] 1974, writ ref'd n.r.e.); *Moore v. Means,* 549 S.W.2d 417 (Tex. Civ. App.—Beaumont 1977, writ ref'd n.r.e.); *LeJeune v. Gulf States Utilities Co.,* 410 S.W.2d 44 (Tex. Civ. App.—Beaumont 1966, writ ref'd n.r.e.). Unlike *Bocanegra,* these cases went to judgment in the first action rather than to settlement. Does the judicial expenditure of time play a role in whether or not the plaintiff is deemed to have made an election in the earlier action? Reconsider the Supreme Court's statement, "[A]n election will bar recovery when the inconsistency in the assertion of a remedy, right, or state of facts is so unconscionable, dishonest, contrary to fair dealing, or so stultifies the legal process or trifles with justice or the courts as to be manifestly unjust." What does this sentence mean? Does the acceptance or nonacceptance of an award make a difference? In *Grimes v. Jalco, Inc.,* 630 S.W.2d 282 (Tex. App.—Houston [1st Dist.] 1981, writ ref'd n.r.e.), the plaintiff was not

deemed to have made an election when he rejected an IAB (now WCC) award obtained on his asserted theory that he was an employee at the time of injury and filed a common law cause of action for negligence asserting he was either an employee or an independent contractor. The *Grimes* court, referring to *Hedgeman, Moore,* and *LeJeune, above*, stated:

> These three cases are distinguishable from our case in that in each instance a final board award had been accepted by the claimant or a final judgment had been entered in the compensation claim. In this case the award by the IAB has been appealed and no final judgment has been entered. Under these circumstances we hold that an election of remedies has not been made by the appellant.

*See also Hanks v. GAB Business Services, Inc., above*, applying the doctrine in a business dispute in which the plaintiff retained assets under one theory and later tried to pursue a different theory resulting in a different remedy.

(3) *Vitality of Election Doctrine.* After *Bocanegra,* how often do you think the court would find the doctrine of election of remedies applicable? Do you think the court would take the same approach in all kinds of cases? What if the plaintiff had not been Mrs. Bocanegra, an employee lacking knowledge of medicine and seeking workers' compensation benefits, but instead had been a business enterprise pursuing redress? The Supreme Court's position in such a case might be considerably different. *See Hanks v. GAB Business Services, Inc.*, 644 S.W.2d 707 (Tex. 1982), *above*.

The Supreme Court in *Bocanegra* found that Mrs. Bocanegra did not have the requisite knowledge regarding the nature of her injury to bind her to an informed election between inconsistent theories and remedies. How uncertain and undetermined were the facts in *Hanks?* Is it any more fair to impute knowledge and understanding of contract law to a business enterprise than it is to impute knowledge of medicine to an injured individual like Mrs. Bocanegra?

How does *Hanks, above*, square with rules allowing pleading of alternative and inconsistent theories of recovery? *See* Tex. R. Civ. P. 48. Did GAB's retention of assets under the first theory it pled hinder the court's willingness to take the liberal stance normally attending pleading rules? If the Supreme Court had found in its favor, would GAB have made the kind of double recovery that the election-of-remedies doctrine would preclude?

(4) *Pleading Requirements.* Note that if the affirmative defense of election of remedies is relied on to defeat recovery, it must be specifically pled. The defense must be presented to the trial court and cannot be urged for the first time on appeal. The *Bocanegra* case demonstrates that the burden of proof on the proponent may be heavy, but, as *Hanks* demonstrates, the doctrine is still viable and should be considered, especially when the doctrine of res judicata is unavailable.

## § 8.04 The Law of the Case Doctrine

### HUDSON v. WAKEFIELD

*711 S.W.2d 628 (Tex. 1986)*

GONZALEZ, Justice.

This case involves the refusal of a bank to honor a check given as earnest money under a contract for the sale of land. The issue presented is whether, under the doctrine of the "law of the case," our "limited remand" of this cause precluded the assertion of additional related legal theories or defenses.

Robert Hudson and Andy Wright (Purchasers) sued to enforce specific performance of a contract for the sale of real property owned by Marion and Jean Wakefield (Sellers). In the original proceeding, the trial court granted sellers' motion for summary judgment on the grounds that the instrument on which specific performance was sought never attained the status of a contract because the check for earnest money was returned due to insufficient funds. The court of appeals affirmed, holding that a condition precedent under the contract was that purchasers fulfill the requirements of the earnest-money provision. 635 S.W.2d 216. We reversed the judgments of the lower courts and remanded, holding that, as a matter of law, the earnest-money provision was only a covenant. We then remanded the cause to the trial court to determine whether "the return of the earnest money check because of insufficient funds was such a material breach of the contract as to warrant sellers' repudiation of same." 645 S.W.2d 427, 431 (Tex. 1983).

On remand, the case was fully litigated to a jury. Prior to submission of the charge, the trial court allowed sellers to file a trial amendment which asserted fraud in the inducement. Purchasers objected to the trial amendment and to the court's submission of issues thereon. The record, however, fails to contain a statement of facts so that we cannot determine if purchasers objected to evidence of fraudulent inducement or if it was tried by consent. That court also allowed purchasers to file a trial amendment alleging a new theory dealing with ratification. The trial court then submitted several issues to the jury. Upon motion, the trial court disregarded two of the jury's findings: one, that sellers had ratified the contract; and two, that there had been no breach of contract by the purchasers. The trial court then rendered judgment *non obstante veredicto* for the sellers. In an unpublished opinion, the court of appeals affirmed the judgment of the trial court. We affirm the judgment of the court of appeals.

The question is whether, under the "law of the case" doctrine, our remand of the cause to the trial court to determine whether "the return of the earnest money check because of insufficient funds was such a material breach of the contract as to warrant sellers' repudiation of the same" precludes sellers' trial amendment and submission of issues on a theory of fraudulent inducement which would defeat the existence of a valid contract. Purchasers argue that when we remanded the case, the existence of a valid contract became the "law of the case;" therefore, the only issue which could be decided on remand was whether the contract breach was material.

### Law of the Case

The "law of the case" doctrine is defined as that principle under which questions of law decided on appeal to a court of last resort will govern the case throughout its subsequent stages. Trevino v. Turcotte, 564 S.W.2d 682, 685 (Tex. 1978); Governing Bd. v. Pannill, 659 S.W.2d 670, 680 (Tex. App.—Beaumont 1983, writ ref'd n.r.e.); Kropp v. Prather, 526 S.W.2d 283 (Tex. Civ. App.—Tyler 1975, writ ref'd n.r.e.). By narrowing the issues in successive stages of the litigation, the law of the case doctrine is intended to achieve uniformity of decision as well as judicial economy and efficiency. Dessommes v. Dessommes, 543 S.W.2d 165, 169 (Tex. Civ. App.—Texarkana 1976, writ ref'd n.r.e.). The doctrine is based on public policy and is aimed at putting an end to litigation. See Barrows v. Ezer, 624 S.W.2d 613, 617 (Tex. App.—Houston [14th Dist.] 1981, no writ); Elliott v. Moffett, 165 S.W.2d 911 (Tex. Civ. App.—Texarkana 1942, writ ref'd w.o.m.).

The doctrine of the law of the case only applies to questions of law and does not apply to questions of fact. Barrows, 624 S.W.2d at 617; Kropp, 526 S.W.2d at 285. Missouri K. & T. Ry. Co. v. Redus, 55 Tex. Civ. App. 205, 118 S.W. 208 (Dallas 1909, writ ref'd). Further, the doctrine does not necessarily apply when either the issues or the facts presented at successive appeals are not substantially the same as those involved on the first trial. Barrows, 624 S.W.2d at 617; Kropp, 526 S.W.2d at 285; Ralph Williams Gulfgate Chrysler Plymouth, Inc. v. State, 466 S.W.2d 639 (Tex. Civ. App.—Houston [14th Dist.] 1971, writ ref'd n.r.e.). Thus, when in the second trial or proceeding, one or both of the parties amend their pleadings, it may be that the issues or facts have sufficiently changed so that the law of the case no longer applies. See Rose v. Baker, 143 Tex. 202, 183 S.W.2d 438 (1944); Seydler v. Keuper, 133 S.W.2d 189 (Tex. Civ. App.—Austin 1939, writ ref'd); Kropp, 526 S.W.2d at 286.

Limited Remand

When this court remands a case and limits a subsequent trial to a particular issue, the trial court is restricted to a determination of that particular issue. Wall v. East Texas Teachers Credit Union, 549 S.W.2d 232 (Tex. Civ. App.—Texarkana 1977, writ ref'd); McConnell v. Wall, 67 Tex. 352, 5 S.W. 681 (1887). Thus, in a subsequent appeal, instructions given to a trial court in the former appeal will be adhered to and enforced. Wall v. Wall, 143 Tex. 418, 186 S.W.2d 57 (1945, opinion adopted); Dessommes, 543 S.W.2d at 169. In interpreting the mandate of an appellate court, however, the courts should look not only to the mandate itself, but also to the opinion of the court. Wells v. Littlefield, 62 Tex. 28 (1884); Seale v. Click, 556 S.W.2d 95, 96 (Tex. Civ. App.—Eastland 1977, writ ref'd n.r.e.). In this regard, we have observed that "the cases are rare and very exceptional in which this court is warranted in limiting the issues of fact, in reversing and remanding a case where the trial has been by jury; and to authorize such interpretation, it must clearly appear from the decision that it was so intended." Cole v. Estell, 6 S.W. 175, 177 (Tex. 1887). See Price v. Gulf Atlantic Life Ins., 621 S.W.2d 185, 187 (Tex. Civ. App.—Texarkana 1981, writ ref'd n.r.e.).

A critical factor in our determination of this case is that in the first appeal we reviewed a summary judgment. On review of summary judgments, the appellate courts are limited in their considerations of issues and facts. In such a proceeding, the movant is not required to assert every theory upon which he may recover or defend.[1] Thus, when a case comes up for a trial on the merits, the parties may be different, the pleadings may be different, and other causes of action may have been consolidated. See Governing Bd. v. Pannill, 659 S.W.2d 670, 680–81 (Tex. App.—Beaumont 1983, writ ref'd n.r.e.). Other distinctions may be drawn; for instance, in reviewing the evidence to determine whether there are any fact issues in dispute, the appellate court must review the evidence in the light most favorable to the party opposing the motion for summary judgment. Gaines v. Hamman, 163 Tex. 618, 358 S.W.2d 557, 562 (1962). Thus, the context of a summary judgment proceeding is distinguishable from a full trial on the merits.

The distinction between a summary judgment and a trial on the merits in regard to the law of the case doctrine was made in Pannill, where the court noted:

> Also, it is apparent that the record presented on this third appeal, being an appeal after a full and lengthy trial on the merits with the jury acting as a finder of facts, differs in a very material sense from the prior limited appeal. There is no error in the action of the trial court in declining to follow the "law of the case" as pronounced by another Court of

[1] It is important to note, that non-movants are required, in a written answer or response to motion, to expressly present to the trial court all issues that would defeat the movants right to a summary judgment, and failing to do so, they cannot later assign them as error on appeal. City of Houston v. Clear Creek Basin Authority, 589 S.W.2d 671, 679 (Tex. 1979).

Civil Appeals on a vastly different record.659 S.W.2d at 681. In the case at hand, the trial amendments by purchasers and sellers changed both the scope and nature of the lawsuit.

Purchasers argue that our remand language established the law of the case as to the existence of a valid contract. Therefore, they contend the trial court erred in allowing seller's trial amendment and issues asserting fraud in the inducement. We disagree.

In this case, sellers moved for summary judgment, asserting breach of contract by purchasers as a defense. In summary judgment proceedings, the movant must conclusively establish the essential elements of his asserted theories of recovery or defense. City of Houston v. Clear Creek Basin Authority, 589 S.W.2d 671, 678 (Tex. 1979). Breach of contract may have been the only theory which sellers believed they could conclusively establish. In regard to this theory, we held, on a single question of law (condition or covenant), that one of the terms of the contract was a covenant; therefore, a fact question existed and summary judgment was improper. Our holding in the first appeal, however, did not preclude sellers from asserting other defensive theories, including those attacking the validity of the contract, at a subsequent trial on the merits. Therefore, in light of the proceeding in which the question first arose, the trial court properly allowed sellers to assert the defense of fraud in the inducement.

The court of appeals correctly determined purchaser's remaining points of error dealing with conflicting jury findings and the propriety of submitting certain issues on fraud.

The judgment of the court of appeals is affirmed.

---

For further consideration of the law of the case doctrine, see Vestal, *Law of the Case: Single-Suit Preclusion,* 1967 Utah L. Rev. 1.

# CHAPTER 9

## DISCOVERY: PURPOSES, SCOPE, AND USES

### SCOPE

This chapter looks at the purpose, scope, and use of discovery: what kind of information is discoverable and what is not. The chapter covers the objectives of discovery, limitations on discovery, policies underlying the discovery rules and procedures, planning discovery in a case, an overview of the discovery devices (though these are covered in depth in Chapter 10), the issue of relevance, and privileges.

## § 9.01 An Introduction to the Purposes and Scope of Discovery

It is difficult to overemphasize the importance of discovery to a trial lawyer. The vast majority of suits involve factual disputes, and even in the minority of suits in which the main question is one of law, the facts must be established. Discovery is the principal means of finding out what the facts are before trial. Therefore, a good trial lawyer must be familiar with the techniques of discovery so that he or she not only understands the rules, but knows how to use them as well.

### [A] Objectives of Discovery

Attorneys in a lawsuit do not use the discovery devices simply to be using them. Discovery is part of the adversary process. Ultimately, the attorney's goal is to win the case. The aims of discovery are subordinate to this ultimate goal.

The primary purpose of discovery is to find out everything possible about the event or transaction that is at the heart of the lawsuit. If, during a deposition, an attorney finds out that the opposing party admits to having driven five miles per hour in excess of the speed limit, the attorney has moved, however slightly, toward winning the suit. But note that the strategy is not limited to the discovery of helpful information. If the opposing party contends that the attorney's client ran a red light, the attorney will also try to discover this claimed fact. Having discovered it, the attorney can consider how to explain, qualify, limit, or destroy the contention. Thus, the attorney seeks to discover unfavorable as well as favorable information. The discovery devices are chiefly a method of finding out as much as possible about the lawsuit.

A second function of discovery is to "freeze" the testimony of harmful witnesses. Does the opposing party claim that the plaintiff was traveling at five miles per hour in excess of the speed limit? In that event, the opponent will have difficulty if he or she testifies at trial that the plaintiff was going "at least 70," and will have even more difficulty in maintaining the position that he or she did not see the plaintiff's vehicle until the accident. The deposition does not prevent such a change in testimony, but it can be used to impeach the credibility of the witness if the witness testifies contrary to it. Consequently, skillful litigators are adept at getting witnesses to give definite, specific, and detailed answers during depositions. Their purpose is to "freeze" the testimony, as far as they are able.

A third purpose of discovery is to put useful evidence in a form admissible at trial. Suppose, for example, that the plaintiff's treating doctor has written plaintiff's attorney a letter summarizing the injuries that are the subject of the suit. The doctor's schedule makes it impossible for the doctor to be available for trial, and a subpoena would be unwise because it would be offensive, and make the doctor a hostile witness. Yet the letter itself is not admissible in evidence (it would be excluded as hearsay at a trial), and therefore the doctor's information must be put in a different form. The plaintiff may wish to take the doctor's deposition—not to discover information this time, and not to freeze the doctor's testimony—but simply because the deposition, unlike the letter, will be admissible at trial.

Sometimes discovery is put to a fourth, and ethically dubious, use: to harass, annoy, or vex an opposing party. In the right kind of case, most skillful litigators could draft interrogatories within an hour that could cost thousands of dollars to answer. Similarly, skillful attorneys in an adversary system might be tempted to expose trade secrets of an opponent or to use discovery in other ways not related to the merits of the case. You cannot understand the function of the rules unless you understand that discovery has the potential for harassment.

### [B] The Scope and Limits of Discovery

Discovery extends to matters that are "relevant to the subject matter of the pending action." Tex. R. Civ. P. 192.3(a). The concept of "relevance" for discovery purposes is broad. For example, discovery is not limited to the issues set forth in the pleadings because it extends to the entire subject matter of the controversy that has given rise to the litigation. Moreover, like its federal counterpart, Civil Procedure Rule 192.3 provides, "It is not a ground for objection that the information sought will be inadmissible at the trial if the information sought appears reasonably calculated to lead to the discovery of admissible evidence." Tex. R. Civ. P. 192.3. For instance, hearsay or opinion matters are usually inadmissible at trial—but they can sometimes be discovered. In a deposition, a lawyer might ask: "What's your opinion as to how the accident happened?" or, "What have you heard other people say about the accident?" The examiner can then inquire into the factual observations underlying the opinion or the names of the other people who said something about the accident. In other words, discovery is a kind of investigatory device, and the rules allow a freer hand than the rules of evidence would at trial.

Nevertheless, there are limits. The information may be so slim or remote that its likelihood of turning up admissible evidence is not "reasonable." In such a case, a court might conclude that the information is not "relevant" in the discovery sense. By the same token, when the burden imposed on the party who is the holder of the information sought to be discovered is heavy, the courts may be inclined to view the relevance question with more strictness. Other limits on the extent of discovery are imposed by Civil Procedure Rule 192. The rule exempts from discovery: (1) an attorney's work product; (2) the identity, mental impressions, and opinions of a consulting expert; and (3) any matter protected from disclosure by privilege. *See* Tex. R. Civ. P. 192. These matters are exempt from discovery, not because the information would be irrelevant to the subject matter involved in the pending action, but on policy grounds. In addition to these exemptions, the trial judge has discretion in the interest of justice to make any order necessary to protect "the movant from undue burden, unnecessary expense, harassment, annoyance, or invasion of personal, constitutional, or property rights." Tex. R. Civ. P. 192.6(b).

### [C] The Ultimate Policies Underlying the Discovery Rules

Aside from the strategies engaged in by trial lawyers, there are certain overarching societal purposes that the discovery rules are designed to serve.

Broad discovery, it is often said, makes the adversary process a better instrument for arriving at the truth. It decreases "Perry Mason" tactics and it discourages trial by ambush. It provides each party with greater knowledge about the case, and thus it arguably leads to fairer trials and, probably, to a higher proportion of disputes settled without trial. The latter result is sometimes said to be reflected in a more efficient system of justice, although this point is the subject of considerable debate.

The limits of discovery are, of course, aimed in part at preventing harassment and undue expense. They are also designed to buttress the adversary nature of the system, in that they limit the extent to which a party may get a "free ride" on investigation done by an opponent. Certain privileges are designed to ensure privacy and protection of desirable interpersonal relationships and to serve other purposes.

The "broad-versus-narrow-discovery" controversy has a long history and is still ongoing. The Texas rules may not be the best possible resolution of this controversy; they are simply one possible resolution.

On January 1, 1999, new rules governing pretrial discovery became effective. Among other goals, these rules were designed to impose limits on the volume of discovery in an attempt to provide adequate access to information without unnecessarily driving up the costs and delays associated with the discovery practice. *See* Explanatory Statement Accompanying the 1999 Amendments to the Rules of Civil Procedure Governing Discovery. *See also* Hecht & Pemberton, A Guide to the 1999 Texas Discovery Rules Revisions (available at www.supreme.courts.state.tx.us/rules/disccle3.htm). As is often true with procedural issues, then, the Texas discovery rules will involve tension between the desire to aid just results and the desire to enhance speed and efficiency.

### [D] Discovery and Attorney Obligations

**W. Dorsaneo, TEXAS LITIGATION GUIDE**

*§ 90.01[4]**

Due to the lack of candor during discovery [*see* Garcia v. Peeples, 734 S.W.2d 343, 347 (Tex. 1987)] and judicial dissatisfaction with litigants' unduly adversarial approach to discovery, there was a fairly active use of sanctions for discovery-related misconduct following the 1984 amendments to the Civil Procedure Rules [*see* Ch. 98, *Discovery Sanctions*; T.R.C.P. 215; *see also* In re Ford Motor Co., — S.W.2d —, —, 41 Sup. Ct. J. 1283, 1285 (Tex. 1998)—Court set out test for imposition of sanctions under Rule 215]. The Texas Supreme Court, through its rule-making authority and power to regulate the practice of law, has addressed attorneys' obligations during discovery in several ways. Civil Procedure Rule 191.2 mandates a certain degree of cooperation among attorneys engaged in discovery, providing [T.R.C.P. 191.2]:

> Parties and their attorneys are expected to cooperate in discovery and to make any agreements reasonably necessary for the efficient disposition of the case. All discovery motions or requests for hearings relating to discovery must contain a certificate by the party filing the motion or request that a reasonable effort has been made to resolve the dispute without the necessity of court intervention and the effort failed.

In addition, Civil Procedure Rule 191.3 requires that all discovery requests, notices, responses, and objections be signed [T.R.C.P. 191.3(a)]. The attorney's signature certifies, among other things, that the discovery request, notice, response, or objection is "not unreasonable or unduly burdensome or expensive, given the needs of the case, the discovery already had in the case, the amount in controversy, and the importance of the issues at stake in the litigation" [T.R.C.P. 191.3(c)(4); *see also* T.R.C.P. 192.4].

Further, the Texas Disciplinary Rules of Professional Conduct, which define proper conduct for attorneys, provide guidelines for proper conduct during discovery. For instance, Rule 3.04 prohibits the habitual violation of established rules of procedure or evidence [State Bar Rules, Art. 10 § 9, Rule 3.04(c)]. A comment to this rule notes that it applies to habitual abuses of procedural rules, including those related to the discovery process [State Bar Rules, Art. 10 § 9, Rule 3.04, Comment ¶ 3]. The Disciplinary Rules also impose duties on lawyers to protect a client's confidential information [*see* State Bar Rules, Art. 10 § 9, Rule 1.05].

Finally, the Texas Lawyer's Creed—A Mandate for Professionalism, adopted by the Supreme Court in 1989, provides that "[a] lawyer should always adhere to the highest principles of professionalism" and sets out standards relating to a lawyer's relationship with his or her client, other lawyers, the judge, and the judicial system. The Lawyer's Creed was a direct result of perceived inappropriate conduct by lawyers in pretrial discovery. Although the Lawyer's Creed is merely aspirational, it sets a standard of conduct that should be followed by attorneys in the conduct of discovery.

## § 9.02 Overall Planning of Discovery

### Morris, STRATEGY OF DISCOVERY

*18 For the Defense 83 (1977)**

[The following outline gives the author's suggestions for the planning of discovery in the defense of a medical malpractice case. You should consider the extent to which it is applicable to other kinds of cases. How, for example, would these approaches have to be adapted if you represented the plaintiff in a medical malpractice case? What about an automobile negligence case in which the damages were small? What about an antitrust case? How would the new disclosure rules change this discovery strategy?]

I. INTRODUCTION

Discovery for the defense begins with the defense—not with the plaintiff

And it begins not with the facts but with the law

For it is the law that determines

(1) What facts are needed

(2) What form these facts must take to be admissible

*Ideally*—defense counsel should know as much about the law of his case before starting discovery as after conclusion of the appeal

---

* Reprinted with the permission of the Practicing Law Institute, copyright © 1977.

## II. THE LAW OF THE CASE

A. *Ways to achieve*

(1) Review the petition and the file and resolve—in your own mind—the legal issues

(2) Review your experiences re trials of similar cases—what were the issues, the necessary proof: a "case-bank" that grows with experience

(3) Review the experience of others in similar cases

(a) *Reported* cases

Read opinions

Read briefs

Read record

Read write-ups—Medical Trial Technique Quarterly—NACCA/ATLA—Defense Research Institute—etc.

(b) *Unreported cases*

Talk to lawyers who tried the case

Talk to judge who presided

B. *Purpose*

(1) *Define the issues*

(a) *re negligence*

Thrust of attack

Thrust of defense

(b) *re responsibility*

Who else involved

By what legal route:

1. Captain of the ship
2. *Respondeat superior*
3. Agency by estoppel
4. Loaned servant
5. Dual employment
6. Joint venture
7. Administrative negligence
   - — defective equipment
   - — improper supervision
8. *Darling* decision
   - — hospital rules
   - — Joint Commission on Accreditation rules
9. Third-party claims

— manufacturer of equipment

— servicer of equipment

— etc.

(2) *Delineate proof needed*

(a) *re substance*

Contractual relationships between the parties

Actual relationship between the parties

Representations to the patient

(b) *re form*

1. Bill to patient for services

— by whom

— in whose name

— how delineated

2. Nurse

— even if private duty, did hospital furnish, did hospital pay, etc.

III. DISCOVERY OF DEFENSE

"Know thyself"

— as completely as possible

*Rules of Thumb*

*Rule 1: Assume nothing*

— Take nothing for granted

— Cross-check everything and everyone including time-honored assumptions

*Rule 2: Be resourceful*

— Use your imagination

— Use your brain

— Use your common sense.

*Rule 3: Be thorough*

— cross-check all sources

*Rule 4: Preserve evidence*

As you go, record:

— identifying information serial numbers, etc.

*Primary sources* (of the fact)

(1) *Records involved*

1. *The hospital record (patient's medical chart)* covering the event in question

(a) Is your copy *complete* — *Caveat:* You must know the format for any hospital records:

— admission sheet

— admitting history and physical

— doctors order sheets

— lab sheets

— nurse's notes etc.

(b) Is your copy *legible* — *Caveat:* What you can't read may be vital

(c) *Understanding your copy*

1. Lay out chronologically

— not easy to do

2. Get doctor to explain significance

— of all recorded events

— of all missing events

2. *Accessory Records*

— Emergency Room records

— Out-Patient records

— Physiotherapy records

— Clinic records

— Pathology records — Autopsy records

3. *Records behind the records*

Original entries in original books from which hospital records are made up:

(a) *Laboratory:*

— Work notebooks

— Log entries

— Routing slips

(b) *Pathology:*

— Work notebooks

— Slides

— Paraffin blocks

— Amputated parts

(c) *Operating Room:*

— Log schedules

— Material schedules

— Financial charges

(d) *Equipment & Supply*

— Purchase orders

— Maintenance and service

— Financial charges

(e) *Financial records:*

— Oxygen given

— R.N. service

— etc.

(f) *X-ray*

— Films

— Therapy dosage

— Charts

(g) *Doctors notes*

— Summaries, etc. (if any)

4. *Legal records*

*Caveat:* Probably privileged from discovery by plaintiffs

*Sierra Vista Hospital v. Superior Court of California* (Ct. App. 1967), 56 Cal. Rptr. 387:

— Hospital's incident report privileged from plaintiff's discovery.

*Brown v. Superior Court* (Dist. Ct. App. 1963) 32 Cal. Rptr. 527:

— Malpractice Committee Review of case privileged from plaintiff's discovery.

(a) Incident report

(b) Correspondence and file, etc.

5. *Medical investigating records reviewing case — Caveat:* Probably privileged from discovery by plaintiffs.

*Judd v. Park Avenue Hospital* (Sup. Ct. N.Y.), 235 N.Y.S.2d 843, *aff'd* 235 N.Y.S.2d 1023:

— "any and all medical staff discussions and meetings of committees" privileged from plaintiff's discovery

(a) *Hospital review committees*

— Tissue committees

— Disciplinary committees

— Mortality committees, etc.

(b) *Outside committees*

— Local Academy of Medicine review

— State Medical Society review

— Maternal Health death reports

*Comment:* Probably privileged from discovery by anyone but may have been published anonymously and can be recognized from factual situation

*cf: Brackenbush v. Southwest Community Hosp.,* (Common Pleas Ct., Cuyahoga County, Ohio, Docket No. 752394):

— Maternal Health Mortality records of Ohio State Medical Association held privileged from plaintiff's discovery on ground of public policy to promote keeping of such records for public's benefit: Courtroom No. 1, Judge Friedman, Journal Entry 11-2-66.

*Supreme Court of Ohio* (Docket No. 40561):

— Demurrers to plaintiff's mandamus petition sustained. Rehearing denied 4-19-67.

*cf: Piotrowski v. Corey Hospital* (Ohio Sup. Ct. 1961), 172 Ohio St. 61; 173 N.E.2d 355:

— Reversible error to admit into evidence collateral write up of the case by medical society investigating same.

(c) *Medical literature*

*Comment:* Occasionally a doctor will have published (before suit filed) an article on the case at bar itself because of its scientific interest

— Check medical literature under authors for doctors' names involved and under subject matter involved from year of incident to date

*Rizzo, Admrx., etc. v. American Cyanamid Co. et al.* (Common Pleas Ct., Cuyahoga County, Ohio, Docket No. 748722):

— Death from allergic reaction to Kynex; prior to suit being filed one of defendant doctors published article about the very case: *JAMA,* 172: 155-57 (1-9-60) "Fatal Thrombocytopenic Purpura after Administration of Sulfamethoxypyridazine."

6. *Regulations applicable*

(a) *Joint Commission on Accreditation*

— Was hospital accredited

— If so, when last inspected

— Report on inspection and recommendations

— Compliance by hospital with recommendations

(b) *Hospital's own regulations*

— Constitution

— Bylaws

— Minutes of meetings of Board of Trustees of Medical Council

— Departmental rules and regulations

— Nursing rules and regulations

(c) *Handbooks*

— Nursing procedures

— Operating procedures

(d) *Standing orders of doctors*

— especially defendant doctor

(2) *Personnel involved*

Each must be identified

Each must be interviewed

1. *Identify*

(a) *Operating room*

— Everyone present at any time

*Prima facie:* Surgeon

1st Asst. Surgeon (resident)

2nd Asst. Surgeon (intern)

Anesthesiologist — including all replacement doctors

Asst. Anesthesiologist (resident) (intern) (R.N.)

Instrument or scrub nurse

Circulating nurse

*Perhaps also present*

Family doctor

Teams of specialists

— heart-lung specialists, etc.

Observers

— doctors

— students

— family of patient

(b) *Laboratories*

— Head of department

— All technicians doing the lab work

— All who had personal contact with the patient

(c) *Nursing and Room Care*

(1) *Hospital Personnel*

*Registered Nurses*

— Supervisor of floor

— All R.N.'s on duty

— All R.N.'s seeing patient

*Licensed Practical Nurses*

— All seeing patient

*Nurse's aides*

— All seeing patient

*Orderlies*

— Any involved

(2) *Non-hospital Personnel*

— Registered nurses

— Licensed practical nurses

— Friends and relatives rendering aid

(3) *Roommates*

— Get addresses from financial records

*Caveat:* In and out

(4) *Visitors*

— Family

— friends

— relations

— priest

— social workers, etc.

*Comment:* Check hospital nurse's note, financial records, and registry of nurses, etc. to locate above

(d) *Medical Care*

Attending physician

— replacement attending physician

Consultants

Family doctor

Specialists

Residents

Interns

Any doctor anywhere in hospital records including nurse's notes, doctor's order sheets, etc.

(e) *Special Departments*

Check all personnel on duty or seeing patient

*Example:* Physiotherapy Department

X-ray Department

Emergency Room

Out-Patient Clinics, etc.

2. *Interview*

(a) Refresh their recollections

— from hospital records, etc.

(b) Commit to writing

— even if negative statement

(c) Inquire re collateral sources

— which may lead to other evidence

(d) Get permanent address

— for later location, including future plans

(e) Ask if they ever gave statement to plaintiffs

(f) Advise need not talk to plaintiff's side if don't want to and contact you if approached

(g) *Qualifications*

— All education

— All positions held

— Professional associations

— Honors

— Board-certified in specialty

(h) All scientific writings by each

(i) Who they recommend to you as expert in their field

(j) Medical theories of case

— theirs

— others they know about

(k) Make them "level" with you re unpleasant facts about case or about themselves you should know

— "cross-examine" them on this

— any colleagues who hate them

3. *Investigate*

(a) *Personnel file*

— Review re each employee of hospital in question

— Review re each doctor on staff of hospital in question

(b) *Talk to colleagues*

— re general reputation of personnel in question

— re specific incident

4. *Equipment involved*

(a) *Identify*

— locate

— examine

— Get copy of instruction manual

*Record*

— Serial number

— Model number

— Type number

— Manufacturer's name

(b) *Preserve* (for trial)

— perhaps photograph

— allow no changes

(c) *Investigate*

— Purchase records

— Maintenance records

— Outside service records

— Adaptations and changes records

— Performance records

— Installation records

(d) *Collateral Investigation*

— State of art of manufacturer at time installed

— Safety features on other makes not on this one

— Later safety features for this one since manufacture but before incident which might have been installed before incident

(e) *Testing*

— Have expert examine and test re alleged incident and re its maintenance status

(f) *Scene of Accident*

Operating room, etc.

(1) Inspect it yourself

(2) Prepare scale diagram, etc.

(3) Photograph

(g) *Third-party suits*

—Discovery may reveal others owing hospital indemnity

(1) Manufacturers of defective equipment

(2) Suppliers of drugs

(3) Independent contractor actors

— Anesthesiologists, etc.

*Secondary Sources* (before the fact) (after the fact)

(1) *Before the fact*

1. Hospital's experience re this type of incident

— re legal "notice" to hospital

— re causes

2. Hospital's experience re this type of equipment

— re notice

— re modifications

3. Hospital experience re this personnel

— *quality* —

— prior training

— prior experience

— record in general

— colleagues' opinions

— *quantity* —

— how much experience with this operation, etc.

(a) Has hospital had

(b) Has this surgeon had

— check hospital index records re this

Incident of this hazard

— What do hospital records show

(a) Re this type of procedure by all surgeons

(b) Re same by this surgeon

(2) *After the fact*

What changes have occurred since this incident which bear on this incident

— In practice

— in procedure

— in rules and regulations

— in personnel

— in equipment etc.

C. *Collateral Sources*

*Comment:* All versions must be checked against independent expert sources to ascertain probable medical truth of matter.

(1) *Experts*

(a) *Quality*

— the best obtainable

(b) *Quantity*

— at least two in each specialty to check on each other

(c) *Review*

— Careful review of all important known data and full hospital records by each expert

(2) *Medical and Scientific literature*

Check it yourself

(a) *Re medicine*

— medical library articles and texts

(b) *Re drugs*

— Manufacturer's brochure

Physicians Desk Reference

Pharmacology Texts

Pharmacologist

Medical literature

(c) *Re equipment*

— manufacturer's brochure

— scientific texts and journals

— scientific experts

IV. DISCOVERY OF THE PLAINTIFF

*Comment:* Now that you "know thyself" you are ready for discovery into plaintiff's case

A. *Discovery is discovery*

— no magic

same as any other lawsuit

(1) *Interrogatories*

Cover all hospital admissions birth to date

Include hospital of birth and all doctors, medications, illnesses, etc.

(2) *Depositions*

(a) Plaintiff-patient especially re alleged verbal admissions by defendants and others

(b) All relatives and friends seeing patient in the hospital

(3) *All Hospital Records*

— a gold mine

Birth to death whether relevant or not

All admissions—all Emergency and Out-patient Departments

C. *Check on plaintiff's version*

(1) With all doctors and hospital personnel

(2) Investigators

Neighborhood checks, etc.

C. Ascertain plaintiff's experts and their theory of case

(1) *Discovery*

(a) interrogatories

(b) motions to produce

*cf: Monier v. Chamberlain* (Ill. 1966), 35 Ill.2d 351; 221 N.E.2d 410

(c) snooping

— gossip

(d) ask your doctors who likely

(e) pre-trial hearings

(2) *Check on plaintiff's expert*

(a) ask other doctors

(b) research literature for his articles

(c) ask local academy re his qualifications

(d) text of medical specialists

*Physical examinations of plaintiff*

(a) Re recovery and present status

(b) Re causation and etiology

(c) Thorough

— all experts necessary

— all tests necessary

Chromosome studies

Allergy studies

X-ray studies

Physical exam

Laboratory studies etc.

*Comment:* Generally, plaintiff's deposition should wait until after defense's discovery of defense is complete.

*Reason:* Operative facts are highly medical and beyond knowledge of plaintiff and within knowledge of defendants

— unlike auto accident case, etc.

*However:* Occasionally, defendant's discovery must begin with plaintiff and plaintiff's witnesses

*Examples:*

(1) Plaintiff's claim Emergency Room treatment — yet defendant hospital has no record of same

*Long v. St. Luke's Hospital* (Common Pleas Ct. Cuyahoga County, Ohio, Docket No. 767933).

(2) Plaintiff claims an R.N. injured his sciatic nerve with I-M injection of medicine and hospital records shows many shots — which does he blame

*Harrell v. St. Luke's Hospital* (Common Pleas Ct. Cuyahoga County, Ohio — Docket No. 781421)

## V. CONCLUSION

Suits against hospitals fall into two main categories

(1) Complicated medical situations

— operating room accidents, etc.

(2) Very simple factual situations

— fall out of bed

— hot water bottle burns etc.

Above format especially important re category (1)

Category (2) may proceed with discovery of plaintiff first

But in both (1) and (2) No substitute for Full discovery of defendant and of plaintiff

Thorough and painstaking discovery and preparation is keynote of success.

1. In the novice — it builds confidence

2. In the expert — it builds reputation

3. In all — prerequisite to continued success.

---

## NOTES AND QUESTIONS

(1) *Discovery Strategy*. Why should discovery by the defense "begin with the defense"? What is the strategic reason for doing so? What is the reason for beginning "not with the facts, but the law"? Is this really "discovery"?

(2) *Volume of Documents*. In a suit involving a "complicated medical situation," as the author puts it, how many documents would you guess might be generated by discovery? Note that the number might be increased by the existence of multiple defendants, cross-claims, addition of claims based on products liability, etc. What problems would be created by the sheer number of documents, and how would the lawyers solve them?

(3) *Interview vs. Deposition*. The author says, "persons involved . . . each must be interviewed." Why "interviewed," rather than "deposed"?

(4) *Thoroughness of Discovery*. Why should interrogatories to plaintiff "cover all hospital admissions, birth to date?" Will plaintiff willingly comply with a request for such information in all cases? What does the author mean by suggesting that plaintiff's hospital records, which he calls a "gold mine," be sought "birth to death whether relevant or not"?

(5) *Corroboration*. Why must "all versions" including, presumably, the client's version and versions of persons friendly to the client, be "checked against independent expert sources to ascertain probable medical truth"? Can't a lawyer assume that a client is telling the truth?

(6) *Cost of Discovery*. What would be the cost of investigation and discovery in a case involving a "complicated medical situation"? What sort of financial resources would plaintiff's lawyers have to have in such a case, and why? Could discovery this thorough be done if the injuries are minor (a case in which potential damages are perhaps $10,000)? Is it possible the defense might engage in discovery that would cause plaintiff to spend many times the $10,000 potentially at stake in such a case? What does this possibility suggest about the way that discovery rules should be written or interpreted?

(7) *Discovery of Privileged Matters*. Note the reference to defense material that may be "privileged," such as internal incident reports, review committee documents and the like. Why would plaintiff want to get such documents? (Note: plaintiff will want them irrespective of whether they contain admissible evidence.) If such documents are privileged, what sort of financial difference might that status make to plaintiff's attorney? Why should they be privileged?

## § 9.03 The Individual Discovery Devices: An Introduction

### [A] The Discovery Devices Provided by the Rules

In the first year of law school you are likely to have had a course covering the federal approach to discovery. Fortunately, although there are important differences, the Texas discovery rules are similar. The discovery rules contemplate discovery among parties to the suit as well as discovery from persons and entities that are not parties. There are six devices that may be used to accomplish formal discovery: (1) requests for disclosure; (2) requests for production and inspection (including pretrial subpoenas) and for entry on land; (3) interrogatories; (4) requests for admissions; (5) depositions (both depositions on oral examination and depositions on written questions); and (6) requests for physical and mental examination. The use of these devices are subject to new numerical limits, depending on the type of case involved. These limits will be discussed in Chapter 10.

1. *Requests for Disclosure*. Beginning in 1999, the discovery rules create a new mechanism requiring, on request, disclosure of basic information described in Civil Procedure Rule 194.2, including identity of parties and potential parties, legal theories, damage calculations, persons with knowledge of relevant facts, information about testifying experts, witness statements, and insurance and settlement agreements. Although they are an entirely new discovery tool, it is likely that they will be used in most cases, especially those with significant limits on the use of other discovery devices.

2. *Oral Depositions*. Depositions are questions asked of a witness before trial in the presence of a court reporter, with opposing parties having the right to be present and ask questions also. The term "deposition" is also used to describe the session at which questions are asked and answered. This type of discovery may be used both as to party and nonparty witnesses. It is set up by a written notice to all other parties and, for a nonparty witness, issuance of a subpoena. Depositions are usually the most effective means for obtaining useful information from adverse witnesses because the examiner may ask follow-up questions in the event of evasive answers.

3. *Depositions on Written Questions*. As an alternative to the oral deposition, a party may send written questions to a person authorized to administer a written deposition to the deponent. The other side may, in response, issue cross-questions. This is a weak form of discovery for several reasons, including the fact that the deposition officer cannot revise the questions or ask follow-up questions. The device was historically used most frequently for authentication of documents. Under the 1999 amendments, however, production of a document authenticates the document for use against the party that produced it unless specific objection procedures are followed. Tex. R. Civ. P. 176.5, 193.7. The deposition on written questions may thus be used less frequently as documents may be acquired from nonparties through subpoena without need for an oral or written deposition. *See* Tex. R. Civ. P. 176, 205. However, deposition of the records custodian may still be required in order to prove that the documents are admissible business records rather than hearsay.

4. *Interrogatories.* Interrogatories are written questions directed by one party to another, to be answered under oath. Because this discovery device allows the opponent leisure to consider the response, and because opposing counsel generally determines the form of the answers, responses are frequently evasive, and thus interrogatories are not an effective method for getting controversial information from an adverse party. However, interrogatories may be an inexpensive way to get basic, background information. Some of the information formally secured through interrogatories will now be sought through requests for disclosure instead. Under the 1999 amendments, parties may serve on any other party no more than 25 written interrogatories (excluding interrogatories asking a party only to identify or authenthenticate specific documents) unless they get court permission. Interrogatories may be directed only to parties. Written discovery from nonparty witnesses must be gotten by the similar but separate mechanism of the deposition on written questions.

5. *Requests for Admissions.* A party opponent may be requested to admit or deny factual propositions submitted to him or her, including the genuineness of documents. This kind of discovery is useful for eliminating issues about which there is no real dispute.

6. *Production and Inspection of Documents, Tangible Things, and Realty.* The request to produce constitutes the basic method for obtaining discovery of documents and other tangible things from other parties to the action. Under the request procedure, a party sends to another party a written request listing the documents, tangible things or realty the party wishes to photograph, copy, or inspect. The request procedure applies to parties only but is similar to the procedure for nonparties. Production of tangible items from nonparties involves the use of a notice and subpoena.

7. *Motions for Physical or Mental Examination.* On motion showing good cause, the court may order that a physical or mental examination be had of a person whose condition is in controversy.

### [B] Basics of Discovery Strategy

In a complicated suit justifying the use of several different kinds of discovery, the "first wave" of discovery, as it is called, usually consists of identifying documents, witnesses, or business entities that need to be investigated. Thus the first devices used may be a request for disclosure and a set of interrogatories, because they are an efficient means for getting background information. In addition to the discovery allowed under the request for disclosure, a party might want further background information such as the identity and location of documents and other tangible things relevant to the case. The opponent may be asked to identify the persons having knowledge of the transaction or occurrence involved in the action, the corporations or other business entities for which they have acted, the officers or employees of those businesses, and the identity and location of any tangible evidence relating to the issues. In a complex suit, such as an antitrust case, the proper conduct of this first wave is essential to a successful effort.

Once the basics are thus established, the "second wave," often consisting of requests for document production, will be conducted. While human testimony may vary, documents contain what they contain, and they are useful to have available when taking depositions.

The "third wave" may be depositions of witnesses or parties who know about the transaction at issue. These depositions may even lead to a fourth or fifth wave of discovery, as the attorneys attempt to discover through depositions not only what the deponents know, but also the existence of other sources of information.

Finally, requests for admissions may be used as a last step in the discovery process to obtain admissions of matters that the discovery process has shown to be undisputed and to secure admissions concerning the authenticity of documents to be introduced at trial.

Of course, cost considerations affect and limit discovery strategy in any given law suit. An automobile accident in which injuries are minor may justify only a brief deposition or two, if even that. An antitrust case, on the other hand, may easily call for the expenditure of hundreds of thousands of dollars in attorney's fees for discovery. It is not unusual for thousands of documents to be produced in such a case.

---

### NOTES AND QUESTIONS

(1) *Use of Discovery Devices.* What device or devices might you use to obtain each of the following items of information? Explain.

(a) Information related to medical expenses of a plaintiff in a suit for personal injuries, including such matters as the doctors consulted, the amount of money paid and the treatment the patient underwent. You represent the defendant.

(b) The bank statements or cancelled checks of the plaintiff for these expenditures.

(c) In an action on a contract, the genuineness of the copy of the contract in your client's possession, which you wish to establish for trial.

(d) In a suit over an automobile accident, the opposing party's version of facts surrounding the accident.

(e) Records maintained by an automobile repair shop, who is not a party to the suit, concerning the condition of the brakes of the automobile driven by the opposing party.

(2) *Defending Discovery Requests.*What would you consider doing in each of the following situations?

(a) In an antitrust case, your opponent subjects your client to interrogatories that, although relevant to the issue of damages, would require disclosure of the names and addresses of all your client's customers, your client's method of doing business, and the process by which your client's product is made.

(b) In a contract action for loss of profits, your opponent seeks production of all your client's income tax records, claiming that they are relevant to the issue of damages.

(c) Your opponent seeks production from your client of "all documents produced as a result of any investigation of the transaction on which this suit is founded."

## § 9.04 The Scope of Discovery: "Relevant" Information, "Not Privileged"

### [A] The Discovery "Relevance" Standard and Information "Reasonably Calculated" to Lead to Admissible Evidence

*Read Tex. R. Civ. P. 192 and accompanying Comments.*

Any analysis of discovery relevance must grow from an understanding of trial relevance. Evidence is relevant for trial purposes if it has "any tendency to make the existence of any fact that is of consequence to the determination of the action more probable or less probable than it would be without the evidence." Tex. R. Evid. 401. This broad standard of relevance must be kept in mind when considering whether information is relevant for purposes of discovery.

Rule 192.3 of the Texas Rules of Civil Procedure defines discovery relevance. Litigants may discover "any matter that . . . is relevant to the subject matter of the pending action, whether it relates to the claim or defense of the party seeking discovery or the claim or defense of any other party." Discovery relevance is broader than trial relevance because trial relevance determinations are based on the issues caused by the parties' pleadings. Moreover, information is not exempt from discovery because it will be inadmissible at trial. Rather, non-privileged information is discoverable if it "appears reasonably calculated to lead to the discovery of admissible evidence."

This broad concept of relevance, however, is limited by the requirement that the information sought be "reasonably" calculated to lead to admissible evidence. In applying this reasonableness test, courts have balanced the probative value of the information sought and the burden upon the party seeking discovery against the burden on the party from whom discovery is sought.

This section examines how Texas courts determine whether requested material is relevant in the discovery sense. It will also examine certain areas that have generated special consideration in the relevance area. Subsection [B] will focus on the privileges recognized by Texas that limit discovery of relevant information. Subsection [C] will look at ways in which privileges can be waived. Subsection [D] examines the proper procedures that parties should follow in asserting their claims in discovery disputes. Finally, Subsection [E] considers the methods for review of discovery orders.

### [1] The Relevance Test Generally

## JAMPOLE v. TOUCHY

*673 S.W.2d 569 (Tex. 1984)*

SPEARS, Justice.

In this original mandamus proceeding, Stanley Jampole asks this court to direct Judge Hugo Touchy of the 129th District Court in Harris County to vacate an order denying certain pre-trial discovery. We conditionally grant the writ of mandamus.

Stanley Jampole brought a products liability suit to recover damages for the death of his wife, Judith Goodley Jampole. Mrs. Jampole died from injuries suffered on April 14, 1979, when her 1976 Chevrolet Vega caught fire after being struck from the rear by another automobile. Mr. Jampole sued the driver of the other car, General Motors Corporation, and the Chevrolet Division of General Motors, but only the latter two ("GMC") are affected by this mandamus proceeding.

The type of accident forming the basis of this suit is commonly known as a post-collision, fuel-fed fire. Jampole seeks to hold GMC liable on theories of strict liability, negligence, and breach of warranty. He alleges that the 1976 Vega hatchback was defectively designed, manufactured, and marketed. Jampole maintains that placing the fuel tank of the Vega between the rear axle and bumper was unreasonably dangerous. He specifically claims that the design made the tank vulnerable to rear-end impacts, resulting in fuel leaking into the passenger compartment and igniting. Jampole alleges that GMC knew of the defect, risks, and safer alternatives, but did nothing. GMC's alleged knowledge and failure to act are asserted as grounds for punitive and exemplary damages.

Jampole seeks a writ of mandamus requiring Judge Touchy to vacate portions of an order that denied Jampole's motion to compel GMC to answer certain interrogatories and requests for production. Jampole originally sought a writ of mandamus on the same basis against Judge Thomas J. Stovall, who first heard and ruled on Jampole's motion. After this court granted Jampole leave to file his petition for writ of mandamus, Judge Touchy replaced Judge Stovall in the 129th District Court. Jampole properly asked this court to delay action on his petition while he requested that Judge Touchy reconsider Judge Stovall's order. *See State v. Olsen*, 163 Tex. 449, 360 S.W.2d 402 (1962). Judge Touchy reaffirmed the prior order, and we granted Jampole's motion to amend his petition to substitute Judge Touchy as respondent.

Jampole complains that the trial court's order denied him discovery of the following types of information: (1) evidence of alternate fuel storage system designs that were known to GMC; (2) installation and assembly diagrams and specifications for 1971–77 Chevrolet Vegas and their counterpart Pontiac Astres; (3) documents revealing how GMC planned to comply with proposed federal motor vehicle safety standards that would have imposed more stringent standards for fuel storage system integrity; (4) documents pertaining to experimental, pre-production, and prototype models of the Vega; and (5) a master index listing all crash test reports available to GMC for 1971–77 Vegas and Astres and any vehicles incorporating certain design alternatives.

In deciding whether a writ of mandamus is appropriate, we recognize that mandamus will not issue unless a clear abuse of discretion is shown. *West v. Solito*, 563 S.W.2d 240 (Tex. 1978); *Allen v. Humphreys*, 559 S.W.2d 798 (Tex. 1977); *Barker v. Dunham*, 551 S.W.2d 41 (Tex. 1977); *Crane v. Tunks*, 160 Tex. 182, 328 S.W.2d 434 (1959). Furthermore, appellate courts will not intervene to control incidental trial court rulings when there is an adequate remedy by appeal. *State Bar v. Heard*, 603 S.W.2d 829 (Tex. 1980); *Werner v. Miller*, 579 S.W.2d 455 (Tex. 1979); *State ex rel. Pettit v. Thurmond*, 516 S.W.2d 119 (Tex. 1974); *Pope v. Ferguson*, 445 S.W.2d 950 (Tex. 1969). We must first consider, then, whether Judge Touchy clearly abused his discretion by denying the requested discovery.

In making this determination, we note that the ultimate purpose of discovery is to seek the truth, so that disputes may be decided by what the facts reveal, not by what facts are concealed. *See West v. Solito,* 563 S.W.2d 240 (Tex. 1978); *Pearson Corp. v. Wichita Falls Boys Club Alumni Ass'n*, 633 S.W.2d 684 (Tex. App.—Fort Worth 1982, no writ). For this reason, discovery is not limited to information that will be admissible at trial. To increase the likelihood that all relevant evidence will be disclosed and brought before the trier of fact, the law circumscribes a significantly larger class of discoverable evidence to include anything reasonably calculated to lead to the discovery of material evidence. *Allen v. Humphreys*, 559 S.W.2d 798, 803 (Tex. 1977); Tex. R. Civ. P. 166b(2). This broad grant is limited, however, by the legitimate interests of the opposing party, for example, to avoid overly-broad requests, harassment, or disclosure of privileged information. *See General Motors Corp. v. Lawrence*, 651 S.W.2d 732 (Tex. 1983).

Jampole filed interrogatories to determine GMC's pre-accident knowledge of alternative designs that would have reduced the risk of fuel escaping from the Vega fuel tank on impact, entering the passenger compartment, and igniting. He specifically requested all impact tests for 1967–79 on vehicles with: (a) above-axle fuel tanks; (b) fuel tanks in other non-production locations; (c) fuel tanks containing flexible liners; (d) fuel tanks that were not made of the standard terne-plated steel (steel coated with a lead/tin alloy); (e) fuel tanks protected by deflector shields;

and (f) fuel tanks equipped with break-away filler necks. Several interrogatories also asked about the design and performance of the 1973–75 Opel Kadetts, small cars manufactured by a foreign subsidiary of GMC and designed with an above-axle fuel tank.

The trial court limited discovery to knowledge and information based on records pertaining to 1971–77 Vegas and Astres. The trial court was persuaded that other vehicles were not substantially similar to the Jampoles' 1976 Vega Hatchback; therefore, he concluded that tests on those vehicles were not relevant.

Jampole contends that it was a clear abuse of discretion for the trial court to deny discovery of alternate design documents. Jampole argues that the requested documents are relevant to his strict liability claim because they could show the availability and feasibility of safer alternatives. In *Boatland of Houston, Inc. v. Bailey*, 609 S.W.2d 743, 746 (Tex. 1980), we held that whether a product is defectively designed must be determined in relation to safer alternatives; thus, evidence of the actual use of, or capacity to use, safer alternatives is relevant. *See also Ford Motor Co. v. Nowak*, 638 S.W.2d 582, 585 (Tex. App.—Corpus Christi 1982, writ ref'd n.r.e.). The basic issue in this lawsuit is whether the 1976 Vega hatchback fuel tank design was defective because it allowed fuel to escape. Other designs that may have prevented fuel escaping are relevant to show that the Vega tank was unreasonably dangerous. Furthermore, the documents showing GMC's knowledge of alternative designs are relevant to show conscious indifference in support of Jampole's claim of gross negligence.

The trial court, in balancing the rights of the parties, took an unduly restrictive view of the degree of similarity necessary for tests on other vehicles to be relevant. The automobiles need not be identical in order for tests on one to be relevant in determining whether the design of another is defective. Design differences between vehicles that might prevent certain alternatives from being adapted to the hatchback design do not necessarily undermine the relevance or discoverability of documents relating to those alternatives. Whether a safer fuel system design suitable for one vehicle is adaptable to another is a question of feasibility to be decided by the trier of fact, not a question to be resolved in ruling on discovery requests. Moreover, if it were impossible to incorporate a safer design in the fuel system of a 1976 Vega Hatchback, the existence of that design would be relevant to establish liability for failure to warn. The time period requested is not overly broad, and Jampole has limited his request to include only tests on GMC passenger cars. There being no valid claim of privilege or limitation invoked, the trial court's denial was a clear abuse of discretion.

GMC argues that because the trial judge conscientiously heard argument from both sides, his order is not an abuse of discretion. The issue, however, is not the degree of care exercised. Rather, the focus is on the effect of the trial court's action on the substantial rights of the parties. The order in this case denied clearly relevant information that is crucial to Jampole's cause of action. Furthermore, although it may be proper in complex litigation such as this to grant discovery in phases, there is no statement anywhere in the trial court order purporting to reserve judgment or postpone any ruling. In unequivocal language, the order states that all of GMC's objections were sustained, except those specifically overruled.

We also reject GMC's argument that because Jampole was free to "come back to the well"— that is, to attempt to persuade the trial court to reconsider—the trial court's action was not an abuse of discretion. First, the statement referred to was not made by Judge Touchy; it was only made by his predecessor, Judge Stovall. Moreover, the trial court's willingness to reconsider does not alter the finality of its ruling. Litigants can always make new arguments that may change the trial court's mind. This does not, however, preclude complaining of the action already taken. It is the court's order that counts, not the stated reasons or oral qualifications. *See In re W.E.R.*, 669 S.W.2d 716 (Tex. 1984) (per curiam); *Kinney v. Shugart*, 234 S.W.2d 451 (Tex. Civ. App.—Eastland 1950, writ ref'd); *Cf. Davis v. Hemphill*, 243 S.W. 691 (Tex. Civ. App —Fort Worth 1922, no writ) (opinion or reasons given by judge constitute no part of judgment); *accord Chandler v. Reder*, 635 S.W.2d 895 (Tex. App.—Amarillo 1982, no writ).

Jampole next complains of the trial court's action in denying discovery of assembly diagrams and instructions. Comparing GMC's assembly instructions and diagrams with the fuel system of the Jampoles' Vega as it was actually manufactured is a proper aid in determining whether manufacturing defects exist. The documents requested are therefore relevant to Jampole's manufacturing defect allegations. GMC's primary objection was not, however, based on lack of relevance. Instead, GMC argued that the diagrams and specifications were competitively sensitive and had proprietary value. The trial court apparently agreed and ruled that GMC was not required to produce any assembly instructions, drawings, or documents.

Although a valid proprietary interest may justify denying or limiting discovery requested by a direct competitor, *Automatic Drilling Machines, Inc. v. Miller*, 515 S.W.2d 256 (Tex. 1974), this is not such a case. Jampole is not GMC's business competitor, and GMC acknowledged that, if the documents were relevant, any proprietary interest could be safeguarded by a protective order. Under these circumstances, it was an abuse of discretion for the trial court to deny discovery of the assembly documents. We do not decide whether GMC has shown a sufficient proprietary interest to justify a protective order. We hold that discovery cannot be denied because of an asserted proprietary interest in the requested documents when a protective order would sufficiently preserve that interest.

Jampole's remaining complaints fail to establish abuses of the trial court's discretion. Jampole argues that he was denied discovery relating to two proposed federal motor vehicle safety standards, GSA 5 15/26 and FMVSS 301. According to Jampole, these federal standards, first proposed in 1967, would have significantly strengthened fuel system integrity requirements. Jampole's expert stated that although the standards were ultimately diluted, until the relaxed standards were adopted, car manufacturers were developing fuel system designs capable of meeting the stricter standards. Jampole requested all documents reflecting GMC's efforts and plans to comply. GMC initially objected, but in its written response GMC agreed to produce certain types of documents relating to the 1976 Vega and public comments prepared by GMC in response to the proposed standards. At the hearing on Jampole's motion, however, the trial judge clearly expressed his understanding and intention that GMC would diligently search for and produce all documents responsive to Jampole's request. Counsel for GMC conceded in oral argument and in their post-submission brief that they were obligated under the trial court's order to fully comply with Jampole's request.

The source of Jampole's concern is that the wording of the trial court's order only requires GMC to produce that which GMC agreed to produce, along with a sworn statement by GMC describing what was being produced. The order does not specify what it was that GMC agreed to produce. Although this language standing alone is unclear, the trial court's intent to give Jampole all he requested is clear. If GMC's production is incomplete or unresponsive, Jampole's remedy is to seek a clarification of the trial court's order and, if necessary, sanctions. A writ of mandamus compelling the trial judge to do that which has already been done, however, is not appropriate.

Jampole also claims the trial court's order denied him discovery of information on experimental, prototype, and pre-production models of the Vega. The order provides: ". . . General Motors' objections are sustained, except that General Motors shall be required to answer the interrogatories and produce documents and things based on a review of its records *pertaining to* the Chevrolet Vega and Pontiac Astre for the model years 1971 through 1977." (emphasis added). This language does not have the effect ascribed to it by Jampole. Documents concerning experimental, prototype, and pre-production models clearly "pertain to" the actual production models, and GMC concedes this is the plain meaning of the trial court's order. We note in passing, however, that requested information is discoverable unless a valid objection is interposed. *See* Tex. R. Civ. P. 167(1)(d); 168(6). For this reason, a better practice would be for the trial court order to state that objections are overruled except for those specifically sustained.

Jampole's final complaint is that he was denied certain master crash test indices. Jampole requested production of "master vehicle crash test indices" listing by test number and type of test the impact tests already requested. On appeal, the parties contest whether any master indices exist and, if so, what the content of such indices is. We do not decide the merits of these arguments, nor do we consider the affidavits and exhibits filed on appeal supporting the parties' positions, because these are factual disputes. *See West v. Solito*, 563 S.W.2d 240, 245 (Tex. 1978). The trial court ordered GMC to produce a listing of all the crash tests that GMC was already required to produce under other provisions of the trial court's order. Although this listing did not require production of any additional material, it gave Jampole exactly what he requested. If indices exist containing information not reached by the trial court's order, Jampole's request does not sufficiently describe them. For this reason, Jampole has failed to show that the trial court abused its discretion. Of course, the wording of the order will cause the list to expand to include tests produced in conformity with this decision.

Having found that the trial court abused its discretion by denying discovery of alternate design and assembly documents, the remaining issue is whether Jampole has an adequate remedy by appeal. . . .

. . . .

[The dissenting opinion of Justice Barrow is omitted.]

---

## K MART CORP. v. SANDERSON

*937 S.W.2d 429 (Tex. 1996)*

PER CURIAM.

. . . .

Stacey Thompson sued K Mart, a Michigan corporation, to recover actual and punitive damages not exceeding $30 million for injuries she received when she was abducted from a K Mart store parking lot in Lufkin and raped. Thompson also sued Weingarten Realty Management Company, a Texas corporation. Thompson alleged that these defendants (to whom we refer collectively as K Mart) and others were negligent and grossly negligent in failing to make adequate provisions for her safety. . . . .

. . . .

Thompson . . . served the three following interrogatories on K Mart:

10. Please describe by date and offense type any criminal conduct that occurred in the K Mart store or parking lot in the shopping center in question during the last seven (7) years.

15. Please list all criminal activities at all property owned, leased or managed by both K Mart Corporation or Weingarten Realty Management Company in the State of Texas during the last seven years that relates in any way to the alleged failure to provide adequate security allegedly resulting in any sort of physical injury to any person.

16. Have there been other incidents at K Mart Stores owned by Weingarten Realty Management Company nationwide in which a person was abducted from the premises and raped? If so, please state the date and location of each such incident that occurred within the last ten years.

Thompson also requested production . . . of all documents related to interrogatory 15. K Mart objected to the interrogatories and request as being overly broad and burdensome. The district court overruled K Mart's objections.

In *Texaco, Inc. v. Sanderson*, plaintiffs claimed damages for exposure to toxic chemicals. At plaintiffs' request, the district court ordered production of all documents written by Texaco's safety director concerning "safety, toxicology, and industrial hygiene, epidemiology, fire protection and training." 898 S.W.2d at 814. We granted mandamus relief, holding the request to be so excessively broad as to be "well outside the bounds of proper discovery." *Id.* at 815. The same may be said of Thompson's interrogatory 10. It would require K Mart to give the date of every shoplifting offense for the past seven years, though shoplifting on K Mart's premises has no apparent connection to Thompson's injury or cause of action.

In *Dillard Department Stores, Inc. v. Hall*, plaintiff sued Dillard for false arrest. At plaintiff's request, the trial court ordered Dillard to produce "every claims file and incident report prepared from 1985 through 1990 in every lawsuit or claim that involved allegations of false arrest, civil rights violations, and excessive use of force" for each of its 227 stores located in twenty states. 909 S.W.2d at 491–492. We granted mandamus relief, holding that the requested discovery was "overly broad as a matter of law." *Id.* At 492. Thompson's interrogatories 15 and 16 are likewise overly broad. The likelihood that criminal conduct on the parking lot of a K Mart store or other property owned by Weingarten in El Paso or Amarillo as long ago as 1989, or outside Texas as long ago as 1986, will have even a minuscule bearing on this case is far too small to justify discovery.

A reference in *Loftin* [*v. Martin*, 776 S.W.2d 145 (Tex. 1989)] suggests that interrogatories and depositions may properly be used for a fishing expedition when a request for production of documents cannot. . . . We reject the notion that any discovery device can be used to "fish." The burden of answering interrogatories like those in this case is hardly less to K Mart than producing documents containing the same information. The district court's order. . . exceeded the bounds of discovery permitted by the rules of procedure and was a clear abuse of discretion.

. . . .

## IN RE AMERICAN OPTICAL CORPORATION

*41 Tex. Sup. Ct. J. 1146 (Tex. 1998)*

PER CURIAM.

This is an original mandamus proceeding. In the underlying case, 140 plaintiffs seek damages for asbetos-related injuries, claiming among other things that relator manufactured and distributed defective respiratory protection products. In response to plaintiffs' document requests, the trial court ordered relator to produce virtually every document ever generated relating to its products, without tying the discovery to the particular products the plaintiffs claim to have used. Because the order requires production well outside the bounds of proper discovery, we conditionally grant mandamus relief.

American Optical Corporation, one of the defendants below, manufactured and distributed a full line of respiratory protection equipment from 1940 until 1990. Plaintiffs, many of whom worked in shipyards, generally contend that they used American Optical's equipment, and that defects in those products contributed to their injuries.

In May 1996, plaintiffs served on American Optical a 76-page document request, containing 221 separately numbered requests. These requests ask for virtually every document which American Optical ever generated regarding its equipment. Some illustrative examples follow:

> 15. All photographs, reproductions, video-tapes, motion picture films, color photographs or color copies of photographs for any of [your respiratory protection products] which lists contain any of the following information: manufacturers' name, brand name, type of product, . . . the contents of the products, and name and address of a distributor of such products. . . .
>
> 18. All documents that set forth the identity of the entitites . . . manufacturing, distributing, relabelling, supplying, selling, assembling, marketing or advertising [your respiratory protection products] which you sold or distributed. . . .
>
> . . .
>
> 28. All documents which describe and all photographs, Xerox copies, color photographs, videotapes, or motion picture films, or color copies of photographs which show the physical appearance of the usual container (i.e. bags, boxes, sacks, etc.) of [your respiratory protection products]. This request includes not only your products, but all such documents in your possession or control.
>
> 29. All documents which set forth the wording of and all photographs which show any label or writing on any container of [your respiratory protection products]. This request includes not only your products, but all such documents in your possession or control.
>
> 33. All documents which would identify the name of each of [your respiratory protection products] which you relabelled after it was relabelled. . . .
>
> 36. All photographs, color copies of photographs, video tapes, films, advertisements, product catalogues, manuals or other documents which show, illustrate, describe, refer to the contracts, refer to the uses, refer to the instructions for use, depict the containers or bags,

contain warnings or cautions, refer to qualities, characteristics, capabilities, capacities and virtues of any of [your respiratory protection products] which were . . . manufactured, distributed, rented, sold, relabelled, assembled, marketed, or advertised by the Defendant or any entity in which Defendant had or has any ownership interest. . . .

108. True, correct and authentic copies of samples of all literature, sales brochures, or any other documents used in any way to advertise, or promote . . . products used for respiratory protection whether written, photographic, video or electronically recorded, or reproduced or otherwise.

American Optical timely objected, contending that the document requests were overbroad because they were not tied to particular products which plaintiffs allegedly used or to the time periods of such use. At the subsequent discovery hearing, the court, with plaintiffs' agreement, modified some of the 221 separate requests. Regarding one part of request 18, for example, where plaintiffs asked for all documents setting forth the identity of distributors, plaintiffs agreed to limit the request to distributors operating in those states where plaintiffs worked. Also, plaintiffs agreed that American Optical could respond to request 18 with a list of entities, rather than producing all documents relating to those entities. The trial court, however, did not significantly limit the other examples quoted above, other than by saying that American Optical need only conduct "reasonable" searches to respond to the expansive requests. Subject to the modifications, the trial court ordered American Optical to produce the requested documents.

American Optical seeks mandamus review. The court of appeals, after initially granting leave to file and hearing oral argument, withdrew leave to file as improvidently granted and denied relief, with one justice dissenting. We have stayed production of the documents.

This Court has repeatedly emphasized that discovery may not be used as a fishing expedition. *See K Mart Corp. v. Sanderson,* 937 S.W.2d 429, 431 (Tex. 1996); *Dillard Dep't Stores, Inc. v. Hall,* 909 S.W.2d 491, 492 (Tex. 1995); *Texaco, Inc. v. Sanderson,* 898 S.W.2d 813, 815 (Tex. 1995). Rather requests must be reasonably tailored to include only matters relevant to the case. *See Texaco*, 898 S.W.2d at 815. For example, in *General Motors Corporation v. Lawrence,* 651 S.W.2d 732, 734 (Tex. 1983), a case alleging the defective design of the fuel filler neck of a particular model truck, we held that requests for fuel filler necks in every vehicle ever manufactured by General Motors were too broad. Similarly, in *Dillard*, a case involving false arrest, we held that a document request from the department store chain for every claims file or incident report over a five-year period involving false arrest, civil rights violations, or excessive use of force was too broad. 909 S.W.2d at 492. *See also Texaco,* 898 S.W.2d at 814–15 (in case alleging exposure to toxic chemicals, request for all documents written by defendant's safety director concerning "safety, toxicology, and industrial hygiene, epidemiology, fire protection and training" was too broad); *K Mart*, 937 S.W.2d at 431 (in case involving abduction from defendant's parking lot, request for a description of all criminal conduct occurring at that location during preceding seven years was too broad). An order compelling discovery that is well outside the proper bounds is reviewable by mandamus. *See K Mart* 937 S.W.2d at 431–32.

Plaintiffs argue that they must be afforded latitude in a mass toxic-tort case such as this involving numerous plaintiffs and defendants. For example, until discovery takes place, individual plaintiffs may be uncertain about precisely what products they used at a particular time. We recognize these problems. This is why trial courts are vested with discretion over the course of discovery. *See Dillard*, 909 S.W.2d at 492 ("The scope of discovery is largely within the discretion of the trial court."). A reasonably tailored discovery request is not overbroad merely because it may include some information of doubtful relevance, and we have specifically recognized that "[p]arties must have some latitude in fashioning proper discovery requests." *Texaco,* 898 S.W.2d at 815.

This latitude is not unlimited, however. The trial court must make an effort to impose reasonable discovery limits. For example, the record reflects that plaintiffs have access to pictures of American Optical's products that may allow them to identify the respirators they used. Also, plaintiffs presumably can identify the facility at which each plaintiff worked and the time-frame of that employment. Notably, American Optical contends that 100 of the 140 plaintiffs worked at one of two facilities, the Todd Shipyard in Galveston and the Ingalls Shipyard in Pascagoula, Mississippi, and that American Optical sold a very limited number of products to those facilities. Preliminary investigation of these background facts could significantly limit the scope of the document production. While the trial court has discretion in fashioning discovery, simply ordering a defendant to produce virtually all documents regarding its products for a fifty-year period is an abuse of that discretion. Plaintiffs' document requests constitute the type of fishing expedition prohibited under *K Mart, Dillard, and Texaco.* The requests are not tied to particular products the plaintiffs claim to have used, and are not limited to time periods such use may have occurred.

American Optical contends that, due to the overbreadth, plaintiffs' entire request for production should be struck. Alternatively, American Optical cites 125 specific requests which it contends are overbroad. The parties have presented general arguments regarding the proper scope of discovery, but have not specifically focused on each of these requests. Under these circumstances, rather than this Court attempting to set the precise bounds of discovery in the first instance, we believe that the trial court should have an opportunity to reconsider its ruling in light of our opinion today.

American Optical also complains about numerous requests seeking documents relating to silica injuries or prior silica cases. American Optical argues that because the plaintiffs in this case allege only asbestos related injuries, any documents relating to silica are not relevant. The record reflects, however, that American Optical did not raise this specific objection in the trial court, either in its written objections or during the trial court hearing. Because this argument was not presented to the trial court, we do not consider it here.

For the foregoing reasons, without hearing oral argument, we conditionally grant mandamus relief compelling the trial court to vacate its November 12, 1996, order compelling production of documents by American Optical. *See* Tex. R. App. P. 59.1. The trial court should reconsider plaintiffs' motion to compel in light of this opinion.

---

## NOTES AND QUESTIONS

(1) *Breadth of Discovery Relevance Test.* How broad is the discovery relevance test in Texas? In determining whether a particular matter is discoverable, would it be proper for a trial judge to deny discovery of marginally relevant information because the burden on the defendant is heavy? Is that what happened in the *K Mart* case, or did the Supreme Court of Texas conclude that the information sought had no logical relevance whatever?

(2) *Burdensomeness Issues.* The burden of retrieving information depends in part on the manner in which the information is stored. Should the court take into consideration that a party's own

decisions about document storage have contributed to the burden of production? *See ISK Biotech Corp. v. Lindsay*, 933 S.W.2d 565 (Tex. App.—Houston [1st Dist.] 1996, no writ).

(3) *The New Proportionality Rule.* The 1999 discovery rule revisions added a new proportionality rule, modeled on the federal discovery provisions, that directly authorizes the court to balance benefit and burden. Tex. R. Civ. P. 192.4. Would this rule have changed the outcome of *Jampole*, *K Mart*, or *American Optical*?

### [2] Special Relevance Issues

Within the generic definition of relevance, there are areas in which there are recurring disputes about the scope of discovery. Some of these areas are directly addressed in the 1999 amendments to the rules regarding relevance and disclosure requests. First, Civil Procedure Rule 192.3 provides that a party may obtain discovery of the name, address, and telephone number of any person having knowledge of relevant facts. In addition, a party is entitled to obtain a brief statement of each identified person's connection with the case. This provision is intended to help parties decide how to allocate limited deposition hours by identifying persons whose connection with the case is more substantial than others. The phrase "connection with the case" does not contemplate a narrative statement of the facts a person knows, but should consist of a few words describing the person's identity as it is relevant to the lawsuit. Examples include: "treating physician," "eyewitness," "director," or "plaintiff's mother and eyewitness to the accident." Tex. R. Civ. P. 192, Comment 3. The new rules also make clear that an expert is a "person with knowledge of relevant facts" if that expert obtained his or her knowledge of the case first hand, not in preparation for trial or in anticipation of litigation.

Second, the 1999 rule amendments allow a party to discover "the statement of any person with knowledge of relevant facts," otherwise called a witness statement. Before the amendments, witness statements were not directly discoverable because they were protected as a species of trial preparation material. A "witness statement" is either a "written statement signed or otherwise adopted or approved in writing by the person making it" or a "stenographic, mechanical, electrical, or other type of recording of a witness's oral statement, or any substantially verbatim transcription of such a recording." Tex. R. Civ. P. 192.3(h). Witness statements must be relevant to be discoverable, and privileges such as the attorney-client privilege may be asserted where applicable. However, no work product objections may be asserted to a request for disclosure of witness statements.

Third, a party may obtain discovery of the name, address, and telephone number of any person who is expected to be called to testify at trial. This specific provision of Rule 192.3(d) should overrule previous cases that protected such information as work product.

Fourth, a party may obtain discovery of any other party's legal contentions and the factual bases for those contentions. Tex. R. Civ. P. 192.3(j). The information may be discovered through either a request for disclosure under Rule 194 or through an interrogatory under Rule 197. Note, however, that a party is not required to marshal all of its available proof or all the proof that party intends to offer at trial. Rather, Comment 5 to Civil Procedure Rule 192 notes that the rules do not "require more than a basic statement of those contentions."

The following Notes and Questions address other recurring issues.

## NOTES AND QUESTIONS

### *Insurance Policies and Settlement Agreements*

(1) *Liability Insurance.* Information concerning the existence of liability insurance and indemnity agreements (including the policy limits of the policies) is discoverable, but its discoverability does not make it admissible. Tex. R. Civ. P. 192.3(f).

(2) *Relevance of Policy Limits.* Why should policy limits be "relevant" in the discovery sense? Most liability insurance policies impose a duty of defense on the insurer, so the defendant's lawyer is likely furnished by the insurer. A plaintiff would want to see the policy because Texas law, like the law of other states, imposes excess liability on an insurer if it fails to settle within policy limits under certain circumstances. *G.A. Stowers Furniture Co. v. American Indemnity Co.*, 15 S.W.2d 544 (Tex. Comm'n App. 1929, opinion adopted). Plaintiff's settlement leverage may be increased if plaintiff can create the potential for *Stowers*-based liability. Why else might a plaintiff want the policy?

(3) *Settlement Agreements.* Civil Procedure Rule 192.3(g) also makes the existence and contents of any settlement agreement discoverable. Tex. R. Civ. P. 192.3(g). As in the case of insurance agreements, its discoverability does not make it admissible. Despite its broad language, this rule has been held to be limited by the general discovery relevance standard. *Palo Duro Pipeline Co. Inc. v. Cochran*, 785 S.W.2d 455, 457 (Tex. App.—Houston [14th Dist.] 1990, orig. proceeding). The court rejected the argument that discovery of settlement agreements is limited to "Mary Carter" agreements (agreements in which a settling defendant retains a financial stake in the plaintiff's recovery against the remaining tortfeasors, and remains a party at trial) or agreements arising out of the same lawsuit. *Id.*

### *Net Worth*

(1) *Relevance of Defendant's Net Worth.* The Supreme Court held in *Lunsford v. Morris*, 746 S.W.2d 471 (Tex. 1988) that information about defendant's net worth is relevant to the issue of punitive damages and is therefore discoverable. Net worth information is not discoverable under *Lunsford* when no proper claim to punitive damages has been made. For example, in *Al Parker Buick Co. v. Touchy*, 788 S.W.2d 129 (Tex. App.—Houston [1st Dist.] 1990, orig. proceeding), plaintiff's petition did not allege a cause of action entitling him to punitive damages against the individual defendant's employer. Because the petition was legally insufficient to support an award of punitive damages, the net worth discovery sought should have been denied.

(2) *Limits on Net Worth Discovery.* Since *Lunsford*, the Supreme Court has considered what type of financial information can be discovered. In *Sears, Roebuck & Co. v. Ramirez*, 824 S.W.2d 558, 559 (Tex. 1992), the Court held that the trial court had abused its discretion in ordering production of Sears' tax returns. Sears had produced annual reports reflecting its net worth and introduced an affidavit claiming that the annual reports were accurate. Further, Sears proffered evidence that it would take an employee two or three weeks to duplicate the requested five years' worth of tax returns. Under these facts, the Supreme Court held that Sears should not have been ordered to produce the returns.

(3) *Bifurcation of Trials: Punitive Damage Claims.* In a case seeking punitive damages, the trial court should bifurcate the trial when presented with a timely motion. *See* C.P.R.C. § 41.009; *Transportation Ins. Co. v. Moriel*, 879 S.W.2d 10, 29–30 (Tex. 1994). This does not mean, however, that discovery of net worth should be postponed until after the first part of the trial. The Houston Court of Appeals has rejected a trial court's attempt to delay the discovery of net worth data until after a finding of liability in a bifurcated trial. *Miller v. O'Neill*, 775 S.W.2d 56 (Tex. App.—Houston [1st Dist.] 1989, orig. proceeding) (also rejecting an overbreadth claim and allowing discovery of income tax returns, financial statements, or net worth statements of defendant and any partnership and professional corporations in which he had an interest for a 10-year period).

*Information Sought Solely for Impeachment*

Special problems arise when information is sought in order to impeach a person who is expected to testify at trial, especially when the person is not a party. The Texas Supreme Court has held that voluminous financial records of a nonparty medical witness were not "discoverable prior to trial in instances where the potential witness is not a party to the lawsuit and whose credibility has not been put in issue and where the records do not relate directly to the subject matter of the pending suit and are sought to be discovered for the sole purpose of impeachment of such witness by showing his bias and prejudice." *Russell v. Young*, 452 S.W.2d 434, 435 (Tex. 1970). Four years later, the court distinguished *Russell* and held that appraisal reports prepared by the government's appraisal witnesses relating to land that was not the subject of the condemnation proceedings in which discovery was sought were discoverable. First, "*Russell* presented an attempt at wholesale discovery of the private records of a non-party . . . . In this case the reports sought are not of a private or personal nature." Second, "[t]he condemning authority has designated the appraisers whose reports are sought as witnesses upon whom they will rely at trial." Third, "the reports are not sought solely, or even primarily, to show bias or prejudice. They are sought as evidence of possible inconsistencies in the appraiser's valuation of other [comparable] properties." *Ex parte Shepperd*, 513 S.W.2d 813, 816 (Tex. 1974).

The Texas Supreme Court returned to the issue of impeachment discovery in *Walker v. Packer*, 827 S.W.2d 833 (Tex. 1992). The Court characterized *Russell* as involving "wholesale discovery of financial records of a potential medical witness who was not a party to the lawsuit." In *Walker*, however, the court noted that the plaintiff had presented the trial court with evidence of specific circumstances that indicated bias. Under these circumstances the Court indicated that some discovery should be allowed:

> [T]he Walkers are not engaged in global discovery of the type disapproved in *Russell*; rather, they narrowly seek information regarding the potential bias suggested by the witness' own deposition testimony and that of his professional colleague. Our rules of civil procedure, and the federal rules upon which they are based, mandate a flexible approach to discovery. . . . Evidence of bias of a witness is relevant and admissible.

Earlier cases suggesting a complete bar to discovery of impeachment materials are therefore incorrect. In addition, the 1999 amendments make information relevant to the bias of an expert witness clearly discoverable. *See* Tex. R. Civ. P. 192.3(e)(5).

### [B] Privileges and Other Limits on Discovery

Even information that is relevant may not be discoverable. There are a number of privileges that, for various policy reasons, protect certain kinds of communications from discovery. These privileges variously come from the procedure rules themselves, from the rules of evidence, from other statutes, and from the U.S. Constitution. This subsection considers the parameters of those privileges, especially those related to trial preparation materials and the attorney-client privilege.

### [1] The Discovery Rule Privileges

*Read Tex. R. Civ. P. 192, 194, 195 and accompanying Comments*

Some of the information that is relevant to a lawsuit is actually generated by the parties and their representatives in the course of preparing for that lawsuit. In the federal courts, communications generated in anticipation of litigation are referred to as "work product," and their discoverability is limited. The United States Supreme Court first considered the issue in *Hickman v. Taylor*, 329 U.S. 495 (1946). The case concerned the sinking of a tugboat, in which five people were killed. The tug owners hired an attorney, who took oral and written statements from witnesses. The controversy before the Supreme Court grew out of a discovery request by a plaintiff's attorney for "copies of all such statements if in writing and, if oral, . . . the exact provisions of such oral statements or reports." The Court rejected an argument that the information requested was covered by the attorney-client privilege, but did create a discovery exemption for the "work product of the lawyer." Note the Texas Supreme Court's discussion of *Hickman* in the *National Tank* opinion below.

Until the 1999 amendments, the Texas Rules of Civil Procedure divided trial preparation materials into four subdivisions, each of which was specifically included in former Civil Procedure Rule 166b(3): (1) work product of an attorney, (2) witness statements, (3) party communications, and (4) information concerning consulting experts who neither testify nor have their work reviewed by testifying experts. The 1999 amendments, however, made a wholesale revision of the trial preparation privileges. Civil Procedure Rule 192 merges the previously undefined "work product" exemption and the party communications exemption into a single "work product" privilege. Significantly, the former separate privileged status for witness statements prepared or taken in anticipation of litigation has been expressly eliminated and witness statements are not work product, even if made in anticipation of litigation. The protection of pure consulting expert information remains, now codified at Civil Procedure Rule 192.3(e).

This section of the chapter examines the work product and expert witness exemptions contained in the discovery rules.

*Work Product*

*Read Tex. R. Civ. P. 192.3(e)(3), (6), 192.5, 194.5.*

Civil Procedure Rule 192.5 provides that work product is not discoverable. "Work product" is defined as material prepared or mental impressions developed in anticipation of litigation or for trial by or for a party or a party's representative. Work product also encompasses a communication made in anticipation of litigation or for trial between a party and a party's representative or among a party's representatives. A party's representatives include the party's attorney's, consultants, sureties, indemnitors, insurers, employees, and agents. Tex. R. Civ. P. 192.5(a).

The primary purpose of the work product rule is to shelter the mental processes, conclusions, and legal theories of the attorney, providing a privileged area in which the lawyer can analyze and prepare the case. *Owens-Corning Fiberglas Corp. v. Caldwell*, 818 S.W.2d 749, 750 (Tex.

1991). The work product exemption protects two related but different concepts. First, the privilege protects the attorney's thought process, which includes strategy decisions and issue formation, and the notes or writing evidencing those mental processes. Second, the privilege protects the mechanical compilation of information in preparation for trial; it protects the documents produced in anticipation of litigation and not the underlying information itself. With respect to an attorney's thought processes, the work product exemption is absolute, subject only to the narrow exceptions listed in Texas Rule of Evidence 503(d). *See* Tex. R. Civ. P. 192.5(c)(5). But with respect to compiled information, the exemption is not absolute. This distinction is carried forward into Civil Procedure Rule 192.5, which draws a distinction between "core work product" and all other work product.

"Core work product" is defined as the work product of an attorney or attorney's representative that contains the attorney's or the attorney's representative's mental impressions, opinions, conclusions, or legal theories. Core work product is not discoverable. Other materials that fall within the definition of work product but do not qualify as core work product (known as "ordinary work product") are discoverable *only* on a showing of substantial need and undue hardship.

Civil Procedure Rule 192.5(c) provides that some types of information are discoverable even if made in anticipation of litigation or for trial: Information discoverable under Rule 192.3 concerning expert witnesses, trial witnesses, witness statements, and contentions. Trial exhibits if ordered disclosed by the trial court. The name, address, and telephone number of any potential party or any person with knowledge of relevant facts. Any photograph or electronic image of underlying facts or a photograph or electronic image of any sort that a party intends to offer into evidence. Any work product created under circumstances within an exception to the attorney-client privilege under the evidence rules.

Difficult issues remain with regard to the duration of the work product exemption: (1) when does a party act in "anticipation of litigation" so as to clothe communications with a discovery exemption; and (2) once it applies, how long does work product protection last? The following case was decided under the pre-1999 rules. As you read it, consider how it will help you to interpret the meaning of the new rules.

---

## NATIONAL TANK CO. v. BROTHERTON

*851 S.W.2d 193 (Tex. 1993)*

PHILLIPS, Chief Justice.

. . . .

An explosion occurred on August 23, 1990, at a Wichita Falls manufacturing facility operated by the National Tank Company (NATCO), Relator in this proceeding. The explosion critically injured Rex Willson, a NATCO employee, and two other persons employed by independent contractors. Willson later died from his injuries. Allen Pease, NATCO's General Counsel and Secretary, learned of the explosion the day it occurred and dispatched Henry Townsend, NATCO's safety and risk control coordinator, to investigate. Although not a lawyer, Townsend was employed in NATCO's legal department under Pease's supervision. Pease also immediately notified David Sneed, a brokerage supervisor with American International Adjustment Company

(AIAC), a representative of NATCO's liability insurers. Pease explained to Sneed the serious nature of the accident, and recommended that AIAC initiate its own investigation, which it did.

Willson's wife, individually and on behalf of her children and the estate, sued NATCO and several other defendants on January 15, 1991. Shortly thereafter, she requested that NATCO produce any reports prepared in connection with the accident investigation. NATCO objected, asserting the attorney-client, work-product, witness-statement, and party-communication privileges. In an order signed July 25, 1991, the trial court overruled NATCO's objections as to documents prepared prior to October 25, 1990, the date NATCO learned that it had been sued by Frank Kroupa, one of the other persons injured in the explosion. The trial court thus ordered NATCO to produce the documents prepared prior to that date. These documents are 1) the transcripts of four interviews of NATCO employees conducted by Henry Townsend shortly after the accident, 2) the transcripts of nine interviews of NATCO employees conducted by Phil Precht, an AIAC employee, shortly after the accident, and 3) three accident reports prepared by Precht and sent to Pease. The trial court, however, stayed the effect of this order to allow NATCO to seek mandamus relief.

. . . .

III

We next consider whether the documents are privileged under Texas Rule of Civil Procedure 166b(3)(a) as "the work product of an attorney." "Work product" has generally been defined as "specific documents, reports, communications, memoranda, mental impressions, conclusions, opinions, or legal theories, prepared and assembled in actual anticipation of litigation or for trial." *Wiley*, 769 S.W.2d at 717; *Brown & Root U.S.A., Inc. v. Moore*, 731 S.W.2d 137, 140 (Tex. App.—Houston [14th Dist.] 1987, orig. proceeding); *Evans v. State Farm Mut. Auto. Ins. Co.*, 685 S.W.2d 765, 767 (Tex. App.—Houston [1st Dist.] 1985, writ ref'd n.r.e.). NATCO argues, however, that the privilege is not limited to documents prepared in anticipation of litigation. This Court has not previously addressed this issue. To do so, it is necessary to examine some of the history of the work product privilege.

The work product doctrine was created by the United States Supreme Court in *Hickman v. Taylor*, 329 U.S. 495, 67 S. Ct. 385, 91 L. Ed. 451 (1947). In *Hickman*, five crew members drowned when the tugboat J.M. Stark sank in the Delaware River. The boat owner's attorney investigated the accident, obtaining signed statements from some of the witnesses and making memoranda of his conversations with the others. The estate of one of the deceased crew members subsequently sued the boat owner and sought by interrogatories to obtain copies of the witness statements and the attorney's memoranda prepared during the investigation. The defendant objected on the grounds that the requests called "for privileged matter obtained in preparation for litigation" and was "an attempt to obtain indirectly counsel's private files." *Id.* at 499, 67 S. Ct. at 388.

The district court ordered production, but the United States Court of Appeals for the Third Circuit reversed and the Supreme Court affirmed the judgment of the appellate court. The Supreme Court could find no existing privilege that applied, but it created a new common law privilege for what it termed the "work product of the lawyer,"[5] consisting of interviews,

[5] The term "work product" was coined during the argument before the Third Circuit in the *Hickman* case. *Hickman v. Taylor*, 153 F.2d 212, 223 (3d Cir. 1945), *aff'd*, 329 U.S. 495, 67 S. Ct. 385, 91 L. Ed. 451 (1947).

memoranda, briefs and other materials prepared "with an eye toward litigation." *Hickman*, 329 U.S. at 511, 67 S. Ct. at 393. The Court justified the privilege as follows:

> Proper preparation of a client's case demands that [the attorney] assemble information, sift what he considers to be the relevant from the irrelevant facts, prepare his legal theories and plan his strategy without undue and needless interference. That is the historical and the necessary way in which lawyers act within the framework of our system of jurisprudence to promote justice and to protect their clients' interests.

*Id.* The Court indicated that the privilege could be overcome as to factual information otherwise unavailable to the opposing party, but not as to the attorney's "mental impressions." *Id.* at 512, 67 S. Ct. at 394.

The *Hickman* work product doctrine was codified in Fed. R. Civ. P. 26(b)(3) in 1970.[6] This rule maintains the distinction between ordinary work product, which is discoverable upon a showing of "substantial need" and "undue hardship," and an attorney's "mental impressions, conclusions, opinions, or legal theories," which are discoverable, if at all, only upon a much higher showing.[7] This latter category has come to be known as "opinion" or "core" work product. *See In re Murphy*, 560 F.2d 326, 329 n. 1 (8th Cir. 1977); Jeff A. Anderson et al., *Special Project, The Work Product Doctrine*, 68 Cornell L. Rev. 760, 817–20 (1983). Federal Rule of Civil Procedure 26(b)(3) has been adopted verbatim by 34 states, and in substantial part by 10 others. *See* Elizabeth Thornburg, *Rethinking Work Product*, 77 Va. L. Rev. 1515, 1520–21 (1991).

The structure of the Texas rule is somewhat different from the federal rule, however, as it simply protects the "work product of an attorney." "Work product" is not defined in the rule, and this Court has never specifically defined the term.

It is important to note that the work product exemption has played a much lesser role in Texas than in the federal system and other states due to the separate privilege in Texas that protects communications between a party's representatives. *See* Tex. R. Civ. P. 166b(3)(d). This privilege, which in one form or another has been part of the Texas Rules of Civil Procedure since their adoption in 1941, is broad enough to protect ordinary work product. *See* Alex W. Albright, *The Texas Discovery Privileges: A Fool's Game?*, 70 Tex. L. Rev. 781, 831 (1992). The specific work product exemption did not appear in the Texas Rules until 1973, [footnote omitted] and there was "a dearth of decisional law" interpreting this exemption prior to 1986, as the work product privilege was often merged with the party communication privilege. *See* James B. Sales,

[6] Fed. R. Civ. P. 26(b)(3) provides:

> Subject to the provisions of subdivision (b)(4) of this rule [regarding experts], a party may obtain discovery of documents and tangible things otherwise discoverable under subdivision (b)(1) of this rule and prepared in anticipation of litigation or for trial by or for another party or by or for that other party's representative (including the other party's attorney, consultant, surety, indemnitor, insurer, or agent) only upon a showing that the party seeking discovery has substantial need of the materials in the preparation of the party's case and that the party is unable without undue hardship to obtain the substantial equivalent of the materials by other means. In ordering discovery of such materials when the required showing has been made, the court shall protect against disclosure of the mental impressions, conclusions, opinions, or legal theories of an attorney or other representative of a party concerning the litigation.

[7] Some courts have held that no showing can overcome the protection of an attorney's mental impressions. *See, e.g., In re Grand Jury Proceedings*, 473 F.2d 840, 848 (8th Cir. 1973). Others have declined to adopt an absolute rule, but recognize that this type of work product would only be discoverable in a "rare situation." *See, e.g., In re Grand Jury Investigation*, 599 F.2d 1224, 1231 (3d Cir. 1979). In *Upjohn Co. v. United States*, 449 U.S. 383, 401, 101 S. Ct. 677, 688, 66 L. Ed. 2d 584 (1981), the Supreme Court recognized this conflict but did not resolve it.

*Pretrial Discovery in Texas Under the Amended Rules: Analysis and Commentary*, 27 S. Tex. L. Rev. 305, 315 (1986). There appears to have been more reliance on the work product privilege since 1986, when the scope of the party communication privilege was narrowed.

NATCO relies on the plain language of Texas Rule of Civil Procedure 166b(3) in arguing that a document need not be prepared in anticipation of litigation to be privileged as work product. NATCO points out that Rule 166b(3)(c) and (d), the witness statement and party communication privileges, expressly require that the statement or communication be made in anticipation of litigation, while Rule 166b(3)(a), the work product privilege, contains no such requirement. This argument, however, is unpersuasive. As discussed below, "work product" by definition applies only to materials prepared in anticipation of litigation.

As indicated, the work product doctrine was firmly established in federal case law and codified in the federal rules when it was adopted in Texas. There is nothing to indicate that the Texas concept of "work product" was intended to be different from that of the federal courts. *See* William W. Kilgarlin et al., *Practicing Law in the "New Age": The 1988 Amendments to the Texas Rules of Civil Procedure*, 19 Tex. Tech. L. Rev. 881, 899 (1988). We have in the past looked to federal precedent in deciding work product questions. *See Garcia v. Peeples*, 734 S.W.2d 343, 348 (Tex. 1987).

There appears to be no doubt that the term "work product" in the federal courts, as well as the courts of other states, applies only to materials prepared in anticipation of litigation. [citations omitted]

Texas courts of appeals have also uniformly held that the privilege applies only to materials prepared in anticipation of litigation. [citations omitted]

We therefore conclude that the term "work product" as used in Rule 166b(3)(a) applies only to materials prepared in anticipation of litigation. It is not necessary to further consider the scope of the work product exemption in Texas,[11] because if the disputed documents were prepared in anticipation of litigation, they are privileged under the witness statement and party communication privileges. . . .

---

[11] It is not clear whether the term "work product" in Rule 166b(3)(a) applies to both opinion and ordinary work product, or whether it is limited to opinion work product. This distinction, which is critical under the federal work product doctrine, is not drawn in the rule and has apparently never been previously recognized by any Texas court. *See Albright, supra* at 829; Robert Ammons, Comment, *Finders Keepers No Longer the Rule: Discovery of Investigatory Materials Under the Texas and Federal Rules of Civil Procedure*, 39 Baylor L. Rev. 271, 282 (1987). We recently noted that "[t]he primary purpose of the work product rule is to shelter the mental processes, conclusions, and legal theories of the attorney," and does not extend to "facts the attorney may acquire." *Owens-Corning Fiberglas*, 818 S.W.2d at 750 & n. 2. *See also Axelson, Inc. v. McIlhany*, 798 S.W.2d 550, 554 n. 8 (Tex. 1990). Also, if Rule 166b(3)(a) applies to ordinary work product, it apparently conflicts with the party communication privilege as to the protection of factual reports that fall under both privileges. The party communication privilege provides for a hardship exception, whereas the work product exemption does not. Commentators have pointed out that ordinary work product should be discoverable upon a showing of substantial need and undue hardship. *Albright, supra*, at 830; *Kilgarlin, supra*, at 899.

We do not now decide this issue, as it is not necessary to do so in deciding this case, and has not been briefed or argued by the parties.

IV

A

Texas Rule of Civil Procedure 166b(3)(c) protects from discovery witness statements "made subsequent to the occurrence or transaction upon which the suit is based and in connection with the prosecution, investigation, or defense of the particular suit, or in anticipation of the prosecution or defense of the claims made a part of the pending litigation. . . ." Texas Rule of Civil Procedure 166b(3)(d) similarly protects communications between agents, representatives or employees of a party when made in anticipation of litigation. The only issue concerning the applicability of these privileges in this case is whether the witness statements and investigative reports generated by NATCO and its insurer were made in anticipation of litigation.

An investigation is conducted in anticipation of litigation if it meets the two-prong test of *Flores v. Fourth Court of Appeals,* 777 S.W.2d 38, 40–41 (Tex. 1989). The first prong of the *Flores* test is objective. The court is required to determine whether a reasonable person, based on the circumstances existing at the time of the investigation, would have anticipated litigation. We stated in *Flores* that "[c]onsideration should be given to outward manifestations which indicate litigation is *imminent.*" *Id.* at 41 (emphasis added). Upon further consideration, however, we conclude that the "imminence" requirement impairs the policy goals of the witness statement and party communication privileges. Serving the function filled in many jurisdictions by the work product doctrine, these privileges seek to strike a balance between open discovery and the need to protect the adversary system. As the Supreme Court noted in *Hickman*, a party[12] must be free to assemble information about the case free of undue interference from the other side:

> Were such materials open to opposing counsel on mere demand, much of what is now put down in writing would remain unwritten. An attorney's thoughts, heretofore inviolate, would not be his own. Inefficiency, unfairness and sharp practices would inevitably develop in the giving of legal advice and in the preparation of cases for trial. The effect on the legal profession would be demoralizing. And the interests of the clients and the cause of justice would be poorly served.

*Hickman*, 329 U.S. at 511, 67 S. Ct. at 393–94. The investigative privileges promote the truthful resolution of disputes through the adversarial process by encouraging complete and thorough investigation of the facts by both sides. *See* Cohn, *supra* note 10, at 919–920; Anderson et al., *supra*, at 785; *see also El Paso Co.*, 682 F.2d at 542; *Coastal States Gas Corp. v. Department of Energy*, 617 F.2d 854, 864 (D.C. Cir. 1980). At the same time, they do not unduly thwart discovery, as they are limited in scope and can be overcome by a showing of substantial need for the information and undue hardship in obtaining it from other sources.

Considering these policies, we conclude that the objective prong of *Flores* is satisfied whenever the circumstances surrounding the investigation would have indicated to a reasonable person that there was a substantial chance of litigation. The confidentiality necessary for the adversary process is not defeated because a party, reasonably anticipating future litigation, conducts an investigation prior to the time that litigation is "imminent." We accordingly modify *Flores* to the extent that it accords protection only to investigations conducted when litigation is imminent.

---

12 Although *Hickman* applied only to materials prepared by an attorney, the federal work product doctrine no longer distinguishes between an investigation conducted by a party and one conducted by its representative. The Texas investigative privileges likewise do not make this distinction.

We agree with the dissenting justices' characterization of "substantial chance of litigation." This does not refer to any particular statistical probability that litigation will occur; rather, it simply means that litigation is "more than merely an abstract possibility or unwarranted fear." 851 S.W.2d at 216. The underlying inquiry is whether it was reasonable for the investigating party to anticipate litigation and prepare accordingly.

The real parties in interest argue, and some courts of appeals have held, that the objective prong of *Flores* may be satisfied only where the *plaintiff* engages in some action indicating an intent to sue. *See, e.g., Boring & Tunneling Co.*, 782 S.W.2d at 287. *Flores*, however, does not hold this. Rather, it requires the trial court to examine the *totality of the circumstances* to determine whether the investigation is conducted in anticipation of litigation. *Flores*, 777 S.W.2d at 41. Requiring that the plaintiff manifest an intent to sue would also be at odds with the policy goals of the witness statement and party communication privileges. These privileges are designed to promote the adversarial process by granting limited protection to investigations conducted in preparation for litigation. Common sense dictates that a party may reasonably anticipate suit being filed, and conduct an investigation to prepare for the expected litigation, before the plaintiff manifests an intent to sue. *See Wiley* 769 S.W.2d at 717; *Smith v. Thornton*, 765 S.W.2d 473, 477 (Tex. App.—Houston [14th Dist.] 1988, no writ); *Lone Star Dodge, Inc. v. Marshall*, 736 S.W.2d 184, 189 (Tex. App.—Dallas 1987, orig. proceeding).

We held in *Stringer v. Eleventh Court of Appeals*, 720 S.W.2d 801 (Tex. 1986), that "[t]he mere fact that an accident has occurred is not sufficient to clothe all post-accident investigations . . . with a privilege." *Id.* at 802. We adhere to this holding, but we disapprove *Stringer* to the extent that it holds that the circumstances surrounding an accident can never by themselves be sufficient to trigger the privilege. If a reasonable person would conclude from the severity of the accident and the other circumstances surrounding it that there was a substantial chance that litigation would ensue, then the objective prong of *Flores* is satisfied.

The second prong of the *Flores* test is subjective. There, we held that the party invoking the privilege must have had "a good faith belief that litigation would ensue." 777 S.W.2d at 41. For the reasons previously discussed with respect to the objective prong, however, we conclude that the subjective prong is properly satisfied if the party invoking the privilege believes in good faith that there is a substantial chance that litigation will ensue. It does not further the policy goals of the privilege to require the investigating party to be absolutely convinced that litigation will occur. Also, although not expressly stated in *Flores*, we believe that the subjective prong plainly requires that the investigation actually be conducted for the purpose of preparing for litigation. An investigation is not conducted "in anticipation of litigation" if it is in fact prepared for some other purpose. As with the objective prong, the court must examine the totality of the circumstances to determine whether the subjective prong is satisfied.

. . . .

The fundamental problem that has plagued other courts is determining whether a "routine" investigation is conducted in anticipation of litigation. The Advisory Committee Notes to the 1970 federal rules amendments provide that "[m]aterials assembled in the ordinary course of business, or pursuant to public requirements unrelated to litigation, or for other nonlitigation purposes" are not protected. Proposed Amendments to the Federal Rules of Civil Procedure Relating to Discovery, 48 F.R.D. 485, 501 (1970). Accordingly, many courts have recognized a bright-line "ordinary course of business" exception.

. . . .

Other courts, however, have rejected a hard and fast ordinary course of business exception, recognizing that a prudent party may routinely prepare for litigation after a serious accident. . . .

. . . .

We agree that there should be no bright-line ordinary course of business exception. It may very well be that a party routinely investigates serious accidents because such accidents routinely give rise to litigation. As with other investigations, an investigation performed in the ordinary course of business is conducted in anticipation of litigation if it passes both prongs of the *Flores* test. With regard to the subjective prong, the circumstances must indicate that the investigation was in fact conducted to prepare for potential litigation. The court therefore must consider the reasons that gave rise to the company's ordinary business practice. If a party routinely investigates accidents because of litigation and nonlitigation reasons, the court should determine the primary motivating purpose underlying the ordinary business practice. [citations omitted][13]

In summary, an investigation is conducted in anticipation of litigation for purposes of Rule 166b(3) when a) a reasonable person would have concluded from the totality of the circumstances surrounding the investigation that there was a substantial chance that litigation would ensue; and b) the party resisting discovery believed in good faith that there was a substantial chance that litigation would ensue and conducted the investigation for the purpose of preparing for such litigation.

. . . .

[The concurring opinion of Justice Gonzalez is omitted.]

DOGGETT, Justice, concurring [footnote omitted] and dissenting.

While a widow plans a funeral, the corporation in whose facility her husband was killed conducts an investigation. While family and friends mourn, the corporation obtains witness statements and prepares reports concerning the circumstances surrounding the death. If this occurrence is ever considered by a judge and jury, they should be able to hear the plain, unvarnished truth—to learn what really happened when memories were fresh and unpolished by counsel.

---

[13] Justice Doggett assumes that all claims investigations conducted by an insurance company will be privileged under today's opinion. 851 S.W.2d at 212–213. This is incorrect. An insurer, like any other party, must establish that the circumstances reasonably indicated a substantial chance of litigation, that the insurer believed in good faith that litigation would ensue, and that the investigation was conducted primarily to prepare for the expected litigation. An insurer routinely investigating a claim to determine whether coverage exists under its policy will in many cases not be able to meet these criteria. We thus do not adopt the "minority" rule referred to in *Langdon v. Champion*, 752 P.2d 999 (Alaska 1988), and cited by Justice Doggett, 851 S.W.2d 212–213, that protects "virtually all insurance carrier investigations." 752 P.2d at 1006.

Justice Doggett also contends that our holding unfairly restricts discovery because "immediate post-accident investigations can uncover fresh evidence from witnesses and the scene that will often not be available at any other time." 851 S.W.2d at 212–213. This analysis ignores the exception to the party-communication and witness-statement privileges set forth in Rule 166b(3)(e), which allows discovery of otherwise privileged materials upon a showing of substantial need and undue hardship in obtaining the substantial equivalent of the materials by other means. This exception, which is patterned after a similar exception in Fed. R. Civ. P. 26(b)(3), has been rarely invoked by parties in Texas seeking discovery.

Justice Doggett further argues that the standard announced today will not be as clear and easy to apply as the "outward manifestations" test attributed to *Flores*, under which the investigatory privilege does not apply until the plaintiff manifests an intent to sue. Whether an investigation is conducted in anticipation of litigation has proved to be an elusive concept, producing a substantial amount of litigation in federal and state courts. Surely *Flores* did not solve this problem, as its standard has also produced substantial litigation.

But now the majority[2] puts a stop to all of that; it approves concealment of this investigation. As the family buries the victim, the corporation can bury any inconvenient facts it has learned. There is certainly nothing improper about the corporation investigating, but justice may well be defeated if the fruits of that investigation are hidden from the victim as well as other parties who may be forced to defend themselves against charges of wrongdoing. Such unwarranted secrecy defeats the search for truth and violates the previous law of Texas, as the trial judge in Wichita properly recognized. Unfortunately, once again neither an explicit procedural rule nor the prior decisions of this court prevent the continued erection of what is essentially a double standard of justice in Texas. Amply displayed here is the added cost and delay resulting from the majority's eagerness to intrude rather than willingness to accept our existing law.[3]

I.

So that the real facts may ultimately be made known, we permit parties discovery before a trial begins. That process is designed to draw no distinction between the weak and the strong. The contrary approach approved today—secrecy—will sometimes benefit one side and sometimes another, [footnote omitted] but it will invariably make truth its first casualty. This court's commitment to openness has previously been firm. [footnote omitted] Most recently in *State v. Lowry*, 802 S.W.2d 669 (Tex. 1991, orig. proceeding), an opinion I authored for a unanimous court, discovery worked to the immediate benefit of the most powerful insurance companies in this country. And, under the circumstances of that case, rightly so. There, as in so many of our prior decisions, this court set forth the principle that should govern the present dispute:

> Affording parties full discovery promotes the fair resolution of disputes by the judiciary. This court has vigorously sought to ensure that lawsuits are "decided by what the facts reveal, not by what facts are concealed." Discovery is thus the linchpin of the search for truth, as it makes "a trial less of a game of blind man's bluff and more a fair contest with the issues and facts disclosed to the fullest practicable extent." In recent years, we have sought to secure this objective through both revision of the Texas Rules of Civil Procedure and our opinions discouraging gamesmanship and secrecy.
>
> Only in certain narrow circumstances is it appropriate to obstruct the search for truth by denying discovery. Very limited exceptions to the strongly preferred policy of openness are recognized in our state procedural rules and statutes. *See* Tex. R. Civ. Evid. 501; Tex. R. Civ. P. 166(b)(3).

802 S.W.2d at 671 (case citations omitted). Today, however, this is all just history, as privileges to hide the truth are unreasonably expanded.

Among "the very limited exceptions to [our] strongly preferred policy of openness," Lowry, 802 S.W.2d at 671, is that for

> written statements of potential witnesses and parties . . . [and] [c]ommunications between agents or representatives or the employees of a party to the action or communications

[2] Although Chief Justice Phillips' writing represents only a plurality opinion, I refer here to the "majority" because my disagreement also applies to the writings of Justices Gonzalez and Hecht.

[3] The lethal explosion occurred on August 23, 1990; Judge Brotherton properly applied Texas law to permit discovery by an order of July 25, 1991; the court of appeals promptly and appropriately rejected mandamus on September 27, 1991. After according National Tank emergency relief in November 1991, this court heard oral argument on March 10, 1992 and now obstructs access to information that could "significantly place the blame for the explosion on . . . National Tank Company. . . ." 851 S.W.2d at 213.

> between a party and that party's agents, representatives or employees, when made subsequent to the occurrence or transaction upon which the suit is based and in connection with the prosecution, investigation or defense of the particular suit, or in anticipation of the prosecution or defense of the claims made a part of the pending litigation.

Tex. R. Civ. P. 166b(3)(c) and (d). Given the persistent efforts of skilled attorneys to employ these provisions to suppress information adverse to their clients, Texas courts have frequently written on this subject. In the most recent attempt to prevent these exceptions from swallowing the rule, our court defined an explicit two part test to ascertain whether an investigation has been conducted in anticipation of litigation. *Flores v. Fourth Court of Appeals*, 777 S.W.2d 38 (Tex. 1989, orig. proceeding). There must be first "an objective examination of the facts surrounding the investigation [that] [c]onsider[s] outward manifestations which indicate that litigation is imminent;" and second, a subjective determination that "the party opposing discovery had a good faith belief that litigation would ensue." *Id.* at 41. We concluded that "[u]nless there is an abuse of discretion, the trial court's ruling should not be disturbed." *Id.* While admitting no abuse of discretion occurred here, the majority nevertheless "disturbs" this litigation in a highly disturbing manner.

As used in the first element of this test, the term "outward manifestations" means that the only investigations that can legitimately be considered to have been made "in anticipation of litigation" are those conducted after a claimant has given some objective indication of an intent to sue. *See Enterprise Prod. Co. v. Sanderson*, 759 S.W.2d 174, 179 (Tex. App.—Beaumont 1988, orig. proceeding); *Foster v. Heard*, 757 S.W.2d 464, 465 (Tex. App.—Houston [1st Dist.] 1988, orig. proceeding); *Texaco Ref. & Mktg., Inc. v. Sanderson*, 739 S.W.2d 493, 495 (Tex. App.—Beaumont 1987, orig. proceeding); *Phelps Dodge Ref. Corp. v. Marsh*, 733 S.W.2d 359, 361 (Tex. App.—San Antonio 1987, orig. proceeding). Such actions by the plaintiff could include "commencing an investigation of the accident, retaining an attorney or private investigator and, of course, making a claim or demand for damages." *Phelps*, 733 S.W.2d at 361. This well-developed rule had already become known as the "outward manifestations" test when we incorporated that term as a part of the standard announced in *Flores*. *See Enterprise Prod.*, 759 S.W.2d at 179.

Previously, in *Stringer v. Eleventh Court of Appeals*, 720 S.W.2d 801 (Tex. 1986, orig. proceeding) (per curiam), we had refused to shield from discovery interviews and an investigation notebook compiled for the Santa Fe Railroad shortly following a train collision which killed a brakeman. Although "any fool" might have known that a lawsuit would result from such an incident, *Flores*, 777 S.W.2d at 43 n. 1 (Gonzalez, J., dissenting), we nonetheless realized that the compelling need for both parties to have equal access to all the facts requires that any exceptions to open discovery be very narrowly drawn. "The mere fact that an accident has occurred is not sufficient to clothe all post-accident investigations, which frequently uncover fresh evidence not obtainable through other sources, with a privilege." *Stringer*, 720 S.W.2d at 802; *see also Robinson v. Harkins & Co.*, 711 S.W.2d 619, 621 (Tex. 1986, orig. proceeding) (per curiam) (pre-suit investigation made after collision between train and a truck not made in anticipation of litigation).

Abruptly abandoning these decisions in a continued disregard of Texas precedent, [footnote omitted] the majority gropes for euphemisms. *Flores* is not overruled; it is "modified," 851 S.W.2d at 195, and "[u]pon further consideration," *id.* at 203, "alter[ed]" beyond recognition. *Id.* at 195. The majority merely "disapprove[s] *Stringer* to the extent [that it applies to] sever[e] accident[s]." *Id.* at 204. [footnote omitted] Yet, had today's opinion been in place, the opposite result would have been required in both *Flores* and *Stringer*. That jurisprudence, as well as the multiple decisions of our courts of appeals are simply replaced with a new rule—corporate clairvoyance. "[A]n investigation [conducted] before the plaintiff manifests an[y] intent to sue"—indeed an investigation conducted before the victim has been buried—can be completely hidden from view. 851 S.W.2d at 204.

. . . .

Much is revealed in the majority's declaration that National Tank Company has no adequate remedy by appeal because the information in the contested statements "could have a significant impact on the assignment of liability." 851 S.W.2d at 207. Thus, while expressly acknowledging the potentially critical relevance of the facts in these documents, the majority contends that such relevance provides greater reason to keep them hidden from other litigants and the factfinder. Because this approach only provides more privileges for the privileged, I dissent.

[An opinion concurring and dissenting by Justice Spector, joined by Justice Gammage, is omitted.]

[A dissenting opinion by Justice Hecht, joined by Justice Cornyn, is omitted.]

---

## NOTES AND QUESTIONS

(1) *Duration of Work Product Protection.* Once it has been created, when does work product protection end? The Supreme Court held in *Owens Corning Fiberglas v. Caldwell*, 818 S.W.2d 749, 751 (Tex. 1991) that the exemption is "perpetual" unless waived. The court believed that this was necessary in order to further the policies underlying the work product doctrine. "Were the work product protection not continuing, a situation would result in which a client's communications to an attorney, which must be full, frank and open, are protected, Tex. R. Civ. Evid. 503, but the same attorney's work product done in furtherance of such attorney-client relationship is not. This anomaly clearly cannot be allowed."

(2) *Relationship to Other Discovery Principles.* The 1999 amendments help to clarify the relationship between work product immunity and other provisions specifically permitting discovery. Civil Procedure Rule 192.3 provides for discovery of information provided to testifying experts, even if made in anticipation of litigation. Under the 1999 discovery rules, even if made or prepared in anticipation of litigation or for trial, information concerning experts that is discoverable under Civil Procedure Rule 192.3 is not work product protected from discovery. Tex. R. Civ. P. 192.5(c). Revised Civil Procedure Rules 194 and 195 control the manner of discovery from testifying experts. For any testifying expert, if the expert is retained by, employed by, or otherwise subject to the control of the responding party, the following information and material provided to the expert must be disclosed in response to a request for disclosure: "all documents, tangible things, reports, models, or data compilations that have been provided to, reviewed by, or prepared by or for the expert in anticipation of the expert's testimony." Tex. R. Civ. P. 194.2(f)(4)(A). Significantly, a response to requested disclosures made in accordance with Civil Procedure Rule 194 may not include an assertion that the information or material to be disclosed constitutes work product. Tex. R. Civ. P. 194.5. Based on these provisions, it

appears that any written material that is furnished to a testifying expert in anticipation of his or her testimony would be discoverable under Civil Procedure Rule 194's procedures, but anything else said to the expert would not be discoverable through that device. However, if the expert's deposition is taken, the additional factual information under Rule 192.3 ("facts [made] known to the expert that relate to or form the basis of the expert's mental impressions and opinions") will also be discoverable. Tex. R. Civ. P. 192.3(e)(3). The question of what materials and information are provided "in anticipation of [the expert's] testimony" and what facts "relate to or form the basis of" the expert's opinions is likely to be a subject of dispute under the new rules. Does it include all information provided to the expert from first contact on? Information provided after the expert is formally retained? Information provided once it is decided that the expert will testify? Which interpretation is most consistent with the purpose behind discovery of expert information?

(3) *Attorney's Notes.* How should a court determine whether an attorney's notes are factual ("other work product") or whether they reveal the attorney's thought processes ("core work product")?

(4) *Discovery of Attorney's Litigation File.* Although it is possible that individual documents located in an attorney's files may be discoverable, the Texas Supreme Court has held that a discovery request for an attorney's "litigation file" is, on its face, an improper invasion of the work product exemption. *National Union Fire Ins. Co. of Pittsburgh v. Valdez*, 863 S.W.2d 458 (Tex. 1993). But an individual document is not privileged simply because it is contained in an attorney's file. A party may not cloak a document with privilege simply by forwarding it to his or her attorney. Thus, although a party may not compel the production of an adverse party's entire file, the party may request individual documents relevant to the case and is entitled to discover nonprivileged documents even if they are kept in the attorney's file.

(5) *The Substantial Need/Undue Hardship Exception.* Work product that is not absolutely protected as "core work product" is subject to discovery if the party seeking discovery "has substantial need of the materials in the preparation of the party's case and . . . is unable without undue hardship to obtain the substantial equivalent of the material by other means." This exception, like the work product doctrine itself, has its origin in the United States Supreme Court's opinion in *Hickman v. Taylor*, 329 U.S. 495, 511–512 (1946). Following *Hickman*, the Federal Rules of Civil Procedure included a substantial need and undue hardship exception in Rule 26(b)(3). A review of federal law, therefore, may help in understanding this exception. In one Texas case, the Texas Supreme Court concluded that both the substantial need and undue hardship requirements were met when the parties seeking discovery attempted to discover information amassed by the state from responses to civil investigative demands made on third parties. *State v. Lowry*, 802 S.W.2d 669, 673 (Tex. 1991). One court of appeals, noting that the exception is underdeveloped in Texas, looked to federal case law to support its determination that credibility issues and the failing memory of a witness who had been interviewed by opposing counsel satisfied the substantial need and undue hardship exception. *Dillard Dep't Stores, Inc. v. Sanderson*, 928 S.W.2d 319, 321 (Tex. App.—Beaumont 1996, leave denied).

(6) *Policy Issues.* Do you agree that the work product exemption is necessary to encourage lawyers to adequately prepare their cases for trial? *Compare* Thornburg, *Rethinking Work Product*, 77 Va. L. Rev. 1515 (1991) *with* Albright, *The Texas Discovery Privileges: A Fool's Game?* 70 Tex. L. Rev. 781 (1992).

---

### *Expert Witnesses*

*Read Tex. R. Civ. P. 192.3(e), 192.5(c)(1), 194.2(f), 195.*

Generally, experts are used in litigation in two ways. First, an expert may help a litigant prepare the case for discovery and trial. Second, an expert may testify at trial as part of a litigant's effort to persuade the trier of fact. The discovery rules are designed to account for the different uses of experts in the litigation process by differentiating between "consulting experts" (those who help litigants prepare the case) and "testifying experts" (those who act as a witness at trial). The discovery rules permit a party to protect from discovery the identity, mental impressions, and opinions of consulting experts, as long as a testifying expert did not review their impressions or opinions. This is in accord with the general theory that a litigant is entitled to prepare for trial without having to disclose his or her trial strategy. Thus, these experts are permitted to work with the litigant and the attorney behind the scenes. However, experts who will play an active role in the trial process receive the opposite treatment. Thus, a person who will testify as an expert at trial is subject to extensive discovery. The same scope of discovery applies to a consulting expert whose mental impressions or opinions have been reviewed by a testifying expert. This is in accord with the general theory of discovery that full disclosure of facts before trial helps achieve justice. Although the 1999 amendments changed the procedure for expert discovery, its scope remains largely unchanged.

The 1999 amendments do, however, change the method and timing of expert discovery. Read and carefully consider Civil Procedure Rules 192.4(f), 195, and the accompanying Comments. Be sure you understand which devices can be used to get information about testifying experts (and consulting experts whose work has been reviewed by testifying experts), the timing of disclosures, and the consequences of providing a report when the expert witness is designated.

Litigation regarding the consulting expert exemption has centered on several issues: (1) when was a consulting expert retained "in anticipation of litigation or preparation for trial"; (2) when can an employee or former employee be designated as a consulting expert; and (3) can an expert be converted from a testifying expert (discoverable) to a consulting expert (exempt) by redesignating the expert's function? The cases that follow show the Texas courts wrestling with these issues.

---

## LINDSEY v. O'NEILL

*689 S.W.2d 400 (Tex. 1985)*

PER CURIAM.

This is an original mandamus action brought by George Lindsey and Betty Lindsey, individually and as next friends of their son, Thomas Daniel Lindsey, to compel Judge O'Neill to rescind his order limiting the scope of their Second Amended Notice of Deposition. This court has jurisdiction over this cause pursuant to Tex. Rev. Civ. Stat. Ann. art. 1733 (Vernon Supp.

1985). Because we believe the trial court's order improperly restricted the scope of discovery as defined by the Texas Rules of Civil Procedure, we conditionally grant the writ.

The Lindseys brought the underlying lawsuit in this cause against several defendants including certain named physicians, several pharmaceutical companies, and Hermann Hospital in Houston, based upon medical malpractice and products liability theories. In the course of conducting pretrial discovery, the Lindseys served their Second Amended Notice of Deposition upon one of the defendants, Travenol Labs, Inc. This deposition notice requested Travenol to produce individuals for deposition on some thirty-nine subject areas. Travenol moved for a protective order and the trial court ordered twenty-one of these subject areas stricken from the notice on the ground that the subjects called for Travenol to produce expert opinion testimony. The trial court struck another eight subjects from the notice on relevancy grounds. As to the remaining subject areas, the trial court limited the scope of permissible inquiry by the Lindseys to only such facts as are, or may lead to, matters relevant to the issues identified by the Lindseys' Seventh Amended Petition. The trial court also quashed the document request which accompanied the deposition notice.

Tex. R. Civ. P. 200 provides that a party may take the deposition of a private or public corporation. Subsection 2b [now Tex. R. Civ. P. 199.2(b)] requires that a deposition notice of a corporation describe with reasonable particularity the matters on which examination is requested. Rule 200 makes no distinction between deposition notices directed toward corporations based upon whether the deposition is to pertain to purely factual matters or matters calling for expert opinion.

. . . .

No provision exists in the Texas Rules of Civil Procedure exempting the mental impressions and opinions of experts from discovery when these mental impressions and opinions were neither acquired nor developed in anticipation of litigation. Before the trial court may hold an entire category of expert opinion evidence exempt from discovery, there must be proof before it that all such evidence was either acquired or developed in anticipation of litigation. Because the trial court excluded from discovery all of the mental impressions and opinions of experts associated with Travenol without any showing that this information was acquired or developed in anticipation of litigation, we find a conflict between the trial court's order and the Texas Rules of Civil Procedure and, hence, an abuse of discretion on the part of the trial court.

With regard to those subject areas either struck from the Lindseys' deposition notice on relevancy grounds or restricted in scope to the facts relevant to the Lindseys' claims, we find no abuse of discretion in the trial court's order.

We grant the motion for leave to file petition for writ of mandamus. Pursuant to Tex. R. Civ. P. 483, without hearing oral argument, we grant the writ. We are confident the trial court will comply with our decision. A writ of mandamus will issue only if it fails to do so.

---

## AXELSON, INC. v. McILHANY

*798 S.W.2d 550 (Tex. 1990)*

GONZALEZ, Justice.

In this mandamus proceeding, we are asked to direct Judge McIlhany to vacate orders denying pretrial discovery. The court of appeals conditionally granted the petition for writ of mandamus on certain points but denied the petition on other points. 755 S.W.2d 170. Among other things, we are requested to grant relief regarding discovery of a kickback investigation and "dual capacity" witnesses. We conditionally grant the writ.

The underlying suit from which this action arises involves what is believed to be the largest gas well blowout in United States history. Key Well 1-11, located in Wheeler County, blew out in October 1981 and was not brought under control for over a year. Apache Corporation operates the well and, together with El Paso Exploration Company (a/k/a Meridian Oil Production, Inc.), owns the working interest. Numerous lawsuits involving over 100 parties have been filed against Apache and El Paso, alleging that their wrongful acts caused the blowout. All suits against Apache and El Paso have been consolidated.

Plaintiffs include Arkla Exploration, Stephens Production Company and Hobart Key, all of whom own mineral interests in the same field. Tom L. Scott, Inc. and other mineral interest holders ("Scott group") [footnote omitted] intervened as plaintiffs, alleging a cause of action against Apache and El Paso only. Apache and El Paso responded by adding numerous third-party defendants. Sooner Pipe & Supply Corporation, Hydril Corporation and Babcock & Wilcox Company ("Sooner") were added because they supplied well equipment that allegedly caused the blowout. Axelson, Inc. and its parent corporation, U.S. Industries, Inc. (USI), were added because Axelson manufactured a relief valve that allegedly should have prevented the blowout.

. . . .

## "DUAL CAPACITY" WITNESSES

Several potential witnesses in this case maintain a dual capacity—possessing firsthand knowledge of relevant facts and serving as consulting-only experts for Apache and El Paso. One of these persons, Paul Douglas Storts, is the petroleum engineer who has been in charge of the well from its inception. He also spearheaded the effort to bring the well under control after the blowout. The others include Richard Biel, Joe Fowler and Tom Hill, who were hired by Apache and El Paso to examine the wellhead equipment and have specific knowledge concerning the chain of custody of the wellhead equipment.

Axelson and USI seek to discover all facts known by Storts and his mental impressions and opinions gained while working on the well and consulting. They seek to discover only chain of custody facts from Biel, Fowler and Hill.

The trial court entered several orders from December 1984 through July 1987 limiting discovery. With regard to Storts, the trial court initially quashed his deposition, but later determined that information gained by him while working on the well was discoverable, but that information he gained while doing a combination of working on the well and consulting was not discoverable. With regard to Biel, Fowler, and Hill, the trial court allowed discovery of facts relating only to the Axelson valve. The court of appeals held that the trial court had not abused its discretion and disallowed all other discovery from these experts. 755 S.W.2d at 176–77. We disagree.

The factual knowledge and opinions acquired by an individual who is an expert and an active participant in the events material to the lawsuit are discoverable. This information is not shielded from discovery by merely changing the designation of a person with knowledge of relevant facts to a "consulting-only expert."

The scope of discovery regarding experts who serve in the dual capacity of fact witness and consulting-only expert has not been addressed thoroughly by Texas courts. Barrow and Henderson, *1984 Amendments to the Texas Rules of Civil Procedure Affecting Discovery,* 15 St. Mary's L.J. 713, 729 (1984). The literal text of the exemption, however, resolves the issue presented in this mandamus. The consulting expert exemption protects the identity, mental impressions and opinions of consulting-only experts; but not the facts. [footnote omitted] The rule we announce today, however, "should not extend to consulting [only] experts . . . whose only source of factual information was the consultation." *Id.* In other words, persons who gain factual information by virtue of their involvement relating to the incident or transaction giving rise to the litigation do not qualify as consulting-only experts because the consultation is not their only source of information. We now separately address Axelson's discovery requests regarding Storts, an employee designated as a consulting-only expert, and Biel, Fowler and Hill, experts designated as consulting-only who have factual knowledge of the well equipment.

STORTS

An employee may be specially employed as a consulting-only expert. *See Barker v. Dunham,* 551 S.W.2d 41, 43–44 (Tex. 1977, orig. proceeding). Nevertheless, all employees do not necessarily qualify as "consulting-only" experts. The rules provide requirements that a consulting-only expert must meet. *See* Tex. R. Civ. P. 166b(3)(b). Rule of Civil Procedure 166b(3)(b) provides:

> 3. Exemptions. The following matters are protected from disclosure by privilege:
>
> b. *Experts.* The identity, mental impressions, and opinions of an expert who has been *informally consulted* or of an expert who has been *retained or specially employed by another party in anticipation of litigation or preparation for trial . . .*

*Id.* (emphasis added). Under this rule, a consulting-only expert must be informally consulted or retained or specially employed in anticipation of litigation. An employee who was employed in an area that becomes the subject of litigation can never qualify as a consulting-only expert because the employment was not in anticipation of litigation. On the other hand, an employee who was not employed in an area that becomes the subject of litigation and is reassigned specifically to assist the employer in anticipation of litigation arising out of the incident or in preparation for trial may qualify as a "consulting-only" expert. In any event, a party may discover facts known by an employee acting as a "consulting-only" expert.

In this case, evidence presented to the trial court suggested that Storts was doing a combination of both working on the well and consulting. Storts was hired to work as a petroleum engineer and he worked on Key Well 1-11 before, during and after the blowout. After litigation began Apache asserted that Storts was a consulting-only expert and resisted all discovery of Storts' mental impressions, opinions and facts. On the record before him, the trial judge abused his discretion in denying discovery of Storts' mental impressions, opinions and facts because Storts did not qualify as a consulting-only expert.

Policies previously enunciated by this court support the decision we reach today. This rule aims to effectuate the ultimate purpose of discovery, which is to seek truth, so that disputes may be decided by those facts that are revealed, rather than concealed. *Jampole,* 673 S.W.2d at 573. Additionally, although Apache and El Paso are defendants in this case, they are pursuing a cross claim and "cannot use one hand to seek affirmative relief in court and with the other lower an iron curtain of silence around the facts of the case." *Ginsburg v. Fifth Court of Appeals,* 686 S.W.2d 105, 108 (Tex. 1985, orig. proceeding).

BIEL, FOWLER, & HILL

Axelson sought only factual discovery from Biel, Fowler and Hill regarding the condition of wellhead equipment in addition to the condition of Axelson's relief valve. The trial judge limited the scope of discovery from these consulting-only experts to the Axelson valve. The trial judge abused his discretion in refusing discovery of these facts because the exemption for consulting-only experts does not extend to facts known to them.

. . .

---

## TOM L. SCOTT, INC. v. McILHANY

*798 S.W.2d 556 (Tex. 1990)*

GONZALEZ, Justice.

This is an original mandamus proceeding involving pretrial discovery of expert witnesses. The relators, Tom L. Scott, Inc. and others, [footnote omitted] seek relief from orders signed by the respondent, the Honorable Grainger W. McIlhany, denying discovery of six experts retained by various parties to the case. By this mandamus, relators seek to obtain the depositions of these experts. The defendants changed the designation of these experts from "testifying" experts to "consulting-only" experts after they settled with some of the plaintiffs and third-party defendants in the underlying suit. The court of appeals denied the petition for writ of mandamus. 753 S.W.2d 214. We hold that the redesignation under the facts before us violates the purpose of discovery enunciated in *Gutierrez v. Dallas Independent School District,* 729 S.W.2d 691, 693 (Tex. 1987), and in *Jampole v. Touchy,* 673 S.W.2d 569, 573 (Tex. 1984, orig. proceeding), and is, therefore, ineffective. Thus we conditionally grant the writ.

[The Court here sets forth the factual background, which is the same as in the preceding case.]

The initial plaintiffs, Arkla, Stephens and Key (Arkla/Key), and third-party defendants, Sooner, Hydril and Babcock & Wilcox, designated the six experts in question as *testifying* experts. [footnote omitted] Allegedly, these experts were prepared to deliver damaging testimony against Apache and El Paso. On the morning the Arkla/Key witnesses' depositions were scheduled, Apache and El Paso settled with these parties on the condition that Apache and El Paso gain control of the experts. Following execution of the settlement, Apache and El Paso, along with the settling parties, redesignated all six as consulting-only experts.

The trial court denied requests by the Scott group to depose the experts. Specifically, the Scott group filed a motion to take depositions of the experts, and Judge McIlhany denied it. . . . We next address the critical question presented in this case—whether a party may obtain an adversary's testifying experts and redesignate them as consulting-only experts to avoid discovery.

Designating these experts as testifying experts subjected their work product to discovery. Texas Rule of Civil Procedure 166b(2)(e)(1) [now Tex. R. Civ. P. 192.3] provides in part:

> A party may obtain discovery of the identity and location (name, address and telephone number) of an expert who may be called as an expert witness, the subject matter on which the witness is expected to testify, the mental impressions and opinions held by the expert and the facts known to the expert (regardless of when the factual information was acquired) which relate to or form the basis of the mental impressions and opinions held by the expert.

. . . .

Upon gaining control of the experts, Apache and El Paso redesignated them as consulting-only experts. The settling parties also redesignated the experts as consulting-only experts. Identities and opinions of experts are nevertheless discoverable if they are not engaged in anticipation of litigation and solely for consultation or if their work product has been reviewed or relied upon by testifying experts. *See* Tex. R. Civ. P. 166b(3)(b) [now Tex. R. Civ. P. 192.3(e)]. [footnote omitted] The trial court allowed the redesignation and refused requests by the Scott group to depose these experts. The Scott group asks us to hold this redesignation invalid.

The primary policy behind discovery is to seek truth so that disputes may be decided by facts that are revealed rather than concealed. *Jampole,* 673 S.W.2d at 573. Privileges from discovery run contrary to this policy but serve other legitimate interests. The policy behind the consulting expert privilege is to encourage parties to seek expert advice in evaluating their case and to prevent a party from receiving undue benefit from an adversary's efforts and diligence. *Werner v. Miller,* 579 S.W.2d 455, 456 (Tex. 1979, orig. proceeding); *see also* D. Keltner, Texas Discovery § 3.110 (1989). But the protection afforded by the consulting expert privilege is intended to be only "a shield to prevent a litigant from taking undue advantage of his adversary's industry and effort, not a sword to be used to thwart justice or to defeat the salutary objects" of discovery. *Williamson v. Superior Court,* 582 P.2d 126, 132 (Cal. 1978); *see also Chuidian v. Philippine Nat'l Bank,* 734 F. Supp. 415, 423 (C.D. Cal. 1990) (interpreting *Williamson* as holding agreements to suppress evidence or conceal discreditable facts are illegal); *Raytheon Co. v. Superior Court,* 256 Cal. Rptr. 425, 427 (Cal. Ct. App. 1989) (interpreting *Williamson* as holding agreements between adversarial codefendants to suppress expert testimony are against public policy).

The redesignation of the experts in this case was an offensive and unacceptable use of discovery mechanisms intended to defeat the salutary objectives of discovery. Attorneys for Apache and El Paso even admitted to the trial judge that the settlements were "expressly contingent" on these experts not being required to give their testimony, and that there might not be a settlement agreement if the depositions were ordered. One of the settling parties expressly told the trial court that he understood the settlement offer would expire upon the depositions being taken. The legitimate purposes and policies behind the consulting expert privilege do not countenance this conduct. We hold that, as a matter of law, the redesignation of experts under the facts of this case violates the policy underlying the rules of discovery and is therefore ineffective. *See Gutierrez,* 729 S.W.2d at 693; *Jampole,* 673 S.W.2d at 573. [footnote omitted] "If we were to hold otherwise, nothing would preclude a party in a multi-party case from in effect auctioning off a witness' testimony to the highest bidder." *Williamson,* 582 P.2d at 132. Because the redesignation of experts under the facts of this case violates the clear purpose and policy underlying the rules of discovery, the trial court abused its discretion in granting the protective order as to these six experts. We are confident Judge McIlhany will vacate his orders denying discovery and will render orders consistent with this opinion. Should he fail to do so, the clerk of the supreme court is directed to issue the writ of mandamus.

### [2] Other Discovery Privileges

The scope of discovery does not include privileged material. Tex. R. Civ. P. 192.3(a). This allows parties resisting discovery to rely on privileges that exist outside the discovery rules themselves. This section of the chapter discusses some of the other privileges that have been applied to the discovery process. They are based in the federal Constitution, the Texas Rules of Evidence, and other Texas statutes.

#### [a] Constitutional Privileges

The privilege against self-incrimination can affect civil cases. That privilege extends to testimonial communications that would sustain a conviction, and also to responses that would furnish a link in the chain of evidence needed to prosecute the person claiming the privilege. The privilege should be sustained unless it clearly appears that the person claiming it is mistaken. *Hoffman v. United States*, 341 U.S. 479, 486–487 (1951). On the other hand, the privilege does not bar the compelled production of a tangible thing, such as a document, that contains no self-incriminating testimonial declaration, unless the act of production itself constitutes an incriminating testimonial communication. *Fisher v. United States*, 425 U.S. 391, 409–411 (1976).

Although a person is never compelled to incriminate him or herself, a plaintiff who invokes this privilege during discovery may suffer sanctions. In other words, the plaintiff has several options: (1) bring the action and disclose self-incriminating matter; (2) limit the action to such matters that, if possible, will not involve disclosure of incriminating material; (3) refrain from suit; or (4) face dismissal or stay on failure to make the required disclosure. In considering the appropriate sanction for a plaintiff asserting privilege, the court must consider a number of factors and must tailor the sanction to the nature of the offensive conduct. *Texas Dep't of Public Safety Officers Ass'n v. Denton*, 897 S.W.2d 757 (Tex. 1995). On the basis that defendants do not have these options, it has been held that a defendant is not subject to sanctions for invoking the privilege. *Duffy v. Currier*, 291 F. Supp. 810, 814 (D. Minn. 1969). The defendant is not, however, the sole judge of the right to invoke the privilege against self-incrimination in a civil case. The judge must decide if the refusal to respond is based on good faith and is justified under the circumstances. *Ex parte Butler*, 522 S.W.2d 196, 197 (Tex. 1975); *Warford v. Beard*, 653 S.W.2d 908, 911 (Tex. App.—Amarillo 1983, no writ). Note also that at trial in civil cases, both the judge and opposing counsel are allowed to comment on a party's claim of the privilege against self-incrimination and suggest that inferences may be drawn from the claim. Tex. R. Evid. 513.

A litigant may also claim a constitutional privilege to challenge discovery requests in violation of First Amendment freedom of association rights. *In re BACALA*, 982 S.W.2d 371 (Tex. 1998); *Tilton v. Moye*, 869 S.W.2d 955 (Tex. 1994); *Ex parte Lowe*, 887 S.W.2d 1 (Tex. 1994). Once the claim of privilege is properly raised, the party seeking associational information has the burden to establish a constitutionally permissible basis justifying its disclosure. *Id.*

#### [b] Privileges Based on the Texas Rules of Evidence

*Read Tex. R. Evid. 501 through 510.*

The Texas Rules of Evidence recognize privileges for required reports privileged by statute (Tex. R. Evid. 502); lawyer-client communications (Tex. R. Evid. 503); husband-wife communications (Tex. R. Evid. 504); communications to clergy (Tex. R. Evid. 505); political vote (Tex. R. Evid. 506); trade secrets (Tex. R. Evid. 507); identity of informers (Tex. R. Evid. 508); physician-patient communications (Tex. R. Evid. 509); and mental health information (Tex. R.

Evid. 510). Some of the privileges are absolute, some are conditional, and all are subject to waiver and exceptions. Most have generated little litigation.

The attorney-client privilege, not surprisingly, has proved the most controversial of the privileges. The privilege protects confidential communications between lawyer and client made for the purpose of receiving legal advice. Until quite recently, there was little litigation in Texas regarding the parameters of the attorney-client privilege. As the exemptions contained in former Civil Procedure Rule 166b, however, lawyers looked with new interest at the attorney-client privilege.

As in all jurisdictions, one of the most difficult privilege questions arises when the "client" is an organization rather than a human being. In such cases, the court must decide who can be a representative of the client, so that communications to and from the representative qualify for the privilege. Different jurisdictions have different approaches to this issue, but they tend to be characterized as falling into two kinds of tests. One approach is the "control group" test. Under a control group analysis, only employees who are quite high in the corporate hierarchy can claim the privilege. While the precise identity of control group employees may be hard to predict, it is generally defined to include those in a position to control or take a substantial part in a decision about any action which the corporation may take on the advice of the attorney. *City of Philadelphia v. Westinghouse Electric Corp.*, 210 F. Supp. 483 (E.D. Pa.), *petition for mandamus and prohibition denied sub. nom., General Electric Co. v. Kirkpatrick*, 312 F.2d 742 (3d Cir. 1962). The pre-1997 version of Evidence Rule 503 was interpreted to adopt a control group approach. *National Tank Co. v. Brotherton*, 851 S.W.2d 193 (Tex. 1993).

The second approach to the attorney-client privilege in the corporate context is referred to as a "subject matter test." The subject matter test provides a privilege to people with whom an attorney needs to communicate in order to render legal services, regardless of their position in the corporate hierarchy. The United States Supreme Court in *Upjohn Co. v. United States*, 449 U.S. 383 (1981) is often said to have used a subject matter approach. There are broader and narrower ways to define a subject matter test, but generally the test will require that the communication with the attorney be made at the direction of an employee's superiors and that the subject matter on which the attorney's advice is sought is the employee's performance of the duties of his employment. *National Tank*, 851 S.W.2d at 198.

Effective March 1, 1998, the Texas Supreme Court amended Evidence Rule 503 to provide coverage to communications made by a lower level employee who "for the purpose of effectuating legal representation for the client, makes or receives a confidential communication while acting in the scope of employment for the client." Tex. R. Evid. 503(a)(2)(B). Before the 1998 amendments to Rule 503, the attorney-client privilege protected only communications made by or received from counsel by employees within the upper echelon of corporate management. *See National Tank Co. v. Brotherton,* 851 S.W.2d 193, 197 (Tex. 1993).

The Texas Supreme Court has recently bolstered the significance of the trade secret privilege. Consider the following case and ask yourself: (1) is the protection for trade secrets a true privilege?; (2) what is a trade secret?; and (3) how would the availability of a protective order and the scope of such an order influence the court's decision about the proper treatment of trade secrets?

---

## IN RE CONTINENTAL GENERAL TIRE, INC.

*979 S.W.2d 609 (Tex. 1998)*

PHILLIPS, Chief Justice, delivered the opinion of the Court, in which GONZALEZ, HECHT, ENOCH, SPECTOR, OWEN, BAKER, and ABBOTT, Justices, join.

Under our rules of evidence, a party has a privilege to refuse to disclose its trade secrets "if the allowance of the privilege will not tend to conceal fraud or otherwise work injustice." See Tex. R. Evid. 507. The issue is whether Rule 507 protects from discovery a tire manufacturer's chemical formula for its "skim stock," a rubber compound used in tire manufacturing. The trial court ordered the manufacturer to produce the formula under a protective order, and the court of appeals denied the manufacturer's requested mandamus relief without opinion. We hold that, when a party resisting discovery establishes that the requested information is a trade secret under Rule 507, the burden shifts to the requesting party to establish that the information is necessary for a fair adjudication of its claim or defense. Because relator established that the formula was a trade secret, and because the real party in interest did not meet its burden of establishing necessity, we conditionally grant mandamus relief. Nothing in the relief we grant prohibits plaintiffs from seeking to discover the formula under the procedure we set forth.

I.

While Kenneth Fisher was driving his pick-up truck on Highway 190, his left front tire blew out, causing him to lose control of the vehicle. Fisher's truck crossed the median and struck Dora Pratt's car, killing Pratt and her passenger. Pratt's heirs, Luz Enid Rivera, Brenda Beatriz Killens, Gilberto DeJesus Cruz, Dora Maria Cruz, and Toribio Nieves, filed the underlying products liability action against Continental General Tire, the manufacturer of the failed tire.

It is undisputed that the tire failed because its tread and outer belt separated from the inner belt. The belts are made from brass-coated steel cords encased in a skim-stock rubber compound. These belts, along with the other tire components, are assembled into a "green tire," to which heat and pressure are applied in a process called "vulcanization." This process causes the components in the tire, including the skim stock, to chemically bond with each other. Plaintiffs contend that either a design or manufacturing defect in the skim stock prevented the belts of Fisher's tire from properly bonding. To secure evidence to prove this claim, plaintiffs requested Continental to produce the chemical formula for the skim stock used on this tire.

Continental objected, claiming that the formula is a trade secret that Texas Rule of Evidence 507 protects. After a hearing, the trial court ordered Continental to produce the formula, subject to a protective order which the trial court had earlier entered for other confidential material produced by Continental.

The trial court stayed its order pending Continental's efforts to obtain mandamus review. After the court of appeals denied relief, we granted Continental's mandamus petition and heard oral argument.

II.

Continental claims that the skim-stock formula is protected by Texas Rule of Evidence 507, which provides in full:

> A person has a privilege, which may be claimed by the person or the person's agent or employee, to refuse to disclose and to prevent other persons from disclosing a trade secret owned by the person, if the allowance of the privilege will not tend to conceal fraud or otherwise work injustice. When disclosure is directed, the judge shall take such protective measure as the interests of the holder of the privilege and of the parties and the furtherance of justice may require.

Tex. R. Evid. 507. This rule, adopted in 1983, is based on Supreme Court Standard 508, a proposed rule of evidence promulgated by the United States Supreme Court in 1969. *See* 3 McLaughlin, Weinstein's Federal Evidence § 508.01, at 508-5 (2d ed. 1998); Preliminary Draft of Proposed Rules of Evidence for the United States District Courts and Magistrates, 46 F.R.D. 161, 270 (1969). Although Congress did not adopt Standard 508 as a federal rule of evidence, see McLaughlin, supra at 508-5, twenty states, including Texas, have adopted some version of it. [footnote omitted]

This Court has never addressed the scope of Rule 507. Moreover, of the other jurisdictions adopting Supreme Court Standard 508, only two have directly considered its scope. *See Bridgestone/Firestone v. Superior Court,* 7 Cal. App. 4th 1384, 9 Cal. Rptr. 2d 709 (Cal. Ct. App. 1992); *Rare Coin-It, Inc. v. I.J.E., Inc.*, 625 So. 2d 1277 (Fla. Ct. App. 1993).

In *Bridgestone/Firestone*, the plaintiffs sued the tire manufacturer for wrongful death caused by a tire failure. Claiming that belt separation caused the tire failure, the plaintiffs sought to discover defendant's compound formula. Defendant asserted California's trade secret privilege, which is virtually identical to our Rule 507. *See* Cal. Evid. Code § 1060. The trial court ordered defendant to produce the formula, and defendant sought interlocutory review.

The court of appeals, in analyzing the rule, first noted that a requesting party must establish more than mere relevance to discover trade secrets, or the statutory privilege would be "meaningless." 9 Cal. Rptr. 2d at 712. "Allowance of the trade secret privilege may not be deemed to'work injustice' within the meaning of Evidence Code section 1060 simply because it would protect information generally relevant to the subject matter of an action or helpful to preparation of a case." *Id.* Rather, to show "injustice," the party seeking to discover a trade secret

> must make a prima facie, particularized showing that the information sought is relevant and necessary to the proof of, or defense against, a material element of one or more causes of action presented in the case, and that it is reasonable to conclude that the information sought is essential to a fair resolution of the lawsuit.

*Id.* at 713. The court perceived this as a balancing process, in which the trial court must weigh the interests of both sides and "must necessarily consider the protection afforded the holder of the privilege by a protective order as well as any less intrusive alternatives to disclosure proposed by the parties." *Id.* Applying these principles, the court noted that plaintiffs' expert, although averring generally that the formula could assist him in determining a defect, did not "describe with any precision how or why the formulas were a predicate to his ability to reach conclusions in the case." *Id.* at 716. The court thus determined that the information, although perhaps useful, was not necessary to the plaintiffs' claim. The court consequently denied the discovery.

Similarly, in *Rare Coin-It*, the court was called upon to interpret section 90.506 of the Florida Statutes, a trade secret privilege identical to ours. The court held:

> When trade secret privilege is asserted as the basis for resisting production, the trial court must determine whether the requested production constitutes a trade secret; if so, the court must require the party seeking production to show reasonable necessity for the requested materials.

625 So. 2d at 1278. [footnote omitted] *See also Inrecon v. Village Homes at Country Walk*, 644 So. 2d 103, 105 (Fla. Ct. App. 1994).

The approach adopted in California and Florida is consistent with the federal courts' treatment of trade secrets. Although Congress did not adopt Supreme Court Standard 508, the federal rules nonetheless allow a court, in the discovery context, to "make any order which justice requires to protect a party or person from . . . undue burden or expense, including... that a trade secret or other confidential research, development, or commercial information not be revealed or be revealed only in a designated way. . . ." Fed. R. Civ. P. 26(c)(7). Federal courts applying this rule recognize that "there is no absolute privilege for trade secrets and similar confidential information." [citations omitted] Rather, federal courts apply a balancing test with shifting burdens, comparable to that articulated by the California appellate court in *Bridgestone/Firestone.*

In federal court, the party resisting discovery must establish that the information sought is indeed a trade secret and that disclosure would be harmful. The burden then shifts to the requesting party to establish that the information is "relevant and necessary" to his or her case. If the trial court orders disclosure, it should enter an appropriate protective order. [citations omitted]

This is ultimately a balancing test, in which the trial court must weigh all pertinent facts and circumstances. *See Wright & Miller*, § 2043 at 559 ("[T]he burden is on the party seeking discovery to establish that the information is sufficiently relevant and necessary to his case to outweigh the harm disclosure would cause to the person from whom he is seeking the information."). *See also Centurion Indus.*, 665 F.2d at 325 ("The district court must balance the need for the trade secrets against the claim of injury resulting from disclosure.").

III.

Our trade secret privilege seeks to accommodate two competing interests. First, it recognizes that trade secrets are an important property interest, worthy of protection. Second, it recognizes the importance we place on fair adjudication of lawsuits. *See* Preliminary Draft of Proposed Rules of Evidence, Advisory Committee's Note to Rule 5-08, 46 F.R.D. at 271 ("The need for accommodation between protecting trade secrets, on the one hand, and eliciting facts required for full and fair presentation of a case, on the other hand, is apparent."). Rule 507 accommodates both interests by requiring a party to disclose a trade secret only if necessary to prevent "fraud" or "injustice." Stated alternatively, disclosure is required only if necessary for a fair adjudication of the requesting party's claims or defenses.

We therefore hold that trial courts should apply Rule 507 as follows: First, the party resisting discovery must establish that the information is a trade secret. The burden then shifts to the requesting party to establish that the information is necessary for a fair adjudication of its claims. If the requesting party meets this burden, the trial court should ordinarily compel disclosure of the information, subject to an appropriate protective order.[3] In each circumstance, the trial court must weigh the degree of the requesting party's need for the information with the potential harm of disclosure to the resisting party.

IV.

Before applying Rule 507 to the facts of this case, we consider various arguments the parties and amicus curiae raise.

A

Plaintiffs first argue that our decisions in *Jampole v. Touchy*, 673 S.W.2d 569 (Tex. 1984), and *Garcia v. Peeples*, 734 S.W.2d 343 (Tex. 1987), require Continental to produce the skim-stock formula. In *Jampole*, a products liability defendant objected to producing its assembly diagrams and instructions, contending that the documents were trade secrets. *See* 673 S.W.2d at 574. After the trial court denied discovery, this Court granted conditional mandamus relief compelling production. The Court reasoned:

> Although a valid proprietary interest may justify denying or limiting discovery requested by a direct competitor, *Automatic Drilling Machines, Inc. v. Miller*, 515 S.W.2d 256 (Tex. 1974), this is not such a case. *Jampole* is not [the defendant's] business competitor, and [the defendant] acknowledged that, if the documents were relevant, any proprietary interest could be safeguarded by a protective order. Under these circumstances, it was an abuse of discretion for the trial court to deny discovery of the assembly documents. We do not decide whether [the defendant] has shown a sufficient proprietary interest to justify a protective order. We hold that discovery cannot be denied because of an asserted proprietary interest in the requested documents when a protective order would sufficiently preserve that interest.

*Id.* at 574–75 (emphasis supplied). According to plaintiffs, *Jampole* stands for the proposition that, in actions that are not between business competitors, the trial court should always require production of relevant trade secrets, subject to an appropriate protective order. *Cf. Federal Open Market Committee v. Merrill*, 443 U.S. 340, 362 n.24, 61 L. Ed. 2d 587, 99 S. Ct. 2800 (1979) ("Actually, orders forbidding any disclosure of trade secrets or confidential commercial information are rare. More commonly, the trial court will enter a protective order restricting disclosure to counsel or to the parties." (citations omitted)). This approach, however, would render the Rule 507 privilege meaningless in noncompetitor cases. Notably, the Court in *Jampole* did not consider Rule 507's effect, presumably because the defendant acknowledged that "any proprietary interest could by safeguarded by a protective order." 673 S.W.2d at 574. *Jampole* thus cannot be read as limiting the privilege's scope.

*Garcia* likewise does not speak to the scope of Rule 507. The issue there was not whether trade secret documents should be produced, but rather the scope of the protective order accompanying the production. *See* 734 S.W.2d at 345. As in *Jampole*, the Court did not consider or apply Rule 507.

Next, plaintiffs argue that a party requesting trade secret documents in a products liability case must show only that the information is relevant to the suit. However, because relevance

[3] In this case, for example, the trial court limited access to the information to the parties in this lawsuit, their lawyers, consultants, investigators, experts and other necessary persons employed by counsel to assist in the preparation and trial of this case. Each person who is given access to the documents must agree in writing to keep the information confidential, and all documents must be returned to Continental at the conclusion of the case.

is the standard for discovery in general, see Tex. R. Civ. P. 166b(2)(a), this approach likewise would render Rule 507 meaningless. See *Bridgestone/Firestone*, 9 Cal. Rptr. 2d at 712. Rule 507 clearly contemplates a heightened burden for obtaining trade secret information.

Finally, plaintiffs argue that because Continental originally sought the confidentiality order for the protection of other documents, Continental has implicitly conceded that the protective order will adequately protect the skim-stock formula as well. However, that Continental was willing to produce certain information under a protective order does not mean that Continental has waived its right to assert Rule 507 about other information which it may regard as more competitively sensitive or less necessary for the plaintiffs' case.

B

Continental and amicus curiae Product Liability Advisory Council present three other arguments about why production is not required in this case.

Continental first argues that, in general, a protective order can never adequately protect a sensitive trade secret because there is always the risk that the receiving party will either deliberately or inadvertently disclose the information. For example, Continental argues that if Robert Ochs, the plaintiffs' expert witness, learns the skim-stock formula, he will be more in demand as an expert witness in other cases, creating incentive for him to disclose the formula. Continental appears to be arguing that the risk of disclosure justifies an absolute trade secret privilege. However, Rule 507 does not support such an approach. It requires production if necessary to prevent fraud or injustice. Of course, the trial court should consider any potential inadequacies of the protective order in weighing the competing interests of the parties under Rule 507. See *Bridgestone/Firestone*, 9 Cal. Rptr. 2d at 713. This is especially true when the trial court has specific, fact-based grounds for believing that trade secrets may be disclosed in violation of its protective order.

Continental next argues that Texas Rule of Civil Procedure 76a may render any protective order for trade secrets ineffective. That rule restricts the circumstances in which trial courts may seal court records, and applies to unfiled discovery "concerning matters that have a probable adverse effect upon the general public health or safety . . . ." Tex. R. Civ. P. 76a(2)(c). Where a trial court has restricted the dissemination of discovery under a protective order, Rule 76a allows any person at any time to argue that the discovery falls within the above definition and therefore must be made public. *See* Tex. R. Civ. P. 76a(7); *General Tire, Inc. v. Kepple*, 970 S.W.2d 520 (Tex. 1998). Continental argues that, if a trial court has determined that trade secrets are "necessary" to a plaintiff's personal injury case under Rule 507, it is likely that the court would also determine that they have a "probable adverse effect upon the general public health or safety" and therefore must be made public under Rule 76a. Thus, Continental argues, any protective order for the documents would be ineffective.

We disagree with Continental's premise that all discoverable trade secrets will likely constitute "court records" under Rule 76a. Moreover, even if a trade secret produced under a protective order is later determined to be a court record, this does not necessarily mean that the information must be made public. Rule 76a allows the information to remain sealed upon a showing that it meets the criteria specified in Rule 76a(1). [footnote omitted] That a document contains trade secret information is a factor to be considered in applying this sealing standard. *See Eli Lilly & Co. v. Marshall*, 829 S.W.2d 157, 158 (Tex. 1992).

Finally, the Product Liability Advisory Council argues that *Automatic Drilling Machines, Inc. v. Miller*, 515 S.W.2d 256 (Tex. 1974), controls this case. That case arose from a suit between direct competitors, in which one side sought discovery of the other side's trade secret documents. After the trial court ordered disclosure, this Court granted mandamus relief, holding that the trial court had abused its discretion. We reasoned:

> Trade secrets and confidential information are not necessarily "privileged" matters within the meaning of Rule 186a. If the information is material and necessary to the litigation and unavailable from any other source, a witness may be required to make disclosure. *Lehnhard v. Moore*, 401 S.W.2d 232. A public disclosure of trade secrets should not be required, however, except "in such cases and to such extent as may appear to be indispensable for the ascertainment of truth." 8 Wigmore, Evidence (McNaughton rev. 1961), § 2212(3). In acting on the motions in this case, it was necessary for the judge to weigh the need for discovery against the desirability of preserving the secrecy of the material in question.

515 S.W.2d at 259. The trial court abused its discretion in compelling disclosure because there had been no showing that the information was "so essential to respondents' investigation and development of their case as to be subject to discovery by them." 515 S.W.2d at 260.

Although the Court decided *Automatic Drilling* before it promulgated Rule 507 in 1983, the decision is consistent with the rule. We recognized in Automatic Drilling that trade secrets should be disclosed only where the information is "material and necessary to the litigation and unavailable from any other source." 515 S.W.2d at 259. We further recognized that the trial court must balance the need for discovery against the need for nondisclosure. As discussed previously, this mirrors the proper approach under Rule 507.

V.

Accordingly, we reject the parties' alternative approaches. Instead, we apply our interpretation of Rule 507 to the facts of this case. Plaintiffs concede for purposes of this proceeding that the compound formula is a trade secret. The burden thus shifted to the plaintiffs to establish that the compound formula is necessary for a fair adjudication of this case. The only evidence that plaintiffs presented was deposition testimony from Continental's expert, Joseph Grant, that a compound that "doesn't have the right ingredients in it" could cause a belt separation. But Grant stated in his affidavit that the physical properties of a tire cannot be determined from an examination of a compound formula; rather, the finished tire itself must be tested. Further, plaintiffs do not contest Continental's assertions that the plaintiffs have no other manufacturers' compound formulas with which to compare Continental's formula. The plaintiffs contended at oral argument before this Court that their expert has found sulfur on the belt surfaces of this tire, and that plaintiffs need Continental's formula to determine whether sulfur is a regular component of the skim stock or whether it was a foreign material improperly introduced during manufacture. Regardless of whether this theory might otherwise justify discovery of the compound formula, an issue on which we express no opinion, plaintiffs presented no evidence supporting this theory to the trial court. Under these circumstances, given the highly proprietary nature of the information, the plaintiffs have not carried their burden under Rule 507 of demonstrating that the information is necessary for a fair trial.

We accordingly conclude that the trial court abused its discretion. Because the trial court has ordered Continental to produce privileged, trade secret information, Continental has no adequate remedy by appeal. *See Walker v. Packer*, 827 S.W.2d 833, 843 (Tex. 1992).

. . . .

For the foregoing reasons, we conditionally grant mandamus relief directing the trial court to vacate its order compelling Continental to produce the belt skim-stock formula. We reiterate that nothing in our decision prohibits plaintiffs from seeking to discover the formula under the procedure we have set forth.

HANKINSON, J., did not participate in the decision.

---

## NOTES AND QUESTIONS

(1) *Breadth of Protection Afforded Corporations.* How broad a protection does the new attorney-client privilege provide for corporate communications? Do you believe that application of the new test will be predictable?

(2) *Satisfaction of Confidentiality Requirement.* Consider the requirement that communications be "confidential." What advice would you give a corporate client about generating, circulating, and storing privileged communications?

(3) *Public Policy Issues.* As a matter of public policy, how broad do you think the corporate attorney-client privilege should be? *Compare* Fried, *The Lawyer as Friend: The Moral Foundations of the Lawyer-Client Relation*, 85 Yale L.J. 1060 (1976) *with* Thornburg, *Sanctifying Secrecy: The Mythology of the Corporate Attorney-Client Privilege*, 69 Notre Dame L. Rev. 157 (1993).

(4) *Exceptions to Attorney-Client Privilege.* Attorney-client communications are not privileged if they fall within certain exceptions, set out in Texas Rule of Evidence 503(d). The most litigated exception is the crime-fraud exception. Tex. R. Evid. 503(d)(1). There is no privilege if the services of counsel were sought or obtained to enable or aid anyone to commit or plan to commit what the client knew or reasonably should have known to be a crime or fraud. The crime-fraud exception applies only when a prima facie case is made of contemplated fraud. In addition, there must be a relationship between the document for which the privilege is challenged and the prima facie proof offered. *Granada Corp. v. First Court of Appeals*, 844 S.W.2d 223, 227–228 (Tex. 1992).

### [c] Other Statutory Privileges

(1) *Hospital Committee Privilege.* In *Barnes v. Whittington*, 751 S.W.2d 493 (Tex. 1988), the Supreme Court interpreted a statutory privilege granted to hospital committee records and proceedings. The Court held that this privilege protects only documents created by or at the direction of the committee for committee purposes. Documents gratuitously submitted to the committee are not protected. Since *Barnes* was decided, the statutory hospital committee privilege has been recodified as Section 161.032 of the Health and Safety Code.

(2) *Judicial or Administrative Proceedings.* The Medical Practice Act also makes the reports, determinations of, and communications to medical peer review committees confidential and privileged in civil judicial or administrative proceedings. As amended in 1987, Article 4495b, Section 5.06(j) of the Medical Practice Act provides as follows:

> Unless disclosure is required or authorized by law, records or determinations of or communications to a medical peer review committee are not subject to subpoena or discovery and are not admissible as evidence in any civil judicial or administrative proceeding without waiver of the privilege of confidentiality executed in writing by the committee.

Any person seeking access to privileged information must plead and prove waiver of the privilege. For example, in one case, the defendant physician and a hospital claimed that a district judge abused his discretion by ordering the production of documents concerning the competency and credentialing of the physician at the hospital, including materials relating to an investigation of the physician's medical conduct and documents concerning any withdrawal of his medical or surgical privileges. *Northeast Community Hosp. v. Gregg,* 815 S.W.2d 320, 321–22 (Tex. App.—Fort Worth 1991, orig. proceeding). The court of appeals concluded that mandamus was appropriate, based in part on the applicability of Article 4495b to hospital peer review committees. Significantly, the court was unwilling to engraft the limitations on the claims of privilege under Article 4495b that are applicable to claims of privilege under Sections 161.031 and 161.032 of the Health and Safety Code. *See also Doctor's Hospital v. West,* 765 S.W.2d 812, 815 (Tex. App.—Houston [1st Dist.] 1988, orig. proceeding).

(3) *Public Health Statutes.* Various other public health statutes contain reporting and confidentiality requirements that might become relevant during discovery disputes. For example, the Communicable Disease Prevention and Control Act contains extensive reporting and confidentiality requirements concerning communicable disease test results. Health & Safety C. § 81.103; *but see Gulf Coast Regional Blood Ctr. v. Houston,* 745 S.W.2d 557 (Tex. App.—Fort Worth 1988, orig. proceeding), holding statute inapplicable to court proceedings.

In addition, another statute makes the medical and donor records of a blood bank confidential. *See* Health & Safety C. § 162.003. However, the statute also provides that the blood bank may be required by a court of competent jurisdiction, after notice and hearing, to provide a recipient of blood from the blood bank with results of tests, with donor identification deleted, of the blood of every donor of blood transfused into the recipient. Health & Safety C. § 162.010. Under certain circumstances, a court may order discovery relating to the donor. Health & Safety C. § 162.011; *see also Gulf Coast Regional Blood Ctr. v. Houston,* 745 S.W.2d 557 (Tex. App.—Fort Worth 1988, orig. proceeding) (pre-statute case; order requiring blood center to identify blood donors in wrongful death action based on blood transfusion resulting in death from AIDS not violation of right to privacy); *Tarrant County Hosp. Dist. v. Hughes,* 734 S.W.2d 675 (Tex. App.—Fort Worth 1987, orig. proceeding)(same).

(4) *Exceptions to Privileges for Medical Records.* A party may be required to disclose medical and mental health records despite assertions of the physician/patient privilege pursuant to Evidence Rule 509 and the confidentiality of mental health information as provided in Evidence Rule 510. Exceptions to the medical and mental health privileges apply when records sought to be discovered are relevant to a condition at issue relied on as part of any party's claim or defense. In this instance, the trial court, on request, is to perform an *in camera* inspection to assure the proper balancing of interest occurs before production is required. If a condition is part of a party's claim or defense, the patient records should be revealed only to the extent necessary to provide relevant evidence pertaining to the alleged condition. The Texas Supreme Court rejected the argument that the 1988 amendments to Evidence Rules 509(d)(4) and 510(d)(5) were meant solely to codify the *Ginsberg* offensive use doctrine, but rather represent "a significant departure from the historical scope of the patient-litigant privilege." The exception terminates

the privilege whenever any party relies upon the condition of the patient as part of its claim or defense even though the patient has not personally placed the condition at issue, and even though the patient is not a party to litigation. This interpretation will abrogate much of the control patients once exercised over the release of their medical records. *R.K. v. Ramirez,* 887 S.W.2d 836, 842 (Tex. 1994).

(5) *Lobbying Activities.* The Government Code prohibits the public disclosure of a written or otherwise recorded communication from a citizen of Texas to a member of the legislature unless either party authorizes disclosure. Gov. C. § 306.004. This provision was held to prevent discovery in a civil case of documents submitted to lobbyists and copies of documents distributed to state representatives in support of proposed legislation. *Inwood West Civic Ass'n v. Touchy,* 754 S.W.2d 276, 278 (Tex. App.—Houston [14th Dist.] 1988, orig. proceeding) (homeowners' associations denied discovery of Houston Cable's lobbying efforts in support of law giving cable companies free access to utility easements across private property).

(6) *Reporter's Privilege.* In *Channel Two Television Co. v. Dickerson,* 725 S.W.2d 470 (Tex. App.—Houston [1st Dist.] 1987, orig. proceeding), the court recognized and applied a qualified privilege protecting information that the press obtains through its investigations. *See also Branzburg v. Hayes,* 408 U.S. 665 (1972). Because of the Texas constitutional provision that "no law shall ever be passed curtailing the liberty of speech or of the press," the court held that, once the privilege is asserted, the party seeking discovery of the reporter's investigative materials must demonstrate that there is a compelling and overriding need for the information. *Channel Two,* 725 S.W.2d at 472. At a minimum, the party seeking discovery must make a "clear and specific showing" that the information sought is: (1) highly material and relevant; (2) necessary to the maintenance of the claim; and (3) not obtainable from other available sources. *Id.* Because no such showing was made in the *Channel Two* case, the reporter's notes, outtakes, records, and other documents were not discoverable. Another court of appeals has questioned whether the plurality opinion in *Branzburg* established a qualified reporter's privilege. *Dolcefino v. Ray,* 902 S.W.2d 163, 164–165 (Tex. App.—Houston [1st Dist.] 1987, orig. proceeding) ("[M]ore than seven years after *Channel Two* was decided, the rules still do not provide any privilege for journalists. We express no opinion, however, on the ultimate question of whether such a privilege exists"); *cf.* State ex rel. Healey v. McMeans, 884 S.W.2d 772, 775 (Tex. Crim. App. 1994) (rejecting reporter's privilege in criminal cases).

(7) *Public Information Act.* The Public Information Act provides for public access to a wide variety of public information maintained by government bodies. *See* Gov. C. § 552.001 et seq. Certain types of information are exempt from the public disclosure requirement. These exceptions from disclosure do not create new privileges from discovery, nor is the Act intended to affect the scope of discovery under the Texas Rules of Civil Procedure. Gov. C. § 552.005. Nevertheless, the Texas Supreme Court has created some privileges based on exceptions to the Act. For example, information held by law enforcement agencies and prosecutors relating to their criminal investigations is privileged from discovery in civil actions against the officers or prosecutors. *Hobson v. Moore*, 734 S.W.2d 340, 341 (Tex. 1987).

### [C] Waiver of Privileges: Offensive Use

Even when a party has a privilege to withhold certain material, that privilege can be waived. Sometimes the waiver results from the party's failure to properly assert or prove the privilege. That situation is discussed in [D], *below*. A party can also lose a privilege by making offensive use of privileged material.

Privileges are created to shield particular kinds of private communications from disclosure in a lawsuit. However, the courts have sometimes found it unacceptable for a party to create a situation in which the privileged information is relevant, but then refuses to disclose that information, claiming privilege. In other words, an evidentiary privilege is intended to be a "shield" but not a "sword," and a person who makes his own privileged communication relevant in the lawsuit may find that he or she has waived that privilege.

Texas first addressed this issue in the context of a psychotherapist-patient privilege. In *Ginsberg v. Fifth Court of Appeals*, 686 S.W.2d 105 (Tex. 1985), the Texas Supreme Court held that when medical records concerning communications between the plaintiff and her psychiatrist regarding a business transaction that was the subject matter of her claim against the discovering party were relevant, the court was within its discretion to hold the medical records discoverable. In *Republic Insurance Co. v. Davis*, 856 S.W.2d 158 (Tex. 1993), the Court applied the doctrine to the attorney-client privilege and articulated a three-pronged test for its application. First, the party asserting the privilege will waive it only if the party is seeking affirmative relief (filing a declaratory judgment action is not seeking affirmative relief). Second, the privileged information must be such that the information, if believed by the fact finder, in all probability would be outcome determinative. It is not enough that the privileged information is relevant, or even that it contradicts a position the party is taking in the current lawsuit. Third, disclosure of the privileged communication must be the only means by which the aggrieved party may obtain the evidence. Texas thus has adopted a more limited offensive use waiver than many states, and shaped it so that plaintiffs are more likely than defendants to find that they have waived a privilege by putting the privileged information in issue. *Compare* Marcus, *The Perils of Privilege: Waiver and the Litigator*, 84 Mich. L. Rev. 1605 (1986) *with* Thornburg, *Attorney-Client Privilege: Issue-Related Waivers*, 50 J. Air L. & Com. 1039 (1985).

The Texas Supreme Court has also discussed the proper procedure to follow when deciding the appropriate sanction for offensive use. *See Texas Dep't of Public Safety Officers Ass'n v. Denton*, 897 S.W.2d 757 (Tex. 1995) (suggesting several factors to consider and requiring that, as with any sanction, a direct relationship must exist between the offensive conduct and the sanction imposed). *See also* Cornell, *Piercing the Iron Curtain of Silence: The Doctrine of Offensive Use Waiver*, 60 Tex. B.J. 304 (April 1997).

### [D] Waiver of Privileges: Failure to Assert or Prove Privilege

*Read Tex. R. Civ. P. 193.*

A lawyer litigating discovery disputes must be aware of the procedures for handling disputes about the scope of discovery. Failure to act properly may waive a party's right to discovery or to assert an objection to discovery. The burdens of making appropriate discovery requests and asserting and proving objections to discovery are the subject of a considerable body of case law. In addition, the 1999 amendments to the discovery rules contain important modifications in existing procedure and information about the waiver of objections.

(1) *Duty to Make Complete Response.* When responding to written discovery, a party must make a complete response, based on all information reasonably available to the responding party or the responding party's attorney at the time the response is made. Tex. R. Civ. P. 193.1. This duty to respond was first made explicit in the 1999 amendments to the rules. In addition, Civil Procedure Rule 191 contains specific provisions regarding the signing of various discovery documents. Signing a disclosure constitutes a certification that "to the best of the signer's

knowledge, information, and belief, formed after a reasonable inquiry, the disclosure is complete and correct as of the time it is made." Tex. R. Civ. P. 191.3(b). Signing a discovery notice, response, or objection constitutes a certification that "to the best of the signer's knowledge, information, and belief, formed after a reasonable inquiry, the notice, response, or objection: (1) is consistent with the rules of civil procedure and [the] discovery rules and warranted by existing law or a good faith argument for the extension, modification, or reversal of existing law; (2) has a good faith factual basis; (3) is not interposed for any improper purpose, such as to harass or to cause unnecessary delay or needless increase in the cost of litigation; and (4) is not unreasonable or unduly burdensome of expensive, given the needs of the case, the discovery already had in the case, the amount in controversy, and the importance of the issues at stake in the litigation." Tex. R. Civ. P. 191.3(c).

(2) *Objecting to Written Discovery.* An individual discovery request may be objectionable for a number of reasons. For example, a request for "all documents relevant to the lawsuit" is overly broad and not in compliance with the rule requiring specific requests for documents. *Loftin v. Martin,* 776 S.W.2d 145, 148 (Tex. 1989). A request may be objectionable because it asks for information or material that is simply not relevant to the subject matter of the pending action, or is not within the scope of discovery, such as a request for the identities of purely consulting experts. Sometimes the request, although overly broad, seeks some discoverable information. For example, a request for income tax returns for a 15-year period may be overly broad, but a request for income tax returns for a five-year period may be appropriate. In addition, the time, manner, and place for complying with the request may be objectionable. A party wanting to assert this kind of objection to a discovery request should do so in writing and should state specifically the legal or factual basis for the objection and the extent to which the party is refusing to comply with the request. A party must make objections to written discovery within the time for making the response. Tex. R. Civ. P. 193.2(a). An objection that is not made within the time required is waived unless the court excuses the waiver for good cause shown.

(3) *Withholding Privileged Information.* After the 1999 amendments to the rules, it is no longer proper to *object* to assert a privilege. Tex. R. Civ. P. 193.2(f). Instead, a claim of privilege is asserted by withholding the privileged information or materials and informing the requesting party that responsive information or materials have been withheld due to privilege. Tex. R. Civ. P. 193.3(a). In addition to withholding the information or material, the party must state: (1) that information or material responsive to the request has been withheld; (2) the request to which the information or material relates; and (3) the privilege or privileges asserted. Tex. R. Civ. P. 193.3(a). Although the rules provide that failure to timely state an objection results in a waiver of the objection, the rules do not set out the consequences for failing to assert a privilege in a timely manner. Under precedent interpreting the rules before the 1999 amendments, failure to timely assert a privilege resulted in waiver of the privilege. In language similar to the current rule, the former rule required a specific pleading of the "particular exemption or immunity from discovery" relied on by the party. Former Tex. R. Civ. P. 166b(4). Failure to specifically state the privilege may result in waiver of the privilege. Note, however, that under the new rules, assertions of privilege should not be made prophylactically against the threat of waiver, but only when the information is actually withheld. Tex. R. Civ. P. 193, Comment 3.

(4) *Request for and Description of Withheld Information and Materials (Privilege Log).* After receiving a response indicating that information or material has been withheld, the party seeking discovery may serve on the withholding party a written request that the withholding party identify

the information and material withheld. Tex. R. Civ. P. 193.3(b). Within 15 days of service of that request, the withholding party must serve a response. The response, often called a "privilege log," must: (1) describe the information or materials withheld, without revealing the privileged information itself or otherwise waiving the privilege, in such a manner as will enable the other parties to assess the applicability of the privilege; and (2) assert a specific privilege for each item or group of items withheld. Tex. R. Civ. P. 193.3(b). *See Weisel Enterprises, Inc. v. Curry*, 718 S.W.2d 56 (Tex. 1986). Under prior law, failure to adequately provide this information could amount to a waiver of the privilege.

(5) *New Exception: Post-Consultation Attorney-Client Communications.* There is one significant exception to the procedure stated in the rule for asserting a privilege. A party need not take any steps to preserve the privilege for a communication to or from a lawyer or lawyer's representative, or a privileged document of a lawyer or lawyer's representative, concerning the litigation in which the discovery is requested if the communication was made or the document was created from the point at which a party consults a lawyer with a view to obtaining professional legal services from the lawyer in the prosecution or defense of a specific claim in the litigation in which discovery is requested. Tex. R. Civ. P. 193.3(c). In other words, a party need not state in the response that such information or document has been withheld, and need not list the information or document in a privilege log. In essence, parties withholding such information assert and rule on their own privilege claims, and the discovering party will not even be informed that the documents exist.

(6) *Inadvertent Production and Compelled Disclosure.* A claim of privilege is not defeated by a disclosure that was compelled erroneously. Tex. R. Evid. 512. The privilege is also not defeated if the disclosure was made without an opportunity to claim the privilege. Tex. R. Evid. 512. A claim that the disclosure was inadvertent does not fall within either of these exceptions. After the 1999 amendments, the discovery rules have a specific provision concerning the inadvertent production of privileged documents. A party who produces material or information "without intending to waive a claim of privilege" does not waive the privilege claim if the producing party amends the response, identifies the material or information produced, and states the privilege asserted. Note that the emphasis is on the intent to *waive*, not the intent to *produce* the material. The amended response must be served within 10 days, or a shorter time if ordered by the court, after the producing party actually discovers the inadvertent production. If the producing party amends the response to assert a privilege, the requesting party must promptly return the specified information or material and any copies, subject to any ruling by the court denying the privilege claim. Tex. R. Civ. P. 193.3(d). This new rule overrules the Texas Supreme Court's decision on this issue in *Granada Corp v. First Court of Appeals*, 844 S.W.2d 223, 227 (Tex. 1992), which had held that a party seeking to protect a privilege after disclosure must show more than inadvertence, instead showing that the circumstances demonstrate the involuntariness of disclosure. Although a party does not have an obligation to notify an opponent that apparently privileged information was inadvertently disclosed, the party should be aware of the implication of the timing rules. For example, if the party holding the material discloses the inadvertent production for the first time at trial, his or her opposing party may demand its return at that time and will preserve the privilege by doing so.

(7) *Hearing and Ruling on Objections and Assertions of Privilege.* Any party may at any reasonable time request a hearing on an objection or claim of privilege. However, a party need not request a ruling on that party's own objection or assertion of privilege to preserve the objection

or privilege. Tex. R. Civ. P. 193.4(b). If there is a hearing, the party making the objection or asserting the privilege must present any evidence necessary to support the objection or privilege, and the burden will be on the objecting party to do so. Failure to meet this burden may also result in waiver of the privilege. The evidence may be in the form of live testimony presented at the hearing or of affidavits. If the evidence is in affidavit form, the affidavits must be served at least seven days before the hearing or at such other reasonable time as the court permits. They may not be tendered for ex parte consideration. Often, the documents themselves are the only evidence of the privilege. They should be submitted to the court for *in camera* inspection. Tex. R. Civ. P. 193.4(a).

(8) *Privileged Material as Evidence.* A decision to use the privileged material as evidence at a trial or hearing also waives the privilege and requires prior disclosure of the material. A party may not use material or information withheld from discovery under a claim of privilege, including a claim sustained by the court, at any hearing or trial without timely revealing the information in an amended or supplemental response to the discovery. Tex. R. Civ. P. 193.4(c).

(9) *Protective Orders.* The 1999 rules conceive of a motion for protective order as a device for objecting to discovery that is distinct from the objection or the assertion of a privilege. Tex. R. Civ. P. 192.6. How was a protective order used in the litigation underlying *Continental General Tire*? Would it be the proper device to use now, given the court's construction of Evidence Rule 507? Civil Procedure Rule 192.6 provides that a person should not move for a protective order "when an objection to written discovery or an assertion of privilege is appropriate." This seems to imply that protective orders are the appropriate procedural device only for material that is discoverable but the person from whom discovery is sought wants to object to something such as the time or place of discovery. Tex. R. Civ. P. 192.6(a). On the other hand, Rule 192.6(b) refers to using a protective order to protect the movant from the invasion of personal, constitutional, or property rights. Is it ultimately helpful to think of "objections," "assertions of privilege," and "motions for protective order" as three separate categories, each with its own rules and procedures?

(10) *Raising and Litigating Trade Secret Claims.* Assuming that trade secrets are "privileged" within the meaning of Civil Procedure Rule 193.3, what procedure should be used to assert trade secret protection in response to a discovery request? How should the party seeking discovery respond? What additional information must the objecting party provide under Rule 193.3(b)? If there is a hearing, what kind of evidence must the objecting party present to show that the information is a trade secret? What kind of evidence must the discovering party present to show that the information is "necessary for a fair adjudication of its claims"? Who has the burden of proving up the appropriate contents of a protective order?

### [E] Review of Discovery Orders

Discovery orders, like other interlocutory orders entered during the course of pretrial proceedings, are not immediately appealable. While it is theoretically possible to secure appellate review of a discovery order after trial, such a postponement may create problems for the party aggrieved by the order. A party ordered to produce information over objection will have to produce it, and a later reversal cannot undo the production. A party denied information will have to complete discovery and try the case without the information; this can cause unnecessary expense and delay. It may even make it impossible to demonstrate to the court of appeals that the discovery error was harmful.

It is sometimes possible to secure immediate review of discovery orders through mandamus. In a mandamus action, the party unhappy with the discovery order (called the "relator") files an action in an appellate court, claiming that the court below (called the "respondent") clearly abused its discretion and that an appeal would provide an inadequate remedy. In *Walker v. Packer*, 827 S.W.2d 833 (Tex. 1992), the Texas Supreme Court discussed the requirements for securing mandamus relief. What follows is the portion of *Walker* discussing both requirements for the mandamus record and the prerequisites for mandamus to be an appropriate remedy in a discovery dispute.

---

## WALKER v. PACKER

*827 S.W.2d 833 (Tex. 1992)*

PHILLIPS, Chief Justice.

This original mandamus action involves two pre-trial discovery requests sought by relators, plaintiffs in a medical malpractice lawsuit. The first discovery dispute involves documents which the plaintiffs seek from one of the defendants, while the second involves documents which they seek from a nonparty for impeachment purposes. As to the first matter, we hold that relators have not presented a sufficient record to demonstrate that the trial court clearly abused its discretion in failing to grant them all requested relief. As to the second, we hold that relators have an adequate remedy by appeal. Thus, mandamus is inappropriate, and we deny the writ.

### The St. Paul and Aetna Records

Catherine Johanna Walker sustained brain damage at birth in January 1983. In January 1985, her parents, Charles F. and Mary Jeanette Walker, sued Dr. Paul Crider, the obstetrician, St. Paul Hospital, where Catherine was born, and Iris Jean White, a nurse attending at the delivery.

In August 1987, the Walkers served on St. Paul their third request for production of documents pursuant to Tex. R. Civ. P. 167. One request asked for:

> Any and all writings, notes, documents, letters, etc., concerning, mentioning, alluding to, or making reference to (either directly or indirectly), the tape recorded statement given by Nurse White to an Aetna adjuster, including but not limited to any notes or entries in any Aetna adjuster's file, any attorney's file, or any file or writing in possession of any employee, representative or agent of St. Paul Hospital. This request is in reference to the tape recorded statement which you have been unable to locate, but which was previously requested. . . .

St. Paul responded as follows:

> In an effort to respond to this request, this Defendant again checked with all appropriate personnel and files at St. Paul Hospital and the law firm of Bailey and Williams. No such statement or taped recording was found. For the third time the Aetna Casualty and Surety Company was asked to check its records and files and a partially transcribed statement was located, a copy of which is attached. No taped recording was located.

Nearly two years later, the Walkers filed a motion to compel under Tex. R. Civ. P. 215, asserting that St. Paul failed to respond completely to the request. [footnote omitted] The Walkers complained that "St. Paul Hospital did not even respond to what was requested in the request for production—that is, writings, notes, and notations in the adjuster's file or attorney's file mentioning, alluding to, or making reference to the tape recorded statement of Nurse White." At about the same time, the Walkers also served on Aetna Casualty and Surety Company, St. Paul's insurer, an "Amended Notice of Intention to Take Deposition Upon Written Questions—Duces Tecum," seeking, among other things, the same documents. Aetna moved to quash the notice.

The trial judge appointed a special master to review the Walkers' motion to compel and Aetna's motion to quash. After an evidentiary hearing on September 5, 1989, the master prepared findings, which formed the basis for two extensive orders signed by the trial court on September 20, 1989. In the first order, the court found that the Walkers were "entitled to all documentation sought in [the request] from the files of Defendant St. Paul or its attorney of record, but not from the files of Aetna Insurance Company, except as they may appear in the files of St. Paul or the attorneys of record of St. Paul." The court also stated that it "has been advised that St. Paul has supplied all documentation that is responsive to [the request], but that additional documentation will be made available to the Court for *in camera* review." The court therefore sustained the Walkers' motion to compel "to the extent that on Friday, September 8, 1989 the Special Master will review in the Chambers of the 134th District Court the relevant portions of the St. Paul files and their attorney [sic] files, which may be in response to Plaintiff's request. . . ." The court, however, did not order St. Paul to produce documents from Aetna's files for *in camera* inspection. [footnote omitted]

After the master's September 8 *in camera* inspection, the court ordered discovery of three additional documents from the files of St. Paul and its attorneys, which it found "relate to the matters sought in discovery and should be supplied after irrelevant portions of such documents are stricken." After unsuccessfully seeking relief in the court of appeals, the Walkers moved for leave to file a petition for writ of mandamus with this court, arguing that the trial court clearly abused its discretion by refusing to order St. Paul to produce the documents from Aetna's files and by ordering that portions of the other responsive documents be stricken. The Walkers contend that the order was a clear abuse of discretion because St. Paul 1) never objected to the Walkers' request for production, 2) had a superior right to the Walkers to compel production of the documents in Aetna's possession, and 3) never asked that any parts of the documents be excised.

The record before us does not include the statement of facts from the evidentiary hearing on the Walkers' motion to compel production. Without it, we cannot determine on what basis the trial judge and the special master reached their conclusions. Since we cannot assess whether or not the trial court's order was correct, we obviously cannot take the additional step of determining that the court's order, if incorrect, constituted a clear abuse of discretion.

As the parties seeking relief, the Walkers had the burden of providing this Court with a sufficient record to establish their right to mandamus relief. Since an evidentiary hearing was held, the Walkers had the burden of providing us not only a petition and affidavit, *see* Tex. R. App. P. 121(a)(2)(C) and (F), but also a statement of facts from the hearing. *See, e.g., Cameron County v. Hinojosa,* 760 S.W.2d 742, 744 (Tex. App.—Corpus Christi 1988, orig. proceeding); *Greenstein, Logan & Co. v. Burgess Mktg. Inc.,* 744 S.W.2d 170, 177 (Tex. App.—Waco 1987, writ denied); *see also Western Casualty & Surety Co. v. Spears,* 730 S.W.2d 821, 822 (Tex. App.—San Antonio 1987, orig. proceeding). [footnote omitted] Having failed to meet this burden, the Walkers have not provided us with a record upon which they can establish their right to mandamus relief against St. Paul.

. . . .

Having concluded that the trial court erred in denying the discovery based solely on *Russell,* we now must determine whether the appropriate remedy lies by writ of mandamus. "Mandamus issues only to correct a clear abuse of discretion or the violation of a duty imposed by law when there is no other adequate remedy by law." *Johnson v. Fourth Court of Appeals,* 700 S.W.2d 916, 917 (Tex. 1985). [footnote omitted] We therefore examine whether the trial court's error in the present case constituted a clear abuse of discretion and, if so, whether there is an adequate remedy by appeal.

*1. Clear Abuse of Discretion*

Traditionally, the writ of mandamus issued only to compel the performance of a ministerial act or duty. *See Wortham v. Walker,* 133 Tex. 255, 277, 128 S.W.2d 1138, 1150 (1939); *Arberry v. Beavers,* 6 Tex. 457 (1851); Helen A. Cassidy, *The Instant Freeze-Dried Guide to Mandamus Procedure in Texas Courts,* 31 S. Tex. L. Rev. 509, 510 (1990); Comment, *The Expanding Use of Mandamus to Review Texas District Court Discovery Orders: An Immediate Appeal Is Available,* 32 Sw. L.J. 1283, 1288 (1979).

Since the 1950's, however, this Court has used the writ to correct a "clear abuse of discretion" committed by the trial court. *See, e.g., Joachim v. Chambers,* 815 S.W.2d 234, 237 (Tex. 1991); *Jampole v. Touchy,* 673 S.W.2d 569, 574 (Tex. 1984); *West v. Solito,* 563 S.W.2d 240, 244 (Tex. 1978); *Womack v. Berry,* 156 Tex. 44, 50, 291 S.W.2d 677, 682 (1956). *See generally,* David W. Holman & Byron C. Keeling, *Entering the Thicket? Mandamus Review of Texas District Court Witness Disclosure Orders,* 23 St. Mary's L.J. 365, 390 (1991); Cassidy, 31 S. Tex. L. Rev. at 510; Note, *The Use of Mandamus to Review Discovery Orders in Texas: An Extraordinary Remedy,* 1 Rev. Litig. 325, 326–27 (1981); Comment, 32 Sw. L.J. at 1290.

A trial court clearly abuses its discretion if "it reaches a decision so arbitrary and unreasonable as to amount to a clear and prejudicial error of law." *Johnson v. Fourth Court of Appeals,* 700 S.W.2d at 917. This standard, however, has different applications in different circumstances.

With respect to resolution of factual issues or matters committed to the trial court's discretion, for example, the reviewing court may not substitute its judgment for that of the trial court. *See Flores v. Fourth Court of Appeals,* 777 S.W.2d 38, 41–42 (Tex. 1989) (holding that determination of discoverability under Tex. R. Civ. P. 166b(3)(d) was within discretion of trial court); *Johnson,* 700 S.W.2d at 918 (holding that trial court was within discretion in granting a new trial "in the interest of justice and fairness"). The relator must establish that the trial court could reasonably have reached only one decision. *Id.* at 917. Even if the reviewing court would have decided the issue differently, it cannot disturb the trial court's decision unless it is shown to be arbitrary and unreasonable. *Johnson,* 700 S.W.2d at 918.

On the other hand, review of a trial court's determination of the legal principles controlling its ruling is much less deferential. A trial court has no "discretion" in determining what the law is or applying the law to the facts. Thus, a clear failure by the trial court to analyze or apply the law correctly will constitute an abuse of discretion, and may result in appellate reversal by extraordinary writ. *See Joachim v. Chambers,* 815 S.W.2d 234, 240 (Tex. 1991) (trial court abused discretion by misinterpreting Code of Judicial Conduct); *NCNB Texas National Bank v. Coker,* 765 S.W.2d 398, 400 (Tex. 1989) (trial court abused discretion by failing to apply proper legal standard to motion to disqualify counsel); *Eanes ISD v. Logue,* 712 S.W.2d 741, 742 (Tex. 1986) (trial court abused discretion by erroneously finding constitutional violation).

In determining whether the trial court abused its discretion in the present case, we treat the trial court's erroneous denial of the requested discovery on the sole basis of *Russell* as a legal conclusion to be reviewed with limited deference to the trial court. This is consistent with our approach in previous mandamus proceedings arising out of the trial court's interpretation of legal rules. *Cf. Axelson, Inc. v. McIlhany,* 798 S.W.2d 550, 555 (Tex. 1990); *Barnes v. Whittington,* 751 S.W.2d 493, 495–96 (Tex. 1988); *Terry v. Lawrence,* 700 S.W.2d 912, 913–14 (Tex. 1985). Under this analysis, the trial court's erroneous interpretation of the law constitutes a clear abuse of discretion.

*2. Adequate Remedy by Appeal*

In order to determine whether the writ should issue, however, we must further decide whether the Walkers have an adequate remedy by appeal.

Mandamus will not issue where there is "a clear and adequate remedy at law, such as a normal appeal." *State v. Walker,* 679 S.W.2d 484, 485 (Tex. 1984). Mandamus is intended to be an extraordinary remedy, available only in limited circumstances. The writ will issue "only in situations involving manifest and urgent necessity and not for grievances that may be addressed by other remedies." *Holloway v. Fifth Court of Appeals,* 767 S.W.2d 680, 684 (Tex. 1989) (quoting James Sales, *Original Jurisdiction of the Supreme Court and the Courts of Appeals of Texas in Appellate Procedure in Texas,* 1.4[1][b] at 47 (2d ed. 1979)). The requirement that persons seeking mandamus relief establish the lack of an adequate appellate remedy is a "fundamental tenet" of mandamus practice. *Holloway,* 767 S.W.2d at 684.

Our requirement that mandamus will not issue where there is an adequate remedy by appeal is well-settled. [footnote omitted] On a few occasions, however, we have not focused on this requirement when applying mandamus review of discovery orders. For example, in *Barker v. Dunham,* 551 S.W.2d 41 (Tex. 1977), the trial court refused to compel defendant's representative to answer certain deposition questions, and the plaintiff applied to this Court for a writ of mandamus. We concluded that the trial court had abused its discretion, and ordered that the writ conditionally issue. We never discussed the well-settled requirement of inadequate remedy by appeal.

A few months later, in *Allen v. Humphreys,* 559 S.W.2d 798 (Tex. 1977), the Court again conditionally issued a writ of mandamus to correct a discovery abuse without considering whether the relator had an adequate remedy by appeal. The real party in interest in *Allen* raised this argument, but the Court avoided the issue by citing *Barker. Id.* at 801.

Commentators quickly criticized the *Barker* and *Allen* opinions: *See* James Sales, *Pre-Trial Discovery in Texas,* 31 Sw. L.J. 1017, 1033 (1977); Comment, *The Expanding Use of Mandamus to Review Texas District Court Discovery Orders: An Immediate Appeal Is Available,* 32 Sw. L.J. 1283, 1300 (1979) (In most cases "forcing a party to await the completion of the trial in order to seek appellate review will not endanger his substantial rights. . . ."); Note, *Mandamus May Issue To Compel A District Judge to Order Discovery,* 9 Tex. Tech. L. Rev. 782 (1978) (mandamus should not be a substitute for appeal).

In *Jampole v. Touchy,* 673 S.W.2d 569 (Tex. 1984), the Court again used the extraordinary writ of mandamus to compel discovery which had been denied by the trial court. Unlike in *Barker* and *Allen,* however, the Court in *Jampole* addressed whether relator had an adequate appellate remedy. The underlying suit in *Jampole* was a products liability action, and the disputed discovery materials included alternate design and assembly documents. The Court held that relator did not have an adequate remedy by appeal because denial of this discovery effectively prevented relator from proving the material allegations of his lawsuit. 673 S.W.2d at 576. Remedy by appeal in a discovery mandamus is not adequate where a party is required "to try his lawsuit, debilitated by the denial of proper discovery, only to have that lawsuit rendered a certain nullity on appeal. . . ." *Id.*

Although the Court in *Jampole* recognized the need to address whether relator had an adequate remedy by appeal, it expressly refused to overrule *Barker* and *Allen. Id.* Perhaps because of this, we have on several occasions since *Jampole* used mandamus to correct discovery errors without considering whether the relator had an adequate appellate remedy. *See Loftin v. Martin,* 776 S.W.2d 145 (Tex. 1989); *Barnes v. Whittington,* 751 S.W.2d 493 (Tex. 1988); *Lunsford v. Morris,* 746 S.W.2d 471 (Tex. 1988); *Turbodyne Corp. v. Heard,* 720 S.W.2d 802 (Tex. 1986); *Terry v. Lawrence,* 700 S.W.2d 912 (Tex. 1985); *Lindsay v. O'Neill,* 689 S.W.2d 400 (Tex. 1985).

On many other occasions, however, we have still required a showing of inadequate remedy by appeal in mandamus proceedings involving other types of pre-trial orders, even those involving discovery. *See, e.g., Transamerican Natural Gas Corp. v. Powell,* 811 S.W.2d 913, 919 (Tex. 1991); *Hooks v. Fourth Court of Appeals,* 808 S.W.2d 56, 59–60 (Tex. 1991); *Bell Helicopter Textron Inc. v. Walker,* 787 S.W.2d 954, 955 (Tex. 1990); *Stringer v. Eleventh Court of Appeals,* 720 S.W.2d 801, 801–02 (Tex. 1986). In *Hooks,* for example, we reaffirmed that the "cost or delay of having to go through trial and the appellate process does not make the remedy at law inadequate." 808 S.W.2d at 60.

The requirement that mandamus issue only where there is no adequate remedy by appeal is sound, and we reaffirm it today. No mandamus case has ever expressly rejected this requirement, or offered any explanation as to why mandamus review of discovery orders should be exempt from this "fundamental tenet" of mandamus practice. Without this limitation, appellate courts would "embroil themselves unnecessarily in incidental pre-trial rulings of the trial courts" and mandamus "would soon cease to be an extraordinary writ." *Braden v. Downey,* 811 S.W.2d 922, 928 (Tex. 1991). We thus hold that a party seeking review of a discovery order by mandamus must demonstrate that the remedy offered by an ordinary appeal is inadequate. We disapprove of *Barker, Allen,* and any other authorities to the extent they might be read as abolishing or relaxing this rule.

We further hold that an appellate remedy is not inadequate merely because it may involve more expense or delay than obtaining an extraordinary writ. As we observed in *Iley v. Hughes,* the "delay in getting questions decided through the appellate process . . . will not justify intervention by appellate courts through the extraordinary writ of mandamus. Interference is justified only when parties stand to lose their substantial rights." 158 Tex. at 368, 311 S.W.2d at 652.

On some occasions, this Court has used, or at least mentioned, the more lenient standard first articulated in *Cleveland v. Ward,* 116 Tex. 1, 14, 285 S.W.2d 1063, 1068 (Tex. 1926), that the remedy by appeal must be "equally convenient, beneficial, and effective as mandamus." *See, e.g., Jampole v. Touchy,* 673 S.W.2d 569, 576 (Tex. 1984); *Crane v. Tunks,* 160 Tex. 182, 190, 328 S.W.2d 434, 439 (Tex. 1959). This standard, literally applied, would justify mandamus review whenever an appeal would arguably involve more cost or delay than mandamus. This is unworkable, both for individual cases and for the system as a whole. Mandamus disrupts the trial proceedings, forcing the parties to address in an appellate court issues that otherwise might have been resolved as discovery progressed and the evidence was developed at trial. Moreover, the delays and expense of mandamus proceedings may be substantial. This proceeding, for example, involving rulings on collateral discovery matters, has delayed the trial on the merits for over two years. The impact on the appellate courts must also be considered. We stated in *Braden* that "[t]he judicial system cannot afford immediate review of every discovery sanction." 811 S.W.2d 922, 928. It follows that the system cannot afford immediate review of every discovery order in general. [footnote omitted] We therefore disapprove of *Cleveland, Crane, Jampole* and any other authorities to the extent that they imply that a remedy by appeal is inadequate merely because it might involve more delay or cost than mandamus.

Justice Doggett's dissent argues that because discovery errors often constitute harmless errors under Tex. R. App. P. 81(b)(1), parties denied mandamus relief will be deprived of any remedy since the error will not provide a basis for appellate reversal. This is nothing more than a thinly disguised attack on the harmless error rule. Avoiding interlocutory appellate review of error that, in the final analysis, will prove to be harmless, is one of the principal reasons that mandamus should be restricted.

Justice Doggett's dissent also suggests that we will be unable to develop a coherent body of discovery law without unrestricted mandamus review. We do not think, however, that losing parties will be reluctant to raise perceived discovery errors on appeal, nor will an appellate court be foreclosed from writing on discovery issues, even when the error may be harmless. *See, e.g., Lovelace v. Sabine Consolidated, Inc.*, 733 S.W.2d 648, 652–53 (Tex. App.—Houston [14th Dist.] 1987, writ denied).

Nor are we impressed with the dissenters' claim that strict adherence to traditional mandamus standards will signal an end to effective interlocutory review for some parties or classes of litigants. There are many situations where a party will not have an adequate appellate remedy from a clearly erroneous ruling, and appellate courts will continue to issue the extraordinary writ. In the discovery context alone, at least three come to mind.

First, a party will not have an adequate remedy by appeal when the appellate court would not be able to cure the trial court's discovery error. This occurs when the trial court erroneously orders the disclosure of privileged information which will materially affect the rights of the aggrieved party, such as documents covered by the attorney-client privilege. *West v. Solito,* 563 S.W.2d 240 (Tex. 1978), or trade secrets without adequate protections to maintain the confidentiality of the information. *Automatic Drilling Machines v. Miller,* 515 S.W.2d 256 (Tex. 1974). As we noted in *Crane:* "After the [privileged documents] had been inspected, examined and reproduced . . . a holding that the court had erroneously issued the order would be of small comfort to relators in protecting their papers." 160 Tex. at 190, 328 S.W.2d at 439. It may also occur where a discovery order compels the production of patently irrelevant or duplicative documents, such that it clearly constitutes harassment or imposes a burden on the producing party far out of proportion to any benefit that may obtain to the requesting party. *See, e.g., Sears, Roebuck & Co. v. Ramirez,* 824 S.W.2d 558 (Tex. 1992) (demand for tax returns); *General Motors Corp. v. Lawrence,* 651 S.W.2d 732 (Tex. 1983) (demand for information about all vehicles for all years).

Second, an appeal will not be an adequate remedy where the party's ability to present a viable claim or defense at trial is vitiated or severely compromised by the trial court's discovery error. It is not enough to show merely the delay, inconvenience or expense of an appeal. Rather, the relator must establish the effective denial of a reasonable opportunity to develop the merits of his or her case, so that the trial would be a waste of judicial resources. We recently held that when a trial court imposes discovery sanctions which have the effect of precluding a decision on the merits of a party's claims—such as by striking pleadings, dismissing an action, or rendering default judgment—a party's remedy by eventual appeal is inadequate, unless the sanctions are imposed simultaneously with the rendition of a final, appealable judgment. *TransAmerican Natural Gas Corp. v. Powell,* 811 S.W.2d 913, 919 (Tex. 1991). Similarly, a denial of discovery going to the heart of a party's case may render the appellate remedy inadequate.

Finally, the remedy by appeal may be inadequate where the trial court disallows discovery and the missing discovery cannot be made part of the appellate record, or the trial court after proper request refuses to make it part of the record, and the reviewing court is unable to evaluate the effect of the trial court's error on the record before it. *See Tom L. Scott, Inc. v. McIlhany,* 798 S.W.2d 556, 558 (Tex. 1990) ("[M]andamus is the only remedy because the protective order shields the witnesses from deposition and thereby prevents the evidence from being part of the record."); *see generally Jampole,* 673 S.W.2d at 576 ("Because the evidence exempted from discovery would not appear in the record, the appellate courts would find it impossible to determine whether denying the discovery was harmful."). If the procedures of Tex. R. Civ. P. 166b(4) are followed, this situation should only rarely arise. If and when it does, however, the court must carefully consider all relevant circumstances, such as the claims and defenses asserted, the type of discovery sought, what it is intended to prove, and the presence or lack of other discovery, to determine whether mandamus is appropriate. [footnote omitted]

In the present case, the Walkers seek documents from the Center to impeach one defendant's expert witness. This information is not privileged, burdensome or harassing, nor does it vitiate or severely compromise the Walkers' ability to present a viable claim. In fact, as we have already noted, the trial court may ultimately conclude that it is not admissible or even discoverable. Finally, although the materials are not before us, they were considered below, and we know of no reason why they would not be available on appeal. Therefore, under our traditional standards of mandamus review, as measured by the factors we mention above, the Walkers have an adequate remedy by appeal and mandamus is inappropriate. For the above reasons, we conclude that the Walkers have not established their right to relief by mandamus on either discovery matter. Therefore, we deny the Walkers' petition for writ of mandamus.

[Concurring and dissenting opinions omitted.]

---

## NOTES AND QUESTIONS

(1) *Availability of Mandamus.* The court's opinion in *Walker* raises a number of questions about the availability of mandamus to review discovery orders. Do you believe that it will reduce the number of mandamus proceedings in the discovery context? For a different view, see Thornburg, *Interlocutory Review of Discovery Orders: An Idea Whose Time Has Come*, 44 Sw. L.J. 1045 (1990). The dissenting justices placed substantial reliance on the article's policy analysis of the need for interim review of discovery orders.

(2) *Changes in Mandamus Procedure.* Since *Walker* was written, the Texas Supreme Court has changed the actual procedures for mandamus, eliminating the two-step process of requesting leave to file a petition for writ of mandamus followed by the petition itself. The new procedure can be found in Tex. R. App. P. 52.

## DISCUSSION PROBLEMS

Opal Allen was shopping at her neighborhood Alpha Omega Grocery Store. She shopped there regularly and knew the store well. On this particular occasion, while shopping in the produce department, Allen slipped and fell, breaking her wrist. She was taken by ambulance to the local hospital, where she was treated and released. Her injury was severe enough that she was unable to return to her job as a secretary for about a month, and she received no pay check during that period. She has now returned to work, but suffers from chronic pain in the injured wrist, and has permanently lost some mobility as well.

Consider the following discovery issues that might arise in a slip and fall case brought by Allen against Alpha Omega. Assume that an "appropriate" discovery request has been made unless the question otherwise specifies.

1. Suppose that you represent Allen. Draft a discovery plan for her case, indicating what information you would seek to discover and what discovery tools you would use to get it.

2. Suppose that you represent Alpha Omega. Draft a discovery plan for its defense, indicating what information you would seek to discover and what discovery tools you would use to get it.

3. Immediately after Allen's fall, Hugh Cumber, a produce department manager, made a list of the names, addresses, and phone numbers of all of the customers in the produce department at the time of the fall. Can Allen discover the list? Can Allen discover the contents of the list?

4. One week after Allen's fall, Alpha Omega's insurer contacted Cumber. The insurance agent questioned Cumber about Allen's accident and tape recorded the conversation. Can Allen discover the recording?

5. Two weeks after Allen's fall, Alpha Omega's insurer contacted Al Gebra, a math teacher who was shopping and witnessed Allen's fall. This conversation was also tape recorded. Can Allen discover the recording? Can Gebra?

6. A month after Allen's fall, after she had recovered somewhat, Allen hired a lawyer to represent her. This lawyer immediately sent a demand letter to Alpha Omega asking it to compensate Allen for her injuries in the fall. After receiving the letter, Alpha Omega's lawyer Dee Fender interviewed everyone on the witness list. She made notes of her interviews, reciting what she had learned. She also interviewed the employees with knowledge of the fall, and wrote a memo to the file describing what she had learned and assessing the probable strengths and weaknesses of the case based on what she heard. These employees included the store manager, the produce manager, and three produce department clerks. Can Allen discover Fender's notes from customer interviews? Can Allen discover Fender's memo about employee interviews? Can Allen take Fender's deposition and ask her about what she learned in the interviews?

7. Alpha Omega employs architects who design its stores and make recommendations about food stocking methods in the stores. They have information about the design of the produce department in this store, including the angle at which produce is displayed and the proper use of safety mats on the floor. Can Allen discover their identity and opinions? They have also tested various types of grocery store furniture and written reports about their findings. Can Allen discover these reports?

8. One of the architects mentioned in the preceding question, Frank Lloyd Wrong, has been particularly critical of the store's practices. To get the benefit of his opinions, Alpha Omega would like to consult with him about Allen's case, but does not want him to testify. Can Alpha Omega designate Wrong as a pure consulting expert and protect his knowledge and opinions from discovery?

9. Two years ago, another shopper slipped and fell in Alpha Omega's produce department. That lawsuit has now been settled. While it was pending, however, the following documents were generated:

a. A statement by Cumber about what caused that customer to fall.

b. A report by the expert witness who would have testified for Alpha Omega.

c. The trial notebook that Dee Fender assembled in preparation for trying the case.

Can Allen discover these documents in her case?

10. Cumber took photographs of the produce department immediately after Allen was taken to the hospital. Are the photographs discoverable? He also took a videotape. Can Allen discover that? Later, in preparing for trial, Fender took photos of the produce department after arranging it to look its best. Can Allen discover these photos?

11. Alpha Omega hired an expert to be its testifying expert. Later it found a different expert whose opinions are more unequivocally supportive. It wants to redesignate the original expert, who has not yet been deposed, as a pure consulting expert. Any problems?

12. Allen sent Alpha Omega a request for production of documents seeking all documents concerning injuries to customers or employees in all Alpha Omega stores in Texas for the last five years. If you represented Alpha Omega, what objection would you make to this request? If you represented Allen, how could you redraft the request to get the most essential information while reducing the probable success of objections?

13. Alpha Omega sent the following interrogatory to Allen: "Please identify, including name, address, and telephone number, all persons who you intend to call as witnesses at the trial of this case." Is this proper? Is an interrogatory the proper discovery device to use to obtain this information?

14. Suppose that Allen has requested all of the notes and memos described in question 6 above. Alpha Omega has asserted privilege and and refused to produce them based on work product protection and attorney-client privilege, and Allen has filed a motion to compel production and set the motion for hearing. What should Alpha Omega's lawyer be prepared to do at the hearing?

15. During document production, Alpha Omega has produced 50 boxes of documents concerning Allen's case in particular and store practices generally. The documents were all reviewed by a paralegal before they were produced to Allen's lawyer. The paralegal was supposed to remove all privileged documents before handing them over and Bates stamp the rest. Allen's lawyer inspected the documents and requested copies of about 1,000 pages, which Alpha Omega provided. After producing those documents, Fender learned at Cumber's deposition that Alpha Omega has unknowingly produced a letter written by Bill Pepper to Fender. Pepper is a produce clerk who was working the day of Allen's accident. The letter informs Fender that before Allen's fall he saw some loose grapes on the floor. He intended to clean them up, but decided to take his break before worrying about it. While he was on his break, Allen fell. Fender believes this letter to be privileged and wants the judge to order Allen's lawyer to return it and never refer to it in the lawsuit. What should Fender do?

16. Alpha Omega would like to know more about Allen's medical treatment and diagnosis. How could it get information from Allen's treating physicians?

17. Cumber used to be a law professor but developed a substance abuse problem. Allen wants to discover his medical records from his treating psychiatrist and possibly take the psychiatrist's deposition. Will the court allow her to do so?

CHAPTER 10

# DISCOVERY: METHODOLOGY OF THE INDIVIDUAL DEVICES

## SCOPE

In Chapter 9, we examined the scope of discovery: what information is discoverable and what is not. This chapter examines the individual discovery devices used to secure discoverable information. The discovery rules allow discovery from both parties and nonparties. This chapter will examine both written and oral discovery devices. It will also discuss the new three-tiered scheme, which creates limits on the use of particular devices depending on the complexity of the case and the "level" of discovery control plan that applies. The chapter also covers the duty to amend or supplement discovery responses, and the sanctions that can be imposed for violations of the discovery rules. As you proceed through the chapter, be sure to refer to the discussion problems in Appendix A and to the sample discovery documents in Appendix B to check your understanding of the material.

## § 10.01 Discovery Devices

### [A] Written Discovery

*Read Tex. R. Civ. P. 176, 193, 194, 196, 197, 198, 205 and accompanying Comments.*

The 1999 amended discovery rules define written discovery as "requests for disclosure, requests for production and inspection of documents and tangible things, requests for entry onto property, interrogatories, and requests for admission." Tex. R. Civ. P. 192.7(a). This section will examine those devices, as well as the use of a subpoena to command the production of documents without the need for a deposition.

#### [1] Requests for Disclosure

The adversarial approach to pretrial discovery is superseded in the new rules by a type of disclosure practice for commonly discoverable matters. The procedural mechanism for implementing this disclosure is a new discovery device: the request for disclosure. Tex. R. Civ. P. 194. Civil Procedure Rule 194.1 specifies the exact language of the request. A standard request for disclosure, which is not subject to objection, allows a party to obtain disclosure of a broad range of information and documents, including the following (Tex. R. Civ. P. 194.2):

(1) The correct names of the parties to the lawsuit.

(2) The name, address, and telephone number of any potential parties.

(3) The legal theories and, in general, the factual bases of the responding party's claims or defenses (although the responding party need not marshal all evidence that may be offered at trial).

(4) The amount and any method of calculating economic damages.

(5) The name, address, and telephone number of persons having knowledge of relevant facts, and a brief statement of each identified person's connection with the case.

(6) Specific information concerning testifying experts.

(7) Any indemnity and insuring agreements described in Rule 192.3(f).

(8) Any settlement agreements described in Rule 192.3(g).

(9) Any witness statements described in Rule 192.3(h).

(10) In a suit alleging physical or mental injury and damages from the occurrence that is the subject of the case, all medical records and bills that are reasonably related to the injuries or damages asserted or, in lieu thereof, an authorization permitting the disclosure of such medical records and bills.

(11) In a suit alleging physical or mental injury and damages from the occurrence that is the subject of the case, all medical records and bills obtained by the responding party by virtue of an authorization furnished by the requesting party.

Disclosure is intended to provide basic discovery of these specific categories of information, not automatically in every case, "but upon request, without preparation of a lengthy inquiry, and without objection or assertion of work product." A responding party may, however, assert applicable privileges other than work product. Tex. R. Civ. P. 194, Comment 1. Generally, a response must be filed within 30 days after service of the request (or 50 days after service for a defendant served before the defendant's answer is due). Tex. R. Civ. P. 194.3. However, a longer period is authorized for a party to designate experts and to furnish expert information. Tex. R. Civ. P. 195.2.

The request for disclosure will tend to replace the use of interrogatories for certain commonly relevant factual matters and, together with a specific rule on discovery regarding testifying expert witnesses, eliminates the use of interrogatories in the discovery process concerning testifying experts. Tex. R. Civ. P. 195.1. This is especially important given the newly reduced limits on the number of interrogatories that can be used in most cases.

Unlike answers to interrogatories, disclosure responses need not be verified, but they are subject to a new general certification requirement contained in Rule 191.3 concerning the propriety, completeness, and accuracy of the response.

---

## NOTES AND QUESTIONS

(1) *Use of Requests.* When might you choose not to use all of the available requests for disclosure?

(2) *Privilege Assertions.* Under what circumstances might you assert a privilege in response to a disclosure request?

(3) *Timing Considerations.* What strategic considerations might affect the timing of your use of requests for disclosure?

(4) *Designation of Experts.* Does a party have to designate experts if that party has never received a request for disclosure under Civil Procedure Rule 194.2(f)? *See also* Tex. R. Civ. P. 195.

### [2] Interrogatories to Parties

Interrogatories are governed by Civil Procedure Rule 197. Interrogatories are written questions that may be served on parties to the lawsuit to inquire about matters within the scope of discovery, except for certain matters with regard to expert witnesses. An interrogatory may request a party to provide the identity and location of relevant documents, inquire whether a party makes a specific legal or factual contention and may ask the responding party to state the legal theories and to describe in general the factual bases for the party's claims or defenses. They may not, however, be used to require the responding party to marshal all of its available proof or the proof the party intends to offer at trial. Tex. R. Civ. P. 197.1.

The responding party must serve a written response within 30 days after service of the interrogatories (except that a defendant served with interrogatories before the defendant's answer is due need not respond until 50 days after the service of the interrogatories). The response must include the party's answers to the interrogatories and may include objections and assertions of privilege. A party's attorney must sign all discovery responses, including interrogatory responses and objections. In addition, the responding party must sign the answers under oath, except: (1) when answers are based on information obtained from other persons, the party may so state; and (2) interrogatories about persons with knowledge of relevant facts, trial witnesses, and legal contentions can be signed by the party's agent or attorney. Tex. R. Civ. P. 197.2. Interrogatory answers can be used only against the responding party. Tex. R. Civ. P. 197.3.

The number of interrogatories that can be directed to a party is limited by the various discovery control plans. *See* § 10.02.

---

## NOTES AND QUESTIONS

(1) *Objections and Privilege Assertions.* A party might object to interrogatories on relevance grounds, or might assert a privilege in response to a particular interrogatory. Neither, however, excuses the responding party from answering the interrogatories to the extent no objection is made. Objections must be in writing and must be made within the time for response. The responding party must state the legal or factual basis for the objection and the extent to which the party is refusing to comply. An objection not made within the time required, or that is obscured by numerous unfounded objections, is waived unless the court excuses the waiver for good cause shown. Tex. R. Civ. P. 193.2. The rules also provide a procedure for asserting privilege claims as to written discovery. *See* Tex. R. Civ. P. 193.3. Any party may at any reasonable time request a hearing on an objection or claim or privilege. Tex. R. Civ. P. 193.4.

(2) *Reference to Business Records.* When the answer to an interrogatory may be derived or ascertained from public records, from the responding party's business records, or from a compilation, abstract, or summary of the responding party's business records, *and* the burden of deriving or ascertaining the answer is substantially the same for the requesting party as for the responding party, the responding party may answer the interrogatory by specifying and, if

applicable, producing the records. Tex. R. Civ. P. 197.2(c). When might you tender business records instead of answering an interrogatory? When would you choose not to do so, even if the Civil Procedure Rules would allow it?

### [3] Production and Inspection of Documents and Tangible Things From Parties

Civil Procedure Rule 196 governs requests for production and inspection sent to parties, as well as requests for entry on land owned by a party or nonparty. To request the production or inspection of a document or tangible thing in another party's possession, custody, or control, the discovering party must serve a request no later than 30 days before the end of the discovery period. The request must specify the items to be produced or inspected, "either by individual item or by category, and describe with reasonable particularity each item and category." If the request is for the medical or mental health records of a nonparty, the requesting party must also serve the nonparty with the request for production. Tex. R. Civ. P. 196.1.

The responding party must serve a written response within 30 days after service of the request (except that a defendant served with a request before the defendant's answer is due need not respond until 50 days after service of the request). The response must state with respect to each item or category of items whatever objections and assertions of privilege the responding party wishes to make. Tex. R. Civ. P. 196.2. In addition, the responding party must produce the requested documents and tangible things not subject to objection or assertion of privilege, and must provide the discovering party with a reasonable opportunity to inspect them. The items produced must be organized either as they are kept in the usual course of business or labeled to correspond with the categories in the request. Tex. R. Civ. P. 196.3. A new provision addresses the problem of data in electronic or magnetic form. *See* Tex. R. Civ. P. 196.4.

Questions often arise as to how specific the requests must be before the responding party has a duty to comply with the request or assert specific objections or privileges. Read the following case, which was decided under the pre-1999 rules.

---

## LOFTIN v. MARTIN

*776 S.W.2d 145 (Tex. 1989)*

SPEARS, Justice.

This is an original mandamus proceeding instituted by Jessie B. Loftin, relator, against respondent, Honorable John Martin, Judge of the Second 9th Judicial District Court of Polk County, Texas. [footnote omitted] Relator seeks a writ of mandamus directing Judge Martin to rescind his order of May 10, 1988 and further directing respondent to allow relator to obtain various reports and documents made during the investigation of relator's underlying claim.

The real party in interest, Lumbermens Mutual Casualty Company (Lumbermens), files suit to set aside an award of the Texas Industrial Accident Board granted to relator, Jessie Loftin. Loftin then brought a counterclaim for an affirmative award of total and permanent incapacity and requested Lumbermens to produce certain documents. Lumbermens filed its objections to three particular requests for production [Request # 2, # 3 and # 4], and a hearing was thereafter set on these discovery matters for February 9, 1988. Although counsel for Lumbermens appeared at the discovery hearing, neither Loftin nor his attorney appeared nor did either notify the court for any reason for their non-attendance. On May 10, 1988, Judge Martin signed an order sustaining Lumbermen's objections to the three requests for production.

Loftin then filed a mandamus petition in the Ninth Court of Appeals seeking to set aside Judge Martin's order of May 10. The court of appeals in an unpublished per curiam opinion held that because the discovery requests were so overly broad and vague it could not say that the trial court abused its discretion, citing *Durham v. Cannan Communications, Inc.*, 645 S.W.2d 845, 848 (Tex. App.—Amarillo 1982, writ dism'd) (the trial court did not abuse its discretion in light of the fact that the disclosure demand was too broad).

. . . .

We first consider whether Judge Martin abused his discretion in sustaining Lumbermens' objection to request for production # 2. Loftin's request # 2 was as follows:

> Request is hereby made that reports be made by all experts you anticipate calling at the trial of this cause to contain all factual observations, tests, supporting data, calculations, photographs and opinions and produced for inspection and copying.

Lumbermens responded as follows:

> The request is objected to on the grounds that it constitutes a request that the Counter-Defendant ask expert witnesses to prepare written reports for the benefit of Counter-Plaintiff, which is outside the scope of discovery under Rule 167. Subject to this objection, Counter-Defendant is unable to comply with the request because it has not yet made a decision on what experts, if any, it will call to testify. However, Counter-Defendant may call to testify any of the physicians who have seen and/or examined Counter-Plaintiff for his alleged injuries and copies of all their written reports are already in your possession.

Rule 166b(2)(e) of the Texas Rules of Civil Procedure governs the discoverability of experts and reports of experts. Basically, it provides for the discovery of facts known, mental impressions and experts' opinions, and the subject matter on which the witness is expected to testify. A request for production of reports of experts, however, must seek an actual document in existence because a party will not be compelled to create or construct it for his opponent. 2 R. McDonald, *Texas Civil Practice in District and County Courts,* Section 10.03 (rev. 1982). The only instance to the contrary is found in Tex. R. Civ. P. 166b(2)(e)(4) which provides:

> If the discoverable factual observations, tests, supporting data . . . of an expert who will be called as a witness have not been recorded and reduced to tangible form, a trial judge may order these matters reduced to tangible form and produced within a reasonable time before the date of trial.

Here, Loftin requested that reports be made by experts, and Lumbermens objected to such request. According to Rule 166b(2)(e)(4), it was incumbent upon Loftin, after Lumbermens objected, to obtain an order from the trial court mandating the creation and production of such reports. No such order has been sought by Loftin nor has such an order been signed by Judge Martin. Accordingly, Loftin's demand for a report is premature because the report is not in existence.

Loftin's request for production # 2 is further premature because no experts had yet been designated by Lumbermens at the time of the discovery hearing. This factor was brought to the attention of the trial court through Lumbermens' objection. It was within the trial court's discretion to disallow the request for production # 2 at least until Lumbermens could designate their experts. According to Rule 166b(2)(e)(3), the trial judge has discretion to compel a party to make the determination and disclosure of whether an expert may be called to testify within a reasonable and specific time before the date of trial.

We therefore hold that Judge Martin was within his discretion in not ordering production of experts' reports when no experts were designated as of the date of the hearing. Thus, Loftin's request for production # 2 was premature.

. . . .

Lumbermens' final objection was made to Loftin's request for production # 4 which demanded:

> all notes, records, memoranda, documents and communications made that the carrier contends supports its allegations [that the award of the Industrial Accident Board was contrary to the undisputed evidence]. Lumbermens objected to request # 4 on the basis that it was so vague, broad and unclear that Lumbermens was unable to determine with reasonable certainty what it was being called upon to produce.

Rule 167 of the Texas Rules of Civil Procedure governs the discovery and production of documents and other tangible things. The 1966 General Commentary to Rule 167, Tex. R. Civ. P., quoted with approval the following from Steely and Gayle, *Operation of the Discovery Rules,* 2 Houston L. Rev. 222, 223 (1964):

> Unlike interrogatories and depositions, Rule 167 is not a fishing rule. It cannot be used simply to explore. You are permitted to fish under deposition procedures, but not under Rule 167. The Motion for Discovery must be specific, must establish materiality, and must recite precisely what is wanted. The Rule does not permit general inspection of the adversary's records.

Loftin has requested all evidence that supports Lumbermens' allegations. The request does not identify any particular class or type of documents but it is merely a request that Loftin be allowed to generally peruse all evidence Lumbermens might have. We hold that such request was vague, ambiguous, and overbroad and that the trial court was within its sound discretion in sustaining Lumbermens' objection. No one seeks to deny Loftin's right to see evidence against him, but he must formulate his request for production with a certain degree of specificity to allow Lumbermens to comply.

. . . .

Dissent by Justice HECHT.

. . . .

The Court holds that the trial court abused its discretion in denying the discovery sought by Loftin without evidence supporting Lumbermens' claim of privilege and without reviewing the documents *in camera.* The Court simply ignores the fact that the trial court did not sustain Lumbermens' claim of privilege. Lumbermens did not even argue its claim of privilege in the trial court. Instead, Lumbermens asserted only its objection as to the scope of Loftin's request. Specifically, Lumbermens' counsel's sole argument to the trial court was that Loftin's request "basically asked me to produce my entire claim file." The trial court sustained Lumbermens' objection on this argument alone. The court of appeals upheld the trial court's ruling by denying the part of Loftin's mandamus application directed to this ruling. Like the trial court, the court of appeals did not hold that Lumbermens' documents are privileged. It held only that Loftin's request was "so overly broad and vague, we cannot say the trial court abused its discretion" in refusing discovery.

This Court, in holding that the trial court abused its discretion in sustaining Lumbermens' objection, never addresses the only grounds Lumbermens argued before the trial court and upon which that court and the court of appeals based their rulings. The Court criticizes the trial court for failing to follow the procedures set out in *Peeples v. Honorable Fourth Supreme Judicial District,* 701 S.W.2d 635 (Tex. 1985), and *Weisel Enterprises, Inc. v. Curry,* 718 S.W.2d 56 (Tex. 1986). The trial court did not follow the procedures outlined in those cases because they simply do not apply. The focus of the objection which Lumbermens chose to argue to the trial court was not the nature of its documents but the breadth of Loftin's request. No *in camera* inspection was necessary for the trial court to determine whether Loftin's request was too broad.

The trial court surely had discretion to hold Loftin's request too broad. A more global request can hardly be imagined. It is not limited to the subject matter of the case but includes all documents made during the investigation of Loftin. It does not exclude privileged documents. It is, as Lumbermens' counsel stated to the trial court, a request for its entire claim file. Texas Rule of Civil Procedure 167 authorizes a request for "designated documents." The commentary to that rule explains:

> The rule permits discovery of "designated" documents, papers, etc. This is an important requirement. The rule does not permit a general inspection of an adversary's records, sometimes referred to as a "fishing expedition." Thus, it has been held that a motion to produce "all written reports, memoranda or other records of conferences of officers or members of the technical staff of defendants" is too general and comprehensive.

. . . .

> Similarly, a motion calling for every writing in the possession of an adversary relating to transactions between it and another over a period of years is too general. . . . The motion should contain a sufficiently explicit designation of the documents intended . . . ..

Tex. R. Civ. P. 167 general commentary—1966 (Vernon 1976). . . .

---

## NOTES AND QUESTIONS

(1) *Requests for "All Documents" Can be Proper.* A request for "any and all documents" does not itself violate the specificity requirements discussed in *Loftin v. Martin,* as long as the request is further restricted to a particular type or class of documents. *Davis v. Pate,* 915 S.W.2d 76, 79 (Tex. App.—Corpus Christi 1996, orig. proceeding) (approving request to "Please produce any and all documents which evidence, reflect or pertain in any way to any lost profits you contend you suffered as a result of the conduct of the Bank of Robstown").

(2) *Avoidance of Overbroad Requests.* In *K Mart Corp. v. Sanderson*, 937 S.W.2d 429 (Tex. 1996), the court considered a challenge based on *Loftin* to plaintiff's request for production of documents. Plaintiff Stacey Thompson was abducted from a K Mart parking lot and raped. She alleged that defendants were negligent and grossly negligent in failing to make adequate provisions for her safety. Thompson requested K Mart to produce all documents "which relate

to, touch or concern the allegations of this lawsuit," all documents "reflecting the incident made the basis of this lawsuit," and any document "which is not work product which relates in any way to this incident." The Texas Supreme Court distinguished these requests from those in the *Loftin* case. "Thompson requested all documents relating to the incident in which she was injured, not all documents which support K Mart's position or which relate to the claims and defenses in the cause of action. Because the incident was an isolated occurrence, we think a reasonable person would understand from the request what documents fit the description. It would be better, of course, to be more specific. We do not hold that a request as broad as Thompson's is proper in every circumstance. Here, however, the district court did not abuse its discretion in enforcing Thompson's requests, except for requiring production of work product." 937 S.W.2d at 430–431.

(3) *No Fishing Expeditions Are Permitted.* The Texas Supreme Court also noted in *K-Mart* that, contrary to the dictum in *Loftin*, no discovery device may be used to "fish." How would you distinguish between "fishing" and "thorough discovery"?

(4) *Drafting Considerations.* How can you draft requests for production that comply with *Loftin's* specificity requirement? Where will you get the necessary information?

### [4] Getting Documents and Things From Nonparties by Subpoena Without Deposition

A new procedural rule governs the issuance, service, and use of subpoenas. Tex. R. Civ. P. 176. A subpoena may be used to command the person to whom it is directed to do either or both of the following: (1) attend and give testimony at a deposition, hearing, or trial; or (2) produce and permit inspection and copying of designated documents or tangible things in the possession, custody, or control of that person. Tex. R. Civ. P. 176.2. Thus, a pretrial subpoena may be used as a separate discovery device for obtaining production of documents from nonparties without taking an oral or written deposition.

The rule provides a subpoena range under which a person "may not be required by subpoena to appear or produce documents or other things in a county that is more than 150 miles from where the person resides or is served" for discovery subpoenas served on persons whose appearance or production may not be compelled by notice alone. Tex. R. Civ. P. 176.3; C.P.R.C. § 22.002. The subpoenas may be issued by a court clerk, a licensed attorney, or an officer authorized to take depositions in Texas. *See* Tex. R. Civ. P. 176.4; C.P.R.C. § 22.001; Gov. C. § 52.021.

A person responding to a subpoena need not appear in person at the time and place of production unless the person is also commanded to attend and give testimony, either in the same subpoena or a separate one. Specific procedures for making objections to a subpoena and for moving for a protective order are set forth in Civil Procedure Rule 176. A person who properly objects or moves for protection "before the time specified for compliance" need not comply with the contested part of the subpoena "unless ordered to do so by the court." Tex. R. Civ. P. 176.6(d). (Note, however, that for oral depositions under Civil Procedure Rule 199.4, a motion for protective order only stays the oral deposition if the motion is filed by the third business day after service of the notice of deposition.) The party requesting the subpoena may seek a court order enforcing it "at any time" after the motion for protection is filed. Tex. R. Civ. P. 176.6(e).

Although the new subpoena rule clearly applies to both parties and nonparties, a separate procedural rule also applies to discovery from nonparties. Tex. R. Civ. P. 205. This new rule requires that a party seeking discovery by subpoena without deposition from a nonparty must serve on the nonparty *and* all parties a copy of the form of notice "required under the rules governing the applicable form of discovery . . . at least ten days before the subpoena compelling production is served." Tex. R. Civ. P. 205.2, 205.3. The new rule also contains other specific provisions concerning the production of documents without depositions and requests for production of medical or mental health records of nonparties.

---

## NOTES AND QUESTIONS

(1) *Need for Testimony.* When using a subpoena to discover documents from a nonparty, when would you need the person subpoenaed to testify in addition to producing the documents?

(2) *Procedural Requirements.* Suppose you want to subpoena nonparty X to testify at a deposition. When do you need to send a deposition notice, and when must the party be subpoenaed? How long a period must you allow between the subpoena and the deposition? What if you also want nonparty X to produce documents at the deposition? Does this change any of the timing requirements?

(3) *Enforcement of Subpoenas.* What happens when a person ignores a subpoena? *See* Tex. R. Civ. P. 176.8. *See also Kieffer v. Miller,* 560 S.W.2d 431 (Tex. Civ. App.—Beaumont 1977, no writ) (refusing to use attachment to enforce the subpoena because the affidavit failed to swear that the witness fee had been tendered).

### [5] Requests for Admissions

Requests for admissions try to identify facts that are not disputed. They are governed by Civil Procedure Rule 198. A party may serve on another party written requests that the other party admit the truth of any matter within the scope of discovery, including statements of opinion or of fact or of the application of law to fact. Each matter for which an admission is requested must be stated separately. Tex. R. Civ. P. 198.1. The responding party must serve a written response on the requesting party within 30 days after service of the request (except that a defendant served with a request before the defendant's answer is due need not respond until fifty days after service of the request). Tex. R. Civ. P. 198.2(a).

Unless the responding party states an objection or asserts a privilege, the responding party must specifically admit or deny the request or explain in detail the reasons that the responding party cannot admit or deny the request. Lack of information or knowledge is not a proper response unless the responding party states that a reasonable inquiry was made but that the information known or easily obtainable is insufficient to enable the responding party to admit or deny. Tex. R. Civ. P. 198.2(a).

If a response is not timely served, the request is considered admitted without the necessity of a court order. Tex. R. Civ. P. 198.2(c). This is a significant consequence, in that a matter admitted under Civil Procedure Rule 198 is conclusively established as to the party making the admission unless the court permits the party to withdraw or amend the admission. The court may permit the party to withdraw or amend the admission if: (1) the party shows good cause for the withdrawal or amendment; and (2) the court finds that the parties relying on the responses and deemed admissions will not be unduly prejudiced and that presentation of the merits of the action will be subserved by permitting the party to amend or withdraw the admission. Tex. R. Civ. P. 198.3. The following case discusses these requirements.

---

## STELLY v. PAPANIA

*927 S.W.2d 620 (Tex. 1996)*

PER CURIAM.

We consider whether a trial court abuses its discretion by allowing a party to withdraw and amend its original answers to a request for admissions. We hold that a trial court does not abuse its discretion when the moving party shows: (1) good cause; (2) that the party relying on the responses will not be unduly prejudiced; and (3) that the withdrawal will serve the purpose of legitimate discovery and the merits of the case. Accordingly, we reverse the judgment of the court of appeals and remand the case to that court to determine the merits of the appeal.

After delivering a pizza to Ermon Stelly's house, Michael Papania slipped on a patch of mud in what he believed to be Stelly's front yard. As a result, he suffered a broken leg. Papania sued Stelly and the City of Port Neches. He alleged that the City created the mud patch when it worked on the sewer line in front of Stelly's home.

Papania sent Requests for Admissions to both Stelly and the City. Stelly mistakingly admitted that he owned the premises on which Papania fell. Papania non-suited the City and the trial court later dismissed all of Papania's claims against the City with prejudice. Later, Stelly discovered that the City owned the land where Papania fell. A surveyor's report revealed that Stelly's boundary line ended seven feet before the street curb.

Stelly moved to withdraw and amend his previous admissions. He also moved for summary judgment on grounds that he did not: (1) own the property by the street; (2) actively cause the alleged defective condition on the City's property; and (3) have a duty to keep the City's land safe.

The trial court granted both motions. The court of appeals reversed and remanded. That court held that the trial court abused its discretion because Stelly did not show that his new responses would not prejudice Papania. Because the new responses formed the basis for Stelly's motion for summary judgment, the court of appeals reversed the judgment and remanded the case for trial.

Stelly argues that the trial court did not abuse its discretion because the surveyor's report about who actually owned the land provided good cause for Stelly to amend his responses to Papania's request for admissions. Stelly also contends that his amended admissions did not prejudice Papania because: (1) Papania's claim against the City was barred because he did not give timely notice under the Texas Tort Claims Act [footnote omitted]; and (2) even if Papania had relied on Stelly's original admission, Stelly's ownership could not absolve the City of responsibility for creating a hazard. We agree.

This case presents a unique situation. We have never considered whether a party can withdraw its original response to a request for admission and substitute it with a new response. Moreover, decisions from the courts of appeals are limited to cases where parties seek to withdraw deemed admissions. *See, e.g., Burden v. John Watson Landscape Illumination, Inc.*, 896 S.W.2d 253, 256 (Tex. App.—Eastland 1995, writ denied); *North River Ins. Co. of New Jersey v. Greene*, 824 S.W.2d 697, 700 (Tex. App.—El Paso 1992, writ denied); *Employers Ins. of Wausau v. Halton*, 792 S.W.2d 462, 465 (Tex. App.—Dallas 1990, writ denied). Although this case does not involve deemed admissions, we find these cases instructive.

A party may withdraw a deemed admission "upon a showing of good cause for such withdrawal . . . if the court finds that the parties relying upon the responses . . . will not be unduly prejudiced and that the presentation of the merits of the action will be subserved thereby." Tex. R. Civ. P. 169(2). After the rule was amended in 1988, "good cause" became the threshold standard for withdrawal of deemed admissions. *Halton*, 792 S.W.2d at 465. A party can establish good cause by showing that its failure to answer was accidental or the result of a mistake, rather than intentional or the result of conscious indifference. *Greene*, 824 S.W.2d at 700; *see Halton*, 792 S.W.2d at 465.

A trial court has broad discretion to permit or deny the withdrawal of deemed admissions. *Halton*, 792 S.W.2d at 464. An appellate court should set aside the trial court's ruling only if, after reviewing the entire record, it is clear that the trial court abused its discretion. *See Simon v. York Crane & Rigging Company, Inc.* 739 S.W.2d 793, 795 (Tex. 1987); *Burden*, 896 S.W.2d at 256. An abuse of discretion occurs when a court acts without reference to guiding rules or principles, or acts arbitrarily or unreasonably. *See Downer v. Aquamarine Operators, Inc.*, 701 S.W.2d 238, 241 (Tex. 1985), *cert. denied*, 476 U.S. 1159, 106 S. Ct. 2279, 90 L. Ed. 2d 721 (1986).

The purpose of the rules of civil procedure is to obtain a just, fair, equitable and impartial adjudication of the litigants' rights under established principles of substantive law. See Tex. R. Civ. P. 1. The "ultimate purpose of discovery is to seek the truth. . . ." *Jampole v. Touchy*, 673 S.W.2d 569, 573 (Tex. 1984). The discovery rules were not designed as traps for the unwary, nor should we construe them to prevent a litigant from presenting the truth. *See Burden*, 896 S.W.2d at 256. As we stated:

> The primary purpose of [Rule 169] is to simplify trials by eliminating matters about which there is no real controversy, but which may be difficult or expensive to prove. It was never intended to be used as a demand upon a plaintiff or defendant to admit that he had no cause of action or ground of defense. *Sanders v. Harder*, 148 Tex. 593, 227 S.W.2d 206, 208 (1950); *see also Birdo v. Parker*, 842 S.W.2d 699 (Tex. App.—Tyler 1992, writ denied).

There is evidence in the record to support the trial court's order allowing Stelly to withdraw his admissions. Stelly presented affidavit testimony that, upon discovering the faulty admissions, he immediately filed his motion to withdraw them and amend his responses. He offered the surveyor's affidavit and report to show "good cause." The report and affidavit showed that he did not own the property where Papania fell. Papania offered no controverting evidence.

Papania was not prejudiced by the withdrawal for two reasons. First, his failure to comply with the notice provision under the Texas Tort Claims Act precluded his suit against the City regardless of who owned the land. [footnote omitted] Secondly, even if Stelly's original admission were true and he did own the land, it would not affect Papania's ability to sue the City for creating the alleged hazard.

Because the trial court properly conducted a hearing on both motions and based its decision on evidence in the record, we cannot say that it abused its discretion. The court of appeals incorrectly concluded that the trial court abused its discretion on a procedural point. It, therefore, declined to consider the merits of Stelly's duty, if any, to Papania. We disagree. Without hearing oral argument the Court remands this case to the court of appeals to determine whether the trial court properly granted Stelly summary judgment. *See* Tex. R. App. P. 170 and 184(c).

---

## NOTES AND QUESTIONS

(1) *Use of Admissions.* Admissions can never be used *by* the party answering them—only *against* that party.

(2) *Improper Refusals to Admit; Sanctions.* Suppose a party denies a request and the matter constituting the subject matter of the request is established in a subsequent trial. Does the requesting party have any recourse? *See* Tex. R. Civ. P. 215.4(b).

(3) *Effect of Admissions.* Admissions are conclusively binding in a way that interrogatories and other forms of discovery are not. They can form the basis of a motion for summary judgment. They can also prevent a party from introducing contradictory evidence at trial. Consider the following opinion regarding the effect of admissions.

---

## MARSHALL v. VISE

*767 S.W.2d 699 (Tex. 1989)*

DOGGETT, Justice.

This appeal presents the issue of whether a party's failure to object at trial to testimony contrary to an opponent's deemed admissions waives the effect of those admissions. Ted Vise sued J. Howard Marshall, II for tortious interference with a business contract. The trial court rendered a take-nothing judgment. The court of appeals, relying on Marshall's deemed admissions, reversed the trial court's judgment and rendered judgment in favor of Vise. 751 S.W.2d 216 (Tex. App. 1988). We reverse the judgment of the court of appeals.

In the course of discovery, Vise submitted a request for admissions to Marshall that was never answered. Marshall filed no motion to withdraw, amend, or extend the time to answer the request. The deemed admissions established the essential elements for Vise's claim of tortious interference with a contract.

Prior to trial, Vise did not move for summary judgment. At trial, Vise did not seek to prevent controverting evidence through a motion in limine nor did he move for a directed verdict based upon the deemed admissions. Instead, Vise commenced the presentation of his case by calling Marshall as an adverse witness. During Vise's direct examination of Marshall, testimony was elicited which directly contradicted the deemed admissions. Marshall testified that Vise was terminated for willful misconduct and gross neglect of duties. Marshall further testified:

> Mr. Vise willfully violated the directions of the Board of Directors in a series of incidents. He was specifically instructed not to open an office in Louisiana. He did. He was specifically

> instructed not to hire [James Cormier]. He hired him anyway. . . . Mr. Vise was specifically again instructed to take competitive bids. . . . He didn't do it.

After all of this testimony was presented, without objection, Vise then moved the court to take judicial notice that the facts contained in the request for admissions were deemed admitted by operation of law. Thereafter, Vise presented additional testimony, and Marshall called three witnesses in rebuttal. During rebuttal Marshall further contradicted the deemed admissions by testifying, without objection, that he neither intentionally interfered with Vise's employment contract, nor acted with any malice toward him.

The trial court rendered a take-nothing judgment and filed findings of fact and conclusions of law in favor of Marshall. On appeal, Vise asserted that the trial court erred in making findings of fact and conclusions of law contrary to the deemed admissions. The court of appeals agreed, and accordingly held that the deemed admissions established as a matter of law Vise's right to recover. 751 S.W.2d at 217. For the reasons discussed below, we reverse the judgment of the court of appeals.

Unanswered requests for admissions are automatically deemed admitted, unless the court on motion permits their withdrawal or amendment. Tex. R. Civ. P. 169. An admission once admitted, deemed or otherwise, is a judicial admission, and a party may not then introduce testimony to controvert it. *See Shaw v. Nat'l County Mut. Fire Ins. Co.*, 723 S.W.2d 236, 238 (Tex. App.—Houston [1st Dist.] 1986, no writ). We have held, however, that a party relying upon an opponent's pleadings as judicial admissions of fact must protect the record by objecting to the introduction of controverting evidence and to the submission of any issue bearing on the facts admitted. *Houston First Am. Sav. v. Musick*, 650 S.W.2d 764, 769 (Tex. 1983).

In the present case, Vise failed to object to the controverting testimony on the ground that he was relying upon Marshall's deemed admissions. In fact, Vise actually elicited much of the contradictory evidence. Vise has waived, therefore, his right to rely upon those admissions which were controverted by testimony admitted at trial without objection. *See Musick*, 650 S.W.2d at 768–69. We hold that a party waives the right to rely upon an opponent's deemed admissions unless objection is made to the introduction of evidence contrary to those admissions.

In reviewing Vise's assertion that the trial court's findings of fact and conclusions of law were contrary to the great weight and preponderance of the evidence, the court of appeals erroneously considered Marshall's deemed admissions to be conclusive. Therefore, we must remand this cause to the court of appeals to consider whether the trial court's findings of fact are against the great weight and preponderance of the evidence. *Pool v. Ford Motor Co.*, 715 S.W.2d 629, 635–36 (Tex. 1986); *Hall v. Villarreal Dev. Corp.*, 522 S.W.2d 195 (Tex. 1975) (per curiam). The judgment of the court of appeals is reversed and the cause is remanded to that court for further consideration in accordance with this opinion.

### [B] Oral and Other Non-Written Discovery

Under the 1999 discovery rules, depositions (oral and on written questions) and motions for physical and mental examinations are governed by different procedures from those specially addressed to written discovery. This section examines these discovery devices.

*Read Tex. R. Civ. P. 176, 191, 193.3, 195.4, 196.2(a), 199, 200, 201, 203 and accompanying Comments.*

### [1] Depositions—General Considerations

Before taking a deposition, an attorney should consider the reasons for choosing the deposition device and for choosing the particular witness. A deposition may serve a variety of purposes. It may be a vehicle for the discovery of facts. It may serve to preserve the testimony of witnesses who may not be available at the time of the trial. It may force witnesses to adopt under oath one particular version of the facts, which may be used for impeachment if the witnesses change their testimony at a later time. Depositions also serve as a forum for the evaluation of an opposing party's witnesses and counsel and for observing one's own client and witnesses under cross-examination.

Before a notice of deposition is prepared, a number of preliminary decisions must be made. The objectives of the particular deposition should be clearly identified. A deposition may, for instance, be exploratory in nature, or it may be intended to cement and preserve a particular witness's testimony. Therefore, consideration should be given to the timing and sequence of depositions. In some cases, early depositions will be necessary; in others depositions will be more productive after other discovery methods are used.

Among the decisions that need to be made are whether the deposition should be taken orally or on written questions. Practical difficulties or the nature of the subject matter may make a deposition on written questions, rather than the more flexible but more expensive oral deposition, the better choice. In light of the variety of recording techniques available, thought must be given to whether a method such as videotaping should be used as a supplement or alternative to the customary stenographic transcription. A videotaped deposition will generally have considerably more impact at trial than a written transcript read into the record.

Finally, the time limits on oral depositions must be considered. Unless otherwise agreed or ordered by the court, oral depositions are limited to six hours per side for each individual witness (Tex. R. Civ. P. 199.5(c)) and are further limited to a total number of hours allowed for all witnesses, depending on the discovery control plan used. *See* § 10.02. Thus, counsel must reserve oral depositions for those witnesses whose testimony is most essential, and obtain information from other individuals through depositions on written questions, which are not so limited, or through other discovery devices.

### [2] Notice and Formalities for Depositions

How do you compel a person to appear for a deposition? The answer to this question depends on whether the deposition witness is a party to the lawsuit. A deposition witness who is a party, or who is retained by, employed by, or otherwise subject to the control of a party, can be compelled to attend merely by serving a notice of oral or written deposition on the party's attorney. Tex. R. Civ. P. 199.3, 200.2. The content of the notice for oral depositions is specified in Rule 199.2. For a deposition on written questions, the direct questions to be propounded to the witness must be attached to the notice. Tex. R. Civ. P. 200.3(a). Below is an example of an oral deposition notice.

| | | |
|---|---|---|
| ______ [*Plaintiff*] | ) | IN THE ______ COURT |
| v. | ) | ______ COUNTY, TEXAS |
| ______ [*Defendant*] | ) | ______ JUDICIAL DISTRICT |

NOTICE OF INTENT TO TAKE ORAL DEPOSITION OF ________ [*name of witness*]

TO: ________ [*Names of witness and of parties to action*] and to their attorneys of record.

PLEASE TAKE NOTICE that ________ [*name of party noticing deposition*] will take the oral deposition of ________ [*name of individual witness or organization*]. The deposition will take place at ________ [*place*] at ________ [*time*] on ________ [*date*]. All parties are invited to attend and examine the witness as prescribed by the Texas Rules of Civil Procedure.

[*Optional. Include if named witness is organization rather than individual*].

We intend to question ________ [*name of organization/witness, e.g., ABC Corporation*] about ________ [*describe with reasonable particularity matters on which examination is requested*]. We therefore request that ________ [*e.g., ABC Corporation*], pursuant to Civil Procedure Rule 199, a reasonable time before the deposition, designate one or more individuals to testify on its behalf and notify us and all other parties of the names of the designated individuals, their position or relationship with ________ [*e.g., ABC Corporation*] and the matters on which each individual will testify.

[*Optional. Include in order to request production of documents or things*]

REQUEST FOR PRODUCTION

Further, ________ [*name of party noticing deposition*] requests that ________ [*name of individual witness or organization*], produce at the deposition the following ________ [*documents or things*] within the witness's possession, custody, or control, as required by the Texas Rules of Civil Procedure: ________ [*list or cross-reference annexed exhibit containing list of documents or items*].

FIRM NAME
________________ [*typed name*]
________________ [*signature of second party*]
________________ [*typed name*]

BY: ________________
[*attorney name*]
________ [*state bar identification number*]
________________ [*address*]
________________ [*phone and fax numbers*]

[*add certificate of service*]

---

## NOTES AND QUESTIONS

(1) *Sufficiency of Deposition Notice.* Does this notice comply with the requirements of the discovery rules? Under what circumstances would additional provisions need to be added?

Suppose you wanted to take the deposition of a corporate party's employee; would this notice be sufficient?

(2) *Production of Documents.* What is the shortest amount of time in which a party could be compelled to appear and produce the requested documents? How specifically would those documents need to be identified?

(3) *Commanding Attendance of Nonparties.* Suppose the witness is a nonparty. What additional steps would the discovering party need to take? *See* Tex. R. Civ. P. 199.3, 205, 176. Below is an example of a subpoena form.

THE STATE OF TEXAS

SUBPOENA REQUIRING APPEARANCE AT
DEPOSITION AND PRODUCTION OF DOCUMENTS OR TANGIBLE EVIDENCE

TO: ________ [*Name and address of person or organization to whom subpoena is directed*]

Greetings: YOU ARE COMMANDED to attend and give testimony at a deposition on oral examination at the following time and place: ________ [*specify*].

YOU ARE ALSO COMMANDED to appear and produce and permit inspection [and copying] of the ________ [*e.g., documents or tangible evidence*] identified in the attached deposition notice at the same time and place.

DUTIES OF PERSON SERVED WITH SUBPOENA

You are advised that under Texas Rule of Civil Procedure 176, a person served with a discovery subpoena has certain rights and obligations. Rule 176.6 provides:

(a) *Compliance required.* Except as provided in this subdivision, a person served with a subpoena must comply with the command stated therein unless discharged by the court or by the party summoning such witness. A person commanded to appear and give testimony must remain at the place of deposition, hearing, or trial from day to day until discharged by the court or by the party summoning the witness.

(b) *Organizations.* If a subpoena commanding testimony is directed to a corporation, partnership, association, governmental agency, or other organization, and the matters on which examination is requested are described with reasonable particularity, the organization must designate one or more persons to testify on its behalf as to matters known or reasonably available to the organization.

(c) *Production of Documents or Tangible Things.* A person commanded to produce documents or tangible things need not appear in person at the time and place of production unless the person is also commanded to attend and give testimony, either in the same subpoena or a separate one. A person must produce documents as they are kept in the usual course of business or must organize and label them to correspond with the categories in the demand. A person may withhold material or information claimed to be privileged but must comply with Rule 193.3. A nonparty's production of a document authenticates the document for use against the nonparty to the same extent as a party's production of a document is authenticated for use against the party under Rule 193.7.

(d) *Objections.* A person commanded to produce and permit inspection and copying of designated documents and things may serve on the party requesting issuance of the subpoena before the time specified for compliance written objections to producing any or all of the designated materials. A person need not comply with the part of a subpoena to which objection is made as provided in this paragraph unless ordered to do so by the court. The party requesting the subpoena may move for such an order at any time after an objection is made.

(e) *Protective Orders.* A person commanded to appear at a deposition, hearing, or trial, or to produce and permit inspection and copying of designated documents and things may move for a protective order under Rule 192.6(b) before the time specified for compliance either in the court in which the action is pending or in a district court in the county where the subpoena was served. The person must serve the motion on all parties in accordance with Rule 21a. A person need not comply with the part of a subpoena from which protection is sought under this paragraph unless ordered to do so by the court. The party requesting the subpoena may seek such an order at any time after the motion for protection is filed.

**Warning**

**Failure by any person without adequate excuse to obey a subpoena served upon that person may be deemed a contempt of the court from which the subpoena is issued or a district court in the county in which the subpoena is served, and may be punished by fine or confinement, or both.**

This subpoena is issued at the request of ________ [*name of party*], a party to the above-described action, whose attorney of record is ________ [*name of attorney*]. Date of Issuance: ________

SUBPOENA ISSUED BY:

________________________ [*signature*]

________________________ [*typed name*]

________________________ [*status, e.g.,* Attorney]

MEMORANDUM OF ACCEPTANCE

I accepted service of a copy of this subpoena on ________ [*date*].

________________________ [*signature of witness*]

RETURN OF SUBPOENA

I certify that I served the annexed subpoena by delivering a copy, together with a fee of $______, to ________ [*name of witness*] in person, at [*address*] on ________ [*date*].

________________________ [*signature*]

________________________ [*typed name*]

________________________ [*title*]

(4) *Contents of Subpoenas.* Consider the text of this subpoena. How informative would it be to a nonlawyer, nonparty who is subpoenaed? Why does it contain the paragraph labeled "Warning"?

(5) *Who May Issue or Serve Subpoenas?* What official position does the person issuing the subpoena need to have? What about the person serving the subpoena? What about the person who will record an oral deposition? *See* Tex. R. Civ. P. 199.1, 176.4, 176.5. Section 52 of the

Texas Government Code provides for the certification of shorthand reporters. It prohibits a person from engaging in shorthand reporting in Texas unless they are certified by the Texas Supreme Court, and defines shorthand reporting as "the practice of shorthand reporting for use in litigation in the courts of this state by making a verbatim record of an oral court proceeding, deposition, or [other proceeding] using written symbols in shorthand, machine shorthand, or oral stenography." Gov. C. § 52.001(5). Civil Procedure Rule 199 specifically allows non-stenographic recording of depositions, but there still must be "a person authorized by law to administer the oath" who will assure "that the recording will be intelligible, accurate, and trustworthy." Tex. R. Civ. P. 199.1(c). However, section 52.021 of the Government Code provides that "all depositions conducted in this state must be recorded by a certified shorthand reporter." How do these laws fit together?

(6) *Written Deposition Practice.* A deposition on written questions of a witness who is alleged to reside or to be located in Texas may be taken by a Texas notary public as well as a clerk of a district or county court and a judge of a county court. *See* C.P.R.C. § 20.001 (reprinted below). A subpoena may be issued by "an officer authorized to take depositions in this state." Tex. R. Civ. P. 176.4. Thus, a Texas notary public may both issue a subpoena and take a deposition on written questions. Although no modern cases address the issue, the Texas Supreme Court has held that an attorney for a party cannot take a written deposition even though the attorney is a notary public because "he must be impartial between the parties, and whatever gives to his relation the character of employment by one party will disqualify the officer and subject the deposition, on proper objection, to be suppressed." *Clegg v. Gulf, C. & S.F. Ry. Co.*, 137 S.W. 109, 111 (Tex. 1911).

(7) *Nonstenographic Recordings.* Consider the rule provisions allowing nonstenographic recording in Rule 199.1(c). If the rule results in both a nonstenographic recording and "another method" of recording the deposition, which is the official record of the deposition? Does it matter? *See* Tex. R. Civ. P. 203.

(8) *Where Can a Deposition be Taken?* This answer also depends on whether the witness is a party or a non-party. Imagine the following situations:

(a) You represent a party in a suit filed in Houston over an automobile accident that happened in Houston. Both you and your client reside in Houston. You receive a notice from the opposition to take your client's oral deposition in the opposing party's lawyer's office, which is in El Paso, where the opponent resides. What would you do in response?

(b) You notice your opponent for deposition in your Houston office. He doesn't want to appear there. What would his lawyer need to do to object to the place of deposition? What options are available to the judge, and how would you expect her to rule?

(c) The only nonparty eyewitness to the accident resides in Dallas. You serve him with a subpoena in Austin while he's on vacation in the state's capital. Where can you take that deposition?

(9) *"Apex" Depositions.* You have seen that a deposing party may notice the deposition of an opposing entity by designating specific subject areas. Tex. R. Civ. P. 199.2(b). But what if you specifically want to depose the CEO? Consider the following case.

## CROWN CENTRAL PETROLEUM CORP. v. GARCIA

*904 S.W.2d 125 (Tex. 1995)*

HIGHTOWER, Justice.

In this original proceeding, we consider the propriety of an "apex" deposition, the deposition of a corporate officer at the apex of the corporate hierarchy. Relators Crown Central Petroleum Corporation and Crown Central Pipeline Company seek a writ of mandamus directing the trial court to vacate its orders of January 18 and 25, 1995 concerning the deposition of Henry Rosenberg, Jr., the chairman of the board and chief executive officer of Crown Central Petroleum Corporation (Crown Central). Today this court adopts guidelines for depositions of persons at the apex of the corporate hierarchy. [footnote omitted] Because these guidelines had not been adopted prior to the trial court's orders, we deny the writ of mandamus without prejudice so that the trial court may reconsider its ruling in light of today's opinion. [footnote omitted]

Otto L. Carl, Jr. was employed by Crown Central at its Pasadena refinery for many years. Carl retired in 1981. In 1992, Carl died of lung cancer allegedly as the result of asbestos exposure. In late 1992, Margaret Carl, individually and as representative of the estate of Otto L. Carl Jr., deceased, Otto L. Carl, III and Margaret E. Nowak (Plaintiffs) sued Crown Central and Crown Central Pipe Line Company for gross negligence. In July 1994, Plaintiffs filed a motion to require Crown Central to produce Rosenberg for a video deposition. The motion also included a subpoena duces tecum for Rosenberg to produce sixteen categories of documents. Crown Central responded with a motion to quash deposition accompanied by Rosenberg's affidavit. Among other things, the affidavit stated: "I have no personal knowledge of Mr. Carl or his job duties, job performance, or any facts concerning alleged exposure to asbestos by Mr. Carl. I was not involved in the day-to-day maintenance decisions at the Refinery. I have no expertise in industrial hygiene, toxicology, or the health effects of asbestos exposure." [footnote omitted] Crown Central complained that Plaintiffs had not exhausted less intrusive means of discovery before attempting to depose Rosenberg and that the motion to produce Rosenberg for a video deposition was filed solely for harassment purposes. Concerning the subpoena duces tecum, Crown Central asserted that Rosenberg was not the custodian of the requested documents and that a substantially identical request was made by the Plaintiffs in a request for production to which Crown Central had responded and filed objections. Neither motion was heard or acted upon. In mid-December 1994, Plaintiffs filed a notice of intention to take the oral deposition of Rosenberg. The notice also included a subpoena duces tecum for Rosenberg to produce thirty-two categories of documents. In late December 1994, Plaintiffs filed their first amended notice of intention to take the oral deposition of Rosenberg which reset the date for Rosenberg's deposition. The notice also included that same subpoena duces tecum concerning thirty-two categories of documents. Crown Central again responded with a motion to quash deposition and a motion for protective order. Crown Central continued to complain about Rosenberg's lack of personal knowledge, the harassment of Rosenberg and the subpoena duces tecum for Rosenberg to produce thirty-two categories of documents.

On January 18, 1995, after a telephone hearing, the court granted Plaintiffs' motion to produce Rosenberg for video deposition and denied Crown Central's motion to quash. The trial court ordered Crown Central to produce Rosenberg for deposition and that Rosenberg produce all documents requested in the subpoena duces tecum. [footnote omitted] On January 20, 1995, Crown Central filed an emergency motion for reconsideration requesting that the trial court quash the deposition, compel the Plaintiffs to serve Rosenberg with written interrogatories concerning the extent of his knowledge concerning this action which would be answered within five days, limit the duration of Rosenberg's deposition to one hour, reconsider its ruling concerning the production of documents in the subpoena duces tecum, and amend its prior order so that neither Crown Central nor Rosenberg would be required to produce any documents requested in the subpoena duces tecum until after they are afforded a reasonable opportunity to have their objections to the production considered by the court. On January 25, 1995, the trial court denied the emergency motion for reconsideration.

I.

Crown Central argues that the trial court abused its discretion when it granted Plaintiffs' motion to produce Rosenberg for video deposition and denied Crown Central's motion to quash.

It is undisputed that a "party is entitled to discovery that is relevant to the subject matter of the claim, and which appears reasonably calculated to lead to the discovery of admissible evidence." *Monsanto Co. v. May*, 889 S.W.2d 274, 276 (Tex. 1994) (Opinion on denial of leave to file petition for writ of mandamus) (Gonzalez, J., joined by Hecht, J., dissenting) (citing Tex. R. Civ. P. 166b(1), (2)(a)). Rule 200 of the Texas Rules of Civil Procedure permits a party to take the deposition of "any person." However, the person noticed for deposition also has the right to protection "from undue burden, unnecessary expense, harassment or annoyance, or invasion of personal, constitutional, or property rights." Tex. R. Civ. P. 166b(5); *Monsanto Co. v. May*, 889 S.W.2d at 276.

Although not previously addressed by this court, the propriety of "apex" depositions—depositions of a corporate officer at the apex of the corporate hierarchy—has been addressed by other courts. [citations omitted]

*Liberty Mutual Ins. Co. v. Superior Court of San Mateo County* is particularly instructive. In *Liberty Mutual Ins. Co.*, the court held:

> that when a plaintiff seeks to depose a corporate president or other official at the highest level of corporate management, and that official moves for a protective order to prohibit the deposition, the trial court should first determine whether the plaintiff has shown good cause that the official has unique or superior personal knowledge of discoverable information. If not, as will presumably often be the case in the instance of a large national or international corporation, the trial court should issue the protective order and first require the plaintiff to obtain the necessary discovery through less-intrusive methods. These would include interrogatories directed to the high-level official to explore the state of his or her knowledge or involvement in plaintiff's case; the deposition of lower-level employees with appropriate knowledge and involvement in the subject matter of the litigation; and the organizational deposition of the corporation itself, which will require the corporation to produce for deposition the most qualified officer or employee to testify on its behalf as the specified matters to be raised at the deposition. Should these avenues be exhausted, and the plaintiff make a colorable showing of good cause that the high-level official possesses necessary information to the case, the trial court may then lift the protective order and allow the deposition to proceed.

13 Cal. Rptr. 2d at 367 (citation omitted).

II.

As virtually every court which has addressed the subject has observed, depositions of persons in the upper level management of corporations often involved in lawsuits present problems which should reasonably be accommodated in the discovery process. From the decisions of these other courts, we distill the following guidelines for addressing the problems.

When a party seeks to depose a corporate president or other high level corporate official and that official (or the corporation) files a motion for protective order to prohibit the deposition accompanied by the official's affidavit denying any knowledge of relevant facts, the trial court should first determine whether the party seeking the deposition has arguably shown that the official has any unique or superior personal knowledge of discoverable information. If the party seeking the deposition cannot show that the official has any unique or superior personal knowledge of discoverable information, the trial court should grant the motion for protective order and first require the party seeking the deposition to attempt to obtain the discovery through less intrusive methods. Depending upon the circumstances of the particular case, these methods could include the depositions of lower level employees, the deposition of the corporation itself, and interrogatories and requests for production of documents directed to the corporation. After making a good faith effort to obtain the discovery through less intrusive methods, the party seeking the deposition may attempt to show (1) that there is a reasonable indication that the official's deposition is calculated to lead to the discovery of admissible evidence, and (2) that the less intrusive methods of discovery are unsatisfactory, insufficient or inadequate. If the party seeking the deposition makes this showing, the trial court should modify or vacate the protective order as appropriate. As with any deponent, the trial court retains discretion to restrict the duration, scope and location of the deposition. If the party seeking the deposition fails to make this showing, the trial court should leave the protective order in place.

Because these guidelines had not been adopted prior to the trial court's orders, we deny the writ of mandamus without prejudice so that the trial court may reconsider its order denying Crown Central's motion to quash Rosenberg's deposition. The stay order previously issued by this court remains in effect only so long as necessary to allow the trial court to act.

---

(10) *Depositions Taken Outside Texas.* The rules also contain special provisions regarding taking depositions outside of Texas. Who can record such a deposition, and what formalities are required? Civil Procedure Rule 201 applies both to oral and written depositions and applies both in sister states and in foreign countries. Comment 1 to this rule notes that the rule itself "does not . . . address whether any of the procedures listed are, in fact, permitted or recognized by the law of the state or foreign jurisdiction where the witness is located. A party must first determine what procedures are permitted by the jurisdiction where the witness is located before using this rule." For example, some civil law countries do not allow the taking of testimony by private attorneys without the involvement of the local judiciary. *See* Bishop, *International Litigation in Texas: Obtaining Evidence in Foreign Countries*, 19 Hous. L. Rev. 361 (1982).

(11) *Issuance of Subpoenas for Witnesses Outside Texas.* Who can issue an enforceable subpoena for an out of state deposition? Presumably, the provision of Rule 176.4 authorizing

"an officer authorized to take depositions in this State" does not provide authority to "any notary public" to issue a subpoena in connection with depositions taken outside of Texas. To answer this question, the law of the place of deposition must be consulted. Many, if not most, other states have statutory or rule provisions similar to Civil Procedure Rule 201.2. This rule provides that a Texas court will enforce a mandate, writ, or commission that requires a witness' oral or written deposition testimony in Texas. As long as the foreign mandate, writ, or commission was issued by a court of record of any other state or foreign jurisdiction, the Texas court will enforce it in the same manner and by the same process used for taking testimony in a Texas proceeding. Tex. R. Civ. P. 201.2.

(12) *Who May be the Deposition Officer Outside Texas?* May a Texas lawyer bring a Texas court reporter along to take a deposition out of state? Civil Procedure Rule 201.1(b) allows a party to "take the deposition by notice in accordance with these rules as if the deposition were taken in the State." It also allows the deposition officer to be a person authorized to administer oaths in the place where the deposition is taken. Rule 201, however, must be read in connection with Section 20.001 of the Civil Practice and Remedies Code. This statute provides:

CIVIL PRACTICE AND REMEDIES CODE

CHAPTER 20. DEPOSITIONS

C.P.R.C. § 20.001. *Persons Who May Take a Deposition.* (a) A deposition on written questions of a witness who is alleged to reside or to be in this state may be taken by: (1) a clerk of the district court; (2) a judge or clerk of a county court; or (3) a notary public of this state.

(b) A deposition of a witness who is alleged to reside or to be outside this state, but inside the United States, may be taken in another state by: (1) a clerk of a court of record having a seal; (2) a commissioner of deeds appointed under the laws of this state; or (3) any notary public.

(c) A deposition of a witness who is alleged to reside or to be outside the United States may be taken by: (1) a minister, commissioner, or charge d'affaires of the United States who is a resident of and is accredited to the country where the deposition is taken; (2) a consul general, consul, vice-consul, commercial agent, vice-commercial agent, deputy consul, or consular agent of the United States who is a resident of the country where the deposition is taken; or (3) any notary public.

Comment 2 to Civil Procedure Rule 201 characterizes C.P.R.C. § 20.001 as providing a "nonexclusive list of persons who are qualified to take a written deposition in Texas and who may take depositions (oral or written) in another state or outside the United States." Taken together, these rules and statutes mean that a Texas notary public may serve as the deposition officer. The Texas certified shorthand reporter statute neither requires nor prohibits Texas certified shorthand reporters from acting as deposition officers for depositions taken outside Texas. If the reporter is a notary public, he or she may take the out of state deposition. For depositions in foreign countries, counsel must also check to see whether a U.S. court reporter would need to have a work visa before being allowed to work as court reporter in that country. To what extent can these limits be circumvented by taking the deposition by "telephone or other remote electronic means" under Civil Procedure Rule 199.1(b)? Will your answer differ for party and nonparty witnesses? What other skills do you need to consider when dealing with an oral deposition?

(13) *Modification of Procedural Requirements by Agreement.* What if the parties would like to extricate themselves from some of the deposition requirements? Civil Procedure Rule 191.1 provides that "[e]xcept where specifically prohibited, the procedures and limitations set forth in the rules pertaining to discovery may be modified in any suit by the agreement of the parties or by court order for good cause." Comment 1 to this rule notes that the parties' ability to vary the rules by agreement is "broad but not unbounded. . . . Thus, for example, parties can agree to enlarge or shorten the time permitted for a deposition and to change the manner in which a deposition is conducted, notwithstanding Rule 199.5, although parties could not agree to be abusive toward a witness." Could you agree to dispense with a certified shorthand reporter? With the requirement that the witness be examined under oath? With the nature of objections allowed? With Rule 199.1's requirement that the person swearing the witness be present with the witness?

### [3] Conduct During Oral Depositions

The 1999 rule changes revised the procedures for oral depositions. Given the time limits on an oral deposition (*See* § 10.02), the new procedures are intended to encourage focused examination and to discourage colloquy between counsel. Under the new rules, regardless of the type of case:

1. No "side" may examine or cross-examine an individual witness for more than six hours. Tex. R. Civ. P. 199.5(c).

2. Private conferences between the witness and the witness's attorney during the actual taking of the deposition are improper except to determine whether a privilege should be asserted. Tex. R. Civ. P. 199.5(d).

3. The language and content of objections is limited. The only approved objections are: "Objection, leading," "Objection, form," and "Objection, nonresponsive." Argumentative or suggestive objections or explanations waive objection and may be grounds for terminating the deposition. Tex. R. Civ. P. 199.5(e).

4. Instructions not to answer are allowed "to preserve a privilege, comply with a court order or these rules, protect a witness from an abusive question or one for which any answer would be misleading, or secure a ruling." Tex. R. Civ. P. 199.5(f). If the time limits for deposition have expired or if the deposition is being conducted or defended in violation of these rules, a party or witness may suspend the deposition to obtain a ruling. Tex. R. Civ. P. 199.5(g).

5. An attorney must not object to a question at oral deposition, instruct the witness not to answer a question, or suspend the deposition unless there is a good faith factual and legal basis for doing so at the time. Nor may the attorney ask a question without a good faith legal basis. Tex. R. Civ. P. 199.5(h).

6. Because the new deposition rules incorporate the procedures and limitations applicable to requests for production or inspection (including the 30-day period for responses by parties to requests for production of documents), party depositions duces tecum can no longer be used to circumvent the 30-day minimum of the document production rule when the witness is a party. Tex. R. Civ. P. 199.2(b)(5).

---

## NOTES AND QUESTIONS

(1) *Coaching.* You are taking a deposition of a party opponent. Suppose that the deponent's lawyer continually carries on whispered conversations with the witness, makes extensive objections that inform the witness of the proper answer, and continually makes time-consuming speeches. What should you do?

(2) *Harassment.* You are representing the witness at a deposition. The lawyer taking the deposition persists in asking your client irrelevant questions about his sex life and medical history, inquiring into conversations between you and your client, and making insulting remarks toward your client. What should you do?

(3) *Corporate Representatives—Time Limits.* You have noticed the deposition of Acme Corporation, specifying the subject matter about which you will inquire. Acme has identified and produced three people to answer various parts of your questions. How much time, absent agreement or court order, do you have to question these Acme deponents? *See* Tex. R. Civ. P. 199.5(c); T.R.C.P. 199, Comment 2.

(4) *Agreements of Counsel.* The discovery rules have long allowed parties to vary the rules regarding making and waiving objections at depositions. Counsel often begin a deposition by entering into a series of stipulations whose explicit purpose is to modify the rules' effect. The form of the stipulations, which are often added to the deposition by the court reporter simply on the direction of the parties that it be prefaced by "the usual agreements," might appear like this:

> It is agreed, stipulated, and understood by and between the parties hereto, acting by and through their respective counsel, that all formalities incident to the taking of the deposition, except for that of the signature of the witness to this deposition, which may be obtained before any notary public or other person authorized to administer oaths, are hereby expressly waived; and that the deposition when so taken may be introduced in evidence by any of the parties on the trial of said cause. It is further agreed, stipulated and understood by and between the parties hereto that all objections may be reserved until the time of trial. The signature of counsel for the respective parties to this agreement and stipulation are hereby expressly waived.

If such a stipulation is entered into at a deposition, what impact will the agreement have on the requirements of Civil Procedure Rules 199.5, 200.3, and 176.6(c)? Remember this problem when considering [4], *below*, regarding use of depositions at hearings and trials. Also keep in mind that the wording of such stipulations is not fixed. The parties may agree, for example, to reserve the right to object until time of trial *except* as to the form of individual questions. Why might this proviso be advisable? Local practice on stipulations differs. A lawyer who is asked by an opponent, "Do you want to make the usual agreements?" and who is uncertain what they are should never hesitate to ask, "What usual agreements do you mean?"

### [4] Use of Depositions at Hearings or Trials

The use of a deposition as evidence at trial is governed by Civil Procedure Rule 203 and by the Texas Rules of Evidence. All or part of a deposition may be used for any purpose in the same proceeding in which it was taken. If the original is not filed, a certified copy may be used. The term "same proceeding" includes a proceeding in a different court but involving the same subject matter and the same parties or their representatives or successors in interest.

A deposition is admissible against a party joined after the deposition was taken only if either (1) the deposition is admissible under the former testimony exception to the hearsay rule, or (2) the party has had a reasonable opportunity to redepose the witness and has failed to do so. The former testimony exception to the hearsay rule allows a deposition to be used if (1) the declarant is unavailable as a witness, and (2) the party against whom the deposition testimony is offered, or a person with a similar interest, had an opportunity and similar motive to develop the testimony by direct, cross, or redirect examination. *See* Tex. R. Evid. 804(b).

A deposition from another proceeding may be used in the current proceeding to the extent permitted by the Texas Rules of Evidence. Generally, depositions taken in a different proceeding are hearsay, but are admissible if they meet the requirements of the "former testimony" exception to the hearsay rule. A declarant is considered "unavailable as a witness" in any of the following situations (Tex. R. Evid. 804(a)):

1. The court rules, on the basis of privilege, to exempt the declarant from testifying concerning the subject matter of the former testimony.

2. The declarant persists in refusing to testify concerning the subject matter of the prior testimony, despite an order of the court to do so.

3. The declarant testifies to a lack of memory of the subject matter of the prior testimony.

4. The declarant is unable to be present or to testify at the hearing because of death or then-existing physical or mental illness or infirmity.

5. The declarant is absent from the hearing, and the proponent of the declarant's statement has been unable to procure the declarant's attendance or testimony by process or other reasonable means.

Before the adoption of the Texas Rules of Evidence, the Texas Supreme Court had held that a witness whose deposition could be taken outside of Texas was not "unavailable." *Hall v. White*, 525 S.W.2d 860, 862 (Tex. 1975). It is probable that this same interpretation will be given to the "or testimony" language of Evidence Rule 804(a)(5).

A declarant is not considered unavailable as a witness if the declarant's exemption, refusal, claim of lack of memory, inability, or absence is due to the procurement or wrongdoing of the proponent of the statement for the purpose of preventing the declarant from attending or testifying. Tex. R. Evid. 804(a).

A nonstenographic recording of an oral deposition, or a written transcription of all or part of the recording, may be used to the same extent as a deposition taken by stenographic means. The trial court has the discretion to find that when a party offers an edited version of a videotape, the edited version would unduly delay the trial, mislead the jury, or needlessly present cumulative evidence. In such a case, the court may decide to admit the full tape under the rule of optional completeness. Tex. R. Evid. 106.

## NOTES AND QUESTIONS

(1) *Tactical Use of Depositions.* In terms of tactics, what sort of witness might you prefer to present by deposition even though available? What sort of witness would you prefer to present live? Suppose that you have an important expert witness who will be unavailable on the day of trial, but you do not wish to lose the impact of his or her personal presentation. What possibility do the rules offer?

(2) *Method of Presenting Deposition Testimony.* How does one actually introduce a deposition into evidence? Unless it is read into evidence or somehow conveyed to the jury, it is not part of the evidence considered by the jury, and unless it is offered, it is not part of the trial record. The usual method is for two people to read the deposition, one reading the questions and the other than answers. Be aware of the possible issues raised by overly dramatic readings or emphasis of parts of the deposition record. One major difficulty with the reading of a deposition before a jury is that it loses much of the impact of live testimony. Indeed, some trial lawyers are concerned that jurors, seeing persons in front of them reading material from a little booklet, may not consider it in the same category as the rest of the evidence. One solution is to have the judge explain the procedure to the jury. The increasing use of videotape depositions also solves some of the problem.

(3) *Available Trial Objections.* Although the deposition as an entirety is admissible, there may still be questions or answers within the deposition that are objectionable. One must therefore also consider whether such objections have been preserved so that they may be raised. Review Rules 199.5 and 203. What objections are required at the deposition? Which ones may be made at trial? Which ones can be made after the deposition but require notice before the trial commences?

### [5] Motions for Physical or Mental Examinations

Unlike the other discovery devices that are designed to work without the intervention of the judge, a requirement that a person subject himself to a mental or physical examination requires a court order. Under the 1999 revisions, the procedures and requirements for motions for physical and mental examinations are contained in Civil Procedure Rule 204.

## COATES v. WHITTINGTON

*758 S.W.2d 749 (Tex. 1988)*

SPEARS, Justice.

At issue in this mandamus proceeding is whether a plaintiff who claims mental anguish damages in a personal injury action may be required to submit to a mental examination. . . . Judge Mark Whittington granted the motion [to compel] and ordered Mrs. Coates to undergo the examination. The court of appeals denied Mrs. Coates' motion for leave to file petition for writ of mandamus. We hold that the trial court abused its discretion by ordering Mrs. Coates to submit to a mental examination. We therefore conditionally grant relator's petition for writ of mandamus.

Mrs. Coates was injured when she inadvertently sprayed her arm with Drackett's "Mr. Muscle Oven Cleaner" while cleaning her stove top. She suffered severe second degree burns and permanent scarring on her left forearm as a result of the incident. Mrs. Coates brought a products liability action against Drackett, seeking damages for pain and suffering, physical impairment, lost earnings, medical expenses, and mental anguish. In response, Drackett pleaded contributory negligence, misuse, and pre-existing condition. Drackett moved for an order compelling Mrs. Coates to submit to a mental examination pursuant to Rule 167a of the Texas Rules of Civil Procedure, claiming that her mental anguish was pre-existing and may have contributed to the incident with the oven cleaner. The trial judge denied the motion. Drackett then sought a rehearing of its motion, asserting that Mrs. Coates had placed her mental condition "in controversy" by pleading mental anguish damages. Drackett also claimed that there was "good cause" for the mental examination because Mrs. Coates alleged that she experienced "depression and general mental problems at the time she used the oven cleaner." Judge Whittington granted Drackett's motion and ordered that Mrs. Coates submit to a mental examination by a court appointed psychologist. Judge Whittington ordered that the examination address: (1) the relationship of Mrs. Coates' prior problems to the occurrence made the basis of the suit, if any; and (2) the relationship of Mrs. Coates' prior problems to the prayer for mental anguish damages, if any. The court of appeals denied Mrs. Coates' motion for leave to file petition for writ of mandamus.

. . . .

Judge Whittington ordered Mrs. Coates to undergo a mental examination with a court appointed examining *psychologist*. Rule 167a expressly requires that a mental examination be conducted by a physician. A "physician" is "a practitioner of medicine" who is skilled in medicine and surgery. 42 Tex. Jur. 3d *Healing Arts and Institutions* § 1 (1985); *Black's Law Dictionary* 1033 (5th ed. 1979); *see also* Tex. Rev. Civ. Stat. Ann. art. 4495b, § 1.01 *et seq.* (Vernon Supp. 1988). A psychologist is not a physician. *Cf. Lenhard v. Butler*, 745 S.W.2d 101, 105–06 (Tex. App.—Fort Worth 1988, writ denied). A psychologist, therefore, may not conduct a compulsory mental examination authorized by Rule 167a. The trial judge's order is invalid in this respect.

The more significant issue in this case, however, is whether the trial court abused its discretion by ordering Mrs. Coates to undergo a mental examination. Rule 167a was derived from Rule 35 of the Federal Rules of Civil Procedure and largely duplicates the language of the original federal rule. [footnote omitted] Historical Note, Tex. R. Civ. P. 167a (Vernon 1976); 28 U.S.C.A. Fed. R. Civ. P. 35 (West 1968). Federal courts' construction of Rule 35 is thus helpful to an analysis of Rule 167a. The United States Supreme Court has held that federal Rule 35 requires an affirmative showing that the party's mental condition is genuinely in controversy and that good cause exists for the particular examination. *Schlagenhauf v. Holder*, 379 U.S. 104, 118 (1964). In *Schlagenhauf*, the Court expressly stated that these two requirements are not met "by mere conclusory allegations of the pleadings—nor by mere relevance to the case." *Id.* Similarly, Rule 167a, by its express language, places an affirmative burden on the movant to meet a two pronged test: (1) the movant must show that the party's mental condition is "in controversy"; and (2) the movant must demonstrate that there is "good cause" for a compulsory mental examination. In the absence of an affirmative showing of both prongs of the test, a trial court may not order an examination pursuant to Rule 167a.

Drackett maintains that Coates' mental condition is in controversy because she has pleaded for mental anguish damages. In support of its position, Drackett relies on *Schlagenhauf*, 379 U.S. at 119, where the United States Supreme Court stated:

> A plaintiff in a negligence action who asserts mental or physical injury . . . places that mental or physical injury in controversy and provides the defendant with good cause for an examination to determine the existence and extent of such asserted injury.

In *Schlagenhauf*, however, the court also warned that sweeping examinations of a party who has not affirmatively put his mental condition in issue may not be routinely ordered simply because the party brings a personal injury action and general negligence is alleged. *Id.* at 121. Further, federal courts that have applied Rule 35 in light of *Schlagenhauf* have consistently distinguished "mental injury" that warrants a psychiatric evaluation from emotional distress that accompanies personal injury. *Compare Anson v. Fickel*, 110 F.R.D. 184, 186 (N.D. Ind. 1986) (mental condition is in controversy when plaintiff claims mental problems that required confinement in a psychiatric hospital) *and Lowe v. Philadelphia Newspapers, Inc.*, 101 F.R.D. 296, 298–99 (E.D. Pa. 1983) (mental condition is in controversy when plaintiff claims severe emotional distress and seeks to prove damages through testimony of psychiatrist) *with Cody v. Marriott Corp.*, 103 F.R.D. 421, 423 (D. Mass. 1984) (mental condition is not in controversy when plaintiff claims emotional distress and does not claim a psychiatric disorder requiring psychiatric or psychological counseling).

In her suit against Drackett, Mrs. Coates asserts that she has suffered the type of emotional distress that typically accompanies a severe second degree burn and permanent scarring. In her deposition, she described her mental anguish as feelings of embarrassment and self-consciousness because the scar is ugly and noticeable in public. She is not alleging a permanent mental injury nor any deep seated emotional disturbance or psychiatric problem. Mrs. Coates' mental anguish claim is, therefore, for the emotional pain, torment, and suffering that a plaintiff who has been burned and scarred would experience in all reasonable probability. Compare Moore v. Lillebo, 722 S.W.2d 683, 688 (Tex. 1986). Further, the record reflects that Mrs. Coates has not sought any type of psychiatric treatment as a result of the incident and, equally important, does not propose to offer psychiatric or psychological testimony to prove her mental anguish at trial.

To permit Drackett to compel a mental examination because Mrs. Coates has claimed mental anguish damages would open the door to involuntary mental examinations in virtually every personal injury suit. Rule 167a was not intended to authorize sweeping probes into a plaintiff' psychological past simply because the plaintiff has been injured and seeks damages for mental anguish as a result of the injury. Plaintiffs should not be subjected to public revelations of the most personal aspects of their private lives just because they seek compensation for mental anguish associated with an injury.

Drackett also contends that Mrs. Coates' mental condition has been placed in controversy by virtue of its contributory negligence claim. With regard to that claim, it is Mrs. Coates' *conduct* that is in controversy. The jury will be asked to decide whether Mrs. Coates was negligent in her use of the oven cleaner. Whatever mental processes underlay her conduct, it is the nature of that conduct, not the reasons for it, that is in issue. Rule 167a clearly does not contemplate that a plaintiff would be subjected to a probing psychiatric incursion into his or her entire psychological past on the strength of a defendant's contributory negligence claim.

The second requirement of Rule 167a is that the movant show "good cause" for compelling an examination. Drackett maintains that it showed good cause by its reference to Mrs. Coates' pre-existing personal problems which, Drackett asserts, may have caused Coates to injure herself with the oven cleaner. Drackett specifically refers to Mrs. Coates' marital problems, her concerns regarding her son's medical problems, and the fact that she had to take a lower paying job when her original employer re-located. Drackett places significance on the fact that Mrs. Coates had seen a doctor two or three times before the incident with the oven cleaner and had complained of depression and problems eating and sleeping. Drackett further emphasizes that on the day of Mrs. Coates' injury, the examining physician in the hospital emergency room noted in the medical record, "Husband states patient depressed—denies suicidal tendencies." Drackett insists that this notation suggests that Mrs. Coates was suicidal and may have misused the oven cleaner intentionally or with indifference to her welfare.

The "good cause" and "in controversy" requirements of Rule 167a are necessarily related. *See Schlagenhauf*, 379 U.S. at 118–19. Mrs. Coates' prior problems are clearly peripheral to the issues in this case, and, consequently, they are not "in controversy." Drackett, however, attempts to meet the "in controversy" requirement by contending that Mrs. Coates' prior problems affected her mental state at the time she used the oven cleaner and they thus provide "good cause" for compelling a mental examination. Mrs. Coates' prior problems and attendant complaints of depression are distinct from the mental anguish she claims as a result of her injury. Drackett has failed to show any connection or "nexus" between Mrs. Coates' pre-injury depression and her post-injury embarrassment.

It is well settled that a tortfeasor takes a plaintiff as he finds him. *Driess v. Friederick*, 73 Tex. 460, 462, 11 S.W. 493, 494 (1889); *Thompson v. Quarles*, 297 S.W.2d 321, 330 (Tex. App.—Galveston 1956, writ ref'd n.r.e.). Regardless of Coates' personal problems at the time of the incident with the oven cleaner, she is entitled to recover the damages resulting from the incident "conditioned as [she] was at the time of the injury." The fact that Mrs. Coates had personal problems at the time of her injury does not, in itself, relieve Drackett of liability, and does not, absent a showing of some connection to her allegation of mental anguish, provide good cause for compelling a mental examination.

A routine allegation of mental anguish or emotional distress does not place the party's mental condition in controversy. The plaintiff must assert mental injury that exceeds the common emotional reaction to an injury or loss. Assuming it is shown that a party has put his mental condition in controversy, good cause for the compelled examination must also be shown. The "good cause" requirement of Rule 167a recognizes that competing interests come into play when a party's mental or physical condition is implicated in a lawsuit—the party's right of privacy and the movant's right to a fair trial. A balancing of the two interests is thus necessary to determine whether a compulsory examination may properly be ordered.

The requirement of good cause for a compulsory mental examination may be satisfied only when the movant satisfies three elements. First, that an examination is relevant to issues that are genuinely in controversy in the case. It must be shown that the requested examination will produce, or is likely to lead to, evidence of relevance to the case. *See Schlagenhauf*, 379 U.S. at 117–18. Second, a party must show a reasonable nexus between the condition in controversy and the examination sought. Neither of these requirements has been satisfied in this case. The mere pleading of mental anguish is inadequate to establish the necessity of plaintiff's submission to a mental examination. Finally, a movant must demonstrate that it is not possible to obtain the desired information through means that are less intrusive than a compelled examination. *See Schlagenhauf*, 379 U.S. at 118; *Marroni v. Matey*, 82 F.R.D. 371, 372 (E.D. Pa. 1979). The movant must demonstrate that the information sought is required to obtain a fair trial and therefore necessitates intrusion upon the privacy of the person he seeks to have examined. *See Lowe v. Philadelphia Newspapers, Inc.*, 101 F.R.D. 296, 298 (E.D. Pa. 1983). Drackett has made no showing that the information it seeks cannot be obtained by other discovery techniques. Mrs. Coates' privacy interests require, at minimum, that Drackett exhaust less intrusive means of discovery before seeking a compulsory mental examination. If, however, a plaintiff intends to use expert medical testimony to prove his or her alleged mental condition, that condition is placed in controversy and the defendant would have good cause for an examination under Rule 167a.

We hold that the trial judge abused his discretion in ordering Mrs. Coates to undergo a mental examination. We conditionally grant Mrs. Coates' petition for writ of mandamus. The writ will issue only if the trial judge refuses to rescind his order.

---

## NOTES AND QUESTIONS

(1) *"Good Cause" and "In Controversy" Requirements.* What does it take, today, to supply these two requirements for a mental or physical examination in Texas? Consider whether the court was correct in holding (1) that Mrs. Coates' pre-existing depression did not put her condition "in controversy" or create "good cause" and (2) that the defendant's inferences that she may have had suicidal tendencies (or other reason for misusing the product) also did not meet the requirements. Try to give an example of evidence that *might* be developed by the defendant, that *would* support an order requiring an examination in this case.

*Schlagenhauf v. Holder*, cited in the principal case, is the leading federal decision on point. The United States Supreme Court there reversed a decision that required a bus driver to submit to examinations in four different specialties, ranging from psychiatry to ophthalmology. The bus driver's deposition showed that on two occasions the driver had driven into other vehicles from the rear in moving traffic while the other vehicles were plainly visible and there was plenty of room to stop. The Court indicated that the only kind of examination that could be ordered under the governing rule was an examination of the driver's eyes.

(2) *Limits on Trial Conduct. C.E. Duke's Wrecker Service, Inc. v. Oakley*, 526 S.W.2d 228 (Tex. Civ. App.—Houston [1st Dist.] 1975, writ ref'd n.r.e.) illustrates another aspect of Civil Procedure Rule 204. What should plaintiff do if plaintiff *offers* to submit to examination, but defendant refuses to undertake any examination and simply argues instead, at trial, that plaintiff's medical witnesses are not credible? Rule 204.3 provides that, in this situation, "the party whose mental or physical condition is in controversy must not comment to the court or jury on the party's willingness to submit to an examination, or on the right or failure of any other party to seek an examination."

In the *Oakley* case, despite this rule, plaintiff's counsel asked his client in the presence of the jury whether she had "been willing to be examined by anyone that [defendant's] counsel might choose in the form of a doctor [to] determine the nature of your injury?" Over objection, plaintiff answered, "Yes." Plaintiff also introduced an interrogatory and answer in which defendant declined to have its physician examine the plaintiff, and plaintiff argued to the jury that if the plaintiff were not injured, defendant "would have got their own doctor." When the defendant appealed a judgment for the plaintiff, the plaintiff argued that this information was appropriately put before the jury to counteract the "unfair and unjust" impression that defendant had created by attacking the credibility of plaintiff's treating doctor (who was plaintiff's brother). Nevertheless, following the rule, the court of appeals reversed.

Consider whether this rule is "unfair" to such a plaintiff, who must produce evidence but cannot point out a defendant's refusal to do likewise. Is this result in accord with the policies underlying discovery? Consider, also, what a plaintiff might lawfully do to counteract the allegedly "unfair and unjust" impression thus created. Could the plaintiff argue, for example, that although the plaintiff has brought expert evidence, the defendant "has brought you absolutely no evidence to contradict the extent of injuries of the plaintiff?" This argument does not appear to violate the letter of Civil Procedure Rule 204, and it is different from that in *Oakley*; is the difference great enough to make a difference in result?

## § 10.02 Limiting the Amount of Discovery: Discovery Control Plans

*Read Tex. R. Civ. P. 190 and accompanying Comments.*

Every case filed on or after January 1, 1999 must be governed by a discovery control plan. In an effort to tailor the amount of discovery to the complexity of the case, there are three levels of discovery plans contained in Civil Procedure Rule 190. Level 1 applies to small cases, Level 2 applies to the majority of cases and is the "default" level, and Level 3 may apply to complex cases (although any case may be governed by a Level 3 plan). Every case must be in some tier at all times. Tex. R. Civ. P. 190.2.

### [A] Level 1 Plans

Level 1 applies to two kinds of cases:

1. Any suit in which all plaintiffs affirmatively plead that they seek only monetary relief aggregating $50,000 or less, excluding costs, prejudgment interest and attorneys' fees; and

2. Any suit for divorce not involving children in which a party pleads that the value of the marital estate is more than zero but not more than $50,000.

Because Level 1 is designed for relatively small cases in which only monetary damages are sought, the amount of discovery that can be taken in a Level 1 case is very limited. Each party may have no more than six hours in total to examine and cross-examine all witnesses in oral depositions. The parties may agree to expand this limit to up to 10 total hours, but cannot agree to more than 10 hours without a court order. In addition, any party may serve on any other party no more than 25 interrogatories, excluding interrogatories asking a party only to identify or authenticate specific documents. Other discovery devices are not limited in Level 1, and a party may take full advantage of requests for disclosure, requests for production and inspection, requests for admissions, requests for entry on land, depositions on written questions, and any other discovery device. The Comments provide, however, that depositions on written questions may not be used to circumvent the limits on interrogatories.

All discovery must be conducted during the "discovery period." The discovery period begins when the suit is filed and continues until 30 days before the date set for trial. For purposes of determining the discovery period, "trial" does not include a hearing on a motion for summary judgment. The discovery devices that permit 30 days for a response (such as requests for disclosure, requests for production of documents, and interrogatories) must be served at least

60 days before the date the case is set for trial so that the responses may be served during the discovery period. *See* Tex. R. Civ. P. 194.1, 196.1, 197.1, 198.1.

In addition to providing a scheme for discovery, Level 1 amends the pleading rules to provide that, without leave of court, a party cannot file an amended or supplemental pleading that would remove the case from Level 1 within 45 days before the date the case is set for trial. Leave may be granted only if good cause for filing the pleading outweighs the prejudice to an opposing party. This is significantly different from the general pleading practice under which a party is entitled to amend pleadings without leave of court up until seven days before trial.

A plaintiff's failure to state in the initial pleading that the case should be in Level 1, as provided in Rule 190.1, does not alone make the case subject to Level 2 because the discovery level is determined by Rule 190.2. A plaintiff's failure to plead as required by Rule 190.1 is subject to special exception.

Litigants must be cautious when proceeding in Level 1. This is because "the relief awarded [in Level 1] cannot exceed the limitations of Level 1," i.e.; $50,000 excluding costs, prejudgment interest, and attorney's fees. Tex. R. Civ. P. 190, Comment 2. In other words, if the plaintiff pleads for damages of $49,000 and discovery is conducted under Level 1, the plaintiff cannot recover more than $50,000 in damages even if the jury awards more. And the plaintiff cannot amend his or her pleadings after verdict to conform the pleadings with the verdict. Comment 2 to Rule 190 specifically provides that "the rule in *Greenhalgh v. Service Lloyds Ins. Co.*, 787 S.W.2d 938 (Tex. 1990) [allowing post-verdict pleading amendments] does not apply." It may be, therefore, that Level 1 will be limited to breach of contract and other similar suits where the damages are subject to an exact calculation, and to small family law cases. Litigants in personal injury and similar suits in which the jury could award damages in excess of $50,000 should probably avoid using Level 1.

### [B] Level 2 Plans

Level 2 applies to all cases that do not proceed under Level 1 or Level 3. It will govern discovery in most cases. Because this is the catch-all tier, the amount of discovery permitted and the period during which the parties may conduct discovery is designed to accommodate most litigation. In Level 2, each side is entitled to no more than 50 hours in oral depositions to examine and cross-examine: (1) parties on the opposing side; (2) experts designated by those parties; and (3) persons who are subject to those parties' control. If one side designates more than two experts, the opposing side may take an additional six hours of total deposition time for each additional expert designated. Other witnesses are not subject to the 50-hour limit. As is the case in Level 1, any party may serve on any other party no more than 25 written interrogatories, excluding interrogatories asking a party only to identify and authenticate specific documents. Other discovery devices are not limited in Level 2.

For purposes of the overall deposition time limit, the term "side" means all litigants with generally common interests in the litigation. Comment 6 to Rule 190 explains that the "concept of 'side' . . . borrows from Rule 233, which governs the allocation of peremptory strikes, and from Fed. R. Civ. P. 30(a)(2). In most cases there are only two sides—plaintiffs and defendants. In complex cases, however, there may be more than two sides, such as when defendants have sued third parties not named by plaintiffs, or when defendants have sued each other." Thus, a defendant who has brought a third-party action or stated a cross-claim against another defendant is entitled to 50 hours in depositions as to the plaintiff on matters in controversy between the defendant and the plaintiff, and another 50 hours in deposition as to the third-party defendant or cross-defendant on matters in controversy between the defendant and the third-party or cross-defendant. It is not clear that a plaintiff will ever be entitled to more than 50 hours in depositions, except that the court may modify the deposition hours on motion by any party, and must do so when a side or party would be given an "unfair advantage" if the deposition limits were not modified.

Discovery in Level 2 must be conducted during the "discovery period." The discovery period for all cases begins when suit is filed. For cases brought under the Family Code, the discovery period continues until 30 days before the date set for trial. In all other cases, the discovery period ends on the *earlier* of 30 days before the date set for trial, nine months after the date of the first oral deposition, or nine months after the due date of the first response to written discovery. As with Level 1, discovery devices that allow a 30-day response time must be served at least 30 days before the end of the discovery period. The "discovery period" may come to a close considerably before trial in some metropolitan areas.

### [C] Level 3 Plans

Level 3 provides for a court-ordered discovery plan. The trial court must, on a party's motion, and may, on its own initiative, order that discovery be conducted in accordance with a discovery control plan tailored to the circumstances of the specific suit. Although Level 3 may be used to provide for additional discovery in complex cases, there is no requirement that the court-ordered plan provide for discovery in excess of Level 1 or Level 2. In fact, Level 3 can be used to limit discovery if a party or the court believes that the discovery allowed by the current level is excessive. Also, a Level 3 plan may simply adopt Level 1 or Level 2 restrictions.

The parties may agree to a Level 3 discovery control plan and may submit an agreed order to the trial court for its consideration. But nothing in the rule requires the court to approve the plan offered by the parties. It is, however, required to render *some* form of Level 3 order if any party moves for one, and to act on the request "as promptly as reasonably possible." Any discovery control plan instituted under Level 3 must include a trial date or date for conference to determine a trial setting, a discovery period during which all discovery must be conducted or all discovery requests must be sent, appropriate limits on the amount of discovery, and deadlines for joining additional parties, amending or supplementing pleadings, and designating expert witnesses. The plan may also address any issue concerning discovery or the matters listed in Civil Procedure Rule 166. In some cases, separate Level 3 plans may be appropriate for different phases of a case.

---

## NOTES AND QUESTIONS

(1) *Choice of Level.* If you represent a plaintiff, what will you consider in initially choosing a level? To what extent can you control the initial level? To what extent is it beyond your control? If you represent a defendant, what will you consider relevant in determining an optimal level? How much control can you exert over the level that applies?

(2) *Moving From Level to Level.* How can cases move among levels? How can a case worth less than $50,000 become a Level 3 case? When would you want it to?

(3) *Modification Orders.* Under what circumstances may a court modify a discovery control plan? When must it do so? May a court who dislikes the new rules simply "opt out" by form order?

(4) *Modification Agreements.* To what extent can parties agree to modify the limits of the various plan levels? Are there matters to which the parties cannot agree? Note that in order to be enforceable, any agreement of the parties must comply with the documentation requirements of Civil Procedure Rule 11.

## § 10.03 Amendment and Supplementation of Discovery Responses

*Read Tex. R. Civ. P. 193.5, 193.6, 195.6 and accompanying Comments.*

---

### ALVARADO v. FARAH MFG. CO., INC.

*830 S.W.2d 911 (Tex. 1992)*

HECHT, Justice.

. . . .

I

While employed by Farah Manufacturing Company, Jose Luis Lerma Alvarado experienced chest pains and was diagnosed as having a pulmonary embolism. Alvarado consulted with an attorney and filed a worker's compensation claim. After receiving medical treatment, Alvarado was released by his physicians to return to work but was restricted from sitting or standing still for long periods of time. This restriction prevented Alvarado from resuming the work he had done before his illness, which required long periods of standing. Farah had other jobs which Alvarado could perform, and he requested reassignment to one of them; but Farah advised him that there were no openings in any of those jobs. In accordance with the collective bargaining agreement which governed Alvarado's employment, Farah placed him on "sustained layoff" status, listing him with other employees in the same status. Whenever a job opening occurred in a particular department, the collective bargaining agreement required that Farah fill the position from the employees on the list, first from those who had worked in that department, by seniority, then from the others on the list, also by seniority. After one year on the list, an employee's seniority and recall rights automatically terminated.

Farah never recalled Alvarado to work, and all his rights under the collective bargaining agreement were eventually terminated. The union did not complain of Alvarado's termination. Nevertheless, Alvarado filed this action for damages against Farah, claiming that Farah had job openings which it should have offered him but did not do so in retaliation for his filing a worker's compensation claim. Thus, Alvarado claims that Farah violated Tex. Rev. Civ. Stat. Ann. article 8307c (Vernon Supp. 1992). [footnote omitted] Farah denies that it violated article 8307c and asserts that it never recalled Alvarado to work because it never had an opening for a job that Alvarado was both physically able to do and eligible to take under the seniority system which Farah had to follow.

Shortly after filing suit, Alvarado directed interrogatories to Farah, the first two of which asked:

1. Please state the name, address, telephone number, and employer of all persons having knowledge of the occurrences made the basis of this suit.
2. Please state the name, address, telephone number, and employer of each potential witness that you may use in the trial of this case.

Farah responded with interrogatories to Alvarado, the first two of which were identical to those quoted above. Neither Alvarado nor Farah objected to these interrogatories; both answered them by identifying several persons.

Six days before trial was set to begin, Alvarado subpoenaed two witnesses to testify who had never been identified in answer to Farah's interrogatories. One of these witnesses, [footnote omitted] Jacqueline Arrambide, had formerly been employed by Farah in a non-union position. Like Alvarado, Arrambide had sued Farah claiming that she had been terminated in retaliation for asserting a claim for worker's compensation benefits. On the first day of trial, before voir dire commenced, Farah moved to exclude the testimony of Arrambide for the reason that she had not been identified in answer to its interrogatories. The trial court denied Farah's motion. After Farah rested its case, Alvarado called Arrambide as a witness on rebuttal. Again Farah objected, and again the trial court overruled, the objection. Arrambide testified that Farah had fired her one week after Farah found out that she had hired an attorney to make a worker's compensation claim for injury to her back. She testified that the reason she was given for her termination was poor attendance at work, even though she had missed only a few days work for medical treatment.

The jury found that Farah violated article 8307c with respect to Alvarado, and that he should be awarded $139,080 actual damages [footnote omitted] and $1,000,000 exemplary damages. The trial court rendered judgment on the verdict.

II

A

Rule 215(5) of the Texas Rules of Civil Procedure states:

> A party who fails to respond to or supplement his response to a request for discovery shall not be entitled to present evidence which the party was under a duty to provide in a response or supplemental response or to offer the testimony of an expert witness or of any other person having knowledge of discoverable matter, unless the trial court finds that good cause sufficient to require admission exists. The burden of establishing good cause is upon the party offering the evidence and good cause must be shown in the record.

To say that this rule has proven to be problematic is perhaps an understatement. On ten occasions in the eight years since the rule was first promulgated in 1984, [footnote omitted] this Court has written on whether a witness not identified in response to a discovery request should have been allowed to testify. *Sharp v. Broadway Nat'l Bank,* 784 S.W.2d 669 (Tex. 1990) (per curiam); *Rainbo Baking Co. v. Stafford,* 787 S.W.2d 41 (Tex. 1990) (per curiam); *McKinney v. National Union Fire Ins. Co.,* 772 S.W.2d 72 (Tex. 1989); *Clark v. Trailways, Inc.,* 774 S.W.2d 644 (Tex. 1989); *Boothe v. Hausler,* 766 S.W.2d 788 (Tex. 1989) (per curiam); *Gee v. Liberty Mut. Fire Ins. Co.,* 765 S.W.2d 394 (Tex. 1989); *E.F. Hutton & Co. v. Youngblood,* 741 S.W.2d 363 (Tex. 1987) (per curiam); *Gutierrez v. Dallas Indep. Sch. Dist.,* 729 S.W.2d 691 (Tex. 1987); *Morrow v. H.E.B., Inc.,* 714 S.W.2d 297 (Tex. 1986) (per curiam); *Yeldell v. Holiday Hills*

*Retirement and Nursing Center, Inc.*, 701 S.W.2d 243 (Tex. 1985). In eight of these cases the trial courts admitted testimony which had not been timely identified in response to discovery requests; in none of them did the Court hold that "good cause sufficient to require admission" was shown.

The trial courts in these cases have given various reasons for allowing testimony despite the failure to comply with discovery rules. These reasons seem to share a basic rationale, sometimes expressed and other times implicit, that admitting the testimony allowed a full presentation of the merits of the case. In the present case, for example, the trial court permitted a previously undisclosed witness to testify "in the interest of justice in getting everything on the table, which this court tries to do when possible. . . ." While it is certainly important for the parties in a case to be afforded a full and fair opportunity to present the merits of their contentions, it is not in the interest of justice to apply the rules of procedure unevenly or inconsistently. It is both reasonable and just that a party expect that the rules he has attempted to comply with will be enforced equally against his adversary. To excuse noncompliance without a showing of good cause frustrates that expectation.

The salutary purpose of Rule 215(5) is to require complete responses to discovery so as to promote responsible assessment of settlement and prevent trial by ambush. *See Clark*, 774 S.W.2d at 646; *Gee*, 765 S.W.2d at 396; *Gutierrez*, 729 S.W.2d at 693. The rule is mandatory, and its sole sanction—exclusion of evidence—is automatic, unless there is good cause to excuse its imposition. The good cause exception permits a trial court to excuse a failure to comply with discovery in difficult or impossible circumstances. *See Clark*, 774 S.W.2d at 647 (inability to locate witness despite good faith efforts or inability to anticipate use of witness' testimony at trial might support a finding of good cause). The trial court has discretion to determine whether the offering party has met his burden of showing good cause to admit the testimony; but the trial court has no discretion to admit testimony excluded by the rule without a showing of good cause.

We have repeatedly addressed what factors, standing alone, are not in themselves good cause. Included among these are inadvertence of counsel, *Sharp*, 784 S.W.2d at 672; *E.F. Hutton*, 741 S.W.2d at 364; lack of surprise, *Sharp*, 784 S.W.2d at 671; *Gee*, 765 S.W.2d at 395 n.2 (lack of surprise is not the standard, but may be a factor); *Morrow*, 714 S.W.2d at 298; and uniqueness of the excluded evidence, *Clark*, 774 S.W.2d at 646. The reasons in each instance are intuitive. If inadvertence of counsel, by itself, were good cause, the exception would swallow up the rule, for there would be few cases in which counsel would admit to making a deliberate decision not to comply with the discovery rules. Determining whether a party is really surprised by an offer of testimony not formally identified in discovery is difficult. The better prepared counsel is for trial, the more likely he is to have anticipated what evidence may be offered against his client, and the less likely he is to be surprised. It would hardly be right to reward competent counsel's diligent preparation by excusing his opponent from complying with the requirements of the rules. As we explained in *Sharp:*

> A party is entitled to prepare for trial assured that a witness will not be called because opposing counsel has not identified him or her in response to a proper interrogatory. Thus, even the fact that a witness has been fully deposed, and only his or her deposition testimony will be offered at trial, is not enough to show good cause for admitting the evidence when the witness was not identified in response to discovery.

784 S.W.2d at 671. Finally, if good cause could be shown simply by establishing the unique importance of the evidence to the presentation of the case, only unimportant evidence would ever be excluded, and the rule would be pointless.

To relax the good cause standard in Rule 215(5) would impair its purpose. Counsel should not be excused from the requirements of the rule without a strict showing of good cause. The difficulty with the rule lies not so much in the requirement of strict adherence, but in the severity of the sanction it imposes for every breach. The consequences of the rule should not be harsher in any case than the vice the rule seeks to correct. The sole sanction should not be the exclusion of all evidence not properly identified in discovery; rather, as with other failures to comply with discovery, the trial court should have a range of sanctions available to it to enforce the rules without injustice. "The punishment should fit the crime." *TransAmerican Natural Gas Corp. v. Powell,* 811 S.W.2d 913, 917 (Tex. 1991).

As written, however, Rule 215(5) prescribes a single sanction for failing to supplement discovery, and we are not free to disregard its plain language. Nor should we revise the rule by opinion. The Legislature has provided that notice be given before rules amendments become effective. Tex. Gov't Code § 22.004. In addition, this Court has structured the rules revision process to encourage advice and comment from the bench and bar, and from the public generally. Any revision in Rule 215(5) should be left to those processes, which are underway.

Last year the Court appointed task forces to study the conduct of discovery and the imposition of sanctions, and to make recommendations for revisions in the rules. The Court's Rules Advisory Committee, the State Bar's Committee on the Administration of Justice, and other groups have undertaken similar studies. While those processes are at work, we adhere to the language of the rule and our consistent precedent.

We note, however, that the trial courts are not without power to prevent the enforcement of Rule 215(5) from operating as an injustice in a particular case. When a party has failed to timely identify evidence in response to discovery requests, the trial court has the discretion to postpone the trial and, under Rule 215(3), to impose an appropriate sanction upon the offending party for abuse of the discovery process. Such sanction may be used to compensate the non-offending party for any wasted expense in preparing for trial. Although the trial court should not allow delay to prejudice the non-offending party, the trial court should ordinarily be able to cure any prejudice by a just imposition of sanctions. [footnote omitted]

B

In the instant case each party inquired of the other the identity of all potential witnesses. Although they might both have successfully objected to the interrogatory, having undertaken to answer it, they were required to do so fully, and to supplement their answers in accordance with the rules. *See Gutierrez,* 729 S.W.2d at 693. Alvarado never supplemented his answers to identify Arrambide as a witness, even though he knew at least six days before trial when he subpoenaed her that she would be a witness. Alvarado does not contend that he did not know of Arrambide until he subpoenaed her. Rather, as good cause to admit Arrambide's testimony over Farah's objection, Alvarado argued at a pretrial hearing that Farah had long known of Arrambide because she had sued Farah herself on a similar claim, that Farah had deposed Arrambide in her own case although not in Alvarado's, and that Arrambide would be called as a rebuttal witness. The trial court did not make a specific finding of good cause but simply overruled Farah's objection. The fact that Farah was aware of Arrambide and had deposed her in another case, is not, either in itself or in the circumstances of this case, good cause for allowing Arrambide to testify. Neither is Alvarado's use of Arrambide as a rebuttal witness. Alvarado was asked to identify "each potential witness that you may use in the trial of this case." Arrambide was clearly a potential witness, at least when Alvarado subpoenaed her, and Alvarado clearly indicated to the trial court prior to trial that he intended to call her to testify. She could just as well have testified during Alvarado's case in chief as in rebuttal. We hold that Alvarado's tactical decision prior to trial to call Arrambide on rebuttal was not good cause for failing to comply with discovery. *See Walsh v. Mullane*, 725 S.W.2d 264, 264–65 (Tex. App.—Houston [1st Dist.] 1986, writ ref'd n.r.e.). To hold otherwise would be to encourage the very kind of gamesmanship that Rule 215(5) is intended to prevent. [footnote omitted]

Later during the trial, when Alvarado called Arrambide to the witness stand and Farah renewed its objection, Alvarado asserted a further reason as good cause for allowing Arrambide to testify. Alvarado argued that Arrambide's testimony was necessary to rebut unexpected testimony by Farah's personnel director during its case in chief that Farah would rehire employees with physical limitations. Even if Alvarado's argument had merit, it could hardly support his pretrial decision to call Arrambide as a rebuttal witness. Moreover, the testimony Alvarado claims was unexpected was essentially immaterial. Regardless of whether Farah would or would not rehire employees with physical limitations, Alvarado asserted, and Farah's personnel director admitted, that Alvarado did not have any such limitations precluding his return to work. Alvarado argues, somewhat inconsistently, that he did not call Arrambide to rebut specific testimony by Farah's personnel director, but to impeach him generally. Farah's personnel director was deposed prior to trial, and his credibility was known to be in issue before trial commenced. To the extent Arrambide's testimony was used generally to impeach him, Alvarado certainly knew before trial that she was a potential witness.

We therefore hold that the trial court erred in admitting Arrambide's testimony. The question remains whether that error was harmful. *See Gee*, 765 S.W.2d at 396 (erroneous admission of surprise witness' testimony is not harmful if that testimony is "merely cumulative of properly admitted testimony"), citing *McInnes v. Yamaha Motor Corp.*, 673 S.W.2d 185, 188 (Tex. 1984), *cert. denied*, 469 U.S. 1107, 105 S. Ct. 782, 83 L. Ed. 2d 777 (1985); *accord*, *McKinney*, 772 S.W.2d at 76. Arrambide testified that she had been fired by Farah one week after the company became aware that she had hired an attorney to file a compensation claim. [footnote omitted] She was the only witness to testify to these facts; her testimony was not cumulative. It was intended to show that Farah had a pattern of firing employees for filing compensation claims. Alvarado's insistence on using her testimony indicates how important he thought it was to his case. Under the circumstances, we hold that the error in admitting Arrambide's testimony was reversible. [footnote omitted]

. . .

Whether Rule 215(5) should be revised is an issue which we leave to the processes which exist to study such matters. In this case, consistent with the plain language of the rule and our prior precedent, we affirm the judgment of the court of appeals.

Justice DOGGETT, J., not sitting.

[The dissent of Justice MAUZY is omitted.]

## NOTES AND QUESTIONS

(1) *Impact of 1999 Amendments.* Since the *Farah* case was decided, the 1999 amendments have codified certain rules and changed others. Specifically:

(a) Amendments or supplementation of responses to written discovery is required "reasonably promptly" on learning that a prior response was "incorrect or incomplete" or is no longer "correct or complete." The "in substance misleading" limit, which itself replaced the former "knowing concealment" standard, is eliminated.

(b) Formal supplementation of responses to written discovery is required for identification of fact witnesses, trial witnesses, or experts.

(c) Informal supplementation of responses to written discovery under a "has been made known" standard applies to other information.

(d) "An amended or supplemental response must be in the same form as the initial response and must be verified by the party if the original response was required to be verified by the party, but the failure to comply with this requirement does not make the amended or supplemental response untimely unless the party making the response refuses to correct the defect within a reasonable time after it is pointed out." *See also State Farm Fire & Cas. Co. v. Morua*, 979 S.W.2d 616 (Tex. 1998) (discussing need to verify supplemental discovery responses).

(e) Amendment or supplementation less than 30 days prior to trial is presumptively not made "reasonably promptly."

(f) A duty exists to supplement the deposition or report of a retained expert, but only with regard to mental impressions and opinions and their basis. There is no general duty to supplement deposition testimony.

(g) A failure to make, amend, or supplement a discovery response in a timely manner precludes introduction of the evidence or testimony of the witness (other than a named party) who was not identified unless the party seeking to introduce the evidence or call the witness establishes good cause *or* the lack of unfair surprise or unfair prejudice. Regardless of whether such a showing is made, the court may grant a continuance or temporarily postpone the trial to allow a response and to allow opposing parties to conduct discovery.

(2) *Exclusion of Depositions.* The deposition of an undisclosed witness should be excluded as well as his or her live testimony. *New Braunfels Factory Outlet Ctr. Inc. v. IHOP Realty Corp.*, 872 S.W.2d 303, 311 (Tex. App.—Austin 1994, no writ).

(3) *Exclusion of Documents.* The duty to supplement also extends to documents requested during discovery, and exclusion is a proper sanction. What if the information that was not produced by the party actually harms that party and *helps* the opponent? Exclusion of the information is not, in that situation, a meaningful sanction. In that situation the court may order other sanctions. *See* § 10.04.

(4) *Effect of Nonsuit.* Sanctions excluding witness testimony or other evidence do not survive a nonsuit and have no effect on a subsequently filed action. *Aetna Casualty & Surety Co. v. Specia*, 849 S.W.2d 805 (Tex. 1993).

(5) *Supplementation of Depositions.* What if a witness has been disclosed and deposed, but his or her testimony is modified within 30 days of trial? Tex. R. Civ. P. 193, Comment 5; Tex. R. Civ. P. 195.6. *See also Exxon Corp. v. West Texas Gathering Co.*, 868 S.W.2d 299, 305 (Tex. 1993) (no exclusion if changes are not material).

(6) *The New "Named Party" Exception.* Suppose a named party is an entity rather than a human. If one of its employees is not disclosed in response to a proper discovery request, will that employee's testimony be allowed as that of a "named party" or is that exception limited to people? Under pre-1999 case law, an undesignated party witness could be allowed to testify "when identity is certain and when his or her personal knowledge of relevant facts has been communicated to all other parties through pleadings by name and response to other discovery at least thirty days in advance of trial." *Smith v. Southwest Feed Yards*, 835 S.W.2d 89, 91–92 (Tex. 1992).

## § 10.04 Sanctions for Failure to Provide Discovery

*Read Tex. R. Civ. P. 215 and accompanying Comment.*

The placement of the theoretically cooperative discovery process within a system that is otherwise adversarial often means that parties fail to comply with the discovery rules, even though the law provides a duty to make discovery. Proper discovery therefore depends on adequate power in the court to enforce the discovery rules.

---

### TRANSAMERICAN NATURAL GAS v. POWELL

*811 S.W.2d 913 (Tex. 1991)*

HECHT, Justice.

In this original mandamus proceeding, TransAmerican Natural Gas Corporation seeks to compel the Hon. William R. Powell, Judge of the 80th District Court, to set aside his orders imposing sanctions for discovery abuse. The district court struck TransAmerican's pleadings, dismissed its action against Toma Steel Supply, Inc., and granted Toma an interlocutory default judgment on its counterclaim against TransAmerican, reserving for trial only the amount of damages due Toma. We conditionally grant the writ of mandamus.

I

The underlying case is a complex, multi-party action arising out of Toma's sale of allegedly defective pipe casing to TransAmerican. TransAmerican withheld payment for the casing, apparently some $2.3 million, and sued Toma in April 1987 for damages allegedly caused by its use. Toma counterclaimed for $52 million damages resulting from TransAmerican's refusal to pay for the casing. Numerous other parties also joined in the litigation.

On July 3, 1988, the district court issued a docket control order pursuant to Rule 166 of the Texas Rules of Civil Procedure, which set a discovery cutoff date of April 3, 1989. The order allowed discovery to be conducted beyond that date only upon agreement of the parties.

On March 7, 1989, Toma noticed the deposition of TransAmerican's president, K. Craig Shephard, to take place March 16. Two days later TransAmerican's counsel, who at that time was one of the attorneys in its legal department, telephoned Toma's counsel to inform him that Shephard could not be available on March 16 because of a previously scheduled deposition in another case. When counsel could not agree on another date for Shephard's deposition, TransAmerica filed a motion for protection to quash the deposition notice and postpone the deposition. The motion stated that it would be submitted to the trial court for ruling on March 17.[1] However, the trial court did not rule on the motion on that date.

Beginning April 3, the deadline set by the district court for completion of discovery, the parties' smoldering discovery problem started to flare. On that date, counsel for TransAmerican and Toma agreed that Shephard would be deposed after April 10 on a date to be agreed upon. Despite this understanding, counsel again failed to agree upon a date, and on April 19 Toma noticed Shephard's deposition for May 2 without TransAmerican's consent. On April 20, upon receipt of this second deposition notice, TransAmerican's counsel wrote a letter to Toma's counsel informing him that Shephard would not be available May 2 because, as before, he already had a deposition in another matter scheduled for that day. Toma's counsel replied by letter that he would not agree to reschedule the deposition. On April 27, TransAmerican reset the date for submission of its motion for protection to the trial court for ruling to May 12. By this time, of course, the motion was moot, and it is not apparent why TransAmerican continued to seek a ruling. TransAmerican did not move the trial court to postpone the May 2 deposition.

Also on April 27, Shephard's other deposition scheduled for May 2 was cancelled, leaving him available to be deposed by Toma. However, Trans-American's counsel did not advise Toma's counsel that Shephard's schedule had changed so that he could be deposed on May 2 after all, nor did Shephard appear on May 2 as noticed. TransAmerican ascribes its failure to produce Shephard for deposition to miscommunication concerning his schedule changes between attorneys in its legal department. Toma alleges that Shephard's failure to appear was purposeful and part of TransAmerican's intentional obstruction of the discovery process.

On May 8, Toma filed a response to TransAmerican's March 14 motion for protective order, even though it acknowledged that that motion was moot. Toma included in its response, however, a motion for sanctions against TransAmerican based on Shephard's failure to appear at the May 2 deposition. In return, TransAmerican filed its own sanctions motion on May 11, urging that Toma's motion for sanctions was itself an abuse of the discovery process. Toma's and TransAmerican's motions for sanctions both stated that they would be submitted to the court for ruling on May 12, the date set for submission of TransAmerican's original motion for protection.

On May 12, without hearing oral argument, [footnote omitted] the district court signed an order granting Toma's motion for sanctions and striking TransAmerican's pleadings in their entirety. TransAmerican moved for reconsideration, which the district court denied after hearing argument of counsel but refusing to hear any evidence. Based upon his May 12 order striking TransAmerican's pleadings, the district court issued an order on October 6 dismissing TransAmerican's action

[1] The local rules governing civil cases in Harris County provide: "Motions shall state a date of submission which shall be at least 10 days from filing, except on leave of court. The motion will be submitted to the court for ruling on that date or later." Rule 3.3.2, Local Rules of the Civil Trial Division of the Harris County District Courts (1987). The March 17 submission date stated in TransAmerican's motion was only three days from the date of filing and the day after the deposition was scheduled.

with prejudice, rendering an interlocutory default judgment against TransAmerican and in favor of Toma on its counterclaim, and setting the case for trial solely on the issue of the damages to be awarded Toma.

TransAmerican sought mandamus relief from the court of appeals to compel the district court to set aside his May 12 and October 6 orders. A divided court of appeals denied TransAmerican leave to file its petition for writ of mandamus in an unpublished per curiam opinion. [footnote omitted] TransAmerican then moved for leave to file its petition in this Court. We granted the motion in order to review the propriety of the discovery sanctions imposed by the district court.

II

The sanctions imposed by the district court are among those authorized for various discovery abuses under Rule 215 of the Texas Rules of Civil Procedure. The district court did not specify what provision of Rule 215 it relied upon. The portions of the rule applicable to the circumstances here are paragraphs 2(b)(5) and 3. Paragraph 2(b)(5) provides in part:

> If a party or an officer . . . of a party . . . fails to comply with proper discovery requests or to obey an order to provide or permit discovery, . . . the court in which the action is pending may, after notice and hearing, make such orders in regard to the failure as are just, and among others the following:
>
> . . .
>
> (5) An order striking out pleadings or parts thereof, . . . or dismissing with or without prejudice the action or proceedings or any part thereof, or rendering a judgment by default against the disobedient party . . . .

At the time of the district court's rulings, paragraph 3 of Rule 215 stated in part:

> If the court finds a party is abusing the discovery process in seeking, making or resisting discovery . . . , then the court in which the action is pending may impose any sanction authorized by paragraphs (1), (2), (3), (4), (5), and (8) of paragraph 2b of this rule. Such order of sanction shall be subject to review on appeal from the final judgment.[4]

Both paragraphs leave the choice of sanctions to the sound discretion of the trial court. *Bodnow Corp. v. City of Hondo*, 721 S.W.2d 839, 840 (Tex. 1986). However, paragraph 2(b) explicitly requires that any sanctions imposed be "just." By referring to paragraph 2(b), paragraph 3 incorporates the same requirement. Thus, whether the district court imposed sanctions under paragraph 2(b) or paragraph 3, we consider whether those sanctions were just.[5] *See Bodnow*, 721 S.W.2d at 840.

---

[4] Rule 215, paragraph 3 was amended, effective September 1, 1990, to require that sanctions be imposed only after notice and hearing and only as "appropriate." (Similar amendments were made at the same time in Rule 13, Tex. R. Civ. P.) However, the requirement that sanctions be appropriate was implicit in the rule before the amendment. *Koslow's v. Mackie*, 796 S.W.2d 700, 703 n. 1 (Tex. 1990). In the context of Rule 215, "appropriate" and "just" are equivalent standards.

[5] TransAmerican contends that Toma's notice to take Shephard's deposition on May 2 was not a "proper" discovery request under Rule 215, paragraph 2(b) because it issued after the discovery cutoff date set by Judge Powell. Toma responds that its request was proper because TransAmerican agreed that Shephard could be deposed after the cutoff, as permitted by the district court's scheduling order. TransAmerican answers even if there were a binding agreement to depose Shephard after the cutoff, no date was ever agreed to.

TransAmerican also contends that the hearing required by Rule 215, paragraph 2(b) is an oral hearing, not merely

In our view, whether an imposition of sanctions is just is measured by two standards. First, a direct relationship must exist between the offensive conduct and the sanction imposed. This means that a just sanction must be directed against the abuse and toward remedying the prejudice caused by innocent party. It also means that the sanction should be visited upon the offender. The trial court must at least attempt to determine whether the offensive conduct is attributable to counsel only, or to the party only, or to both. This we recognize will not be an easy matter in many instances. On the one hand, a lawyer cannot shield his client from sanctions; a party must bear some responsibility for its counsel's discovery abuses when it is or should be aware of counsel's conduct and the violation of discovery rules. On the other hand, a party should not be punished for counsel's conduct in which it is not implicated apart from having entrusted to counsel its legal representation. The point is, the sanctions the trial court imposes must relate directly to the abuse found.

Second, just sanctions must not be excessive. The punishment should fit the crime. A sanction imposed for discovery abuse should be no more severe than necessary to satisfy its legitimate purposes. It follows that courts must consider the availability of less stringent sanctions and whether such lesser sanctions would fully promote compliance.

These standards set the bounds of permissible sanctions under Rule 215 within which the trial court is to exercise sound discretion.[6] The imposition of very severe sanctions is limited, not only by these standards, but by constitutional due process. The sanctions the district court imposed against TransAmerican are the most devastating a trial court can assess against a party. When a trial court strikes a party's pleadings and dismisses its action or renders a default judgment against it for abuse of the discovery process, the court adjudicates the party's claims without regard to their merits but based instead upon the parties' conduct of discovery. "[T]here are constitutional limitations upon the power of courts, even in aid of their own valid processes, to dismiss an action without affording a party the opportunity for a hearing on the merits of his cause." *Societe Internationale v. Rogers,* 375 U.S. 197, 209–10 (1958), *citing Hammond Packing Co. v. Arkansas,* 212 U.S. 322, 350–51 (1909), and *Hovey v. Elliot,* 167 U.S. 409 (1897); *accord Insurance Corp. of Ireland, Ltd. v. Compagnie des Bauxites de Guinee,* 456 U.S. 694, 705–06 (1982). Discovery sanctions cannot be used to adjudicate the merits of a party's claims or defenses unless a party's hindrance of the discovery process justifies a presumption that its claims or defenses lack merit. *Insurance Corp. of Ireland,* 456 U.S. 694, 705–06 (1982); *Rogers,* 357 U.S. at 209–10; *Hammond Packing,* 212 U.S. at 350–51. However, if a party refuses to

---

a submission of the issue on written motion and response, and that it was denied such a hearing before the imposition of sanctions. Further, TransAmerican argues that the notice required by Rule 215, paragraph 2(b) is at least ten days' notice, and that Toma's motion for sanctions was filed only four days before the district court ruled on it. Toma responds that TransAmerican did not request an oral hearing, that an oral hearing was not necessary and is not required by the rule, and that in any event, TransAmerican received an oral hearing on its motion to reconsider, thus satisfying any requirement of the rule. Toma also argues that Rule 215, paragraph 2(b), requires only reasonable notice, and that four days' notice to TransAmerican in this case was reasonable because TransAmerican was able to respond fully to the motion before the district court ruled.

Our resolution of the matter before us does not require that we address these arguments, and we express no view on any of them.

[6] Justice Gonzalez' concurring opinion sets out guidelines for assessing sanctions which have been identified in the context of applying Rule 11, Fed. R. Civ. P. *Post,* at 920–922. Our analysis of this case does not require us to consider whether those factors or others are appropriate considerations in imposing sanctions. However, we do subscribe to the principle, inherent in the effort to state guidelines, that the trial court's discretion in assessing sanctions must be guided by a reasoned analysis of the purposes sanctions serve and the means of accomplishing those purposes.

produce material evidence, despite the imposition of lesser sanctions, the court may presume that an asserted claim or defense lacks merit and dispose of it. *Insurance Corp. of Ireland*, 456 U.S. at 705–06. Although punishment and deterrence are legitimate purposes for sanctions, *National Hockey League v. Metropolitan Hockey Club, Inc.*, 427 U.S. 639 (1976) (per curiam); *Bodnow Corp. v. City of Hondo*, 721 S.W.2d at 840 (Tex. 1986), they do not justify trial by sanctions, *Hammond Packing*, 212 U.S. at 350–51; *Hovey*, 167 U.S. at 413–14. Sanctions which are so severe as to preclude presentation of the merits of the case should not be assessed absent a party's flagrant bad faith or counsel's callous disregard for the responsibilities of discovery under the rules. *See National Hockey League*, 427 U.S. at 642–643.[7]

In the present case, it is not clear whether TransAmerican or its counsel or both should be faulted for Shephard's failure to attend his deposition. Moreover, there is nothing in the record to indicate that the district court considered imposition of lesser sanctions or that such sanctions would not have been effective. If anything, the record strongly suggests that lesser sanctions should have been utilized and perhaps would have been effective. The district court could have ordered Shephard's deposition for a specific date and punished any failure to comply with that order by contempt or another sanction. He also could have taxed the costs of the deposition against TransAmerican and awarded Toma attorney fees. The range of sanctions available to the district court under Rule 215 is quite broad. The district court dismissed TransAmerican's claims against Toma and rendered default judgment for Toma on its counterclaim solely because, as the record before us establishes, TransAmerican's president failed to present himself for his deposition.[8] Nothing in the record before us even approaches justification for so severe a sanction.[9]

We recognize that we affirmed a similar sanction in *Downer v. Aquamarine Operators, Inc.*, 701 S.W.2d 238, 241–42 (Tex. 1985), *cert. denied*, 476 U.S. 1159 (1986). In that case the trial court struck defendant's answer and rendered a default judgment against it based upon the failure

---

[7] *National Hockey League* cites *Rogers* but not *Hammond Packing*, and does not refer to the rule of the latter that discovery sanctions cannot be used to dispose of the merits of a claim or defense unless the offending party's withholding of evidence warrants a presumption that its claim or defense is without merit. Nevertheless, the conduct sanctioned in *National Hockey League* was so egregious that it clearly would have justified the same ultimate sanctions under *Hammond Packing*. The *Hammond Packing* rule is not in doubt. That it has not been abandoned is further demonstrated in *Insurance Corp. of Ireland*, which came after *National Hockey League* and reasserted the rule of *Hammond Packing*.

[8] Toma's motion for sanctions was based solely upon Shephard's failure to attend his deposition. As Toma itself stated in its response to TransAmerican's motion to refile its pleadings after they were struck: "On May 12, 1989, the Court granted (Toma's) Motion for Sanctions against (TransAmerican) for TransAmerican's refusal to agree to a date certain for Mr. Craig Shephard's deposition and for the failure of its President, Mr. Craig Shephard, to appear for a properly noticed deposition on May 2, 1989, and struck TransAmerican's pleadings in their entirety." Notwithstanding this rather clear statement in the trial court, during this mandamus proceeding Toma has suggested that the district court properly sanctioned TransAmerican because it had abused the discovery process on other occasions. TransAmerican disputes Toma's assertions. While the district court would have been entitled to consider a pattern of discovery abuse in imposing sanctions, the record does not reveal the existence of any such pattern, Toma did not complain of one, and the district court does not appear to have found one.

[9] The district court made no findings to support the sanctions imposed. Rule 215 does not require a trial court to make findings before imposing discovery sanctions, and we do not add such a requirement here. We note only that we do not have the benefit of any explanation by the district court for the severity of its ruling. It would obviously be helpful for appellate review of sanctions, especially when severe, to have the benefit of the trial court's findings concerning the conduct which it considered to merit sanctions, and we commend this practice to our trial courts. *See Thomas v. Capital Security Services, Inc.*, 836 F.2d 866, 882–883 (5th Cir. 1988). Precisely to what extent findings should be required before sanctions can be imposed, however, we leave for further deliberation in the process of amending the rules of procedure.

of defendant and his employees to appear for their deposition on three separate occasions without explanation. Even assuming that *Downer* was correctly decided, the instant case does not show the same pattern of abuse present in *Downer.* Furthermore, *Downer's* approval of the sanction of default judgment was specifically based upon the facts of that case, and the holding in that case is limited to those facts. Rendition of default judgment as a discovery sanction ought to be the exception rather than the rule.

There are cases, of course, when striking pleadings, dismissal, rendition of default and other such extreme sanctions are not only just but necessary. *See National Hockey League,* 427 U.S. at 642. In this case, however, the record before us establishes that the severe sanctions the district court imposed against TransAmerican were manifestly unjust in violation of Rule 215.

III

We next consider whether TransAmerican has an adequate remedy by appeal. If it does, then the writ of mandamus must be denied. *State v. Walker,* 679 S.W.2d 484, 485 (Tex. 1984). Rule 215 paragraph 3 states that orders imposing discovery sanctions "shall be subject to review on appeal from the final judgment." Today we have held in *Braden v. Downey,* 811 S.W.2d 922 (Tex. 1991), that sanctions should not be imposed in such a way that effective appellate review is thwarted. Whenever a trial court imposes sanctions which have the effect of adjudicating a dispute, whether by striking pleadings, dismissing an action or rendering a default judgment, but which do not result in rendition of an appealable judgment, then the eventual remedy by appeal is inadequate. Specifically, in this case TransAmerican does not have an adequate remedy by appeal because it must suffer a trial limited to the damages claimed by Toma. The entire conduct of the litigation is skewed by the removal of the merits of TransAmerican's position from consideration and the risk that the trial court's sanctions will not be set aside on appeal. Resolution of matters in dispute between the parties will be influenced, if not dictated, by the trial court's determination of the conduct of the parties during discovery. Some award of damages on Toma's counterclaim is likely, leaving TransAmerican with an appeal, not on whether it should have been liable for those damages, but on whether it should have been sanctioned for discovery abuse. This is not an effective appeal.

We therefore hold that when a trial court imposes discovery sanctions which have the effect of precluding a decision on the merits of a party's claims—such as by striking pleadings, dismissing an action, or rendering default judgment—a party's remedy by eventual appeal is inadequate, unless the sanctions are imposed simultaneously with the rendition of a final, appealable judgment. If such an order of sanctions is not immediately appealable, the party may seek review of the order by petition for writ of mandamus. Although not every such case will warrant issuance of the extraordinary writ, this case does. TransAmerican's remedy by appeal from a final judgment eventually to be rendered in Toma's favor is inadequate.

. . .

Accordingly, we hold that TransAmerican is entitled to the mandamus relief it seeks. We are confident that Judge Powell will vacate his orders of May 12 and October 6, after which he may conduct further proceedings consistent with this opinion. Our writ of mandamus will issue only in the event he fails promptly to comply.

[The concurring opinions of Justices Gonzalez and Mauzy are omitted.]

## NOTES AND QUESTIONS

*Imposing Death Penalty Sanctions*

(1) *Just Sanctions Must Not be Excessive.* The Texas Supreme Court further limited the trial court's ability to impose death penalty sanctions in *Chrysler Corp. v. Blackmon*, 841 S.W.2d 844 (Tex. 1992). In that case, plaintiff accused Chrysler of needless delay, failing to produce crash tests and other requested information, and falsely stating that Chrysler had fully complied with discovery requests. The trial court made findings supporting plaintiff's accusations, and struck Chrysler's pleadings and rendered a default judgment against Chrysler on all issues. The Supreme Court found this to be an abuse of discretion for four reasons:

> First, there is no direct relationship between the offensive conduct and the sanction imposed. As we stated in *Transamerican*, the sanction must be directed against the abuse and toward remedying the prejudice caused an innocent party. We do not doubt that a failure to produce documents can prejudice a party's efforts to assert or defend a claim. But here, there has simply been no showing that the Garcias are unable to prepare for trial without the additional crash-test reports they seek. Furthermore, the record fails to demonstrate Chrysler's ability to produce the missing crash-test reports. There is no evidence in the record that the missing tests exist or are within Chrysler's possession, custody, or control, either actual or constructive. A party cannot be penalized for failure to produce documents under such circumstances. *See* Tex. R. Civ. P. 166b(2)(b).
>
> The Garcias also contend that Chrysler failed to disclose all similar lawsuits, pointing to the omission of a single lawsuit. Chrysler explains that this omission occurred because the case was classified on its computer as an "air bag" case, rather than a "seatbelt" case. Once Chrysler was advised that the Garcias considered their request to include this type of suit, it made an additional search and disclosed ten air bag suits in advance of the April 1st deadline. The Garcias have made no showing as to how they have been hindered in their preparation for trial by this omission.
>
> It seems obvious that the Garcias would be prejudiced by the expenditure of attorneys' fees and expenses in pursuing motions to compel discovery and sanctions. However, reimbursement of those expenses would appear to be better calculated to remedy such prejudice than would death penalty sanctions. [footnote omitted]
>
> Second, striking Chrysler's pleadings and rendering a default judgment on liability is more severe than necessary to satisfy the legitimate purposes of sanctions for discovery abuse. Judge Blackmon himself conceded as much in his letter to counsel . . . requesting alternative sanction proposals. [footnote omitted]
>
> Third, no lesser sanction was first imposed. Although potentially exposed to a substantial daily fine, such fine was never imposed because there was no judicial determination that Chrysler failed to meet Judge Dunham's deadline for production of the items specified in his Order. Thus, we do not consider the conditional fine to be, as the Garcias argue, an imposition of a required lesser sanction.
>
> Fourth and perhaps most significantly, death penalty sanctions should not be used to deny a trial on the merits unless the court finds that the sanctioned party's conduct "justifies a

> presumption that its claims or defenses lack merit" and that "it would be unjust to permit the party to present the substance of that position [which is the subject of the withheld discovery] before the court." [Citations omitted.] This record contains no evidence to justify such a presumption. In fact, the record conclusively refutes any such suggestion. [footnote omitted] Nor do we find any evidence in the record of flagrant bad faith or counsel's callous disregard for the obligations of discovery.

841 S.W.2d at 849–850.

(2) *"Lesser" Sanctions Must be "Tested."* Also in *Chrysler*, the Supreme Court clarified that a trial court may not impose death penalty sanctions without first imposing lesser sanctions:

> Sanctions that by their severity, prevent a decision on the merits of a case cannot be justified "absent a party's flagrant bad faith or counsel's callous disregard for the responsibilities of discovery under the rules." Even then, lesser sanctions must first be tested to determine whether they are adequate to secure compliance, deterrence, and punishment of the offender.

841 S.W.2d 844, 849, quoting *TransAmerican,* 811 S.W.2d at 918. *See also Humphreys v. Meadows,* 938 S.W.2d 750 (Tex. App.—Fort Worth 1996, writ denied).

(3) *Role of Trial Judge's Factual Findings.* In *TransAmerican*, the Court had suggested that trial court findings would be helpful in determining whether the sanctions imposed were within the trial court's discretion. However, in *Chrysler v. Blackmon*, 841 S.W.2d 844 (Tex. 1992), the Court addressed the issue of the appellate treatment of such findings:

> Although the trial court made extensive findings, only two appear pertinent to the *Transamerican* standards: whether Chrysler's discovery abuse justifies the presumption that its defenses to the suit lack merit; and, whether the conditional monetary sanctions order . . . can be fairly characterized as a lesser sanction. We have reviewed the entire record and conclude that it contains no evidence that would justify the presumption of lack of merit of Chrysler's defense; [footnote omitted] further, we conclude that the conditional monetary sanctions order is not the type of lesser sanction required before the imposition of death penalty sanctions, which we contemplated in *Transamerican* . . . . While trial court findings in a death penalty sanctions case can be helpful in demonstrating how the court's discretion was guided by a reasoned analysis of the purposes sanctions serve and the means of accomplishing those purposes, especially in complex cases where the record is voluminous, such findings must be pertinent to the *Transamerican* standards and supported by the record. Findings specifically tied to an appropriate legal standard are the only type of findings that can be truly beneficial to appellate review.

841 S.W.2d at 852–853.

(4) *The 1999 Amendments.* The 1999 amendments to the discovery rules do not make any substantive changes in Rule 215 except for the elimination of subdivision 5 of former Rule 215 (failure to respond to or supplement discovery) and the inclusion of former Rule 203 (failure of party or witness to attend or seek subpoena; expenses) as a part of Rule 215. Discovery sanctions were treated as a separate problem by the Supreme Court Advisory Committee and a separate Task Force on Discovery Sanctions. Thus, it is anticipated that Rule 215 will be revised substantially within the foreseeable future.

(5) *Understanding Civil Procedure Rule 215.* Read Tex. R. Civ. P. 215. What kinds of sanctions are available to the trial court? What should the court consider in determining which sanction(s) to apply?

(6) In *Braden v. Downey*, 811 S.W.2d 922 (Tex. 1991), the court characterized the sanction of ordering the attorney to perform community service as "creative." It noted, however, that should the attorney wish to challenge the imposition of this type of sanction the trial court should defer the time for performance until after an opportunity to appeal.

(7) In *Firestone Photographs, Inc. v. Lamaster*, 567 S.W.2d 273 (Tex. App.—Texarkana 1978, no writ), the court ordered a defendant who refused to produce a witness for deposition to pay a daily fine (with the amount of the fine doubling periodically) for each day of noncompliance. When the case was called to trial, plaintiff waived all of the relief asked for in the petition and sought judgment for the accumulated sanctions, up to the amount originally sought by plaintiff. The court entered judgment for plaintiff for $65,245 in sanctions, plus attorney's fees. The court of appeals found this sanction to be within the discretion of the trial court.

## APPENDIX A, CHAPTER 10

## DISCUSSION PROBLEMS

Opal Allen was shopping at her neighborhood Alpha Omega Grocery Store. She shopped there regularly and knew the store well. On this particular occasion, while shopping in the produce department, Allen slipped and fell, breaking her wrist. She was taken by ambulance to the local hospital, where she was treated and released. Her injury was severe enough that she was unable to return to her job as a secretary for about a month, and she received no pay check during that period. She has now returned to work, but suffers from chronic pain in the injured wrist, and has permanently lost some mobility as well.

Considering the following discovery issues that might arise in a slip and fall case brought by Allen against Alpha Omega.

(1) You represent Allen. What discovery level will best meet your needs for information and your litigation budget? What steps will you take to try to establish the case at that level?

(2) You represent Alpha Omega. What discovery limits would you find appropriate for this lawsuit? If you are unhappy with the initial level, as determined by the pleadings, what steps can you take to change the discovery control plan to one that better suits your client's needs?

(3) You represent Alpha Omega. You have received a disclosure requests that reads, in part: "Pursuant to Rule 194, you are requested to disclose, within 30 days of service of this request, the information or material described in Rule 194.2(c)."

How much do you have to reveal about your basis for denying Allen's claim?

(4) You represent Alpha Omega. You were served with interrogatories one day before the day your Answer was due. How long do you have to answer those interrogatories?

(5) You represent Allen. You're concerned about the limits on discovery. You have always used interrogatories to get (cheaply) much of the information you need to prove your case. You would like to ask a separate interrogatory asking Alpha Omega to identify all documents relevant to each factual claim that it has made in its answer or its responses to the request for disclosure. Further, you would like to define "identify" to require Alpha Omega to list the documents individually, give the name, address, and phone number of the person who possesses that document, and specify the physical location of that document. How would such questions affect your interrogatory limit?

(6) You represent Allen. You have received a combination discovery request that consists of 50 requests for admission and two interrogatories. The interrogatories read:

> (a) For any request to admit that has not been unqualifiedly admitted, please identify all documents that form the basis of or otherwise relate to the denial or other answer.
>
> (b) For any request to admit that has not been unqualifiedly admitted, please state all facts that form the basis of or otherwise relate to the denial or other answer.

How many interrogatories is this? Do they all "count" against the 25 interrogatory limit? Do you see any other problems? What should you do?

(7) You represent Alpha Omega. You have received a document production request from Allen that, read fairly, requires production of a very damaging internal memo. You wish it were

privileged, but it is not. You would like to place it in the middle of a very large file full of grape invoices. Do the discovery rules allow that?

(8) You represent Alpha Omega. You have received a document production request from Allen that, read fairly, requires production of a memo written from the produce department manager to the produce clerks the week before Allen fell. You believe, probably incorrectly, that this memo is protected as work product. What steps do you have to take to avoid producing this document to Allen?

(9) You represent Brock O. Lee, a produce company delivery man. He delivered a large quantity of pre-bagged grapes to Alpha Omega on the day of Allen's fall. Lee has been served with a subpoena to produce all documents reflecting his delivery of grapes to Alpha Omega from 1990 to the present. One of these documents is a letter from his employer's lawyer to all delivery people describing possible company liability if the grapes are not properly handled. Lee never throws much of anything away, and has boxes of this stuff in his garage. However, he doesn't keep his business records separate from his personal records and it is all mixed up with old birthday cards, newspapers, and tax returns. Advise Lee on his possible responses to the subpoena.

(10) You represent Allen. You have received the following Request for Production of Documents from Alpha Omega: "Please produce any and all books, records, reports, or other documents in your possession, custody, or control that relate to Allen's claim in this case."

Any problems? What should you do?

(11) You represent Allen. You have learned from your neighbor, a former Alpha Omega employee, that Alpha Omega maintains an extensive national database: (1) describing every incident in which a customer has fallen in an Alpha Omega store; (2) identifying each Alpha Omega employee who has ever been reprimanded or discharged for failure to follow store safety policies; and (3) listing all products used by various Alpha Omega stores to maximize produce department safety. You would love to get at this information, and would be even more ecstatic if you could search it on your own computer. What will you do to maximize your chance of getting this information, and getting it in usable form?

(12) You represent Allen. In addition to suing Alpha Omega you have sued Produce R Us, the company that you believed manufactured the produce bins that allowed slippery fruit to fall to the floor. Before the statute of limitations ran, you sent Produce R Us a request to admit that they manufactured the bins in the Alpha Omega store in which Allen fell. They failed to respond. Now, after it is too late to sue anyone else, they have requested permission to withdraw the deemed admission. It turns out that the bins were actually manufactured by Grapes to Go, an unrelated entity. What will you argue to the judge in opposition to the Produce R Us motion for leave to withdraw the deemed admission?

(13) You represent Allen. You will be using expert witnesses at trial to testify about grocery store safety, about Allen's medical condition, and about her lost income. When are you required to submit them for deposition by Alpha Omega's attorneys? How will you decide whether to furnish reports (and how detailed those reports will be)? When must the materials identified in Rule 194.2(f)(4)(A) be produced? When will you get to learn about and depose Alpha Omega's experts?

(14) You represent Allen. Alpha Omega's lawyers have taken the deposition of the economist who will be your expert on lost income. He has sent you a substantial bill for his time in preparing for and giving the deposition. Mrs. Allen is quite poor. Who must pay this bill?

(15) Alpha Omega has brought a third-party action against FruitSafe, the company that manufactured the mats used on the floor in the produce section of this Alpha Omega store. If this case is proceeding under a Level 2 discovery control plan, how many hours of deposition time does each party get, and on what issues?

(16) Ruby Humphreys, another Alpha Omega customer, also slipped and fell in the same Alpha Omega store when trying to pull a grocery cart out of the stack. Humphreys has her own lawsuit pending against Alpha Omega. In that lawsuit, she took the deposition of Alpha Omega's national store design consultant. His testimony turned out to be very damaging to Alpha Omega. Unfortunately, the consultant has enlisted in the army and been sent to Kosovo. Allen would like to use the consultant's deposition testimony in the trial of her case. Should she be allowed to?

(17) The deposition of Allen's husband has been taken by videotape. Since his health is poor, it will be very difficult for him to testify at trial. The following exchanges are contained within the transcript of his deposition. You may assume that there were no agreements modifying the usual deposition rules. Do you see any problems?

1. Q (by Allen's lawyer): So, Mr. Allen, wouldn't you agree that your wife is in constant terrible pain?

A: Yes, I would agree with that.

2. Q (by Alpha Omega's lawyer): Mr. Allen, what has your lawyer told you about your probable success in this case?

A: My wife's lawyers say that slip and fall cases are hard to win.

3. Q (by Alpha Omega's lawyer): Mr. Allen, what did you tell your wife's lawyer about her symptoms?

Q (by Allen's lawyer): Objection. Attorney-client privilege.

Q (by Alpha Omega's lawyer): The court reporter isn't a judge, Mr. Allen, so please answer my question.

A (by witness): I told him that she can still mow the lawn, run the vacuum cleaner, and do the laundry.

(18) Allen v. Alpha Omega is now in the middle of trial. During discovery, Allen sent a request for disclosure including all of the topics allowed under Civil Procedure Rule 194. Alpha Omega provided a list of persons having knowledge of relevant facts, but did not include the name of Al Gebra, a customer who witnessed the accident. Alpha Omega's lawyer did orally mention Gebra to Allen's lawyer during a telephone conversation a couple of months before trial. Alpha Omega is now attempting to call Gebra as a witness at trial. Under what circumstances should the trial judge allow Gebra to testify?

(19) Alpha Omega's testifying expert was deposed about a month before trial. At that time he testified that he had not yet completed his analysis, but believed that Alpha Omega took adequate precautions to prevent falls. During the deposition, Allen's lawyer punched significant holes in the basis for that testimony. Now, at trial, the expert wants to testify about additional tests that he did between deposition and trial. Should he be allowed to testify about these tests and their effect on his opinion?

(20) Assume that the trial court allowed Gebra to testify. His testimony mirrored that of Hugh Cumber, an Alpha Omega employee. The jury found that Allen's negligence was 55 percent

responsible for her injuries, and thus she collects nothing. You represent Allen on appeal. What will you have to show to secure reversal on the ground that Gebra should not have been allowed to testify?

(21) Before trial, Allen's lawyer intended to take the deposition of Mack N. Tosh, another Alpha Omega Customer. He sent the proper notice of deposition to all parties. Unfortunately, he did not subpoena Tosh who, being unenthusiastic about this deposition thing, failed to show up to be deposed. The Alpha Omega lawyer, however, traveled from his office in the big city to Tosh's hometown, where the deposition was to be taken, and while he was traveling his hourly fee meter was running. What sanctions are available to Alpha Omega?

(22) When Kay Rett, the manager of the Alpha Omega store, was being deposed, she was asked the question: "Has anyone ever fallen in your produce department before?" She answered the question, "No," because she was mentally interpreting the phrase "produce department" to exclude the adjoining bakery. Allen's lawyer later learns from other sources that there have been three falls in the area where the fruit and bagel areas meet. Are any sanctions appropriate or available?

(23) There was another problem with Rett's deposition. She waited for about 30 seconds after each question was asked (apparently considering it carefully), asked for many words to be defined for her, talked *really* slowly, had numerous "off the record" conversations with Alpha Omega's attorney, fumbled through the documents needed to answer various questions, and generally ran out the clock. After six hours of this, Allen's attorney still had a number of questions he wanted to answer, but Alpha Omega's lawyer called time and terminated the deposition. Does Allen have any recourse?

(24) Alpha Omega sent interrogatories to Allen. She failed to answer interrogatory number 20, which read, "Please describe in detail anything you remember about the causes of your fall." Alpha Omega really wants this information. What can they do?

## APPENDIX B, CHAPTER 10

## THE USE OF DISCOVERY IN PRACTICE—PURPOSES, SCOPE, AND TECHNIQUES

The following materials pertain to two kinds of discovery devices—depositions and interrogatories. Their purpose is not merely to show you nitty-gritty aspects of discovery. Each item also raises interesting questions of relevance, privilege, and the scope and purposes of discovery. You should be considering these "abstract" matters at the same time that you review the mechanical aspects of the discovery process.

## CHECKLIST

### TAKING PLAINTIFF'S DEPOSITION

STATE BAR OF TEXAS, PRACTICE SKILLS COURSE

By Josh H. Groce, San Antonio, Texas*

This is not intended to be all-inclusive. Each case, of course, requires an interrogation indicated largely by the investigation file, but this is intended to give pointers that are sometimes overlooked.

1. Ask the (1) name; (2) social security number; (3) exact date of birth of the witness; (4) and whether he has ever gone under any other name; (5) or different spelling of the same name.
2. General history of the witness, including: (1) where he was born; (2) all places where he has lived; (3) names and location of (a) father; (b) mother; (c) brothers and (d) sisters; (4) education.
3. Marital history—(1) whether he is married or divorced; (2) where marriage or marriages took place; (3) and if divorced how many times; (4) how many children; (5) where former spouse or spouses can be located; (6) their maiden and present name; (7) and where divorce was granted.
4. (1) Description of the accident, letting witness first describe it in narrative form; (2) and then questioning him specifically; (3) condition of the street or other scene of accident; (4) weather condition.
5. Names and addresses of all witnesses known to plaintiff. Pin him down as to who saw the accident.
6. Whether or not any statements were made at the time of the accident or any admissions were made by any of the parties to the accident.
7. What occurred immediately after the accident; whether claimant went to the hospital and, if so, how.
8. Names and addresses of all doctors who have treated him prior and subsequent to the accident and who selected such doctors. He should identify his "family doctor," if he has one, and just what treatments for anything that he has received.

---

* Reprinted permission of the State Bar of Texas, Professional Development Program.

9. Have witness sign authorization in the following form: "All doctors who have treated me and all hospitals in which I have ever been a patient are hereby authorized to give to the bearer of this authorization or of any facsimile copy hereof, all information relative to my physical condition, past, present or future." This should be dated and signed by the witness and witnessed by his attorney.

10. Ask if claimant is willing to submit to a medical examination by doctors of defendant's selection and if not then will he agree to an examination by doctors selected by the court.

11. Ask witness whether he or any member of his family, as far as he knows, has ever had a claim for personal injury against any person, firm, corporation or governmental agency, and follow this up, depending upon the answer of the witness.

12. (1) Ask the witness whether he has ever had any previous accidents or injuries of any character; (2) any subsequent accidents or injuries to this one; (3) does he have any health and accident insurance paying money for prior injuries or the injury made the basis of this suit; (4) is he receiving any government benefits for disability, unemployment, etc. (5) has he applied for any jobs or insurance that required a physical examination either shortly before or at any time after the accident.

13. (1) Determine the nature of previous jobs; (2) how much he was making; (3) for whom he was working; (4) why employment was terminated; (5) what qualifications and experience the witness had for the type of work he was doing when injured; (6) and ask what income tax he paid, demand a copy of return; (7) inquire as to what work witness has done since accident, and describe just what his duties are or were; (8) determine his employers and earnings with particular care for the year preceding his injury.

14. (1) Definitely determine what part or parts of the witness' body were injured and eliminate all other portions; (2) if there is any particular member of the body injured, have him state what he can or cannot do with that particular member; (3) go into detail as to what witness can and cannot do. This becomes important when movies are used.

15. (1) Ask for his status during the last war; (2) where his draft board was, and (3) if he was turned down, why; (4) obtain a signed authorization permitting bearer to review his army records and examine his records at any Veterans' Administration hospital; (5) obtain his service serial number and Veterans Administration Claim Number for identification purposes.

16. Inquire whether witness has ever been arrested, indicted or convicted of felony or crime, offense or misdemeanor and whether or not he has ever been in jail or prison. Geographically locate where the offenses occurred.

17. In automobile cases (1) obtain his drivers license number; (2) ask if his license has ever been revoked, suspended or put on probation together with details; (3) ask for history of all prior automobile accidents and moving traffic violations.

18. Explain to plaintiff that the purpose of the deposition is to bring out all the relevant facts from the plaintiff's standpoint and then ask: "Is there any other fact relevant to this matter about which I have not asked but which might have a bearing on this case?"

## NOTES AND QUESTIONS

(1) Consider the last item on the above checklist (the inquiry as to whether there is "any other fact relevant to this matter"). Imagine that you represent the plaintiff who is being deposed and that this question is asked of him in your presence. What would you do? (Hint: if you have interviewed the plaintiff yourself and discussed the case with him, what is the probable source of answers he would likely give as to what is "relevant?" Isn't there a difference between asking a litigant to state a relevant fact and asking a litigant to judge whether any "relevant" fact is left out?) If you decide that this question is outside the bounds of discovery, on what ground? How would you enforce your rights in this situation?

(2) Aside from the last item on the checklist (the general inquiry into "any other relevant fact"), are there other items on the checklist that you would consider outside the bounds of discovery if you represented the deponent?

(3) What happens if a question is asked that is outside the bounds of discovery but the deponent's attorney does nothing? What happens if there is a genuine difference of opinion between the two attorneys as the proper bounds (as there may be with several items here?)

(4) What is the relevance of questions about deponent's family? Education? Military history? Whether he has ever been in jail? Are all of these items discoverable?

(5) How does the substantive law control or influence the nature of the examination?

(6) In connection with the inquiry into the accident or event itself, the writer advises the examiner to let the "witness first describe it in narrative form." Only after that is done does the writer advise "questioning him specifically." Why? What would be lost if the examiner began with pointed questions of a leading nature? How will this examination differ from the cross-examination of this witness at trial (would a skillful cross-examiner simply ask the witness to describe the accident in his or her own words)? What does this tell you about the aims and goals of taking a deposition?

(7) Suppose you are trying to get the witness to describe the accident "in narrative form," as the writer here advises, and the witness responds with a brief and incomplete statement. What would you do? Would you then go to pointed and specific questions, or would you try again to get a complete narrative (and if so, by what techniques)?

(8) Notice that there is an effort to find out about all witnesses, statements, or other sources of information. Why?

(9) Try to describe all the purposes or goals the writer's advice might achieve. Compare the advice given against the statement of purposes of discovery that began this chapter.

(10) The following is an actual deposition taken in the case of *Obiedio v. J. Weingarten, Inc.* You have seen the pre-litigation documents and pleadings in previous chapters. Analyze the scope, purposes and techniques of examination in light of what you have learned from this checklist and from this chapter.

---

## SAMPLE DEPOSITION

(Taken from D. Crump, *The Anatomy of a Civil Case: Obiedio v. J. Weingarten, Inc.* (1977))*

In approximately early April of 1971, Mr. Thompson and Mr. Elder, by telephone, agreed at Mr. Thompson's request to a date for the taking of Mrs. Obiedio's deposition. As a result of that conversation, Mr. Thompson sent the following LETTER CONFIRMING DEPOSITION SCHEDULE:

April 8, 1971

Mr. Elder
301 Houston First Savings Building
Houston, Texas 77002

Re: Delfina Obiedio
vs.
J. Weingarten, Inc.

Dear Steve:

This will confirm our agreement to take Mrs. Obiedio's deposition in your office at 3:00 P. M. on May 6, 1971.

I will furnish the court reporter.

Very truly yours,

VINSON, ELKINS, SEARLS & SMITH
By ____________________
Raybourne Thompson, Jr.

cc: Boland & O'Neal

Mr. Elder, by letter, replied that "I will see you on the 6th."

NO. 862,428

DELFINA OBIEDIO ) IN THE DISTRICT COURT OF
VS. ) HARRIS COUNTY, TEXAS
J. WEINGARTEN, INC. ) F-125TH JUDICIAL DISTRICT

DEPOSITIONS OF DELFINA OBIEDIO AND HENRY OBIEDIO

On the 6th day of May, 1971, at the offices of Stephen T. Elder, 301 Houston First Savings Building, Houston, Harris County, Texas, Delfina Obiedio and Henry Obiedio appeared before me, Howard J. Boland, a notary public of Harris County, Texas, and being by me first duly sworn, testified by their oral depositions as hereinafter set out, pursuant to agreement of counsel for the respective parties that:

---

All formalities precedent to and incident to the taking and return of the depositions were waived; without making any objection at the time of taking, either party to the suit should have the right at the time of trial to urge objections to questions or answers appearing in the depositions;

The depositions might be filed in court unsigned, the signatures of the witnesses being waived.

DEPOSITION OF DELFINA OBIEDIO

EXAMINATION BY MR. THOMPSON:

Q: Would you state your full name, please, ma'am?

A: Delfina Obiedio.

Q: How old a lady are you, Mrs. Obiedio?

A: 60 right now.

Q: Mrs. Obiedio, my name is Ray Thompson, and I represent Weingarten's in this suit that you filed against them. Do you understand that?

A: Yes, sir.

Q: I am going to ask you some questions. If you don't understand any question, please stop me and I'll be happy to repeat it. If you do understand my question, I'll expect you to go ahead and answer it accordingly.

Has your attorney explained to you what a deposition is?

A: Yes.

Q: You understand that testimony that you give here today is subject to the same pains and penalties for perjury as if you were testifying in a court of law before a judge and jury; do you understand that?

A: Yes, sir.

Q: This gentleman here is taking down your testimony in writing, so that he is not able to look at you. So don't shake your head yes or no but answer yes or no so that we can get it down on paper. All right?

A: Okay.

Q: Where do you presently live, Mrs. Obiedio?

A: 3906 Citte.

Q: Okay. How long have you lived at that address, Mrs. Obiedio?

A: A year.

Q: Where did you live before that?

A: 1003 James.

Q: Is that in Houston, too?

A: Yes, sir.

Q: How many children do you have?

A: One daughter.

Q: What is your husband's name?

A: Henry.

Q: How long have you been married to Henry Obiedio?

A: 27 years.

Q: Is this your only marriage?

A: Yes, sir.

Q: How much education do you have?

A: I went through junior school.

Q: Went through junior high school?

A: Uh-huh.

Q: Are you presently employed?

A: No, sir.

Q: When was the last time that you were employed?

A: '46.

Q: What have you been doing since 1946, just been a housewife?

A: That's right.

Q: What is your daughter's name?

A: Thelma Ramirez.

Q: Does she live here in Houston?

A: Yes, sir.

Q: What's her address?

A: I can't remember her address right now, sir.

Q: What is her husband's name?

A: Lupe.

Q: Have you ever had your deposition taken before?

A: No, sir.

Q: Have you ever made any claim against anyone for any sort of injuries or anything of this nature before this claim?

A: Yes, I did one time.

Q: Tell me about that, please.

A: That was when I hurt my leg.

Q: Where did you hurt your leg?

A: In Weingarten's, the same store.

Q: When was that?

A: I don't remember what year it was. It's been a long time.

Q: Did you file a lawsuit?

A: Yes, sir.

Q: Was the case tried or settled?

A: It was settled in the lawyer's office.

Q: Was it 10 years ago or more?

A: It's more than 10 years.

Q: On what date did this present accident happen?

A: On May 7th 1969.

Q: Have you ever made claim against anyone other than Weingarten's?

A: No, sir.

Q: Have you ever been involved in an automobile accident or anything like that that you made a claim for?

A: No, sir.

Q: Do you drive a car?

A: No, sir.

Q: What day of the week was May 7th 1969?

A: It was a Thursday.

Q: Why were you in the store?

A: I was doing—going to do our shopping.

Q: Had you done your shopping or were you starting?

A: I was going to get a basket to do some shopping when it happened.

Q: Tell me what happened.

A: I walked in the store, and I was going to get my basket. And they was all stuck together. And I pulled with my right hand and they were all, at the beginning—

Q: In other words, they were inside each other, like they stack them?

A: Yes. And I pulled with my right hand. Here come three or four baskets and they pushed me down. And I put my right hand on the floor to think to keep from falling down, and that was when I broke my hand.

Q: Let me back up for just a minute and run through this piece by piece here.

You came into the store and you went through the turnstile, didn't you?

A: Yes, sir.

Q: And you went over to where they stack the baskets?

A: That's right.

Q: And these baskets are stuck one inside each other, they stack them?

A: Uh-huh.

Q: And you reached over with your hand?

A: With my right hand.

Q: Right hand. To pull the basket loose?

A: Yes, sir.

Q: And about three or four baskets came out, and the basket ran over you and you lost your balance, is that right?

A: That's right, yes.

Q: And you fell down, and when you landed, you landed—

A: On my right hand.

Q: —on your right hand?

A: The first thing I knew, my hand was turned backwards and was all purple and I was just in pain. I couldn't stand it! I went through a lot of pain.

Q: Do you know why the baskets stuck together?

A: Sir?

Q: Do you know why the baskets stuck together?

A: No. In the beginning they have all baskets there, sir.

Q: They always stack them in the same way inside each other?

A: Yes.

Q: And you have shopped in that store every week, haven't you?

A: Yes.

Q: And every week when you go in there, the baskets are stacked in the same way?

A: Yes, sir.

Q: And this was no different; they were stacked in the same way, inside each other?

A: But they were too tight. And I just lost my balance and the baskets came toward my body.

Q: The only difference between this time and any other time that you'd been in the store and getting a basket was when you pulled this time about two or three or four baskets came out instead of just one; isn't that right?

A: Yes. sir.

Q: That's the only difference?

A: Yes.

Q: And you don't have any idea why the two or three or four of them stayed together?

A: No, sir.

Q: Was there anything else that caused you to fall other than these baskets?

A: It had rained that day, and the floor was kind of damp and that was what made me fell down, too.

Q: The floor was wet?

A: Yes. Kind of damp. Not exactly wet, but damp, people going in and out.

Q: People were walking in and out and it was raining that day?

A: It wasn't raining when I went in, but it had rained that day.

Q: You testified, I believe, that these baskets kind of made you lose your balance and you fell because the baskets made you lose your balance?

A: Yes.

Q: Did your feet slip?

A: No. I slipped after the basket pushed me down.

Q: So, then, the water on the floor really didn't cause you to fall; the baskets caused you to fall?

A: Yes, you can say the baskets.

Q: And you have already testified, Mrs. Obiedio, that you didn't slip, that you lost your balance when you pulled these baskets out and about three or four baskets came out at you?

A: Yes.

Q: And that is what caused you to fall and land on the floor?

A: Yes.

Q: You said that the floor was kind of damp?

A: Yes, sir.

Q: Can you describe it any more than that "just kind of damp"?

A: No. Just kind of damp. That's all I can tell you.

Q: You didn't look at the floor to determine whether it was dirty or clean or anything like that?

A: No. I was concerned about my hand, that's all, my hand, the way it was.

Q: Outside was damp; isn't this correct?

A: Yes.

Q: Because it had just stopped raining?

A: Yes, sir.

Q: But you wouldn't have fallen if the baskets the three or four baskets, had not come out?

A: No, sir.

Q: That was what caused you to fall?

A: Yes, sir.

Q: Did you ever make any sort of inspection of the baskets?

A: No, sir.

Q: Were you taken to the doctor?

A: Dr. Elliott at Memorial Hospital.

Q: Had you been to Dr. Elliott before?

A: Yes, sir.

Q: When had you been to Dr. Elliott before?

A: When I had that fall.

Q: Who sent you to Dr. Elliott?

A: I went on my own.

Q: Who recommended Dr. Elliott when you had that fall?

A: A friend of mine.

Q: All right. Who is the friend?

A: I couldn't remember, sir.

Q: It was not your lawyer?

A: No, sir.

[At this point, Mr. Thompson asked a number of questions as to when the witness saw Dr. Elliott, when he released her, how often she went to see him, what hospitals she was in, and the like. The witness's testimony, in substance, was that she went every week during the first month after the accident; then the doctor removed the cast and found her hand and arm swelling and put her in the hospital for two weeks at Memorial Baptist Hospital in downtown Houston. Thereafter, she continued to see the doctor every "two months or every three weeks." She ceased to see Dr. Elliott when he released her. The witness stated, "I can't remember" whether the release date was one year ago or three.]

Q: Do you know how much your medical bills have been?

A: Yes. I got them over here in my purse, the bills.

Q: Will you look at them and see how much they are?

A: Dr. Elliott is 285 and Dr. Brady is $96.00.

Q: That was the X-ray doctor or the anesthesiologist?

A: The one that give me some kind of shot in my arm to get the swelling out.

Q: And that was $85?

A: No. $96.

Q: $96.

A: And the hospital, my insurance paid some, and the balance is $696.30.

Q: Do you know how much your insurance paid?

A: Sir?

Q: Do you know how much your insurance paid?

A: 85—$89.25. That was all my insurance paid.

Q: So, your total hospital bill was in the amount of about $785?

A: Yes. And the balance is $696.30. And then for the first night I went in the hospital it was $95.25 when I broke my hand. Dr. Elliott kept me that night overnight in the hospital.

Q: Did your insurance pay any portion of Dr. Elliott's bill?

A: A hundred.

Q: The $285 you gave me, is that the balance?

A: That's the balance.

Q: Well, did your insurance pay any amount of Dr. Brady's bill?

A: No, sir.

Q: And did your insurance pay any amount of the first hospital bill?

A: No, sir.

Q: Is this all of your bills?

A: That's right.

Q: And you have any other out-of-pocket expenses other than Dr. Elliott's and Dr. Brady's and those hospital bills?

A: No. Except my husband taking a lot of days off to take me to the doctor. He used to take off from work and didn't get no pay.

[Here, Mr. Thompson asks questions to pin down the employment and wage rate of the witness's husband. The witness states that her husband works at Paramount Floor Company and that company would have records of his employment. He earns $3.25 per hour. He is a floor finisher. When she went to the hospital, the witness testifies, her husband would lose a day's work and wages.]

Q: And you haven't seen any doctors other than Dr. Brady and Dr. Elliott?

A: No, sir.

Q: You were speaking a moment ago of dampness on the floor. Do you know how long this dampness had been on the floor?

[Here Mr. Thompson established that the dampness was caused by people walking in with wet shoes; that the witness herself walked outside where it was wet before coming in, though "not too much;" that the witness "would drag some of this wetness in, wouldn't you?" "Yes, sir;" and that the witness had no idea how long the dampness had been there and didn't know how it could have gotten there other than by customers tracking it in.]

Q: But, Mrs. Obiedio, as I understand your testimony, you did not slip; you lost your balance because of these buggies; isn't that right?

A: Yes, sir.

Q: So this damp floor didn't have anything to do with your falling, did it?

A: No.

Q: Was anyone with you in the store that day?

A: No, I went in by myself.

Q: Mrs. Obiedio, when you go into the Weingarten store, as you walk into where the buggy area is, you go through a turnstile, don't you, or turntable?

. . . .

Q: When you check out of the store, Mrs. Obiedio—not this time but on previous occasions when you have shopped there—you get a basket; what do you do when you get to the check-out area and you don't need the basket? Don't you take and put the stuff down on the counter and push your basket over into the basket area?

A: No, sir. We always leave it right there by the checker and the boy came and get all the baskets.

Q: The boys come and get all the baskets?

A: Yes, the boys work in the store.

Q: Have you ever seen customers putting baskets in and taking baskets out of the area where the baskets are kept?

A: Well, I haven't noticed that.

Q: You haven't noticed that?

A: No, sir.

Q: They could; you just haven't noticed it; is that correct?

A: Well, I don't know.

Q: Now, is it your testimony that you pulled the basket with your right hand and then placed your right hand down and it broke it?

A: Yes, sir.

Q: You didn't pull the baskets with your left hand?

A: No. I pulled it with my right hand.

Q: Were you looking at the baskets when you pulled them?

A: Yes, sir, I was.

Q: Were you stopped?

A: Yes, sir.

Q: Was there anyone else around you that came up to you and tried to help you?

A: No, sir, there was nobody there.

Q: There was nobody in the immediate area that saw the fall?

A: No, sir, I don't think so. I didn't see anybody there, sir.

Q: And I believe you have already testified you don't know what caused the buggies to stick together?

A: Well, you can put it that way.

Q: Do you know what caused them to stick together?

A: Well, they were just all stuck together, that's all I can explain to you.

Q: In other words, you don't know why they were stuck together?

A: No, sir.

Q: They were just stuck together?

A: Yes.

Q: And three or four of them came out when you pulled?

A: That's right.

Q: You didn't see them tied together or anything like that?

A: No, I didn't see whether they were tied or what, sir.

[Here Mr. Thompson asked whether the witness had "ever had any trouble with the police" ("No, sir"); had a social security number (she did, but did not have the card or know the number); had a driver's license (No); had any hobbies, either before or after the accident ("No, sir"); knew how much time her husband had missed from work taking her to the doctor ("No, sir"); and finally, whether she had understood his questions ("Yes, sir").]

MR. THOMPSON: I don't have anything further.

Let me ask a couple of Mr. Obiedio.

DEPOSITION OF HENRY OBIEDIO

EXAMINATION BY MR. THOMPSON:

[The deposition of Henry Obiedio was considerably shorter than that of Ms. Obiedio; it occupies only three pages of type. Mr. Thompson asked questions about the work the witness did, how long he had been employed, where the company was located, how much time he lost from work, whether he was docked, how many hours a day he worked, what hours those were, whether he got a vacation, whether the work was steady, whether his employment and pay depended upon the business the company had, whether he or his wife had incurred any other bills or losses than those already mentioned, and whether the witness had ever had any lawsuits or claims. The witness testified that he worked at Paramount Floor Co. at 4701 Fulton, had worked there 11 years, had lost about a week and "when I am off, like today I'm off on account of this, I ain't getting paid." He further stated that he worked steady, though it depended upon the volume of business, and he worked "52 weeks a year" with no vacation, from 7:30 a.m. to 4 p.m. The bills and losses mentioned, he said, were the only ones, and he had never had a claim or suit.] [Following the deposition of Mr. Obiedio, Mr. Elder, the plaintiffs' attorney, resumed the deposition of Ms. Obiedio to ask his own questions, as follows.]

DELFINA OBIEDIO

EXAMINATION BY MR. ELDER:

Q: Mrs. Obiedio, what is the main use of those carts that you were talking about?

A: You mean those wagons?

Q: Yes.

A: Well, they were all kind of stuck up together.

Q: No. No. No. What's the main use of them, the main function you saw them being put to in the store?

A: Could you repeat that question?

Q: Weren't those carts primarily to carry groceries inside the store?

A: Well, sometimes the people leave them outside.

Q: But the primary function—did you ever see them taken outside?

A: Yes.

Q: Did you ever see them taken outside onto the parking lot?

A: Yes. Some of the kids take them outside and play with them.

. . . .

Q: Did you ever see anyone abandon a cart out there and leave it out in the parking lot?

A: I see a lot of people.

Q: Did you ever see these grocery baskets anywhere else in the neighborhood?

A: Yes. Around the neighborhood. Over there in January there was wagons all over the street down there. Especially on weekends. The kids would be playing with them up and down the street.

Q: You saw kids playing with the wagons?

A: Yes.

Q: What sort of games would they play with them?

A: Running them up and down the street.

Q: Did they ever run them into each other?

A: Yes.

Q: Did they ever fall down with them?

A: No. I watch them outside.

Q: Did you ever see one of the baskets falling down, laying on its side?

A: Yes, sir.

. . . .

Q: How long had you and your family been shopping there?

A: About 10 or 11 years.

Q: During that 10 or 11 years, had they used the same carts?

A: Yes, sir.

Q: Did you ever notice that the carts were bent?

A: Sometimes. I didn't pay any attention.

Q: Did you ever notice the carts were in less than perfect condition?

A: Yes, sir, because the wheel would go this way and that way, wouldn't go straight.

Q: So, it would be fair to say that the carts were pretty old and rundown?

A: That's right.

Q: And in all that time, Mrs. Obiedio, did you ever know Weingarten's to replace any of the carts?

A: Not in that store.

Q: Did you ever know them to repair any of the carts?

A: No, sir.

Q: Had you ever before had them to break loose in a whole row like this time when three or four carts came loose at once? Had they ever happened to you before?

A: No, sir, that's the first time it ever happened to me like that.

MR. ELDER: That's all.

EXAMINATION BY MR. THOMPSON:

Q: Mrs. Obiedio, you never saw Weingarten's repairing the carts; this is your testimony?

A: Yes. Not in that store.

Q: You wouldn't know whether they repaired them or not, would you?

A: No, sir.

MR. THOMPSON: I don't have anything further.

[END OF DEPOSITIONS. The reporter's notes reflect the waiver of signatures. On the next page is the reporter's certificate that the transcript was dictated and transcribed from his shorthand under his supervision and is a correct record of the proceedings.]

## NOTES AND QUESTIONS

(1) Discuss the use of the following techniques or tactics in the examination:

(a) Asking the witness a general question calling for a narrative, followed up by more specific questions.

(b) Repetition.

(c) Leading questions.

(d) Discovery regarding damages as a separate item from liability.

(e) Methods of dealing with ambiguous answers or answers in which the witness has apparently failed to understand the question.

(f) Making sure the witness knows the nature of the proceeding and that this knowledge is on the record.

(g) Getting the witness to talk freely. (Was this done well?)

(2) Ordinarily, one does not depose one's own client. In this instance, Mr. Elder asked a few, brief, leading questions of his client. Why do you suppose he did so? (Hint: if the record were left in the state it was in when Mr. Thompson finished his examination—with the witness having said that she did not see the baskets and knew of no one who saw them, and that the damp floor had nothing to do with the fall—what might Thompson have done at the pretrial stage to dispose of the case by a favorable judgment? Would the record have supported him? Do Elder's questions prevent Thompson from doing so?)

(3) Discuss the relevance and discoverability of the following subjects inquired into:

(a) Ms. Obiedio's past, including her education.

(b) Ms. Obiedio's daughter's name and address.

(c) Ms. Obiedio's having filed a previous lawsuit against Weingarten (note that the prior claim is not admissible in evidence at trial).

## PREPARING A CLIENT TO BE DEPOSED

From what you have read thus far, you should have gathered that the best way to get information from an opposing party is the deposition. It is also the best way to derogate the credibility of an opposing party. A skillful deposer can obtain information from a witness, even if the witness is truthful, tending to embarrass the witness at trial—for the simple reason that no one has a perfect memory. Ambiguities in language also tend to create credibility difficulties with truthful witnesses. Therefore, the question arises: what does one do to prepare a client to be deposed?

The preparation of a client for deposition is as much an art as taking a deposition. The opponent is an educated and trained lawyer; the client often is less than articulate. The following ideas may help:

(a) Explain to the witness the purpose of the taking of the deposition. It is to help the other side, not the client.

(b) Anticipate the areas of questions, tell the client what you anticipate, and discuss the answers he or she gives.

(c) Explain how questions are asked—general questions, leading questions, and the like.

(d) Give the client specific advice on the deposition procedure, on how to act and on the format that questions and answers should take. Simulation is helpful and appropriate.

(e) Be express and emphatic in advising the client to tell the truth.

Many litigators give their clients written advice. The following, used by the law office of Montgomery & Lee, is a sample. What additions or modifications might you make to it?

MONTGOMERY & LEE
ATTORNEYS AT LAW
5512 CHAUCER
HOUSTON, TX 77005
(713) 528-2878

**Your Deposition**

**What is a Deposition?**

In its simplest form, a deposition is the oral testimony of a witness, taken under oath, before trial. The basic rule is that the questions asked need only address themselves to information which is relevant to the case or to discovering relevant facts. The rules by which Texas courts operate allow either side in a law suit to take a deposition of the other side and/or of any witness. Your deposition may be taken in our office, the office of the opposing attorney, a courtroom, or some other place. We will tell you where to be and when. There will be no judge present. However, what you say *will* be recorded, either by shorthand, court reporter, or perhaps videotape. We represent you in this important matter, but it is *your* deposition. We cannot answer the questions for you, and depending upon how you answer the questions and your attitude, your truthfulness, and your appearance, *your* case will be helped or hurt!

You can help us, but more importantly you can help yourself, by reading the following *carefully:*

**Purpose**

Why is your deposition being taken? That's simple—the opposing side wants to "pick your mind!" They want to find out what facts you know regarding this law suit and they want to pin you down to a specific story. If you answer a question one way during the deposition and another way during the trial, you will make it very difficult for us to help you. So we can avoid such difficulties, here are a few "DOs" and "DON'Ts" to remember:

1. DON'T hurry—DO take your time answering all questions; speak slowly and clearly.
2. DON'T volunteer—DO answer the question you are asked and *stop* talking. Never try to explain your answer. If you can answer "yes" or "no," do so and *stop.*
3. DON'T get excited or angry—DO relax and listen calmly. The opposing attorney may try to make you angry in hopes you will say something you will regret later (like at trial!).

4. DON'T guess—which means don't speculate; don't give your "opinion;" and don't estimate things like time, speed, or distance unless you have a good reason for knowing such matters. DO stick to the basic facts and testify only to that which you *personally* know.

5. DON'T fib—which is a nice way of saying *don't lie!* (DO believe us when we say the truth, in a law suit, never is as damaging as a lie!)

6. DON'T joke—while you may think a particular question or a possible answer to a question is cute or funny, we doubt you think your law suit is funny. DO treat the whole deposition seriously.

7. DON'T memorize—DO just answer the questions to the best of your ability.

8. DON'T worry—especially if you honestly don't know the answer to a question. If you don't, then admit it with the simple response, "I don't know."

9. DON'T be chummy—either with the opponents or their attorneys, before, during, and after the deposition. DO be on guard. Remember, the *other* attorney is your "legal enemy." Do not let his friendly manner cause you to drop your guard or become chatty. A deposition is *not* a social event!

10. DON'T magnify your injuries or losses. DO be conservative in describing them, but don't leave any out.

### Your Attitude & Appearance

The first opportunity the opposing attorney has to see you usually comes at the deposition. He or she will use the occasion to try and size up you and your case. Therefore, it is important that you make a good impression, you should prepare as if you were going to trial, and that means *you should:*

1. Be clean and neat and wear clean and neat clothing.
2. Treat all persons in the deposition room with respect.
3. Come prepared to exhibit any and all injuries which you have suffered.
4. Bring facts and figures with respect to the time you lost from work, amount of wages lost, doctor bills, hospital bills, and any other information pertaining to your law suit.

---

## SAMPLE INTERROGATORIES

The following interrogatories, used by Houston attorney Michael Bell of the firm of Baker, Brown, Sharman, Wise & Stephens, concern a wrongful death case in which plaintiff's decedent's automobile was struck by a truck driven by defendant's driver when it turned suddenly into the lane of oncoming traffic. A first set of interrogatories had already been sent, followed by the deposition of defendant's driver. That deposition disclosed that the driver had a record of traffic offenses and convictions. It also disclosed the driver's contention that the brakes on defendant's truck failed immediately before the collision.

Defendant's answers to this second set of interrogatories, which are a follow-up to the deposition, are inserted in the interrogatories themselves, after each question. Several are objected to.

As you read the interrogatories and answers, you should bear in mind the following questions:

1. What are the strategies of each side in drafting and answering each question?
2. What controls the choice of discovery method used?
3. What is the relevance of each of the requested items?
4. What privileges are expressly asserted? What others, if any, might be argued? What is your evaluation of the merits of the privileges?
5. Assume (as was the fact) that inspection of the brakes was done after the incident at the instance of defendant or its insurers. Assume further that the brakes have since been serviced, rendering inspection by the plaintiff impossible. Do these further facts affect the discoverability of the information? Should they? If the information is nondiscoverable, what tactics would you think the plaintiff might consider at trial with reference to the brake inspection and repair?

NO. 78-2788

| | | |
|---|---|---|
| LAVOIS LOFTON | ) | IN THE DISTRICT COURT OF |
| v. | ) | HARRIS COUNTY, TEXAS |
| MARKLE STEEL COMPANY | ) | 61st JUDICIAL DISTRICT |
| ET AL | ) | |

PLAINTIFF'S SECOND INTERROGATORIES

TO: MARKLE STEEL COMPANY,
by and through its attorneys of record . . .:

Pursuant to Rule 197 of the Texas Rules of Civil Procedure, LAVOIS LOFTON, Plaintiff herein, files the following Second Interrogatories to Markle Steel Company, one of the Defendants herein, and advises that such answers must be made separately, fully, completely and under oath. Plaintiff further advises that said answers should be furnished to Plaintiff, by and through her attorney of record, within thirty (30) days from the date hereof.

As used herein, the term "subject accident" refers to the accident which occurred on January 4, 1978 on U. S. Highway 90 in Harris County, Texas, between a vehicle being driven by Robert Lofton and a tractor-trailer being driven by James Miller, Sr., as more particularly described in Plaintiff's Original Petition on file herein.

As used herein, the term "tractor-trailer vehicle" shall refer to a 1969 Chevrolet model L-60, identification number C639T805481, license plate number 2DB-557 and the trailer which was attached to the tractor at the time of the subject accident, having license plate number Z19-32.

As used herein the term "you" shall refer to Markle Steel Company, its employees, officers, directors, shareholders, attorneys, insurers, agents or representatives.

1. Have you or any person or entity acting on your behalf made any investigation of any kind regarding the subject accident?

[Objection—This is privileged and work product.]

2. If your answer to the above interrogatory is yes, please state the following:

[Objection—This is privileged and work product.]

a. The names, job titles, and current addresses of all persons participating to any extent in such investigation.

b. The names and addresses of all persons who were interviewed in connection with such investigation.

c. The description of any and all documentation which was reviewed in connection with such investigation.

d. A description of any and all property of any kind which was inspected and/or examined in connection with such investigation.

e. Whether a written report or summary of any such investigation was prepared.

f. If your answer to the above interrogatory 2(e) is yes, will you attach a copy of any such written report to your answers without the necessity of a motion to compel?

g. If your answer to the above interrogatory 2(e) is no, please set forth in detail the substance of the findings of the investigation.

3. Please list the factors which you consider in attempting to determine whether you should employ a job applicant as a truck driver. [Experience, work habits, personal interview, substance of driving record recommendations, desires of driver and information listed on the application.]

4. Do you maintain any written pamphlets, rules, regulations, books or documents of any kind setting forth your criteria for hiring truck drivers? If you will agree to produce any such written material without a formal motion, please attach same to these interrogatories. [No. We do pass out to our personnel information from Hartford Insurance Company. We do not retain a file on this and, therefore, do not have copies. We also post safety posters.]

5. Please state the name and current address of your employee who was responsible for hiring truck drivers as of January 1, 1974. If such person is no longer employed by you in such capacity, please state the name and address of each person so employed from 1974 to the present.

[Roger T. Kircus, 2517 Patricia Manor, Houston, Texas 77012; Mr. Walter B. Abbott, Markle Steel; Brooks Williams, Markle Steel]

6. Please state whether or not your truck driver employees received any driver education, instruction or courses prior to or during their performance of job duties with your company.

[Yes.]

7. If your answer to the above interrogatory is yes, please state the following:

a. Describe in detail the particular type of training or education received by such truck drivers. [Road test; Questionnaire concerning driving habits and government rules and regulations; distribution information for Hartford Insurance Company; instruction concerning use of various equipment.]

b. Are written documents or materials of any kind distributed to the truck drivers in connection with their driver education or training? If so, will you agree to attach such materials to your answers to these interrogatories without a formal motion to produce? [Yes. See No. 4 and No. 7(a) above.]

c. If there are no such written materials, please describe the specific method for instructing your drivers on driving tractor-trailer vehicles. [See No. 4 and No. 7 above.]

8. Do you maintain any rules and regulations governing job performance of your truck drivers? If so please state: [Yes.]

a. Whether such rules and regulations are in written form and, if you will do so without a motion to produce, attach copies hereto. [No.]

b. The substance of any such rules and regulations, including the particular rules or regulations and the sanctions available for enforcing such rules and regulations. [Basic common sense rules of operation plus daily driving record of drivers.]

9. Please state, by name and address, each and every location where the tractor-trailer in question was taken following the accident. If any work of any kind was performed on the tractor-trailer please describe the nature of such work and the name and address of the person performing same. [Taken from scene to Bryant Auto Parts & Service by wrecker, 4806 Highway 90 at Crosby, Texas. Then was taken to Markle Steel, 1709 Delano, Houston, Texas. 77003 by Bratten Wrecker Service and Roger T. Kircus. Tractor sold to Jesse Finch unrepaired. Trailer still in use by Markle Steel.]

10. Please state whether or not the tractor-trailer vehicle is currently in service for you. If so, please state the date when the tractor-trailer returned to service and the person or persons who have been assigned to drive it since the accident in question.

[Answer: *See* No. 9 above. Trailer put in use day following accident.]

. . . .

---

## SAMPLE MOTION TO QUASH SUBPOENA

The following motion, which is similar in effect to a Motion for Protective Order, is directed to the discretion of the court. As you read the motion, consider the legal standard by which the judge should decide the motion (hint: the standard may be vague), the strategies of each side and the appropriate ruling on the merits.

CAUSE NO. 1,152,525

| | | |
|---|---|---|
| NANETTE ENTZMINGER, | ) | |
| A WIDOW, ET AL. | ) | IN THE DISTRICT COURT OF |
| VS. | ) | HARRIS COUNTY, TEXAS |
| GENERAL AMERICAN | ) | 55TH JUDICIAL DISTRICT |
| TRANSPORTATION | ) | |
| COMPANY, ET AL. | | |

MOTION TO QUASH THE ORAL DEPOSITIONS OF JOE WOOD, EDWARD L. JENKINS, JAMES E. JENNINGS, NEIL D. LEECH, JOHN WISE AND KENNETH SARKEY

To the Honorable Judge of said Court:

THE BENDIX CORPORATION, one of the Defendants herein, files this its motion to quash the taking of certain oral depositions by Plaintiffs set for May 24–25, 1978 at the Federal Courthouse at Tinker Air Force Base, Oklahoma and in support of this motion would respectfully show this Honorable Court the following:

I.

This is a lawsuit arising out of the crash of a jet aircraft at Ellington Air Force Base on February 18, 1976, resulting in the death of the two crewmen aboard the aircraft. This Defendant is one of 19 Defendants sued in connection with the claims that one or more of the products supplied by one or more of these Defendants was involved in the cause of the crash. Plaintiffs have sued all of the Defendants based on negligence and strict tort liability.

II.

On April 13, 1978 this Defendant served interrogatories to the Plaintiffs providing for answers to the interrogatories within thirty-three (33) days of date of service. The interrogatories were received by counsel for Plaintiffs on April 14, 1978. The Plaintiffs have not objected to this Defendant's interrogatories and have wholly failed to respond to the interrogatories within the prescribed time period. These interrogatories are extremely important to this Defendant in order to properly investigate the case and to prepare for depositions of any witnesses in connection with the accident. Defendant's interrogatories are designed to determine, inter alia, the Bendix product in question, the alleged "defect" thereof, and the involvement, if any, of the Defendant Bendix in this matter.

III.

The Plaintiffs noticed the taking of the oral depositions of Joe Wood, Edward L. Jenkins, James E. Jennings, Neil D. Leech, John Wise and Kenneth Sarkey by giving notice to this Defendant on May 13, 1978. This defendant says that it cannot properly prepare for participation in the taking of these depositions without the benefit of answers to its previously filed interrogatories to the Plaintiffs. It would be extremely unfair and burdensome to require this Defendant to participate in the taking of depositions of witnesses without the benefit of key information which would be available if its interrogatories were answered.

WHEREFORE, Premises Considered, this Defendant prays that Plaintiff's notice to take the oral depositions of the individuals enumerated be quashed and for such other and further relief as the Court may deem appropriate under all the circumstances.

Respectfully submitted,
[Signature block]

# CHAPTER 11

## DISPOSITION WITHOUT TRIAL

### SCOPE

This chapter covers the disposition of a case without a trial. Procedures discussed include judgment by default, dismissal for want of prosecution, summary judgment, settlement, nonsuits, and consent judgments. "Mary Carter" agreements are discussed, as are settlement negotiation and counseling, and methods of alternative dispute resolution.

### § 11.01 Judgment by Default

*Read Tex. R. Civ. P. 239 through 243.*

There are three types of judgments that are similar to each other and to which the term "default judgment" has been applied from time to time by Texas courts. The true default judgment exists when the defendant has failed to appear on "answer day," the result being the entry of an interlocutory or final judgment. *Frymire Eng'g Co., Inc. v. Grantham,* 524 S.W.2d 680 (Tex. 1975). A nihil dicit judgment exists when the defendant has appeared (usually by filing a dilatory plea or motion) but has had a plea or motion not dealing with the merits of the case overruled, leaving the defendant with no answer. *See Butler v. Butler,* 577 S.W.2d 501 (Tex. Civ. App.—Texarkana 1978, writ dism'd). A failure to appear at trial case is different from both of the foregoing in that the only "default" is a failure to appear at trial in response to a proper trial setting notice. *See* Tex. R. Civ. P. 245; *Smith v. Smith,* 544 S.W.2d 121 (Tex. 1977). Generally speaking, the true default and the nihil dicit cases are similar. There is an admission of liability but not damages, unless the damages are liquidated and proved by an instrument in writing. If damages are unliquidated or not proved by an instrument in writing or both, then "the court shall hear evidence as to damages." *See* Tex. R. Civ. P. 243.

In the failure-to-appear-at-trial case, there is no admission of liability because there is an answer on the merits, *i.e.*, plaintiff must prove both liability and damages. Of course, the answer might itself be an insufficient response. *See, e.g.*, Tex. R. Civ. P. 185. A decision of the Texas Supreme Court appears to hold that a failure to appear at trial case (characterized by the Court as a post-answer-default-judgment case) is to be treated the same as a *no-answer*-default-judgment case with respect to the requirement that the petition (or other pleading for affirmative relief) must give "fair notice" of the claims for relief. *See Stoner v. Thompson,* 578 S.W.2d 679, 685 (Tex. 1979).

---

## MORGAN v. COMPUGRAPHIC CORP.

*675 S.W.2d 729 (Tex. 1984)*

RAY, Justice.

Margie F. Morgan brought this suit against Compugraphic Corporation and Solutek Corporation under theories of negligence and strict liability, alleging that the two corporations were jointly and severally liable for injuries she had incurred as a result of inhaling chemical fumes emitted from a typesetting machine installed in her office. Solutek timely answered, but Compugraphic filed no answer. After hearing evidence as to damages pursuant to Texas Rule of Civil Procedure 243, the trial court rendered default judgment against Compugraphic in the amount of $200,000 and then severed Morgan's cause of action against Compugraphic from her suit against Solutek. Compugraphic appealed by writ of error to the Dallas Court of Appeals. The court of appeals reversed and remanded the cause for a trial on the merits,[1] holding that: (1) Morgan had the burden of proving that her injuries were proximately caused by the acts of Compugraphic; (2) Morgan had presented no competent evidence of proximate cause; and (3) the trial court's severance of Morgan's suit against Compugraphic from her suit against Solutek was improper. 656 S.W.2d 530.

Morgan contests the correctness of each of these holdings before this court. Upon consideration of the court of appeals holding that it was incumbent upon Morgan to prove proximate cause, we reach the somewhat different conclusion that Morgan was required to prove a causal nexus between her injuries and her exposure to chemical fumes. We find some competent evidence in the record which establishes such a causal nexus. We further find that the court of appeals erred in holding that the trial court's severance of Morgan's causes of action was improper. We reverse the judgment of the court of appeals and remand the cause to that court for a determination of whether there was factually sufficient evidence to support an award of $200,000.

The only evidence as to the facts of this case consists of Morgan's testimony before the trial court at the assessment of damages hearing, at which Compugraphic did not appear. Morgan is a secretary employed by Frito-Lay, Inc. Morgan testified that she had always been in good health prior to returning to work from a vacation in November of 1979. Upon her return to work, Morgan found that a typesetting machine had been installed near her desk. The machine was manufactured and installed by Compugraphic and used chemicals manufactured by Solutek. Morgan testified that the machine was positioned in such a way that the back of it was only two inches from her face as she worked. Soon after Morgan came back to work, she began to develop problems with her breathing. After working four or five days near the machine, she began to experience blurred vision, headaches, stomach problems, and swelling of the eyes, lips, and nasal passages. About a month after she began to suffer these symptoms, Morgan learned that two chemical leaks in the typesetter had been discovered and repaired. Morgan's health

---

[1] One associate justice filed a dissenting opinion in which he agreed with the majority that the judgment of the trial court should be reversed, but differed with the majority in stating that the court of appeals should render judgment that Morgan take nothing.

continued to decline after the repair. She testified that she began to develop frequent skin rashes as well as a number of problems with her circulatory, digestive and nervous systems. She further testified that she has to administer histamine shots to herself twice each day.

We first reach the question of whether a party who secures a default judgment against a non-answering defendant must, at a Rule 243 hearing, present evidence proving the cause of the damages. Rule 243 reads as follows:

> If the cause of action is unliquidated or be not proved by an instrument in writing, the court shall hear evidence as to damages and shall render judgment therefor, unless the defendant shall demand and be entitled to a trial by jury in which case the judgment by default shall be noted, a writ of inquiry awarded, and the cause entered on the jury docket.

At issue in this case is the meaning of the phrase "the court shall hear evidence as to damages." Morgan contends that "evidence as to damages" refers only to evidence establishing the fact of damages and does not include evidence pertaining to the cause of those damages. Morgan cites as support two long-standing rules of Texas jurisprudence. One rule is that a judgment taken by default on an unliquidated claim admits all allegations of fact set out in the petition, except the amount of damages. *See Stoner v. Thompson*, 578 S.W.2d 679, 684 (Tex. 1979); *Long v. Wortham*, 4 Tex. 381 (1849). The other rule, a corollary of the first, holds that if the facts set out in the petition allege a cause of action, a default judgment conclusively establishes the defendant's liability. *Tarrant County v. Lively*, 25 Tex.—Supp. 399 (1860); *Clark v. Compton*, 15 Tex. 32 (1855); *Wall v. Wall*, 630 S.W.2d 493, 496 (Tex. Civ. App.—Fort Worth 1982, writ ref'd n.r.e.).

Morgan's argument is flawed because it combines two distinct aspects of causation which exist in a personal injury case such as this. In a personal injury case, the plaintiff typically alleges that the defendant's conduct caused an event—an automobile accident, a fall, or in this case, the release of chemical fumes—and that this event caused the plaintiff to suffer injuries for which compensation in damages should be paid. Thus, at trial the plaintiff must establish two causal nexuses in order to be entitled to recovery: (a) a causal nexus between the defendant's conduct and the event sued upon; and (b) a causal nexus between the event sued upon and the plaintiff's injuries.[2]

The causal nexus between the defendant's conduct and the event sued upon relates to the liability portion of plaintiff's cause of action. Here, we use the term "liability" to mean legal responsibility for the event upon which suit is based. In a negligence action, liability is usually established by proving that the defendant's negligence was a proximate cause of the event sued

---

[2] The distinction between these two causal nexuses is illustrated by contrasting the standard jury issues regarding proximate and producing cause with the issue regarding damages for personal injuries. The issues on proximate and producing cause inquire as to the defendant's liability for the event upon which suit is based: Proximate Cause Issue: "Do you find from a preponderance of the evidence *that such action was a proximate cause of the occurrence in question*?" 1 State Bar of Texas, *Texas Pattern Jury Charges* PJC 3.01 (1969) (emphasis supplied).

Producing Cause Issue: "Was that defect *a producing cause of the occurrence in question*?" 3 State Bar of Texas, *Texas Pattern Jury Charges* PJC 71.01A (1982) (emphasis supplied).

The damages issue inquires as to whether there is a causal link between the event sued upon and the plaintiff's injuries:

> Find from a preponderance of the evidence what sum of money, if any, if paid now in cash, would fairly and reasonably compensate [plaintiff] for his *injuries*, if any, *resulting from the occurrence in question*.

*Id.*, PJC 80.03 (emphasis supplied).

upon; in a products liability action in which a manufacturing defect is alleged, liability is established by proving that a product was placed in the stream of commerce containing a defect which was a producing cause of the event made the basis of suit. It is this causal nexus between the conduct of the defendant and the event sued upon that is admitted by default. From the rule that a default judgment conclusively establishes the defendant's liability, it follows that a default judgment admits that the defendant's conduct caused the event upon which the plaintiff's suit is based.

Whether the event sued upon caused any injuries to the plaintiff is another matter entirely. The causal nexus between the event sued upon and the plaintiff's injuries is strictly referable to the damages portion of the plaintiff's cause of action. Even if the defendant's liability has been established, proof of this causal nexus is necessary to ascertain the amount of damages to which the plaintiff is entitled. This is true because the plaintiff is entitled to recover damages only for those injuries caused by the event made the basis of suit; that the defendant has defaulted does not give the plaintiff the right to recover for damages which did not arise from his cause of action. *See Mitchell v. Town of Akoskie*, 190 N.C. 235, 129 S.E. 626 (1925). To hold, as we do, that a defaulting defendant does not admit that the event sued upon caused any of plaintiff's alleged injuries is entirely consistent with the rule that a judgment taken by default admits all allegations of fact set out in the petition, except for the amount of damages. Proving that the event sued upon caused the plaintiff's alleged injuries is part and parcel of proving the amount of damages to which the plaintiff is entitled. The causal nexus between the event sued upon and the plaintiff's injuries must be shown by competent evidence. *See Gerland's Food Fair, Inc. v. Hare*, 611 S.W.2d 113 (Tex. Civ. App.—Houston [1st Dist.] 1980, writ ref'd n.r.e.). *Accord Smith v. Sayles*, 637 S.W.2d 714 (Mo. App. 1982). We conclude that the mandate of Rule 243 that the court hear "evidence as to damages" makes it incumbent upon a party who obtains a default judgment in a personal injury action to present competent evidence of a causal nexus between the event sued upon and the party's alleged injuries.

It remains to apply the rules set forth in the foregoing discussion to the case before us. Morgan alleged in her petition that Compugraphic negligently installed a typesetting machine, or, alternatively, installed a defective typesetting machine, and that as a result of this conduct chemical fumes were released into Morgan's office, causing her a variety of injuries. The event sued upon is thus the release of chemical fumes into Morgan's office. By its default, Compugraphic admitted that its negligence was a proximate cause of the release of chemical fumes into Morgan's office. Compugraphic further admitted by its default that a defect in the typesetting machine was a producing cause of that event. However, Compugraphic's default did not establish that the release of chemical fumes caused Morgan any injuries. At the Rule 243 hearing, Morgan had the burden of presenting competent evidence of a causal nexus between the release of chemical fumes and her alleged injuries.

This brings us to the issue of whether Morgan presented some competent evidence that her alleged injuries were caused by the release of chemical fumes into her office. We do not attempt here to detail all such evidence; rather, our task is to determine if there is some evidence to support the trial court's judgment. As stated previously, Morgan's testimony was the only evidence presented at the Rule 243 hearing. Morgan concedes that she is a layperson not qualified to give expert medical testimony. Lay testimony is adequate to prove causation in those cases in which general experience and common sense will enable a layman to determine, with reasonable probability, the causal relationship between the event and the condition. *Lenger v.*

*Physician's General Hospital, Inc.*, 455 S.W.2d 703, 706 (Tex. 1970). Generally, lay testimony establishing a sequence of events which provides a strong, logically traceable connection between the event and the condition is sufficient proof of causation. *Griffin v. Texas Employers' Insurance Association*, 450 S.W.2d 59, 61 (Tex. 1969). *See, e.g., Insurance Company of North America v. Kneten*, 440 S.W.2d 52 (Tex. 1969); *Fidelity & Guaranty Insurance Underwriters, Inc. v. Rochelle*, 587 S.W.2d 493 (Tex. Civ. App.—Dallas 1979, writ ref'd n.r.e.); *Coca Cola Bottling Co. of Plainview v. White*, 545 S.W.2d 279 (Tex. Civ. App.—Waco 1976, no writ); *Northern Assurance Company of America v. Taylor*, 540 S.W.2d 832 (Tex. Civ. App.—Texarkana 1976, writ ref'd n.r.e.); *Coca Cola Bottling Co. of Fort Worth v. McAlister*, 256 S.W.2d 654 (Tex. Civ. App.—Fort Worth 1953, no writ); *United States Casualty Co. v. Vance*, 91 S.W.2d 465 (Tex. Civ. App.—San Antonio 1936, writ ref'd).

In the instant case, the evidence shows that Morgan had always been in good health prior to returning to work from her vacation. Upon returning to her job, she worked with her face two inches from a typesetting machine which, it is admitted by default, was leaking chemical fumes. Soon after resuming her employment, that is, soon after being exposed to the fumes emanating from the typesetting machine, Morgan experienced problems with "breathing and swelling and the like." After four or five days of being constantly exposed to these fumes during her working hours, Morgan developed symptoms such as watering of the eyes, blurred vision, headaches and swelling of the breathing passages. We believe this evidence establishes a sequence of events from which the trier of fact may properly infer, without the aid of expert medical testimony, that the release of chemical fumes from the typesetting machine caused Morgan to suffer injury. We thus conclude that there is some evidence in the record to support the trial court's award of damages. *See Hurst v. Sears, Roebuck & Co.*, 647 S.W.2d 249, 253 (Tex. 1983).

. . . .

We reverse the judgment of the court of appeals and remand the cause to that court for a consideration of Compugraphic's point of error asserting that the evidence is factually insufficient to support an award of $200,000.

---

## NOTES AND QUESTIONS

(1) *Proving Damages in a Default Judgment Case.* Why does Justice Ray conclude that evidence of causation is part of proof of damages? How difficult a burden does this conclusion impose on plaintiffs in personal injury cases?

What is a writ of inquiry? Is there a true hearing under Civil Procedure Rule 243? Must notice of the hearing be given to the defendant? *See* Tex. R. Civ. P. 245. Is it a "trial"? Is the case a contested case within Civil Procedure Rule 245? Notwithstanding a prior demand for a jury trial, under Civil Procedure Rule 220, a party who commits a post-answer default by failing to appear at trial waives the right to a jury trial. *Bradley Motors, Inc. v. Mackey*, 878 S.W.2d 140, 141 (Tex. 1994). You should note that the Court's attitude about the sufficiency of the plaintiff's testimony to prove a causal nexus between the event and her injuries is possibly not consistent with the Court's more recent decisions. *See, e.g., Broders v. Heise*, 924 S.W.2d 148, 151–154 (Tex. 1996); *cf. Uniroyal Goodrich Tire Co. v. Martinez*, 977 S.W.2d 328, 338–339 (Tex. 1998).

(2) *Reversal of a Default Judgment Due to Lack of a Proper Record.* A party who obtains a default judgment by presenting evidence of unliquidated damages must ensure that a reporter's record is available to the defaulted party. This means that a court reporter must be present to take down the necessary testimony presented by the plaintiff at the default hearing. *See, e.g., Morgan Express, Inc. v. Elizabeth-Perkins, Inc.*, 525 S.W.2d 312 (Tex. Civ. App.—Dallas 1975, writ ref'd).

(3) *The Court Reporter's Duty.* In *Rogers v. Rogers,* 561 S.W.2d 172 (Tex. 1978), the Texas Supreme Court explains that the principle that a "defaulted" party is not required to rely on the unaided memory of the trial judge does not rest on the court reporter statute (which was amended before *Rogers* was filed to provide that the reporter need only be present "on request"). Judge Chadick states that it rests on the following language from *Robinson v. Robinson,* 487 S.W.2d 713 (Tex. 1972): "if an appellant exercises due diligence and through no fault of his own is unable to obtain a proper record of the evidence introduced, this may require a new trial where his right to have the case reviewed on appeal can be preserved in no other way." *Id.* at 714.

Does this mean a court reporter must always be present even though the reporter only has a duty to attend on request? Is this sensible? Are there any other methods to make a record of the testimony?

## § 11.02 Dismissal for Want of Prosecution

*Read Tex. R. Civ. P. 165a, 306a, 329b.*

### MEMORIAL HOSP. v. GILLIS

*741 S.W.2d 364 (Tex. 1987)*

PER CURIAM.

Forty days after the trial court had dismissed her worker's compensation suit for want of prosecution, Zelma Lee Gillis filed an unverified motion to reinstate. Gillis' motion stated the nature of her action, explained the cause for the delay in prosecution, and claimed that her suit had merit. Following a hearing on her motion, the trial court reinstated her action. The record does not reflect what transpired at that hearing, and the order reinstating the cause does not recite the trial court's findings or the grounds for reinstatement. The action later went to trial, where Gillis had judgment on a jury verdict awarding some $52,000 for her injuries. The court of appeals affirmed. 731 S.W.2d 692. On September 16, 1987, we refused Memorial Hospital's application for writ of error, finding no reversible error. The court grants Memorial Hospital's motion for rehearing, and without hearing oral argument reverses the judgment of the court of appeals and vacates the judgment of the trial court. The opinion of the court of appeals conflicts with Tex. R. Civ. P. 306(a).

The procedure for obtaining relief from a dismissal for want of prosecution is set forth in Tex. R. Civ. P. 165a. In pertinent part, Rule 165a states:

> [a] motion to reinstate shall set forth the grounds therefor and be verified by the movant or his attorney. It shall be filed with the clerk within 30 days after the order of dismissal is signed or within the period provided by Rule 306a.

It is undisputed that Gillis' motion was not filed within thirty days of the signing of the order dismissing her action. The question is whether it was filed within the time period provided by

Tex. R. Civ. P. 306a. Rule 306a provides that a party who did not have notice or knowledge of a judgment or order may be afforded thirty days from the date he acquired such notice or knowledge in order to invoke the trial court's plenary jurisdiction, provided that he can:

> . . . prove in the trial court, on sworn motion and notice, the date on which the party or his attorney first either received a notice of the judgment or acquired actual knowledge of the signing and that this date was more than twenty days after the judgment was signed.

Tex. R. Civ. P. 306a(5). Compliance with the time periods prescribed by these rules is a jurisdictional prerequisite. Unless a party establishes in the manner prescribed by the rule that he had no notice or knowledge of the judgment, the general rule prevails: a trial court's power to reinstate a cause after dismissal expires thirty days after the order of dismissal is signed. *Harris County v. Miller*, 576 S.W.2d 808 (Tex. 1979).

There is nothing in the record to indicate that Gillis sustained her burden of proving to the trial court that she had no notice or knowledge of the order dismissing her cause within twenty days of its rendition. In her motion for reinstatement, Gillis did not allege that she had no notice or knowledge of the order. The order granting her motion for reinstatement does not recite that Gillis had no notice or knowledge of the dismissal. No statement of facts has been brought before us that would indicate that Gillis sustained her burden of proof at the reinstatement hearing. Gillis supplied the court of appeals with a supplemental transcript, which contained a copy of the postcard notices sent by the district clerk to the attorneys for the parties in order to notify them of the dismissal. *See* Tex. R. Civ. P. 306a(3). The postcards indicate the date of dismissal and the date upon which the postcards were sent. However, there is nothing to indicate that the trial court considered these postcard notices at the hearing, nor is there anything in the record to negate the possibility that Gillis or her attorney acquired actual knowledge of the dismissal within twenty days of its signing. Rule 306a plainly requires that this proof be made in the trial court, not the court of appeals. Since Gillis did not establish the applicability of Rule 306a(4) in the trial court in the manner prescribed by the rule, the trial court was without jurisdiction to reinstate her cause upon a motion filed forty days after dismissal. The subsequent judgment in Gillis' favor was therefore a nullity, and the court of appeals erred in affirming it.

The judgment of the court of appeals is reversed, and the judgment of the trial court in Gillis' favor is vacated. The trial court's order dismissing Gillis' cause for want of prosecution is reinstated.

---

## NOTES AND QUESTIONS

(1) *The Motion to Reinstate Must be Verified and Timely.* What should have been done to invoke the court's jurisdiction to reinstate? Civil Procedure Rule 165a provides that "[n]otice of the court's intention to dismiss and the date and place of the dismissal hearing shall be sent by the clerk to each attorney . . . by posting same in the United States Postal Service. At the dismissal hearing, the court shall dismiss for want of prosecution unless there is good cause for the case to be maintained on the docket." Tex. R. Civ. P. 165a(1). What constitutes "good cause"? *See* Tex. R. Civ. P. 165a(3) (second paragraph); *see also S. B. & T. Gem Imports, Inc. v. Creswell*, 671 S.W.2d 145, 147 (Tex. App.—Houston [1st Dist.] 1984, no writ). What happens if the case

is retained on the docket? What is the role played by the Texas Supreme Court's Administrative Rules? *See* Texas Rule of Judicial Administration 6, providing for disposition of civil jury cases within 18 months from the appearance date.

(2) *Ruling on a Motion to Reinstate.* What period of time does the trial judge have to rule on a timely reinstatement motion? The judge is to set a hearing on the motion "as soon as practicable." The motion is deemed overruled by operation of law if it "is not decided by signed written order within seventy-five days after the judgment is signed, or, within such other time as may be allowed by Rule 306a." Tex. R. Civ. P. 165a(3). What is the effect of an oral order setting aside an order of dismissal for want of prosecution? *See Walker v. Harrison*, 597 S.W.2d 913 (Tex. 1980) (oral pronouncement in open court is not sufficient in absence of timely, written order bearing judge's signature).

(3) *Refiling the Dismissed Action.* What is the effect of a dismissal for want of prosecution? What if the dismissal is drafted erroneously so that the case is dismissed "with prejudice"? *See El Paso Pipe v. Mountain States Leasing*, 617 S.W.2d 189, 190 (Tex. 1981) (holding that order is res judicata and not subject to collateral attack).

(4) *An Oral Hearing Is Required for Motions Under Rule 165a.* Civil Procedure Rule 165a says that the trial court "shall set a hearing on the motion [to reinstate] as soon as practicable." In *Gulf Coast Investment Corp. v. Nasa 1 Business Center*, 754 S.W.2d 152 (Tex. 1988), the Texas Supreme Court held that this language referred to an oral hearing. Ordinarily, such a hearing is not required even if a given rule refers to "a hearing"; the Court noted that Texas Rule of Judicial Administration 7 encourages judges to use expeditious means, including "telephone or mail in lieu of personal appearance [f]or motion hearings." But if the "language or context of the particular rule" so requires, the hearing must be oral. The Court supported its holding by noting that Rule 165a requires the trial court to give the parties notice of the "date, time and place of the hearing."

(5) *Inherent Power to Dismiss.* A trial court may have inherent power to dismiss a case that is not prosecuted with due diligence regardless of the provisions of Civil Procedure Rule 165a, even though the permissible time periods provided by the Texas Supreme Court's time standards have not been exceeded. *City of Houston v. Robinson*, 837 S.W.2d 262, 264–265 (Tex. App.—Houston [1st Dist.] 1992, no writ).

(6) *Local Rules and "Dismissal Dockets."* Local rules figure prominently in some dismissals. In fact, some courts have "dismissal dockets."

---

## STROMBERG CARLSON v. CENTRAL WELDING

*750 S.W.2d 862 (Tex. App.—Houston [14th Dist.] 1988, no writ)*

ELLIS, Justice.

Appellant and lessor, Stromberg Carlson Leasing Corporation ["Stromberg"], appeals from a judgment of dismissal for want of prosecution. Appellant sought damages from the appellees, Central Welding Supply Co. and its successor-in-interest, Amerigas, Inc., who had leased telecommunications equipment through Stromberg since 1974 pursuant to a written contract.

Appellant's point of error alleges the trial court abused its discretion by dismissing its case for want of prosecution and failing to grant its motion to reinstate. We affirm.

After a dispute arose over payments allegedly due Stromberg, it filed suit against the appellees on October 19, 1982. They followed their November 15, 1982 general denial with a third party action filed on February 4, 1983. That action impleaded and sought damages from third party defendants, Stromberg-Carlson Communications Corporation, vendor of the equipment leased, and General Dynamics Corporation, parent company of both appellant and the vendor. On April 22, 1983, the third party defendants answered with a general denial which also raised lack of notice and limitations issues.

Stromberg and the appellees both agree that Stromberg requested interrogatories and documents from appellee in May of 1983. Both parties also agree that appellees noticed the depositions of the third party defendants' chief executive officers, that those officers failed to appear, and that appellees thereafter filed a motion for sanctions, which the trial court did not hear. Stromberg contends the appellees withdrew their motion for sanctions by agreement while the appellees state they merely failed to urge their motion. There is nothing in the record to show that the appellees actually withdrew their motion for sanctions, or that the parties filed an agreement with the court.

No further activity occurred until March 23, 1987, when appellant received notice that its case had been placed on the Harris County annual dismissal docket scheduled for April 4, 1987. Appellant filed a verified motion in which it asked the trial court to retain the case on its trial docket. Appellant did not request a hearing on the motion. Pursuant to the court order of the Harris County dismissal docket entered on April 13, 1987, the case was dismissed for want of prosecution. On May 13, 1987, Stromberg filed a timely and verified motion to reinstate to which the appellees filed a response. Without holding a hearing, the trial court denied the motion to reinstate on June 4, 1987.

Texas trial courts have inherent discretion to dismiss for failure to prosecute. *Veteran's Land Board v. Williams*, 543 S.W.2d 89, 90 (Tex. 1976) (per curiam). In addition, Tex. R. Civ. P. 165a and Local Rule 7 (now Rule 3.6) specifically authorize Harris County trial courts to dismiss a case which a party has failed to prosecute diligently. As appellant acknowledges, it carries the heavy burden of establishing a clear abuse of discretion in order for this court to reverse a dismissal for want of prosecution, whether the trial court acted pursuant to its express or inherent authority, and whether appellant complains of the order of dismissal or the denial of its motion to reinstate. *See State v. Rotello*, 671 S.W.2d 507, 509 (Tex. 1984); [citations omitted] The controlling question is whether appellant exhibited due diligence in prosecuting its case. [citations omitted] In assessing appellant's diligence this court may properly consider the entire history of the case. [citation omitted]

We first address the contention that the trial court abused its discretion by dismissing appellant's case. Appellant's March 23 motion asked the court to retain the case, alleged it had completed discovery, was ready for trial, and was willing to produce "suitable representatives" should appellees require their depositions, and requested that the case be placed on the trial docket. Appellant alleged the appellees had withdrawn their motion for sanctions after the parties came to an agreement that the appellees would request, and appellant would produce, "appropriate corporate officials with knowledge of the issues involved in the case." In short, appellant alleged it was anticipating and awaiting promised action by the appellees.

It is undisputed that appellant received notice of its case having been placed on the April 4, 1987 annual dismissal docket. Pursuant to former Harris County Local Rule 7(A) (now Rule 3.6), if a case on file for more than four years had not yet been *set*, it would be dismissed for want of prosecution without further notice at the annual dismissal docket unless a party showed good cause to prevent the dismissal. Local Rule 7 therefore defined what a Harris County litigant must do to keep his case retained: either succeed in setting the case for trial or show good cause why its case should not be dismissed.

The version of Tex. R. Civ. P. 165a(1) in effect on April 13, 1987, the date of dismissal, authorized trial courts to dismiss a case for want of prosecution if a party failed "to request a hearing or *take other action specified by the court*" by the fifteenth day following receipt of the court's notice of intent to dismiss (emphasis added). . . .

Since Local Rule 7 applied only to cases which had not been set for trial, appellant clearly had a duty to request a trial setting in order to avoid dismissal. . . .

Harris County local rules have consistently required that requests for a trial setting state a date certain. *See* former Local Rule 3(B) (now Rule 3.4.2). Although appellant's motion to retain claimed it was ready for trial and willing to accommodate party opponents, and also requested placement on the trial docket, the motion was not a request for a trial setting at a date certain. *Compare Moore*, 660 S.W.2d at 578. In addition, appellant could not show any activity following the appellees' request for sanctions other than its alleged readiness to provide witnesses for deposition in the event of a request by the appellees. The alleged agreement to supply witnesses merely attempts to explain appellant's failure to request a setting. In view of the rapidly approaching "set or risk dismissal" deadline established by Local Rule 7, the alleged agreement does not adequately explain appellant's lack of diligence in procuring a setting and moving its case to trial.

Although appellant was in the unfortunate position of waiting for the appellees to perform, that position resulted from appellant's claimed response to the appellees' motion for sanctions. In view of Harris County Local Rule 7 and Tex. R. Civ. P. 165a, appellant should have done more in order to establish that it had diligently prosecuted the case. . . .

. . . .

Because appellant's motion failed to demonstrate its own diligence in moving its case to trial and procuring a setting, we find no clear abuse of discretion in the trial court's dismissing the case.

The trial court denied appellant's motion to reinstate on June 4, 1987. A motion for reinstatement essentially provides an opportunity for the dismissed plaintiff to explain his failure to prosecute with due diligence and to request the court to reconsider its decision to dismiss, in much the same manner as a motion for a new trial. Tex. R. Civ. P. 165a establishes specific requirements and timetables governing motions to reinstate and the reinstatement procedure.

Subsection (2) of Rule 165a (so numbered when the court entered its dismissal order), required a trial court to reinstate a case dismissed for want of prosecution if it determined that a party's "failure" was either reasonably explained or the result of mistake or accident. . . . As our previous discussion indicates, the court based the order which dismissed the case on the failure of the appellant's motion to establish that it had prosecuted its case with sufficient diligence to prevent dismissal.

Appellant argues it satisfied the "reasonable explanation" prong of former Tex. R. Civ. P. 165a(2). It offered the following excuse for its failure to prosecute: it failed to request a trial setting in an attempt to accommodate appellees, having agreed to furnish appropriate witnesses in exchange for the appellees' withdrawing their motion for sanctions. The motion to reinstate repeated the allegations of the motion to retain, requested a trial setting, recited that the case had been placed on the dismissal docket only once, stated that appellant's rights might be jeopardized, and alleged the dismissal was due to accident or mistake. The appellees then filed a response in which they alleged that Stromberg's only action, other than filing suit and serving interrogatories and requests for production in 1983, was its refusal to comply with the appellees' deposition request.

Of the several grounds alleged, appellant places great reliance on its alleged "agreement" with the appellees. As a preliminary matter, we note that appellant should not now attempt to enforce an alleged "agreement" which has no support in the record. *See* Tex. R. Civ. P. 11; . . . But because appellant cites *S.B. & T. Gem Imports, Inc. v. Creswell*, 671 S.W.2d 145 (Tex. App.—Houston [1st Dist.] 1984, no writ), also an appeal from a dismissal for want of prosecution, we will address its arguments in greater detail. Appellant claims *Creswell* supports its premise that this court may presume the truth of the allegations, made in its motions to the trial court and in its brief to this court, concerning its purported agreement with the appellees. We disagree.

In *Creswell* the court of appeals . . . accepted the appellant's version of the facts, after pointing out that the appellee had failed to file a brief controverting the appellant's factual assertions. 671 S.W.2d at 146. In the case at hand, we note that appellees' brief could have been more specific in controverting appellant's asserting it had agreed to furnish suitable deponents in return for the appellees' agreeing to withdraw their motion for sanctions. Nonetheless, the appellees' brief does address the motion for sanctions by stating they merely failed to urge it without waiving the right to re-urge it, and simply allowed the time for hearing on the motion to lapse. Additionally, counsel for the appellees denied knowledge of the alleged agreement when questioned during oral submission of this case. Moreover, the defendants-appellees responded to the motion to reinstate, whereas in *Creswell*, the trial court considered only the sworn allegations the plaintiff-appellant made in its motion for rehearing of the order of dismissal. 671 S.W.2d at 146.

We find the appellees sufficiently controverted appellant's factual assertions and conclude that Tex. R. App. P. 74(f) and *Creswell* do not apply. Instead, because the record appellant presents fails to evidence an agreement between the parties, we hold that Tex. R. Civ. P. 11 and Tex. R. App. P. 50(d) prevent appellant from relying on a purported agreement with the appellees in order to excuse its own lack of diligence in prosecuting this case.

. . . .

Appellant also stresses that its case was on file only four years and that it had come up for dismissal only once. Because Local Rule 7(B) (now Rule 3.6) charged parties with notice of the annual dismissal docket, and because lack of due diligence is the sole determiner of the propriety of a dismissal, we find no merit in these arguments or in appellant's unsupported allegations of accident or mistake.

We hold the trial properly dismissed appellant's case based on its failure to prosecute it diligently, and properly denied its motion for reinstatement without holding a hearing.

We overrule appellant's point of error and affirm the judgment of the trial court.

## § 11.03 Summary Judgment

### [A] Standards and Procedure for Granting

#### [1] Ordinary Motions

*Read Tex. R. Civ. P. 166a(a), (b), (c), (e).*

**CITY OF HOUSTON v. CLEAR CREEK BASIN AUTHORITY**

*589 S.W.2d 671 (Tex. 1979)*

SPEARS, Justice

Respondent Clear Creek Basin Authority, a statutory governmental entity existing under article 8280-311 (1965), sued the City of Houston for injunctive relief and statutory penalties, alleging the unlawful discharge of waste waters by treatment plants operated by the City in violation of chapter 26 of the Texas Water Code. [footnote omitted] The trial court granted summary judgment for the City of Houston, but the court of civil appeals reversed and remanded. 573 S.W.2d 839.

Two questions are presented: (1) whether the respondent, Clear Creek Basin Authority, properly presented its objections to the summary judgment under rule 166-A(c) which provides that only "expressly presented" issues may be considered on appeal as grounds for reversal; and (2) whether the respondent Clear Creek, plaintiff below, has standing to sue under the provisions of the Texas Water Code § 26.001 et seq., which prohibits the unauthorized discharge of polluting waste waters, for discharges occurring upstream and *outside* its territorial boundaries. Because the answer to both questions is "no," we reverse the court of civil appeals and affirm the summary judgment entered by the trial court.

Clear Creek's suit alleges numerous violations of waste control orders of the Texas Water Quality Board and a common law nuisance as a result of the discharge of sewage into waters which ultimately flow into Galveston Bay. The Attorney General of Texas, on behalf of the Texas Water Quality Control Board and the State of Texas, intervened as a necessary party-plaintiff pursuant to the requirement of the Texas Water Code.

Clear Creek alleged in its first amended original petition that the City of Houston had committed numerous violations at 31 different locations. Defendant City admitted that four of these plants discharging effluent are situated within the territorial boundaries of Clear Creek Basin Authority set forth in section 2 of Article 8280-311, *supra,* and that these four plants exceeded the terms of the City's permit from the Water Quality Control Board during the periods of 1974 and 1976. The remaining plants were located upstream and outside of Clear Creek's territorial jurisdiction.

The City of Houston filed a motion for summary judgment, alleging three grounds:

> 1. The matters upon which Clear Creek bases its claims for relief fall within the primary jurisdiction of the Texas Water Quality Board; Clear Creek has failed to exhaust its administrative remedies; and that neither the Texas Water Quality Board nor the Texas Department of Water Resources has authorized the bringing of this action;
>
> 2. As a matter of law, Clear Creek cannot obtain relief for violations of the Texas Water Code which occur outside the territorial jurisdiction of the Authority; and

3. The action represents an attempt by Clear Creek to perform a function or service which the City of Houston is authorized to perform without the written consent of the governing body of the City of Houston, all in violation of Article 8280-311, sec. 5.

Clear Creek filed this response to the motion:

I.

The only issue before this Court is a question of law: can a downstream victim of pollution sue an upstream polluter?

II.

The City has admitted that its sewer plants exceed the parameters of its permits on a regular basis. See Answers to Admissions and Interrogatories.

III.

The City's effluent is flushed into Clear Lake on a daily basis and causes pollution there. See deposition testimony of Sidney H. Tanner and Affidavits on file.

There is no *verbatim* record of the hearing on the motion, but the trial court's judgment recites that at the hearing, Clear Creek withdrew its common law cause of action in open court and announced its desire to proceed only on the basis of its claims under chapter 26 of the Texas Water Code. It further recites that the City of Houston withdrew paragraphs 1 and 3 of its motion for summary judgment and desired to proceed to hearing only on paragraph 2 challenging Clear Creek's right to sue for violations outside its jurisdictional boundaries. In this context, the trial court granted the City's motion for summary judgment. [footnote omitted]

In the meantime, and apart from the summary judgment proceeding, the City of Houston and the state Attorney General worked out a settlement agreement between them to which Clear Creek was not a party. The settlement agreement was incorporated in the trial court's final judgment but was made expressly contingent upon the judgment that Clear Creek take nothing being upheld on appeal. The settlement provided for an agreed injunction judgment obligating the City to construct and place into operation some $500,000,000 worth of additional waste water treatment plants, sludge disposal plants, and sewage diversion lines with a reporting schedule to the Texas Department of Water Resources and to the trial court.

The court of civil appeals, in reversing and remanding the cause for trial, held that a fact issue existed as to the alleged violations occurring *within* Clear Creek's territorial boundaries. The court reasoned that even if the admitted fact of those violations was not presented to the trial court at the hearing on summary judgment, this part of Clear Creek's cause of action was not waived because there was no written agreement of waiver filed under rule 11. The court said that the City had not carried its burden and was not entitled to a summary judgment despite Clear Creek's failure to specify the reasons why the motion should not be granted.

Petitioner City of Houston asserts nine points of error. The first alleged error is that the judgment of the court of civil appeals is erroneous for the reason that it is contrary to the requirement of rule 166-A, that "[i]ssues not expressly presented to the trial court by written motion, answer or other response, shall not be considered on appeal as grounds for reversal." The remaining points claim that Clear Creek waived and abandoned any fact issue and that it is estopped from asserting any complaints of violations occurring within the geographical boundaries of the Clear Creek Basin Authority.

The first question is whether the 1978 amendment to rule 166-A(c), providing that issues not expressly presented to the trial court may not be considered on appeal as grounds for reversal, precludes the court of civil appeals from reversing the summary judgment when the non-movant agreed to the submission to the trial court of a single issue of law. We hold that because the parties agreed on the submission of only one issue to the trial court and its ruling on that issue constituted the basis of the granting of the motion for summary judgment, Clear Creek is precluded from later urging on appeal the issue not presented, *i.e.*, the violations of the four plants located within Clear Creek's boundaries.

A history of the summary judgment rule, rule 166-A, reflects that the high hopes of increasing judicial efficiency advanced by the proponents of the rule did not materialize. While no summary judgment rule was included in the initial promulgation of the rules of civil procedure in 1940, after considerable urging by legal scholars and commentators and by the Texas Civil Judicial Council, rule 166-A was adopted by this court, effective March 1, 1950. Pittsford and Russell, *Summary Judgment in Texas: A Selective Survey,* 14 Hous. L. Rev. 854 (1977). Despite predictions of success by its supporters, the rule has been fraught with misunderstanding. One prominent writer observed in 1961 that a poll of district judges throughout the state reflected many were skeptical about the efficacy of the rule because of frequent reversals by appellate courts. McDonald, *The Effective Use of Summary Judgment,* 15 Sw. L.J. 365, 373–4 (1961). In 1977, a survey concluded that fewer than two percent of the civil cases disposed of in Texas in the six preceding years were decided by summary judgment. *See* Pittsford and Russell, *supra* at 854. Another survey of the cases decided by this court between 1968 and 1976 reflected that when a summary judgment was granted in the trial court, seventy percent of those cases were reversed and remanded for trial. Sheehan, *Summary Judgment: Let the Movant Beware,* 8 St. Mary's L. J. 253, 254 (1976).

Attempts within the bar to clarify summary judgment practice began to gain momentum in the early 1970's. After several unsuccessful attempts at revision, the Committee on the Administration of Justice of the State Bar of Texas voted in March of 1976 to recommend changes in rule 166-A that would require the non-movant to provide some assistance to the trial judge in narrowing the issues to be decided. That proposal was then considered by the Supreme Court Advisory Committee in March of 1977, and after several changes, was recommended to this court for adoption. The proposal recommended significant change in section (c), primarily by requiring the nonmovant to "define specifically in writing" the controverted issues and defects in the movant's proof that would defeat the motion. The recorded minutes of the Advisory Committee reflect a prevailing sentiment to change the rule, to make summary judgments a more useful procedure in judicial administration, to require non-movant to specify his opposition to the motion, and to prevent the non-movant from "laying behind the log" with his objections until appeal. [footnote omitted]

A comparison of section (c) of the rule as it existed before January 1, 1978, and as amended demonstrates the significance of the change in the mechanics of the summary judgment procedure. The new rule adopts the objectives of the Advisory Committee, but goes even further by precluding from consideration on appeal grounds not raised in the trial court in opposition to a summary judgment motion. The pre-1978 summary judgment rule had a chilling effect on the willingness of trial courts to utilize the intended benefits of the procedure. *See* McDonald, *The*

*Effective Use of Summary Judgment,* 15 Sw. L. J. 365, 375-382 (1961). The new rule attempts to encourage the trial court to utilize the summary judgment in appropriate cases.

Prior to January 1, 1978, section (c) read:

> (c) Motion and Proceedings Thereon. The motion for summary judgment shall state the specific grounds therefor. The motion shall be served at least ten days before the time specified for the hearing. The adverse party prior to the day of hearing may serve opposing affidavits. No oral testimony shall be received at the hearing. The judgment sought shall be rendered forthwith if the pleadings, depositions, answers to interrogatories, and admissions on file, together with the affidavits, if any, show that, except as to the amount of damages, there is no genuine issue as to any material fact and that the moving party is entitled to a judgment as a matter of law.

Section (c) now reads:

> (c) Motion and Proceedings Thereon. The motion for summary judgment shall state the specific grounds therefor. Except on leave of court, the motion shall be served at least twenty-one days before the time specified for the hearing. Except on leave of court, the adverse party, not later than seven days prior to the day of hearing may serve opposing affidavits or other written response. No oral testimony shall be received at the hearing. The judgment sought shall be rendered forthwith if the pleadings, depositions, answers to interrogatories, admissions and affidavits, if any, on file at the time of the hearing, or filed thereafter and before the judgment with permission of the court, show that, except as to the amount of damages, there is no genuine issue as to any material fact and the moving party is entitled to judgment as a matter of law on the issues as expressly set out in the motion or in an answer or any other response. *Issues not expressly presented to the trial court by written motion, answer or other response shall not be considered on appeal as grounds for reversal.* A summary judgment may be based on uncontroverted testimonial evidence of an interested witness, or of an expert witness as to subject matter concerning which the trier of fact must be guided solely by the opinion testimony of experts, if the evidence is clear, positive and direct, otherwise credible and free from contradictions and inconsistencies, and could have been readily controverted. (emphasis added)

A concomitant change to section (e) of the rule added this sentence:

> Defects in the form of affidavits or attachments will not be grounds for reversal unless specifically pointed out by objection by an opposing party with opportunity, but refusal, to amend.

Responding to the criticism that a nonmovant could "lay behind the log" in the trial court and urge deficiencies for the first time on appeal, the new section (c) specifically prohibits this tactic by clearly requiring:

> . . . Issues not expressly presented to the trial court by *written* motion, answer or other response shall not be considered on appeal as grounds for reversal. (emphasis added)

The word "written" modifies not only the word "motion," but also the words "answer" and "other response." The "issues" required by the rule to be "expressly presented" are those pointed out to the trial court in written motions, written answers or written responses to the motion. The term "answer" in the context of the rule refers to an answer to the motion, not an answer generally filed in response to a petition. *Feller v. Southwestern Bell Tel. Co.,* 581 S.W.2d 775 (Tex. Civ.

App.—Houston [14th Dist.] 1979, no writ). The movant must also expressly set out his grounds in writing:

> . . . The judgment sought shall be rendered forthwith if . . . and the moving party is entitled to judgment as a matter of law *on the issues as expressly set out in the motion or in an answer or any other response.* (emphasis added)

Thus, both the reasons for the summary judgment and the objections to it must be in writing and before the trial judge at the hearing. The appellate court which must later decide whether the issue was actually presented to and considered by the trial judge will then be able to examine the transcript and make its determination. To permit "issues" to be presented orally would encourage parties to request that a court reporter record summary judgment hearings, a practice neither necessary nor appropriate to the purposes of such a hearing. *Richards v. Allen,* 402 S.W.2d 158, 161 (Tex. 1966); rule 166-A(c).

If the issues are to be further restricted or expanded by the parties beyond those "expressly presented" by the written motion, the answer to the motion, or any other written response, the change must meet the requirements of rule 11 which provides:

> No agreement between attorneys or parties touching any suit pending will be enforced unless it be in writing, signed and filed with the papers as a part of the record, *or unless it be made in open court and entered of record.* (emphasis added)

The City of Houston contends that the parties orally agreed in open court at the hearing on the motion to narrow the issue to a single question of law—does Clear Creek have standing under the code to sue for pollution originating outside its territorial boundaries? The City further maintains that if that agreement must comply with rule 11, the recitations in the judgment satisfy the requirements of the rule.

We agree that the parties in open court should be able to narrow the issues presented to the trial court provided the agreement is reduced to writing, signed, and filed with papers or "entered of record." If a party represents to the court that he waives a ground or objection that he has previously asserted in a written motion or response and agrees that a certain issue is the only issue before the court, rule 11 is satisfied if the oral waiver or agreement made in open court is described in the judgment or an order of the court. Rule 11 expressly approves this procedure.

The trial court's judgment [footnote omitted] reflects that the parties by agreement expressly presented only one issue to the court, and the requirements of rule 11 were met when the agreement was reflected in the judgment. Counsel for the City announced in open court that he was withdrawing grounds 1 and 3 of its motion for summary judgment. Clear Creek agreed to withdraw its common law cause of action, and the City of Houston agreed not to object to its revival if the case were remanded for a new trial. The only issue then remaining to be determined at the hearing on the motion for summary judgment, taking into consideration the motion, the written response, and the open court representations of counsel recited in the judgment, was the second ground asserted by the City's motion—the standing of Clear Creek to file a suit under the Texas Water Code for violations which occur upstream and *outside* the jurisdictional boundaries of the Clear Creek Basin Authority. No other issues were presented to the trial court by either party, and he ruled on no others.

Clear Creek next argues that its pleadings on file in the case adequately assert its claim of violations by the four plants located within its territorial boundaries, that its response to the City's motion for summary judgment does not supersede Clear Creek's previous pleadings, and that it should not have to replead in its response to the motion what it had already pled.

Pleadings do not constitute summary judgment proof. *Hidalgo v. Sur. Sav. & Loan Assn.*, 462 S.W.2d 540 (Tex. 1971). The new rule requires that contentions be expressly presented in the written motion or in a written answer or response to the motion, and pleadings are not to be considered in determining whether fact issues are expressly presented in summary judgment motions. The terms "answer" and "response" as used in the context of the rule clearly refer to the motion and not to the pleadings generally. *Feller v. Southwestern Bell Tel. Co., supra.* To hold otherwise would be to perpetuate the evil the rule change was designed to eliminate. The written answer or response to the motion must fairly appraise the movant and the court of the issues the non-movant contends should defeat the motion.

We are not to be understood, however, as shifting the burden of proof that exists in summary judgment proceedings.The trial court may not grant a summary judgment by default for lack of an answer or response to the motion by the non-movant when the movant's summary judgment proof is legally insufficient. [footnote omitted] The movant still must establish his entitlement to a summary judgment on the issues expressly presented to the trial court by conclusively proving all essential elements of his cause of action or defense as a matter of law. *See Swilley v. Hughes.* 488 S.W.2d 64, 67 (Tex. 1972). Summary judgments must stand on their own merits, and the non-movant's failure to answer or respond cannot supply by default the summary judgment proof necessary to establish the movant's right.

While it would be prudent and helpful to the trial court for the non-movant always to file an answer or response, the non-movant needs no answer or response to the motion to contend on appeal that the grounds expressly presented to the trial court by the movant's motion are insufficient *as a matter of law* to support summary judgment. The non-movant, however, may not raise any *other* issues as grounds for reversal. Under the new rule, the non-movant may not urge on appeal as reason for reversal of the summary judgment any and every *new* ground that he can think of, nor can he resurrect grounds that he abandoned at the hearing.

With the exception of an attack on the legal sufficiency of the grounds expressly raised by the movant in his motion for summary judgment, the non-movant must expressly present to the trial court any reasons seeking to *avoid* movant's entitlement, such as those set out in rules 93 and 94, and he must present summary judgment proof when necessary to establish a fact issue. No longer must the movant negate all possible issues of law and fact that *could* be raised by the non-movant in the trial court but were not. *See, e.g., "Moore" Burger Inc. v. Phillips Petroleum Co.*, 492 S.W.2d 934 (Tex. 1972); *Doyle v. USAA*, 482 S.W.2d 849 (Tex. 1972); *Hidalgo v. Sur. Sav. & Loan Assn.*, 462 S.W.2d 540 (Tex. 1971); *Womack v. Allstate Ins. Co.*, 156 Tex. 467, 296 S.W.2d 233 (1957). In cases such as *Torres v. Western Cas. & Sur. Co.*, 457 S.W.2d 50 (Tex. 1970) (existence of good cause for late filing of worker's compensation claim), and *Gardner v. Martin*, 162 Tex. 156, 345 S.W.2d 274 (1961) (failure of movant to attach certified copies of prior case to establish res judicata), the nonmovant must now, in a written answer or response to the motion, expressly present to the trial court those issues that would defeat the movant's right to a summary judgment and failing to do so, may not later assign them as error on appeal.

Having held that Clear Creek is not entitled to defeat the summary judgment by raising a fact issue for the first time on appeal which was not expressly presented to the trial court, we now determine if the City of Houston is entitled to its summary judgment as a matter of law for the reason asserted in its motion. Specifically, the question is whether under the Texas Water Code, Clear Creek Basin Authority can sue to enforce the Code provisions prohibiting unauthorized discharges of polluting waste into the waters of the state when those discharges occur upstream and *outside* the territorial jurisdiction of the Clear Creek Basin Authority. As we have said, this issue was the only question before the trial court.

[The court cites portions of the Code providing that a local government can sue for violations "occurring . . . within" its jurisdiction. "Violations" include the "discharge" of various kinds of effluent or the commission of "any other act . . . which . . . will cause pollution." Discharge, says the court, "is not a process that continues to the sea but an 'act,' and 'an act can only occur where it actually takes place.' " Furthermore, the Water Code vests statewide authority in the Department of Water Resources, allowing local governments to operate only within their boundaries to prevent overlap and conflicts. The legislative history of the Code also confirms that a downstream government cannot sue an upstream one for acts occurring outside the plaintiff government's territorial jurisdiction.]

The judgment of the court of civil appeals is reversed, and the judgment of the trial court is affirmed.

---

## NOTES AND QUESTIONS

(1) *Filing a Response to Summary Judgment Motions.* After *Clear Creek,* when will you file an answer or response to a motion for summary judgment? What should you say in the answer or response? Why?

(2) *No Genuine Issue as to Any Material Fact.* What is necessary to establish entitlement to judgment "as a matter of law"? Assume plaintiff A sues B on a promissory note. If A fails to provide summary judgment evidence that A is the owner and holder of the note, can the defendant raise the absence of such proof for the first time on appeal? *See Combs v. Fantastic Homes, Inc.,* 584 S.W.2d 340, 342–343 (Tex. Civ. App.—Dallas 1979, writ ref'd n.r.e.). Under Civil Procedure Rule 166a(c), when is proof only sufficient to raise a fact issue because of the source of the evidence?

(3) *Defendant's Motion Based on an Affirmative Defense.* Suppose a defendant seeks a summary judgment on the basis of an affirmative defense; what summary judgment proof should the defendant provide? *See Swilley v. Hughes,* 488 S.W.2d 64, 67 (Tex. 1972) ("When a defendant moves for summary judgment on the basis of his affirmative defense, he must, therefore, conclusively prove all essential elements of that defense").

(4) *Avoidance of an Affirmative Defense.* Torres v. Western Cas. & Sur. Co., 457 S.W.2d 50, 53 (Tex. 1970), contains the following paragraph:

> There is one situation where the opponent of a summary judgment motion must come forward himself to raise a fact issue by proof rather than allegation, the movant having presented no proof on the issue, and that is to support the non-movant's own affirmative defense. . . . Affirmative defenses are well recognized under our rules. It would unduly confuse summary judgment practice to reshape our previous holdings so as to shift the burden of presenting proof to levels of avoidance of an opponent's proof.

What does this mean? A plaintiff who is a nonmovant and wants to defeat a summary judgment in the context of a defendant's motion based on an affirmative defense must raise a matter in avoidance of the affirmative defense by proof rather than by allegation. *See Nichols v. Smith*, 507 S.W.2d 518 (Tex. 1974), in which the plaintiff alleged fraudulent concealment to avoid a defense of limitations. Plaintiff's pleading of fraudulent concealment was held insufficient. Summary judgment evidence *sufficient to raise a fact issue* was required on each component element to avoid summary judgment. *See also Zale Corp. v. Rosenbaum*, 520 S.W.2d 889 (Tex. 1975); *"Moore" Burger, Inc. v. Phillips Petroleum Co.*, 492 S.W.2d 934 (Tex. 1973) (promissory estoppel avoids affirmative defense of statute of frauds).

### [2] No Evidence Motions

*Read Tex. R. Civ. P. 166a(i) and Comment to 1997 change.*

The Texas Supreme Court amended the summary judgment rule effective September 1, 1997, to embrace the federal approach to motions that are based on challenges to a ground of recovery or defense on which the nonmovant would have the burden of proof at trial. Formerly, in order for a defendant to be entitled to summary judgment, he or she was required, by competent proof, to disprove as a matter of law at least one of the essential elements of the plaintiff's cause of action (*Lear Siegler, Inc. v. Perez*, 819 S.W.2d 470, 471 (Tex. 1991)) or establish one or more affirmative defenses as a matter of law. *Jennings v. Burgess*, 917 S.W.2d 790, 793 (Tex. 1996). By this amendment, the Texas Supreme Court is reversing the position taken in *Casso v. Brand*, 776 S.W.2d 551 (Tex. 1989), rejecting the approach adopted by the United States Supreme Court in *Celotex Corp. v. Catrett*, 477 U.S. 317 (1986). In *Celotex*, Chief Justice Rehnquist wrote that "the plain language of [federal] Rule 56(c) mandates the entry of summary judgment, after adequate time for discovery and upon motion, against a party who fails to make a showing sufficient to establish the existence of an element essential to that party's case, and on which that party will bear the burden of proof at trial." 477 U.S. at 322. In *Casso v. Brand*, the Texas Supreme Court held that "we never shift the burden of proof to the non-movant unless and until the movant has 'establish[ed] his entitlement to a summary judgment on the issues expressly presented to the trial court by conclusively proving all essential elements of his cause of action. . . .' " 776 S.W.2d at 556.

As a result of the amendment, a defendant may obtain a summary judgment without conclusively negating an element of the plaintiff's cause of action.

---

## MOORE v. K MART CORP.

*981 S.W.2d 266 (Tex. App.—San Antonio 1998, no pet. h.)*

HARDBERGER, Chief Justice.

Appellant, Janet K. Moore ("Moore"), appeals the trial court's summary judgment granted in favor of K Mart Corporation d/b/a K Mart Super Center ("Kmart"). Moore brought suit against Kmart for the personal injuries she allegedly sustained when she tripped and fell on Kmart's premises. Kmart filed a no-evidence motion for summary judgment, asserting that there was no evidence that a dangerous condition existed on its premises or, alternatively, there was no evidence that Kmart had actual or constructive knowledge of any such condition.

## PROCEDURAL HISTORY

Moore filed suit against Kmart on September 11, 1996. In her petition, Moore alleged that on April 8, 1996, she was walking to the photograph counter when she tripped and fell where the carpet and floor tile inside Kmart's store was separated by a black rubber border. Moore contended that the carpet area next to the border depressed lower than the border when she stepped onto the carpet, causing her to trip on the border. Moore asserted that the depression of the carpet in this manner was a condition on Kmart's premises that posed an unreasonable risk of harm to her, and Kmart had actual or constructive knowledge of the condition. Moore further contended that one of Kmart's employees created the condition by pushing shopping carts across the border. [footnote omitted] Moore concluded that the condition proximately caused her fall, resulting in her injury.

On September 18, 1997, Kmart moved for summary judgment under rule 166a(i) of the Texas Rules of Civil Procedure. Kmart asserted that no evidence of any dangerous condition existed. If the court found that such a condition did exist, Kmart argued in the alternative that it did not have actual or constructive knowledge of such a condition. Although not required by the rule, Kmart attached deposition excerpts in support of its position.

The first excerpt attached to Kmart's motion was from Moore's deposition. Moore testified that on the date that she fell, she did not go back and see what had caused her to trip and she did not tell anyone that the border had caused her to fall. Moore stated that she knew the black border caused her to trip because there was "nothing else there."

The second excerpt attached to Kmart's motion was from the deposition of Estella Duque, the Kmart employee to whom Moore reported the incident several days later. Duque stated that she personally inspected the carpet and did not see anything wrong with the border. Duque stated that she could not move the border with her hand, and the border did not move even after she kicked it with her foot.

In response to Kmart's motion, Moore filed the following summary judgment evidence: (1) her opposing affidavit; (2) excerpts from her deposition; and (3) excerpts from two other Kmart employees' depositions, together with an exhibit from one of those depositions. In her affidavit, Moore stated that she returned to the store three days after her fall and stepped on the carpet by the black border where she fell. Moore further stated that the depression of the carpet at least one half inch below the black border caused her to stumble because there was nothing else in the area that could have caused her fall. Two weeks after her fall, Moore again returned to the store and noticed the black border was pulled away from the carpet in the shopping cart area, which was 18-20 feet from where she fell. Because dust and debris were on the tile floor where the border had pulled away from the carpet, Moore believed the black border had been pulled away for at least two weeks. Moore contended that the border being pulled away from the carpet created the same condition that had caused her to fall. In her deposition, Moore stated that she could tell that the border had been pulled away from the carpet in the shopping cart area for some time because there were footprints on the exposed tile area.

Moore also relied upon excerpts from the depositions of Derrick Hayes and Robert Bender, who were both Kmart employees. Hayes stated that the carpet and floor tile were inspected by taking a couple of shopping baskets and running them over the edging every other day. Bender testified that the carpet had pulled away from the border in the shopping cart area. Bender stated that the condition was caused by the carts pushing against the border as they were turned into the shopping cart area. Bender estimated that the condition had existed for two days, and when he noticed it, he pushed the border back under the carpet because it was still tacky. Bender stated that other than this one occurrence, he had never seen this condition on the border. Bender also admitted that another person had reported tripping or stumbling at the border area in August of 1996, and when Bender inspected the area, he saw that the border had slightly separated from the carpet.

## STANDARD OF REVIEW

"A no-evidence summary judgment is essentially a pretrial directed verdict," and we apply the same legal sufficiency standard in reviewing a no-evidence summary judgment as we apply in reviewing a directed verdict. Judge David Hittner and Lynne Liberto, *No-Evidence Summary Judgments Under the New Rule*, in State Bar of Texas Prof. Dev. Program, 20 Advanced Civil Trial Course D, D-5 (1997). We review the evidence in the light most favorable to the respondent against whom the no-evidence summary judgment was rendered, disregarding all contrary evidence and inferences. *Merrell Dow Pharmaceuticals, Inc. v. Havner*, 953 S.W.2d 706, 711 (Tex. 1997); *Connell v. Connell*, 889 S.W.2d 534, 538 (Tex. App.—San Antonio 1994, writ denied). A no-evidence summary judgment is improperly granted if the respondent brings forth more than a scintilla of probative evidence to raise a genuine issue of material fact. Tex. R. Civ. P. 166a(i); Judge David Hittner and Lynne Liberato, *No-Evidence Summary Judgments Under the New Rule, in* State Bar of Texas Prof. Dev. Program, 20 Advanced Civil Trial Course D, D-5 (1997); *see also Merrell Dow Pharmaceuticals, Inc. v. Havner*, 953 S.W.2d at 711. Less than a scintilla of evidence exists when the evidence is "so weak as to do no more than create a mere surmise or suspicion" of a fact. *Kindred v. Con/Chem, Inc.*, 650 S.W.2d 61, 63 (Tex.1983). More than a scintilla of evidence exists when the evidence "rises to a level that would enable reasonable and fair-minded people to differ in their conclusions." *Merrell Dow Pharmaceuticals, Inc. v. Havner*, 953 S.W.2d at 711.

Having set forth the standard we must apply in reviewing a no-evidence summary judgment, we must further understand the meaning of the terms "genuine" and "material fact," as they are used in rule 166a(i). For clarification of these terms, we turn to federal law. *See* Judge David Hittner and Lynne Liberato, *No-Evidence Summary Judgments Under the New Rule, in* State Bar of Texas Prof. Dev. Program, 20 Advanced Civil Trial Course D, D-5 (1997).

Materiality is a criterion for categorizing factual disputes in relation to the legal elements of the claim. *Anderson v. Liberty Lobby, Inc.*, 477 U.S. 242, 249, 106 S. Ct. 2505, 91 L. Ed. 2d 202 (1986). The materiality determination rests on the substantive law, and only those facts identified by the substantive law to be critical are considered material. *See id.* Stated differently, "[o]nly disputes over facts that might affect the outcome of the suit under the governing law will properly preclude the entry of summary judgment." *Id.*

A material fact issue is genuine if the evidence is such that a reasonable jury could find the fact in favor of the non-moving party. *Anderson*, 477 U.S. at 249, 106 S. Ct. 2505; *Matsushita Electric Industrial Co., Ltd. v. Zenith Radio Corp.*, 475 U.S. 574, 588, 106 S. Ct. 1348, 89 L. Ed. 2d 538 (1986). If the evidence simply shows that some metaphysical doubt as to the fact exists, or if the evidence is not significantly probative, the material fact issue is not "genuine."

*Anderson*, 477 U.S. at 250–51, 106 S. Ct. 2505; *Matsushita Electric Industrial Co., Ltd.*, 475 U.S. at 587–88, 106 S. Ct. 1348.

DISCUSSION

The elements in a premises liability negligence case are as follows:

(1) Actual or constructive knowledge of some condition on the premises;

(2) That the condition posed an unreasonable risk of harm;

(3) That the owner/operator did not exercise reasonable care to reduce or eliminate the risk; and

(4) That the owner/operator's failure to use such care proximately caused the plaintiff's injuries.

*Motel 6 G.P., Inc. v. Lopez*, 929 S.W.2d 1, 3 (Tex. 1996). With regard to Moore's claim, Kmart's motion for summary judgment asserted that there was no evidence of the following elements: (1) the existence of a condition that posed an unreasonable risk of harm; and (2) actual or constructive knowledge of the condition.

1. Condition Posing Unreasonable Risk of Harm

Viewing the evidence in the light most favorable to Moore, Moore stated that she tripped over the border separating the floor tile and carpet. Three days after she fell, she went back to the store, stepped on the carpet by the border where she fell, and the carpet depressed at least one half inch below the border. Moore stated that if the border had been under the edge of the carpet, the carpet would not have depressed, and she would not have stumbled and fallen. Although a Kmart employee testified that she did not discover such a condition when she inspected the area, we must disregard her testimony as contrary. *Merrell Dow Pharmaceuticals, Inc. v. Havner*, 953 S.W.2d 706. The Kmart employee designated as safety coordinator was responsible for checking the border by running shopping carts over the edging or border throughout the store every other day. One Kmart employee testified that when the carpet is pulled away from the border it is a potential trip hazzard.

Moore testified that the carpet depressed because the border was not under the edge of the carpet. Moore's testimony that this condition existed at the location where she fell three days after her fall is evidence that "rises to a level that would enable reasonable and fair-minded people to differ in their conclusions" with respect to whether the condition existed at the time Moore fell. *Merrell Dow Pharmaceuticals, Inc. v. Havner*, 953 S.W.2d at 711. Moore's testimony, coupled with the Kmart employees' actions and testimony that recognize this condition to be a potential trip hazzard, is some evidence that a condition existed that posed an unreasonable risk of harm.

2. Actual or Constructive Knowledge of the Condition

Moore relies on the Texarkana court's decision in *K Mart Corp. v. Rhyne*, 932 S.W.2d 140 (Tex. App.—Texarkana 1996, no writ), in support of her contention that Kmart had actual or constructive knowledge of the condition. In *Rhyne*, the plaintiff slipped and fell on a three-inch metal plate protruding from the concrete floor. *Id.* at 142. The metal plate was embedded in the middle of a concrete walkway and was used to hold a pipe that ran between the concrete and the fence to stabilize the fence. *Id.* The assistant manager, who completed an accident report, admitted that the metal plate was a dangerous and hazardous condition and that it was Kmart's responsibility to repair the condition. *Id.*

The case was tried to a jury, which awarded damages to the plaintiff. *See id* at 141. On appeal, Kmart argued that there was legally insufficient evidence for the jury to infer Kmart's actual or constructive knowledge of the condition that injured the plaintiff. *Id.* at 142. The appellate court noted that the assistant manger testified that the most probable explanation for the condition was that a Kmart employee in a fork lift truck broke the pipe while setting tables in the garden area. *Id.* at 142–43. The assistant manager further testified that the employee must have hit the pipe with great force to dislodge it and, therefore, should have assessed the situation after the impact. The Texarkana court held that the jury could have inferred actual or constructive knowledge from the assistant manager's testimony that the Kmart employee working in the area should have known of the condition based on the likely cause of the condition or from the physical condition of the metal plate itself, which extended three inches up from the floor in the middle of the aisle. *See id.* at 143.

In this case, there is no evidence Kmart had actual knowledge of the condition. However, in order for Kmart to prevail in a no-evidence summary judgment, there also must be no evidence that Kmart had constructive knowledge of the border condition. *Motel 6 G.P., Inc.*, 929 S.W.2d at 3–4.

Unlike the evidence in *Rhyne*, the evidence in this case does not support an inference that Kmart should have known of the condition based on the physical nature of the condition itself. However, constructive knowledge can be found if a reasonably careful inspection would have revealed an unreasonable risk. *Corbin v. Safeway Stores, Inc.*, 648 S.W.2d 292, 295 (Tex. 1983); *Johnson v. Tom Thumb Stores, Inc.*, 771 S.W.2d 582, 587 (Tex. App.—Dallas 1989, writ denied).

A Kmart employee inspected the edging every other day. The nature of this inspection was described as follows:

Q. Okay. Do you know—do you have any personal knowledge of how they would do inspections of he [sic] carpet and floor tile?

A. Robert Bender—I have knowledge of Robert Bender. He would come and our [sic] the store—whole store daily. He'd take a couple of baskets and run it over the tile and see how it would handle up—how it would hold up to the baskets running over it.

Q. And he would do this every day?

A. He would do it approximately every other day.

Q. Every other day?

A. Yes.

Q. And what I'm understanding is he would take a cart and kind of roll it across the floor tile and the carpet both?

A. The edging.

Q. The edging?

A. Uh-huh. And the carpet.

Q. Would he do this everywhere the edging was in the store?

A. Yes, sir.

Q. And he would do this like every other day?

A. Yes, sir.

While this is evidence that an inspection was undertaken based on the possibility that the border might pull away from the carpet, there is no evidence that such an inspection revealed or should have revealed the border condition that allegedly caused Moore to fall. Although an inference could be made that the inspections undertaken by Kmart in this manner were not reasonable, *see Johnson*, 771 S.W.2d at 589, there is no evidence that a different, reasonably careful inspection would have revealed the condition. Therefore, we agree with the trial court that Moore presented no evidence of actual or constructive knowledge and affirm the trial court's judgment.

---

## NOTES AND QUESTIONS

(1) *Sufficiency of No Evidence Motions.* A comment to the 1997 amendments to Civil Procedure Rule 166a states that "[p]aragraph (i) authorizes a motion for summary judgment based on the assertion that, after adequate time for discovery, there is no evidence to support one or more specified elements of an adverse party's claim or defense. . . . The motion must be specific in challenging the evidentiary support for an element of a claim or defense; paragraph (i) does not authorize conclusory motions or general no-evidence challenges to an opponent's case." Does this comment mean that the movant must only identify one or more elements of the plaintiff's claim and assert that, after adequate time for discovery, no evidence has been discovered that would be sufficient to authorize submission of the claim to the jury? Does it mean more than that? How does this differ from the former practice? See *In re Mohawk Rubber Co.*, 982 S.W.2d 494, 497–498 (Tex. App.—Texarkana 1998, no pet. h.) ("The rule requires a motion to be specific in alleging a lack of evidence on an essential element of the plaintiffs' alleged cause of action, but it does not require that the motion specifically attack the evidentiary components that may prove an element of the cause of action. The specificity requirement is designed to avoid conclusory no-evidence challenges to an opponent's cause of action. The rule requires a specific challenge to the evidentiary support for an element of a claim or defense. Causation is a specific element of tort liability.")

(2) *Defending the No Evidence Motion.* The comment to Rule 166a also states that "[t]o defeat a motion made under paragraph (i), the respondent is not required to marshal its proof; its response need only point out evidence that raises a fact issue on the challenged elements. The existing rules continue to govern the general requirements of summary judgment practice. A motion under paragraph (i) is subject to sanctions provided by existing law (Tex. Civ. Prac. & Rem. Code §§ 9.001–10.006) and rules (Tex. R. Civ. P. 13)." What does new paragraph (i) require of the plaintiff if the defendant challenges the proximate cause element in a negligence case involving an unreasonably dangerous condition of the defendant's premises? *See Nixon v. Mr. Property Management*, 690 S.W.2d 546, 548–549 (Tex. 1985). Does the "summary judgment evidence" need to be in admissible form? For example, if you were the claimant would you need to obtain an affidavit from a disinterested witness who provided a witness statement containing information that would be sufficient to raise a fact issue, if given as the witness' trial testimony, or could you use the witness' statement to show that a genuine issue for trial exists?

It is interesting to note that Chief Justice Rehnquist's majority opinion in *Celotex* provides:

"We do not mean that the nonmoving party must produce evidence in a form that would be admissible at trial in order to avoid summary judgment. Obviously, Rule 56 does not require the nonmoving party to depose her own witnesses. Rule 56(e) permits a proper summary judgment motion to be opposed by any of the kinds of evidentiary materials listed in Rule 56(c), except the mere pleadings themselves, and it is from this list that one would normally expect the nonmoving party to make the [required] showing. . . ." 477 U.S. at 324.

Although proposals for amending Civil Procedure Rule 166a to embrace the federal approach had been pending before the Texas Supreme Court for a number of years, the 1997 amendment's adoption was motivated by the filing of House Bill No. 95 "relating to summary judgments in civil actions" by Representative Joe M. Nixon of Houston. Representative Nixon's bill (which was withdrawn due to the amendment) would have superseded Civil Procedure Rule 166a, if it had become law. Under the bill, which would have become Chapter 40 of the Civil Practice and Remedies Code:

> If a motion by a defendant is based on absence of proof on a claim or issue with respect to which the claimant has the burden of proof, the claimant must respond with evidence sufficient to entitle the claimant to submission of the claim or issue to the jury. If the claimant does not respond as required by this subsection, the court shall grant summary judgment in favor of the defendant.

Proposed C.P.R.C. § 40.001(c) (H.B. 95 by Nixon). Is Representative Nixon's bill consistent with the approach taken in the amended rule? Is it consistent with the Supreme Court's decision in *Celotex*?

### [B] Procedure and Evidence

*Read Tex. R. Civ. P. 166a(d), (f), (g), (h).*

## MATHIS v. BOCELL

*982 S.W.2d 52 (Tex. App.—Houston [1st Dist.] 1998, no pet. h.)*

HEDGES, Justice.

In this medical malpractice case, Nancy Mathis, M.D. and Gary Mathis ("plaintiffs") appeal from a summary judgment granted in favor of appellees, James R. Bocell, M.D. and Thomas Cain, M.D. In their sole point of error, Nancy and Gary Mathis complain that (1) the summary judgment evidence did not establish the absence of material fact issues and (2) the affidavits of Drs. Bocell and Cain were legally insufficient to support a summary judgment. We reverse and remand.

### BACKGROUND

[In September, 1992, Nancy Mathis had arthroscopic knee surgery, during which the surgeon placed ethibond sutures over Mathis' meniscal tear. After the surgery and in the following months, Mathis continued to have swelling and an apparent infection in the knee. Mathis went to Dr. Bocell for treatment on many occasions, complaining of swelling. Bocell prescribed antibiotics and provided follow-up care, including an aspiration of the knee and an arthroscopic examination to determine whether infection was present. Bocell found no sutures and believed the tissue was in good condition. Mathis later sought treatment from Dr. Cain, still complaining of swelling. Dr. Cain also performed an arthroscopy and claimed to have removed two ethibond sutures. Mathis continued to have problems until November, 1993, when a third doctor performed an arthroscopy and removed two sutures.]

## PROCEDURAL HISTORY

In their original petition, Nancy and Gary Mathis sued Bocell alleging that Bocell failed to (1) properly diagnose, manage, and treat Nancy's post-operative infection and knee, (2) timely perform a subsequent irrigation and debridement of her knee in face of her recurring infection, and (3) use reasonable skill, care, and diligence to correctly perform a thorough irrigation and debridement of her knee in March 1993. Bocell moved for summary judgment arguing that nothing he did fell below the standard of care so as to cause or contribute to the damages of which plaintiffs complained. In support of his motion for summary judgment, Bocell attached his own affidavit.

Plaintiffs filed a response arguing that genuine issues of fact exist as to whether Bocell was negligent and whether that negligence caused Nancy Mathis' injury. Plaintiffs attached the affidavit of their expert, Dr. Julio V. Westerband, to controvert the facts stated in Bocell's affidavit. In his reply to plaintiffs' response, Bocell argued that Westerband's affidavit was fatally defective because plaintiffs did not attach the medical records upon which Westerband relied in forming his opinion. In response, plaintiffs filed a motion for leave to supplement Westerband's affidavit with those medical records. The record does not indicate whether the trial court ruled on this motion. The trial court granted Bocell's motion for summary judgment but did not rule on Bocell's objection to Westerband's affidavit.

While Bocell's motion for summary judgment was pending, plaintiffs amended their petition, adding Cain as a defendant. . . .

Cain moved for summary judgment arguing that he did not breach the relevant standard of care. In support of his motion for summary judgment, Cain attached his own affidavit. In their response to that motion for summary judgment, plaintiffs argued that (1) Cain's affidavit did not detail the standards of reasonably prudent orthopedic care and treatment for patients like Nancy Mathis; (2) Cain's affidavit did not detail how he met the standards of reasonably prudent orthopedic care; (3) Cain's affidavit was based on medical records not attached as summary judgment proof; (4) Cain's affidavit was conclusory; (5) genuine issues of material fact existed on negligence and causation because of inconsistencies between Cain's affidavit and the medical records; and (6) Westerband's affidavit, which was attached to the response along with the medical records he relied upon in forming his opinion, created genuine fact issues regarding whether Cain breached the standard of care and whether that breach caused her injuries. In his reply, Cain argued that Westerband's affidavit lacked credibility and did not raise a fact issue because Westerband never reviewed Cain's records.

The trial court granted Cain's motion for summary judgment, overruled plaintiffs' procedural and evidentiary objections to Cain's motion for summary judgment, and granted Cain's objections to the conclusory nature of Westerband's affidavit.

## STANDARD OF REVIEW

In reviewing a summary judgment, we must take all evidence favorable to the nonmovant as true and grant every reasonable inference in favor of the nonmoving party. *Nixon v. Mr.*

*Property Management Co.*, 690 S.W.2d 546, 548–49 (1985). If differing inferences may reasonably be drawn from the summary judgment evidence, a summary judgment should not be granted. *Id.* at 549. The movant's own evidence may establish the existence of a genuine issue of material fact on the plaintiff's claim. *Armbruster v. Memorial Southwest Hosp.*, 857 S.W.2d 938, 941 (Tex. App.—Houston [1st Dist.] 1993, no writ).

The elements of a medical negligence claim are: (1) a duty to conform to a certain standard of care; (2) a failure to conform to the required standard; (3) actual injury; and (4) a reasonably close causal connection between the conduct and the injury. *Armbruster*, 857 S.W.2d at 940. A defendant seeking a summary judgment must prove conclusively that the plaintiff cannot prevail. *Griffin v. Rowden*, 654 S.W.2d 435, 435–36 (Tex. 1983); *Armbruster*, 857 S.W.2d at 940. This may be accomplished by proving at least one element of the claim conclusively against the plaintiff. *Gray v. Bertrand*, 723 S.W.2d 957, 958 (Tex. 1987); *Armbruster*, 857 S.W.2d at 940–41. If the movant negates an element of the plaintiff's claim, the plaintiff must produce controverting evidence raising a fact issue on the element or elements negated. *Armbruster*, 857 S.W.2d at 941. The plaintiff must prove by competent medical evidence either that the defendant did something other health care providers using ordinary care would not have done or that it failed to do something they would have done under the same circumstances. *Birchfield v. Texarkana Memorial Hosp.*, 747 S.W.2d 361, 366 (Tex. 1987); *Armbruster*, 857 S.W.2d at 941.

## SUMMARY JUDGMENT FOR THE APPELLEES

The threshold question in a medical malpractice case is the standard of care, which must be established so the fact finder can determine if the defendant deviated from it. *Armbruster*, 857 S.W.2d at 941. In such cases, the court must be guided solely by an expert's opinion. Id. A summary judgment may be based on an expert's uncontroverted testimony if the testimony is clear, positive, direct, otherwise credible, free from inconsistencies, and capable of being readily controverted. Tex. R. Civ. P. 166a(c). The affidavit of an interested expert who is also a party to the case can support summary judgment if it meets these requirements. *Anderson v. Snider*, 808 S.W.2d 54, 55 (Tex. 1991). However, an expert cannot merely state that he knows the standard of care and conclude that it was met. *Armbruster*, 857 S.W.2d at 941.

### Dr. Bocell

In addition to setting out his credentials and qualifications in orthopedic surgery, Bocell's affidavit [described Nancy Mathis's condition on each visit, described the medical care provided on each visit, stated his familiarity with the standard of care involved in orthopedic and arthroscopic surgery, and stated his reasons for believing he had met the standard of care.]

Plaintiffs contend that Bocell's affidavit did not specifically establish the orthopedic standard of care and, therefore, is insufficient to sustain the summary judgment. We disagree. An interested expert's affidavit is sufficient to establish compliance with the standard of care if the affiant (1) states that he is familiar with the applicable standard of care, (2) states with specificity each examination and treatment performed, (3) states that the acts of the physician were consistent with the appropriate standard of care, and (4) states that there was no causal connection between the physician's acts and the plaintiff's injury. *Griffin v. Methodist Hosp.*, 948 S.W.2d 72, 74 (Tex. App.—Houston [14th Dist.] 1997, no writ); *see also Wheeler v. Aldama-Luebbert*, 707 S.W.2d 213, 215–17 (Tex. App.—Houston [1st Dist.] 1986, no writ) (expert affidavit stated with specificity each examination, each operative procedure, and each treatment administered to plaintiff; affidavit stated that expert knew what standard of care was for plaintiff and that treatment and diagnosis of plaintiff was standard of care and was same standard of care used by other reasonably prudent physicians acting under same or similar circumstances).

In this case, Bocell's affidavit met the requirements set out in *Griffin*. First, Bocell's affidavit described with specificity each examination and treatment he performed on Nancy Mathis from September 1992, through September 1993. Second, Bocell's affidavit stated he was familiar with the standard of care involved in orthopedic surgery, pre-operative assessment of patients, the technical aspect of orthopedic surgery, post-operative care, and the recognition and treatment of complications. Third, Bocell's affidavit stated that the standard of medical doctors in his field of practice requires patients such as Nancy Mathis to be "evaluated, diagnosed, and for treatment recommendations to be made to the patient and treatment rendered as required in accordance with the patient and the manor [sic] in which the patient is presented." Fourth, Bocell's affidavit stated that the evaluation, diagnosis, and treatment of Nancy Mathis, which he described in the affidavit, met or exceeded the standard of care in Houston. Finally, Bocell's affidavit states there was no causal connection between the infectious process in Nancy Mathis' knee and the presence of sutures during his treatment of her. We conclude that Bocell's affidavit was sufficient to establish compliance with the standard of care.

Plaintiffs also contend that fact issues exist as to whether Bocell was negligent in failing to remove the ethibond sutures and whether such failure to remove these sutures proximately caused Nancy Mathis' injuries. They assert that although Bocell denied that he was negligent and that he proximately caused Nancy Mathis' injuries, Westerband's controversion of Bocell's testimony raised genuine issues of material fact. Before we examine whether the Westerband affidavit raised a fact issue, we must decide whether the Westerband affidavit is proper summary judgment evidence.

Rule 166a requires that certified or sworn copies of all records or papers referred to in a supporting or opposing affidavit be attached to the affidavit. Tex. R. Civ. P. 166a(f). The last sentence of rule 166a(f) provides: "Defects in the form of affidavits or attachments will not be grounds for reversal unless specifically pointed out by objection by an opposing party with opportunity, but refusal, to amend." Plaintiffs argue that Bocell waived his objections to the defective nature of Westerband's affidavit because Bocell did not get a written ruling on his objection to plaintiffs' failure to attach medical records to Westerband's affidavit. A party must also obtain a ruling on an objection as to defects of form of an affidavit, or the objection is waived. *McConnell v. Southside Indep. Sch. Dist.*, 858 S.W.2d 337, 343 n. 7 (Tex. 1993); *Roberts v. Friendswood Dev. Co.*, 886 S.W.2d 363, 365 (Tex. App.—Houston [1st Dist.] 1994, writ denied). Thus, Bocell waived his objection to the lack of medical records attached to Westerband's affidavit if the defect is of the type that a party must object to and receive a ruling.

There is conflicting authority concerning the difference between a defect of substance and a defect of form in summary judgment evidence. Among the courts of appeals, there is contradiction, if not confusion, distinguishing the two. Rule 166a(f) refers only to "defect of form": there is no mention of its counterpart, defect of substance. The application of one or the other is crucial because formal defects must be objected to and ruled upon by the trial court, while substantive defects may be raised for the first time on appeal.

The concept of defect in form in summary judgment proof first appeared in *Youngstown Sheet & Tube Co. v. Penn*, 363 S.W.2d 230, 234 (Tex. 1962). The movant's summary judgment affidavits were allegedly defective because (1) they did not state that they were made on the personal knowledge of the affiants; (2) they did not affirmatively show that the affiants were competent to testify to the matters stated therein; (3) sworn or certified copies of the documents referred to in the affidavit were not attached; and (4) they contained conclusions and hearsay. The nonmovant failed to object on any grounds in the trial court. The supreme court found that although there was no merit to the fourth ground, the affidavits were defective based on the other three grounds. The court concluded that "The deficiencies which [nonmovant] now urges appear to be purely formal, and it may be assumed that they would have been corrected upon proper exception in the trial court." *Id.* at 234. It went on to state that "objections of this kind may not be raised for the first time on appeal when it fairly appears from the record that there is no genuine issue as to any material fact and that the moving party is entitled to judgment as a matter of law." *Id.*

The first mention of "substantive defect" appeared in *Landscape Design and Construction, Inc. v. Warren*, 566 S.W.2d 66, 67 (Tex. Civ. App.—Dallas 1978, no writ). In that case, the nonmovant argued that the movant's affidavit was defective because it did not reflect whether the affiant had personal knowledge of the facts recited in the affidavit supporting the motion for summary judgment. The movant urged that the defect was a mere formal defect which was waived by the defendant's failure to object in the trial court. The appellate court rejected that argument, explaining that "[a] defect is rendered'formal' only when it fairly appears *from the record* that, despite the deficiency, there is no genuine issue as to any material fact and that the moving party is entitled to judgment as a matter of law." *Id.* at 67 (emphasis in the original). The court concluded that the defect was "substantive," rather than "formal" and that no objection to the affidavit was necessary to preserve error on appeal. *Id.*

In interpreting rule 166a(f), several courts have held that the failure to attach copies of the documents relied upon in forming an expert opinion is a defect in substance, and therefore, can be raised for the first time on appeal. *See, e.g., Gorrell v. Texas Utils. Elec. Co.*, 915 S.W.2d 55, 60 (Tex. App.—Fort Worth 1995) (failure to attach sworn or certified affidavits of the extraneous documents referred to in the affidavit was defect in substance and trial court was not required to give offering party the chance to amend), *writ denied*, 954 S.W.2d 767 (Tex. 1997) ("We neither approve nor disapprove of the conclusion of the court of appeals that the failure to attach copies of documents referenced in the affidavit of an expert witness 'constituted a defect in the substance of the affidavit.' "); *Rodriquez v. Texas Farmers Ins. Co.*, 903 S.W.2d 499, 506 (Tex. App.—Amarillo 1995, writ denied) ("Failure to attach copies of the documents relied upon in forming . . . [expert's] opinion was a fatal defect in the substance of the affidavit, and the trial court properly excluded it from consideration"); *Ceballos v. El Paso Health Care Sys.*, 881 S.W.2d 439, 444–45 (Tex. App.—El Paso 1994, writ denied) ("The failure to attach to, or serve with, Dr. Krumlovsky's and Nurse Williams' affidavits sworn or certified copies of the medical chart or other record referred to therein is not simply a *defect in the form of his affidavit*, but rather is a *defect in the substance* thereof. This is true because there is no way to tell from these affidavits on what specific entries, notations or statements entered on the medical chart they are basing their respective opinions.") (emphasis in original).

Other courts have held that the failure to attach copies of the documents relied upon in forming an expert opinion is a waivable defect in form. *See, e.g., Martin v. Durden*, 965 S.W.2d 562, 565, (Tex. App.—Houston [14th Dist.] 1997, pet. filed) ("[W]e find the failure to attach sworn or certified copies of documents relied upon in expert opinion is merely a defect in form which is waived on appeal if not raised in the trial court."); *Noriega v. Mireles*, 925 S.W.2d 261, 265–66

(Tex. App.—Corpus Christi 1996, writ denied) ("If there is a dispute as to what is contained in the medical records, we agree that the failure to attach the medical records to the summary judgment affidavit would be a substantive defect. . . . [W]here there is no dispute regarding the contents of the medical records and the treatment the patient received, and in which the disputed issue relates to additional treatment that the patient clearly did not receive but arguably should have, the failure to attach the relevant medical records to the expert witness's affidavit is a formal, rather than a substantive defect."); *Knetsch v. Gaitonde*, 898 S.W.2d 386, 389–90 (Tex. App.—San Antonio 1995, no writ) (characterizing the failure to attach documents to summary judgment affidavit as a defect in form but ultimately disposing of case on substantive ground that affidavit itself raised issue of material fact).

How can this conflict be resolved? We believe that the best way to analyze these defects is on the basis of admissibility versus competency of evidence. A defect is substantive if the evidence is incompetent, and it is formal if the evidence is competent but inadmissible. *See* Address by Justice Sarah B. Duncan, *No-Evidence Motions for Summary Judgment: Harmonizing Rule 166a(i) and its Comment*, 21st Annual Page Keeton Products Liability and Personal Injury Law Conference (November 20–21, 1997) 25–26. Formal defects may be waived by failure to object, and if waived, the evidence is considered. Substantive defects are never waived because the evidence is incompetent and cannot be considered under any circumstances. *See* Address by Justice Sarah B. Duncan at 26 ("If evidence is incompetent, it necessarily has no probative value because it either does not relate to a controlling fact, or, if material, does not tend to make the existence of that fact more or less probable; therefore, there is no need to object to the erroneous introduction of incompetent evidence either to preserve the error in its admission or to ensure it is not treated as 'some evidence.' ") (citing *Aetna Ins. v. Klein*, 160 Tex. 61, 325 S.W.2d 376 (1959)).

Following this reasoning, we conclude that the failure of Westerband to attach the medical records on which he relied is a defect of form. Clearly, the affidavit is competent: it recites Mathis' medical history; it establishes the affiant as an expert in the field in which he is testifying; and it presents his expert opinion. The lack of underlying documents on which he relied makes the evidence inadmissible, not incompetent. Therefore, Bocell waived his objection when he failed to obtain a ruling by the trial court.

Having determined that Bocell waived his objection to the failure to attach the medical records to Westerband's affidavit, we will now examine whether Westerband's affidavit raises fact issues regarding whether Bocell was negligent and whether such negligence proximately caused Mathis' injury. . . .

. . . . According to Westerband, had Bocell been aware that he should have been looking for ethibond sutures, which are nonabsorbable, he might have meticulously scrutinized the knee to find the presence of such sutures. Nevertheless, Bocell opined that it "would have been an inappropriate course of action to have removed the good tissue visualized . . . in order to get down to the underlying sutures with no signs of infection, redness or irritation in the tissue."

Contrary to Bocell's assertion that there was no evidence of any infectious process relating to the presence of sutures during his treatment of Nancy Mathis, Westerband opined that Nancy Mathis suffered a chronic infection as a result of the retained ethibond sutures. Given these two contradicting statements as well as the inconsistencies regarding whether Bocell should have scrutinized the tissue more closely for the presence of ethibond sutures, we conclude that material fact issues exist. Thus, the trial court erred in granting summary judgment in favor of Bocell.

Dr. Cain

In response to Cain's motion for summary judgment, plaintiffs again relied on the affidavit of Westerband. Attached to Westerband's affidavit were the medical records upon which Westerband relied in forming his opinion. Plaintiffs argue that material fact issues exist as to whether Cain was negligent . . . .

. . . .

Contrary to Cain's assertion that the infection, if any, in Nancy Mathis' knee did not relate to the presence of sutures in her knee, Westerband opined that the failure to remove the retained ethibond sutures caused and prolonged Nancy Mathis' infection. Given these two contradicting statements as well as the inconsistencies in the number or type of sutures removed, we conclude that material fact issues exist. Thus, the trial court erred in granting summary judgment in favor of Cain.

CONCLUSION

We sustain point of error one. We reverse the summary judgments granted in favor of Bocell and Cain and remand the cause for further proceedings.

---

## NOTES AND QUESTIONS

At what point in the summary judgment proceeding does waiver of formal defects occur?

(1) *Drafting the Motion for Summary Judgment.* The grounds for a summary judgment must be expressly set forth in the motion itself. *See* Tex. R. Civ. P. 166a(c). Although exceptions should be urged in the trial court if the grounds for summary judgment are only expressed in an accompanying brief, failure to except does not result in waiver. *See McConnell v. Southside School Dist.*, 858 S.W.2d 337, 341–342 (Tex. 1993). Summary judgment evidence need not be referenced in the motion itself. *Wilson v. Burford*, 904 S.W.2d 628, 629 (Tex. 1995).

(2) *Role of Pleadings.* In general, summary judgment is not usually granted "on the pleadings," as the preceeding materials show. They may, however, form the basis for a summary judgment by defining the issues to which the summary judgment evidence is relevant, as when summary judgment is granted for a defendant when the plaintiff states no cause of action other than those that are defeated by the defendant's summary judgment materials. In *Hidalgo v. Surety Savings & Loan Ass'n*, 462 S.W.2d 540, 543 n.1 (Tex. 1971), the Supreme Court explained as follows:

> We are not to be understood as holding that summary judgment may not be rendered, when authorized, *on the pleadings*, as, for example, when suit is on a sworn account under Rule 185, Texas Rules of Civil Procedure, and the account is not denied under oath as therein provided, or when the plaintiff's petition fails to state a legal claims or cause of action. In such cases summary judgment does not rest on proof supplied by pleading, sworn or unsworn, but on deficiencies in the opposing pleading.

(3) *Summary Judgment Proof.* Neither a motion for summary judgment nor the response constitutes summary judgment proof. Civil Procedure Rule 166a provides that summary judgment

proof may be made by: (1) affidavits; (2) discovery on file; (3) stipulations; and (4) certified or sworn records. Tex. R. Civ. P. 166a(c). The motion for summary judgment and supporting proof is to be filed and served no later than 21 days before the hearing. If service of the motion is by mail, the motion must be served no later than 24 days before the hearing under Tex. R. Civ. P. 4. *Lewis v. Blake*, 876 S.W.2d 314, 316 (Tex. 1994). A response in opposition and any supporting proof is to be filed and served no later than seven days before the hearing. Late filed proof will not be considered on appeal, unless leave of the trial court appears of record or in a written agreement of counsel.

(4) *Formal and Substantive Defects.* What is the difference between a formal defect in summary judgment proof and a substantive defect? *See Trimble v. Gulf Paint & Battery, Inc.*, 728 S.W.2d 887, 888 (Tex. App.—Houston [1st Dist.] 1987, no writ)—holding that absence of jurat on affidavit is substantive defect. What if the movant's affidavit is conclusory or based on hearsay? *See Brownlee v. Brownlee*, 665 S.W.2d 111, 112 (Tex. 1984); Tex. R. Evid. 802.

(5) *Affidavits of Marginal "Experts": A Controversial Issue.* What should happen if the nonmovant, to dispute the movant's summary judgment evidence, offers an affidavit of an "expert"—but the court considers the expert clearly unqualified? Or, what if the "expert's" opinions are based on data for which there is no apparent basis other than the expert's imagination? *Cf. In re "Agent Orange" Products Liability Litigation*, 611 F. Supp. 1223 (E.D.N.Y. 1985); *In re "Agent Orange" Products Liability Litigation*, 611 F. Supp. 1267 (E.D.N.Y. 1985) (summary judgment granted because court refused even to consider opposing affidavits in which physicians made diagnoses on basis of written questionnaires and failed to consider what court believed were relevant epidemiologic studies).

(6) *Reliance on Deposition Excerpts.* Authentication is not required as a condition to the use of deposition excerpts as summary judgment proof. *McConathy v. McConathy*, 869 S.W.2d 341, 342 (Tex. 1994). The excerpts need not include a copy of the court reporter's certificate or an original affidavit of counsel certifying the accuracy of the copied deposition testimony. The 1990 amendments to Civil Procedure Rule 166a dispensed with the necessity of authenticating deposition excerpts for use as summary judgment evidence. *See* Tex. R. Civ. P. 166a(d). However, two courts of appeals have concluded that a litigant must present to the court deposition testimony on which the motion for summary judgment relies. In *E.B. Smith Co. v. USF & G,* 850 S.W.2d 621 (Tex. App.—Corpus Christi 1993, writ denied), the court interpreted the term "specific references" in Civil Procedure Rule 166a(d) to require that the party "show the court language from an unfiled deposition or other unfiled discovery document before the court rules on the summary judgment motion." *E.B. Smith Co. v. USF & G*, 850 S.W.2d 621, 624 (Tex. App.—Corpus Christi 1993, writ denied). *Accord Salmon v. Miller,* 958 S.W.2d 424, 428 (Tex. App.—Texarkana 1997, writ denied). Thus, the prudent practitioner filing a summary judgment motion will attach copies of unfiled discovery products on which the motion relies.

(7) *Is an Oral Hearing Required?* There is no live testimony at the summary judgment hearing, only the argument of counsel. (All proof is written and is required to be timely filed well in advance of the hearing.) May the trial court dispense with the hearing? The Texas Supreme Court denied application for writ of error to review a summary judgment rendered without affording a hearing, despite the nonmovant's request for a hearing. *See Adamo v. State Farm Lloyd's Co.*, 864 S.W.2d 491, 492 (Tex. 1993) (Doggett, J., dissenting).

## § 11.04 Settlement, Nonsuits, and Consent Judgments

### [A] General Attributes of Settlement Agreements

Most legal disputes are resolved before litigation. Most lawsuits are settled before trial. Indeed, a large portion of the pretrial process could be characterized as preparation for settlement rather than preparation for trial. Consider the following excerpt from Dorsaneo, *Texas Litigation Guide*:

**W. Dorsaneo, TEXAS LITIGATION GUIDE**

*§ 102.01* *

From the very moment that a trial lawyer undertakes a case, the possibility of settlement is a consideration. Factors of time and expense encourage both lawyer and client to work toward termination of a dispute short of an actual trial. Certainly, a plaintiff seeking money damages would prefer the cash in hand today rather than after the levy of execution on a judgment. Many defendants would prefer to compromise and substitute a certain result for the uncertainty involved in placing the dispute in the jury's hands. Obviously, neither side intends to "sell out," and the satisfactory settlement, like the trial of a lawsuit, depends upon a proper functioning of the adversary system.

In negotiating the compromise and settlement of a legal dispute, attorneys are, in effect, selling, buying, and bargaining. As salesmen or negotiators, they must know their "product" well. Preparation for settlement negotiations will vary depending upon the amount or extent of the matter at stake and the probabilities of successfully advocating the client's cause in court.

Timing the commencement of settlement negotiations may well depend upon the scope of counsel's preparation and investigation. Many successful plaintiff's attorneys work toward settlement before suit is filed by accumulating statements, reports, photographs, and medical bills into a settlement brochure by which the defense can "see the product" underlying the plaintiff's demands. Others may deliver to their adversary a copy of a petition and memorandum of law when the theory of the cause of action is important to the dispute. Once suit is filed and appearances made by all parties, skillful use of pretrial procedures may prepare counsel for settlement negotiations. Depositions and other discovery devices not only reveal the essential facts, but also provide an opportunity to determine the impression the parties and witnesses will have upon the trier of fact. Other procedures, such as special exceptions, partial summary judgment, or severance of claims or parties, may narrow the issues in aid of compromise.

Alternative dispute resolution procedures designed to aid the settlement process may also provide an opportunity to settle or to enhance the likelihood of settlement of the claims made in litigation. The Texas Alternative Dispute Resolution Procedures Act allows a court, on its own motion or the motion of a party, to refer a pending dispute to an appropriate alternative dispute resolution procedure, to be determined by the court after conferring with the parties [C.P.R.C. § 154.021].

During the preparation process, the trial lawyer should ascertain the positive and negative factors affecting the client's position and evaluate the client's chances of recovery or defense. The lawyer must be prepared not only to zealously try the case but also to advance the client's cause in negotiations knowledgeably and realistically, seeking a result that is advantageous to the client but consistent with requirements of honest dealing with others [*see* State Bar Rules, Art. 10 § 9, Preamble: A Lawyer's Responsibilities, Comment 2]. The lawyer must be prepared to advise the client of the reasonableness and effects of any proposed settlement, for it is the client's decision whether to accept a settlement offer [*see* State Bar Rules, Art. 10 § 9, Rule 1.02(a)(2); *but see* State Bar Rules, Art. 10 § 9, Rule 1.02, Comment 3—rights of client may be limited in class actions, insurance defense cases, and cases in which client has waived right of consent; T.R.C.P. 42(a)—court approval required for settlement of shareholder derivative suit; *see also* Liberty Steel Co. v. Guardian Title Co., 713 S.W.2d 358, 361 (Tex. App.—Dallas 1986, no writ)—when settling party is indemnitee, third-party indemnitor has right, if granted in indemnity contract, to approve any settlement before it becomes final].

---

Of course, a settlement agreement is a type of contract. Hence, the law of contracts, including principles of offer, acceptance, and consideration apply to settlement agreements. *See Stewart v. Mathes*, 528 S.W.2d 116, 118 (Tex. Civ. App.—Beaumont 1975, no writ). Settlement agreements frequently contain releases. Consider the following agreement, reprinted from Dorsaneo, *Texas Litigation Guide*:

**W. Dorsaneo, TEXAS LITIGATION GUIDE**

*§ 102.100[2]**

NO. ______

| | | |
|---|---|---|
| ______ [*plaintiff*] | ) | IN THE ______ COURT |
| v. | ) | ______ COUNTY, TEXAS |
| ______ [*defendant*] | ) | [______ JUDICIAL DISTRICT] |

COMPROMISE SETTLEMENT AGREEMENT

THIS AGREEMENT is between:

__________ [*Name*], __________ [*status or capacity, e.g.*, an individual *or* a Texas corporation *or* individually and as independent executor of the Estate of John Doe, deceased], who is referred to in this agreement as __________ [*abbreviated reference, e.g.*, plaintiff]

and

__________ [*Name*], __________ [*status or capacity, e.g.*, a Texas corporation *or* individually and as next friend of __________, a minor], who is referred to in this agreement as __________ [*abbreviated reference, e.g.*, defendant].

RECITALS

1. There is a dispute between the parties to this agreement that arose when __________ [*describe transaction or occurrence giving rise to litigation, e.g.*, plaintiff and defendant were involved in an automobile collision on __________ (*date*) at the intersection of Fourth and Main in Hillsboro, Texas].

2. Litigation was instituted as a result of this dispute. In particular, ________ [*name*] instituted a suit in the ________ Court of ________ County on ________ [*date*], in which ________ [he *or* she] claimed damages as a result of the transaction or occurrence described above. [*Add, if appropriate*: ________ [*name*] filed a counterclaim in that suit against ________ in which ________ (he *or* she) claimed damages as a result of the transaction or occurrence described above].

3. Both parties to this agreement concede that bona fide disputes and controversies exist between them both as to liability and the amount of damages, if any, that are due because of the disputes between them.

4. Both parties desire to dispose of the entire controversy and dispute between them, including all claims and causes of action of any kind that currently exist or that may exist in the future that relate in any way to the transaction or occurrence described in this agreement. The parties recognize that there may be claims or injuries arising out of the transaction or occurrence described in this agreement that are unknown to the parties at the time of execution of this agreement, or that may arise in the future. However, the parties have negotiated this agreement in full knowledge of the possibility of additional claims or injuries, and intend this agreement to settle and finally dispose of all such claims or injuries arising out of the described transaction or occurrence, whether known or unknown.

________ [*Continue with additional recitals as needed, e.g., describing consideration to be transferred:* Defendant warrants that she is the lawful owner, in fee simple, of that certain tract or parcel of real property situated in Hill County, Texas, that is described in Exhibit A. Exhibit A is attached to an made a part of this agreement].

## TERMS OF AGREEMENT

IN CONSIDERATION OF the mutual promises and agreements contained in this agreement, including the recitals set forth above, the parties agree as follows:

1. At the closing, ________ [*name of party, e.g.*, defendant] agrees to ________ [*state agreed obligation of party named, e.g.*, pay plaintiff the sum of $10,000 and dismiss its counterclaim in the court action described above or transfer to plaintiff all of her interest in that certain tract or parcel of real property situated in Hill County, Texas, that is described in Exhibit A]. A substantial portion of the consideration agreed to be paid in this agreement is for the express purpose of disposing of claims or injuries that may arise from the transaction or occurrence described in this agreement, but that are unknown to the parties as of the date that this agreement is made.

2. In exchange, at the closing ________ [*name of other party, e.g.*, plaintiff] agrees to ________ [*state agreed obligation of other party, e.g.*, execute and deliver to defendant a full and complete release in the form attached to this agreement as Exhibit ________ or release defendant from any and all claims, known and unknown, arising from the occurrence or transaction described in this agreement]. ________ [*Name, e.g.*, plaintiff] agrees and understands that this release covers claims and injuries of all types, including claims and injuries that are unknown to the parties at the time this agreement is made.

3. The lawsuit described in this agreement will be ________ [*describe agreed disposition, e.g.*, mutually dismissed, with prejudice, each party to bear its own costs or dismissed as to all claims and causes of action between plaintiff and defendant, after presentation to the court of

an agreed order severing all causes and claims against by plaintiff against defendant from any other cause or claim asserted by plaintiff against any other party].

4. The "closing" referred to in this agreement will take place ________ [*date*], at ________ [a.m. *or* p.m.], at ________ [*address, e.g.*, Stewart Title Company, 1206 Main Street, Hillsboro, Hill County, Texas].

5. This agreement is a compromise of doubtful and disputed claims. Nothing in this agreement is an admission of liability by any party, and nothing in this agreement may be interpreted as an admission of liability. Each party to this agreement expressly denies liability to every other party to this agreement.

6. This agreement is made according to the laws of the State of Texas. The parties expressly agree that this agreement is governed by, and will be construed and enforced in accordance with Texas law.

7. This agreement is binding on and inures to the benefit of the parties and their respective heirs, representatives, successors, and assigns.

8. This agreement contains the entire agreement between the parties. It supersedes any and all prior agreements, arrangements, or understandings between the parties on all subjects in any way related to the transaction or occurrence described in this agreement. No oral understandings, statements, promises, or inducements contrary to or consistent with the terms of this agreement exist. This agreement is not subject to any modification, waiver, or addition that is made orally. This agreement is subject to modification, waiver, or addition only by means of a writing signed by all parties.

9. This agreement may be executed in a number of identical counterparts, each of which shall be deemed an original for all purposes.

The parties have executed this agreement on ________ [*date*].

________________ [*signature of first party*]
________________________ [*typed name*]
______________ [*signature of second party*]
________________________ [*typed name*]

APPROVED AS TO FORM:

______ [*signature of attorney for first party*]
________________________ [*typed name*]
Attorney for ________________________
____ [*signature of attorney for second party*]
________________________ [*typed name*]
Attorney for ________

[*Optional*]

ACKNOWLEDGMENT

THE STATE OF TEXAS )
COUNTY OF ________ )

Before me, the undersigned Notary Public, on this day personally appeared __________ [*name*] and __________ [*name*], both __________ [known to me *or* proved to me on the oath of __________ (*name*) or proved to me through __________ (*description of identity card or other document*)] to be the persons whose names are subscribed to the attached agreement. They acknowledged to me that they have executed the attached agreement for purposes and consideration expressed in the attached agreement.

GIVEN under my hand and seal of office on __________ [*date*].

[*Seal*]

Notary Public in and for
Benson County, TEXAS
______________________________ [*signature*]
______________________________ [*typed name*]

Notary Public in and for the State of Texas
My commission expires ____________________
[*date*]

[*OR*]

CORPORATE ACKNOWLEDGMENT

STATE OF TEXAS )
)
COUNTY OF __________ )

Before me, the undersigned Notary Public, on this day personally appeared __________ [*name*], __________ [known to me *or* proved to me on the oath of __________ (*name*) or proved to me through __________ (*description of identity card or other document*)] to be the person and officer whose name is subscribed to the attached agreement. __________ [He *or* She] acknowledged to me that __________ [he *or* she] executed and is duly authorized to execute the attached agreement in the name of and on behalf of __________ [*name of corporation*], for purposes and consideration expressed in the attached agreement.

GIVEN under my hand and seal of office on __________ [*date*].

[*Seal*]

______________________________ [*signature*]
______________________________ [*typed name*]

Notary Public in and for the State of Texas
[*date*]

### [B] The Adjudicative Effects of Settlement

#### [1] General Principles

**McMILLEN v. KLINGENSMITH**

*467 S.W.2d 193 (Tex. 1971)*

POPE, Justice.

Joyce Lynn McMillen and husband sued Dr. William Klingensmith and Dr. Henry E. Martinez for negligence in the treatment of Joyce McMillen's injuries which she suffered in an automobile collision with a car driven by William Robert Perkins. Mrs. McMillen and her husband released Perkins from all claims upon his payment of $7,900. The McMillens then instituted suit against the two physicians who moved for summary judgment grounded upon the release. The trial court and the court of civil appeals rendered judgment for the defendant doctors, holding that the release of the original tort-feasor operated to release the subsequent tort-feasors also. 454 S.W.2d 424. We reverse those judgments and remand the cause to the trial court.

The collision occurred on June 2, 1967. Mrs. McMillen was hospitalized in Clarendon, Texas, for emergency treatment, including an emergency tracheostomy. She was then transferred to an Amarillo hospital where the two defendant physicians treated her. On June 9, 1967, Mrs. McMillen was released from the hospital, and accompanied by a nurse, returned to her home in California.

On May 2, 1968, Mrs. McMillen and her husband, upon receipt of $7,900, signed a release which named Perkins only and discharged him

> "from any and all actions, causes of action, claims, demands, damages, costs, loss of services, expenses and compensation, on account of, or in any way growing out of, any and all known AND UNKNOWN personal injuries and property damage resulting or to result from the accident that occurred on or about the 2nd day of June, 1967, at or near Clarendon, Texas.
>
> I/we hereby declare and represent that the injuries sustained are permanent and progressive and that recovery therefrom is uncertain and indefinite, and in making this release and agreement it is understood and agreed that I/we rely wholly upon my/our own judgment, belief and knowledge of the nature, extent and duration of said injuries,. . . .
>
> . . . .
>
> This release contains the ENTIRE AGREEMENT between the parties hereto, and the terms of this release are contractual and not a mere recital."

On May 22, 1969, the McMillens filed suit against Doctors Klingensmith and Martinez, asserting that their negligent diagnoses and treatment resulted in permanent damage to her larynx. The two doctors answered and moved for summary judgment, contending that the release of Perkins was also a release of them. The legal question presented is whether the McMillens may maintain an action for damages against the doctors for malpractice after releasing from liability the named tort-feasor whose conduct made the services of the doctors necessary.

Both parties before us recognize the significance of Cannon v. Pearson, 383 S.W.2d 565 (Tex. 1964), in deciding the issue in this case. We granted the application for writ of error in that case believing that the issue stated above was presented for decision. However, we ultimately concluded that the trial pleadings and the summary judgment proofs were not directed to that issue.

In Cannon v. Pearson, *supra,* we reviewed the rule that a release of an original named tort-feasor also operates to release an unnamed negligent doctor, citing three Texas cases which had followed the rule. Those cases are, Sims v. Auringer, 301 S.W.2d 286 (Tex. Civ. App. 1957, writ ref. n.r.e.); Borden v. Sneed, 291 S.W.2d 485 (Tex. Civ. App. 1956, writ ref. n.r.e.); Phillips v. Wright, 81 S.W.2d 129 (Tex. Civ. App. 1935, writ dis.). We then said that the rule had been disavowed by a number of jurisdictions and wrote that the modern tendency "is to treat the older rule as an illegitimate off-spring of the rule that release of one joint tort-feasor releases all, which rule is itself condemned by some of our ablest scholars on the theory that the courts have confused release of a party with satisfaction of a cause of action."

We cited a number of precedents which had adopted or changed to the rule that the release of the original named tort-feasor did not necessarily release an unnamed subsequent tort-feasor. In addition to the cases cited in Cannon v. Pearson, *supra,* we now add Dickow v. Cookinham, 123 Cal. App. 2d 81, 266 P.2d 63, 40 A.L.R.2d 1066 (1954); Kyte v. McMillion, 256 Md. 85, 259 A.2d 532 (1969); Smith v. Conn., 163 N.W.2d 407 (Iowa 1968); Steeves v. Irwin, 233 A.2d 126 (Me. 1967); Galloway v. Lawrence, 263 N.C. 433, 139 S.E.2d 761 (1965); DeNike v. Mowery, 69 Wash. 2d 357, 418 P.2d 1010 (1966); Rudick v. Pioneer Memorial Hosp., 296 F.2d 316 (9th Cir. 1961); Leech v. Bralliar, 275 F. Supp. 897 (D. Ariz. 1967).

The rule that a release of an original tort-feasor also releases a malpracticing physician finds its basis in the broader common-law rule known as the unity of release rule. The unity of release rule is based upon the idea that there is such a unity of the obligation or injury that a release of one is release of all. After a re-examination of this common-law rule, we have now determined to place our decision in this case upon a broader base than that expressed by our dictum in Cannon v. Pearson.

The legal basis for the unity of release rule has been challenged by every legal scholar who has examined it. 4 Corbin, Contracts, Sec. 931–935 (1951); 1 Harper and James, The Law of Torts, Sec. 10.1 (1956); Prosser, Law of Torts, Sec. 46 (3d ed. 1964); Prosser, Joint Torts and Several Liability, 25 Cal. L. Rev. 413 (1937); Salmond, Torts, p. 90 (11 ed. 1953); Throckmorton's Cooley on Torts, Sec. 80 (1930); 2 Williston, Contracts, Sec. 338A (3d ed. 1959); Note, 17 Ill. L. Rev. 563 (1923).

Underlying much of the criticism is the idea mentioned in Cannon v. Pearson, *supra*, that there has been a confusion of satisfaction of a claim with release of a cause of action. As expressed by Prosser: "A satisfaction is an acceptance of full compensation for the injury; a release is a surrender of the cause of action, which might be gratuitous, or given for inadequate consideration." Prosser, Joint Torts and Several Liability, 25 Cal. L. Rev. 413, 423 (1937). Unless the settlement with one of the tort-feasors fully satisfies the injured party, the release of one party should, according to Prosser, release only the tort-feasor who makes the partial settlement.

Those jurisdictions which purport to follow the unity of release rule have, nevertheless, looked with favor upon devices, such as the "covenant not to sue" or a reservation of a cause against others, which are used to skirt the rule. Texas is among those jurisdictions which hold that such devices will save the cause against another tort-feasor when a release would be fatal to it. . . .

These judicial efforts to avoid the harsh common-law rule have also been challenged for their artificial reasoning. They have been declared by the scholars cited above to be less than forthright, judicial fudging, and a trap for the unwary who do not notice in a document such nice distinctions. Breen v. Peck, 28 N.J. 351, 146 A.2d 665, 73 A.L.R.2d 390 (1958).

Mr. Justice Rutledge, while serving on the court of appeals for the District of Columbia wrote McKenna v. Austin, 77 U.S. App. D.C. 228, 134 F.2d 659, 148 A.L.R. 1253 (1943). He thoroughly examined the foundation and rationale of the unity of release rule. He said that it arose historically by an inappropriate transference of the metaphysics of the property concepts of joint estates and survivorship to the law of obligations independent of property. He summarized the practical reasons for abandoning the rule by saying:

> The rule's results are incongruous. More often than otherwise they are unjust and unintended. Wrongdoers who do not make or share in making reparation are discharged,

> while one willing to right the wrong and no more guilty bears the whole loss. Compromise is stifled, first, by inviting all to wait for the others to settle and, second, because claimants cannot accept less than full indemnity from one when doing that discharges all. Many, not knowing this, accept less only to find later they have walked into a trap. The rule shortchanges the claimant or overcharges the person who settles, as the recurring volume and pattern of litigation show. Finally, it is anomalous in legal theory, giving tortfeasors an advantage wholly inconsistent with the nature of their liability.

The Supreme Court of Alaska, writing in Young v. State, 455 P.2d 889 (Alaska 1969), reviewed the several alternatives which that jurisdiction could adopt, and it chose the path of simplicity. It wrote:

> In our opinion the rule which will bring most clarity to this area of ambiguous and conflicting release rules is one under which a release of one tort-feasor does not release other joint tort-feasors unless such tort-feasors are specifically named in the release. We are of the further view that adoption of this rule will insure that the intent of the parties to the release is given effect and will greatly minimize the possibility of any party being misled as to the effect of the release.

The rule is a simple one. Unless a party is named in a release, he is not released. A rule of this type is fairer and easier to apply. It avoids many of the problems arising from the present rule which often requires proof by parol evidence of the releasor's subjective intent at the time the release was executed. With a slight modification we adopt the rule suggested by the Alaska court. We hold that a release of a party or parties named or otherwise specifically identified fully releases only the parties so named or identified, but no others. Our holding in this case shall not affect releases presently in existence where it appears from the language of the release and other circumstances that it was the intention of the releasor to release the named parties and other persons generally identified. The release presently before us names only William Robert Perkins and makes no reference to any other parties.

In holding as we do, we preserve the rule that a claimant in no event will be entitled to recover more than the amount required for full satisfaction of his damages. Bradshaw v. Baylor University, 126 Tex. 99, 84 S.W.2d 703 (1935). One of the problems considered by the court in McKenna v. Austin, supra, was that of disturbing the law concerning the adjustment of rights between tort-feasors after a release of one tort-feasor. In deciding McKenna both Justice Rutledge for the majority and Judge Stephens in dissent, discussed this problem in connection with their choice of the better rule. We regard this as less a problem in Texas than in McKenna by reason of our decision in Palestine Contractors, Inc. v. Perkins, 386 S.W.2d 764 (Tex. 1965) which concerned true joint tort-feasors. See also, Hodges, Contribution and Indemnity Among Tortfeasors, 26 Tex. L. Rev. 150, 170–172 (1947). We feel that these authorities are also instructive on the effects of a release on the relative rights and liabilities of successive tort-feasors. The impact of a release effective only as to the named original tort-feasor on the extent of the liability of the successive tort-feasor is not yet before us. We reserve judgment on that problem.

We disapprove the holdings in Sims v. Auringer, 301 S.W.2d 286 (Tex. Civ. App. 1957, writ ref. n.r.e.); Borden v. Sneed, 291 S.W.2d 485 (Tex. Civ. App. 1956, writ ref. n.r.e.); and Phillips v. Wright, 81 S.W.2d 129 (Tex. Civ. App. 1935, writ dis.). We overrule Riley v. Industrial Finance Service Co., 157 Tex. 306, 302 S.W.2d 652 (1957) and the other Texas decisions insofar as they approved the common-law unity of release rule, but only in that respect.

This case is before us as a result of the trial court's judgment sustaining the defendant physicians' motion for summary judgment. This judgment was based solely on the conclusion that the release, which named only Perkins, released all other tort-feasors including the doctors. Under our present decision disapproving the unity of release rule, this conclusion was erroneous and the summary judgment for the doctors must fall. The judgments of the courts below are reversed and the cause is remanded for trial.

---

## NOTES

(1) *The New Rule: Parties Not Identified in a Release Are Not Released.* Before the decision of the Texas Supreme Court in *Knutson v. Morton Foods, Inc.*, 603 S.W.2d 805 (Tex. 1980), it was held that if the liability of a person not named in the release was strictly vicarious, the release of the active tortfeasor would serve as a release of the party whose liability was derivative or vicarious. *See Spradley v. McCrackin*, 505 S.W.2d 955–959 (Tex. Civ. App.—Tyler 1974, writ ref'd n.r.e.). In *Knutson*, the Supreme Court held that the release of an employee (Chastain) did not operate as a release of the employer (Morton Foods) despite the fact that the employer was entitled to indemnity from the employee. The Court justified its conclusion in the following terms:

> The Chastains may, as argued, be subjected to an indemnity suit by Morton Foods. It is true that the Chastains are not completely protected from all liability arising out of the accident. Moreover the Knutsons, under their agreement to indemnify the Chastains up to $10,000, may have to return that sum to the Chastains. Morton Foods says, therefore, that this suit by the Knutsons, a subsequent claim for indemnity by Morton Foods against Chastain, and the Chastains' claim for indemnity up to $10,000 against the Knutsons, presents an undesirable circuity of action and undermines the original settlement if Knutson has to give back the $10,000.
>
> There are reasons, however, which favor a recognition of partial settlements and the application of *Klingensmith* to this case and situation. We have long recognized that encouraging settlement and compromise is in the public interest. *Gilliam v. Alford*, 69 Tex. 267, 6 S.W. 757 (1887); *Fidelity-Southern Fire Ins. Co. v. Whitman*, 422 S.W.2d 552 (Tex. Civ. App.—Houston [14th Dist.] 1967, writ ref'd n.r.e.). The instant decision will aid in the achievement of that goal. A plaintiff will be able to settle with a tortfeasor who acts for another without being fearful of losing his cause of action against the party who may be liable under *respondeat superior*. At the same time, the party who is liable under *respondeat superior* will retain complete access to the courts for a full adjudication of his liabilities and his rights to indemnification.
>
> The Knutsons and Chastains knew about these possibilities, and they were exposed to these obligations to indemnify when they executed the release. They contracted with those possibilities in mind. Paragraph IV of the release, quoted above, fully states the rights of the parties. Only the Knutsons and the Chastains will be affected by the fact that this agreement may fail to protect the Chastains from all future liability, or may subject the Knutsons to a circuitous course of litigation resulting in the return of the $10,000 to the Chastains. Ironically, the only party that is troubled by the incompleteness, or wisdom, of

this release is Morton Foods. Morton Foods, however, neither participated in the negotiation of this instrument, nor paid any consideration for its release from liability.

Morton Foods, who was not a party to the settlement agreement, is the only one who does not want to give it the force expressed in the document, but it is no more prejudiced by the settlement than if none had been made. Morton Foods has actually been benefitted since the partial settlement made by the Chastains to the plaintiffs reduces Morton Foods' liability. We see no reason why we should be more concerned with the potential problems that the Knutsons and Chastains may encounter as a result of this settlement than they were at the time they executed the release. Accordingly, we conclude that the policies expressed in *Klingensmith* outweigh the perceived dangers in permitting parties to enter into an incomplete release, or one that may lead to a circuity of action, when the parties themselves are not disturbed by those possibilities.

In *Klingensmith* we adopted, with slight modifications, the rule that was proposed by the Alaska Supreme Court in *Young v. State,* 455 P.2d 889 (Alaska 1969). In *Alaska Airlines, Inc. v. Sweat,* 568 P.2d 916 (Alaska 1977), the Alaska Supreme Court addressed the exact question that is posed in this case; whether the rule established in *Young* and *Klingensmith,* requiring the identification of a party in a release before his liability would be extinguished, should be extended to include cases in which the non-released defendant was liable solely under the theory of *respondeat superior.* In answering the question affirmatively, as we do, that court declared:

> [B]ased on our reasoning in *Young,* we would reach the same result at common law by giving effect to the obvious intent of the parties to the covenant. The policy favoring termination of litigation and encouraging settlement agreements should here prevail.

568 P.2d at 930.

We disapprove the holding in *Spradley v. McCrackin,* 505 S.W.2d 955 (Tex. Civ. App.—Tyler 1974, writ ref'd n.r.e.).

(2) *A Party Not Named Must be Otherwise Specifically Identified to be Released.* The *McMillen* case abolished the unity of release rule in favor of a rule that only a "party or parties named or otherwise specifically identified" in a release are released. This formulation of the release rule differs from the Alaska approach and has produced its own difficulties. When are unnamed parties "otherwise specifically identified"? The Texas Supreme Court answered the question in *Duncan v. Cessna Aircraft Co.,* 665 S.W.2d 414 (Tex. 1984). Agreeing with the court of appeals' interpretation that "otherwise specifically identified" means "sufficiently particular so that a stranger to the release could readily identify the released party even though the party's name is lacking," the Supreme Court held that merely naming a general class of tortfeasors, e.g., "all corporations," in a release would not absolve all persons literally encompassed in the general language. Rather, the tortfeasor must be identified by name or "with such descriptive particularity that his identity or his connection with the tortious event is not in doubt."

In another case cited with approval in *Duncan,* a release executed by a patient that named and released a doctor "as well as all other persons, firms and corporations of an [sic] from all claims and causes of action arising from as in any way connected with medical treatment by the said [doctor] and the claims and causes of action . . . which were or could have been asserted in said cause No. 77-653 in the District Court of Guadalupe County, Texas" was held not to specifically identify a second doctor who failed to diagnose the problem caused by the first doctor's medical treatment. Although the release was signed after the second doctor's treatment had occurred, it was made before a lawsuit was filed against the second doctor and in connection with a settlement of a lawsuit which had been brought against the doctor who was named in the release. *Lloyd v. Ray,* 606 S.W.2d 545, 546–547 (Tex. Civ. App.—San Antonio 1980, writ ref'd n.r.e.).

### [2] Evolving Approaches to Settlement Problems: Which Rules Apply?

A complex body of legal rules developed during the 20th century concerning the effect that a settlement with a tortfeasor may have on the liability to the plaintiff of other tortfeasors. Currently, several statutory approaches exist, depending on the date the action accrued, the date the suit was filed, and the theory or theories of liability. The main approach applicable to most tort cases appears in Chapter 33 of the Civil Practice and Remedies Code in the 1995 "proportionate responsibility" statute, which applies to causes of action accruing after September 1, 1995, or any case filed after September 1, 1996. *See* C.P.R.C. § 33.001 et seq.

Current Chapter 33 carries forward the approach taken in the 1987 "comparative responsibility" statute in negligence actions as well as in actions for products liability, grounded on strict tort liability, strict products liability, or breach of warranty under Chapter 2 of the Business and Commerce Code. The 1987 "comparative responsibility" statute, which was also codified as Chapter 33 of the Civil Practice and Remedies Code, applies to cases based on these theories if the action was filed on or after September 2, 1987, and if the action accrued before September 1, 1995, and was filed before September 1, 1996. Acts 1995, 74th Leg. Ch. 136 § 3; Acts 1987, 70th Leg., 1st Called Sess., ch. 2 § 4.05. However, the 1987 version of Chapter 33 does not apply to intentional torts, actions brought under Chapter 21 of the Insurance Code, or actions brought under the Deceptive Trade Practices Act that do not involve death or bodily injury. *See* former C.P.R.C. § 33.002 (b)(2); Bus. & Com. C. § 17.50(b)(1).

Under both the 1987 comparative responsibility statute and the 1995 proportionate responsibility statute, a nonsettling defendant may elect to receive a dollar credit or a formula credit by filing a written election before the case is submitted to the trier of fact. C.P.R.C. § 33.014. An election by one defendant is binding on all other defendants unless another defendant elects a different method. In the event of a conflicting election or if no election is made by any defendant, all defendants are considered to have elected the statutory formula credit. C.P.R.C. § 33.014.

Actions filed after September 1, 1987, that are not covered by either the proportionate responsibility statute or the comparative responsibility statute appear to be governed by the 1917 contribution statute codified in Chapter 32 of the Civil Practice and Remedies Code. *See* C.P.R.C. § 32.001 et seq.; *see also Stewart Title Guar. Co. v. Sterling,* 822 S.W.2d 1, 5–9 (Tex. 1991). Under this approach, the adjudicative effect of the settlement can be devastating for a claimant because the settlement may extinguish a larger part of the claim than the dollar value of the settlement. For example, under the *Palestine Contractors* rule, the settlement and release of one of two joint tortfeasors releases one half of the claimant's damages, the release of one of three tortfeasors releases one third of the damages, and so on, depending on the number of tortfeasors, regardless of the dollar value of the settlement. *See Palestine Contractors, Inc. v. Perkins,* 386 S.W.2d 764, 766, 773 (Tex. 1964). The passage of time has all but eliminated the importance of the 1917 statute because of the broad coverage of the 1995 proportionate responsibility statute.

### [C] The Consent Judgment/Enforcement of the Settlement

*Read Tex. R. Civ. P. 11.*

## LEAL v. CORTEZ

*569 S.W.2d 536 (Tex. Civ. App.—Corpus Christi 1978, no writ)*

BISSETT, Justice.

The question presented by this appeal is whether the trial judge rendered judgment in accordance with an agreement between the parties which was dictated into the record. Fidel Leal and wife, Magdalena Leal, brought this suit against Narciso Cortez and other named defendants, where, among other things, they sought a recovery of certain lands. During the course of a jury trial all parties announced in open court that they had reached a settlement of the lawsuit. The terms of the settlement were then dictated into the record and the jury was discharged. Several months later a dispute arose between the parties as to whether a certain promissory note was to be made payable to Gloria Leal Cortez, as insisted by plaintiffs, or to the Cortez Trust, as contended by defendants. Following a hearing relating to the sole issue in disagreement, judgment was rendered that the note be made payable to the Cortez Trust. Plaintiffs have appealed.

Two points of error are brought forward. Plaintiffs contend that the trial court erred: 1) in rendering judgment when neither they nor the defendants mutually agreed upon all the terms of the judgment; 2) in not rendering a judgment which conformed to all of the terms of the agreement. They ask that the judgment of the trial court be reversed and the cause remanded, or, in the alternative, that the judgment be reversed and judgment rendered in accordance with the settlement agreement as the same appears in the record.

Rule 11, T.R.C.P., provides:

> "No agreement between attorneys or parties touching any suit pending will be enforced unless it be in writing, signed and filed with the papers as part of the record, or unless it be made in open court and entered of record."

In a judgment by consent, the terms must have been definitely agreed upon by all parties, and either reduced to writing, signed by all parties and filed among the papers of the case, or made in open court and dictated into the record. *McIntyre v. McFarland,* 529 S.W.2d 857 (Tex. Civ. App.—Tyler 1975, no writ); *Behrens v. Behrens,* 186 S.W.2d 697 (Tex. Civ. App.—Austin 1945, no writ).

It is absolutely essential that the parties themselves agree upon all the terms, provisions and conditions of the agreed settlement; the trial court has no power to supply terms, provisions or conditions not previously agreed to by the parties; and the trial court is without authority to render an agreed judgment that does not fall strictly within the terms of the agreement dictated into the record by the parties themselves. *Matthews v. Looney,* 123 S.W.2d 871 (Tex. Com. App. 1939, opinion adopted); *Pope v. Powers,* 132 Tex. 80, 120 S.W.2d 432 (Tex. Com. App. 1938, opinion adopted); *Wyss v. Bookman,* 235 S.W. 567 (Tex. Com. App. 1921, opinion adopted); *Farr v. McKinzie,* 477 S.W.2d 672 (Tex. Civ. App.—Houston [14th Dist.] 1972, writ ref'd n.r.e.). Further, it is not sufficient that a party's consent to the agreed judgment may at one time have been given; consent must exist at the very moment the trial court undertakes to make the agreement the judgment of the court. *Burnaman v. Heaton,* 150 Tex. 333, 240 S.W.2d 288 (1951);

*Wilmer-Hutchins Independent Sch. Dist. v. Blackwell,* 529 S.W.2d 575 (Tex. Civ. App.—Dallas 1975, writ dism'd).

In the case at bar, on the morning of April 13, 1977, during the trial before the jury, Mr. Hollis Rankin, Jr., counsel for plaintiffs, and Mr. Tony Martinez, counsel for defendants, announced that they had reached a settlement of all matters in dispute. The trial judge then instructed counsel for the parties to dictate into the record the terms of settlement. This was done. It was agreed by both Mr. Rankin and Mr. Martinez, who represented to the court that each had full authority from his respective clients to settle the suit, that Gloria Leal Cortez was to be conveyed as her sole and separate estate free and clear of all indebtedness approximately 100 acres of land, and the remainder of the lands in dispute was to be conveyed by the Cortez Trust to the plaintiff Fidel Leal for the total consideration of $130,000.00, to be paid $13,000.00 in cash and the execution and delivery of a note for the remaining balance of $117,000.00, to be paid in 15 equal annual installments, with interest at 7 1/2% per annum; it was further agreed that a second lien on the land to be conveyed by the Cortez Trust to Leal "will be given on this land to Gloria Leal Cortez as her sole and separate property to secure this."

A short time after the agreement was dictated into the record, and before the jury was discharged, counsel advised the trial court that they had decided to change some of the terms of the original agreement of settlement. The following statements were then dictated into the record:

> "MR. RANKIN: The agreement that we have heretofore dictated is the same with the exception that the property will be conveyed to the Cortez Trust.
>
> MR. MARTINEZ: All right. The property previously described as the property going to Gloria Leal Cortez.
>
> MR. RANKIN: The hundred-acre tract.
>
> MR. MARTINEZ: Right. Shall remain in the Cortez Trust; either way, as we see fit to do.
>
> MR. RANKIN: I would prefer to deed it.
>
> MR. MARTINEZ: As you wish. It shall be deeded to the trust.
>
> THE COURT: All right, Gentlemen, have you recited the amendment in the agreement now?
>
> MR. RANKIN: Yes, sir.
>
> THE COURT: Now, do I understand now that as amended the agreement now comprises the settlement entered into by all parties?
>
> MR. RANKIN: That is correct, Your Honor.
>
> MR. MARTINEZ: Yes, sir.
>
> THE COURT: And that you have settled all your differences?
>
> MR. RANKIN: We have settled the differences. The only change was that the hundred acres is to be deeded directly to the Cortez Trust.
>
> THE COURT: And the necessary instruments will be executed by all parties by agreement to effect the agreement, the settlement; is that correct?
>
> MR. RANKIN: Yes, Your Honor.

MR. MARTINEZ: Yes, Your Honor.

THE COURT: Any reason why the jury should not be discharged?

MR. RANKIN: No, Your Honor.

MR. MARTINEZ: No, Your Honor."

Whereupon, the jury was discharged. Later, and before judgment was rendered, a dispute arose with respect to the identity of the payee of the note. Plaintiffs contended that the payee, under the terms of the agreement, was Gloria Leal Cortez. Defendants contended that all parties to the original agreement, as amended, agreed that the Cortez Trust was to be the named payee. On September 26, 1977, a hearing was had, wherein the following statements were made:

> "THE COURT: All right, Gentlemen, the Court set a hearing for today with respect to an agreement that had been entered into while a jury was waiting in this cause, and I will hear from you.
>
> What seems to be your differences, Gentlemen?
>
> MR. MARTINEZ: Your Honor, on behalf of Dr. Cortez, I guess we tried this way back in April, but since that time Mr. Rankin had submitted to me a proposed judgment in this cause in accordance with our agreement and, obviously, there was a discrepancy in understanding exactly what was meant or said back on April the 13th of 1977 with regard to a note for a hundred and thirty thousand dollars.
>
> It was my understanding and the way that I read the notes of the court reporter from that time that the note was to be payable to the Cortez Trust, and the Cortez Trust would, in turn, deed the properties over to Mr. and Mrs. Leal.
>
> Mr. Rankin feels that the note was meant to have been to Gloria Leal Cortez, and that is our sole and only dispute that we have as of right now. And my client's understanding at that time was that it was going to go strictly to the Cortez Trust and he is staunch about the fact that it should so reflect in the judgment.
>
> MR. RANKIN: Your Honor, my recollection of the record—and Your Honor has it before you—was that we dictated an agreement providing that certain land, roughly a hundred and one and a fraction acres and a note for a hundred and thirty thousand or a hundred and thirty thousand dollars payable $13,000.00 down and the balance over a period of years at a certain percent should be given to Gloria Cortez as her sole and separate estate, and certain other terms and conditions, and this was dictated into the record.
>
> THE COURT: Yes. As I look at the recitations with which I have been favored now, and as I recall this situation, you gentlemen agreed that everything was going to go to Gloria Leal Cortez in her separate right.
>
> MR. RANKIN: Yes, sir.
>
> THE COURT: And that then a phone call was made in between and then the agreement was off.
>
> MR. RANKIN: He said it was off.
>
> THE COURT: And it came back because of the fact that the Defendant Narciso Cortez would not agree.
>
> MR. RANKIN: That is right. Unless she agreed to convey to—

THE COURT: You then came back and returned and at that time Mr. Leal had taken ill the day before.

MR. RANKIN: Yes, sir.

THE COURT: And then everybody returned and said it would go to the trust.

MR. RANKIN: The land, Your Honor.

THE COURT: Well, as I noticed, the record only made reference to the land specifically.

MR. RANKIN: That is right, sir.

THE COURT: But I remember the holdup between the parties was the fact that there was a projection by which she was to receive everything in her separate right. This was disagreeable. And then they talked to Mr. Leal and you came back and said that—so the problem as between both parties appears to be as to whether a hundred thirty thousand dollars was a part of the land.

MR. RANKIN: That is right.

THE COURT: I will give you one of two choices: I will declare a mistrial and we'll start trying this case again, or I will rule on the motion for a verdict from the evidence I heard in the case.

There was perjury in this case, my recollection is. I will give you one of two choices.

MR. RANKIN: Your Honor, let me talk to my clients and I will give you a—

THE COURT: Go ahead and discuss it, but I was very displeased by the fact that there was perjury."

After a short recess, the hearing continued, and the following statements were made:

"THE COURT: All right, Gentlemen, I will hear you.

MR. RANKIN: All right, Your Honor. For the plaintiffs, as I understand, the Court said that he would declare a mistrial or the Court would enter a judgment in accordance with his understanding of the agreement, and we are prepared for the Court to enter a judgment in accordance with the agreement as it was made and appears in the record.

THE COURT: Very well. Both sides ready, Gentlemen?

MR. MARTINEZ: Yes, sir.

THE COURT: Both sides ready?

MR. MARTINEZ: Yes, sir.

MR. RANKIN: Yes, sir.

THE COURT: All right. It is my opinion from all of the circumstances that took place at that time that it was the intention of the parties that all of the matters go into the Cortez Trust.

That is my opinion, Gentlemen, and I am going to so rule."

A judgment was then rendered which stated that the parties "had reached an agreement and settlement of this lawsuit," wherein the said 100 acres "is to be conveyed" to the Cortez Trust, and the Cortez Trust will convey certain described lands to plaintiffs, and that "plaintiffs shall give defendant Cortez Trust a note for $117,000.00," payable in 15 equal annual installments, "and further the sum of $13,000.00 should be paid to defendant Cortez Trust by plaintiffs."

It is plaintiffs' position that in the original agreement of settlement, it was agreed by all parties that the 100 acres would be conveyed to Gloria Leal Cortez free and clear of liens and as her separate property and estate and that the remaining lands (544 acres) would be conveyed by the Cortez Trust to Fidel Leal; and, also, that $13,000.00 in cash was to be paid to Gloria Leal Cortez and a note in the amount of $117,000.00 was to be executed to her as payee, which was to be secured by a second lien on the 544 acres. They admit that the original agreement was amended so as to provide that the 100 acres would be conveyed to the Cortez Trust instead of to Gloria Leal Cortez, but say that this was the only change made by the amendment. They further contend that at the hearing on September 26, 1977, that they agreed to the rendition of a judgment in accordance with the agreement as it was made and appears in the record, and did not agree to a rendition of judgment based on the trial judge's interpretation of the agreement.

The original agreement does not specifically provide that the note in question shall be made payable to Gloria Leal Cortez. With respect to the original agreement, all that was said concerning any deferred consideration for the transaction was:

> "[t]he total consideration will be $130,000.00, $13,000.00 cash, the balance in 15 equal installments, with interest at 7 1/2 per cent per annum, and a second lien will be given on this land to Gloria Leal Cortez as her sole and separate property to secure the payment of this."

The implication from the above-quoted statement is that the parties agreed that a note payable to Gloria Leal Cortez would be executed. Further, after the statement was dictated into the record, counsel for both plaintiffs and defendants, in the initial settlement agreement, used the word "note" in their discussions clarifying some of the terms of settlement, and agreed that the "note" would be an "on or before note" which would contain a "prepayment clause." No mention of the note was made when the agreement was amended.

We tend to agree with plaintiffs' contention that the trial court, in rendering judgment, failed to follow the final agreement made by the parties. Statements by counsel for each side have already been delineated. The amendment to the initial settlement did not refer to the note in question. The amendment affected only the disposition of the 100 acres. This is made clear by the last part of Mr. Rankin's statement, which was not contradicted by Mr. Martinez, when he represented unto the trial court:

> "We have settled the differences. The only change was that the hundred acres is to be deeded directly to the Cortez Trust."

After the trial court told the parties that they had a choice of either a mistrial or the rendition of judgment "from the evidence I heard in the case," Mr. Rankin said:

> "[w]e are prepared for the court to enter a judgment in accordance with the agreement as it was made and appears in the record."

There was no agreement by counsel for plaintiffs to be bound by the judgment of the trial court according to the trial court's understanding of the settlement terms. The court below had no power to alter the agreement or supply additional terms; it only had the power to put the agreement as made by the parties themselves into judgment form. The trial court may not enter a valid consent judgment when consent of one of the parties is lacking. *Burnaman v. Heaton, supra*. A judgment by agreement must fall strictly within the stipulations and agreements of the parties. *Edwards v. Gifford*, 137 Tex. 559, 155 S.W.2d 786, 788 (1941). Where the trial court undertakes to make an agreement of the parties the judgment of the court, and consent is lacking in the case, the judgment of the trial court must be reversed and the cause remanded for a new trial. *Carter v. Carter*, 535 S.W.2d 215, 217 (Tex. Civ. App.—Tyler 1976, writ ref'd n.r.e.). Accordingly, we sustain plaintiff's first point of error.

The circumstances suggest that the parties were not in agreement as to the identity of the payee of the note in question. It is apparent that both defendants' counsel and the trial judge were under the impression that the settlement agreement, as finally reached, provided that the note would be payable to the Cortez Trust. It is likewise apparent that plaintiffs' counsel was under the impression that the final settlement provided that the note would be made payable to Gloria Leal Cortez.

We hold that the judgment was not in accordance with the agreement of the parties which was dictated into the record. Plaintiffs' second point is sustained.

An argument can be made that we should reverse the judgment of the trial court with respect to the note in question. However, we do not believe that we should do so under the record here presented. Since it is evident that there was an honest misunderstanding between the parties, we believe, and so hold, that the ends of justice would be better served by a reversal and remand of the case for a new trial. *See*: *Morrow v. Shotwell,* 477 S.W.2d 538 (Tex. Sup. 1972); *National Life and Accident Insurance Co. v. Blagg,* 438 S.W.2d 905 (Tex. Sup. 1969).

Reversed and Remanded.

---

## NOTES AND QUESTIONS

(1) *The Burnaman Rule: A Consent Judgment Cannot be Rendered if Consent of One of the Parties Is Lacking.* Notice that there is a difference between a settlement agreement and an agreed judgment. Just what is the difference? *See Burnaman v. Heaton,* 150 Tex. 333, 240 S.W.2d 288 (1951), cited in *Leal, above*.

An agreed judgment, as the preceding case shows, cannot be rendered unless both parties are in agreement at the time the judgment is made. What if the settlement agreement does not satisfy the technical requirements of Civil Procedure Rule 11? Rule 11 imposes other distinct requirements. The Texas Supreme Court has held that such an agreement may not be enforced in derogation of Rule 11's requirements. *See Kennedy v. Hyde*, 682 S.W.2d 525, 528–529, 530 (Tex. 1984)—holding that compliance with Rule 11 and the *Burnaman* rule are both necessary because "Rule 11 is a minimum requirement for enforcement of all agreements concerning pending suits, including but not limited to, agreed judgments." A settlement agreement, on the other hand, can be enforced contractually if it has been properly made under contract law.

With this distinction in mind, consider the following hypothetical situation. Plaintiff and defendant enter into a complete settlement agreement, unambiguous in its terms, and they shake hands and sign it. The agreement provides for an agreed take-nothing judgment to be rendered on joint motion of the parties in exchange for a payment by defendant. The parties begin to walk down to the courthouse carrying a proposed form of agreed order, but the plaintiff begins thinking that the settlement does not provide him with enough money. As the parties stand before the judge, the plaintiff states, outright, "I've changed my mind and I no longer agree to the settlement." What courses of action are available to the defendant now?

(2) *Rationale of Leal v. Cortez.* What is the basis of the decision in *Leal v. Cortez?* Is it that the judgment was not what the parties agreed? Is it that the agreement to the judgment was not in effect at the time of the entry of judgment? Is it that there never *was* an enforceable agreement in the first place? Is it a combination of these rationales?

What should be done next by the parties relying on the "settlement"?

(3) *A Settlement Agreement May be Enforced Over One Party's Objection.* Although a party may revoke consent to settlement any time before the trial court's rendition of judgment, liability may still result for breach of contract. *S & A Restaurant Corp. v. Leal*, 892 S.W.2d 855, 857 (Tex. 1995). Thus, a Rule 11 agreement to settle is enforceable even though a party withdraws consent before the agreement is filed with the court. *Padilla v. LaFrance*, 907 S.W.2d 454, 461 (Tex. 1995). For a case in which a settlement agreement was enforced, see *National Maritime Union v. Altman,* 568 S.W.2d 441 (Tex. Civ. App.—Beaumont 1978, no writ). Plaintiff sued for certain pension benefits. After some discovery and while a trial setting was pending, the parties agreed orally on a settlement. Plaintiff then sent a letter to defendant offering to settle for $12,000. Defendant responded with a letter enclosing a proposed judgment, a proposed set of releases and a letter stating that if the papers met with plaintiff's approval, plaintiff should return them signed, and defendant would enter them and send a check. Plaintiff signed and returned the papers. Defendant then discovered that its records showed plaintiff was owed a lesser sum, and it repudiated the settlement agreement. Plaintiff then filed a motion to enforce the settlement agreement contractually, and the trial court did so, entering a judgment substantially similar to that proposed initially by defendant. The court of civil appeals affirmed. It pointed out that there was no question of lack of authority by the attorney, no question of overreaching and no contractual defense. The court emphasized the distinction between "the *Burnaman Rule* and the enforcement of an agreement to settle a case." The agreement here was contractually enforceable, and the judgment was not made as an agreed judgment. Hence, *Burnaman* did not apply.

## § 11.05 "Mary Carter" Agreements

### ELBAOR v. SMITH

*845 S.W.2d 240 (Tex. 1992)*

GONZALEZ, Justice.

In this medical malpractice case we consider: 1) whether the trial court should have submitted to the jury a requested issue concerning the plaintiff's contributory negligence; and 2) whether Mary Carter agreements are void as contrary to public policy. The trial court rendered judgment in favor of the plaintiff, and the court of appeals affirmed. 845 S.W.2d 282. We hold that the trial court committed reversible error in refusing to submit an issue on the plaintiff's contributory negligence. We further hold that Mary Carter agreements are void as against public policy. [footnote omitted] We thus reverse the judgment of the court of appeals and remand this cause to the trial court for a new trial.

I.

At 2:00 a.m. on May 8, 1985, Carole Smith was seriously injured in a single vehicle accident when the Corvette she was driving left the highway and collided with a tree. She received emergency treatment at the Dallas Fort Worth Medical Center-Grand Prairie ("D/FW Medical

Center") from Dr. Abraham Syrquin for multiple injuries including a compound fracture of her left ankle. In an effort to stop the bleeding, Dr. Syrquin performed emergency surgery closing the ankle wound. Ms. Smith remained under Dr. Syrquin's treatment for eight days at D/FW Medical Center after which time she was transferred to the care of Dr. James Elbaor, an orthopedic surgeon, at Arlington Community Hospital ("ACH").

While Ms. Smith was at ACH, she was treated by a team of physicians including Dr. Elbaor, Dr. Joseph Stephens, a plastic surgeon, and Dr. Bienvenido Gatmaitan, an infectious disease specialist. Upon admission to ACH, Ms. Smith was evaluated by Dr. Gatmaitan and placed on intravenous antibiotics. During the course of her stay, Dr. Stephens performed two debridements of the ankle wound. [footnote omitted] Although the issue of whether Ms. Smith's ankle was infected was hotly contested at trial, Dr. Stephens' progress notes following both debridement procedures indicated that there was no active infection present in the ankle. On June 3, Ms. Smith was transferred to the care of Dr. Wayne Burkhead at Baylor University Medical Center ("Baylor"). Four days after admission, Dr. Burkhead removed a two inch section of bone from Ms. Smith's ankle. Ms. Smith received treatment from several orthopedic specialists over the next three years which ultimately led to the fusion of her ankle joint.

Ms. Smith's medical records from D/FW Medical Center and ACH indicate that she refused to cooperate with the instructions of her doctors and nurses. She frequently refused to take her antibiotics, and directed family members to remove weights from her femoral traction device. Some time later, Ms. Smith was transferred to another hospital for surgery to shorten and fuse the bone, leaving her permanently disabled.

Ms. Smith filed suit against D/FW Medical Center, ACH, Drs. Syrquin, Elbaor, Stephens, and Gatmaitan. Sometime before trial, Ms. Smith entered into Mary Carter agreements with Dr. Syrquin, Dr. Stephens, and ACH.[3] The Mary Carter agreements provided for payments to Ms. Smith of $350,000 from Dr. Syrquin, $75,000 from ACH, and $10 from Dr. Stephens. Under the terms of each agreement, the settling defendants were required to participate in the trial of the case. The agreements also contained pay-back provisions whereby Dr. Syrquin and ACH would be reimbursed all or part of the settlement money paid to Ms. Smith out of the recovery against Dr. Elbaor.

Ms. Smith nonsuited her claim against Dr. Gatmaitan and settled and dismissed her claim against D/FW Medical Center. Dr. Elbaor filed a cross claim against Dr. Stephens, Dr. Gatmaitan, [footnote omitted] Dr. Syrquin, and ACH. He alleged that in the event he was found liable to Ms. Smith, that he was entitled to contribution from these defendants. Furthermore, Dr. Elbaor requested that the trial court hold the Mary Carter agreements void as against public policy, and alternatively, to dismiss the settling defendants from the suit. The trial court denied this request. The suit proceeded to trial against Dr. Elbaor and the cross defendants.

At trial, the jury found that Ms. Smith's damages totaled $2,253,237.07, of which Dr. Elbaor was responsible for eighty-eight percent, and Dr. Syrquin for twelve percent. After deducting all credits for Dr. Syrquin's percentage of causation and settlements with other defendants, the trial court rendered judgment against Dr. Elbaor for $1,872,848.62.

---

[3] These agreements acquired their name from a case out of Florida styled *Booth v. Mary Carter Paint Co.*, 202 So. 2d 8, 10–11 (Fla. App. 1967). When the Florida Supreme Court finally addressed Mary Carter agreements, it noted their potential to skew the trial process and thus established supervisory guidelines to limit their ill effects. *See Ward v. Ochoa*, 284 So. 2d 385 (Fla. 1973).

. . . .

III.

As previously noted, Ms. Smith entered into Mary Carter agreements with Dr. Syrquin, ACH, and Dr. Stephens. [footnotes omitted] Under the terms of the agreements, the settling defendants were required to participate in the trial of the case. The agreements also contained pay-back provisions whereby Dr. Syrquin and ACH would be reimbursed for all or part of the settlement money paid to Ms. Smith out of the recovery against Dr Elbaor.

Dr. Syrquin had performed emergency surgery on Ms. Smith's ankle. Testimony at trial revealed that Dr. Syrquin, who was not an orthopedic specialist, committed malpractice by closing the ankle too soon after debriding it. Eight days after the surgery, Dr. Syrquin recommended transferring Ms. Smith to ACH where she came under the care of, among others, Dr. Elbaor, an orthopedic specialist. At ACH, Dr. Elbaor observed but did not participate in two additional debridements of Ms. Smith's ankle which were performed by Dr. Stephens, a plastic surgeon. Dr. Stephens sought to explore and alleviate any infection in Ms. Smith's ankle. Additional expert medical testimony elicited during the trial demonstrated that, in all probability, Ms. Smith's ankle was beyond restoration by the time she arrived at ACH. Arguably neither the subsequent surgeries performed at ACH nor the care she received there could have remedied the damage caused by Dr. Syrquin's malpractice.

Although the Mary Carter agreements were not entered into evidence, the trial judge was troubled by them and he took remedial measures to mitigate their harmful effects by reapportioning the peremptory challenges, changing the order of proceedings to favor Dr. Elbaor, allowing counsel to explain the agreements to the jury, and instructing the jury regarding the agreements. [footnote omitted]

During the trial, the settling defendants' attorneys, who sat at the table with Dr. Elbaor's attorneys, vigorously assisted Ms. Smith in pointing the finger of culpability at Dr. Elbaor. This created some odd conflicts of interest and some questionable representations of fact. For example, although Ms. Smith's own experts testified that Dr. Syrquin committed malpractice, her attorney stated during voir dire and in her opening statement that Dr. Syrquin's conduct was "heroic" and that Dr. Elbaor's negligence caused Ms. Smith's damages. And during her closing argument, Ms. Smith's attorney urged the jury to find that Dr. Syrquin had not caused Ms. Smith's damages. This is hardly the kind of statement expected from a plaintiff's lawyer regarding a named defendant. ACH and Drs. Syrquin and Stephens had remained defendants of record, but their attorneys asserted during voir dire that Ms. Smith's damages were "devastating," "astoundingly high," and "astronomical." Furthermore, on cross examination they elicited testimony from Ms. Smith favorable to her and requested recovery for pain and mental anguish. The settling defendants' attorneys also abandoned their pleadings on Ms. Smith's contributory negligence, argued that Ms. Smith should be awarded all of her alleged damages, and urged that Dr. Elbaor was 100 percent liable.

A.

The term "Mary Carter agreement" has been defined in different ways by various courts and commentators.[13] This Court has yet to definitively define the requisite elements of a Mary Carter agreement—our prior pronouncements utilized different definitions of the term. *Compare General Motors Corp. v. Simmons,* 558 S.W.2d 855 (Tex. 1977) (a Mary Carter agreement is a settlement where the settling defendant remains a party at trial and retains a financial stake in the plaintiff's recovery), *overruled,* on other grounds by *Duncan v. Cessna Aircraft Co.,* 665 S.W.2d 414 (Tex. 1984) *with Bristol-Myers Co. v. Gonzales,* 561 S.W.2d 801, 805 (Tex. 1978) (a Mary Carter agreement is a settlement where the settling defendant retains a financial interest in the plaintiff's recovery). Today we clarify what we mean by the term "Mary Carter agreement." A Mary Carter agreement exists when the settling defendant retains a financial stake in the plaintiff's recovery *and* remains a party at the trial of the case. This definition comports with both the present majority view and the original understanding of the term. [footnotes omitted]

A Mary Carter agreement exists, under our definition, when the plaintiff enters into a settlement agreement with one defendant and goes to trial against the remaining defendant(s). The settling defendant, who remains a party, guarantees the plaintiff a minimum payment, which may be offset in whole or in part by an excess judgment recovered at trial. *See General Motors Corp. v. Simmons,* 558 S.W.2d 855, 858 (Tex. 1977), *overruled,* on other grounds by *Duncan v. Cessna Aircraft Co.,* 665 S.W.2d 414, 427 (Tex. 1984). This creates a tremendous incentive for the settling defendant to ensure that the plaintiff succeeds in obtaining a sizable recovery, and thus motivates the defendant to assist greatly in the plaintiff's presentation of the case (as occurred here). Indeed, Mary Carter agreements generally, but not always, contain a clause requiring the settling defendant to participate in the trial on the plaintiff's behalf.

Given this Mary Carter scenario, it is difficult to surmise how these agreements promote settlement. Although the agreements do secure the partial settlement of a lawsuit, they nevertheless nearly always ensure a trial against the non-settling defendant. *Bedford School Dist. v. Caron Constr. Co.,* 367 A.2d 1051, 1054 (N.H. 1976) (agreement required plaintiff to prosecute claim against remaining defendant and plaintiff could not settle the claim for under $20,000 without the consent of the settling defendant); *Lum v. Stinnet,* 488 P.2d 347, 348 (Nev. 1971) (same). Mary Carter agreements frequently make litigation inevitable, because they grant the settling defendant veto power over any proposed settlement between the plaintiff and any remaining defendant. *See Bass v. Phoenix Seadrill/78 Ltd.,* 749 F.2d 1154, 1156 (5th Cir. 1985) (Mary Carter agreement gave settling defendant veto power). Thus, "[o]nly a mechanical

[13] The majority of cases and commentators define "Mary Carter agreement" as one in which the settling defendant possesses a financial stake in the outcome of the case and the settling defendant remains a party to the litigation. *See Ward v. Ochoa,* 284 So. 2d 385, 387 (Fla. 1973); *General Motors Corp. v. Lahocki,* 286 Md. 714, 410 A.2d 1039, 1042 (1980); *Johnson v. Moberg,* 334 N.W.2d 411, 415 (Minn. 1983); *Bedford School Dist. v. Caron Constr. Co.,* 116 N.H. 800, 367 A.2d 1051, 1053 (1976); *Cox v. Kelsey-Hayes Co.,* 594 P.2d 354, 357 (Okla. 1978); *General Motors Corp. v. Simmons,* 558 S.W.2d 855, 858 (Tex. 1977); *Vermont Union School Dist. v. H.P. Cummings Constr. Co.,* 143 Vt. 416, 469 A.2d 742, 748 (1983); John E. Benedict, Note, *It's a Mistake to Tolerate the Mary Carter Agreement,* 87 Columbia L. Rev. 368, 369–70 (1987); David R. Miller, Comment, *Mary Carter Agreements: Unfair and Unnecessary,* 32 Sw. L.J. 779, 783–84 (1978). Many cases also describe other requisite elements of a Mary Carter agreement, such as secrecy. *See, e.g., Ward,* 284 So. 2d at 387. Other cases and commentators argue that a Mary Carter agreement exists any time the settling defendant possesses a financial interest in the plaintiff's recovery. *See Bristol-Myers Co. v. Gonzales,* 561 S.W.2d 801, 805 (Tex. 1978); Robin Renee Green, Comment, *Mary Carter Agreements: The Unsolved Evidentiary Problems in Texas,* 40 Baylor L. Rev. 449, 451 (1988).

jurisprudence could characterize Mary Carter arrangements as promoting compromise and discouraging litigation—they plainly do just the opposite." *Stein v. American Residential Mgmt.*, 781 S.W.2d 385, 389 (Tex. App.—Houston [14th Dist.] 1989), *writ denied per curiam*, 793 S.W.2d 1 (Tex. 1990).

In his concurring opinion in *Scurlock Oil Co. v. Smithwick*, 724 S.W.2d 1, 8 (Tex. 1986) (on motion for rehearing), Justice Spears pointed out that "Mary Carter Agreements should be prohibited because they are inimical to the adversary system, and they do not promote—settlement their primary justification." The truth of this statement has been recognized by commentators and has been proven by the subsequent history regarding the use of Mary Carter agreements. [footnote omitted]

The dissent approves of the supervisory guidelines suggested in the *Smithwick* concurrence, but his opinion misses the point. These guidelines were suggested as a stop-gap measure to ameliorate the harmful effects of Mary Carter agreements until this court finally ruled on the agreements' propriety. Our inaction has created confusion because the question as to whether Mary Carter agreements are valid has remained open. *See, e.g., Stein*, 781 S.W.2d at 388 ("Texas Supreme Court has not passed squarely on the question of [Mary Carter agreements'] validity"); *Adams v. Petrade Int'l, Inc.*, 754 S.W.2d 696, 718 (Tex. App.—Houston [1st Dist.] 1988, writ denied) ("the Texas Supreme Court has not held that such settlements are invalid"); *Lubbock Mfg. Co. v. Perez*, 591 S.W.2d 907, 920 (Tex. Civ. App.—Waco 1979, dism. arg.) (whether Mary Carter agreements are against public policy is "matter for determination by our Supreme Court of Texas").

B.

Many jurisdictions have decided to tolerate the ill effects of Mary Carter agreements, presumably because they believe that the agreements promote settlement. Some have sought to mitigate the agreements' harmful skewing of the trial process by imposing prophylactic protections. [footnote omitted] Indeed, Texas previously has taken such an approach. *See Stein*, 781 S.W.2d at 389 (problematic incentives created by Mary Carter agreements require supervisory guidelines enabling trial judges to "keep a short leash on Mary Carter agreements' potential for wreaking havoc on the civil justice system"); *Smithwick*, 724 S.W.2d at 8–12 (Spears, J., concurring). [footnote omitted] These protective measures generally seek to remove the secrecy within which Mary Carter agreements traditionally have been shrouded. *See Slusher v. Ospital*, 777 P.2d 437, 440 (Utah 1977) (secrecy is the essence of a Mary Carter agreement).

Justice Spears rightly noted in *Smithwick* the falsity of the premise upon which the prophylactic protection approach is founded, namely, the promotion of equitable settlements. *Id.* at 8. Mary Carter agreements instead:

> present to the jury a sham of adversity between the plaintiff and one co-defendant while these parties are actually allied for the purpose of securing a substantial judgment for the plaintiff and, in some cases, exoneration for the settling defendant.

June F. Entman, *Mary Carter Agreements: An Assessment of Attempted Solutions,* 38 U. Fla. L. Rev. 521, 574 (1986); *see also General Motors Corp. v. Lahocki,* 410 A.2d 1039, 1046 (Md. 1980). The agreements pressure the "settling" defendant to alter the character of the suit by contributing discovery material, peremptory challenges, trial tactics, supportive witness examination, and jury influence to the plaintiff's cause. *See* John E. Benedict, Note, *It's A Mistake to*

*Tolerate the Mary Carter Agreement*, 87 Columbia L. Rev. 368, 372–73 (1987). These procedural advantages distort the case presented before a jury that came "to court expecting to see a contest between the plaintiff and the defendants [and] instead see[s] one of the defendants cooperating with the plaintiff." *Smithwick*, 724 S.W.2d at 9 (Spears, J., concurring).

Mary Carter agreements not only allow plaintiffs to buy support for their case, [footnote omitted] they also motivate more culpable defendants to "make a 'good deal' [and thus] end up paying little or nothing in damages." *Id.; cf. Slayton v. Ford Motor Co.*, 435 A.2d 946, 947 (Vt. 1981) (jury may infer that non-settling defendant was the most culpable defendant because plaintiff did not settle with that defendant). Remedial measures cannot overcome nor sufficiently alleviate the malignant effects that Mary Carter agreements inflict upon our adversarial system. No persuasive public policy justifies them, and they are not legitimized simply because this practice may continue in the absence of these agreements. The Mary Carter agreement is simply an unwise and champertous device that has failed to achieve its intended purpose. *See Lum*, 488 P.2d at 351 (Mary Carter agreements essentially champertous because settling defendant retains financial interest in plaintiff's success against non-settling defendant); *cf. Monjay v. Evergreen School Dist.*, 537 P.2d 825, 830 (Wash. App. 1975).

IV.

The case before us reveals yet another jury trial and verdict distorted by a Mary Carter agreement. The trial judge, who fully grasped the detrimental effect these agreements could have on the outcome, attempted to monitor the lawsuit by assiduously applying the guidelines suggested in the *Smithwick* concurrence. The conduct of this trial, however, confirms the apprehension expressed by Justice Spears in *Smithwick* that these remedial measures would only mitigate and not eliminate the unjust influences exerted on a trial by Mary Carter agreements. Equalizing peremptory strikes, reordering proceedings, thoroughly disclosing the true alignment of the parties, and revealing the agreement's substance cannot overcome collusion between the plaintiff and settling defendants who retain a financial interest in the plaintiff's success. In fact, Mary Carter agreements may force attorneys into questionable ethical situations under Rule 3.05 of the Texas Disciplinary Rules of Professional Conduct, which is titled "Maintaining the Impartiality of the Tribunal." Comment 2 to that rule notes, regarding alternate methods of dispute resolution (like Mary Carter agreements), that "a lawyer should avoid any conduct that is or could reasonably be construed as being intended to corrupt or to unfairly influence the decisionmaker." *See* Supreme Court of Texas, Texas Disciplinary Rules of Professional Conduct art. X, 9 (1990); *cf.* Model Code of Professional Responsibility EC—720 (1979) (attorneys responsible for upholding adversarial system). The dissent acknowledges that Mary Carter agreements skew the trial process. This effect reasonably could be construed as unfairly influencing the decisionmaker.

As a matter of public policy, this Court favors settlements, but we do not favor partial settlements that promote rather than discourage further litigation. And we do not favor settlement arrangements that skew the trial process, mislead the jury, promote unethical collusion among nominal adversaries, and create the likelihood that a less culpable defendant will be hit with the full judgment. The bottom line is that our public policy favoring fair trials outweighs our public policy favoring partial settlements.

This case typifies the kind of procedural and substantive damage Mary Carter agreements can inflict upon our adversarial system. Thus, we declare them void as violative of sound public policy.

However, we do recognize the hardships that our decision today will create on our already burdened courts. Thus, we must decide whether our decision voiding Mary Carter agreements will apply prospectively or retrospectively. Although our decisions usually apply retrospectively, exceptions are recognized when considerations of fairness and policy dictate prospective effect only. *Duncan v. Cessna Aircraft Co.,* 665 S.W.2d 414, 434 (Tex. 1984). In *Carrollton Farmers Branch Ind. School Dist. v. Edgewood Ind. School Dist.,* 826 S.W.2d 489, 518–19 (Tex. 1992), we adopted the three factors from the United States Supreme Court's decision in *Chevron Oil Co. v. Huson,* 404 U.S. 97, 106–07 (1971) to determine whether to apply a decision prospectively or retroactively. These factors are: (1) whether the decision establishes a new principle of law by either overruling clear past precedent on which litigants may have relied or by deciding an issue of first impression whose resolution was not clearly foreshadowed; (2) whether prospective or retroactive application of the particular rule will further or retard its operation through an examination of the history, purpose, and effect of the rule; and (3) whether retroactive application of the rule could produce substantial inequitable results. *Id.*

The first and the third of these factors weigh clearly in favor of a determination of prospective application. This case represents an issue of first impression whose resolution was not clearly foreshadowed. Although commentators have routinely criticized the Mary Carter agreement, only a couple of states have previously held that such agreements are void. [footnote omitted] The only Texas opinion which even hinted that such agreements might be void was Justice Spear's concurrence in *Scurlock Oil Co. v. Smithwick,* 724 S.W.2d 1, 8 (Tex. 1986) (on motion for rehearing). Therefore, we conclude that the first factor weighs heavily in favor of prospective application. The third factor likewise weighs heavily in favor of prospective application because retroactive application would create substantial inequitable results for litigants who would have to re-try their cases and re-enter the clogged court dockets of this state when they could not have known that such agreements would be held to be void as against public policy. The second factor favors retroactive application of the rule since the rule is designed to prevent unfair trials resulting from the use of Mary Carter agreements. However, as we discussed in *Edgewood,* 826 S.W.2d at 519 n.36, all *Chevron* factors are not required to favor prospectivity: we engage in a broad balancing of the factors to determine the ultimate considerations of fairness and policy. We conclude that the strength of the first and third factors outweigh the second factor. [footnote omitted] Thus, we declare, as a matter of sound administration and fairness, that this holding shall be applicable only in the present case, to those cases in the judicial pipeline where error has been preserved, and to those actions tried on or after December 2, 1992. [footnote omitted]

V.

In short, the evidence in the record creates a fact issue of comparative causation. The jury should have been allowed to pass not only on Drs. Elbaor's, Syrquin's, and Stephens' alleged negligence, but also on Ms. Smith's alleged negligence. Under this record, the trial court should have left these fact issues for the jury's resolution within the framework of our well-established comparative negligence law. The failure to submit the issues was calculated to cause, and probably did cause, the rendition of an improper judgment in this case. Tex. R. App. P. 81. The danger in allowing the trial court's action to stand uncorrected is that this would indicate that patients who refuse to take medication necessary to their recovery are not contributorily negligent even though their unwillingness may have causally contributed to their injuries. Additionally, the judgment in this case was fundamentally driven by Mary Carter agreements. However, because of the existence of a severability clause in some of the agreements but not others and the creation of a financial stake for some defendants in Ms. Smith's lawsuit but not in others, they must be treated separately.

*Agreement between Ms. Smith and Arlington Community Hospital*: Because of the severability clause, the portion of the agreement between Ms. Smith and ACH creating ACH's financial stake in the outcome of the case and requiring ACH to participate in the trial is severed from the rest of the agreement and held null and void.

*Agreement between Ms. Smith and Dr. Syrquin*: This agreement did not contain a severability clause, but Dr. Syrquin retained a financial stake in Ms. Smith's lawsuit and was required to participate in the trial. The portion of the agreement granting Dr. Syrquin a financial stake in Ms. Smith's lawsuit is nonetheless held null and void. So as not to interfere with the parties' right to contract, we leave it to the parties, if they choose, to develop before the trial court whether this void provision is severable, or whether the entire agreement must fail.

*Agreement between Ms. Smith and Dr. Stephens*: This agreement did not create a financial stake for Dr. Stephens in Ms. Smith's lawsuit. Thus, this agreement does not meet the test for a Mary Carter agreement.

In summary, a settling defendant may not participate in a trial in which he or she retains a financial interest in plaintiff's lawsuit. Since Dr. Stephens does not have a financial interest in Ms. Smith's lawsuit, there is no impediment for him to participate fully in the re-trial of this case as any other party. ACH possesses a financial interest in Ms. Smith's lawsuit, but it can also participate in the re-trial of the case because we have severed the portion of the agreement creating ACH's financial stake in the outcome of the case from the remainder of the settlement. Likewise, Dr. Syrquin does have a financial interest in Ms. Smith's lawsuit and was required to participate in the trial. We have held the portion of the agreement granting Dr. Syrquin a financial interest in Ms. Smith's cause of action against Dr. Elbaor null and void. However, his future participation in the re-trial of this case has yet to be determined. After a hearing, if the trial court invalidates the entire agreement for lack of consideration or for some other reason, Ms. Smith is obligated to return the settlement funds to Dr. Syrquin and he is free to participate in the re-trial of this cause as any other party. Accordingly, we reverse the judgment of the court of appeals and remand this cause to the trial court for further proceedings consistent with this opinion.

[The dissenting opinion of Justice DOGGETT, in which Justices MAUZY and GAMMAGE join, is omitted.]

## § 11.06 Settlement Negotiation and Counseling

### HOW DOES LITIGATION GET SETTLED? NEGOTIATING TECHNIQUES AND THEIR PLACE IN THE SETTLEMENT PROCESS

Just how do lawsuits get settled? We all are aware that most disputes are settled, not tried. How does it happen?

It can happen at almost any stage of the proceedings, in almost any kind of case and in almost any way. The case can be settled before suit is filed, or it may be settled after the supreme court has denied certiorari. Small claims cases are settled, and so are death penalty criminal cases. Settlement may be precipitated by a telephone call from defendant to plaintiff, to set up a discovery schedule, culminating in the offhand question: "What will it take to settle this case?"

Or it may be precipitated by the stern commands of an irascible federal judge to "sit down and settle this case," together with an implied (or explicit) threat to hold the failure to do so against any party appearing recalcitrant.

There are many ways to study negotiation. One can study the sociological, psychological, or ethical aspects of it. Sociologically, negotiation is a process in which two or more persons make an agreement for their mutual benefit. The aim of a negotiation is always, in a larger sense, a mutual benefit; if this aim were not available, the dispute would be resolved in a different way, such as by a test of strength. Psychologically, one may attempt to learn why negotiating techniques work. Ethically, one can recognize that negotiation is an adversary process, often involving concealment or falsehood, but to which there are limits imposed by custom.

The description that follows attempts to catalog and explain certain negotiation techniques. The inclusion of a given technique does not necessarily imply endorsement of its use. Some of the listed techniques are ethically dubious. However, even an ethical negotiator needs to know *all* of the "tricks of the trade," so that he or she can recognize and deal with improper ones when they are used by others. Also, this catalog includes several techniques that are successful only if skillfully employed and several that can only be used in very limited situations. Finally, no claim is made of completeness. Completeness would be impossible because the varieties of successful negotiating behaviors are infinite.

1. *Refusal to Bargain: The "Firm, Fair Offer."* Conceptually, the simplest negotiating technique is to determine a satisfactory point of resolution, communicate it to one's adversary and refuse to bargain about it. There are situations in which this technique is the only reasonable approach. For example, the Charles Manson murder case was not plea-bargained, and it could not have been unless the defendant had been willing to accept liability for the maximum sentence. Historically, the "firm, fair offer" is associated with a General Electric Company labor negotiator named Boulware, who customarily figured an acceptable settlement point and communicated it, along with his refusal to bargain, to the union. Irrespective of its success as a negotiating technique, the technique was so successful at undermining the union's authority that the refusal to bargain has since become the archetypical unfair labor practice. It is sometimes known as "Boulwareism."

The refusal to bargain is effective only if it is convincing enough so that rational negotiators will capitulate to it. Even then, unless the process is perceived as fair by adversaries, one may have to litigate often. And if one deals each time with a different adversary who has no reason to know or be convinced of one's track record, the firm, fair offer will not be an effective technique, because many will interpret it as an invitation to bargain further. An institutional litigator with a large volume of claims may successfully use the technique. For example, a retail outlet with a large number of slip-and-fall cases may pursue a policy of offering only out-of-pocket medical expenses when negligence proof is weak. The result will be that the litigant will have to try many cases that might more rationally be settled, but it may believe that its "tough" reputation among plaintiff's attorneys has offsetting value.

Frequently, a prosecutor's office may be in a position to use a modified "firm, fair offer" approach. Interestingly, when given descriptions of such a system, law students generally appear to consider it ethically superior for a prosecutor's office, on the theory that variations in sentences owing to negotiating ability should be minimized. But there are situations, too, when the firm, fair offer can be ethically dubious, such as when an insurer engages in the unfair settlement practice of offering unrealistically low amounts upon pain of forcing economically impractical litigation.

2. *Concealment of One's Own Settlement Point.* This is the opposite result from the firm, fair offer, and in a world of strangers negotiating for maximum advantage, it is generally the more successful approach. The technique works because an opponent who does not know the negotiator's true settlement point may have undervalued his or her own position, or overvalued the resistance of the negotiator, so that the opponent may make greater concessions than are really necessary to settle the dispute to the satisfaction of the negotiator. Conversely, a negotiator who discloses his or her true settlement point has indicated to the opponent the maximum concession the opponent need make. An opponent may not believe a statement of one's "true" settlement point and may require one to decide between further concessions and litigation.

3. *Inducing the Opponent to Start the Bargaining.* There is an advantage to having the opponent state his or her position first. By doing so, a negotiator not only can avoid giving away his or her own settlement point, but can also begin to assemble data from which to infer the opponent's settlement point.

An inexperienced opponent may be induced to make the first offer by being asked the question, "What will it take to settle this case?" One with more experience is likely to respond differently, by making a first offer that is unrealistically high, concealing the knowledge that it is unrealistically high, and by thus avoiding disclosing any information about a settlement point, shift the responsibility back to the opponent, requiring the opponent to begin true bargaining. This tactic—that of making an unreasonable offer as the first statement of position and communicating a belief that it is reasonable—is so common that it might be deemed *the* fundamental negotiating technique. The belief in reasonableness (which is frequently deceptive) may be stated explicitly, or it may be implied in non-verbal conduct, but it is an essential part of the technique.

Many people dislike negotiating because of the prevalence and undeniable success of this simple but seemingly dishonest technique. Several ethical theories have been advanced to justify the technique, including the argument that negotiation is a separate endeavor with rules different from that of other human activity, the argument that there may be an element of "self-fulfilling prophecy" in the mere statement of one's true position because it sets, instead, the perimeter of the opponent's maximum concession, and similar arguments.

4. *The Appearance of Irrationality.* Negotiation is a rational process. It depends on the willingness of both parties to concede something to get something in return. If one of the parties is irrational, no negotiation can take place. A person confronted by a hungry tiger in the jungle would not attempt to pursuade the tiger to restrain its appetite on promise of a larger amount of food at a later time. In the same manner, a person negotiating with another perceived as "crazy" may understand that he or she will have to make greater concessions than against a rational opponent, or will have resort to a test of force.

Anger, cantankerousness, indifference to consequences, and ignorance in some cases enhance a negotiator's bargaining strength. In part, they do so because they communicate irrationality to the opponent. It follows that the *appearance* of anger, cantankerousness, indifference to consequences, or ignorance may likewise create a bargaining advantage. Successful negotiators are often good actors. They are able to break off discussions with an appearance of anger that is not really anger at all but the application of a negotiating technique.

5. *Blaming the Client or Some Other Person Over Whom One Has No Control.* This technique is really a different form of irrationality. It puts the opponent in the position of arguing with a rational person, namely oneself, but with the final result to be determined by another person impervious to rational arguments. "It's entirely up to him, and he refuses your offer," is a typical way of invoking this technique. In some instances, the outsider may be a third person not closely identified with the lawyer. For example, settlement of a claim with the government may require approval of an agency independent of the one concerned in the primary dispute, and this requirement adds settlement leverage. For settlement to be reached, it must appeal not only to the primary disputants but to some third party whose interests may be different. The "Mutt and Jeff Routine" (in which one of a team of negotiators is rational but uses the feigned irrationality of another on the same team to induce concessions) is another example.

It should go without saying that blaming it on the client may be a statement of the true facts. But the point is that it may also be a pure negotiating technique. The client may have already given settlement authority to the lawyer or, more likely, would accept the advice of the lawyer, but the lawyer pretends that the client is independent.

6. *Using a Mediator.* Sometimes, a person confronted with an ostensibly irrational opponent may call in a neutral third person to help dispose of the claim. Not infrequently in lawsuit litigation, the trial judge can be induced to occupy this role (assuming the judge does not naturally undertake it). A mediator is a useful countervailing tool against most of the preceding techniques, undercutting the effort to avoid stating a realistic position as well as blaming the client.

7. *Appeals to the Merits.* Inexperienced negotiators tend to place more stock in statements about the merits of the dispute than do experienced negotiators. However, there is advantage to having one's opponent know the facts advantageous to one's position. Accordingly, even experienced negotiators often take great pains to ensure that the opposing side is aware of all evidence and law that could possibly be helpful. The difference between the inexperienced and experienced negotiator is the former's belief that the latter will accept such information as dispositive.

Experienced negotiators do, however, do a fair amount of posturing over the merits of the suit. This posturing often takes the form of expressing unshakable conviction in the prediction that one will prevail. This approach is an effort to shore up the appearance of reasonableness that is essential to the unrealistically high offer technique. The experienced negotiator will also take a position more extreme than that of the inexperienced negotiator on the merits, and will advance it with ironclad certainty. These approaches are part of the strategies of irrationality and concealment of position.

8. *Throwing Oneself on the Opponent's Mercy.* A negotiator may say, "We can't possibly dispute your claim. You've got us over a barrel. Please don't take advantage of your superior position and punish us." Although the technique is reserved to peculiar situations, specifically those in which one has little or no bargaining strength and the opponent does not seem cold blooded enough to take absolute advantage, it does work sometimes in such situations.

What must be borne in mind is that throwing oneself on the mercy of the opponent is a bargaining technique, and it has a relationship with other bargaining techniques. For example, it is not unheard of for a person using this gambit, and who is successful in inducing a "merciful" offer, to respond by saying, "Oh! That doesn't seem fair. What I had in mind was the following," and then state an unreasonably high counteroffer, having thus induced the opponent to make the first step in the bargaining.

9. *Inducing the Opponent to Bargain Against Herself.* Sometimes, an inexperienced opponent, having made the first offer, can be induced to make the first concession too. The methodology is familiar: "Your offer is not even in the ballpark. Come up with something more realistic and then we'll talk."

In doing so, the negotiator may have induced the opponent to move early from a reasonable bargaining position to one that is even more favorable to the negotiator. Further, a pattern of concessions by one party not matched by the other tends to carry over into later stages of the process.

10. *Forcing Two Opponents to Bargain Against Each Other.* This technique is often used by experienced negotiators in sales situations, sometimes with a "phantom" second bidder. In lawsuits, it requires the presence of multiple parties. The "Mary Carter" agreement, named after a case in which the Mary Carter Paint Company was one of the litigants, enables a plaintiff to settle with one of multiple defendants on the condition that the settling defendant will be repaid out of any recovery from others. *See* § 11.05. In such a situation, each of the defendants is exposed to the implied threat that such an agreement will be made with the others. Plaintiff may make the threat explicit, saying, "If you don't settle the case for X amount, I'll make an agreement with the other defendant and that will give me a war chest to go after you."

11. *"Ganging Up."* The Mary Carter agreement or the multiple-party situation in general carries another implied threat. A settling defendant may be retained in the lawsuit and may assist the plaintiff in pinning blame on the other defendant. A third party impleaded by a defendant may threaten, "If you don't release me, I'm going to cooperate with the Plaintiff in pinning blame on you."

12. *Flattery, Clubbiness, and Other Attitudes.* Experienced negotiators sometimes resort to flattery ("You're too good a lawyer to be handling this kind of case"). Or the negotiator may depict himself and the opposing lawyer as having more in common than the opponent and his client ("You have my sympathies in having to deal with a person as crazy as that. I've been in that situation too. I know what you must be going through."). Behind these statements lies the psychological truth that it is easier for a person to make concessions in an atmosphere of dignity and in the belief that he or she is respected by peers.

13. *Timing.* Time is usually on one side or the other in a negotiation. A person who can afford to wait, who can give the appearance of being able to afford to wait, or who forces himself or herself to wait, has an advantage. Another aspect of the timing of settlement negotiations is that it is advantageous to settle the case when the opponent is facing a time of difficulty or expense. A litigant who has just been ordered to prepare a pretrial order that will require the assimilation and labeling of 100,000 documents may be more willing to settle at a reasonable figure than one who has done the work and is prepared for trial.

Another aspect of timing in settlement negotiation is the closing and reopening of settlement negotiations with intervening time. Bargaining terminated with all parties angry may be resumed at a later session with time having erased the rancor from the process. Experienced negotiators know how to wait. They also know that repeated statements of the same position, made in several separate sessions with intervening periods of waiting, is an effective negotiating technique.

14. *Activity.* Vigorous and aggressive activity moving the litigation toward a point of conclusion can have advantageous effects. Many cases settle on the courthouse steps. To put the matter differently, in many cases, the factor precipitating settlement is the opponent's realization that

unless the case is settled now, a trial will be necessary. The initiation of sequential steps before trial, including discovery, a motion for summary judgment, and like steps, communicating to the opponent a determination to resolve the case and forcing the opponent, repeatedly, to confront and evaluate the situation, is an effective means of precipitating settlement.

At the same time, however, activity must be undertaken with the realization that it often costs money. A litigant who undertakes vigorous and purposeful activity, only to find that he or she has spent large amounts of money in discovery and unsuccessful pretrial motions, may find the opponent's settlement position unaffected. Activity must therefore be undertaken with an eye toward its economic feasibility in the case as well as the likelihood that it will move the case closer to resolution.

15. *Collateral Consequences to the Opponent.* There are many litigants whose initial reaction is to "fight it all the way to the supreme court" until educated as to the cost of doing so. Some negotiators, taking this fact one step further, tend to increase expense to the opponent by causing collateral consequences to ensue. The drafting of interrogatories that are expensive to answer, the taking of lengthy depositions that tie up the time of the opposing lawyer or make the client realize how much time is being wasted, or the use of discovery to embarrass, threaten trade secrets, and the like are all examples. The filing of multiple suits in different forums and even, unfortunately, use of grievance processes against opposing attorneys are all a part of the negotiation process to some litigants. The technique is that of making any alternative but settlement unduly unpleasant or expensive. Many of these tactics are ethically dubious, but they are nevertheless common.

16. *Deadlines and "Locking In."* Some negotiators place deadlines on the acceptance of a given offer to avoid the opponent's "riding" the case to get the benefit of future developments. Thus one may say, "If you wait until discovery is finished and I'm ready for trial, my settlement offer is going to go up by $10,000." The effectiveness of this technique depends on its credibility. It is a variant of the "firm, fair offer," and, like that technique, depends on the opponent's belief that one is indeed "locked in" to the deadline and to the promised refusal to bargain.

17. *Focal Point Solutions.* As differences narrow in the negotiation process, the likelihood of a "splitting of the difference" or adoption of some "standard" solution close to the bargaining position of the parties increases. Round numbers are more likely resolutions, as are multiples of 10. The experienced negotiator is aware of this phenomenon, and attempts to make and elicit offers aiming for the elusive "point in the middle" that is advantageous. For example, if the parties' latest positions are $5,000 and $12,000, respectively, the latter negotiator, if experienced, will try to keep his or her position a respectable increment over $10,000, so that this figure, rather than, say, $7,500, will be the natural focal point.

18. *Drafting the Agreement.* In a straight monetary claim situation, the drafting of the agreement may not be highly important.But in litigation involving a multiplicity of issues, such as a divorce or employment discrimination case, it can be a significant advantage to be the drafter. There are frequently minor points that are incompletely negotiated. The drafter, naturally, drafts these so as to resolve them in his or her favor. There is always the likelihood that the opponent will not notice the difference, which may depend on nuances in words, or that the opponent may consider some objections too small, in the scheme of things, to make.

19. *Control of the Agenda.* In a litigation matter with many issues to resolve, the person who sets the order of discussion may have an advantage. For some reason, concessions seem to come more easily at the beginning of a negotiation process (or at its end, when agreement is

approached). Thus the experienced negotiator attempts to cause the most important matters to be considered early, or may insist that the resolution of a particularly important point is a "precondition" to further negotiation. Conversely, the negotiator may suggest with reference to an important, but sticky, point, "Let's put that issue to the side and come back to it later," believing that the opponent will, in the meantime, acquire such a stake in preserving agreement that the issue will be favorably resolved.

20. *The "Bargaining Chip" or the False Demand.* One may ask for something one does not really want or expect so that one may appear to give it up in exchange for something else. If this happens, one has gained a concession without really making one. Sometimes, for example, a party to a divorce case who really wants a reasonable property settlement and visitation schedule will demand custody as well. This technique (like the unrealistically high offer) depends on the concealment of one's true position; *i.e.*, it depends on the opponent's belief that the bargaining chip represents a real desire conceded.

21. *"Reverse Psychology."* Against a perverse opponent (one expected to take a contrary position simply because it is contrary) one can occasionally get what one wants by asking for the opposite. "The last thing we want is custody. My client wants to be free of the responsibility." Obviously, this technique is useful in its purest form only in very limited situations.

22. *Physical Factors.* Negotiating on familiar ground, among familiar people, and under familiar conditions gives one a psychological edge. Consequently, a negotiator who induces the opponent to come to an unfamiliar place, who physically outnumbers the opponent with others on his or her team, or who persuades the opponent to engage in unfamiliar areas of bargaining discussion may have an advantage.

23. *Direct Involvement of the Principal.* Occasionally, a negotiator may see some advantage in having the opponent and his or her principal communicate directly. The opponent may have undervalued the determination or persuasiveness of the principal (or vice versa). In some situations, *e.g.* criminal defense or personal injury plaintiff's litigation, exposure of the opponent to the human qualities of the principal may have a moderating influence. Sometimes direct communication facilitates balanced concessions that would be difficult to obtain through an intermediary. In a divorce case, for example, the "four parties meeting" (with both attorneys and both clients present) may be a way of cutting through the posturing, distrust, and animosity that stands as the final obstacle to agreement.

24. *Making the Opponent Feel He Has Negotiated Capably.* An experienced negotiator generally refrains from "crowing" about an attractive result. Knowing that she may have to meet this opponent again, she instead makes the opponent feel that the result was advantageous to him.

25. *The Test of Strength, Total or Partial.* It is worth reemphasizing that not every dispute can be settled by negotiation. Some require a total—or partial—test of strength. The willingness to "go to the mat" is part of the arsenal of the skillful negotiator. However, the hallmark of the good negotiator is the settlement, without the delay or expense or trauma of litigation, of that vast majority of disputes that can be settled. It is the wisdom, in other words, to know the difference.

## NOTES AND QUESTIONS

(1) *Negotiating Techniques.* Identify the technique that is being used in each of the following negotiation statements, why the technique may work, when it would be useful, and how it might be defended against.

(a) "When we have a case that we don't think there's a good chance of liability on, we always take the position of offering out-of-pocket medical expenses only."

(b) "This lawsuit's going to cost a lot just to try. Why don't you get with your man and tell me your best shot, the bottom dollar you can settle it for, and I'll see if I can get my people to take it."

(c) "My client is being totally unreasonable about this case. He just doesn't trust me. I'd almost be willing to recommend your last offer, but what it amounts to is that you're really not dealing with me, you're dealing with him. I do think I can get him to take it if you up the offer another $5,000, though."

(d) "Well, you keep telling me that we can't win on the merits of the case. Frankly, outside the courtroom, I'll admit you're probably right. But let's put the lawsuit to the side for a minute and talk about what's right. The suit's incidental to the fact that your folks know they owe my man something. Why don't you approach it on that basis? I'm sure my man will take anything that is fair."

(e) "If you guys don't come up with at least $100,000, I'm going to be forced to make a deal with the other defendant and have them testify at the trial." (The same thing is being said to the other side).

(f) "My client really doesn't want the corporation to buy his stock back, even though that's what he's suing for, because then he'd miss out on what looks like a real good deal. The last thing he really wants is to be cashed out."

(2) *Ethical Considerations in Negotiations.* Most of the preceding discussion has been done without consideration of the ethical aspects of each technique. Most books on negotiation undertake the study of the subject in this manner, because it is easier to assess the ethics of a negotiating technique if one understands its use and its relation to other techniques. Nevertheless, the impression should not be left that ethical considerations are somehow irrelevant.

Accordingly, it seems appropriate to ask which of the preceding techniques seem most vulnerable to ethical criticisms? Which, if any, are so ethically suspect that they should not be used under any circumstances? As to those that seem ethical in some circumstances, are there other circumstances in which they should not be used?

Actually, the preceding discussion omits some of the most dubious tactics. One team of writers posits the following technique: "After agreement has been reached, have your client reject it and raise his demands." Meltsner & Schrag, *Negotiating Techniques for Legal Services Lawyers,* 7 Clearinghouse Rev. 262 (1973). The authors acknowledge that "This is the most ethically dubious of the tactics listed, but there will be occasions where a lawyer will have to defend against it or even employ it."

(3) *Negotiating Skills Are Critical.* How important are negotiation skills to practicing lawyers? Decotiis and Steele observed a sample of skilled general practitioners and recorded how the practitioners spent their professional time. Decotiis & Steele, *The Skills of the Lawyering Process,* 40 Tex. B.J. 483 (1977). They conclude that negotiation is "the most highly developed skill" employed by the lawyers observed.

(4) *Of Cows and Settlements.* Evidence of the infinite variety of negotiating behaviors is furnished by the following excerpt from Judge Jerry Buchmeyer's book, *et cetera,* pp. 62–64.* What techniques discussed above are exemplified here?

## ET CETERA

*Settlement techniques*—"this is my final offer," "I'd like to offer more, but my client just won't give me the authority," etc.—need not be repetitive and routine. Consider this example—contributed by *Lee Simpson* (passed down by his father, an attorney with the Missouri Pacific Railroad)—of a truly imaginative and, no doubt, effective technique used in September of 1917 by William H. Peterman, an attorney in Alexandria, Louisiana.

The plaintiff's claim: $100.00 for the alleged value of a cow killed by defendant's train. The "final offer" by the plaintiff's attorney: $75.00. The $50.00 counteroffer by the defendant's attorney and the devastating spiel:

> [I offer you $50.00], simply in the way of a compromise for the railroad company in making this offer does not acknowledge liability.
>
> I say to you, confidentially of course, that *the animal in question undoubtedly committed suicide.* The statements furnished me show that she hid behind a cattleguard fence, evidently by design and quietly awaited the approach of the train in order to leap in front of it and end her life. What her thoughts must have been as she thus calmly waited for death, we will not inquire. The subject is too painful.
>
> There must have been some powerful motive that actuated her in taking this dreadful course. Possibly she was afflicted with some incurable disease and saw only a future of suffering. Possibly, again, she suffered from the pangs of unrequited love; or, it may be, she sacrificed her virtue to the blandishments of some scoundrelly young bull of the neighborhood and could not survive the disgrace of exposure.
>
> Now, if you will take $50.00, I will see to it that this secret of her suicide will be sacredly guarded. If you decline it and the case is aired in the Courts, her family will be dishonored and her memory stained, and for this, your client will be answerable."

The letter continues with a somewhat more traditional justification, and supposedly practical matter, which might appeal to the plaintiff "if he is not susceptible to the appeals of sentiment":

> It is this: If he will take $50.00 he will get it now. If he sues and obtains a judgment, say for double this amount, when and how will he obtain payment? He cannot issue execution, for the railroad is in the hands of receivers. He must await action by a Federal Court. These courts move leisurely. You don't know the height and the depth and the length and the breadth of the word "leisure," unless you have had dealings with a Federal Court. If your client insists on $100.00 his grandchildren may enjoy disbursing it. If he takes $50.00 now, there is no telling how much it will yield if judiciously invested in cotton futures.

---

Or, if he is not of a speculative turn, let him buy a heifer or two and he will have a herd of milk cows before any judgment he may secure will be collectible.

Think of these things, dear friend and let me hear from you.

Is this letter a joke? If so, is it a joke with an ulterior motive? Does it look as though it would work? Why or why not?

## § 11.07 Alternate Dispute Resolution

In 1987, the 70th Legislature enacted a number of statutes providing for Alternative Dispute Resolution. *See* C.P.R.C. §§ 154.001–154.073. The following excerpt analyzes and summarizes the legislation.

### Krier and Nadig, 1987 ALTERNATIVE DISPUTE RESOLUTION PROCEDURES ACT: AN OVERVIEW

*51 Tex. B.J. 22–24 (1988).**

. . . .

The Act is found beginning at Section 154.001 of the Texas Civil Practice and Remedies Code. Significantly, the act begins by clearly stating, "It is the policy of the State to encourage the peaceable resolution of disputes . . . and the early settlement of pending litigation through voluntary settlement procedures." It is the responsibility of the courts—appellate, district, county, family, probate, municipal, and justice of the peace—to carry out this policy.

To implement the policy, the Act allows a court, on its own motion, or the motion of a party, to refer a pending dispute to an ADR procedure and to appoint neutral third parties to preside over such procedures. The court must confer with the parties to determine the most appropriate ADR procedure and notify the parties of its determination. The parties have 10 days after receipt of the notice to file a written objection to the referral. If the court finds a reasonable basis exists for an objection, an ADR referral may not be used.

Sections 154.023–027 contain broad descriptions of a number of ADR procedures such as mediation, mini-trial, moderated settlement conferences, summary jury trials, and arbitration. This list, however, is not inclusive. Flexibility exists to adapt procedures to individual disputes. The descriptions also will serve as a useful source for both judges and attorneys as ADR procedures are integrated into the Texas judicial system. It is important to note that each section stresses that the results of an ADR procedure are not binding on the parties. Therefore, while participation can be required, acceptance of the outcome is not.

Section 154.052 addresses the qualifications of impartial third parties in ADR procedures, an area which received careful review. The Act requires a minimum of 40 hours of training in dispute resolution techniques and 24 additional hours for those involved in parent-child disputes. Waivers, however, may be based on other training and experience. While these qualifications give the parties and the judge broad latitude in selecting a neutral third party, it is important that those selected have the qualifications to perform competently.

The list of duties of neutral third parties contained in Section 154.053 is equally important because it helps to maintain the uniformity of the procedures and it gives notice to everyone

---

involved of what should be expected. Only when these conditions are met will ADR be successfully integrated into Texas' court system. The duties emphasize "encouraging" and "assisting" a settlement and strictly forbid coercion. Finally, the Act specifies that a written ADR agreement is enforceable as any other written contract and may be incorporated in the court's final decree and that communications during the procedure are strictly confidential.

Assessing the impact of this legislation, especially at this early stage, presents a challenge. It is important that we, as members of the Texas Bar, look at this not as a change to be feared but rather as an opportunity. As former Texas Chief Justice John Hill has pointed out, ADR does not deny rights; it adds options. Under this Act, due process rights are protected. While the parties can be directed to participate, they are free to reject the results and are not thereafter prejudiced.

We are convinced of ADR's potential. Its impact in Texas will be significant if the Bar will help it to reach its full potential. . . .

. . . .

We doubt there is a person reading this journal who is unaware of or unconcerned by the too-often negative public perception of the legal profession. The judicial system is viewed as being too fraught with complexities, delays, expenses, and various other obstacles. It is too often perceived not as a place to solve problems, but as a place which causes or adds to problems. We must change that perception and that will require substantive change in the way we settle disputes.

ADR can be part of that change—that progress—by providing every person access to justice through the most expeditious, inexpensive, and appropriate process. The continued development of alternatives is vital to our judicial system. If we do this, not only ADR, but our entire judicial system, can be brought to its full potential and help us to meet the growing demands of society.

---

In light of the foregoing, consider the following case:

## J.B.J. DISTRIBUTORS, INC. v. JAIKARAN

*744 S.W.2d 379 (Tex. App.—Houston [1st Dist.] 1988, no writ)*

EVANS, Chief Justice.

The parties have filed a joint motion to dismiss as a result of a settlement reached following a Moderated Settlement Conference Procedure, that was conducted pursuant to the provisions of the Tex. Civ. Prac. & Rem. Code Ann. secs. 154.001 et seq. (Alternative Dispute Resolution Procedures Act) (Vernon Supp. 1988).

The appellee, Dr. Jacques Jaikaran, recovered $178,000 in damages from the appellants, J.B.J. Distributors, Inc., and Joel E. Morrow, based on his claims of breach of contract, fraud, and violations of the Deceptive Trade Practices Act. He alleged that he had purchased for $10,600 a wrist watch from the appellants, that they represented to be an authentic Rolex watch. He asserted that contrary to the defendants' representations, the watch was not an authentic Rolex watch and was not subject to that manufacturer's warranty. After a non-jury trial, the court found all essential facts in favor of the appellee and on January 23, 1987, entered judgment awarding to Jaikaran $178,000. This amount represented $10,600 as actual damages, $35,670 for lost wages, $25,000 for mental anguish, $50,000 for exemplary damages, and $56,755 for attorney's fees.

On appeal, the appellants bring six points of error, challenging (1) the legal and factual sufficiency of the evidence to support the trial court's award of actual damages, (2) the court's award of lost wages, (3) the legal and factual sufficiency of the court's award of damage for mental anguish, (4) the court's award of punitive damages, (5) the award of attorney's fees, and (6) the trial court's findings that the non-conformity of the wrist watch substantially impaired its value and that revocation occurred before the watch changed substantially.

The 1987 Alternative Dispute Resolution Procedures Act implements the policy of this State to encourage the peaceable resolution of disputes and the early settlement of pending litigation through voluntary settlement procedures. Tex. Civ. Prac. & Rem. Code Ann. sec. 154.002. Under this Act, all courts, including appellate courts, have been given the responsibility to carry out that policy. Tex. Civ. Prac. & Rem. Code sec. 154.001.

Both parties to this appeal made written requests for oral argument, and the case was duly set for oral submission on January 26, 1988. The Court, after reviewing the case file, advised counsel of its responsibility under the Act, suggested that the case might be appropriate for referral to some alternative dispute resolution procedure, and indicated that the Court would conduct a telephone conference with counsel to discuss the potential for such referral. *See* Tex. Civ. Prac. & Rem. Code Ann. secs. 154.002, 154.022. As a result of that telephone conference, the lawyers agreed to attend, with their clients, a Moderated Settlement Conference Procedure, to be conducted in the courtroom of this Court on January 25, 1988. The Court entered an order of referral, confirming the time and place and directing that each party to the appeal (or their representative having settlement authority) attend the conference with their counsel of record. In its order, the court appointed three impartial attorneys whom the Court found to be fully qualified to serve as moderators. *See* Tex. Civ. Prac. & Rem. Code Ann. secs. 154.051–154.054. The appointed moderators were: The Honorable Barbara Clark, The Honorable Ronald Hayes, and The Honorable Roy Ashe.

Additionally, the referral order directed that the Moderated Settlement Conference was to be conducted pursuant to the provisions of the Act, and that all matters, including the conduct and demeanor of the parties and their counsel, would remain confidential and would not be disclosed to anyone, including the Court. *See* Tex. Civ. Prac. & Rem. Code Ann. sec. 154.073. The Court further specified that the referral would not delay or modify any time period relating to the disposition of the case, unless expressly ordered by a subsequent ruling by the Court.

The Moderated Settlement Conference was conducted pursuant to this order, and following that conference, counsel for both parties advised the clerk of this Court that they had reached a settlement of their dispute and intended to dismiss the appeal. Thereafter, on January 27, 1988, the parties filed a joint motion to dismiss the appeal.

We conclude that the settlement conference was duly conducted pursuant to the provisions of Tex. Civ. Prac. & Rem. Code Ann. sec. 154.051 *et seq.*, and that the appeal should be dismissed in accordance with Tex. R. App. P. 59(a)(1)(A). We further conclude that this opinion should be published under authority of Tex. R. App. P. 90 and that the disposition should be reported to the Texas Supreme Court. Tex. Civ. Prac. & Rem. Code Ann. sec. 154.072.

The parties' joint motion to dismiss the appeal is granted, and the appeal is ordered dismissed. In accordance with the parties' agreed motion, the supersedeas bond is ordered released immediately. Costs of appeal are divided equally between the parties.

## APPENDIX, CHAPTER 11

This appendix contains selected materials and practice problems associated with settlement. You will also see documents related to composition and extension agreements. You should find the documents contained in this appendix extremely relevant, especially those dealing with settlement. As stated in § 11.04, settlement represents the avoidance of dispute resolution through a trial. Usually it means the satisfactory culmination of pretrial activities that were directed toward settlement at least as much as toward trial.

## SAMPLE SETTLEMENT PAPERS AND PRACTICE PROBLEMS

### Problem: Settlement Proposal Between Wilson and Keywest Savings

Sometimes it is surprising to new lawyers how complicated settlement papers can be. In the following set of papers, you should assume that the facts are as follows: plaintiff has sued a builder, a savings and loan association, and several other individuals and entities concerning a building that he claims was improperly built. He refused to make payments required by a note to the savings and loan association, whereupon it foreclosed a deed of trust lien securing the indebtedness. The suit seeks cancellation of the foreclosure, damages, and other relief from each of the parties (it is alleged that the savings and loan and builder were acting together). The allegations about improper building, complicity of the savings and loan association, and most other material facts are hotly contested. In this state of affairs, plaintiff has come to an oral agreement with the defendant savings and loan association to the effect that, for $19,000, the case will be settled as to the savings and loan, a notice of lis pendens will be removed, plaintiff will indemnify the savings and loan from contribution to other defendants if it is claimed, and plaintiff may pursue his claims against the other defendants for what they are worth.

Analyze the papers. Consider whether you understand the function of each paper and each clause. Decide what you would advise your client. Note that your client has already decided that the settlement amount is desirable, and you may assume that you have exacted top dollar from the defendant. The problem is based on the facts and documents of a real dispute, though names, numbers, and other particulars have been changed. Below is a transmittal letter enclosing the documents.

---

Sandy Q. Student
Attorney at Law
2235 Brazos Blvd.
Suite 400
London, Texas 71728

Re: *Settlement with my client, Keywest Savings Ass'n, in cause no. 4972536, Norman J. Wilson, et ux v. Andrew G. Stornbeck, et al.*

Dear Sir or Madam:

I apologize for the delay in getting these papers to you but, as I believe you will see from a review of them, the matter was of some complexity.

I enclose various proposed documents in connection with our settlement of the case. The Release and Settlement Agreement is self-explanatory. If you have any questions or wish any changes, please call me.

The Motion and Order to Cancel the Lis Pendens are also self-explanatory. Please note that this particular motion, as well as the Release and Settlement Agreement, requires the signatures of the Wilsons.

The Motion to Sever and Judgment are in the usual form.

If you have any questions or suggestions regarding any of the above, please feel free to call me. If the enclosed documents meet with your approval, contact me and I will arrange for a check in the amount of NINETEEN THOUSAND AND NO/100 ($19,000.00) DOLLARS to be forwarded to you. I would request that you then obtain the signatures of the Wilsons on the various papers necessary and then return them to me so that I may set the appropriate motions and notify all parties of a hearing date.

Thank you for your attention to the above.

Sincerely,
Thomas W. Harding

---

## RELEASE AND SETTLEMENT AGREEMENT

THE STATE OF TEXAS )
)
COUNTY OF BENSON )

That we, Norman J. Wilson and Patricia A. Wilson, in consideration of the sum of NINETEEN THOUSAND AND NO/100 ($19,000.00) DOLLARS, paid to us by KEYWEST SAVINGS ASSOCIATION, receipt of which is hereby acknowledged, do for ourselves our heirs, executors, administrators, legal representatives, successors, and assigns, release, acquit, and forever discharge KEYWEST SAVINGS ASSOCIATION, all principals, agents, and employees of same, and all heirs, executors, administrators, legal representatives, successors, and assigns of same, from any and all claims, demands, damages, losses, costs, expenses, actions, and causes of action of whatsoever nature, whether known or unknown, whether in contract or in tort, that have accrued or may ever accrue to us, our heirs, executors, administrators, legal representatives, successors, or assigns arising or to arise, in whole or in part, out of or in consequence of the acquisition of Lots 33 and 35, Block 4, Section II, Shores of Matagorda, Benson County, Texas, more commonly known as 8319 and 8323 Pike's Drive, Benson County, and the construction of a house on such land and the foreclosure on such land and house and subsequent sale of such land and house and all occurrences and transactions in connection with any and all of the above, and any and all matters arising out of, resulting from or relating to the above, including, but expressly not limited to, any claim based upon any State or Federal statute, ordinance, regulation, or provision of any law, or any breach of any contract.

The payment of such sum of money by KEYWEST SAVINGS ASSOCIATION is not to be construed as an admission of liability of any sort, which liability has been denied by KEYWEST SAVINGS ASSOCIATION.

We have heretofore brought suit in the 31st District Court of Benson County, Texas in Cause No. 4,972,536, styled Norman J. Wilson and wife, Patricia A. Wilson vs. Stornbeck, et al, to obtain various remedies as the result of certain alleged losses sustained by us arising out of the above described transactions. The payment mentioned above is accepted by us in full compromise and settlement of all claims, actions and causes of action, being asserted in said suit against KEYWEST SAVINGS ASSOCIATION or that might have been asserted in said suit against KEYWEST SAVINGS ASSOCIATION and we agree that a Judgment may be entered in that suit, denying us any recovery against KEYWEST SAVINGS ASSOCIATION.

As further part of the consideration of the payment of the above sum of money by KEYWEST SAVINGS ASSOCIATION to us, we agree to waive, and do so hereby waive, any and all claims, rights, and title to, and any interest in, the above described property that we may have had in the past, or that we may currently have, or that we may ever hereafter acquire as the result of this suit or of any of the facts, transactions, circumstances or occurrences made the basis of same. We also agree to waive, and do so hereby waive, all remedies we now seek or could seek in the above described suit that would or could affect in any way any title to, or ownership or possession of, the above described property. Should we seek to continue the above described suit against any other entity, we hereby agree to amend our pleadings and delete all requests for any remedy that could affect title to, or ownership or possession of, the above described property. We agree to cause the Notice of Lis Pendens previously filed by us against the above described property under County Clerk's File No. G210468, Film Code No. 141-61-3290, Real Property Records of Benson County, Texas, to be cancelled and agree to perform whatever acts are necessary to accomplish same.

We agree that the payment of the above sum of NINETEEN THOUSAND AND NO/100 ($19,000.00) DOLLARS is a full payment to us for any and all claims to or rights, title, or interest we may have or hereafter acquire in the above described property as the result of this suit or of any of the facts, transactions, circumstances, or occurrences made the basis of this suit. We agree that should we hereafter acquire any right, title, or interest in or to said property arising out of, in connection with, or resulting from, the above described suit, we will, without any additional consideration, execute a deed in a form acceptable to KEYWEST SAVINGS ASSOCIATION conveying to KEYWEST SAVINGS ASSOCIATION or its designee all such right, title, or interest.

As further part of the consideration for the payment of the above sum of money by KEYWEST SAVINGS ASSOCIATION, we have expressly warranted and represented and do hereby for ourselves, successors, and assigns, expressly warrant and represent to each and all of the parties hereby released that: (1) we are legally competent to execute this agreement and release, and (2) we have not assigned, pledged, or otherwise in any manner whatsoever sold or transferred, either by instrument in writing or otherwise any right, title, interest, or claim that we have or may have by reason of any of the above described, and (3) KEYWEST SAVINGS ASSOCIATION shall have no liability for, nor be responsible for, the payment of any sums of money, including fees, to any of our counsel.

As further part of the consideration for the payment of the above sum of money by KEYWEST SAVINGS ASSOCIATION, we, for ourselves, our heirs, executors, administrators, legal representatives, successors, and assigns, do hereby agree to indemnify and hold harmless KEYWEST SAVINGS ASSOCIATION from any and all claims, demands, damages, losses, expenses, actions, and causes of action of whatsoever nature or character which have been or which may hereafter be asserted by any person, firm, corporation, or any other legal entity whatsoever resulting from either or both of (1) a claim through or under either or both of us arising out of, relating to, in connection with or resulting from the above described, including, but expressly not limited to, any claim for contribution in the above described or any subsequent suit, or (2) a breach by either or both of us of any part of this agreement.

As further part of the consideration for the payment of the sum of money by KEYWEST SAVINGS ASSOCIATION, we specifically agree that this instrument, as well as any judgment or order of dismissal used in connection herewith, will not be used in any existing or subsequent legal proceedings asserted against us resulting from the occurrences or transactions herein described, as a plea of res judicata, compulsory counterclaim, estoppel by judgment, or any similar doctrine of defense.

We expressly warrant and represent to the parties hereby released, as part of the consideration for the payment of the above mentioned sum of money by KEYWEST SAVINGS ASSOCIATION, that before executing this instrument we have fully informed ourselves of its terms, contents, conditions, and effects; that in making this settlement we have had the benefit of the advice of an attorney of our own choosing; that no promise or representation of any kind has been made to us by the parties hereby released or any agent acting for them, except as is expressly stated in this instrument; that we have relied solely and completely upon our own judgment, and the advice of our counsel, in making this settlement; and that we fully understand that this is a full, complete and final settlement and release between us and KEYWEST SAVINGS ASSOCIATION, and that the sum of money mentioned above is all the money that is to be paid to us from or through KEYWEST SAVINGS ASSOCIATION as a result of any of the above described.

Executed on this the ______ day of ______, 1999.

______________________________
Norman J. Wilson

______________________________
Patricia A. Wilson

______________________

THE STATE OF TEXAS )
)
COUNTY OF BENSON )

BEFORE ME, the undersigned authority, a Notary Public in and for the State of Texas and County of Benson, on this day personally appeared NORMAN J. WILSON, known to me to be the person whose name is subscribed to the foregoing instrument, and he acknowledged to me that he executed the same for the purposes and consideration therein expressed.

Given under my hand and seal of office this the ______ day of ______, 1999.

______________________________

Notary Public in and for
Benson County, TEXAS

---

THE STATE OF TEXAS )
)
COUNTY OF BENSON )

BEFORE ME, the undersigned authority, a Notary Public in and for the State of Texas and the County of Benson, on this day personally appeared PATRICIA A. WILSON, known to me to be the person whose name is subscribed to the foregoing instrument, and she acknowledged to me that she executed the same for the purposes and consideration therein expressed.

Given under my hand and seal of office this the ______ day of ______, 1999.

______________________________

Notary Public in and for
Benson County, TEXAS

---

NO. 4,972,536

| | | |
|---|---|---|
| NORMAN J. WILSON, ET UX | ) | IN THE DISTRICT COURT OF |
| V. | ) | BENSON COUNTY, TEXAS |
| ANDREW G. STORNBECK, ET | ) | 31st JUDICIAL DISTRICT |
| AL | ) | |

JUDGMENT

BE IT REMEMBERED that on this the ______ day ______, 1999, came on to be heard and considered the above entitled and numbered cause, NORMAN J. WILSON and wife, PATRICIA A. WILSON and KEYWEST SAVINGS ASSOCIATION, appeared by and through their respective attorneys of record, and the parties having announced ready for trial, and the Court having proceeded to hear such cause, when the parties announced to the Court that they had entered into a settlement in this cause, and the consideration of such settlement had been paid in full, and the parties having agreed that the Judgment should be entered in favor of KEYWEST SAVINGS ASSOCIATION and against NORMAN J. WILSON and wife, PATRICIA A. WILSON;

It is accordingly, ORDERED, ADJUDGED, and DECREED that the Plaintiffs, NORMAN J. WILSON and wife, PATRICIA A. WILSON, take nothing from KEYWEST SAVINGS ASSOCIATION by reason of this suit, and that KEYWEST SAVINGS ASSOCIATION be discharged, and that such Defendant, stands fully released, discharged, and acquitted.

Any relief not herein granted is hereby specifically denied.

SIGNED and ENTERED this the ______ day of ______, 1999.

______________________________
JUDGE PRESIDING

APPROVED AND AGREED TO
BOTH AS TO FORM
AND AS TO SUBSTANCE:

| | |
|---|---|
| BY______________________________ | BY ______________________________ |
| SANDY Q. STUDENT | THOMAS W. HARDING |
| Attorney for Plaintiffs, | Attorney for Defendant, |
| Norman J. and | Keywest Savings Associ |
| Patricia A. Wilson | ation |

______________________

NO. 4,972,536

| | | |
|---|---|---|
| NORMAN J. WILSON, ET UX | ) | IN THE DISTRICT COURT OF |
| VS. | ) | BENSON COUNTY, TEXAS |
| ANDREW G. STORNBECK, | ) | 31st JUDICIAL DISTRICT |
| ET AL | ) | |

## MOTION TO CANCEL LIS PENDENS

COME NOW NORMAN J. WILSON and wife, PATRICIA A. WILSON, Plaintiffs in the above entitled and numbered cause, and would file this their Motion for cancellation of Lis Pendens and as grounds thereof would show unto the Court as follows:

I.

Plaintiffs, Norman J. Wilson and wife, Patricia A. Wilson, and Defendant, Keywest Savings Association, have entered into a settlement of all matters between them. In connection with such settlement, Plaintiffs herein, Norman J. Wilson and wife, Patricia A. Wilson, have waived any and all claims, rights, titles, or interest in or to Lots 33 and 34 Block 4, Section II, Shores of Matagorda Subdivision, Benson County Texas, more commonly known as 8319 and 8323 Pike's Drive, Benson County, Texas, which they may have had in the past or which they may currently have, or which they may ever hereafter acquire as the result of this suit or of any of the facts, transactions, circumstances or occurrences made the basis of this suit. As a result, Plaintiffs herein move the Court for an Order cancelling the Notice of Lis Pendens against the described property previously filed by them under County Clerk's File No. G210468, Film Code No. 141-61-3290, Real Property Records of Benson County, Texas.

WHEREFORE, PREMISES CONSIDERED, Plaintiffs move that this Court enter an Order cancelling the Notice of Lis Pendens previously filed by Plaintiffs herein along with such other and further relief, both general and special, at law and equity, to which Plaintiffs may show themselves to be justly entitled.

Respectfully submitted,

______________________________

SANDY Q. STUDENT
2235 Brazos Blvd., Suite 400
London, Texas 71728
(801) 693-1212
Attorney for Plaintiffs,
NORMAN J. AND
PATRICIA A. WILSON

---

NO. 4,972,536

| | | |
|---|---|---|
| NORMAN J. WILSON, ET UX | ) | IN THE DISTRICT COURT OF |
| VS. | ) | BENSON COUNTY, TEXAS |
| ANDREW G. STORNBECK, | ) | 31st JUDICIAL DISTRICT |
| ET AL | ) | |

ORDER

Be it remembered that on the ______ day of ______, 1999, Plaintiffs in the above entitled and numbered cause, Norman J. Wilson and wife, Patricia A. Wilson, moved the Court for an Order cancelling the Notice of Lis Pendens filed with the County Clerk of Benson County, Texas. The Court, having heard and considered the Motion, and the evidence presented thereon, and the arguments of counsel is of the opinion that Plaintiffs are entitled to an Order granting same. It is therefore,

ORDERED, ADJUDGED, and DECREED that Plaintiff's Motion to Cancel the Notice of Lis Pendens filed under County Clerk's File No. G210468, Film Code No. 141-61-3290, Real Property Records of Benson County, Texas, be granted and it is further,

ORDERED, ADJUDGED, and DECREED that said notice should be, and thc same is hereby, cancelled, voided and nullified, and it is further,

ORDERED, ADJUDGED, and DECREED that the County Clerk of Benson County, Texas, cancel from the Real Property Records of Benson County, Texas the Notice of Lis Pendens previously entered in this action.

SIGNED and ENTERED on this the ______ day of ______, 1999.

______________________________

JUDGE PRESIDING

APPROVED AND AGREED TO
BOTH AS TO FORM

AND AS TO SUBSTANCE:

______________________________

SANDY Q. STUDENT
Attorney for Plaintiffs,
Norman J. Wilson and wife,
Patricia A. Wilson

______________________________

THOMAS W. HARDING
COOPER, BOLT & BENNET
Attorney for Defendant,
Keywest Savings Association

______________________________ ______________________________

NORMAN J. WILSON PATRICIA A. WILSON

______________________________

NO. 4,972,536

| | | |
|---|---|---|
| NORMAN J. WILSON, ET UX | ) | IN THE DISTRICT COURT OF |
| VS. | ) | BENSON COUNTY, TEXAS |
| ANDREW G. STORNBECK, | ) | 31st JUDICIAL DISTRICT |
| ET AL | ) | |

MOTION TO SEVER

TO THE HONORABLE JUDGE OF SAID COURT:

COMES NOW KEYWEST SAVINGS ASSOCIATION, Defendant herein, and files this its Motion to Sever and as grounds therefore would show unto the Court as follows:

I.

All matters between Plaintiffs, Norman J. Wilson and wife, Patricia A. Wilson, and Defendant, Keywest Savings Association, have been settled and a Judgment has been submitted to the Court for signature. Defendant, Keywest Savings Association, requests the Court to sever the above captioned lawsuit against Defendant, Keywest Savings Association, out of the case in order that the Judgment in favor of Defendant, Keywest Savings Association, becomes final.

WHEREFORE, PREMISES CONSIDERED, Defendant, Keywest Savings Association, prays that this Court sever this Defendant from the above captioned lawsuit, and that this Defendant be awarded such other and further relief, both general and special, at law and equity, to which they may show themselves justly entitled.

Respectfully submitted,

______________________________

THOMAS W. HARDING
COOPER, BOLT, & BENNET
1612 Crockett Street
Suite 806
London, Texas 71735
(801) 555-63001

CERTIFICATE OF SERVICE

A true and correct copy of the above Motion to Sever was mailed this ______ day of May, 1999, to opposing counsel of record, certified, return receipt requested.

______________________________

Thomas W. Harding

---

| | | |
|---|---|---|
| NORMAN J. WILSON, ET UX | ) | IN THE DISTRICT COURT OF |
| VS. | ) | BENSON COUNTY, TEXAS |
| ANDREW G. STORNBECK, | ) | 31st JUDICIAL DISTRICT |
| ET AL | ) | |

ORDER ON MOTION TO SEVER

BE IT REMEMBERED THAT ON THE ______, day of ______, 1999, came on to be heard by the Court, Defendant KEYWEST SAVINGS ASSOCIATION'S Motion to Sever the claim of Norman J. Wilson and wife, Patricia A. Wilson, against Keywest Savings Association, from the above numbered and entitled cause, and after due and proper notice to all parties, and after the attorneys for Keywest Savings Association having appeared, and the Court having read the appropriate Motions and heard the arguments of counsel, and the Court being of the opinion said Motion is good and should be granted,

It is, therefore, ORDERED, ADJUDGED, and DECREED that the cause of action of NORMAN J. WILSON, ET UX against KEYWEST SAVINGS ASSOCIATION, be, and is now and hereby, severed from the original suit, and the Clerk of this Court is hereby ORDERED to:

1. Docket the cause of NORMAN J. WILSON, ET UX vs. KEYWEST SAVINGS ASSOCIATION, under Cause No. 4,972,536-A, with Norman J. Wilson, ET UX as Plaintiff and KEYWEST SAVINGS ASSOCIATION as Defendant; and

2. Prepare certified copies of the following pleadings and orders and file such certified copies in Cause No. 4,972,536-A:

    1. Certified copy of Plaintiff's Second Amended Original Petition; and

2. A certified copy of the Motion and Order of Severance; and
3. A certified copy of Keywest Savings Association's First Amended Original Answer; and
4. Certified copy of Judgment.

Cost of all certified copies ordered prepared are charged to Defendant, KEYWEST SAVINGS ASSOCIATION.

SIGNED and ENTERED this ______, day of ______, 1999.

______________________________

JUDGE PRESIDING

APPROVED AS TO SUB-
STANCE AND FORM:

______________________________

THOMAS W. HARDING
COOPER, BOLT, & BENNET
1612 Crockett Street, Suite 806
London, Texas 71735
Attorney for Defendant.

______________________________

SANDY Q. STUDENT
2235 Brazos Blvd., Suite 400
London, Texas 71728
Attorney for Plaintiffs.

---

## MARY CARTER AGREEMENT IN *GREER v. BUTLER EQUIPMENT CO.* *

As you read the following, you will notice that it is considerably more than an ordinary settlement agreement between Greer and Butler, the ostensible parties to it. Although settling the suit between those parties is part of its purpose, there are other purposes that relate to the other parties to the suit. There are in the agreement recitals of facts, statements about probable liability, and estimates of the severity of damages—recitals that do not appear in most two-party settlement documents. As you read the agreement, you should ask yourself why these recitals appear, what terms of agreement are unusual, and how the law should treat such an agreement.

NO. 20,462

| | | |
|---|---|---|
| GREGG GREER | ) | |
| VS. | ) | |
| R.B. BUTLER EQUIPMENT | ) | IN THE DISTRICT COURT OF |
| CO., INC. AND THE | ) | BRAZOS COUNTY, TEXAS |
| HARNISCHFEGER | ) | 85th JUDICIAL DISTRICT |
| CORPORATION | ) | |

* Reprinted from Fisher, Compromise Settlement Agreements, in State Bar of Texas, Advanced Civil Trial Course R-37 to R-45 (1978).

## AGREEMENT

On August 1, 1985, GREGG GREER sustained serious and grotesque injuries as a result of being electrocuted when a crane came in contact with a high-voltage electric wire.

The circumstances surrounding this tragic event are such that GREGG GREER has causes of action against the manufacturer of the crane, THE HARNISCHFEGER CORPORATION, and the owner and lessor of the crane, BUTLER EQUIPMENT COMPANY, and a potential cause of action, even though it has not yet been asserted, against the distributor, MOODY-DAY CO., INC.

After an investigation of the facts surrounding this most unfortunate event, it is readily apparent that the manufacturer, THE HARNISCHFEGER CORPORATION, failed to equip and install upon the crane in question any type of high-voltage proximity warning device that would have warned the operator of the crane that the crane or its cable was approaching contact with a high-voltage wire and would have warned persons working in the vicinity of the crane, such as GREGG GREER, that the crane was moving dangerously close to the source of the electrostatic field. There is no question but that a crane sold without a safety device is dangerous to intended users working in the area of voltage lines. Moreover, the manufacturer failed to furnish BUTLER EQUIPMENT COMPANY with any information regarding the existence of high-voltage proximity warning devices and failed to furnish any information that such safety devices were available either by written or oral communications. It is painfully clear that the presence of a high-voltage proximity warning device on the crane would have prevented the terrible injuries and massive damages suffered by GREGG GREER.

An investigation of the facts has also revealed that the manufacturer of the crane failed to furnish any type of insulated link device to be used with the crane and failed to design the crane in such a manner that an insulated link could have been safely carried upon such crane at all times, and failed to furnish any information whatsoever regarding the existence of insulated links and failed to furnish any instructions regarding how and when insulated links were to be used in connection with the crane in question. It is apparent that the presence of an insulated link attached above the lifting hook mechanism would have prevented the terrible injuries and massive damages suffered by GREGG GREER.

Although GREGG GREER may, from a technical standpoint, have a cause of action against BUTLER EQUIPMENT COMPANY for failure to equip the crane with a high-voltage proximity warning device (even though the manufacturer had failed to furnish adequate information regarding such device to BUTLER EQUIPMENT COMPANY) and for failure to install an insulated link on the crane, it is now obvious that the real fault and responsibility for GREGG GREER's injuries and damages lies primarily upon THE HARNISCHFEGER CORPORATION, the designer, manufacturer and seller of this type of equipment. Under the facts which exist, BUTLER EQUIPMENT COMPANY is entitled to indemnity from THE HARNISCHFEGER CORPORATION even if a finding should be made by the Jury that would, from a technical standpoint, impose legal liability upon BUTLER EQUIPMENT COMPANY.

The parties to this Agreement agree that GREGG GREER contends that his damages are at least the sum of TWO MILLION SEVEN HUNDRED FIFTY THOUSAND AND NO/100 ($2,750,000.00) based upon the fact that 7,500 volts of electricity passing through his body caused him severe electrical burns over at least 30% of his body and the amputation of his right arm;

further, GREGG GREER is going to have to undergo a series of operations in an attempt to prevent the amputation of his left leg but he has been advised that no assurance can be given that the leg can be saved even after suffering through a series of very painful operations that will cause tremendous mental anguish. The parties to this Agreement agree that a Jury of reasonable jurors will probably determine that GREGG GREER's legal damages are at least the sum of TWO MILLION SEVEN HUNDRED FIFTY THOUSAND AND NO/100 DOLLARS ($2,750,000.00), as set forth in his pleadings.

THE HARNISCHFEGER CORPORATION, the manufacturer of the crane, and its insurance carriers, have already indicated that they deny any responsibility for GREGG GREER's injuries and deny that the crane was unreasonably dangerous for use around high-voltage lines without a high-voltage proximity warning device by the manufacturer, and THE HARNISCHFEGER CORPORATION has been totally unreasonable, unfair and calloused in evaluating their exposure.

BUTLER EQUIPMENT COMPANY recognizes that in the trial of this case, even though the evidence is strong in its favor that would entitle it to indemnity from the manufacturer, there is always some risk that a Jury unknowingly might make findings that would compel the Court to enter a judgment which would permit the manufacturer to avoid what the parties to this Agreement believe to be its true responsibility in this matter.

BUTLER EQUIPMENT COMPANY firmly believes that in designing and manufacturing a crane without safety equipment which is known by and available to fabricators of cranes, the manufacturer, THE HARNISCHFEGER CORPORATION, is responsible for the injuries suffered by GREGG GREER and accordingly has or will file cross-actions against the manufacturer.

BUTLER EQUIPMENT COMPANY seeks to protect both itself and GREGG GREER in such a way as will permit him to proceed to trial wherein he may seek full compensation for his damages; and BUTLER EQUIPMENT COMPANY, because of its high regard for GREGG GREER, an employee of one of its related companies, hereby attempts to discharge, in part, what it believes to be a moral obligation to him.

It is agreed by the parties hereto as follows:

1) BUTLER EQUIPMENT COMPANY, and its insurers, guarantee GREGG GREER a minimum recovery of SEVEN HUNDRED FIFTY THOUSAND AND NO/100 DOLLARS ($750,000.00), which unfortunately would not begin to compensate him for his damages and losses caused by the horrible injuries inflicted upon him; and GREGG GREER, in turn, guarantees BUTLER EQUIPMENT COMPANY, and its insurers, that under no circumstances would they ever be required to pay more than the total sum of SEVEN HUNDRED FIFTY THOUSAND AND NO/100 DOLLARS ($750,000.00) in the disposition of this case. In connection with this guarantee, BUTLER EQUIPMENT COMPANY, and its insurers, represent and warrant to GREGG GREER that they do not have any written contracts whereby they are obligated to indemnify THE HARNISCHFEGER CORPORATION or MOODY-DAY CO., INC.

2) The parties to this Agreement have learned that prior to GREGG GREER's injuries other persons have also been electrocuted and severely burned because of this failure of THE HARNISCHFEGER CORPORATION to install high-voltage proximity warning devices and insulated links upon its cranes. THE HARNISCHFEGER CORPORATION has taken the position in the past that it has no responsibility for those occurrences and that those tragedies were caused by parties other than THE HARNISCHFEGER CORPORATION.

THE HARNISCHFEGER CORPORATION, and its insurance carriers, have already demonstrated they intend to employ the same type of defensive tactics they have previously used to attempt to escape responsibility for the unreasonably dangerous cranes. THE HARNISCHFEGER CORPORATION has stated in paragraph II of its Original Answer that:

"Defendant says that the sole proximate cause or in the alternative a proximate cause of the accident in question was the negligence of R.B. Butler Equipment Company, or alternatively the misuse of Harnischfeger's product by R.B. Butler Equipment Company or others not presently known to this defendant at the time of preparing this answer."

In the highly unlikely event that THE HARNISCHFEGER CORPORATION is able to convince a Jury to make findings which would entitle THE HARNISCHFEGER CORPORATION to contribution or indemnity from BUTLER EQUIPMENT COMPANY, then BUTLER EQUIPMENT COMPANY will, in that event pay a sum, never to exceed SEVEN HUNDRED FIFTY THOUSAND AND NO/100 DOLLARS ($750,000.00), which, when added to the sums to be paid by any other parties, will result in and guarantee GREGG GREER a recovery of at least ONE MILLION AND NO/100 DOLLARS ($1,000,000.00) over and above the amount of workmen's compensation benefits which have to be repaid under the law to the workmen's compensation insurance carrier. If, after applying the law of Contribution and Indemnity, GREGG GREER is entitled to recovery from any parties other than BUTLER EQUIPMENT COMPANY, of at least the sum of ONE MILLION AND NO/100 DOLLARS ($1,000,000.00) over and above the total of all workmen's compensation benefits, then, in that event, BUTLER EQUIPMENT COMPANY shall not be obligated to make any payments to GREGG GREER under this Agreement.

3) It is hereby agreed BUTLER EQUIPMENT COMPANY, and their insurers, will become obligated to pay GREGG GREER pursuant to the guarantees set forth herein upon final judgment of this case.

4) It is distinctly understood and agreed and stipulated that this instrument is not a settlement or release, but rather a guarantee in which the sums to be paid, if any, are indeterminable until a judgment becomes final and the obligation to actually make payment to GREGG GREER, if any be required, does not occur until a judgment becomes final.

5) It is further understood and agreed that it is the intent of all parties to this agreement that GREGG GREER specifically reserves all of his causes of action against THE HARNISCHFEGER CORPORATION, MOODY-DAY CO., INC. and/or any other potentially responsible parties, even though they have not yet been named in any pleadings filed on behalf of GREGG GREER, and specifically reserves all his causes of action and rights against any and all such persons, firms or corporations.

6) Finally, in the event that the Jury should mistakenly place some of the fault for this occurrence on BUTLER EQUIPMENT COMPANY, and only in that event, GREGG GREER agrees to indemnify and hold harmless BUTLER EQUIPMENT COMPANY from any liability of any kind or character to any other party seeking contribution or indemnity from BUTLER EQUIPMENT COMPANY for any sum over SEVEN HUNDRED FIFTY THOUSAND AND NO/100 DOLLARS ($750,000.00). It is the intent of this Agreement to clearly set forth that BUTLER EQUIPMENT COMPANY will, under no circumstances, ever have to pay anyone over SEVEN HUNDRED FIFTY THOUSAND

AND NO/100 DOLLARS ($750,000.00). It is further clearly understood that GREGG GREER's damages are very substantially in excess of such sum, and this Agreement is not intended in any way to limit his right to the recovery of his full and complete damages against parties other than BUTLER EQUIPMENT COMPANY.

EXECUTED THIS ______ day of ______, 1986.

[Signatures omitted]

---

## NOTE—OUTCOME OF THE CASE

The jury rendered a verdict for $1,735,000 in favor of Gregg Greer against the manufacturer. The judge rendered judgment for indemnity in favor of Butler Equipment Co. Thus plaintiff recovered judgment of $1,735,000, and Butler became liable for nothing. What function did the agreement play?

---

## COMPOSITION AND EXTENSION AGREEMENTS ("PAYOUT AGREEMENTS")

A "composition" is an agreement by which creditors agree to accept less than the sum owing on an indebtedness. An "extension" agreement is one by which the terms of payment are changed, usually to allow the debtor more time to pay. An agreement can be, and frequently is, a combination of both.

The following agreement is for the payment of a judgment. It prescribes payment in full, on a time schedule, and hence is an extension rather than a composition. Agreements of this sort, however, can be written at many stages of trial and in many ways. How, for example, would the agreement differ if the case was still pending on the docket? If suit had not yet been filed?

MATHEW, MANNING, LEE, SMITH & HOOKS
Attorneys at Law
1000 Langley Building
Princeton, Texas 77123

February 25, 1986

Mr. Edward L. Calloway
Calloway, Schultz & Price
2150 Chamber of Commerce Bldg.
914 Rusk Street
Princeton, Texas 77123

Re: No. 75-223019—L. J.
Sledge
Inc. vs. Cecil M. Brown, Sr.
and Winston Westly

Dear Sir:

As you are aware, we have obtained a Final Judgment against Defendants Cecil M. Brown, Sr. and Winston Westly in the above-styled cause. This Judgment is in the principal amount of $33,621.92 plus interest of $4,771.50 accruing until February 16, 1986, interest after February 16, 1986 accruing at the rate of $9.29 per day, and attorneys' fees of $3,500.00. This Judgment bears interest at the rate of 10% per annum. The total amount of the Judgment is $41,893.42. At a rate of 10% per annum, this Judgment will accumulate interest per day at the rate of $11.48.

Pursuant to our conversations, I would like to propose the following terms of payments and conditions. If these are amenable to you, will you please indicate your approval by signing your name and having Mr. Westly and Mr. Smith sign their names in the appropriate places at the bottom of the letter and return a copy of the letter to me.

1. *Payment of Interest on the Judgment.*

Cecil M. Brown, Sr. and Winston Westly agree to pay to L. J. Sledge & Co., Inc. quarterly interest accruing on the judgment at the rate of 10% per annum from the date of entry of the judgment until the judgment is satisfied in full. Payments of interest shall be made on the following dates of each year until said judgment is paid in full:

1. June 1
2. September 1
3. December 1
4. March 1

The first interest payment shall be due on or before June 1, 1986.

2. *Payments to Principal from February 26, 1986–May 26, 1986.*

In addition, Mr. Brown and Mr. Westly will make the following payments in the following amounts as a reduction of the principal amount of the judgment:

A $200.00 payment on or before February 26, 1986;

A $200.00 payment on or before March 26, 1986;

A $200.00 payment on or before April 26, 1986;

A $200.00 payment on or before May 26, 1986;

If said interest and principal payments are paid on or before the above described dates, L. J. Sledge & Co., Inc. agrees not to abstract, record, index, execute, or otherwise file any action for attachment or garnishment based on the judgment rendered in this case. If such payments are not timely made by Cecil M. Brown, Sr. and Winston Westly, L. J. Sledge & Co., Inc. reserves the right to abstract, record, index, execute, or otherwise file any action for attachment or garnishment against Cecil M. Brown, Sr. and Winston Westly or their assets.

3. Payments to Principal from July 1, 1986 Until Paid in Full.

After July 1, 1986, L. J. Sledge & Co., Inc. reserves the right to periodically re-examine the financial ability of Mr. Brown and Mr. Westly and require that they increase their monthly payments on the principal amount of the judgment and to abstract, execute, index, record, or otherwise enforce this judgment by any legal means should Mr. Brown and Mr. Westly not meet the monthly payments on or before the 26th of each month that are demanded by L. J. Sledge

& Co., Inc. No consideration has been given to L. J. Sledge & Co., Inc. in return for its agreement to not demand payment of the judgment in full after July 1, 1976.

# INDEX

[References are to pages.]

## A

[References are to pages.]

[References are to pages.]

[References are to pages.]

[References are to pages.]

[References are to pages.]

[References are to pages.]



## R

[References are to pages.]

## S

[References are to pages.]

# TABLE OF CASES

[References are to text sections.]

[References are to text sections.]



## C

[References are to text sections.]

[References are to text sections.]

[References are to text sections.]

## F



## G

[References are to text sections.]



## H

[References are to text sections.]

[References are to text sections.]

[References are to text sections.]



## N

[References are to text sections.]



## O



## P

[References are to text sections.]



## Q



## R



## S

[References are to text sections.]

[References are to text sections.]

[References are to text sections.]



## W



## Y



## Z